# VISUAL BASIC 6
# HOW TO PROGRAM

## Deitel & Deitel
## Books and Cyber Classrooms
published by
## Prentice Hall

### *How to Program* Series
*C How to Program, 2/E*
*C++ How to Program, 2/E*
*Java How to Program, 2/E*
*Java How to Program with an Introduction to Visual J++ (1.0), 1/E*
*Visual Basic 6 How to Program, 1/E*

### *Multimedia Cyber Classroom* Series
*C & C++ Multimedia Cyber Classroom, 2/E*
*Java Multimedia Cyber Classroom, 2/E*
*Visual Basic 6 Multimedia Cyber Classroom, 1/E*

### *A Complete Training Course* Series
*A Complete C++ Training Course, 2/E*
*A Complete Java Training Course, 2/E*
*A Complete Visual Basic 6 Training Course, 1/E*

For continuing updates on Prentice Hall and Deitel & Associates, Inc. publications
visit the Prentice Hall web site

`http//www.prenhall.com/deitel`

To communicate with the authors, send email to:

`deitel@deitel.com`

For information on corporate on-site seminars and public seminars offered by
Deitel & Associates, Inc. worldwide, visit:

`http://www.deitel.com`

# VISUAL
# BASIC™ 6
## HOW TO
## PROGRAM

### H. M. Deitel
Deitel & Associates, Inc.

### P. J. Deitel
Deitel & Associates, Inc.

### T. R. Nieto
Deitel & Associates, Inc.

PRENTICE HALL, Upper Saddle River, New Jersey 07458

Library of Congress Cataloging in Publication Data

Deitel, Harvey M.
   Visual Basic 6 how to program / H. M. Deitel, P. J. Deitel, Tem Nieto
     p. cm. --
   Includes bibliographical references and index.
   ISBN 0-13-456955-5
   1. Microsoft Visual Basic  2. BASIC (Computer program language)
I. Deitel, Paul J.  II. Nieto, Tem. III. Title.
QA76.73.B3D46  1999
005.26'8--dc21                                           98-44388
                                                            CIP

Acquisitions Editor: *Laura Steele*
Production Editor: *Camille Trentacoste*
Chapter Opener and Cover Designer: *Tamara Newnam Cavallo*
Buyer: *Pat Brown*
Editorial Assistant: *Kate Kaibni*

The authors and publisher of this book have used their best efforts in preparing this book. These efforts include the development, research, and testing of the theories and programs to determine their effectiveness. The authors and publisher make no warranty of any kind, expressed or implied, with regard to these programs or to the documentation contained in this book. The authors and publisher shall not be liable in any event for incidental or consequential damages in connection with, or arising out of, the furnishing, performance, or use of these programs.

Many of the designations used by manufacturers and sellers to distinguish their products are claimed as trademarks and registerd trademarks. Where those designations appear in this book, and Prentice-Hall and the autors were aware of a trademark claim, the designations have been printed in initial caps or all caps. All product names mentioned remain trademarks or registered trademarks of thier respective owners.

Printed in the United States of America

10 9 8 7 6 5 4 3 2 1

ISBN 0-13-456955-5

Prentice-Hall International (UK) Limited, London
Prentice-Hall of Australia Pty. Limited, Sydney
Prentice-Hall Canada Inc., Toronto
Prentice-Hall Hispanoamericana, S.A., Mexico
Prentice-Hall of India Private Limited, New Delhi
Prentice-Hall of Japan, Inc., Tokyo
Simon & Schuster of Asia Pte. Ltd., Singapore
Editora Prentice-Hall do Brasil, Ltda., Rio de Janeiro

TO

Susanne Peterson

*Manager of University Curriculum Programs*
*Microsoft Research Unit*
*Microsoft Corporation*

and our mentor at Microsoft. Thank you for your extraordinary efforts in the conception and implementation of our

*Visual Studio Series*

of academic textbooks including

*Visual Basic 6 How to Program*

and our forthcoming titles

*Visual J++ 6 How to Program*
*Visual C++ 6 How to Program*
*Visual InterDev 6 How to Program.*

Your enthusiasm, expertise, market savvy and commitment to this series has made creating these books a sheer joy.

Thank you for being the special person that you are.

*Harvey, Paul and Tem*

# Contents

# Illustrations

# Preface

*Live in fragments no longer. Only connect.*
Edward Morgan Forster

Welcome to Visual Basic 6 and the exciting world of Internet and World Wide Web programming! This book is by an old guy and two young guys. The old guy [HMD; Massachusetts Institute of Technology (MIT) 1967] has been programming and/or teaching programming for 37 years. The two young guys [PJD; MIT 1991 and TRN; MIT 1992] have each been programming for 15 years and have caught the teaching and writing "bug." The old guy programs and teaches from experience; the young guys do so from an inexhaustible reserve of energy. The old guy wants clarity; the young guys want performance. The old guy seeks elegance and beauty; the young guys want results. We got together to produce a book we hope you will find informative, interesting, challenging and entertaining.

## Why We Wrote Visual Basic 6 How to Program

Dr. Harvey M. Deitel taught introductory programming courses in universities for 20 years with an emphasis on developing clearly written, well-structured programs. Much of what is taught in these courses is the basic principles of programming with an emphasis on the effective use of control structures, primitive data types, arrays, functions and the program development process.

We present these topics in *Visual Basic 6 How to Program* exactly the way HMD has done in his university courses. Our experience has been that students handle the material in the early chapters on primitive data types, control structures, procedures and arrays in about the same manner as they handle introductory Pascal or C courses. There is one noticeable difference though: students are highly motivated by the fact that they are learning a leading-edge language (Visual Basic 6) and leading-edge programming paradigms (event-driven programming and object-oriented programming) that will be immediately useful to them as they leave the university environment. This increases their enthusiasm for the material. Students quickly discover that they can do great things with Visual Basic 6, so they are willing to put incredible effort into their courses.

Our goal was clear: produce a Visual Basic 6 textbook for introductory university-level courses in computer programming for students with little or no programming experience, yet offer the depth and the rigorous treatment of theory and practice demanded by traditional, upper-level C and C++ courses and that satisfies professionals' needs. To meet these goals, we produced a comprehensive book because our text also patiently teaches the principles of control structures, event-driven programming, object-oriented programming and the Visual Basic 6 language.

*Visual Basic 6 How to Program* was written fresh on the heels of *C How to Program: Second Edition*, *C++ How to Program: Second Edition* and *Java How to Program: Second Edition*, each of which has become the world's leading introductory textbook in its respective field. Hundreds of thousands of students and professional people worldwide have learned C, C++ and Java from these texts. Upon publication in November, 1998 *Visual Basic 6 How to Program* will be used in universities, professional schools and corporate training programs worldwide.

We have prepared an interactive multimedia CD-ROM edition of this book—the *Visual Basic 6 Multimedia Cyber Classroom*. Prentice Hall offers a "value pack" edition of both *Visual Basic 6 How to Program* and the *Visual Basic 6 Multimedia Cyber Classroom* called *The Complete Visual Basic 6 Training Course* at a discount for people who want to use both the book and the multimedia CD. Please see the last few pages of this book for ordering instructions. *The Complete Visual Basic 6 Training Course* is discussed in more detail later in this Preface.

We believe in Visual Basic 6. Its conceptualization by Microsoft®, the creators of Visual Basic 6, is brilliant: Base a language on one of the world's most widely known languages, Basic. Endow the language with the ability to conveniently build applications for Microsoft Windows®—the world's most widely used platform. Provide the kinds of heavy duty, high-performance capabilities needed for enterprise systems development. Make the language appropriate for implementing Internet-based and World-Wide-Web-based applications, and build in the features people really need such as **String**s, graphics, graphical user interface components, error handling, multimedia (audio, images, animation and video), file processing, database processing, Internet-based client/server networking, World Wide Web browsing, World Wide Web document enhancement with Visual Basic Script (VBScript), and prepackaged components. Make the language extensible so that independent software vendors (ISVs) can provide componentry for a vast array of application arenas. These features are precisely what businesses and organizations need to meet today's information processing requirements.

Visual Basic 6 empowers programmers to unleash their creativity. Once Visual Basic 6 students enter lab, instructors will not be able to hold the students back. They will be eager to experiment and explore. They will quickly produce applications that go well beyond anything they would have produced in introductory programming courses in procedural languages like C, Pascal and non-visual versions of Basic.

The computer field has never seen anything like the Internet/World Wide Web "explosion" occurring today. People want to communicate. People need to communicate. Sure they have been doing that since the dawn of civilization, but computer communications have been mostly limited to digits, alphabetic characters and special characters passing back and forth. The next major wave is surely multimedia. People want to transmit pictures and they want those pictures to be in color. They want to transmit voices, sounds and audio clips. They want to transmit full-motion color video. And at some point, they will insist on three-dimensional, moving-image transmission. Our current flat, two-dimensional televisions will eventually be replaced with three-dimensional versions that turn our living rooms into "theaters in the round." Actors will perform their roles as if we were watching live theater. Our living rooms will be turned into miniature sports stadiums. Our business offices will enable video conferencing among colleagues half a world apart as if they were sitting around one conference table. The possibilities are intriguing and Visual Basic 6 is sure to play a key role in making many of these possibilities become reality.

There have been predictions that the Internet will eventually replace the telephone system. Well, why stop there? It could also replace radio and television as we know them today. It's not hard to imagine the Internet replacing the newspaper with completely electronic news media. This textbook you are reading may someday appear in a museum alongside radios, TVs and newspapers in an "early media of ancient civilization" exhibit.

## Teaching Approach

*Visual Basic 6 How to Program* contains a rich collection of examples, exercises, and projects drawn from many fields to provide the student with a chance to solve interesting real-world problems. The book concentrates on the principles of good software engineering and stresses program clarity. We avoid arcane terminology and syntax specifications in favor of teaching by example. Each of our code examples has been carefully tested.

This book is written by three educators who spend most of their time teaching edge-of-the-practice topics in industry classrooms worldwide. The text emphasizes pedagogy.

### Live-Code Teaching Approach

The book is loaded with live-code examples. This is the focus of the way we teach and write about programming, and the focus of each of our multimedia *Cyber Classrooms* as well. Virtually every new concept is presented in the context of a complete, working Visual Basic 6 program immediately followed by one or more windows showing the program's output. We call this style of teaching and writing our *live-code approach. We use the language to teach the language.* Reading these programs is much like entering and running them on a computer.

### World Wide Web Access

All of the code for *Visual Basic 6 How to Program* is on the Internet at the Prentice Hall Web site **http://www.prenhall.com/deitel** and at the Deitel & Associates, Inc. Web site **http://www.deitel.com**. Please download all the code then run each program as you read the text. Make changes to the code examples and see what happens. See how the Visual Basic 6 compiler "complains" when you make various kinds of errors. Immediately see the effects of making changes to the code. It's a great way to learn programming by doing programming. [You must respect the fact that this is copyrighted material. Feel free to use it as you study Visual Basic 6, but you may not republish any portion of it without explicit permission from the authors and Prentice Hall.]

### Objectives

Each chapter begins with a statement of *Objectives*. This tells the student what to expect and gives the student an opportunity, after reading the chapter, to determine if he or she has met these objectives. It is a confidence builder and a source of positive reinforcement.

### Quotations

The learning objectives are followed by quotations. Some are humorous, some are philosophical and some offer interesting insights. Our students enjoy relating the quotations to the chapter material. The quotations are worth a "second look" after you read each chapter.

### Outline

The chapter *Outline* helps the student approach the material in top-down fashion. This, too, helps students anticipate what is to come and set a comfortable and effective learning pace.

### 7806 lines of code in 178 Example Programs (with Program Outputs)

We present Visual Basic 6 features in the context of complete, working Visual Basic 6 programs. This is the focus of our teaching and our writing. We call it our "live-code" approach. Each program is followed by a window with the output produced when the program runs. This enables the student to confirm that the programs run as expected. Reading the book carefully is much like entering and running these programs on a computer. The programs range from just a few lines of code to substantial examples with several hundred lines of code. Students should download all the code for the book from our Web sites and run each program while studying that program in the text. The programs are available at both **http://www.deitel.com** and **http://www.prenhall.com/deitel**.

### 558 Illustrations/Figures

An abundance of charts, line drawings and program outputs is included. The discussion of control structures, for example, features carefully drawn flowcharts. [Note: We do not teach the use of flowcharting as a program development tool, but we do use a brief, flowchart-oriented presentation to specify the precise operation of Visual Basic 6's control structures.]

### 412 Programming Tips

We include programming tips to help students focus on important aspects of program development. We highlight hundreds of these tips in the form of *Good Programming Practices, Common Programming Errors, Look-and-Feel Observations, Testing and Debugging Tips, Performance Tips, Portability Tips*, and *Software Engineering Observations*. These tips and practices represent the best we have gleaned from a combined six decades of programming and teaching experience. One of our students—a mathematics major—told us recently that she feels this approach is like the highlighting of axioms, theorems and corollaries in mathematics books; it provides a basis on which to build good software.

### 78 Good Programming Practices

When we teach introductory courses, we state that the "buzzword" of each course is "clarity," and we highlight as *Good Programming Practices* techniques for writing programs that are clearer, more understandable, more debuggable and more maintainable.

### 155 Common Programming Errors

Students learning a language tend to make certain errors frequently. Focusing the students' attention on these *Common Programming Errors* helps students avoid making the same errors. It also helps reduce the long lines outside instructors' offices during office hours!

### 14 Look-and-Feel Observations

We provide *Look-and-Feel Observations* to highlight Windows graphical user interface conventions. These observations help students design their applications to "look" and "feel" like typical Windows programs.

### 39 Performance Tips

In our experience, teaching students to write clear and understandable programs is by far the most important goal for a first programming course. But students want to write the programs that run the fastest, use the least memory, require the smallest number of keystrokes, or dazzle in other nifty ways. Students really care about performance. They want to know what they can do to "turbo charge" their programs, so we have included extensive *Performance Tips*.

### 15 Portability Tips

We include *Portability Tips* to help students write portable code, i.e., code that is designed to run on a variety of platforms. These tips highlight issues that may affect how Visual Basic 6 programs run on Windows systems with different hardware devices. We also consider internationalization issues.

### 76 Software Engineering Observations

Event-driven programming and object-oriented programming require a complete rethinking about the way we build software systems. Visual Basic 6 is an effective language for performing good software engineering. The *Software Engineering Observations* highlight architectural and design issues that affect the construction of software systems, especially large-scale systems. Much of what the student learns here will be useful in upper-level courses and in industry as the student begins to work with large, complex real-world systems.

### 40 Testing and Debugging Tips

When we first designed this "tip type," we thought we would use it strictly to tell people how to test and debug Visual Basic 6 programs. In fact, many of the tips describe aspects of Visual Basic 6 that reduce the likelihood of "bugs" and thus simplify the testing and debugging process for Visual Basic 6 programs.

## Summary

Each chapter ends with additional pedagogical devices. We present a thorough, bullet-list-style *Summary* of the chapter. On average, there are 38 summary bullets per chapter. This helps the students review and reinforce key concepts.

## Terminology

We include in a *Terminology* section an alphabetized list of the important terms defined in the chapter—again, further reinforcement. On average, there are 94 terms per chapter.

## Summary of Tips, Practices, and Errors

For ease of reference, we collect and reiterate the *Good Programming Practices, Common Programming Errors, Look-and-Feel Observations, Testing-and-Debugging Tips, Performance Tips, Portability Tips,* and *Software Engineering Observations.*

## 406 Self-Review Exercises and Answers (Count Includes Separate Parts)

Extensive self-review exercises and answers are included for self study. This gives the student a chance to build confidence with the material and prepare for the regular exercises. Students should be encouraged to do all the self-review exercises and to check their answers.

## 819 Exercises (Solutions in Instructor's Manual; Count Includes Separate Parts)

Each chapter concludes with a substantial set of exercises including simple recall of important terminology and concepts; writing individual Visual Basic 6 statements; writing small portions of Visual Basic 6 procedures and modules; writing complete Visual Basic 6 procedures, classes, applications; and writing major term projects. The large number of exercises across a wide variety of areas enables instructors to tailor their courses to the unique needs of their audiences and to vary course assignments each semester. Instructors can use these exercises to form homework assignments, short quizzes, and major examinations. The solutions for the exercises are included in the *Instructor's Manual* and on the disks *available only to instructors* through their Prentice-Hall representatives. [**NOTE: Please do not write to us requesting the instructor's manual. Distribution of this publication is strictly limited to college professors teaching from the book. Instructors may obtain the solutions manual only from their regular Prentice Hall representatives.**] Solutions to many of the exercises are included on the *Visual Basic 6 Multimedia Cyber Classroom* CD; please see the last few pages of this book for ordering instructions [or call 1-800-811-0912 and ask for ISBN# 0-13-083116-6].

## Approximately 5150 Index Entries (with approximately 7400 Page References)

We have included an extensive *Index* at the back of the book. This helps the student find any term or concept by keyword. The *Index* is useful to people reading the book for the first time and is especially useful to practicing programmers who use the book as a reference. Most of the 2078 terms in the *Terminology* sections appear in the *Index* (along with many more index items from each chapter). Students can use the *Index* in conjunction with the *Terminology* sections to be sure they have covered the key material of each chapter.

*Bibliography*

A bibliography is included to encourage further reading. Excellent additional bibliographic information on Visual Basic 6 is available on the World Wide Web. The bibliography includes a summary of the Visual Basic 6 on-line documentation that comes with the Standard, Professional and Enterprise editions of Visual Basic 6 (but which, unfortunately, does not come with the Working Model Edition software included with this book).

*Additional Resources for Instructors and Students*

We have prepared an Adobe Acrobat PDF-format slide show including all the illustrations, tables, program listings and program output windows in *Visual Basic 6 How to Program*. We will post regular announcements on our web sites

```
http://www.deitel.com
http://www.prenhall.com/deitel
```

about additional instructor and student resources, including errata, FAQs, test banks, syllabi and other forthcoming resources.

## A Tour of the Book

**Chapter 1—Computers Concepts**—discusses what computers are, how they work and how they are programmed. It introduces the notion of structured programming and explains why this set of techniques has fostered a revolution in the way programs are written. The chapter gives a brief history of the development of programming languages from machine languages to assembly languages to high-level languages. The origin of the Visual Basic 6 programming language is discussed.

**Chapter 2—Integrated Development Environment**—overviews the Visual Basic 6 Integrated Development Environment (IDE) which is used to create Windows programs. The IDE is a graphical environment containing an editor for writing Visual Basic 6 code, a compiler, and a debugger. The Toolbox, **Properties** window, **Project** window, form window, tool bars and menus are discussed. This chapter familiarizes students with the IDE. Students are also introduced to the concept of *visual programming*—the ability to create programs by writing little code and sometimes no code at all.

**Chapter 3—Introduction to Visual Basic Programming**—gives a concise introduction to writing Visual Basic 6 programs. Detailed discussions of event-driven programming, decision making, arithmetic operations and operator precedence are presented. After studying this chapter, the student will understand how to write simple, but complete, Visual Basic 6 programs.

**Chapter 4—Control Structures: Part I**—focuses on the program development process. The chapter discusses how to take a problem statement (i.e., a requirements document) and from it develop a working Visual Basic 6 program, including performing intermediate steps in pseudocode. The chapter introduces some fundamental data types and simple control structures used for decision making (**If/Then** and **If/Then/Else**) and repetition (**While**, **Do While** and **Do Until**). The chapter uses simple flowcharts to show the flow of control through each of the control structures. We examine counter-controlled repetition and sentinel-controlled repetition. We have had a positive experience assigning problems 4.16 through 4.19 in our introductory courses. Since these four problems have similar structure, doing all four is a nice way for students to "get the hang of" the program development process. Students will enjoy the challenges of the "mystery programs." The more mathematically inclined students will enjoy problems on encryption and decryption and determining how many digits in a five-digit number are 7s.

**Chapter 5—Control Structures: Part II**—continues the discussion of Visual Basic 6's sequence, selection (**Select Case**) and repetition (**For/Next**, **Do/Loop While** and **Do/Loop Until**) control structures. This chapter also uses simple flowcharts to show the flow of control through each of the control structures. The techniques discussed in Chapter 4 and Chapter 5 constitute a large part of what has been traditionally taught in the universities under the topic of structured programming. Chapter 5 examines repetition in detail and compares the alternatives of counter-controlled loops and sentinel-controlled loops. This chapter helps the student develop good programming habits in preparation for dealing with the more substantial programming tasks in the remainder of the text. The chapter also introduces logical operators—**And** (logical AND), **Or** (logical OR), and **Not** (logical NOT), constants, and Visual Basic 6 data types. There is a substantial exercise set including mathematical and graphical applications. The more mathematically inclined students will enjoy problems on calculating the trigonometric sine of a number with an infinite series, Pythagorean triples and De Morgan's Laws. Our students particularly enjoy the challenges of triangle-printing and diamond-printing in Exercises 5.16, 5.17 and 5.21; these problems really help students learn to program nested repetition structures—a complex topic to master in introductory courses.

**Chapter 6—Sub Procedures and Function Procedures**—takes a deeper look at procedures. We explore procedures in depth and include a discussion of procedures that "call themselves," so-called *recursive* procedures. We discuss Visual Basic 6 procedures, programmer-defined procedures and recursion. The techniques presented in Chapter 6 are essential to the production of properly structured programs, especially the kinds of larger programs and software that application programmers are likely to develop in real-world applications. The "divide and conquer" strategy is presented as an effective means for solving complex problems by dividing them into simpler interacting components. Students enjoy the treatment of random numbers and simulation, and they appreciate the discussion of the dice game of craps that makes elegant use of control structures (this is one of our most successful lectures in our introductory courses). The chapter offers a solid introduction to recursion. Some texts leave recursion for a chapter late in the book; we feel this topic is best covered gradually throughout the text. The extensive collection of exercises at the end of the chapter includes several classical recursion problems such as the *Towers of Hanoi*; the reader may want to revisit this problem later in the text and employ graphics, animation and sound to make the problem "come alive." There are many mathematical and graphical examples. Our students particularly enjoy the development of a "Computer-Assisted Instruction" system in Exercises 6.19 through 6.21.

**Chapter 7—Arrays**—explores the processing of data in lists and tables of values. We discuss the structuring of data into arrays, or groups, of related data items of the same type. The chapter presents numerous examples of both one-dimensional arrays and two-dimensional arrays. It is widely recognized that structuring data properly is just as important as using control structures effectively in the development of properly structured programs. Examples in the chapter investigate various common array manipulations, printing histograms, sorting data, passing arrays to procedures and an introduction to the field of survey data analysis (with simple statistics). A feature of this chapter is the discussion of elementary sorting and searching techniques and the presentation of binary searching as a dramatic improvement over linear searching. The 32 end-of-chapter exercises include a variety of interesting and challenging problems such as improved sorting techniques, the design of an airline reservations system, an introduction to the concept of turtle graphics (made famous in the LOGO programming language) and the Knight's Tour and Eight Queens problems that introduce the notions of heuristic programming so widely employed in the field of artificial intelligence. The exercises contain a series of recursion problems including the selection sort, linear search, binary search and quick sort.

**Chapter 8—Strings, Dates, and Times**—deals with processing words, sentences, characters, groups of characters, dates and times. For each example we provide extensive live-code examples demonstrating appropriate Visual Basic 6 functions "in action." We show output windows so the reader can see the precise effects of each of the string and character manipulations we discuss. Students will enjoy the card shuffling and dealing example (which they will enhance in the exercises). A key feature of the chapter is an extensive collection of challenging string-manipulation exercises related to limericks, text analysis, word processing, printing dates in various formats, check protection, writing the word equivalent of a check amount, Morse Code, card shuffling and dealing, encryption, hangman, cryptograms and metric-to-English conversions. Students will enjoy the challenges of developing their own spell checker and crossword puzzle generator.

## Advanced Topics

**Chapter 9—Graphics**—begins a run of chapters that present the multimedia "sizzle" of Visual Basic 6. We consider Chapters 9 through 21 to be the book's advanced material. Professors who have been teaching C and/or C++ at the introductory level will find that the Visual Basic 6 topics open all kinds of opportunities to explore new areas. This is "fun stuff." We discuss drawing graphical shapes (e.g., lines, circles, etc.), manipulating colors, images, and printing. The chapter illustrates each of these graphics capabilities with live-code examples, appealing screen outputs, detailed features tables and detailed line art. The exercises challenge students to draw various geometric shapes, manipulate images and create a graphical version of the game of hangman.

**Chapter 10—Basic Graphical User Interface Concepts**—introduces the creation of applications with user-friendly graphical user interfaces (GUIs). GUI development is a huge topic, so we divided it into two chapters. These chapters cover the material in depth to enable you to build "industrial-strength" GUI interfaces. Through its programs, tables and line drawings, the chapter illustrates GUI design principles, **ListBox**es, **TextBox**es, **ComboBox**es, **MaskedEdit** controls, scrollbars, **Slider**s, menus, pop-up menus, and **MsgBox**es. Some of the exercises challenge the student to use various controls to format inputs, create GUIs and sort stored strings to facilitate searching. The chapter exercises include a delightful simulation of the classic race between the tortoise and the hare.

A special section entitled "Building Your Own Computer" explains machine-language programming and proceeds with the design and implementation of a computer simulator that allows the reader to write and run machine-language programs. This unique feature of the text will be especially useful to the reader who wants to understand how computers really work. Our students enjoy this project and often implement substantial enhancements; several enhancements are suggested in the exercises.

**Chapter 11—Advanced Graphical User Interface Concepts**—continues the detailed walkthrough of Visual Basic 6's GUI capabilities. The examples walk the reader through the manipulation of more advanced GUI controls including `RichTextBox`, `UpDown`, `ImageList`, `ImageCombo`, and `FlatScrollBar`. Single document interface (SDI) and multiple document interfaces (MDI) are discussed. The chapter concludes with a discussion of native-code compilation. The exercises encourage the reader to develop more substantial GUIs with the advanced components presented in the chapter.

**Chapter 12—Mouse and Keyboard**—discusses handling mouse and keyboard events. Topics discussed include drag-and-drop, changing the mouse-pointer shape, distinguishing which mouse button was pressed, intercepting key events (from the keyboard) and distinguishing which keyboard key was pressed. The chapter provides several nice examples—including a drag-and-drop example that allows the user to move a Knight chess piece around a chess board.

**Chapter 13—Error Handling and Debugging**—is one of the most important chapters in the book from the standpoint of building so-called "mission-critical" or "business-critical" applications that require high degrees of robustness and fault tolerance. Things do go wrong, and at today's computer speeds—commonly hundreds of millions of operations per second—if they can go wrong they will, and rather quickly at that. Programmers are often a bit naive about using components. They ask, "How do I request that a component do something for me?" They also ask "What value(s) does that component return to me to indicate it has performed the job I asked it to do?" But programmers also need to be concerned with, "What happens when the component I call on to do a job experiences difficulty? How will that component signal that it has a problem?" In Visual Basic 6, when a component (i.e., a procedure) encounters difficulty, it can "raise an error." The environment of that component is programmed to "handle" that error and deal with it. To use a Visual Basic 6 component, you need to know not only how that component behaves when "things go well," but also what errors that component raises when "things go poorly." The chapter discusses the vocabulary of error handling. The **On Error** block executes program code that may execute properly or may raise an error if something goes wrong. Associated with an **On Error** block are one or more handlers that process raised errors and attempt to restore order and keep systems "up and running" rather than letting them "crash." Even if order can not be fully restored, the handlers may perform operations that enable a system to continue executing, albeit at reduced levels of performance—such activity is often referred to as "graceful degradation."

The chapter also introduces the reader to the Visual Basic 6 debugger. We discuss the **Debug** menu and debug tool bar commands (used to control the debugging session), the **Locals** window (used to display local variable values), the **Watch** window (used to view both local and module variables) and the **Call Stack** window (used to view a list of all the procedures that were called in order to reach the selected line).

**Chapter 14—Sequential File Processing**—deals with input/output that is accomplished through streams of data directed to and from files. This is one of the most important chapters for programmers who will be developing commercial applications. The chapter introduces the data hierarchy from bits, to bytes, to fields, to records, to files. Next, Visual Basic 6's simple view of files and streams is presented. We show how programs pass data to secondary storage devices like disks and how programs retrieve data already stored on those devices. Sequential-access files are discussed using a series of programs that show how to open and close files, how to store data sequentially in a file and how to read data sequentially from a file. This chapter uses the new **FileSystem** object model of Visual Basic 6 which allows files, directories and drives to be conveniently manipulated. We also discuss controls for graphically manipulating files, directories and drives.

**Chapter 15—Records and Random-Access Files**—Random-access files are discussed using a series of programs that show how to sequentially create a file for random access, how to read and write data to a file with random access, and how to read data sequentially from a randomly accessed file. The last random-access program combines many of the techniques of accessing files both sequentially and randomly into a complete transaction-processing program. We discuss the notion of User-Defined Types (UDTs)—Visual Basic's equivalent of records. We explain how these records can be output to, and input from, secondary storage devices. Students in our industry seminars have told us that after studying the material on file processing, they were able to produce substantial file-processing programs that were immediately useful to their organizations. The exercises ask the student to implement a variety of programs that build and process random-access files.

**Chapter 16—Object-Oriented Programming**—begins our discussion of class modules. The chapter represents a wonderful opportunity for teaching data abstraction the "right way." The chapter focuses on the essence and terminology of classes and objects. What is an object? What is a class of objects? What does the inside of an object look like? How are objects created? How are they destroyed? How do objects communicate with one another? Why are classes such a natural mechanism for packaging software as reusable componentry? The chapter discusses implementing abstract data types (ADTs) as Visual Basic 6 classes, accessing class members, enforcing information hiding with **Private** instance variables, separating interface from implementation, using access methods and utility methods, and initializing objects. The chapter discusses composition—the process of building classes that have references to objects as members, dynamic memory allocation, interface inheritance, and delegation. The chapter compares inheritance ("is a" relationships) with composition ("has a" relationships). A feature of the chapter is its several substantial case studies. In particular, a lengthy case study implements a point, circle and cylinder class hierarchy. Another lengthy case study implements an employee, boss, commission worker, piece worker and hourly worker class hierarchy.

The chapter explains polymorphic behavior. In object-oriented languages in general, when many subclasses are related through inheritance to a common superclass, each subclass object may be treated as a superclass object. This enables programs to be written in a general manner independent of the specific types of the subclass objects. New kinds of objects can be handled by the same program, thus making systems more extensible. Polymorphism enables programs to eliminate complex **Select Case** logic in favor of simpler "straight-line" logic. A screen manager of a video game, for example, can simply send a "draw" message to every object in a linked list of objects to be drawn. Each object knows how to draw itself. A new type of object can be added to the program without modifying that program as long as that new object also knows how to draw itself. This style of programming is typically used to implement today's popular GUIs. Visual Basic 6 does not support conventional implementation inheritance (as Java and C++ do, for example), but does allow polymorphism through interface inheritance. The chapter introduces interfaces—sets of methods that must be defined by any class that **Implements** the interfaces. Interfaces are useful for providing a basic set of methods to classes throughout the hierarchy. A feature of the chapter is its major polymorphism case studies.

The chapter exercises ask the student to discuss several conceptual issues and approaches, work with interfaces, modify the chapter's employee class—and pursue all these projects with polymorphic programming. The exercises also ask the student to compare the creation of new classes by inheritance vs. composition; to extend the inheritance hierarchies discussed in the chapter; to write an inheritance hierarchy for quadrilaterals, trapezoids, parallelograms, rectangles and squares; and to create an automobile hierarchy. Additional exercises challenge the student to develop classes for complex numbers, rational numbers, times, dates, Tic-Tac-Toe, a savings account and sets of integers.

**Chapter 17—ActiveX**—introduces the student to Microsoft's broad range of distributed computing technologies called ActiveX. The chapter discusses the foundations of ActiveX—Microsoft's component object model (COM), Microsoft's distributed component model (DCOM), and object linking and embedding (OLE).

In previous chapters, the student becomes familiar with using ActiveX controls to create GUIs and to perform other tasks. This chapter carefully demonstrates how to create ActiveX controls. We discuss the types of ActiveX controls that can be created using Visual Basic 6. We also discuss the key events in the lifetime of an ActiveX control.

Two key examples in the chapter create a **LabelScrollbar** control and digital **Clock** control. The **LabelScrollbar** combines a **Label** control and a scrollbar control. The digital **Clock** control draws the time on the control every second with the assistance of a **Timer** control. Each of these controls is written from "scratch."

We also introduce the **ActiveX Control Interface Wizard** for rapidly creating simple controls and for creating the foundation of more complex controls. We provide a step-by-step example that uses the **ActiveX Control Interface Wizard** to aid in the creation of the same **LabelScrollbar** created earlier in the chapter.

Special windows, called *property pages*, that contain a list of properties are also discussed. Many ActiveX controls provide property pages to allow the developer to conveniently set groups of properties. We demonstrate how to create property pages for the **LabelScrollbar** control using the **Property Page Wizard**.

The chapter also demonstrates how a Visual Basic 6 program can control Microsoft **Word** through a process called automation. In one example, we create a **Word** document without explicitly opening **Word**. In another example we use **Word**'s spelling checker to determine if a word is spelled correctly.

The exercises also ask the reader to create several controls as well as to enhance both the **LabelScrollbar** and **Clock** controls.

**Chapter 18—Database Management**—discusses how Visual Basic 6 can be used to access relational databases. Visual Basic 6 provides a variety of database-aware controls for displaying and manipulating database data. In this chapter we primarily focus on the **Microsoft ADO Data** control and the **Microsoft DataGrid** control. The examples in the chapter use the **Biblio.mdb** sample database provided with Visual Basic 6. For accessing the **Biblio.mdb** database, we provide an overview of *Structured Query Language* (*SQL*). We discuss the **Hierarchical FlexGrid** control, **DataList** control and **DataCombo** controls. We also discuss the **Data Environment Designer** for rapidly designing and implementing data-driven Visual Basic 6 applications.

**Chapter 19—Networking, the Internet and the World Wide Web**—deals with programs that can communicate over computer networks. What is a client? What is a server? How do clients ask servers to perform their services? How do servers give results back to clients? What is a URL (uniform resource locator)? How can a program load World Wide Web pages? How can I use Visual Basic 6 to develop collaborative applications?

This chapter gives you what you need to begin implementing client/server networked Visual Basic 6 programs immediately. We show how to write programs that "walk the Web." We discuss manipulating URLs, using a URL stream connection to read a file on a server, establishing simple clients and simple servers using stream sockets, client/server interaction with stream sockets and connectionless client/server interaction with datagrams.

The chapter concludes with a discussion of *Visual Basic Scripting* (*VBScript*) for enhancing World Wide Web documents. VBScript is a subset of Visual Basic 6. The chapter has a nice collection of exercises including several suggested modifications to the server examples.

If this is your first Visual Basic 6 book and you are an experienced computing professional, you may well be thinking, "Hey, this just keeps getting better and better. I can't wait to get started programming in this language. It will let me do all kinds of stuff I'd like to do, but that was never easy for me to do with the other languages I've used." You've got it right. Visual Basic 6 is an enabler. So if you liked the ActiveX and networking discussions, hold onto your hat, because Visual Basic 6 will also let you program multimedia applications.

**Chapter 20—Multimedia: Images, Animation and Audio**—deals with Visual Basic 6's capabilities for making computer applications come alive. It is remarkable that students in first programming courses will be writing applications with all these capabilities. The possibilities are intriguing. Imagine having access (over the Internet and through CD-ROM technology) to vast libraries of graphics images, audios and videos and being able to weave your own together with those in the libraries to form creative applications. Already more than half the new computers sold come "multimedia equipped." Within just a few years, new machines equipped for multimedia will be as common as machines with floppy disks today. We can't wait to see the kinds of term papers and classroom presentations students will be making when they have access to vast public domain libraries of images, drawings, voices, pictures, videos, animations and the like.

A "paper" when most of us were in the earlier grades was a collection of characters, possibly handwritten, possibly typewritten. A "paper" in just a few short years will become a multimedia "extravaganza" that makes the subject matter come alive. It will hold your interest, pique your curiosity, make you feel what the subjects of the paper felt when they were making history. Multimedia will make your science labs much more exciting. Textbooks will come alive. Instead of looking at a static picture of some phenomenon, you will watch that phenomenon occur in a colorful, animated, presentation with sounds, videos and various other effects. It will leverage the learning process. People will be able to learn more, learn it in more depth and experience more viewpoints.

The chapter discusses images and image manipulation, audios and animation. A feature of this chapter is an example that uses the **Microsoft Agent** control which allows the user to choose one of three predefined characters—*Merlin*, *Genie* and *Robby the Robot*. These characters actually speak and move (e.g., Robby the Robot removes his head and fixes himself with a screwdriver). Another key example of this chapter is the **Multimedia MCI** control—which we use to create a CD player and an AVI file player. We demonstrate the **RealAudio** control for receiving streaming audio and video from the Internet. We also demonstrate the **Marquee** control for scrolling an image from a specified URL. The chapter concludes with a discussion of the **ActiveMovie** control which enables an application to play video and sound in many different formats (i.e., MPEG, AVI, WAV, etc.).

Once you have read the chapter, you will be eager to try out these techniques, so we have included extensive exercises to challenge and entertain you; many of these make interesting term projects:

| Multimedia exercises | | |
| --- | --- | --- |
| Analog Clock | Dynamic Newsletter | On-Line Product Catalog |
| Artist | Horse Race | One-Armed Bandit |
| Automated Teller Machine | Image Flasher | Physics Demo: Kinetics |
| Background Audio | Image Zooming | Reaction Time Precision Tester |
| Calendar/Tickler File | Karaoke | Story Teller |
| Calling Attention to an Image | Limericks | Text Flasher |
| Digital Clock | Simpletron Simulator | Towers of Hanoi |
| Audio/Graphical Kaleidoscope | | |

You are going to have a great time attacking some of these problems! Some will take a few hours and some are great term projects. We see all kinds of opportunities for multimedia electives starting to appear in the university computing curriculum. You might compete with your classmates to develop the best solutions to several of these problems.

**Chapter 21—Data Structures, Collections, Dictionaries**—is particularly valuable in second- and third-level university courses. The chapter discusses the techniques used to create and manipulate dynamic data structures such as linked lists, stacks, queues (i.e., waiting lines) and trees. The chapter begins with discussions of self-referential classes and dynamic memory allocation. We proceed with a discussion of how to create and maintain various dynamic data structures. For each type of data structure, we present live-code programs and show sample outputs. The **Collection** object—an array-like object that can dynamically grow and shrink—is also discussed. We also discuss the **Dictionary** object for storing key/value pairs.

One problem when working with references is that students may have trouble visualizing the data structures and how their nodes are linked together. So we have included illustrations that show the links and the sequence in which they are created. The binary tree example is a nice capstone for the study of references and dynamic data structures. This example creates a binary tree; enforces duplicate elimination; and introduces recursive preorder, inorder and postorder tree traversals. Students have a genuine sense of accomplishment when they study and implement this example. They particularly appreciate seeing that the inorder traversal prints the node values in sorted order. The chapter exercises include a supermarket simulation using queueing, recursively searching a list, recursively printing a list backwards, binary tree deletion, level-order traversal of a binary tree, printing trees, inserting/deleting anywhere in a linked list, analyzing the performance of binary tree searching and sorting and implementing an indexed list class.

**Appendix A—Operator Precedence Chart**—lists each of the Visual Basic 6 operators and indicates their relative precedence. We list each operator and its full name on a separate line.

**Appendix B—ANSI Character Set**—lists the characters of the ANSI (American National Standards Institute) character set and indicates the character code value for each. ANSI includes ASCII (American Standard Code for Information Interchange) as a subset.

**Appendix C—Visual Basic Internet and World Wide Web Resources**—presents the best resources Abbey Deitel was able to track down for you on the Web. This is a great way for you to get into the "world of Visual Basic." The appendix lists various Visual Basic resources such as consortia, journals and companies that make various key Visual Basic-related products. The following chart summarizes the resources you will find by visiting the URLs Abbey recommends.

| | |
|---|---|
| add-ins | examples and demos |
| ActiveX controls | FAQs |
| books | games |
| *Carl and Gary's Visual Basic Home Page* | *Inside Visual Basic* |
| COM | jobs |
| **comp.lang.basic.visual** newsgroups | links |
| custom controls | mailing lists |
| *Developer.com* | *Microsoft COM home page* |
| DCOM | *Microsoft Developer Network (MSDN)* |
| COM+ | **microsoft.public.vb** newsgroups |
| conferences | *Microsoft Scripting Technologies VBScript site* |
| DirectX | *Microsoft Transaction Server* |
| discussion groups | *Microsoft VBA web site* |
| documentation | *Microsoft Visual Basic home page* |
| downloads | *MSDN Visual Basic page* |

| | |
|---|---|
| news | training information |
| newsgroups | tutorials |
| on-line help | user groups |
| product information | *VB Area* |
| publications | *VB Helper* |
| references | *VB Pro* |
| samples | *VBxtras* |
| shareware | *Visual Basic Developers Resource Centre* |
| source code | *Visual Basic Explorer* |
| support | *Visual Basic FAQs* |
| technical articles | *Visual Basic Game Programming* |
| *The Experts Exchange* | *Visual Basic On-line Magazine* |
| third party tools | *Visual Basic Tips and Tricks* |
| tips and tricks | |

**Appendix D—Number Systems—**discusses the binary (base 2), decimal (base 10), octal (base 8) and hexadecimal (base 16) number systems. This material is valuable for introductory courses in computer science and computer engineering. The appendix is presented with the same pedagogic learnings aids as the chapters of the book. A nice feature of the appendix is its 33 exercises, 19 of which are self-review exercises with answers.

## The Complete Visual Basic 6 Training Course

We have implemented an interactive, CD-ROM-based, software version of *Visual Basic 6 How to Program* called *The Visual Basic 6 Multimedia Cyber Classroom.* It is loaded with features for learning and reference. The *Cyber Classroom* is normally wrapped with *Visual Basic 6 How to Program* in the product called *The Complete Visual Basic 6 Training Course.* If you have already purchased the textbook, you can get a copy of the *Cyber Classroom* CD directly from Prentice Hall. Please call 1-800-811-0912 and ask for ISBN# 0-13-083116-6.

The *Visual Basic 6 Multimedia Cyber Classroom* contains an introductory presentation in which we overview the *Cyber Classroom* features. The live-code Visual Basic 6 example programs in the textbook truly "come alive" in the *Cyber Classroom.* We have placed executables for all these example programs "under the hood" of the *Cyber Classroom*, so if you are viewing a program and want to execute it, you simply click the lightning bolt icon and the program executes. You immediately see—and hear for the audio-based multimedia programs—the program's outputs. If you want to modify a program and see and hear the effects of your changes, simply click the floppy-disk icon that causes the source code to be "lifted off" the CD and "dropped into" one of your own directories so you can edit the program, recompile the program and try out your new version. Click the audio icon and Tem Nieto or Paul Deitel will talk about the program and "walk you through" the code. We provided line numbers in the source code listings to help you follow the audio discussions.

The *Cyber Classroom* contains a set of interactive, self-review questions that reinforce your understanding of the material. These questions are provided at the end of most sections. Also, solutions to many of the end-of-chapter exercises are provided. Please note that we cannot provide complete solutions to all the exercises as this product is a college textbook and the exercises are used by professors for homework assignments and exams. For professors, the *Instructor's Manual* provides a list of the solved exercises provided with the *Cyber Classroom*. **Again, please do not ask us for the Instructor's Manual. It is only available to college instructors teaching from the book. It can only be obtained by faculty members from Prentice Hall field representatives.**

The *Visual Basic 6 Multimedia Cyber Classroom* also provides many navigational aids including extensive hyperlinking. The *Cyber Classroom* remembers in a "history list" recent sections you have visited and allows you to move forward or backward in that history list. The thousands of index entries are hyperlinked to their text occurrences. Using the full-text-search feature, you can type a term and the *Cyber Classroom* will locate the occurrences of the term throughout the text. The *Table of Contents* entries are "hot," so clicking a chapter name immediately takes you to that chapter. The **Contents** menu provides direct access to all the sections in the current chapter, every chapter, every appendix, the *Bibliography* and the *Index*. Many people like to browse through our programming tips—*Common Programming Errors, Good Programming Practices, Look-and-Feel Observations, Performance Tips, Portability Tips, Software Engineering Observations* and *Testing-and-Debugging Tips*. The tips are all accessible via icons at the bottom of each chapter page.

Students and professional users of our *Multimedia Cyber Classrooms* tell us they like the interactivity and that the *Cyber Classrooms* are effective reference tools because of the extensive hyperlinking and other navigational features. We recently had an email from a person who said that he lives "in the boonies" and can not take a live course at a university, so the *Cyber Classroom* was the solution to his educational needs.

Professors have sent us emails indicating their students enjoy using the *Cyber Classrooms*, spend more time on the courses and master more of the material than in textbook-only courses. Also, the *Cyber Classroom* helps shrink lines outside professors' offices during office hours. Our other *Cyber Classrooms* include the *C & C++ Multimedia Cyber Classroom: Second Edition*, the *Java Multimedia Cyber Classroom: Second Edition* and plan to publish *Cyber Classroom* editions of our forthcoming *Visual J++ 6 How to Program* and *Visual C++ 6 How to Program* textbooks.

## Visual Basic 6.0 Working Model Edition Software

This book contains a CD-ROM that includes Microsoft's *Visual Basic 6.0 Working Model Edition* and the examples from the book. The CD also contains an HTML web page that you can load into your World Wide Web browser. The page contains links to the Deitel & Associates, Inc. web site, the Prentice Hall web site and the web sites listed in Appendix C.

The *Visual Basic 6.0 Working Model Edition* allows the reader to create and execute Visual Basic 6 programs. Although the *Working Model Edition* does not support every Visual Basic 6 feature presented in this book, it does support the vast majority of the features discussed. Some features covered in this book are specific to the *Professional Edition* or the *Enterprise Edition*.

We carefully tested every one of the 178 examples in the book using the *Visual Basic 6.0 Working Model Edition* and have compiled for you in the following table a list of the 7 programs that cannot be created/executed using this software and notes on six other examples that will run but may require special handling:

| Chapter | Figure | Problem |
|---------|--------|---------|
| Chapter 17 | 17.2 | Requires Microsoft **Word** to be installed with Service Release 1 (SR-1). |
| | 17.15, 17.33, 17.34, 17.45 | These work correctly, but may issue various error messages when the projects are loaded into the *Visual Basic 6.0 Working Model*. Simply dismiss the dialogs that are displayed. |
| | 17.47 and 17.50 | *Visual Basic 6.0 Working Model* does not allow the programmer to create ActiveX DLLs. |
| | 17.52 and 17.54 | The ActiveX features of these examples are only available in the Professional and Enterprise editions of Visual Basic. |
| | 17.55 | The ActiveX features of this example are only available in the Professional and Enterprise editions of Visual Basic. |
| Chapter 18 | 18.19 | The **Data Environment Designer** is only provided with the Professional and Enterprise editions of Visual Basic. |
| Chapter 20 | 20.1 | Microsoft Agent must be installed before this program can execute. Refer to the discussion in the text for more information on downloading Microsoft Agent. |
| | 20.9 | The **Animation** control is only provided with the Professional and Enterprise editions of Visual Basic. |

The following are the minimum system requirements to use the *Visual Basic 6 Working Model Edition:*

- A personal computer with a 486DX/66 processor. A Pentium 90 or higher microprocessor is recommended.
- Microsoft Windows 95, Windows 98 or Windows NT® 4.0 with service pack 3 (or later) installed.
- The minimum system memory for Windows 95, Windows 98 or Windows NT 4.0 is 24 MB. Microsoft recommends 32 MB or higher for all versions of Windows.
- The hard-disk space required is 52 MB for the typical installation and 65 MB for the maximum installation.
- Microsoft Internet Explorer™ 4.01 with Service Pack 1 (included). The additional hard disk space required for Microsoft Internet Explorer is 43 MB for the typical installation and 59 MB for the maximum installation.
- A CD-ROM drive.
- A monitor with VGA or higher-resolution (Super VGA recommended).
- Microsoft Mouse or a compatible pointing device.

### Installing the Visual Basic 6 Working Model Edition

On most Windows 95, Windows 98 and Windows NT 4.0 computers, the *Visual Basic 6 Working Model Edition* software begins its installation program automatically when the CD-ROM is inserted, so you can simply answer the questions asked by the installation program. In the event that the installation program does not execute automatically, run the **Setup.exe** program from the *Visual Basic 6 Working Model Edition* CD-ROM, then answer the questions asked by the installation program.

### Documentation for the Visual Basic 6 Working Model Edition

Microsoft provides the full documentation for Visual Basic on the World Wide Web at the *Microsoft Developer Network* web site

**http://msdn.microsoft.com/developer/default.htm**

When you browse this site, click the link *MSDN Library Online*. If you have not already registered for the *Microsoft Developer Network*, you will be asked to register now. Registration is free and you can only access the documentation if you register first. After you register, go back to the *Microsoft Developer Network* web site home page and click *MSDN Library Online*. You should now see the *MSDN Library Online* page. The documentation is arranged hierarchically. You can find the Visual Basic documentation under

```
Microsoft Developer Network Library Online
      Developer Products
         Visual Studio 6.0
            Visual Basic 6.0
```

## Acknowledgments

One of the great pleasures of writing a textbook is acknowledging the efforts of many people whose names may not appear on the cover, but whose hard work, cooperation, friendship, and understanding were crucial to the production of the book.

Three other people at Deitel & Associates, Inc. devoted long hours to this project. We would like to acknowledge the efforts of Chris Poirier, Barbara Deitel and Abbey Deitel.

Mr. Chris Poirier, a junior majoring in Computer Science at the University of Rhode Island, created many of the graphical illustrations presented in this book.

Barbara Deitel managed the preparation of the manuscript and coordinated with Prentice Hall the production of the book. Barbara's efforts are by far the most painstaking of what we do to develop books. She has infinite patience. She handled the endless details involved in publishing a 1000-page, two-color book; a 500-page instructor's manual and the 650 megabyte CD—*Visual Basic 6 Multimedia Cyber Classroom.* She used FrameMaker page-composition software to prepare the book. Barbara mastered this complex software package and did a marvelous job giving the book its clean style. She spent long hours researching the quotes at the beginning of each chapter. Barbara prepared every one of the 7800 page references in the 46-page index. She did all this in parallel with handling her extensive financial and administrative responsibilities at Deitel & Associates, Inc.

Abbey Deitel, a graduate of Carnegie Mellon University's industrial management program, and now pursuing a management career with Deitel & Associates, Inc., wrote Appendix C, "Visual Basic Internet and World Wide Web Resources" and suggested the title for the book. We asked Abbey to surf the World Wide Web and track down the best Visual Basic 6 sites. She used every major Web search engine and collected this information for you in Appendix C. For each resource and demo, Abbey has provided a brief explanation. She will be maintaining current versions of these resources and demo listings on our Web sites `http://www.prenhall.com/deitel` and `http://www.deitel.com` She asks that you send URLs for your favorite sites to her by email at `deitel@deitel.com` and she will post links to these on our sites.

We are fortunate to have been able to work on this project with a talented and dedicated team of publishing professionals at Prentice Hall. This book happened because of the encouragement, enthusiasm, and persistence of our computer science editor, Laura Steele, and her boss—our mentor at Prentice Hall one of the best friends we've ever had in publishing—Marcia Horton, Editor-in-Chief of Prentice-Hall's Engineering and Computer Science Division. Camille Trentacoste did a marvelous job as production manager.

The *Visual Basic 6 Multimedia Cyber Classroom* was developed in parallel with *Visual Basic 6 How to Program*. We sincerely appreciate the "new media" insight, savvy and technical expertise of our editor Mark Taub, Editor-in-Chief of Multimedia and Distance Learning and his able colleague, Karen McLean. Mark and Karen did a remarkable job bringing the *Visual Basic 6 Multimedia Cyber Classroom,* to publication under a tight schedule.

We owe special thanks to the creativity of Tamara Newnam Cavallo who did the art work for our programming tips icons and the cover. She created the delightful creature who shares with you the book's programming tips. Please help us name this endearing little bug.

We sincerely appreciate the efforts of our reviewers:

> Sean Alexander (Microsoft Corporation)
> Dave Glowacki (Microsoft Corporation)
> Phil Lee (Microsoft Corporation)
> William Vaughn (Microsoft Corporation)
> Scott Wiltamuth (Microsoft Corporation)
>
> Mehdi Abedinejad (Softbank Marketing Services, Inc.)
> David Bongiovanni (Bongiovanni Research & Technology, Inc.)
> Rockford Lhotka

Under an especially tight time schedule, they scrutinized every aspect of the text and made countless suggestions for improving the accuracy and completeness of the presentation.

We would like to acknowledge the extraordinary efforts of Susanne Peterson, our mentor at Microsoft. All the nice things we said about Susanne on the book's dedication page are absolutely true!

Our single most important source of information was Microsoft's *Visual Basic 6 Documentation* from the *Microsoft Developer Network (MSDN) Library for Visual Studio 6.0* which we worked from mostly during the beta releases of Visual Basic 6. We list the key portions of this documentation in the *Bibliography* at the end of this book. The single most valuable source of information for us within this documentation set was the *Visual Basic 6 Programmer's Guide*.

We would sincerely appreciate your comments, criticisms, corrections, and suggestions for improving the text. Please send your suggestions for improving and adding to our list of *Good Programming Practices, Common Programming Errors, Look-and-Feel*

*Observations, Testing-and-Debugging Tips, Performance Tips, Portability Tips* and *Software Engineering Observations.* We will acknowledge all contributors in the next edition of our book. Please address all correspondence to our email address:

**deitel@deitel.com**

We will respond immediately. Well, that's it for now. Welcome to the exciting world of Visual Basic 6 programming. We hope you enjoy this look at contemporary computer applications development using multimedia, databases, ActiveX, the Internet and the World Wide Web. Good luck!

*Dr. Harvey M. Deitel*
*Paul J. Deitel*
*Tem R. Nieto*

*Sudbury, Massachusetts*
*October, 1998*

## About the Authors

**Dr. Harvey M. Deitel**, CEO of Deitel & Associates, Inc., has 37 years experience in the computing field including extensive industry and academic experience. He is one of the world's leading computer science instructors and seminar presenters. Dr. Deitel earned B.S. and M.S. degrees from the Massachusetts Institute of Technology and a Ph.D. from Boston University. He worked on the pioneering virtual memory operating systems projects at IBM and MIT that developed techniques widely implemented today in systems like UNIX, Windows NT and OS/2. He has 20 years of college teaching experience including earning tenure and serving as the Chairman of the Computer Science Department at Boston College before founding Deitel & Associates, Inc. with Paul J. Deitel. He is author or co-author of several dozen books and multimedia packages and is currently writing many more. With translations published in Japanese, Russian, Spanish, Basic Chinese, Advanced Chinese, Korean, French, Polish and Portuguese. Dr. Deitel's texts have earned international recognition. Dr. Deitel has delivered professional seminars internationally to major corporations, government organizations and various branches of the military.

    **Paul J. Deitel**, Executive Vice President of Deitel & Associates, Inc., is a graduate of the Massachusetts Institute of Technology's Sloan School of Management where he studied Information Technology. Through Deitel & Associates, Inc. he has delivered Java, C and C++ courses for industry clients including Digital Equipment Corporation, Sun Microsystems, Rogue Wave Software, Software 2000, Computervision, Stratus, Fidelity, Cambridge Technology Partners, Open Environment Corporation, One Wave, Hyperion Software, Lucent Technologies, Adra Systems, Entergy, CableData Systems, NASA at the Kennedy Space Center, the National Severe Storm Laboratory and IBM. He has lectured on C++ and Java for the Boston Chapter of the Association for Computing Machinery. He teaches satellite-based Java courses through a cooperative venture of Deitel & Associates, Inc., Prentice Hall and the Technology Education Network. He is the co-author of fifteen books and multimedia packages with Harvey Deitel and is currently writing five more.

The Deitels are co-authors of the world's best-selling introductory college programming language textbooks, *C How to Program: Second Edition*, *C++ How to Program: Second Edition* and *Java How to Program: Second Edition*. The Deitels are also co-authors of the *C & C++ Multimedia Cyber Classroom: Second Edition*—Prentice Hall's first multimedia-based textbook, the *Java Multimedia Cyber Classroom: Second Edition* and the *Visual Basic 6 Multimedia Cyber Classroom* co-authored with their colleague Tem R. Nieto.

**Tem R. Nieto**, Senior Instructor with Deitel & Associates, Inc., is a graduate of the Massachusetts Institute of Technology where he studied engineering and computing. Through Deitel & Associates, Inc. he has delivered courses for industry clients including Sun Microsystems, Digital Equipment Corporation, Compaq, Stratus, Fidelity, Art Technology, Progress Software, Toys "R" Us, Operational Support Facility of the National Oceanographic and Atmospheric Administration, Jet Propulsion Laboratory, Nynex, Motorola, Federal Reserve Bank of Chicago, Banyan, Schlumberger, University of Notre Dame, NASA, various military installations and many others.

## About Deitel & Associates, Inc.

Deitel & Associates, Inc. is an internationally recognized corporate training and publishing organization specializing in programming languages, Internet/World Wide Web technology and object technology education. The company provides courses on Visual Basic, C++, Visual C++, Visual J++, C, Java, Internet and World Wide Web programming, and Object-Oriented Analysis and Design. The principals of Deitel & Associates, Inc. are Dr. Harvey M. Deitel and Paul J. Deitel. The company's clients include some of the world's largest computer companies, government agencies, branches of the military and business organizations. Through its publishing partnership with Prentice Hall, Deitel & Associates, Inc. publishes leading-edge programming textbooks, professional books, interactive, CD-ROM based multimedia *Cyber Classrooms*, satellite courses and World Wide Web courses. Deitel & Associates, Inc. and each of the authors can be reached via email at

        `deitel@deitel.com`

To learn more about Deitel & Associates, Inc., its public seminar schedule and its worldwide on-site course curriculum, visit:

        `http://www.deitel.com`

To learn more about Deitel & Deitel/Prentice Hall publications, visit:

        `http://www.prenhall.com/deitel`

For a current list of Deitel/Prentice Hall publications including textbooks and multimedia packages, and for complete worldwide ordering information, please see the last few pages of this book.

# 1

# Computing Concepts

## Objectives

- To understand fundamental computer concepts.
- To understand the notions of personal computing, distributed computing and client/server computing.
- To become familiar with different types of programming languages.
- To become familiar with the history of the Visual Basic programming language.
- To understand the role Visual Basic and VBScript play in developing applications for the Internet and the World Wide Web.
- To understand the kinds of multimedia applications you can create with Visual Basic, including graphics, images, animation, audio and video.
- To understand the role ActiveX components play in developing Visual Basic Applications.

*High thoughts must have high language.*
Aristophanes

*Our life is frittered away by detail ... Simplify, simplify.*
Henry Thoreau

*Things are always at their best in their beginning.*
Blaise Pascal

## Outline

## 1.1 Introduction

Welcome to Visual Basic! We have worked hard to create what we hope will be an informative, entertaining and challenging learning experience for you. The core of the book emphasizes achieving program clarity through the proven techniques of structured programming, event-driven programming and object-oriented programming. Nonprogrammers will learn programming the right way from the beginning. We have attempted to write in a clear and straightforward manner. The book is abundantly illustrated. Perhaps most important, the book presents hundreds of working Visual Basic programs and shows the outputs produced when those programs are run on a computer.

The first five chapters introduce the fundamentals of computers, computer programming, and the Visual Basic computer programming language. Novices who have taken our courses tell us that the material in those chapters presents a solid foundation for the deeper treatment of Visual Basic in Chapters 6 through 21. Experienced programmers typically read the first five chapters quickly and then find that the treatment of Visual Basic in Chapters 6 through 21 is both rigorous and challenging.

Many experienced programmers have told us that they appreciate our treatment of structured programming. Often they have been programming in structured languages like COBOL or Pascal, but because they were never formally introduced to the principles of structured programming, they are not writing the best possible code in these languages. As they review structured programming in the early chapters of this book, they are able to improve their programming styles. So whether you are a novice or an experienced programmer, there is much here to inform, entertain, and challenge you.

Most people are familiar with the exciting things computers do. Using this textbook, you will learn how to command computers to do those things. It is *software* (i.e., the instructions you write to command the computer to perform *actions* and make *decisions*) that controls computers (often referred to as *hardware*), and Visual Basic is one of today's most popular software development languages.

The use of computers is increasing in almost every field of endeavor. In an era of steadily rising costs, computing costs have been decreasing dramatically because of the rapid developments in both hardware and software technology. Computers that might have filled large rooms and cost millions of dollars 15 years ago can now be inscribed on the surfaces of silicon chips smaller than a fingernail that cost perhaps a few dollars each. Ironically, silicon is one of the most abundant materials on the earth—it is an ingredient in common sand. Silicon chip technology has made computing so economical that more than 200 million general-purpose computers are in use worldwide, helping people in business, industry, government and their personal lives. That number could easily double in the next few years.

Your peers from just a few years ago probably learned the programming methodology called *structured programming*. You will learn structured programming as well as the exciting newer methodologies *event-driven programming and object-oriented programming*. Why do we teach these methodologies? We certainly anticipate that object-oriented programming and event-driven programming will be the key programming methodologies for the next decade. So you will work with many objects and events in this course. But you will discover that the internal structure of those objects is often best built using structured programming techniques. Also, the logic of manipulating objects is occasionally best expressed with structured programming.

## 1.2  What Is a Computer?

A *computer* is a device capable of performing computations and making logical decisions at speeds millions, and even billions, of times faster than human beings can. For example, many of today's personal computers can perform hundreds of millions of additions per second. A person operating a desk calculator might require a lifetime to complete the same number of calculations that a powerful personal computer can perform in 1 second. (Points to ponder: How would you know whether the person added the numbers correctly? How would you know whether the computer added the numbers correctly?) Today's fastest *supercomputers* can perform hundreds of billions of additions per second—about as many calculations as hundreds of thousands of people could perform in one year! And trillion-instruction-per-second computers are already functioning in research laboratories!

Computers process *data* under the control of sets of instructions called *computer programs*. These computer programs guide the computer through orderly sets of actions specified by people called *computer programmers*.

The various *devices* (such as the *keyboard*, *screen*, *disks*, *memory* and *processing units*) that comprise a computer system are referred to as *hardware*. The computer programs that run on a computer are referred to as *software*. Hardware costs have been declining dramatically in recent years, to the point that personal computers have become a commodity. Unfortunately, software development costs have been rising steadily as programmers develop ever more powerful and complex applications without being able to improve the technology of software development. In this book you will learn proven software development methods that can reduce software development costs—*structured programming, top-down stepwise refinement, functionalization, event-driven programming* and *object-oriented programming*.

## 1.3 Computer Organization

Regardless of differences in physical appearance, virtually every computer may be envisioned as being divided into six *logical units* or sections. These are:

1. *Input unit.* This is the "receiving" section of the computer. It obtains information (data and computer programs) from various *input devices* and places this information at the disposal of the other units so that the information may be processed. Most information is entered into computers today through typewriter-like keyboards and "mouse" devices. In the future, perhaps most information will be entered by speaking to your computer and by video.

2. *Output unit.* This is the "shipping" section of the computer. It takes information that has been processed by the computer and places it on various *output devices* to make the information available for use outside the computer. Most information output from computers today is displayed on screens, printed on paper, or used to control other devices.

3. *Memory unit.* This is the rapid access, relatively low-capacity "warehouse" section of the computer. It retains information that has been entered through the input unit so that the information may be made immediately available for processing when it is needed. The memory unit also retains information that has already been processed until that information can be placed on output devices by the output unit. The memory unit is often called either *memory* or *primary memory*.

4. *Arithmetic and logic unit (ALU).* This is the "manufacturing" section of the computer. It is responsible for performing calculations such as addition, subtraction, multiplication, and division. It contains the decision mechanisms that allow the computer for example, to compare two items from the memory unit to determine whether or not they are equal.

5. *Central processing unit (CPU).* This is the "administrative" section of the computer. It is the computer's coordinator and is responsible for supervising the operation of the other sections. The CPU tells the input unit when information should be read into the memory unit, tells the ALU when information from the memory unit should be utilized in calculations, and tells the output unit when to send information from the memory unit to certain output devices.

6. *Secondary storage unit.* This is the long-term, high-capacity "warehousing" section of the computer. Programs or data not actively being used by the other units are normally placed on secondary storage devices (such as disks) until they are again needed, possibly hours, days, months, or even years later. Information in secondary storage takes much longer to access than information in primary memory. The cost per unit of secondary storage is much less than the cost per unit of primary memory.

## 1.4 Evolution of Operating Systems

Early computers were capable of performing only one *job* or *task* at a time. This form of computer operation is often called single-user *batch processing*. The computer runs a single program at a time while processing data in groups or *batches*. In these early systems, users generally submitted their jobs to the computer center on decks of punched cards. Users often had to wait hours or even days before printouts were returned to their desks.

Software systems called *operating systems* were developed to help make it more convenient to use computers. Early operating systems managed the smooth transition between jobs. This minimized the time it took for computer operators to switch between jobs, and hence increased the amount of work, or *throughput*, computers could process.

As computers became more powerful, it became evident that single-user batch processing rarely utilized the computer's resources efficiently. Instead, it was thought that many jobs or tasks could be made to *share* the resources of the computer to achieve better utilization. This is called *multiprogramming*. Multiprogramming involves the "simultaneous" operation of many jobs on the computer—the computer shares its resources among the jobs competing for its attention. With early multiprogramming operating systems, users still submitted jobs on decks of punched cards and waited hours or days for results.

In the 1960s, several groups in industry and the universities pioneered *timesharing* operating systems. Timesharing is a special case of multiprogramming in which users access the computer through *terminals*, typically devices with keyboards and screens. In a typical timesharing computer system, there may be dozens or even hundreds of users sharing the computer at once. The computer does not actually run all the users simultaneously. Rather, it runs a small portion of one user's job and then moves on to service the next user. The computer does this so quickly that it may provide service to each user several times per second. Thus the users' programs *appear* to be running simultaneously. An advantage of timesharing is that the user receives almost immediate responses to requests rather than having to wait long periods for results as with previous modes of computing.

## 1.5 Personal Computing, Distributed Computing, and Client/Server Computing

In 1977, Apple Computer popularized the phenomenon of *personal computing*. Initially, it was a hobbyist's dream. Computers became economical enough for people to buy them for their own personal or business use. In 1981, IBM, the world's largest computer vendor, introduced the IBM Personal Computer. Literally overnight, personal computing became legitimate in business, industry and government organizations.

But these computers were "stand-alone" units—people did their work on their own machines and then transported disks back and forth to share information (sometimes called "sneakernet"). Although early personal computers were not powerful enough to timeshare several users, these machines could be linked together in computer networks, sometimes over telephone lines and sometimes in *local area networks* (*LANs*) within an organization. This led to the phenomenon of *distributed computing* in which an organization's computing, instead of being performed strictly at some central computer installation, is distributed over networks to the sites at which the real work of the organization is performed. Personal computers were powerful enough to handle the computing requirements of individual users, and to handle the basic communications tasks of passing information back and forth electronically.

Today's most powerful personal computers are as powerful as the million-dollar machines of just a decade ago. The most powerful desktop machines—called *workstations*—provide individual users with enormous capabilities. Information is easily shared across computer networks where computers called *servers* offer a common store of programs and data that may be used by *client computers* distributed throughout the network, hence the term *client/server computing*. C and C++ have become the programming languages of choice for writing software for operating systems, for computer networking and for distributed client/server applications. Today's popular operating systems, such as UNIX and Windows NT, provide the kinds of capabilities discussed in this section. Visual Basic has become the premier client/server applications development language on Microsoft-based systems.

## 1.6 Machine Languages, Assembly Languages, and High-level Languages

Programmers write instructions in various programming languages, some directly understandable by the computer and others that require intermediate *translation* steps. Hundreds of computer languages are in use today. These may be divided into three general types:

1.  Machine languages

2.  Assembly languages

3.  High-level languages

Any computer can directly understand only its own *machine language*. Machine language is the "natural language" of a particular computer. It is defined by the hardware design of that computer. Machine languages generally consist of strings of numbers (ultimately reduced to 1s and 0s) that instruct computers to perform their most elementary operations one at a time. Machine languages are *machine-dependent* (i.e., a particular machine language can be used on only one type of computer). Machine languages are cumbersome for humans, as can be seen by the following section of a machine language program that adds overtime pay to base pay and stores the result in gross pay:

```
+1300042774
+1400593419
+1200274027
```

As computers became more popular, it became apparent that writing machine language programs was simply too slow and tedious a process for most programmers. Instead of using the strings of numbers that computers could directly understand, programmers began using English-like abbreviations to represent the elementary operations of the computer. These English-like abbreviations formed the basis of *assembly languages. Translator programs* called *assemblers* were developed to convert assembly language programs to machine language at computer speeds. The following section of an assembly language program also adds overtime pay to base pay and stores the result in gross pay, but more clearly than its machine language equivalent:

```
LOAD    BASEPAY
ADD     OVERPAY
STORE   GROSSPAY
```

Although such code is clearer to humans, it is incomprehensible to computers until translated to machine language.

Computer usage increased rapidly with the advent of assembly languages, but these still required many instructions to accomplish even the simplest tasks. To speed the programming process, *high-level languages* were developed in which single statements could be written to accomplish substantial tasks. The translator programs that convert high-level language programs into machine language are called *compilers*. High-level languages allow programmers to write instructions that look almost like everyday English and contain commonly used mathematical notations. A payroll program written in a high-level language might contain a statement such as

```
grossPay = basePay + overTimePay
```

Obviously, high-level languages are much more desirable from the programmer's standpoint than either machine languages or assembly languages. Visual Basic is the world's most widely used high-level language.

The process of compiling a high-level language program into machine language can take a considerable amount of computer time. *Interpreter* programs were developed that can directly execute high-level language programs without the need for compiling those programs into machine language. Although interpreted programs run slower than compiled programs, interpreted programs begin execution immediately without suffering a some-times substantial compilation delay. Visual Basic is an example of an interpreted language. Interpreters are popular in program-development environments in which programs are recompiled frequently and executed only briefly as new features are added and errors are corrected. Once a program is developed, a compiled version can be produced to run most efficiently. With recent versions of Visual Basic, programmers can compile Visual Basic programs to produce machine language *executables* that run at the high speeds previously attributed only to languages like C and C++. This and the many exciting new Visual Basic 6 features will secure Visual Basic's position as the world's foremost application development language for many years to come.

## 1.7  History of Visual Basic

Visual Basic evolved from BASIC (Beginner's All-purpose Symbolic Instruction Code). BASIC was developed in the mid-1960s by Professors John Kemeny and Thomas Kurtz of Dartmouth College as a language for writing simple programs. BASIC's primary purpose was to help people learn how to program.

The widespread use of BASIC with various types of computers (sometimes called hardware platforms) led to many enhancements to the language. With the development of the Microsoft Windows *graphical user interface* (*GUI*) in the late 1980s and the early 1990s, the natural evolution of BASIC was Visual Basic, which was created by Microsoft Corporation in 1991.

Until Visual Basic appeared, developing Microsoft Windows-based applications was a difficult and cumbersome process. Visual Basic greatly simplifies Windows application development. Since 1991 six versions have been released, with the latest—Visual Basic 6—appearing in September 1998.

## 1.8   Other High-level Languages

Hundreds of high-level languages have been developed, but only a few have achieved broad acceptance. *FORTRAN* (FORmula TRANslator) was developed by IBM Corporation between 1954 and 1957 to be used for scientific and engineering applications that require complex mathematical computations. FORTRAN is still widely used, especially in engineering applications.

*COBOL* (COmmon Business Oriented Language) was developed in 1959 by a group of computer manufacturers and government and industrial computer users. COBOL is used primarily for commercial applications that require precise and efficient manipulation of large amounts of data. Today, about half of all business software is still programmed in COBOL. Approximately 1 million people are actively writing COBOL programs. Use of COBOL had been declining dramatically for many years. But in the late 1990s COBOL programmers were once again in big demand to help repair the many software systems from the widely publicized "Year 2000" computer problem (or glitch).

*C* was developed by Dennis Richie at Bell Laboratories in 1972. C is one of the most popular system implementation languages in industry; it was first used to develop the UNIX operating system.

*Pascal* was designed at about the same time as C. It was created by Professor Nicklaus Wirth and was intended for academic use. We will say more about Pascal in the next section.

*C++*, an extension of C, was developed by Bjarne Stroustrup in the early 1980s at Bell Laboratories. C++ provides a number of features that "spruce up" the C language and add capabilities for doing so-called object-oriented programming (OOP). Many people believe that OOP can greatly improve the software development process. C++ has become the dominant systems implementation language.

The languages mentioned above are *text-based languages*. Text-based languages do not allow the user to work directly with graphics. A special software package is often required to "add" the graphical elements. These software packages often require the programmer to write many lines of code in addition to normal program code.

Visual Basic is an example of a *graphical-based language*. A graphical-based language allows the user to work directly with graphics. Graphical-based languages can be used to develop Windows programs quickly without having to learn an additional software package.

*Java* was developed by Sun Microsystems and released in 1995. Java is based on C and C++ and incorporates a number of features from other object-oriented languages. Java includes extensive libraries for doing multimedia, networking, multithreading, graphics, graphical user interface development, database access, distributed computing and much more. Microsoft's version of Java is called Visual J++. Many people believe that Java and Visual J++ will be the most significant long-term competitors to Visual Basic.

*PowerBuilder*, developed by Powersoft Corporation, and *Delphi,* developed by Borland International, are languages that compete with Visual Basic but that have a much smaller market share.

## 1.9 Structured Programming

During the 1960s, many large software development efforts encountered severe difficulties. Software schedules were typically late, costs greatly exceeded budgets, and the finished products were unreliable. People began to realize that software development was a far more complex activity than they had imagined. Research activity in the 1960s resulted in the evolution of *structured programming*—a disciplined approach to writing programs that are clearer than unstructured programs, easier to test and debug, and easier to modify.

Chapters 4 and 5 discuss the principles of structured programming with Visual Basic's control structures.

One of the more tangible results of this research was the development of the Pascal programming language by Nicklaus Wirth in 1971. Pascal, named after the seventeenth-century mathematician and philosopher Blaise Pascal, was designed for teaching structured programming in academic environments and rapidly became the preferred programming language in most colleges. Unfortunately, the language in its early years lacked many features needed to make it useful in commercial, industrial, and government applications, so it did not become widely accepted in these environments.

The *Ada* programming language was developed under the sponsorship of the United States Department of Defense (DOD) during the 1970s and early 1980s. Hundreds of separate languages were being used to produce DOD's massive command-and-control software systems. DOD wanted a single language that would fulfill most of its needs. Pascal was chosen as a base, but the final Ada language is quite different from Pascal. The language was named after Lady Ada Lovelace, daughter of the poet Lord Byron. Lady Lovelace is generally credited with writing the world's first computer program in the early 1800s (for the Analytical Engine, a mechanical computing device designed by Charles Babbage). One important capability of Ada is *multitasking (called multithreading in other languages)*; this allows programmers to specify that many activities are to occur in parallel in individual programs. The other high-level languages we have discussed generally allow programs to perform only one activity at a time. (Remember that Java does support multithreading.)

Visual Basic does not directly support multithreading, but multithreaded Visual Basic programs can be created using *Win32 Application Programming Interface (API)* functions. The Win32 API is part of Windows and can be used by any Windows program.

## 1.10  What Is Visual Basic?

Visual Basic is a Microsoft Windows programming language. Visual Basic programs are created in an *Integrated Development Environment (IDE)*. The IDE allows the programmer to create, run and debug Visual Basic programs conveniently. IDEs allow a programmer to create working programs in a fraction of the time that it would normally take to code programs without using IDEs. We discuss the Visual Basic IDE in Chapter 2. The process of rapidly creating an application is typically referred to as *Rapid Application Development (RAD)*. Visual Basic is the world's most widely used RAD language.

Visual Basic is derived from the BASIC programming language. Visual Basic is a distinctly different language providing powerful features such as graphical user interfaces, event handling, access to the Win32 API, object-oriented features, error handling, structured programming, and much more.

*Software Engineering Observation 1.1*

*The Visual Basic IDE allows Windows programs to be created without the need for the programmer to be a Windows programming expert.*

Microsoft provides several versions of Visual Basic, namely the *Learning Edition*, the *Professional Edition* and the *Enterprise Edition*. The Learning Edition provides fundamental programming capabilities. The Professional Edition provides a much richer set of programming capabilities than the Learning Edition and is the choice of many programmers to write Visual Basic applications. The Enterprise Edition is used for developing large-scale computing systems that meet the needs of substantial organizations. Students using this book will prefer the Learning Edition or the Professional Edition. Programmers working in industry will prefer the Professional Edition or the Enterprise Edition.

Visual Basic is an interpreted language. However, the Professional and Enterprise Edition allows Visual Basic code to be compiled to *native code* (i.e., machine language code).

## 1.11  General Notes About Visual Basic and This Book

Experienced programmers sometimes take pride in being able to create some weird, contorted, convoluted usage of a language. This is a poor programming practice. It makes programs more difficult to read, more likely to behave strangely, more difficult to test and debug, and more difficult to adapt to changing requirements. This book is geared for novice programmers, so we stress *clarity*. The following is our first "good programming practice."

**Good Programming Practice 1.1**

*Write your Visual Basic programs in a simple and straightforward manner. This is sometimes referred to as KIS ("keep it simple"). Do not "stretch" the language by trying bizarre usages.*

We will include many of these tips throughout the text to highlight those practices that can help you write programs that are clearer, more understandable, higher in performance, more maintainable and easier to test and debug. These practices are only guidelines; you will, no doubt, develop your own preferred programming style. We will also highlight *Common Programming Errors* (problems to watch out for so you do not make these errors in your programs), *Performance Tips* (techniques that will help you write programs that run faster and use less memory), *Portability Tips* (techniques that will help you write programs that can run, with little or no modification, on a variety of computers), *Software Engineering Observations* (thoughts and concepts that affect and improve the overall architecture of a software system, and particularly, of large software systems), *Testing and Debugging Tips* (techniques that will help you remove bugs from your programs and, more important, techniques that will help you write bug-free programs to begin with) and *Look-and-Feel Observations* (explanations of how to write Visual Basic programs that conform to accepted standards in the appearance and operation of Microsoft Windows programs).

We have done a careful walkthrough of Microsoft Visual Basic documentation and audited our presentation against it for completeness and accuracy. However, Visual Basic is a rich language, and there are some subtleties in the language and some advanced subjects we have not covered. If you need additional technical details, we suggest that you read the most current draft of the Microsoft documentation.

**Portability Tip 1.1**

*Some features of the current versions of Visual Basic are not compatible with older Visual Basic implementations, so you may find that some of the programs in this text do not work with older versions.*

**Good Programming Practice 1.2**

*Read the documentation for the version of Visual Basic you are using. Refer to these manuals frequently to be sure that you are aware of the rich collection of Visual Basic features and are using these features correctly.*

## 1.12  A Tour of the Book

You are about to study the most widely used Microsoft Windows programming language in the world. Mastering Visual Basic will help you develop powerful business and personal computer applications software. In this section we take a tour of the many exciting capabilities of Visual Basic you will study in *Visual Basic 6 How to Program*.

### *Chapter 1: Computing Concepts*

Chapter 1, "Computing Concepts," discusses the history of computing and introduces key basic computing concepts. You do not do any programming in Chapter 1. Rather, you are introduced to the "lingo" of the field to help you appreciate the material in the remaining chapters.

### *Chapter 2: Integrated Development Environment*

Of course, you are reading this book to learn how to program computers with Visual Basic 6. Visual Basic uses a technique called *visual programming* which makes developing Windows-based programs fun to do as well as a more productive and efficient process. Chapter 2, "Integrated Development Environment," discusses Visual Basic's Integrated Development Environment (IDE) tools and walks you step-by-step through a simple example of visual programming. You will be amazed at how easy it is to develop programs visually. In this example, we will let Visual Basic do most of the work for you.

### *Chapter 3: Introduction to Visual Basic Programming*

In Chapter 3, "Introduction to Visual Basic Programming," we begin the serious discussion of programming in Visual Basic. You will learn how to read (or *input*) data from the keyboard, perform simple calculations, and write (or *output*) data to the screen. You will also learn about how data is represented inside computers as integers, numbers with decimal points, character strings and the like.

### *Chapters 4 and 5: Control Structures Parts I and II*

When we write computer programs, we are concerned primarily with two things, namely the *actions* we would like the computer to perform and the *order* in which we would like the computer to perform those actions. In Chapter 4, "Control Structures: Part I," and Chapter 5, "Control Structures: Part II," we discuss various types of actions, including *input actions*, *calculation actions* and *output actions*. We also discuss how to specify the order in which a program's actions should be performed. This is done by using *control structures*, namely *sequence structures* (which specify several actions should be performed one after the other "in sequence"), *selection structures* (which enable a program to choose among different actions to be performed under different conditions) and *repetition structures* (which enable a program to repeat actions until the program determines that no further repetitions are needed).

### *Chapter 6: Sub Procedures and Function Procedures*

Most programs that students write are small. But "real-world" programs that programmers write in industry can be quite large. Experience has shown that writing large programs as one large piece, so-called *monolithic construction*, can be a recipe for disaster. Such programs are hard to write, test, debug, document and update with new features (such updating is often called *program maintenance*). It is best to break large programs into sets of small, simple, cooperating components, a technique called *divide and conquer*. Chapter 6, "Sub Procedures and Function Procedures," discusses the packaging of these small cooperating pieces into units called *procedures*. Programs written this way are often much easier to develop and maintain than monolithic programs.

### Chapter 7: Arrays
The pieces of data that our programs process are sometimes quite independent of one another, such as a person's weight and a salesperson's sales for last month. Often, however, programs process data items that are closely related, such as the weights of all the players on one team, or the set of a salesperson's monthly sales figures for the last twelve months. In Visual Basic programs it is common to store sets of related data items in *arrays*. Chapter 7, "Arrays," discusses how to create and manipulate the data we store in arrays.

### Chapter 8: Strings, Dates and Times
We all use characters, words and sentences. Computers do not just process numeric data. Chapter 8, "Strings, Dates and Times" explains how to manipulate individual characters as well as strings of characters that form units like words and sentences. These techniques are especially useful to application developers who create software like word processors, electronic mail packages and the page composition packages like the one we used to write and typeset this book.

### Chapter 9: Graphics
Everyone loves to draw. Chapter 9, "Graphics," discusses how to create Visual Basic programs that draw. You can create programs that let the user draw with devices like the mouse. You will learn how to command Visual Basic to draw lines, arcs, circles, ellipses, rectangles and many other common shapes. Today, many artists (including the one who created the cover of this book and our friendly bug characters) generate their art with the assistance of graphics software packages.

### Chapter 10: Basic Graphical User Interface Concepts and Chapter 11: Advanced Graphical User Interface Concepts
People communicate with the world around them through the five senses of sight, sound, smell, touch and taste. Strangely, until only 15 years ago, most people communicated with computers through typing and reading individual characters. This is extremely slow (referred to as "low bandwidth" in computer parlance) because most of us are not particularly good typists and because individual characters do not convey much information. It is also slow because commanding the computer by typing characters requires computer users to memorize long lists of complicated commands, so users are often forced to plow through lengthy documentation to locate the appropriate keystroke sequences. In 1984, this situation changed dramatically when *Apple Computer* introduced *graphical user interface (GUI)* technology with its *Macintosh* line of personal computers. This technology, based on pioneering research done at *Xerox's Palo Alto Research Center (PARC)* in the early 1970s, made it much easier for users to communicate with computers. People began using the *mouse* device to point to things on the screen representing the actions the computer should take (such as opening, saving, printing or closing a file), and clicking a mouse button to select a desired action. The term *user friendly* became extremely popular and within a few years Microsoft followed with its Windows operating system, bringing user-friendly graphical user interfaces to the vast majority of personal computers. Chapter 10, "Basic

Graphical User Interface Concepts," and Chapter 11, "Advanced Graphical User Interface Concepts," discuss how to create user-friendly graphical user interfaces with Visual Basic. You will learn how to display *menus*, *buttons*, *text boxes* and many other *GUI components* (also called *controls*) to make your applications user friendly. Hold onto your seats, though, because as powerful as GUI is, it is not the "ultimate" user interface. We will say more about this when we discuss Chapter 20, "Multimedia," below.

### Chapter 12: Mouse and Keyboard

In Chapter 12, "Mouse and Keyboard," you will learn much more about working with the mouse and the keyboard. We discuss how to change the shape of the *mouse pointer*, how to process *mouse events* (such as *pressing a mouse button down*, *releasing a mouse button* and *moving the mouse*), how to interact with mouse devices that have several buttons, how to use the mouse to *drag* items on the screen and *drop* them somewhere else, and how to respond to various *keyboard events*.

### Chapter 13: Error Handling and Debugging

Most of us are familiar with "Murphy's Law," which states: "If something can go wrong it will, and probably at the most inopportune time." Given that many of today's computers perform hundreds of millions of operations per second, things can go wrong awfully fast and incredibly often. Chapter 13, "Error Handling and Debugging," discusses how to track down and remove errors from Visual Basic programs (a processing called *debugging*). Perhaps even more important, the chapter discusses how to deal with exceptional situations that occur as a program runs. The point is that we need our systems to keep running, even in the face of problems that may develop as the programs run. Businesses such as supermarkets depend on computers to keep running to prevent customers from being inconvenienced, so we build business-critical systems. Organizations in the United States like NASA (the National Aeronautics and Space Administration) and the FAA (Federal Aviation Administration) have a deeper responsibility. If computers guiding spaceflights or commercial airliners fail, human lives could be lost, so NASA, the FAA, the military and other organizations are concerned with *mission-critical computing*. Visual Basic is a serious programming language for developing business-critical applications. Mission-critical applications are still more likely to be programmed in languages like C, C++ and Ada. Chapter 13 discusses Visual Basic features that improve program reliability.

### Chapter 14: Sequential File Processing

When we use computers to process information, we may need to store that information for long periods of time on the computer. Such information is said to be *persistent* and is typically stored in *files* on devices like *hard disks*. Perhaps the simplest way to store persistent information is in *sequential files*. These files are organized to be processed in much the same way as you would read a novel. You read the first chapter first, the next chapter second, the next chapter third, etc. Chapter 14, "Sequential File Processing," discusses how to create and manipulate sequential files. Sequential files are appropriate when you are going to process most or all of the data in the file when you run a particular application.

### Chapter 15: Records and Random-Access Files

Another popular means for storing files is *random-access files,* in which individual pieces of data may be referenced without having to process sequentially all of the information that precedes that data in the file. Random-access files are particularly effective for *transaction-*

*processing systems* such as point-of-sale systems in stores and supermarkets. When a checkout person runs your milk carton by a bar-code reader, a computer system "looks up" the number coded in the bar code in a local random-access file to determine the name of the product and its price. This information is then used to prepare your receipt and determine your total bill. One store could have tens of thousands of different items. Sequential files would be inappropriate for this type of application because reading virtually every entry in the file before the one you need could take a great deal of time, creating long lines at checkout counters. Chapter 15, "Records and Random-Access Files," presents several live-code examples of creating and manipulating data stored in random-access files.

### Chapter 16: Object-Oriented Programming

People time is precious. Programmer time is precious. Programmers need programming languages that will enable them to design and build systems quickly and effectively. If the people who build houses had to work with the individual molecules that go into all the components of a house, it would take forever to build houses. Home builders have long recognized that it is best to build houses from two-by-fours, bricks, doors, windows and other prebuilt components, rather than working directly with the molecules that comprise these components. Strangely, programmers have tended to build computer software systems from "software molecules." Given the complexity and volume of software we need to build to meet the world's software demand, it is no longer feasible for us to work at this level of detail. We need to work at the levels of "software doors, windows, bricks and two-by-fours." This is what object technology lets us do, namely work with software components, many that are prebuilt and others that we build ourselves and share with our colleagues. This enables us to build software faster, and if we use high-quality components, better. Chapter 16, "Object-Oriented Programming," discusses programming with components, both the kinds you create yourselves and the kinds that other people have created and you can reuse.

### Chapter 17: ActiveX

For many of our readers, Chapter 17, "COM, DCOM and ActiveX," is the most important chapter in the book. In Chapter 16, we discuss the virtues of object technology. Chapter 17 discusses Microsoft's object packaging technology called *ActiveX*. Visual Basic 6 enables you to build your own ActiveX components and to reuse the thousands of ActiveX components that have been created by other programmers worldwide and made available either free or for a fee. ActiveX components make programming more pleasant. They give you access to powerful, reusable, reliable software components that perform a great variety of the most common software tasks. *Component-oriented software construction* can be tens or even hundreds of times faster than conventional software development methods. Not only can you program faster with ActiveX components, but you can also program in areas in which you may not have a great deal of expertise. ActiveX components *encapsulate*, or hide, complexity from programmers in much the same way that a car hides complexity from a driver. Despite the fact that we know very little about how cars work "on the inside," we are able to drive safely and effectively by performing simple actions such as pressing the accelerator peddle, pressing the brake peddle and turning the steering wheel. This is what object technology and ActiveX components are all about. To be able to use a car effectively, we take courses like "Driver's Ed," rather than taking courses in mechanical engineering that explain the internal operation of cars. To be able to use ActiveX components effectively, we study how to use them, rather than their internal construction. We will learn that ActiveX components are more than just the "raw objects" we discuss in Chapter 16—ActiveX components are packaged for ease of use over the Internet! To make ActiveX technology even more powerful, you can build ActiveX components with any of Microsoft's key programming languages like Visual Basic, Visual C++ and Visual J++. Also, no matter which of these languages is used to build an ActiveX component, the component can be used in any of them. Thus, when you learn ActiveX technology, you are gaining access to a huge world of component-oriented software construction.

### Chapter 18: Database Management
We've mentioned in Chapters 14 and 15 how data is stored and manipulated in sequential files and random-access files. These are "physical" views. They are oriented to the actual way the data is physically stored and made available. The trend in the computer field is to get away from how things are represented in the computer, and instead focus on the way information is used in real-world applications. Let's stop thinking about the computer's needs and start concentrating on people's needs. Hardware costs have come crashing down and they continue declining. People costs keep rising. Today, it is the programmer's and user's time that is precious, not the computer's time. Database technology gives organizations easier and faster access to their information than was possible with low-level file-processing techniques. *Relational databases* (the kind we most often use with Visual Basic) do consist of files, but relational database systems provide a friendlier, more applications-oriented view to the application developer. Chapter 18, "Database Management," explains how to use Visual Basic to create and manipulate databases. Note that most of the database manipulations we present are done with the convenience and power of easy-to-use ActiveX controls rather than direct Visual Basic programming.

### Chapter 19: Networking, the Internet and the World Wide Web
Chapter 19, "Networking, the Internet and the World Wide Web," is a great opportunity for you to create applications that operate across the Internet and the World Wide Web. As we enter the next millennium, the Internet and the World Wide Web (which operates over the Internet) will surely be listed among the most important and profound creations of humankind. In the past, most computer applications ran on one computer. Today's applications can be written to communicate among the world's hundreds of millions of computers. The Internet mixes computing and communications technologies. It makes our work easier. It makes information instantly and conveniently accessible worldwide. It makes it possible for individuals and local small businesses to get worldwide exposure. It is changing the nature of the way business is done. People can search for the best prices on virtually any product or service. Special-interest communities can stay in touch with one another. Researchers can be made instantly aware of the latest developments internationally. In this chapter you will learn how to develop Internet-based applications. You will learn how to program computers to communicate over the Internet and to search the World Wide Web for information. In the past, this type of network programming was considered to be so complex that most programmers would not even consider building these kinds of applications without enlisting the help of experts in the field. Today, through the convenience and power of ActiveX controls like those we discuss in Chapter 19, Visual Basic programmers can develop powerful Internet- and World-Wide-Web-based applications. The controls

presented in this chapter enable you to incorporate World Wide Web browsing capabilities into any application, to communicate between applications using the popular protocols of the Internet and the Web and to download files and HTML documents. This chapter also introduces you to Visual Basic Script (VBScript). VBScript is a subset of Visual Basic that is used to enhance the functionality of Web documents being viewed in a Web browser and to enhance the functionality of applications running on server computers around the world.

### Chapter 20: Multimedia: Images, Animation, Audio

We all listen to music, watch television and movies, and enjoy animated characters. Wouldn't it be great if we could incorporate those technologies into our computer applications? Well, with Visual Basic 6 we can make our applications display animations, play sounds, music and videos, and process two- and three-dimensional graphics. Chapter 20, "Multimedia: Images, Animation, Audio," discusses each of these technologies and provides numerous live-code examples on which you can model your code. You will learn how to create and manipulate 3D cartoon characters that look like a genie, Merlin the magician, and a robot. You will learn how to make these characters jump and dance and talk. The technology is even available to make them recognize your spoken commands! Imagine that. You can write your own computer applications that will listen to your voice and obey your spoken commands! In the overview of Chapters 10 and 11, we discussed the notion of graphical user interfaces. Well, it is our firm belief that within just a few years, users will no longer be willing to settle for just GUIs. We believe they will demand MUIs (multimedia user interfaces). Once and for all people will be able to communicate with computers the way people communicate with one another, using relatively "wide bandwidth" means such as speech, sight and the other senses. These technologies are in use today, but they will become pervasive over the next decade. The possibilities are mind boggling. Once again, just a few years back, programmers would not even consider developing multimedia applications. The technologies were simply far too complex. Today, through the convenience and power of ActiveX controls like those we discuss in Chapter 20, Visual Basic programmers can develop powerful multimedia-based applications.

### Chapter 21: Data Structures, Collections, Dictionaries

Programmers write action statements that process data. In the early years of computing, the focus of attention was on these actions. Quickly, programmers realized that arranging data into certain kinds of data structures (such as lists, queues, stacks, trees and others) simplifies program development and improves program performance. Chapter 21, "Data Structures, Collections, Dictionaries," discusses many popular data structures, and shows how to build and use them. Actually, the chapter presents two views. It shows you how to build key data structures yourself. It also shows you how to implement these data structures simply by reusing Visual Basic Collection and Dictionary prebuilt components.

Many readers will already have our interactive multimedia CD software version of *Visual Basic 6 How to Program*. This Windows 95/98/NT-based software product is called the *Visual Basic 6 Multimedia Cyber Classroom* and it accompanies this textbook in our Prentice Hall publication called *The Complete Visual Basic 6 Training Course*. The *Visual Basic 6 Multimedia Cyber Classroom* contains extensive interactivity features, including hyperlinking, text searching and audio walkthroughs of most of the code examples in *Visual Basic 6 How to Program*. It also contains solutions to many of the exercises in the book. Ordering instructions for this CD product are given in the last few pages of this book.

Well, there you have it! We have worked hard to create this book and the optional Cyber Classroom version of the book for you. The book is loaded with live-code examples, programming tips, self-review exercises and answers, challenging exercises and projects, and numerous study aids to help you master the material. Despite the word "basic" in its name, Visual Basic is a serious programming language that will help you write Microsoft Windows-based programs quickly and effectively. And Visual Basic is a language that scales nicely into the realm of enterprise systems development to help organizations build their key business systems. As you read the book, if something is not clear, or if you find an error, please write to us at **deitel@deitel.com**. We will make every effort to respond promptly, and we will post corrections and clarifications on our Web site, **www.deitel.com**. We hope you enjoy learning with *Visual Basic 6 How to Program* as much as we enjoyed writing it!

## Summary

- A computer is a device capable of performing computations and making logical decisions at speeds millions, and even billions, of times faster than human beings can.

- It is software (i.e., the instructions you write to command the computer to perform actions and make decisions) that controls computers (often referred to as hardware).

- Computers process data using sets of instructions called computer programs. Computer programs guide the computer through sets of actions specified by people called computer programmers.

- The various devices (such as the keyboard, screen, disks, memory and processing units) that comprise a computer system are referred to as hardware.

- The computer programs that run on a computer are referred to as software.

- The input unit is the "receiving" section of the computer. It obtains information (data and computer programs) from various input devices.

- The output unit is the "shipping" section of the computer. It takes information that has been processed by the computer and places it on various output devices.

- The memory unit is the rapid access, relatively low-capacity "warehouse" section of the computer. The memory unit is often called either memory or primary memory.

- The arithmetic and logic unit (ALU is the "manufacturing" section of the computer. It is responsible for performing calculations and making decisions.

- The central processing unit (CPU) is the "administrative" section of the computer. It is the computer's coordinator and supervises the operation of the other sections.

- The secondary storage unit is the long-term, high-capacity "warehousing" section of the computer. Programs or data not actively being used by the other units are normally placed on secondary storage devices (such as disks) until they are again needed.

- Software systems called operating systems were developed to make it more convenient to use computers and increase the amount of work, or throughput, computers process.

- Timesharing is a special case of multiprogramming in which users access the computer through terminals, typically devices with keyboards and screens. The computer runs a small portion of one user's job and then moves on to service the next user. The computer does this so quickly that the users' programs appear to be running simultaneously.

- In 1977, Apple Computer popularized the phenomenon of personal computing.

- In 1981, IBM, the world's largest computer vendor, introduced the IBM Personal Computer. This made personal computing legitimate in business, industry and government.

- With distributed computing, an organization's computing, instead of being performed strictly at some central computer installation, is distributed over networks to various work sites.
- Information is easily shared across computer networks where some computers called servers offer a common store of programs and data that may be used by client computers distributed throughout the network, hence the term client/server computing.
- C and C++ are the programming languages of choice for writing software for operating systems, for computer networking, and for distributed client/server applications.
- Visual Basic is the premier client/server applications development language on Microsoft-based systems.
- Machine languages generally consist of strings of numbers (ultimately reduced to 1s and 0s) that instruct computers to perform their most elementary operations one at a time. Machine languages are machine-dependent (i.e., a machine language can be used on only one type of computer).
- English-like abbreviations form the basis of assembly languages. Translator programs called assemblers convert assembly language programs to machine language at computer speeds.
- The translator programs that convert high-level language programs into machine language are called compilers. High-level languages allow programmers to write instructions that look like English and contain commonly used mathematical notations. Visual Basic is the world's most widely used high-level language.
- Interpreter programs can directly execute high-level language programs without compiling those programs into machine language. Historically, Visual Basic has been an interpreted language. Visual Basic programmers can now compile programs to produce machine language executables that run at high speeds (as is true with C and C++).
- FORTRAN is used for mathematical, scientific and engineering applications that require complex computations. COBOL is used for commercial applications that require precise and efficient manipulation of large amounts of data.
- C is one of the most popular system implementation languages in industry; it was first used to develop the UNIX operating system.
- C++, an extension of C, provides a number of features that "spruce up" the C language and add capabilities for doing object-oriented programming (OOP). C++ has become the dominant systems implementation language.
- Graphical languages like Visual Basic are used to develop Windows programs quickly.
- Java was developed by Sun Microsystems. Java is based primarily on C and C++. Java includes extensive libraries for doing multimedia, networking, multithreading, graphics, graphical user interface development, database access, distributed computing and much more.
- The Pascal programming language was designed for teaching structured programming.
- One important capability of Ada is multitasking (often called multithreading); this allows programmers to specify that many activities are to occur in parallel.
- Visual Basic does not directly support multithreading, but multithreaded programs can be created using Win32 Application Programming Interface (API) functions. The Win32 API is part of Microsoft Windows and can be used by any Windows program.
- Visual Basic is a Microsoft Windows programming language.
- Visual Basic programs are created in an integrated development environment (IDE), which allows programmers to create, run and debug Visual Basic programs conveniently without being Windows programming experts.
- The process of rapidly creating an application is typically referred to as Rapid Application Development (RAD). Visual Basic is the world's most widely used RAD language.

- When we write computer programs, we specify the actions we would like the computer to perform and the order in which we would like the computer to perform those actions.

- Various types of actions are input actions, calculation actions and output actions.

- We specify the order in which a program's actions should be performed by using control structures, namely sequence structures (which specify several actions should be performed one after the other "in sequence"), selection structures (which enable a program to choose among different actions to be performed under different conditions) and repetition structures (which enable a program to repeat actions until the program determines that no further repetitions are needed).

- It is best to break large programs into sets of small, simple, cooperating components called procedures, a technique called divide and conquer.

- In Visual Basic programs it is common to store sets of related data items in arrays.

- Words and sentences are represented in Visual Basic as strings of characters.

- Visual Basic can draw lines, arcs, circles, ellipses, rectangles and other shapes.

- Graphical user interface (GUI) technology made it easier for users to communicate with computers. People use the mouse to point to things on the screen representing actions the computer should take (such as opening, saving, printing or closing a file).

- The process of tracking down and removing errors from programs is called debugging.

- Visual Basic is used for developing business-critical applications. Mission-critical applications are still programmed in languages like C and C++.

- Sequential files are appropriate when you process most or all of the data in a file when you run an application. Random-access files are effective for transaction-processing systems such as point-of-sale systems.

- Object technology lets us work with prebuilt software components. This enables us to build software faster, and if we use high-quality components, better.

- You can build your own ActiveX components and reuse thousands of ActiveX components created by other programmers and made available either free or for a fee.

- ActiveX components make programming more pleasant. They give you access to powerful, reusable software components that perform many common software tasks.

- Component-oriented software construction can be tens or even hundreds of times faster than conventional software development methods.

- With ActiveX components, you can program in areas in which you have little expertise.

- ActiveX components are more than just "raw objects"—ActiveX components are packaged for ease of use over the Internet.

- You can build and use ActiveX components interchangeably with any of Microsoft's key programming languages like Visual Basic, Visual C++ and Visual J++.

- Database technology gives organizations easier and faster access to their information than was possible with low-level file-processing techniques.

- Visual Basic enables you to create applications for the Internet and the World Wide Web.

- The Internet mixes computing and communications technologies. It makes information instantly and conveniently accessible worldwide. Through ActiveX controls, Visual Basic programmers can develop powerful Internet and World-Wide-Web-based applications.

- Application users will soon demand MUIs (multimedia user interfaces). People will be able to communicate with computers the way people communicate with one another, using relatively "wide bandwidth" means such as speech, sight and the other senses. With ActiveX controls, Visual Basic programmers can develop powerful multimedia-based applications.

- Arranging data into certain kinds of data structures, such as lists, queues, stacks, trees and others, can simplify program development and improve program performance.

- You can build key data structures yourself or you can implement these data structures simply by reusing Visual Basic Collection and Dictionary prebuilt components.

- VBScript is a subset of Visual Basic. DHTML is related to HTML (the Hypertext Markup Language so crucial to World-Wide-Web-based applications). These technologies are used to create more interactive and "dynamic" Web pages.

## *Terminology*

| | |
|---|---|
| actions | FORTRAN |
| ActiveX controls | graphical user interface (GUI) |
| Ada | graphics |
| ALU | hardware |
| animation | high-level language |
| Apple Computer | HTML (Hypertext Markup Language) |
| application programming interface (API) | IBM |
| arithmetic and logic unit (ALU) | IBM Personal Computer |
| array | input device |
| assembler | input unit |
| assembly language | integrated development environment (IDE) |
| audio | Internet |
| batch processing | interpreter |
| building block approach | Java |
| business-critical computing | keyboard |
| C | Learning Edition of Visual Basic |
| C++ | local area network (LAN) |
| central processing unit (CPU) | logical units |
| clarity | machine dependent |
| client computer | machine language |
| client/server computing | memory |
| COBOL | memory unit |
| compiler | Microsoft |
| component-oriented software construction | mission-critical computing |
| computer | mouse pointing device |
| computer program | multimedia |
| computer programmer | multimedia user interface (MUI) |
| control structures | multitasking |
| CPU | multithreading |
| data | object |
| database | object-oriented programming (OOP) |
| debugging | operating system |
| decisions | output device |
| DHTML (Dynamic HTML) | output unit |
| disk | Pascal |
| distributed computing | personal computing |
| divide and conquer | Powerbuilder |
| Enterprise Edition of Visual Basic | prebuilt components |
| environment | primary memory |
| event-driven programming | procedure |
| executable | Professional Edition of Visual Basic |

| | |
|---|---|
| program | throughput |
| programmer | timesharing |
| programming languages | translation steps |
| random-access file | translator programs |
| rapid application development (RAD) | UNIX |
| repetition structure | user friendly |
| screen | VBScript |
| secondary storage unit | Video |
| selection structure | Visual Basic |
| sequence structure | Visual C++ |
| sequential file | Visual J++ |
| server | visual programming |
| software | Win32 Application Programming Interface (API) |
| software reusability | Windows |
| string | Windows NT |
| structured programming | workstation |
| supercomputer | World Wide Web |

## Good Programming Practices

**1.1** Write your Visual Basic programs in a simple and straightforward manner. This is sometimes referred to as KIS ("keep it simple"). Do not "stretch" the language by trying bizarre usages.

**1.2** Read the documentation for the version of Visual Basic you are using. Refer to these manuals frequently to be sure that you are aware of the rich collection of Visual Basic features and are using these features correctly.

## Portability Tip

**1.1** Some features of the current versions of Visual Basic are not compatible with older Visual Basic implementations, so you may find that some of the programs in this text do not work with older versions.

## Software Engineering Observation

**1.1** The Visual Basic IDE allows Windows programs to be created without the need for the programmer to be a Windows programming expert.

## Self-Review Exercises

**1.1** Fill in the blanks in each of the following:
   a) The company that popularized personal computing was _____.
   b) The computer that made personal computing legitimate in business and industry was the _____.
   c) Computers process data under the control of sets of instructions called computer _____.
   d) The six key logical units of the computer are the _____, _____ , _____, _____, _____ and _____.

**1.2** Fill in the blanks in each of the following:
   a) The three classes of languages discussed in the chapter are _____, _____ and _____.
   b) The programs that translate high-level language programs into machine language are called_____.

c) C is widely known as the development language of the _____ operating system.

d) The_____ language was developed by Wirth for teaching structured programming in universities.

e) The Department of Defense developed the Ada language with a capability called _____, which allows programmers to specify that many activities can proceed in parallel.

**1.3**    Fill in the blanks in each of the following sentences.

a) The editions of Visual Basic are _____, _____ and _____.

b) RAD is short for _____.

c) API is short for _____.

d) _____ corporation created Visual Basic.

e) IDE is short for _____.

**1.4**    Fill in the blanks in each of the following statements.

a) Visual Basic programs are created in an _____, which allows programmers to create, run and debug Visual Basic programs conveniently without being Windows programming experts.

b) _____ is the world's most widely used Rapid Application Development (RAD) language.

c) We specify the order in which a program's actions should be performed by using _____ structures, namely sequence structures, selection structures and repetition structures.

d) The technique of breaking large programs into sets of small, simple, cooperating components called procedures is called _____.

e) In Visual Basic programs it is common to store sets of related data items in_____.

f) Words and sentences are represented in Visual Basic as _____ of characters.

g) The process of tracking down and removing errors from programs is called_____.

h) _____ technology gives organizations easier and faster access to their information than was possible with low-level file-processing techniques.

i) Application users will soon demand _____ user interfaces (MUIs). Once and for all people will be able to communicate with computers the way people communicate with one another, using relatively "wide bandwidth" means such as speech, sight and the other senses.

**1.5**    State whether each of the following is *true* or *false*. If *false*, explain why.

a) Computing costs have been increasing dramatically.

b) Visual Basic does not directly support multithreading, but multithreaded programs can be created using Win32 Application Programming Interface (API) functions.

c) The company that performed the pioneering research on graphical user interfaces (GUIs) was Apple Computer.

d) The preferred language for developing mission-critical applications is Visual Basic.

## Answers to Self-Review Exercises

**1.1**    a) Apple. b) IBM Personal Computer. c) programs. d) input unit, output unit, memory unit, arithmetic and logic unit, central processing unit, secondary storage unit.

**1.2**    a) machine languages, assembly languages, high-level languages. b) compilers. c) UNIX. d) Pascal. e) multitasking.

**1.3**    a) Learning, Professional, Enterprise. b) rapid application development. c) application programming interface. d) Microsoft. e) integrated development environment.

**1.4** a) integrated development environment. b) Visual Basic. c) control. d) divide and conquer. e) arrays. f) strings. g) debugging. h) Database. i) multimedia.

**1.5**
a)  False. Costs have been decreasing dramatically due to developments in technology.
b)  True.
c)  False. It was Xerox.
d)  False. C, C++ and Ada are preferred for mission-critical applications.

## Exercises

**1.6**   Categorize each of the following items as either hardware or software.
a)  CPU
b)  Visual Basic IDE
c)  ALU
d)  mouse
e)  input unit
f)  Windows operating system
g)  Monitor
h)  CD-ROM/DVD player

**1.7**   Fill in the blanks in each of the following statements.
a)   Which logical unit of the computer receives information from outside the computer for use by the computer? _____.
b)   The process of instructing the computer to solve specific problems is called_____.
c)   What type of computer language uses English-like abbreviations for machine language instructions? _____.
d)   Which logical unit of the computer sends information that has already been processed by the computer to various devices so that the information may be used outside the computer? _____.

**1.8**   Fill in the blanks in each of the following statements.
a)   Which logical unit of the computer retains information?_____.
b)   Which logical unit of the computer performs calculations?_____.
c)   Which logical unit of the computer makes logical decisions?_____.
d)   The level of computer language most convenient to the programmer for writing programs quickly and easily is _____.
e)   The only language that a computer can directly understand is called that computer's _____.
f)   Which logical unit of the computer coordinates the activities of all the other logical units? _____.

**1.9**   Fill in the blanks in each of the following statements.
a)   The most powerful desktop machines are called _____.
b)   Information is easily shared across computer networks, where some computers called file servers offer a common store of programs and data that may be used by client computers distributed throughout the network, hence the term _____.
c)   Any computer can directly understand only its own _____ language.
d)   Translator programs called _____ convert assembly language programs to machine language at computer speeds.
e)   The translator programs that convert high-level language programs into machine language are called _____.
f)   _____ is the preferred programming language for scientific and engineering applications that require complex mathematical computations.

g)  _____ is the popular system implementation language that was first used to develop the UNIX operating system.

h)  _____, an extension of C, provides a number of features that "spruce up" the C language and add capabilities for doing object-oriented programming (OOP).

i)  The _____ programming language was developed by Sun Microsystems, is based on C and C++ and incorporates features from other object-oriented languages.

**1.10**  State whether each of the following is *true* or *false*. If *false*, explain why.

a)  Sequential files are preferred in transaction-processing systems like point-of-sale systems.

b)  You can build ActiveX components with any of Microsoft's key programming languages, like Visual Basic, Visual C++ and Visual J++. No matter which of these languages is used to build an ActiveX component, the component can be used by any of them.

c)  The trend in the computer field is to get away from how things are represented in the computer, and instead, focus on the way information is used in real-world applications.

d)  The programmer's and user's time is more precious than the computer's time.

# Integrated Development Environment

### Objectives

- To become familiar with the integrated development environment.
- To be able to create a standard executable.
- To be able to identify the controls in the toolbox.
- To be able to understand the types of commands contained in the menus and the tool bar.
- To be able to customize the form using properties.
- To be able to customize the form using controls.
- To be able to customize controls using properties.
- To be able to save a project.
- To be able to execute a simple program.
- To understand the difference between design mode and run mode.

*Seeing is believing.*
Proverb

*Form ever follows function.*
Louis Henri Sullivan

*Intelligence. . . is the faculty of making artificial objects, especially tools to make tools.*
Henri-Louis Bergson

*Our life is frittered away by detail . . . Simplify, simplify.*
Henry Thoreau

# Outline

## 2.1 Introduction

Visual Basic's *Integrated Development Environment* (*IDE*) allows the programmer to create, run and debug Windows programs in one application (e.g., Visual Basic) without the need to open additional programs (i.e., a program to create the program, a program that executes the program, a program that debugs the program, etc.). In this chapter, we overview the Visual Basic IDE features and discuss how to create and execute a simple program.

## 2.2 Integrated Development Environment Overview

When Visual Basic is loaded, the **New Project** *dialog* shown in Fig. 2.1 is displayed. The **New Project** dialog allows the programmer to choose what type of Visual Basic program to create. **Standard EXE**, which is highlighted by default, allows the programmer to create a *standard executable* (i.e., a program that uses the most common Visual Basic features). We use **Standard EXE** for the majority of examples and exercises in this book, although later in the book you will learn about some of the other types.

Each type listed in Fig. 2.1 describes a group of related files called a *project*. Collectively, the project files form a Visual Basic program. The *project types* listed in Fig. 2.1 are the "Visual" in Visual Basic, because they contain predefined features for designing Windows programs. The programmer can use or leverage these existing project types to create powerful Windows applications in a fraction of the time it would normally take to create the same applications in other programming languages.

The **New Project** dialog contains three tabs—**New** for creating a new project, **Existing** for opening an existing project and **Recent** for opening a project that has been previously loaded into the IDE. Note that the **New Project** dialog is displayed every time Visual Basic is executed unless the **Don't show this dialog in the future** *checkbox* (in the lower-left portion of Fig. 2.1) is checked. The number and names of the types appearing in the window can differ depending on the version of Visual Basic. Figure 2.1 shows *Visual Basic Enterprise Edition* project types (you may be working with another version of Visual Basic 6 that shows fewer project types).

A project type is opened by either double-clicking its icon with the left mouse button or by single-clicking the icon with the left mouse button and pressing **Open**. Opening a project type closes the **New Project** dialog and loads the features associated with the selected project type into the IDE.

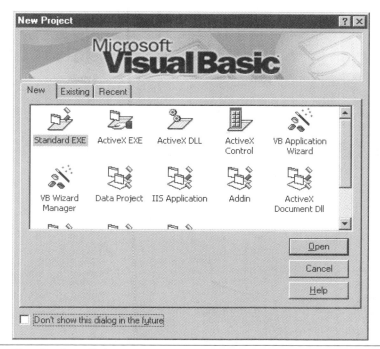

**Fig. 2.1     New Project** dialog.

Pressing ***Cancel*** closes the **New Project** dialog without opening a project type. Pressing **Help** opens the on-line assistance. We refer to single-clicking with the left mouse button as *selecting* or *clicking,* and we refer to double-clicking with the left mouse button simply as *double-clicking.*

Figure 2.2 shows the IDE after **Standard EXE** is selected. The top of the IDE window (the *title bar*) displays **Project1 - Microsoft Visual Basic [design]**. The environment consists of various windows, a *menu bar* and a *tool bar.* The menu bar contains several menus (**File**, **Edit**, **View**, etc.), each of which we overview shortly. The tool bar contains several icons that provide quick access to commonly used features. We discuss several of these tool bar icons in this chapter and others later in the book.

A **Standard EXE** project contains the following windows:

- **Project1 - Form1** (**Form**)
- **Form Layout**
- **Properties - Form1**
- **Project - Project1**
- Toolbox

The **Project - Form1** *(***Form***)* window contains a *form* named **Form1**, which is where the program's *Graphical User Interface* (*GUI*) will be displayed. A GUI is the visual portion of the program (i.e., buttons, etc.)–this is where the user enters data (called *inputs*) to the program and where the program displays its results (called *outputs*) for the user to read. We refer to the **Form1** window simply as "the form.*"*

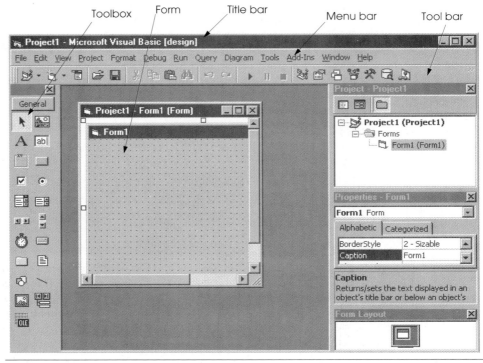

**Fig. 2.2**    IDE with a **Standard EXE** project open.

The **Form Layout** window enables the user to specify the form's position on the screen when the program is executed.

The **Properties - Form1** window displays form attributes or *properties* (i.e., color, font style, size, etc.). The **Project - Project1** window groups the project's files by type.

The toolbox contains *controls* for customizing the GUI (i.e., the form). Controls are GUI components such as buttons and checkboxes. We discuss a simple example at the end of this chapter that customizes a form with a control from the toolbox. We discuss toolbox controls throughout the book, especially in Chapters 10 and 11.

In the remainder of this chapter, we use these windows to create, manage and execute our first Visual Basic program.

## 2.3 Project Window

The window titled **Project - Project1** (Fig. 2.3) is called the ***Project Explorer*** and contains the project files. We refer to the **Project Explorer** window simply as the ***Project*** window.

The **Project** window's tool bar contains three *buttons*, namely **View Code**, **View Object** and **Toggle Folders**. When pressed, the **View Code** button displays a window for writing Visual Basic code. Writing code is the main subject of this book. **View Object**, when pressed, displays the form. Double-clicking **Form1 (Form1)** also displays the form. Both **View Code** and **View Object** are initially *disabled* (i.e., the buttons appear gray and pressing them has no effect) unless **Form1 (Form1)** is selected (i.e., highlighted) as it is in Fig. 2.3. Figure 2.4 shows both the **View Code** and **View Object** buttons disabled. The **Toggle Folders** button *toggles* (i.e., alternately hides or shows) the *Forms* folder. When shown as in Fig. 2.3, the folder is visible, and when hidden as in Fig. 2.4, the folder is invisible. The **Forms** folder contains a listing of all forms in the current project. Early in the book our projects will have only one form.

Later in this chapter we will save projects and forms with more meaningful names. The current names **Project1**, **Form1**, etc. are default names provided by Visual Basic to help you get started. Visual Basic does many things automatically to minimize the amount of work you must do to create applications. In this regard, Visual Basic is the world's most popular *RAD (Rapid Applications Development)* programming language. The **Project** window becomes an important project management tool as projects become more complex (i.e., contain more forms and other support files).

## 2.4 Toolbox

The toolbox (Fig. 2.5) contains *controls* used to customize forms. Controls are prepackaged components that you reuse instead of writing them yourself–this helps you write programs faster. In this chapter, we overview the toolbox controls and in later chapters we discuss these controls in greater detail. Notice the box named **Data** displayed at the bottom of Fig. 2.5 when the *mouse pointer* (i.e., the **white arrow**) rests on the **Data** control. These boxed descriptions, called *tool tips*, are displayed by Visual Basic to tell you what each icon means. Tool tips are also displayed for many IDE features besides the toolbox. Figure 2.6 summarizes the toolbox controls.

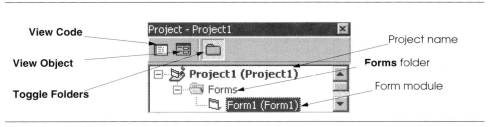

**Fig. 2.3     Project** window.

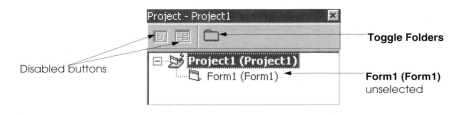

**Fig. 2.4     Project** window with disabled buttons and **Toggle Folders** set to off.

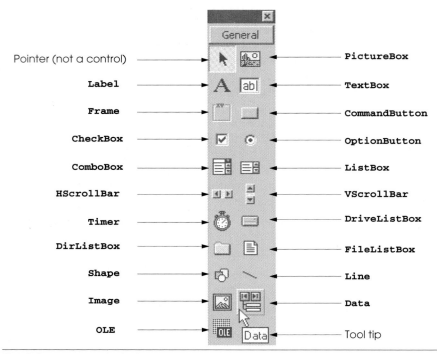

**Fig. 2.5     Toolbox** window.

| Control | Description |
|---|---|
| Pointer | Used to interact with the controls on the form (i.e., resize them, move them, etc.). The pointer is not a control. |
| **PictureBox** | A control that displays images. |
| **Label** | A control that displays uneditable text to the user. |
| **TextBox** | A control for accepting user input. **TextBox**es can also display text. |
| **Frame** | A control for grouping other controls. |
| **CommandButton** | A control that represents a button. The user presses or clicks to initiate an action. |
| **CheckBox** | A control that provides the user with a toggle choice (checked or unchecked). |
| **OptionButton** | A "radio button." **OptionButtons** are used in groups where only one at a time can be **True** (i.e., on)—like the buttons on a car radio. |
| **ListBox** | A control that provides a list of items. |
| **ComboBox** | A control that provides a short list of items. |

**Fig. 2.6**     Toolbox control summary (part 1 of 2).

| Control | Description |
|---------|-------------|
| **HScrollBar** | A horizontal scrollbar. |
| **VScrollBar** | A vertical scrollbar. |
| **Timer** | A control that performs a task at programmer-specified intervals. A **Timer** is not visible to the user. |
| **DriveListBox** | A control for accessing the system disk drives (**C:**, **A:**, etc.). |
| **DirListBox** | A control for accessing directories on a system. |
| **FileListBox** | A control for accessing files in a directory. |
| **Shape** | A control for drawing circles, rectangles, squares or ellipses. |
| **Line** | A control for drawing lines. |
| **Image** | A control for displaying images. The **Image** control does not provide as many capabilities as a **PictureBox**. |
| **Data** | A control for connecting to a database. |
| **OLE** | A control for interacting with other window applications. |

**Fig. 2.6**    Toolbox control summary (part 2 of 2).

## 2.5  Form Layout Window

The **Form Layout** window (Fig. 2.7) specifies a form's position on the screen at runtime. The **Form Layout** window consists of an image representing the screen and the form's relative position on the screen. With the mouse pointer positioned over the form image, *drag* (i.e., hold down the left mouse button, then move the mouse and release the button) the form to a new location. Note that the mouse pointer changes shape when over the image representing the form. Later in the book we discuss the various shapes that the mouse pointer can assume.

## 2.6  Properties Window

The **Properties** window (Fig. 2.8) displays the *properties* for a form or control. Properties are attributes such as size, position, etc. Like a form, each control type has its own set of properties. Some properties, like **Width** and **Height**, such as, are common to both forms and controls, while other properties are unique to a form or control. Controls often differ in the number and type of properties.

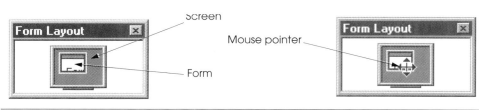

**Fig. 2.7**    **Form Layout** window.

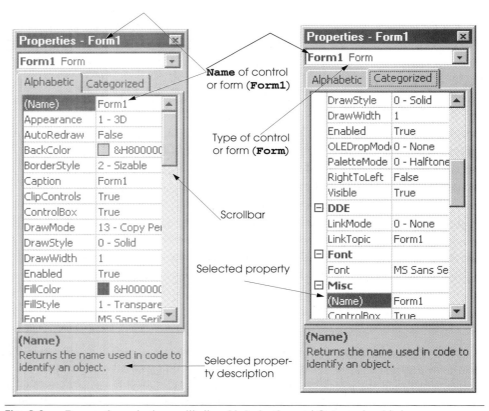

**Fig. 2.8**   **Properties** window with the **Alphabetic** and **Categorized** tabs.

Properties are listed either alphabetically (by selecting the **_Alphabetic_** tab) or categorically (by selecting the **_Categorized_** tab). **Alphabetic** lists the properties in alphabetical order and is the default. Clicking the **Categorized** tab lists properties by categories, such as **Appearance**, **Behavior**, **DDE**, **Font**, **Misc**, etc. The scrollbar can be used to scroll through the list of properties (by dragging the scrollbar up or down). We discuss setting individual properties later in this chapter and throughout the book.

## 2.7 Menu Bar and Tool Bar

Commands for developing, maintaining and executing programs are contained in the IDE's menus. Figure 2.9 shows the menus displayed on the *menu bar* for a **Standard EXE** project. Menus contain groups of related capabilities from which the user may select appropriate choices. The menus of Fig. 2.9 are summarized in Fig. 2.10. Note: Your version of Visual Basic may not have some of these menus.

**Fig. 2.9**   IDE menu bar.

| Menu | Description |
|------|-------------|
| File | Contains options for opening projects, closing projects, printing projects, etc. |
| Edit | Contains options such as cut, paste, find, undo, delete, etc. |
| View | Contains options for displaying IDE windows and tool bars. |
| Project | Contains options for adding features such as forms to the project. |
| Format | Contains options for aligning and locking a form's controls. |
| Debug | Contains options for debugging. |
| Run | Contains options for executing a program, stopping a program, etc. |
| Query | Contains options for manipulating data retrieved from a database. |
| Diagram | Contains options for editing and viewing the design of databases. |
| Tools | Contains options for IDE tools and options for customizing the environment. |
| Add-Ins | Contains options for using, installing and removing add-ins. Add-ins are typically independent software vendor (ISV) products that extend Visual Basic's features. |
| Windows | Contains options for arranging and displaying windows. |
| Help | Contains options for getting help. |

**Fig. 2.10**   Menu summary.

Rather than having to navigate the menus for certain commonly used commands, the programmer can select them from the *tool bar* (Fig. 2.11). The tool bar is comprised of pictures called *icons* that represent commands. Figure 2.11 shows the *standard tool bar* (i.e., the default tool bar). The figure indicates which menus contain the equivalent commands and it shows a few specific icons related to displaying the IDE windows.

## 2.8  A Simple Program: Displaying a Line of Text

In this section, we will create a program that displays the text "**Welcome to Visual Basic!**" on the form. The program consists of one form and uses one **Label** control to display the text. The program is a **Standard EXE**. We do not write a single line of program code. Instead, we introduce the techniques of *visual programming in which through various programmer gestures (such as using the mouse for pointing, clicking, dragging and*

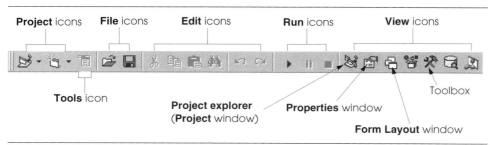

**Fig. 2.11**   Tool bar icons.

*dropping) we provide Visual Basic with sufficient information so that it can automatically generate all or a major portion of the program code for our program.* Figure 2.12 shows the program at runtime. In the next chapter, we begin our discussion of writing program code. Throughout the book we will produce increasingly substantial and powerful programs. Visual Basic programming involves a combination of writing a portion of the program code yourself and having Visual Basic generate the remaining code automatically.

Here are the steps you perform to create, run and terminate this first program:

1. *Setting the form's title bar.* The form's **Caption** *property* determines what is displayed in the form's title bar. In the **Properties** window, set the **Caption** property to **Fig. 2.12: A Simple Program**. To change the value of this property, click in the field next to **Caption** (this field displays **Form1**). Delete the existing value using the *Backspace* key or *Delete* key and enter the new value. Hit the *Enter* key (*Return* key). Note: As you enter a new value for the **Caption** property the form's title bar changes in response to what you are typing.

2. *Setting the form's **Name** property.* The **Name** *property* identifies a form or control. Set the **Name** property to **frmFig02_12**. After the property is set, note the changes to the **Properties** window and **Project** window as shown in Fig. 2.13.

Title bar ——→

**Fig. 2.12**   Program at run-time.

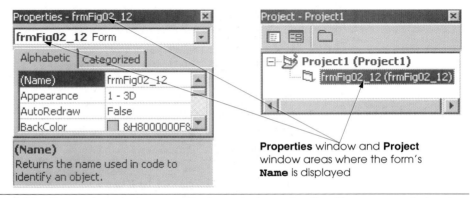

**Properties** window and **Project** window areas where the form's **Name** is displayed

**Fig. 2.13**   **Properties** window and **Project** window after the **Name** property is set.

*Good Programming Practice 2.1*

*Prefix the **Name** of each form with **frm** to make form objects easy to identify.*

3. *Resizing the form.* Click and drag one of the form's *enabled sizing handles* (the small squares around the form shown in Fig. 2.14). White sizing handles are *disabled* and the programmer cannot use them to resize the form. Sizing handles that are black are enabled and can be used for resizing. Size the form according to your own preference. Sizing handles are not visible during program execution.

4. *Centering the form.* Center the form using the **Form Layout** window (Fig. 2.15). This causes the form to display in the center of the monitor when the program is executed.

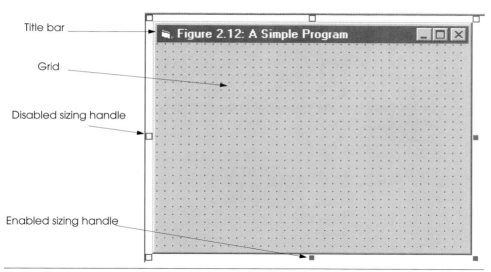

**Fig. 2.14**   Form with sizing handles.

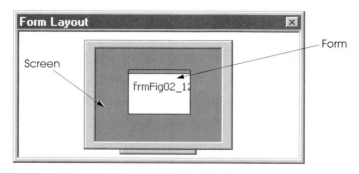

**Fig. 2.15   Form Layout** window with form centered.

5. *Changing the form's background color.* The **BackColor** *property* specifies a form or control's background color. Clicking **BackColor** in the **Properties** window causes a *down-arrow* button to appear next to the property value as shown in Fig. 2.16. When clicked, the down arrow displays a window with the tabs *System* (the default) and *Palette*. Click the **Palette** tab to display the *palette* (a group of colors from which the user selects one by clicking). Select the box representing yellow. The palette disappears and the form's background color changes to yellow. Note that **BackColor** displays a small rectangle representing the current color.

6. *Adding a **Label** control to the form.* Double-click the toolbox's **Label** control to create a **Label** with sizing handles in the center of the form (Fig. 2.17). The **Label** displays the word **Label1** by default. Double clicking any toolbox control results in a control being created and placed in the center of the form. When the sizing handles appear around the **Label**, the **Properties** window displays the **Label**'s properties. Clicking the form causes the form's properties to be displayed in the **Properties** window.

7. *Setting the **Label**'s display.* The **Label**'s **Caption** property determines what text (if any) the **Label** displays. The form and **Label** each have their own **Caption** property—with each being completely independent of the other. Forms and controls can have properties with the same name without conflict. Set the **Label**'s **Caption** property to **Welcome to Visual Basic!** (Fig. 2.18). The **Label** displays each character as it is typed. Note that when the edge of the **Label** is reached, the text automatically wraps to the next line.

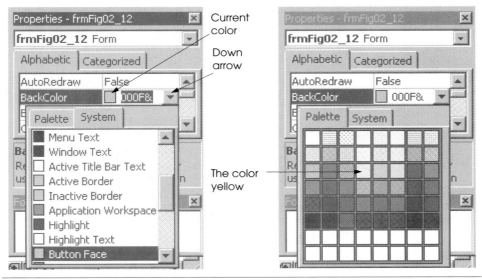

**Fig. 2.16**    Changing the **BackColor**.

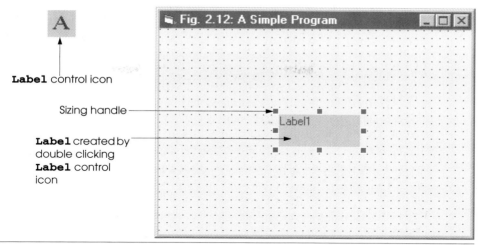

**Fig. 2.17** A **Label** placed on the form.

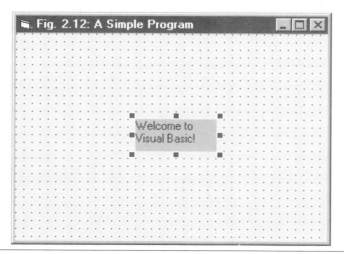

**Fig. 2.18** The **Caption** property set for the **Label**.

8. *Naming the **Label***. The **Label**'s **Name** property is used to identify the **Label**. The default name for the **Label** we just created is **Label1**. Set the **Name** property to **lblWelcome**.

*Good Programming Practice 2.2*

*Prefix the **Name** of each **Label** with **lbl** to make **Label** objects easy to identify.*

*Good Programming Practice 2.3*

*Following widely accepted naming conventions can make your program clearer—especially to other people.*

9. *Customizing the **Label**'s colors.* Like a form, a control's **BackColor** is gray by default, and we wish to change it to yellow. There are two ways to accomplish this using the **Label**'s properties. One way is to change the **Label**'s **BackColor** property to yellow—which works well as long as the form's **BackColor** does not change. If the form's **BackColor** changes, the **Label BackColor** remains yellow. The second way is to change the **Label**'s *BackStyle* property from *Opaque* (i.e., solid) to *Transparent* (i.e., see through). The **Label**'s *ForeColor* *property* determines the color in which text is displayed. Set the **ForeColor** to blue using the techniques discussed in Step 5.

10. *Setting the **Label**'s font size and aligning the **Label**'s text.* Clicking the *Font* *property* value causes an *ellipsis* button to appear (Fig. 2.20). When this button is pressed, the *Font* window of Fig. 2.21 appears. The font name (**MS Sans Serif**, **Serif**, etc.), font style (**Regular**, **Bold**, etc.) and font size (**8**, **10**, etc.) can be selected. The current font is applied to the text in the **Sample** area. Under the **Size** category select **24** and press **OK**. Next, select the *Alignment property*—which determines how the text is aligned within the **Label** boundaries. The three **Alignment** choices are *Left Justify* (the default), *Right Justify* and *Center*. Select **Center**. At this point, you might notice that the **Label** size is too small for the font size. In the next step we will resize the **Label**.

11. *Positioning and resizing the **Label**.* Resize the **Label** using the **Label**'s sizing handles, such that the **Label** appears similar to that of Fig. 2.22. Note the change in the mouse pointer when it is placed over a sizing handle. Center the **Label** on the form by dragging the **Label**. The *grid* dots on the background of the form are used for aligning controls and are only visible at design time.

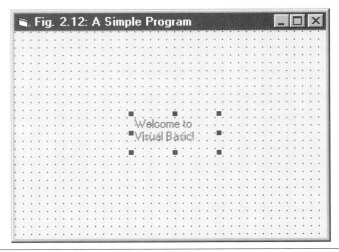

**Fig. 2.19**   Transparent **Label** with yellow **ForeColor**.

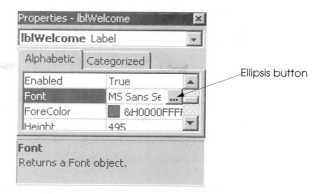

**Fig. 2.20**   **Properties** window displaying the **Label**'s properties.

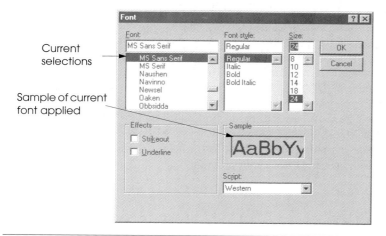

**Fig. 2.21**   **Font** window for selecting fonts, styles and sizes.

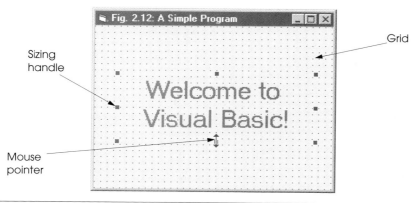

**Fig. 2.22**   Resizing the **Label**.

12. *Saving the project.* Click the **Save Project** *tool bar icon* (Fig. 2.23) or select **Save Project / Save Project As...** from the **File** menu to display the **Save File As...** dialog (Fig. 2.23). The **Save File As...** dialog specifies the *form file name* that will store all the form's information (i.e., properties, etc.). We save our file in the **c:\books\vbhtp\examples\chap02\fig02_12** directory. You are free to choose whatever directory you want. The window provides the capabilities to visually navigate the directories and to create new folders. After specifying the name and directory, click the **Save** button.

The next dialog that appears is the **Save Project As...** dialog. The features of this dialog are identical to the features of the **Save File As...** dialog, except that now we specify the *project file name*. The project file stores the name and location of every file in the project. We save the project in the same directory as the form (**c:\books\vbhtp\examples\chap02\fig02_12**). Again you are free to save the project file in any directory you choose. Figure 2.25 shows the **Project** window after the project is saved.

13. *Running the program.* Prior to this step, we have been working in the IDE *design mode* (i.e., the program is not executing). While in design mode, the programmer has access to all the environment windows (i.e., toolbox and **Properties**), menus, tool bars, etc. While in *run mode* the program is executing and the user can only interact with a few IDE features. Features that are not available are disabled. To execute or run your program, click the **Start** button or select **Start** from the **Run** menu. Figure 2.26 shows the IDE in run mode. Note that the IDE title bar displays **[Run]** and that most tool bar icons are disabled. Also note that the **Immediate** window appears at runtime. The **Immediate** window is primarily used for debugging (i.e., removing errors from your program) and is discussed in Chapter 13.

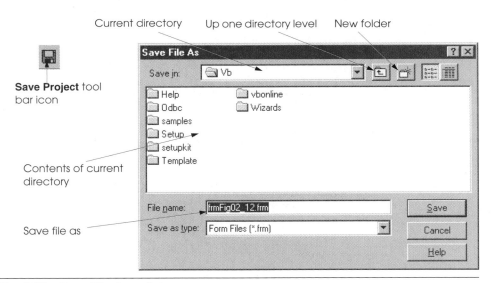

**Fig. 2.23   Save File As...** dialog.

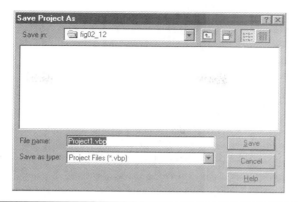

**Fig. 2.24    Save Project As...** dialog.

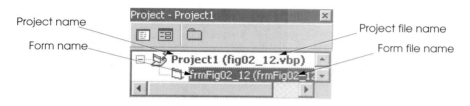

**Fig. 2.25    Project** window after saving project.

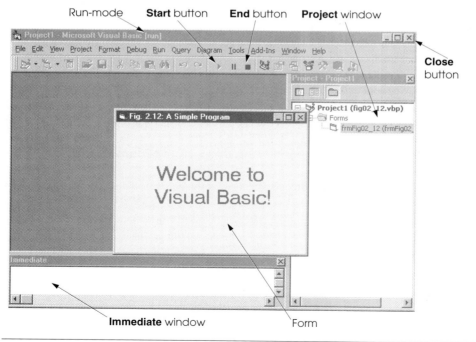

**Fig. 2.26    IDE** during execution.

14. *Terminating execution.* Clicking form's **Close** button icon (i.e., the "X" at the top right corner of Fig. 2.26) or by clicking the tool bar's **End** button terminates program execution and places the IDE in design mode.

## Summary

- The Visual Basic Integrated Development Environment (IDE) allows the programmer to create, run and debug Windows programs.
- The **New Project** dialog allows the programmer to choose what type of Visual Basic program to create. **Standard EXE** allows the programmer to create a standard executable (i.e., a program that uses the most common Visual Basic features).
- The **New Project** dialog contains three tabs—**New** for creating a new project, **Existing** for opening an existing project and **Recent** for opening a project that has been previously loaded into the IDE.
- We refer to single clicking with the left mouse button as selecting or clicking, and we refer to double-clicking with the left mouse button simply as double-clicking.
- A **Standard EXE** project contains the following windows: **Project1 - Form1 (Form)**, **Form Layout**, **Properties - Form1**, **Project - Project1** and the toolbox.
- The **Project - Form1 (Form)** window contains a child window named **Form1**, which is where the program's Graphical User Interface (GUI) will be displayed. A GUI is the visual portion of the program (i.e., buttons, checkboxes, etc.)–this is where the user enters data (called inputs) to the program and where the program displays its results (called outputs) for the user to read.
- The **Form Layout** window enables the user to specify the form's position on the screen when the program is executed.
- The **Properties - Form1** window displays form attributes or properties (i.e., color, font style, size, etc.).
- The toolbox contains controls for customizing the GUI (i.e., the form). Controls are GUI components such as buttons and checkboxes.
- The window titled **Project - Project1** (Fig. 2.3) is called the **Project Explorer** and contains the project files. We refer to the **Project Explorer** window simply as the **Project** window.
- The **Project** window's tool bar contains three buttons, namely **View Code**, **View Object** and **Toggle Folders**. When pressed, the **View Code** button displays a window for writing Visual Basic code.
- **View Object**, when pressed, displays the form. Double-clicking **Form1 (Form1)** also displays the form.
- Both **View Code** and **View Object** are initially disabled (i.e., the buttons appear gray and pressing them has no affect) unless **Form1 (Form1)** is selected (i.e., highlighted).
- The **Toggle Folders** button toggles (i.e., alternately hides or shows) the **Forms** folder.
- The **Forms** folder contains a listing of all forms in the current project.
- Visual Basic does many things automatically to minimize the amount of work you must do to create applications. In this regard, Visual Basic is the world's most popular RAD (Rapid Applications Development) programming language.
- The **Project** window becomes an important project management tool as projects become more complex (i.e., contain more forms and other support files).
- The toolbox contains controls used to customize forms. Controls are prepackaged components that you reuse instead of writing them yourself–this helps you write programs faster.

- Tool tips are displayed by Visual Basic to tell you what each icon means.
- The pointer is used to interact with the controls on the form (i.e., resize them, move them, etc.). The pointer is not a control.
- A **PictureBox** is a control that displays images.
- A **Label** is a control that displays uneditable text to the user.
- A **TextBox** is a control for accepting user input. **TextBox**es can also display text.
- A **Frame** is a control for grouping other controls.
- A **CheckBox** is a control that provides the user with a toggle choice (checked or unchecked).
- An **OptionButton** is a "radio button." **OptionButtons** are used in groups where only one at a time can be **True** (i.e., on), just like the buttons on a car radio.
- **ListBox** is a control that provides a list of items.
- A **ComboBox** is a control that provides a short list of items.
- An **HScrollBar** is a horizontal scrollbar.
- A **VScrollBar** is a vertical scrollbar.
- A **Timer** is a control that performs a task at programmer-specified intervals. A **Timer** is not visible to the user.
- A **DriveListBox** is a control for accessing the system disk drives (**C:**, **A:**, etc.).
- A **DirListBox** is a control for accessing directories on a system.
- A **FileListBox** is a control for accessing files in a directory.
- A **Shape** is a control for drawing circles, rectangles, squares or ellipses.
- A **Line** is a control for drawing lines.
- An **Image** is a control for displaying images. The **Image** control does not provide as many capabilities as a **PictureBox**.
- A **Data** control provides a means for connecting to a database.
- An **OLE** control for interacting with other Windows applications.
- The **Form Layout** window specifies a form's position on the screen at run-time. The **Form Layout** window consists of an image representing the screen and the form's relative position on the screen. To reposition the form on the screen, position the mouse pointer over the form image, then drag (i.e., hold down the left mouse button, then move the mouse and release the button) the form to a new location.
- The **Properties** window displays the properties for a forms and controls.
- Properties are attributes such as size, position, etc. Like a form, each control type has its own set of properties. Some properties, such as, **Width** and **Height**, are common to both forms and controls, while other properties are unique to a form or control. Controls often differ in the number and type of properties.
- Properties are listed either alphabetically (by selecting the **Alphabetic** tab) or categorically (by selecting the **Categorized** tab). **Alphabetic** lists the properties in alphabetical order and is the default. Clicking the **Categorized** tab lists properties by categories, such as **Appearance**, **Behavior**, **DDE**, **Font**, **Misc**, etc. The scrollbar can be used to scroll through the list of properties (by dragging the scrollbar up or down).
- Commands for developing, maintaining and executing programs are contained in the IDE's menus. Menus contain groups of related capabilities from which the user may select appropriate choices.

- The **File** menu contains options for opening projects, closing projects, printing projects, etc.
- The **Edit** menu contains options such as cut, paste, find, undo, delete, etc.
- The **View** menu contains options for displaying IDE windows and tool bars.
- The **Project** menu contains options for adding features such as forms to the project.
- The **Format** menu contains options for aligning and locking a form's controls.
- The **Debug** menu contains options for debugging.
- The **Run** menu contains options for executing a program, stopping a program, etc.
- The **Query** menu contains options for manipulating data retrieved from a database.
- The **Diagram** menu contains options for editing and viewing the design of databases.
- The **Tools** menu contains options for IDE tools and options for customizing the environment.
- The **Add-Ins** menu contains options for using, installing and removing add-ins. Add-ins are typically independent software vendor (ISV) products that extend the features of Visual Basic.
- The **Windows** menu contains options for arranging and displaying windows.
- The **Help** menu contains options for getting help.
- Rather navigating the menus for certain commonly used commands, the programmer can select them from the tool bar. The tool bar is comprised of pictures called icons that represent commands.
- We do not write a single line of code—instead, we introduce the technique of visual programming.
- The form's **Caption** property determines what is displayed in the form's title bar.
- To change the value of the **Caption** property, click in the field next to **Caption**. Delete the existing value using the Backspace key or Delete key and enter the new value. Hit the Enter key (Return key). As you enter a new value for the **Caption** property the form's title bar changes in response to what you are typing.
- The **Name** property identifies a form or control.
- To resize a form, click and drag one of the form's enabled sizing handles (the small squares around the form). White sizing handles are disabled and the programmer cannot use them to resize the form. Sizing handles that are black are enabled and can be used for resizing. Sizing handles are not visible during program execution.
- A form can be centered by using the **Form Layout** window.
- The **BackColor** property specifies a form or control's background color. Clicking **BackColor** in the **Properties** window causes a down-arrow button to appear next to the property value. When clicked, the down arrow displays a window with the tabs **System** (the default) and **Palette**. Click the **Palette** tab to display the palette (a group of colors from which the user selects one by clicking). The **BackColor** displays a small rectangle representing the current color.
- To add a **Label** control to a form, double-click the toolbox's **Label** control to create a **Label** with sizing handles in the center of the form. The **Label** displays the word **Label1** by default. Double-clicking any toolbox control results in a control being created and placed in the center of the form. When the sizing handles appear around the **Label**, the **Properties** window displays the **Label** properties. Clicking the form causes the form's properties to be displayed in the **Properties** window.
- The **Label**'s **Caption** property determines what text (if any) the **Label** displays. The form and **Label** each have their own **Caption** property—with each being completely independent of the other. Forms and controls can have properties with the same name without conflict. The **Label** displays each character as it is typed. Note that when the edge of the **Label** is reached, the text automatically wraps to the next line.

- A control's **BackColor** is gray by default.

- A **Label** has a **BackColor** property. A **Label**'s **BackStyle** property can be **Opaque** (i.e., solid) or **Transparent** (i.e., see through).

- A **Label**'s **ForeColor** property determines the color in which text is displayed.

- Clicking a **Label**'s **Font** property value causes an ellipsis button to appear. When this button is pressed, the **Font** dialog appears. The font name (**MS Sans Serif**, **Serif**, etc.), font style (**Regular**, **Bold**, etc.) and font size (**8**, **10**, etc.) can be selected. The current font is applied to the text in the **Sample** area.

- A **Label**'s **Alignment** property determines how text is aligned within the **Label** boundaries. The three **Alignment** choices are **Left Justify** (the default), **Right Justify** and **Center**.

- A **Label** can be resized using its sizing handles. The shape of the mouse pointer changes when it is placed over a sizing handle. The grid dots on the background of the form are used for aligning controls at design time.

- Click the **Save Project** tool bar icon or select **Save Project / Save Project As...** from the **File** menu to display the **Save File As...** dialog. The **Save File As...** dialog specifies the form file name that will store all the form's information (i.e., properties, etc.) as well as its directory location.

- The **Save Project As...** dialog's features are identical to those of the **Save File As...** dialog, except that you use it to specify the project file name. The project file stores the name and location of every file in the project.

- In IDE design mode, the program is not executing. While in design mode, the programmer has access to all the environment windows (i.e.f, toolbox and **Properties**, menus, tool bars, etc.).

- While in run mode the program is executing and the user can interact with only a few IDE features. Features that are not available are disabled.

- To execute or run a program, click the **Start** button or select **Start** from the **Run** menu. Note that the IDE title bar displays **[Run]** and that most tool bar icons are disabled. Also note that the **Immediate** window appears at run-time. The **Immediate** window is primarily used for debugging.

- Clicking form's **Close** button icon (i.e., the "X" at the form's top-right corner or clicking the tool bar's **End** button terminates program execution and places the IDE in design mode.

## *Terminology*

| | |
|---|---|
| active window | checkbox |
| **Add-Ins** menu | click and drag |
| **Alignment** property of a **Label** | clicking |
| **Alignment** property's **Left Justify** value | **Close** button |
| **Alignment** property's **Right Justify** value | controls |
| **Alphabetic** tab of **Properties** window | **Debug** menu |
| **BackColor** property of a **Form** | *Delete* key |
| *Backspace* key | design mode |
| **BackStyle** property | design time |
| button | disabled button |
| **Cancel** button | disabled sizing handle |
| **Caption** property | **Don't show this dialog in the future** |
| **Categorized** tab of a **Properties** window | double-clicking |
| **Center** value of **Alignment** property | down-arrow button |

dragging
**Edit** menu
ellipsis button
enabled sizing handle
**End** button
*Enter* key
*Enterprise Edition*
**Existing** tab of **New Project** dialog
**File** menu
focus
font
**Font** property of a **Label**
**Font** window
**ForeColor** property of a **Label**
form
**Format** menu
**Form Layout** window
**Forms** folder
graphical user interface (GUI)
grid
**Height** property
**Help** menu
icons
**Immediate** window
integrated development environment (IDE)
**Label** control
menu
menu bar
mouse pointer
**Name** property
**New Project** dialog
**New** tab of **New Project** dialog
**Opaque** value of **Back Style** property
**Open** button
palette of colors
**Palette** tab
project
**Project Explorer** window
**Project** menu
project types

**Project** window
properties
**Properties** window
RAD (Rapid Applications Development)
radio buttons
**Recent** tab of **New Project** dialog
*Return* key
**Run** menu
run mode
run-time
**Sample** area of **Font** window
**Save** button
**Save File As...** dialog
**Save Project As...** dialog
**Save Project** tool bar icon
selecting
sizing handle
**Standard EXE** project type
standard executable
standard tool bar
standard Visual Basic executable
**Start** button
**System** tab
title bar
toggle
**Toggle Folders** button in **Project** window
tool bar
toolbox
**Toolbox** window
**Tools** menu
tool tips
**Transparent** value
**VB Application Wizard** project type
**VB Learning Edition Controls** project type
**View Code** button in **Project** window
**View** menu
**View Objects** button in **Project** window
visual programming
**Width** property
**Window** menu

## Good Programming Practices

**2.1**   Prefix the **Name** of each form with **frm** to make form objects easy to identify.

**2.2**   Prefix the **Name** of each **Label** with **lbl** to make **Label** objects easy to identify.

**2.3**   Following widely accepted naming conventions can make your program clearer—especially to other people.

## Self-Review Exercises

**2.1**   Fill in the blanks in each of the following:
    a)   A _____ is a customizable window.

b) The form's _____ is used to visually align controls.

c) The form's _____ property specifies the text for the form's title bar.

d) The _____ window has a dark-colored title bar and is said to have the _____.

e) The _____ window determines where a form will appear on the screen at execution.

f) The _____ window contains the program files.

**2.2** State whether each of the following is *true* or *false*. If *false*, explain why.

a) The tool bar contains the control icons.

b) The **Project** window is also called the **Project Explorer**.

c) The tool bar provides a convenient way to execute certain menu commands.

d) The **Properties** window is also called the **Immediate** window.

e) A form's sizing handles are always enabled.

f) The pointer is not a control.

**2.3** Match the control name with the proper toolbox icon in Fig. 2.27. Note that **OLE** is not shown.

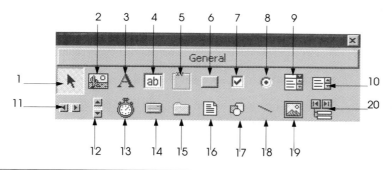

**Fig. 2.27**  Toolbox.

a) **CommandButton**
b) **OptionButton**
c) **Label**
d) **Line**
e) **Frame**
f) **Image**
g) **PictureBox**
h) **VScrollBar** (Vertical scrollbar)
i) Pointer
j) **ComboBox**

k) **TextBox**
l) **HScrollBar** (Horizontal scrollbar)
m) **DriveListBox**
n) **Shape**
o) **CheckBox**
p) **Data**
q) **FileListBox**
r) **ListBox**
s) **Timer**
t) **DirListBox** (Directory list box)

## Answers to Self-Review Exercises

**2.1**    a) form. b) grid. c) **Caption**. d) active, focus. e) **Form Layout**. f) **Project** or **Project Explorer**.

**2.2**    a) False. The toolbox contains the control icons.

b) True.

c) True.

d) False. The **Immediate** window is a distinctly different window.

e) False. Some of the form's sizing handles are disabled.

f) True.

**2.3**    a) 6.  b) 8.  c) 3.  d) 18.  e) 5.  f) 19.  g) 2.  h) 12.  i) 1.  j) 9.  k) 4.  l) 11.  m) 14.  n) 17.  o) 7.
p) 20.  q) 16.  r) 10.  s) 13.  t) 15.

## Exercises

**2.4**    Fill in the blanks in each of the following statements:
   a) The _____ contains a variety of colors, from which the programmer selects one.
   b) The three values of the **Alignment** property are _____, _____ and _____.
   c) The _____ property changes a control's foreground color.
   d) IDE is an abbreviation for _____.
   e) Clicking the _____ on the toolbar executes the program.
   f) The _____ property identifies a form and is often prefixed with **frm**.
   g) GUI is an abbreviation for _____.
   h) A _____ is a group of related files.

**2.5**    State which of the following are *true* and which are *false*. If *false*, explain why.
   a) At run-time, a form's grid is visible.
   b) A tool tip identifies an IDE feature.
   c) A **Label**'s **Text** property determines what text is displayed to the user.
   d) At design-time, almost every IDE feature is available.
   e) When placed over an enabled sizing handle, the mouse pointer changes.
   f) A **Label** displays uneditable text to the user.
   g) A form and **Label** have an identical set of properties.

**2.6**    Build the following GUIs (you need not provide any functionality). Execute each program
and determine what happens when a control is clicked with the mouse.
   a) This GUI consists of three **Label**s colored yellow, red and black.

   b) This GUI consist of one **Label** and eighteen **CommandButton**s. Note: You must mod-
      ify the **Label**'s **BorderStyle** property. Also note that the dotted line around the six
      (**6**) button (it can be any of your buttons) appears during run mode.

c) The following GUI consists of one **Label**, one **CommandButton** and four **Option-Button**s. Note: The black dot in **Dog** automatically appears at run-time but may appear in a different one of your buttons.

d) The following GUI consists of three **VScrollBar**s and two **Label**s. Note: One **Label** requires its **BorderStyle** property changed. Also note that one **VScrollBar**'s *scroll box* automatically flashes at run-time.

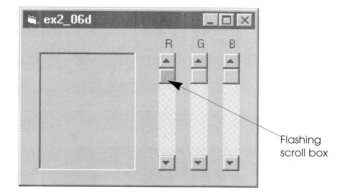

Flashing scroll box

**2.7** Briefly describe each of the following IDE features:
a) tool bar
b) menu bar
c) toolbox
d) control
e) form
f) project
g) title bar

**2.8** Briefly describe the differences between design mode and run mode.

**2.9** Compare a form's properties to a **Label**'s properties. Make a list of all the properties that are common to both. Now, summarize only the properties on the list we have discussed in this chapter.

**2.10** Why do you think that the toolbox, the form and the **Properties** window are crucial to the concept of visual programming?

# 3

# Introduction to Visual Basic Programming

## Objectives

- To write simple programs in Visual Basic.
- To become familiar with fundamental data types.
- To understand computer memory concepts.
- To be able to use arithmetic operators.
- To understand the precedence of arithmetic operators.
- To be able to write simple decision-making statements.

*"Where shall I begin, please your majesty?" she asked.*
*"Begin at the beginning," the king said, very gravely, "and go on till you come to the end; then stop."*
Lewis Carroll

*It is a capital mistake to theorize before one has data.*
Arthur Conan Doyle

*. . . the wisest prophets make sure of the event first.*
Horace Walpole

*An actor entering through the door, you've got nothing. But if he enters through the window, you've got a situation.*
Billy Wilder

*You shall see them on a beautiful quarto page, where a neat rivulet of text shall meander through a meadow or margin.*
Richard Brinsley Sheridan

*Exit, pursued by a bear.*
William Shakespeare

# Outline

## 3.1 Introduction

The Visual Basic language facilitates a structured and disciplined approach to computer program design. In this chapter we introduce Visual Basic programming and present several examples that illustrate many important features. Each example is carefully analyzed one statement at a time. In Chapters 4 and 5 we present an introduction to structured programming.

## 3.2 Visual Programming and Event-Driven Programming

With visual programming, the programmer has the ability to create graphical user interfaces (GUIs) by pointing and clicking with the mouse. Visual programming eliminates the need for the programmer to write code that generates the form, code for all the form's properties, code for form placement on the screen, code to create and place a **Label** on the form, code to change foreground and background colors, etc. All of this code is provided as part of the project. The programmer does not need to be an expert Windows programmer to create functional Windows programs. The programmer creates the GUI and writes code to describe what happens when the user interacts (clicks, presses a key, double-clicks, etc.) with the GUI. These notifications, called *events*, are passed into the program by Microsoft's Windows operating system.

Programming the code that responds to these events is called *event-driven programming*. With event-driven programs, the user dictates the order of program execution—not the programmer. Instead of the program "driving" the user, the user "drives" the program. With the user in control, using a computer becomes a much more user-friendly process. Consider, for example, a web browser. When opened, the web browser may or may not load a page by default. After the browser is loaded, it just "sits there" with nothing else happening. The browser will stay in this *event monitoring* state (i.e., listening for events) indefinitely. If the user presses a button, the browser then performs some action, but as soon as the browser is done performing the action it returns to the event monitoring state. Thus, user actions determine browser activity.

*Event procedures* are Visual Basic procedures that respond to events and are automatically generated by the Visual Basic. The programmer adds code to respond to specific events. Only events that are relevant to a program need be coded. In the next section we demonstrate how to locate event procedures and add code to respond to events.

## 3.3 A Simple Program: Printing a Line of Text on the Form

Consider a simple program that prints a line of text on the form. The GUI contains two buttons, **Print** and **Exit**, and is shown in the left picture of Fig. 3.1. The right picture of Fig. 3.1 shows the result after **Print** is pressed many times.

Figure 3.2 lists the *object* (i.e., form, **CommandButton**, etc.) and some property settings. We have only listed the properties we changed. We also provide a brief property description.We refer to **CommandButton**s simply as *button*s.

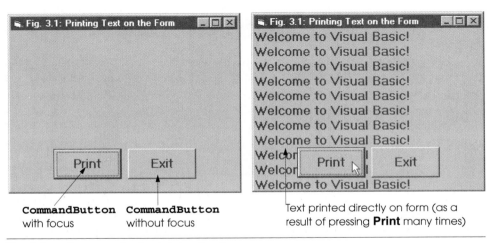

Fig. 3.1     Program that prints on the form.

| Object | Property | Property setting | Description |
|---|---|---|---|
| form | **Name** | **frmWelcome** | Identifies the form. |
| | **Caption** | **Fig. 3.1: Printing Text on the Form** | Form title bar display. |
| | **Font** | **MS Sans Serif Bold 12 pt** | Font for display on the form. |
| **Print** button | **Name** | **cmdPrint** | Identifies **Print** button. |
| | **Caption** | **Print** | Text that appears on button. |
| | **Font** | **MS Sans Serif Bold 12 pt** | **Caption** text font. |
| | **TabIndex** | **0** | Tab order number. |

Fig. 3.2     Object property settings (part 1 of 2).

| Object | Property | Property setting | Description |
|--------|----------|------------------|-------------|
| **Exit** button | `Name` | `cmdExit` | Identifies **Exit** button. |
| | `Caption` | `Exit` | Text that appears on button. |
| | `Font` | `MS Sans Serif Bold 12` pt | `Caption` text font. |
| | `TabIndex` | `1` | Tab order number. |

**Fig. 3.2**    Object property settings (part 2 of 2).

*Good Programming Practice 3.1*

*Prefix the name of* **CommandButton**s *with* **cmd**. *This allows easy identification of* **CommandButton**s.

The **Properties** window contains the ***Object box*** that determines which object's properties are displayed (Fig. 3.3). The **Object box** lists the form and all objects on the form. A selected object's properties are displayed in the **Properties** window.

The ***TabIndex*** property determines which control gets the *focus* (i.e., becomes the active control) when the *Tab* key is pressed at runtime. The control with a **TabIndex** value of **0** gets the initial focus. Pressing the *Tab* key at runtime transfers the focus to the control with a **TabIndex** of **1**. Eventually, if the *Tab* key is pressed enough times, the focus is transferred back to the control with a **TabIndex** of **0**. The focus for each control is displayed differently. For buttons, the one with the focus has a darker border around it and a dotted inner square on its face as shown in Fig. 3.1. Some controls, such as **Label**s, have a **TabIndex** property but are not capable of receiving the focus. In this situation, the next control (based upon **TabIndex** values) capable of receiving the focus gets it. By default, a control receives a **TabIndex** value based on the order in which it is added to the form. The first control added gets **0**, the next control added gets **1**, etc. A control's **TabIndex** property can be changed in the **Properties** window.

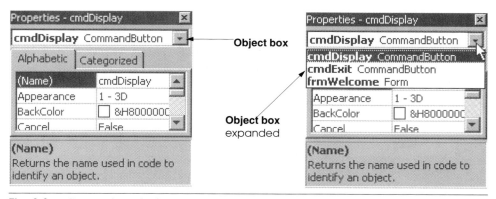

**Fig. 3.3    Properties** window.

We now switch over from the visual programming side to the event-driven programming side. If our program is going to print on the form, we must write code to accomplish this. With GUI and event-driven programming, the user decides when text is printed on the form by pressing **Print**. Each time **Print** is pressed, our program must respond by printing to the form. When the button is pressed does not matter; the fact that the button is pressed matters. Code must be written for the **Print** button's event procedure that receives this clicking (i.e., pressing) event.

When pressed, the **End** button terminates the program. Code must be written for the **End** button's event procedure that receives this clicking event. This event procedure for **End** is completely separate from the event procedure for **Print**. Separate event procedures make sense, because each button needs to respond differently.

Code is written in the **Code** window (Fig. 3.4). The **Code** window is displayed by either clicking the **Properties** window's **View Code** button or by double-clicking an object. The **View Code** button is disabled unless the form is visible. Figure 3.4 is the result of double-clicking the **Print** button at design time.

The code shown in Fig. 3.4 is generated by Visual Basic. The line

```
Private Sub cmdDisplay_Click()
```

begins the event procedure definition and is called the *procedure definition header*. The event procedure's name is **cmdDisplay_Click** (the parentheses **()** are necessary for syntax purposes). Visual Basic creates the event procedure name by appending the *event type* (**Click**) to the property **Name** with an underscore (_) added. ***Private Sub*** marks the beginning of the procedure. The ***End Sub*** statement marks the end of the procedure. Code that the programmer wants executed when **Print** is pressed is placed between the procedure definition header and the end of the procedure (i.e., **End Sub**). Figure 3.5 shows the **Code** window with code. We will discuss the code momentarily.

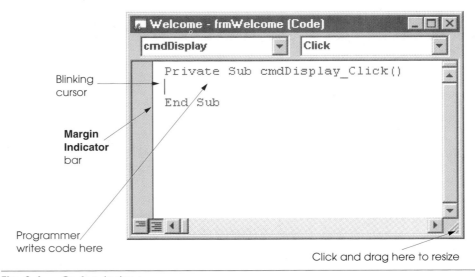

**Fig. 3.4    Code** window.

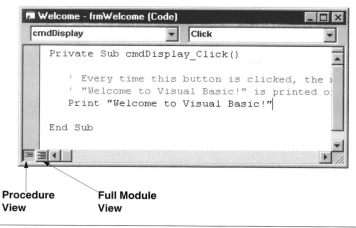

Procedure
View

Full Module
View

**Fig. 3.5**    **Code** window displaying code.

Figure 3.6 labels two buttons **_Procedure View_** and **_Full Module View_**. **Procedure View** lists only one procedure at a time. **Full Module View** lists the complete code for the whole *module* (the form in this example) as shown in Fig. 3.6. The **_Procedure Separator_** separates one procedure from another. The default is **Full Module View**. We pressed the **Procedure View** button in Fig. 3.5. Any object's code can be accessed with the **Code** window's **Object box** and **_Procedure box_**. The **Object box** lists the form and all objects associated with the form. The **Procedure box** lists the procedures associated with the object displayed in the **Object box**.

Object box            Procedure Separator            Procedure box

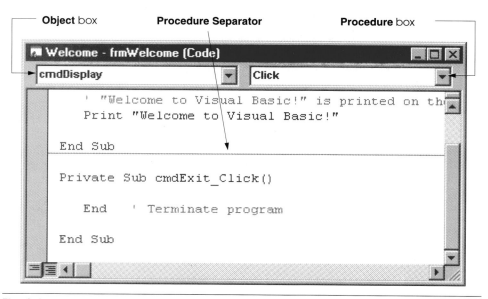

**Fig. 3.6**    **Code** window with **Full Module View** selected.

The program code is shown in Fig. 3.7. The line numbers to the left of the code are not part of the code but are placed there for reference purposes.

Procedure **cmdDisplay_Click** executes when button **Print** is pressed. The lines

```
' Every time this button is clicked, the message
' "Welcome to Visual Basic!" is printed on the form
```

are *comments*. Programmers insert comments to document programs and improve program readability. Comments also help other people read and understand your program code. Comments do not cause the computer to perform any action when a program is run. A comment can begin with either **'** or **_Rem_** (short for "remark") and is a *single-line comment* that terminates at the end of the current line. Most programmers use the single-quote style.

*Good Programming Practice 3.2*

*Comments written to the right of a statement should be preceded by several spaces to enhance program readability.*

*Good Programming Practice 3.3*

*Visual Basic statements can be long. You might prefer to write comments above the line(s) of code you are documenting.*

*Good Programming Practice 3.4*

*Precede comments that occupy a single line with a blank line. The blank line makes the comment stand out and improves program readability.*

The line

```
Print "Welcome to Visual Basic!"
```

prints the text "**Welcome to Visual Basic!**" on the form using the **_Print_** *method*. Each time this *statement* executes, the text is displayed on the next line. Method **Print** is a feature of the Visual Basic language and is unrelated to **cmdDisplay**'s **Caption** (**Print**).

*Good Programming Practice 3.5*

*Indent statements inside the bodies of event procedures. We recommend three spaces of indentation. Indenting statements increases program readability.*

```
1   Private Sub cmdDisplay_Click()
2
3      ' Every time this button is clicked, the message
4      ' "Welcome to Visual Basic!" is printed on the form
5      Print "Welcome to Visual Basic!"
6
7   End Sub
8
9   Private Sub cmdExit_Click()
10
11     End     ' Terminate program
12
13  End Sub
```

**Fig. 3.7**   Program code.

Drawing directly on the form using **Print** is not the best way of displaying information, especially if the form contains controls. As is shown in Fig. 3.1, a control can hide text that is displayed with **Print**. This problem is solved by displaying the text in a control. We demonstrate this in the next example.

The only statement in the **cmdExit_Click** event procedure is

```
End       ' Terminate program
```

The **End** statement terminates program execution (i.e., places the IDE in design mode). Note the comment's placement in the statement.

**Software Engineering Observation 3.1**

*Even though multiple **End** statements are permitted, use only one. Normal program termination should occur in only one place.*

When the user types a line of code and presses the *Enter* key, Visual Basic responds either by generating a *syntax error* (also called a *compile error*) or by changing the colors on the line. Colors may or may not change depending on what the user types.

A syntax error is a violation of the language syntax (i.e., a statement is not written correctly). Syntax errors occur when statements are missing information, when statements have extra information, when names are misspelled, etc. When a syntax error occurs, a *dialog* like Fig. 3.8 is displayed. Note that some syntax errors are not generated until the programmer attempts to enter run mode.

**Testing and Debugging Tip 3.1**

*As Visual Basic processes the line you typed, it may find one or more syntax errors. Visual Basic will display an error message indicating what the problem is and where on the line the problem is occurring.*

If a statement does not generate syntax errors when the *Enter* key is pressed, a coloring scheme (called *syntax color highlighting*) is imposed on the line of code. Comments are changed to green. The event procedure names remain black. Words recognized by Visual Basic (called *keywords* or *reserved words*) are changed to blue. Keywords (i.e., **Private**, **Sub**, **End**, **Print**, etc.) cannot be used for anything other than for the feature they represent. In addition to syntax color highlighting, Visual Basic may convert some lowercase letters to uppercase, and vice versa.

**Common Programming Error 3.1**

*Using a keyword as a variable name is a syntax error.*

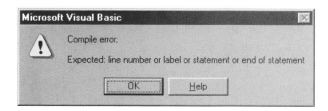

**Fig. 3.8**    Syntax error dialog.

*Testing and Debugging Tip 3.2*

*Syntax color highlighting helps the programmer avoid using keywords accidentally.*

The colors used for comments, keywords, etc. can be set using the ***Editor Format*** *tab* in the ***Options*** dialog (from the **Tools** menu). The **Option** dialog displaying the **Editor Format** tab is shown in Fig. 3.9.

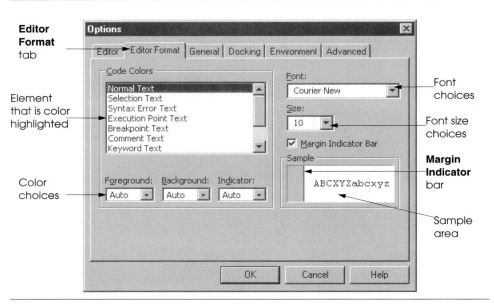

**Fig. 3.9**   **Options** dialog displaying **Editor Format** tag.

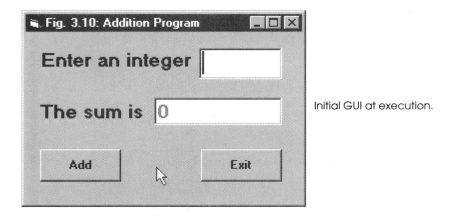

Initial GUI at execution.

**Fig. 3.10**   Program that adds **Integer**s (part 1 of 3).

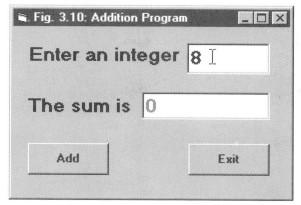

GUI after user has entered **8** in the first **TextBox**.

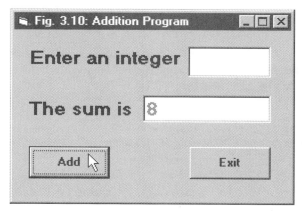

GUI after user has pressed **Add**. The value 8 is added to the sum and the sum is displayed in the second **TextBox**. The first **TextBox** is cleared.

GUI after user has entered **22** in the first **TextBox**.

**Fig. 3.10**    Program that adds **Integer**s (part 2 of 3).

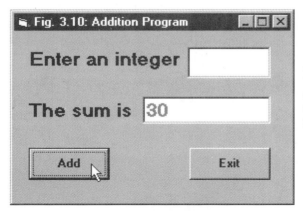

GUI after user has pressed **Add**.
The value 22 is added to the sum
and the sum is displayed in the
second **TextBox**. The first **Text-
Box** is cleared.

**Fig. 3.10**   Program that adds **Integer**s (part 3 of 3).

## 3.4  Another Simple Program: Adding `Integers`

Our next program obtains **Integer**s from the user, computes their sum and displays the
result. The GUI consists of two **Label**s, two **TextBox**es and two buttons as shown in Fig.
3.10. The object properties are listed in Fig. 3.11 and the program is shown in Fig. 3.12.

| Object | Icon | Property | Property setting | Property description |
|--------|------|----------|------------------|----------------------|
| form | | **Name** | **frmAddition** | Identifies the form. |
| | | **Caption** | **Fig. 3.10: Addition Program** | Form title bar display. |
| **Add** button | | **Name** | **cmdAdd** | Identifies **Add** button. |
| | | **Caption** | **Add** | Text that appears on button. |
| **Exit** button | | **Name** | **cmdExit** | Identifies **Exit** button. |
| | | **Caption** | **Exit** | Text that appears on button. |
| **Label** | A | **Name** | **lblSum** | Identifies the **Label**. |
| | | **Caption** | **The sum is** | Text **Label** displays. |
| **Label** | A | **Name** | **lblPrompt** | Identifies the **Label**. |
| | | **Caption** | **Enter an integer** | Text **Label** displays. |

**Fig. 3.11**   Object properties (part 1 of 2).

| Object | Icon | Property | Property setting | Property description |
|--------|------|----------|------------------|----------------------|
| **TextBox** | `ab\|` | **Name** | **txtSum** | Identifies **TextBox**. |
| | | **Font** | **MS San Serif Bold 14** pt | Font for **TextBox**. |
| | | **Text** | **0** | Text that is displayed. |
| | | **Enabled** | **False** | Enabled/disabled. |
| **TextBox** | `ab\|` | **Name** | **txtInput** | Identifies **TextBox**. |
| | | **Font** | **MS San Serif Bold 14** pt | Font for **TextBox**. |
| | | **MaxLength** | **5** | Maximum length of character input. |
| | | **TabIndex** | **0** | Tab order. |
| | | **Text** | (empty) | Text that is displayed. |

**Fig. 3.11**   Object properties (part 2 of 2).

```
1   Dim sum As Integer              ' Declare an Integer
2
3   Private Sub cmdAdd_Click()
4       sum = sum + txtInput.Text    ' Add to sum
5       txtInput.Text = ""           ' Clear TextBox
6       txtSum.Text = sum            ' Display sum in TextBox
7   End Sub
8
9   Private Sub cmdExit_Click()
10      End                          ' Terminate execution
11  End Sub
```

**Fig. 3.12**   Program code.

*Good Programming Practice 3.6*

*Prefix the name of **TextBox**es with **txt** to allow easy identification of **TextBox**es.*

The **TextBox** control is introduced in this example. This is the primary control for obtaining user input. **TextBox**es can also be used to display text. In our program one **TextBox** accepts input from the user and the other outputs the sum.

Like other controls, **TextBox**es have many properties. **Text** is the most commonly used **TextBox** property. The **Text** property stores the text for the **TextBox**. **TextBox**es have their **Enabled** *property* set to **True** by default. If the **Enabled** property is set to **False**, the user cannot interact with the **TextBox** and any text displayed in the **TextBox** is grayed. Object **txtSum** has its **Enabled** property set to **False**. Note that the text representing the sum appears gray, indicating that it is disabled.

The **MaxLength** property value limits how many characters can be entered in a **TextBox**. The default value is **0**, which means that any number of characters can be input. We set **txtInput**'s **MaxLength** value to **5**.

The first line of code resides in the *general declaration*. Statements placed in the general declaration are available to every event procedure. The general declaration can be accessed with the **Code** window's **Object box**. The statement

```
Dim sum As Integer
```

declares a variable named **sum**. A *variable* is a location in the computer's memory where a value can be stored for use by a program. A variable name is any valid *identifier. Variable names cannot be keywords and must begin with a letter.* The maximum length of a variable name is 255 characters containing only letters, numbers, and underscores. Visual Basic is not case-sensitive—uppercase and lowercase letters are treated the same, so **a1** and **A1** are considered identical. Keywords appear to be case-sensitive but they are not. Visual Basic automatically sets to uppercase the first letter of keywords, so typing **dim** would be changed to **Dim**.

**Good Programming Practice 3.7**

*Begin each identifier with a lowercase letter. This will allow you to distinguish between a valid identifier and a keyword.*

**Common Programming Error 3.2**

*Attempting to declare a variable name that does not begin with a letter is a syntax error.*

**Good Programming Practice 3.8**

*Choosing meaningful variable names helps a program to be "self-documenting." A program becomes easier to understand simply by reading the code rather than having to read manuals or having to use excessive comments.*

Keyword **Dim** *explicitly* (i.e., formally) declares variables. The clause beginning with the keyword **As** is part of the declaration and describes the *variable's type (i.e., what type of information can be stored)*. **Integer** means that the variable holds **Integer** values (i.e., whole numbers such as 8, –22, 0, 31298). **Integer**s are stored in two bytes of memory and have a range of –32767 to +32768. **Integer** variables are initialized to **0** by default. We discuss other data types in the next several chapters.

**Common Programming Error 3.3**

*Exceeding an **Integer**'s range is a run-time error.*

Variables can also be declared using special symbols called *type declaration characters*. For example, the declaration

```
Dim sum As Integer
```

could also be written as

```
Dim sum%
```

The *percent sign*, **%**, is the **Integer** *type declaration character*. Not all types have type declaration characters.

***Common Programming Error 3.4***

*Attempting to use a type declaration character and keyword **As** together is a syntax error.*

Variables can also be declared *implicitly* (without giving them a formal type) by mentioning the name. For example, consider the line

```
someVariable% = 8   ' Implicitly declare an Integer variable
```

which declares and initializes **someVariable**. When Visual Basic executes this line, **someVariable** is declared and given a value of **8** with *assignment operator =*. Visual Basic provides a means of forcing explicit declaration which we discuss later in this chapter.

***Good Programming Practice 3.9***

*Explicitly declaring variables makes programs clearer.*

If a variable is not given a type when its declared, its type defaults to ***Variant***. The **Variant** data type can hold any type of value (i.e., **Integer**s, **Single**s, etc.). Although the **Variant** type seems like a convenient type to use, it can be very tricky determining the type of the value stored. We discuss the **Variant** type in Chapter 4.

***Common Programming Error 3.5***

*It is an error to assume that the **As** clause in a declaration distributes to other variables on the same line. For example, writing the declaration **Dim x As Integer, y** and assuming that both **x** and **y** would be declared as **Integer**s would be incorrect, when in fact the declaration would declare **x** to be an **Integer** and **y** (by default) to be a **Variant**.*

Line 4

```
sum = sum + txtInput.Text
```

gets **txtInput**'s text and adds it to **sum**, storing the result in **sum**. To access a property, use the object's name followed by a period and the property name. Before the *addition operator*, **+**, adds the value input, the **Text** property value must be converted from a *string* (i.e., text) to an **Integer**. The conversion is done implicitly—no code need be written to force the conversion.

***Common Programming Error 3.6***

*Expressions or values that cannot be implicitly converted result in run-time errors.*

The previous assignment statement could have been written as

```
Let sum = sum + txtInput.Text
```

which uses keyword **Let**. When writing an assignment statement, keyword **Let** is optional. Our convention is to omit the keyword **Let**.

The lines

```
txtInput.Text = ""
txtSum.Text = sum
```

"clear" the characters from **txtInput** and display text in **txtSum**. The pair of double quotes, **""**, assigned to **txtInput.Text** is called an *empty string*. Assigning an empty string to **txtInput.Text** clears the **TextBox**. When **sum** (an **Integer**) is assigned to **txtSum.Text**, Visual Basic implicitly converts **sum**'s value to a string.

## 3.5 Memory Concepts

Variable names such as **sum** actually correspond to locations in the computer's memory. Every variable has a name, a type, a size and a value. In the addition program of Fig. 3.12, the statement

```
sum = sum + txtInput.Text
```

places into **sum**'s memory location the result of adding **sum** to **txtInput.Text**. Suppose the value of **txtInput.Text** is **"22"**. Visual Basic converts the string **"22"** to the **Integer 22** and adds it to the value contained in **sum**'s memory location. The result is then stored in **sum**'s memory location as shown in Fig. 3.13.

Whenever a value is placed in a memory location, the value replaces the previous value in that location. The process of storing a value in a memory location is known as *destructive read-in*. The statement

```
sum = sum + txtInput.Text
```

that performs the addition involves destructive read-in. This occurs when the result of the calculation is placed into location **sum** (destroying the previous value in **sum**).

Variable **sum** is used on the right side of the assignment expression. The value contained in **sum**'s memory location must be read in order to do the addition operation. Thus, when a value is read out of a memory location, the original value is preserved and the process is *nondestructive*.

## 3.6 Arithmetic

Most programs perform arithmetic calculations. The *arithmetic operators* are summarized in Fig. 3.14. Note the use of various special symbols not used in algebra. The *caret* ( ^ ) indicates exponentiation, and the *asterisk* ( * ) indicates multiplication. The **Integer** *division operator* ( \ ) and the *modulus* ( **Mod** ) operator will be discussed shortly. Most arithmetic operators are *binary operators* because they each operate on two *operands*. For example, the expression **sum + value** contains the binary operator **+** and the two operands **sum** and **value**.

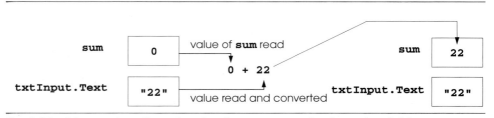

**Fig. 3.13**    Memory locations showing the names and values of variables.

| Visual Basic operation | Arithmetic operator | Algebraic expression | Visual Basic expression |
|---|---|---|---|
| Addition | + | $x + y$ | x + y |
| Subtraction | - | $z - 8$ | z - 8 |
| Multiplication | * | $yb$ | y * b |
| Division (float) | / | $v / u$ or $\dfrac{v}{u}$ | v / u |
| Division (**Integer**) | \ | none | v \ u |
| Exponentiation | ^ | $q^p$ | q ^ p |
| Negation | - | $-e$ | -e |
| Modulus | **Mod** | $q \bmod r$ | q Mod r |

**Fig. 3.14**　Arithmetic operators.

Visual Basic has separate operators for **Integer** division (the backslash, **\**) and floating-point division (the forward slash, **/**). **Integer** division yields an **Integer** result; for example, the expression **7 \ 4** evaluates to **1**, and the expression **17 \ 5** evaluates to **3**. Note that any fractional part in **Integer** division is rounded before the division takes place. For example, the expression **7.7 \ 4** would yield **2**. The value **7.7** is rounded to **8**. The expression **7.3 \ 4** would yield **1**. The value **7.3** is rounded to **7**.

Floating-point division yields a *floating-point number* (i.e., a number with a decimal point such as 7.7). We will discuss floating-point numbers in Chapter 4.

The *modulus operator*, *Mod*, yields the **Integer** remainder after **Integer** division. Like the **Integer** division operator, the modulus operator rounds any fractional part before performing the operation. The expression **x Mod y** yields the remainder after **x** is divided by **y**. A result of 0 indicates that **y** divides evenly into **x**. Thus, 20 **Mod** 5 yields 0, and 7 **Mod** 4 yields 3.

The *negation operator*, **-**, changes the sign of a number from positive to negative (or from negative to positive). The expression **-8** changes the sign of 8 to negative, which yields **-8**. The negation operator is said to be a *unary operator*, because it operates on only one operand. The operand must appear to the right of the negation operator.

Arithmetic expressions must be written in *straight-line form* when entering programs into the computer. Thus, expressions such as "*a* raised to the power *b*" must be written as

　　　a ^ b

so that all constants, variables and operators appear in a straight line. The algebraic notation
　　　$a^b$
is generally not acceptable to compilers, although some special-purpose software packages do exist that support more natural notation for complex mathematical expressions.

Parentheses are used in expressions in much the same manner as in algebraic expressions. For example, to multiply **b** times the quantity **e + n** we write

　　　b * (e + n)

## 3.7 Operator Precedence

Visual Basic applies the operators in arithmetic expressions in a sequence determined by the following rules of *operator precedence*, which are similar to those followed in algebra:

1. Operators in expressions contained within pairs of parentheses are evaluated first. Thus, *parentheses may be used to force the order of evaluation to occur in any sequence desired by the programmer.* Parentheses are said to be at the "highest level of precedence." In cases of *nested* or *embedded* parentheses, the operators in the innermost pair of parentheses are applied first.

2. Exponentiation is applied next. If an expression contains several exponentiation operations, operators are applied from left to right.

3. Negation is applied next. If an expression contains several negation operations, operators are applied from left to right.

4. Multiplication and floating-point division operations are applied next. If an expression contains several multiplication and floating-point division operations, operators are applied from left to right. Multiplication and floating-point division are said to be on the same level of precedence.

5. **Integer** division is applied next. If an expression contains several **Integer** division operations, operators are applied from left to right.

6. Modulus operators are applied next. If an expression contains several modulus arithmetic operations, operators are applied from left to right.

7. Addition and subtraction operations are applied last. If an expression contains several addition and subtraction operations, operators are applied from left to right. Addition and subtraction also have the same level of precedence.

The rules of operator precedence enable Visual Basic to apply operators in the correct order. Figure 3.15 summarizes these rules of operator precedence. This table will be expanded as we introduce additional Visual Basic operators. A complete precedence chart is included in the Appendices.

| Operator(s) | Operation(s) | Order of evaluation (precedence) |
| --- | --- | --- |
| ( ) | Parentheses | Evaluated first. If the parentheses are nested, the expression in the innermost pair is evaluated first. If there are several pairs of parentheses "on the same level" (i.e., not nested), they are evaluated left to right. |
| ^ | Exponentiation | Evaluated second. If there are several, they are evaluated left to right. |
| – | Negation | Evaluated third. If there are several, they are evaluated left to right. |
| * or / | Multiplication and floating-point division | Evaluated fourth. If there are several, they are evaluated left to right. |

**Fig. 3.15**   Precedence of arithmetic operators.

| Operator(s) | Operation(s) | Order of evaluation (precedence) |
|---|---|---|
| \ | Division (**Integer**) | Evaluated fifth. If there are several, they are evaluated left to right. |
| **Mod** | Modulus | Evaluated sixth. If there are several, they are evaluated left to right. |
| **+** or **−** | Addition and subtraction | Evaluated last. If there are several, they are evaluated left to right. |

**Fig. 3.15**   Precedence of arithmetic operators.

Now let us consider several expressions in light of the rules of operator precedence. Each example lists an algebraic expression and its Visual Basic equivalent.

The following is an example of an arithmetic mean (average) of five terms:

Algebra:   $m = \dfrac{a + b + c + d + e}{5}$

Visual Basic:   **m = (a + b + c + d + e) / 5**

The parentheses are required because floating-point division has higher precedence than addition. The entire quantity **(a + b + c + d + e)** is to be divided by 5. If the parentheses are erroneously omitted, we obtain **a + b + c + d + e / 5**, which evaluates as

$$a + b + c + d + \frac{e}{5}$$

The following is the equation of a straight line:

Algebra:   $y = mx + b$

Visual Basic:   **y = m * x + b**

No parentheses are required. Multiplication has a higher precedence than addition and is applied first.

The following example contains exponentiation, multiplication, floating-point division, addition and subtraction operations:

*Algebra:*   $z = pr^q + w/x - y$

Visual Basic:   **z = p * r ^ q + w / x − y**
          ⑥    ②    ①    ④    ③    ⑤

The circled numbers under the statement indicate the order in which the operators are applied. The exponentiation operator is evaluated first. The multiplication and floating-point division operators are evaluated next in left-to-right order since they have higher precedence than assignment, addition and subtraction. Addition and subtraction operators are evaluated next in left-to-right order (addition followed by subtraction). The assignment operator is evaluated last.

Not all expressions with several pairs of parentheses contain nested parentheses. For example, the expression

```
a * (b + c) + c * (d + e)
```

does not contain nested parentheses. Rather, the parentheses are said to be on the same level of precedence.

To develop a better understanding of the rules of operator precedence, consider how a second-degree polynomial is evaluated.

The circled numbers under the statement indicate the order in which Visual Basic applies the operators.

Suppose that variables **a**, **b**, **c** and **x** are initialized as follows: **a = 2**, **b = 3**, **c = 7** and **x = 5**. Figure 3.16 illustrates the order in which the operators are applied in the preceding second-degree polynomial.

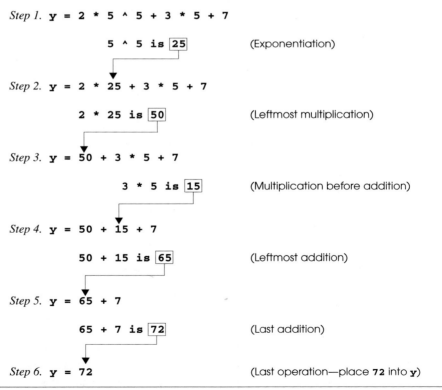

**Fig. 3.16**    Order in which operators in a second-degree polynomial are evaluated.

As in algebra, it is acceptable to place extra parentheses in an expression to make the expression clearer. Unnecessary parentheses are also called *redundant parentheses*. For example, the preceding assignment statement could be parenthesized as follows without changing its meaning:

```
y = (a * x ^ 2) + (b * x) + c
```

*Good Programming Practice 3.10*

*Placing extra parentheses in an expression can make that expression clearer.*

## 3.8 Decision Making: Comparison Operators

This section introduces a simple version of Visual Basic's *If/Then structure* that allows a program to make a decision based on the truth or falsity of some *condition*. If the condition is met (i.e., the condition is **True**), the statement in the body of the **If/Then** structure is executed. If the condition is not met (i.e., the condition is **False**), the body statement is not executed.

Conditions in **If/Then** structures can be formed by using the *comparison operators* summarized in Fig. 3.17. The comparison operators all have the same level of precedence.

*Common Programming Error 3.7*

*Reversing the order of the symbols in the operators <>, >= and <= as in ><, => and =<, respectively, are each syntax errors.*

*Common Programming Error 3.8*

*Writing a statement such as* **x = y = 0** *and assuming that the variables* **x** *and* **y** *are both assigned zero, when in fact comparisons are taking place, can lead to subtle logic errors.*

*Good Programming Practice 3.11*

*Refer to the operator precedence chart when writing expressions containing many operators. Confirm that the operators in the expression are performed in the order you expect. If you are uncertain about the order of evaluation in a complex expression, use parentheses to force the order, exactly as you would do in algebraic expressions.*

| Standard algebraic equality operator or relational operator | Visual Basic comparison operator | Example of Visual Basic condition | Meaning of Visual Basic condition |
|---|---|---|---|
| = | = | d = g | d is equal to g |
| ≠ | <> | s <> r | s is not equal to r |
| > | > | y > i | y is greater than i |
| < | < | p < m | p is less than m |
| ≥ | >= | c >= e | c is greater than or equal to e |
| ≤ | <= | m <= s | m is less than or equal to s |

**Fig. 3.17**  Comparison operators.

The next example uses six **If/Then** statements to compare two numbers input by the user. The GUI is shown in Fig. 3.18, the properties in Fig. 3.19 and the code in Fig. 3.20.

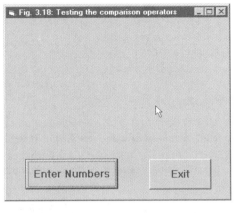

Initial GUI at execution.

First input dialog displayed for user input. User inputs **8** before pressing **OK**.

Second input dialog displayed for user input. User inputs **22** before pressing **OK**.

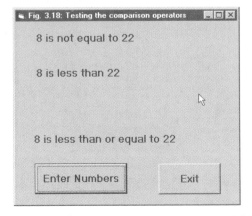

GUI after second input dialog is closed.

**Fig. 3.18** GUI for program that compares two **Integer**s.

| Object | Icon | Property | Property setting | Property description |
|---|---|---|---|---|
| form | | `Name` | `frmIfThen` | Identifies the form. |
| | | `Caption` | `Fig. 3.18: Testing the comparison operators` | Form title bar display. |
| **Enter Numbers** button | | `Name` | `cmdEnterNumbers` | Identifies **Enter Numbers** button. |
| | | `Caption` | `Enter Numbers` | Text that appears on button. |
| | | `Font` | `MS Sans Serif bold 12` pt | Font for text on button's face. |
| **Exit** button |  | `Name` | `cmdExit` | Identifies **Exit** button. |
| | | `Caption` | `Exit` | Text that appears on button. |
| | | `Font` | `MS Sans Serif bold 12` pt | Font for text on button's face. |
| `Label` |  A | `Name` | `lblDisplay1` | Identifies the **Label**. |
| | | `Caption` | (empty) | Text **Label** displays. |
| | | `Font` | `MS Sans Serif bold 12` pt | Font **Label** for **Label** display. |
| `Label` |  A | `Name` | `lblDisplay2` | Identifies the **Label**. |
| | | `Caption` | (empty) | Text **Label** displays. |
| | | `Font` | `MS Sans Serif bold 12` pt | Font **Label** for **Label** display. |
| `Label` |  A | `Name` | `lblDisplay3` | Identifies the **Label**. |
| | | `Caption` | (empty) | Text **Label** displays. |
| | | `Font` | `MS Sans Serif bold 12` pt | Font **Label** for **Label** display. |
| `Label` |  A | `Name` | `lblDisplay4` | Identifies the **Label**. |
| | | `Caption` | (empty) | Text **Label** displays. |
| | | `Font` | `MS Sans Serif bold 12` pt | Font **Label** for **Label** display. |

**Fig. 3.19**　Object properties for program that compares two `Integer`s.

```
1   ' Code listing for Fig. 3.18
2   ' Program compares two numbers
3   Option Explicit     ' Force explicit declarations
4
5   Private Sub cmdEnterNumbers_Click()
6      Dim num1 As Integer, num2 As Integer
7
8      ' Clear Labels
9      lblDisplay1.Caption = ""
10     lblDisplay2.Caption = ""
11     lblDisplay3.Caption = ""
12     lblDisplay4.Caption = ""
13
14     ' Get values from user
15     num1 = InputBox("Enter first integer", "Input")
16     num2 = InputBox("Enter second integer", "Input")
17
18     ' Test the relationships between the numbers
19     If num1 = num2 Then
20        lblDisplay1.Caption = num1 & " is equal to " & num2
21     End If
22
23     If num1 <> num2 Then
24        lblDisplay1.Caption = num1 & " is not equal to " & num2
25     End If
26
27     If num1 > num2 Then
28        lblDisplay2.Caption = num1 & " is greater than " & num2
29     End If
30
31     If num1 < num2 Then
32        lblDisplay2.Caption = num1 & " is less than " & num2
33     End If
34
35     If num1 >= num2 Then
36        lblDisplay3.Caption = num1 & _
37                             " is greater than or equal to " _
38                             & num2
39     End If
40
41     If num1 <= num2 Then
42        lblDisplay4.Caption = num1 & _
43                             " is less than or equal to " & num2
44     End If
45
46   End Sub
47
48   Private Sub cmdExit_Click()
49      End
50   End Sub
```

**Fig. 3.20**  Program that compares two **Integer**s.

The statement

```
Option Explicit
```

forces variables to be explicitly declared. The **Option Explicit** statement is always placed in the general declaration. **Option Explicit** can either be typed directly into the general declaration or placed there by Visual Basic when the ***Require Variable Declaration*** *checkbox* is checked. The ***Require Variable Declaration*** checkbox is on the **Options** dialog ***Editor*** *tab,* as shown in Fig. 3.21. The **Options** dialog is displayed when the **Tool** menu's **Options** menu item is selected. ***Require Variable Declaration*** is unchecked by default. Once checked, each new form associated with a project includes **Option Explicit** in the general declaration. Note: If ***Require Variable Declaration*** is unchecked and the form already exists, **Option Explicit** will not be added to the general declaration. The programmer must type it in the general declaration. However, each time a new form is created, **Option Explicit** is added by Visual Basic.

***Testing and Debugging Tip 3.3***

*Force variable declarations by using* **Option Explicit***.*

***Common Programming Error 3.9***

*If variable names are misspelled when not using* **Option Explicit***, a misspelled variable name will be declared and initialized to zero, usually resulting in a run-time logic error.*

Note that Fig. 3.21 labels a few **Editor** tab features relevant to our earlier discussion of **Full Module View** (Fig. 3.6). The user can also set the number of spaces that corresponds to a tab in the ***Tab Width*** **TextBox.**

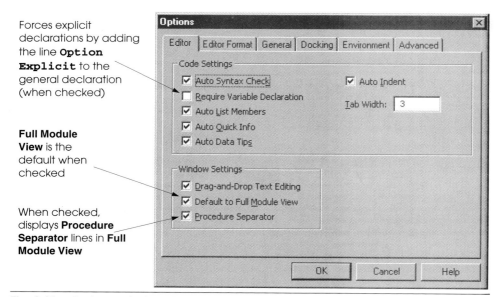

Forces explicit declarations by adding the line **Option Explicit** to the general declaration (when checked)

**Full Module View** is the default when checked

When checked, displays **Procedure Separator** lines in **Full Module View**

**Fig. 3.21**    **Options** window displaying **Editor** tab.

In procedure **cmdEnterNumbers_Click**, variables **num1** and **num2** are declared as **Integer**s. Variables can be declared just about anywhere in a procedure. Variables may be declared on separate lines or on a single line.

**Good Programming Practice 3.12**

*If you prefer to place declarations at the beginning of a procedure, separate those declarations from executable statements in that procedure with one blank line to highlight where the declarations end and the executable statements begin.*

**Good Programming Practice 3.13**

*Always place a blank line before and after a group of declarations that appears between executable statements in the body of a procedure. This makes the declarations stand out in the program and contributes to program readability.*

*Function* **InputBox** is used to get the values for **num1** and **num2** with the lines

```
num1 = InputBox("Enter first integer", "Input")
num2 = InputBox("Enter second integer", "Input")
```

Function **InputBox** displays an *input dialog,* which is shown in Fig. 3.22. The first argument (i.e., **"Enter first integer"**) is the prompt and the second argument (i.e., **"Input"**) determines what is displayed in the input dialog's title bar. When displayed, the dialog is *modal*—the user cannot interact with the form until the dialog is closed.

The input dialog contains a **Label**, two buttons and a **TextBox**. The **Label** displays the first argument passed to **InputBox**. The user clicks the **OK** button after entering a value in the **TextBox**. The **Cancel** button is pressed to cancel input. For this example, the values returned by successive calls to **InputBox** are assigned to **Integer**s **num1** and **num2**. The text representation of a number is implicitly converted (i.e., **"78"** is converted to **78**). If a value entered cannot be properly converted, a run-time error occurs. Pressing **Cancel** also creates a run-time error, because the empty string cannot be converted to an **Integer**. We discuss handling run-time errors in Chapter 13.

The line

```
If num1 = num2 Then
```

compares the contents of **num1** to the contents of **num2** for equality. If **num1** is equivalent to **num2**, the statement

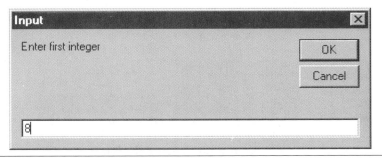

**Fig. 3.22** Dialog displayed by function **InputBox**.

```
lblDisplay1.Caption = num1 & " is equal to " & num2
```

is executed. The *string concatenation operator*, **&**, concatenates the implicitly converted values of **num1** and **num2** to strings. Keywords ***End If*** mark the end of the **If/Then** block. Since there is one statement in the body of the **If/Then**, the statement could be re-written on a single line as

```
If num1 = num2 Then lblDisplay1 = num1 & " is equal to " & num2
```

**End If** is not required to terminate a single-line **If/Then**. We will use the **End If** convention throughout this book. If the condition is **False**, the next **If/Then** is tested. Note that in the above statement, we mentioned **lblDisplay1**, not **lblDisplay1.Caption**. Each control has a *default property* (a property that is used when only the control's **Name** is used). A **Label**'s default property is **Caption**.

*Good Programming Practice 3.14*

*Write each **If/Then** structure on multiple lines using the **End If** to terminate the condition. Indent the statement in the body of the **If/Then** structure to highlight the body of the structure and to enhance program readability.*

*Good Programming Practice 3.15*

*Explicitly writing the default property improves program readability. Since default properties are different for most controls, omitting the property name can make the code more difficult to read.*

Notice the use of spacing in Fig. 3.20. *White-space characters* such as tabs and spaces are normally ignored by the compiler (except when placed inside a set of double quotes). Statements may be split over several lines if the *line-continuation character*, _, is used (e.g., lines 36-38). A minimum of one white-space character must precede the line-continuation character.

*Common Programming Error 3.10*

*Splitting a statement over several lines without the line-continuation character is a syntax error.*

*Common Programming Error 3.11*

*Not preceding the line-continuation character with at least one white-space character is a syntax error.*

*Common Programming Error 3.12*

*Placing anything, including comments, after a line-continuation character is a syntax error.*

Several statements may be combined onto a single line by using a colon, **:**, between the statements. For example, the two statements

```
square = number ^ 2
cube = number ^ 3
```

could be combined on the single line

```
square = number ^ 2 : cube = number ^ 3
```

Statements can be spaced according to the programmer's preferences.

*Common Programming Error 3.13*

*Splitting an identifier or a keyword is a syntax error.*

*Good Programming Practice 3.16*

*Even though Visual Basic provides the colon to combine multiple statements on a single line, writing only one statement per line improves program readability.*

## Summary

- With visual programming, the programmer has the ability to create graphical user interfaces (GUIs) by pointing and clicking with the mouse.

- Visual programming eliminates the need for the programmer to write code that generates the form, code for all the form's properties, code for form placement on the screen, code to create and place a **Label** on the form, code to change foreground and background colors, etc.

- The programmer creates the GUI and writes code to describe what happens when the user interacts (clicks, presses a key, double-clicks, etc.) with the GUI. These interactions, called events, are passed into the program by the Windows operating system.

- With event-driven programs, the user dictates the order of program execution.

- Event procedures are bodies of code that respond to events and are automatically generated by the IDE. All the programmer need do is locate them and add code to respond to the events. Only events relevant to a particular program need be coded.

- The **Properties** window contains the **Object box** that determines which object's properties are displayed. The **Object box** lists the form and all objects on the form. An object's properties are displayed in the **Properties** window when an object is clicked.

- Property **TabIndex** determines which control gets the focus (i.e., becomes the active control) when the Tab key is pressed at runtime. The control with a **TabIndex** value of **0** gets the initial focus. Pressing the Tab key at runtime transfers the focus to the control with a **TabIndex** of **1**.

- Pressing the **End** button terminates the program.

- Code is written in the **Code** window. The **Code** window is displayed by clicking the **Properties** window's **View Code** button.

- Visual Basic creates the event procedure name by appending the event type (**Click**) to the property **Name** (with an underscore _ added). **Private Sub** marks the beginning of the procedure. The **End Sub** statement marks the end of the procedure. Code the programmer wants executed is placed between the procedure definition header and the end of the procedure (i.e., **End Sub**).

- The **Object box** lists the form and all objects associated with the form. The **Procedure box** lists the procedures associated with the object displayed in the **Object box**.

- Programmers insert comments to document programs and improve program readability. Comments also help other people read and understand the program code. Comments do not cause the computer to perform any action when a program is run. A comment can begin with either **'** or **Rem** (for "remark") and is a single-line comment that terminates at the end of the current line.

- A program can print on the form using the **Print** method. Drawing directly on the form using **Print** is not the best way of displaying information, especially if the form contains controls because a control can hide text that is displayed with **Print**. This problem is solved by displaying the text in a control.

- The **End** statement terminates program execution (i.e., places the IDE in design mode).

- When a line of code is typed and Enter pressed, Visual Basic responds either by generating a syntax error (also called a compile error) or by changing the colors on the line.

- A syntax error is a violation of the language syntax (i.e., a statement is not written correctly). As a general rule, syntax errors tend to occur when statements are missing information, statements have extra information, names are misspelled, etc.

- If a statement does not generate syntax errors when the Enter key is pressed, a coloring scheme (called syntax-color highlighting) is imposed on the line of code. Comments are changed to green. The event procedure names remain black. Words recognized by Visual Basic are called keywords (also called reserved words) and appear blue.

- Keywords (i.e., **Private**, **Sub**, **End**, **Print**, etc.) cannot be used for anything other than for the feature they represent. Any improper use results in a syntax error. In addition to syntax color highlighting, Visual Basic may convert some lowercase letters to uppercase, and vice versa. The colors used for comments, keywords, etc. can be set using the **Editor Format** tab in the **Options** dialog (from the **Tools** menu).

- The **TextBox** control is the primary control for obtaining user input. **TextBox**es can also be used to display text.

- **Text** is the most commonly used **TextBox** property. The **Text** property stores the text for the **TextBox**. **TextBox**es have their **Enabled** property set to **True** by default. If the **Enabled** property is **False**, the user cannot interact with the **TextBox**.

- The **MaxLength** property value limits how many characters can be entered in a **TextBox**. The default value is **0**, which means that any number of characters can be input.

- Code that resides in the general declaration is available to every event procedure. The general declaration can be accessed with the **Code** window's **Object box**.

- A variable is a location in the computer's memory where a value can be stored for use by a program. A variable name is any valid identifier. Variable names cannot be keywords and must begin with a letter. The maximum length of a variable name is 255 characters containing only letters, numbers and underscores.

- Visual Basic is not case-sensitive—uppercase and lowercase letters are treated the same.

- Keyword **Dim** explicitly declares variables. Keyword **As** describes the variable's type (i.e., what type of information can be stored). **Integer** means that the variable holds **Integer** values (i.e., whole numbers such as 8, –22, 0, 31298). **Integer**s have a range of +32768 to –32767. **Integer** variables are initialized to **0** by default.

- Variables can also be declared special symbols called type-declaration characters such as the percent sign, **%**, for **Integer**. Not all types have type declaration characters.

- If a variable is not given a type when its declared, its type defaults to **Variant**. The **Variant** data type can hold any type of value (i.e., **Integer**s, **Single**s, etc.).

- When writing an assignment statement, the keyword **Let** is optional.

- The pair of double quotes, **""**, is called an empty string. Assigning an empty string to a **TextBox**'s **Text** property "clears" the **TextBox**.

- Variable names correspond to locations in the computer's memory. Every variable has a name, a type, a size and a value.

- Whenever a value is placed in memory, the value replaces the previous value in that location. Storing a value in a memory location is known as destructive read-in. When a value is read out of a memory location, the process is nondestructive.

- Caret (**^**) indicates exponentiation and asterisk (**\***) indicates multiplication.

- Most of the arithmetic operators are binary operators because they each operate on two operands.

- Visual Basic has separate operators for **Integer** and floating-point division. **Integer** division yields an **Integer** result. Fractional parts in **Integer** division are rounded before the division.

- Floating-point division yields a floating-point result (with a decimal point).

- The modulus operator, **Mod**, yields the **Integer** remainder after **Integer** division. Like the **Integer** division operator, the modulus operator rounds any fractional part before performing the operation. The expression **x Mod y** yields the remainder after **x** is divided by **y**. A remainder of 0 indicates that **y** divides evenly into **x**.

- The negation operator, **–**, changes the sign of a number from positive to negative (or a vice versa). The negation operator is a unary operator; it operates on one operand.

- Arithmetic expressions must be written in straight-line form.

- Parentheses are used in expressions much as in algebraic expressions.

- Parentheses may be used to force the order of evaluation to occur in any sequence desired by the programmer. Parentheses are said to be at the "highest level of precedence." Operators in the innermost pair of parentheses are applied first.

- As in algebra, it is acceptable to place extra parentheses in an expression to make the expression clearer. Unnecessary parentheses are also called redundant parentheses.

- The **If/Then** structure makes a decision based on the truth or falsity of some condition. If the condition is **True**, the statement in the body of the **If/Then** structure is executed. If the condition is **False**, the body statement is not executed.

- Conditions in **If/Then** structures can be formed by using the comparison operators.

- The **Option Explicit** statement forces variables to be explicitly declared. The **Option Explicit** statement is placed in the general declaration. **Option Explicit** can either be typed directly into the general declaration or placed there by Visual Basic when the **Require Variable Declaration** checkbox is checked.

- You can set the number of spaces that correspond to a tab in the **Tab Width TextBox**.

- Variables can be declared almost anywhere in a procedure. Variables may be declared on separate lines or on a single line.

- Function **InputBox** displays an input dialog. The first argument is the prompt and the second determines what is displayed in the input dialog's title bar. When displayed, the dialog is modal—the user cannot interact with the form until the dialog is closed.

- The ampersand operator, **&**, concatenates strings.

- Keywords **End If** mark the end of the **If/Then** block. **End If** is not required to terminate a single-line **If/Then**.

- Each control has a default property (a property that is used when only the control's **Name** is used). A **Label**'s default property is **Caption**.

- White-space characters such as tabs and spaces are normally ignored by the compiler.

- Statements may be split over several lines if the line-continuation character, **_**, is used. A minimum of one white-space character must precede the line-continuation character.

- Statements may be combined onto a line by using a colon, **:**, between the statements.

- It is incorrect to split identifiers and keywords.

## Terminology

| | |
|---|---|
| addition operator, **+** | binary operator |
| arithmetic operators | button |
| **As** keyword | **Cancel** button |
| assignment operator, **=** | caret, **^** |
| asterisk, **\*** | **Code** window |

colon, **:**
comments
comparison operators
compile error
condition
default property
destructive read-in
**Editor** tab
**Editor Format** tab
embedded parentheses
empty string
**Enabled** property
End If
**End** keyword
**End Sub**
event
event-driven programming
event monitoring
event procedure
event type
explicit declaration
**False** keyword
floating-point number
focus
**Full Module View**
general declaration
identifier
**If/Then** structure
implicit declaration
**InputBox** function
**Integer** division operator, **\**
**Integer** keyword
keyword
**Let** keyword
line-continuation character, **_**
**Margin Indicator** bar
**MaxLength** property
modal
modulus operator, **Mod**

negation operator, **–**
nested parentheses
nondestructive read-in
object
**Object box**
OK button
operand
operator
operator precedence
**Option Explicit**
Options dialog
percent sign, **%**
**Print** method
**Procedure box**
procedure definition header
**Procedure Separator**
**Procedure View**
Require Variable Declaration checkbox
**Rem**
reserved word
single-line comment
statement
string
string concatenation operator, **&**
**Sub** keyword
syntax color highlighting
syntax error
**TabIndex** property
*Tab* key
**Tab Width TextBox**
text
**TextBox** control
**Text** property
**True** keyword
type
type declaration character
unary operator
variable
**Variant**

## Common Programming Errors

**3.1**   Using a keyword as a variable name is a syntax error.

**3.2**   Attempting to declare a variable name that does not begin with a letter is a syntax error.

**3.3**   Exceeding an **Integer**'s range is a run-time error.

**3.4**   Attempting to use a type declaration character and keyword **As** together is a syntax error.

**3.5**   It is an error to assume that the **As** clause in a declaration distributes to other variables on the same line. For example, writing the declaration **Dim x As Integer**, **y** and assuming that both **x** and **y** would be declared as **Integer**s would be incorrect, when in fact the declaration would declare **x** to be an **Integer** and **y** (by default) to be a **Variant**.

**3.6**   Expressions or values that cannot be implicitly converted result in run-time errors.

**3.7**    Reversing the order of the symbols in the operators `<>`, `>=` and `<=` as in `><`, `=>` and `=<`, respectively, are syntax errors.

**3.8**    Writing a statement such as `x = y = 0` and assuming that the variables `x` and `y` are both assigned zero, when in fact comparisons are taking place. This can lead to subtle logic errors.

**3.9**    If variable names are misspelled when not using **Option Explicit**, a misspelled variable name will be declared and initialized to zero, usually resulting in a run-time logic error.

**3.10**   Splitting a statement over several lines without the line-continuation character is a syntax error.

**3.11**   Not preceding the line-continuation character with at least one white-space character is a syntax error.

**3.12**   Placing anything, including comments, after a line-continuation character is a syntax error.

**3.13**   Splitting an identifier or a keyword is a syntax error.

## Good Programming Practices

**3.1**    Prefix the name of **CommandButton**s with **cmd**. This allows easy identification of **CommandButton**s.

**3.2**    Comments written to the right of a statement should be preceded by several spaces to enhance program readability.

**3.3**    Visual Basic statements can be long. You might prefer to write comments above the line(s) of code you are documenting.

**3.4**    Precede comments that occupy a single line with a blank line. The blank line makes the comment stand out and improves program readability.

**3.5**    Indent statements inside the bodies of event procedures. We recommend three spaces of indentation. Indenting statements increases program readability.

**3.6**    Prefix the name of **TextBox**es with **txt** to allow easy identification of **TextBox**es.

**3.7**    Begin each identifier with a lowercase letter. This will allow you to distinguish between a valid identifier and a keyword.

**3.8**    Choosing meaningful variable names helps a program to be "self-documenting." A program becomes easier to understand simply by reading the code rather than having to read manuals or having to use excessive comments.

**3.9**    Explicitly declaring variables makes programs clearer.

**3.10**   Placing extra parentheses in an expression can make that expression clearer.

**3.11**   Refer to the operator precedence chart when writing expressions containing many operators. Confirm that the operators in the expression are performed in the order you expect. If you are uncertain about the order of evaluation in a complex expression, use parentheses to force the order, exactly as you would do in algebraic expressions.

**3.12**   If you prefer to place declarations at the beginning of a procedure, separate those declarations from executable statements in that procedure with one blank line to highlight where the declarations end and the executable statements begin.

**3.13**   Always place a blank line before and after a group of declarations that appears between executable statements in the body of a procedure. This makes the declarations stand out in the program and contributes to program readability.

**3.14**   Write each **If/Then** structure on multiple lines using the **End If** to terminate the condition. Indent the statement in the body of the **If/Then** structure to highlight the body of the structure and to enhance program readability.

**3.15**   Explicitly writing the default property improves program readability. Since default properties are different for most controls, omitting the property name can make the code more difficult to read.

**3.16**   Even though Visual Basic provides the colon to combine multiple statements on a single line, writing only one statement per line improves program readability.

## Testing and Debugging Tips

**3.1** As Visual Basic processes the line you typed, it may find one or more syntax errors. Visual Basic will display an error message indicating what the problem is and where on the line the problem is occurring.

**3.2** Syntax color highlighting helps the programmer avoid using keywords accidentally.

**3.3** Force variable declarations by using **Option Explicit**.

## Software Engineering Observation

**3.1** Even though multiple **End** statements are permitted, use only one. Normal program termination should occur in only one place.

## Self-Review Exercises

**3.1** Fill in the blanks in each of the following:

a) Keywords _____ begin the body of an event procedure and keywords _____ end the body of an event procedure.

b) When a value is placed into a memory location, it is known as _____ read-in.

c) What arithmetic operation(s) is/are on the same level of precedence as multiplication?_____

d) When parentheses are nested in an arithmetic expression, which set of parentheses is evaluated first? _____

e) A location in a computer's memory that may contain different values at various times throughout program execution is called a _____.

f) By default, **Integer** variables are initialized to the value _____.

**3.2** State whether each of the following is *true* or *false*. If *false*, explain why.

a) A comment's text is printed on the form as the comment is executed.

b) The **Rem** statement stores a string in the Visual Basic variable **Remark**.

c) **Option Explicit** forces explicit variable declaration.

d) All variables, when declared explicitly, must be given a data type either by using the **As** keyword or by using a type-declaration character (if the data type has one).

e) The variables **number** and **NuMbEr** are identical.

f) Declarations can appear almost anywhere in the body of an event procedure.

g) The modulus operator, **Mod**, can be used only with **Integer** operands. Attempts to use floating-point numbers (e.g., 19.88, 801.93, 3.14159, etc.) are syntax errors.

h) The arithmetic operators **\***, **/** and **\** all have the same level of precedence.

i) Visual Basic syntax always requires arithmetic expressions to be enclosed in parentheses—otherwise, syntax errors occur.

**3.3** Fill in the blanks in each of the following:

a) The _____ property limits the number characters input in a **TextBox**.

b) The default data type is _____.

c) The _____ character is the symbol for the string concatenation operator.

d) When a value is read out of a memory location, it is known as _____ readout.

**3.4** Write a single statement to accomplish each of the following:

a) Explicitly declare the variables **cj**, **ventor** and **num** to be of type **Integer**.

b) Assign "**Hello!**" to the **Label lblGreeting**.

c) Combine the following three lines into a single line:

```
' Initialization
total% = 0
counter% = 1
```

d) Assign the sum of **x**, **y** and **z** to the variable **sum**. Assume that each variable is of type **Integer**.

e) Decrement the variable **count** by 1, then subtract it from the variable **total**, and assign the result to the variable **u**. Assume all variables to be of type **Integer**.

f) Assign the product of the **Integer** variables **r**, **i**, **m**, **e** and **s** to the variable **g**.

g) Calculate the remainder after **total** is divided by **counter** and assign the result to **remainder**. Assume the variables to be of type **Integer**.

h) Assign the value returned from function **InputBox** to the variable **userInput**. The function **InputBox** should display the message "**Enter your data.**" The Input-Box's title bar should display "**Data Input.**" Assume the variable **userInput** to be of type **Integer**.

**3.5**   Write a statement or comment to accomplish each of the following:

a) State that a program will calculate the product of three **Integer**s.

b) Print the message "**printing to the form**" on the form using the **Print** method.

c) Force variable declarations.

d) Compute the **Integer** average of the three **Integer**s contained in variables **x**, **y** and **z**, and assign the result to the **Integer** variable **result**.

e) Print on the form "**The product is**" followed by the value of the **Integer** variable **result**.

f) Compare the **Integer** variables **sum1** and **sum2** for equality. If the result is true, set the **Integer** variable **flag** to 76.

**3.6**   Identify and correct the error(s) in each of the following statements:

a) `Dim False As Integer`

b) `Dim variable, inputValue As Integers`

c) `Integer oscii      Rem   declare variable`

d) `a + b = c      ' add a, b and assign result to c`

e) `d = t Modulus r + 50`

f) `variable = -65800      ' variable is of type Integer`

g) `" Change BackColor property's value`

h) `If (x > y)`
       `frmMyForm.Print x`

i) `Dim triplett As Integer, picks As Integer, End As Integer`

j) `triplett = picks = 10      ' Initialize both variables to 10`

k) `x : y = oldValue      Rem assign oldValue to both x and y`

**3.7**   Given the equation $b = 8e^5 - n$, which of the following, if any, are correct statements for this equation?

a) `b = 8 * e ^ 5 - n`

b) `b = ( 8 * e ) ^ 5 - n`

c) `b = 8 * ( e ^ 5 ) - n`

d) `b = 8 * e ^ ( 5 - n )`

e) `b = ( 8 * e ) ^ ( ( 5 ) - n )`

f) `b = 8 * e * e ^ 4 - n`

**3.8**   State the order of evaluation of the operators in each of the following statements, and show the value of **m** after each statement is performed. Assume **m** to be an **Integer** variable.

a) `m = 7 + 3 * 6 \ 2 - 1`

b) `m = 2 Mod 2 + 2 * 2 - 2 / 2`

c) `m = 8 + 10 \ 2 * 5 - 16 \ 2`

d) `m = -5 - 8 Mod 4 + 7 * (2 ^ 2 + 2)`

e) `m = 10 Mod 3 ^ 1 ^ 2 - 8`

## Answers to Self-Review Exercises

**3.1**  a) **Sub**, **End Sub**. b) destructive. c) floating-point division (**/**). d) innermost. e) variable. f) zero.

**3.2**  a) False. Comments are not executable statements; nothing is printed.
  b) False. **Rem** is simply another way of writing a comment.
  c) True.
  d) False. If a variable is not explicitly given a type, then it is given the default data type of **Variant**.
  e) True. Visual Basic is not case-sensitive.
  f) True.
  g) False. Floating-point numbers are rounded to **Integer**s before **Mod** is performed.
  h) False. Multiplication (**\***) and floating-point division (**/**) have the same precedence. **Integer** division (**\**) has a lower precedence.
  i) False. Visual Basic does not require all expressions to use parentheses.

**3.3**  a) **MaxLength**. b) **Variant**. c) ampersand, **&**. d) nondestructive.

**3.4**  a) `Dim cj As Integer, ventor As Integer, num As Integer`
  b) `lblGreeting.Caption = "Hello!"`
  c) `total% = 0 : counter% = 1      ' Initialization`
  d) `sum = x + y + z`
  e) `u = total - (count - 1)`
  f) `g = r * i * m * e * s`
  g) `remainder = total Mod counter`
  h) `userInput = InputBox("Enter your data", "Data Input")`

**3.5**  a) `' This program will calculate the product of three integers`
  b) `Print "printing to the form"`
  c) `Option Explicit   ' In general declaration`
  d) `result = (x + y + z) / 3`
  e) `Print "The product is " & result`
  f) `If sum1 = sum2 Then`
     `    flag = 76`
     `End If`

**3.6**  a) **False** is a keyword and may not be used as an identifier. Use a non-keyword as the variable name.
  b) **Integers** should be **Integer**.
  c) A variable cannot be declared this way. Correction: **Dim oscii As Integer**.
  d) The variable storing the result of the assignment (**c**) must be the left operand of the assignment operator. The statement should be rewritten as **c = a + b**.
  e) **Modulus** should be **Mod**.
  f) The number –65800 is out of range for an **Integer**. The value being assigned should be in the range –32,768 to 32,767.
  g) The double quotes should be single quotes or **Rem** to form a comment.
  h) The **Then** keyword is missing and the statement should either be contained on one line or be terminated by **End If**.
  i) **End** is a keyword and may not be used as an identifier.
  j) A comparison is being made rather than an assignment. Each assignment should be done separately.
     `    triplett = 10`
     `    picks = 10`

      k)  Invalid syntax. Each assignment must be done separately.

```
x = oldValue
y = oldValue
```

**3.7**     a, c, f.

**3.8**     a)
```
m = 7 + 3 * 6 \ 2 - 1
m = 7 + 18 \ 2 - 1
m = 7 + 9 - 1
m = 16 - 1
m = 15
```
       b)
```
m = 2 Mod 2 + 2 * 2 - 2 / 2
m = 2 Mod 2 + 4 - 2 / 2
m = 2 Mod 2 + 4 - 1
m = 0 + 4 - 1
m = 4 - 1
m = 3
```
       c)
```
m = 8 + 10 \ 2 * 5 - 16 \ 2
m = 8 + 10 \ 10 - 16 \ 2
m = 8 + 1 - 16 \ 2
m = 8 + 1 - 8
m = 9 - 8
m = 1
```
       d)
```
m = -5 - 8 Mod 4 + 7 * (2 ^ 2 + 2)
m = -5 - 8 Mod 4 + 7 * (4 + 2)
m = -5 - 8 Mod 4 + 7 * 6
m = -5 - 8 Mod 4 + 42
m = -5 - 0 + 42
m = -5 + 42
m = 37
```
       e)
```
m = 10 Mod 3 ^ 1 ^ 2 - 8
m = 10 Mod 3 ^ 1 - 8
m = 10 Mod 3 - 8
m = 1 - 8
m = -7
```

## Exercises

**3.9**     Identify and correct the error(s) in each of the following statements:

       a)  Assume that **Option Explicit** has been set.

```
' Event code for procedure
Private Sub cmdDisplay_Click()
   value1 = 5 : value2 = 10

   If value1 > value2 Then
      Print value1
   End If
End Sub
```

       b)  Assume that **Option Explicit** has not been set.

```
' Event code for procedure
Private Sub lblGreeting_Click()
    Low1Val = 8

    ' Display the value in lblGreeting's Caption property
    lblGreeting = LowlVal
End Sub
```

c) `animalName = "Giant " Cat "Parrot"`    `' Concatenate strings`

d) `thisIsAnIncrediblyLongVariableNameOf45Letters As Integer`

e) Assume that the **Integer** variables **c** and **j** are declared and initialized to **47** and **55**, respectively.

```
Dim x As Integer

If c =< j Then
    x = 79
    frmMyForm.Print x
End If
```

f) Assume that the variables **q**, **pcm** and **qp** are declared as **Integer**s.

```
' Executable statement
q = 76 ; qp =    ' Hard return after =
78 ; pcm = 61
```

**3.10** Write a single statement or line that accomplishes each of the following:

a) Print the message **"Visual Basic 6!!!!"** on the form.

b) Assign the product of variables **width22** and **height88** to variable **area51**.

c) State that a program performs a sample payroll calculation (i.e., use text that helps to document a program).

d) Calculate the area of a circle and assign it to the **Integer** variable **circleArea**. Use the formula $area = (\pi r^2)$, the variable **radius** and the value 3.14159 for $\pi$.

e) Concatenate the following two strings using the string concatenation operator and assign the result to **Label lblHoliday**'s **Caption**: **"Merry Christmas"** and **" and a Happy New Year"**.

**3.11** Fill in the blanks in each of the following:

a) _____ are used to document a program and improve its readability.

b) A statement that makes a decision is _____.

c) Calculations are normally performed by _____ statements.

d) The _____ statement terminates program execution.

e) The _____ method is used to display information to the form.

f) A _____ is a message to the user indicating that some action is required.

**3.12** State which of the following are *true* and which are *false*. If *false*, explain why.

a) **Integer** division has the same precedence as floating-point division.

b) The following are all valid variable names: **_under_bar_**, **m928134**, **majestic12**, **her_sales**, **hisAccountTotal**, **cmdWrite**, **b**, **creditCardBalance1999**, **YEAR_TO_DATE**, **__VoLs__LiSt__**.

c) The statement **squareArea = side ^ 2** is a typical example of an assignment statement.

    d)  A valid arithmetic expression with no parentheses is evaluated from left to right regard-less of the operators used in that expression.

    e)  The following are all invalid variable names: **2quarts**, **1988**, **&67h2**, **vols88**, **\*true_or_FALSE**, **99_DEGREES**, **_this**, **Then**.

    f)  Visual Basic automatically generates the beginning and end code of event procedures.

**3.13**     Given the following declarations, list the type for each variable declared.
    a)  `Dim traveler88 As Integer`
    b)  `number% = 76`
    c)  `Dim cars As Integer, trucks`
    d)  `Dim touchDowns, fieldGoals As Integer`
    e)  `portNumber = 80      ' Implicit declaration`

**3.14**     Given the equation $y = ax^3 + 7$, which of the following, if any, are correct statements for this equation?
    a)  `y = a * ( x ^ 3 + 7 )`
    b)  `y = ( a * x ) ^ 3 ) + 7`
    c)  `y = ( a * x * x * x + 7 )`
    d)  `y = ( a * ( x * ( x * x ) ) + 7 )`
    e)  `y = ( a * ( x * x ) ^ 2 ) + 7`
    f)  `y = (a) * (x) * (x) * (x) + (7)`

**3.15**     State the order of evaluation of the operators in each of the following statements, and show the value of **x** after each statement is performed. Assume **x** to be an **Integer** variable.
    a)  `x = ( 3 * 9 * ( 3 + ( 9 * 3 / ( 3 ) ) ) )`
    b)  `x = 1 + 2 * 3 - 4 / 4 - 12 \ 6 * 6`
    c)  `x = ( ( 10 - 4 * 2 ) \ 2 + ( 13 - 2 * 5 ) ) ^ 2`
    d)  `x = 8.2 Mod 3 + 2 / 2 - -3`
    e)  `x = -2 + 7.4 \ 5 - 6 / 4 Mod 2`

**3.16**     Which, if any, of the following statements contain variables involved in destructive read-in?
    a)  `myVariable = txtTextBox.Text`
    b)  `V = O + L + S + 8 * 8`
    c)  `Print "Destructive read-in"`
    d)  `Print "a = 8"`
    e)  `Print x = 22`
    f)  `Print userName`

**3.17**     What, if anything, prints when each of the following statements is performed? If nothing prints, then answer "nothing." Assume that **x = 2** and **y = 3**.
    a)  `Print x`
    b)  `Print -y ^ 2`
    c)  `Print x + x`
    d)  `Print "x ="`
    e)  `txtTextBox.Text = "x + y"`
    f)  `z = x + y`
    g)  `Print x + y * 4 ^ 2 / 4 & " is the magic number!"`

**3.18**     Write a program that inputs three different **Integer**s using function **InputBox** and prints the sum, the average, the product, the smallest and the largest of these numbers on the form using **Print**. Use only the single-selection version of the **If/Then** statement you learned in this chapter.

Provide an **Exit** button to terminate program execution. (Hint: Each `Print` statement is similar to `Print "Sum is "; sum`. The semicolon (`;`) instructs Visual Basic to print the variable's value immediately after the last character printed.)

**3.19**    Write a program that reads in the radius of a circle as an `Integer` and prints the circle's diameter, circumference and area to the form using the `Print` method. Do each of these calculations inside a `Print` statement. Use the following formulas ($r$ is the radius): *diameter = 2r*, *circumference = 2πr*, *area = πr²*. Use the value 3.14159 for π. (Note: In this chapter, we have discussed only `Integer` variables. In Chapter 4 we will discuss floating-point numbers (i.e., values that can have decimal points and data type `Single`).

**3.20**    Enhance Exercise 3.19 by displaying the diameter, circumference and area in `Label`s.

**3.21**    Write a temperature conversion program that converts a Fahrenheit temperature to a Celsius temperature. Provide a `TextBox` for user input and a `Label` for displaying the converted temperature. Provide a **Input** button to read the value from the `TextBox`. Also provide the user with an **Exit** button to end program execution. Use the following formula: *Celsius = 5 / 9 x (Fahrenheit – 32)*.

**3.22**    Enhance Exercise 3.21 to provide a conversion from Fahrenheit to Kelvin. Display the converted Kelvin temperature in a second `Label`. Use the formula: *Kelvin = Celsius + 273*.

**3.23**    Modify Exercise 3.21 to use function `InputBox` for input.

# 4

# Control Structures: Part I

## Objectives

- To understand basic problem-solving techniques.
- To be able to develop algorithms through the process of top-down, stepwise refinement.
- To be able to use the **If/Then** and **If/Then/Else** selection structures to choose between alternative actions.
- To be able to use the **While/Wend**, **Do While/Loop** and **Do Until/Loop** repetition structures.
- To understand counter-controlled repetition and sentinel-controlled repetition.
- To understand the concept of nested control structures.

*Use it up, wear it out;*
*Make it do, or do without.*
Anonymous

*Eternity is a terrible thought. I mean, when's it going to end?*
Tom Stoppard

*If you don't know where you're going, you will probably end up somewhere else.*
*The Peter Principle* [1969]
Laurence Johnston Peter

# Outline

## 4.1 Introduction

Before writing a program to solve a particular problem, it is essential to have a thorough understanding of the problem and a carefully planned approach to solving the problem. When writing a program, it is equally essential to understand the types of building blocks that are available and to employ proven program construction principles. In this chapter we discuss these issues in our presentation of the theory and principles of structured programming. The techniques that you will learn here are applicable to most high-level languages, including Visual Basic. In this and the next two chapters, we discuss techniques that facilitate the development of structured programs. In Section 5.12, we present a summary of structured programming that ties together the techniques developed here and in Chapter 5.

## 4.2 Algorithms

Any computing problem can be solved by executing a series of actions in a specific order. A procedure for solving a problem in terms of

     1. the *actions* to be executed, and

     2. the *order* in which these actions are to be executed

is called an *algorithm*. The following example demonstrates that correctly specifying the order in which actions are to be executed is important.

     Consider the "rise-and-shine algorithm" followed by one junior executive for getting out of bed and going to work:

     1. get out of bed

2. take off pajamas

3. take a shower

4. get dressed

5. eat breakfast

6. carpool to work

This routine gets the executive to work well prepared to make critical decisions. Suppose, however, that the same steps are performed in a slightly different order:

1. get out of bed

2. take off pajamas

3. get dressed

4. take a shower

5. eat breakfast

6. carpool to work

In this case, our junior executive shows up for work soaking wet! Specifying the order in which statements are to be executed in a computer program is called *program control*. In this chapter, we investigate the program control capabilities of Visual Basic.

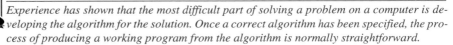

**Software Engineering Observation 4.1**

*Experience has shown that the most difficult part of solving a problem on a computer is developing the algorithm for the solution. Once a correct algorithm has been specified, the process of producing a working program from the algorithm is normally straightforward.*

## 4.3 Pseudocode

*Pseudocode* is an artificial and informal language that helps programmers develop algorithms. Pseudocode particularly useful for developing algorithms that will be converted to structured programs. Pseudocode is similar to everyday English; it is convenient and user-friendly although it is not an actual computer programming language.

Pseudocode programs are not actually executed on computers. Rather, they help the programmer "think out" a program before attempting to write it in a programming language such as Visual Basic. In this chapter, we give several examples of how pseudocode may be used effectively in developing structured programs.

The style of pseudocode we present consists purely of characters, so programmers may conveniently type pseudocode programs using an editor program. The computer can display a fresh copy of a pseudocode program on demand. A carefully prepared pseudocode program may be converted easily to a corresponding Visual Basic program.

Pseudocode consists only of executable statements—those that are executed when the program has been converted from pseudocode to Visual Basic and is run. Declarations are not executable statements. For example, the declaration

```
Dim number1 As Integer
```

simply tells the compiler the type of variable **number1** and instructs the compiler to reserve space in memory for the variable. But this declaration does not cause any action—

such as input, output, or a calculation—to occur when the program is executed. Some programmers choose to list variables and briefly mention the purpose of each at the beginning of a pseudocode program.

**Software Engineering Observation 4.2**

*Many experienced programmers write programs without ever using program development tools like pseudocode. These programmers feel that their ultimate goal is to solve the problem on a computer, and that writing pseudocode merely delays the production of final outputs. Although this may work for simple and familiar problems, it can cause confusion and serious errors on large, complex projects.*

## 4.4  Introduction to Control Structures

Normally, statements in a program are executed one after the other in the order in which they are written. This is called *sequential execution.* Various statements we will soon discuss enable the programmer to specify that the next statement to be executed may be other than the next one in sequence. This is called *transfer of control.*

During the 1960s, it became clear that the indiscriminate use of transfers of control was the root of much difficulty experienced by software development groups. The finger of blame was pointed at the **goto** *statement,* which allows the programmer to specify a transfer of control to one of a wide range of possible destinations in a program. The notion of so-called *structured programming* became almost synonymous with "*goto elimination*" or "*goto-less*" programming.

The research of Bohm and Jacopini[1] had demonstrated that programs could be written without any **goto** statements. The challenge of the era became for programmers to shift their styles to "**goto**-less programming." It was not until the 1970s that programmers started taking structured programming seriously. The results have been impressive, as software development groups have reported reduced development times, more frequent on-time delivery of systems, and more frequent within-budget completion of software projects. The key to these successes is that structured programs are clearer, easier to debug and modify, and more likely to be bug-free in the first place.

Bohm and Jacopini's work demonstrated that all programs could be written in terms of only three control structures, namely the *sequence structure*, the *selection structure* and the *repetition structure.* The sequence structure is built into Visual Basic—unless directed otherwise, the computer executes Visual Basic statements one after the other in the order in which they are written.

A *flowchart* is a graphical representation of an algorithm or of a portion of an algorithm. Flowcharts are drawn using certain special-purpose symbols such as rectangles, diamonds, ovals, and small circles; these symbols are connected by arrows called *flowlines.*

Like pseudocode, flowcharts are useful for developing and representing algorithms, although pseudocode is preferred by most programmers. Flowcharts show clearly how control structures operate; that is all we use flowcharts for in this text.

Consider the flowchart segment for the sequence structure in Fig. 4.1 in which two calculations are performed in order. We use the *rectangle symbol*, also called the *action symbol*, to indicate any type of action, including a calculation or an input/output operation.

---

1.  Bohm, C., and G. Jacopini, "Flow Diagrams, Turing Machines, and Languages with only Two Formation Rules," *Communications of the ACM*, Vol. 9, No. 5, May 1966, pp. 336-371.

The flowlines in the figure indicate the order in which the actions are to be performed—first, **grade** is to be added to **total**, then **1** is to be added to **counter**. Visual Basic allows us to have as many actions as we want in a sequence structure. As we will soon see, anywhere a single action may be placed, we may place several actions in sequence.

When drawing a flowchart that represents a complete algorithm, an *oval symbol* containing the word "Begin" (or a synonym such as "Start") is the first symbol used in the flowchart; an oval symbol containing the word "End" (or a synonym such as "Finish") is the last symbol used. When drawing only a portion of an algorithm as in Fig. 4.1, the oval symbols are omitted in favor of using small circle symbols also called *connector symbols*.

Perhaps the most important flowcharting symbol is the *diamond symbol*, also called the *decision symbol*, which indicates that a decision is to be made. We discuss the diamond symbol in the next section.

Visual Basic provides three types of selection structures; we discuss two of these in this chapter. The ***If/Then*** *selection structure* either performs (selects) an action if a condition is **True** or skips the action if the condition is **False**. The ***If/Then/Else*** *selection structure* performs an action if a condition is **True** and performs a different action if the condition is **False**.

The **If/Then** structure is called a *single-selection structure* because it selects or ignores a single action. The **If/Then/Else** structure is called a *double-selection structure* because it selects between two different actions. The third selection structure is a *multiple-selection structure* discussed in Chapter 5 called ***Select Case***.

Visual Basic provides six types of repetition structures, namely ***While***, ***Do While***, ***Do Until***, ***Do Loop/While***, ***Do Loop/Until*** and ***For/Next***. We will discuss the last three repetition structures in Chapter 5. Each of the words **If**, **Then**, **Else**, **While**, **Do**, **Until**, **Loop**, **Select**, **Case**, **For**, and **Next** are keywords.

Visual Basic has ten control structures: the sequence structure, three types of selection structures and six types of repetition structures. Each program is formed by combining as many of each type of control structure as is appropriate for the algorithm the program implements. As with the sequence structure of Fig. 4.1, we will see that each control struc-

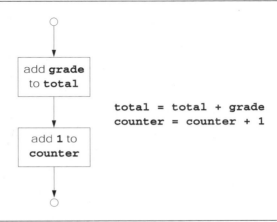

total = total + grade
counter = counter + 1

**Fig. 4.1**    Flowcharting Visual Basic's sequence structure.

ture is flowcharted with two small circle symbols, one at the *entry point* to the control structure and one at the *exit point*. These *single-entry/single-exit control structures* make it easy to build programs—the control structures are attached to one another by connecting the exit point of one control structure to the entry point of the next. This is similar to the way a child stacks building blocks, so we call this *control-structure stacking*. There is only one other way that control structures may be connected—a method called *control-structure nesting* (which we discuss in Section 4.12). Thus, any program to be written can be constructed from only ten different types of control structures combined in only two ways, stacking and nesting.

## 4.5  If/Then Selection Structure

A selection structure is used to choose among alternative courses of action. For example, suppose the passing grade on an exam is 60. The pseudocode statement

> *If student's grade is greater than or equal to 60*
>     *Display "Passed"*

determines if the condition "student's grade is greater than or equal to 60" is **True** or **False**. If the condition is **True**, then "Passed" is displayed, and the next pseudocode statement in order is "performed" (remember that pseudocode is not a real programming language). If the condition is **False**, the display statement is ignored, and the next pseudocode statement in order is performed.

The preceding pseudocode **If/Then** statement may be written in Visual Basic as

```
If grade >= 60 Then
    lblStatus.Caption = "Passed"
End If
```

Notice that the code corresponds closely to the pseudocode. This is one of the properties of pseudocode that makes it such a useful program development tool.

**Software Engineering Observation 4.3**

*Pseudocode is often used to "think out" a program during the program design process. Then the pseudocode program is converted to Visual Basic.*

The flowchart of Fig. 4.2 illustrates the *single-selection If/Then structure*. This flowchart contains what is perhaps the most important flowcharting symbol—the *diamond symbol*, also called the *decision symbol*, which indicates that a decision is to be made. The decision symbol contains an expression, such as a condition, that can be either **True** or **False**. The decision symbol has two flowlines emerging from it. One indicates the direction to be taken when the expression in the symbol is **True**; the other indicates the direction to be taken when the expression is **False**. We learned in Chapter 3 that decisions can be made based on conditions containing comparison operators.

Note that the **If/Then** structure, too, is a single-entry/single-exit structure. We will soon learn that the flowcharts for the remaining control structures also contain (besides small circle symbols and flowlines) only rectangle symbols to indicate the actions to be performed, and diamond symbols to indicate decisions to be made. This is the *action/decision model of programming* we have been emphasizing.

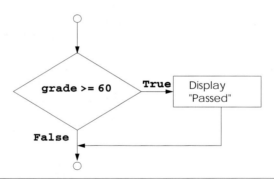

**Fig. 4.2**    Flowcharting of the single-selection **If/Then** structure.

Envision ten bins, each containing only control structures of one of the ten types. These control structures are empty—nothing is written in the rectangles or in the diamonds. The programmer's task is assembling a program from as many of each type of control structure as the algorithm demands, combining those control structures in only two possible ways (stacking or nesting), and filling in the actions and decisions in a manner appropriate for the algorithm. We will discuss many ways in which actions and decisions can be written.

## 4.6 **If/Then/Else** Selection Structure

The **If/Then** selection structure performs an indicated action only when the condition is **True**; otherwise the action is skipped. The **If/Then/Else** selection structure allows the programmer to specify that a different action is to be performed when the condition is **True** than when the condition is **False**. For example, the pseudocode statement

> *If student's grade is greater than or equal to 60*
> > *Display "Passed"*
> *Else*
> > *Display "Failed"*

displays "Passed" if the student's grade is greater than or equal to 60 and displays "Failed" if the student's grade is less than 60. In either case, after the display occurs, the next pseudocode statement in sequence is "performed." Note that the body statements of this selection structure are indented. Such indentation is optional, but it is highly recommended because it emphasizes the inherent structure of structured programs. The compiler ignores whitespace characters (blanks, tabs and newlines) used for indentation and vertical spacing.

 *Good Programming Practice 4.1*

*Whatever indentation convention you choose should be uniformly applied throughout your programs. It is difficult to read programs that do not obey uniform spacing conventions.*

The preceding pseudocode **If/Then/Else** structure may be written as

```
If grade >= 60 Then
    lblStatus.Caption = "Passed"
Else
    lblStatus.Caption = "Failed"
End If
```

Note that each **If/Then** or **If/Then/Else** spanning multiple lines must end in **End If** unless the line-continuation character, _ is used. The last **End If** always matches up with the previous **If/Then** or **If/Then/Else**.

The flowchart of Fig. 4.3 illustrates the flow of control in the **If/Then/Else** selection structure. Once again, note that (besides small circles and arrows) the only symbols in the flowchart are rectangles (for actions) and a diamond (for a decision). We continue to emphasize this action/decision model of computing. Imagine a deep bin containing as many empty double-selection structures as might be needed to build any program. The programmer's job is to assemble these selection structures (by stacking and nesting) with any other control structures required by the algorithm, and to fill in the empty rectangles and empty diamonds with actions and decisions appropriate to the algorithm being implemented.

Visual Basic provides *function* **IIf**, which is closely related to the **If/Then/Else** structure. Function **IIf** takes three arguments—the condition, the value returned when the condition is **True** and the value returned when the condition is **False**. For example, the output statement

```
lblStatus.Caption = IIf(grade >= 60, "Passed", "Failed")
```

prints "**Passed**" if **grade** is greater than or equal to **60** and prints "**Failed**" if **grade** is less than **60**. Thus, the function call performs essentially the same as the preceding **If/ Then/Else** statement.

*Good Programming Practice 4.2*

*Indent both body statements of an* ***If/Then/Else*** *structure.*

Nested **If/Then/Else** structures test for multiple cases by placing **If/Then/Else** structures inside **If/Then/Else** structures. For example, the following pseudocode statement will print **A** for exam grades greater than or equal to 90, **B** for grades in the range 80 to 89, **C** for grades in the range 70 to 79, **D** for grades in the range 60 to 69, and **F** for all other grades.

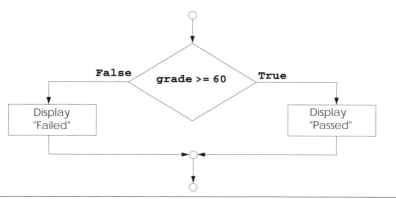

**Fig. 4.3**　　Flowcharting the double-selection **If/Then/Else** structure.

> *If student's grade is greater than or equal to 90*
>> *Display "A"*
> *Else*
>> *If student's grade is greater than or equal to 80*
>>> *Display "B"*
>> *Else*
>>> *If student's grade is greater than or equal to 70*
>>>> *Display "C"*
>>> *Else*
>>>> *If student's grade is greater than or equal to 60*
>>>>> *Display "D"*
>>>> *Else*
>>>>> *Display "F"*

This pseudocode may be written in Visual Basic as

```
If grade >= 90 Then
    lblStudentGrade.Caption = "A"
Else
    If grade >= 80 Then
        lblStudentGrade.Caption = "B"
    Else
        If grade >= 70 Then
            lblStudentGrade.Caption = "C"
        Else
            If grade >= 60 Then
                lblStudentGrade.Caption = "D"
            Else
                lblStudentGrade.Caption = "F"
            End If
        End If
    End If
End If
```

If **grade** is greater than or equal to 90, the first four conditions will be **True**, but only the statement after the first test will be executed. After the assignment is executed, the **Else**-part of the "outer" **If/Then/Else** statement is skipped, in fact skipping the entire remainder of the preceding code segment. Most programmers prefer to write the preceding **If/Then/Else** structure as

```
If grade >= 90 Then
    lblStudentGrade.Caption = "A"
ElseIf grade >= 80 Then
    lblStudentGrade.Caption = "B"
ElseIf grade >= 70 Then
    lblStudentGrade.Caption = "C"
ElseIf grade >= 60 Then
    lblStudentGrade.Caption = "D"
Else
    lblStudentGrade.Caption = "F"
End If
```

which uses the keyword ***ElseIf***. Both forms are equivalent. The latter form is popular because it avoids the deep indentation of the code to the right and does not require multiple

**End If** statements. Such indentation often leaves little room on a line, which decreases program readability.

*Good Programming Practice 4.3*

*Placing a blank line before and after every control structure makes control structures stand out in a program.*

Visual Basic provides *function* **Switch**, which is related to the **If/Then/Else** structure. Each argument passed to **Switch** is either a condition or a value. Any number of condition-value pairs can be passed to **Switch**. If a condition is **True**, the value associated with that condition is returned. If no condition is **True**, **Switch** returns *Null*. Function **Switch** does not provide **Else** functionality; a value must be paired with a condition. For example, the assignment

```
lblStudentGrade.Caption = Switch(grade >= 90, "A", _
                                 grade >= 80, "B", _
                                 grade >= 70, "C", _
                                 grade >= 60, "D", _
                                 grade < 60, "F")
```

assigns a string representing a letter grade to **lblStudentGrade**'s **Caption**. This call to function **Switch** approximates the **If/Then/Else** logic presented earlier.

*Common Programming Error 4.1*

*Not providing a condition for a Switch function value is a run-time error.*

The **If/Then** selection structure, when written on a single line, normally expects only one statement in its body. To include several statements in the body of an **If/Then**, write the statements between the **If/Then** and **End If** keywords. A control structure's multiple statement body is often called a *block*.

*Good Programming Practice 4.4*

*If there are several levels of indentation, each level should be indented the same additional amount of space.*

*Software Engineering Observation 4.4*

*The body of a control structure may contain one or more statements.*

The following code includes two statements in the **Else** block of an **If/Then/Else** structure.

```
If grade >= 60 Then
   lblStatus.Caption = "Passed."
Else
   lblStatus.Caption = "Failed. Repeat course."
   currentYear = 1999
End If
```

In this case, if **grade** is less than 60, the program executes both statements in the body of the **Else** and displays

```
Failed. Repeat course.
```

Multiple-line **If/Then** or **If/Then/Else** statements must terminate with **End If**. If the **End If** is accidentally omitted, a syntax error is generated.

*Testing and Debugging Tip 4.1*

Syntax errors *are generally caught by the compiler.* Logic errors *have their effects at run time.* Fatal logic errors *cause programs to fail and terminate prematurely.* Nonfatal logic errors *allow programs to continue executing, but produce incorrect results.*

## 4.7 While/Wend Repetition Structure

A repetition structure allows the programmer to specify that an action is to be repeated based on the truth or falsity of some condition. The pseudocode statement

> *While there are more items on my shopping list*
> *Purchase next item and cross it off my list*

describes the repetition that occurs during a shopping trip. The condition, "there are more items on my shopping list" may be **True** or **False**. If it is **True**, then the action, "Purchase next item and cross it off my list" is performed. This action will be performed repeatedly while the condition remains **True**. Eventually, the condition will become **False** (when the last item on the shopping list has been purchased and crossed off the list). At this point, the repetition terminates, and the first pseudocode statement after the repetition structure is executed.

*Common Programming Error 4.2*

*Not providing in the body of a* **While/Wend** *structure an action that eventually causes the condition in the* **While/Wend** *to become* **False***. Will normally result in a repetition structure that will never terminate—an error called an "infinite loop."*

As an example of an actual **While/Wend**, consider a program segment designed to find the first power of 2 larger than 1000. Suppose the **Integer** variable **product** has been initialized to 2. When the following **While/Wend** repetition structure finishes executing, **product** will contain the desired answer:

```
Dim product As Integer
product = 2

While product <= 1000
   product = product * 2
Wend
```

A **While/Wend** repetition structure may have one or more statements in its body. The keyword **Wend** terminates the **While/Wend** structure. The flowchart of Fig. 4.4 illustrates the flow of control in the **While/Wend** repetition structure. Once again, note that (besides small circles and arrows) the flowchart contains only a rectangle symbol and a diamond symbol. Imagine, again, a deep bin of empty **While/Wend** structures that may be stacked and nested with other control structures to form a structured implementation of an algorithm's flow of control. The empty rectangles and diamonds are then completed by filling in appropriate actions and decisions. The flowchart clearly shows the repetition. The flowline emerging from the rectangle wraps back to the decision, which is tested each time through the loop until the decision eventually becomes **False**. At this point, the **While/Wend** structure is exited and control passes to the next statement in the program.

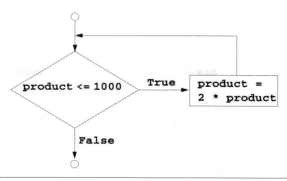

**Fig. 4.4**    Flowcharting the **While/Wend** repetition structure.

When the **While/Wend** structure is entered, the value of **product** is 2. Variable **product** is repeatedly multiplied by 2, taking on the values 4, 8, 16, 32, 64, 128, 256, 512 and 1024. When **product** becomes 1024, the condition, **product <= 1000**, becomes **False**. This terminates the repetition, with the final **product** value of 1024. Execution continues with the next statement after the **While/Wend**.

## 4.8 Do While/Loop Repetition Structure

Visual Basic provides another form of repetition called the **Do While/Loop** repetition structure. The **Do While/Loop** behaves like the **While/Wend** repetition structure. The flowchart of Fig. 4.5 illustrates the flow of control. Note that the flow of control is identical to the flow of control in Fig. 4.4.

As an example of a **Do While/Loop**, consider the program segment designed to find the first power of 2 larger than 1000.

```
Dim product As Integer
product = 2

Do While product <= 1000
   product = product * 2
Loop
```

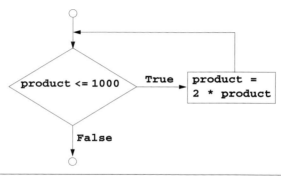

**Fig. 4.5**    Flowcharting the **Do While/Loop** repetition structure.

When the **Do While/Loop** structure is entered, the value of product is 2. The variable **product** is repeatedly multiplied by 2, taking on the values 4, 8, 16, 32, 64, 128, 256, 512 and 1024 successively. When product becomes 1024, the condition in the **Do While/Loop** structure, **product <= 1000**, becomes **False**. This terminates the repetition, with the final value of **product** being 1024. Program execution continues with the next statement after the **Do While/Loop**.

*Common Programming Error 4.3*

*Not providing in the body of a **Do While/Loop** structure an action that eventually causes the condition in the **Do While/Loop** to become **False** creates an infinite loop.*

## 4.9 Do Until/Loop Repetition Structure

Unlike the **Do While/Loop** and **While/Wend** repetition structures, the **Do Until/Loop** repetition structure tests a condition for falsity. Statements in the body of a **Do Until/Loop** are executed repeatedly as long as the loop-continuation test evaluates to **False**. The **Do Until/Loop** repetition structure should be used when it is more natural to express a condition "in the negative." The flowchart of Fig. 4.6 illustrates the flow of control.

As an example of a **Do Until/Loop** repetition structure, once again consider a program segment designed to find the first power of 2 larger than 1000.

```
Dim product As Integer
product = 2

Do Until product > 1000
    product = product * 2
Loop
```

*Common Programming Error 4.4*

*Not providing in the body of a **Do Until/Loop** structure an action that eventually causes the condition in the **Do Until/Loop** to become **True** creates an infinite loop.*

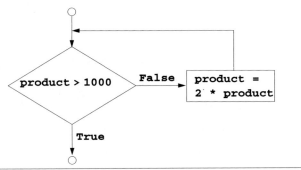

**Fig. 4.6**   Flowcharting the **Do Until/Loop** repetition structure.

## 4.10  Formulating Algorithms: Case Study 1 (Counter-Controlled Repetition)

To illustrate how algorithms are developed, we solve several variations of a drawing problem. Consider the following problem statement:

> *Create a program that displays in a **Label** up to nine "#" characters. The user inputs a number (from 1 to 9) indicating the number of "#" characters to display.*

The algorithm for solving this problem on a computer requires that a **Label** displays up to nine "#" characters from the value input by the user.

Let us use pseudocode to list the actions to be executed and specify the order in which these actions should be executed. We use *counter-controlled repetition* to set the display **Label** to the proper number of "#"s. This technique uses a variable called a *counter* to control the number of times a set of statements should execute. In this example, repetition terminates when the counter is 0. Counter-controlled repetition is often called *definite repetition* because the number of repetitions is known before the loop begins executing. We will study *indefinite repetition* in Section 4.11.

In this section, we present a pseudocode algorithm (Fig. 4.7), the GUI (Fig. 4.8), a properties list (Fig. 4.9), and the corresponding program code (Fig. 4.10). In the next section, we show how pseudocode algorithms are developed. Note the references in the algorithm to a variable (**counter**) used to count—in this case, to count the number of # characters for display.

---

*Prompt the user to enter a number*
*Assign the number input to counter*
*Clear the text in the display **Label***

*While counter is greater than 0*
    *Concatenate a # character to the display **Label***
    *Subtract one from counter*

---

**Fig. 4.7**    Pseudocode algorithm that uses counter-controlled repetition.

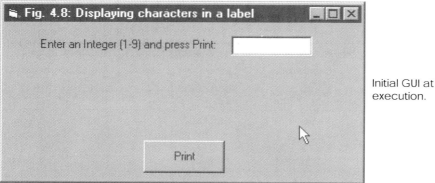

Initial GUI at execution.

**Fig. 4.8**    GUI for program that displays #s in a **Label** (part 1 of 2).

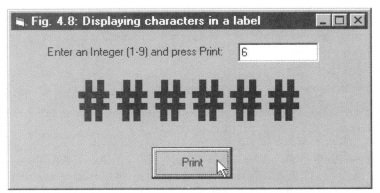

GUI after the user has entered **6** and pressed **Print**.

**Fig. 4.8**   GUI for program that displays #s in a **Label** (part 1 of 2).

| Object | Icon | Property | Property setting | Property description |
|---|---|---|---|---|
| form | | **Name** | **frmDisplay** | Identifies the form. |
| | | **Caption** | **Fig. 4.8: Displaying characters in a label** | Form title-bar display. |
| **Print** button | | **Name** | **cmdPrint** | Identifies **Print** button. |
| | | **Caption** | **Print** | Text that appears on button. |
| **Label** | A | **Name** | **lblPrompt** | Identifies the **Label**. |
| | | **Caption** | **Enter an Integer (1-9) and press Print** | Text **Label** displays. |
| **Label** | A | **Name** | **lblDisplay** | Identifies the **Label**. |
| | | **Alignment** | **2 (Center)** | Alignment of text. |
| | | **Caption** | (empty) | Text **Label** displays. |
| | | **Font** | **Courier bold 48** pt | **Label** text font. |
| **TextBox** | abl | **Name** | **txtInput** | Identifies **TextBox**. |
| | | **MaxLength** | **1** | Limits character input. |

**Fig. 4.9**   Property listing for the program of Fig. 4.8.

```
1    ' Fig 4.8
2    ' Program displays #'s in a Label
3    Option Explicit                    ' General Declaration
4
5    Private Sub cmdPrint_Click()
6        Dim counter As Integer          ' Declaration
7
8        counter = txtInput.Text         ' Get number of characters
9        lblDisplay.Caption = ""         ' Clear Label
10
11       ' Repeat the statements between Do While and Loop
12       ' until counter has a value of 0.
13       Do While counter > 0
14           lblDisplay.Caption = lblDisplay.Caption & "#"
15           counter = counter - 1       ' Decrement number
16       Loop
17
18   End Sub
```

**Fig. 4.10**   Code listing for Fig. 4.8.

For this example, we do not provide code to ensure that the user input is within the proper range of values (i.e., 1 through 9). We leave this to the reader as an exercise. Lines 13 through 16,

```
Do While counter > 0
    lblDisplay.Caption = lblDisplay.Caption & "#"
    counter = counter - 1       ' Decrement number
Loop
```

perform the repetition part of the program. While the condition **counter > 0** is **True**, the two statements in the loop body are executed. With each iteration of the loop, **counter** is decremented by one. Eventually, **counter** is assigned the value zero, which causes the loop-continuation test to become **False**, thus terminating the loop.

## 4.11   Formulating Algorithms with Top-down, Stepwise Refinement: Case Study 2 (Sentinel-Controlled Repetition)

Let us generalize a class average problem. Consider the following problem:

*Develop a class averaging program that will process an arbitrary number of grades each time the program is run.*

In the statement, no indication is given of how many grades are to be entered. The program must process an arbitrary number of grades. How can the program determine when to stop the input of grades? How will it know when to calculate and display the class average?

One way to solve this problem is to use a special value called a *sentinel value* (also called a *signal value*, a *dummy value*, or a *flag value*) to indicate "end of data entry." The user types grades in until all legitimate grades have been entered. The user then either types the sentinel value to indicate that the last grade has been entered or presses a particular button to indicate that the data entry is complete. Sentinel-controlled repetition is often called *indefinite repetition* because the number of repetitions is not known before the loop begins executing.

Clearly, the sentinel value must be chosen so that it cannot be confused with an acceptable input value. Because grades on a quiz are normally nonnegative integers, –1 would be an acceptable sentinel value for this problem. Thus, a run of the class average program might process a stream of inputs such as 95, 96, 75, 74, 89 and –1. The program would then compute and display the class average for the grades 95, 96, 75, 74 and 89 (–1 is the sentinel value, so it should not enter into the averaging calculation).

**Common Programming Error 4.5**

*Choosing a sentinel value that is also a legitimate data value is a logic error.*

We approach the class average program with a technique called *top-down, stepwise refinement*, a technique that is essential to the development of well-structured programs. We begin with a pseudocode representation of the top:

*Determine the class average for the quiz*

The *top* is a single statement that conveys the overall function of the program. As such, the top is, in effect, a complete representation of a program. Unfortunately, the top (as in this case) rarely conveys a sufficient amount of detail from which to write the program. So we begin the refinement process. We divide the top into a series of smaller tasks listed in the order in which they need to be performed. This results in the following first refinement.

*Initialize variables*
*Input, sum, and count the quiz grades*
*Calculate and display the class average*

Here, only the sequence structure has been used—the steps listed are to be executed in order, one after the other.

**Software Engineering Observation 4.5**

*Many programs can be divided logically into three phases: an* initialization phase *that initializes the program variables; a* processing phase *that inputs data values and adjusts program variables accordingly; and a* termination phase *that calculates and prints the final results.*

**Software Engineering Observation 4.6**

*Each refinement, as well as the top itself, is a complete specification of the algorithm; only the level of detail varies.*

To proceed to the next level of refinement (i.e., the second refinement), we commit to specific variables. We need a running total of the numbers, a count of how many numbers have been processed, a variable to receive the value of each grade as it is input and a variable to hold the calculated average. The pseudocode statement

*Initialize variables*

may be refined as follows:

*Initialize total to zero*
*Initialize counter to zero*

Notice that only variables *total* and *counter* need to be initialized before they are used; the variables *average* and *grade* (the calculated average and the user input) need not be initialized because their values will be written over as they are calculated or input.

The pseudocode statement

*Input, sum, and count the quiz grades*

requires a repetition structure (i.e., a loop) that successively inputs each grade. Because we do not know in advance how many grades are to be processed, we will use sentinel-controlled repetition. The user will type legitimate grades in one at a time. After the last legitimate grade is typed, the user will type either the sentinel value or press a button. The program will test for the sentinel value after each grade is input and will terminate the loop when the sentinel value is entered by the user. The second refinement of the preceding pseudocode statement is then

*Prompt for first grade*
*Input the first grade (possibly the sentinel)*

*While the user has not as yet entered the sentinel*
     *Add this grade to the running total*
     *Add one to the grade counter*
     *Prompt for the next grade*
     *Input the next grade (possibly the sentinel)*

Notice that in pseudocode, we do not write **Wend** or **Loop** to terminate the body of the repetition structure. At this stage, we need not be concerned about what specific loop will be used. We simply indent all these statements under the *While* to show that they all belong to the *While*. Again, pseudocode is only an informal program development aid.

The pseudocode statement

*Calculate and display the class average*

may be refined as follows:

*If the counter is not equal to zero*
     *Set the average to the total divided by the counter*
     *Display the average*
*Else*
     *Display "No grades were entered"*

Notice that we are being careful here to test for the possibility of division by zero—a fatal logic error that if undetected would cause the program to fail (often called "bombing" or "crashing"). The complete second refinement of the pseudocode for the class average problem is shown in Fig. 4.9.

***Common Programming Error 4.6***

*An attempt to divide by zero is a fatal error.*

***Testing and Debugging Tip 4.2***

*When performing division by an expression whose value could be zero, explicitly test for this case and handle it appropriately in your program (such as printing an error message) rather than allowing the fatal error to occur.*

*Initialize total to zero*
*Initialize counter to zero*

*Prompt for first grade*
*Input the first grade (possibly the sentinel)*

*While the user has not as yet entered the sentinel*
 *Add this grade to the running total*
 *Add one to the grade counter*
 *Prompt for the next grade*
 *Input the next grade (possibly the sentinel)*

*If the counter is not equal to zero*
 *Set the average to the total divided by the counter*
 *Print the average*
*Else*
 *Print "No grades were entered"*

---

**Fig. 4.11** Pseudocode algorithm that uses sentinel-controlled repetition to solve the class average problem.

In Figs. 4.7 and 4.11, we included blank lines in the pseudocode to make it more readable. The blank lines separate these programs into their various phases. Note the references in the algorithm to a total and a counter. A *total* is a variable used to accumulate the sum of a series of values. A counter is a variable used to count—in this case, to count the number of grades entered. Variables used to store totals should normally be initialized to 0 before being used in program; otherwise the sum could contain previously stored values (often called *garbage values*). Although Visual Basic initializes **Integer** types to 0, it is a good practice to explicitly initialize total variables to 0. Counter variables are normally initialized to zero or one, depending on their use.

*Software Engineering Observation 4.7*

*The programmer terminates the top-down, stepwise refinement process when the pseudocode algorithm is specified in sufficient detail for the programmer to be able to convert the pseudocode to Visual Basic. Implementing the Visual Basic program is then normally straightforward.*

This algorithm was developed after only two levels of refinement. Sometimes more levels are necessary. The next step is to convert the pseudocode to Visual Basic. The GUI is shown in Fig. 4.12, properties in Fig. 4.13, and program code in Fig. 4.14.

Although only **Integer** grades are entered, the averaging calculation is likely to produce a number with a decimal point (i.e., a real number). Type **Integer** cannot represent real numbers. The program introduces data type ***Single*** to handle numbers with decimal points (also called *floating-point numbers*). The line

```
Dim average As Single
```

declares **Single** variable **average**. **Single**s store values in the range $-3.402823E38$ (i.e., $-3.402823 \infty 10^{38}$) to $-1.401298E\text{--}45$ (i.e., $-1.401298 \infty 10^{-45}$) for negative numbers and $1.401298E\text{--}45$ (i.e., $1.401298 \infty 10^{-45}$) to $3.402823E38$ (i.e., $3.402823 \infty 10^{38}$) for positive values. The *!* (exclamation point) is the **Single** type-declaration character.

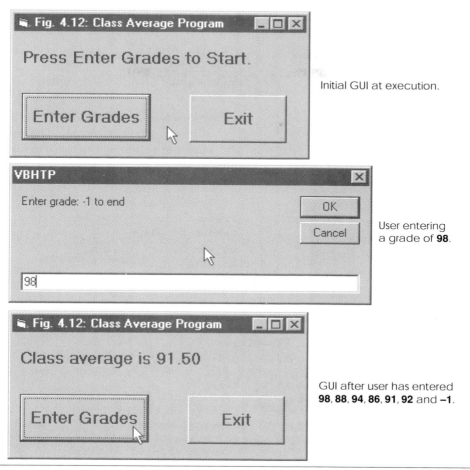

Fig. 4.12   Class averaging program GUI.

| Object | Icon | Property | Property setting | Property description |
|--------|------|----------|------------------|----------------------|
| form | | **Name** | **frmAverage** | Identifies the form. |
| | | **Caption** | **Fig. 4.12: Class Averaging Program** | Form title-bar display. |
| **Exit** button | | **Name** | **cmdExit** | Identifies **Exit** button. |
| | | **Caption** | **Exit** | Text that appears on button. |

Fig. 4.13   Property listing for the program of Fig. 4.12 (part 1 of 2).

| Object | Icon | Property | Property setting | Property description |
|--------|------|----------|------------------|---------------------|
| | | Font | `MS Sans Serif bold 12` pt | Font for button text. |
| **Enter Grades** button | | Name | `cmdEnterData` | Identifies **Enter Grades** button. |
| | | Caption | `Enter Grades` | Text that appears on button. |
| | | Font | `MS Sans Serif bold 12` pt | Font for button text. |
| `Label` | A | Name | `lblAverage` | Identifies the **Label**. |
| | | Caption | `Press Enter Grades to Start` | Text **Label** displays. |
| | | Font | `MS San Serif bold 12` pt | **Label** text font. |

**Fig. 4.13**   Property listing for the program of Fig. 4.12 (part 2 of 2).

```
1   ' Fig. 4.12
2   ' Class average program with
3   ' sentinel-controlled repetition
4   Option Explicit     ' General declaration
5
6   Private Sub cmdEnterData_Click()
7       Dim total As Integer    ' Sum of all grades input
8       Dim counter As Integer  ' Number of grades input
9       Dim grade As Integer    ' Current grade
10      Dim average As Single   ' Floating-point average
11      Dim message As String   ' Text displayed in Label
12
13      ' Initialization phase
14      total = 0
15      counter = 0
16
17      ' Processing phase
18      grade = InputBox("Enter grade: -1 to end", "VBHTP")
19
20      ' Loop until grade has a -1 value
21      Do Until grade = -1
22         total = total + grade      ' Add grade to total
23         counter = counter + 1      ' Increment counter
24
25         ' Input the next grade. When -1 is assigned,
26         ' the loop continuation condition becomes True
27         grade = InputBox("Enter grade: -1 to end", "VBHTP")
28      Loop
```

**Fig. 4.14**   Class averaging program with sentinel-controlled repetition (part 1 of 2).

```
29
30        ' Termination phase
31        If counter <> 0 Then              ' Prevent division by zero
32          average = total / counter  ' Floating-point division
33          message = "Class average is "
34
35          ' Format average and concatenate to message
36          message = message & Format$(average, "Fixed")
37          lblAverage.Caption = message
38        Else      ' counter is 0
39          lblAverage.Caption = "No grades were entered."
40        End If
41
42    End Sub
43
44    Private Sub cmdExit_Click()
45        End
46    End Sub
```

**Fig. 4.14**  Class averaging program with sentinel-controlled repetition (part 2 of 2).

*Common Programming Error 4.7*

*Using floating-point numbers in a manner that assumes they are represented precisely can lead to incorrect results. Floating-point numbers are represented only approximately by most computers. Soon we will introduce a more accurate type called **Currency** for handling monetary amounts precisely.*

Type **String** is also introduced in this example. A **String** is a sequence of characters enclosed in a set of double quotes **""**. The **$** is the **String** type-declaration character.

Function **InputBox** is used to input the first grade (line 18). The **Do Until/Loop** provides the repetition by executing the lines

```
total = total + grade
counter = counter + 1
grade = InputBox("Enter grade: -1 to end", "VBHTP")
```

The first statement adds the **grade** and **total** and stores the result into **total**. As each **grade** is input, **counter** is incremented by one. The last line inputs the next **grade**.

*Look-and-Feel Observation 4.1*

*In a sentinel-controlled loop, the prompts requesting data entry should explicitly remind the user what the sentinel value is.*

The **If/Then/Else** determines the proper action to take if **counter** is zero (which occurs if the user enters **-1** on line 18). If **counter** is not zero, the lines

```
average = total / counter
message = "Class Average is "
message = message & Format$(average, "Fixed")
lblAverage.Caption = message
```

are executed. The floating-point division operator, **/**, is used to get a floating-point result from the division. We do not use the **Integer** division operator, **\**, because it returns a whole number (i.e., a number without a decimal place).

***Common Programming Error 4.8***

*Using the* **Integer** *division operator,* **\**, *when the floating-point division operator,* **/**, *is needed is often a logic error.*

Despite the fact that floating-point numbers are not always "100% precise," they have numerous applications. For example, when we speak of a "normal" body temperature of 98.6° we do not need to be precise to a large number of digits. When we view the temperature on a thermometer and read it as 98.6°, it may actually be 98.5999473210643°. The point here is that calling this number simply 98.6° is fine for most applications.

Another way floating-point numbers develop is through division. When we divide 10 by 3, the result is 3.3333333… with the sequence of 3s repeating infinitely. The computer allocates only a fixed amount of space to hold such a value, so clearly the stored floating-point value can only be an approximation.

The line

```
message = message & Format$(average, "Fixed")
```

concatenates to **message** (which contains the **String "Class average is"**) the formatted **average**. *Function* ***Format$*** returns a formatted **String**. The first argument, **average**, is the *expression* to which the formatting is to be applied, and the second argument, ***Fixed***, is the *format*. **Fixed** has two digits to the right of the decimal point and at least one digit to the left of the decimal point. Note that **Fixed** automatically "rounds" numbers so, for example, **7.76** is printed by the expression

```
Print Format$(7.756, "Fixed")
```

## 4.12 Formulating Algorithms with Top-down, Stepwise Refinement: Case Study 3 (Nested Control Structures)

Let us work another complete problem. We will once again formulate the algorithm using pseudocode and top-down, stepwise refinement, and write the corresponding program. We have seen that control structures may be stacked on top of one another (in sequence) just as a child stacks building blocks. In this case study we will see the only other structured way control structures may be combined, namely through nesting of one control structure inside another.

Consider the following problem statement:

*Write a program that draws a square of $ characters on the form. The side of the square (i.e., the number of $ characters to be printed side by side) should be input by the user and should be in the range 1 through 12.*

Your program should draw the square as follows:

1. Input the side of the square.

2. Validate that the side is in the range 1 through 12.

3. Use repetition to draw the square on the form.

After reading the problem statement carefully, we make the following observations (in no particular order):

1. The program must draw *n* (the value input by the user) rows each with *n* $ characters. Counter-controlled repetition will be used.

2. Each time a value is input for the side, a test must be made to ensure that the value is in the range 1 through 12.

3. Three variables will be used—one that represents the side of the square, one that represents the row where each $ will appear, and one that represents the column where each $ will appear.

Let us proceed with top-down, stepwise refinement. We begin with a pseudocode representation of the top:

*Draw a square of $ characters on the form*

Once again, it is important to emphasize that the top is a complete representation of the program, but several refinements are likely to be needed before the pseudocode can be naturally evolved into a program. Our first refinement is

*Initialize variables*
*Prompt for the side of the square*
*Input the side of the square*
*Validate that the side is within the proper range*
*Print the square*

Here, too, even though we have a complete representation of the entire program, further refinement is necessary. We now commit to specific variables. A variable is needed to store the side, a variable is needed to store the row where printing is occurring, and a variable is needed to store the column where the printing is occurring. The pseudocode statement

*Initialize variables*

may be refined as follows:

*Initialize side to the value input*
*Initialize row to one*
*Initialize column to one*

The pseudocode statement

*Input the side of the square*

requires that a value be obtained from a **TextBox** (or **InputBox**). The pseudocode statement

*Validate that input is within the proper range*

may be refined as

*If side is less than or equal to 12 then*
    *If side is greater than 0 then*

which explicitly tests whether *side is less than or equal to 12* and whether *side is greater than 0*. If the first condition (i.e., *side is less than or equal to 12*) is true, the next condition (i.e., *side greater than 0*) is tested. If the first condition is false, the second condition is not tested. These two control structures are said to be *nested*—because one is inside the body of the other.

The pseudocode statement

*Print the square*

can be implemented by using nested loops to draw the square. Here it is known in advance that there are precisely *n* $ characters, so counter-controlled repetition is appropriate. One loop will control the row on which each **$** is drawn. This loop does not do the actual drawing. Inside this loop (i.e., nested within this loop) a second loop will draw each individual **$**. The refinement of the preceding pseudocode statement is then

*While row is less than or equal to side*
    *Set column to one*

    *While column is less than or equal to side*
        *Print $*
        *Increment column by one*

    *Print*
    *Increment row by one*

After *column* is set to one, the inner loop executes to completion (i.e., until *column* exceeds *side*). Each iteration of the inner loop results in a single $ being printed. *Print* specifies that the next printing operation is to occur on the next row. Variable *row* is incremented by one. If the outer loop condition allows the body of the loop to be executed, *column* is reset to one because we want the inner loop to execute again and print another row of $ characters. *Print* specifies that the next printing operation is to occur on the next line. Variable *row* is incremented by one. This process is repeated until the value of *row* exceeds *side*.

The complete second refinement appears in Fig. 4.15. Notice that blank lines are used to separate the nested repetition structures for program readability. Also notice *row* is initialized after the nested *If* statements determine that *row* is valid. This was done for performance reasons—why take the time to initialize *rows* unless we are going to use *rows*?

**Performance Tip 4.1**

*Often, particular performance enhancements may seem nominal. But constantly focusing on performance can lead to significant performance enhancements.*

Now we convert the pseudocode algorithm to a Visual Basic program. The GUI is shown in Fig. 4.16, the properties are listed in Fig. 4.17, and the code is shown in Fig. 4.18. In the code we introduce the **Beep** statement, which sounds a beep through the computer speaker.

**Portability Tip 4.1**

*The frequency and duration of* **Beep** *is hardware and system dependent.*

**Good Programming Practice 4.5**

*Too many levels of nesting can make a program difficult to understand. As a general rule, try to avoid using more than three levels of nesting.*

*Initialize side to the value input*

*If side is less than or equal to 12 then*
    *If side is greater than 0 then*
        *Initialize row to one*

        *While row is less than or equal to side*
            *Set column to one*

            *While column is less than or equal to side*
                *Print $*
                *Increment column by one*

            *Print*
            *Increment row by one*
    *Else*
        *Print "Side too small"*
*Else*
    *Print "Side too large"*

**Fig. 4.15**  Second refinement of square problem pseudocode.

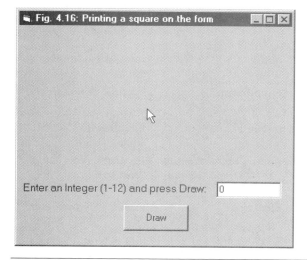

Initial GUI at execution.

**Fig. 4.16**  Square-drawing program GUI (part 1 of 2).

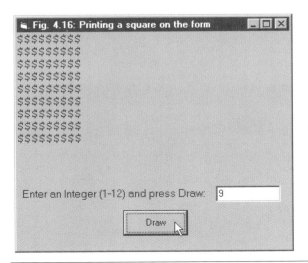

GUI after user enters **9** and presses the **Draw** button.

**Fig. 4.16**   Square-drawing program GUI (part 2 of 2).

| Object | Icon | Property | Property setting | Property description |
|---|---|---|---|---|
| form | | Name | `frmDraw` | Identifies the form. |
| | | Caption | `Fig. 4.16: Printing a square on the form` | Form title-bar display. |
| | | Font | Courier Regular 11 pt | Font for text drawn on form. |
| **Draw** button | | Name | `cmdDraw` | Identifies **Draw** button. |
| | | Caption | `Draw` | Text that appears on button. |
| **TextBox** | abl | Name | `txtPrompt` | Identifies **TextBox**. |
| | | BorderStyle | 0 - None | **TextBox** does not display a border. |
| | | Text | `Enter an Integer (1-12) and press Draw` | Text that appears in **TextBox** |
| **TextBox** | abl | Name | `txtInput` | Identifies the **TextBox**. |
| | | Text | `0` | Text **TextBox** displays. |

**Fig. 4.17**   Property listing for the program of Fig. 4.16.

```
1    ' Fig. 4.16
2    ' Program draws a square of $ on the form
3    Option Explicit                        ' In general Declaration
4
5    Private Sub cmdDraw_Click()
6       Dim side As Integer, row As Integer, column As Integer
7
8       side = txtInput.Text ' Get user input from TextBox
9       Cls                  ' Clear the form
10
11      If side <= 12 Then   ' If True, the next If is tested
12         If side > 0 Then
13            row = 1        ' Executed only if the two previous
14                           ' If conditions are True.
15
16            ' Use repetition to draw square of $
17            While row <= side          ' Controls the row
18               column = 1
19
20               ' This loop will print one "row" of $ characters.
21               ' Each iteration of the loop prints a single $.
22               While column <= side
23                  Print "$";   ' Print one $ on the same line
24                  column = column + 1
25               Wend
26
27               Print              ' Print to next line
28               row = row + 1  ' Increment row
29            Wend
30
31         Else  ' Condition (side > 0) is False
32            Print "Side too small."
33            Beep
34         End If
35
36      Else      ' Condition (side <= 12) is False
37         Print "Side too large."
38         Beep
39      End If
40
41   End Sub
```

**Fig. 4.18**   Code listing for Fig. 4.16.

## Summary

- Before writing a program to solve a particular problem, it is essential to have a thorough understanding of the problem and a carefully planned approach to solving the problem.

- When writing a program, it is equally essential to understand the types of building blocks that are available and to employ proven program construction principles.

- Any computing problem can be solved by executing a series of actions in a specific order. A procedure for solving a problem in terms of the actions to be executed and the order in which these actions are to be executed is called an algorithm.

- Pseudocode is an artificial and informal language that helps programmers develop algorithms. Pseudocode is similar to everyday English; it is convenient and user-friendly although it is not an actual computer programming language.

- Pseudocode helps the programmer "think out" a program before attempting to write it in a programming language. A carefully prepared pseudocode program may be converted easily to a corresponding Visual Basic program.

- Statements are executed one after the other in the order in which they are written. This is called sequential execution. Various statements enable the programmer to specify that the next statement to be executed may be other than the next one in sequence. This is called transfer of control.

- The notion of so-called structured programming has become almost synonymous with "goto elimination" or "goto-less" programming.

- Structured programs are clearer and easier to debug and modify.

- Bohm and Jacopini's work demonstrated that all programs could be written in terms of the sequence structure, the selection structure and the repetition structure.

- The sequence structure is built in—unless directed otherwise, the computer executes Visual Basic statements one after the other in the order in which they are written.

- A flowchart is a graphical representation of an algorithm or of a portion of an algorithm. Flowcharts are drawn using certain special-purpose symbols such as rectangles, diamonds, ovals, and small circles; these symbols are connected by arrows called flowlines.

- The rectangle symbol, also called the action symbol, indicates any type of action, including a calculation or an input/output operation. Flowlines indicate the order in which the actions are to be performed. Visual Basic allows us to have as many actions as we want in a sequence structure.

- An oval symbol containing the word "Begin" (or a synonym such as "Start") is the first symbol used in the flowchart; an oval symbol containing the word "End" (or a synonym such as "Finish") is the last symbol used.

- When drawing only a portion of an algorithm the oval symbols are omitted in favor of using small circle symbols, also called connector symbols.

- Perhaps the most important flowcharting symbol is the diamond symbol, also called the decision symbol, which indicates that a decision is to be made.

- The **If/Then** selection structure either performs (selects) an action if a condition is **True** or skips the action if the condition is **False**. The **If/Then/Else** selection structure performs an action if a condition is **True** and performs a different action if the condition is **False**.

- The **If/Then** structure is a single-selection structure because it selects or ignores one action. The **If/Then/Else** structure is a double-selection structure because it selects between two different actions. The multiple-selection structure is called **Select Case**.

- Visual Basic has ten control structures: sequence, three types of selection and six types of repetition. Each program is formed by combining as many of each control structure as is appropriate for the algorithm the program implements.

- Single-entry/single-exit control structures make it easy to build programs—control structures are attached by connecting the exit point of one to the entry point of the next—called control-structure stacking. Control structures may be connected by control-structure nesting. Any program can be constructed from ten different control structures combined in two ways, stacking and nesting.

- A selection structure is used to choose among alternative courses of action.

- The single-selection **If/Then** structure flowchart contains the diamond flowcharting symbol, also called the decision symbol, which indicates that a decision is to be made. The decision symbol contains an expression, such as a condition, that is either **True** or **False**. The decision symbol has two flowlines emerging from it. One indicates the direction to be taken when the expression in the symbol is **True**; the other indicates the direction to be taken when the expression is **False**.

- The programmer's task is assembling a program from as many of each type of control structure as the algorithm demands, combining those control structures in only two possible ways (stacking or nesting), and then filling in the actions and decisions in a manner appropriate for the algorithm.

- The **If/Then** structure performs an indicated action only when the condition is **True**; otherwise the action is skipped. The **If/Then/Else** structure allows the programmer to specify that a different action is to be performed when the condition is **True** than when the condition is **False**.

- The compiler ignores whitespace characters like blanks, tabs and newlines used for indentation and vertical spacing.

- Each **If/Then** or **If/Then/Else** spanning multiple lines must end in **End If**. The last **End If** always matches up with the previous **If/Then** or **If/Then/Else**.

- Function **IIf** takes three arguments—the condition, the value returned when the condition is **True** and the value returned when the condition is **False**.

- Nested **If/Then/Else** structures test for multiple cases by placing **If/Then/Else** structures inside **If/Then/Else** structures.

- Function **Switch** is related to the **If/Then/Else** structure. Each argument passed to **Switch** is either a condition or a value. Any number of condition-value pairs can be passed to **Switch**. If a condition is **True**, the value associated with that condition is returned. If no condition is **True**, **Switch** returns **Null**. Function **Switch** does not provide **Else** functionality.

- The **If/Then** structure, when written on a single line, expects only one statement in its body. To include several statements in the body of an **If/Then**, write the statements between the **If/Then** and **End If** keywords. A control structure's multiple statement body is often called a block.

- A repetition structure allows the programmer to specify that an action is to be repeated based on the truth or falsity of some condition.

- A **While/Wend** repetition structure may have one or more statements in its body. The keyword **Wend** terminates the **While/Wend** structure.

- Visual Basic also provides the **Do While/Loop** repetition structure, which behaves like the **While/Wend** repetition structure.

- Statements in the body of a **Do Until/Loop** are executed repeatedly as long as the loop continuation test evaluates to **False**. The **Do Until/Loop** repetition structure should be used when it is more natural to express a condition "in the negative."

- Counter-controlled repetition uses a variable called a counter to control the number of times a set of statements should execute. Counter-controlled repetition is called definite repetition because the number of repetitions is known before the loop begins.

- A sentinel value (also called a signal value, a dummy value, or a flag value) can indicate "end of data entry." Sentinel-controlled repetition is called indefinite repetition because the number of repetitions is not known before the loop begins executing. A sentinel value must be chosen so that it cannot be confused with acceptable input values.

- The top is a single statement that conveys the overall function of the program. As such, the top is, in effect, a complete representation of a program. Unfortunately, the top rarely conveys enough detail, so the programmer performs a refinement process.

- Division by zero is a fatal logic error that if undetected would cause the program to fail (often called "bombing" or "crashing").

- Variables used to store totals should normally be initialized to 0; otherwise the sum could contain previously stored values (often called garbage values). Although Visual Basic initializes **Inte-**

**ger** types to 0, it is a good practice to explicitly initialize total variables to 0. Counter variables are normally initialized to zero or one, depending on their use.

- Type **Single** represents floating-point numbers. **Single** variables store numeric values in the range –3.402823E38 to –1.401298E–45 for negative numbers and 1.401298E–45 to 3.402823E38 for positive values. The **!** (exclamation point) is the **Single** type-declaration character.

- A **String** is a sequence of characters enclosed in a set of double quotes **""**. The **$** is the **String** type-declaration character.

- The floating-point division operator, **/**, is used to get a floating-point result from division. The **Integer** division operator, **\**, returns a whole number (i.e., a number without a decimal point).

- Function **Format$** returns a formatted **String**. The first argument is the expression to which the formatting is to be applied, and the second argument is the format. Format **Fixed** has two digits to the right of the decimal point and at least one digit to the left.

## Terminology

| | |
|---|---|
| action | **Format$** function |
| action/decision model | function **Format$** |
| action symbol | function **IIF** |
| algorithm | function **Switch** |
| **Beep** method | garbage values |
| block | **goto** statement |
| bombing | **If/Then** control structure |
| **Case** statement | **If/Then/Else** control structure |
| **Cls** method | **IIf** function |
| connector symbol | indefinite repetition |
| control-structure nesting | logic error |
| control-structure stacking | **Loop** keyword |
| counter | multiple-selection structure |
| counter-controlled repetition | nonfatal logic error |
| crashing | **Null** keyword |
| decision symbol | order |
| default data type | pseudocode |
| definite repetition | rectangle symbol |
| diamond symbol | repetition structure |
| dollar sign (**$**) type-declaration character | **Select Case** |
| double-selection structure | selection structure |
| **Do Until/Loop** control structure | sequence structure |
| **Do While/Loop** control structure | signal value |
| dummy value | **Single** |
| **ElseIf** | single-entry/single-exit |
| **End If** | single-selection structure |
| entry point | **String** |
| exclamation point (**!**) type-declaration character | **Switch** function |
| exit point | syntax error |
| fatal logic error | top |
| **Fixed** | top-down, stepwise refinement |
| flag value | total |
| flowchart | **Wend** keyword |
| flowline | **While** keyword |
| **For** control structure | **While/Wend** control structure |

## Common Programming Errors

**4.1**   Not providing a condition for a **Switch** function value is a run-time error.

**4.2**   Not providing in the body of a **While** structure an action that eventually causes the condition in the **While** to become **False** will normally result in a repetition structure that will never terminate—an error called an "infinite loop."

**4.3**   Not providing in the body of a **Do While/Loop** structure an action that eventually causes the condition in the **Do While/Loop** to become **False** creates an infinite loop.

**4.4**   Not providing in the body of a **Do Until/Loop** structure an action that eventually causes the condition in the **Do Until/Loop** to become **True** creates an infinite loop.

**4.5**   Choosing a sentinel value that is also a legitimate data value is a logic error.

**4.6**   An attempt to divide by zero is a fatal error.

**4.7**   Using floating-point numbers in a manner that assumes they are represented precisely can lead to incorrect results. Floating-point numbers are represented only approximately by most computers. Soon we will introduce a more accurate type called **Currency** for handling monetary amounts precisely.

**4.8**   Using the **Integer** division operator,**\**, when the floating-point division operator,**/**, is needed is often a logic error.

## Good Programming Practices

**4.1**   Whatever indentation convention you choose should be uniformly applied throughout your programs. It is difficult to read programs that do not obey uniform spacing conventions.

**4.2**   Indent both body statements of an **If/Then/Else** structure.

**4.3**   Placing a blank line before and after every control structure makes control structures stand out in a program.

**4.4**   If there are several levels of indentation, each level should be indented the same additional amount of space.

**4.5**   Too many levels of nesting can make a program difficult to understand. As a general rule, try to avoid using more than three levels of nesting.

## Look-and-Feel Observation

**4.1**   In a sentinel-controlled loop, the prompts requesting data entry should explicitly remind the user what the sentinel value is.

## Performance Tip

**4.1**   Often, particular performance enhancements may seem nominal. But constantly focusing on performance can lead to significant performance enhancements.

## Portability Tip

**4.1**   The frequency and duration of **Beep** is hardware and system dependent.

## Software Engineering Observations

**4.1**   Experience has shown that the most difficult part of solving a problem on a computer is developing the algorithm for the solution. Once a correct algorithm has been specified, the process of producing a working program from the algorithm is normally straightforward.

**4.2**   Many experienced programmers write programs without ever using program development tools like pseudocode. These programmers feel that their ultimate goal is to solve the problem on a computer, and that writing pseudocode merely delays the production of final outputs. Although this may work for simple and familiar problems, it can cause confusion and serious errors on large, complex projects.

**4.3**    Pseudocode is often used to "think out" a program during the program design process. Then the pseudocode program is converted to Visual Basic.

**4.4**    The body of a control structure may contain one or more statements.

**4.5**    Many programs can be divided logically into three phases: an initialization phase that initializes the program variables; a processing phase that inputs data values and adjusts program variables accordingly; and a termination phase that calculates and prints the final results.

**4.6**    Each refinement, as well as the top itself, is a complete specification of the algorithm; only the level of detail varies.

**4.7**    The programmer terminates the top-down, stepwise refinement process when the pseudocode algorithm is specified in sufficient detail for the programmer to be able to convert the pseudocode to Visual Basic. Implementing the Visual Basic program is then normally straightforward.

## Testing and Debugging Tips

**4.1**    Syntax errors are generally caught by the compiler. Logic errors have their effects at run time. Fatal logic errors cause programs to fail and terminate prematurely. Nonfatal logic errors allow programs to continue executing, but produce incorrect results.

**4.2**    When performing division by an expression whose value could be zero, explicitly test for this case and handle it appropriately in your program (such as printing an error message) rather than allowing the fatal error to occur.

## Self-Review Exercises

**4.1**    Answer each of the following questions.
  a) The _____ selection structure is used to execute one action when a condition is **True** and another action when that condition is **False**.
  b) Repetition of a set of instructions a specific number of times is called_____ repetition.
  c) When it is not known in advance how many times a set of statements will be repeated, a _____ value can be used to terminate the repetition.
  d) A procedure for solving a problem in terms of the actions to be executed and the order in which the actions should be executed is called an _____.
  e) The _____ structure specifies that statements are to be executed one after the other in order as written.
  f) _____ is an artificial and informal language that helps programmers develop algorithms.

**4.2**    Write statements to accomplish each of the following:
  a) Test if the value of the variable **count** is greater than 10. If it is, print **"Count is greater than 10"** in **Label lblDisplayCount**'s **Caption** property.
  b) Write a statement to test the variable **dayOfMonth** against the value 1 for equality. If it is, beep and print the message **"First of the Month"** to the form.
  c) Assign the **String "Cubicle 007"** to the **String** variable **employeeAddress**.

**4.3**    Identify and correct the error(s) in each of the following (you may simply need to add code):
  a) Assume that **z** has been initialized to 50. The values from 0 to 50 should be totaled.

```
While (z >= 0)
    sum = sum + z
```

  b) Assume that **w** is an **Integer** and initialized to 0.

```
Do Until w = 88 Print w : w = w + 1 : Loop
```

c) Assume that **y** and **total** are declared as **Integer**s.

```
total = 0

Do Until y = -1
   Print y
   y = InputBox("Enter a value, value input")
   total = total + y
Loop
```

d) The following code should print the squares of 1 to 10 on the form.

```
Dim n As Integer

n = 1

Do While n < 10
   Print n ^ 2
Wend
```

e) Assume **x** to be declared as an **Integer**. The code should print the values 888 to 1000.

```
x = 888

While x <= 1000
    x = x - 1
Wend
```

**4.4**   State whether the following are *true* or *false*. If the answer is *false*, explain why.
a) Pseudocode is a structured programming language.
b) The body of a **Do While** is only executed if the loop continuation test is **False**.
c) The body of a **While** is only executed if the loop continuation test is **False**.
d) The body of a **Do Until** is only executed if the loop continuation test is **False**.
e) Data type **Single** stores floating-point numbers.

**4.5**   Write a statement or a set of statements to accomplish each of the following:
a) Sum the odd **Integer**s between 1 and 99 using a **While** structure. Assume that variables **sum** and **count** have been declared explicitly as **Integer**s.
b) Sum the squares of even numbers between 1 and 15 using a **Do While** repetition structure. Assume that the **Integer** variables **sum** and **count** have been declared and initialized to 0 and 2, respectively.
c) Print the numbers from 20 to 1 on the form using a **Do Until** loop and **Integer** counter variable **x**. Assume that the variable **x** is initialized to 20.
d) Repeat Exercise 4.5 (c) using a **Do While** structure.

## Answers to Self-Review Exercises

**4.1**   a) **If/Then/Else**.
b) counter-controlled (or definite).
c) sentinel.
d) algorithm.
e) sequence.
f) pseudocode.

**4.2**   a) ```If count > 10 Then
        lblDisplayCount.Caption = "Count is greater than 10"
     End If```

b) ```
If dayOfMonth = 1 Then
    Beep
    Print "First of Month"
End If
```
c) ```
employeeAddress = "Cubicle 007"
```

**4.3**    a) ```
While (z >= 0)
    sum = sum + z
    z = z - 1
Wend
```
b) The **Do Until w = 88** statement must be a separate statement. One way to correct this error is to insert a **:** between the **88** and the **Print** statement. The other way to correct it is to move the **Print** statement to the next line.
c) ```
Dim y As Integer, total As Integer
total = 0
y = InputBox("Enter a value", "value input")

Do Until y = -1
    Print y
    total = total + y
    y = InputBox("Enter a value", "value input")
Loop
```
d) ```
Dim n As Integer
n = 1

Do While n <= 10
    Print n ^ 2
    n = n + 1
Loop
```
e) ```
x = 888

While x <= 1000
    x = x + 1
    Print x
Wend
```

**4.4**    a) False. Pseudocode is not a programming language.
b) False. The loop condition must evaluate to **True** for the body to be executed.
c) False. The loop condition must evaluate to **True** for the body to be executed.
d) True.
e) True.
f) True.

**4.5**    a) ```
count = 1
sum = 0

While count <= 99
    sum = sum + count
    count = count + 1
Wend
```
```

b) 
```
Do While count <= 15
   sum = sum + count ^ 2
   count = count + 2
Loop
```
c) 
```
Do Until x = 1
   Print x
   x = x - 1
Loop
```
d) 
```
Do While x >= 1
   Print x
   x = x - 1
Loop
```

## Exercises

**4.6**    Identify and correct the error(s) in each of the following:

a) Assume that the variable **age** is declared and has a valid value.

```
If age >= 65
   lblAge = "Age is greater than or equal to 65"
Else
   lblAge.Caption = Age is less than 65
```

b) Assume that the variable **x** is declared and initialized to 1. The loop should iterate from 1 to 10.

```
Dim total As Integer

Do Until x <= 10
   total = total + x
   x = x + 1
```

c) Assume that the variable **y** is declared and initialized to 1. The loop should sum the numbers from 1 to 100.

```
While y <= 100
   total = total + y
Wend

y = y + 1
```

d) Assume that the variable **z** is declared and initialized to 1000. The loop should iterate from 1000 to 1.

```
While (z > 0)
   Print z
   z = z + 1
Wend
```

e) Assume that the variable **k** is declared as an **Integer**. The loop should iterate until –1 is input.

```
Do While k <> -1
   InputBox("Enter a number -1 to quit:", VB6)
Loop
```

    f)  Assume that **u** and **t** are declared as **Integer**s.

```
Let u = 8
Let t = 22

' If u is not equal to t then print t; otherwise print
' the value of u.
If u <> t Then Print t : Print u
```

**4.7**    What does the following event procedure do?

```
Private Sub CommandButton1_Click()
   Dim y As Integer, x As Integer, mysteryValue As Integer

   x = 1
   mysteryValue = 0

   While x <= 10
      y = x ^ 2
      Print y
      mysteryValue = mysteryValue + y
      x = x + 1
   Wend

   Caption = "Value is " & mysteryValue
End Sub
```

**4.8**    Fill in the blanks in each of the following:

    a)  The solution to any problem involves performing a series of actions in a specific _____.

    b)  A variable that accumulates the sum of several numbers is called a _____.

    c)  A special value used to indicate "end of data entry" is called a _____, a _____, a _____ or a _____ value.

    d)  A _____ is a graphical representation of an algorithm.

    e)  The item written inside a decision symbol is called a _____.

    f)  In a flowchart, the order in which the steps should be performed is indicated by _____ symbols.

    g)  The termination symbol indicates the _____ and _____ of every algorithm.

    h)  Rectangle symbols correspond to calculations that are normally performed by _____ statements.

**4.9**    State which of the following are *true* and which are *false*. If *false*, explain why.

    a)  Experience has shown that the most difficult part of solving a problem on a computer is producing a working program from an algorithm.

    b)  A sentinel value must be a value that cannot be confused with a legitimate data value.

    c)  Flowlines indicate the actions to be performed.

    d)  In top-down stepwise refinement, each refinement is a complete representation of the algorithm.

    e)  Conditions written inside decision symbols always contain arithmetic operators (i.e., **+, -, /, \, ^,** etc.).

    f)  The **!** is the type declaration character for type **Single**.

    g)  Function **Format$** returns a formatted **Single**.

**4.10**    Write a single pseudocode statement to accomplish each of the following:

    a)  Display the message **"Enter two numbers"** on the form.

    b) Assign the sum of the variables **x**, **y**, **z** to variable **p**.

    c) The following condition is to be tested in an **If/Then/Else** selection structure: The current value of variable **m** is greater than twice the current value of variable **v**. If the condition is **True**, print the value of **m** to the form. Otherwise print twice the value of **v** to the form.

    d) Obtain values for variables **r**, **y** and **u** from the user.

**4.11** Formulate a pseudocode algorithm for each of the following:

    a) Obtain two numbers from the user, compute the sum of the numbers and display the result.

    b) Obtain two numbers from the user, and determine and display which (if either) is the larger of the two numbers.

    c) Obtain a series of positive numbers from the user, and determine and display the sum of the numbers. Assume that the user types the sentinel value **−1** to indicate "end of data entry."

**4.12** Convert each of the following **While** loops to **Do While** loops.

    a)
```
While x > 500
      Print x;
      x = x - 5
Wend
```

    b)
```
While pcm = q
      qFactor = qFactor + pcm
      pcm = txtInput.Text
Wend
```

    c)
```
While J <> hugeJ
      largeJ = largeJ + J
      J = J Mod bigJ
Wend
```

    d)
```
While n <= display
      Print "Visual Basic 6 How To Program!"
      n = n * 7
Wend
```

**4.13** Convert each **While** loop in Exercise 4.12 to a **Do Until** loop.

**4.14** Convert the pseudocode statements you wrote in Exercise 4.10 to Visual Basic code.

**4.15** Convert the pseudocode algorithms you wrote in Exercise 4.11 to Visual Basic code.

**For Exercises 4.16 to 4.19, perform each of these steps:**

    1. Read the problem statement.

    2. Formulate the algorithm using pseudocode and top-down stepwise refinement.

    3. Write a Visual Basic program.

    4. Test, debug and execute the program.

**4.16** Drivers are concerned with the mileage obtained by their automobiles. One driver has kept track of several tankfuls of gasoline by recording miles driven and gallons used for each tankful. Develop a program that will input the miles driven and gallons used for each tankful. The program should calculate and display the miles per gallon obtained for each tankful. After processing all input information, the program should calculate and print the combined miles per gallon obtained for all tankfuls.

**4.17**    Develop a program that will determine if a department store customer has exceeded the credit limit on a charge account. For each customer, the following facts are available:

1.  Account number.

2.  Balance at the beginning of the month.

3.  Total of all items charged by this customer this month.

4.  Total of all credits applied to this customer's account this month.

5.  Credit limit.

The program should input each of these facts, calculate the new balance (= *beginning balance + charges – credits*) and determine if the new balance exceeds the customer's credit limit. For those customers whose credit limit is exceeded, the program should beep and display the message **"Credit Limit Exceeded."**

**4.18**    One large chemical company pays its salespeople on a commission basis. The salespeople receive $200 per week plus 9 percent of their gross sales for that week. For example, a salesperson who sells $5000 worth of chemicals in a week receives $200 plus 9 percent of $5000, or a total of $650. Develop a program that will input each salesperson's gross sales for last week and will calculate and display the salesperson's earnings. Process one salesperson's figures at a time.

**4.19**    The simple interest on a loan is calculated by the formula

$$interest = principal \times rate \times days \div 365$$

The preceding formula assumes that rate is the annual interest *rate*, and therefore includes the division by 365 (days). Develop a program that will input principal, rate and days for several loans, and will calculate and display the simple interest for each loan, using the preceding formula. Use **TextBox**es for input and **Label**s for display.

**4.20**    Develop a program that will determine the gross pay for each of several employees. The company pays "straight-time" for the first 40 hours worked by each employee and pays "time-and-a-half" for all hours worked in excess of 40 hours. You are given a list of employees of the company, the number of hours each employee worked last week and the hourly rate of each employee. Your program should input this information for each employee, and should determine and display the employee's gross pay. Use **TextBox**es for input and **Label**s for display.

**4.21**    The process of finding the largest number (i.e., the maximum of a group of numbers) is used frequently in computer applications. For example, a program that determines the winner of a sales contest would input the number of units sold by each salesperson. The salesperson who sells the most units wins the contest. Write a program that inputs a series of 10 numbers, and determines and prints the largest of the numbers. Hint: Your program should use three variables as follows:

1.  **counter**:    A counter to count 10 (i.e., to keep track of how many numbers have been input, and to determine when all 10 numbers have been processed).

2.  **number**:    The current number input to the program.

3.  **largest**:    The largest number found so far.

**4.22**     What does the following event procedure do?

```
Private Sub cmdDisplay_Click()
   Dim count As Integer

   count = 1

   While count <= 10
      Print IIf(count Mod 2, "$$$$", "????????")
      count = count + 1
   Wend

End Sub
```

**4.23**     What does the following event procedure do?

```
Private Sub cmdDisplay_Click()
   Dim row As Integer, column As Integer

   row = 10

   Do While row >= 1
      column = 1

      Do While column <= 10

         If row Mod 2 Then
            Print "j";
         Else
            Print "c";
         End If

         column = column + 1
      Loop

      row = row - 1
      Print
   Loop
End Sub
```

**4.24**     Write a program that prints a hollow square on the form. The square length should be input in a **TextBox**.

**4.25**     Write a program that keeps printing to the form powers of 2, namely 2, 4, 8, 16, 32, 64, etc. Your loop should not terminate (i.e., you should create an infinite loop). What happens when you run this program?

**4.26**     A company wants to transmit data over the telephone, but they are concerned that their phones may be tapped. All of their data is transmitted as four-digit **Integer**s. They have asked you to write a program that will encrypt their data so that it may be transmitted more securely. Your program should read a four-digit **Integer** and encrypt it as follows: Replace each digit by (the sum of that digit plus 7) modulus 10. Then, swap the first digit with the third, and swap the second digit with the fourth. Then print the encrypted **Integer**.

**4.27**     Write a program that takes an encrypted **Integer** from Exercise 4.26 and decrypts it.

**4.28**    Write a program that reads in one five-digit **Integer** and determines and prints how many digits in the **Integer** are 7s. Use a loop to solve the problem. Note: The range for an **Integer** is −32,768 to 32,767.

**4.29**    Modify Exercise 4.28 so that it determines and prints the number of 7s for any number of digits up to five digits. Use a **TextBox** for input and a **Label** for display.

**4.30**    How can you determine how fast your machine operates? Write a program with the **Do While** loop that counts from 1 to 50,000,000 by 1s. Every time the count reaches a multiple of 10,000,000, print that number to the form. Use your watch to time how long each 10 million repetitions of the loop takes. Use the **Single** variable **counter** to do the counting. Today's personal computers execute so quickly that you might need to count each 20 million, 50 million or even 100 million items to be able to time the intervals manually.

**4.31**    Write a program that prints 100 asterisks to the form one at a time. After every tenth asterisk, your program should print a blank line. (Hint: Count from 1 to 100. Use the modulus operator to recognize each time the counter reaches a multiple of 10.) Note: You should change the **Font** property of the form to **Courier**.

**4.32**    Modify the program of Fig. 4.8 to perform validation on the user input. Invalid input should be rejected. Note: this may require you to rewrite portions of the example code.

# Control Structures: Part II

## Objectives

- To be able to use the **For/Next**, **Do/Loop While** and **Do/Loop Until** repetition structures.
- To understand multiple selection using the **Select Case** multiple selection structure.
- To be able to use the **Exit Do** and **Exit For** statements.
- To be able to use the **Boolean** data type.
- To be able to create and use constant variables.
- To be able to use the logical operators to combine conditions.
- To understand how control structures can be combined in a structured program.
- To become familiar with the data types available in Visual Basic.

*Who can control his fate?*
William Shakespeare, *Othello*

*Man is a tool-making animal.*
Benjamin Franklin

*Intelligence ... is the faculty of making artificial objects, especially tools to make tools.*
Henri Bergson

## Outline

## 5.1 Introduction

At this point, the reader should be comfortable with the process of writing simple but complete programs. In this chapter, repetition is considered in greater detail, and additional repetition control structures, namely the **For/Next** structure, the **Do/Loop While** and the **Do/Loop Until** structures, are presented. The **Select Case** multiple selection structure is introduced. We discuss the **Exit Do** and **Exit For** statements for exiting immediately and rapidly from repetition structures. The chapter discusses the logical operators used for combining conditions, and concludes with a summary of the principles of structured programming as presented in this chapter as well as Chapters 3 and 4.

## 5.2 Essentials of Counter-Controlled Repetition

Counter-controlled repetition requires:

1. The *name of a control variable* (or loop counter).

2. The *initial value* of the control variable.

3. The *increment* (or *decrement*) by which the control variable is modified each time through the loop.

4. The *condition* that tests for the final value of the control variable (i.e., whether looping should continue).

5. Consider the simple program shown in Fig. 5.1, which prints the even numbers from 2 through 20. The lines

```
Dim counter As Integer
counter = 2
```

name the control variable (**counter**), declare it to be an **Integer**, reserve space for it in memory and set it to an initial value of **2**. The declaration is not executable, but the assignment is executable.

The statement

```
counter = counter + 2
```

increments the loop counter by **2** each time the loop is performed. The *loop-continuation condition* in the **Do While/Loop** structure tests if the value of the control variable is less than or equal to 20 (the last value for which the condition is **True**). Note that the body of this **Do While/Loop** is performed even when the control variable is 20. The loop terminates when the control variable exceeds 20 (i.e., **counter** becomes 22).

*Common Programming Error 5.1*

*Because floating-point values may be approximate, controlling counting loops with floating-point variables may result in imprecise counter values and inaccurate tests for termination.*

*Testing and Debugging Tip 5.1*

*Control counting loops with **Integer** values.*

*Good Programming Practice 5.1*

*Indent the statements in the body of each control structure.*

*Good Programming Practice 5.2*

*Put a blank line before and after each control structure to make it stand out in the program.*

*Good Programming Practice 5.3*

*Vertical spacing above and below control structures, and indentation of the bodies of control structures within the control structure headers, give programs a two-dimensional appearance that greatly improves readability.*

```
1    Private Sub cmdButton_Click()
2       Dim counter As Integer
3
4       counter = 2                  ' Initialization
5
6       Do While counter <= 20       ' Repetition condition
7          Print counter
8          counter = counter + 2     ' Increment
9       Loop
10
11   End Sub
```

**Fig. 5.1**    Counter-controlled repetition.

## 5.3 `For/Next` Repetition Structure

The *For/Next repetition structure* handles all the details of counter-controlled repetition. To illustrate the power of **For/Next**, let us rewrite the event procedure of Fig. 5.1. The result is shown in Fig. 5.2.

The program operates as follows. When the **For/Next** structure begins executing, the control variable **counter** is initialized to **2**. Then, the implied loop-continuation condition, **counter <= 20**, is tested by Visual Basic. The *To* keyword in the **For/Next** structure is required. The optional *Step* keyword specifies the increment (i.e., how much will be added to **counter** each time the **For/Next** body is executed). If **Step** and the value following it are omitted, the increment defaults to **1**. Programmers typically omit the **Step** portion for increments of **1**.

Because the initial value of **counter** is **2**, the condition is satisfied, so the body statement prints **counter**'s value, namely **2**. Variable **counter** is then incremented in the expression **Next counter**, and the loop begins again with the implied loop-continuation test. The required keyword *Next* marks the end of the **For/Next**.

*Good Programming Practice 5.4*

*Including the **For/Next** loop's control variable name after the **Next** statement is optional but doing so improves program readability.*

*Common Programming Error 5.2*

*Using the wrong variable name in a **Next** statement is a syntax error.*

*Common Programming Error 5.3*

*Not terminating a **For/Next** with **Next** is a syntax error.*

Note that the incrementing is implied. Because the control variable is now equal to **4**, the final value of **20** is not exceeded, so the program performs the body again. This process continues until **counter** is incremented to **22**—this causes the loop-continuation test to fail and repetition terminates.

Figure 5.3 takes a closer look at the **For/Next** structure of Fig. 5.2. Notice that the **For/Next** structure "does it all"—it specifies each of the items needed for counter-controlled repetition with a control variable.

```
1   Sub cmdButton_Click()
2      Dim counter As Integer
3
4      ' Initialization, repetition condition, and incrementing
5      ' are all included in the For structure header.
6      For counter = 2 To 20 Step 2
7         Print counter
8      Next counter
9
10  End Sub
```

**Fig. 5.2**   Counter-controlled repetition with the **For/Next** structure.

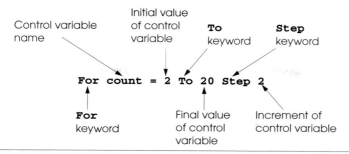

**Fig. 5.3**   Components of a typical **For/Next** header.

In most cases the **For/Next** structure can be represented with any other repetition structure. For example, an equivalent **Do While/Loop** structure is

*variable = start*

**Do While** *variable* **<=** *end*
   *statement*
   *variable* **=** *variable* **+** *increment*
**Loop**

The starting value, ending value, and increment portions of a **For/Next** structure can contain arithmetic expressions. For example, assume that **x = 2** and **y = 10**. The statement

        **For j = x To 4 \* x \* y Step y \ x**

is equivalent to the statement

        **For j = 2 To 80 Step 5**

The "increment" of a **For/Next** structure may be negative, in which case it is really a decrement and the loop actually counts downwards.

*Common Programming Error 5.4*

*In nested **For/Next** loops, using the same control variable name for more than one loop is a syntax error.*

If the loop-continuation condition is initially **False** (i.e., the starting value is greater than the ending value and the increment is positive), the **For/Next**'s body is not performed. Instead, execution proceeds with the statement following the **For/Next**.

*Common Programming Error 5.5*

*When your program should be counting downwards it is a logic error to have a positive increment in a **For/Next** loop, when the starting value is greater than the ending value.*

*Common Programming Error 5.6*

*When your program should be counting upwards it is a logic error to have a negative increment in a **For/Next** loop, when the starting value is less than the ending value.*

The control variable is frequently printed or used in calculations in the **For/Next** body, but it does not have to be. It is common to use the control variable for controlling repetition while never mentioning it in the **For/Next** body.

*Testing and Debugging Tip 5.2*

*Although the value of the control variable can be changed in the body of a **For/Next** loop, avoid doing so because this practice can lead to subtle errors.*

*Testing and Debugging Tip 5.3*

*Use a **For/Next** loop for counter-controlled repetition. Off-by-one errors (i.e., the process of looping one more iteration or one less iteration than necessary) tend to disappear, because the terminating value is not ambiguous.*

The **For/Next** structure is flowcharted much like the **Do While/Loop** structure. For example, the flowchart of the **For/Next** statement

```
For counter = 2 To 20 Step 2
    Print counter
Next counter
```

is shown in Fig. 5.4. This flowchart makes it clear that the initialization occurs only once and that incrementing occurs each time after the body is executed. Note that (besides small circles and arrows) the flowchart contains only rectangle symbols and a diamond symbol.

Imagine, again, that the programmer has access to a deep bin of empty **For/Next** structures—as many as the programmer might need to stack and nest with other control structures to form a structured implementation of an algorithm's flow of control. And again, the rectangles and diamonds are then filled with actions and decisions appropriate to the algorithm.

## 5.4  Examples Using the `For/Next` Repetition Structure

The following examples show methods of varying the control variable in a **For/Next** structure. In each case, we write the appropriate **For/Next** header.

1.  Vary the control variable from 1 to 100 in increments of 1.

    ```
    For a = 1 To 100
    ```

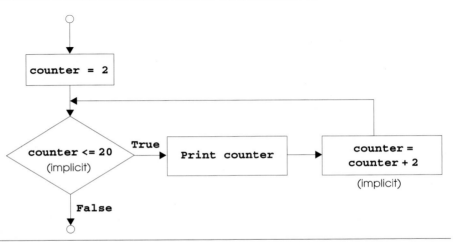

**Fig. 5.4**   Flowcharting a typical **For/Next** repetition structure.

2. Vary the control variable from 100 to 1 in increments of –1 (decrements of 1).

```
For b = 100 To 1 Step -1
```

3. Vary the control variable from 7 to 77 in increments of 7.

```
For c = 7 To 77 Step 7
```

4. Vary the control variable from 20 to 2 in decrements of 2.

```
For d = 20 To 2 Step -2
```

5. Vary the control variable over the following sequence of values: 2, 5, 8, 11, 14, 17, 20.

```
For e = 2 To 20 Step 3
```

6. Vary the control variable over the following sequence of values: 99, 88, 77, 66, 55, 44, 33, 22, 11, 0.

```
For f = 99 To 0 Step -11
```

The next example computes compound interest using the **For/Next** structure. Consider the following problem statement:

*A bank wishes to develop a program that will calculate the amount of money on deposit at the end of 10 years. The bank's representative enters the initial deposit amount and the fixed interest rate. The amount of money on deposit at the end of each year is to be calculated and displayed. Neither the initial deposit amount nor the interest accumulated can be withdrawn until 10 years has elapsed. The following formula is used to determine the amount of money on deposit at the end of each year:*

$$a = p\,(1 + r)^n$$

*where*

> *p* is the original amount invested (i.e., the principal)
> *r* is the annual interest rate
> *n* is the number of years
> *a* is the amount on deposit at the end of the $n^{th}$ year.

This problem involves a loop that performs the indicated calculation for each of the 10 years the money remains on deposit. The GUI is shown in Fig. 5.5, properties in Fig. 5.6 and the program code in Fig. 5.7.

Four variables are declared **years**, **interestRate**, **amount** and **principal**. Variable **interestRate** is declared as *Double*. Data type **Double** is a floating-point type much like **Single**, but a variable of type **Double** can store a value of greater magnitude with greater precision. The **Double** type declaration character is **#**. A **Double** is stored in eight bytes. Interest rates are generally fractional values between 0 and 1. We use data type **Double** here for greater precision.

Variables **amount** and **principal** are declared as *Currency*. Type **Currency** is useful for monetary calculations. **Currency**'s type declaration character is **@** and is stored in eight bytes. We will soon discuss why **Currency** variables are preferable to **Single** and **Double** variables for monetary amounts.

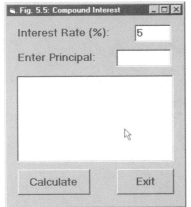

Initial GUI at execution.

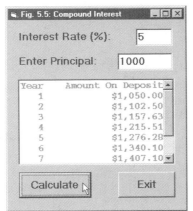

GUI after user enters **1000** and presses **Calculate**.

**Fig. 5.5** Compound interest program GUI.

| Object | Icon | Property | Property setting | Property description |
|---|---|---|---|---|
| form | | **Name** | **frmCompound** | Identifies the form. |
| | | **Caption** | **Fig 5.5: Compound Interest** | Form title bar display. |
| **Calculate** button | | **Name** | **cmdCalculate** | Identifies **Calculate** button. |
| | | **Caption** | **Calculate** | Text that appears on button. |
| | | **Font** | **MS San Serif Bold 12 pt** | Font applied to button text. |

**Fig. 5.6** Properties listing (part 1 of 2).

| Object | Icon | Property | Property setting | Property description |
|--------|------|----------|------------------|----------------------|
| **Exit** button | | `Name` | `cmdExit` | Identifies **Exit** button. |
| | | `Caption` | `Exit` | Text that appears on button. |
| | | `Font` | `MS San Serif Bold 12 pt` | Font applied to button text. |
| `Label` | A | `Name` | `lblInterest` | Identifies **Label**. |
| | | `Caption` | `Interest Rate (%):` | Text that appears in the **Label**. |
| | | `Font` | `MS San Serif Bold 12 pt` | Font applied to **Label** text. |
| `Label` | A | `Name` | `lblAmount` | Identifies **Label**. |
| | | `Caption` | `Enter Principal:` | Text that appears in the **Label**. |
| | | `Font` | `MS San Serif Bold 12 pt` | Font applied to **Label** text. |
| `ListBox` | | `Name` | `lstDisplay` | Identifies **ListBox**. |
| | | `Enabled` | `False` | Disable **ListBox**. |
| | | `Font` | `Courier Bold 12 pt` | Font applied to **List-Box** text. |
| `TextBox` | abl | `Name` | `txtDisplay` | Identifies **TextBox**. |
| | | `Font` | `MS Sans Serif 12 pt` | Font applied to text. |
| | | `MaxLength` | `2` | Maximum number of characters that can be input. |
| | | `Text` | `5` | Text that appears in **TextBox**. |
| `TextBox` | abl | `Name` | `txtAmount` | Identifies **TextBox**. |
| | | `Font` | `MS Sans Serif 12 pt` | Font applied to text. |
| | | `Text` | `(empty)` | Text that appears in **TextBox**. |

**Fig. 5.6**    Properties listing (part 2 of 2).

```
1    ' Fig. 5.5
2    ' Calculating compound interest.
3    Option Explicit              ' General Declaration
4
5    Private Sub cmdCalculate_Click()
6       Dim years As Integer
7       Dim interestRate As Double
8       Dim amount As Currency
9       Dim principal As Currency
10
11       lstDisplay.Clear        ' Clear list box
12       years = 10              ' Initialize variable
13
14       ' Get information from text boxes
15       principal = txtAmount.Text
16       interestRate = txtInterest.Text / 100
17
18       ' Display header in list box
19       lstDisplay.AddItem "Year" & vbTab & "Amount On Deposit"
20
21       For years = 1 To 10
22          amount = principal * (1 + interestRate) ^ years
23          lstDisplay.AddItem Format$(years, "@@@@") & vbTab & _
24                             Format$(Format$(amount, "Currency"), _
25                             String$(17, "@"))
26       Next years
27
28    End Sub
29
30    Private Sub cmdExit_Click()
31       End
32    End Sub
```

**Fig. 5.7**     Calculating compound interest.

The line

      **lstDisplay.Clear**

uses method **Clear** to empty the contents of **ListBox lstDisplay**. Every time the **Calculate** button is pressed, **lstDisplay** is cleared (i.e., does not display anything). A **ListBox** is a control that displays a series of **String**s.

*Good Programming Practice 5.5*

*Prefix the name of **ListBox**es with **lst**. This allows **ListBox**es to be identified easily.*

The statement

      **lstDisplay.AddItem "Year" & vbTab & "Amount On Deposit"**

displays a **String** in **lstDisplay**. Method **AddItem** adds an item (a **String**) to **lstDisplay**. Constant variable **vbTab** represents a tab. A *constant variable* is a variable whose value cannot be changed. Visual Basic provides constants for many commonly used features. Visual Basic constants are prefixed with **vb**. We discuss constant variables in greater detail in Section 5.10.

The **For/Next** structure executes the body of the loop 10 times, varying a control variable from **1** to **10** in increments of **1** (again **1** is the default when **Step** is omitted). The amount on deposit at the end of each year is calculated with the line

```
amount = principal * (1 + interestRate) ^ years
```

A formatted **String** containing the year and the amount on deposit at the end of that year is displayed in **lstDisplay** with the line

```
lstDisplay.AddItem Format$(years, "@@@@") & vbTab & _
                   Format$(Format$(amount, "Currency"), _
                   String$(17, "@"))
```

We now examine each key formatting item of the previous line, starting with

```
Format$(years, "@@@@")
```

Function ***Format$*** returns a formatted **String**. The first argument passed, **years**, is the *expression* to format. The second argument, **"@@@@"**, is a **String** that describes the *format*. The *at sign character*, **@**, specifies that either a character or a space is displayed. The **@** character here is unrelated to the **Currency** type declaration character. The number of **@** characters determine the number of spaces that appear in the formatted **String**.

For example, **years** is assigned the value **1** in the loop. The number **1** consists of one character, so the formatted **String** returned by **Format$** is **"   1"**. Three spaces precede the **1** character—which indicates *right-justification* (the default). *Left-justification* is accomplished by preceding the first **@** character with an **!** character. Thus,

```
Format$(years, "!@@@@")
```

returns the formatted **String "1    "**. Three spaces are after the **1**.

The next formatting piece contains three function calls. We have placed this piece on one line and added spacing for emphasis. The code segment

```
Format$(  Format$(amount, "Currency"), String$(17, "@")   )
```

formats the expression

```
Format$(amount, "Currency")
```

using the format

```
String$(17, "@")
```

Function ***String$*** creates a **String** containing 17 **@** characters. Note the change in the second argument of

```
Format$(amount, "Currency")
```

We previously had used **"Fixed"**, but since we are dealing with dollar amounts, format **"*Currency*"** is appropriate. Format **"Currency"** displays a dollar sign, **$**, displays two places to the right of the decimal point and displays commas after every three digits. The resulting **String** returned is then formatted with the 17 **@** character **String**.

Notice that we have declared the variables **amount** and **principal** to be of type **Currency**. We have done this for simplicity because we are dealing with dollars and we need a type that allows decimal points in its values. We could have declared the variables as either **Single** or **Double**, which could result in problems. Here is a simple explanation of what can go wrong when using **Single** or **Double** to represent dollar amounts (assuming formatting is done with **Format$(variable, "Fixed")**). Two **Single** dollar amounts stored in the machine could be 14.234 (which prints as 14.23) and 18.673 (which prints as 18.67). When these amounts are added, they produce the internal sum 32.907, which prints as 32.91. Thus your printout could appear as

```
    14.23
+   18.67
  -------
    32.91
```

but a person adding the individual numbers as printed would expect the sum 32.90! You have been warned!

*Good Programming Practice 5.6*

*Do not use variables of type **Single** or **Double** to perform monetary calculations. The imprecision of floating-point numbers can cause errors that will result in incorrect monetary values. Type **Currency** should be used for monetary amounts.*

Note that the calculation **1 + interestRate** is contained in the **For/Next**'s body. In fact, this calculation produces the same result each time through the loop, so repeating the calculation is wasteful.

*Performance Tip 5.1*

*Placing expressions whose values do not change inside loops can decrease performance.*

## 5.5 Select Case Multiple-Selection Structure

We have discussed the **If/Then** single-selection structure and the **If/Then/Else** double-selection structure. We also discussed multiple selection using the **If/Then/Else**, which used keyword **ElseIf**. Although **If/Then/Else** multiple-selection structures and **Select Case** multiple-selection structures perform equivalently, many programmers prefer to use **Select Case**. The **Select Case** structure can be used with any data type and is flowcharted in Fig. 5.8.

Again, note that (besides small circles and arrows) the flowchart contains only rectangle and diamond symbols. Imagine, again, that the programmer has access to a deep bin of empty **Select Case** structures—as many as the programmer might need to stack and nest with other control structures to form a structured implementation of an algorithm's flow of control. And again, the rectangles and diamonds are then filled with actions and decisions appropriate to the algorithm. Nested control structures are common, but it is rare to find nested **Select Case** structures in a program.

The next example uses a **Select Case** statement to check an access code entered on a security keypad. Consider the following problem statement:

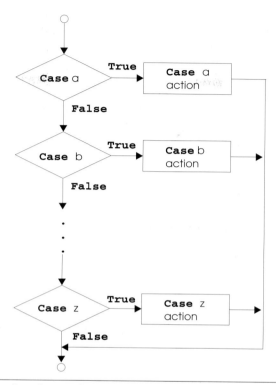

**Fig. 5.8**    Flowcharting the **Select Case** multiple-selection structure.

*A government lab wants to install a security keypad outside a laboratory room. Only authorized personnel may enter the lab, using their security codes. The following are valid security codes:*

| | |
|---|---|
| *1645 - 1689* | *Technicians* |
| *8345* | *Custodians* |
| *55875* | *Special Services* |
| *999898* | *Chief Scientist* |
| *1000006 - 1000008* | *Scientists* |

*As an added security measure, the keypad treats any access less than 1000 as a panic code by sounding a single beep. Although access is denied, security is notified immediately. Once an access code is entered, access is either granted or denied. All access attempts are written to a window below the keypad. If access is granted, the date, time, and group (i.e., scientist, custodian, etc.) are written to the window. If access is denied, the date, time and the message "Access Denied" are written to the window.*

The GUI is shown in Fig. 5.9, properties in Fig. 5.10 and the code in Fig. 5.11.

Text entered in a **TextBox** can be *masked* using the character specified in property **PasswordChar**. Rather than displaying the exact character the user types, the masking character is displayed instead. The actual value being input is retained and is unaffected by the masking character.

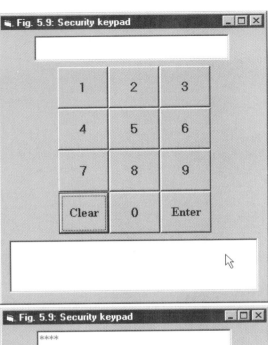

Initial GUI at execution.

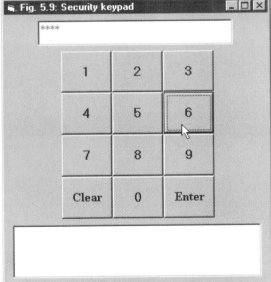

User entering an access code.

**Fig. 5.9**    Security keypad program GUI (part 1 of 2).

*Software Engineering Observation 5.1*

*Masking is commonly used for passwords or other sensitive pieces of information that should not be observed by other people.*

Note that we only listed the properties for **cmdZero** in Fig. 5.10. Although we did not list the other "numbered" buttons, they have the same property settings.

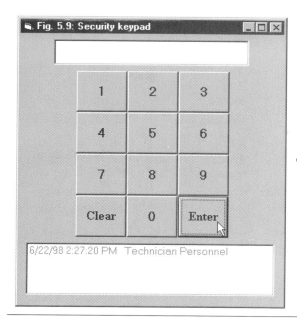

GUI after user has pressed **Enter**.

**Fig. 5.9**    Security keypad program GUI (part 2 of 2).

| Object | Icon | Property | Property setting | Property description |
|--------|------|----------|------------------|----------------------|
| form | | `Name` | `frmSecurity` | Identifies the form. |
| | | `Caption` | `Fig 5.9:`<br>`Security keypad` | Form title bar display. |
| **Clear** button | | `Name` | `cmdClear` | Identifies **Clear** button. |
| | | `Caption` | `Clear` | Text that appears on button. |
| **Enter** button | | `Name` | `cmdEnter` | Identifies **Enter** button. |
| | | `Caption` | `Enter` | Text that appears on button. |
| **0** button | | `Name` | `cmdZero` | Identifies **0** button. |
| | | `Caption` | `0` | Text that appears on button. |
| | | `Font` | `MS San Serif`<br>`Bold 12 pt` | Font applied to button text. |

**Fig. 5.10**    Properties listing.

| Object | Icon | Property | Property setting | Property description |
|---|---|---|---|---|
| ListBox | | Name | lstLogEntry | Identifies **ListBox**. |
| | | Enabled | False | Disable **ListBox**. |
| TextBox | | Name | txtDisplay | Identifies **TextBox**. |
| | | Enabled | False | Disable **TextBox**. |
| | | Font | Times Bold 10 pt | Font applied to text. |
| | | PasswordChar | * | Masking character. |
| | | Text | (empty) | Text in **TextBox**. |

**Fig. 5.10**  Properties listing.

```
1   ' Fig. 5.9
2   ' Security keypad program
3   Option Explicit           ' General Declaration
4   Dim mAccessCode As Long    ' General Declaration
5
6   Private Sub cmdEnter_Click()
7      Dim message As String
8
9      mAccessCode = txtDisplay.Text
10     txtDisplay.Text = ""
11
12     Select Case mAccessCode
13        Case Is < 1000                ' Panic codes
14           message = "Access Denied"
15           Beep
16        Case 1645 To 1689
17           message = "Technician Personnel"
18        Case 8345
19           message = "Custodial Services"
20        Case 55875
21           message = "Special Services"
22        Case 999898, 1000006 To 1000008
23           message = "Scientific Personnel"
24        Case Else
25           message = "Access Denied"
26     End Select
27
28     lstLogEntry.AddItem Now & Space$(3) & message
29   End Sub
30
31   Private Sub cmdZero_Click()
32      txtDisplay.Text = txtDisplay.Text & "0"
33   End Sub
```

**Fig. 5.11**  Code Listing (part 1 of 2).

```
34
35    Private Sub cmdOne_Click()
36        txtDisplay.Text = txtDisplay.Text & "1"
37    End Sub
38
39    Private Sub cmdTwo_Click()
40        txtDisplay.Text = txtDisplay.Text & "2"
41    End Sub
42
43    Private Sub cmdThree_Click()
44        txtDisplay.Text = txtDisplay.Text & "3"
45    End Sub
46
47    Private Sub cmdFour_Click()
48        txtDisplay.Text = txtDisplay.Text & "4"
49    End Sub
50
51    Private Sub cmdFive_Click()
52        txtDisplay.Text = txtDisplay.Text & "5"
53    End Sub
54
55    Private Sub cmdSix_Click()
56        txtDisplay.Text = txtDisplay.Text & "6"
57    End Sub
58
59    Private Sub cmdSeven_Click()
60        txtDisplay.Text = txtDisplay.Text & "7"
61    End Sub
62
63    Private Sub cmdEight_Click()
64        txtDisplay.Text = txtDisplay.Text & "8"
65    End Sub
66
67    Private Sub cmdNine_Click()
68        txtDisplay.Text = txtDisplay.Text & "9"
69    End Sub
70
71    Private Sub cmdClear_Click()
72        txtDisplay.Text = ""
73    End Sub
```

**Fig. 5.11**   Code Listing (part 2 of 2).

We begin by looking at the general declaration. The line

```
Dim mAccessCode As Long
```

declares the variable **mAccessCode** as type **Long**. Like type **Integer**, **Long** stores whole numbers (numbers without a decimal point). The range of values that can be stored in a **Long** are –2,147,483,648 to 2,147,483,647. **Long**'s type declaration character is **&**.

Placing a declaration in the general declaration, as we have done, creates a *module-level variable*. A module-level variable is accessible to other procedures. For example, line 9 uses **mAccessCode**. We will discuss the merit of module-level variables and alternative ways of accomplishing the same thing in Chapter 6.

*Testing and Debugging Tip 5.4*

*Prefixing module-level variables with* **m** *allows them to be identified easily.*

The line

```
Select Case mAccessCode
```

begins the **Select Case** structure. The value of **mAccessCode** will be compared sequentially with each **Case** until either a match occurs or the **End Select** statement is executed. Execution of a particular **Case** statement causes program control to proceed with the first statement after the **Select Case** structure.

The first **Case** statement,

```
Case Is < 1000
```

tests if **mAccessCode** is less than **1000**. Keyword *Is* along with the comparison operator, **<**, specifies the range of values to test.

The next **Case** statement,

```
Case 1645 To 1689
```

checks if the value of **mAccessCode** is between **1645** and **1689** inclusive. Keyword **To** is used to specify the range. This is the same keyword **To** that is used with the **For/Next** structure.

*Common Programming Error 5.7*

*Placing a larger value on the left side of keyword* **To** *in a* **Case** *statement is a logic error and is ignored at run-time.*

The next two **Case** statements check for specific numbers. If **mAccessCode** matches the value of either, the code in that particular **Case** is executed. Specifying a single value in a **Case** statement is quite common.

*Common Programming Error 5.8*

*Duplicate* **Case** *statements are logic errors. At run-time the first matching* **Case** *is executed.*

The next **Case** statement,

```
Case 99989, 1000006 To 1000008
```

checks if **mAccessCode** is **99989** or between **1000006** and **1000008** inclusive. When several non-consecutive values are tested for in a **Case** statement, the values are separated by commas.

The

```
Case Else
```

statement is the optional default **Case**. **Case Else** is executed when a match has not occurred for any previous **Case**. If used, the **Case Else** is always specified as the last **Case**.

*Common Programming Error 5.9*

*When using the optional* **Case Else** *statement in a* **Select Case** *structure, not placing the* **Case Else** *as the last statement is a syntax error.*

*Testing and Debugging Tip 5.5*

*Provide a* **Case Else** *in* **Select Case** *structures.* **Case**s *not explicitly tested in a* **Select Case** *structure without a* **Case Else** *are ignored. Including a* **Case Else** *statement focuses the programmer on the need to process exceptional conditions. In some situations, no* **Case Else** *processing is needed.*

The required **End Select** terminates the **Select Case** structure. Note the indentation of the **Select Case** structure. Such indentation improves program readability.

*Good Programming Practice 5.7*

*Consistently applying reasonable indentation conventions throughout your programs greatly improves program readability. We suggest a fixed-size tab of about 1/4 inch or three blanks per indent.*

The statement

```
lstLogEntry.AddItem Now & Space$(3) & message
```

displays a **String** in **lstLogEntry** consisting of the current system date and time, three spaces, and either the text "**Access Denied**" or the text "**Access Granted**." Function *Now* returns the current system time and date. Function *Space$* creates and returns a **String** containing spaces—the value passed to **Space$** specifies the number of spaces to create.

Function *Choose* is related to the **Select Case** statement. The first argument is an **Integer** that specifies the index of any argument after the first argument. Any number of items (of any type) can be provided after the first argument. Index values start at 1. Consider the statement

```
Print Choose(x, "Red", "Green", "Blue")
```

which prints either **Red**, **Green** or **Blue** depending on the value of **x**. If **x** is **1**, **Red** is displayed. If **x** is **2**, **Green** is displayed, and if **x** is **3**, **Blue** is displayed. **Choose** returns *Null* (i.e., which represents no valid data) if **x** has a value that is not between **1** and **3** inclusive. If a floating-point number is passed as the first argument, it is rounded to the nearest **Integer**.

## 5.6 Do/Loop While Repetition Structure

The **Do/Loop While** repetition structure is similar to the **Do While/Loop** structure. In the **Do While/Loop** structure, the loop-continuation condition is tested at the beginning of the loop before the body of the loop is performed. The **Do/Loop While** structure tests the loop-continuation condition after the loop body is performed, thus executing the loop body at least once. When a **Do/Loop While** terminates, execution continues with the statement after the **Loop While** clause. The program in Fig. 5.12 uses a **Do/Loop While** structure to print the numbers from 1 to 10.

```
1    ' Fig. 5.12
2    ' Demonstrating the Do/Loop While repetition structure
3    Option Explicit     ' General Declaration
4
5    Private Sub cmdPrint_Click()
6        Dim counter As Integer
7
8        counter = 1
9
10       Do
11           Print counter & Space$(2);
12           counter = counter + 1
13       Loop While counter <= 10
14
15       Print
16   End Sub
```

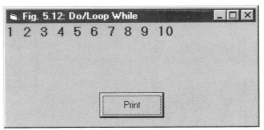

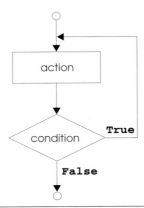

GUI after user has pressed **Print**.

**Fig. 5.12**   Using the **Do/Loop While** structure.

The **Do/Loop While** structure is flowcharted in Fig. 5.13. This flowchart makes it clear that the loop-continuation condition is not executed until after the action is performed at least once. Again, note that (besides small circles and arrows) the flowchart contains only a rectangle symbol and a diamond symbol.

**Fig. 5.13**   Flowcharting the **Do/Loop While** repetition structure.

Imagine that the programmer has access to a deep bin of empty **Do/Loop While** structures—as many as needed to stack and nest with other control structures to form a structured implementation of an algorithm's flow of control. And again, the rectangles and diamonds are then filled with actions and decisions appropriate to the algorithm.

**Testing and Debugging Tip 5.6**

*Infinite loops are caused when the loop-continuation condition in a **While/Wend**, **Do While/Loop** or **Do/Loop While** structure never becomes **False**. In a counter-controlled loop, make sure the control variable is incremented (or decremented) in the body of the loop. In a sentinel-controlled loop, make sure the sentinel value is eventually input.*

**Common Programming Error 5.10**

*Using an incorrect relational operator or an incorrect final value of a loop counter in the condition of a **Do While/Loop** or **Do/Loop While** structure can cause off-by-one errors.*

## 5.7 Do/Loop Until Repetition Structure

The **Do/Loop Until** structure is similar to **Do Until/Loop**. In the **Do Until/Loop** structure, the loop-continuation condition is tested at the beginning of the loop before the body of the loop is performed. **Do/Loop Until** tests the loop-continuation condition after the loop body is performed; therefore, the loop body executes at least once. When a **Do/Loop Until** terminates, execution continues with the statement after the **Do/Loop Until** clause. Figure 5.14 uses a **Do/Loop Until** structure to print the numbers from 1 to 9.

```
1   ' Fig. 5.14
2   ' Demonstrating the Do/Loop Until repetition structure
3   Option Explicit      ' General Declaration
4   Private Sub cmdPrint_Click()
5      Dim counter As Integer
6
7      counter = 1
8
9      Do
10        Print counter & Space$(2);
11        counter = counter + 1
12     Loop Until counter = 10
13
14     Print
15  End Sub
```

GUI after user has pressed **Print**.

**Fig. 5.14**   Using the **Do/Loop Until** structure.

The **Do/Loop Until** structure is flowcharted in Fig. 5.15. This flowchart makes it clear that the loop-continuation condition is not executed until after the action is performed at least once. Again, note that (besides small circles and arrows) the flowchart contains only a rectangle symbol and a diamond symbol.

Imagine, again, that the programmer has access to a deep bin of empty **Do/Loop Until** structures—as many as the programmer might need to stack and nest with other control structures to form a structured implementation of an algorithm's flow of control. And again, the rectangles and diamonds are then filled with actions and decisions appropriate to the algorithm.

***Common Programming Error 5.11***

*Using an incorrect relational operator or using an incorrect final value of a loop counter in the condition of a **Do Until/Loop** or **Do/Loop Until** structure can cause off-by-one errors.*

***Testing and Debugging Tip 5.7***

*Infinite loops are caused when the loop-continuation condition in a **Do Until/Loop** or **Do/Loop Until** structure never becomes true. In a counter-controlled loop, make sure the control variable is incremented (or decremented) in the body of the loop. In a sentinel-controlled loop, make sure the sentinel value is eventually input.*

***Testing and Debugging Tip 5.8***

*Using the final value in the condition of a **Do While/Loop**, **Do/Loop While**, **Do Until/Loop** or **Do/Loop Until** structure and using the **<=** relational operator can help avoid off-by-one errors. For a loop used to print the values 1 to 10, for example, the loop-continuation condition should be counter **<= 10** rather than counter **< 10** (which is an off-by-one error) or counter **< 11** (which is nevertheless correct).*

***Common Programming Error 5.12***

*Not using the proper relational operator in the loop-continuation condition of a loop that counts downwards (such as using **counter <= 1** in a loop counting down to **1** instead of using **counter >= 1**) is an error.*

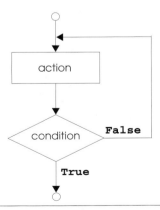

**Fig. 5.15**   Flowcharting the **Do/Loop Until** repetition structure.

## 5.8 **Exit Do** and **Exit For** Statements

The **Exit Do** and **Exit For** statements alter the flow of control. The **Exit Do** statement, when executed in a **Do While/Loop, Do/Loop While, Do Until/Loop** or **Do/Loop Until**, causes immediate exit from that structure. Program execution continues with the first statement after the structure. Figure 5.16 demonstrates the **Exit Do** statement in a **Do/Loop While** repetition structure. When the **If/Then** structure detects that **x** is 5, the **Exit Do** statement executes to terminate the **Do/Loop While** structure. The program continues with the **Print** after the **Do/Loop While**. The loop executes only four times.

The **Exit For** statement causes immediate exit from the **For/Next** structure. Program execution continues with the first statement after the **For/Next** structure. Figure 5.17 demonstrates the **Exit For** statement. When the **If/Then** structure detects that **y** has become 5, the **Exit For** statement is executed. This terminates the **For/Next** structure and the program continues with the **Print** after the **For/Next**. The loop executes only four times.

```
1   ' Fig. 5.16
2   ' Demonstrating Exit Do.
3   Option Explicit      ' General Declaration
4
5   Private Sub cmdPrint_Click()
6      Dim x As Integer
7
8      x = 1
9
10     Do
11
12        If x = 5 Then
13           Exit Do     ' Exit loop only if x = 5
14        End If
15
16        Print x & Space$(2);
17        x = x + 1
18     Loop While x <= 10
19
20     Print "Exited loop at x = " & x
21  End Sub
```

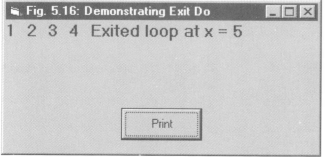

GUI after user has pressed **Print**.

**Fig. 5.16** Using the **Exit Do** statement in a **Do/Loop While** structure.

**Software Engineering Observation 5.2**

*Some programmers feel that **Exit Do** and **Exit For** violate structured programming. Because the effects of these statements can be achieved by structured programming techniques we will soon learn, these programmers do not use **Exit Do** and **Exit For**.*

**Performance Tip 5.2**

*The **Exit Do** and **Exit For** statements, when used properly, perform faster than the corresponding structured techniques we will soon learn.*

**Software Engineering Observation 5.3**

*There is a tension between achieving quality software engineering and achieving the best-performing software. Often, one of these goals is achieved at the expense of the other.*

**Testing and Debugging Tip 5.9**

*During the debugging process it is often helpful to comment out selected portions of your code that you suspect may contain an error. Running your program with selected lines commented repeatedly will often allow you to "zero-in" on an error.*

```
1    ' Fig. 5.17
2    ' Demonstrating Exit For.
3    Option Explicit    ' General Declaration
4
5    Private Sub cmdPrint_Click()
6       Dim x As Integer
7
8       For x = 1 To 10
9
10         If x = 5 Then
11            Exit For     ' Exit loop only if x = 5
12         End If
13
14         Print x & Space$(2);
15      Next x
16
17      Print "Exited loop at x = " & x
18   End Sub
```

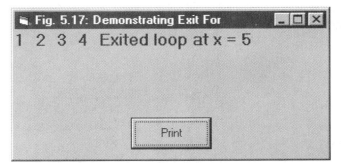

GUI after user has pressed **Print**.

**Fig. 5.17**   Using the **Exit For** statement in a **For/Next** structure.

## 5.9 Data Type `Boolean`

Visual Basic provides data type ***Boolean*** for storing boolean values. A *boolean value* is represented by either the keywords ***True*** or ***False*** or by a non-zero or zero value. For example, the non-zero value **–9** is equivalent to **True** and **0** is equivalent to **False**. **Boolean**s are stored in two bytes and do not have a type-declaration character. When an **Integer** value is explicitly assigned to a **Boolean**, the **Integer** value is implicitly converted to **True** or **False**. The following program demonstrates the use of **Boolean**s. The GUI is shown in Fig. 5.18, properties in Fig. 5.19 and code in Fig. 5.20.

The declaration

```
Dim bool As Boolean
```

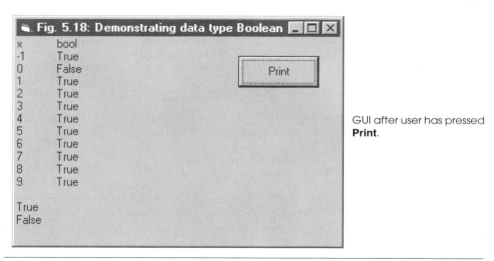

GUI after user has pressed **Print**.

Fig. 5.18   **Boolean** program GUI.

| Object | Icon | Property | Property setting | Property description |
|--------|------|----------|------------------|----------------------|
| form |  | **Name** | **frmBoolean** | Identifies the form. |
|  |  | **Caption** | **Fig. 5.18: Demonstrating data type Boolean** | Form title bar display. |
| **Print** button |  | **Name** | **cmdPrint** | Identifies **Print** button. |
|  |  | **Caption** | **Print** | Text that appears on button. |

Fig. 5.19   Object properties.

```
1   ' Fig. 5.18
2   ' Demonstrating data type Boolean
3   Option Explicit                      ' General declaration
4
5   Private Sub cmdPrint_Click()
6       Dim bool As Boolean
7       Dim x As Integer
8
9       x = -1                           ' Initialize x to -1
10      Print "x" & vbTab & "bool"       ' Print Header
11
12      Do Until x = 10
13         bool = x                      ' Implicit conversion
14         Print x & vbTab & bool        ' Print True or False
15         x = x + 1                     ' Increment x
16      Loop
17
18      Print                            ' Print blank line
19      bool = True                      ' Assign True
20      Print bool                       ' Print True or False
21      bool = False                     ' Assign False
22      Print bool                       ' Print True or False
23   End Sub
```

**Fig. 5.20**  Code listing.

declares **Boolean** variable **bool**. **Integer x** is also declared and initialized to **−1**. The statement

> ```
> Print "x" & vbTab & "bool"
> ```

prints **x** and **bool** separated by a tab on the form. The **Do Until/Loop** repetition structure iterates until **x** is **10**. Each iteration assigns **x**'s value to **bool** with the statement

> ```
> bool = x
> ```

The value of **x** is implicitly converted to **True** or **False**. A nonzero value converts to
**True** and a zero value converts to **False**. Both **x** and **bool** are output on line 14. When
**x** is output, an **Integer** is displayed. Printing **bool** results in either **True** or **False** being displayed. Variable **x** is then incremented by one.

The statement

> ```
> bool = True
> ```

explicitly assigns **True** to **bool**. Variable **bool** is then output.

*Good Programming Practice 5.8*

*Using **True** and **False** in preference to 0 and non-zero improves program readability.*

## 5.10 Constant Variables

Visual Basic allows programmer to create variables whose values cannot change during
program execution. These special types of variables are called *constant variables*. The term

"constant variable" is an oxymoron—a contradiction in terms—like "jumbo shrimp" or "freezer burn." Constant variables are often used to make a program more readable. The program of Fig. 5.21 demonstrates using constant variables.

Lines 6 and 7 create constant variables **year**, **version** and **pi** using keyword **Const**. Although **version** is not immediately preceded by **Const**, it is a constant variable because **Const** begins the declaration. Constant variables must be initialized with a constant expression when they are declared and cannot be modified thereafter. The value of each constant is displayed and the **Print** button disabled.

*Common Programming Error 5.13*

*Attempting to declare a constant variable without assigning it a value in the declaration is a syntax error.*

*Common Programming Error 5.14*

*Assigning a value to a constant variable in an executable statement is a run-time error.*

*Common Programming Error 5.15*

*Using **Dim** with **Const** in a declaration is a syntax error.*

```
1   ' Fig. 5.21
2   ' Constant Variables
3   Option Explicit              ' General declaration
4
5   Private Sub cmdPrint_Click()
6       Const year As Integer = 1998, version As Single = 2.22
7       Const pi As Double = 3.14159
8
9       Print "Constant variable year is " & year
10      Print "Constant variable version is " & version
11      Print "Constant variable pi is " & pi
12
13      cmdPrint.Enabled = False    ' Disable button
14  End Sub
```

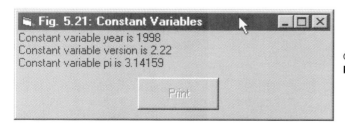

GUI after user has pressed **Print**.

**Fig. 5.21**   Demonstrating constant variables.

## 5.11 Logical Operators

So far we have studied only simple conditions such as **counter <= 10**, **total > 1000** and **number <> sentinelValue**. We have expressed these conditions in terms of the relational operators **>**, **<**, **>=** and **<=**, and the equality operators **=** and **<>**. Each decision tested precisely one condition. If we wanted to test multiple conditions in the process of making a decision, we had to perform these tests in several **If/Then** or **If/Then/Else** statements.

*Logical operators* may be used to form more complex conditions by combining simple conditions. The logical operators are **And** (*logical AND*), **Or** (*logical OR*) and **Not** (*logical NOT*—also called *logical negation*). We will consider examples of each of these.

Suppose we wish to ensure at some point in a program that two conditions are both **True** before we choose a certain path of execution. In this case we can use the logical **And** operator as follows:

```
If partNumber = 5526 And inventory > 0 Then
    Print "Part is in stock"
End If
```

This **If/Then** statement contains two simple conditions. The condition **part-Number = 5526** might be evaluated, for example, to determine if a store carries a particular part. The condition **inventory > 0** is evaluated to determine if a part's **inventory** is greater than zero. The two simple conditions are evaluated first because the precedences of **=** and **>=** are both higher than the precedence of **And**. The **If/Then** statement then considers the combined condition

```
partNumber = 5526 And inventory > 0
```

This condition is **True** if and only if both of the simple conditions are **True**. Finally, if this combined condition is indeed **True**, then the message "**Part is in stock**" is printed on the form. If either or both of the simple conditions are **False**, then the program skips the printing and proceeds to the statement following the **If/Then**. The preceding combined condition can be made more readable by adding redundant parentheses:

```
( partNumber = 5526 ) And ( inventory > 0 )
```

The table of Fig. 5.22 summarizes the **And** operator. The table shows all four possible combinations of **False** and **True** values for *expression1* **And** *expression2*. Such tables are often called *truth tables*.

| Expression1 | Expression2 | Expression1 And Expression2 | Result |
|---|---|---|---|
| False | False | False And False | False |
| False | True | False And True | False |
| True | False | True And False | False |
| True | True | True And True | True |

**Fig. 5.22**   Truth table for operator **And**.

Now let us consider operator **Or**. Suppose we wish to ensure at some point in a program that either or both of two conditions are **True** before we choose a certain path of execution. In this case we use operator **Or** as in the following program segment:

```
If semesterAverage >= 90 Or finalExam >= 90 Then
    Print "Student grade is A"
End If
```

This statement also contains two simple conditions. The condition **semesterAverage >= 90** is evaluated to determine if the student deserves an "A" in the course because of a solid performance throughout the semester. The condition **finalExam >= 90** is evaluated to determine if the student deserves an "A" in the course because of an outstanding performance on the final exam. The **If/Then** statement then considers the combined condition

```
semesterAverage >= 90 Or finalExam >= 90
```

and awards the student an "A" if either or both of the simple conditions are **True**. Note that the message "**Student grade is A**" is not printed only when both of the simple conditions are **False**. Figure 5.23 is a truth table for operator **Or**.

Operator **And** has a higher precedence than operator **Or**. Each condition involving operators **And** and **Or** is always evaluated in its entirety—regardless if truth or falsity is known. Thus, evaluation of the expression

```
partNumber = 5526 And inventory > 0
```

evaluates both conditions. If **partNumber** is **9999**, falsity is established and the condition **inventory > 0** is still tested.

Operator **Not** (logical negation operator) enables a programmer to "reverse" the meaning of a condition. Unlike operators **And** and **Or**, which combine two conditions and are therefore binary operators, **Not** has only a single condition as an operand and is therefore a unary operator. When we are interested in choosing a path of execution when a condition is **False**, operator **Not** is placed before the condition as in the following program segment:

```
If Not( grade = sentinelValue ) Then
    Print "The next grade is " & grade
End If
```

| Expression1 | Expression2 | Expression1 Or Expression2 | Result |
|---|---|---|---|
| False | False | False Or False | False |
| False | True | False Or True | True |
| True | False | True Or False | True |
| True | True | True Or True | True |

**Fig. 5.23**  Truth table for operator **Or**.

The parentheses around the condition **grade** = **sentinelValue** are not needed because comparison operators have a higher precedence than logical operators. The parentheses are added for clarity. Figure 5.24 is a truth table for the logical negation operator.

In most cases, the programmer can avoid using logical negation by expressing the condition differently with an appropriate relational or equality operator. For example, the preceding statement may also be written as follows:

```
If grade <> sentinelValue Then
    Print "The next grade is " & grade
End If
```

This flexibility can often help a programmer express a condition in a more "natural" or convenient manner.

Figure 5.25 lists the operators introduced to this point. The operators are shown from top to bottom in decreasing order of precedence.

| Expression | Not expression | Result |
|---|---|---|
| **True** | **Not True** | **False** |
| **False** | **Not False** | **True** |

**Fig. 5.24**    Truth table for operator **Not**.

| Operator | Type | Name(s) |
|---|---|---|
| ( ) | Parentheses | Parentheses |
| ^ | Arithmetic | Exponent |
| − | Arithmetic | Negation (unary) |
| * / | Arithmetic | Multiplication, floating-point division |
| \ | Arithmetic | **Integer** division |
| **Mod** | Arithmetic | Modulus |
| + − | Arithmetic | Addition, subtraction |
| & | Concatenation | **String** concatenation |
| = <> <= >= > < | Comparison (all have the same level of precedence) | Equal to, not equal to, less than or equal to, greater than or equal to, greater than, less than |
| **Not** | Logical | Logical negation |
| **And** | Logical | Logical **And** |
| **Or** | Logical | Logical **Or** |

**Fig. 5.25**    Precedence and associativity of the operators discussed so far.

## 5.12 Structured Programming Summary

Just as architects design buildings by employing the collective wisdom of their profession, so should programmers design programs. Our field is younger than architecture is, and our collective wisdom is considerably sparser. We have learned that structured programming produces programs that are easier than unstructured programs to understand and hence are easier to test, debug, modify, and even prove correct in a mathematical sense.

Figures 5.26 and 5.27 summarize Visual Basic's control structures. Small circles are used in the figure to indicate the single entry point and the single exit point of each structure. Connecting individual flowchart symbols arbitrarily can lead to unstructured programs. Therefore, the programming profession has chosen to combine flowchart symbols to form a limited set of control structures, and to build structured programs by properly combining control structures in two simple ways. For simplicity, only single-entry/single-exit control structures are used—there is only one way to enter and only one way to exit each control structure. Connecting control structures in sequence to form structured programs is simple—the exit point of one control structure is connected directly to the entry point of the next control structure, i.e., the control structures are simply placed in sequence (i.e., one after another in a program); we have called this "control structure stacking." The rules for forming structured programs also allow for control structures to be nested.

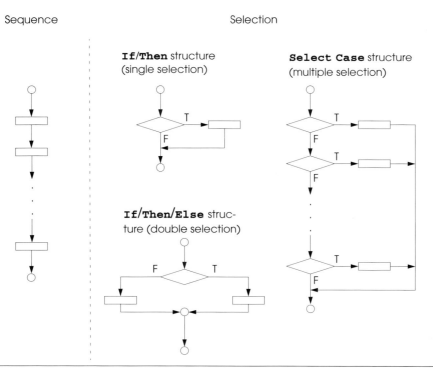

**Fig. 5.26**   *Visual Basic's single-entry/single-exit sequence and selection structures.*

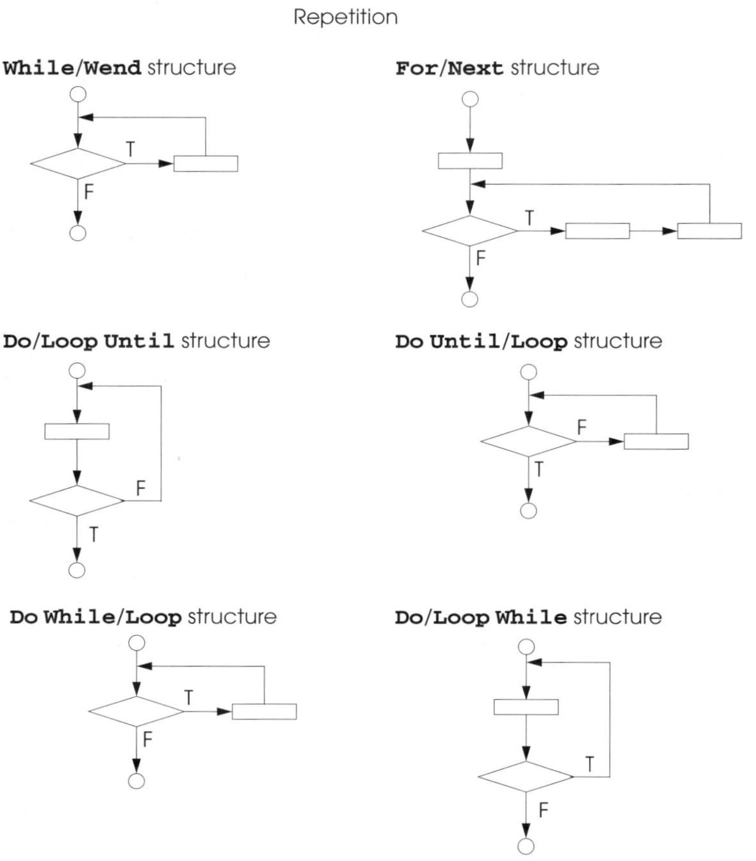

Repetition

**Fig. 5.27**  Visual Basic's single-entry/single-exit repetition structures.

Figure 5.28 shows the rules for forming properly structured programs. The rules assume that the rectangle flowchart symbol may be used to indicate any action, including input/output.

---

**Rules for Forming Structured Programs**

1. Begin with the "simplest flowchart" (Fig. 5.29).
2. Any rectangle (action) can be replaced by two rectangles (actions) in sequence.
3. Any rectangle (action) can be replaced by any control structure (sequence, **If/Then**, **If/Then/Else**, **Select Case**, **While/Wend**, **Do While/Loop**, **Do Loop/While**, **Do Until/Loop**, **Do Loop/Until** or **For/Next**).
4. Rules 2 and 3 may be applied as often as you like and in any order.

**Fig. 5.28**  Rules for forming structured programs.

Applying the rules of Fig. 5.28 always results in a structured flowchart with a neat, building-block appearance. For example, repeatedly applying rule 2 to the simplest flowchart (Fig. 5.29) results in a structured flowchart containing many rectangles in sequence (Fig. 5.30). Notice that rule 2 generates a stack of control structures; so let us call rule 2 the *stacking rule*.

Rule 3 is the *nesting rule*. Repeatedly applying rule 3 to the simplest flowchart results in a flowchart with neatly nested control structures. For example, in Fig. 5.31, the rectangle in the simplest flowchart is first replaced with a double-selection (**If/Then/Else**) structure. Then rule 3 is applied again to both of the rectangles in the double-selection structure, replacing each of these rectangles with double-selection structures. The dashed boxes around the double-selection structures represent the rectangles that were replaced.

Rule 4 generates larger, more involved, and more deeply nested structures. The flowcharts that emerge from applying the rules in Fig. 5.28 constitute the set of all possible structured flowcharts and hence the set of all possible structured programs.

The beauty of the structured approach is that we use only ten simple single-entry/single-exit pieces, and we assemble them in only two simple ways. Figure 5.32 shows the kinds of stacked building blocks that emerge from applying rule 2 and the kinds of nested building blocks that emerge from applying rule 3. The figure also shows the kind of overlapped building blocks that cannot appear in structured flowcharts (because of the elimination of the **goto** statement).

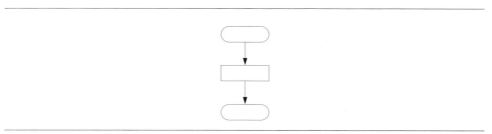

**Fig. 5.29**   The simplest flowchart.

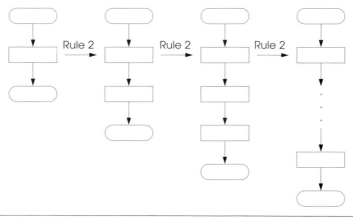

**Fig. 5.30**   Repeatedly applying rule 2 of Fig. 5.28 to the simplest flowchart.

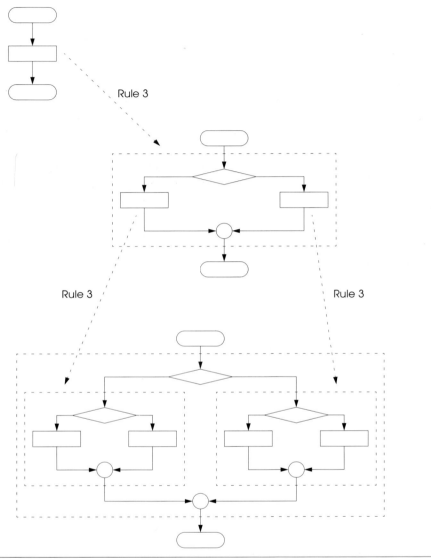

**Fig. 5.31**    Applying rule 3 of Fig. 5.28 to the simplest flowchart.

If the rules in Fig. 5.28 are followed, an unstructured flowchart (such as that in Fig. 5.33) cannot be created. If you are uncertain if a particular flowchart is structured, apply the rules of Fig. 5.28 in reverse to try to reduce the flowchart to the simplest flowchart. If the flowchart is reducible to the simplest flowchart, the original flowchart is structured; otherwise, it is not.

Structured programming promotes simplicity. Bohm and Jacopini have given us the result that only three forms of control are needed:

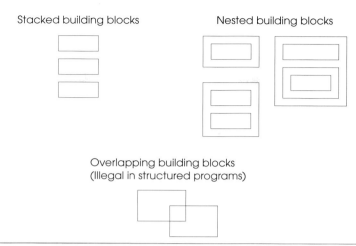

**Fig. 5.32**   Stacked building blocks, nested building blocks and overlapped building blocks.

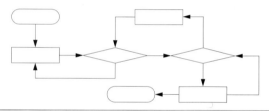

**Fig. 5.33**   An unstructured flowchart (i.e., one that cannot be reduced to the "simplest flowchart").

- Sequence
- Selection
- Repetition

Sequence is trivial. Selection is implemented in one of three ways:

- **If/Then** structure (single selection)
- **If/Then/Else** structure (double selection)
- **Select Case** structure (multiple selection)

In fact, it is straightforward to prove that the simple **If/Then** structure is sufficient to provide any form of selection—everything that can be done with the **If/Then/Else** structure and the **Select Case** structure can be implemented by combining **If/Then** structures (although perhaps not as smoothly).

- Repetition is implemented in one of six ways:
- **While/Wend** structure
- **Do While/Loop** structure

- **Do/Loop While** structure

- **Do Until/Loop** structure

- **Do/Loop Until** structure

- **For/Next** structure

It is straightforward to prove that the **While/Wend** structure is sufficient to provide any form of repetition. Everything that can be done with the **Do While/Loop** structure, **Do/Loop While** structure, **Do Until/Loop** structure, **Do/Loop Until** structure and the **For/Next** structure can be done with the **While/Wend** structure (although perhaps not as smoothly).

Combining these results illustrates that any form of control ever needed in a program can be expressed in terms of:

- sequence

- **If/Then** structure (selection)

- **While/Wend** structure (repetition)

And these control structures can be combined in only two ways—stacking and nesting. Indeed, structured programming promotes simplicity.

In this chapter, we discussed how to compose programs from control structures containing only actions and decisions. In Chapter 6, we introduce two new program structuring units—the **Sub** procedure and the **Function** procedure. We will learn to compose large programs by combining **Sub** procedures and/or **Function** procedures, which, in turn, are composed of control structures. We will also discuss how using **Sub** procedures and **Function** procedures promotes software reusability.

## 5.13 Visual Basic Data Types

In Chapters 3 through 5, we have introduced several Visual Basic data types. Data types describe the information that a variable stores. For example, **Integer** variables store whole numbers (i.e., non-floating point numbers). Data types also describe how many bytes of memory are required to represent a type (e.g., **Integer** requires 2 bytes).

The number of bytes determine the range of values that can be stored. For example, an **Integer** can store a value in the range –32768 to 32767 and a **Long**, which is 4 bytes, can store a value in the range –2147483648 to 2147483647.

 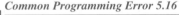

*Common Programming Error 5.16*

*Attempting to assign any value outside a data type's range is a run-time error.*

Visual Basic provides a variety of data types, which are listed in Fig. 5.34. For each type we list the number of bytes required and the range of values the type is capable of storing. Note: The byte sizes and range values are fixed. The programmer cannot change them.

| Data type | Bytes | Range |
|---|---|---|
| Boolean | 2 | **True** or **False** |
| Byte | 1 | 0 to 255 |
| Currency | 8 | –922337203685477.5808 to 922337203685477.5807 |
| Date | 8 | 1 January 100 to 31 December 9999<br>0:00:00 to 23:59:59 (discussed in Chapter 8). |
| Double | 8 | –1.79769313486232E308 to –4.94065645841247E–324 (negative)<br>1.79769313486232E308 to 4.94065645841247E–324 (positive) |
| Integer | 2 | –32768 to 32767 |
| Long | 4 | –2147483648 to 2147483647 |
| Object | 4 | Any **Object** type (discussed in Chapter 16). |
| Single | 4 | –3.402823E38 to –1.401298E–45 (negative)<br>3.402823E38 to 1.401298E–45 (positive) |
| String | 10+ | 0 to ~2000000000 characters. |
| Variant | 16 | Any value within the ranges listed above (discussed in Chapter 21). |

**Fig. 5.34**  Visual Basic data types.

Data type **Boolean** represents **True/False** values. The *Byte* data type stores one byte of information. **Currency** is a precise data type for storing monetary values. *Date* stores date and time formats. We discuss **Date** in Chapter 8. *Double* represents double-precision floating-point numbers. **Long** stores a whole number which can have a greater magnitude than **Integer**. **Single** represents single-precision floating-point numbers. **String** stores a series of characters. **Variant** stores any type of data and is the default Visual Basic data type. Using **Variant**s can be tricky, so we defer our discussion of **Variant** until Chapter 21.

Not all Visual Basic data types have a type declaration character (e.g., **Boolean**). Figure 5.35 lists the data types that have type declaration characters.

| Data type | Type-declaration character | Example expression |
|---|---|---|
| Currency | At sign, **@**. | `cash@ = cash@ - fee@` |
| Double | Pound sign, **#**. | `circleArea# = PI# * r# ^ 2` |
| Integer | Percent sign, **%**. | `total% = total% + grade%` |
| Long | Ampersand, **&**. | `Print diskspace&` |
| Single | Exclamation point, **!**. | `area! = width! * height!` |
| String | Dollar sign, **$**. | `ColorName$ = "yellow"` |

**Fig. 5.35**  Data types that have type-declaration characters.

## Summary

- The **For/Next** repetition structure handles all the details of counter-controlled repetition.

- Data type **Double** is a floating-point type stored in eight bytes. A **Double** stores a value of greater magnitude and precision than a **Single**. The **Double** type declaration character is **#**.

- Type **Currency** is stored in eight bytes and is used for monetary calculations. **Currency**'s type declaration character is **@**.

- A **ListBox** control displays a list of **String**s which are added individually to the **ListBox** by calling method **AddItem**. The entire **ListBox** contents can be removed by calling method **Clear**.

- A constant variable is a variable whose value cannot be changed. Visual Basic constants are prefixed with **vb**. Constant variable **vbTab**, which represents a tab, is an example of a Visual Basic constant variable.

- Function **Format$** returns a formatted **String**. The first argument passed is the expression to format, and the second argument passed describes the format. The **String** displayed is either right- or left-justified.

- Function **String$** creates a **String** of characters. The first argument specifies the number of characters, and the second argument specifies the character.

- **Select Case** is a multiple-selection control structure that can be used with any data type.

- Text entered in a **TextBox** can be masked using the character specified in property **Password-Char**.

- Data type **Long** stores whole numbers (numbers without a decimal point). The range of values that can be stored in a **Long** are –2,147,483,648 to 2,147,483,647. **Long**'s type declaration character is **&**.

- A module-level variable is accessible to other event procedures in the same module. Module-level variables are declared in the general declaration.

- Function **Now** returns the current system time and date.

- Function **Space$** creates and returns a **String** containing spaces. The value passed to **Space$** specifies the number of spaces to create.

- Function **Choose** returns an item from a list of items. The first argument specifies the item's index. Successive arguments that follow are items. After the first argument any number of arguments can be provided. Choose returns **Null** if an invalid index is used.

- The **Do/Loop While** structure tests the loop-continuation condition after the loop body is performed.

- The **Exit Do** statement, when executed in a **Do While/Loop, Do/Loop While, Do Until/Loop** or **Do/Loop Until**, causes immediate exit from that structure.

- The **Exit For** statement causes immediate exit from the **For/Next** structure.

- Data type **Boolean** stores boolean values. A boolean value is represented by either the keywords **True** or **False** or by a non-zero or zero value.

- Programmer-defined constant variables are created using keyword **Const**. Constant variables must be initialized with a constant expression when they are declared and cannot be modified thereafter.

- Logical operators may be used to form more complex conditions by combining simple conditions. The logical operators are **And** (logical AND), **Or** (logical OR) and **Not** (logical NOT—also called logical negation).

## Terminology

| | |
|---|---|
| **AddItem** method | **ListBox** control |
| **And** logical operator | logical **And** |
| at (**@**) character with **Format$** function | logical negation (Not) |
| **Boolean** data type | logical operators |
| **Byte** data type | logical **Or** |
| **Case Else** | loop continuation condition |
| **Case** in a **Select Case** statement | masking text in a **TextBox** control |
| **Choose** function | module-level variable |
| **Clear** method | nesting control structures |
| constant variable | nesting rule |
| **Const** keyword | **Not** logical operator |
| control variable | **Now** Function |
| counter-controlled repetition | **Null** keyword |
| **Currency** data type | **Object** data type |
| **Date** data type | off-by-one error |
| decrement a control variable | **Or** logical operator |
| **Do/Loop Until** repetition structure | **PasswordChar** property |
| **Do/Loop While** repetition structure | **Select Case** multiple-selection structure |
| **Double** data type | **Single** data type |
| **ElseIf** keyword | single-entry/single-exit control structures |
| **Enabled** property | stacking control structures |
| **End Select** in a **Select Case** statement | stacking rule |
| **Exit Do** statement | **Step** keyword in a **For/Next** structure |
| **Exit For** statement | **String** data type |
| **False** value of **Boolean** data type | structural programming |
| **Format$** function | **To** keyword in a **For/Next** structure |
| **For/Next** repetition structure | **True** value of **Boolean** data type |
| general declaration | truth table |
| increment a control variable | **Variant** data type |
| infinite loop | **vb** prefix |

## Common Programming Errors

**5.1**      Because floating-point values may be approximate, controlling counting loops with floating-point variables may result in imprecise counter values and inaccurate tests for termination.

**5.2**      Using the wrong variable name in a **Next** statement is a syntax error.

**5.3**      Not terminating a **For/Next** with **Next** is a syntax error.

**5.4**      In nested **For/Next** loops, using the same control variable name for more than one loop is a syntax error.

**5.5**      When your program should be counting downwards it is a logic error to have a positive increment in a **For/Next** loop, when the starting value is greater than the ending value.

**5.6**      When your program should be counting upwards it is a logic error to have a negative increment in a **For/Next** loop, when the starting value is less than the ending value.

**5.7**      Placing a larger value on the left side of keyword **To** in a **Case** statement is a logic error and is ignored at run-time.

**5.8**      Duplicate **Case** statements are logic errors. At run-time the first matching **Case** is executed.

**5.9**      When using the optional **Case Else** statement in a **Select Case** structure, not placing the **Case Else** as the last statement is a syntax error.

5.10    Using an incorrect relational operator or an incorrect final value of a loop counter in the condition of a **Do While/Loop** or **Do/Loop While** structure can cause off-by-one errors.

5.11    Using an incorrect relational operator or using an incorrect final value of a loop counter in the condition of a **Do Until/Loop** or **Do/Loop Until** structure can cause off-by-one errors.

5.12    Not using the proper relational operator in the loop-continuation condition of a loop that counts downwards (such as using **counter <= 1** in a loop counting down to **1** instead of using **counter >= 1**) is an error.

5.13    Attempting to declare a constant variable without assigning it a value in the declaration is a syntax error.

5.14    Assigning a value to a constant variable in an executable statement is a run-time error.

5.15    Using **Dim** with **Const** in a declaration is a syntax error.

5.16    Attempting to assign any value outside a data type's range is a run-time error.

## Good Programming Practices

5.1    Indent the statements in the body of each control structure.

5.2    Put a blank line before and after each control structure to make it stand out in the program.

5.3    Vertical spacing above and below control structures, and indentation of the bodies of control structures within the control structure headers, give programs a two-dimensional appearance that greatly improves readability.

5.4    Including the **For/Next** loop's control variable name after the **Next** statement is optional but doing so improves program readability.

5.5    Prefix the name of **ListBox**es with **lst**. This allows **ListBox**es to be identified easily.

5.6    Do not use variables of type **Single** or **Double** to perform monetary calculations. The imprecision of floating-point numbers can cause errors that will result in incorrect monetary values. Type **Currency** should be used for monetary amounts.

5.7    Consistently applying reasonable indentation conventions throughout your programs greatly improves program readability. We suggest a fixed-size tab of about 1/4 inch or three blanks per indent.

5.8    Using **True** and **False** in preference to 0 and non-zero improves program readability.

## Performance Tips

5.1    Placing expressions whose values do not change inside loops can decrease performance.

5.2    The **Exit Do** and **Exit For** statements, when used properly, perform faster than the corresponding structured techniques.

## Software Engineering Observations

5.1    Masking is commonly used for passwords or other sensitive pieces of information that should not be observed by other people.

5.2    Some programmers feel that **Exit Do** and **Exit For** violate structured programming. Because the effects of these statements can be achieved by structured programming techniques, these programmers do not use **Exit Do** and **Exit For**.

5.3    There is a tension between achieving quality software engineering and achieving the best-performing software. Often, one of these goals is achieved at the expense of the other.

## Testing and Debugging Tips

5.1    Control counting loops with **Integer** values.

5.2    Although the value of the control variable can be changed in the body of a **For/Next** loop, avoid doing so because this practice can lead to subtle errors.

**5.3**   Use a **For/Next** loop for counter-controlled repetition. Off-by-one errors (i.e., the process of looping one more iteration or one less iteration than necessary) tend to disappear, because the terminating value is not ambiguous.

**5.4**   Prefixing module-level variables with **m** allows them to be identified easily.

**5.5**   Provide a **Case Else** in **Select Case** structures. **Case**s not explicitly tested in a **Select Case** structure without a **Case Else** are ignored. Including a **Case Else** statement focuses the programmer on the need to process exceptional conditions. In some situations, no **Case Else** processing is needed.

**5.6**   Infinite loops are caused when the loop-continuation condition in a **While/Wend**, **Do While/Loop** or **Do/Loop While** structure never becomes **False**. In a counter-controlled loop, make sure the control variable is incremented (or decremented) in the body of the loop. In a sentinel-controlled loop, make sure the sentinel value is eventually input.

**5.7**   Infinite loops are caused when the loop-continuation condition in a **Do Until/Loop** or **Do/ Loop Until** structure never becomes true. In a counter-controlled loop, make sure the control variable is incremented (or decremented) in the body of the loop. In a sentinel-controlled loop, make sure the sentinel value is eventually input.

**5.8**   Using the final value in the condition of a **Do While/Loop**, **Do/Loop While**, **Do Until/ Loop** or **Do/Loop Until** structure and using the **<=** relational operator can help avoid off-by-one errors. For a loop used to print the values 1 to 10, for example, the loop-continuation condition should be counter **<= 10** rather than counter **< 10** (which is an off-by-one error) or counter **< 11** (which is nevertheless correct).

**5.9**   During the debugging process it is often helpful to comment out selected portions of your code that you suspect may contain an error. Running your program with selected lines commented repeatedly will often allow you to "zero-in" on an error.

## Self-Review Exercises

**5.1**   Write a statement or a set of statements to accomplish each of the following:
   a)  Declare the variables **bankBalance** and **discountPrice** to be of type **Currency**.
   b)  Declare the variables **catalogNumber** and **versionNumber** to be of type **Double**.
   c)  Print the system date and time to the form, using the **Print** method.
   d)  Print the **Integer**s from 1 to 20 using a **Do/Loop While** repetition structure and the counter variable **x**. Assume that the variable **x** has been declared as an **Integer**, but not initialized.
   e)  Repeat Exercise 5.1 (d) using a **For/Next** structure.
   f)  Sum the odd **Integer**s between 1 and 99 using a **For/Next** structure. Assume that the **Integer** variables **sum** and **count** have been declared and initialized to 0 and 1, respectively.

**5.2**   Answer each of the following questions.
   a)  Keyword _____ is used to declare a constant variable.
   b)  The _____ data type stores whole numbers in the approximate range ±2.1 billion.
   c)  The type declaration character for the **Double** type is _____.
   d)  Method _____ clears a **ListBox**.
   e)  Control structures can be combined either by _____ or _____.

**5.3**   Identify and correct the error(s) in each of the following:
   a)  Assume that the variable **p** is declared as **Integer**.

```
For p = 1 <= 100
   Print p * 1202
Next p
```

b) `Dim taxRefund As Money   Rem use fundamental data type`

c) Assume that the variable **y** has been declared as **Variant**.

```
For y = 0.1 To 1.0 Step .2
    Print y
Next .2
```

d) `Dim Const GOLDEN_RATIO as Double = 1.618 ' Declare constant`

e) Assume that the variables **u**, **x** and **c** have been declared and initialized.

```
' Condition should contain both Not operators
If Not Not u Or x = 78 And c <> 1.9 Then
    Print "Condition satisfied."
Else
    Print "Condition not satisfied."
```

f) Assume that the variable **testVariable** has been declared as **Integer**.

```
Do Loop Not testVariable
    Print "Inside of Loop."
Until
```

**5.4** State whether the following are *true* or *false*. If the answer is *false*, explain why.

a) The **Case Else** statement is required in the **Select Case** structure.

b) The **Exit For** statement is required in the **For/Next** repetition structure.

c) The expression (**x > y And a < b**) is **True** if either **x > y** is **True** or **a < b** is **True**.

d) An expression containing operator **Or** is **True** if either or both of its operands is **True**.

e) The **Case Else** statement can appear as any of the **Case**s in a **Select Case** structure.

f) A module-level variable is declared in the general declaration.

g) Keyword **To** is required when writing a **For/Next** loop.

**5.5** What does the following event procedure do?

```
Private Sub cmdButton_Click()
    Dim b As Integer, e As Integer
    Dim a As Integer, r As Integer

    r = 1
    b = InputBox("Enter a number:", "One")
    e = InputBox("Enter a number:", "Two")

    For a = 1 To e
        r = r * b
    Next a

    lblDisplayValue.Caption = "Mystery is " & r
End Sub
```

## Answers to Self-Review Exercises

**5.1**    a) `Dim bankBalance As Currency, discountPrice As Currency`

b) `Dim catalogNumber As Double, versionNumber As Double`

c) `Print Now`

d) `x = 1`

```
Do Loop
    Print x
    x = x + 1
While x <= 20
```
e) `For x = 1 To 20`
```
    Print x
Next x
```
f) `For count = 1 To 99 Step 2`
```
    sum = sum + count
Next count
```

**5.2**   a) `Const`
    b) `Long`
    c) `#`
    d) `Clear`
    e) stacking, nesting

**5.3**   a) The `<=` operator should be replaced with `To`.
```
For p = 1 To 100
    Print p * 1202
Next p
```
    b) The `Money` type does not exist and should be replaced with `Currency`.
```
Dim taxRefund As Currency  Rem use fundamental data type
```
    c) Floating-point numbers should not be used.
```
For y = 1 To 10 Step 2
    Print y / 10
Next y
```
    d) `Dim` and `Const` cannot be used together. `Dim` should be removed.
```
Const GOLDEN_RATIO as Double = 1.618   ' Declare constant
```
    e) `End If` is missing.
```
' Condition should contain both Not operators
If Not Not u Or x = 78 And c <> 1.9 Then
    Print "Condition satisfied."
Else
    Print "Condition not satisfied."
End If
```
    f) The `Not testVariable` should be placed after the `Until`.
```
Do Loop
    Print "Inside of Loop."
Until Not testVariable
```

**5.4**   a) False. `Case Else` is optional.
    b) False. `Exit For` is optional.
    c) False. Both conditions must be `True`.
    d) True.
    e) False. `Case Else` must appear last.
    f) True.
    g) True.

**5.5**   Program simulates exponentiation by multiplying the variable **r** by **b** **e** times.

## Exercises

**5.6**    Identify and correct the error(s) in each of the following:

a)  Assume that the variable **x** is declared as **Integer**.

```
For x = 100 To 1
   Print x
```

b)  The following code should print whether **Integer value** is odd or even:

```
Select (value Mod 2)
   Case 0
      Print "Even integer"
   Case 1
      Print "Odd integer"
Select End
```

c)  The following code should output the odd **Integer**s from 19 to 1:

```
For (x = 19 To 1 Step 2)
   Print x
Next
```

d)  The following code should output the even **Integer**s from 2 to 100:

```
counter = 2

Do Loop
   counter = counter + 2
   Print counter
While counter < 100
```

e)  **lstMyListBox.AddItem = "adding a string!"**

f)  Assume that variables **a**, **b** and **j** are declared as **Integer**.

```
For j = 1 To 200

   For j = 11 To 777 Step 11
      Print a * b
   Next j

Next j
```

g)  Assume that the variables **x**, **y** and **z** are declared as **Integer**s.

```
For x = 800 To 900

   For y = -50 To 150
      Print z + 8 * y + x - 3
   Next x

Next z
```

**5.7**    State whether the following are *true* or *false*. If the answer is *false*, explain why.

a)  The **$** is the type declaration character for the **Currency** type.

b)  A **Do Loop/Until** structure may be used to replace a **For/Next** structure.

   c) A **Do Loop/While** structure may be used to replace a **For/Next** structure.

   d) Keyword **Is** may be used in a **Select Case** structure.

   e) A module-level variable is accessible to multiple event procedures in the same module.

   f) **Case** statements are tested sequentially until either a match occurs or the **End Select** is executed.

**5.8**    Write a statement or a set of statements to accomplish each of the following:

   a) Declare the variable **nationalDebtInterest** as a **Long**.

   b) Declare constant variable **general76** as an **Integer** and assign it the value **76**.

   c) Print the value of **mDie1** using the **Print** method. Variable **mDie1** contains a number in the range 1 to 6.

   d) Write a **Select Case** structure that tests variable **s** against the odd numbers between 1 and 10. If **s** is indeed an odd number in the range 1 to 10, print value of **s** as "**One**," "**Three**," etc. Otherwise, print "**Out of range**."

   e) Add **"Sorted Values are: "** to ListBox **lstSortedNames**.

**5.9**    Answer each of the following questions.

   a) Of the three logical operators introduced in this chapter, _____ has the highest precedence.

   b) The _____ statement causes an immediate exit from a **Do While/Loop**, **Do Loop/ While/Wend**, **Do Until/Loop** and **Do Loop/Until**.

   c) Operator _____ reverses the result of a condition.

   d) Visual Basic constant _____ represents a tab character.

**5.10**    What does the following event procedure do?

```
Private Sub cmdButton_Click()
    Dim x As Integer, y As Integer
    Dim i As Integer, j As Integer

    x = InputBox("Enter a number in the range 1-20:")
    y = InputBox("Enter a number in the range 1-20:")

    For i = 1 To y
        For j = 1 To x
            Print "&";
        Next j

        Print
    Next i

End Sub
```

**5.11**    What does the following do?

```
For i = 1 To 2
    For j = 1 To 3
        For k = 1 To 4
            Print "*";
        Next k

        Print
    Next j
Next i
```

**5.12**    What does the following print?

---

```
1   Dim p As Integer, c As Integer, m As Integer
2
3   For p = 0 To 4
4
5      While c < p
6
7         Select Case (p + c - 1)
8            Case -1 Or 0
9               m = m + 1
10            Case 1, 2, 3
11               m = m + 2
12            Case Else
13               m = m + 3
14         End Select
15
16         Print m, ;
17         c = c + 1
18      Wend
19
20   Next p
21
22   Print
23   Print m
```

**5.13**    What does the following print?

---

```
1   Dim e As Integer, b As Integer
2   Dim t As Integer, w As Integer
3
4   For e = 4 To 0 Step -1
5
6      For b = 0 To e - 1
7         t = e + b + 1
8
9         If Not t Mod 2 Then
10            w = w + t
11         ElseIf Not t Mod 3 Then
12            w = w + t - 2
13         End If
14
15         lstListBox.AddItem w
16      Next b
17
18   Next e
19
20   lstListBox.AddItem w & "*"
```

**5.14**    Assume that $a = 1$, $b = 2$, $c = 3$ and $d = 2$. What does each of the following statements print? Are the parentheses necessary in each case?

a) **Print ( a = 1 )**

b) **Print ( b = 3 )**

```
c) Print ( a >= 1 And b < 4 )
d) Print ( d <= 99 And c < d )
e) Print ( b >= a Or c = d )
f) Print ( c + d < b Or 3 - b >= c )
g) Print ( True )
h) Print ( ( False ) + False )
i) Print ( Not( c > d ) )
```

**5.15** (*De Morgan's Laws*) In this chapter, we discussed the logical operators **And**, **Or** and **Not**. De Morgan's Laws can sometimes make it more convenient for us to express a logical expression. These laws state that the expression **Not**(condition1 **And** condition2) is logically equivalent to the expression (**Not** condition1 **Or Not** condition2). Also, the expression **Not** (condition1 **Or** condition2) is logically equivalent to the expression (**Not** condition1 **And Not** condition2). Use De Morgan's Laws to write equivalent expressions for each of the following. (Note: In some cases there may be more than one correct answer.)

```
a) Not ( x < 5 ) And Not ( y >= 7 )
b) Not ( a = b ) Or Not ( g <> 5 )
c) Not ( ( x <= 8 ) And ( y > 4 ) )
d) Not ( ( i > 4 ) Or ( j <= 6 ) )
```

**5.16** Write a program that prints the following patterns separately on the form each time a button is pressed. Provide four buttons **A**, **B**, **C** and **D**. When button **A** is pressed, the triangle shown in part (A) is printed, etc. Use **For/Next** loops to generate the patterns. Each triangle's asterisks (**\***) should be printed by a single statement of the form **Print "\*";** (this causes the asterisks to print side by side). Hint: The last two patterns require that each line begin with an appropriate number of blanks. Set the form's **Font** to **Courier Bold**.

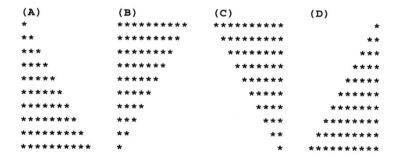

**5.17** Combine your code from the four separate problems of Exercise 5.16 into a single program that prints all four patterns side by side on the form by making clever use of nested **For/Next** loops.

**5.18** A criticism of the **Exit Do** statement and the **Exit For** statement is that each is unstructured. Actually, **Exit Do** statements and **Exit For** statements can always be replaced by structured statements, although doing so can be awkward. Describe in general how you would remove any **Exit Do** statement from a loop in a program and replace that statement with some structured equivalent. (Hint: The **Exit Do** statement leaves a loop from within the body of the loop. The other way to leave is by failing the loop-continuation test. Consider using in the loop-continuation test a second test that indicates "early exit because of an "exit" condition.") Use the technique you developed here to remove the **Exit Do** statement from the program of Fig. 5.13 and the **Exit For** statement from the program of Fig. 5.14.

**5.19**    Using the series

$$\sin(x) = x - x^3 / 3! + x^5 / 5! - x^7 / 7! + \ldots$$

calculate the sine $x$ to $n$ terms. The GUI should consist of two **TextBox**es, three **Label**s and a button. One **TextBox** should allow the user to input the value of $x$ in radians ($2\pi$ radians in a circle). The second **TextBox** should allow the user to input the number of terms $n$. The larger the term, the more accurate the value. Display the results in a **Label**. The other two **Label**s should be used as prompts. The calculation should be performed and displayed when the button is pressed.

**5.20**    (*Pythagorean Triples*) A right triangle can have sides that are all **Integer**s. The set of three **Integer** values for the sides of a right triangle is called a Pythagorean triple. These three sides must satisfy the relationship that the sum of the squares of two of the sides is equal to the square of the hypotenuse. Write a program to find all Pythagorean triples for **side1**, **side2** and the **hypotenuse**, all no larger than 500. Use a triple-nested **For/Next** loop that tries all possibilities. This is an example of "brute force" computing. You will learn in more advanced computer science courses that there are large numbers of interesting problems for which there is no known algorithmic approach other than using sheer brute force.

**5.21**    Write a program that prints the following diamond shape. You may use an output statement that prints a single asterisk (**\***). Maximize your use of repetition (with nested **For/Next** structures) and minimize the number of output statements. Print the diamond on the form. Set the form's **Font** to **Courier Bold**.

**5.22**    Modify the program you wrote in Exercise 5.21 to allow the user to input an odd number in the range 1 to 25. The odd number input specifies the number of rows in the diamond. Your program should provide a button which when clicked displays the diamond on the form.

# 6

# **Sub** Procedures And **Function** Procedures

## Objectives

- To understand how to construct programs modularly from procedures and functions.
- To be able to create new procedures and functions.
- To understand the mechanisms used to pass information between procedures and functions.
- To understand the **Exit Sub** and **Exit Function** statements.
- To understand how the visibility of indentifiers is limited to specific regions of programs.
- To introduce simulation using random numbers.
- To understand recursion.
- To understand and be able to use **Optional** arguments and named arguments.
- To be able to use Visual Basic math functions.
- To be able to create and use code modules.

*Form ever follows function.*
Louis Henri Sullivan

*O! call back yesterday, bid time return.*
William Shakespeare, *Richard II*

*Call me Ishmael.*
Herman Melville, *Moby-Dick*

*When you call me that, smile.*
Owen Wister

# Outline

## 6.1  Introduction

Most computer programs that solve real-world problems are much larger than those presented in the first few chapters. Experience has shown that the best way to develop and maintain a large program is to construct it from smaller pieces each of which is more manageable than the original program. This technique is called *divide and conquer*. This chapter describes many key features that facilitate the design, implementation, operation and maintenance of large programs.

## 6.2  Form Modules

A project is made up of *modules*—such as *form modules*. Form modules consist of smaller pieces called *procedures*. Four types of procedures exist: *event procedures*, *Visual Basic procedures*, **Sub** *procedures* and **Function** *procedures*. Event procedures respond to events (i.e., pressing a button, etc.). Visual Basic procedures (i.e., **Format$**, **IIf**, **Load-Picture**, etc.) are provided by Microsoft to perform common tasks. Because Visual Basic cannot provide every conceivable feature a programmer may want, Visual Basic allows programmers to create their own procedures (called **Sub** procedures and **Function** procedures) to meet the unique requirements of the problems they solve. Throughout this chapter we simply use the term *procedure* to refer to both **Sub** procedures and **Function** procedures unless otherwise indicated.

**Software Engineering Observation 6.1**

*Familiarize yourself with the rich collection of Visual Basic procedures. Avoid reinventing the wheel. When possible, use Visual Basic procedures instead of writing new procedures. This reduces program development time.*

**Performance Tip 6.1**

*Visual Basic procedures will normally execute faster than "equivalent" programmer-defined procedures that most programmers would write.*

Programmers can write procedures to define specific tasks that may be used at many points in a program. The actual statements defining the procedure are written only once.

**Software Engineering Observation 6.2**

*Each procedure should be limited to performing a single well-defined task, and should effectively express that task. This promotes software reusability.*

**Software Engineering Observation 6.3**

*A procedure should usually be no longer than one page. Better yet, a procedure should usually be no longer than half a page. Regardless of how long a procedure is, it should perform one task well. Small procedures promote software reusability.*

A procedure is *invoked* (i.e., made to perform its designated task) by a *procedure call*. The call specifies the procedure name and provides information (as arguments) that the *callee* needs to do its job.

A common analogy for this is the hierarchical form of management. A boss (the *caller*) asks a worker (the callee) to perform a task and *return* (i.e., report back) the results when the task is done. The boss does not know how the worker performs its designated tasks. The worker may call other workers—the boss will be unaware of this. We will soon see how this *hiding of implementation details* promotes good software engineering.

Figure 6.1 shows a procedure **Boss** communicating with several worker procedures in a hierarchical manner. Note that **Worker1** acts as a boss procedure to **Worker4** and **Worker5**, and that **Worker2** and **Worker3** act as bosses to **Worker6**. Relationships among procedures may be other than the hierarchical structure shown in this figure. Procedure **Boss** (as well as any worker procedure) can be an event procedure, **Sub** procedure or **Function** procedure.

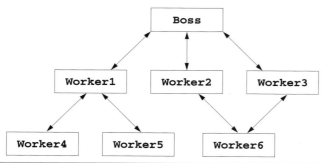

**Fig. 6.1**    Hierarchical boss procedure/worker procedure relationship.

There are several motivations for "dividing" code into procedures. The divide-and-conquer approach makes program development more manageable. Another motivation is *software reusability*—using existing procedures as building blocks for new programs. With proper naming and definition, programs can be created from standardized pieces that accomplish specific tasks, rather than being built with customized code. A third motivation is to avoid repeating code in a program. Packaging code as a procedure allows it to be executed from several locations in a program simply by calling or *invoking* the procedure.

**Common Programming Error 6.1**

*Writing executable code outside a procedure is a syntax error.*

**Testing and Debugging Tip 6.1**

*Small procedures are easier than large procedures to test and debug.*

## 6.3 Sub Procedures

**Sub** procedures are created with the ***Add Procedure*** dialog (displayed when ***Add Procedure*** is selected from the ***Tools*** menu). The **Add *Procedure*** menu item is grayed unless the **Code** window is visible. Figure 6.2 displays the **Add Procedure** dialog.

The procedure name is entered in **TextBox *Name*** and can be any valid identifier. **Frame *Type*** contains radio buttons for selecting the procedure type (***Sub*** or ***Function***); we discuss procedure types **Property** and **Event** later in the book.

**Software Engineering Observation 6.4**

*Since procedures operate on data, procedure names tend to be verbs. It is a Visual Basic convention to begin programmer-defined procedures with an uppercase first letter. For example, a procedure that sends an email message might be named **Send** or **SendEmail**.*

**Frame *Scope*** contains radio buttons for selecting keyword **Public** or keyword **Private** that will precede the procedure name. **Public** is selected by default. For now as a good practice, we will use keyword **Private**, which also preceded our event procedures. Later in the chapter we discuss both **Private** and **Public** in detail.

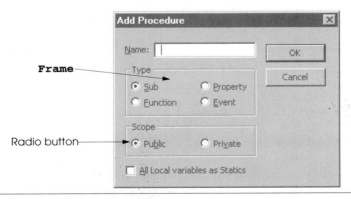

**Fig. 6.2    Add Procedure** dialog.

Checking **CheckBox All Local variables as Statics** adds keyword **Static** to the procedure created with **Add Procedure**. For now, we will not use this feature. In Section 6.7, we discuss keyword **Static**.

Once a valid name has been typed into **TextBox *Name*** and **Ok** has been pressed, the procedure appears in the **Code** window. Figure 6.3 shows procedure **MyProcedure**, which we created with the **Add Procedure** dialog. The code representing **MyProcedure** in Fig. 6.3 is called the *Sub procedure definition*.

**Sub** procedures can also be created by typing the **Sub** procedure directly into the **Code** window. Once a line such as

```
Private Sub AnotherProcedure()
```

is typed and the *Enter* key pressed, Visual Basic automatically creates the **End Sub** line. Figure 6.4 shows the results when **AnotherProcedure** is typed directly into the **Code** window.

The line

```
Private Sub AnotherProcedure()
```

is the *Sub procedure header*. The header contains keyword **Private**, keyword **Sub**, the procedure name, and parentheses. Any declarations and statements the programmer places between the header and **End Sub** form the *Sub procedure body*. Every time the **Sub** procedure is *called* (or *invoked*) the body is immediately executed. **AnotherProcedure** is invoked with the line

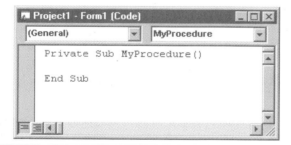

**Fig. 6.3**     A **Sub** procedure created with the **Add Procedure** dialog.

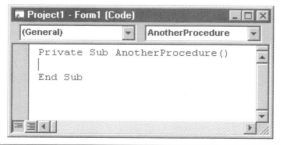

**Fig. 6.4**     A **Sub** procedure created by typing directly into the **Code** window.

```
AnotherProcedure
```

Execution of the **Sub** procedure terminates when **End Sub** is reached. Program execution then continues with the statement immediately following the call to **AnotherProcedure**.

*Software Engineering Observation 6.5*

*If you cannot choose a concise name that expresses what the procedure does, it is possible that your procedure is attempting to perform too many diverse tasks. It is often best to break such a procedure into several procedures.*

All **Sub** procedure definitions contain parentheses which may be empty (e.g., **AnotherProcedure**) or may contain a list of variable declarations (called a *parameter list*). Consider the following **Sub** procedure:

```
Private Sub PrintPay(hours As Single, wage As Currency)
    Print hours * wage
End Sub
```

which declares two *parameter variables*, **hours** and **wage**, in the parameter list. *Parameter variables* are declared using the **As** keyword or a type-declaration character (if one exists). Parameter variables are not explicitly given a type default to **Variant**. Parameter variables receive their values from the procedure call and are used in the procedure body.

*Software Engineering Observation 6.6*

*Choosing meaningful procedure names and meaningful parameter variable names makes programs more readable and helps avoid excessive use of comments.*

*Common Programming Error 6.2*

*Attempting to give a variable the same name as a procedure name is a syntax error.*

Procedure **PrintPay** is called with the line

```
PrintPay 40, 10.00
```

which provides (i.e., *passes* into **PrintPay**) values for parameter **hours** and parameter **wage**. The value **40** is stored in **hours** and the value **10.00** is stored in **wage**. These values are multiplied together to calculate the pay, which is then **Print**ed.

*Software Engineering Observation 6.7*

*A procedure requiring a large number of arguments may be performing too many tasks. Consider dividing the procedure into smaller procedures that perform the separate tasks.*

*Common Programming Error 6.3*

*Not passing the correct number of arguments to a procedure is a syntax error.*

*Software Engineering Observation 6.8*

*When it makes sense to do so, Visual Basic will implicitly convert arguments from one type to another in a procedure call. For example, a procedure that declares **Integer** variable u would receive 56 when passed 55.77; indeed, Visual Basic rounds rather than truncating when converting numbers with decimal points to **Integer**s.*

*Common Programming Error 6.4*

*Passing an argument that cannot be implicitly converted is a run-time error.*

The call to **PrintPay** could also have be written as

```
Call PrintPay(40, 10.00)
```

which uses keyword **Call** and encloses the *arguments* passed in a set of parentheses. The arguments passed can be variable names as well. For example, the call

```
Call PrintPay(x, y)          •
```

would pass **x** and **y** to **PrintPay**.

*Good Programming Practice 6.1*

*When calling a **Sub** procedure, use keyword **Call** and enclose argument(s) being passed in parentheses. This makes **Sub** procedure calls stand out and improves program readability.*

*Common Programming Error 6.5*

*Not enclosing the arguments being passed in parentheses when using keyword **Call** or enclosing the arguments passed in parentheses and not providing keyword **Call** are each syntax errors.*

Fig. 6.5 uses a programmer-defined **Sub** procedure **Minimum** to determine the smallest of three **Integer**s. The smallest value is displayed in a **Label**.

```
1   ' Fig. 6.5
2   ' Program finds the minimum of three numbers input
3   Option Explicit      ' General declaration
4
5   Private Sub cmdSmallest_Click()
6      Dim value1 As Long, value2 As Long, value3 As Long
7      value1 = txtOne.Text
8      value2 = txtTwo.Text
9      value3 = txtThree.Text
10
11     Call Minimum(value1, value2, value3)
12  End Sub
13
14  Private Sub Minimum(min As Long, y As Long, z As Long)
15
16     If y < min Then
17        min = y
18     End If
19
20     If z < min Then
21        min = z
22     End If
23
24     lblSmallest.Caption = "Smallest value is " & min
25  End Sub
```

**Fig. 6.5**    Program that determines the smallest of three numbers (part 1 of 2).

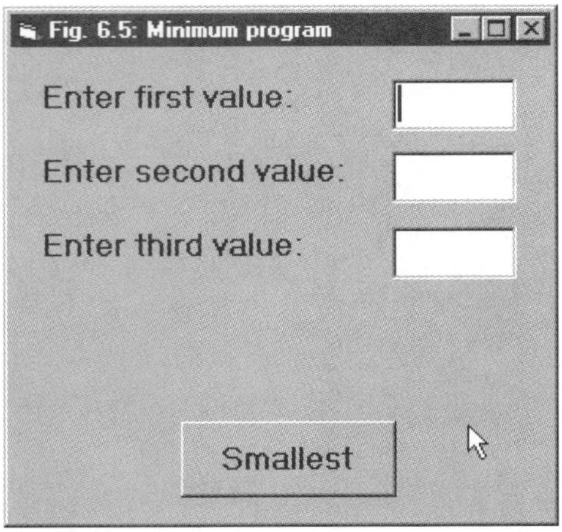

Initial GUI at execution.

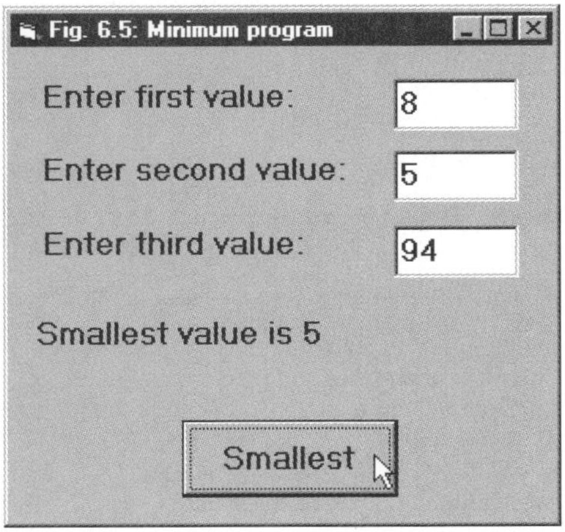

GUI after user has entered three numbers and pressed **Smallest**.

**Fig. 6.5**    Program that determines the smallest of three numbers (part 2 of 2).

The statement

```
Call Minimum(value1, value2, value3)
```

calls **Minimum** passing **value1**, **value2** and **value3** as arguments. Variables **min, y** and **z** are declared in **Minimum** to store the values of **value1**, **value2** and **value3**, respectively. Two **If/Then** statements ensure that **min** contains the smallest value. Variable **min**'s contents are displayed in a **Label**.

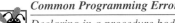

*Common Programming Error 6.6*

*Declaring in a procedure body a variable with the same name as a parameter variable is a syntax error.*

The Visual Basic IDE provides many features for creating programs rapidly. *Auto list members* is one such feature that automatically displays an object's properties and methods. When the period, **.**, is typed after an object name, a window appears as shown in Fig. 6.6

that lists the properties and methods for that object. *Auto list members* allows the programmer to quickly find a property or method. A property or method is selected by double-clicking with the mouse or by pressing the *Tab* key or the *Enter* key.

Another useful IDE feature is *auto quick info* for displaying procedure information (i.e., argument names and types) for both Visual Basic procedures and programmer-defined procedures. Figure 6.7 shows auto quick info for programmer-defined procedure **Minimum**. *Auto quick info* is displayed automatically when the opening parenthesis that follows a procedure name is typed.

Both *auto list members* and *auto quick info* can be disabled by unchecking **Auto List Members** and **Auto Quick Info** in the **Options** dialog (displayed when the **Tools** menu **Options...** command is selected).

*Testing and Debugging Tip 6.2*

*Using auto list members and auto quick info eliminates calls to non-existent procedures and methods by allowing the programmer to validate calls.*

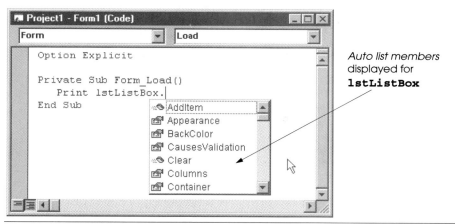

**Fig. 6.6**   *Auto list members* displayed for a **ListBox** object.

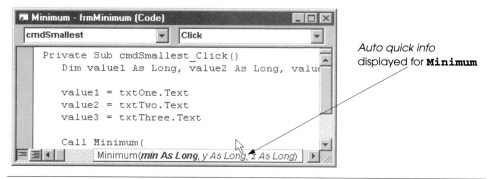

**Fig. 6.7**   *Auto quick info* for programmer-defined **Sub** procedure **Minimum**.

## 6.4 Function Procedures

**Function** procedures and **Sub** procedures share the same characteristics, with one important difference—**Function** procedures *return* a value (i.e., give a value back) to the caller, whereas **Sub** procedures do not. Most procedures provided by Visual Basic are **Function** procedures. For example, **Format$** returns a formatted **String**. Throughout this book, we simply refer to Visual Basic procedures as *Visual Basic functions*.

Programmer-defined **Function** procedures can be created with the **Add Procedure** dialog shown in Fig. 6.2 by selecting *Function*. Figure 6.8 shows a **Function** procedure, **IsVolunteer88**, created with the **Add Procedure** dialog. **IsVolunteer88** implicitly returns **Variant**. We will also discuss how to specify a return type explicitly. **IsVolunteer88** could also have been created by typing the **Function** procedure directly into the **Code** window.

The line

```
Private Function IsVolunteer88()
```

is the **Function** *procedure header*. The header contains the keyword **Function**, the function name and parentheses. The declarations and statements that the programmer will insert between the header and **End Function** form the **Function** *procedure body*. **IsVolunteer88** is invoked with the line

```
returnValue = IsVolunteer88()
```

When a **Function** *procedure* name (such as **IsVolunteer88**) is encountered at runtime, the **Function** *procedure* is called, causing its body statements to execute. Consider the complete definition for **IsVolunteer88**:

```
Private Function IsVolunteer88()
    ' mIdNumber is module variable
    IsVolunteer88 = IIf(mIdNumber, True, False)
End Function
```

**IsVolunteer88** returns either **True** or **False** to the caller. A **Function** *procedure*'s return value is specified in the body by assigning a value to the **Function** *procedure* name, as in

```
IsVolunteer88 = IIf(mIdNumber, True, False)
```

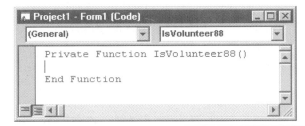

**Fig. 6.8**   **Function** procedure created with the **Add Procedure** dialog.

which returns either **True** or **False**. Control then returns (along with the value returned) to the calling statement

```
returnValue = IsVolunteer88()
```

and the return value, **True** or **False**, is assigned to variable **returnValue**. Program execution then continues with the next statement after the call to **IsVolunteer88**.

All **Function** procedure definitions contain parentheses. The parentheses may be empty (e.g., **IsVolunteer88**) or may contain one or parameter variable declarations. Consider the following **Function** procedure:

```
Private Function Area(s1 As Single, s2 As Single)
    Area = s1 * s2    ' return the area
End Sub
```

which declares two parameter variables **s1** and **s2**. **Area**'s return type is **Variant**.

**Area** is called with the statement

```
squareFtNeeded = Area(8.5, 7.34)
```

which passes **8.5** and **7.34** to **Area**. The value **8.5** is stored in **s1** and the value **7.34** is stored in **s2**. These values are multiplied together to calculate the area, which is returned and assigned to **squareFtNeeded**. When one or more arguments are passed to a **Function** procedure, parentheses are required. A **Function** procedure that does not take any arguments need not have parentheses in the call.

*Common Programming Error 6.7*

*Calling a **Function** procedure without enclosing its argument(s) in parentheses is a syntax error.*

Return types can be explicitly stated in the **Function** procedure header using either the **As** keyword or a type declaration character (if one exists). For example, we could rewrite the definition of **Area** to explicitly return a **Single** as follows:

```
Private Function Area!(s1 as Single, s2 As Single)
```

or

```
Private Function Area(s1 as Single, s2 As Single) As Single
```

*Common Programming Error 6.8*

*Placing a type-declaration character for the return type after the parentheses of the parameter list is a syntax error.*

*Common Programming Error 6.9*

*Placing the **As** return type between the function name and the parentheses of the parameter list is a syntax error.*

We could also rewrite the definition of **IsVolunteer88** as

```
Private Function IsVolunteer88() As Boolean
```

In this situation we cannot use a type declaration character because **Boolean** does not have one.

Throughout the book, we display various images for dice, the mouse, etc. We created these images using graphics programs like Microsoft **Paint**, Adobe **Photoshop**, etc. Microsoft **Paint** ships with Windows. Adobe **Photoshop** and many other graphical software packages must be purchased. The images we created are available for downloading at **www.prenhall.com/deitel**. Figure 6.9 uses several of our dice images.

Consider a program that uses programmer-defined **Function** procedure **GetImage** to return the proper image to draw on a button. Figure 6.9 shows the program GUI, Fig. 6.10 lists the properties and Fig.6.11 lists the program code.

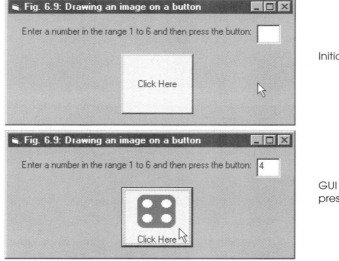

Initial GUI at execution.

GUI after user enters **4** and presses **Click Here**.

**Fig. 6.9**   Drawing an image on a button.

| Object | Icon | Property | Property setting | Property description |
|--------|------|----------|------------------|----------------------|
| form |  | **Name** | **frmButtonDraw** | Identifies the form. |
|  |  | **Caption** | **Fig. 6.9: Drawing an image on a button** | Form title bar display. |
| **Click Here** button |  | **Name** | **cmdButton** | Identifies **Click Here** button. |
|  |  | **BackColor** | light yellow | Button's background color. |
|  |  | **Caption** | **Click Here** | Text on the button. |
|  |  | **Style** | **1 - Graphical** | Style of button. |

**Fig. 6.10**   Properties listing (part 1 of 2).

| Object | Icon | Property | Property setting | Property description |
|---|---|---|---|---|
| Label |  A | Name | lblPrompt | Identifies **Label**. |
| | | Caption | Enter a number in the range 1 to 6 and then press the button: | Text that appears in the **Label**. |
| TextBox |  abl | Name | txtInput | Identifies **TextBox**. |
| | | Text | (empty) | Text that appears in **TextBox**. |

**Fig. 6.10**　Properties listing (part 2 of 2).

**CommandButton** property *Style* specifies whether or not graphics can be drawn on a **CommandButton**. Graphics cannot be drawn with the default *Standard* setting, but can be drawn with the *Graphical* setting. Visual Basic constants **vbButton-Standard** and **vbButtonGraphical** can also be used to explicitly set property **Style** within the code.

```
1   ' Fig. 6.9 code listing
2   ' Using a programmer-defined function
3   Option Explicit           ' General declaration
4
5   Private Sub cmdButton_Click()
6      Dim value As Integer, name As String
7
8      value = txtInput.Text
9
10     If value >= 1 And value <= 6 Then
11        name = GetImage(value)    ' Invoke function getImage
12        cmdButton.Picture = LoadPicture(name)
13     Else
14        txtInput.Text = ""        ' Clear txtInput
15     End If
16
17  End Sub
18
19  ' GetImage is a programmer defined function
20  Private Function GetImage(n As Integer) As String
21     GetImage = "d:\images\common\die" & n & ".gif"
22  End Function
```

**Fig. 6.11**　Code listing.

**GetImage** is invoked by **cmdButton_Click** with the call

```
name = GetImage(value)
```

**GetImage** receives **value** as variable **n** and returns a **String** describing the name and location of the image which is then assigned to **name**. Note: You may need to alter the path specified in **GetImage** to match the directory structure or your machine. The statement

```
cmdButton.Picture = LoadPicture(name)
```

draws the image onto **cmdButton**. The *Picture* property specifies which image **cmdButton** displays. The **Style** property is set to **Graphical** to display the image. Visual Basic function *LoadPicture* loads the specified image into memory. The value returned from **LoadPicture** is assigned to **cmdButton**'s **Picture** property, resulting in the image being drawn on **cmdButton**.

*Software Engineering Observation 6.9*

*Procedures can call event procedures.*

## 6.5  Call-by-Value vs. Call-by-Reference

Two ways to invoke procedure calls in most programming languages are *call-by-value* and *call-by-reference*. Each of the arguments that have been passed in the programs in this chapter so far have been passed call-by-reference—the default for all arguments passed. With call-by-reference, the caller gives the called procedure the ability to directly access the caller's data, and to modify that data if the called procedure so chooses. When an argument is passed call-by-value, a copy of the argument's value is passed. The called procedure can manipulate that copy but cannot manipulate the caller's data.

*Performance Tip 6.2*

*Call-by-reference is good for performance because it can eliminate the overhead of copying large amounts of data.*

*Software Engineering Observation 6.10*

*Call-by-reference can weaken security because the called procedure can modify the caller's data at will, possibly changing that data.*

*Software Engineering Observation 6.11*

*When an argument is passed call-by-value, a copy of that argument's value is made and passed. Changes to the copy do not affect the original variable's value in the caller. This prevents accidental side effects that so greatly hinder the development of correct and reliable software systems.*

*Performance Tip 6.3*

*Call-by-value is potentially bad for performance if the data being passed is large, because making a copy of that data takes time and consumes memory.*

An argument can be passed call-by-value either by using keyword *ByVal* or by enclosing that argument in parentheses, **()**. To pass an argument call-by-value, precede the corresponding parameter variable in the procedure definition with keyword **ByVal**. Otherwise, call-by-reference is implied. The following header declares two variables:

> ### Function Foo(ByVal x As Long, y As Boolean) As Double

**Foo** receives **x** by value and **y** by reference. Visual Basic also provides keyword **ByRef**, so **Foo** could be rewritten as

> ### Function Foo(ByVal x As Long, ByRef y As Boolean) As Double

which also indicates that **x** is received call-by-value and **y** is received by call-by-reference. **ByRef** is the default, so programmers rarely use it. The call

> ### doubleValue = Foo(passACopy, passOriginal)

does not use keyword **ByVal** or **ByRef**. Arguments passed **ByVal** can be enclosed in an optional set of parentheses, as in

> ### doubleValue = Foo((passACopy), passOriginal)

which passes **passACopy** by value and **passOriginal** by reference.

*Good Programming Practice 6.2*

*When passing arguments call-by-value, use the optional parentheses around the arguments being passed and the **ByVal** keyword in the procedure header. This makes it absolutely clear that arguments are being passed call-by-value.*

*Common Programming Error 6.10*

*Assuming the **ByVal** keyword applies to more than one parameter is a logic error. For example, **ByVal** in the header of **Function Foo(ByVal x As Long, y As Boolean)** applies to **x** and not to **y**.*

*Common Programming Error 6.11*

*Using the **ByVal** or **ByRef** keywords outside a procedure header is a syntax error.*

The program of Fig. 6.12 demonstrates call-by-value and call-by-reference. The program contains three procedures that receive arguments call-by-value and two procedures that receive an argument call-by-reference.

```
1   ' Fig. 6.12
2   ' Demonstrating passing arguments by value and by reference
3   Option Explicit           ' General declaration
4
5   Private Sub cmdPrint_Click()
6      Dim a As Integer
7
8      Call Cls
9      a = 1       ' Initialize a
10
11     ' Call CallByValue1
12     Print "Value of a before CallByValue1 is " & a
13     Call CallByValue1(a)   ' ByVal in parameter list
14     Print "Value of a after CallByValue1 is " & a
15     Print
```

**Fig. 6.12**   Demonstrating call-by-value versus call-by-reference (part 1 of 3).

```
16
17        ' Call CallByValue2
18        Print "Value of a before CallByValue2 is " & a
19        Call CallByValue2((a)) ' Parentheses for call-by-value
20        Print "Value of a after CallByValue2 is " & a
21        Print
22
23        ' Call CallByValue3
24        Print "Value of a before CallByValue3 is " & a
25        Call CallByValue3((a)) ' Parentheses for call-by-value
26        Print "Value of a after CallByValue3 is " & a
27        Print
28
29        ' Call CallByReference
30        Print "Value of a before CallByReference is " & a
31        Call CallByReference(a) ' Default call-by-reference
32        Print "Value of a after CallByReference is " & a
33        Print
34
35        ' Call CallByReference2
36        Print "Value of a before CallByReference2 is " & a
37        Call CallByReference2(a) ' Default call-by-reference
38        Print "Value of a after CallByReference2 is " & a
39     End Sub
40
41     Private Sub CallByValue1(ByVal x As Integer)
42        Print "Initial value of x in CallByValue1 is " & x
43        x = x * 3    ' Modifying x does not modify caller's a
44        Print "Last value of x in CallByValue1 is " & x
45     End Sub
46
47     Private Sub CallByValue2(y As Integer)
48        Print "Initial value of y in CallByValue2 is " & y
49        y = y * 4    ' Modifying y does not modify caller's a
50        Print "Last value of y in CallByValue2 is " & y
51     End Sub
52
53     ' Parentheses around argument in call and ByVal in header
54     Private Sub CallByValue3(ByVal z As Integer)
55        Print "Initial value of z in CallByValue3 is " & z
56        z = z * 5    ' Modifying z does not modify caller's a
57        Print "Last value of z in CallByValue3 is " & z
58     End Sub
59
60     ' Implicit call-by-reference
61     Private Sub CallByReference(r As Integer)
62        Print "Initial value of r in CallByReference is " & r
63        r = r * 9    ' Modifying r does modify caller's a
64        Print "Last value of r in CallByReference is " & r
65     End Sub
66
```

**Fig. 6.12**   Demonstrating call-by-value versus call-by-reference (part 2 of 3).

```
67   ' Explicit call-by-reference using ByRef in the header
68   Private Sub CallByReference2(ByRef r2 As Integer)
69      Print "Initial value of r2 in CallByReference2 is " & r2
70      r2 = r2 * 2  ' Modifying r does modify caller's a
71      Print "Last value of r2 in CallByReference2 is " & r2
72   End Sub
```

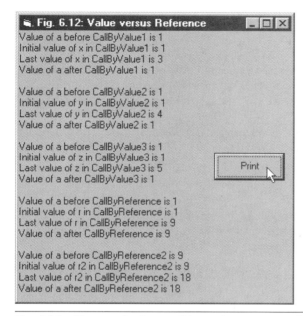

Fig. 6.12   Demonstrating call-by-value versus call-by-reference (part 3 of 3).

Variable **a** is declared and initialized to **1** in **cmdPrint_Click**. Variable **a**'s value is output, and a copy of **a**'s value is passed call-by-value to **CallByValue1**. Argument **a** is passed call-by-value because keyword **ByVal** is specified in the procedure definition header. The value **1** (a copy of **a**'s value) is stored in **x** and **x** is multiplied by **3**. When **End Sub** is reached, control is returned to **cmdPrint_Click**, where the value of **a** is printed and still has value **1** despite the calculations performed in **CallByValue1** (which were done on a copy of **a**).

Next **a** is passed call-by-value to **CallByValue2**. Parentheses around **a** in the call to **CallByValue2** specify call-by-value. Procedure **CallByValue2** stores the copy of **a**, **1**, in variable **y**. Variable **y** is multiplied by **4**. When **End Sub** is reached, control is returned to **cmdPrint_Click**, where **a**'s value, **1**, is printed.

Next **a** is passed call-by-value to **CallByValue3**. Parentheses around **a** in the call to **CallByValue3** specify call-by-value. Keyword **ByVal** is also used in the procedure definition header. Procedure **CallByValue3** stores the copy of **a**, **1**, in variable **z**. Variable **z** is multiplied by **5**. **End Sub** is then reached and control is returned to **cmdPrint_Click**, where **a**'s value, **1**, is printed.

The call to **CallByReference** passes **a** call-by-reference. The call does not enclose **a** in parentheses and the procedure definition does not use keyword **ByVal**. Variable **r** in the called procedure becomes a synonym, alias or "nickname" for **a**. Changing the value of

**r** actually changes the value of **a**. So multiplying **r** by **9** really multiplies **a** by **9**. **End Sub** is reached and control is returned to **cmdPrint_Click**, where **a**'s value, **9**, is printed.

The call to **CallByReference2** passes **a** call-by-reference. The call does not enclose **a** in parentheses and the procedure definition uses keyword **ByRef**. Variable **r2** in **CallByReference2** changes the value of **a** by multiplying **a** by **2**. **End Sub** is reached and control is returned to **cmdPrint_Click**, where **a**'s value, **18**, is printed.

## 6.6  **Exit Sub** and **Exit Function**

Statements **Exit Sub** and **Exit Function** alter the flow of control. Executing **Exit Sub** in a **Sub** procedure causes an immediate exit from that procedure. Control is returned to the caller and the next statement in sequence after the call is executed. Figure 6.13 demonstrates **Exit Sub**.

When the **If/Then/Else** statement determines that **number** is less than **0**, **Exit Sub** is executed and control is transferred to line

        **Next x**

where execution resumes.

Statement **Exit Function** causes immediate exit from a **Function** procedure. Control is returned to the caller and the next statement in sequence after the call is executed. Figure 6.14 demonstrates **Exit Function**.

```
1   ' Fig. 6.13
2   ' Demonstrating Exit Sub
3   Option Explicit      ' General declaration
4
5   Private Sub cmdBegin_Click()
6      Dim x As Integer
7
8      For x = 5 To -1 Step -1
9         Call PrintNumbers(x)
10     Next x
11
12     cmdBegin.Enabled = False    ' Disable button
13  End Sub
14
15  Private Sub PrintNumbers(number As Integer)
16
17     If number >= 0 Then
18        Print number
19     Else
20        Print "Exiting Sub with number = " & number
21        Exit Sub    ' Exit procedure
22     End If
23
24  End Sub
```

**Fig. 6.13**  Demonstrating **Exit Sub** (part 1 of 2).

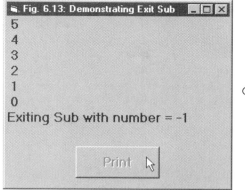

GUI after user has pressed **Print.**

**Fig. 6.13**   Demonstrating **Exit Sub** (part 2 of 2).

```
1    ' Fig. 6.14
2    ' Demonstrating Exit Function
3    Option Explicit        ' General declaration
4
5    Private Sub cmdDivide_Click()
6       Dim numerator As Integer, denominator As Integer
7       Dim result As String
8
9       numerator = txtNum.Text
10      denominator = txtDen.Text
11      result = Divide(numerator, denominator)
12
13      ' Value of result is "" if Exit Function executed
14      If result = "" Then
15         lblThree.Caption = "Divide by zero attempted!"
16      Else
17         lblThree.Caption = result    ' Display the String returned
18      End If
19
20   End Sub
21
22   Private Function Divide(n As Integer, d As Integer) As String
23
24      If d = 0 Then
25         Exit Function    ' Exit the function returns ""
26         Print "After Exit Function Line"    ' Never executed
27      Else
28         Divide = "Division yields " & n / d
29      End If
30
31   End Function
```

**Fig. 6.14**   Demonstrating **Exit Function** (part 1 of 2).

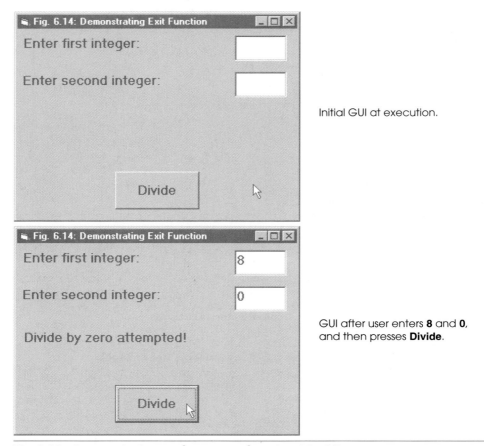

Initial GUI at execution.

GUI after user enters **8** and **0**, and then presses **Divide**.

**Fig. 6.14**   Demonstrating **Exit Function** (part 2 of 2).

When the **If/Then/Else** structure in **Divide** detects that **d** is **0**, **Exit Function** is executed, resulting in an *empty string*, **" "**, value being returned. An empty string simply means the **String** does not have a value. Executing **Exit Function** in a **Function** procedure that has a **String** return type returns an empty string. Executing **Exit Function** in a **Function** procedure that has a numeric return type (i.e., **Integer**, **Single**, etc.) returns **0**. The line

```
Print "After Exit Function Line"
```

is never executed, because **Exit Function** causes an immediate return to the caller.

*Software Engineering Observation 6.12*

*Some programmers feel that **Exit Sub** and **Exit Function** violate the spirit of structured programming. Because the effects of these statements can be achieved by structured programming techniques, these programmers do not use **Exit Sub** and **Exit Function**.*

*Performance Tip 6.4*

The **Exit Sub** and **Exit Function** *statements, when used properly, perform faster than the corresponding structured techniques we will soon learn.*

*Testing and Debugging Tip 6.3*

The **Exit Sub** and **Exit Function** *statements are often used to exit procedures and functions to avoid potential run-time errors such as division by zero.*

## 6.7 Storage Classes

In Chapters 3 through 5, we have used identifiers for variable names. The attributes of variables include *name*, *type*, *size* and *value*. In this chapter, we also use identifiers as names for programmer-defined procedures. Actually, each identifier in a program has other attributes, including *storage class* and *scope*.

An identifier's storage class determines the period during which that identifier exists in memory. Some identifiers exist briefly, some are repeatedly created and destroyed, and others exist for the entire program execution. A variable's storage class is sometimes referred to as its *lifetime*.

An identifier's *scope* is the region in a program in which the identifier can be referenced. Some identifiers can be referenced throughout a program, while others can be referenced from only limited portions of a program. This section discusses storage class. Section 6.8 discusses scope.

Visual Basic provides two storage class specifiers: automatic and **Static**. An identifier's storage class specifier helps determine its storage class and scope.

Non-**Static** local variables (also called *automatic variables*) have automatic storage class by default and are created when the procedure becomes active. Automatic variables exist until the procedure is exited. Memory allocated for automatic variables is reclaimed by the system (i.e., variable contents are not preserved).

Keyword **Static** is used to declare identifiers for variables and procedures of the **Static** storage class. For **Static** variables, storage is allocated and initialized once when the form is created. For **Static** procedures, all variables in the procedure are **Static** variables—regardless of whether or not the variables are explicitly declared **Static**. For example, the procedure

```
Private Static Sub AllVariablesAreStatic()
    Dim q, a, s;     ' declaration
    ...              ' Other statements in body
End Sub
```

implicitly declares variables **q**, **a** and **s** as having **Static** storage class. To make a procedure **Static**, either place **Static** between the **Private** and **Sub** keywords or check the **Add Procedure** dialog's (Fig. 6.2) **All Local variables as Statics CheckBox**. Applying **Static** to a procedure that has variables explicitly declared **Static** in its body is not an error; keyword **Static** in the body is simply redundant.

*Software Engineering Observation 6.13*

*Even though **Static** variables exist at form creation, this does not mean that these variables can be used throughout the program. Storage class and scope (where a name can be used) are separate issues.*

There are two types of identifiers with **Static** storage class: *external identifiers* (such as module variables and procedure names) and local variables declared with the storage class specifier **Static**.

Local variables declared with keyword **Static** are still known only in the procedure in which they are defined, but unlike automatic variables, **Static** variables retain their value when the procedure is exited. The next time the procedure is called, the **Static** local variable contains the value it had when the procedure last exited.

All numeric variables of the **Static** storage class are initialized to zero. The following statement declares local variable **count** to be **Static** (and implicitly initializes **count** to **0**):

> **Static count As Integer**

When declaring a **Static** local variable, **Static** can be used in place of **Dim** or in combination with **Dim**. The declaration

> **Static Dim count As Integer**

also declares **count** as a **Static** variable. In this declaration, **Dim** is redundant.

*Performance Tip 6.5*
*Using **Static** only for variables that must retain their value between calls conserves memory.*

*Common Programming Error 6.12*
*Forgetting to reinitialize a **Static** variable that needs to be reinitialized can lead to logic errors.*

*Common Programming Error 6.13*
*Attempting to declare a **Static** variable outside a procedure is a syntax error.*

## 6.8 Scope Rules

The *scope* of an identifier is the region of a project in which that identifier can be referenced. For example, when we declare a local variable in a procedure, it can be referenced only in that procedure. The three scopes for an identifier are *local scope*, *module scope* and ***Public*** *scope*.

Local scope applies to variables declared in a procedure's body. Local variables can be referenced from the point at which they are declared through **End Sub** (or **End Function**). Module scope applies to variables declared in the general declaration with **Dim**. By default, module variables can only be referenced in the module in which they are declared. Module scope is sometimes called ***Private*** *scope*. **Public** scope refers to module variables that are declared **Public**. Module variables that are **Public** are accessible to all modules. We discuss **Public** variables in detail in Section 6.17 and in Chapter 16.

When an identifier in an outer scope (such as module scope) has the same name as an identifier in an inner scope (such as local scope), the identifier in the outer scope is "hidden" until the inner scope terminates. This means that while executing in the inner scope, the inner scope sees the value of its own identifier and not the value of the identically named identifier in the outer scope.

*Testing and Debugging Tip 6.4*

*Avoid variable names that hide names in outer scopes. This can be accomplished simply by avoiding the use of duplicate variable names in a program. This can help eliminate subtle bugs in which the programmer may think that code in a procedure references a variable in an outer scope when that code is really referencing code in the inner scope.*

Local variables declared **Static** still have local scope even though they exist from the time the form is loaded into memory. Thus, storage duration does not affect the scope of an identifier.

The program of Fig. 6.15 demonstrates scoping issues with module variables, local variables and **Static** local variables.

```
1    ' Fig. 6.15
2    ' Scoping example
3    Option Explicit      ' General declaration
4    Dim x As Integer     ' Module variable in general declaration
5
6    Private Sub cmdGo_Click()
7       Dim x As Integer       ' Local variable
8
9       x = 6
10      Print "Local x is " & x & " on entering cmdGo_Click()"
11      Print
12
13      ' Call procedures
14      Call One
15      Call Two
16      Call Three
17
18      ' Call procedures again
19      Call One
20      Call Two
21      Call Three
22      Print "Local x is " & x & " on exiting cmdGo_Click()"
23      cmdGo.Enabled = False
24   End Sub
25
26   Private Sub One()
27      Dim x As Integer
28
29      x = 26
30      Print "Local x is " & x & " on entering One"
31      x = x + 1
32      Print "Local x is " & x & " on exiting One"
33      Print
34   End Sub
35
36   Private Sub Two()
37      Static x As Integer
38
```

**Fig. 6.15**   Scoping example (part 1 of 2).

```
39          Print "Local static x is " & x & " on entering Two"
40
41          ' Initialize local static x to 60
42          ' the first time into the procedure
43          If x = 0 Then
44             x = 60
45          End If
46
47          x = x + 1
48          Print "Local static x is " & x & " on exiting Two"
49          Print
50       End Sub
51
52       Private Sub Three()
53          Print "Module x is " & x & " on entering Three"
54          x = x + 5
55          Print "Module x is " & x & " on exiting Three"
56          Print
57       End Sub
```

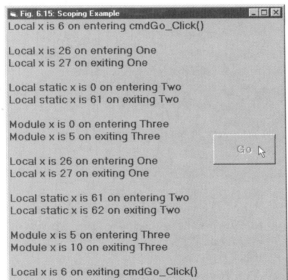

GUI after user has pressed **Go**.

**Fig. 6.15**   Scoping example (part 2 of 2).

Module variable **x** is declared and initialized to **0** in the general declaration. Module variable **x** is hidden in any procedure in which a local variable named **x** is declared.

In **cmdGo_Click**, a local variable **x** is declared and initialized to **6**. Local variable **x** is then printed with the statement

```
Print "Local x is " & x & " on entering cmdGo_Click"
```

Local variable **x** hides module variable **x**.

The program defines three procedures that do not take arguments. **One** declares local automatic variable **x** and initializes it to **26**. When **One** is called, **x** is printed, incremented and printed again before exiting the procedure. Each time this procedure is called, variable **x** is recreated and initialized to **26**. Local variable **x** has automatic storage class and hides module variable **x**.

**Two** declares local **Static** variable **x** and initializes it to **60** the first time **Two** is entered. Local variables declared as **Static** retain their values even when they are out of scope (i.e., when the procedure is not being executed). When **Two** is called, **x** is printed, incremented and printed again before exiting the procedure. Upon exiting the procedure **x** has a value of **61**. When **Two** is called again, **x**'s value is initially **61**.

**Three** does not declare any local variables. When **x** is used, the module variable **x** is printed, incremented by **5** and printed again before exiting the procedure. The next time procedure **Three** is called, the module variable **x** is initially **5**.

## 6.9 Random Number Generation

We now take a brief and hopefully entertaining diversion into a popular programming application, namely simulation and game playing. In this section and the next, we will develop a game-playing program that includes several of the control structures we have studied.

There is something in the air of a gambling casino that invigorates every type of person, from the high-rollers at the plush mahogany-and-felt craps tables to the quarter-poppers at the one-armed bandits. It is the element of chance, the possibility that luck will convert a pocketful of money into a mountain of wealth. The element of chance can be introduced into computer applications by using Visual Basic function *Rnd*, which returns a **Single** random number that is always in the range

```
0 ≤ Rnd < 1
```

If **Rnd** truly produces random numbers, every number between 0 and 1 (but not including 1) has an equal chance (or probability) of being chosen each time **Rnd** is called. Multiple calls to **Rnd** should not generate any predictable pattern of numbers.

The range of values produced by **Rnd** is often different from that needed in a specific application. For example, a program that simulates coin tossing might require only 0 for "heads" and 1 for "tails." A program that simulates rolling a six-sided die would require random **Integer**s in the range 1 to 6. A program that randomly predicts the next type of spaceship (out of 10 possibilities) that will fly across the horizon in a video game might require random **Integer**s in the range 1 through 10.

To demonstrate **Rnd**, let us develop code to simulate one roll of a six-sided die. We use the multiplication operator, **\***, and Visual Basic functions *Int* and **Rnd** as follows:

```
dieFace = Int(6 * Rnd())
```

to produce **Integer**s in the range 0 to 5. This is called *scaling*. The number 6 is called the *scaling factor*.

We then *shift* the range of numbers produced by adding **1**, the *shift adjustment*, to our previous result, as demonstrated in the statement

```
dieFace = 1 + Int(6 * Rnd())
```

Function **Int** returns the **Integer** part of the argument passed to it. So passing a value of **8.567** to **Int** returns 8. If we do not use function **Int**, as in

```
dieFace = 6 * Rnd()
```

**dieFace** gets a value in the range $0 \le$ **dieFace** $\le 6$. Numbers such as **5.923** are rounded to **6** during the implicit conversion from **Single** to **Integer**.

We now present a program that simulates rolling 12 six-sided dice each time **Roll** is pressed. We graphically draw each die image in an **Image** control. The **Picture** property of control **Image** displays the image. The program GUI is shown in Fig. 6.16 and the code is listed in Fig. 6.17.

Procedure **DisplayDie** is called 12 times when **cmdRoll_Click** is executed. Controls, like variables, can be passed to procedures. Each **Image** control (i.e., **imgDie1**, **imgDie2**, etc.) is passed to **DisplayDie**.

*Good Programming Practice 6.3*

*Prefix the name of **Image** controls with **img**. This allows **Image** controls to be identified easily.*

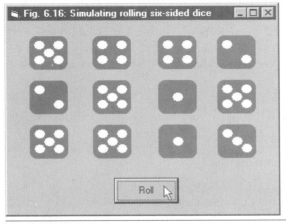

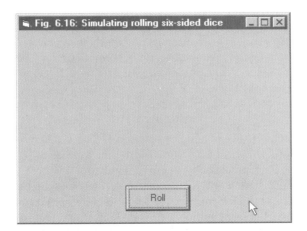

Initial GUI at execution.

GUI after user has pressed **Roll**.

**Fig. 6.16**   Simulating rolling 12 six-sided dice.

```
1    ' Fig. 6.16
2    ' Six-sided die simulation
3    Option Explicit      ' General declaration
4
5    Private Sub cmdRoll_Click()
6
7        ' Pass Image controls to Sub procedure DisplayDie
8        Call DisplayDie(imgDie1)
9        Call DisplayDie(imgDie2)
10       Call DisplayDie(imgDie3)
11       Call DisplayDie(imgDie4)
12       Call DisplayDie(imgDie5)
13       Call DisplayDie(imgDie6)
14       Call DisplayDie(imgDie7)
15       Call DisplayDie(imgDie8)
16       Call DisplayDie(imgDie9)
17       Call DisplayDie(imgDie10)
18       Call DisplayDie(imgDie11)
19       Call DisplayDie(imgDie12)
20   End Sub
21
22   Private Sub DisplayDie(imgDie As Image)
23       Dim face As Integer
24
25       face = 1 + Int(6 * Rnd())
26       imgDie.Picture = LoadPicture("d:\images\common\die" _
27                                    & face & ".gif")
28   End Sub
```

**Fig. 6.17**  Code listing.

Sub procedure **DisplayDie** declares local **Image** variable **imgDie**, which is an "alias" to the passed **Image**. Local variable **face** is assigned a random number between 1 and 6. **LoadPicture** loads the image into **imgDie**'s **Picture** property.

To show that these numbers occur approximately with equal likelihood, let us modify the program of Fig. 6.17 to keep some simple statistics. The frequency of each face value (**1** through **6**) should be approximately the same. The GUI shown in Fig. 6.18 displays the results after clicking **Roll** 10 times. The code is shown in Fig. 6.19.

As the program output shows, by scaling and shifting we have utilized function **Rnd** to realistically simulate the rolling of a six-sided die (i.e., over a large number of die rolls, each of the six possible faces from 1 through 6 appears with equal likelihood about one-sixth of the time). Note that no **Case Else** is provided in the **Select Case** structure. This, of course, assumes that our random number generation formula is working correctly. After we study arrays in Chapter 7, we will show how to replace the entire **Select Case** structure elegantly with a single-line statement.

Executing the program of Fig. 6.18 again produces the results shown in Fig. 6.20. Notice that exactly the same sequence of values was printed. How can these be random numbers? Ironically, this repeatability is an important characteristic of function **Rnd**. When debugging a program, this repeatability is essential for proving that corrections to a program work properly.

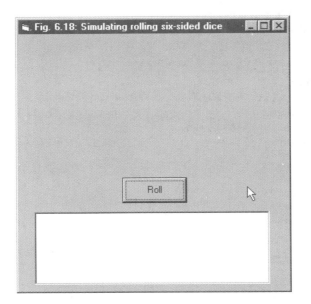

Initial GUI at execution.

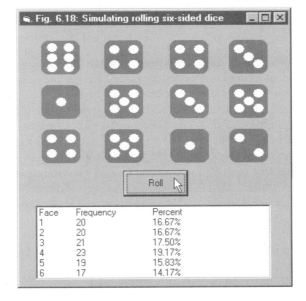

GUI after user has pressed **Roll** 10 times.

**Fig. 6.18**   Simulating rolling 12 six-sided dice.

```
1    ' Fig. 6.19
2    ' Six-sided die simulation
3    Option Explicit      ' General declaration
4
5    ' Declare module variables
6    Dim mFace1 As Integer, mFace2 As Integer    ' General declaration
7    Dim mFace3 As Integer, mFace4 As Integer
8    Dim mFace5 As Integer, mFace6 As Integer
9    Dim mTotalRolls As Integer
10
11   Private Sub cmdRoll_Click()
12       mTotalRolls = mTotalRolls + 12
13
14       Call DisplayDie(imgDie1)
15       Call DisplayDie(imgDie2)
16       Call DisplayDie(imgDie3)
17       Call DisplayDie(imgDie4)
18       Call DisplayDie(imgDie5)
19       Call DisplayDie(imgDie6)
20       Call DisplayDie(imgDie7)
21       Call DisplayDie(imgDie8)
22       Call DisplayDie(imgDie9)
23       Call DisplayDie(imgDie10)
24       Call DisplayDie(imgDie11)
25       Call DisplayDie(imgDie12)
26
27       Call lstStatistics.Clear
28       Call DisplayStats
29   End Sub
30
31   Private Sub DisplayDie(imgDie As Image)
32       Dim face As Integer
33
34       face = 1 + Int(6 * Rnd())
35
36       Select Case face
37          Case 1
38             mFace1 = mFace1 + 1
39          Case 2
40             mFace2 = mFace2 + 1
41          Case 3
42             mFace3 = mFace3 + 1
43          Case 4
44             mFace4 = mFace4 + 1
45          Case 5
46             mFace5 = mFace5 + 1
47          Case 6
48             mFace6 = mFace6 + 1
49       End Select
50
51       imgDie.Picture = LoadPicture("d:\images\common\die" _
52                                  & face & ".gif")
53   End Sub
```

**Fig. 6.19**   Simulating rolling 12 six-sided dice (part 1 of 2).

```
54
55  Private Sub DisplayStats()
56      lstStatistics.AddItem "Face" & vbTab & "Frequency" & _
57                          vbTab & "Percent"
58      lstStatistics.AddItem 1 & vbTab & mFace1 & vbTab & vbTab & _
59                          Format$(mFace1 / mTotalRolls, "Percent")
60      lstStatistics.AddItem 2 & vbTab & mFace2 & vbTab & vbTab & _
61                          Format$(mFace2 / mTotalRolls, "Percent")
62      lstStatistics.AddItem 3 & vbTab & mFace3 & vbTab & vbTab & _
63                          Format$(mFace3 / mTotalRolls, "Percent")
64      lstStatistics.AddItem 4 & vbTab & mFace4 & vbTab & vbTab & _
65                          Format$(mFace4 / mTotalRolls, "Percent")
66      lstStatistics.AddItem 5 & vbTab & mFace5 & vbTab & vbTab & _
67                          Format$(mFace5 / mTotalRolls, "Percent")
68      lstStatistics.AddItem 6 & vbTab & mFace6 & vbTab & vbTab & _
69                          Format$(mFace6 / mTotalRolls, "Percent")
70  End Sub
```

**Fig. 6.19**  Simulating rolling 12 six-sided dice (part 2 of 2).

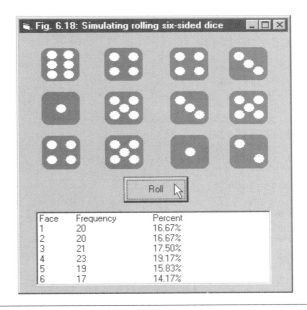

**Fig. 6.20**  Results of running the dice-rolling program of Fig. 6.18 again.

Function **Rnd** actually generates *pseudo-random numbers*. Calling **Rnd** repeatedly produces a sequence of numbers that appears to be random. However, the sequence repeats itself each time the program is executed. Once a program has been thoroughly debugged, it can be conditioned to produce a different sequence of random numbers for each execution. This is called *randomizing*, and is accomplished with the **Randomize** statement. **Randomize** "seeds" function **Rnd** to produce a different sequence of random numbers each time **Randomize** is used. The *seed* is the initial number that the random number generator uses to produce a series of random numbers and receives its value from the system clock (which of course changes each time the program is run).

Figure 6.21 lists the code for **cmdRoll_Click**, which is identical to the code listed in Fig. 6.19 except that Fig. 6.21 includes the **Randomize** statement (line 5).

```
1    ' Fig. 6.21
2    ' All other code is identical to the code listed in Fig. 6.19
3
4    Private Sub cmdRoll_Click()
5        Call Randomize        ' Seed function Rnd
6        mTotalRolls = mTotalRolls + 12
7
8        Call DisplayDie(imgDie1)
9        Call DisplayDie(imgDie2)
10       Call DisplayDie(imgDie3)
11       Call DisplayDie(imgDie4)
12       Call DisplayDie(imgDie5)
13       Call DisplayDie(imgDie6)
14       Call DisplayDie(imgDie7)
15       Call DisplayDie(imgDie8)
16       Call DisplayDie(imgDie9)
17       Call DisplayDie(imgDie10)
18       Call DisplayDie(imgDie11)
19       Call DisplayDie(imgDie12)
20
21       Call lstStatistics.Clear
22       Call DisplayStats
23   End Sub
```

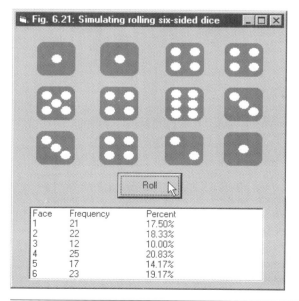

GUI after the user has pressed **Roll** 10 times.

**Fig. 6.21**   Randomizing the die program.

Let us run the program several times and observe the results. Notice that a different sequence of random numbers is produced when **Roll** is pressed 10 times. The statement

```
Call Randomize
```

obtains the value for the seed automatically from Visual Basic function **Timer**. The seed used by the random number generator is the current time (expressed as the number of seconds elapsed since midnight).

Previously we demonstrated how to write a single statement to simulate the rolling of a six-sided die with the statement

```
dieFace = 1 + Int(6 * Rnd())
```

which always assigns an **Integer** (at random) to variable **dieFace** in the range

$$1 \leq \text{dieFace} \leq 6$$

Note that the *width* of this range (i.e., the number of consecutive **Integer**s in the range) is 6 and the starting number in the range is 1. Referring to the preceding statement, we see that the range width is determined by the number used to scale **Rnd** with the multiplication operator (i.e., **6**), and the starting number of the range is equal to the number (i.e., **1**) that is added to **6 * Rnd()**. We can generalize this result as follows:

```
n = a + Int(b * Rnd())
```

where **a** is the shift adjustment (which is equal to the first number in the desired range of consecutive **Integer**s), and **b** is the scaling factor (which is equal to the width of the desired range of consecutive **Integer**s).

*Testing and Debugging Tip 6.5*

*Do not call* **Randomize** *until you are satisfied that your program is working correctly.*

## 6.10  Example: A Game of Chance

One of the most popular games of chance is a dice game known as "craps," which is played in casinos and back alleys throughout the world. The rules of the game are straightforward:

> *A player rolls two dice. Each die has six faces. These faces contain 1, 2, 3, 4, 5 and 6 spots. After the dice have come to rest, the sum of the spots on the two upward faces is calculated. If the sum is 7 or 11 on the first throw, the player wins. If the sum is 2 ("snake eyes"), 3 ("trey") or 12 ("boxcars") on the first throw (called "craps"), the player loses (i.e., the "house" wins). If the sum is 4, 5, 6, 8, 9 or 10 on the first throw, then that sum becomes the player's "point." To win, you must continue rolling the dice until you "make your point." The player loses by rolling a 7 before making the point.*

The GUI is shown in Fig. 6.22, properties in Fig. 6.23 and the code is listed in Fig. 6.24. The program introduces the **Frame** control, which groups other controls placed inside the frame. Controls grouped inside a **Frame** cannot be separated from the **Frame**. The **Frame fraPoint** groups two **Image** controls that graphically display the sum needed for a point.

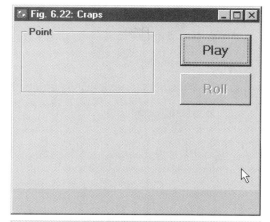

Initial GUI at execution.

GUI after user has pressed **Play**. A 6 is rolled and becomes the player's point. The **Play** button is grayed and the user is instructed to roll again.

GUI after user has pressed **Roll**. The user has rolled an 8, which is neither a win (i.e., a 6) nor a loss (i.e., 7), so the user is instructed to roll again.

**Fig. 6.22**   Craps program (part 1 of 2).

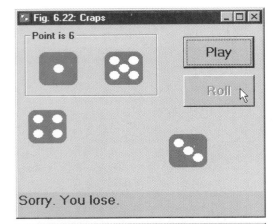

GUI after user presses **Roll**. A 7 is rolled and the player loses. The game is completed and the **Roll** button disabled.

GUI after user presses **Play**. The user wins because an 11 is rolled on the first roll.

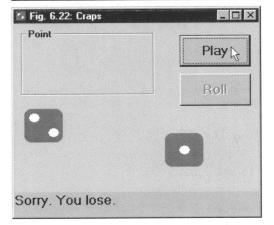

GUI after user presses **Play**. The user loses because a three is rolled on the first roll.

**Fig. 6.22**  Craps program (part 2 of 2).

*Good Programming Practice 6.4*

*Prefix the name of* **Frame** *controls with* **fra***. This allows* **Frame** *controls to be identified easily.*

| Object | Icon | Property | Property setting | Property description |
|--------|------|----------|------------------|----------------------|
| form | | **Name** | **frmCraps** | Identifies the form. |
| | | **BackColor** | light green | Background color. |
| | | **Caption** | **Fig 6.22: Craps** | Form title bar display. |
| **Play** button | | **Name** | **cmdPlay** | Identifies **Play** button. |
| **Roll** button | | **Name** | **cmdRoll** | Identifies **Roll** button. |
| **Exit** button | | **Name** | **cmdExit** | Identifies **Exit** button. |
| **Label** | A | **Name** | **lblStatus** | Identifies **Label**. |
| | | **Caption** | (empty) | Text that appears in the **Label**. |
| | | **Font** | **MS Sans Serif Bold 12** pt | Font for **Label** text. |
| **Frame** | | **Name** | **fraPoint** | Identifies **Label**. |
| | | **BackColor** | light green | Background color. |
| | | **Caption** | **Point** | Text that appears in the **Label**. |
| **Image** | | **Name** | **imgDie1** | Identifies **Image**. |
| **Image** | | **Name** | **imgDie2** | Identifies **Image**. |
| **Image** | | **Name** | **imgPointDie1** | Identifies **Image**. |
| **Image** | | **Name** | **imgPointDie2** | Identifies **Image**. |

**Fig. 6.23**    Properties listing for the craps program of Fig. 6.22.

```
1    ' Fig. 6.24
2    ' Craps program
3    Option Explicit      ' General declaration
4
5    ' Declare module variables
6    Dim mMyPoint As Integer      ' General declaration
7    Dim mDie1 As Integer         ' General declaration
8    Dim mDie2 As Integer         ' General declaration
9
10   Enum DiceNames
11       snakeEyes = 2    ' Explicitly assign 2
12       trey             ' Implicitly assign 3 (snakeEyes + 1)
13       [yo leven] = 11  ' Explicitly assign 11
14       boxCars          ' Implicitly assign 12 ([yo leven] + 1)
15   End Enum
16
17   Private Sub Form_Load()
18       Icon = LoadPicture("d:\images\ch06\die.ico")
19   End Sub
20
21   Private Sub cmdPlay_Click()
22       Dim sum As Integer
23
24       ' initialization
25       mMyPoint = 0
26       fraPoint.Caption = "Point"
27       lblStatus.Caption = ""
28       imgPointDie1.Picture = LoadPicture("")
29       imgPointDie2.Picture = LoadPicture("")
30       Call Randomize
31
32       sum = RollDice()        ' Invoke rollDice
33
34       ' Determine outcome of first roll
35       Select Case sum
36          Case 7, [yo leven]
37             cmdRoll.Enabled = False   ' Disable Roll button
38             lblStatus.Caption = "You Win!!!"
39          Case snakeEyes, trey, boxCars
40             cmdRoll.Enabled = False
41             lblStatus.Caption = "Sorry. You lose."
42          Case Else
43             mMyPoint = sum
44             fraPoint.Caption = "Point is " & sum
45             lblStatus.Caption = "Roll Again."
46             Call DisplayDie(imgPointDie1, mDie1)
47             Call DisplayDie(imgPointDie2, mDie2)
48             cmdPlay.Enabled = False   ' Disable Play button
49             cmdRoll.Enabled = True    ' Enable Roll button
50       End Select
51
52   End Sub
53
```

**Fig. 6.24**   Code listing (part 1 of 2).

```
54  Private Sub cmdRoll_Click()
55     Dim sum As Integer
56
57     sum = RollDice()              ' Invoke rollDice
58     ' Check for a win or loss
59     If sum = mMyPoint Then           ' Win
60        lblStatus.Caption = "You Win!!!"
61        cmdRoll.Enabled = False
62        cmdPlay.Enabled = True
63     ElseIf sum = 7 Then              ' Loss
64        lblStatus.Caption = "Sorry. You lose."
65        cmdRoll.Enabled = False
66        cmdPlay.Enabled = True
67     End If
68
69  End Sub
70
71  Private Sub DisplayDie(imgDie As Image, face As Integer)
72     imgDie.Picture = LoadPicture("d:\images\" & _
73                                  "common\die" & face & ".gif")
74
75  End Sub
76
77  Private Function RollDice() As Integer
78     Dim die1 As Integer, die2 As Integer, dieSum As Integer
79     Dim a As Integer, b As Integer
80
81     die1 = 1 + Int(6 * Rnd())        ' Roll die1
82     die2 = 1 + Int(6 * Rnd())        ' Roll die2
83
84     Call DisplayDie(imgDie1, die1) ' Draw die1 image
85     Call DisplayDie(imgDie2, die2) ' Draw die2 image
86
87     mDie1 = die1                     ' Store die1 value
88     mDie2 = die2                     ' Store die2 value
89     dieSum = die1 + die2             ' Sum dice
90     RollDice = dieSum                ' Return dieSum to caller
91  End Function
```

**Fig. 6.24**   Code listing (part 2 of 2).

The lines

```
Enum DiceNames
   snakeEyes = 2
   trey
   [yo leven] = 11
   boxCars
End Enum
```

create a *user-defined type* called an *enumeration*. An enumeration—introduced by keyword **Enum** and followed by a type name (in this case, **DiceNames**)—is a set of **Long** constants represented by identifiers. The values of *enumeration constants* (also called *named constants*) start at **0**, unless specified otherwise, and are incremented by **1**. In the preceding enumeration, **snakeEyes** is assigned a value of **2**, **trey** a value of **3**, **[yo leven]** a value of **11** and **boxCars** a value of **12**. Enumeration constants containing one or more spaces—such as **[yo leven]**—must be enclosed in brackets, **[]**. The identifiers in an enumeration must be unique, but separate enumeration constants can have the same positive or negative **Long** value. Keywords ***End Enum*** terminate the enumeration. Enumerations must have module scope.

*Common Programming Error 6.14*

*Attempting to define an enumeration in a scope other than the module scope is a syntax error.*

*Common Programming Error 6.15*

*Attempting to modify an enumeration constant's value is a syntax error.*

In **Form_Load**, we change the image the form title bar displays to a die by setting the form's ***Icon*** property to an *icon image* (i.e., a graphics file with the **.ico** extension). Changing the icon image adds a "nice touch" to the program.

The player rolls two dice on the first roll and all subsequent rolls. Pressing **Play** begins a new game of craps. Event procedure **cmdPlay_Click** calls **RollDice**. The sum of the two die are returned from **RollDice** and assigned to the variable **sum**. A **Select Case** determines the outcome of the first roll. If a 7 or 11 is rolled, button **Roll** is disabled and a message is displayed indicating that the player has won. If a 2, 3 or 12 is rolled, button **Roll** is disabled and a message is displayed indicating that the player has lost. If a "point" has occurred, **Case Else** is executed. **Play** is disabled and **Roll** is enabled. **Roll** is pressed when attempting to make a "point."

We define **RollDice** to roll the dice and compute and return their sum. **RollDice** is defined once, but it is called from two places in the program. Interestingly, **RollDice** takes no arguments, so we have an empty parameter list. **RollDice** returns the sum of the two dice, so a return type of **Integer** is indicated in the function header. **RollDice** calls a utility procedure **DisplayDie**. A *utility procedure* assists another procedure in completing a specific task and is only called by that procedure. We define utility procedure **DisplayDie** to handle the drawing of the dice images.

The game is reasonably involved. The player may win or lose on the first roll, or may win or lose on any subsequent roll. When the game is won, **lblStatus.Caption** displays that the game has been won. When the game is lost, **lblStatus.Caption** displays that the game has been lost. Otherwise, **Roll** must be pressed to roll the dice.

Note the interesting use of the various program control mechanisms we discussed. The craps program uses one **Function** procedure—**RollDice**—and one **Sub** procedure—**DisplayDie**. The program also uses the **Select Case** and **If/Then/Else** structures. In the exercises, we investigate various interesting characteristics of the game of craps.

## 6.11 Recursion and the Factorial Function

For some types of problems, it is actually useful to have procedures call themselves. A *recursive procedure* calls itself either directly or indirectly through another call. In this section and the next, several examples of recursion are presented.

We consider recursion conceptually first, and then present several recursive programs. Recursive problem-solving approaches have a number of elements in common. A recursive procedure is called to solve a problem. The procedure actually knows how to solve only the *simplest case*(s), or so-called *base case*(s). If called with a base case, the procedure stops recursively calling itself and simply returns to its caller. If called with a more complex problem, the procedure divides the problem into two conceptual pieces: a piece that it knows how to do and a piece that it does not know how to do.

To make recursion feasible, the latter piece must resemble the original problem, but be a slightly simpler or slightly smaller version of the original problem. Because this new problem looks like the original problem, the procedure *launches* (calls) a fresh copy of itself to go to work on the smaller problem—this is referred to as a *recursive call* and is also called the *recursion step*. The recursion step also includes keywords **Exit Sub** for **Sub** procedures, and either keywords **Exit Function** or assignment to the **Function** procedure name for **Function** procedures.

The recursion step executes while the original call to the procedure is still "open" (i.e., it has not yet finished executing). The recursion step can result in many more such recursive calls as the procedure divides each new subproblem into two conceptual pieces. In order for the recursion to eventually terminate, each time the procedure calls itself with a slightly simpler version of the original problem, this sequence of smaller and smaller problems must eventually converge on the base case. At that point, the procedure recognizes the base case, returns a result to the previous copy of the procedure and a sequence of returns ensues all the way up the line until the original procedure call eventually returns the final result.

All of this sounds quite exotic compared to the kind of conventional problem-solving techniques we have been using to this point. As an example of these concepts at work, let us write a recursive program to perform a popular mathematical calculation.

The factorial of a nonnegative **Integer** $n$, written $n!$ (and pronounced "$n$ factorial"), is the product

$$n \cdot (n - 1) \cdot (n - 2) \cdot \ldots \cdot 1$$

with $1!$ equal to 1, and $0!$ defined to be 1. For example, $5!$ is the product $5 \cdot 4 \cdot 3 \cdot 2 \cdot 1$, which is equal to 120.

The *factorial* of an **Integer** number, greater than or equal to 0, can be calculated iteratively (nonrecursively) using a **For** loop as follows:

```
factorial = 1

For counter = number To 1 Step -1
   factorial = factorial * counter
Next counter
```

A recursive definition of the factorial procedure is arrived at by observing the following relationship:

$$n! = n \cdot (n - 1)!$$

For example, $5!$ is clearly equal to $5 \cdot 4!$, as is shown by the following:

$$5! = 5 \cdot 4 \cdot 3 \cdot 2 \cdot 1$$
$$5! = 5 \cdot (4 \cdot 3 \cdot 2 \cdot 1)$$
$$5! = 5 \cdot (4!)$$

The evaluation of $5!$ would proceed as shown in Fig. 6.25. Figure 6.25 part (a) shows how the succession of recursive calls proceeds until $1!$ is evaluated to be 1, which terminates the recursion. Figure 6.25 part (b) shows the values returned from each recursive call to its caller until the final value is calculated and returned.

The program of Fig. 6.26 uses recursion to calculate and print the factorials of the number entered in a **TextBox**. Programmer-defined recursive **Function** procedure **Factorial** first tests to see if a terminating condition is **True** (i.e., is a number less than or equal to **1**). If **number** is indeed less than or equal to **1**, **Factorial** returns **1**, no further recursion is necessary and the program terminates. If **number** is greater than **1**, the statement

```
Factorial = number * Factorial(number - 1)
```

expresses the problem as the product of **number** and a recursive call to **Factorial** evaluating the factorial of **number - 1**. Note that **Factorial(number - 1)** is a slightly simpler problem than the original calculation **Factorial(number)**.

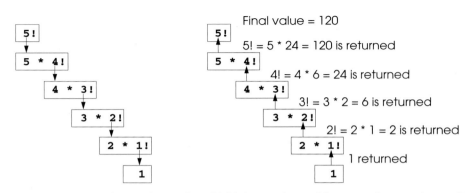

(a) Procession of recursive calls    (b) Values returned from each recursive call

**Fig. 6.25**    Recursive evaluation of *5!*.

```
1   ' Fig. 6.26
2   ' Program recursively calculates factorials
3   Option Explicit          ' General declaration
4
5   Private Sub cmdCalculate_Click()
6      Dim x As Integer, n As Integer
7
8      Call lstValues.Clear        ' Clear lstValues
9      n = txtInput.Text           ' Get input
10
11     ' Calculate factorial(s)
12     For x = 0 To n
13        lstValues.AddItem Format$(x, "@@") & "! = " & _
14                          Factorial((x))   ' Call-by-value
15     Next x
16
17  End Sub
```

**Fig. 6.26**    Calculating factorials with procedure **Factorial** (part 1 of 2).

```
18
19   Private Function Factorial(ByVal y As Double) As Double
20
21      If y <= 1 Then
22         Factorial = 1                     ' Base case
23      Else
24         Factorial = y * Factorial(y - 1)  ' Recursive step
25      End If
26
27   End Function
```

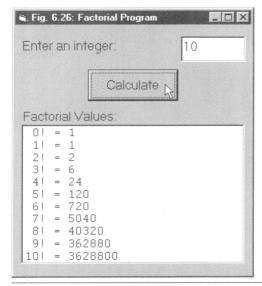

GUI after user enters **10** and presses **Calculate**.

**Fig. 6.26**   Calculating factorials with procedure **Factorial** (part 2 of 2).

**Factorial** receives a parameter of type **Double** and returns a result of type **Double**. We use **Double** because factorial values become large quickly and **Double** is the data type capable of holding the largest values. Unfortunately, **Factorial** produces large values so quickly that even **Double** does not help us print many factorial values before the size of a **Double** variable is exceeded—which results in an over-flow error.

*Common Programming Error 6.16*

*Either omitting the base case, or writing the recursion step incorrectly so that it does not converge on the base case, will cause infinite recursion, eventually exhausting memory. This is analogous to the problem of an infinite loop in an iterative (nonrecursive) solution.*

## 6.12 Another Recursion Example: The Fibonacci Series

The Fibonacci series

0, 1, 1, 2, 3, 5, 8, 13, 21, …

begins with 0 and 1 and has the property that each subsequent Fibonacci number is the sum of the previous two Fibonacci numbers.

The series occurs in nature and, in particular, describes a form of spiral. The ratio of successive Fibonacci numbers converges on a constant value of 1.618.... This number, too, repeatedly occurs in nature and has been called the *golden ratio* or the *golden mean*. Humans tend to find the golden mean aesthetically pleasing. Architects often design windows, rooms and buildings whose length and width are in the ratio of the golden mean. Postcards are often designed with a golden mean length/width ratio.

The Fibonacci series may be defined recursively as follows:

*Fibonacci(0) = 0*
*Fibonacci(1) = 1*
*Fibonacci(n) = Fibonacci(n – 1) + Fibonacci(n – 2)*

The program of Figure 6.27 calculates the $i^{th}$ Fibonacci number recursively using programmer-defined **Function** procedure **Fibonacci**. Notice that Fibonacci numbers tend to become large quickly. Therefore, we have once again chosen the data type **Double** as the parameter type and as the return type.

```
1    ' Fig. 6.27
2    ' Recursively generating Fibonacci numbers
3    Option Explicit        ' General declaration
4
5    Private Sub cmdCalculate_Click()
6        Dim fibonacciValue As Double
7
8        lblValue.Caption = ""        ' Clear lblValue Caption
9
10       ' Change the mouse pointer to an hourglass shape
11       ' so user will know the Fibonacci value is being
12       ' calculated. For small numbers input, evaluation
13       ' occurs quickly and the user is not likely to see
14       ' the hourglass cursor.
15       Screen.MousePointer = vbHourglass
16
17       fibonacciValue = Fibonacci(txtInput.Text)
18       lblValue.Caption = "Fibonacci Value is " & fibonacciValue
19
20       ' Change the mouse pointer to the default
21       Screen.MousePointer = vbDefault
22   End Sub
23
24   Private Function Fibonacci(n As Double) As Double
25
26       If (n = 0 Or n = 1) Then
27           Fibonacci = n    ' Base Case
28       Else
29           ' Recursive step
30           Fibonacci = Fibonacci(n - 1) + Fibonacci(n - 2)
31       End If
32
33   End Function
```

**Fig. 6.27** Demonstrating recursive procedure **Fibonacci** (part 1 of 2).

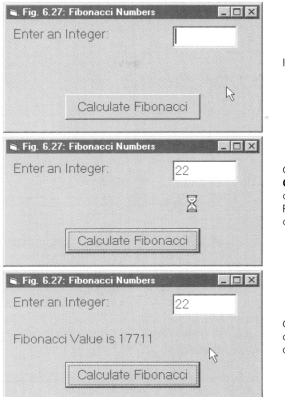

Initial GUI at execution.

GUI after user enters **22** and presses **Calculate Fibonacci**. Cursor changes to an hourglass while the Fibonacci value is being calculated.

GUI after Fibonacci calculation is complete. Cursor changes back to default cursor.

**Fig. 6.27**   Demonstrating recursive procedure **Fibonacci** (part 2 of 2).

Pressing **Calculate Fibonacci** begins the Fibonacci calculation, which can take several seconds to evaluate depending on the number input. The line

```
Screen.MousePointer = vbHourglass
```

changes the mouse pointer to the hourglass icon. The **Screen** object represents the environment display and allows the programmer to set the shape of the mouse pointer with property **MousePointer**. During the calculation we set the mouse pointer to Visual Basic constant **vbHourglass**. When the calculation completes, we set the mouse pointer to the default value **vbDefault**. The hourglass mouse pointer indicates that the program is busy and may take some time before allowing the user to interact with the GUI.

The call to **Fibonacci** from **cmdCalculate_Click** is not a recursive call, but all subsequent calls to **Fibonacci** are indeed recursive. Each time **Fibonacci** is invoked, it immediately tests for the base case—**n** equal to 0 or 1. If **True**, **n** is returned. Interestingly, if **n** is greater than 1, the recursion step generates two recursive calls, each of which is for a slightly simpler problem than the original **Fibonacci** call. Figure 6.28 shows how **Function** procedure **Fibonacci** would evaluate **Fibonacci(3)**—we abbreviate **Fibonacci** as **F** to make the figure more readable.

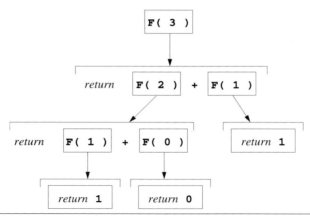

**Fig. 6.28**   Set of recursive calls to **Function** procedure **Fibonacci**.

A word of caution is in order about recursive programs like the one we use here to generate Fibonacci numbers. Each level of recursion in **Fibonacci** has a doubling effect on the number of calls (i.e., the number of recursive calls that will be executed to calculate the $n^{th}$ Fibonacci number is on the order of $2^n$). This rapidly gets "out of hand." Calculating only the $20^{th}$ Fibonacci number would require on the order of $2^{20}$ or about a million calls, calculating the $30^{th}$ Fibonacci number would require on the order of $2^{30}$ or about a billion calls and so on. Computer scientists refer to this as *exponential complexity*. Problems of this nature humble even the world's most powerful computers!

*Performance Tip 6.6*

*Avoid Fibonacci-style recursive programs that result in an exponential "explosion" of calls.*

## 6.13 Recursion vs. Iteration

In the previous sections, we studied two **Function** procedures that can easily be implemented recursively or iteratively. In this section, we compare the two approaches and discuss why we might choose one approach over the other in a particular situation.

Both iteration and recursion are based on a control structure: Iteration uses a repetition structure; recursion uses a selection structure. Both iteration and recursion involve repetition: Iteration explicitly uses a repetition structure; recursion achieves repetition through repeated procedure calls. Iteration and recursion each involve a termination test: Iteration terminates when the loop-continuation condition fails; recursion terminates when a base case is recognized. Iteration with counter-controlled repetition and recursion each gradually approach termination: Iteration keeps modifying a counter until the counter assumes a value that makes a loop-continuation condition fail; recursion keeps producing simpler versions of the original problem until the base case is reached. Both iteration and recursion can occur infinitely: An infinite loop occurs with iteration if the loop-continuation test never becomes **False**; infinite recursion occurs if the recursion step does not reduce the problem each time in a manner that converges on the base case.

Recursion has many negatives. It repeatedly invokes the mechanism, and consequently the overhead, of procedure calls. This can be expensive in both processor time and memory.

Each recursive call causes another copy of the procedure (actually only the data) to be created; this can consume considerable memory. Iteration normally occurs within a procedure, so the overhead of repeated calls and extra memory is omitted. So why choose recursion?

**Software Engineering Observation 6.14**

*Any problem that can be solved recursively can also be solved iteratively (nonrecursively). A recursive approach is normally chosen in preference to an iterative approach when the recursive approach more naturally mirrors the problem and results in a clearer program that is easier to understand and debug. Another reason to choose a recursive solution is that an iterative solution may not be apparent.*

**Performance Tip 6.7**

*Avoid using recursion in performance situations. Recursive calls take time and consume additional memory.*

Let us reconsider some observations that we make repeatedly throughout the book. Good software engineering is important. High performance is often important. Unfortunately, these goals are often at odds with one another. Good software engineering is key to making more manageable the task of developing the larger and more complex software systems we need. High performance in these systems is key to realizing the systems of the future that will place ever-greater computing demands on hardware. Where do procedures fit in here?

**Software Engineering Observation 6.15**

*Dividing a program into a neat, hierarchical set of cooperating procedures promotes good software engineering. But it has a price.*

**Performance Tip 6.8**

*A program composed of many cooperating procedures—as compared to a monolithic (i.e., one-piece) program without procedures—makes potentially large numbers of procedure calls and these consume execution time and memory. But monolithic programs are difficult to program, test, debug, maintain and evolve.*

So divide your programs into procedures judiciously, always keeping in mind the delicate balance between performance and good software engineering.

## 6.14 Optional Arguments

Visual Basic allows programmers to create procedures that take one or more *optional arguments*. With an optional argument, the caller has the *option* of passing that particular argument. Optional arguments are specified in the procedure header with keyword **Optional**. For example, the procedure header

```
Private Sub FooBar(y As Boolean, Optional z As Long)
```

specifies that the last argument is **Optional**. Any procedure calling **FooBar** must pass at least one argument to **FooBar** in order to avoid syntax errors. If the caller so chooses, a second argument can be passed to **FooBar**. Consider the following calls to **FooBar**:

```
Call FooBar
Call FooBar(True)
Call FooBar(False, 10)
```

The first call to **FooBar** generates a syntax error because a minimum of one argument is required. The second call to **FooBar** is valid because one argument is being passed. The **Optional** argument is not provided. The last call to **FooBar** is also valid—**False** is passed as the one required argument and **10** is passed as the **Optional** argument.

*Common Programming Error 6.17*

*Not passing a required argument to a procedure is a syntax error.*

In the preceding **Call** in which the only one argument, **True**, is passed to **FooBar**, **z** defaults to **0**. Numeric types default to **0** and **Boolean**s default to **False**.

*Default values* for **Optional** arguments can be set explicitly using the assignment operator along with the value. For example, the header

```
Private Function Foo(Optional x As Integer = 8) As Double
```

sets **8** as the default value for **x**. Default values can only be used with **Optional** arguments.

*Common Programming Error 6.18*

*Attempting to use default arguments without the **Optional** keyword is a syntax error.*

The program of Fig. 6.29 demonstrates **Optional** arguments and default arguments with programmer-defined **Sub** procedure **BoxVolume**.

```
1   ' Fig. 6.29
2   ' Demonstrating optional arguments
3   Option Explicit                    ' General declaration
4
5   Private Sub cmdPrint_Click()
6       Call Cls
7
8       Call BoxVolume              ' Default three arguments
9       Call BoxVolume(0)           ' Default rightmost two arguments
10      Call BoxVolume(6, 7)        ' Default rightmost argument
11      Call BoxVolume(6, 4, 5)  ' Pass three arguments
12      Call BoxVolume(5, , 9)      ' Default second argument
13      Call BoxVolume(, 7)         ' Default first and third arguments
14      Call BoxVolume(, , 8)       ' Default first two arguments
15   End Sub
16
17   Private Sub BoxVolume(Optional x As Integer = 1, _
18                         Optional y As Integer = 3, _
19                         Optional z As Integer = 2)
20
21       Print "Dimensions: " & x & ", " & y & ", " & z & Space$(5) & _
22                         "Volume: " & (x * y * z)
23   End Sub
```

Fig. 6.29   Demonstrating **Optional** arguments (part 1 of 2).

```
Fig. 6.29: Demonstrating Optional Arguments  _ □ X
Dimensions: 1, 3, 2      Volume: 6
Dimensions: 0, 3, 2      Volume: 0
Dimensions: 6, 7, 2      Volume: 84
Dimensions: 6, 4, 5      Volume: 120
Dimensions: 5, 3, 9      Volume: 135
Dimensions: 1, 7, 2      Volume: 14
Dimensions: 1, 3, 8      Volume: 24
                  Print
```

GUI after user presses **Print**.

**Fig. 6.29**   Demonstrating **Optional** arguments (part 2 of 2).

**BoxVolume** defines three **Optional** arguments, which default to **1**, **3** and **2**, respectively. When declaring **Optional** variables in a procedure header, all variable declarations to the right of an **Optional** variable must be declared **Optional**. For example, the header

```
Private Sub Bad(Optional x As Integer = 1, y As Integer, _
                Optional z As Integer = 1)
```

would generate a syntax error because **y** is not declared as **Optional**.

> *Common Programming Error 6.19*
>
> *Attempting to declare in a procedure header non-Optional arguments to the right of an Optional argument is a syntax error.*

## 6.15  Named Arguments

Named arguments simplify procedure calls that specify a large number of **Optional** arguments. With *named arguments* the programmer specifies in the call the name of the argument and the value being passed into that argument. For example, the header

```
Private Sub K(Optional a As Integer, _
              Optional b As Integer, _
              Optional c As Integer)
```

declares three **Integer Optional** arguments. If **K**'s caller only wants to pass a value of **20** to **c**, values for **a** and **b** still must be passed. We could accomplish this with either

```
Call K(0, 0, 20)
```

or

```
Call K(, , 20)
```

The call is simplified if we use named arguments. Rewriting the call to **K** as

```
Call K(c:=20)
```

specifies that **c** is to be passed a value of **20**. A named argument is specified in a procedure call by writing the parameter variable name followed by **:=** and the parameter variable's value. Using *auto quick info* allows the programmer to see the parameter variable names.

**Common Programming Error 6.20**

*Using = instead of := when specifying a named argument is a syntax error. Note: if a local variable has the same name as the named argument specified in the call then a logic error occurs.*

**Common Programming Error 6.21**

*Using a variable name for a named argument that is not declared in the procedure header is a syntax error.*

Named arguments can be used with procedures that do not specify **Optional** arguments. This allows the programmer to pass arguments in any order. For example, the header

```
Private Sub Display(flag As Boolean, number As Long, _
                    message As String)
```

specifies the argument order as **Boolean**, **Long** and **String**. Now consider the following call using named arguments:

```
Call Display(message:="Named Arguments", flag:=True, _
             number:=1000000)
```

which passes the arguments as **String**, **Boolean** and **Long**. Any order for the three arguments is possible because named arguments are used. Variable **flag** always gets the value **True**, regardless of the order in which it is passed. The same is true for **message** and **number**.

The program of Fig. 6.30 demonstrates the use of named arguments with two **Sub** procedures **Display1** and **Display2**. **Display1** does not use **Optional** arguments, while **Display2** does use **Optional** arguments. The call to **Display1** demonstrates that named arguments can be passed in any order, and the call to **Display2** demonstrates that any **Optional** variable can be assigned a value using named arguments.

```
1   ' Fig. 6.30
2   ' Demonstrating named arguments
3   Option Explicit        ' General declaration
4
5   Private Sub cmdPrint_Click()
6      Call Cls
7
8      ' Invoke Display1. Argument list is String, Boolean, Long
9      Call Display1(message:="Named Arguments", flag:=True, _
10               number:=1000000)
11
12     ' Invoke Display2. Give number2 a value.
13     Call Display2(number2:=2000000)
14  End Sub
15
16  ' Note the order of declaration: Boolean, Long, String
17  Private Sub Display1(flag As Boolean, number As Long, _
18                  message As String)
```

**Fig. 6.30** Demonstrating named arguments (part 1 of 2).

```
19
20      Print "flag is " & flag
21      Print "number is " & number
22      Print "message is " & message
23   End Sub
24
25   Private Sub Display2(Optional flag2 As Boolean, _
26                       Optional number2 As Long, _
27                       Optional money As Currency)
28
29      Print       ' Blank line
30      Print "flag2 is " & flag2
31      Print "number2 is " & number2
32      Print "money is " & money
33   End Sub
```

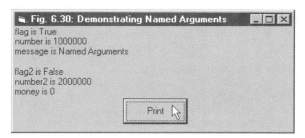

GUI after user presses **Print**.

**Fig. 6.30** Demonstrating named arguments (part 2 of 2).

## 6.16 Visual Basic Math Functions

Visual Basic math functions allow the programmer to perform certain common mathematical calculations. Figure 6.30 summarizes some Visual Basic math functions.

| Function | Description | Example |
|---|---|---|
| **Abs(x)** | Absolute value of **x** | if **x** < 0 then **Abs(x)** is **x**<br>if **x** = 0 then **Abs(x)** is 0<br>if **x** > 0 then **Abs(x)** is **x** |
| **Atn(x)** | Trigonometric arctangent of **x** (in radians) | **Atn(1)\*4** is 3.14159265358979 |
| **Cos(x)** | Trigonometric cosine of **x** (in radians) | **Cos(0)** is 1 |
| **Exp(x)** | Exponential function $e^x$ | **Exp(1.0)** is 2.71828<br>**Exp(2.0)** is 7.38906 |
| **Int(x)** | Returns the whole-number part of **x** | **Int(-5.3)** is –6<br>**Int(0.893)** is 0<br>**Int(76.45)** is 76 |

**Fig. 6.31** Visual Basic math functions (part 1 of 2).

| Function | Description | Example |
|----------|-------------|---------|
| `Fix(x)` | Returns the whole-number part of **x** (Note: **Fix** and **Int** are different only when **x** is negative. **Int** rounds to the next smallest number, while **Fix** rounds to the next-largest number.) | `Int(-5.3)` is –5<br>`Int(0.893)` is 0<br>`Int(76.45)` is 76 |
| `Log(x)` | Natural logarithm of **x** (base *e*) | `Log(2.718282)` is 1.0<br>`Log(7.389056)` is 2.0 |
| `Round(x, y)` | Rounds **x** to **y** decimal places. If **y** is omitted, **x** is returned as an **Integer**. | `Round(4.844)` is 4<br>`Round(5.73839, 3)` is 5.738 |
| `Sgn(x)` | Sign of **x** | `Sgn(-1988)` is –1<br>`Sgn(0)` is 0<br>`Sgn(3.3)` is 1 |
| `Sin(x)` | Trigonometric sine of **x** (in radians) | `Sin(0)` is 0 |
| `Sqr(x)` | Square root of **x** | `Sqr(900.0)` is 30<br>`Sqr(9.0)` is 3.0 |
| `Tan(x)` | Trigonometric tangent of **x** (in radians) | `Tan(0)` is 0 |

**Fig. 6.31**    Visual Basic math functions (part 2 of 2).

## 6.17 Code Modules

Our discussions thus far have centered on the form module. This section introduces the *code module (also called a standard module),* which does not have a GUI and can contain only code. Procedures the programmer wishes to use in multiple projects are often placed in code modules. Code modules are created by selecting **Add Module** from the **Project** menu. When **Add Module** is selected, the ***Add Module*** *dialog* is displayed (Fig. 6.32).

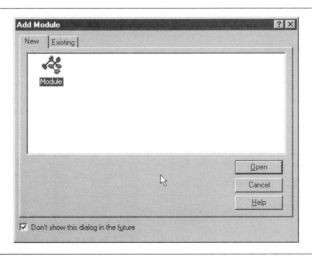

**Fig. 6.32    Add Module** dialog.

*Software Engineering Observation 6.16*

*Code modules promote software reusability. Code modules conveniently package procedures for reuse in multiple projects.*

The programmer can choose to open a **New** or an **Existing** code module. Pressing **Open** opens a code module. Pressing **Cancel** closes the dialog without opening a code module. On-line help is displayed when **Help** is pressed.

Code modules are maintained in a separate folder in the **Project** explorer window, as shown in Fig. 6.33. Double-clicking a code module name (or highlighting the code module name and pressing the **View Code** button) in the **Project** explorer window displays the code module's **Code** window. Code modules do not have a GUI, so the **View Object** button is always grayed.

Like a form module, a code module has a general declaration. Variables, **Option Explicit**, **Enum**s, etc. are placed in the general declaration. Procedures are added using the techniques described in Sections 6.3 and 6.4. Code module file names end in **.bas**. A project can have multiple code modules (as well as multiple form modules). Code modules and form modules can always be added to a project or removed from a project. To remove a code module or form module from a project, highlight the module name in the **Project** explorer window and select **Remove** from the **Project** menu.

In order to use code modules effectively, the programmer must understand scoping rules. By default, module variables and event procedures are **Private** to the module in which they are defined. A **Private** variable or procedure can only be used within the module where it is declared. If the programmer wishes to allow another module to use a variable or procedure, keyword **Public** is used in the declaration. **Public** variables and procedures are accessible to every module in the project. Procedures that other modules are expected to use are made **Public** by the programmer and utility procedures are generally made **Private**. We use **Public** and **Private** in detail in Chapter 16.

*Software Engineering Observation 6.17*

*If you do not expect to use a procedure outside a code module, make the procedure **Private**. This reduces the accessibility of the procedure and avoids potential naming conflicts when other modules are added.*

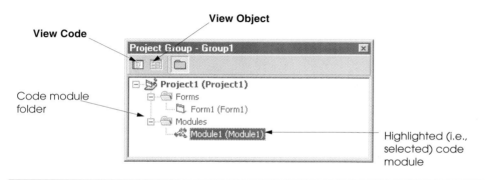

**Fig. 6.33    Project** explorer window displaying the code module's folder.

The program of Fig. 6.34 contains one form module and one code module. Clicking the form's **Print** button calls the code module's programmer-defined **Public Sub** procedure **ModulePrint**, which displays text.

***Common Programming Error 6.22***

*Attempting to use **Dim** with **Public** or with **Private** is a syntax error.*

***Common Programming Error 6.23***

*Attempting to access **Private** variables or call **Private** procedures in another module is a syntax error.*

***Common Programming Error 6.24***

*Attempting to declare local variables as **Private** or **Public** is a syntax error.*

***Common Programming Error 6.25***

*Declaring a **Public** procedure in one code module that has the same name as another procedure in another code module in the same project is a syntax error.*

```
1   ' Fig. 6.34
2   ' Using a code module
3   Option Explicit
4
5   Private Sub cmdPrint_Click()
6       ' ModulePrint is defined in code module modModule.bas
7       Call ModulePrint
8   End Sub
```

**Fig. 6.34**   Calling a **Public** procedure defined in a code module (part 1 of 2).

```
9   ' modModule.bas
10  ' modModule code module
11  Option Explicit     ' General declaration
12
13  Public Sub ModulePrint()
14      frmForm.Print "ModulePrint"
15  End Sub
```

GUI after user has pressed **Print** several times.

**Fig. 6.34**   Calling a **Public** procedure defined in a code module (part 2 of 2).

## Summary

- Experience has shown that the best way to develop and maintain a large program is to construct it from smaller pieces, each of which is more manageable than the original program. This technique is called divide and conquer.

- Four types of procedures exist: event procedures, Visual Basic procedures, **Sub** procedures and **Function** procedures. Event procedures respond to events. Forms and controls predefine their event procedures. Visual Basic procedures are provided by Microsoft to perform common tasks. Programmers can create their own procedures to meet the requirements of the problems they solve.

- A procedure is invoked by a call. The call specifies the procedure name and provides information (as arguments) that the callee (i.e., the called procedure) needs to do its job.

- **Sub** procedures and **Function** procedures can either be created with the **Add Procedure** dialog or typed directly into the **Code** window.

- The **Sub** procedure header contains the keyword **Sub**, the procedure name and parentheses. The declarations and statements between the header and **End Sub** form the **Sub** procedure body. Every time the **Sub** procedure is called the body is executed.

- When a **Sub** procedure name is encountered at run-time, the **Sub** procedure's body is immediately executed. **Sub** procedure execution terminates when **End Sub** is reached. Program execution continues with the next statement immediately following the call.

- Parameter variables can be declared using keyword **As** or a type-declaration character (if one exists). Parameter variables default to **Variant** if they are not explicitly given a type. Parameter variables receive their values from the caller and are used in the procedure body.

- Auto list members automatically displays an object's properties and methods.

- Auto quick info displays procedure arguments for Visual Basic procedures and for programmer-defined procedures.

- **Function** procedures and **Sub** procedures share the same characteristics, with one important difference—**Function** procedures return a value to the caller.

- **Function** procedures contain the keyword **Function**, the function name, and parentheses. The declarations and statements between the header and **End Function** form the **Function** procedure body. Every time the **Function** procedure is invoked the body is executed.

- When a **Function** procedure name is encountered at run-time, the **Function** procedure is called. A **Function** procedure's return value is specified by assigning a value to the **Function** procedure name in the body. Return types can be explicitly stated in the **Function** procedure header using either the **As** keyword or a type declaration character (if one exists).

- When arguments are passed to a **Function** procedure, parentheses are required in the call. For a **Function** procedure with no arguments, parenthesesare not required.

- **CommandButton** property **Style** specifies whether or not graphics can be drawn on a **CommandButton**. Graphics cannot be drawn with the default **Standard** setting, but can be drawn with the **Graphical** setting. Visual Basic constants **vbButtonStandard** and **vbButtonGraphical** can also be used to explicitly set the **Style** property.

- The **Picture** property specifies which image a **CommandButton** displays. The **Style** property must be set to **Graphical** to display an image. Visual Basic function **LoadPicture** loads a specified image into memory.

- Call-by-reference allows the called procedure to directly access the caller's data and modify that data. When an argument is passed call-by-value, a copy of the argument's value is passed. The called procedure can only manipulate that copy; the called procedure cannot manipulate the caller's data. By default Visual Basic arguments are passed call-by-reference.

- Arguments can be passed call-by-value by using keyword **`ByVal`** for each call-by-value argument in the procedure header or by enclosing the procedure call's argument(s) in parentheses, **`()`**.

- Visual Basic provides keyword **`ByRef`** for explicitly passing arguments call-by-reference, but **`ByRef`** is the default, so it is rarely used.

- **`Exit Sub`** and **`Exit Function`** alter the flow of control. **`Exit Sub`**, when executed in a **`Sub`** procedure causes an immediate exit from that procedure. Control is returned to the caller and the next statement in sequence after the call is executed.

- **`Exit Function`** causes immediate exit from a **`Function`** procedure. Control is returned to the caller and the next statement in sequence after the call is executed.

- An identifier's storage class determines the period during which that identifier exists in memory. A variable's storage class is sometimes referred to as its lifetime.

- An identifier's scope is the region in a program in which the identifier can be referenced.

- Non-**`Static`** local variables (also called automatic variables) have automatic storage class by default. Automatic variables defined within a procedure are created when that procedure becomes active. Automatic variables exist until the procedure is exited. Memory allocated for automatic variables is reclaimed by the system.

- Keyword **`Static`** is used to declare identifiers for variables and procedures of the **`Static`** storage class. For **`Static`** variables, storage is allocated and initialized once when the form is created. For **`Static`** procedures, all their variables are **`Static`** variables—regardless of whether or not the variables are explicitly declared **`Static`**.

- Local variables declared with the keyword **`Static`** are known only in the procedure in which they are defined, but unlike automatic variables, **`Static`** variables retain their value when the procedure is exited. All numeric variables of the **`Static`** storage class are initialized to zero.

- The scopes for an identifier are local scope, module scope and **`Public`** scope. Local scope applies to local variables declared in a procedure's body. Module scope applies to variables declared in the general declaration. **`Public`** scope refers to module variables that are declared **`Public`**.

- Visual Basic function **`Rnd`** returns a **`Single`** random number in the range $0 \le x < 1$. Function **`Rnd`** generates pseudo-random numbers.

- Visual Basic Function **`Int`** returns the **`Integer`** part of the argument passed to it.

- **`Randomize`** "seeds" function **`Rnd`** to produce a different sequence of random numbers each time **`Rnd`** is called. The seed value is obtained from Visual Basic function **`Timer`**, which returns the current time expressed as the number of seconds elapsed since midnight.

- Controls grouped inside a **`Frame`** cannot be separated from the **`Frame`**.

- The icon in the form title bar is set with the form's **`Icon`** property.

- A utility procedure is a **`Private`** procedure that assists other procedures in completing a task.

- An enumeration is a set of **`Long`** constants represented by identifiers. Values for enumeration constants start at **`0`**, unless specified otherwise, and are incremented by **`1`**. The identifiers in an enumeration must be unique, but separate enumeration constants can have the same positive or negative **`Long`** value. Enumerations must have module scope.

- A recursive procedure calls itself either directly or indirectly through another call. A recursive procedure knows how to solve only the simplest case(s), or so-called base case(s). If called with a base case, the procedure stops recursively calling itself and simply returns to its caller. If called with a more complex problem, the procedure divides the problem into two conceptual pieces: a piece that it knows how to do and a piece that it does not know how to do.

- The **`Screen`** object represents the display environment and allows the programmer to set the shape of the mouse pointer with the **`MousePointer`** property.

- Optional arguments give the caller the option of passing arguments. Optional arguments are specified in a procedure header with keyword **Optional**.

- **Optional** argument default values can be set using the assignment operator along with a value. Default values can only be used with **Optional** arguments.

- Named arguments allow the programmer to specify in the call the argument name and the argument's value.

- Visual Basic math functions allow the programmer to perform many common mathematical calculations.

- Code modules do not have a GUI. Code module file names end in **.bas**. A project can have multiple code modules and multiple form modules. Code modules and form modules can always be added to a project or removed from a project.

- By default, module variables and event procedures are **Private** to the module in which they are declared. A **Private** variable or procedure can only be used within the module where it is declared. **Public** variables and procedures are accessible to every module in the project.

## Terminology

:= to assign a value to a named argument
**.bas**
**.ico**
Abs function
**Add Module** dialog
**Add Procedure** dialog
**All Local Variables as Statics Checkbox**
argument
**As** keyword
assign return value to **Function** name
**Atn** function
*auto list members*
automatic variables
*auto quick info*
braces, **[]**
**ByRef** keyword
**ByVal** keyword
call a procedure
call-by-reference
call-by-value
callee
caller
**Call** keyword
**Clear** method
code module
**Cos** function
default values for **Optional** arguments
divide-and-conquer
**End Enum**
**End Function**
**End Sub**
**Enum** keyword
enumeration

enumeration constants
equal likelihood
event procedure
**Exit Function**
**Exit Sub**
**Exp** function
exponential complexity
**Factorial** function
factorial of an **Integer**
Fibonacci series
**Fix** function
form module
**Frame** control
**Function** procedure
**Function** procedure body
**Function** procedure header
golden mean
golden ratio
**Graphical** setting of **Style** property
hiding implementation details
icon image
**Icon** property
infinite recursion
**Int** function
invoke a procedure
iteration
**LoadPicture** function
**Log** function
module
**MousePointer** property
named arguments
named constants
optional arguments

**Optional** keyword
parameter
parameter list
parentheses, **()**
**Picture** property
**Private** keyword
procedure
procedure definition
procedure header
programmer-defined procedure
pseudo-random numbers
**Public** keyword
**Randomize** statement
randomizing
random number generation
recursion
recursion step
recursion vs. iteration
return a value
**Rnd** function
**Round** function
scaling factor
scope
**Screen** object

seed
**Sgn** function
shift adjustment
simplest case
**Sin** function
software reusability
**Sqr** function
standard module
**Standard** setting of **Style** property
**Static** keyword
storage class
**Style** property
**Sub** procedure
**Sub** procedure body
**Sub** procedure header
**Tan** function
type name
user-defined type
utility procedure
**vbButtonGraphical** constant
**vbButtonStandard** constant
**vbDefault** constant
**vbHourglass** constant
Visual Basic function

## Common Programming Errors

**6.1**    Writing executable code outside a procedure is a syntax error.

**6.2**    Attempting to give a variable the same name as a procedure name is a syntax error.

**6.3**    Not passing the correct number of arguments to a procedure is a syntax error.

**6.4**    Passing an argument that cannot be implicitly converted is a run-time error.

**6.5**    Not enclosing the arguments being passed in parentheses when using keyword **Call** or enclosing the arguments passed in parentheses and not providing keyword **Call** are each syntax errors.

**6.6**    Declaring in a procedure body a variable with the same name as a parameter variable is a syntax error.

**6.7**    Calling a **Function** procedure without enclosing its argument(s) in parentheses is a syntax error.

**6.8**    Placing a type-declaration character for the return type after the parentheses of the parameter list is a syntax error.

**6.9**    Placing the **As** return type between the function name and the parentheses of the parameter list is a syntax error.

**6.10**   Assuming the **ByVal** keyword applies to more than one parameter is a logic error. For example, **ByVal** in the header of **Function Foo(ByVal x As Long, y As Boolean)** applies to **x** and not to **y**.

**6.11**   Using the **ByVal** or **ByRef** keywords outside a procedure header is a syntax error.

**6.12**   Forgetting to reinitialize a **Static** variable that needs to be reinitialized can lead to logic errors.

**6.13**   Attempting to declare a **Static** variable outside a procedure is a syntax error.

**6.14**   Attempting to define an enumeration in a scope other than the module scope is a syntax error.

**6.15**     Attempting to modify an enumeration constant's value is a syntax error.

**6.16**     Either omitting the base case, or writing the recursion step incorrectly so that it does not converge on the base case, will cause infinite recursion, eventually exhausting memory. This is analogous to the problem of an infinite loop in an iterative (nonrecursive) solution.

**6.17**     Not passing a required argument to a procedure is a syntax error.

**6.18**     Attempting to use default arguments without the **Optional** keyword is a syntax error.

**6.19**     Attempting to declare in a procedure header non-**Optional** arguments to the right of an **Optional** argument is a syntax error.

**6.20**     Using = instead of := when specifying a named argument is a syntax error. Note: if a local variable has the same name as the named argument specified in the call then a logic error occurs.

**6.21**     Using a variable name for a named argument that is not declared in the procedure header is a syntax error.

**6.22**     Attempting to use **Dim** with **Public** or with **Private** is a syntax error.

**6.23**     Attempting to access **Private** variables or call **Private** procedures in another module is a syntax error.

**6.24**     Attempting to declare local variables as **Private** or **Public** is a syntax error.

**6.25**     Declaring a **Public** procedure in one code module that has the same name as another procedure in another code module in the same project is a syntax error.

## Good Programming Practices

**6.1**     When calling a **Sub** procedure, use keyword **Call** and enclose argument(s) being passed in parentheses. This makes **Sub** procedure calls stand out and improves program readability.

**6.2**     When passing arguments call-by-value, use the optional parentheses around the arguments being passed and the **ByVal** keyword in the procedure header. This makes it absolutely clear that arguments are being passed call-by-value.

**6.3**     Prefix the name of **Image** controls with **img**. This allows **Image** controls to be identified easily.

**6.4**     Prefix the name of **Frame** controls with **fra**. This allows **Frame** controls to be identified easily.

## Performance Tips

**6.1**     Visual Basic procedures will normally execute faster than "equivalent" programmer-defined procedures that most programmers would write.

**6.2**     Call-by-reference is good for performance because it can eliminate the overhead of copying large amounts of data.

**6.3**     Call-by-value is potentially bad for performance if the data being passed is large, because making a copy of that data takes time and consumes memory.

**6.4**     The **Exit Sub** and **Exit Function** statements, when used properly, perform faster than the corresponding structured techniques we will soon learn.

**6.5**     Using **Static** only for variables that must retain their value between calls conserves memory.

**6.6**     Avoid Fibonacci-style recursive programs that result in an exponential "explosion" of calls.

**6.7**     Avoid using recursion in performance situations. Recursive calls take time and consume additional memory.

**6.8**     A program composed of many cooperating procedures—as compared to a monolithic (i.e., one-piece) program without procedures—makes potentially large numbers of procedure calls and these consume execution time and memory. But monolithic programs are difficult to program, test, debug, maintain and evolve.

## Software Engineering Observations

**6.1**    Familiarize yourself with the rich collection of Visual Basic procedures. Avoid reinventing the wheel. When possible, use Visual Basic procedures instead of writing new procedures. This reduces program development time.

**6.2**    Each procedure should be limited to performing a single well-defined task, and should effectively express that task. This promotes software reusability.

**6.3**    A procedure should usually be no longer than one page. Better yet, a procedure should usually be no longer than half a page. Regardless of how long a procedure is, it should perform one task well. Small procedures promote software reusability.

**6.4**    Since procedures operate on data, procedure names tend to be verbs. It is a Visual Basic convention to begin programmer-defined procedures with an uppercase first letter. For example, a procedure that sends an email message might be named **Send** or **SendEmail**.

**6.5**    If you cannot choose a concise name that expresses what the procedure does, it is possible that your procedure is attempting to perform too many diverse tasks. It is often best to break such a procedure into several procedures.

**6.6**    Choosing meaningful procedure names and meaningful parameter variable names makes programs more readable and helps avoid excessive use of comments.

**6.7**    A procedure requiring a large number of arguments may be performing too many tasks. Consider dividing the procedure into smaller procedures that perform the separate tasks.

**6.8**    When it makes sense to do so, Visual Basic will implicitly convert arguments from one type to another in a procedure call. For example, a procedure that declares **Integer** variable **u** would receive **56** when passed **55.77**; indeed, Visual Basic rounds rather than truncating when converting numbers with decimal points to **Integer**s.

**6.9**    Procedures can call event procedures.

**6.10**    Call-by-reference can weaken security because the called procedure can modify the caller's data at will, possibly changing that data.

**6.11**    When an argument is passed call-by-value, a copy of that argument's value is made and passed. Changes to the copy do not affect the original variable's value in the caller. This prevents accidental side effects that so greatly hinder the development of correct and reliable software systems.

**6.12**    Some programmers feel that **Exit Sub** and **Exit Function** violate the spirit of structured programming. Because the effects of these statements can be achieved by structured programming techniques, these programmers do not use **Exit Sub** and **Exit Function**.

**6.13**    Even though **Static** variables exist at form creation, this does not mean that these variables can be used throughout the program. Storage class and scope (where a name can be used) are separate issues.

**6.14**    Any problem that can be solved recursively can also be solved iteratively (nonrecursively). A recursive approach is normally chosen in preference to an iterative approach when the recursive approach more naturally mirrors the problem and results in a clearer program that is easier to understand and debug. Another reason to choose a recursive solution is that an iterative solution may not be apparent.

**6.15**    Dividing a program into a neat, hierarchical set of cooperating procedures promotes good software engineering. But it has a price.

**6.16**    Code modules promote software reusability. Code modules conveniently package procedures for reuse in multiple projects.

**6.17**    If you do not expect to use a procedure outside a code module, make the procedure **Private**. This reduces the accessibility of the procedure and avoids potential naming conflicts when other modules are added.

## Testing And Debugging Tips

**6.1** Small procedures are easier than large procedures to test and debug.

**6.2** Using auto list members and auto quick info can eliminate calls to non-existent procedures and methods by allowing the programmer to validate calls.

**6.3** The **Exit Sub** and **Exit Function** statements are often used to exit procedures and functions to avoid potential run-time errors such as division by zero.

**6.4** Avoid variable names that hide names in outer scopes. This can be accomplished simply by avoiding the use of duplicate variable names in a program. This can help eliminate subtle bugs in which the programmer may think that code in a procedure references a variable in an outer scope when that code is really referencing code in the inner scope.

**6.5** Do not call **Randomize** until you are satisfied that your program is working correctly.

## Self-Review Exercises

**6.1** Answer each of the following:
 a) Two types of modules introduced in this chapter are _____ modules and _____ modules.
 b) A procedure is invoked with a _____.
 c) A variable that is known only within the procedure in which it is defined is called a _____.
 d) The _____ of an identifier is the portion of the program in which the identifier can be used.
 e) Two ways to return control from a **Sub** procedure to a caller are _____ and _____.
 f) Visual Basic function _____ is used to produce pseudo-random numbers.
 g) _____ sets the random number seed to randomize a program so that a different sequence of random numbers is produced by **Rnd**.
 h) For a local variable in a procedure to retain its value between calls, it must be declared with keyword _____.
 i) The three possible scopes of an identifier are _____ scope, _____ scope and _____ scope.

**6.2** For each of the following, state the scope (either local scope, module scope or **Public** scope) of each of the following elements.
 a) Variable **z** declared in the general declaration of **M.BAS** with keyword **Public**.
 b) Variable **x** declared inside procedure **Cube**.
 c) Variable **y** declared in the general declaration of **M1.BAS** with keyword **Dim**.
 d) Variable **calendarYear** declared in the general declaration of form module **FRMSCD.FRM** with keyword **Dim**.
 e) **Function** procedure **CalculateSum** in the code module **BIGT.BAS**.
 f) **Public Sub** procedure **Cube3Numbers** in the code module **ILANA.BAS**.
 g) **Static** variable **c** declared in procedure **PCM**.
 h) Variable **w** declared in event procedure **Form_Load**.
 i) Variable **cat** declared in **Private** procedure **Gft** in code module **J.BAS**.
 j) Enumeration **LotNumbers** in code module **INVEST.BAS**.

**6.3** Write the procedure header for each of the following (assume that all headers are preceded by keyword **Private**):
 a) **Hypotenuse** takes two **Double** arguments, **s1** and **s2**, and returns a **Double** result.
 b) **Smallest** takes two **Single**s, **x**, **y**, and returns a **Currency** result.
 c) **Instructions** does not receive any arguments and does not return a value.

d) **IntToSingle** takes an **Integer** argument, **number** and returns a **Single** result. The procedure header should also indicate that **number** is passed call-by-value.

e) **PrintMessage** takes a **String** argument, **message** and does not return a value.

**6.4**   Write a declaration for each of the following:

a) Monetary variable **creditLimit** that is accessible to all form and code modules.

b) **Single** variable **lastVal** that is to retain its value between calls to the procedure in which it is defined.

c) **Integer number** whose scope should be restricted to the form module in which it is defined.

**6.5**   Find the error(s) in each of the following program segments. If an error can be corrected, explain how the error can be corrected:

a)
```
Private Procedure HugeJ(p As Currency) As Variant
    Dim p As Single
    p = p * 10
    Print "p is " & p
    HugeJ = p
End Procedure
```

b)
```
Enum X
    xFactor1 = "VB6 How To Program"
    xFactor2 = -2838
End X
```

c)
```
Private Function Sum(x As Long, y As Long) As Long
    Enum Codes
        Emergency = 911
        GeneralInformation = 411
    End Enum

    Sum = x + y + Emergency + GeneralInformation
End Function
```

d)
```
Sub (a As Single) As
    Static b As Single

    b = b + 1
    Print a, b
    F = a ^ 2
End Sub
```

e)
```
Public Function Product() As Long
    Dim a As Integer, b As Integer, c As Integer
    Dim result As Integer

    a = 1: b = 2: c = 3
    result = a * b * c
    Product = result
End Function
```

f)
```
Private Sub General76(Optional flag As Boolean, _
                        ByVal q As Integer) As String
    If flag Then End Sub
    Print "False " & q & " time(s) in a row!!"
End Sub
```

```
g) Private Sub Y2K(t As Integer = 1) As String
       Dim c As Integer

       For c = 1 To t
           Print "Its a massive problem!!!"
       Next c

       Y2K = "Problem has not been solved..."
   End Sub
```

## Answers to Self-Review Exercises

**6.1**   a)  form, code.
    b)  call.
    c)  local variable.
    d)  scope.
    e)  **End Sub**, **Exit Sub**.
    f)  **Rnd**.
    g)  **Randomize**.
    h)  **Static**.
    i)  local, module, **Public**.

**6.2**   a) **Public** scope. b) local scope. c) module scope.  d) module scope.  e) module scope.
f) **Public** scope. g) local scope. h) local scope. i) local scope.  j) module scope.

**6.3**   a) `Function Hypotenuse(s1 As Double, s2 As Double) As Double`
    b) `Function Smallest(x As Single, y As Single) As Currency`
    c) `Sub Instructions()`
    d) `Function IntToSingle(ByVal number As Integer) As Single`
    e) `Sub PrintMessage(message As String)`

**6.4**   a) `Public creditLimit As Currency`      ` ' in a code module`
    b) `Static lastVal As Single`         ` ' local declaration`
    c) `Dim number As Integer`            ` ' in a form module`

**6.5**   a)  Variable **p** is declared twice. **Function** should be used instead of **Procedure** because a value is being returned.

```
       Private Function HugeJ(p As Currency) As Variant
           p = p * 10
           Print "p is " & p
           HugeJ = p
       End Function
```

    b)  Enumeration constant **xFactor1** should be assigned a **Long** value, not a **String**. Enumeration should be terminated with **End Enum**.
    c)  Enumerations cannot have local scope. Moving the enumeration to the general declaration corrects the problem.
    d)  Procedure should be a **Function** procedure. Procedure name **F** is missing from the header. Return type is missing.

```
       Function F(a As Single) As Single
           Static b As Single
           b = b + 1
           Print a, b
           F = a ^ 2
       End Function
```

e) **Public** variables must be declared in the general declaration. Changing **Public** to **Dim** corrects the problem. Note that moving the declaration of **result** to the general declaration would also solve this particular problem.

```
Public Function Product() As Long
    Dim a As Integer, b As Integer, c As Integer
    Dim result As Integer

    a = 1: b = 2: c = 3
    result = a * b * c
    Product = result
End Function
```

f) Argument **flag** is **Optional**; therefore, **q** must be **Optional**. **Sub** procedures cannot specify return types in the header. The **If/Then** statement's **End Sub** should be **Exit Sub**.

```
Private Sub General76(Optional flag As Boolean, _
                      Optional ByVal q As Integer)
    If flag Then Exit Sub
    Print "False " & q & " time(s) in a row!!"
End Sub
```

g) Should be a **Function** procedure. Default values can only be used with **Optional** arguments.

```
Private Function Y2K(Optional t As Integer = 1) As String
    Dim c As Integer

    For c = 1 To t
        Print "Its a massive problem!!!"
    Next c

    Y2K = "Problem has not been solved..."
End Function
```

## Exercises

**6.6** State whether each of the following is *true* or *false*. If *false*, explain why.

a) All procedure calls pass arguments call-by-value by default.

b) **Rnd** returns a number in the range $0 < x < 1$.

c) Keyword **Static** may be applied to procedures.

d) Keyword **ByVal** applies to all variables in the parameter list that follow it.

e) **Static** variables are always declared in a procedure.

f) In a **Function** procedure call, the argument(s) passed are enclosed in parentheses.

g) A variable's storage class is determined by its scope.

h) A control may be passed to a procedure as an argument.

i) **Static** may not be applied to a procedure that has **Static** variables declared in the body.

j) To pass arguments call-by-value to a procedure, keyword **ByVal** is used in the call.

**6.7** Answer the following questions about enumeration **Z**:

```
Enum Z
    value1
    value2
    value3 = -6
    value4
```

```
    value5 = value2
    value6
End Enum
```

a) What is the value of **value1**?

b) What is the value of **value2**?

c) What is the value of **value4**?

d) What is the value of **value5**?

e) What is the value of **value6**?

f) What happens if another enumeration constant, **value4**, is added to the existing enumeration, which already contains an enumeration constant **value4**?

**6.8**     Determine if the following program segments contain error(s). For each error, explain how it can be corrected. Note: For a particular program segment, it is possible that no errors are present in the segment.

a)
```
Call ByRef MyProcedure(1, 2, 3)
```

b)
```
Call RXZ 9, 8, 7
```

c)
```
Call ANLT(varOne=:100)
```

d)
```
Public Sub C(number As Single)
    lstValue.AddItem number & "*"
    Exit Sub
End Sub
```

e) Assume that the following declaration resides in a code module's general declaration.
```
Static Public gMyNumber As Double
```

f)
```
Private Sub R(number As Integer ByVal, s As String)
    Print s & number
End Sub
```

g)
```
Public Function RedLineIX(x%, y%, z%)%
    Print x: Print y: Print z
    RedLineIX = x * y * z
End Function
```

h)
```
Private Function PrintResults(x&, y As Long) As Long
    Print "The sum is " & x + y
    PrintResults = x + y
End Function
```

i)
```
Private Static Function Square(number As Long) As Long
    Dim number As Long, temp As Long

    temp = number ^ 2
    Function Square = temp
End Function
```

j)
```
Private Static Bft(x%, y%)
    Static z as Integer
    Print x; y

    If z = 0 Then
        z = 100
    End If

    z = z + 1
End Sub
```

k)
```
Call Static Procedure003(x, y)
```

**6.9**   Answer each of the following questions.
   a)   What does it mean to choose numbers "at random"?
   b)   Why is **Rnd** useful for simulating games of chance?
   c)   Why would you randomize a program by using **Randomize**? Under what circumstances is it desirable not to randomize?
   d)   Why is it often necessary to scale and/or shift the values produced by **Rnd**?
   e)   How does using the **Int** instead of the **Fix** affect the random numbers generated by **Rnd**?
   f)   Why is computerized simulation of real-world situations a useful technique?

**6.10**   Write statements that assign random **Integer**s to the variable **n** in the following ranges:
   a)   $1 \le n \le 2$
   b)   $1 \le n \le 100$
   c)   $0 \le n \le 9$
   d)   $1000 \le n \le 1112$
   e)   $-1 \le n \le 1$
   f)   $-3 \le n \le 11$

**6.11**   For each of the following sets of **Integer**s, write a single **Print** statement that will print a number at random from the set.
   a)   2, 4, 6, 8, 10.
   b)   3, 6, 7, 9, 11.
   c)   6, 10, 14, 18, 22.

**6.12**   Find the error(s) in the following recursive **Function** procedure and explain how to correct it/them:

```
Private Function Sum(n As Integer) As Integer
    If (n = 0) Then
        Exit Function
    Else
        Sum = n + Sum(n)
    End If
End Function
```

**6.13**   What does the following **Function** procedure do?

```
' Parameter b must be a positive Integer
' to prevent infinite recursion
Public Function Mystery(a As Integer, b As Integer) As Integer
    If b = 1 Then
        Mystery = a
        Exit Function
    Else
        Mystery = a + Mystery(a, b - 1)
    End If
End Function
```

**6.14**   After you determine what the procedure of Exercise 6.13 does, modify it to operate properly after removing the restriction of the second argument being non-negative.

**6.15**   Write a program that simulates coin tossing. For each toss of the coin the program should print **Heads** or **Tails**. Let the program toss the coin 100 times, and count the number of times each side of the coin appears. Print the results. The program should call a separate **Function** procedure

**Flip** that takes no arguments and returns **0** for tails and **1** for heads. Note: If the program realistically simulates the coin tossing, then each side of the coin should appear approximately half the time.

**6.16**    Write a program that obtains a character and an **Integer** from the user and displays a square out of whatever character is contained in character parameter **fillCharacter**. Thus if side is 6 and **fillCharacter** is "**#**", then this procedure should print

```
#####
#####
#####
#####
#####
```

Note: The form's **Font** property should be changed to **Courier**.

**6.17**    A mail order house sells five different products whose retail prices are product 1— $2.98, product 2—$4.60, product 3—$9.98, product 4—$4.49 and product 5—$6.87. Write a program that reads a series of pairs of numbers as follows:

1.  Product number

2.  Quantity sold for one day

Your program should use a **Select Case** statement in a programmer-defined procedure to help determine the retail price for each product. Your program should calculate and display the total retail value of all products sold last week.

**6.18**    A parking garage charges a $6.00 minimum fee to park for up to three hours. The garage charges an additional $1.50 per hour for each hour or part thereof in excess of three hours. The maximum charge for any given 24-hour period is $25.00. Assume that no car parks for longer than 24 hours at a time. Write a program that will calculate and print the parking charges for each customer who parked his or her car in this garage yesterday. You should enter the hours parked for each customer. Your program should print the results in a neat tabular format and should calculate and print the total of yesterday's receipts. The program should use the procedure **CalculateCharges** to determine the charge for each customer.

**6.19**    Computers are playing an increasing role in education. Write a program that will help an elementary school student learn multiplication. Use **Rnd** to produce two positive one-digit **Integer**s. It should then type a question such as

```
How much is 6 times 7?
```

The student then types the answer. Your program checks the student's answer. If it is correct, print **"Very good!"** and then ask another multiplication question. If the answer is wrong, print **"No. Please try again."** and then let the student try the same question again repeatedly until the student finally gets it right.

**6.20**    The use of computers in education is referred to as computer-assisted instruction (CAI). One problem that develops in CAI environments is student fatigue. This can be eliminated by varying the computer's dialogue to hold the student's attention. Modify the program of Exercise 6.19 so that the various comments are printed for each correct answer and each incorrect answer as follows:

Responses to a correct answer

```
Very good!
Excellent!
Nice work!
Keep up the good work!
```

Responses to an incorrect answer

```
No. Please try again.
Wrong. Try once more.
Don't give up!
No. Keep trying.
```

Use the random number generator to choose a number from 1 to 4 to select an appropriate response to each answer. Use a **Select Case** structure to issue the responses. Your solution should use programmer-defined procedures.

**6.21**    More sophisticated computer-aided instruction systems monitor the student's performance over a period of time. The decision to begin a new topic is often based on the student's success with previous topics. Modify the program of Exercise 6.20 to count the number of correct and incorrect responses typed by the student. After the student types 10 answers, your program should calculate the percentage of correct responses. If the percentage is lower than 70 percent, your program should print "**Please ask your instructor for extra help**."

**6.22**    Write a program that plays the game of "guess the number" as follows: Your program choose-es the number to be guessed by selecting an **Integer** at random in the range 1 to 1000. The program then types:

```
I have a number between 1 and 1000.
Can you guess my number?
Please enter your first guess.
```

The player then types a first guess. The program responds with one of the following:

```
Excellent! You guessed the number!
Would you like to play again (y or n)?

Too low. Try again.

Too high. Try again.
```

If the player's guess is incorrect, your program should loop until the player finally gets the number right. Your program should keep telling the player "**Too high**" or "**Too low**" to help the player "ze-ro in" on the correct answer.

**6.23**    Modify the program of Exercise 6.22 to count the number of guesses the player makes. If the number is 10 or fewer, print "**Either you know the secret or you got lucky!**" If the player guesses the number in 10 tries, then print "**Ahah! You know the secret!**" If the player makes more than 10 guesses, then print "**You can do better!**" Why should it take no more than 10 guesses? Well, with each "good guess" the player should be able to eliminate half of the numbers. Now show why any number 1 to 1000 can be guessed in 10 or fewer tries.

**6.24**    Modify the craps program of Fig. 6.22 to allow wagering. Package as multiple procedures the portion of the program that runs the game of craps. Initialize variable **bankBalance** to 1000 dollars. Prompt the player to enter a **wager**. Use a loop to check that **wager** is less than or equal to **bankBalance** and if not, prompt the user to reenter **wager** until a valid **wager** is entered. Also check for **wager**s less than or equal to zero. After a correct **wager** is entered, allow the player to play a game of craps.

If the player wins, increase **bankBalance** by **wager** and display the new **bankBalance**. If the player loses, decrease **bankBalance** by **wager**, display the new **bankBalance**, check if **bankBalance** has become zero, and if so, print the message "**Sorry. You busted!**" The game should continue until either the player runs out of money or the player quits.

Write a procedure called **Chatter** that displays various messages as the game progresses to create some "chatter" such as "**Oh, you're going for broke, huh?**", or "**Aw cmon, take a chance!**", or "**You're up big. Now's the time to cash in your chips!**" Procedure **Chatter** should use random number generation and a **Select Case** structure to display the chatter. Note: The chatter does not have to be relevant to what is occurring in the game.

**6.25**    Modify Exercise 6.24 to support up to four different players. Allow each player to enter his or her name. Each player's name and bank balance should be displayed at all times.

**6.26**    Procedures are capable of returning enumeration constants. Write a **Function** procedure that returns an enumerated constant representing the month of the year. Create an enumeration, **MonthsOfYear**, which defines enumerated constants **Jan**, **Feb**, etc. Both the procedure and enumeration should reside in a code module. Write a program which verifies that the procedure is properly written.

**6.27**    Write a procedure **Maximum3** that returns the largest of three **Single** numbers. Use Visual Basic function **IIf** to implement **Maximum3**. Write a program which verifies that the procedure is properly written.

**6.28**    Write a procedure that takes an **Integer** value and returns the number with its digits reversed. For example, given the number 8456, the procedure should return 6548. Write a program which verifies that the procedure is properly written.

**6.29**    Write a program that uses a programmer-defined procedure called **CircleArea** to calculate and print the area of a circle. The user should input the radius in a **TextBox**.

**6.30**    The *greatest common divisor (GCD)* of two **Integer**s is the largest **Integer** that evenly divides each of the two numbers. Write a procedure **Gcd** that returns the greatest common divisor of two **Integer**s. Incorporate the procedure into a program that reads two values from the user.

**6.31**    Write a recursive version of the **Gcd** procedure you developed in Exercise 6.30. The **Gcd** of **x** and **y** is defined recursively as follows: If **y** is equal to **0**, then **Gcd(x, y)** is **x**; otherwise, **Gcd(x, y)** is **Gcd(y, x Mod y)**, where **Mod** is the modulus operator.

**6.32**    *(Towers of Hanoi)* Every budding computer scientist must grapple with certain classic problems, and the Towers of Hanoi (see Fig. 6.35) is one of the most famous of these. Legend has it that in a temple in the Far East, priests are attempting to move a stack of disks from one peg to another. The initial stack had 64 disks threaded onto one peg and arranged from bottom to top by decreasing size. The priests are attempting to move the stack from this peg to a second peg under the constraints that exactly one disk is moved at a time, and at no time may a larger disk be placed above a smaller disk. A third peg is available for temporarily holding disks. Supposedly the world will end when the priests complete their task, so there is little incentive for us to facilitate their efforts.

Let us assume that the priests are attempting to move the disks from peg 1 to peg 3. We wish to develop an algorithm that will print the precise sequence of peg-to-peg disk transfers.

If we were to approach this problem with conventional methods, we would rapidly find ourselves hopelessly knotted up in managing the disks. Instead, if we attack the problem with recursion in mind, it immediately becomes tractable. Moving $n$ disks can be viewed in terms of moving only $n - 1$ disks (and hence the recursion) as follows:

a)   Move $n - 1$ disks from peg 1 to peg 2, using peg 3 as a temporary holding area.
b)   Move the last disk (the largest) from peg 1 to peg 3.
c)   Move the $n - 1$ disks from peg 2 to peg 3, using peg 1 as a temporary holding area.

The process ends when the last task involves moving $n = 1$ disk (i.e., the base case). This is accomplished by trivially moving the disk without the need for a temporary holding area.

**Fig. 6.35**   The Towers of Hanoi for the case with four disks.

Write a program to solve the Towers of Hanoi problem. Allow the user to enter the number of disks in a **TextBox**. Use a recursive **Tower** procedure with four parameters:

a)  The number of disks to be moved
b)  The peg on which these disks are initially threaded
c)  The peg to which this stack of disks is to be moved
d)  The peg to be used as a temporary holding area

Your program should display in a **ListBox** the precise instructions it will take to move the disks from the starting peg to the destination peg. For example, to move a stack of three disks from peg 1 to peg 3, your program should print the following series of moves:

$1 \rightarrow 3$ (This means move one disk from peg 1 to peg 3.)
$1 \rightarrow 2$
$3 \rightarrow 2$
$1 \rightarrow 3$
$2 \rightarrow 1$
$2 \rightarrow 3$
$1 \rightarrow 3$

**6.33**   Any program that can be implemented recursively can be implemented iteratively, although sometimes with more difficulty and less clarity. Try writing an iterative version of the Towers of Hanoi. If you succeed, compare your iterative version with the recursive version you developed in Exercise 6.32. Investigate issues of performance, clarity and your ability to demonstrate the correctness of the programs.

**6.34**   Write a procedure **IntegerPower(base, exponent)** that returns the value of

$base \ ^{exponent}$

For example, **IntegerPower(3, 4) = 3 * 3 * 3 * 3**. Assume that **exponent** is a positive, non-zero **Integer**, and **base** is an **Integer**. Procedure **IntegerPower** should use a loop to control the calculation. Do not use any Visual Basic math functions. Incorporate this procedure into a program that reads **Integer** values from **TextBox**es for **base** and **exponent** from the user and performs the calculation with procedure **IntegerPower**.

**6.35**   Write a recursive version of procedure **IntegerPower** that you developed in Exercise 6.34. The recursion step would use the relationship

$base \ ^{exponent} = base \cdot base \ ^{exponent - 1}$

and the terminating condition occurs when **exponent** is equal to **1** because

$$base^1 = base$$

Incorporate this procedure into a program that enables the user to enter the **base** and **exponent**.

**6.36**    An **Integer** number is said to be a *perfect number* if its factors, including 1 (but not the number itself), sum to the number. For example, 6 is a perfect number because $6 = 1 + 2 + 3$. Write a procedure **Perfect** that determines if parameter **number** is a perfect number. Use this procedure in a program that determines and prints all the perfect numbers between 1 and 1000. Print the factors of each perfect number to confirm that the number is indeed perfect. Challenge the computing power of your computer by testing numbers much larger than 1000.

**6.37**    An **Integer** is said to be *prime* if it is divisible only by 1 and itself. For example, 2, 3, 5 and 7 are prime, but 4, 6, 8 and 9 are not.
  a) Write a procedure that determines if a number is prime.
  b) Use this procedure in a program that determines and prints all the prime numbers between 1 and 10000. How many of these 10000 numbers do you really have to test before being sure that you have found all the primes?
  c) Initially you might think that $n/2$ is the upper limit for which you must test to see if a number is prime, but you need only go as high as the square root of $n$. Why? Rewrite the program, and run it both ways. Estimate the performance improvement.

**6.38**    Write program segments that accomplish each of the following:
  a) Calculate the **Integer** part of the quotient when **Integer a** is divided by **Integer b**.
  b) Calculate the **Integer** remainder when **Integer a** is divided by **Integer b**.
  c) Use the program pieces developed in a) and b) to write a procedure **DisplayDigits** that receives an **Integer** between **1** and **99999** and prints it as a series of digits, each pair of which is separated by two spaces. For example, the **Integer 4562** should be printed as
       **4  5  6  2**.
  d) Incorporate the procedure developed in part (c) into a program that inputs an **Integer** from the user and invokes **DisplayDigits** from a button's **Click** event procedure by passing the procedure the **Integer** entered.

**6.39**    Implement the following **Integer** procedures:
  a) Procedure **Celsius** returns the Celsius equivalent of a Fahrenheit temperature using the calculation

       ```
       C = 5 / 9 * (F - 32)
       ```

  b) Procedure **Fahrenheit** returns the Fahrenheit equivalent of a Celsius temperature.

       ```
       F = 9 / 5 * C + 32
       ```

  c) Use these procedures to write a program that enables the user to enter either a Fahrenheit temperature and display the Celsius equivalent or enter a Celsius temperature and display the Fahrenheit equivalent.

**6.40**    Write a procedure **Multiple** that determines for a pair of **Integer**s whether the second **Integer** is a multiple of the first. The procedure should take two **Integer** arguments and return **True** if the second is a multiple of the first, and **False** otherwise. Incorporate this procedure into a program that inputs a series of **Integer** pairs (one pair at a time using **TextBox**es).

**6.41**    Write a program that inputs **Integer**s (one at a time) and passes them one at a time to procedure **IsEven**, which uses the modulus operator to determine if an **Integer** is even. The procedure should take an **Integer** argument and return **True** if the **Integer** is even and **False** otherwise.

**6.42**    Write a **Function** procedure that takes two **String** arguments representing a first name and a last name, concatenates the two **String**s to form a new **String** representing the full name and returns the concatenated **String**.

**6.43**    Write a procedure that keeps count of how many times it is called. Write this procedure two different ways. First, use a module value to keep count. Then write a version that uses a static local variable to keep count. In what situations might the programmer prefer to write the procedure one way versus the other?

**6.44**    Write a **Function** procedure **ToMorseCode** that takes one **String** argument (containing either a single letter or digit) and returns a **String** containing the Morse code equivalent. Figure 6.36 lists the Morse code for letters and digits.

| Character | Code | Character | Code |
|---|---|---|---|
| A | . – | T | – |
| B | – . . . | U | . . – |
| C | – . – . | V | . . . – |
| D | – . . | W | . – – |
| E | . | X | – . . – |
| F | . . – . | Y | – . – – |
| G | – – . | Z | – – . . |
| H | . . . . | | |
| I | . . | Digits | |
| J | . – – – | 1 | . – – – – |
| K | – . – | 2 | . . – – – |
| L | . – . . | 3 | . . . – – |
| M | – – | 4 | . . . . – |
| N | – . | 5 | . . . . . |
| O | – – – | 6 | – . . . . |
| P | . – – . | 7 | – – . . . |
| Q | – – . – | 8 | – – – . . |
| R | . – . | 9 | – – – – . |
| S | . . . | 0 | – – – – – |

**Fig. 6.36**    The letters of the alphabet as expressed in international Morse code.

# 7

# Arrays

## Objectives

- To introduce the array data structure.
- To understand the use of arrays to store, sort, and search lists and tables of values.
- To understand how to declare an array, initialize an array, and refer to individual elements of an array.
- To be able to pass arrays to procedures.
- To understand basic sorting techniques.
- To be able to create and manipulate multidimensional arrays.
- To be able to create and use control arrays.
- To understand how to create, use, and redimension dynamic arrays.
- To be able to use **ParamArray** and **Array**.

*With sobs and tears he sorted out*
*Those of the largest size*
Lewis Carroll

*Attempt the end, and never stand to doubt;*
*Nothing's so hard, but search will find it out.*
Robert Herrick

*Now go, write it before them in a table,*
*and note it in a book.*
Isaiah 30:8

# Outline

## 7.1 Introduction

This chapter serves as an introduction to the important topic of data structures. *Arrays* are data structures consisting of related data items of the same type. In Chapter 15 we discuss the notions of *user-defined types*—capable of holding related data items of possibly different types. A *fixed-size array*'s size does not change during program execution; a *dynamic array*'s size can change during execution.

## 7.2 Arrays

An array is a consecutive group of memory locations that all have the same name and the same type. To refer to a particular location or element in the array, we specify the array name and the array element *position number*. Arrays are named like any other variable.

Figure 7.1 shows a *six-element* **Integer** array named **numbers**. Any one of these elements may be referred to by giving the array name followed by the element position number in parentheses, **()**. The first array element is at position number zero. Thus, the first element of **numbers** is referred to as **numbers(0)**, the second element of **numbers** is referred to as **numbers(1)**, the third element of **numbers** is referred to as **numbers(2)**, the fourth element of **numbers** is referred to as **numbers(3)**, and, in general, the $i^{th}$ element of **numbers** is referred to as **numbers(i-1)**.

The position number contained within parentheses is more formally called an *index*. An index must be a **Long** or a **Long** expression in the range –2,147,483,648 to 2,147,483,648 (any floating-point number is rounded to the nearest whole number). We will discuss ways to have indexes begin at numbers other than 0 later in the chapter.

If a program uses an expression as a index, then the expression is evaluated to determine the value of index. For example, if we assume that **a** is 1 and **b** is 2, then the statement

```
numbers(a + b) = numbers(a + b) + 2
```

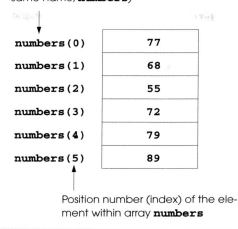

Name of array (Note that all elements of this array have the same name, **numbers**)

| | |
|---|---|
| **numbers(0)** | 77 |
| **numbers(1)** | 68 |
| **numbers(2)** | 55 |
| **numbers(3)** | 72 |
| **numbers(4)** | 79 |
| **numbers(5)** | 89 |

Position number (index) of the element within array **numbers**

**Fig. 7.1**    A six-element array.

adds **2** to **numbers(3)**.

Let us examine array **numbers** in Fig. 7.1 more closely. The array name is **numbers**. Its six elements are referred to as **numbers(0)**, **numbers(1)**, **numbers(2)**, **numbers(3)**, **numbers(4)** and **numbers(5)**. The value of **numbers(0)** is 77, the value of **numbers(1)** is 68, the value of **numbers(2)** is 55, the value of **numbers(3)** is 72, the value of **numbers(4)** is 79 and the value of **numbers(5)** is 89. To print the sum of the values contained in the first three elements of **numbers**, we write

```
Print numbers(0) + numbers(1) + numbers(2)
```

To divide the value of element 3 (where element indexes begin at 0) of **numbers** by 2 and assign the result to the variable **x**, we would write

```
x = numbers(3) \ 2
```

*Testing and Debugging Tip 7.1*

*It is important to note the difference between the "seventh element of the array" and "array position number seven." Because array indexes may begin at 0, the "seventh element of the array" has an index of 6, while "array position number seven" has an index of 7 and is actually the eighth element of the array. This is a source of "off-by-one" errors.*

## 7.3 Declaring Arrays

Arrays occupy space in memory. The programmer specifies the array *type* and the number of elements required by the array so that the compiler may reserve the appropriate amount of memory. Arrays may be declared as **Public** (in a code module), module or local. *Module arrays* are declared in the general declarations using keyword **Dim** or **Private**. *Local arrays* are declared in a procedure using **Dim** or **Static**. Arrays must be declared explicitly with keyword **As**.

*Common Programming Error 7.1*

*Attempting to declare an array implicitly is a syntax error.*

*Common Programming Error 7.2*

*Attempting to declare a **Public** array in a form module is a syntax error.*

*Testing and Debugging Tip 7.2*

*Assuming that elements of a local **Static** array are initialized to zero every time a procedure is called can result in logic errors.*

The declaration

```
Dim numbers(5) As Integer
```

tells the compiler to reserve six elements for **Integer** array **numbers**. The value **5** defines the *upper bound* (i.e., the highest valid index) of **numbers**. The *lower bound* (the lowest valid index) of **numbers** defaults to **0**. When an upper bound is specified in the declaration, a fixed-size array is created.

*Common Programming Error 7.3*

*Attempting to access an index that is smaller than the lower bound or greater than the upper bound is a run-time error.*

Memory may be reserved for several arrays with a single declaration. The declaration

```
Dim b(99) As Integer, x(26) As Long, s(14) As String, a@(4)
```

reserves 100 elements for **Integer** array **b**, 27 elements for **Long** array **x**, 15 elements for **String** array **s** and four elements for **Currency** array **a**.

Individual numeric array elements are initialized to zero by default. The programmer can explicitly initialize the array with assignment statements. For example, the lines

```
numbers(0) = 77
numbers(1) = 68
numbers(2) = 55
numbers(3) = 72
numbers(4) = 79
numbers(5) = 89
```

would initialize **numbers** to the values shown in Fig. 7.1. Repetition statements can also be used to initialize arrays. For example, the **For**

```
For x = 0 to 30 Step 3
    h(i) = x
    i = i + 1
Next x
```

initializes the elements of **h** to the values 0, 3, 6, 9, ..., 30.

*Common Programming Error 7.4*

*Not initializing the elements of an array whose elements should be initialized is a logic error.*

## 7.4 Examples Using Arrays

The program in Fig. 7.2 uses a **For** to print the contents of ten-element **Integer** array **n**. By default, each element of **n** is initialized to zero. The program introduces functions **LBound** and **UBound**. Function **LBound** returns the lower bound (i.e., the lowest-numbered index value) and function **UBound** returns the upper bound (i.e., the highest-numbered index value).

```
1   ' Fig. 7.2
2   ' Initializing array elements to 0
3   Option Explicit      ' General declaration
4
5   Private Sub cmdPrint_Click()
6       Dim n(9) As Integer      ' 10 Elements
7       Dim x As Integer
8
9       Call Cls
10      Print "Index" & Space$(3) & "Value"
11
12      ' Ouput values. By default array n has
13      ' each element initialized to 0
14      For x = LBound(n) To UBound(n)
15          Print Space$(2) & x & Space$(7) & n(x)
16      Next x
17
18  End Sub
19
20  Private Sub cmdExit_Click()
21      End
22  End Sub
```

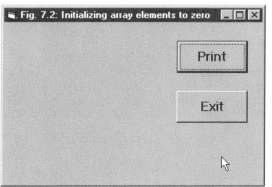

Initial GUI at execution.

**Fig. 7.2**    Printing the elements of an array (part 1 of 2).

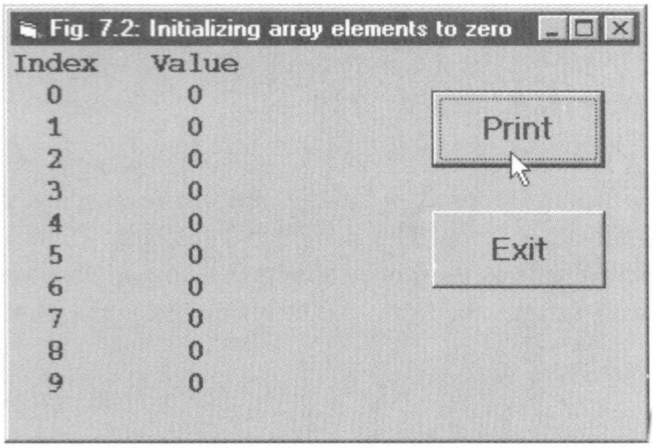

GUI after user has pressed **Print**.

**Fig. 7.2**   Printing the elements of an array (part 2 of 2).

The program in Fig. 7.3 initializes the elements of a ten-element array **s** to the **Integer**s 2, 4, 6, …, 20, and prints the array element contents in a tabular format. The numbers are generated by multiplying each successive value of the loop counter by 2 and adding 2.

```
1   ' Fig. 7.3
2   ' Initializing an array
3   Option Explicit        ' General declaration
4
5   Private Sub cmdPrint_Click()
6      Dim s(9) As Integer
7      Dim x As Integer
8
9      Call Cls
10
11     ' Initialize array to even elements
12     For x = LBound(s) To UBound(s)
13        s(x) = 2 + 2 * x
14     Next x
15
16     Print "Index" & Space$(3) & "Value"
17
18     For x = LBound(s) To UBound(s)
19        Print Space$(2) & x & Space$(7) & s(x)
20     Next x
21
22   End Sub
23
24   Private Sub cmdExit_Click()
25      End
26   End Sub
```

**Fig. 7.3**   Initializing an array to even **Integer**s (part 1 of 2).

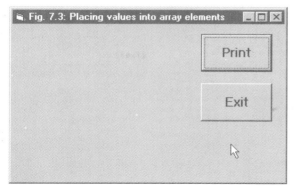

Initial GUI at execution.

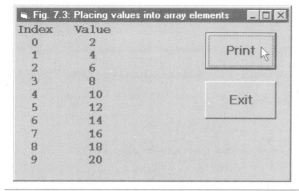

GUI after user presses **Print**.

Fig. 7.3    Initializing an array to even **Integer**s (part 2 of 2).

Our next example uses arrays to summarize the results of data collected in a survey. Consider the problem statement:

*Forty students were asked to rate the quality of the food in the student cafeteria on a scale of 1 to 10 (1 means awful and 10 means excellent). Place the 40 responses in an Integer array and summarize the results of the poll.*

This is a typical array application (see Fig. 7.4). We wish to summarize the number of responses of each type (i.e., 1 through 10). The array **responses** is a 40-element array of the students' responses. We randomly generate the poll data. Ten-element array **frequency** counts the number of occurrences of each response.

Up to this point, we have used the default lower bound of 0. We could ignore the first element, **frequency(0)**, because it is more logical to have the first response increment **frequency(1)** than **frequency(0)**. This would require oversizing the array by one element. A more convenient solution is to use the **Option Base** statement. **Option Base** sets the lower bound to **0** or **1** and is placed in the general declaration. This allows us to use each response directly as the index in the **frequency** array.

*Common Programming Error 7.5*

*Placing an array declaration before the Option Base statement is a syntax error.*

*Common Programming Error 7.6*

*Attempting to give **Option Base** a value other than **0** or **1** is a syntax error.*

*Testing and Debugging Tip 7.3*

*Array lower bounds and upper bounds can vary. Use functions **LBound** and **UBound** to ensure that each index is in range (i.e., within the bounds of the array).*

```
1   ' Fig. 7.4
2   ' Student poll summation program
3   Option Explicit                      ' General declaration
4
5   ' Set default lower bound to 1
6   Option Base 1                        ' General declaration
7
8   Dim mResponses(40) As Integer   ' General declaration
9
10  Private Sub Form_Load()
11     Dim x As Integer
12
13     ' Generate survey data
14     For x = LBound(mResponses) To UBound(mResponses)
15        mResponses(x) = 1 + Int(Rnd() * 10)
16     Next x
17
18  End Sub
19
20  Private Sub cmdPrint_Click()
21     Dim frequency(10) As Integer ' 10 Elements
22     Dim x As Integer
23
24     Call Cls
25     Call Randomize
26
27     ' Calculate results
28     For x = LBound(mResponses) To UBound(mResponses)
29        frequency(mResponses(x)) = frequency(mResponses(x)) + 1
30     Next x
31     Print "Rating" & Space$(3) & "Frequency"
32     For x = LBound(frequency) To UBound(frequency)
33        Print Space$(3) & x & vbTab & vbTab & frequency(x)
34     Next x
35     cmdPrint.Enabled = False
36  End Sub
37
38  Private Sub cmdExit_Click()
39     End
40  End Sub
```

**Fig. 7.4**    A student poll analysis program (part 1 of 2).

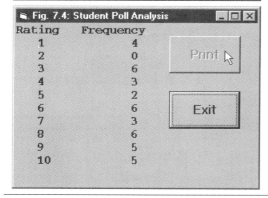

**Fig. 7.4**    A student poll analysis program (part 2 of 2).

    *Software Engineering Observation 7.1*

*Strive for program clarity. It is sometimes worthwhile to trade off the most efficient use of memory or processor time in favor of writing clearer programs.*

    *Performance Tip 7.1*

*Sometimes performance considerations outweigh clarity considerations.*

The program introduces event procedure **Form_Load**, which is called by Visual Basic when the form is created at run time. During the form's lifetime, **Form_Load** is called only once by Visual Basic. In **Form_Load**, we randomly generate the data that represent the student poll responses and place them into **mResponses**.

Procedure **cmdPrint_Click** calculates and prints the frequency of each response. The first **For** loop takes each responses from **mResponses** and increments one of the ten frequency counters (**frequency(1)** to **frequency(10)**) with the statement

```
frequency(mResponses(x)) = frequency(mResponses(x)) + 1
```

This statement increments the appropriate **frequency** counter depending on the value of **mResponses(x)**. For example, when the counter **x** is 1, **mResponses(x)** is 1, so **frequency(mResponses(x))** is actually interpreted as

```
frequency(1) = frequency(1) + 1
```

which increments array index one. When **x** is 1, **mResponses(x)** is 2, so **frequency(mResponses(x))** is interpreted as

```
frequency(2) = frequency(2) + 1
```

which increments array index two. When **x** is 2, **mResponses(x)** is 6, so **frequency(mResponses(x))** is interpreted as

```
frequency(6) = frequency(6) + 1
```

which increments array index six, and so on. Note that regardless of the number of responses processed in the survey, only a ten-element array is required to summarize the results. If the data contained invalid values such as 13, the program would attempt to add 1 to **frequency(13)**. This would be outside the bounds of the array, which is a run-time error. Thus, an executing program can walk off either end of an array without warning.

*Testing and Debugging Tip 7.4*

*The program should be written to ensure that all array indexes remain within the bounds of the array.*

*Testing and Debugging Tip 7.5*

*Programs should validate the correctness of all input values to prevent erroneous information from affecting a program's calculations.*

In Chapter 6 we stated that we would show a more elegant method of writing the dice-rolling program of Fig. 6.20. The program rolls 12 six-sided dice each time the **Roll** button is pressed. A more compact version of this program that uses arrays is shown in Fig. 7.5.

```
1   ' Fig. 7.5
2   ' Six-sided die simulation
3   Option Explicit
4
5   ' Declare module variables
6   Dim mFrequency(1 To 6) As Integer
7   Dim mTotalRolls As Integer
8
9   Private Sub cmdRoll_Click()
10     Call Randomize                          ' Seed function Rnd
11     mTotalRolls = mTotalRolls + 12
12
13     Call DisplayDie(imgDie1)
14     Call DisplayDie(imgDie2)
15     Call DisplayDie(imgDie3)
16     Call DisplayDie(imgDie4)
17     Call DisplayDie(imgDie5)
18     Call DisplayDie(imgDie6)
19     Call DisplayDie(imgDie7)
20     Call DisplayDie(imgDie8)
```

**Fig. 7.5** Rolling 12 six-sided dice (part 1 of 3).

```
21        Call DisplayDie(imgDie9)
22        Call DisplayDie(imgDie10)
23        Call DisplayDie(imgDie11)
24        Call DisplayDie(imgDie12)
25
26        Call lstStatistics.Clear
27        Call DisplayStats
28     End Sub
29
30     Private Sub DisplayDie(imgDie As Image)
31        Dim face As Integer
32
33        face = 1 + Int(Rnd() * 6)
34
35        ' Replaces Select Case structure
36        mFrequency(face) = mFrequency(face) + 1
37        imgDie.Picture = LoadPicture("d:\images\common\die" _
38                                     & face & ".gif")
39     End Sub
40
41     Private Sub DisplayStats()
42        Dim x As Integer
43
44        lstStatistics.AddItem "Face" & vbTab & "Frequency" & _
45                               vbTab & "Percent"
46
47        ' Replaces multiple output statements
48        For x = LBound(mFrequency) To UBound(mFrequency)
49           lstStatistics.AddItem x & vbTab & mFrequency(x) & vbTab _
50                                 & vbTab & Format$(mFrequency(x) / _
51                                 mTotalRolls, "Percent")
52        Next x
53     End Sub
```

**Fig. 7.5**    Rolling 12 six-sided dice (part 2 of 3).

The declaration

```
    Dim mFrequency(1 To 6) As Integer
```

declares **Integer** array **mFrequency**. Keyword **To** is used to set the lower bound to **1** and the upper bound to **6**. Keyword **To** provides the greatest flexibility for setting array index ranges. Lower bound values set with **To** are not affected by **Option Base** (i.e., **mFrequency**'s lower bound is always **1** even if **Option Base** is **0**).

*Common Programming Error 7.7*

*Placing a value on the left side of **To** greater than the value on the right side of **To** is a syntax error.*

In **DisplayDie**, the statement

```
    mFrequency(face) = mFrequency(face) + 1
```

replaces the **Select Case** structure of Fig. 6.20. In **DisplayStats**, several **Print** statements are replaced with a **For** loop that **Print**s each array element.

Initial GUI at execution.

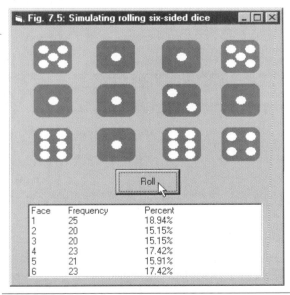

GUI after user has pressed **Roll** 11 times.

**Fig. 7.5** Rolling 12 six-sided dice (part 3 of 3).

## 7.5 Passing Arrays to Procedures

To pass an array argument to a procedure, specify the name of the array followed by a pair of empty parentheses. For example, if array **hourlyTemperatures** is declared as

```
Dim hourlyTemperatures(24) As Integer
```

the call

> **Call ModifyArray(hourlyTemperatures())**

passes array **hourlyTemperatures** to procedure **ModifyArray**. Arrays are automatically passed call-by-reference—the callee can modify the element values in the caller's original array.

*Performance Tip 7.2*

*Passing arrays call-by-reference makes sense for performance reasons. If arrays were passed call-by-value, a copy of each element would be passed. For large, frequently passed arrays, this would be time consuming and would consume considerable storage for the copies of the array elements.*

Individual array elements are also passed call-by-reference. To pass an element of an array to a procedure, use the array element as an argument in the call. For example, the call

> **Call PassOneElement(hourlyTemperatures(5))**

would pass the array element corresponding to index **5** to **PassOneElement**.

For a procedure to receive an array through a call, the parameter list must specify that an array will be received. For example, the procedure header for **ModifyArray** might be written as

> **Private Sub ModifyArray(a() As Integer)**

indicating that **ModifyArray** expects to receive an **Integer** array in parameter **a**. The size of the array is not specified between the array parentheses. Because arrays are passed call-by-reference, when the callee uses the array name **a**, it will in fact be referring to the actual array in the caller (array **hourlyTemperatures** in the preceding call).

*Common Programming Error 7.8*

*Placing any number in the parentheses of an array parameter variable is a syntax error.*

For a procedure to receive an array element from a call, the procedure declares a variable of the type passed. For example, the procedure header for **PassOneElement** might be written as

> **Private Sub PassOneElement(k as Integer)**

Variable **k** refers to **hourlyTemperatures(5)**.

There may be situations in which a procedure should not be allowed to modify array elements. Because arrays are always passed call-by-reference, modification of array values is difficult to control. One solution is to pass each element individually call-by-value, but remember that this can cause performance problems.

*Common Programming Error 7.9*

*Attempting to pass an array call-by-value is a syntax error.*

Array elements are passed call-by-value with keyword **ByVal** or parentheses. For example, to pass the eighth index of **hourlyTemperatures** call-by-value to procedure **TempGauge**, we write

```
        Call TempGauge((hourlyTemperatures(8)))
```

or we write

```
        Private Sub TempGauge(ByVal hourlyTemp as Integer)
```

which uses keyword **ByVal**. The parentheses in the call and keyword **ByVal** in the declaration can be used together or separately.

The program of Fig. 7.6 demonstrates passing an array and passing array elements to a procedure.

```
1    ' Fig. 7.6
2    ' Passing array elements and individual array
3    ' elements to procedures
4    Option Explicit             ' General declaration
5
6    ' Declare array with indexes between -5 and 5
7    Dim mArray(-5 To 5) As Integer    ' General declaration
8
9    Private Sub cmdDisplay_Click()
10      Dim x As Integer
11
12      ' Initialize array and list boxes
13      Call Initialize
14
15      ' Pass whole array call-by-reference
16      Call ModifyArray(mArray())
17
18      ' Print modified values to list box
19      Call PrintModified
20   End Sub
21
22   Private Sub cmdElement_Click()
23      Dim x As Integer
24
25      ' Initialize array
26      Call Initialize
27
28      For x = LBound(mArray) To UBound(mArray)
29
30         ' Pass each element call-by-reference
31         Call ModifyElement(mArray(x))
32      Next x
33
34      Call PrintModified
35   End Sub
36
37   Private Sub cmdExit_Click()
38      End
39   End Sub
40
```

**Fig. 7.6**　Passing an array to a procedure (part 1 of 3).

```
41   Private Sub Initialize()
42      Dim x As Integer
43
44      ' Clear list boxes
45      lstOriginal.Clear
46      lstModified.Clear
47
48      ' Place value into array
49      For x = LBound(mArray) To UBound(mArray)
50         mArray(x) = x
51         lstOriginal.AddItem mArray(x)
52      Next x
53
54   End Sub
55
56   Private Sub PrintModified()
57      Dim x As Integer
58
59      For x = LBound(mArray) To UBound(mArray)
60         lstModified.AddItem mArray(x)
61      Next x
62
63   End Sub
64
65   Private Sub ModifyArray(a() As Integer)
66      Dim x As Integer
67
68      For x = LBound(a) To UBound(a)
69         a(x) = a(x) * 2
70      Next x
71
72   End Sub
73
74   Private Sub ModifyElement(element As Integer)
75      element = element * 5
76   End Sub
```

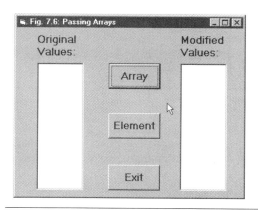

Initial GUI at execution.

**Fig. 7.6**    Passing an array to a procedure (part 2 of 3).

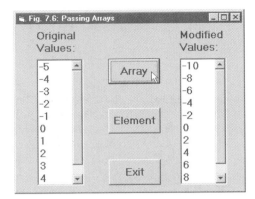

GUI after user presses **Array**.

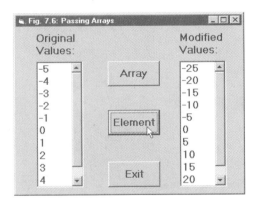

GUI after user presses **Element**.

**Fig. 7.6**   Passing a array to a procedure (part 3 of 3).

Line 16's procedure call,

```
Call ModifyArray(mArray())
```

passes **mArray** by-reference to **ModifyArray**, where **mArray**'s elements are then multiplied by **2**. When control is returned to **cmdDisplay_Click**, procedure **PrintModified** is called to update **ListBox lstModified**.

Event procedure **cmdElement_Click**'s call,

```
Call ModifyElement(mArray(x))
```

passes each individual array element one at a time to **ModifyElement**. Each element is passed call-by-reference. Procedure **ModifyElement** multiplies each element by **5** and stores the result in the element. When control is returned to **cmdElement_Click**, procedure **PrintModified** is called to update **ListBox lstModified**.

## 7.6 Sorting Arrays

*Sorting* data (i.e., placing the data into some particular order such as ascending or descending) is one of the most important computing applications. A bank sorts all checks by account number so that it can prepare individual bank statements at the end of each month. Telephone companies sort their lists of accounts in telephone books by last name and, within that, by first name to make it easy to find phone numbers. Virtually every organization must sort some data and, in many cases, massive amounts of data. Sorting data is an intriguing problem that has attracted intense research efforts in the field of computer science. In this chapter we discuss the simplest known sorting scheme, and in the exercises we investigate more complex schemes that yield superior performance.

*Performance Tip 7.3*

*Sometimes the simplest algorithms perform poorly. Their virtue is that they are easy to write, test and debug. However, more complex algorithms are often needed to realize maximum performance.*

The program in Fig. 7.7 sorts the values of the ten-element array **mArray** into ascending order. The technique we use is called the *bubble sort* or the *sinking sort* because smaller values gradually "bubble" their way to the top of the array like air bubbles rising in water and larger values "sink" to the bottom of the array. The technique is to make several passes through the array. On each pass, successive pairs of elements are compared. If a pair is in increasing order (or the values are identical), we leave the values as they are. If a pair is in decreasing order, we swap the values in the array. **Sub** procedure **BubbleSort** performs the sort. For reusability, we place **BubbleSort** in a code module.

```
1    ' Fig. 7.7
2    ' Bubble Sort
3    Option Explicit
4    Option Base 1
5    Dim mArray(10) As Integer
6
7    Private Sub cmdGenerate_Click()
8        Dim x As Integer
9
10       Call Randomize          ' Randomize Rnd
11       Call lstOriginal.Clear  ' Clear data
12       Erase mArray            ' Clear array
13
```

**Fig. 7.7**   Bubble sort program (part 1 of 4).

```
14      ' Generate numbers
15      For x = LBound(mArray) To UBound(mArray)
16         mArray(x) = 1 + Int(100 * Rnd())
17         Call lstOriginal.AddItem(mArray(x))
18      Next x
19
20      Call lstSorted.Clear      ' Clear ListBox
21      cmdSort.Enabled = True    ' Enable Sort button
22   End Sub
23
24   Private Sub cmdSort_Click()
25      Dim x As Integer
26
27      Call lstSorted.Clear      ' Clear ListBox
28      Call BubbleSort(mArray)  ' Sort the array
29
30      For x = 1 To UBound(mArray)
31         Call lstSorted.AddItem(mArray(x))
32      Next x
33
34      cmdSort.Enabled = False
35   End Sub
36
37   Private Sub cmdExit_Click()
38      End
39   End Sub
```

**Fig. 7.7**    Bubble sort program (part 2 of 4).

```
40   ' Module modBubble.bas
41   Option Explicit
42
43   Public Sub BubbleSort(theArray() As Integer)
44      Dim pass As Integer, compare As Integer
45      Dim hold As Integer
46
47      For pass = 1 To (UBound(theArray) - 1)
48
49         For compare = 1 To (UBound(theArray) - 1)
50
51            If theArray(compare) > theArray(compare + 1) Then
52               hold = theArray(compare)
53               theArray(compare) = theArray(compare + 1)
54               theArray(compare + 1) = hold
55            End If
56
57         Next compare
58
59      Next pass
60
61   End Sub
```

**Fig. 7.7**    Bubble sort program (part 3 of 4).

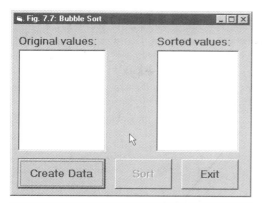

Initial GUI at execution.

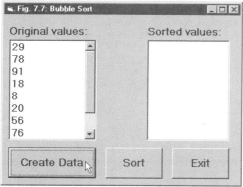

GUI after user presses **Create Data**.

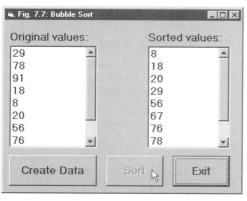

GUI after user presses **Sort**.

**Fig. 7.7**    Bubble sort program (part 4 of 4).

In **cmdSort_Click**, **BubbleSort** is called and passed **mArray**. **BubbleSort** declares parameter variable **theArray** to refer to **mArray**. All comparisons and swaps are done using **theArray**—which is an alias for **mArray**.

First **BubbleSort** compares **theArray(1)** to **theArray(2)**, then **theArray(2)** to **theArray(3)**, then **theArray(3)** to **theArray(4)**, and so on until it completes the pass by comparing **theArray(9)** to **theArray(10)**. Although there are ten elements, only nine comparisons are performed. Because of the way the successive comparisons are made, a large value can move down the array many positions on a single pass, but a small value can move up only one position. On the first pass, the largest value is guaranteed to sink to the bottom element of the array, **theArray(10)**. On the second pass, the second-largest value is guaranteed to sink to **theArray(9)**. On the ninth pass, the ninth-largest value sinks to **theArray(2)**. This leaves the smallest value in **theArray(1)**, so only nine passes are needed to sort a ten-element array.

The sorting is performed by nested **For** loops. If a swap is necessary, it is performed by the three assignments

```
hold = theArray(compare)
theArray(compare) = theArray(compare + 1)
theArray(compare + 1) = hold
```

where the extra variable **hold** temporarily stores one of the two values being swapped. The swap cannot be performed with only the two assignments

```
theArray(compare) = theArray(compare + 1)
theArray(compare + 1) = theArray(compare)
```

If, for example, **theArray(compare)** is 7 and **theArray(compare + 1)** is 5, after the first assignment both values will be 5 and the value 7 will be lost. Hence the need for the extra variable **hold**.

The chief virtue of the bubble sort is that it is easy to program. However, the bubble sort runs slowly. This becomes apparent when sorting large arrays. In the exercises, we will develop more efficient versions of the bubble sort and investigate sorts that are far more efficient than the bubble sort.

## 7.7 Searching Arrays: Linear Search and Binary Search

Often, a programmer will be working with large amounts of data stored in arrays. It may be necessary to determine whether an array contains a value that matches a certain *key value*. The process of finding a particular element of an array is called *searching*. In this section we discuss the simplest searching technique—the *linear search*. The linear search works well for small arrays or for unsorted arrays, but linear searching is inefficient for large, sorted arrays. If the array is sorted, the high-speed binary search technique can be used.

The linear search (Fig. 7.8) compares each element of the array with the *search key*. Since the array is not in any particular order, it is just as likely that the value will be found in the first element as in the last. On average, therefore, the program compares the search key with half the elements of the array to locate a value in the array. To determine that a value is not in the array, the program compares the search key to every array element.

The binary search algorithm removes from consideration one half of the elements in the array being searched after each comparison. The algorithm locates the middle element of the array and compares it to the search key. If they are equal, the search key is found and the array index of that element is returned. Otherwise, the problem is reduced to searching one half of the array. If the search key is less than the middle element of the array, the first half of the array is searched, otherwise the second half of the array is searched. If the search key is not the middle element in the specified subarray (piece of the original array), the algorithm is repeated on one quarter of the original array, then one eighth, then one sixteenth, and so on. The search continues until the search key is equal to the middle element of a subarray or until the subarray consists of one element that is not equal to the search key (i.e., the search key is not found).

```
1    ' Fig. 7.8
2    ' Demonstrating a linear search
3    Option Explicit
4    Option Base 1
5    Dim mArray(10) As Integer
6
7    Private Sub cmdSearch_Click()
8       Dim searchKey As Integer    ' Value to search for
9       Dim element As Integer      ' Index of Value
10
11      lblResult.Caption = ""
12      searchKey = txtKey.Text
13
14      ' Call LinearSearch and pass array and key
15      element = LinearSearch(mArray(), searchKey)
16
17      If element <> -1 Then
18         lblResult.Caption = "Value was found."
19      Else
20         lblResult.Caption = "Value was not found."
21      End If
22
23   End Sub
24
25   Private Sub Form_Load()
26      Call lstData_Click
27   End Sub
28
29   Private Sub lstData_Click()
30      Dim x As Integer
31
32      Call Randomize
33      Call lstData.Clear
34      lblResult.Caption = ""
35
36      ' Generate some random data
37      For x = LBound(mArray) To UBound(mArray)
38         mArray(x) = 1 + Int(10000 * Rnd())
39         Call lstData.AddItem(mArray(x))
40      Next x
41
42   End Sub
43
44   Private Sub cmdExit_Click()
45      End
46   End Sub
```

**Fig. 7.8**   Linear search program (part 1 of 3).

```
47  ' Code module modLinear.bas
48  Option Explicit
49
50  Function LinearSearch(a() As Integer, key As Integer) As Integer
51     Dim x As Integer
52
53     For x = LBound(a) To UBound(a)
54
55        If a(x) = key Then
56           LinearSearch = x     ' Return index
57           Exit Function
58        End If
59
60     Next x
61
62     LinearSearch = -1          ' Value not found
63  End Function
```

**Fig. 7.8**   Linear search program (part 2 of 3).

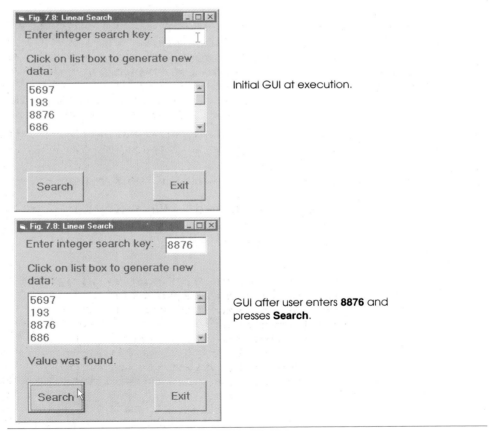

Initial GUI at execution.

GUI after user enters **8876** and presses **Search**.

**Fig. 7.8**   Linear search program (part 3 of 3).

In a worst-case scenario, searching an array of 1024 elements will take only ten comparisons using a binary search. Repeatedly dividing 1024 by 2 (because after each comparison we are able to eliminate half of the array) yields the values 512, 256, 128, 64, 32, 16, 8, 4, 2 and 1. The number 1024 ($2^{10}$) is divided by 2 only ten times to get the value 1. Dividing by 2 is equivalent to one comparison in the binary search algorithm. An array of one billion elements takes a maximum of 30 comparisons to find the search key. This is a tremendous increase in performance over the linear search that required comparing the search key on average to half the elements in the array. For a one billion-element array, this is the difference between an average of 500 million comparisons and a maximum of 30 comparisons! The maximum number of comparisons needed for the binary search of any sorted array can be determined by finding the first value of the power of 2 greater than or equal to the number of elements in the array.

*Performance Tip 7.4*

*The tremendous performance gains of the binary search over the linear search do not come without a price. Sorting an array is an expensive operation compared to searching an entire array once for an item. The overhead of sorting an array becomes worthwhile when the array will need to be searched many times at high speed.*

Figure 7.9 presents the iterative version of function **BinarySearch**. If the **searchKey** does not match the **middle** element of a subarray, the **low** index or **high** index is adjusted so that a smaller subarray can be searched. If the **searchKey** is less than the **middle** element, the **high** index is set to **middle – 1**, and the search is continued on the elements from **low** to **middle – 1**. If the **searchKey** is greater than the **middle** element, the **low** index is set to **middle + 1**, and the search is continued on the elements from **middle + 1** to **high**. The program uses an array of 15 elements. The first power of 2 greater than the number of elements in this array is 16 ($2^4$), so a maximum of four comparisons are required to find the **searchKey**. Procedure **PrintHeader** prints the array indexes and procedure **PrintRow** prints each subarray during the binary search process. The **middle** element in each subarray is marked with an asterisk, **\***, to indicate the element to which the **searchKey** is compared.

```
1   ' Fig. 7.9
2   ' Demonstrating a binary search
3   Option Explicit              ' General declaration
4   Option Base 1                ' General declaration
5   Dim mArray(15) As Integer    ' General declaration
6   Dim mLowBound As Integer     ' General declaration
7   Dim mUpperBound As Integer   ' General declaration
8
9   Private Sub Form_Load()
10      Dim x As Integer
11
12      mLowBound = LBound(mArray)
13      mUpperBound = UBound(mArray)
14
```

**Fig. 7.9**   Binary search program (part 1 of 4).

```
15      ' Generate some array data
16      For x = mLowBound To mUpperBound
17          mArray(x) = 2 * x
18      Next x
19
20   End Sub
21
22   Private Sub cmdSearch_Click()
23      Dim x As Integer
24
25      Call Cls
26
27      ' Print blanks so printing does not
28      ' print behind Label and TextBox
29      For x = 1 To 5
30          Print
31      Next x
32
33      Call BinarySearch
34   End Sub
35
36   Private Sub BinarySearch()
37      Dim middle As Integer
38      Dim low As Integer, high As Integer
39      Dim searchKey As Integer
40
41      low = mLowBound
42      high = mUpperBound
43      Call PrintHeader
44      searchKey = txtKey.Text
45
46      Do While (low <= high)
47         middle = (low + high) \ 2
48
49         Call PrintRow(low, middle, high)
50
51         If (searchKey = mArray(middle)) Then
52            Print "Found " & searchKey & " in " _
53                   & "index " & middle
54            Exit Sub
55         ElseIf searchKey < mArray(middle) Then
56            high = middle - 1
57         Else
58            low = middle + 1
59         End If
60
61      Loop
62
63      Print searchKey & " not found."
64   End Sub
65
66   Private Sub PrintHeader()
67      Dim x As Integer
```

**Fig. 7.9**    Binary search program (part 2 of 4).

```
68
69       Print "Indexes:"
70       For x = mLowBound To mUpperBound
71           Print Format$(x, "!@@@@");
72       Next x
73
74       Print
75       For x = mLowBound To 4 * mUpperBound
76           Print "-";
77       Next x
78
79       Print
80    End Sub
81
82    Private Sub PrintRow(low As Integer, middle As Integer, _
83                         high As Integer)
84       Dim x As Integer
85
86       For x = mLowBound To mUpperBound
87
88          If (x < low Or x > high) Then
89             Print Space$(4);
90          ElseIf (x = middle) Then
91             Print Format$(mArray(x) & "*", "!@@@@");
92          Else
93             Print Format$(mArray(x), "!@@@@");
94          End If
95
96       Next x
97
98       Print
99    End Sub
```

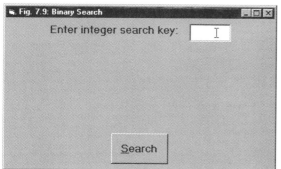

Initial GUI at execution.

**Fig. 7.9**  Binary search program (part 3 of 4).

## 7.8 Multidimensional Arrays

Arrays can have multiple dimensions. A common use of *multidimensional* arrays is to represent *tables* of values consisting of information arranged in *rows* and *columns*. To identify a particular table element, we must specify two indexes: The first (by convention) identifies the element's row and the second (by convention) identifies the element's column.

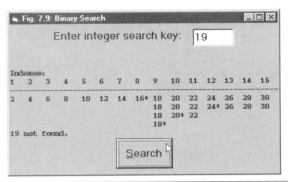

GUI after user has entered **19** and pressed **Search**.

**Fig. 7.9** Binary search program (part 4 of 4).

Tables or arrays that require two indexes to identify a particular element are called *two-dimensional arrays*. Note that multidimensional arrays can have more than two dimensions. Visual Basic supports at least 60 array dimensions, but most people will need to use no more than two- or three-dimensional arrays.

Figure 7.10 illustrates a two-dimensional array, **u**. If **Option Base** has a default value of **0**, the array contains three rows and four columns, so it is said to be a 3-by-4 array. In general, an array with *m* rows and *n* columns is called an *m-by-n* array.

Every element in array **u** is identified in Fig. 7.10 by an element name of the form **u(i, j)**; **u** is the name of the array, and **i** and **j** are the indexes that uniquely identify each element in **u**. Notice that the names of all the elements in row **0** all have a first index of **0**; the names of all the elements in the column **3** all have a second index of **3**.

*Common Programming Error 7.10*

*Referencing a two-dimensional array element **u(x, y)** incorrectly as **u(x)(y)** is a syntax error.*

A multidimensional array is declared much like a one-dimensional array. For example, a two-dimensional array **b** could be declared as

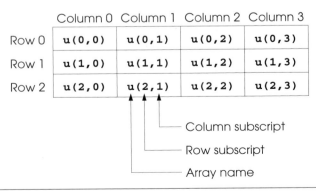

**Fig. 7.10** A two-dimensional array with three rows and four columns.

```
Dim b(2, 2) As Integer
```

Like one-dimensional arrays, multidimensional arrays can have **Public** module, and local scope. **Option Base** determines the lower bound of each dimension. Keyword **To** can be used to specify the index range for one or more dimensions. For example, the declaration

```
Dim tripleArray(50 To 100, 8, 7 To 15)
```

explicitly sets two of the three lower bounds to **50** and **7**, respectively.

Functions **UBound** and **LBound** can also be used with multidimensional arrays. When calling **UBound** or **LBound**, the dimension is passed as the second argument. If a dimension is not provided, the default dimension 1 is used. For example, the **For** header

```
For x = LBound(tripleArray, 3) To UBound(tripleArray, 3)
```

would increment **x** from the third dimension's lower bound, **7**, to the third dimension's upper bound, **15**.

Although any repetition structure can be used, many common array manipulations use **For** structures. One-dimensional arrays need one **For** loop to access all the elements. Two-dimensional arrays need two **For** loops (one nested inside the other) to access all the elements. In general, the number of array dimensions determines the number of **For** loops needed to access all the elements. One- and two-dimensional arrays are commonly used. Three-dimensional arrays are rare. Arrays larger than three dimensions are seldom used.

The program of Fig. 7.11 calls procedure **PrintArray** to output each element of a two-dimensional array.

```
1   ' Fig. 7.11
2   ' Printing a two-dimensional array
3   Option Explicit      ' General declaration
4   Option Base 1        ' General declaration
5
6   ' Declare two-dimensional array
7   Dim mArray(2, 3) As Integer    ' General declaration
8
9   Private Sub Form_Load()
10     Dim x As Integer, y As Integer
11     Call Randomize
12
13     For x = LBound(mArray) To UBound(mArray)
14
15        For y = LBound(mArray, 2) To UBound(mArray, 2)
16           mArray(x, y) = 10 + Int(89 * Rnd())
17           Call lstValues.AddItem(mArray(x, y))
18        Next y
19
20     Next x
21
22   End Sub
23
```

**Fig. 7.11**   Multidimensional array program (part 1 of 3).

```
24   Private Sub cmdDisplay_Click()
25       cmdDisplay.Enabled = False
26       Call PrintArray(mArray)
27   End Sub
28
29   Private Sub cmdExit_Click()
30       End
31   End Sub
32
33   Private Sub PrintArray(a() As Integer)
34       Dim row As Integer, col As Integer
35       Dim temp As String
36
37       temp = "Col 1 Col 2 Col 3"
38       Call lstDisplay.AddItem(Space$(6) & temp)
39
40       For row = LBound(mArray) To UBound(mArray)
41          temp = "Row " & row & " "
42          For col = LBound(mArray, 2) To UBound(mArray, 2)
43             temp = temp & Space$(3) & a(row, col) & " "
44          Next col
45
46          Call lstDisplay.AddItem(temp)
47       Next row
48
49   End Sub
```

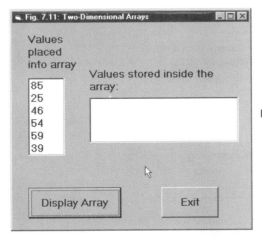

**Fig. 7.11**   Multidimensional array program (part 2 of 3).

## 7.9 Control Arrays

*Control arrays* group together controls that provide similar functionality. As with arrays, every element of a control array must have the same type. Each control array element maintains its own properties, but shares its event procedure code with the other control array elements.

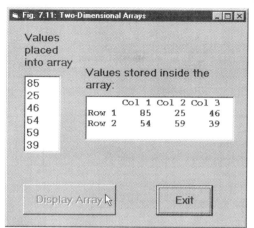

GUI after user presses **Display Array**.

**Fig. 7.11**  Multidimensional array program (part 3 of 3).

*Performance Tip 7.5*

*Control arrays use fewer resources than the equivalent controls maintained separately. Control array elements share code, whereas separate controls do not.*

Control arrays have a minimum lower bound of 0 and a maximum upper bound of 32767. Control array bounds are not affected by **Option Base**—unless the programmer specifies otherwise, 0 is always the lower bound. Each control array element is uniquely identified by its **Integer Index** property.

*Common Programming Error 7.11*

*Attempting to set a control's **Index** property to a value less than 0 or greater than 32767 is a run-time error.*

Control arrays can be created several ways, either by giving a control the same name as another control or by copying a form's control and pasting the copy on the form. Control arrays can also be created by explicitly setting a control's **Index** property. Visual Basic usually prompts the user as to whether or not a control array is to be created with the dialog of Fig. 7.12. We call this dialog the "create control array option dialog."

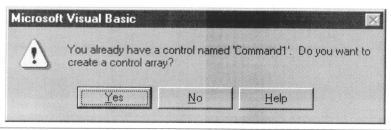

**Fig. 7.12**  Create control array option dialog.

Pressing **Yes** results in the **Index** property being set by Visual Basic to a value one more than the previous control's Index. Pressing **No** results in the control receiving a default name—the control is not part of a control array. Pressing **Help** displays a help dialog. The create control array option dialog is only displayed when the control array is initially created and is not displayed when a control array is created by explicitly setting the control's **Index** property. Control array elements do not have to have consecutive **Index**es. For example, three-element control array **imgDisplay** might have elements with **Index**es of 7, 89 and 2022.

Once a control array has been created, the number of control array elements is retrieved using the *Count* property. Properties **UBound** and **LBound** return the control array's upper and lower bounds, respectively. So, for example, if **lblLabels** control array exists, then the statement

```
Print lblLabels.Count,lblLabels.UBound, lblLabels.LBound
```

would print the number of control array elements in **lblLabels**, the upper bound and the lower bound. Any individual control in a control array can be accessed using method *Item*. For example, the statement

```
lblLabels.Item(33).Caption = "My Control Index is 33!"
```

sets the **Caption** property for the control array element with an **Index** of **33**.

The program of Fig. 7.13 is a rewrite of Fig. 5.9. In this version, the buttons that have numeric values on their faces are placed in a control array named **cmdButton**.

```
1   ' Fig. 7.13
2   ' Security keypad program
3   Option Explicit            ' General Declaration
4   Dim mAccessCode As Long    ' General Declaration
5
6   Private Sub cmdEnter_Click()
7      Dim message As String
8
9      mAccessCode = txtDisplay.Text
10     txtDisplay.Text = ""
11
12     Select Case mAccessCode
13        Case Is < 1000                ' Panic codes
14           message = "Access Denied"
15           Beep
16        Case 1645 To 1689
17           message = "Technician Personnel"
18        Case 8345
19           message = "Custodial Services"
20        Case 55875
21           message = "Special Services"
22        Case 999898, 1000006 To 1000008
23           message = "Scientific Personnel"
```

**Fig. 7.13** Security program that uses control arrays (part 1 of 2).

```
24          Case Else
25              message = "Access Denied"
26      End Select
27
28      Call lstLogEntry.AddItem(Now & Space$(3) & message)
29  End Sub
30
31  Private Sub cmdClear_Click()
32      txtDisplay.Text = ""
33  End Sub
34
35  Private Sub cmdButton_Click(Index As Integer)
36      txtDisplay.Text = txtDisplay.Text & Index
37  End Sub
```

Initial GUI at execution.

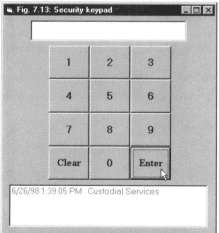

GUI after user has entered a code and pressed **Enter**.

**Fig. 7.13**   Security program that uses control arrays (part 2 of 2).

The event procedure

```
Private Sub cmdButton_Click(Index As Integer)
    txtDisplay.Text = txtDisplay.Text & Index
End Sub
```

replaces 10 event procedures. Control array event procedures receive parameter **Index**. The value of **Index** identifies which button (control element) was pressed.

*Common Programming Error 7.12*

*Attempting to access a control array element that does not exist is a run-time error.*

## 7.10 Dynamic Arrays

Arrays that grow and shrink at run-time are called *dynamic arrays (also called redimmable arrays)*. Dynamic arrays are more flexible than fixed-sized arrays, because they can be resized anytime to accommodate new data. Like fixed-sized arrays, dynamic arrays have either **Public** (in code modules), module or local scope. Module dynamic arrays are declared using keyword **Dim** or **Private**. Local dynamic arrays are declared with either **Dim** or **Static**.

*Performance Tip 7.6*

*Dynamic arrays allow the programmer to manage memory more efficiently than with fixed-size arrays.*

A dynamic array is not given a size when declared. For example, the line

```
Dim dynamicArray() As Double
```

would declare **dynamicArray** as a dynamic array of **Double**s. The size of a dynamic array is specified at run-time with keyword *ReDim* and the memory for the array is then allocated. The statement

```
ReDim dynamicArray(9)
```

would allocate ten elements for **dynamicArray** using **ReDim** (**Option Base** is **0**). If **Option Base** is **1**, the preceding **ReDim** would allocate nine elements whose indices range from 1 to 9.

*Common Programming Error 7.13*

*Attempting to use *ReDim* outside a procedure is a syntax error.*

*Common Programming Error 7.14*

*Attempting to use *ReDim* on a fixed-size array is a syntax error.*

A dynamic array's size can be changed anytime with **ReDim**. For example, the line

```
ReDim dynamicArray(19)
```

changes the number of elements allocated from 10 to 20 (if the lower bound is 0). **ReDim** can also be used to change the index bounds. The line

```
ReDim dynamicArray(50 To 100)
```

changes the lower bound from 0 to 50 and the upper bound from 19 to 100. The total number of dimensions cannot be changed by **ReDim** (i.e., if the array is a two-dimensional array, it cannot become a three-dimensional array). The first time **ReDim** is used—the number of dimensions for the array becomes fixed.

*Performance Tip 7.7*

*Resizing dynamic arrays consumes processor time and can slow a program's execution speed.*

When **ReDim** is executed, all values contained in the array are lost. Numeric values are reset to zero and **String**s are reset to a zero-length **String**. Values can be retained by using keyword **Preserve** with **ReDim**. For example, the line

```
ReDim Preserve dynamicArray(50 To 150)
```

resizes **dynamicArray**—preserving (i.e., retaining) the original values in the array.

*Common Programming Error 7.15*

*Attempting to change the total number of dimensions of a dynamic array is a run-time error.*

The lines

```
ReDim threeD(11, 8, 1)
ReDim Preserve threeD(11, 8, 2)
```

would change the upper bound of the third dimension from 1 to 2—retaining all the values previously stored in all dimensions.

*Common Programming Error 7.16*

*Using **ReDim** without **Preserve** and assuming that the array still contains previous values is a logic error.*

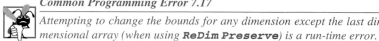

*Common Programming Error 7.17*

*Attempting to change the bounds for any dimension except the last dimension in a multidimensional array (when using **ReDim Preserve**) is a run-time error.*

*Testing and Debugging Tip 7.6*

*Failure to **Preserve** array data can result in unexpected loss of data at run-time.*

Memory allocated for a dynamic array can be *deallocated* (*released*) at run-time using keyword **Erase**. A dynamic array that has been deallocated must be redimensioned with **ReDim** before it can be used again. **Erase** can also be used with fixed-sized arrays to initialize all the array elements to 0.

*Common Programming Error 7.18*

*Accessing a dynamic array that has been deallocated is a run-time error.*

The next example dynamically allocates memory for an array, populates the array with values and displays the index and value of each element in a **ListBox**. The program also allows the user to redimension the array. Array contents can be preserved by checking the **Preserve CheckBox**. The user can also deallocate the array by pressing **Erase**. The GUI is shown in Fig. 7.14, properties in Fig. 7.15, and code in Fig. 7.16.

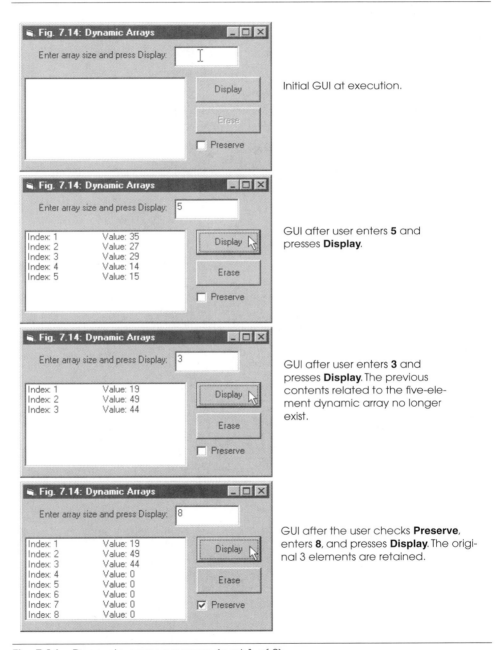

**Fig. 7.14**   Dynamic array program (part 1 of 2).

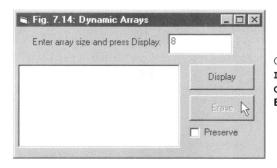

GUI after the user presses **Erase**. The **ListBox** is cleared, the **Preserve** **CheckBox** is unchecked, and the **Erase** button disabled.

**Fig. 7.14** Dynamic array program (part 2 of 2).

The program introduces the **CheckBox** control. **CheckBox**es are commonly used to express optional features. If checked, the feature is used and if unchecked the feature is not used. A **CheckBox**'s **Value** property determines whether a **CheckBox** is checked or unchecked. Visual Basic constant **vbChecked**, 1, represents a checked state and constant of **vbUnchecked**, 0, represents unchecked state.

| Object | Icon | Property | Property setting | Property description |
|---|---|---|---|---|
| form | | Name | frmDynamic | Identifies the form. |
| | | Caption | Fig 7.14: Dynamic arrays | Form title bar display. |
| **Erase** button | | Name | cmdErase | Identifies **Erase** button. |
| | | Caption | Erase | Text that appears on button. |
| | | Enabled | False | Disables button. |
| **Display** button | | Name | cmdPrint | Identifies **Display** button. |
| | | Caption | Display | Text that appears on button. |
| Label | A | Name | lblPrompt | Identifies **Label**. |
| | | Caption | Enter array size and press Display: | Text that appears in the **Label**. |
| CheckBox | ☑ | Name | chkPreserve | Identifies **CheckBox**. |
| ListBox | | Name | lstValues | Identifies **ListBox**. |

**Fig. 7.15** Properties listing (part 1 of 2).

| Object | Icon | Property | Property setting | Property description |
|--------|------|----------|------------------|----------------------|
| TextBox |  | Name | txtInput | Identifies TextBox. |

**Fig. 7.15**  Properties listing (part 2 of 2).

*Good Programming Practice 7.1*

*Prefixing CheckBox controls with chk allows CheckBox controls to be identified easily.*

```
1   ' Fig. 7.14
2   ' Demonstrating dynamic arrays
3   Option Explicit      ' General declaration
4   Option Base 1        ' General declaration
5   Dim mDynamic() As Integer
6
7   Private Sub cmdErase_Click()
8      Erase mDynamic          ' Free memory
9      Call lstValues.Clear
10     cmdErase.Enabled = False
11     chkPreserve.Value = vbUnchecked   ' Uncheck Preserve
12  End Sub
13
14  Private Sub cmdPrint_Click()
15     Dim arrayLength As Integer, x As Integer
16
17     Call lstValues.Clear
18     arrayLength = txtInput.Text
19
20     ' Determine state of CheckBox
21     If chkPreserve.Value = vbUnchecked Then   ' Unchecked
22        ReDim mDynamic(arrayLength)            ' Allocate memory
23        Call InitArray                         ' Initialize
24     ElseIf chkPreserve.Value = vbChecked Then ' Checked
25        ' Allocate memory and preserve contents
26        ReDim Preserve mDynamic(arrayLength)
27     End If
28
29     ' Display index and array contents in ListBox
30     For x = LBound(mDynamic) To UBound(mDynamic)
31        Call lstValues.AddItem("Index: " & x & vbTab & _
32                        vbTab & "Value: " & mDynamic(x))
33     Next x
34
35     cmdErase.Enabled = True
36  End Sub
37
```

**Fig. 7.16**  Program that demonstrates dynamic arrays (part 1 of 2).

```
38   Private Sub InitArray()
39      Dim x As Integer
40
41      ' Generate some data
42      For x = LBound(mDynamic) To UBound(mDynamic)
43         mDynamic(x) = Int(51 * Rnd())
44      Next x
45
46   End Sub
```

**Fig. 7.16**  Program that demonstrates dynamic arrays (part 2 of 2).

When **Display** is pressed, the value entered in **txtInput** is retrieved and assigned to **arrayLength**. The **If/Then/ElseIf** structure tests the state of **chkPreserve**. If unchecked the lines

```
        ReDim mDynamic(arrayLength)
        Call InitArray
```

are executed. **ReDim** dynamically sizes **mDynamic** to **arrayLength** elements (**Option Base** is **1**). Procedure **InitArray** is called to populate the array. If **chkPreserve** is checked, the line

```
    ReDim Preserve mDynamic(arrayLength)
```

is executed. Array **mDynamic** is resized to **arrayLength** elements and any contents in the array are preserved. If **ReDim** creates a larger array, the elements beyond the last **arrayLength** contain zeros and if a smaller array is created, the previous values are retained for those elements.

The **Erase** button when pressed releases the memory allocated with the statement

```
    Erase mDynamic
```

The **ListBox** is cleared and **Erase** is disabled. Preserving the array contents is no longer necessary, so **chkPreserve**'s **Value** is set to unchecked.

Dynamic arrays can be assigned to other dynamic or fixed-size arrays. The program of Fig. 7.17 assigns a fixed-size array returned from function **GetArray** to dynamic array **x**.

```
1    ' Fig. 7.17
2    ' Returning an array from function
3    Option Explicit       ' General declaration
4
5    Private Sub cmdPrint_Click()
6       Dim x() As Integer    ' Dynamic array
7       Dim i As Integer      ' Looping variable
8
9       Call Cls              ' Clear form
10      x = GetArray          ' Assign returned array
11                            ' to x
12
```

**Fig. 7.17**  Assigning an array to a dynamic array (part 2 of 2).

```
13      Print "In cmdPrint_Click array x contains:"
14
15      For i = LBound(x) To UBound(x)
16          Print x(i), ;
17      Next i
18
19  End Sub
20
21  Private Function GetArray() As Integer()
22      Dim y(5) As Integer      ' Fixed-size array
23      Dim j As Integer         ' Looping variable
24
25      Print "In GetArray array y contains:"
26
27      ' Generate data
28      For j = LBound(y) To UBound(y)
29          y(j) = Int(10 * Rnd())
30          Print y(j), ;
31      Next j
32
33      Print
34      GetArray = y             ' Return array
35  End Function
```

Initial GUI at execution.

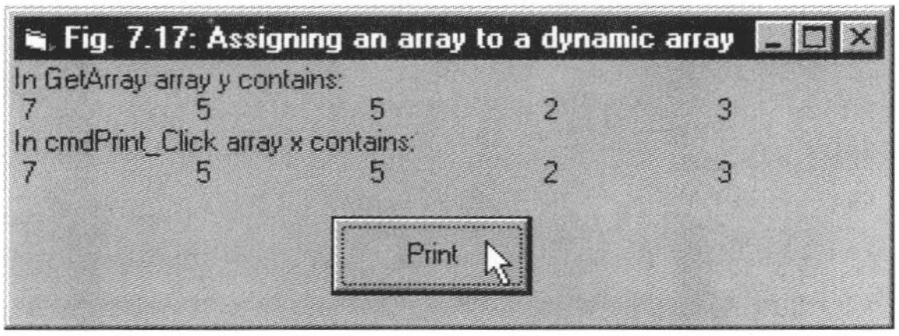

GUI after user presses **Print**.

**Fig. 7.17**   Assigning an array to a dynamic array (part 2 of 2).

In **cmdPrint_Click**, dynamic array **x** is assigned the **Integer** array returned from **GetArray** with the line

```
x = GetArray
```

**GetArray**'s function definition header is defined as

```
Private Function GetArray() As Integer()
```

Return type **Integer()** indicates that **GetArray** returns an **Integer** array. Line 22 declares fixed-size local array **y**. A **For** loop places values from 1 to 10 in array **y** and prints each element. The array is returned from **GetArray** with **GetArray = y**.

*Common Programming Error 7.19*

*Attempting to assign an array to a fixed-size array is syntax error.*

## 7.11 Variable-Length Arguments: **ParamArray**

It is possible to create procedures that receive an unspecified number of arguments. Key-word **ParamArray** in a procedure definition header indicates that the procedure receives a variable number of arguments. **ParamArray** precedes the declaration of a **Variant** array. The program of Fig. 7.18 calls programmer-defined procedure **AnyNumberArguments** four times, passing a different number of values each time. The values passed into **AnyNumberArguments** are stored in **Variant** array **x**.

*Common Programming Error 7.20*

*Attempting to declare a variable in a procedure header to the right of the **ParamArray** array is a syntax error.*

```
1   ' Fig. 7.18
2   ' Passing a variable number of arguments
3   Option Explicit
4
5   Private Sub Form_Load()
6       Call AnyNumberArguments
7       Call AnyNumberArguments(1)
8       Call AnyNumberArguments(2, 3)
9       Call AnyNumberArguments(4, 5, 6)
10      Call AnyNumberArguments(7, 8, 9, 10, 11, 12)
11  End Sub
12
13  Private Sub AnyNumberArguments(ParamArray x() As Variant)
14      Dim y As Integer
15
16      Print "Procedure AnyNumberArguments received "
17      For y = LBound(x) To UBound(x)
18          Print x(y) & Space$(4);
19      Next y
20
21      Print
22  End Sub
```

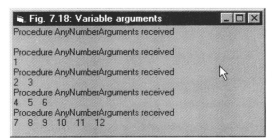

GUI at execution.

**Fig. 7.18** Demonstrating variable-length argument list.

*Common Programming Error 7.21*

*Attempting to declare a non-array variable with* **ParamArray** *is a syntax error.*

*Common Programming Error 7.22*

*Attempting to use* **ParamArray** *with an array type other than* **Variant** *is a syntax error.*

## 7.12 Function **Array**

Function **Array** creates and returns a **Variant** array at execution time. The values passed to **Array** specify element values in the returned array. The returned array's lower bound is either **0** or **1** depending on **Option Base**. Function **Array** uses **ParamArray** to create the **Variant** array. Figure 7.19 demonstrates function **Array**.

## Summary

- Arrays are data structures consisting of related data items of the same type. Visual Basic provides a fixed-size array, whose size does not change during program execution, and a dynamic array, whose size can change during execution.

```
1    ' Fig. 7.19
2    ' Demonstrating function Array.
3    Option Explicit          ' General declaration
4    Option Base 1            ' General declaration
5
6    Private Sub cmdPrint_Click()
7       Dim v As Variant, x As Integer
8
9       v = Array(7, 5, 6, 9, 3, 0)     ' Returns Variant array
10      Print "Variant array values are: ";
11      For x = LBound(v) To UBound(v)
12         Print Format$(v(x), "@@@");
13      Next x
14
15      Print
16      v = Array("hello", "bye", "hi")  ' Return Variant array
17      Print "Variant array values are: ";
18      For x = LBound(v) To UBound(v)
19         Print v(x) & Space$(2);
20      Next x
21
22      Print
23      v = Array(1.1, 2.2, 3.3, 4.4)      ' Return Variant array
24      Print "Variant array values are: ";
25      For x = LBound(v) To UBound(v)
26         Print v(x) & Space$(2);
27      Next x
28
29      cmdPrint.Enabled = False
30   End Sub
```

**Fig. 7.19**  Demonstrating function **Array** (part 1 of 2).

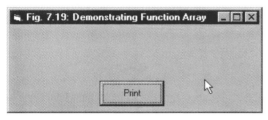

Initial GUI at execution.

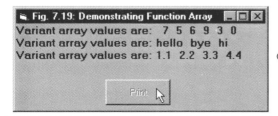

GUI after user presses **Print**.

**Fig. 7.19**   Demonstrating function **Array** (part 2 of 2).

- An array is a contiguous group of memory locations that all have the same name and the same type.
- An array index must be a **Long** or a **Long** expression in the range –2,147,483,648 to 2,147,483,648.
- Arrays may be declared as **Public** (in code modules), module or local. Module arrays are declared in the general declarations using **Dim** or **Private**. Local arrays are declared in a procedure body with **Dim** or **Static**. Arrays must be declared explicitly with keyword **As**.
- Array elements are initialized to zero by default.
- Function **LBound** returns the lowest-numbered index value and function **UBound** returns the highest-numbered index value.
- **Option Base** sets the lower bound to **0** or **1** and is placed in the general declaration.
- Keyword **To** sets the lower bound and upper bound. Lower-bound values set with **To** are not affected by **Option Base**.
- Array arguments are passed to procedures by specifying the name of the array followed by a pair of empty parentheses. Arrays are automatically passed call-by-reference.
- Individual array elements are call-by-reference. Individual array elements are passed to procedures by specifying the array name followed by the index in parentheses.
- Individual array elements are passed call-by-value with keyword **ByVal** or parentheses.
- Sorting data is the process by which data is arranged into some particular order such as ascending or descending.
- The bubble sort is easy to program but executes slowly compared to other sorting algorithms.
- The process of finding a particular element of an array is called searching.
- Linear search works well for small arrays or for unsorted arrays, but linear searching is inefficient for large, sorted arrays.
- Binary search works well for large, sorted arrays. The binary search algorithm removes from consideration one half of the elements in the array being searched after each comparison.
- Visual Basic supports at least 60 array dimensions. Unless keyword **To** is used in the declaration, **Option Base** determines the lower bound of each dimension.

- Control arrays group together controls that provide similar functionality. Each control array element maintains its own properties but shares its event procedures with the other control array elements. Control arrays have a minimum lower bound of 0 and a maximum upper bound of 32767. Control array bounds are not affected by **Option Base**. Each control array element is uniquely identified by its **Integer Index** property.

- A control array's **Count** property contains the number of control array elements. Properties **UBound** and **LBound** return the control array's upper and lower bounds. Method **Item** returns a control array element (i.e., a control).

- Dynamic arrays grow and shrink at run-time and are not given a size when declared. Dynamic arrays are sized and given memory at run-time with keyword **ReDim**.

- Memory allocated for a dynamic array can be deallocated (released) at run-time using keyword **Erase**. A dynamic array that has been deallocated must be redimensioned with **ReDim** before it can be used again. **Erase** can also be used with fixed-sized arrays to initialize all the array elements to 0.

- **CheckBox**es are commonly used to express optional features. If checked, the feature is used, and if unchecked, the feature is not used. A **CheckBox**'s **Value** property determines whether a **CheckBox** is checked or unchecked. Visual Basic constant **vbChecked** represents a checked state and constant of **vbUnchecked** represents unchecked state

- Dynamic arrays can be assigned to other dynamic or fixed-size arrays.

- Functions can return arrays.

- Keyword **ParamArray** in a procedure definition header indicates that the procedure receives a variable number of arguments. **ParamArray** precedes the declaration of a **Variant** array.

- Function **Array** returns a **Variant** array at run-time.

## *Terminology*

| | |
|---|---|
| **a(i)** | **LBound** method |
| **a(i, j)** | **LBound** property |
| array | linear search |
| **Array** function | lower bound of an array |
| assign an array to a dynamic array | m-by-n array |
| binary search | multidimensional array |
| bounds checking | name of an array |
| bubble sort | off-by-one error |
| **CheckBox** control | **Option Base 1** |
| column of a table | **Option Base 0** |
| control array | **ParamArray** keyword |
| **Count** property | parentheses |
| deallocate memory for a dynamic array | pass an array to a procedure |
| declare an array | pass-by-reference |
| **Dim** keyword (dimension an array) | pass of a bubble sort |
| dynamic array | position number |
| element of an array | **Preserve** with **ReDim** |
| **Erase** statement | **ReDim** keyword (redimension an array) |
| fixed-size array | redimmable array |
| function **Array** | release memory for a dynamic array |
| index | returning an array from a **Function** procedure |
| initialize an array | row of a table |
| **Item** method | search an array |

| | |
|---|---|
| search key | **UBound** method |
| sinking sort | **UBound** property |
| sort an array | upper bound of an array |
| **Space$** function | value of an element |
| table of values | variable arguments |
| tabular format | variable-length string |
| temporary area for exchange of values | **vbChecked** constant |
| three-dimensional array | **vbUnchecked** constant |
| **To** keyword | "walk off" an array |
| two-dimensional array | zeroth element |

## Common Programming Errors

**7.1**   Attempting to declare an array implicitly is a syntax error.

**7.2**   Attempting to declare a **Public** array in a form module is a syntax error.

**7.3**   Attempting to access an index that is smaller than the lower bound or greater than the upper bound is a run-time error.

**7.4**   Not initializing the elements of an array whose elements should be initialized is a logic error.

**7.5**   Placing an array declaration before the **Option Base** statement is a syntax error.

**7.6**   Attempting to give **Option Base** a value other than **0** or **1** is a syntax error.

**7.7**   Placing a value on the left side of **To** greater than the value on the right side of **To** is a syntax error.

**7.8**   Placing any number in the parentheses of an array parameter variable is a syntax error.

**7.9**   Attempting to pass an array call-by-value is a syntax error.

**7.10**  Referencing a two-dimensional array element **u(x, y)** incorrectly as **u(x)(y)** is a syntax error.

**7.11**  Attempting to set a control's **Index** property to a value less than 0 or greater than 32767 is a run-time error.

**7.12**  Attempting to access a control array element that does not exist is a run-time error.

**7.13**  Attempting to use **ReDim** outside a procedure is a syntax error.

**7.14**  Attempting to use **ReDim** on a fixed-size array is a syntax error.

**7.15**  Attempting to change the total number of dimensions of a dynamic array is a run-time error.

**7.16**  Using **ReDim** without **Preserve** and assuming that the array still contains previous values is a logic error.

**7.17**  Attempting to change the bounds for any dimension except the last dimension in a multidimensional array (when using **ReDim Preserve**) is a run-time error.

**7.18**  Accessing a dynamic array that has been deallocated is a run-time error.

**7.19**  Attempting to assign an array to a fixed-size array is syntax error.

**7.20**  Attempting to declare a variable in a procedure header to the right of the **ParamArray** array is a syntax error.

**7.21**  Attempting to declare a non-array variable with **ParamArray** is a syntax error.

**7.22**  Attempting to use **ParamArray** with an array type other than **Variant** is a syntax error.

## Good Programming Practice

**7.1**   Prefixing **CheckBox** controls with **chk** allows **CheckBox** controls to be identified easily.

## Performance Tips

**7.1**   Sometimes performance considerations outweigh clarity considerations.

**7.2**   Passing arrays call-by-reference makes sense for performance reasons. If arrays were passed call-by-value, a copy of each element would be passed. For large, frequently passed arrays, this would be time consuming and would consume considerable storage for the copies of the array elements.

**7.3**  Sometimes the simplest algorithms perform poorly. Their virtue is that they are easy to write, test and debug. However, more complex algorithms are often needed to realize maximum performance.

**7.4**  The tremendous performance gains of the binary search over the linear search do not come without a price. Sorting an array is an expensive operation compared to searching an entire array once for an item. The overhead of sorting an array becomes worthwhile when the array will need to be searched many times at high speed.

**7.5**  Control arrays use fewer resources than the equivalent controls maintained separately. Control array elements share code, whereas separate controls do not.

**7.6**  Dynamic arrays allow the programmer to manage memory more efficiently than with fixed-size arrays.

**7.7**  Resizing dynamic arrays consumes processor time and can slow a program's execution speed.

## Software Engineering Observation

**7.1**  Strive for program clarity. It is sometimes worthwhile to trade off the most efficient use of memory or processor time in favor of writing clearer programs

## Testing and Debugging Tips

**7.1**  It is important to note the difference between the "seventh element of the array" and "array position number seven." Because array indexes may begin at 0, the "seventh element of the array" has an index of 6, while "array position number seven" has an index of 7 and is actually the eighth element of the array. This is a source of "off-by-one" errors.

**7.2**  Assuming that elements of a local **Static** array are initialized to zero every time a procedure is called can result in logic errors.

**7.3**  Array lower bounds and upper bounds can vary. Use functions **LBound** and **UBound** to ensure that each index is in range (i.e., within the bounds of the array).

**7.4**  The program should be written to ensure that all array indexes remain within the bounds of the array.

**7.5**  Programs should validate the correctness of all input values to prevent erroneous information from affecting a program's calculations.

**7.6**  Failure to **Preserve** array data can result in unexpected loss of data at run-time.

## Self-Review Exercises

**7.1**  Answer each of the following:
  a)  Lists and tables of values are stored in _____.
  b)  The elements of an array are related by the fact that they all have the same _____ and _____.
  c)  The number used to refer to a particular element of an array is called its _____.
  d)  The process of placing the elements of an array in order is called _____ the array.
  e)  Determining if an array contains a certain key value is called _____ the array.
  f)  An array that uses two sets of indexes is referred to as a _____ array.

**7.2**  State whether the following are *true* or *false*. If *false*, explain why.
  a)  A **Variant** array can store many different types of values.
  b)  An array index should be of data type **Single**.
  c)  A fixed-size array can be assigned to another fixed-size array.
  d)  A fixed-size array can be assigned to a dynamic array.
  e)  A dynamic array can be assigned to a fixed-size array.

   f)  A dynamic array can be assigned to another dynamic array.
   g)  A procedure can return an array.

**7.3**    Write a statement or series of statements to accomplish each of the following.
   a)  Force the array indexes to begin at 1.
   b)  Define a constant variable **SIZE** initialized to 10.
   c)  Declare array **pcm** to have **SIZE** elements and be of type **Single**. Explicitly initialize
       the array elements to 0.
   d)  Refer to array element 7.
   e)  Assign the value 1.667 to element 9.
   f)  Print array elements 6 and 9.
   g)  Print all the elements of the array using a **For** repetition structure. Use **Integer** vari-
       able **x** as the looping variable. Show the output.

**7.4**    Answer the following questions or write statement(s) regarding an array called **table**. Assume that array indexes begin with 0.
   a)  Declare **table** to be an **Integer** array using 3 for the rows and 3 for the columns.
   b)  How many elements does **table** contain?
   c)  Use a **For** repetition structure to initialize each element of **table** to the sum of its in-
       dexes (i.e., current row + current column). Assume that **Integer** variables **x** and **y** are
       declared for use as looping variables.

**7.5**    Find the error(s) in each of the following program segments. If possible, correct the error(s).
   a)  **a.Item(50000).Enabled = True    ' a is a control array**
   b)  **Option Base 8    ' Begin indexes at 8**
   c)  **Dim x%(20), array, q, parameterArray(45) as Boolean**

## Answers to Self-Review Exercises

**7.1**    a) arrays.  b) name, type.  c) index.  d) sorting.  e) searching.  f) two-dimensional.

**7.2**    a)  True.
   b)  False. The index value should be within the range of a **Long**.
   c)  False. This type of assignment is not permitted.
   d)  False. This type of assignment is not permitted.
   e)  True.
   f)  True.
   g)  True.

**7.3**    a)  **Option Base 1**
   b)  **Const SIZE As Integer = 10**
   c)  **Dim pcm(SIZE) As Single**

```
    For c = LBound(pcm) to UBound(pcm)
       pcm(c) = 0
    Next c
```
   d)  **pcm(7)**
   e)  **pcm(9) = 1.667**
   f)  **Print pcm(6), pcm(9)**
   g)  **For x = LBound(pcm) to UBound(pcm)**
```
       Print pcm(x) & " ";
    Next x
```
       Output: **0 0 0 0 0 0 0 0 0 0**

**7.4**    a) `Dim table(3, 3) As Integer`
      b) 16.
      c) `For x = LBound(table) To UBound(table)`
           `For y = LBound(table, 2) To UBound(table, 2)`
             `table(x, y) = x + y`
           `Next y`
        `Next x`

**7.5**    a) The index passed to **Item** exceeds 32767—the limit for control arrays.
      b) **Option Base** can only have a value of **1** or **2**.
      c) **Array** is a keyword and cannot be used as a programmer-defined identifier.

## Exercises

**7.6**    Fill in the blanks in each of the following:
      a) The elements of an array are related by the fact that they _____.
      b) When referring to an array element, the position number contained within parentheses is called a _____.
      c) Naming an array, stating its type, and specifying the number of elements in the array is called _____ the array.
      d) The process of placing the elements of an array into either ascending or descending order is called _____.
      e) In a two-dimensional array, the first index (by convention) identifies the _____ of an element, and the second index (by convention) identifies the _____ of an element.
      f) An *m*-by-*n* array contains _____ rows, _____ columns and _____ elements.

**7.7**    State which of the following are *true* and which are *false*. If *false*, explain why.
      a) To refer to a particular location or element within an array, we specify the name of the array and the value of the particular element.
      b) An array declaration reserves space for the array.
      c) To indicate that 100 locations should be reserved for **Integer** array **p**, the programmer could write the declaration (**Option Base** is **1**)
          `Static p[100] As Integer`
      d) A program that initializes the elements of a 15-element array to 0 must contain at least one **For** statement.
      e) A program that totals the elements of a two-dimensional array must contain nested **For** statements.

**7.8**    Write statement(s) that perform the following one-dimensional array operations:
      a) Initialize the 10 elements of **Integer** array **counts** to zeros.
      b) Add 1 to each of the 15 elements of **Integer** array **bonus**.
      c) Print the 12 values of **Single** array **monthlyTemperatures**.

**7.9**    Find the error(s) in each of the following statements and if possible, correct the error(s).
      a) `Print Count(x)     ' Print total elements in control array x`
      b) `Print b.Caption.Item(1) ' b is a control array of TextBoxes`
      c) `Print UBound(c), LBound(c); "**" ' c is a control array`

**7.10**    Label the elements of 3-by-5 two-dimensional array **sales** to indicate the order in which they are set to 0 by the following program segment (**Option Base** is **0**):

```
For row = 0 To 3
   For column = 0 To 5
      sales(row, column) = 0
   Next column
Next row
```

**7.11**   Write statement(s) to accomplish each of the following (assume that indexes begin at 1):
   a)   Display the value of the seventh element of **String** array **f**.
   b)   Place the value 762 into element 7 of one-dimensional **Single** array **b**.
   c)   Initialize each of the five elements of one-dimensional **Integer** array **g** to 8.
   d)   Total and print the 100 elements of **Currency** array **c**.
   e)   Copy array **a** into the first portion of array **b**. Assume that **a(11)** and **b(37)** are declared as fixed-size **Double** arrays.
   f)   Print the smallest and largest values contained in 99-element **Long** array **w**.

**7.12**   Consider a 2-by-3 **Integer** array **t** (assume that **Option Base** is **1**):
   a)   Write a local declaration for **t**.
   b)   How many rows does **t** have?
   c)   How many columns does **t** have?
   d)   How many elements does **t** have?
   e)   Write the names of all the elements in the second row of **t**.
   f)   Write the names of all the elements in the third column of **t**.
   g)   Write a single statement that sets the element of **t** in row 1 and column 2 to 0.
   h)   Write a statement that initializes each element of **t** to 0. Do not use a repetition structure.
   i)   Write a nested **For** statement that initializes each element of **t** to 0.

**7.13**   Use a one-dimensional array to solve the following problem. A company pays its salespeople on a commission basis. The salespeople receive $200 per week plus 9 percent of their gross sales for that week. For example, a salesperson who grosses $5000 in sales in a week receives $200 plus 9 percent of $5000, or a total of $650. Write a program (using an array of counters) that determines how many of the salespeople earned salaries in each of the following ranges (assume that each salesperson's salary is truncated to an **Integer** amount):

   1.   $200–$299

   2.   $300–$399

   3.   $700–$799

   4.   $500–$599

   5.   $600–$699

   6.   $700–$799

   7.   $800–$899

   8.   $900–$999

   9.   $1000 and over

**7.14**   Use a one-dimensional array to solve the following problem. Read in 20 numbers, each of which is between 10 and 100, inclusive. As each number is input, print it only if it is not a duplicate of a number already input. Provide for the "worst case" in which all 20 numbers are different.

**7.15**   Write a program that simulates the rolling of two dice. The program should use function **Rnd** to roll the first die, and should use **Rnd** again to roll the second die. The sum of the two values should then be calculated. Note: Since each die can show an **Integer** value from 1 to 6, the sum of the two values will vary from 2 to 12, with 7 being the most frequent sum and 2 and 12 being the least frequent sums. Figure 7.20 shows the 36 possible combinations of the two dice. Your program should roll the

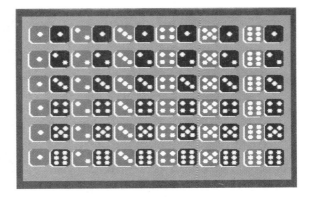

**Fig. 7.20** The 36 possible outcomes of rolling two dice.

two dice 36,000 times. Use a one-dimensional array to tally the number of times each possible sum appears. Print the results in a tabular format. Also, determine if the totals are reasonable (i.e., there are six ways to roll a 7), so approximately one sixth of all the rolls should be 7.

**7.16** Write a program that runs 1000 games of craps and uses arrays to answer the following questions:

    a) How many games are won on the first roll, second roll, …, twentieth roll, and after the twentieth roll?

    b) How many games are lost on the first roll, second roll, …, twentieth roll, and after the twentieth roll?

    c) What are the chances of winning at craps? (Note: You should discover that craps is one of the fairest casino games. What do you suppose this means?)

    d) What is the average length of a game of craps?

    e) Do the chances of winning improve with the length of the game?

**7.17** (*Airline Reservations System*) A small airline has just purchased a computer for its new automated reservations system. You have been asked to program the new system. You are to write a program to assign seats on each flight of the airline's only plane (capacity: 10 seats).

Your program should display the following menu of alternatives:

        **Please type 1 for "smoking"**
        **Please type 2 for "nonsmoking"**

If the person types 1, then your program should assign a seat in the smoking section (seats 1-5). If the person types 2, then your program should assign a seat in the nonsmoking section (seats 6-10). Your program should then print a boarding pass indicating the person's seat number and whether it is in the smoking or nonsmoking section of the plane.

Use a one-dimensional array to represent the seating chart of the plane. Initialize all the elements of the array to 0 to indicate that all seats are empty. As each seat is assigned, set the corresponding elements of the array to 1 to indicate that the seat is no longer available.

Your program should, of course, never assign a seat that has already been assigned. When the smoking section is full, your program should ask the person if it is acceptable to be placed in the nonsmoking section (and vice versa). If yes, then make the appropriate seat assignment. If no, then print the message "Next flight leaves in 3 hours."

**7.18**    Use a two-dimensional array to solve the following problem. A company has four salespeople (with salesperson numbers 1 to 4) who sell five different products (with product numbers 1 to 5).
Once a day, each salesperson passes in a slip for each different type of product sold. Each slip contains:

1.  The salesperson number

2.  The product number

3.  The total dollar value of that product sold that day

Thus, each salesperson passes in 0 to 5 sales slips per day. Assume that the information from all of
the slips for last month is available. Write a program that will read all this information for last month's
sales and summarize the total sales by salesperson by product. All totals should be stored in the two-
dimensional array **sales**. After processing all the information for last month, print the results in tabular format with each of the columns representing a particular salesperson and each of the rows representing a particular product. Cross total each row to get the total sales of each product for last
month; cross total each column to get the total sales by salesperson for last month. Your neat tabular
printout should include these cross totals to the right of the totaled rows and to the bottom of the totaled columns.

**7.19**    (*Knight's Tour*) One of the more interesting puzzlers for chess buffs is the Knight's Tour
problem, originally proposed by the mathematician Euler. The question is this: Can the chess piece
called the knight move around an empty chessboard and touch each of the 64 squares once and only
once? We study this intriguing problem in depth here.

The knight makes L-shaped moves (over two in one direction and then over one in a perpen-
dicular direction). Thus, from a square in the middle of an empty chessboard, the knight can make
eight different moves (numbered 0 through 7), as shown in Fig. 7.21.

   a)  Draw an 8-by-8 chessboard on a sheet of paper and attempt a Knight's Tour by hand. Put
       a 1 in the first square you move to, a 2 in the second square, a 3 in the third, etc. Before
       starting the tour, estimate how far you think you will get, remembering that a full tour
       consists of 64 moves. How far did you get? Was this close to your estimate?

   b)  Now let us develop a program that will move the knight around a chessboard. The board
       is represented by an 8-by-8 two-dimensional array board. Each of the squares is initial-
       ized to zero. We describe each of the eight possible moves in terms of both their horizon-
       tal and vertical components. For example, a move of type 0 as shown in Fig. 7.21 consists
       of moving two squares horizontally to the right and one square vertically upward. Move
       2 consists of moving one square horizontally to the left and two squares vertically up-
       ward. Horizontal moves to the left and vertical moves upward are indicated with negative
       numbers. The eight moves may be described by two one-dimensional arrays, horizontal
       and vertical, as shown in Fig. 7.22.

       Let the variables **currentRow** and **currentColumn** indicate the row and col-
       umn of the knight's current position. To make a move of type **moveNumber**, where
       **moveNumber** is between 0 and 7, your program uses the statements

```
currentRow = currentRow + vertical(moveNumber)
currentColumn = currentColumn + horizontal(moveNumber)
```

       Keep a counter that varies from 1 to 64. Record the latest count in each square the knight
       moves to. Remember to test each potential move to see if the knight has already visited
       that square. And, of course, test every potential move to make sure that the knight does
       not land off the chessboard. Now write a program to move the knight around the chess-
       board. Run the program. How many moves did the knight make?

**Fig. 7.21** The eight possible moves of the knight.

| Horizontal component | Vertical component |
|---|---|
| horizontal(0) = 2 | vertical(0) = -1 |
| horizontal(1) = 1 | vertical(1) = -2 |
| horizontal(2) = -1 | vertical(2) = -2 |
| horizontal(3) = -2 | vertical(3) = -1 |
| horizontal(4) = -2 | vertical(4) = 1 |
| horizontal(5) = -1 | vertical(5) = 2 |
| horizontal(6) = 1 | vertical(6) = 2 |
| horizontal(7) = 2 | vertical(7) = 1 |

**Fig. 7.22** Arrays that describe the knight's move.

c) After attempting to write and run a Knight's Tour program, you have probably developed some valuable insights. We will use these to develop a heuristic (or strategy) for moving the knight. Heuristics do not guarantee success, but a carefully developed heuristic greatly improves the chance of success. You may have observed that the outer squares are more troublesome than the squares nearer the center of the board. In fact, the most troublesome, or inaccessible, squares are the four corners.

Intuition may suggest that you should attempt to move the knight to the most troublesome squares first and leave open those that are easiest to get to so that when the board gets congested near the end of the tour there will be a greater chance of success.

We may develop an "accessibility heuristic" by classifying each of the squares according to how accessible they are, and then always moving the knight to the square (within the knight's L-shaped moves, of course) that is most inaccessible. We label a two-dimensional array accessibility with numbers indicating from how many squares each particular square is accessible. On a blank chessboard, each center square is rated as 8, each corner square is rated as 2, and the other squares have accessibility numbers of 3, 4 or 6, as shown in Fig. 7.23.

**Fig. 7.23**   Accessibility numbers for Knight's Tour heuristic.

Write a version of the Knight's Tour program using the accessibility heuristic. At any time, the knight should move to the square with the lowest accessibility number. Therefore, the tour may begin in any of the four corners. In case of a tie, the knight may move to any of the tied squares. (Note: As the knight moves around the chessboard, your program should reduce the accessibility numbers as more and more squares become occupied. At any given time during the tour, each available square's accessibility number reflects the precise number of squares from which that square may be reached.) Run this version of your program. Did you get a full tour? Now modify the program to run 64 tours, one starting from each square of the chessboard. How many full tours did you get?

d) Write a version of the Knight's Tour program which, when encountering a tie between two or more squares, decides what square to choose by looking ahead to those squares reachable from the "tied" squares. Your program should move to the square for which the next move would arrive at a square with the lowest accessibility number.

**7.20**   (*Knight's Tour: Brute Force Approaches*) In Exercise 7.19 we developed a solution to the Knight's Tour problem. The approach used, called the "accessibility heuristic," generates many solutions and executes efficiently.

As computers continue increasing in power, we will be able to solve more problems with sheer computer power and relatively unsophisticated algorithms. Let us call this approach "brute force" problem solving.

a) Use random number generation to enable the knight to walk around the chessboard (in its legitimate L-shaped moves, of course) at random. Your program should run one tour and print the final chessboard. How far did the knight get?

b) Most likely, the preceding program produced a relatively short tour. Now modify your program to attempt 1000 tours. Use a one-dimensional array to keep track of the number of tours of each length. When your program finishes attempting the 1000 tours, it should print this information in neat tabular format. What was the best result?

c) Most likely, the preceding program gave you some "respectable" tours but no full tours. Now "pull all the stops out" and simply let your program run until it produces a full tour. (Caution: This version of the program could run for hours on a powerful computer.) Once again, keep a table of the number of tours of each length, and print this table when the first full tour is found. How many tours did your program attempt before producing a full tour? How much time did it take?

    d)  Compare the brute force version of the Knight's Tour with the accessibility heuristic version. Which required a more careful study of the problem? Which algorithm was more difficult to develop? Which required more computer power? Could we be certain (in advance) of obtaining a full tour with the accessibility heuristic approach? Could we be certain (in advance) of obtaining a full tour with the brute force approach? Argue the pros and cons of brute force problem solving in general.

**7.21**    (*Knight's Tour: Closed Tour Test*) In the Knight's Tour, a full tour occurs when the knight makes 64 moves touching each square of the chessboard once and only once. A closed tour occurs when the 64th move is one move away from the location in which the knight started the tour. Modify the Knight's Tour program you wrote in Exercise 7.19 (or Exercise 7.20) to test for a closed tour if a full tour has occurred.

**7.22**    (*Eight Queens*) Another puzzler for chess buffs is the Eight Queens problem. Simply stated: Is it possible to place eight queens on an empty chessboard so that no queen is "attacking" any other (i.e., no two queens are in the same row, the same column, or along the same diagonal)? Use the thinking developed in Exercise 7.19 to formulate a heuristic for solving the Eight Queens problem. Run your program. (Hint: It is possible to assign a value to each square of the chessboard indicating how many squares of an empty chessboard are "eliminated" if a queen is placed in that square. Each of the corners would be assigned the value 22, as in Fig. 7.24.) Once these "elimination numbers" are placed in all 64 squares, an appropriate heuristic might be: Place the next queen in the square with the smallest elimination number. Why is this strategy intuitively appealing?

**7.23**    (*Eight Queens: Brute Force Approaches*) In this exercise you will develop several brute force approaches to solving the Eight Queens problem introduced in Exercise 7.22.
    a)  Solve the Eight Queens exercise using the random brute force technique developed in Exercise 7.20.
    b)  Use an exhaustive technique (i.e., try all possible combinations of eight queens on the chessboard).
    c)  Why do you suppose the exhaustive brute force approach may not be appropriate for solving the Knight's Tour problem?
    d)  Compare and contrast the random brute force and exhaustive brute force approaches in general.

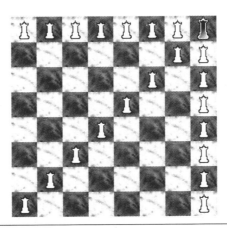

**Fig. 7.24**  The 22 squares eliminated by placing a queen in the upper right corner.

**7.24**    Modify the die-rolling program of Fig. 7.5 to use a control array for the **Image**s.

**7.25**    The bubble sort presented in Fig. 7.7 is inefficient for large arrays. Make the following simple modifications to improve the performance of the bubble sort.

   a) After the first pass, the largest number is guaranteed to be in the highest-numbered element of the array; after the second pass, the two highest numbers are "in place," and so on. Instead of making nine comparisons on every pass, modify the bubble sort to make eight comparisons on the second pass, seven on the third pass, and so on.

   b) The data in the array may already be in the proper order or near-proper order, so why make nine passes if fewer will suffice? Modify the sort to check at the end of each pass if any swaps have been made. If none has been made, then the data must already be in the proper order, so the program should terminate. If swaps have been made, then at least one more pass is needed.

**7.26**    (*Selection Sort*) A selection sort searches an array looking for the smallest element in the array. Then, the smallest element is swapped with the first element of the array. The process is repeated for the subarray beginning with the second element of the array. Each pass of the array results in at least one more element being placed into its proper location. This sort performs comparably to the bubble sort—for an array of $n$ elements, $n - 1$ passes must be made, and for each subarray, $n - 1$ comparisons must be made to find the smallest value. When the subarray being processed contains one element, the array is sorted. Write a program to perform this algorithm.

**7.27**    (*Bucket Sort*) A bucket sort begins with a one-dimensional array of positive **Integer**s to be sorted and a two-dimensional array of **Integer**s with rows indexed from 0 to 9 and columns indexed from 0 to $n - 1$, where n is the number of values in the array to be sorted. Each row of the two-dimensional array is referred to as a "bucket." Write a function **BucketSort** that takes an integer array and the array size as arguments and performs as follows:

   1. Place each value of the one-dimensional array into a row of the bucket array based on the value's ones digit. For example, 97 is placed in row 7, 3 is placed in row 3 and 100 is placed in row 0. This is called a "distribution pass."

   2. Loop through the bucket array row-by-row and copy the values back to the original array. This is called a "gathering pass." The new order of the preceding values in the one-dimensional array is 100, 3 and 97.

   3. Repeat this process for each subsequent digit position (tens, hundreds, thousands, etc.).

   4. On the second pass, 100 is placed in row 0, 3 is placed in row 0 (because 3 has no tens digit) and 97 is placed in row 9. After the gathering pass, the order of the values in the one-dimensional array is 100, 3 and 97. On the third pass, 100 is placed in row 1, 3 is placed in row zero and 97 is placed in row zero (after the 3). After the last gathering pass, the original array is now in sorted order.

Note that the two-dimensional array of buckets is ten times the size of the **Integer** array being sorted. This sorting technique provides better performance than a bubble sort, but requires much more memory. The bubble sort requires space for only one additional element of data. This is an example of the space-time trade-off: The bucket sort uses more memory than the bubble sort, but performs better. This version of the bucket sort requires copying all the data back to the original array on each pass. Another possibility is to create a second two-dimensional bucket array and repeatedly swap the data between the two bucket arrays.

**7.28**    (*Quicksort*) In this chapter and previous exercises, we discussed the sorting techniques of bubble sort, bucket sort, and selection sort. We now present the recursive sorting technique called Quicksort. The basic algorithm for a one-dimensional array of values is as follows:

   a) *Partitioning Step:* Take the first element of the unsorted array and determine its final location in the sorted array (i.e., all values to the left of the element in the array are less than the element, and all values to the right of the element in the array are greater than the element). We now have one element in its proper location and two unsorted subarrays.

b) *Recursive Step:* Perform step 1 on each unsorted subarray.

Each time step 1 is performed on a subarray, another element is placed in its final location of the sorted array, and two unsorted subarrays are created. When a subarray consists of one element, it must be sorted; therefore, that element is in its final location.

The basic algorithm seems simple enough, but how do we determine the final position of the first element of each subarray? As an example, consider the following set of values (the element in bold is the partitioning element—it will be placed in its final location in the sorted array):

**37**  2  6  4  89  8  10  12  68  45

a) Starting from the rightmost element of the array, compare each element to **37** until an element less than **37** is found, then swap **37** and that element. The first element less than **37** is 12, so **37** and 12 are swapped. The new array is:

*12*  2  6  4  89  8  10  **37**  68  45

Element 12 is in italic to indicate that it was just swapped with **37**.

b) Starting from the left of the array, but beginning with the element after 12, compare each element to **37** until an element greater than **37** is found, then swap **37** and that element. The first element greater than **37** is 89, so **37** and 89 are swapped. The new array is

12  2  6  4  **37**  8  10  *89*  68  45

c) Starting from the right, but beginning with the element before 89, compare each element to **37** until an element less than **37** is found, then swap **37** and that element. The first element less than **37** is 10, so **37** and 10 are swapped. The new array is

12  2  6  4  *10*  8  **37**  89  68  45

d) Starting from the left, but beginning with the element after 10, compare each element to **37** until an element greater than **37** is found, then swap **37** and that element. There are no more elements greater than **37**, so when we compare **37** to itself we know that **37** has been placed in its final location of the sorted array.

Once the partition has been applied on the above array, there are two unsorted subarrays. The subarray with values less than 37 contains 12, 2, 6, 4, 10 and 8. The subarray with values greater than 37 contains 89, 68 and 45. The sort continues with both subarrays being partitioned in the same manner as the original array.

Based on the preceding discussion, write recursive function **QuickSort** to sort a one-dimensional **Integer** array. The function should receive as arguments an **Integer** array, a starting index and an ending index. Function **Partition** should be called by **QuickSort** to perform the partitioning step.

**7.29**    (*Turtle Graphics*) The Logo language, which is particularly popular among personal computer users, made the concept of turtle graphics famous. Imagine a mechanical turtle that walks around the room under the control of a Visual Basic program. The turtle holds a pen in one of two positions, up or down. While the pen is down, the turtle traces out shapes as it moves; while the pen is up, the turtle moves about freely without writing anything. In this problem you will simulate the operation of the turtle and create a computerized sketchbook as well.

Use a 20-by-20 array **floor** which is initialized to zeros. Read commands from an array that contains them. Keep track of the current position of the turtle at all times and whether the pen is currently up or down. Assume that the turtle always starts at position 0,0 of the floor with its pen up. The set of turtle commands your program must process are as follows:

| Command | Meaning |
|---------|---------|
| 1 | Pen up |
| 2 | Pen down |
| 3 | Turn right |
| 7 | Turn left |
| 5,10 | Move forward $n$ spaces (in this case 10) |
| 6 | Print the 20-by-20 array |
| 9 | End of data (sentinel) |

Suppose that the turtle is somewhere near the center of the floor. The following "program" would draw and print a 12-by 12-square leaving the pen in the up position:

2

5,12

3

5,12

3

5,12

3

5,12

1

6

9

As the turtle moves with the pen down, set the appropriate elements of array **floor** to 1s. When the 6 command (print) is given, wherever there is a 1 in the array, display an asterisk, or some other character you choose. Wherever there is a zero display a blank. Write a program to implement the turtle graphics capabilities discussed here. Write several turtle graphics programs to draw interesting shapes. Add other commands to increase the power of your turtle graphics language.

**7.30**    Write a recursive version of the **LinearSearch** discussed in Fig. 7.8.

**7.31**    Write a recursive version of the **BinarySearch** discussed in Fig. 7.9.

**7.32**    The Fibonacci series

0, 1, 1, 2, 3, 5, 8, 13, 21, ...

begins with the terms 0 and 1 and has the property that each succeeding term is the sum of the two preceding terms. (a) Write a nonrecursive procedure **Fibonacci** that calculates the $n^{th}$ Fibonacci number. (b) Determine the largest Fibonacci number that can be calculated on your system. Use data type **Double**.

# Strings, Dates and Times

## Objectives

- To use the string concatenation operators.
- To be able to compare strings and search strings for substrings.
- To be able to manipulate the characters in a string using a variety of functions.
- To be able to convert values to and from strings and other data types.
- To be able to use the date and time functions.
- To be able to format strings, dates and times.

*The chief defect of Henry King*
*Was chewing little bits of string.*
Hilaire Belloc

*Vigorous writing is concise. A sentence should contain no unnecessary words, a paragraph no unnecessary sentences.*
William Strunk, Jr.

*I have made this letter longer than usual, because I lack the time to make it short.*
Blaise Pascal

*The difference between the almost-right word & the right word is really a large matter—it's the difference between the lightning bug and the lightning.*
Mark Twain

*Mum's the word.*
Miguel de Cervantes, *Don Quixote de la Mancha*

# Outline

## 8.1  Introduction

With this chapter we begin our study of more advanced topics. At this point in the text, the reader should have a thorough understanding of fundamental programming concepts and should be well prepared for investigating more substantial programming applications.

In this chapter, we introduce Visual Basic's string and character processing capabilities. The techniques discussed here are appropriate for developing text editors, word processors, page layout software, computerized typesetting systems, and other kinds of text-processing software. In this chapter we discuss in detail the capabilities of data type **String** and the many **String**, **Date**, **Time** and conversion functions available in Visual Basic.

String manipulation features of the Visual Basic language permit the programmer to write programs that process letters, words, sentences, names, addresses, descriptive data, and special symbols (such as +, –, *, /, $, etc.).

The importance of string manipulation has been greatly underscored by developments in the area of word processing. Word processing involves many office tasks related to automatic letter writing systems, text editing systems, document preparation systems, etc. This chapter illustrates many of the text manipulation methods that are useful in word processing systems.

## 8.2 Fundamentals of Characters and **Strings**

Characters are the fundamental building blocks of Visual Basic source programs. Every program is composed of a sequence of characters that—when grouped together meaningfully—is interpreted by the computer as a series of instructions used to accomplish a task. Each character is represented internally as a small integer in the range 0 to 255 (e.g., 65 represents the uppercase letter **A**, 66 represents the uppercase letter **B**, 97 represents the lowercase letter **a**, 98 represents the lowercase letter **b**, etc.). The set of the small integer values used by Visual Basic is called the *American National Standards Institute (ANSI) character set* (see Appendix B).

The first 128 ANSI characters (i.e., small integer values from 0 to 127) correspond to "*American Standard Code for Information Interchange (ASCII)* values. ANSI values from 128 to 255 represent a variety of special characters, accents, fractions, currency symbols and international characters.

A string is a series of characters treated as a single unit. A string may include letters, digits and various *special characters* such as **+**, **-**, **\***, **/**, **$** and others. A string in Visual Basic is of data type **String**. *String literals* or *string constants* in Visual Basic are written as a sequence of characters in double quotation marks as follows:

| | |
|---|---|
| `"John Q. Doe"` | (a name) |
| `"9999 Main Street"` | (a street address) |
| `"Somewhere, Massachusetts"` | (a city and state) |
| `"(555) 555-5555"` | (a telephone number) |

String manipulations inside the computer actually involve the manipulation of the appropriate numeric codes (i.e., the small integers we have been discussing) and not the characters themselves. When a computer compares two strings, it actually compares the underlying numeric codes that make up the characters in the strings.

From this point forward, we shall refer to string values (or string constants) simply as strings. Visual Basic also provides for *string variables* that may contain different strings at different times during a particular execution of a program. The dollar sign, **$**, is the type declaration character for a **String**.

## 8.3 `String` Data Type

Visual Basic provides data type ***String*** to declare *string variables* in a program. Two types of strings that can be declared: *variable-length strings* and *fixed-length strings.* Variable-length strings are composed of up to 2,147,483,648 characters. Fixed-length strings are composed of up to 65,536 characters. A **String** consists of characters with numeric values in the range 0 – 255.

> *Good Programming Practice 8.1*
>
> *Variables that will only contain strings should be declared as* ***String****.*

By default, **String** variables represent variable-length strings that grow and shrink dynamically based on the strings that are assigned to them, as in the lines

```
Dim s as String
s = "blue"
```

that declare **s** as a **String** and assign **s** the string **"blue"**.

Fixed-length strings are declared as follows:

```
Dim variableName As String * size
```

For example, to declare a string that represents a social security number in the form 111-11-1111 (a total of 11 characters), use the declaration

```
Dim socialSecurityNumber As String * 11
```

If the string assigned to **socialSecurityNumber** is fewer than 11 characters, the string is padded with trailing spaces so that the total number of characters is 11. For strings larger than the fixed-length string, Visual Basic truncates the characters so that the length matches the length of the fixed-length string.

## 8.4 String Concatenation with & and +

Larger strings can be constructed by combining several smaller strings. This process, called *string concatenation,* is indicated with a *plus sign ( +)* or an *ampersand ( &)* as follows:

```
s1 = "Pro"
s2 = "gram"
s3 = s1 & s2
```

*or*

```
s3 = s1 + s2
```

The above statements would concatenate (or append) **s2** to the right of **s1** to create an entirely new string, **s3**, containing **Program**.

If both operands of the concatenation operators are strings, these two operators can be used interchangeably. However, if the + operator is used in an expression consisting of varying data types, there can be a problem. For example, in the statement

```
s1 = "hello" + 22
```

Visual Basic first tries to convert the string **"hello"** to a number, then add **22** to it. The string **"hello"** cannot be converted to a number, so a type mismatch error occurs at execution time. For this reason, the **&** operator should be used for string concatenation.

*Good Programming Practice 8.2*

*Always use the ampersand (**&**) operator for string concatenation.*

## 8.5 Comparing Character Strings

In string manipulation applications, it is frequently necessary to compare two strings. Visual Basic allows all of the relational and equality operators to be used to compare strings.

The program in Fig. 8.1 demonstrates string comparisons using function *StrComp* and the relational (**<**, **<=**, **>**, **>=**) and equality (**=**, **<>**) operators. The user interface for this program consists of several **Label**s, two **TextBox**es, a **CommandButton** and a **List**. To compare two strings, type the strings into the two **TextBox**es, then click the **Compare** button (this calls event procedure **cmdCompare_Click** at line 6). The program then compares the strings, displays the results of using **StrComp** below the **Compare** button and displays the results of using the relational and equality operators in the **List** at the bottom of the window.

```
1   ' Fig. 8.1
2   ' Comparing strings with StrComp,
3   ' relational and equality operators
4   Option Explicit
5
6   Private Sub cmdCompare_Click()
7      Dim result As Integer
8
9      result = StrComp(txtInput1.Text, txtInput2.Text)
10
11     If result = -1 Then
12        lblOutput.Caption = _
13           "The first string is less than the second string"
14     ElseIf result = 1 Then
15        lblOutput.Caption = _
16           "The first string is greater than the second string"
17     Else
18        lblOutput.Caption = "The strings are equal"
19     End If
20
21     Call lstOutput.Clear
22
23     If txtInput1.Text = txtInput2.Text Then
24        Call lstOutput.AddItem(txtInput1.Text & " is equal to " & _
25                               txtInput2.Text)
26     End If
27
```

**Fig. 8.1**   Comparing strings (part 1 of 3).

```
28        If txtInput1.Text <> txtInput2.Text Then
29            Call lstOutput.AddItem(txtInput1.Text & _
30                              " is not equal to " & txtInput2.Text)
31        End If
32
33        If txtInput1.Text < txtInput2.Text Then
34            Call lstOutput.AddItem(txtInput1.Text & _
35                              " is less than " & txtInput2.Text)
36        End If
37
38        If txtInput1.Text > txtInput2.Text Then
39            Call lstOutput.AddItem(txtInput1.Text & _
40                              " is greater than " & txtInput2.Text)
41        End If
42
43        If txtInput1.Text <= txtInput2.Text Then
44            Call lstOutput.AddItem(txtInput1.Text & _
45                              " is less than or equal to " & _
46                              txtInput2.Text)
47        End If
48
49        If txtInput1.Text >= txtInput2.Text Then
50            Call lstOutput.AddItem(txtInput1.Text & _
51                              " is greater than or equal to " & _
52                              txtInput2.Text)
53        End If
54
55    End Sub
```

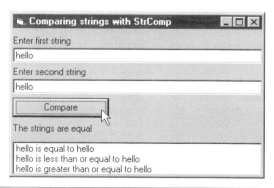

**Fig. 8.1**    Comparing strings (part 2 of 3).

Line 9,

```
result = StrComp(txtInput1.Text, txtInput2.Text)
```

uses function **StrComp** to compare the strings in the **txtInput1** and **txtInput2** **TextBox**es. Based on the **result**, the **If/ElseIf/Else** structure at lines 11 through 19 assigns a string indicating the result to **lblOutput.Caption**. Function **StrComp** returns **0** if the strings are equal, **-1** if the first string is less than the second and **1** if the first string is greater than the second.

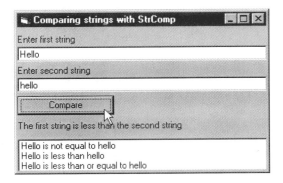

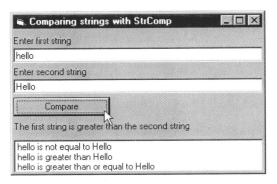

**Fig. 8.1**   Comparing strings (part 3 of 3).

To understand just what it means for one string to be "greater than" or "less than" another string, consider the process of alphabetizing a series of last names. The reader would, no doubt, place "Jones" before "Smith" because the first letter of "Jones" comes before the first letter of "Smith" in the alphabet. But the alphabet is more than just a list of 26 letters—it is an ordered list. Each of the letters occurs in a specific place in the ordering. "Z" is more than merely a letter of the alphabet. More specifically, it is the twenty-sixth letter of the alphabet.

How does the computer know that one particular letter comes before another? All characters are represented inside the computer as numeric codes; when the computer compares two strings, it actually compares these numeric codes.

Function **StrComp** can receive an optional third argument that indicates the comparison type. Possible values for this argument are shown in Fig. 8.2.

Type **vbUseCompareOption** indicates that the comparison type is specified in a module-level *Option Compare* statement of the form

```
Option Compare type
```

where type is *Binary*, *Text* or *Database*. If an **Option Compare** statement is not used, the default comparison type is **Binary**.

The **If** structures at lines 23 through 51 use the **=**, **<>**, **<**, **>**, **<=** and **>=** operators to compare the strings. For each **True** condition, an item is added to **lstOutput**.

| Comparison type | Description |
| --- | --- |
| **vbUseCompareOption** | Use the comparison type specified in the **Option Compare** statement. |
| **vbBinaryCompare** | Perform a case-sensitive comparison (i.e., **A** and **a** are compared using their ASCII values to determine that they are not equal). |
| **vbTextCompare** | Perform a case-insensitive comparison (i.e., **A** and **a** are equal). |
| **vbDatabaseCompare** | Perform comparisons based on information from a Microsoft Access database. |

**Fig. 8.2**    Types of comparisons.

The outputs in Fig. 8.1 show several string comparisons. In the first screen capture, both strings are "**hello**," so the strings compare as equal. In the second screen capture, the string "**Hello**" is considered to be less than the string "**hello**" (because "**H**" comes before "**h**" in the ASCII character set). In the third screen capture, the string "**hello**" is considered to be greater than the string "**Hello**" (because "**h**" comes after "**H**" in the ASCII character set). Note that the computer considers the string "**j**" to be less than the string "**john**." This corresponds to the ordering the reader would use in alphabetizing names of different lengths. If one name is equivalent to the leftmost portion of another name, the shorter name would come before the longer name in an alphabetical sequence.

## 8.6 Operator **Like**

Operator **Like** provides another way to compare two strings. **Like** allows the programmer to compare patterns of characters as well as strings. For example,

        **"HBLT55DD" Like "HBLT55DD"**

and

        **"HBLT55DD" Like "HBLT*"**

are both **True**. The first comparison tests the two strings for equality. The second comparison tests to see if **HBLT55DD** is a string that begins with **HBLT**. The *asterisk*, **\***, is a *pattern matching character* that indicates any number of characters can follow.

Pattern matching character **?** indicates that a single character can be any type of character (i.e., letter, digit, etc.) and pattern matching character **#** indicates that a single character can be a digit. For example,

        **"HBLT55DD" Like "?#LT55DD"**

is **False** because the second letter of **HBLT55DD** is not a digit. The operation

        **"HBLT55DD" Like "?BLT5#DD"**

is **True** because the first letter of **HBLT55DD** can be any character and the sixth character is a **5**. A series of characters can also be provided for the pattern matching character using square brackets, *[]*. For example,

```
"HBLT55DD" Like "H[A-F]LT55DD"
```

is **True** because the second character in **HBLT55DD** is within the range **A** through **F**. The operation

```
"HBLT55DD" Like "H[A-F]LT[!4-7]5DD"
```

is **False** because the fifth character is within the range **4** through **7**. The *exclamation point*, *!*, behaves like operator **Not** when placed inside the square brackets.

The program of Fig. 8.3 allows the user to determine if a string matches the pattern of characters in another string.

```
1   ' Fig. 8.3
2   ' Demonstrating operator Like
3   Option Explicit
4
5   Private Sub Form_Load()
6       Call lstPatterns.AddItem("  ?         Any one character")
7       Call lstPatterns.AddItem("  *         Multiple characters")
8       Call lstPatterns.AddItem("[chars]   Any one character " & _
9                               "in chars")
10      Call lstPatterns.AddItem("[!chars]  Any one character " & _
11                              "not in chars")
12  End Sub
13
14  Private Sub cmdTest_Click()
15      Dim b As Boolean
16
17      b = txtString.Text Like txtPattern.Text
18      lblResult.Caption = txtString.Text & " Like " & _
19                          txtPattern.Text & " is " & b
20  End Sub
```

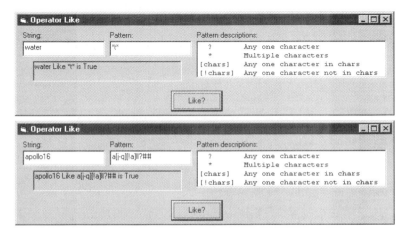

**Fig. 8.3**   Demonstrating operator **Like**.

## 8.7 Manipulating the Individual Characters in a String: `Mid$`

Visual Basic provides several different means for referencing the individual characters in a string. The next several examples introduce these techniques.

Figure 8.4 demonstrates function **_Mid$_** for selecting substrings from a string. The program allows the user to type a string and reverses the characters. To be able to spell a word or a phrase backwards, we need the ability to extract one character at a time from a string. In particular, we need to obtain the last character of the string, then the next preceding character, then the next, etc. The **Mid$** function is appropriate for this purpose.

The crux of the program is the **For** loop. The loop counts backwards from the highest-numbered position in the string to 1. Function **_Len_** (for "length") is used to determine the length of **phrase**. Function **Mid$** is then used to extract one character at a time from **phrase**.

```
1    ' Fig. 8.4
2    ' Using Mid$ and Len to reverse a string
3    Option Explicit
4
5    Private Sub cmdReverse_Click()
6       Dim phrase As String, position As Integer
7
8       txtOutput.Text = ""
9       phrase = txtInput.Text
10
11      For position = Len(phrase) To 1 Step -1
12         txtOutput.Text = txtOutput.Text & _
13            Mid$(phrase, position, 1)
14      Next
15
16   End Sub
```

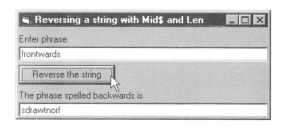

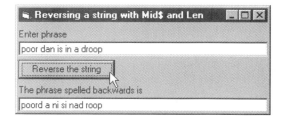

**Fig. 8.4**    Using functions **Mid$** and **Len** (part 1 of 2).

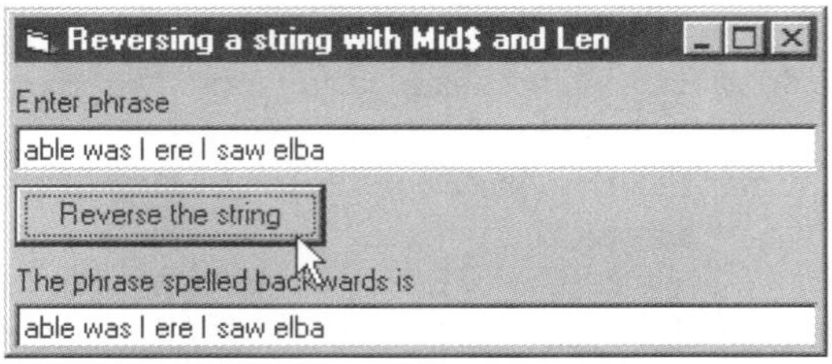

**Fig. 8.4**    Using functions **Mid$** and **Len** (part 2 of 2).

The user interface of the program consists of **Label**s, two **TextBox**es and a **CommandButton**. The user types a phrase in the first **TextBox** and presses the **Reverse the String** button to reverse the string. Event procedure **cmdReverse_Click** at line 5 executes and displays the result in the second **TextBox**. Line 9,

```
phrase = txtInput.Text
```

assigns the text the user typed to **phrase**. Lines 12 and 13,

```
txtOutput.Text = txtOutput.Text & _
    Mid$(phrase, position, 1)
```

append one character to the end of the string in **txtOutput**. The **&** *string concatenation operator* concatenates two strings by appending the characters of its second operand at the end of the characters in its first operand. The result of the operation is a new string that can be stored by assigning it to a string variable (**txtOutput.Text** in this case).

Function **Mid$** takes three arguments—the source string from which a substring will be selected, the starting character position in the string and the number of characters to select. If the last argument is omitted or if the number of characters remaining is fewer than the number of characters to select, the remainder of the string from the starting character position is returned. In this statement, the **1** character at **position** of **phrase** is selected and returned.

**Mid$** can also be used to replace a portion of a string with another string. For example, the statements

```
x = "Visual Basic 6!"
Mid$(x, 2, 3) = "xxx"
```

change the contents of **x** to "**Vxxxal Basic 6!**".

## 8.8 Left$, Right$ and InStr

Let us consider three additional Visual Basic functions, namely **Left$**, **Right$** and **InStr**, which are useful for manipulating and searching strings.

**Left$** selects the leftmost portion of a string. For example, if **s1** and **s2** are **String** variables, the statements

```
s1 = "ABCDEF"
s2 = Left$(s1, 4)
```

would select the leftmost four characters of **s1** and assign the string **ABCD** to **s2**. **Right$** selects the rightmost portion of a string. For example, the statements

```
s1 = "ABCDEF"
s2 = Right$(s1, 4)
```

would select the rightmost four characters of **s1** and assign the string **CDEF** to **s2**.

Function **InStr** is useful for searching through one string, called the *base string*, to determine if it contains another string, called the *search string*. If the second string is found, the starting character location of that string is returned. If the second string is zero length (i.e., it contains no characters) the starting position is returned. For example, the statements

```
s1 = "AEIOU"
s2 = "IOU"
result = InStr(1, s1, s2)
```

would determine that **s2** (the search string) is indeed contained within **s1** (the base string), at position 3. Function **InStr** returns the starting position of **s2** within **s1**; in this case **3**, and **3** is assigned to **result**. In this **InStr** example, **1** indicates that the search for **s2** is to begin at position **1** of **s1**. It is possible to begin the search at any position within **s1**. The first argument can be omitted if the search should begin from the start of the base string. Note that if **InStr** determines that the search string is not contained within the base string, then **InStr** returns zero. For example, the following statements each result in zero being returned and assigned to **result**:

```
result = InStr(1, "aeiou", "aeb")
result = InStr(4, "aeiou", "iou")
result = InStr(1, "aeiou", "aeiouy")
```

The program of Fig. 8.5 uses the **Left$**, **Right$** and **InStr** functions to encode English language phrases into pig Latin. Pig Latin is a form of coded language often used for amusement. Many variations exist in the methods used to form pig Latin phrases. For simplicity, use the following algorithm:

> *To form a pig Latin phrase from an English language phrase, the translation proceeds one word at a time. To translate an English word into a pig Latin word, place the first letter of the English word at the end of the English word, and add the letters "**ay**." Thus, the word "**jump**" becomes "**umpjay**," the word "**the**" becomes "**hetay**," and the word "**computer**" becomes "**omputercay**." Blanks between words remain as blanks. Make the following assumptions: the English phrase consists of words separated by blanks, there are no punctuation marks and all words have two or more letters.*

```
1   ' Fig. 8.5
2   ' Demonstrating Left$, Right$ and InStr
3   Option Explicit
4
5   Private Sub cmdConvert_Click()
6      Dim phrase As String, nextWord As String, _
7         blankPosition As Integer
```

**Fig. 8.5**    A pig Latin program (part 1 of 2).

```
 8
 9        txtOutput.Text = ""
10        phrase = txtInput.Text
11        blankPosition = InStr(1, phrase, " ")
12
13        While blankPosition <> 0
14           nextWord = Left$(phrase, blankPosition - 1)
15
16           Call DisplayLatinWord(nextWord)
17           phrase = Right$(phrase, Len(phrase) - blankPosition)
18           blankPosition = InStr(1, phrase, " ")
19        Wend
20
21        nextWord = phrase
22        Call DisplayLatinWord(nextWord)
23     End Sub
24
25     Private Sub DisplayLatinWord(word As String)
26        txtOutput.Text = txtOutput.Text & _
27           Right$(word, Len(word) - 1) & _
28           Left$(word, 1) & "ay "
29     End Sub
```

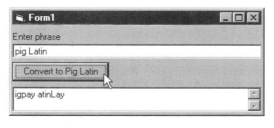

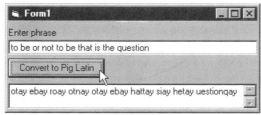

**Fig. 8.5**    A pig Latin program (part 2 of 2).

The user interface of the program consists of a **Label**, two **TextBox**es and a **CommandButton**. The second **TextBox** is a multiline **TextBox** with a vertical scrollbar. The user types a phrase in the first **TextBox** and presses the **Convert to Pig Latin** button to reverse the string. Event procedure **cmdConvert_Click** at line 5 executes and displays the result in the second **TextBox**.

Line 10,

```
phrase = txtInput.Text
```

obtains an English phrase from **txtInput** and assigns it to **phrase**.

Line 11,

```
blankPosition = InStr(1, phrase, " ")
```

uses function **InStr** to locate the first blank in **phrase** (if there are any blanks).
Line 14,

```
nextWord = Left$(phrase, blankPosition - 1)
```

in the **While** structure uses function **Left$** to "pick off" one word at a time from **phrase** and places the word in **nextWord**. Line 16 calls procedure **DisplayLatin-Word** (line 25) to append the pig Latin equivalent of the word to **txtOutput**.

After a word is processed, the program "shrinks" the original English phrase by removing that word from **phrase**.
Line 17,

```
phrase = Right$(phrase, Len(phrase) - blankPosition)
```

uses function **Right$** to return the remainder of **phrase** from the character after **blankPosition**. Line 18 locates the next blank if there is one.

Eventually, **phrase** will shrink to a single word. This causes a zero to be assigned **blankPosition** and causes termination of the **While** structure. The program then processes the last word in the phrase and prints its pig Latin equivalent.

In procedure **DisplayLatinWord**, lines 26 through 28,

```
txtOutput.Text = txtOutput.Text & _
   Right$(word, Len(word) - 1) & _
   Left$(word, 1) & "ay "
```

append to the text in **txtOutput.Text** by using function **Right$** to append all but the first character of word, using function **Left$** to append the first character of word and appending the string **"ay "** to complete the current pig Latin word.

## 8.9 Searching for Substrings in **Strings** Using **InStr** and **InStrRev**

Most word processors support searching for strings from the beginning and end of a document. Functions **InStr** and **InStrRev** search for substrings in a string from the start and end of the string, respectively. As we showed in Section 8.7, function **InStr** can search from any location in a string. Similarly, **InStrRev** can search from the end or any other position in a string. Both functions take an optional fourth argument that specifies the type of comparison to use while searching. Constants for this argument are shown in Fig. 8.2.

Function **InStrRev**'s arguments are a base string, a search string and the starting character position in the base string. If the search string is found, the starting character location of that string is returned. If the search string is *zero length* (i.e., it contains no characters) the starting position is returned. For example, if **s1** and **s2** are **String**s, the statements

```
s1 = "abcdefghijklmnop"
s2 = "m"
result = InStrRev(s1, s2, Len(s1))
```

would determine that **s2** (the search string) is contained in **s1** (the base string) at position 13. Function **InStrRev** returns the starting position of **s2** in **s1**, in this case **13**, and **13** is assigned to **result**. In this **InStrRev** example, **Len(s1)** indicates that the search for **s2** begins at the end of **s1**. It is possible to begin the search at any position in **s1**. The third argument can be omitted if the search begins from the end of the base string. Note that if **InStrRev** determines that the search string is not contained within the base string, then **InStrRev** returns zero. For example, the following statements each result in zero:

```
result = InStr("aeiou", "aeb")
result = InStr("aeiou", "iou", 2)
result = InStr("aeiou", "aeiouy")
```

The program of Fig. 8.6 allows the user to enter two strings into **TextBox**es. When the user presses the **Search** button, the program searches for the second string in the first string and displays the results of the search in two **Label**s at the bottom of the window.

When the user clicks the **Search** button, event procedure **cmdSearch_Click** at line 5 executes. Line 8,

```
forwardResult = InStr(txtInput1.Text, txtInput2.Text)
```

uses function **InStr** to locate the first occurrence of **txtInput2.Text** in **txtInput1.Text** starting from the beginning of **txtInput1.Text**.

```
1   ' Fig. 8.6
2   ' Using InStr and InStrRev to search a string for a substring
3   Option Explicit
4
5   Private Sub cmdSearch_Click()
6      Dim forwardResult As Integer, backwardResult As Integer
7
8      forwardResult = InStr(txtInput1.Text, txtInput2.Text)
9
10     If forwardResult <> 0 Then
11        lblOutput1.Caption = "Forward search: " & _
12           "The text was found at position " & forwardResult
13     Else
14        lblOutput1.Caption = "Forward search: " & _
15           "The text was not found"
16     End If
17
18     backwardResult = InStrRev(txtInput1.Text, txtInput2.Text)
19
20     If backwardResult <> 0 Then
21        lblOutput2.Caption = "Backward search: " & _
22           "The text was found at position " & backwardResult
23     Else
24        lblOutput2.Caption = "Backward search: " & _
25           "The text was not found"
26     End If
27  End Sub
```

**Fig. 8.6**   Searching strings with **InStr** and **InStrRev** (part 1 of 2)

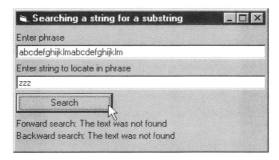

**Fig. 8.6**    Searching strings with **InStr** and **InStrRev** (part 2 of 2)

Line 18,

```
backwardResult = InStrRev(txtInput1.Text, txtInput2.Text)
```

uses function **InStrRev** to locate the last occurrence of **txtInput2.Text** in **txtInput1.Text** starting from the end of **txtInput1.Text**.

## 8.10 LTrim$, RTrim$ and Trim$

Functions *LTrim$*, *RTrim$* and *Trim$* remove leading spaces at the left side of a string, trailing spaces at the right side of a string, and spaces on both the left and the right side of a string, respectively. These functions are particularly useful for removing extra space characters used to pad a fixed-length string so that the string occupies the total space allocated for it. Figure 8.7 allows the user to type a string with leading and trailing spaces in a **Text-Box**. When the user clicks button **Trim space characters**, event procedure **cmd-Trim_Click** executes and adds three items to the **ListBox lstOutput**. Each item is preceded and followed by **\*\*\*** so you can see the results of removing the spaces. The three items are the results of the **LTrim$**, **RTrim$** and **Trim$** operations, respectively.

## 8.11 String$ and Space$

Functions *String$* and *Space$* create strings of a specified number of characters. Function *String$* creates a string of a specified character. Function *Space$* creates a string of spaces. The program of Fig. 8.8 demonstrates these functions. When the program loads, three items are added to **ListBox lstOutput**. In line 6,

```
1   ' Fig. 8.7
2   ' Using LTrim, RTrim and Trim to remove
3   ' leading and trailing spaces on a string
4   Option Explicit
5
6   Private Sub cmdTrim_Click()
7       Call lstOutput.Clear
8       Call lstOutput.AddItem ("***" & LTrim$(txtInput.Text) & _
9                                "***")
10      Call lstOutput.AddItem ("***" & RTrim$(txtInput.Text) & _
11                               "***")
12      Call lstOutput.AddItem ("***" & Trim$(txtInput.Text) & _
13                               "***")
14  End Sub
```

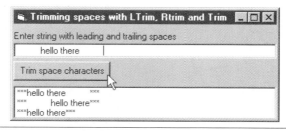

**Fig. 8.7**   Demonstrating **LTrim$**, **RTrim$** and **Trim$**.

```
1   ' Fig. 8.8
2   ' Using String and Space
3   Option Explicit
4
5   Private Sub Form_Load()
6       Call lstOutput.AddItem("10 A's: " & String$(10, "A"))
7       Call lstOutput.AddItem("5 a's: " & String$(5, 97))
8       Call lstOutput.AddItem("5 a's preceded by 5 spaces: " & _
9                               Space$(5) & String$(5, "a"))
10  End Sub
```

**Fig. 8.8**   Demonstrating functions **String$** and **Space$**.

       **String$(10, "A")**

creates a string containing **10** of the letter **A**. In line 7,

       **String$(5, 97)**

creates a string containing **5** of the character with numeric code **97** (the letter **a**). In line 9,

       **Space$(5) & String$(5, "a")**

creates a string containing **5** spaces and appends to it a string containing **5** of the letter **a**.

## 8.12 Replacing Substrings in a `String` with Function `Replace`

Word processors typically provide a capability to search for a string and replace one or more occurrences of that string. Function *Replace* provides that capability in Visual Basic. The program of Fig. 8.9 demonstrates function **Replace**. When the user clicks the **Replace spaces with two periods** button, event procedure **cmdReplace_Click** executes the statement

```
lblOutput.Caption = Replace(txtInput.Text, " ", "..")
```

The first argument to **Replace** is the string in which substrings will be replaced. The second argument is the substring to locate and replace. The third argument is the replacement string. In this example, every space character is replaced with two periods. The resulting string is assigned to **Label lblOutput**'s **Caption** property and displayed below the **CommandButton**.

Function **Replace** has three optional arguments also. The fourth argument is used to indicate the starting character position for the search. The fifth argument is used to specify the number of replacements to perform. The sixth argument specifies the comparison type by using one of the comparison constants in Fig. 8.2.

## 8.13 Reversing `Strings` with Function `StrReverse`

In Fig. 8.4, we demonstrated function *Mid$* by using it to reverse a string. Visual Basic provides **StrReverse** exactly for this purpose. Fig. 8.10 demonstrates function *StrReverse*. When the user types a string in the **TextBox** and clicks the **Reverse the string** button, event procedure **cmdReverse_Click** executes the statement

```
txtOutput.Text = StrReverse(txtInput.Text)
```

to reverse the string and assign the result to **txtOutput.Text**.

```
1   ' Fig. 8.9
2   ' Using Replace to replace substrings in a string
3   Option Explicit
4
5   Private Sub cmdReplace_Click()
6       lblOutput.Caption = Replace(txtInput.Text, " ", "..")
7   End Sub
```

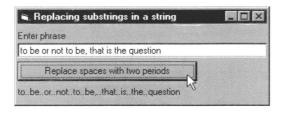

**Fig. 8.9**    Demonstrating function **Replace**.

```
1   ' Fig. 8.10
2   ' Using StrReverse to reverse the characters in a string
3   Option Explicit
4
5   Private Sub cmdReverse_Click()
6       txtOutput.Text = StrReverse(txtInput.Text)
7   End Sub
```

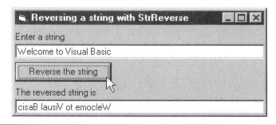

**Fig. 8.10**   Reversing strings with function **StrReverse**.

## 8.14 Converting Strings to Uppercase and Lowercase

Functions **UCase$** and **LCase$** convert strings to all uppercase letters and all lowercase letters, respectively. In the program of Fig. 8.11, the user enters a string in the first **TextBox** and clicks the **Convert** button to execute event procedure **cmdConvert_Click** at line 5. The lines

```
txtUpperCase.Text = UCase$(txtInput.Text)
txtLowerCase.Text = LCase$(txtInput.Text)
```

convert the strings and assign the results to the **TextBox**es **txtUpperCase** and **txtLowerCase**, respectively.

```
1   ' Fig. 8.11
2   ' Demonstrating UCase$ and LCase$
3   Option Explicit
4
5   Private Sub cmdConvert_Click()
6       txtUpperCase.Text = UCase$(txtInput.Text)
7       txtLowerCase.Text = LCase$(txtInput.Text)
8   End Sub
```

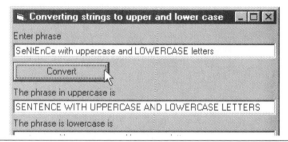

**Fig. 8.11**   Demonstrating **UCase$** and **LCase$**.

## 8.15  Conversion Functions

Visual Basic provides a variety of conversion functions for strings and other data types. Each of these functions is presented in the next several sections.

### 8.15.1  Asc and Chr$

Function **Asc** returns the ASCII code corresponding to a given character. For example,

```
Asc("a")
```

returns 97, the ASCII code for lowercase **"a"**. If the given string contains more than one character, **Asc** returns the ASCII code of the first character only. Function **Chr$** complements function **Asc**. **Chr$** returns the string corresponding to an ASCII code. The program of Fig. 8.12 demonstrates these functions.

The top half of the GUI for the program allows the user to enter an ASCII value in a **TextBox**. When the user clicks button **Show corresponding character**, event procedure **cmdConvertInt_Click** at line 5 executes to convert the **Integer** to a character and displays the result in the **TextBox txtOutputChar**. If the user types a non-numeric value, a run-time error occurs.

```
1   ' Fig. 8.12
2   ' Demonstrating
3   Option Explicit
4
5   Private Sub cmdConvertInt_Click()
6      txtOutputChar.Text = _
7         "The character value of " & txtInputInt.Text & _
8         " is " & Chr$(txtInputInt.Text)
9   End Sub
10
11  Private Sub cmdConvertChar_Click()
12     txtOutputInt.Text = _
13        "The ASCII value of " & txtInputChar.Text & " is " & _
14        Asc(txtInputChar.Text)
15  End Sub
```

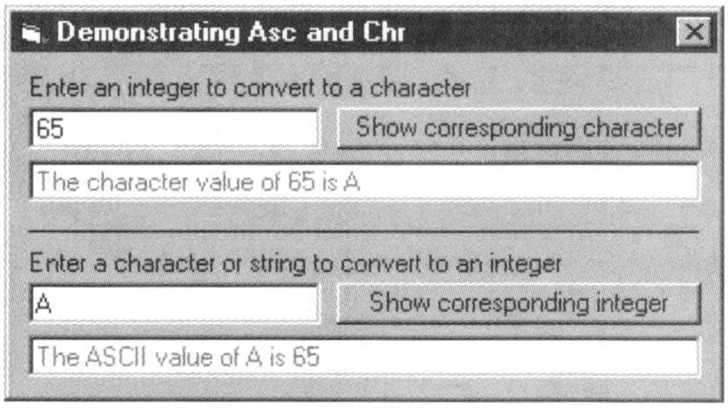

**Fig. 8.12**  Demonstrating **Asc** and **Chr$**.

The bottom half of the GUI for the program allows the user to enter a character value in a **TextBox**. When the user presses **Show corresponding integer**, event procedure **cmdConvertChar_Click** at line 11 executes to convert the character to an **Integer** and displays the result in the **TextBox txtOutputInt**. If the user types a non-numeric value, a run-time error occurs.

**Chr$** is often used to return a double quote character, **"**. For example, the statement

```
Print "B is " & Chr$(34) & "greater than" & Chr$(34) & " A"
```

uses **Chr$** twice to print double quote characters. When executed, the statement outputs

```
B is "greater than" A
```

## 8.15.2 IsNumeric, Val and Str$

Functions *IsNumeric*, *Val* and *Str$* are useful for converting between numbers and strings. Function **Val** converts strings to numbers. Function **Str$** is the complement of **Val**—it converts numbers to strings. Function **IsNumeric** returns **True** if a string can represent a number. The program of Fig. 8.13 demonstrates these functions.

```
1   ' Fig. 8.13
2   ' Using IsNumeric, Val and Str$
3   Option Explicit
4
5   Private Sub cmdIsNumeric_Click()
6      If IsNumeric(txtInput.Text) Then
7         lblOutput.Caption = txtInput.Text & " + 10 is " & _
8                             Str$(Val(txtInput.Text) + 10)
9      Else
10        lblOutput.Caption = txtInput.Text & " is not a number"
11     End If
12  End Sub
```

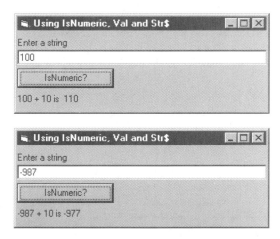

**Fig. 8.13**   Demonstrating **IsNumeric**, **Val** and **Str$** (part 1 of 2).

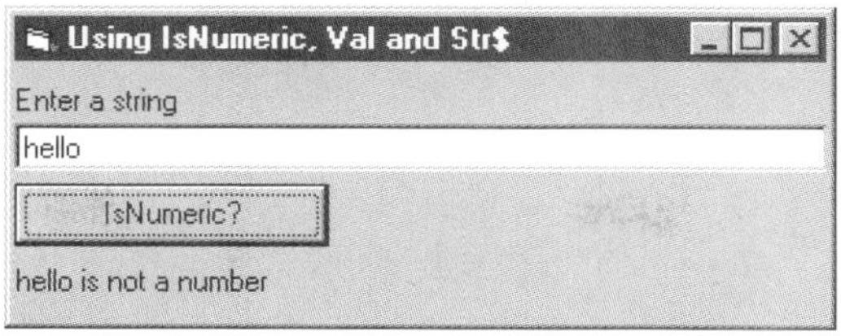

Fig. 8.13    Demonstrating **IsNumeric**, **Val** and **Str$** (part 2 of 2).

The GUI of this program allows the user to enter a string in a **TextBox**. When the user clicks button **IsNumeric?**, event procedure **cmdIsNumeric_Click** at line 5 executes. Line 6 uses function **IsNumeric** to determine if **txtInput.Text** is a string that can be converted to an **Integer**. If so, lines 7 and 8,

```
lblOutput.Caption = txtInput.Text & " + 10 is " & _
                    Str$(Val(txtInput.Text) + 10)
```

convert the string to a number, add 10 to the value and convert the new value to a string with the expression

```
Str$(Val(txtInput.Text) + 10)
```

Function **Val** converts every digit character in a string until it encounters the first non-digit character. Valid characters are the digits 0–9, the sign (+ or −) and the decimal point (**.**). Also, **Val** can convert hexadecimal values that are preceded by **&H** and octal values that are preceded by **&O**. Function **Str$** converts numbers to strings. The resulting string includes a leading space character for the sign of the number. For negative values, a minus sign appears rather than a leading space.

### 8.15.3 Hex$ and Oct$

Functions **Hex$** and **Oct$** convert numbers to hexadecimal (base 16) format strings and octal (base 8) format strings, respectively. Each function can receive either a number or a string containing a number as its argument. Figure 8.14 demonstrates these two functions.

When the user enters a number in the top **TextBox** and clicks the **Convert to Hex and Oct** button, event procedure **cmdConvert_Click** at line 5 executes. Lines 6 and 7,

```
1  ' Fig. 8.14
2  ' Demonstrating Hex$ and Oct$
3  Option Explicit
4
5  Private Sub cmdConvert_Click()
6      txtHex.Text = Hex$(txtInput.Text)
7      txtOct.Text = Oct$(txtInput.Text)
8  End Sub
```

Fig. 8.14    Demonstrating **Hex$** and **Oct$** (part 1 of 2).

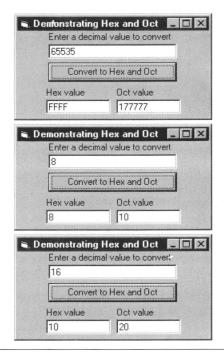

**Fig. 8.14**   Demonstrating **Hex$** and **Oct$** (part 2 of 2).

```
txtHex.Text = Hex$(txtInput.Text)
txtOct.Text = Oct$(txtInput.Text)
```

convert the number to hexadecimal format and octal format, respectively. The results are assigned to the **Text** properties of the **txtHex** and **txtOct TextBox**es.

## 8.15.4 Type Conversion Functions

Visual Basic provides functions for converting string and numeric expressions to many different data types. The program of Fig. 8.15 demonstrates these functions.

When the user types a string in the **TextBox** and presses button **Convert**, event procedure **cmdConvert_Click** at line 5 attempts to convert the string using each of the conversion functions. Any errors occurring during conversions is a run-time error.

Line 7 uses *function CBool* to convert the string to a **Boolean**. Any numeric value or numeric string representation of zero returns **Boolean** value **False**. All other numeric values or numeric string representations return **Boolean** value **True**.

Line 8 uses *function CByte* to convert the string to a value from 0 to 255. Any numeric value or numeric string representation in this range of values returns a **Byte** containing 0 to 255. All other numeric values or numeric string representations result in an error.

Line 9 uses *function CCur* to convert the string to a **Currency** value for use in precise monetary calculations. Any numeric value or numeric string representation of a currency value returns a value of type **Currency**. All other numeric values or numeric string representations result in an error.

```
1   ' Fig. 8.15
2   ' Demonstrating type conversion functions
3   Option Explicit
4
5   Private Sub cmdConvert_Click()
6       Call lstOutput.Clear
7       Call lstOutput.AddItem("CBool: " & CBool(txtInput.Text))
8       Call lstOutput.AddItem("CByte: " & CByte(txtInput.Text))
9       Call lstOutput.AddItem("CCur: " & CCur(txtInput.Text))
10      Call lstOutput.AddItem("CDate: " & CDate(txtInput.Text))
11      Call lstOutput.AddItem("CDbl: " & CDbl(txtInput.Text))
12      Call lstOutput.AddItem("CDec: " & CDec(txtInput.Text))
13      Call lstOutput.AddItem("CInt: " & CInt(txtInput.Text))
14      Call lstOutput.AddItem("CLng: " & CLng(txtInput.Text))
15      Call lstOutput.AddItem("CSng " & CSng(txtInput.Text))
16      Call lstOutput.AddItem("CStr: " & CVar(txtInput.Text))
17      Call lstOutput.AddItem("CVar: " & CVar(txtInput.Text))
18  End Sub
```

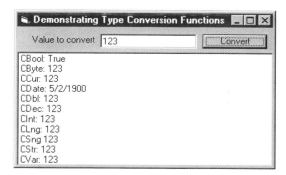

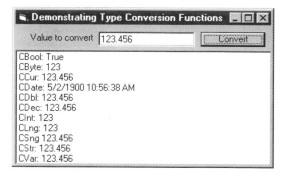

**Fig. 8.15**   Demonstrating the type conversion functions (part 1 of 2).

Line 10 uses *function **CDate*** to convert the string to a **Date** value. Any numeric value or numeric string representation of a date returns a **Date** value. All other numeric values or numeric string representations result in an error.

Line 11 uses *function **CDbl*** to convert the string to a **Double** value representing a double-precision, floating-point value. If the string is not a number, an error occurs.

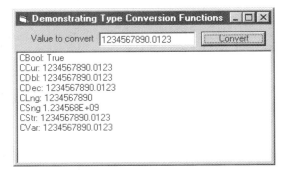

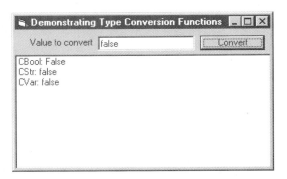

**Fig. 8.15**    Demonstrating the type conversion functions (part 2 of 2).

Line 12 uses *function* **CDec** to convert the string to a **Decimal** value representing the number. If the string is not a number, an error occurs.

Line 13 uses *function* **CInt** to convert the string to an **Integer** value. If the string is not a number, an error occurs.

Line 14 uses *function* **CLng** to convert the string to a **Long** value. If the string is not a number, an error occurs.

Line 15 uses *function* **CSng** to convert the string to a **Single** value representing a single-precision, floating-point value. If the string is not a number, an error occurs.

Line 16 uses *function* **CStr** to convert the string to a **CStr** value. If the argument is a **Date**, the string contains the short format date representation for your system (discussed later in this chapter). If the argument is a **Boolean**, the string **True** or **False** is returned. If the argument is a number, the string representation of the number is returned. If the argument is an **Error**, the corresponding error message is returned. If the argument is **Null**, an error occurs.

Line 17 uses *function CVar* to convert the string to a **Variant**. For numeric values, the result is a **Double**. For non-numeric values, the result is a **String**.

## 8.16 String Formatting

Precise string formatting is accomplished with many functions in Visual Basic. This section demonstrates many of these features. Later in the chapter we discuss dates and times. At that point we will introduce precise data and time formatting. Note: The format displayed by **Format$**, **FormatNumber**, **FormatCurrency**, and **FormatPercent** is dependent on the country specified in the Windows **Control Panel**'s **Regional Settings**. Our machines are set to **English (United States)**.

### 8.16.1 Function Format$ and Named Numeric Formats

The majority of Visual Basic's formatting capabilities are provided by function **Format$**. Function **Format$** provides for both pre-defined formats and user-defined formats.

The program of Fig. 8.16 demonstrates the pre-defined numeric formats known as the *named numeric formats*. Each of the formatted values is added as an item in a **List** for output purposes.

```
1   ' Fig. 8.16
2   ' Demonstrating named numeric formats
3   Option Explicit
4
5   Private Sub Form_Load()
6      Call lstOutput.AddItem("General Number: " & _
7             Format$(123456.789, "General Number"))
8      Call lstOutput.AddItem("Currency: " & _
9             Format$(123456.789, "Currency"))
10     Call lstOutput.AddItem("Fixed: " & _
11            Format$(123456.789, "Fixed"))
12     Call lstOutput.AddItem("Standard: " & _
13            Format$(123456.789, "Standard"))
14     Call lstOutput.AddItem("Scientific: " & _
15            Format$(123456.789, "Scientific"))
16     Call lstOutput.AddItem("Percent: " & _
17            Format$(0.05475, "Percent"))
18     Call lstOutput.AddItem("Yes/No: " & _
19            Format$(0, "Yes/No"))
20     Call lstOutput.AddItem("Yes/No: " & _
21            Format$(1, "Yes/No"))
22     Call lstOutput.AddItem("True/False: " & _
23            Format$(0, "True/False"))
```

**Fig. 8.16**   Demonstrating function **Format$** and the named numeric formats (part 1 of 2).

```
24      Call lstOutput.AddItem("True/False: " & _
25            Format$(1, "True/False"))
26      Call lstOutput.AddItem("On/Off: " & _
27            Format$(0, "On/Off"))
28      Call lstOutput.AddItem("On/Off: " & _
29            Format$(1, "On/Off"))
30   End Sub
```

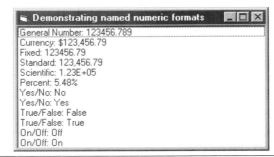

**Fig. 8.16**   Demonstrating function **Format$** and the named numeric formats (part 2 of 2).

Line 7,

**Format$(123456.789, "General Number")**

formats a number using the ***"General Number"*** *named numeric format*. This displays the number with no separators for thousands.

Line 9,

**Format$(123456.789, "Currency")**

formats a number using the ***"Currency"*** *named numeric format*. This displays the number with a currency symbol, separators for thousands (if appropriate) and two digits to the right of the decimal separator.

Line 11,

**Format$(123456.789, "Fixed")**

formats a number using the ***"Fixed"*** *named numeric format*. This displays the number with at least one digit to the left of the decimal separator and two digits to the right of the decimal separator.

Line 13,

**Format$(123456.789, "Standard")**

formats a number using the ***"Standard"*** *named numeric format*. This displays the number with separators for thousands (if appropriate), at least one digit to the left of the decimal separator and two digits to the right of the decimal separator.

Line 15,

**Format$(123456.789, "Scientific")**

formats a number using the ***"Scientific"*** *named numeric format*. This displays the number in scientific notation with two digits to the right of the decimal separator.
Line 17,

```
Format$(0.05475, "Percent")
```

formats a number using the ***"Percent"*** *named numeric format*. This format multiplies the number by 100, displays a **%** to the right of the number and displays two digits to the right of the decimal separator.
Lines 19 and 21,

```
Format$(0, "Yes/No")
Format$(1, "Yes/No")
```

format a number using the ***"Yes/No"*** *named numeric format*. This displays **No** if the number is **0** and **Yes** otherwise.
Lines 23 and 25,

```
Format$(0, "True/False")
Format$(1, "True/False")
```

format a number using the ***"True/False"*** *named numeric format*. This displays **False** if the number is **0** and **True** otherwise.
Lines 27 and 29,

```
Format$(0, "On/Off")
Format$(1, "On/Off")
```

format a number using the **"On/Off"** *named numeric format*. This displays **Off** if the number is **0** and **On** otherwise.

## 8.16.2 Function `Format$` and User-Defined Numeric Formats

The program of Fig. 8.17 demonstrates user-defined numeric formats. The formats are constructed by creating strings containing *formatting flags*. Note that the format flags we demonstrate can be used in almost any combination. Each of the formatted values in this example is added as an item in a **List** for output purposes.

```
1   ' Fig. 8.17
2   ' Demonstrating user-defined numeric formats
3   Option Explicit
4
5   Private Sub Form_Load()
6       Call lstOutput.AddItem("No format: " & _
7           Format$(1123456.789))
8       Call lstOutput.AddItem("No format: " & _
9           Format$(-1123456.789))
10      Call lstOutput.AddItem("No format: " & Format$(0.789))
11      Call lstOutput.AddItem("0: " & Format$(1123456.789, "0"))
12      Call lstOutput.AddItem("0: " & Format$(-1123456.789, "0"))
```

**Fig. 8.17**   Demonstrating function **Format$** and the user-defined numeric formats (part 1 of 3).

```
13      Call lstOutput.AddItem("0: " & Format$(0.789, "0"))
14      Call lstOutput.AddItem("0.00: " & _
15         Format$(1123456.789, "0.00"))
16      Call lstOutput.AddItem("0.00: " & _
17         Format$(-1123456.789, "0.00"))
18      Call lstOutput.AddItem("0.00: " & Format$(0.789, "0.00"))
19      Call lstOutput.AddItem("#,##0.00: " & _
20         Format$(1123456.789, "#,##0.00"))
21      Call lstOutput.AddItem("#,##0.00: " & _
22         Format$(-1123456.789, "#,##0.00"))
23      Call lstOutput.AddItem("#,##0.00: " & _
24         Format$(0.789, "#,##0.00"))
25      Call lstOutput.AddItem("$#,##0.00: " & _
26         Format$(1123456.789, "$#,##0.00"))
27      Call lstOutput.AddItem("$#,##0.00: " & _
28         Format$(-1123456.789, "$#,##0.00"))
29      Call lstOutput.AddItem("$#,##0.00: " & _
30         Format$(0.789, "$#,##0.00"))
31      Call lstOutput.AddItem("0%: " & Format$(2.789, "0%"))
32      Call lstOutput.AddItem("0%: " & Format$(-2.789, "0%"))
33      Call lstOutput.AddItem("0%: " & Format$(0.789, "0%"))
34      Call lstOutput.AddItem("0.00%: " & _
35         Format$(2.789, "0.00%"))
36      Call lstOutput.AddItem("0.00%: " & _
37         Format$(-2.789, "0.00%"))
38      Call lstOutput.AddItem("0.00%: " & _
39         Format$(0.789, "0.00%"))
40      Call lstOutput.AddItem("0.00E+00: " & _
41         Format$(1123456.789, "0.00E+00"))
42      Call lstOutput.AddItem("0.00E+00: " & _
43         Format$(-1123456.789, "0.00E+00"))
44      Call lstOutput.AddItem("0.00E+00: " & _
45         Format$(0.789, "0.00E+00"))
46      Call lstOutput.AddItem("0.00E-00: " & _
47         Format$(1123456.789, "0.00E-00"))
48      Call lstOutput.AddItem("0.00E-00: " & _
49         Format$(-1123456.789, "0.00E-00"))
50      Call lstOutput.AddItem("0.00E-00: " & _
51         Format$(0.789, "0.00E-00"))
52      Call lstOutput.AddItem("$#,##0.00;($#,##0.00): " & _
53         Format$(1123456.789, "$#,##0.00;($#,##0.00)"))
54      Call lstOutput.AddItem("$#,##0.00;($#,##0.00): " & _
55         Format$(-1123456.789, "$#,##0.00;($#,##0.00)"))
56   End Sub
```

**Fig. 8.17**  Demonstrating function **Format$** and the user-defined numeric formats (part 2 of 3).

Lines 6 through 10,

```
Call lstOutput.AddItem("No format: " & _
   Format$(1123456.789))
Call lstOutput.AddItem("No format: " & _
   Format$(-1123456.789))
Call lstOutput.AddItem("No format: " & Format$(0.789))
```

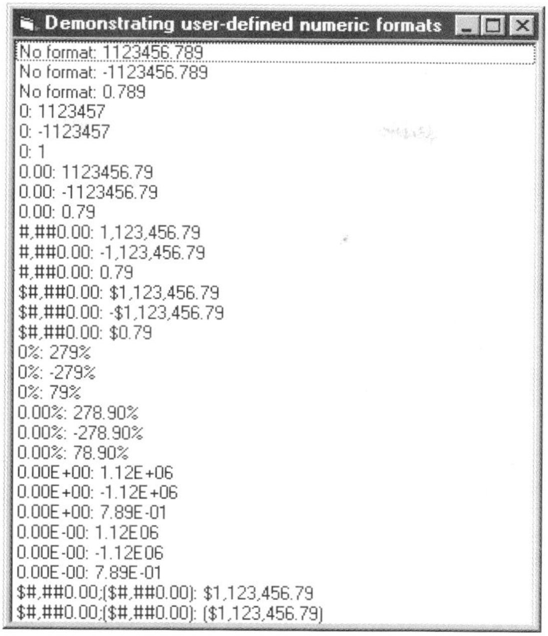

**Fig. 8.17** Demonstrating function **Format$** and the user-defined numeric formats (part 3 of 3).

do not format the numbers. If no format string is specified, the number is returned in its original format.

Lines 11 through 13,

```
Call lstOutput.AddItem("0: " & Format(1123456.789, "0"))
Call lstOutput.AddItem("0: " & Format$(-1123456.789, "0"))
Call lstOutput.AddItem("0: " & Format$(0.789, "0"))
```

use the format string **"0"**. The *format flag* **0** represents a required digit position. This format specifies that the number should be displayed as a whole number value with at least one digit. Floating-point values are automatically rounded.

Lines 14 through 18,

```
Call lstOutput.AddItem("0.00: " & _
    Format$(1123456.789, "0.00"))
Call lstOutput.AddItem("0.00: " & _
    Format$(-1123456.789, "0.00"))
Call lstOutput.AddItem("0.00: " & Format$(0.789, "0.00"))
```

use the format string **"0.00"**. The flag **0** represents a required digit position. The flag **.** represents where the decimal separator should be placed in the formatted number. This format specifies that the number should be displayed with at least one digit to the left of the decimal separator and should display exactly two digits to the right of the decimal separator. Floating-point values are automatically rounded.

Lines 19 through 24,

```
lstOutput.AddItem("#,##0.00: " & _
   Format$(1123456.789, "#,##0.00"))
lstOutput.AddItem("#,##0.00: " & _
   Format$(-1123456.789, "#,##0.00"))
lstOutput.AddItem("#,##0.00: " & _
   Format$(0.789, "#,##0.00"))
```

use the format string **"#,##0.00"**. The *flag* **#** represents a digit placeholder. If there is a digit in this position in the number being formatted, it is displayed; otherwise nothing appears. The *flag* **,** indicates that a thousands separator should be displayed when the number is 1000 or greater. This format specifies that the number should be displayed with at least one digit to the left of the decimal separator, a thousands separator when necessary and exactly two digits to the right of the decimal separator.

Lines 25 through 30,

```
Call lstOutput.AddItem("$#,##0.00: " & _
   Format$(1123456.789, "$#,##0.00"))
Call lstOutput.AddItem("$#,##0.00: " & _
   Format$(-1123456.789, "$#,##0.00"))
Call lstOutput.AddItem("$#,##0.00: " & _
   Format$(0.789, "$#,##0.00"))
```

use the format string **"$#,##0.00"**. This format is the same as the format for lines 19 through 24 except that it displays a literal **$** before the formatted number. Other valid literal characters are **-**, **+**, **(** and **)**. Other literals can be displayed by preceding the character with a backslash (**\**) in the format string.

Lines 31 through 33,

```
Call lstOutput.AddItem("0%: " & Format$(2.789, "0%"))
Call lstOutput.AddItem("0%: " & Format$(-2.789, "0%"))
Call lstOutput.AddItem("0%: " & Format$(0.789, "0%"))
```

use the format string **"0%"**. The flag **%** indicates that the number should be multiplied by 100 and a percent sign should appear at the specified position in the string. This format specifies that the number should be output as a whole number percentage.

Lines 34 through 39,

```
Call lstOutput.AddItem("0.00%: " & _
   Format$(2.789, "0.00%"))
Call lstOutput.AddItem("0.00%: " & _
   Format$(-2.789, "0.00%"))
Call lstOutput.AddItem("0.00%: " & _
   Format$(0.789, "0.00%"))
```

use the format string **"0.00%"**. This format specifies that the number should be output as a percentage with two digits to the right of the decimal format.

Lines 40 through 45,

```
Call lstOutput.AddItem("0.00E+00: " & _
   Format$(1123456.789, "0.00E+00"))
Call lstOutput.AddItem("0.00E+00: " & _
   Format$(-1123456.789, "0.00E+00"))
```

```
Call lstOutput.AddItem("0.00E+00: " & _
    Format$(0.789, "0.00E+00"))
```

use the format string **"0.00E+00"**. The *flag E+00* indicates that the number should be formatted in scientific notation with at least two digits in the exponent. Positive exponents are displayed with a + sign and negative exponents are displayed with a – sign. Other scientific notation format flags include **e+** (the same as **E+**, but a lowercase **e** is displayed), **E–** and **e–**. The last two flags indicate that only negative exponents should be preceded by a sign.

Lines 46 through 51,

```
Call lstOutput.AddItem("0.00E-00: " & _
    Format$(1123456.789, "0.00E-00"))
Call lstOutput.AddItem("0.00E-00: " & _
    Format$(-1123456.789, "0.00E-00"))
Call lstOutput.AddItem("0.00E-00: " & _
    Format$(0.789, "0.00E-00"))
```

use the format string **"0.00E-00"** to illustrate scientific notation where only negative exponents should be preceded by a sign.

Lines 52 through 55,

```
Call lstOutput.AddItem("$#,##0.00;($#,##0.00): " & _
    Format$(1123456.789, "$#,##0.00;($#,##0.00)"))
Call lstOutput.AddItem("$#,##0.00;($#,##0.00): " & _
    Format$(-1123456.789, "$#,##0.00;($#,##0.00)"))
```

illustrate using different formats for non-negative values and negative values. The format **"$#,##0.00;($#,##0.00)"** specifies that non-negative values should be formatted with **$#,##0.00**, and negative values should be formatted with **($#,##0.00)**. Semicolons (**;**) are used to separate the formats. Actually, up to four separate formats can be specified. If there are three, the first is for positive values, the second is for negative values and the third is for zero values. If there are four, the fourth is for **Null** values.

## 8.16.3 Function **FormatNumber**

The program of Fig. 8.18 demonstrates function ***FormatNumber*** for formatting numeric values. The user enters a number in the **TextBox** at the top of the window, then clicks the **Format** button to call event procedure **cmdFormat_Click** (line 5) to format the number and display the result in the other **TextBox**. Formatting is performed based on the states of the other GUI components in the window.

```
1   ' Fig. 8.18
2   ' Demonstrating the FormatNumber function
3   Option Explicit
4
5   Private Sub cmdFormat_Click()
6       Dim numDigits As Integer, leadDigit As Boolean, _
7           parens As Boolean, group As Boolean
```

**Fig. 8.18**   Demonstrating function **FormatNumber** (part 1 of 2).

```
8
9       numDigits = cboNumDigits.Text
10      leadDigit = chkLeadDigit.Value
11      parens = chkParentheses.Value
12      group = chkGroupDigits.Value
13      txtOutput.Text = FormatNumber(txtInput.Text, _
14                      numDigits, leadDigit, parens, group)
15  End Sub
```

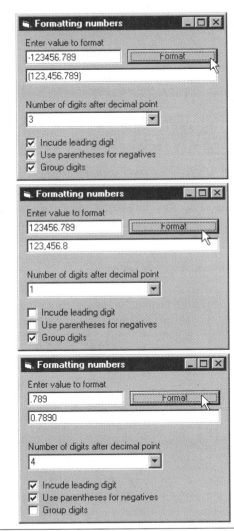

**Fig. 8.18**  Demonstrating function **FormatNumber** (part 2 of 2).

Lines 6 and 7,

```
Dim numDigits As Integer, leadDigit As Boolean, _
    parens As Boolean, group As Boolean
```

declare several local variables. Variable **numDigits** is used to store the number of digits to the right of the decimal separator. Variable **leadDigit** is a **Boolean** indicating if floating-point values less than 1 should be displayed with a leading **0**. Variable **parens** is a **Boolean** indicating if negative numbers should be displayed in parentheses. Variable **group** is a **Boolean** indicating if numbers 1000 and greater should be displayed with thousands separators.

Line 9,

```
numDigits = cboNumDigits.Text
```

gets the value of the string currently selected in **ComboBox cboNumDigits** and assigns it to **numDigits**. This value is used as the second argument to **FormatNumber**.

Line 10,

```
leadDigit = chkLeadDigit.Value
```

determines if **CheckBox chkLeadDigit** is checked and assigns the result to **leadDigit**. This value is used as the third argument to **FormatNumber**.

Line 11,

```
parens = chkParentheses.Value
```

determines if **CheckBox chkParentheses** is checked and assigns the result to **parens**. This value is used as the fourth argument to **FormatNumber**.

Line 12,

```
group = chkGroupDigits.Value
```

determines if **CheckBox chkGroupDigits** is checked and assigns the result to **group**. This value is used as the fifth argument to **FormatNumber**.

Lines 14 and 15,

```
txtOutput.Text = FormatNumber(txtInput.Text, _
                 numDigits, leadDigit, parens, group)
```

set **TextBox txtOutput**'s **Text** property to the formatted value returned by function **FormatNumber**. The first argument to **FormatNumber** is the numeric expression to format. The last four arguments specify the number of digits to the right of the decimal point, whether or not a leading 0 is displayed for numbers less than zero, whether or not parentheses are displayed around negative values and whether or not numbers greater than or equal to 1000 are displayed with thousands separators. The last four arguments are all optional.

## 8.16.4 Function **FormatCurrency**

The program of Fig. 8.19 demonstrates function *FormatCurrency* for formatting **Currency** values. The user enters a number in the **TextBox** at the top of the window, then clicks the **Format** button to call event procedure **cmdFormat_Click** (line 5) to format the number and display the result in the other **TextBox**. Formatting is performed based on the states of the other GUI components in the window.

```
1   ' Fig. 8.19
2   ' Demonstrating the FormatCurrency function
3   Option Explicit
4
5   Private Sub cmdFormat_Click()
6       Dim numDigits As Integer, leadDigit As Boolean, _
7           parens As Boolean, group As Boolean
8
9       numDigits = cboNumDigits.Text
10      leadDigit = chkLeadDigit.Value
11      parens = chkParentheses.Value
12      group = chkGroupDigits.Value
13      txtOutput.Text = FormatCurrency(txtInput.Text, _
14                      numDigits, leadDigit, parens, group)
15  End Sub
```

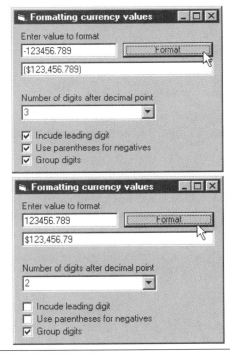

**Fig. 8.19**   Demonstrating function **FormatCurrency** (part 1 of 2).

Lines 6 and 7,

```
Dim numDigits As Integer, leadDigit As Boolean, _
    parens As Boolean, group As Boolean
```

declare several variables. Variable **numDigits** stores the number of digits to the right of the decimal separator. Variable **leadDigit** is a **Boolean** indicating if floating-point values less than 1 are displayed with a leading **0**. Variable **parens** is a **Boolean** indicating if negative numbers should be displayed in parentheses. Variable **group** is a **Boolean** indicating if numbers 1000 and greater should be displayed with thousands separators.

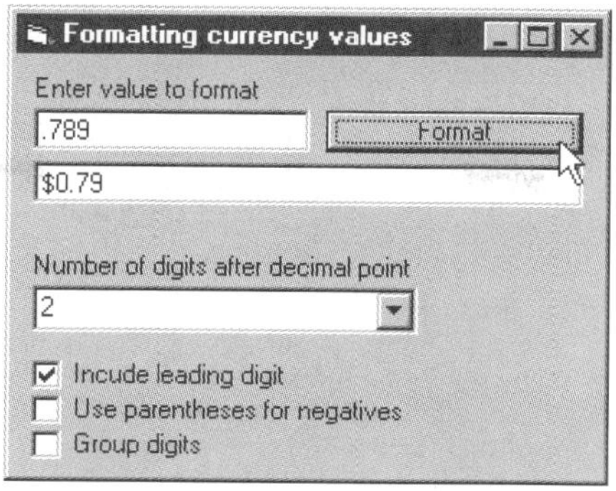

**Fig. 8.19**  Demonstrating function **FormatCurrency** (part 2 of 2).

Line 9,

```
numDigits = cboNumDigits.Text
```

gets the value of the string currently selected in **ComboBox cboNumDigits** and assigns it to **numDigits**. This value is used as the second argument to **FormatCurrency**.
Line 10,

```
leadDigit = chkLeadDigit.Value
```

assigns **chkLeadDigit**'s **Value** to **leadDigit**. This value is used as the third argument to **FormatCurrency**.
Line 11,

```
parens = chkParentheses.Value
```

assigns **chkParentheses**'s **Value** to **parens**. This value is used as the fourth argument to **FormatCurrency**.
Line 12,

```
group = chkGroupDigits.Value
```

assigns **chkGroupDigits**'s **Value** to **group**. This value is used as the fifth argument to **FormatCurrency**.
Lines 13 and 14,

```
txtOutput.Text = FormatNumber(txtInput.Text, _
                 numDigits, leadDigit, parens, group)
```

set **TextBox txtOutput**'s **Text** property to the formatted value returned by function **FormatCurrency**. The first argument to **FormatCurrency** is the numeric expression to format. The last four arguments specify the number of digits to the right of the decimal point, whether or not a leading **0** is displayed for numbers less than zero, whether or not parentheses are displayed around negative values and whether or not numbers greater than or equal to 1000 are displayed with thousands separators. The last four arguments are all optional.

### 8.16.5 Function `FormatPercent`

The program of Fig. 8.20 demonstrates function *FormatPercent* for formatting percentages. The user enters a number in the **TextBox** at the top of the window, then clicks the **Format** button to call event procedure **cmdFormat_Click** (line 5) to format the number and display the result in the other **TextBox**. Formatting is performed based on the states of the other GUI components in the window.

```
1   ' Fig. 8.20
2   ' Demonstrating the FormatPercent function
3   Option Explicit
4
5   Private Sub cmdFormat_Click()
6       Dim numDigits As Integer, leadDigit As Boolean, _
7           parens As Boolean, group As Boolean
8
9       numDigits = cboNumDigits.Text
10      leadDigit = chkLeadDigit.Value
11      parens = chkParentheses.Value
12      group = chkGroupDigits.Value
13
14      txtOutput.Text = FormatPercent(txtInput.Text, _
15                          numDigits, leadDigit, parens, group)
16  End Sub
```

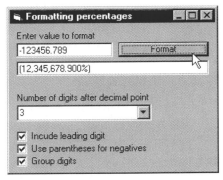

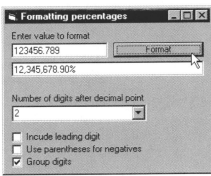

**Fig. 8.20**    Demonstrating function **FormatPercent** (part 1 of 2).

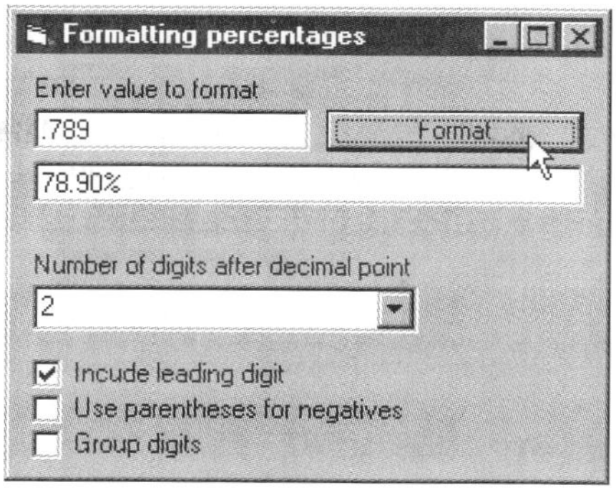

**Fig. 8.20**   Demonstrating function **FormatPercent** (part 2 of 2).

Lines 6 and 7,

```
Dim numDigits As Integer, leadDigit As Boolean, _
    parens As Boolean, group As Boolean
```

declare several local variables. Variable **numDigits** is used to store the number of digits to the right of the decimal separator. Variable **leadDigit** is a **Boolean** indicating if floating-point values less than 1 should be displayed with a leading **0**. Variable **parens** is a **Boolean** indicating if negative numbers should be displayed in parentheses. Variable **group** is a **Boolean** indicating if numbers 1000 and greater should be displayed with thousands separators.

Line 9,

```
numDigits = cboNumDigits.Text
```

gets the value of the string currently selected in **ComboBox cboNumDigits** and assigns it to **numDigits**. This value is used as the second argument to **FormatPercent**.

Line 10,

```
leadDigit = chkLeadDigit.Value
```

assigns **chkLeadDigit**'s **Value** to **leadDigit**. This value is used as the third argument to **FormatPercent**.

Line 11,

```
parens = chkParentheses.Value
```

assigns **chkParentheses**'s **Value** to **parens**. This value is used as the fourth argument to **FormatPercent**.

Line 12,

```
group = chkGroupDigits.Value
```

assigns **chkGroupDigits**'s **Value** to **group**. This value is used as the fifth argument to **FormatPercent**.

Lines 14 and 15,

```
txtOutput.Text = FormatNumber(txtInput.Text, _
    numDigits, leadDigit, parens, group)
```

set **TextBox txtOutput**'s **Text** property to the formatted value returned by function **FormatPercent**. The first argument to **FormatPercent** is the numeric expression to format. The last four arguments (all four are optional) specify the number of digits to the right of the decimal point, whether or not a leading 0 is displayed for numbers less than zero, whether or not parentheses are displayed for negative values, and whether or not numbers greater than or equal to 1000 are displayed with thousands separators.

## 8.17 Date and Time Processing

Managing dates and times is a much more sophisticated task than most programmers realize. Visual Basic provides many date- and time-related functions and the **Date** data type to help programmers standardize and ensure the completeness of their dates and times. Over the next several examples, we demonstrate the date and time functions and the date and time formatting capabilities.

The program of Fig. 8.21 demonstrates functions *Now*, *Date*, *Day*, *Weekday*, *WeekdayName*, *Month*, *MonthName* and *Year*. When this program executes, items are added to **ListBox lstOutput** that illustrate the results of these functions.

Line 6,

```
Call lstOutput.AddItem("Current date and time: " & Now)
```

uses function **Now** to get the current system date and time.

```
1   ' Fig. 8.21
2   ' Demonstrating Date, Day, Month and Year functions
3   Option Explicit
4
5   Private Sub Form_Load()
6      Call lstOutput.AddItem("Current date and time: " & Now)
7      Call lstOutput.AddItem("Date: " & Date)
8      Call lstOutput.AddItem("Day: " & Day(Date))
9      Call lstOutput.AddItem("Weekday: " & Weekday(Date))
10     Call lstOutput.AddItem("WeekdayName: " & _
11                         WeekdayName(Weekday(Date)))
12     Call lstOutput.AddItem("WeekdayName abbrieviated: " & _
13                         WeekdayName(Weekday(Date), True))
14     Call lstOutput.AddItem("Month: " & Month(Date))
15     Call lstOutput.AddItem("MonthName: " & _
16                         MonthName(Month(Date)))
17     Call lstOutput.AddItem("MonthName abbrieviated: " & _
18                         MonthName(Month(Date), True))
19     Call lstOutput.AddItem("Year: " & Year(Date))
20     Call lstOutput.AddItem(#3/2/1976#)   ' Date literal
21   End Sub
```

**Fig. 8.21**   Demonstrating functions **Now**, **Date**, **Day**, **Weekday**, **WeekdayName**, **Month**, **MonthName** and **Year** (part 1 of 2).

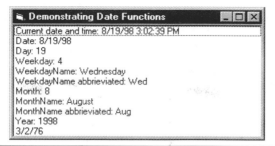

**Fig. 8.21** Demonstrating functions **Now**, **Date**, **Day**, **Weekday**, **WeekdayName**, **Month**, **MonthName** and **Year** (part 2 of 2).

Line 7,

```
Call lstOutput.AddItem("Date: " & Date)
```

uses *function* **Date** to get the current system date. Line 8,

```
Call lstOutput.AddItem("Day: " & Day(Date))
```

uses *function* **Day** to get the day of the month as an **Integer** in the range 1 to 31. The argument to function **Day** is any string or numeric expression that represents a date.

Line 9,

```
Call lstOutput.AddItem("Weekday: " & Weekday(Date))
```

uses *function* **WeekDay** to get the day of the week as an **Integer** in the range 1 to 7 as represented by the constants **vbSunday**, **vbMonday**, **vbTuesday**, **vbWednesday**, **vbThursday**, **vbFriday** and **vbSaturday**, respectively. The argument to function **WeekDay** is any string or numeric expression that represents a date. By default, the first day of the week is Sunday. However, any of the preceding constants can be passed as an optional second argument to **WeekDay** to specify a customized first day of the week.

Lines 10 and 11,

```
Call lstOutput.AddItem("WeekdayName: " & _
                     WeekdayName(Weekday(Date)))
```

use *function* **WeekDayName** to get the name of the day of the week as string. The argument to function **WeekDayName** is the number that represents the day of the week.

Lines 12 and 13,

```
Call lstOutput.AddItem("WeekdayName abbrieviated: " & _
                     WeekdayName(Weekday(Date), True))
```

use *function* **WeekDayName** with a second argument of **True** that indicates an abbreviated name should be returned. For example, if the day name is **Sunday**, **Sun** is returned. This function has an optional third argument to specify a customized first day of the week.

Line 14,

```
Call lstOutput.AddItem("Month: " & Month(Date))
```

uses *function* **Month** to get the day of the month as an integer in the range 1 to 12. The argument to function **Month** is any string or numeric expression that represents a date.

Lines 15 and 16,

```
Call lstOutput.AddItem("MonthName: " & _
                       MonthName(Month(Date)))
```

uses *function* **MonthName** to get the name of the month as string. The argument to function **MonthName** is the number that represents the month (1 for January, 2 for February, etc.). Both **WeekDayName** and **MonthName** display **String**s in the language specified in the Windows **Control Panel**'s **Regional Settings TextBox**.

Lines 17 and 18,

```
Call lstOutput.AddItem("MonthName abbrieviated: " & _
                       MonthName(Month(Date), True))
```

use function **MonthName** with a second argument of **True** which indicates that an abbreviated name should be returned (e.g., if the month name is **January**, **Jan** is returned).

Line 19,

```
Call lstOutput.AddItem("Year: " & Year(Date))
```

uses *function* **Year** to get the year as an **Integer**. The argument to function **Year** is any string or numeric expression that represents a date.

Line 20

```
Call lstOutput.AddItem(#3/2/1976#)   ' Date literal
```

adds a **Date** *literal* to **lstOutput**. **Date** literals consist of a date enclosed within two pound sign, **#**, characters.

*Portability Tip 8.1*

**Date** *literals implicitly convert to the date format of the locale specified in the* **Control Panel**'s **Regional Settings TextBox**. *For example,* **English (United States)** *prints* **#5/16/1984#** *as* **5/16/84** *and* **German (Standard)** *prints* **#5/16/1984#** *as* **16.05.84**.

The program of Fig. 8.22 demonstrates functions *IsDate*, *DateValue* and *Date-Serial*. When this program executes, items are added to **List lstOutput** that illustrate the results of these functions.

```
1   ' Fig. 8.22
2   ' Demonstrating IsDate, DateValue and DateSerial functions
3   Option Explicit
4
5   Private Sub Form_Load()
6      Call lstOutput.AddItem("IsDate(123456): " & _
7                        Format(IsDate(123456), "True/False"))
```

**Fig. 8.22**  Demonstrating functions **IsDate**, **DateValue** and **DateSerial** (part 1 of 2).

```
 8      Call lstOutput.AddItem("IsDate(2/15/73): " & _
 9                        Format(IsDate("2/15/73"), "True/False
10      Call lstOutput.AddItem("DateValue(2-15-73): " & _
11                        DateValue("2-15-73"))
12      Call lstOutput.AddItem("DateValue(February 15, 1973): " & _
13                        DateValue("February 15, 1973"))
14      Call lstOutput.AddItem("DateValue(15-Feb-73): " & _
15                        DateValue("15-Feb-73"))
16      Call lstOutput.AddItem("DateSerial(1998, 8, 2): " & _
17                        DateSerial(1998, 8, 2))
18   End Sub
```

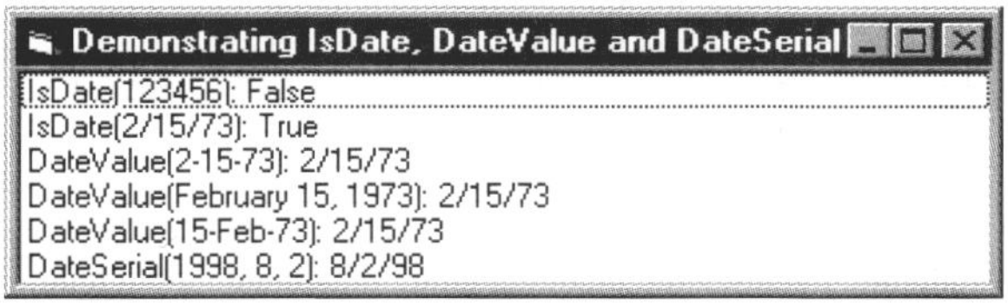

```
Demonstrating IsDate, DateValue and DateSerial
IsDate(123456): False
IsDate(2/15/73): True
DateValue(2-15-73): 2/15/73
DateValue(February 15, 1973): 2/15/73
DateValue(15-Feb-73): 2/15/73
DateSerial(1998, 8, 2): 8/2/98
```

**Fig. 8.22**  Demonstrating functions **IsDate**, **DateValue** and **DateSerial**
(part 2 of 2).

Lines 6 through 9,

```
Call lstOutput.AddItem("IsDate(123456): " & _
                  Format(IsDate(123456), "True/False"))
Call lstOutput.AddItem("IsDate(2/15/73): " & _
                  Format(IsDate("2/15/73"), "True/False"))
```

use *function* **IsDate** to determine if a string or date can be converted to a date. The function returns **True** if the expression can be converted, **False** otherwise.

Lines 10 through 15,

```
Call lstOutput.AddItem("DateValue(2-15-73): " & _
                  DateValue("2-15-73"))
Call lstOutput.AddItem("DateValue(February 15, 1973): " & _
                  DateValue("February 15, 1973"))
Call lstOutput.AddItem("DateValue(15-Feb-73): " & _
                  DateValue("15-Feb-73"))
```

use *function* **DateValue** to convert a string into a **Date**. This function recognizes dates in the range January 1, 100 to December 31, 9999 and recognizes many formats, including

```
January 1, 1999
Jan 1, 1999
1/1/1999
1/1/99
1-Jan-99
1-Jan-1999
```

If no year is specified, the current year specified by the system is used.

Lines 16 through 19,

```
Call lstOutput.AddItem("DateSerial(1998, 8, 2): " & _
                  DateSerial(1998, 8, 2))
```

```
tOutput.AddItem("DateSerial(1998, -2, -15): " & _
                DateSerial(1998, -2, -15))
```

*ateSerial* to create dates. The function receives three arguments—the
.nd day. The arguments can represent relative values by adding or subtracting
with each of the arguments.

8.23 demonstrates function **DatePart**. When this program executes, items are
**ListBox lstOutput** that illustrate the results of these functions.
.e 6,

```
Call lstOutput.AddItem("Year: " & DatePart("yyyy", Now))
```

uses *function DatePart* to get the year from the current date and time returned by **Now**.
Function **DatePart** receives two arguments—a string indicating the part of the date to
return and a date expression. The string **"yyyy"** indicates that the year should be returned.
There are two optional arguments to **DatePart**—the third argument is a constant indicating the first day of the week (as discussed for function **Weekday**) and the fourth argument
is a constant indicating the first week of the year. The possible values are *vbFirstJan1*
(week in which January 1 occurs), *vbFirstFourDays* (first week with at least four days
in the new year) and *vbFirstFullWeek* (the first full week of the year).

Line 7,

```
Call lstOutput.AddItem("Quarter: " & DatePart("q", Now))
```

```
1   ' Fig. 8.23
2   ' Demonstrating DatePart
3   Option Explicit
4
5   Private Sub Form_Load()
6       Call lstOutput.AddItem("Year: " & DatePart("yyyy", Now))
7       Call lstOutput.AddItem("Quarter: " & DatePart("q", Now))
8       Call lstOutput.AddItem("Month: " & DatePart("m", Now))
9       Call lstOutput.AddItem("Day of year: " & DatePart("y", Now))
10      Call lstOutput.AddItem("Day: " & DatePart("d", Now))
11      Call lstOutput.AddItem("Weekday: " & DatePart("w", Now))
12      Call lstOutput.AddItem("Week: " & DatePart("ww", Now))
13      Call lstOutput.AddItem("Hour: " & DatePart("h", Now))
14      Call lstOutput.AddItem("Minute: " & DatePart("n", Now))
15      Call lstOutput.AddItem("Second: " & DatePart("s", Now))
16  End Sub
```

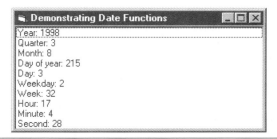

**Fig. 8.23**  Demonstrating function **DatePart**.

uses function **DatePart** to get the current quarter (**"q"**) as a value from 1 to 4.
Line 8,

```
Call lstOutput.AddItem("Month: " & DatePart("m", Now))
```

uses function **DatePart** to get the current month (**"m"**) as a value from 1 to 12.
Line 9,

```
Call lstOutput.AddItem("Day of year: " & DatePart("y", Now))
```

uses function **DatePart** to get the current day of the year (**"y"**).
Line 10,

```
Call lstOutput.AddItem("Day: " & DatePart("d", Now))
```

uses function **DatePart** to get the current day of the month (**"d"**) as a value from 1 to 31.
Line 11,

```
Call lstOutput.AddItem("Weekday: " & DatePart("w", Now))
```

uses function **DatePart** to get the current weekday (**"w"**) as a value from 1 to 7.
Line 12,

```
Call lstOutput.AddItem("Week: " & DatePart("ww", Now))
```

uses function **DatePart** to get the current week (**"ww"**) as a value from 1 to 52.
Line 13,

```
Call lstOutput.AddItem("Hour: " & DatePart("h", Now))
```

uses function **DatePart** to get the current hour (**"h"**) as a value from 0 to 23.
Line 14,

```
Call lstOutput.AddItem("Minute: " & DatePart("n", Now))
```

uses function **DatePart** to get the current minute (**"n"**) as a value from 0 to 59.
Line 15,

```
Call lstOutput.AddItem("Second: " & DatePart("s", Now))
```

uses function **DatePart** to get the current second (**"s"**) as a value from 0 to 59.

The program of Fig. 8.24 demonstrates adding and subtracting dates with functions **DateAdd** and **DateDiff**. When this program executes, items are added to **List lstOutput** that illustrate the results of these functions.

Lines 7 and 8,

```
Call lstOutput.AddItem("Now + 3 years: " & _
                 DateAdd("yyyy", 3, Now))
```

use *function* **DateAdd** to add to a date. The function takes three arguments—the interval, the value to add and the date. The interval is a string indicating the part of the date that will be modified. For example, the string **"yyyy"** indicates that the second argument should be added to the year. The strings for the interval argument are identical to those used in Fig. 8.23 for function **DatePart**.

```
 1    ' Fig. 8.24
 2    ' Adding and subtracting dates
 3    Option Explicit
 4
 5    Private Sub Form_Load()
 6       Call lstOutput.AddItem("Now: " & Now)
 7       Call lstOutput.AddItem("Now + 3 years: " & _
 8                              DateAdd("yyyy", 3, Now))
 9
10       Call lstOutput.AddItem("Days between now and 12/31/98: " & _
11                              DateDiff("d", Now, "12/31/98"))
12       Call lstOutput.AddItem("Days between 1/1/98 and now: " & _
13                              DateDiff("d", "1/1/98", Now))
14       Call lstOutput.AddItem("Days between 1/1/98 and " & _
15               "12/31/98: " & DateDiff("d", "1/1/98", "12/31/98"))
16    End Sub
```

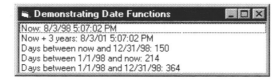

**Fig. 8.24**    Demonstrating functions **DateAdd** and **DateDiff**.

Lines 10 through 15,

```
Call lstOutput.AddItem("Days between now and 12/31/98: " & _
                       DateDiff("d", Now, "12/31/98"))
Call lstOutput.AddItem("Days between 1/1/98 and now: " & _
                       DateDiff("d", "1/1/98", Now))
lstOutput.AddItem("Days between 1/1/98 and " & _
        "12/31/98: " & DateDiff("d", "1/1/98", "12/31/98"))
```

use *function **DateDiff*** to subtract dates. The function takes three arguments—the interval, the first date and the second date. The interval is a string indicating the part of the date that will be modified. For example, the string **"d"** indicates that the difference between the second and third arguments should be determined based on the day of the month. The strings for the interval argument are identical to those used in Fig. 8.23 for function **DatePart**. Function **DateDiff** has two optional arguments—the fourth argument is a constant indicating the first day of the week (as discussed for function **Weekday**) and the fifth argument is a constant indicating the first week of the year (as discussed for function **DatePart**).

The program of Fig. 8.25 demonstrates functions ***Time***, ***Hour***, ***Minute***, ***Second***, ***Timer***, ***TimeSerial*** and ***TimeValue***. When this program executes, items are added to **ListBox lstOutput** that illustrate the results of these functions.

Line 6,

```
Call lstOutput.AddItem("Time: " & Time)
```

uses function **Time** to get the current system time.

```
1   ' Fig. 8.25
2   ' Demonstrating the Time functions
3   Option Explicit
4
5   Private Sub Form_Load()
6       Call lstOutput.AddItem("Time: " & Time)
7       Call lstOutput.AddItem("Hour: " & Hour(Time))
8       Call lstOutput.AddItem("Minute: " & Minute(Time))
9       Call lstOutput.AddItem("Second: " & Second(Time))
10      Call lstOutput.AddItem("Seconds since midnight: " & Timer)
11      Call lstOutput.AddItem("TimeSerial(0,0,90): " & _
12                          TimeSerial(0, 0, 90))
13      Call lstOutput.AddItem("TimeSerial(13,0,90): " & _
14                          TimeSerial(13, 0, 90))
15      Call lstOutput.AddItem("TimeSerial(0,90,0): " & _
16                          TimeSerial(0, 90, 0))
17      Call lstOutput.AddItem("3:33PM as a Time is: " & _
18                          TimeValue("3:33PM"))
19      Call lstOutput.AddItem("15:33 as a Time is: " & _
20                          TimeValue("15:33"))
21  End Sub
```

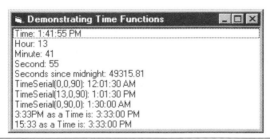

**Fig. 8.25** Demonstrating functions **Time**, **Hour**, **Minute**, **Second**, **Timer**, **TimeSerial** and **TimeValue**.

Line 7,

```
Call lstOutput.AddItem("Hour: " & Hour(Time))
```

uses *function **Hour*** to get the hour from its numeric or string argument.
Line 8,

```
Call lstOutput.AddItem("Minute: " & Minute(Time))
```

uses *function **Minute*** to get the minute from its numeric or string argument.
Line 9,

```
Call lstOutput.AddItem("Second: " & Second(Time))
```

uses *function **Second*** to get the second from its numeric or string argument.
Line 10,

```
Call lstOutput.AddItem("Seconds since midnight: " & Timer)
```

uses *function **Timer*** to get the number of seconds since midnight.

Lines 11 through 18,

```
Call lstOutput.AddItem("TimeSerial(0,0,90): " & _
                       TimeSerial(0, 0, 90))
Call lstOutput.AddItem("TimeSerial(13,0,90): " & _
                       TimeSerial(13, 0, 90))
Call lstOutput.AddItem("TimeSerial(0,90,0): " & _
                       TimeSerial(0, 90, 0))
```

use *function* **TimeSerial** to return a **Date** containing the specified time. The first argument represents the hour as a value from 0 to 23. The second and third arguments represent the minute and second as any value in the range –32,768 to 32,767. For example, a value of 90 for the minute is interpreted as 1 hour and 30 minutes. Also, relative times can be specified by adding or subtracting an **Integer** with the minute or second.

Lines 19 through 22,

```
Call lstOutput.AddItem("3:33PM as a Time is: " & _
                       TimeValue("3:33PM"))
Call lstOutput.AddItem("15:33 as a Time is: " & _
                       TimeValue("15:33"))
```

use *function* **TimeValue** to return a **Date** containing the specified time. Any time in the range 0:00:00 (12 AM) to 23:59:59 (12:59:59 PM) is valid as the argument.

## 8.18 Date and Time Formatting

Visual Basic provides numerous pre-defined date and time formats and user-defined date and time formats. The next two programs illustrate these capabilities.

The program of Fig. 8.26 demonstrates function **FormatDateTime** and the named date and time formats of the **Format** function.

```
1  ' Fig. 8.26
2  ' Formatting dates and times with the FormatDateTime function
3  ' and the named date/time formats of the Format function
4  Option Explicit
5
6  Private Sub Form_Load()
7     Call lstOutput.AddItem("vbGeneralDate: " & _
8                            FormatDateTime(Now, vbGeneralDate))
9     Call lstOutput.AddItem("vbLongDate: " & _
10                           FormatDateTime(Now, vbLongDate))
11    Call lstOutput.AddItem("vbLongTime: " & _
12                           FormatDateTime(Now, vbLongTime))
13    Call lstOutput.AddItem("vbShortDate: " & _
14                           FormatDateTime(Now, vbShortDate))
15    Call lstOutput.AddItem("vbShortTime: " & _
16                           FormatDateTime(Now, vbShortTime))
17    Call lstOutput.AddItem("")
```

**Fig. 8.26**   Demonstrating function **FormatDateTime** and the named date/time formats of function **Format** (part 1 of 2).

```
18    Call lstOutput.AddItem("General Date: " & _
19                           Format(Now, "General Date"))
20    Call lstOutput.AddItem("Long Date: " & _
21                           Format(Now, "Long Date"))
22    Call lstOutput.AddItem("Medium Date: " & _
23                           Format(Now, "Medium Date"))
24    Call lstOutput.AddItem("Short Date: " & _
25                           Format(Now, "Short Date"))
26    Call lstOutput.AddItem("Long Time: " & _
27                           Format(Now, "Long Time"))
28    Call lstOutput.AddItem("Medium Time: " & _
29                           Format(Now, "Medium Time"))
30    Call lstOutput.AddItem("Short Time: " & _
31                           Format(Now, "Short Time"))
32    End Sub
```

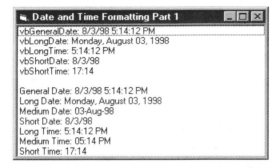

**Fig. 8.26**  Demonstrating function **FormatDateTime** and the named date/time formats of function **Format** (part 2 of 2).

For each of the formats discussed below, refer to the screen capture of Fig. 8.26 to see the actual formatted output.

Lines 7 and 8,

```
Call lstOutput.AddItem("vbGeneralDate: " & _
    FormatDateTime(Now, vbGeneralDate))
```

use function **FormatDateTime** to format the current date and time (**Now**) as a general date which displays both the date and time. The function receives two arguments—the expression to format and a constant representing the format (**vbGeneralDate** in this case).

Lines 9 and 10,

```
Call lstOutput.AddItem("vbLongDate: " & _
    FormatDateTime(Now, vbLongDate))
```

use function **FormatDateTime** to format the current date and time (**Now**) as a long date (**vbLongDate**) which displays only the date in long format.

Lines 11 and 12,

```
Call lstOutput.AddItem("vbLongTime: " & _
    FormatDateTime(Now, vbLongTime))
```

use function **FormatDateTime** to format the current date and time (**Now**) as a long time (**vbLongTime**) which displays only the time in long format.

Lines 13 and 14,

```
Call lstOutput.AddItem("vbShortDate: " & _
   FormatDateTime(Now, vbShortDate))
```

use function **FormatDateTime** to format the current date and time (**Now**) as a short date (**vbShortDate**) which displays only the date in short format.

Lines 15 and 16,

```
Call lstOutput.AddItem("vbShortTime: " & _
   FormatDateTime(Now, vbShortTime))
```

use function **FormatDateTime** to format the current date and time (**Now**) as a short time (**vbShortTime**) which displays only the time in short format.

Lines 18 and 19,

```
Call lstOutput.AddItem("General Date: " & _
   Format(Now, "General Date"))
```

use function **Format** to format the current date and time (**Now**) as a general date which displays both the date and time. The function receives two arguments—the expression to format and a string representing the format (**"General Date"** in this case).

Lines 20 and 21,

```
Call lstOutput.AddItem("Long Date: " & _
   Format(Now, "Long Date"))
```

use function **Format** to format the current date and time (**Now**) as a long date (**"Long Date"**) which displays only the date in long format.

Lines 22 and 23,

```
Call lstOutput.AddItem("Medium Date: " & _
   Format(Now, "Medium Date"))
```

use function **Format** to format the current date and time (**Now**) as a medium date (**"Medium Date"**) which displays only the date in medium format.

Lines 24 and 25,

```
Call lstOutput.AddItem("Short Date: " & _
   Format(Now, "Short Date"))
```

use function **Format** to format the current date and time (**Now**) as a short date (**"Short Date"**) which displays only the date in short format.

Lines 26 and 27,

```
Call lstOutput.AddItem("Long Time: " & _
   Format(Now, "Long Time"))
```

use function **Format** to format the current date and time (**Now**) as a long time (**"Long Time"**) which displays only the time in long format.

Lines 28 and 29,

```
Call lstOutput.AddItem("Medium Time: " & _
    Format(Now, "Medium Time"))
```

use function **Format** to format the current date and time (**Now**) as a medium time (***"Medium Time"***) which displays only the time in medium format.

Lines 30 and 31,

```
Call lstOutput.AddItem("Short Time: " & _
    Format(Now, "Short Time"))
```

use function **Format** to format the current date and time (**Now**) as a short time (***"Short Time"***) which displays only the time in short format.

The program of Fig. 8.27 demonstrates the user-defined date and time formats of the **Format** function.

Line 8,

```
Call lstOutput.AddItem("m/d/yy: " & Format(Now, "m/d/yy"))
```

uses function **Format** to format the current date and time (**Now**) using the format string **"m/d/yy"**, which displays the month, day and a two-digit year separated by slashes.

---

```
1   ' Fig. 8.27
2   ' Formatting dates and times user-defined date/time
3   ' formats of the Format function
4   Option Explicit
5
6   Private Sub Form_Load()
7       Call lstOutput.AddItem("DATE FORMATS")
8       Call lstOutput.AddItem("m/d/yy: " & Format(Now, "m/d/yy"))
9       Call lstOutput.AddItem("d-mmm-yy: " & _
10                                  Format(Now, "d-mmm-yy"))
11      Call lstOutput.AddItem("d-mmmm-yy: " & _
12                                  Format(Now, "d-mmmm-yy"))
13      Call lstOutput.AddItem("mmmm d, yyyy: " & _
14                                  Format(Now, "mmmm d, yyyy"))
15      Call lstOutput.AddItem("ddd: " & Format(Now, "ddd"))
16      Call lstOutput.AddItem("dddd: " & Format(Now, "dddd"))
17      Call lstOutput.AddItem("ddddd: " & Format(Now, "ddddd"))
18      Call lstOutput.AddItem("dddddd: " & Format(Now, "dddddd"))
19      Call lstOutput.AddItem("")
20      Call lstOutput.AddItem("TIME FORMATS")
21      Call lstOutput.AddItem("Hh:Nn:Ss AM/PM: " & _
22                                  Format(Now, "Hh:Nn:Ss AM/PM"))
23      Call lstOutput.AddItem("ttttt: " & Format(Now, "ttttt"))
24      Call lstOutput.AddItem("")
25      Call lstOutput.AddItem("DATE/TIME FORMAT")
26      Call lstOutput.AddItem("c: " & Format(Now, "c"))
27   End Sub
```

---

**Fig. 8.27**  Demonstrating the user-defined date and time formats of function **Format** (part 1 of 2).

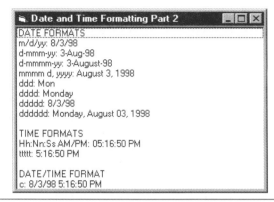

**Fig. 8.27**    Demonstrating the user-defined date and time formats of function **Format** (part 2 of 2).

Lines 9 and 10,

```
Call lstOutput.AddItem("d-mmm-yy: " & _
                        Format(Now, "d-mmm-yy"))
```

uses function **Format** to format the current date and time (**Now**) using the format string **"d-mmm-yy"**, which displays the day, abbreviated month name and a two-digit year separated by dashes.

Lines 11 and 12,

```
Call lstOutput.AddItem("d-mmmm-yy: " & _
                        Format(Now, "d-mmmm-yy"))
```

use function **Format** to format the current date and time (**Now**) using the format string **"d-mmmm-yy"**, which displays the day, full month name and a two-digit year separated by dashes.

Lines 13 and 14,

```
Call lstOutput.AddItem("mmmm d, yyyy: " & _
                        Format(Now, "mmmm d, yyyy"))
```

use function **Format** to format the current date and time (**Now**) using the format string **"mmmm d, yyyy"**, which displays the full month name, a space, the day and a four-digit year separated by dashes.

Line 15,

```
Call lstOutput.AddItem("ddd: " & Format(Now, "ddd"))
```

uses function **Format** to format the current date and time (**Now**) using the format string **"ddd"**, which displays an abbreviated day name.

Line 16,

```
Call lstOutput.AddItem("dddd: " & Format(Now, "dddd"))
```

uses function **Format** to format the current date and time (**Now**) using the format string **"dddd"**, which displays a full day name.

Line 17,

```
Call lstOutput.AddItem("ddddd: " & Format(Now, "ddddd"))
```

uses function **Format** to format the current date and time (**Now**) using the format string **"ddddd"**, which displays the date in short format (as shown in line 8).
Line 18,

```
Call lstOutput.AddItem("dddddd: " & Format(Now, "dddddd"))
```

uses function **Format** to format the current date and time (**Now**) using the format string **"dddddd"**, which displays the date in long format.
Lines 21 and 22,

```
Call lstOutput.AddItem("Hh:Nn:Ss AM/PM: " & _
                Format(Now, "Hh:Nn:Ss AM/PM"))
```

use function **Format** to format the current date and time (**Now**) using the format string **"Hh:Nn:Ss AM/PM"**, which displays the time in 12-hour format with two digits for the hour, minute and second and an AM or PM indication.
Line 23,

```
Call lstOutput.AddItem("ttttt: " & Format(Now, "ttttt"))
```

uses function **Format** to format the current date and time (**Now**) using the format string **"ttttt"**, which displays the time in 12-hour format with the hour, two-digit minute and two-digit second and an AM or PM indication.
Line 26,

```
Call lstOutput.AddItem("c: " & Format(Now, "c"))
```

uses function **Format** to format the current date and time (**Now**) using the format string **"c"**, which displays the date in short format and the time in 12-hour format with the hour, two-digit minute and two-digit second and an AM or PM indication.

## 8.19 String Arrays

A **String** array is an array whose elements are **String**s. A particular element (or **String**) within a **String** array is referred to by giving the name of the **String** array followed by the index (enclosed in parentheses). For example, the fifth element or **String** within array **mMonth** is referred to as **mMonth(4)** (in a 0-based array). The $i^{th}$ element or **String** within array **part** is referred to as **part(**$i$ **- 1)** (in a 0-based array). Various Visual Basic functions, such as the concatenation function *Join*, take a **String** array as an argument. For example the statements

```
Dim a(1) As String, b As String
a(0) = "Hello "
a(1) = "There!"
b = Join(a)
```

take the **String** elements of **a** and create a new **String** ("**Hello There!**"). **String b** is a concatenation of **a(0)** and **a(1)**. Both **a(0)** and **a(1)** are not modified.

In this section we provide two examples that use **String** arrays and in Section 8.19.1 we utilize **String** arrays in a card shuffling and dealing simulation. Our first example, Fig. 8.28, calls Visual Basic function ***Filter*** twice. Once to extract all occurrences of the **String** "Visual Basic 6" from a **String** array and a second time to extract every **String** other than "Visual Basic 6" from the same **String** array. Line 19

```
b = Filter(a, "Visual Basic 6")
```

calls **Filter** to search **String** array **a** for "**Visual Basic 6**". **Filter** returns a **String** array that is assigned to array **b**. Each element of **b** stores the **String** "**Visual Basic 6**". Array **b** is then passed to **Sub** procedure **PrintStrings** where each element of **b** is printed to the form. Line 23 uses the **Erase** statement to release **b**'s memory.

```
1   ' Fig. 8.28
2   ' Demonstrating function Filter
3   Option Explicit
4   Private Sub Form_Load()
5       Dim a(9) As String, b() As String
6
7       a(0) = "Java"
8       a(1) = "Visual Basic 6"
9       a(2) = "Visual Basic 5"
10      a(3) = "C++"
11      a(4) = "Visual Basic 6"
12      a(5) = "Visual Basic 5"
13      a(6) = "Visual Basic 6"
14      a(7) = "Visual C++ 6"
15      a(8) = "Visual J++ 6"
16      a(9) = "Visual Basic 6"
17      Print "Filtering for the string: " & Chr$(34) & _
18              "Visual Basic 6" & Chr$(34)
19      b = Filter(a, "Visual Basic 6")
20      Call PrintStrings(b)
21
22      Print
23      Erase b
24
25      Print "Filtering for strings other than: " & Chr$(34) & _
26              "Visual Basic 6" & Chr$(34)
27      b = Filter(a, "Visual Basic 6", False)
28      Call PrintStrings(b)
29  End Sub
30
31  Private Sub PrintStrings(c() As String)
32      Dim z As Integer
33
34      For z = 0 To UBound(c)
35          Print c(z)
36      Next z
37
38  End Sub
```

**Fig. 8.28**  Using function **Filter** (part 1 of 2).

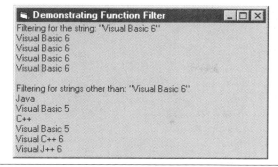

**Fig. 8.28**  Using function **Filter** (part 2 of 2).

Line 27

```
b = Filter(a, "Visual Basic 6", False)
```

calls **Filter** again. The third argument is an optional **Boolean** value that indicates whether or not the second argument is included in the filtering. When **True** (the default), the second argument is included in the filtering. When **False**, the second argument is excluded. String "**Visual Basic 6**" is excluded and every string other than "**Visual Basic 6**" is assigned to **b**. **PrintStrings** is called again to print the elements of **b**.

    **Filter** takes a fourth optional argument that determines the type of comparison to use. The default is **vbBinaryCompare**, but other values from Fig. 8.2 may be used.

    Our next example uses a Visual Basic tokenization function called **Split**. Figure 8.29 uses function **Split** to extract the words from a sentence.

Line 10

```
x = Split(y)
```

```
1   ' Fig. 8.29
2   ' Using function Split
3   Option Explicit
4
5   Private Sub Form_Load()
6       Dim x() As String, y As String
7       Dim z As Integer
8
9       y = "This is a sentence with 7 tokens"
10      x = Split(y)
11
12      For z = LBound(x) To UBound(x)
13          Print x(z)
14      Next z
15
16  End Sub
```

**Fig. 8.29**  Using function **Split** (part 1 of 2).

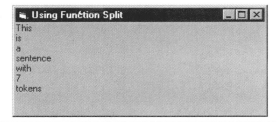

**Fig. 8.29**    Using function **Split** (part 2 of 2).

calls **Split** to extract all substrings (or *tokens*) from **String** array **y**. A substring in this particular case is any character or group of characters separated by a space character. **Split** returns a one-dimensional array (which is zero based) containing the substrings.

By default, **Split** uses a space character as the *delimiter* (i.e., the character that separates the substrings), returns all substrings, and uses **vbBinaryCompare**. The general form of **Split** is

$$\textbf{Split}(\textit{string, delimiter=" ", count=-1, compare=}\textbf{vbBinaryCompare})$$

The last three optional arguments represent the delimiter character, the number of substrings to return, and the type of comparison to use.

### 8.19.1 A Card Shuffling and Dealing Simulation

In this section, we use **String** arrays to develop a card shuffling and dealing simulation program. This program can then be used to implement programs that play specific card games. To reveal some subtle performance problems, we have intentionally used sub-optimal shuffling and dealing algorithms. In the exercises, we develop more efficient algorithms. We develop a program that will shuffle a deck of 52 playing cards, and then deal each of the 52 cards.

We use a 4-by-13 two-dimensional array **mDeck** to represent the deck of playing cards (Fig. 8.30). The rows correspond to the suits—row 1 corresponds to hearts, row 2 to diamonds, row 3 to clubs and row 4 to spades. The columns correspond to the face values of the cards—columns 1 through 10 correspond to faces ace through ten, respectively, and columns 11 through 13 correspond to jack, queen and king. We shall load **String** array **mSuit** with **String**s representing the four suits and **String** array **mFace** with **String**s representing the thirteen face values.

This simulated deck of cards may be shuffled as follows. First the array **mDeck** is cleared to zeros. Then, a **row** (1 – 4) and a **column** (1 – 13) are each chosen at random. The number 1 is inserted in array element **mDeck(row, column)** to indicate that this card is going to be the first one dealt from the shuffled deck. This process continues with the numbers 2, 3, …, 52 being randomly inserted in the **mDeck** array to indicate which cards are to be placed second, third, …, and fifty-second in the shuffled deck. As the **mDeck** array begins to fill with card numbers, it is possible that a card will be selected twice (i.e., **mDeck(row, column)** will be nonzero when it is selected). This selection is simply ignored and other **row**s and **column**s are repeatedly chosen at random until an unselected card is found. Eventually, the numbers 1 through 52 will occupy the 52 slots of the **mDeck** array. At this point, the deck of cards is fully shuffled.

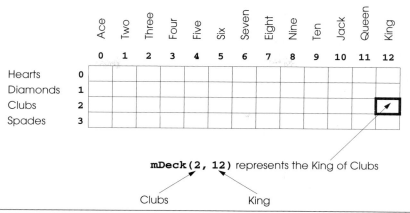

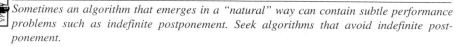

**Fig. 8.30**    Two-dimensional array representation of a deck of cards.

This shuffling algorithm could execute for an indefinitely long period of time if cards that have already been shuffled are repeatedly selected at random. This phenomenon is known as *indefinite postponement.* In an exercise later in the book, we discuss a better shuffling algorithm that eliminates the possibility of indefinite postponement.

**Performance Tip 8.1**

*Sometimes an algorithm that emerges in a "natural" way can contain subtle performance problems such as indefinite postponement. Seek algorithms that avoid indefinite postponement.*

To deal the first card we search the array for **mDeck(row, column)** matching **1**. This is accomplished with a nested **For** structure that varies **row** from 1 to 4 and **column** from 1 to 13. What card does that slot of the array correspond to? The **mSuit** array has been preloaded with the four suits, so to get the suit we print the **String mSuit(row)**. Similarly, to get the face value of the card, we print the **String mFace(column)**. We also print the **String "of"**. Printing this information in the proper order enables us to print each card in the form "**King of Clubs**," "**Ace of Diamonds**," and so on.

Note that this program is more efficient if the shuffle and deal portions of the algorithm are combined so each card is dealt as it is placed in the deck. We have chosen to program these operations separately because normally cards are dealt after they are shuffled (not as they are shuffled).

The card shuffling and dealing program is shown in Fig. 8.31. There is a weakness in the dealing algorithm. Once a match is found, even if it is found on the first try, the two inner **For** structures continue searching the remaining elements of **mDeck** for a match. In the exercises, we ask the reader to correct this deficiency.

When the program loads, lines 4 and 5 dimension the **mSuit**, **mFace** and **mDeck** arrays. Procedure **Form_Load** (line 7) assigns the **String**s representing the suits of the cards to the **suit** array, assigns the **String**s representing the faces of the cards to the **face** array and calls **Randomize** so the program produces different outputs each time it executes.

```
1    ' Fig. 8.31
2    ' A card shuffling and dealing simulation
3    Option Explicit
4    Dim mSuit(1 To 4) As String, mFace(1 To 13) As String
5    Dim mDeck(1 To 4, 1 To 13) As Integer
6
7    Private Sub Form_Load()
8        mSuit(1) = "Hearts"
9        mSuit(2) = "Diamonds"
10       mSuit(3) = "Clubs"
11       mSuit(4) = "Spades"
12
13       mFace(1) = "Ace"
14       mFace(2) = "Deuce"
15       mFace(3) = "Three"
16       mFace(4) = "Four"
17       mFace(5) = "Five"
18       mFace(6) = "Six"
19       mFace(7) = "Seven"
20       mFace(8) = "Eight"
21       mFace(9) = "Nine"
22       mFace(10) = "Ten"
23       mFace(11) = "Jack"
24       mFace(12) = "Queen"
25       mFace(13) = "King"
26
27       Call Randomize
28   End Sub
29
30   Private Sub cmdShuffle_Click()
31       Call lstOutput.Clear
32       Call Shuffle
33       Call Deal
34   End Sub
35
36   Private Sub Shuffle()
37       Dim card As Integer, row As Integer, column As Integer
38
39       Call ZeroDeckArray
40
41       For card = 1 To 52
42          Do
43             row = 1 + Int(Rnd() * UBound(mSuit))
44             column = 1 + Int(Rnd() * UBound(mFace))
45          Loop While mDeck(row, column) <> 0
46
47          mDeck(row, column) = card
48       Next
49
50   End Sub
51
```

**Fig. 8.31**   Card shuffling and dealing program (part 2 of 2).

```
52   Private Sub Deal()
53      Dim card As Integer, row As Integer, column As Integer
54
55      For card = 1 To 52
56         For row = LBound(mSuit) To UBound(mSuit)
57            For column = LBound(mFace) To UBound(mFace)
58
59               If mDeck(row, column) = card Then
60                  lstOutput.AddItem ( _
61                     mFace(column) & " of " & mSuit(row))
62               End If
63
64            Next column
65         Next row
66      Next card
67
68   End Sub
69
70   Private Sub ZeroDeckArray()
71      Dim row As Integer, column As Integer
72
73      For row = LBound(mSuit) To UBound(mSuit)
74         For column = LBound(mFace) To UBound(mFace)
75            mDeck(row, column) = 0
76         Next column
77      Next row
78
79   End Sub
```

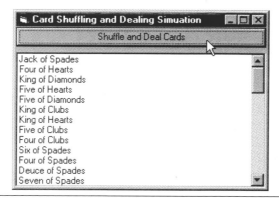

**Fig. 8.31**   Card shuffling and dealing program (part 2 of 2).

To make the program more dynamic, we provide a command button for the user to press to shuffle and deal the cards. Each time the button is pressed, event procedure **cmdShuffle_Click** (line 30) executes and calls **Shuffle** (line 36) to shuffle the cards and **Deal** (line 52) to deal the cards.

## Summary

• Characters are represented in memory by numeric values in the range 0-255. The values from 0 to 127 represent the ASCII character set.

- A string is a series of characters treated as a single unit. A string may include letters, digits, and various special characters such as **+**, **-**, **\***, **/**, **$** and others. Strings are enclosed in a set of double quotation marks.

- Visual Basic provides variable-length strings and fixed-length strings.

- Fixed-length strings are declared as follows:

      **Dim** *variableName* **As String** * *size*

  where *variableName* is the declared variable and *size* is the number of characters in the string.

- String concatenation is indicated with either a plus sign (**+**) or an ampersand (**&**).

- The relational and equality operators can be used to compare strings.

- Function **StrComp** returns **0** if the two strings it compares are equal, **-1** if the first string is less than the second and **1** if the first string is greater than the second. **StrComp** has an optional third argument that indicates the comparison type.

- The comparison type can be specified in a module-level **Option Compare** statement of the form

      **Option Compare** *type*

  where *type* is **Binary** (the default), **Text** or **Database**.

- When the computer compares two strings, it actually compares the numeric codes that make up the characters in the strings.

- Function **Mid$** takes three arguments—the source string from which a substring will be selected, the starting character position in the string and the number of characters to select. If the last argument is omitted or if the number of characters remaining is fewer than the number of characters to select, the remainder of the string from the starting character position is returned.

- **Left$** selects the leftmost portion of a string. **Right$** selects the rightmost portion of a string.

- Function **InStr** is useful for searching through one string, called the base string, to see if it contains another string, called the search string. An optional first argument is an **Integer** indicating the starting character position. Function **InStrRev**'s arguments are a base string, a search string and the starting character position in the base string. This function searches from the end of the base string toward the beginning of the string. Both functions take an optional fourth argument that specifies the type of comparison to use while searching.

- Functions **LTrim$**, **RTrim$** and **Trim$** remove leading spaces at the left side of a string, trailing spaces at the right side of a string and spaces on both the left and the right side of a string.

- Function **String$** creates a string of a specified character.

- Function **Space$** creates a string of spaces.

- Function **Replace** provides the ability to search for a string and replace one or more occurrences of that string.

- Function **StrReverse** reverses the characters in a string.

- Functions **UCase$** and **LCase$** convert strings to all uppercase letters and all lowercase letters, respectively.

- Function **Asc** returns the ASCII code corresponding to a given character. **Chr$** returns the string corresponding to an ASCII code.

- Function **Val** converts strings to numbers. Function **Str$** converts numbers to strings. Function **IsNumeric** returns **True** if a string can represent a number.

- Functions **Hex$** and **Oct$** convert numbers to hexadecimal (base 16) format strings and octal (base 8) format strings, respectively.

- Function **CBool** converts a value to a **Boolean**. Any numeric value or numeric string representation of zero returns **False**. All others return **True**.
- Function **CByte** converts a value to a value in the range 0 to 255.
- Function **CCur** converts a value to a **Currency** value for use in precise monetary calculations.
- Function **CDate** converts a value to a **Date** value.
- Function **CDbl** converts a value to a **Double** value representing a double-precision, floating-point value.
- Function **CDec** converts a value to a **Decimal** value representing the number.
- Function **CInt** converts a value to an **Integer** value.
- Function **CSng** converts a value to a **Single** value representing a single-precision, floating-point value.
- Function **CStr** converts a value to a **CStr** value.
- Function **CVar** converts a value to a **Variant**.
- Function **Format$** provides for both pre-defined formats (the named numeric formats and user-defined formats). Named numeric formats include **"General Number"**, **"Currency"**, **"Fixed"**, **"Standard"**, **"Scientific"**, **"Percent"**, **"Yes/No"**, **"True/False"** and **"Yes/No"**.
- Function **FormatNumber** formats numeric values.
- Function **FormatCurrency** formats currency values.
- Function **FormatPercent** formats percentages.
- Function **Now** gets the current system date and time.
- Function **Date** gets the current system date.
- Function **Day** gets the day of the month as an integer in the range 1 to 31.
- Function **WeekDay** gets the day of the week as an integer in the range 1 to 7.
- Function **WeekDayName** gets the name of the day of the week as string.
- Function **Month** gets the day of the month as an integer in the range 1 to 12.
- Function **Year** gets the year as an **Integer**.
- Function **IsDate** determines if a string or date can be converted to a **Date**.
- Function **DateValue** converts a string into a **Date**.
- Function **DateSerial** creates dates representing the year, month and day.
- Function **DatePart** returns parts of a date or time by specifying a string that represents the part of the date or time to return.
- Function **DateAdd** adds an integer to a date. Function **DateDiff** subtracts dates.
- Function **Time** gets the current system time.
- Function **Hour** gets the hour from its numeric or string argument.
- Function **Minute** gets the minute from its numeric or string argument.
- Function **Second** gets the second from its numeric or string argument.
- Function **Timer** gets the number of seconds since midnight.
- Function **TimeSerial** creates a **Date** containing the specified time.
- Function **TimeValue** returns a **Date** containing the specified time.
- Function **FormatDateTime** and **Format$** format dates and times.

## Terminology

**Trim$** function
**UCase$** function
user-defined numeric format
**Val** function
variable length string
**vbBinaryCompare** constant
**vbDatabaseCompare** constant
**vbFirstFourDays** constant
**vbFirstFullWeek** constant
**vbFirstJan1** constant
**vbFriday** constant
**vbGeneralDate** constant
**vbLongDate** constant
**vbLongTime** constant

**vbMonday** constant
**vbSaturday** constant
**vbShortDate** constant
**vbShortTime** constant
**vbSunday** constant
**vbTextCompare** constant
**vbThursday** constant
**vbTuesday** constant
**vbUseCompareOption** constant
**vbWednesday** constant
**Weekday** function
**WeekdayName** function
**Year** function

## Good Programming Practices

**8.1** Variables that will only contain strings should be declared as **String** data type.

**8.2** Always use the ampersand (**&**) operator for string concatenation.

## Performance Tip

**8.1** Sometimes an algorithm that emerges in a "natural" way can contain subtle performance problems such as indefinite postponement. Seek algorithms that avoid indefinite postponement.

## Portability Tip

**8.1** **Date** literals implicitly convert to the date format of the locale specified in the **Control Panel**'s **Regional Settings TextBox**. For example, **English (United States)** prints **#5/16/1984#** as **5/16/84** and **German (Standard)** prints **#5/16/1984#** as **16.05.84**.

## Self-Review Exercises

**8.1** State whether the following are *true* or *false*. If the answer is *false*, explain why.
  a) Function **Asc** returns the string representation of a numeric character representation.
  b) Only function **StrComp** can be used to compare strings in Visual Basic.
  c) Both the **+** and **&** operators can be used to concatenate strings.

**8.2** For each of the following, write a single statement that performs the indicated task.
  a) Compare the string in **s1** to the string in **s2** for equality using an operator.
  b) Append the string **s2** to the string **s1**.
  c) Determine the length of the string in **s1**.
  d) Determine the hour in the current system time two different ways.
  e) Determine the month in the current system date two different ways.

## Answers to Self-Review Exercises

**8.1** a) False. Function **Asc** returns the ASCII value of a character.
  b) False. Strings can also be compared using the relational and equality operators.
  c) True.

**8.2** a) **s1 = s2**
  b) **s1 = s1 & s2**

    c) `Len(s1)`
    d) `Hour(Now)`
       `Hour(Time)`
    e) `Month(Now)`
       `Month(Date)`

## Exercises

**8.3**    Suppose that you are interested in determining how many commonly used three-letter words there are in the English language that begin with a particular letter. Write a program that obtains the first letter of the three-letter words from the user, and then generates all possible three-letter words beginning with the letter typed by the user. Use function **Mid$** to extract the individual letters from a string containing the alphabet.

**8.4**    Write a program that reads a five-letter word from the user and produces all possible three-letter words that can be derived from the letters of the five-letter word. For example, the three-letter words produced from the word "bathe" include the commonly used words

      `ate`    `bat`    `bet`    `tab`    `hat`    `the`    `tea`

**8.5**    Use the techniques for comparing strings developed in Section 8.5 and the techniques for sorting arrays developed in Chapter 7 to write a program that alphabetizes a list of strings. Use the names of 10 or 15 towns in your area as input data to your program.

**8.6**    The chart in Appendix A shows the numeric code representations for many of the characters in the ASCII character set. Study this appendix carefully and then state whether each of the following is *true* or *false*.
    a)   The letter "A" comes before the letter "B."
    b)   The digit "9" comes before the digit "0."
    c)   The commonly used symbols for addition, subtraction, multiplication and division in Visual Basic all come before any of the digits.
    d)   The digits come before the letters.
    e)   If a sort program sorts strings into ascending sequence, the program will place the symbol for a right parenthesis before the symbol for a left parenthesis.

**8.7**    Write a program that reads a series of strings from the user and displays only those strings beginning with the letter "b."

**8.8**    Write a program that reads a series of strings from the user and prints only those strings that end with the letters "ED."

**8.9**    Write a program that generates all possible three-digit codes in the range 000 to 255 and attempts to print the corresponding characters using **Chr$**. What happens when this program is run?

*NOTE: Exercises 8.10 through 8.13 are reasonably challenging. Once you have done these problems, you ought to be able to implement most popular card games easily.*

**8.10**    Modify the program in Fig. 8.29 so that the card dealing method deals a five-card poker hand. Then write the following additional procedures:
    a)   Determine if the hand contains a pair.
    b)   Determine if the hand contains two pairs.
    c)   Determine if the hand contains three of a kind (e.g., three jacks).
    d)   Determine if the hand contains four of a kind (e.g., four aces).
    e)   Determine if the hand contains a flush (i.e., all five cards of the same suit).

    f)  Determine if the hand contains a straight (i.e., five cards of consecutive face values).

    g)  Determine if the hand contains a full house (i.e., two cards of one face value and three cards of another face value).

**8.11**    Use the procedures developed in Exercise 8.10 to write a program that deals two five-card poker hands, evaluates each hand and determines which is the better hand.

**8.12**    Modify the program developed in Exercise 8.11 so that it can simulate the dealer. The dealer's five-card hand is dealt "face down" so the player cannot see it. The program should then evaluate the dealer's hand and, based on the quality of the hand, the dealer should draw one, two or three more cards to replace the corresponding number of unneeded cards in the original hand. The program should then reevaluate the dealer's hand. (*Caution:* This is a difficult problem!)

**8.13**    Modify the program developed in Exercise 8.12 so that it can handle the dealer's hand automatically, but the player is allowed to decide which cards of the player's hand to replace. The program should then evaluate both hands and determine who wins. Now use this new program to play 20 games against the computer. Who wins more games, you or the computer? Have one of your friends play 20 games against the computer. Who wins more games? Based on the results of these games, make appropriate modifications to refine your poker playing program (this, too, is a difficult problem). Play 20 more games. Does your modified program play a better game?

**8.14**    Write a program that uses random number generation to create sentences. Use four arrays of **String**s called **article**, **noun**, **verb** and **preposition**. Create a sentence by selecting a word at random from each array in the following order: **article**, **noun**, **verb**, **preposition**, **article** and **noun**. As each word is picked, concatenate it to the previous words in the sentence. The words should be separated by spaces. When the sentence is output, it should start with a capital letter and end with a period. The program should generate 20 sentences and output them to a **List**.

    The arrays should be filled as follows: the **article** array should contain the articles **"the"**, **"a"**, **"one"**, **"some"** and **"any"**; the **noun** array should contain the nouns **"boy"**, **"girl"**, **"dog"**, **"town"** and **"car"**; the **verb** array should contain the verbs **"drove"**, **"jumped"**, **"ran"**, **"walked"** and **"skipped"**; the **preposition** array should contain the prepositions **"to"**, **"from"**, **"over"**, **"under"** and **"on"**.

    After the preceding program is written, modify the program to produce a short story consisting of several of these sentences. (How about the possibility of a random story writer!)

**8.15**    (*Limericks*) A limerick is a humorous five-line verse in which the first and second lines rhyme with the fifth, and the third line rhymes with the fourth. Using techniques similar to those developed in Exercise 8.14, write a program that produces random limericks. Polishing this program to produce good limericks is a challenging problem, but the result will be worth the effort!

**8.16**    Write a program that inputs a telephone number as a string in the form **(555) 555-5555**. The program should use functions **Mid$**, **Left$** and **Right$** to extract the area code, the first three digits of the phone number and the last four digits of the phone number. The seven digits of the phone number should be concatenated into one string. The program should convert the area code string and the phone number string to **Integer**s. Both the area code and the phone number should be printed.

**8.17**    Write a program that inputs a line of text, breaks the string into substrings (called "tokenizing" the string) representing each word and outputs the substrings in reverse order.

**8.18**    Rewrite the program of Exercise 8.17 using function **Split**. Function **Split** returns a one dimensional array of **String**s (starting at element 0) based on its two arguments—the string to be tokenized and the delimiter character. The delimiter character is the character that is used to determine where a "token" begins and ends. If the second argument is omitted, the default delimiter character is the space character.

**8.19**   Write a program that inputs several lines of text and a search character, and uses function **InStr** to determine the number of occurrences of the character in the text.

**8.20**   Write a program based on the program of Exercise 8.19 that inputs several lines of text and uses function **InStr** to determine the total number of occurrences of each letter of the alphabet in the text. Uppercase and lowercase letters should be counted together. Store the totals for each letter in an array, and display the values in tabular format after the totals have been determined.

**8.21**   (*Printing Dates in Various Formats*) Dates are represented in several common formats. Two of the more common formats are:

**07/21/55** and **July 21, 1955**

Write a program that reads a date in the first format and displays that date in the second format.

**8.22**   (*Simple Encryption*) Some information on the Internet may be encrypted with a simple algorithm known as "rot13"—which rotates each character by 13 positions in the alphabet. Thus, **'a'** corresponds to **'n'**, **'x'** corresponds to **'k'**. Rot13 is an example of *symmetric key encryption*. With symmetric key encryption, both the encrypter and decrypter use the same key.
   a)   Write a program that encrypts a message using rot13.
   b)   Write a program that decrypts the scrambled message using 13 as the key.
   c)   After writing the programs of part (a) and part (b), briefly answer the following question: If you did not know the key for part (b), how difficult do you think it would be to break the code using any resources available? What if you had access to substantial computing power (e.g., Cray supercomputers)?

**8.23**   (*Hangman*) Write a program that plays the game of hangman. The program should pick a word (which is coded directly into the program) and display the following:

**Guess the word:     XXXXXX**

Each **X** represents a letter. If the user guesses correctly, the program should display

**Congratulations!!! You guessed my word. Play again? yes/no**

The appropriate response **yes** or **no** should be input. If the user guesses incorrectly, display the appropriate body part.

After seven incorrect guesses, the user should be hung. The display should look like

After each guess you want to display all their guesses.

**8.24**   (*Cryptograms*) Write a program that creates a cryptogram out of a **String**. A cryptogram is a message or word, where each letter is replaced with another letter. For example, the **String**

**The birds name was squawk**

might be scrambled to form

**xms kbypo zhqs fho obrhfu**

Note that spaces are not scrambled. In this particular case, **T** was replaced with **x**, each **a** was replaced with **h**, etc. Uppercase letters and lowercase letters should be treated the same.

**8.25**     Modify Exercise 8.24 to allow a user to solve the cryptogram by inputting two characters. The first character specifies the letter in the cryptogram, and the second letter specifies the user's guess. For example, if the user inputs **r g**, the user is guessing that the letter **r** is really a **g**.

**8.26**     Write a program that inputs a sentence and counts the number of palindromes in the sentence. A palindrome is a word that reads the same backwards and forwards. For example, **"tree"** is not a palindrome but **"noon"** is.

**8.27**     Write a program that inserts the characters **"*$$*"** in the middle of a **String**.

**8.28**     Write a program that generates from the string **"abcdefghijklmnopqrstuvwxyz{"** the following:

```
              a
             bcb
            cdedc
           defgfed
          efghihgfe
         fghijkjihgf
        ghijklmlkjihg
       hijklmnonmlkjih
      ijklmnopqponmlkji
     jklmnopqrsrqponmlkj
    klmnopqrstutsrqponmlk
   lmnopqrstuvwvutsrqponml
  mnopqrstuvwxyxwvutsrqponm
 nopqrstuvwxyz{zyxwvutsrqpon
```

**8.29**     Modify Fig. 8.29 to **Deal** the cards more efficiently. Only rewrite **Deal** and use only the topics discussed in Chapters 1 through 8.

**8.30**     Law enforcement agencies often get partial descriptions of suspect license plate numbers and have to search for license plate numbers that match the description. Create a program that will allow a local law enforcement agency to determine how many license plate numbers match a partial description. Randomly create 500 6-character long license plate numbers and store them in an array. Allow the user to search for partial plate numbers of 3 or 4 digits. Note: License plate numbers can contain both digits and letters.

### Special Section: Advanced String Manipulation Exercises

The preceding exercises are keyed to the text and designed to test the reader's understanding of fundamental string manipulation concepts. This section includes a collection of intermediate and advanced string manipulation exercises. The reader should find these problems challenging, yet entertaining. The problems vary considerably in difficulty. Some require an hour or two of program writing and implementation. Others are useful for lab assignments that might require two or three weeks of study and implementation. Some are challenging term projects.

**8.31**     *(Text Analysis)* The availability of computers with string manipulation capabilities has resulted in some rather interesting approaches to analyzing the writings of great authors. Much attention has been focused on whether William Shakespeare ever lived. Some scholars believe there is substantial evidence indicating that Christopher Marlowe or other authors actually penned the masterpieces attributed to Shakespeare. Researchers have used computers to find similarities in the writings of these two authors. This exercise examines three methods for analyzing texts with a computer.

    a)   Write a program that reads several lines of text from the keyboard and displays a table indicating the number of occurrences of each letter of the alphabet in the text. For example, the phrase

**To be, or not to be: that is the question:**

contains one "a," two "b's," no "c's," etc.

b) Write a program that reads several lines of text and displays a table indicating the number of one-letter words, two-letter words, three-letter words, etc. appearing in the text. For example, the phrase

**Whether 'tis nobler in the mind to suffer**

contains

| Word length | Occurrences |
|---|---|
| 1 | 0 |
| 2 | 2 |
| 3 | 2 |
| 4 | 2 (including 'tis) |
| 5 | 0 |
| 6 | 2 |
| 7 | 1 |

c) Write a program that reads several lines of text and displays a table indicating the number of occurrences of each different word in the text. The first version of your program should include the words in the table in the same order in which they appear in the text. For example, the lines

**To be, or not to be: that is the question:**
**Whether 'tis nobler in the mind to suffer**

d) contain the words "to" three times, the word "be" two times, the word "or" once, etc. A more interesting (and useful) printout should then be attempted in which the words are sorted alphabetically.

**8.32**   *(Check Protection)* Computers are frequently employed in check-writing systems such as payroll applications and accounts payable applications. Many strange stories circulate regarding weekly paychecks being printed (by mistake) for amounts in excess of $1 million. Incorrect amounts are printed by computerized check-writing systems because of human error and/or machine failure. Systems designers build controls into their systems to prevent erroneous checks from being issued.

Another serious problem is the intentional alteration of a check amount by someone who intends to cash a check fraudulently. To prevent a dollar amount from being altered, most computerized check-writing systems employ a technique called *check protection.*

Checks designed for imprinting by computer contain a fixed number of spaces in which the computer may print an amount. Suppose a paycheck contains eight blank spaces in which the computer is supposed to print the amount of a weekly paycheck. If the amount is large, then all eight of those spaces will be filled, for example:

```
1,230.60 (check amount)
--------
12345678 (position numbers)
```

On the other hand, if the amount is less than $1000, then several of the spaces would ordinarily be left blank. For example,

```
   99.87
--------
12345678
```

contains three blank spaces. If a check is printed with blank spaces, it is easier for someone to alter the amount of the check. To prevent a check from being altered, many check-writing systems insert *leading asterisks* to protect the amount, as follows:

```
***99.87
--------
12345678
```

Write a program that inputs a dollar amount to be printed on a check, and then prints the amount in check-protected format with leading asterisks if necessary. Assume that nine spaces are available for printing the amount.

**8.33**    *(Writing the Word Equivalent of a Check Amount)* Continuing the discussion of Exercise 8.30, we reiterate the importance of designing check-writing systems to prevent alteration of check amounts. One common security method requires that the check amount be written both in numbers and "spelled out" in words as well. Even if someone is able to alter the numerical amount of the check, it is extremely difficult to change the amount in words.

Many computerized check-writing systems do not print the amount of the check in words. Perhaps the main reason for this omission is the fact that most high-level languages used in commercial applications do not contain adequate string manipulation features. Another reason is that the logic for writing word equivalents of check amounts is somewhat involved.

Write a program that inputs a numeric check amount and writes the word equivalent of the amount. For example, the amount 112.43 should be written as

```
ONE HUNDRED TWELVE and 43/100
```

**8.34**    *(Morse Code)* Perhaps the most famous of all coding schemes is the Morse code, developed by Samuel Morse in 1832 for use with the telegraph system. The Morse code assigns a series of dots and dashes to each letter of the alphabet, each digit, and a few special characters (such as period, comma, colon, and semicolon). In sound-oriented systems, the dot represents a short sound and the dash represents a long sound. Other representations of dots and dashes are used with light-oriented systems and signal-flag systems.

Separation between words is indicated by a space, or, quite simply, the absence of a dot or dash. In a sound-oriented system, a space is indicated by a short period of time during which no sound is transmitted. The international version of the Morse code appears in Fig. 6.44.

Write a program that reads an English language phrase and encodes the phrase into Morse code. Also write a program that reads a phrase in Morse code and converts the phrase into the English language equivalent. Use one blank between each Morse-coded letter and three blanks between each Morse-coded word.

**8.35**    *(A Metric Conversion Program)* Write a program that will assist the user with metric conversions. Your program should allow the user to specify the names of the units as strings (i.e., centimeters, liters, grams, etc. for the metric system and inches, quarts, pounds, etc. for the English system) and should respond to simple questions such as

```
"How many inches are in 2 meters?"
"How many liters are in 10 quarts?"
```

Your program should recognize invalid conversions. For example, the question

> **"How many feet are there in 5 kilograms?"**

is not a meaningful question because **"feet"** are units of length while **"kilograms"** are units of mass.

## Special Section: Challenging String Manipulation Projects

**8.36**   *(Project: A Spelling Checker)* Many popular word processing software packages have built-in spell checkers.

In this project, you are asked to develop your own spell-checker utility. We make suggestions to help get you started. You should then consider adding more capabilities. Use a computerized dictionary (if you have access to one) as a source of words.

Why do we type so many words with incorrect spellings? In some cases, it is because we simply do not know the correct spelling, so we make a "best guess." In some cases, it is because we transpose two letters (e.g., "defualt" instead of "default"). Sometimes we double-type a letter accidentally (e.g., "hanndy" instead of "handy"). Sometimes we type a nearby key instead of the one we intended (e.g., "biryhday" instead of "birthday"). And so on.

Design and implement a spell-checker program in Visual Basic. Your program should maintain an array **wordList** of strings. Enable the user to enter these strings. Note: In Chapters 14, 15 and 19 we introduce file processing and networking. Once you have these capabilities, you can obtain the words for the spell checker from a computerized dictionary stored in a file.

Your program should ask a user to enter a word. The program should then look up that word in the **wordList** array. If the word is present in the array, your program should print '**Word is spelled correctly**."

If the word is not present in the array, your program should print '**word is not spelled correctly**." Then your program should try to locate other words in **wordList** that might be the word the user intended to type. For example, you can try all possible single transpositions of adjacent letters to discover that the word "default" is a direct match to a word in **wordList**. Of course, this implies that your program will check all other single transpositions, such as "edfault," "dfeault," "deafult," "defalut" and "defautl." When you find a new word that matches one in **wordList**, print that word in a message such as, '**Did you mean "default?"**"

Implement other tests, such as replacing each double letter with a single letter and any other tests you can develop to improve the value of your spell checker.

**8.37**   *(Project: A Crossword Puzzle Generator)* Most people have worked a crossword puzzle, but few have ever attempted to generate one. Generating a crossword puzzle is suggested here as a string manipulation project requiring substantial sophistication and effort.

There are many issues the programmer must resolve to get even the simplest crossword puzzle generator program working. For example, how does one represent the grid of a crossword puzzle inside the computer? Should one use a series of strings, or should double-subscripted arrays be used?

The programmer needs a source of words (i.e., a computerized dictionary) that can be directly referenced by the program. In what form should these words be stored to facilitate the complex manipulations required by the program?

The really ambitious reader will want to generate the "clues" portion of the puzzle, in which the brief hints for each "across" word and each "down" word are printed for the puzzle worker. Merely printing a version of the blank puzzle itself is not a simple problem.

# Graphics

## Objectives

- To understand coordinate systems.
- To understand coordinate system scales.
- To be able to use method **Line**.
- To be able to use method **Circle**.
- To be able to use the **Line** control.
- To be able to use the **Shape** control.
- To understand and be able to manipulate colors.
- To understand the different image formats supported by Visual Basic.
- To be able to incorporate images into a program.
- To understand and be able to use the **Printer** object.

*One picture is worth ten thousand words.*
Chinese proverb

*Treat nature in terms of the cylinder, the sphere, the cone, all in perspective.*
Paul Cezanne

*Nothing ever becomes real till it is experienced—even a proverb is no proverb to you till your life has illustrated it.*
John Keats

*Capture its reality in paint!*
Paul Cézanne

# Outline

## 9.1 Introduction

Graphics convey information and make programs visually appealing. Everywhere we look
we see graphics—video games, billboards, movies, etc. One of the best examples is World
Wide Web pages. The majority of pages have some form of graphics. Pictures are one form
of graphics commonly found on a Web page. Pictures provide an enormous quantity of information. Graphics are more than just pictures. Graphics are the elements of a picture. Colors, lines, rectangles, patterns, text, etc. are all graphics. Graphics are visual.

Visual Basic provides graphics capabilities for drawing shapes in different colors and
patterns. Visual Basic is also capable of displaying many popular image formats. Although
the graphics capabilities may not be as feature rich as graphics software programs, Visual
Basic's graphic capabilities are integral to creating polished Windows applications.

## 9.2 Coordinate Systems

To draw in Visual Basic, we must understand Visual Basic's *coordinate system* (Fig. 9.1),
that identifies points on the screen (or objects such as forms, **PictureBox**es, etc.). By default, the upper-left point on the screen has coordinate *(0, 0),* which is commonly called the
*origin.* A coordinate pair is composed of an *x coordinate* (the *horizontal coordinate*) and a
*y coordinate* (the *vertical coordinate*). The *x* coordinate is the horizontal distance on the *x*
axis from the origin. The *y* coordinate is the vertical distance on the *y* axis from the origin.

The unit that a coordinate system is measured in is called a *scale.* Visual Basic provides eight coordinate system scales, which are shown in Fig. 9.2. Most controls as well as
the form use *twips* by default. Property **ScaleMode** specifies the scale.

*Portability Tip 9.1*

*Pixels are a device-dependent unit of measurement. The number of pixels varies with screen
size and resolution.*

*Portability Tip 9.2*

*The twip is a device-independent unit of measurement.*

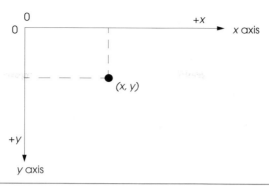

**Fig. 9.1**    Coordinate system.

| Scale | Constant | Value | Description |
|-------|----------|-------|-------------|
| User defined | **vbUser** | 0 | Scale defined by the programmer. |
| Twips | **vbTwips** | 1 | Default for forms and most controls. 1440 twips per inch. 567 twips per centimeter. 20 twips per point. |
| Points | **vbPoints** | 2 | Commonly used for fonts. 72 points per inch. |
| Pixels | **vbPixels** | 3 | Commonly used with images. Represents the smallest unit of resolution on a screen. |
| Characters | **vbCharacters** | 4 | 120 twips horizontally. 240 twips vertically (12 points). |
| Inches | **vbInches** | 5 | Physical inch. |
| Millimeters | **vbMillimeters** | 6 | Physical millimeter. |
| Centimeters | **vbCentimeters** | 7 | Physical centimeter. |

**Fig. 9.2**    Visual Basic coordinate system scales.

For maximum programming flexibility, coordinate systems can be changed. Consider a program that draws at the origin a circle with radius 10. If the default coordinate system is used when the circle is drawn, a quarter of the circle is visible (Fig. 9.3a). A user-defined coordinate system allows the programmer to relocate the origin such that the whole circle is visible (Fig. 9.3b). In both coordinate systems, the origin remains *(0, 0)*.

User-defined coordinates are defined using method ***Scale***. Two sets of coordinates define the scale. The first coordinate set defines the upper-left corner and the second coordinate set defines the lower-right corner. For example, the statement

```
Scale (-500, 250) - (500, -250)
```

changes the form's coordinate system to a user-defined scale of 1000 by 500. The upper-left corner has the coordinate *(–500, 250)* and the lower-right corner has the coordinate *(500, –250)*. Upon execution of method **Scale**, the **ScaleMode** property is set to **vbUser** by Visual Basic.

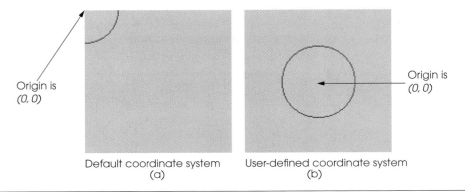

Origin is
(0, 0)

Origin is
(0, 0)

Default coordinate system            User-defined coordinate system
              (a)                                   (b)

**Fig. 9.3**    Default coordinates versus user-defined coordinates.

Calling method **Scale** is equivalent to setting properties *ScaleTop*, *ScaleLeft*, *ScaleWidth* and *ScaleHeight*. The call to **Scale** could have been written as

```
ScaleTop = -500
ScaleLeft = 250
ScaleWidth = 500
ScaleHeight = -250
```

Changing any one of these four properties sets the **ScaleMode** property to **vbUser**, **0**.

Methods *ScaleX* and *ScaleY* convert between scales. For example, the statement

```
Print ScaleX(1, vbCentimeters, vbTwips)
```

displays 567 (which is consistent with Fig. 9.2). One unit of **vbCentimeters** is converted to **vbTwips**.

## 9.3  Drawing Methods

Visual Basic provides methods *Print*, *Line*, *Circle* and *Pset* for drawing on forms and controls (Fig. 9.4). We begin our discussion of drawing methods with **Print**.

In previous chapters, we used statements such as

```
Print "VB6 How To Program"
```

| Method | Description |
|--------|-------------|
| **Print** | Draws text on a form or control. |
| **Line** | Draws lines on a form or control. Can also be used to draw rectangles. |
| **Circle** | Draws circles on a form or control. Can also be used to draw ellipses, arcs and sectors. |
| **Pset** | Sets a point's color. |

**Fig. 9.4**    Common drawing methods.

to draw text on the form. The default *x* coordinate is 0 and Visual Basic automatically increments the *y* coordinate to draw on the next line. The current drawing coordinates are stored in properties **CurrentX** and **CurrentY**. The drawn text's width and height can be retrieved with methods **TextWidth** and **TextHeight**, useful for aligning the text.

Figure 9.5 draws "**VB6 How To Program**" on the form at random coordinates. Note that text drawn near the edges of the form is *clipped*; drawing does not automatically wrap to the next line.

Method **Line** draws lines and rectangles between two sets of coordinates. The first set of coordinates is the starting point and the second is the ending point. For rectangles (also called *boxes*) the first coordinate set specifies the upper-left corner and the second specifies the lower-left corner. For example, the statements

```
1   ' Fig. 9.5
2   ' Printing to the form
3   Option Explicit          ' General declaration
4
5   Private Sub cmdPrint_Click()
6      Call Randomize
7
8      ' Randomly pick coordinates at which to draw
9      CurrentX = Rnd() * Width
10     CurrentY = Rnd() * Height
11
12     ' Print at (CurrentX, CurrentY)
13     Print "VB6 How To Program"
14  End Sub
```

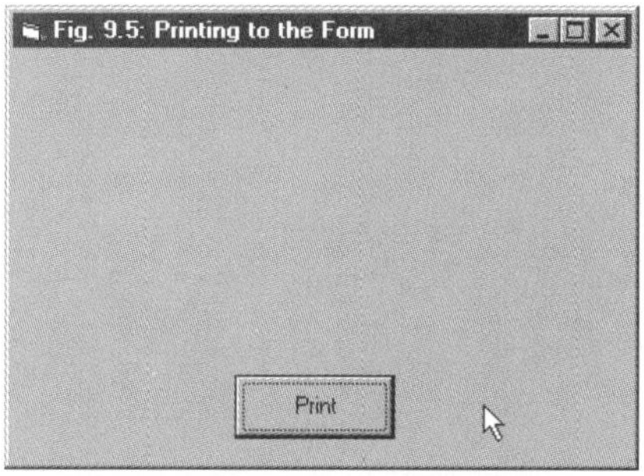

Inital GUI at execution.

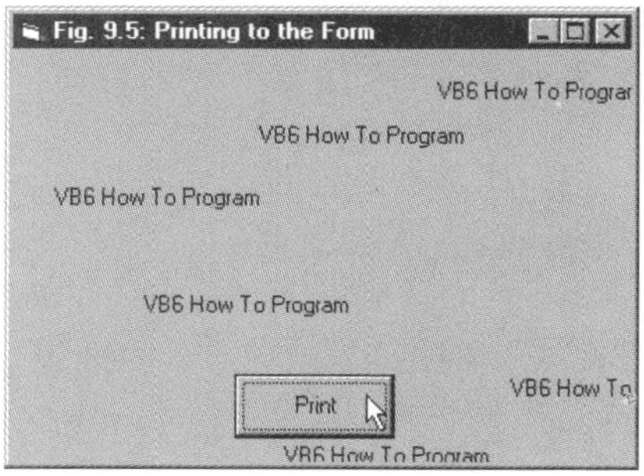

GUI after user has pressed **Print** several times.

**Fig. 9.5**    Drawing text with method **Print**.

```
Line (0, 0) - (100, 100)
Line (0, 0) - (55, 21), vbRed, B
Line (25, 50) - (500, 300), vbRed, BF
```

draw two lines and one rectangle. **Line**'s second argument specifies a color, in this case the Visual Basic constant **vbRed**, which represents the color red. We discuss colors in greater detail later in this chapter. The third argument, **B**, indicates that the method should draw a rectangle. A third argument of **BF** would indicate that the rectangle should be *filled* (i.e., solid). The three statements above draw a line between *(0, 0)* and *(100, 100)*, a red rectangle 55 by 21 with an upper-left corner of *(0, 0)* and a lower-right corner of *(55, 21)* and a filled red rectangle 475 by 250 with an upper-left corner of *(25, 50)* and a lower-right corner of *(500, 300)*. Any coordinates off the form or control are clipped.

The program of Fig. 9.6 draws lines and rectangles on the form. Pressing **Print** results in the program drawing either a black line or a red rectangle. Drawing coordinates are randomly calculated using the form's **Width** and **Height**.

Method **Circle** draws circles, ellipses, arcs, and sectors (Fig. 9.7a). A circle's *radius* is the distance from the circle's center to any circle point. An ellipse differs from a circle in that its *aspect ratio* (i.e., the ratio of width to height) is not 1. Ellipses with aspect ratios less than 1 are taller than they are wide, and ellipses with aspect ratios greater than 1 are wider than they are tall. *Sectors* are wedge-shaped pieces of a circle. Arcs are the curved portions of sectors.

*Testing and Debugging Tip 9.1*

*Visual Basic defines the radius in units of the horizontal scale. In user-defined coordinate systems, these scales can be different, resulting in distorted graphics.*

```
1   ' Fig. 9.6
2   ' Printing lines and rectangles to the form
3   Option Explicit
4
5   Private Sub cmdPrint_Click()
6      Dim x1 As Single, y1 As Single
7      Dim x2 As Single, y2 As Single
8
9      Call Randomize
10
11     ' Randomly pick values to draw at
12     x1 = Rnd() * Width
13     y1 = Rnd() * Height
14     x2 = Rnd() * Width
15     y2 = Rnd() * Height
16
17     ' Randomly decide which shape
18     If (Rnd() < 0.5) Then
19        Line (x1, y1)-(x2, y2)                ' Line
20     Else
21        Line (x1, y1)-(x2, y2), vbRed, B      ' Rectangle
22     End If
23   End Sub
```

**Fig. 9.6**    Drawing lines and rectangles (part 1 of 2).

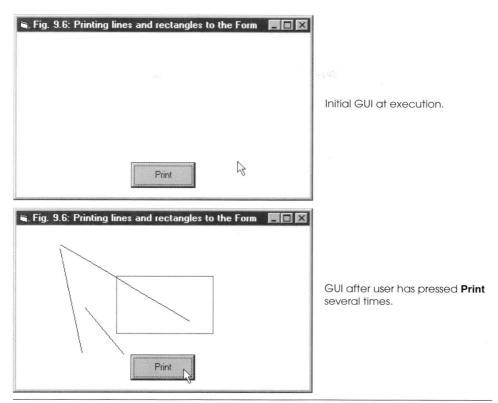

Initial GUI at execution.

GUI after user has pressed **Print** several times.

**Fig. 9.6**    Drawing lines and rectangles (part 2 of 2).

Circles are often measured in *degrees* (360 degrees total). A circle can also be measured in *radians* [$2\pi$ radians total—*pi* ($\pi$) has an approximate value of 3.14159] as shown in Fig. 9.7b. Radians must be used for sector and arc angles. Degrees can be converted to radians using the following formula: *radians = degrees* $\times \pi / 180$.

The statements

```
' PI is equivalent to 4 * Atn(1)
Circle (50, 50), 25                              ' Circle
Circle (0, 0), 1, vbRed, -PI / 2, -PI            ' Sector
Circle (1.5, 1.2), 1, vbRed, 3 * PI / 2, 0       ' Arc
Circle (10, 10), 5, vbRed, , , 1.5               ' Ellipse
```

draw a circle of radius 25 centered at *(50, 50)*, a red sector centered at *(0, 0)* with a radius of 1 that *sweeps* from $\pi/2$ radians to $\pi$ radians, a red arc centered at *(1.5, 1.2)* with a radius of 1 that sweeps from $3\pi/4$ radians to zero radians and a red ellipses at *(10, 10)* with a radius of 5 and an aspect ratio of 1.5. This ellipse is 1.5 times as wide as it is high. The expression **4 * Atn(1)** evaluates to pi. Note that the difference between drawing a sector and an arc is the *minus sign character*, **-**. The minus sign does not correspond to negative angles (which are not supported by Visual Basic).

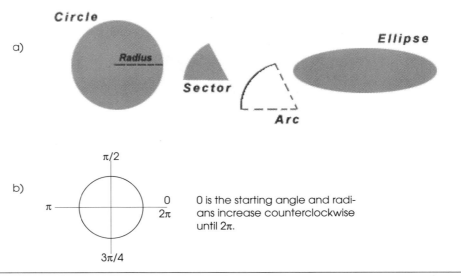

**Fig. 9.7**   Circles, ellipses, arcs and sectors.

 ***Common Programming Error 9.1***

*When drawing an ellipse, not providing four commas between the radius and the aspect ratio is a logic error.*

The program of Fig. 9.8 draws circles, ellipses, sectors and arcs on the form. Pressing **Print** results in either a circle, ellipse, sector or arc being drawn. The *x* coordinate, *y* coordinate and radius are randomly generated. All shapes are drawn in black with the exception of sectors and arcs, which are drawn in red.

```
1   ' Fig. 9.8
2   ' Using method Circle
3   Option Explicit          ' General declaration
4
5   Private Sub cmdPrint_Click()
6       Dim x As Single, y As Single
7       Dim r As Single
8
9       Call Randomize
10
11      ' Randomly pick values to draw at
12      x = Rnd() * 5
13      y = Rnd() * 5
14      r = Rnd() * 2.5
15
16      Scale (-1, 5)-(5, -5)
17
```

**Fig. 9.8**   Drawing circles, ellipses, sectors, and arcs (part 1 of 2).

```
18       ' Randomly decide which shape
19       Select Case Int(Rnd() * 5)
20          Case 0    ' Circle
21             Circle (x, y), r
22          Case 1    ' Ellipse
23             Circle (x, y), r, , , , 1.5
24          Case 2    ' Ellipse
25             Circle (x, y), r, , , , 0.5
26          Case 3    ' Sector
27             Circle (x, y), r, vbRed, -2 * Atn(1), -4 * Atn(1)
28          Case 4    ' Arc
29             Circle (x, y), r, vbRed, 2 * Atn(1), 4 * Atn(1)
30       End Select
31
32    End Sub
```

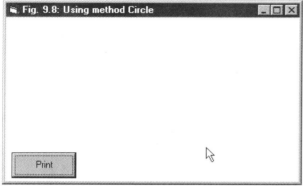

Initial GUI at execution.

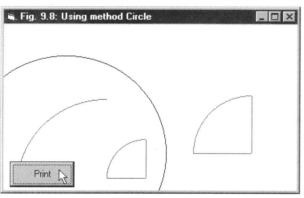

GUI after user has pressed **Print** several times.

**Fig. 9.8**    Drawing circles, ellipses, sectors, and arcs (part 2 of 2).

Method **PSet** turns on a point by changing the color at that point. For example, the statements

```
PSet(100, 200)
Pset(120, 220), vbRed
```

change the color of *(100, 200)* to black (the default) and the color of *(120, 220)* to red.

Graphics programming can involve complex calculations. In the next example and examples that follow we use mathematical equations that involve trigonometry to generate interesting graphical shapes. The reader need not be concerned with the mathematical specifics of the problem, only the Visual Basic feature we are demonstrating. Following the next example (Fig. 9.9) we provide a brief discussion of the equation used in the program.

The program of Fig. 9.9 draws shapes on the form when the mouse is clicked. In this example, we introduce the **Form_Click** event procedure, which is called when the user clicks the mouse on the form. Method **Pset** is used to draw the shapes.

```
1   ' Fig. 9.9
2   ' Demonstrating method PSet
3   Option Explicit
4
5   Private Sub Form_Click()
6       Call DrawShape
7   End Sub
8
9   Private Sub DrawShape()
10      Dim x As Single, y As Single
11      Dim totalRadians As Single, r As Single
12      Dim a As Single, theta As Single
13
14      Call Randomize
15      Scale (3, -3)-(-3, 3)              ' Change scale
16      totalRadians = 8 * Atn(1)         ' Circle in Radians
17
18      a = 3 * Rnd()  ' Offset used in equation
19
20      For theta = 0.001 To totalRadians Step 0.01
21          r = 2 * a / Sin(2 * theta)
22          x = r * Cos(theta)                    ' y coordinate
23          y = r * Sin(theta)                    ' x coordinate
24          PSet (x, y)                           ' Turn pixel on
25      Next theta
26
27  End Sub
```

Initial GUI at execution.

**Fig. 9.9**    Using **PSet** to draw shapes (part 1 of 2).

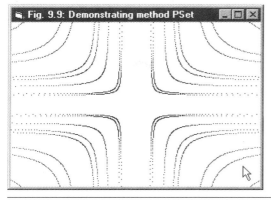

GUI after the user has clicked the
mouse several times.

**Fig. 9.9**    Using `PSet` to draw shapes (part 2 of 2).

In Visual Basic, the programmer uses *rectangular coordinates* (i.e., *x*-coordinates and *y*-coordinates as shown in Fig. 9.1). Some equations are specified in different coordinate systems, such as *polar coordinates,* which are shown in Fig. 9.10. In a polar coordinate system, any point can be described by rotating a *Pole* along the *Polar axis* through theta, θ, radians. The distance, *r*, from the polar origin, along with theta, describe a point.

In the example of Fig. 9.9, the equation

is expressed in polar coordinates which are converted to rectangular coordinates using the following two formulas:

(line 22 in the example)

and

(line 23 in the example)

We use these formulas to convert from polar to rectangular coordinates to graph many interesting shapes in this chapter.

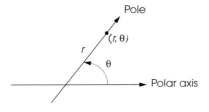

**Fig. 9.10**    Polar coordinate system.

Up to this point we have been working with *absolute coordinates,* which are always measured from the origin. Both the **Line** method and the **Circle** method support an optional keyword called ***Step*** for specifying *relative coordinates* (coordinates that are measured from a location other than the origin). Relative coordinates are often used to draw *polylines* (a series of connected lines where the end point of one line is the starting point of the next line) or other potentially closed shapes.

First let us consider two method calls to **Line**:

```
Line (500, 500) - (700, 600)
Line (500, 500) - Step (200, 100)
```

The first call to **Line** uses absolute coordinates to draw a line between points *(500, 500)* and *(700, 600)*. The second call also draws a line between *(500, 500)* and *(700, 600)*. The values following ***Step*** do not define the coordinate *(200, 100)*; rather, they specify the distance from *(500, 500)*.

Keyword ***Step*** can also precede the first set of values as in

```
Line Step (500, 500) - (700, 600)
```

which specifies that the first coordinate is a distance of 500 from **CurrentX** and the second coordinate is a distance 500 from **CurrentY**. The line is drawn between the points *(**CurrentX** + 500, **CurrentY** + 500)* and *(700, 600)*.

## 9.4 Drawing Properties

Several drawing properties can be used with the drawing methods. In this section, we introduce properties ***AutoRedraw***, ***DrawMode***, ***DrawStyle***, ***DrawWidth*** and ***FillStyle***. (Fig. 9.11).

Figure 9.12 describes the 16 different **DrawMode** values. Constants are specified in the left column, the equivalent value in the middle column and a brief description in the right column. **DrawMode**'s default is **vbCopyPen, 13**.

| Property | Description |
|---|---|
| **AutoRedraw** | A **Boolean** value that determines whether or not a copy of all graphical elements drawn is stored in memory. |
| **DrawMode** | An **Integer** value that specifies how new points generated from **Line**, **Circle** and **Pset** are drawn (see Fig. 9.12). |
| **DrawStyle** | An **Integer** value that specifies how new points generated from **Line**, **Circle** and **Pset** are drawn (see Fig. 9.13). |
| **DrawWidth** | An **Integer** value in the range 1 to 32767 that specifies the drawing width in pixels. |
| **FillStyle** | An **Integer** value that specifies how new points generated from **Line**, **Circle** and **Pset** are drawn (see Fig. 9.14). |

**Fig. 9.11**    Common properties related to drawing graphics.

A *pen* corresponds to the graphical characteristics (i.e., color, etc.) set by **Pset**, **Line**, **Circle**, etc. The term *inverse* refers to the opposite color. For example, the inverse of black is white and the inverse of green is magenta. Later in the chapter we demonstrate how to inverse an image.

Figure 9.13 describes the seven different **DrawStyle** values. Constants are specified in the left column, the equivalent constant value in the middle column and a brief description in the right column. **DrawStyle**'s default value is **vbSolid**, 0.

| Constant | Value | Description |
|---|---|---|
| **vbBlackness** | 1 | (Blackness) Drawing is done in black. |
| **vbNotMergePen** | 2 | (Not Merge Pen) Inverse of **vbMergePen**, **15**. |
| **vbMaskNotPen** | 3 | (Mask Not Pen) Combines colors common to the inverse pen's background color. |
| **vbNotCopyPen** | 4 | (Not Copy Pen) Inverse of **vbCopyPen**, **13**. |
| **vbMaskPenNot** | 5 | (Mask Pen Not) Combines the colors common to both the pen and the inverse of the display. |
| **vbInvert** | 6 | (Inverse) Inverse of the display color. |
| **vbXorPen** | 7 | (Xor Pen) Combines the colors in the pen and in the display color, but not in both. |
| **vbNotMaskPen** | 8 | (Not Mask Pen) Inverse of **vbMaskPen**, **9**. |
| **vbMaskPen** | 9 | (Mask Pen) Combines the colors common to both the pen and the display. |
| **vbNotXorPen** | 10 | (Not Xor Pen) Inverse of **vbXorPen**, **7**. |
| **vbNop** | 11 | (No Operation) Turns drawing off. |
| **vbMergeNotPen** | 12 | (Merge Not Pen) Combines the display color and the inverse of the pen color. |
| **vbCopyPen** | 13 | (Copy Pen) Default. Drawing is done in the **ForeColor**. |
| **vbMergePenNot** | 14 | (Merge Pen Not) Combines the pen color and the inverse of the display color. |
| **vbMergePen** | 15 | (Merge Pen) Combines the pen color and the display color. |
| **vbWhiteness** | 16 | (Whiteness) Drawing is done in white. |

**Fig. 9.12**    **DrawMode** property constants.

| Constant | Value | Description |
|---|---|---|
| **vbSolid** | 0 | (Solid) Default. Drawing is done as a solid. |
| **vbDash** | 1 | (Dash) Drawing is done as a series of dashes. |
| **vbDot** | 2 | (Dot) Drawing is done as a series of dots. |

**Fig. 9.13**    **DrawStyle** property constants (part 1 of 2).

| Constant | Value | Description |
|---|---|---|
| VbDashDot | 3 | (Dash Dot) Drawing is done as a series of dash and dot combinations. |
| vbDashDotDot | 4 | (Dash Dot Dot) Drawing is done as a series of dash, dot, dot combinations. |
| vbInvisible | 5 | (Invisible) Drawing is invisible (i.e., transparent). |
| vbInsideSolid | 6 | (Inside Solid) Drawing is done inside the solid. |

Fig. 9.13  **DrawStyle** property constants (part 2 of 2).

Figure 9.14 describes the **FillStyle** values. Constants are specified in the left column, the equivalent constant value in the middle column, and a brief description in the right column. **FillStyle**'s default value is **vbFSTransparent, 1**.

The program of Fig. 9.15 draws circles of random sizes in a **PictureBox**. The user specifies the **DrawMode**, **DrawStyle** and **FillStyle** values.

| Constant | Value | Description |
|---|---|---|
| vbFSSolid | 0 | (Solid) The fill is solid. |
| vbFSTransparent | 1 | (Transparent) Default. The fill is not visible. |
| vbFSHorizontalLine | 2 | (Horizontal Line) The fill is a series of horizontal lines. |
| VbVerticalLine | 3 | (Vertical Line) The fill is a series of vertical lines. |
| vbUpwardDiagonal | 4 | (Upward Diagonal) The fill is a series of diagonal lines. |
| vbDownwardDiagonal | 5 | (Downward Diagonal) The fill is a series of diagonal lines. |
| vbCross | 6 | (Crossing Lines) The fill is a series of crossing horizontal and vertical lines. |
| vbDiagonalCross | 7 | (Diagonal Crossing Lines) The fill is a series of upward and downward diagonal crossing lines. |

Fig. 9.14  **FillStyle** property constants.

```
1   ' Fig. 9.15
2   ' DrawMode, DrawStyle, and FillStyle properties
3   Option Explicit
4
5   Private Sub Form_Load()
6       picPicture.ForeColor = vbRed    ' Set drawing color
7   End Sub
8
```

Fig. 9.15  Demonstrating **DrawMode**, **DrawStyle** and **FillStyle** properties (part 1 of 3).

```vb
9    Private Sub chkAutoRedraw_Click()
10       ' Update picPicture's AutoRedraw
11       picPicture.AutoRedraw = chkAutoRedraw.Value
12   End Sub
13
14   Private Sub cmdClear_Click()
15       ' Enable AutoRedraw so the PictureBox can
16       ' be cleared with a call to Cls
17       picPicture.AutoRedraw = True
18       Call picPicture.Cls
19
20       ' Uncheck CheckBox and set AutoRedraw to False.
21       chkAutoRedraw.Value = vbUnchecked
22       picPicture.AutoRedraw = False
23   End Sub
24
25   Private Sub cmdDraw_Click()
26       Dim v As Integer
27
28       Call Randomize
29       v = txtDrawMode.Text
30
31       If v >= vbBlackness And v <= vbWhiteness Then
32          picPicture.DrawMode = v
33       Else
34          picPicture.DrawMode = vbCopyPen
35          txtDrawMode.Text = vbCopyPen
36       End If
37
38       v = txtDrawStyle.Text
39
40       If v >= vbSolid And v <= vbInsideSolid Then
41          picPicture.DrawStyle = v
42       Else
43          picPicture.DrawStyle = vbSolid
44          txtDrawStyle.Text = vbSolid
45       End If
46
47       v = txtFillStyle.Text
48
49       If v >= vbFSSolid And v <= vbDiagonalCross Then
50          picPicture.FillStyle = v
51       Else  ' Out of range reset to defaults
52          picPicture.FillStyle = vbFSTransparent
53          txtFillStyle.Text = vbFSTransparent
54       End If
55
56       ' Draw the circle
57       picPicture.Circle (picPicture.Width / 2, _
58                          picPicture.Height / 2), _
59                          Int(2000 * Rnd())
60   End Sub
```

**Fig. 9.15** Demonstrating **DrawMode**, **DrawStyle** and **FillStyle** properties (part 2 of 3).

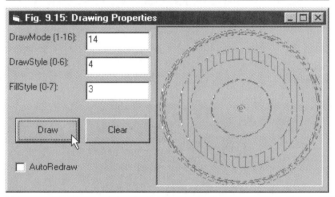

Initial GUI at execution.

GUI after user has set the **DrawMode**, **DrawStyle** and **FillStyle** and pressed **Draw** several times.

**Fig. 9.15**   Demonstrating **DrawMode**, **DrawStyle** and **FillStyle** properties (part 3 of 3).

In **Form_Load**, the **ForeColor** is set to **vbRed**. By changing the drawing color to a color other than black (the default), certain styles such as **vbXorPen** are more pronounced. All drawing in the **PictureBox** is performed in **cmdDraw_Click**.

When **CheckBox AutoRedraw** is clicked, the state of the **PictureBox**'s **AutoRedraw** property is set to the **CheckBox Value**. If the **PictureBox**'s **AutoRedraw** property is **True**, a separate offscreen image (i.e., not visible to the user) is created by Visual Basic. Anything drawn on **PictureBox** is also drawn on the offscreen image. Every time the **PictureBox** needs to be refreshed (e.g., the **PictureBox** is covered by another window) Visual Basic displays the off-screen image in the **PictureBox**.

*Performance Tip 9.1*

*Setting **AutoRedraw** to **True** decreases performance because a separate copy of an image is maintained in memory.*

Pressing **Clear** calls **cmdClear_Click**, which sets the **PictureBox**'s **AutoRedraw** property to **True** and calls **Cls** on the **PictureBox**. In order to clear the off-screen image, **AutoRedraw** must be **True**.

## 9.5 `Line` Control and `Shape` Control

The *Line* control and *Shape* control provide another way of drawing graphics. Figure 9.16 shows the toolbox icons for the **Line** control and the **Shape** control. These controls do not have event procedures. We first discuss drawing lines with the **Line** control.

Unlike method **Line**, which must be used at run-time, the **Line** control can be used at design-time. Lines can also be drawn at run-time with the **Line** control.

A line's color is specified using **Line** control's *BorderColor* property and a line's style is specified by setting the *Line* control's *BorderStyle* property (Fig. 9.17).

**Line** control line width (or thickness) is specified by setting the *BorderWidth* property to an **Integer** value between 1 and 32767 (if the **BorderWidth** is greater than 1, some **BorderStyle** values are ignored). Line length and position are specified using properties *X1*, *Y1*, *X2* and *Y2*. **X1** and **Y1** specify the starting coordinates. **X2** and **Y2** specify the ending coordinates. **Line** control lines are not affected by **AutoRedraw** being **False**—like other controls they repaint themselves.

The program of Fig. 9.18 allows the user to change the width of a **Line** control line to a value in the range 1 to 100.

**Line** control                                        **Shape** control

**Fig. 9.16**  **Line** control and **Shape** control.

| Constant | Value | Description |
|---|---|---|
| **vbTransparent** | 0 | Transparent. |
| **vbBSSolid** | 1 | Default. Solid. |
| **vbBSDash** | 2 | Dash. |
| **vbBSDot** | 3 | Dot. |
| **vbBSDashDot** | 4 | Dash-Dot. |
| **vbBSDashDotDot** | 5 | Dash-Dot-Dot. |
| **vbBSInsideSolid** | 6 | Pattern is inside solid. |

**Fig. 9.17**  Some **BorderStyle** constants.

```
1   ' Fig. 9.18
2   ' Using the Line control
3   Option Explicit
4
5   Private Sub cmdButton_Click()
6       Dim v As Integer
```

**Fig. 9.18**  Demonstrating the **Line** control (part 1 of 3).

```
7
8        v = txtStyle.Text
9
10       If v >= 0 And v <= 6 Then
11          linLine.BorderStyle = v
12       Else
13          linLine.BorderStyle = 1
14          txtStyle.Text = 1
15       End If
16
17       v = txtWidth.Text
18
19       If v >= 1 And v <= 100 Then
20
21          ' If v is greater than 1 some BorderStyle
22          ' properties are ignored
23          linLine.BorderWidth = v
24       Else
25          linLine.BorderWidth = 1
26          txtWidth.Text = 1
27       End If
28
29    End Sub
```

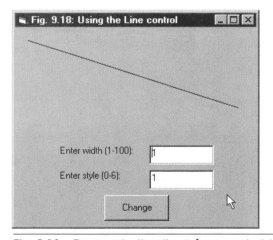

Initial GUI at execution.

**Fig. 9.18**    Demonstrating the **Line** control (part 2 of 3).

*Good Programming Practice 9.1*

*Prefixing **Line** controls with **lin** allows them to be identified easily.*

The **Shape** control can be used to draw rectangles, ellipses, rounded rectangles, squares, circles and rounded squares. The ***Shape*** property (Fig. 9.19) specifies which shape is drawn.

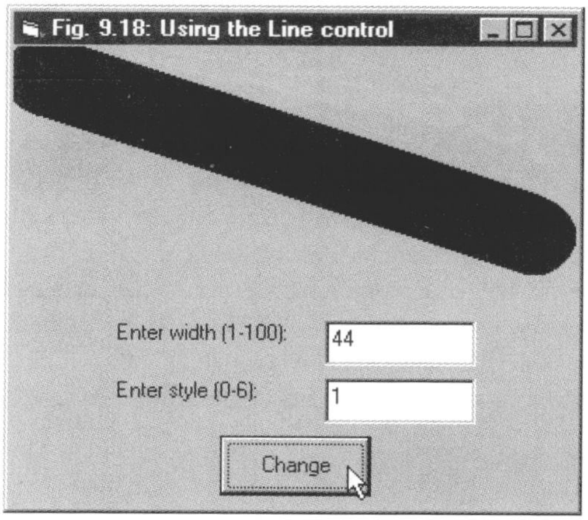

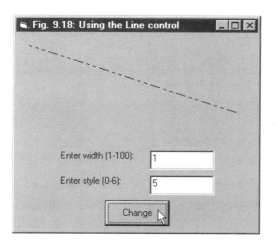

GUI after user has entered **44** and pressed **Change**.

GUI after user has entered **1** and **5** and then pressed **Change**.

**Fig. 9.18**  Demonstrating the **Line** control (part 3 of 3).

| Constant | Value | Description |
|---|---|---|
| **vbShapeRectangle** | 0 | Rectangle. |
| **vbShapeSquare** | 1 | Square. |
| **vbShapeOval** | 2 | Oval (i.e., an ellipse). |
| **vbShapeCircle** | 3 | Circle. |
| **vbShapeRoundedRectangle** | 4 | Rounded rectangle. |
| **vbShapeRoundedSquare** | 5 | Rounded square. |

**Fig. 9.19**  **Shape** property constants.

*Good Programming Practice 9.2*

*Prefixing **Shape** controls with **shp** allows them to be identified easily.*

**Shape** control property **FillStyle** (Fig. 9.14) specifies how the shape is to be filled. The **BorderStyle** property specifies the style using the values of Fig. 9.17. **BackColor**, *FillColor* and **BorderColor** specify coloring. **DrawMode** values of Fig. 9.12 specify the drawing mode. Note that **FillColor** and **BackColor** are ignored when either **FillStyle** or **BackStyle** is **vbTransparent**. Property **Border-Width** changes the width of the lines.

The program of Fig. 9.20 displays the six different **Shape** control shapes. Each **Shape** control shape's **BorderWidth** is **8**. No code is written for this example.

## 9.6 Colors

Colors enhance a program's output and convey meaning. Visual Basic provides properties, constants, and functions for manipulating colors.

Every color is created from an *RGB value* (Red/Green/Blue) consisting of three **Integer** numbers in the range 0 to 255. The first number specifies the *red intensity*, the second specifies the *green intensity* and the third specifies the *blue intensity*. An intensity value of 0 indicates the absence of a color, and an intensity value of 255 indicates *saturation*. Visual Basic enables the programmer to choose from $256 \times 256 \times 256$ (approximately 16 million) colors. Visual Basic provides constants for several common colors (Fig. 9.21).

*Software Engineering Observation 9.1*

*Some computers are not capable of displaying all the Visual Basic colors. If a color cannot be displayed, the computer displays the closest color possible.*

Programmers can use function *RGB* to create their own custom colors. Function **RGB** takes three **Integer** arguments and returns a **Long** value representing the color. For example, the programmer may create the color pink with the statement

```
pinkColor = RGB(255, 175, 175)
```

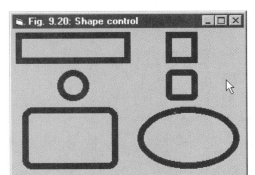

GUI at execution. The user cannot interact with the shapes.

**Fig. 9.20** Using the **Shape** control.

| Constant | Color | RGB value |
|----------|-------|-----------|
| `vbBlack` | black | 255, 255, 255 |
| `vbBlue` | blue | 0, 0, 255 |
| `vbCyan` | cyan | 0, 255, 255 |
| `vbGreen` | green | 0, 255, 0 |
| `vbYellow` | yellow | 255, 255, 0 |
| `vbWhite` | white | 0, 0, 0 |
| `vbRed` | red | 255, 0, 0 |
| `vbMagenta` | magenta | 255, 0, 255 |

Fig. 9.21   Visual Basic color constants.

where **pinkColor** is a **Long**. Variable **pinkColor** can then be assigned to a form's or control's **ForeColor** property, **BackColor** property, etc.

*Common Programming Error 9.2*

*Passing a value less than 0 or greater than 255 to function **RGB** is a run-time error.*

Figure 9.22 draws spirals in random colors and introduces the **Timer** control that monitors the system clock and raises an event after a specified number of milliseconds (set in the **Timer**'s **Interval** property). When an event is raised, the appropriate event procedure executes to handle the event. We set the **Interval** property to **500**.

```
1   ' Fig. 9.22
2   ' Demonstrating function RGB
3   Option Explicit        ' General declaration
4
5   Private Sub DrawShape()
6      Dim x As Single, y As Single
7      Dim totalRadians As Single, r As Single
8      Dim a As Single, theta As Single
9      Dim x1 As Single, y1 As Single
10
11     Call Randomize
12     Scale (3, -3)-(-3, 3)          ' Change scale
13     totalRadians = 8 * Atn(1)      ' Circle in Radians
14
15     ForeColor = RGB(Rnd() * 256, Rnd() * 256, Rnd() * 256)
16
17     a = 3 * Rnd()  ' Offset used in equation
18
19     For theta = 0.001 To totalRadians Step 0.01
20        r = Sqr(a ^ 2 / theta)
21        x = r * Cos(theta)        ' y coordinate
```

Fig. 9.22   Drawing spirals in random colors (part 1 of 2).

```
22          y = r * Sin(theta)      ' x coordinate
23          x1 = -r * Cos(theta)    ' y coordinate
24          y1 = -r * Sin(theta)    ' x coordinate
25          PSet (x, y)             ' Turn pixel on
26          PSet (x1, y1)           ' Turn pixel on
27       Next theta
28
29    End Sub
30
31    Private Sub tmrTimer_Timer()
32       Call DrawShape    ' Call when time interval expires
33    End Sub
```

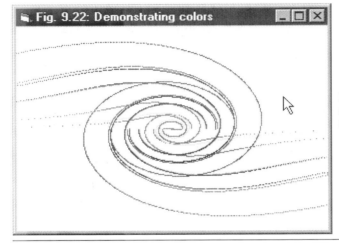

Program at run-time. Every 500 milliseconds new spirals are added.

**Fig. 9.22**   Drawing spirals in random colors (part 2 of 2).

**Timer** controls are visible only at design-time (Figure 9.23). **Timer**s can be placed anywhere on the form—even on top of other controls—without affecting the GUI.

**Timer** control →

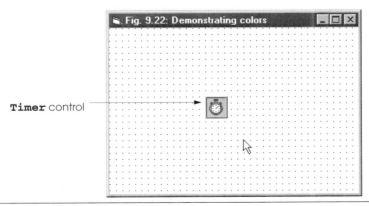

**Fig. 9.23**   Figure 9.22 program GUI at design time.

After the time specified in the **Interval** property has elapsed, Visual Basic calls the **Timer**'s *Timer* event procedure. In Fig. 9.22, the **Timer** event procedure is called after every 500 milliseconds. **Timer**s can be disabled by setting their **Enabled** property to **False**, and **Timer**s can be enabled by setting their **Enabled** property to **True**.

*Good Programming Practice 9.3*

*Prefixing **Timer** controls with **tmr** allows them to be identified easily.*

Visual Basic also provides function *QBColor* for creating colors. Function **QBColor** takes one **Integer** argument, in the range **0** to **15**, and returns a **Long** representing the color. Figure 9.24 list the colors supported by **QBColor**.

*Common Programming Error 9.3*

*Passing a value less than 0 or greater than 15 to function **QBColor** is a run-time error.*

The program of Fig. 9.25 draws a flower shape on the screen. Function **QBColor** is used to set the drawing color.

| Value | Color | Value | Color |
|---|---|---|---|
| 0 | black | 8 | gray |
| 1 | blue | 9 | light blue |
| 2 | green | 10 | light green |
| 3 | cyan | 11 | light cyan |
| 4 | red | 12 | light red |
| 5 | magenta | 13 | light magenta |
| 6 | yellow | 14 | light yellow |
| 7 | white | 15 | bright white |

**Fig. 9.24**   **QBColor** argument values.

```
1   ' Fig. 9.25
2   ' Demonstrating function QBColor
3   Option Explicit        ' General declaration
4
5   Private Sub DrawShape()
6      Dim x As Single, y As Single
7      Dim totalRadians As Single, r As Single
8      Dim a As Single, theta As Single
9
10     Call Randomize
11     Scale (3, -3)-(-3, 3)           ' Change scale
12     totalRadians = 8 * Atn(1)       ' Circle in Radians
13
```

**Fig. 9.25**   Demonstrating function **QBColor** (part 1 of 2).

```
14        ForeColor = QBColor(Rnd() * 15)
15
16        a = 3 * Rnd()    ' Offset used in equation
17
18        For theta = 0 To totalRadians Step 0.01
19            r = a * Sin(10 * theta) ' Multi-Leaved Rose
20            x = r * Cos(theta)      ' y coordinate
21            y = r * Sin(theta)      ' x coordinate
22            PSet (x, y)             ' Turn pixel on
23        Next theta
24
25    End Sub
26
27    Private Sub tmrTimer_Timer()
28        Call DrawShape    ' Call when time interval expires
29    End Sub
```

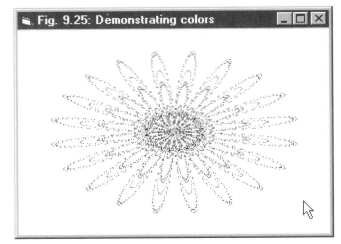

Program at run-time.
Layers are added to the
flower every 500
milliseconds.

**Fig. 9.25**   Demonstrating function **QBColor** (part 2 of 2).

Colors can also be specified using the **Common Dialog** control, which is not part of the **Standard EXE** toolbox. The **Common Dialog** control is added to the toolbox by checking **Microsoft Common Dialog Control 6.0** in the **Components** dialog (Fig. 9.26) and pressing **OK**. Selecting **Components** from the **Project** menu displays the **Components** dialog.

The program of Fig. 9.29 displays a **Color** dialog (generated by the **Common Dialog** control) when the user presses the **Color** button. The **Color** dialog is *modal*—other Visual Basic windows in the same application will not respond to events until the **Color** dialog is closed. Like the **Timer** control, the **Common Dialog** control is visible only at design-time. Figure 9.27 shows the form at design time, and Fig. 9.28 lists the properties.

*Good Programming Practice 9.4*

*Prefixing **Common Dialog** controls with **dlg** allows them to be identified easily.*

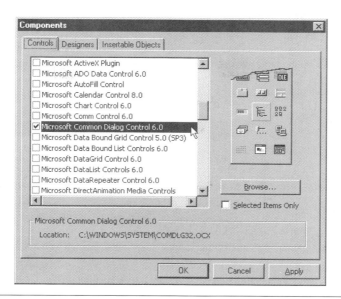

**Fig. 9.26**   **Components** dialog with **Microsoft Common Dialog Control 6.0** selected.

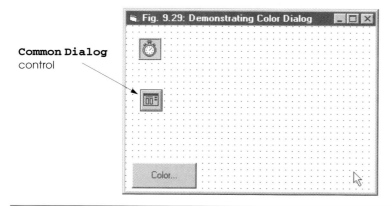

**Fig. 9.27**   GUI at design time showing a **Timer** and a **Common Dialog** control.

| Object | Icon | Property | Property setting | Property description |
|--------|------|----------|------------------|---------------------|
| form   |      | **Name** | **frmComDlg** | Identifies the form. |
|        |      | **BackColor** | white | Background color. |
|        |      | **Caption** | **Fig 9.29: Demonstrating Color Dialog** | Form title bar display. |

**Fig. 9.28**   Properties listing (part 1 of 2).

| Object | Icon | Property | Property setting | Property description |
|--------|------|----------|------------------|---------------------|
| **Color** button | | `Name` | `cmdColorChoose` | Identifies **Color** button. |
| | | `Caption` | `Color` | Text that appears on button. |
| `Timer` | | `Name` | `tmrTimer` | Identifies **Timer**. |
| | | `Interval` | `500` | Interval for event. |
| `Common Dialog` | | `Name` | `dlgColor` | Identifies **Common Dialog**. |

**Fig. 9.28** Properties listing (part 2 of 2).

```
1   ' Fig. 9.29
2   ' Demonstrating the color Common Dialog
3   Option Explicit          ' General declaration
4
5   Private Sub DrawShape()
6      Dim x As Single, y As Single
7      Dim totalRadians As Single, r As Single
8      Dim a As Single, theta As Single
9      Dim b As Single
10
11     Call Randomize
12     Scale (3, -3)-(-3, 3)        ' Change scale
13     totalRadians = 8 * Atn(1)    ' Circle in Radians
14
15     a = 3 * Rnd()  ' Offset used in equation
16     b = 2 * Rnd()  ' Offset used in equation
17
18     For theta = 0 To totalRadians Step 0.01
19        r = b - a * Cos(theta)
20        x = r * Cos(theta)        ' y coordinate
21        y = r * Sin(theta)        ' x coordinate
22        PSet (x, y)               ' Turn pixel on
23     Next theta
24  End Sub
25
26  Private Sub tmrTimer_Timer()
27     Call DrawShape    ' Call when time interval expires
28  End Sub
29
30  Private Sub cmdColorChoose_Click()
31     dlgColor.ShowColor            ' Display color common dialog
32     ForeColor = dlgColor.Color  ' Assign color to ForeColor
33  End Sub
```

**Fig. 9.29** Demonstrating the **Color Common Dialog** (part 1 of 2).

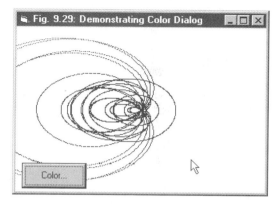

Program at run-time. A new shape is
drawn every 500 milliseconds.

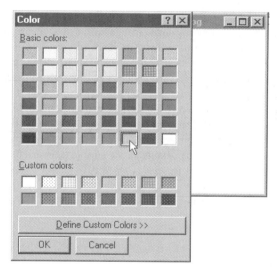

The **Color** dialog displayed when **Color**
is pressed. **AutoRedraw** is **False**, so
the shapes drawn beneath the **Color**
are not preserved when the **Color** dialog is closed.

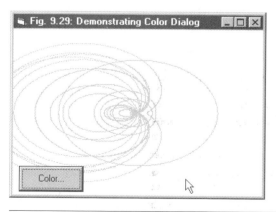

Shapes are drawn in the
selected color.

**Fig. 9.29**   Demonstrating the **Color Common Dialog** (part 2 of 2).

Pressing **Color** results in **cmdColorChoose_Click** being called. The line

    **dlgColor.ShowColor**

calls **Common Dialog** method *ShowColor* to display the modal **Color** dialog. The line

    **ForeColor = dlgColor.Color**

assigns the color, as a **Long**, from the **Common Dialog**'s *Color* property to the form's **ForeColor** property.

*Look-and-Feel Observation 9.1*

*Most Windows programs display* **Common Dialog***s for* **Color***,* **Fonts***, etc. Using the* **Common Dialog** *control provides a program with a Windows look-and-feel.*

## 9.7 Images

In previous chapters, we incorporated images into our programs. Images provide a means of graphically displaying information. One feature all image formats have in common is *color depth*—the number of colors the image supports. Color depth is often mentioned in terms of bits. The higher the number of bits, the greater the color depth and therefore the image quality. Images with color depths of one bit are *monochrome images* (black-and-white images). Images with color depths of eight bits have 256 colors and are often called *palette images*. Images with a color depth of 16 bits, called *high color images*, have 65536 colors. Images with a color depth of 24 bits are *true color images* (i.e., the colors are not approximated and every possible color can be represented). Visual Basic supports a variety of image formats, from monochrome images to true color images (Fig. 9.30).

*Look-and-Feel Observation 9.2*

*Images are used frequently in Windows applications to convey information to the user. Images give programs a Windows look-and-feel.*

| Type | File extension | Description |
|------|----------------|-------------|
| GIF image | **.gif** | Graphics Interchange Format image type that supports 256 or fewer colors. |
| Bitmap image | **.bmp** | Device-dependent bitmap. Image type that supports 1-bit, 4-bit, 8-bit, 16-bit and 24-bit color depths. |
| Bitmap image | **.dib** | Device-independent bitmap type that supports 1-bit, 4-bit, 8-bit, 16-bit and 24-bit color depths. |
| Icon image | **.ico** | Icon. Image type composed of approximately 16 colors. Typically sized at 32-by-32 pixels. |
| Cursor image | **.cur** | Cursor. A special bitmap type commonly used to represent the mouse pointer. |
| Windows meta file and Enhanced windows meta file | **.wmf** **.emf** | Graphical images that describe a picture in terms of geometric shapes (i.e., lines, circles, etc.) |

**Fig. 9.30**    Image types supported by Visual Basic (part 1 of 2).

| Type | File extension | Description |
|---|---|---|
| RLE images | .rle | Run-Length Encoding. A compressed image type. |
| JPEG image | .jpg | Joint Photographic Experts Group. Supports true color images and palette images. |

**Fig. 9.30**   Image types supported by Visual Basic (part 2 of 2).

Images are usually displayed in either **Image** controls or **PictureBox** controls—although images can be displayed using the form's **Picture** property. **Image** controls and **PictrureBox** controls have many similar properties. **PictureBox** controls have additional properties (i.e., **BackColor**) and event procedures (i.e., **Click**) that **Image** controls do not.

*Performance Tip 9.2*

**PictureBox** *controls consume more resources than* **Image** *controls. Use* **PictureBox** *controls in preference to* **Image** *controls when their special properties or event procedures are needed.*

Figure 9.31 loads an image into a **PictureBox** and generates the inverse of the image when the user presses **Inverse**. The program also saves the inverse image.

Event procedure **cmdInvert_Click** calls method *PaintPicture* to display the inverse of the image in the **PictureBox**. **PaintPicture**'s first argument specifies the **Picture** to draw. The second and third arguments specify the *x* coordinate and *y* coordinate where image's upper-left corner is displayed. **PaintPicture** has seven optional arguments for various special effects (many of these special effects apply only to bitmaps). We ask the reader to explore these special effects in the exercises. The last argument is a **Long** value that specifies the operation to perform. We pass *RasterOp* constant *vbDst-Invert* to perform an inverse operation on the bitmap. Method *SavePicture* saves **Picture**s to disk. The method takes two arguments—a **Picture** and a **String**. The **String** specifies the location and file name of the **Picture** to save.

```
1  ' Fig. 9.31
2  ' Generating the inverse of an image
3
4  Private Sub Form_Load()
5      picPicture.Picture = LoadPicture("d:\images\ch09\cool.bmp")
6  End Sub
7
8  Private Sub cmdInvert_Click()
9      Call picPicture.PaintPicture(picPicture.Picture, 0, 0, _
10                                   , , , , , , vbDstInvert)
11
12     Call SavePicture(picPicture, "d:\images\ch09\" & _
13                      "cool_inverse.bmp")
14 End Sub
```

**Fig. 9.31**   Generating the inverse of an image (part 1 of 2).

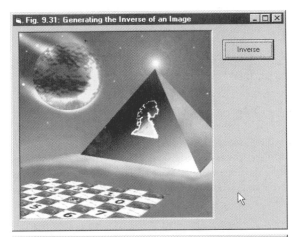

Initial GUI at execution.

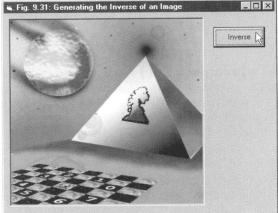

GUI after user has pressed **Inverse**.

**Fig. 9.31**   Generating the Inverse of an image (part 2 of 2).

## 9.8 `Printer` Object

The *Printer* object allows the programmer to send text and graphics to a printer. By default the **Printer** object's properties correspond to the default printer (which is set in the Windows Control Panel). Figure 9.32 lists several **Printer** object properties.

| Property | Description |
|---|---|
| `Copies` | The number of copies to print. |
| `DeviceName` | The name of the device supported by the printer driver. |
| `DriverName` | The unique printer driver name. |

**Fig. 9.32**   Some **Printer** properties (part 1 of 2).

| Property | Description |
|----------|-------------|
| Orientation | The page orientation defined by constants **vbPRORPortrait** and **vbPRORLandscape**. |
| Port | The port used to send the data to the printer. |
| PrintQuality | The print quality defined by constants **vbPRPQDraft**, **vbPRPQLow**, **vbPRPQMedium** and **vbPRPQHigh**. |
| TrackDefault | If the default printer is changed in the Windows Control Panel and **TrackDefault** is **True**, the **Printer** object properties refer to the new printer. Otherwise, if the default printer is changed in the Windows Control Panel and **TrackDefault** is **False**, the **Printer** object properties do not change. |
| Zoom | Percentage that the printed output is scaled. |

**Fig. 9.32**   Some **Printer** properties (part 2 of 2).

*Portability Tip 9.3*

*The **Printer** object is a device-independent drawing area. Windows performs the translation from this drawing space to match the printer's abilities.*

*Portability Tip 9.4*

*The effect of setting a **Printer** object's properties is dependent on the printer driver. Different drivers can produce different effects.*

Figure 9.33 lists several **Printer** methods and one related printing method. Note that the **Print**, **Circle**, **Line** and **PSet** methods are the same as those discussed earlier in the chapter.

| Method | Description |
|--------|-------------|
| EndDoc | Sends the print job to disk or memory until the printer is ready for the print job. Called automatically if program terminates without **EndDoc** being explicitly called. |
| NewPage | Starts printing on the next page. |
| KillDoc | Terminates the print job. Cannot be used if the print job was initiated with method **PrintForm**. |
| Print | Prints text as shown in Section 9.3. |
| Circle | Prints graphical shapes as shown in Section 9.3. |
| Line | Prints lines as shown in Section 9.3. |
| Pset | Prints a point (i.e., turns on a pixel) as shown in Section 9.3. |
| PrintForm | (Not a **Printer** method) Prints a graphical representation of the form interior (i.e., the border and title bar are not printed). |

**Fig. 9.33**   Method **PrintForm** and **Printer** methods.

The program of Fig. 9.34 prints the form and prints the printer driver name, port, and number of copies. Two pages are printed—a graphical representation of the form and a page of text (with the printer driver name, etc.).

## Summary

- The upper-left point on the screen has the coordinates (0, 0), which is commonly called the origin. A coordinate pair is composed of an x coordinate (the horizontal coordinate) and a y coordinate (the vertical coordinate). The x coordinate is the horizontal distance on the x axis. The y coordinate is the vertical distance on the y axis.
- The unit that a coordinate system is measured in is called a scale. Most controls as well as the form use twips. Property **ScaleMode** sets the scale.
- User-defined coordinate systems allow the programmer to relocate the origin. User-defined scales are defined using method **Scale**. Calling method **Scale** is equivalent to setting the properties for methods **ScaleTop**, **ScaleLeft**, **ScaleWidth** and **ScaleHeight**. Executing method **Scale** results in the **ScaleMode** property being set to **vbUser** by Visual Basic.
- Methods **ScaleX** and **ScaleY** convert between coordinate systems.
- Methods **Print**, **Line**, **Circle** and **Pset** draw graphical shapes on forms and controls.
- Current drawing coordinates are stored in properties **CurrentX** and **CurrentY**. Drawn text's width and height are retrieved with calls to methods **TextWidth** and **TextHeight**.
- Method **Line** draws lines and rectangles between two sets of coordinates.
- Method **Circle** draws circles, ellipses, arcs and sectors.
- Method **PSet** turns on a point.
- Keyword **Step** is used to specify relative coordinates.
- Properties **AutoRedraw**, **DrawMode**, **DrawStyle**, **DrawWidth** and **FillStyle** are used with the drawing methods.
- The **Line** control draws lines. These controls do not have event procedures and can be used at design time. Line length and position are specified using properties **X1**, **Y1**, **X2** and **Y2**.
- The **Shape** control draws rectangles, ellipses, rounded rectangles, squares, circles and rounded squares. The **Shape** property specifies which shape is drawn.

```
1   ' Fig. 9.34
2   ' Demonstrating method PrintForm and the Printer object
3   Option Explicit
4
5   Private Sub cmdPrint_Click()
6       Call PrintForm        ' Print the form
7
8       ' Printing appears on a separate page
9       Printer.PrintQuality = vbPRPQDraft
10      Printer.Print "Some Printer property values: "
11      Printer.Print "DriverName: " & Printer.DriverName
12      Printer.Print "Port: " & Printer.Port
13      Printer.Print "Copies: " & Printer.Copies
14      Printer.EndDoc        ' Send to printer
15  End Sub
```

**Fig. 9.34**   Demonstrating method **PrintForm** and the **Printer** object.

- Every color is created from an RGB value (Red/Green/Blue) consisting of three `Integer`s numbers in the range 0 to 255. The first number specifies the red intensity, the second specifies the green intensity and the third specifies the blue intensity.
- Function `RGB` takes three `Integer` arguments and returns a `Long` value representing a color.
- `Timer` controls monitor the system clock and generate an event after a certain number of milliseconds. `Timer` controls are only visible at design time.
- Function `QBColor` takes one `Integer` argument, in the range `0` to `15`, and returns a `Long` representing the color.
- The `Common Dialog` control is added to the toolbox by checking **Microsoft Common Dialog Control 6.0** in the **Components** dialog and pressing **OK**. Selecting **Components** from the **Project** menu displays the **Components** dialog. The `Common Dialog` control is visible only at design-time.
- Images with color depths of one bit are monochrome images. Images with color depths of eight bits have 256 colors and are often called palette images. High color images have a color depth of 16 bits (65536 colors). Images with a color depth of 24 bits are true color images.
- The `Printer` object allows the programmer to send text and graphics to a printer. By default the `Printer` object's properties correspond to the default printer (which is set in the Windows **Control Panel**).

## Terminology

| | |
|---|---|
| `.bmp` images | coordinate system |
| `.cur` images | `Copies` property |
| `.dib` images | `CurrentX` property |
| `.emf` images | `CurrentY` property |
| `.gif` images | cursor file (`.cur`) |
| `.jpg` images | degree |
| `.rle` images | `DeviceName` property |
| `.wmf` images | `DrawMode` property |
| absolute coordinates | `DrawStyle` property |
| arc | `DrawWidth` property |
| aspect ratio | `DriverName` property |
| `AutoRedraw` property | ellipses |
| `B` argument | `EndDoc` method |
| `BackColor` property | `FillColor` property |
| `BF` argument | filled |
| bitmap file (`.bmp`) | `FillStyle` property |
| `BorderColor` property | `ForeColor` property |
| `BorderStyle` property | `Form_Click` event procedure |
| `BorderWidth` property | `Height` property |
| boxes | high color image |
| centimeter scale | horizontal coordinate |
| `Circle` method | icon file |
| clipping | `Image` control |
| color depth | Inch scale |
| **Color** dialog | `Interval` property |
| `Color` property | `KillDoc` method |
| `Common Dialog` control | `Line` control |
| **Components** dialog | `Line` method |

**vbPRPQHigh** constant
**vbPRPQLow** constant
**vbPRPQMedium** constant
**vbRed** constant
**vbShapeCircle** constant
**vbShapeOval** constant
**vbShapeRectangle** constant
**vbShapeRoundedRectangle** constant
**vbShapeRoundedSquare** constant
**vbShapeSquare** constant
**vbSolid** constant
**vbTransparent** constant
**vbTwips** constant
**vbUpwardDiagonal** constant
**vbUser** constant

**vbVerticalLine** constant
**vbWhiteness** constant
**vbXorPen** constant
**vbYellow** constant
vertical coordinate
width
**Width** property
windows metafile
*x*-axis
*x* coordinate
**X1** property
**X2** property
**Y1** property
**Y2** property
**Zoom** property

## Common Programming Errors

**9.1**  When drawing an ellipse, not providing four commas between the radius and the aspect ratio is a logic error.

**9.2**  Passing a value less than 0 or greater than 255 to function **RGB** is a run-time error.

**9.3**  Passing a value less than 0 or greater than 15 to function **QBColor** is a run-time error.

## Good Programming Practices

**9.1**  Prefixing **Line** controls with **lin** allows them to be identified easily.

**9.2**  Prefixing **Shape** controls with **shp** allows them to be identified easily.

**9.3**  Prefixing **Timer** controls with **tmr** allows them to be identified easily.

**9.4**  Prefixing **Common Dialog** controls with **dlg** allows them to be identified easily.

## Look-and-Feel Observations

**9.1**  Most Windows programs display **Common Dialog**s for **Color**, **Fonts**, etc. Using the **Common Dialog** control provides a program with a Windows look-and-feel.

**9.2**  Images are used frequently in Windows applications to convey information to the user. Images give programs a Windows look-and-feel.

## Performance Tips

**9.1**  Setting **AutoRedraw** to **True** decreases performance because a separate copy of an image is maintained in memory.

**9.2**  **PictureBox** controls consume more resources than **Image** controls. Use **PictureBox** controls in preference to **Image** controls when their special properties or event procedures are needed.

## Portability Tips

**9.1**  Pixels are a device-dependent unit of measurement. The number of pixels varies with screen size and resolution.

**9.2**  The twip is a device-independent unit of measurement.

**9.3**  The **Printer** object is a device-independent drawing area. Windows performs the translation from this drawing space to match the printer's abilities.

**9.4**  The effect of setting a **Printer** object's properties is dependent on the printer driver. Different drivers can produce different effects.

## Software Engineering Observation

**9.1** Some computers are not capable of displaying all the Visual Basic colors. If a color cannot be displayed, the computer displays the closest color possible.

## Testing and Debugging Tip

**9.1** Visual Basic defines the radius in units of the horizontal scale. In user-defined coordinate systems, these scales can be different resulting in distorted graphics.

## Self-Review Exercises

**9.1** Fill in the blanks in each of the following:
   a) **Common Dialog** control method _____ displays a **Color** dialog.
   b) Methods _____ and _____ convert from one scale unit to another.
   c) A _____ is a "pie"-shaped wedge.
   d) Method _____ draws lines and boxes.
   e) **Printer** method _____ specifies that printing is to occur on the beginning of the next page.
   f) Method _____ returns an individual pixel's color represented as a **Long**.

**9.2** State which of the following are *true* and which are *false*. If *false*, explain why.
   a) Method **Line** is not a method of the **Line** control.
   b) Method **Shape** draws ovals, rectangles, etc.
   c) Degrees are used specify a sector's angle.
   d) **PrintForm** is not a **Printer** method.
   e) An ellipse with an aspect ratio of 0.854 has a greater width than height.
   f) Method **Circle** can be used to draw arcs.

## Answers to Self-Review Exercises

**9.1** a) **ShowColor**.
   b) **ScaleX, ScaleY**.
   c) sector.
   d) **Line**.
   e) **NewPage**.
   f) **Point**.

**9.2** a) True.
   b) False. The **Shape** control or the **Circle** method draws ovals, rectangles, etc.
   c) False. Radians are used.
   d) True.
   e) False. An ellipse with an aspect ratio of 0.854 has a greater height than width.
   f) True.

## Exercises

**9.3** Fill in the blanks in each of the following:
   a) The _____ property determines how "thick" a **Line** control line is.
   b) The curved portion of a sector is an _____.
   c) RGB is short for _____, _____ and _____.
   d) Most graphical images are measured in units of _____.
   e) **Printer** method _____ kills a print job.

**9.4** State which of the following are *true* and which are *false*. If *false*, explain why.
  a) A bit has a value of either 0 or 1.
  b) Visual Basic's default coordinate system is polar coordinates.
  c) **Line** controls are not affected by **AutoRedraw**.
  d) Method **Circle** can be used to draw sectors.
  e) **PictureBox** controls are simplified **Image** controls.
  f) The pixel coordinate *(0, 0)* is located at the exact center of the screen.

**9.5** Write a program that draws a tetrahedron (i.e., a pyramid).

**9.6** Write a program that draws a solid cube. Each of the visible faces should be a different color.

**9.7** Write a program that displays four triangles of different sizes. Each triangle should be filled with a different color (or pattern).

**9.8** Write a program that draws a series of lines of different lengths in different colors.

**9.9** Write a program that draws a series of eight concentric circles each separated by 10 pixels.

**9.10** Write a program that reads four numbers from the user and graphs the numbers as a pie chart.

**9.11** Modify Exercise 9.10 to graph the numbers as a bar graph.

**9.12** Write a program that flips a bitmap image horizontally.

**9.13** Write a program that flips a bitmap image vertically.

**9.14** Write a program that displays a linear gradient.

**9.15** Write a program that displays a circular gradient.

**9.16** Write a program that draws a grid over an image displayed in a **PictureBox**. Provide a **CheckBox** that controls when the grid is visible.

**9.17** Write a program that draws each **Shape** control shape with a different **BorderStyle**, **FillStyle** and **FillColor**.

**9.18** Write a program that displays a **Line** control line and allows the user to move the line by specifying values for **X1**, **Y1**, **X2** and **Y2**.

**9.19** Modify either Fig. 9.9, 9.22, 9.25 or 9.29 to send the shape to the printer. If the example you are modifying uses a **Timer**, remove the **Timer** and replace it with a button. Each time the user presses the button, send the shape to the printer. Use the **Zoom** property to increase the size of the displayed image.

**9.20** Although not discussed in line in the chapter, the **Common Dialog** control is capable of displaying a **Printer Common Dialog**. Modify Fig. 9.34 to display the **Printer Common Dialog** before information is sent to the printer. What is printed when the user changes the copies in the **Common Dialog** to an **Integer** value greater than 1?

**9.21** Write a program that creates a tiled background (i.e., the same image repeated over the entire background) on the form using method **PaintPicture**.

**9.22** Write a program that centers text input by the user on the form. Each time text is input, the background should be cleared before the centered text is drawn.

**9.23** Write a program that draws a box, an oval, an arrow, and a diamond on the form.

**9.24** (*Hangman*) Write a graphical version of Exercise 8.23. Use the drawing techniques discussed in this chapter to draw the person and the gallows.

**9.25** Write a program that allows the user to demonstrate the various **RasterOp** constants used with **PaintPicture**. Consult the on-line documentation for the available **RasterOp** constants.

# 10

# Basic Graphical User Interface Concepts

## Objectives

- To understand how to add ActiveX controls to a project.
- To be able to use the **TextBox** control to receive user input and display text.
- To be able to use the **MaskedEdit** control to receive formatted input from the user.
- To be able to use the **ComboBox** control and **ListBox** control to allow the user to select from a list of options.
- To be able to use the scrollbar controls and **Slider** control to select from ranges of values.
- To be able to create menus and pop-up menus to enhance an application's GUI.
- To be able to use the **MsgBox** function to display information to the user.

*All the better to see you with my dear.*
The Big Bad Wolf to Little Red Riding Hood

*...The user should feel in control of the computer; not the other way around. This is achieved in applications that embody three qualities: responsiveness, permissiveness, and consistency.*
*Inside Macintosh, Volume 1*
Apple Computer, Inc. 1985

# Outline

## 10.1  Introduction

A graphical user interface (GUI) presents a pictorial interface to a program. A GUI (pronounced "GOO-EE") gives a program a distinctive "look" and "feel." By providing applications with a consistent set of intuitive GUI components, GUIs allow the user to spend less
time trying to remember which keystroke sequences do what and spend more time using
programs in a productive manner. Consistent GUIs also enable users to learn new applications faster. Interaction between users and programs is through the GUI.

GUI are built from *controls*. A control is an object with which the user interacts via the
mouse or keyboard. In this chapter we discuss controls in more detail. In the next chapter
we discuss more advanced GUI controls and concepts.

## 10.2  Controls

Controls are reusable, predefined components used for visual programming. Controls serve
as building blocks that can be quickly combined to create a working application. Visual Basic controls exist in two varieties–*intrinsic controls* and *ActiveX controls*. Intrinsic controls
(also called *standard controls*) are the default controls provided in the Visual Basic toolbox. Intrinsic controls are summarized in Fig. 10.1.

| Control | Icon | Preferred Prefix | Description |
|---------|------|------------------|-------------|
| **CheckBox** | ☑ | **chk** | Acts as a toggle. (Ch. 7) |

**Fig. 10.1**   Intrinsic controls (part 1 of 2).

| Control | Icon | Preferred Prefix | Description |
|---------|------|-----------------|-------------|
| **ComboBox** |  | **cbo** | **Displays a drop-down list. (Ch. 10)** |
| **Data** |  | **dat** | Navigates data in a database. |
| **DirListBox** |  | **dir** | Displays a directory box. (Ch. 14) |
| **DriveListBox** |  | **drv** | Displays a drive list box. (Ch. 14) |
| **FileListBox** |  | **fil** | Displays a file list box. (Ch. 14) |
| **Frame** | 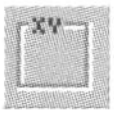 | **fra** | Acts as a container for other controls. (Ch. 6) |
| **Image** |  | **img** | Displays images. (Ch. 9) |
| **Label** |  A | **lbl** | Displays static text. (Ch. 2) |
| **Line** | 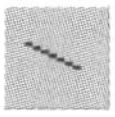 | **lin** | Draws lines. (Ch. 9) |
| **ListBox** |  | **lst** | Displays a list. (Ch. 10) |
| **OLE** |  | **ole** | Acts as an OLE container. |
| **OptionButton** | 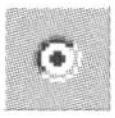 | **opt** | Displays options from which the user can choose only one. (Ch. 10) |
| **PictureBox** |  | **pic** | Displays images. Also acts as a container for other controls. (Ch. 9) |
| scrollbars |   | **hsb, vsb** | Specify a range of values. (Ch. 10) |
| **Shape** |  | **shp** | Draws graphical shapes. (Ch. 9) |
| **TextBox** |  abl | **txt** | Control for user input. (Ch. 10) |
| **Timer** |  | **tmr** | Raises an event after a specified interval. (Ch. 9) |

**Fig. 10.1**    Intrinsic controls (part 2 of 2).

ActiveX controls must be loaded into the Visual Basic project with the **Components** dialog (Fig. 10.2). The **Components** dialog is displayed when the **Project** menu's **Components** menu item is selected. Checking an ActiveX control item's **CheckBox** and pressing **OK** loads the control. An icon representing the control is added to the toolbox.

Other than the loading process, ActiveX controls are used in the same manner as intrinsic controls—ActiveX controls have properties, methods and event procedures, and display an icon in the toolbox when loaded. Figure 10.3 lists some of the ActiveX controls discussed in this book and the chapters where they are introduced. We use additional ActiveX controls for networking (Chap. 19) and multimedia (Chap. 20) which are not listed in Fig. 10.3. Figure 10.4 presents the database controls presented in Chapter 18. Note that some controls are specific to the Professional and Enterprise editions of Visual Basic and are not available in the Learning Edition.

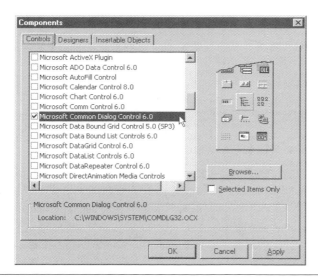

**Fig. 10.2**    **Components** dialog.

| Control | Icon | Preferred Prefix | Description |
|---------|------|------------------|-------------|
| **CommonDialog** | | **dlg** | Provides several common dialog boxes such as **Open**, **Save**, etc. (Ch. 9) |
| **FlatScrollBar** | | **fsb** | A scrollbar that provides a visual response when the mouse is positioned over the scrollbar. (Ch. 11) |
| **ImageCombo** | | **imgcbo** | An enhanced **ComboBox** that is capable of displaying images and text. (Ch. 11) |

**Fig. 10.3**    Some ActiveX controls discussed in this book (part 1 of 2).

| Control | Icon | Preferred Prefix | Description |
|---|---|---|---|
| **ImageList** | | **ils** | Stores a series of images. (Ch. 11) |
| **MaskedEdit** | | **msk** | An enhanced **TextBox** that can control the format of text entered by the user. (Ch. 10) |
| **RichTextBox** | | **rtf** | An enhanced **TextBox** that provides basic text editor capabilities. (Ch. 11) |
| **Slider** | | **sld** | Represents a range of values. (Ch. 10) |
| **UpDown** | | **upd** | Allows scrolling through a set of values. (Ch. 11) |

**Fig. 10.3**    Some ActiveX controls discussed in this book (part 2 of 2).

| Control | Icon | Preferred Prefix | Description |
|---|---|---|---|
| **ADO Data Control** | | **ado** | Supports connecting to a database. |
| **DataCombo** | | **dbc** | An enhanced **ComboBox** that is populated automatically with data from a database. |
| **DataGrid** | | **dgd** | A table that is populated automatically with data from a database. |
| **DataList** | | **dbl** | An enhanced **ListBox** that is populated automatically with data from a database. |
| **Hierarchical FlexGrid** | | **flex** | A table that is populated automatically with data from a database. This table is read-only (data cannot be modified). |

**Fig. 10.4**    Database ActiveX Controls presented in Chapter 18.

Many *independent software venders* (*ISV*s) specialize in creating ActiveX controls using Visual C++, Visual J++, Visual Basic and various non-Microsoft development tools. We discuss ActiveX controls in greater detail in Chapter 17.

## 10.3 **TextBox** Control

***TextBox***es are intrinsic controls in which text is either input or displayed. Figure 10.5 summarizes common **TextBox** properties and methods. The program of Fig. 10.6 demonstrates the use of **TextBox**es.

| Property/method | Description |
|---|---|
| *Properties* | |
| **Enabled** | Specifies whether or not the user can interact with the control. |
| **Index** | Specifies the control array index. |
| **Locked** | **Boolean**. Specifies whether or not the user can type in the **TextBox**. |
| **MaxLength** | Specifies the maximum number of characters input. Default of **0** corresponds to any number of characters. |
| **MousePointer** | Specifies the shape of the mouse pointer when over a **TextBox**. |
| **Multiline** | Specifies whether or not the **TextBox** contains more than one line. |
| **PasswordChar** | Specifies the masking character for text displayed in the **TextBox**. |
| **Scrollbars** | Specifies either horizontal scrollbars, vertical scrollbars or both horizontal and vertical scrollbars for the **TextBox**. This property is used with the **Multiline** property. |
| **Text** | Specifies the **TextBox** text. |
| **ToolTipText** | Specifies what text is displayed as the **TextBox**'s tool tip. |
| **Visible** | Specifies whether or not the **TextBox** is visible. |
| *Method* | |
| **SetFocus** | Transfers focus to the **TextBox**. |
| *Event Procedures* | |
| **Change** | Called when text in **TextBox** changes. |
| **Clicked** | Called when **TextBox** is clicked with the mouse. |
| **GotFocus** | Called when **TextBox** receives the active focus. |
| **LostFocus** | Called when **TextBox** loses the active focus. |
| **KeyDown** | Called when a key is pressed while the **TextBox** has the focus. |
| **KeyUp** | Called when a key is released while the **TextBox** has the focus. |

**Fig. 10.5**    Common **TextBox** properties and methods.

Figure 10.6 creates **TextBox**es **txtDisplay**—with its *Multiline* property set to **True**—and **txtInput**—with its **Multiline** property set to **False**. When text is input in **txtInput**, the text is copied to **txtDisplay** in **txtInput**'s *Change* event procedure. Event **Change** is raised every time the **TextBox Text** changes. The program also introduces the *ToolTipText* property that displays a text message (called a *tool tip*) when the mouse pointer rests in the control's area. We use property *MousePointer* to change the shape of the mouse pointer icon. We discuss mouse interactions in detail in Chapter 12. Both property *ToolTipText* and property *MousePointer* were set at design-time. Property *Scrollbars* was set at design-time for a vertical scrollbar.

**Common Programming Error 10.1**

*Not setting the **Multiline** property to **True** for a **TextBox** that has its **Scrollbars** property set to a non-zero value is a logic error. The scrollbars are not visible.*

```
1   ' Fig. 10.6
2   ' Demonstrating the TextBox Control
3   Option Explicit     ' General declaration
4
5   Private Sub txtInput_Change()
6       txtDisplay.Text = txtInput.Text    ' Copy to other TextBox
7   End Sub
```

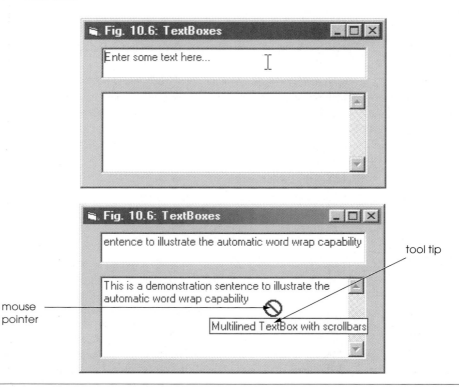

**Fig. 10.6**   Program that demonstrates using **TextBox** controls.

When text is typed or copied into the multilined **TextBox**, the text automatically wraps to the next line when the right edge of the **TextBox** is reached. Text also automatically wraps for multilined **TextBox**es without vertical scrollbars.

*Good Programming Practice 10.1*

*Prefixing **TextBox**es with **txt** allows them to be identified easily.*

## 10.4 **MaskEdit** Control

The ***MaskEdit*** ActiveX control is a specialized version of a **TextBox**. **MaskEdit**s allow for validation of input by ensuring that only data in the correct format is input. Figure 10.7 shows the **MaskEdit** control selected in the **Components** dialog.

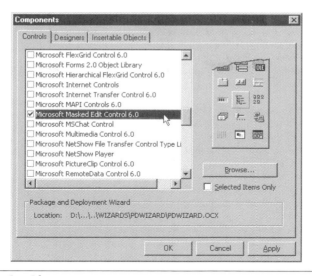

Fig. 10.7    **MaskEdit** control in the **Components** dialog.

Most ActiveX controls provide the ability to set control properties through *property pages*. Once the ActiveX control has been placed on the form, the control's property page is accessed through a pop-up menu. Clicking the control once with the right mouse button displays the pop-up menu. Figure 10.8 shows the pop-up menu displayed when a **MaskEdit** control is clicked with the right mouse button.

When **Properties** is selected, the property page is displayed as a **Property Pages** dialog, as shown in Fig. 10.9. Property pages typically contain tabs that group related categories. Different ActiveX controls will have different properties, and the number of tabs and the number of properties per tab can vary. The property page only displays certain properties. Property pages are a convenient way for users to access common properties. All properties, including those not listed in the properties page, are accessible in the **Properties** window.

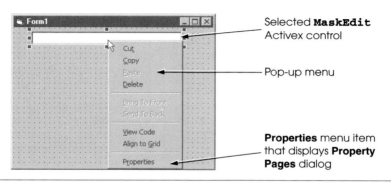

Fig. 10.8    Pop-up menu displayed when a **MaskEdit** control is clicked with the right mouse button.

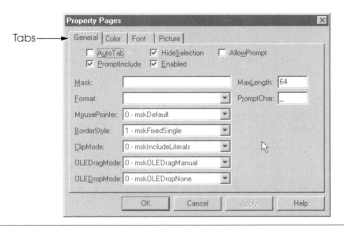

**Fig. 10.9** **Property Pages** dialog for the **MaskEdit** control.

The **Property Pages** dialog for the **MaskEdit** control contain four tabs: **General**, **Color**, **Font** and **Picture**. The most important properties are listed on the **General** tab. We summarize some of these properties as well as other properties not listed in the properties page in Fig. 10.10.

**MaskEdit** methods and event procedures are generally the same as those of a **TextBox**. Selected **TextBox** methods and event procedures are shown in Fig. 10.5.

**MaskEdit** controls are useful for ensuring that information is input in the proper format. Consider a program that requires a phone number to be input in the format:

    **(210) 555-7373**

| Property | Description |
| --- | --- |
| **AllowPrompt** | Specifies whether or not the prompt character is acceptable input. |
| **AutoTab** | Specifies whether or not the focus is transferred to the next contol in the tab order when the required number of characters is input. |
| **Enabled** | Specifies whether or not the user is allowed to interact with the control. |
| **Format** | The format the text is displayed in when the control does not have the focus. |
| **HideSelecton** | Specifies whether or not the selected text appears highlighted when the control loses focus. |
| **Mask** | A **String** that describes the input mask. Masking characters are shown in Fig. 10.11. |
| **MaxLength** | Maximum number of characters allowed as input. |
| **MousePointer** | Specifies the shape of the mouse pointer. |
| **Text** | Text displayed in control. |

**Fig. 10.10** Some **MaskEdit** control properties.

| Mask character | Description |
|---|---|
| # | A numeric character is required in this position. |
| . | A decimal point which is treated as a literal (a character that is simply displayed in the **MaskEdit** control. |
| , | A thousands separator which is treated as a literal. |
| / | A date separator which is treated as a literal. |
| : | A time separator which is treated as a literal. |
| \ | The character immediately following the backslash is treated as a literal. Backslash is often used with the other mask symbols: **a**, **A**, etc. |
| & | An ANSI character in the ranges 32 to 126 and 128 to 255 (see Appendix B for a complete listing of the ANSI character set). |
| > | Converts characters to uppercase. |
| < | Converts characters to lowercase. |
| A | An alphanumeric character is required at this position. |
| a | An alphanumeric character is optional at this position. |
| 9 | A numeric character is optional at this position. |
| ? | An alpha character is required in this position. |

**Fig. 10.11**  Some common mask characters.

The user might not type the phone number in the required format. Extra code would be needed to perform the validation. Suppose we could change the appearance of the way we prompt the user to the following:

(____)  ____-_____

The **MaskEdit** control provides this capability by using the mask characters listed in Fig. 10.11. When using a mask, we can exclude improper characters from being input—such as letters or other non-numeric characters. To set the mask, we change the **Mask** property in the **Property Pages** dialog to the following:

(###)  ###-####

The parentheses, **()**, and hyphen, **-**, are *literal characters* (also called non-masking characters) displayed. Non-masking characters are displayed as literals by the **MaskEdit** control. The user cannot modify literal characters. The pound sign (**#**) characters required digits (a number from 0 to 9). Figure 10.12 shows the mask in the control at design time.

The user does not see the mask characters, only the prompt character in the locations where input is allowed. The **MaxLength** property ensures that the user will not input more characters than allowed. Figure 10.13 shows the phone number mask at run-time.

For completeness, the **Property Pages** dialog (Fig. 10.14) is shown for the **MaskEdit** control of Figs. 10.12 and 10.13.

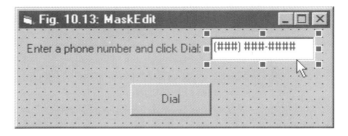

**Fig. 10.12** **MaskEdit** control at design time.

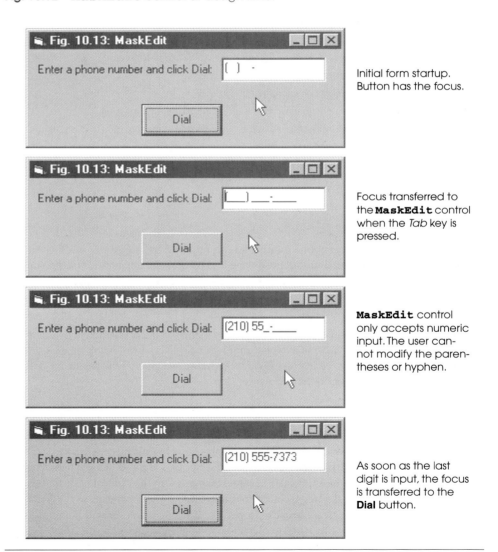

**Fig. 10.13** Demonstrating the **MaskEdit** control.

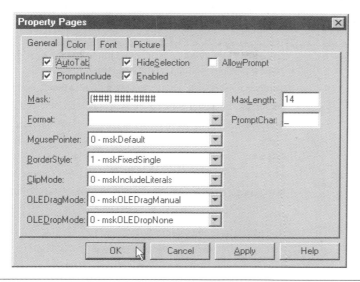

**Fig. 10.14**   **Property Pages** dialog for **MaskEdit** control of Figs. 10.12 and 10.13.

*Good Programming Practice 10.2*

*Prefix **MaskEdit** controls with **msk** to allow them to be identified easily.*

## 10.5  **ComboBox** Control

The **ComboBox** is an intrinsic control that combines **TextBox** features with a short drop-down list. Figure 10.15 lists some of the common **ComboBox** properties and methods.

| Property/method | Description |
| --- | --- |
| *Properties* | |
| **Enabled** | **Boolean**. Specifies if the user can interact with the **ComboBox**. |
| **Index** | **Integer**. Specifies the control array index. |
| **List** | **String** array. Contains the **String**s displayed in the drop-down list. Starting array index is **0**. |
| **ListCount** | **Integer**. Contains the number of drop-down list items. |
| **ListIndex** | **Integer**. Contains the index of the selected **ComboBox** item. If an item is not selected, **ListIndex** is **-1**. |
| **Locked** | **Boolean**. Specifies whether or not the user can type data in the **ComboBox**. |
| **MousePointer** | **Integer**. Specifies the shape of the mouse pointer when over the area of the **ComboBox**. |

**Fig. 10.15**   Common **ComboBox** properties, methods and events (part 1 of 2).

| Property/method | Description |
|---|---|
| **NewIndex** | **Integer**. Index of last item added to the **ComboBox**. If the **ComboBox** does not contain any items, **NewIndex** is **-1**. |
| **Sorted** | **Boolean**. Specifies whether or not a **ComboBox**'s items are sorted. |
| **Style** | **Integer**. Specifies the **ComboBox** appearance. (See Fig. 10.16.) |
| **TabStop** | **Boolean**. Determines whether or not the **ComboBox** receives the focus. |
| **Text** | **String**. Specifies the **ComboBox**'s selected item. |
| **ToolTipText** | **String**. Specifies what text is displayed as the **ComboBox**'s tool tip. |
| **Visible** | **Boolean**. Specifies whether or not the **ComboBox** is visible. |
| *Methods* | |
| **AddItem** | Adds an item to the **ComboBox**. |
| **Clear** | Removes all items from the **ComboBox**. |
| **RemoveItem** | Removes the specified item from the **ComboBox**. |
| **SetFocus** | Transfers focus to the **ComboBox**. |
| *Event Procedures* | |
| **Change** | Called when text in **ComboBox** changes. |
| **DropDown** | Called when the **ComboBox** drop-down list is displayed. |
| **GotFocus** | Called when **ComboBox** receives the focus. |
| **LostFocus** | Called when **ComboBox** loses the focus. |

**Fig. 10.15** Common **ComboBox** properties, methods and events (part 2 of 2).

**ComboBox**es can have three different visual appearances (controlled by the *Style* property) as shown in Fig. 10.16. The **Style** property is set to either **0** (*vbComboDropDown*), **1** (*vbComboSimple*) or **2** (*vbComboDropDownList*). Style **vbComboDropDown** is the default and allows the user to type data directly into the **ComboBox** and to select items from the drop-down list. Style **vbComboSimple** has the visual appearance of a **TextBox**—a drop-down list never appears. Style **vbComboDropDownList** does not allow the user to enter data in the **ComboBox**. The user can only select items from the drop-down list.

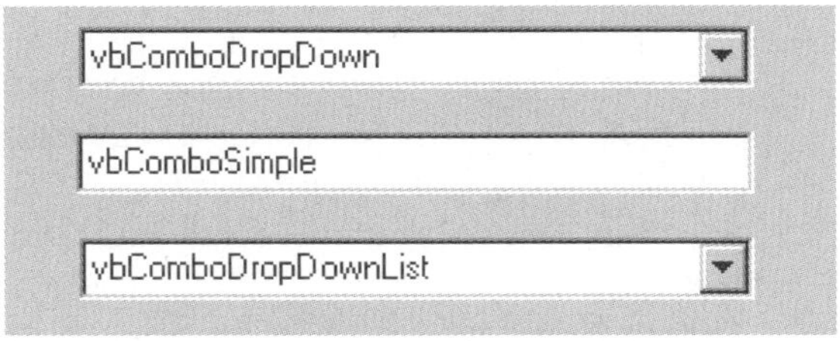

**Fig. 10.16** **ComboBox** styles.

Figure 10.17 allows the user to add and remove items from a **ComboBox**. **String**s are added to the **ComboBox** drop-down list by entering data in a **TextBox** and pressing **Add**. A **ComboBox** item is removed by selecting it from the drop-down list and pressing **Remove**. The program also allows the user to remove all items in the **ComboBox** by pressing **Clear**.

After text has been typed into the **TextBox**, pressing the **Add** button causes the line

```
Call cboCombo.AddItem(txtInput.Text)
```

```
1   ' Fig. 10.17
2   ' Demonstrating the ComboBox control.
3   Option Explicit          ' General declaration
4
5   Private Sub cmdInput_Click()
6
7       ' Add item to cboCombo drop-down list
8       Call cboCombo.AddItem(txtInput.Text)
9
10      ' Display input in cboCombo's text area
11      cboCombo.Text = txtInput.Text
12
13      Call UpdateLabel      ' Display stats
14      txtInput.Text = ""    ' Clear user input
15  End Sub
16
17  Private Sub UpdateLabel()     ' Programmer defined procedure
18      lblStats.Caption = "ListCount: " & cboCombo.ListCount & _
19                         " ListIndex: " & cboCombo.ListIndex & _
20                         " New Index: " & cboCombo.NewIndex
21  End Sub
22
23  Private Sub cboCombo_LostFocus()
24
25      ' When cboCombo loses focus call updateLabel
26      Call UpdateLabel
27  End Sub
28
29  Private Sub cmdClear_Click()
30      cboCombo.Clear      ' Clear all items
31      Call UpdateLabel    ' Display stats
32  End Sub
33
34  Private Sub cmdRemove_Click()
35
36      ' Remove item from cboCombo
37      Call cboCombo.RemoveItem(cboCombo.ListIndex)
38
39      ' Display cboCombo item 0
40      cboCombo.Text = cboCombo.List(0)
41  End Sub
```

**Fig. 10.17**   Demonstrating the **ComboBox** control (part 1 of 3).

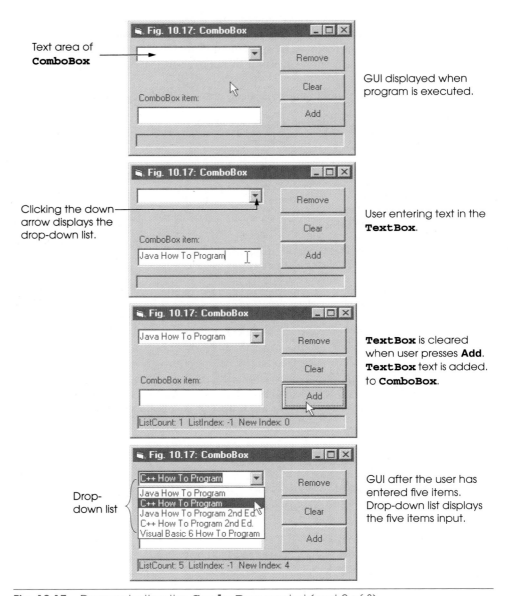

**Fig. 10.17**    Demonstrating the **ComboBox** control (part 2 of 3).

to execute. Method **AddItem** adds **txtInput.Text**'s **String** to **ComboBox cboCombo**. Technically, the **String** is really added to an array of **String**s that the **ComboBox** uses to populate its drop-down list. Next, line 11,

```
cboCombo.Text = txtInput.Text
```

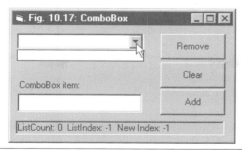

GUI displayed after the user pressed **Clear**. Drop-down list indicates **ComboBox** is empty.

**Fig. 10.17**   Demonstrating the **ComboBox** control (part 3 of 3).

displays **txtInput.Text** in the text area of the **ComboBox**. The programmer must explicitly write this line; otherwise the text area portion remains empty until the user either types text or a selection is made from the drop-down list. The programmer-defined procedure **updateLabel** is then called to display the number of items in the **ComboBox** (the *ListCount* property), the current selected index (by accessing the *ListIndex* property) and the value of the last created index (by accessing the *NewIndex* property).

Clicking the small, down arrowhead on the **ComboBox** displays the drop-down list and gives the **ComboBox** the focus. The user can *scroll* through the list with the mouse. When the mouse pointer passes over an item, the item is highlighted. A drop-down list member is selected with the mouse by a single click. The selected item appears in the text area of the **ComboBox**.

When the focus is directed at another control, the system raises the *LostFocus* event and the **ComboBox**'s **LostFocus** event procedure executes to handle the event. Our event handler calls procedure **UpdateLabel** to display the new **ListIndex** value.

Once a **ComboBox** item is selected it can be deleted by clicking **Remove** (that raises the **Click** event). Event procedure **cmdRemove_Click** executes the line

```
Call cboCombo.RemoveItem(cboCombo.ListIndex)
```

which calls method *RemoveItem* to delete the item selected. The argument passed to **RemoveItem** is an **Integer** corresponding to the item to delete. In order to avoid an empty text area, we display the first item in the drop-down list with the assignment

```
cboCombo.Text = cboCombo.List(0)
```

The *List* method provides access to the array of **String**s that stores the **ComboBox** items. This array begins with a default index of **0**. Pressing the **Clear** button calls method *Clear* to delete all items from the **ComboBox**.

*Good Programming Practice 10.3*

*Prefixing* **ComboBox***es with* **cbo** *allows them to be identified easily.*

## 10.6 **ListBox** Control

The *ListBox* intrinsic control allows the user to view a list of items. **ListBox** controls often allow the user to select one or more items. Figure 10.18 lists some of the common

**ListBox** properties and methods. Many **ListBox** properties and methods are the same as those for the **ComboBox**.

| Property/method | Description |
| --- | --- |
| *Properties* | |
| Columns | **Integer**. Specifies whether or not **ListBox** contents are listed vertically. When **0**, items are listed vertically. A value greater than **0** specifies the number of columns in which items are listed horizontally. |
| Enabled | **Boolean**. Specifies if the user can interact with the **ListBox**. |
| Index | **Integer**. Specifies the control array index. |
| List | **String** array. Contains the **String**s displayed in the **ListBox**. Starting array index is **0**. |
| ListCount | **Integer**. Contains the number of **ListBox** items. |
| ListIndex | **Integer**. Contains the index of the selected **ListBox** item. If an item is not selected, **ListIndex** is **-1**. |
| MousePointer | **Integer**. Specifies the shape of the mouse pointer when over the area of the **ListBox**. |
| MultiSelect | **Integer**. Specifies whether or not the user can select more than one item at a time from the **ListBox**. (See Fig. 10.20.) |
| NewIndex | **Integer**. Index of last item added to the **ListBox**. If the **ListBox** does not contain any items, **NewIndex** is **-1**. |
| SelCount | Integer. Contains the number of **ListBox** items selected. |
| Sorted | **Boolean**. Specifies whether or not a **ListBox**'s items are sorted. |
| Style | **Integer**. Specifies the **ListBox** appearance. (See Fig. 10.19.) |
| TabStop | **Boolean**. Determines whether or not the **ListBox** receives the focus. |
| Text | **String**. Specifies the **TextBox**'s selected item. |
| ToolTipText | **String**. Specifies what text is displayed as the **ListBox**'s tool tip. |
| Visible | **Boolean**. Specifies whether or not the **ListBox** is visible. |
| *Methods* | |
| AddItem | Adds an item to the **ListBox**. |
| Clear | Removes all items from the **ListBox**. |
| RemoveItem | Removes one item from the **ListBox**. |
| SetFocus | Transfers focus to the **ListBox**. |
| *Event Procedures* | |
| Click | Called when the user clicks once on a **ListBox** item. |
| DblClick | Called when the user double clicks on a **ListBox** item. |
| GotFocus | Called when **ListBox** receives the focus. |
| LostFocus | Called when **ListBox** loses the focus. |

Fig. 10.18   Common **ListBox** properties and methods.

Visual Basic provides two styles of **ListBox**es, shown in Fig. 10.19. **ListBox** styles are set using the *Style* property. A value of **0**, *vbListBoxStandard*, specifies a standard **ListBox** style that is found in most Windows applications. A value of **1**, *vbListBoxCheckBox*, specifies a **ListBox** containing a **CheckBox** in front of each item.

Property *MultiSelect* determines whether or not the user can select multiple items from a **vbListBoxStandard ListBox**. Visual Basic does not allow multiple selection in **vbListBoxCheckBox ListBox**es. Figure. 10.20 shows a **ListBox** with multiple items selected, and Fig. 10.21 summarizes **MuliSelect** values.

The program of Fig. 10.22 allows the user to add items, remove items, and clear a **ListBox**. The **ListBox** does not allow multiple selections and has its **Sorted** property set to **True**. The program uses the same **AddItem**, **RemoveItem** and **Clear** methods introduced in Section 10.5. The program also introduces the concept of *access keys* (*Alt* key plus another key) to execute a command. Access keys are created by preceding a character in the **Caption** property with an *ampersand*, **&**.

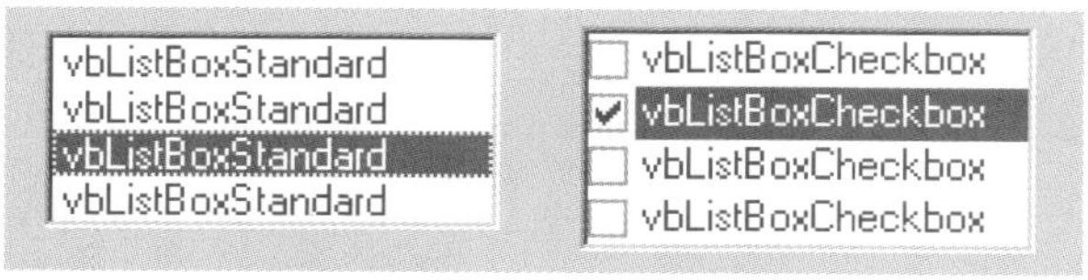

**Fig. 10.19**   **ListBox** styles.

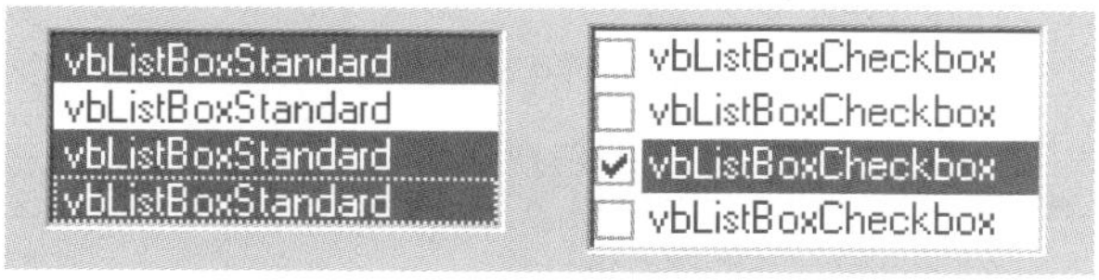

**Fig. 10.20**   Multiple selection in a **ListBox**.

| Value | Description |
|---|---|
| **0 (None)** | **ListBox** does not allow multiple selections. |
| **1 (Simple)** | **ListBox** allows multiple selections. Items are selected/deselected with either the mouse or the *Space* bar. |
| **2 (Extended)** | **ListBox** allows multiple selections. Items are selected/deselected with either the mouse or the *Space* bar. Holding the *Shift* key and selecting an item selects all items between the last selection and the current selection. The arrow keys can also be used with *Shift*. Holding the *Ctrl* key and selecting an item selects/deselects that item. |

**Fig. 10.21**   **MultiSelect** property values.

Note: Some properties (such as **ListBox** property **Sorted**) are read-only properties at run time—they can only be assigned values at design time (called *design-time properties*). Similarly, some properties can only be set at run time (called *run-time properties*). Run-time properties do not appear in the **Properties** window, but are visible with *Auto Quick Info* in the Visual Basic editor.

**Good Programming Practice 10.4**

*Prefixing **ListBox**es with **lst** allows them to be identified easily.*

```
1   ' Fig. 10.22
2   ' Demonstrating the ListBox control
3   Option Explicit            ' General declaration
4
5   Private Sub cmdAdd_Click()
6       Call lstList.AddItem(txtInput.Text)   ' Add Text to ListBox
7       txtInput.Text = ""         ' Clear TextBox
8   End Sub
9
10  Private Sub cmdRemove_Click()
11
12      ' If an item is selected then delete it
13      If lstList.ListIndex <> -1 Then
14          Call lstList.RemoveItem(lstList.ListIndex)
15      End If
16
17  End Sub
18
19  Private Sub cmdClear_Click()
20      Call lstList.Clear    ' Remove all list items
21  End Sub
22
23  Private Sub cmdExit_Click()
24      End     ' Terminate execution
25  End Sub
```

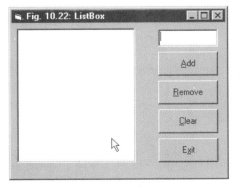

Initial GUI at execution. The lines on the face of the buttons indicate access keys. *Alt* + *A* is equivalent to pressing **Add**, *Alt* + *R* is equivalent to pressing **Remove**, etc.

**Fig. 10.22**    Demonstrating the **ListBox** control (part 1 of 3).

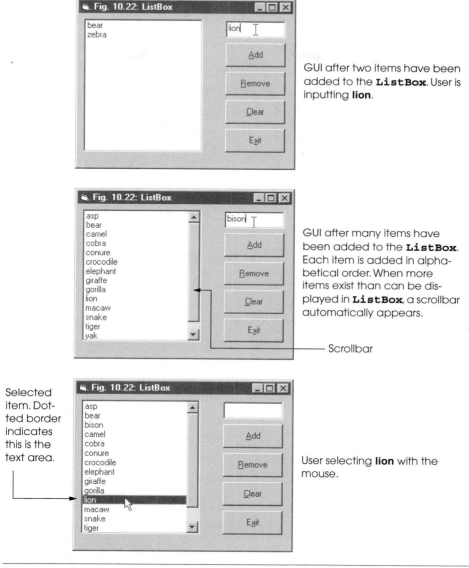

**Fig. 10.22**    Demonstrating the **ListBox** control (part 2 of 3).

## 10.7 Scrollbars

*Scrollbar* controls are intrinsic controls that allow the user to access a range of **Integer** values. Visual Basic provides two types of scrollbar controls *HScrollBar* and *VScrollBar*. **HScrollBar**s are horizontal scrollbars and **VScollBar**s are vertical scrollbars. Figure 10.23 displays an **HScrollBar**. Figure 10.24 lists the common scrollbar properties and methods.

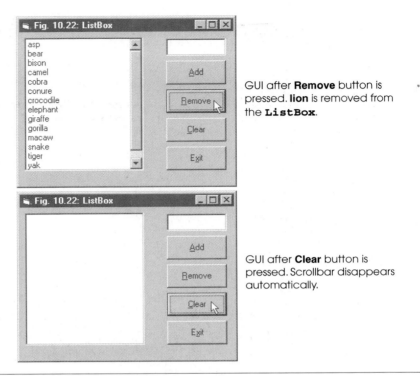

GUI after **Remove** button is pressed. **lion** is removed from the **ListBox**.

GUI after **Clear** button is pressed. Scrollbar disappears automatically.

**Fig. 10.22**   Demonstrating the **ListBox** control (part 3 of 3).

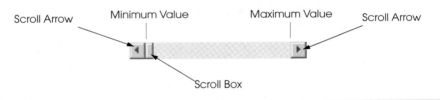

**Fig. 10.23**   **HScrollBar** control.

| Property/method | Description |
|---|---|
| *Properties* | |
| **Enabled** | **Boolean**. Specifies whether or not the user is allowed to interact with the scrollbar. |
| **Index** | **Integer**. Specifies the control array index. |
| **LargeChange** | **Integer**. Amount the property **Value** changes by when the area between the scroll box and scroll arrow is clicked. |
| **Max** | **Integer**. The largest value that property **Value** can have. |

**Fig. 10.24**   Common scrollbar properties and methods (part 1 of 2).

| Property/method | Description |
|---|---|
| Min | **Integer**. The smallest value that property **Value** can have. |
| MousePointer | **Integer**. Specifies the shape of the mouse pointer when over the area of the scrollbar. |
| SmallChange | **Integer**. Amount the property **Value** changes by when a scroll arrow is pressed. |
| TabStop | **Boolean**. Determines whether or not the scrollbar receives the focus. |
| Value | **Integer**. The position of the scroll box. |
| Visible | **Boolean**. Specifies whether or not the scrollbar is visible. |
| *Method* | |
| SetFocus | Transfers focus to the scrollbar. |
| *Event Procedures* | |
| Change | Called when the scrollbar **Value** property changes (i.e., the scroll box has moved). |
| GotFocus | Called when scrollbar receives the focus. |
| LostFocus | Called when scrollbar loses the focus. |
| Scroll | Called repeatedly when the scroll box is *clicked and dragged* (clicking the scroll box and holding the mouse button, then moving the mouse). |

**Fig. 10.24**  Common scrollbar properties and methods (part 2 of 2).

The program of Fig. 10.25 displays a **PictureBox** and two scrollbars–one horizontal and one vertical. The program is a simple variation of a popular toy that allows pictures to be drawn from lines. Each scrollbar controls the line drawn in the **PictureBox**. The program uses drawing units of **Pixel**s. Both the form and **PictureBox** have their **ScaleMode** set to **Pixel**s.

```
1   ' Fig. 10.25
2   ' Demonstrating Scrollbars
3   Option Explicit        ' General declarations
4
5   Private Sub Form_Load()
6      ' Set maximum values for scrollbars
7      hsbScroll.Max = picPicture.Width
8      vsbScroll.Max = picPicture.Height
9   End Sub
10
11  Private Sub hsbScroll_Change()
12     ' Turn pixel on when horizontal scrollbar value changes
13     picPicture.PSet (hsbScroll.Value, vsbScroll.Value)
14  End Sub
```

**Fig. 10.25**  Demonstrating scrollbars (part 1 of 2).

```
15
16   Private Sub vsbScroll_Change()
17       ' Turn pixel on when vertical scrollbar value changes
18       picPicture.PSet (hsbScroll.Value, vsbScroll.Value)
19   End Sub
20
21   Private Sub hsbScoll_Scroll()
22       picPicture.PSet (hsbScroll.Value, vsbScroll.Value)
23   End Sub
24
25   Private Sub vsbScroll_Scroll()
26       picPicture.PSet (hsbScroll.Value, vsbScroll.Value)
27   End Sub
```

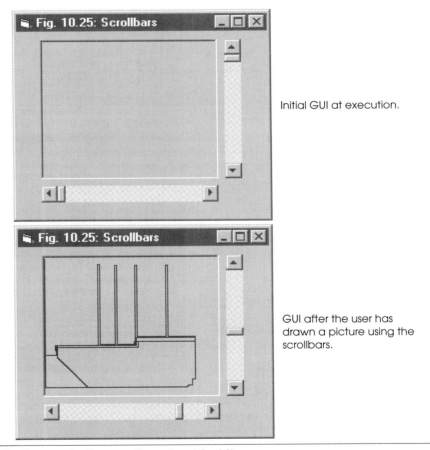

Initial GUI at execution.

GUI after the user has drawn a picture using the scrollbars.

**Fig. 10.25**  Demonstrating scrollbars (part 2 of 2).

In the **Form_Load** event procedure, the horizontal scrollbar **hsbScroll**'s *Max* property is set to the **Width** of **picPicture** and vertical scrollbar **vsbScroll**'s **Max** property is set to the **Height** of **picPicture**. Both **hsbScroll** and **vsbScroll** use the default value **0** for **Min**.

***Common Programming Error 10.2***

*Attempting to assign a value outside the range of an **Integer** to a scrollbar's **Max** or **Min** property is a run-time error (the program terminates).*

Each time a **Change** event or **Scroll** event is raised for the scrollbars, the statement

```
picPicture.PSet (hsbScroll.Value, vsbScroll.Value)
```

executes. The pixel located at (**hsbScroll.Value**, **vsbScroll.Value**) changes to the default color—black.

***Good Programming Practice 10.5***

*Prefixing horizontal scrollbars with **hsb** allows them to be identified easily.*

***Good Programming Practice 10.6***

*Prefixing vertical scrollbars with **vsb** allows them to be identified easily.*

## 10.8 **Slider** Control

The ***Slider*** *ActiveX control* provides the same type of functionality as a scrollbar. **Slider**s do provide a different user interface than scrollbars, as shown in Fig. 10.26. Like scrollbars, **Slider**s can either be horizontal or vertical. Figure 10.27 lists common **Slider** properties and methods.

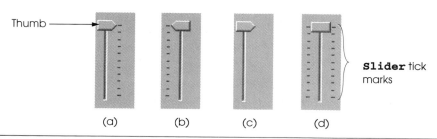

**Fig. 10.26   Slider**s.

| Property/method | Description |
| --- | --- |
| *Properties* | |
| **Enabled** | **Boolean**. Specifies whether or not the user is allowed to interact with the **Slider**. |
| **GetNumTicks** | **Long**. Contains the number of ticks on the **Slider**. |
| **Index** | **Integer**. Specifies the control array index. |

**Fig. 10.27**   Common **Slider** properties and methods (part 1 of 2).

| Property/method | Description |
| --- | --- |
| LargeChange | **Integer.** Amount the property **Value** changes by when the area between the thumb and the end/beginning of the **Slider** is clicked. |
| Max | **Integer.** The largest value that property **Value** can have. |
| Min | **Integer.** The smallest value that property **Value** can have. |
| MousePointer | **Integer.** Specifies the shape of the mouse pointer when over the **Slider.** |
| Orientation | **Integer.** Specifies whether or not **Slider** is horizontal or vertical. |
| SmallChange | **Integer.** Amount the property **Value** changes by when the **Slider** is clicked. |
| TabStop | **Boolean.** Determines whether or not the **Slider** receives the focus. |
| TickFrequency | **Long.** Specifies the number of units between each tick mark. |
| TickStyle | **Integer.** Describes if and where tick marks are displayed. (See Fig. 10.28.) |
| Value | **Integer.** The position of the thumb. |
| Visible | **Boolean.** Specifies whether or not the **Slider** is visible. |
| *Method* | |
| SetFocus | Transfers focus to the **Slider.** |
| *Event Procedures* | |
| Change | Called when the **Slider Value** property changes (i.e., moving the thumb, or assigning a number to **Value**). |
| GotFocus | Called when **Slider** receives the focus. |
| LostFocus | Called when **Slider** loses the focus. |
| Scroll | Called when the thumb is *clicked-and-dragged* (clicking the thumb and holding the mouse button, then moving the mouse). |

**Fig. 10.27**  Common **Slider** properties and methods (part 2 of 2).

Property *TickStyle* determines whether or not the **Slider** displays *tick marks*. If tick marks are to be displayed, the **TickStyle** property also specifies where the tick marks are positioned. Figure 10.28 lists the **TickStyle** property values.

*Look-and-Feel Observation 10.1*
*Displaying tick marks gives **Slider**s a more professional appearance.*

The program of Fig. 10.29 displays a **Slider** representing a volume control. The **Slider Value** is displayed in a **Label**. **Slider**'s **Max** property is set to **20** and **Slider**'s **Min** property is **0**. **LargeChange** is **5** and **SmallChange** is **1**.

*Common Programming Error 10.3*
*Attempting to assign a value outside the range of an **Integer** to a **Slider**'s **Max** or **Min** property is a run-time error.*

| Constant | Value | Description |
|---|---|---|
| `sldBottomRight` | 0 | Ticks are displayed by default on the bottom of horizontal **Slider**s and to the right of vertical **Slider**s (Fig. 10.26a). |
| `sldTopLeft` | 1 | Ticks are displayed on top of horizontal **Slider**s and to the left of vertical **Slider**s (Fig. 10.26b). |
| `sldBoth` | 2 | Ticks are displayed on both sides of the **Slider** (Fig. 10.26d). |
| `sldNoTicks` | 3 | Ticks are not displayed (Fig. 10.26c). |

**Fig. 10.28**   `TickStyle` property values .

```
1   ' Fig. 10.29
2   ' Demonstrating the Slider control
3   Option Explicit      ' General declaration
4
5   Private Sub sldVolume_Change()
6      lblDb.Caption = sldVolume.Value & " dB"
7   End Sub
8
9   Private Sub sldVolume_Scroll()
10     lblDb.Caption = sldVolume.Value & " dB"
11  End Sub
```

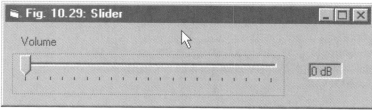

Initial GUI at execution.

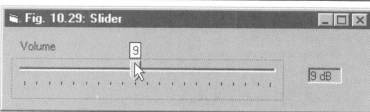

User dragging the thumb. The **Value** of the **Slider** is displayed above the thumb (**TextPosition** property).

**Fig. 10.29**   Demonstrating the **Slider** control.

*Good Programming Practice 10.7*

*Prefixing **Slider**s with **sld** allows them to be identified easily.*

## 10.9 Menus

Windows applications provide groups of related commands in *menus*. These commands depend on the application, but some—such as **Open** and **Save**—are frequently found in applications. Visual Basic provides an easy way to create menus with the modal **Menu Editor** dialog, Fig. 10.30. The dialog is displayed when **Menu Editor** is selected from the **Tools** menu. The **Menu Editor** command is grayed unless the form is visible. The **Menu Editor** dialog can also be displayed by right-clicking the form and selecting **Menu Editor**. In this section we discuss some of the **Menu Editor** features.

The **Menu Editor** dialog contains the **TextBox**es *Caption* and *Name*. The value entered in the **Caption TextBox** is the menu name the user sees. The value entered in the **Name TextBox** is the variable name the programmer uses. Every menu must have a **Caption** and a **Name**.

*Good Programming Practice 10.8*

*Prefixing menus with* **mnu** *allows them to be identified easily.*

*Common Programming Error 10.4*

*Not providing a value for either the* **Menu Editor***'s* **Name** *or the* **Caption TextBox**es is *a syntax error.*

Menus are like other controls in that they have properties and events. The **Menu Editor** is a way of setting select properties for a menu. Once a menu is created, its properties can be viewed in the **Properties** window and its events in the **Code** window.

The programmer can create menu control arrays. The *Index* **TextBox** specifies the menu's index in the control array.

Figure 10.31 shows an *expanded* menu that lists various *commands* (called *menu items*) as well as other *submenus* (i.e., a menu in a menu). Menus that are not top-level menus can have *shortcut keys* (combinations of *Ctrl*, *Shift*, *Alt*, function keys (i.e., *F1*, *F2*, etc.) and letter keys). Shortcut keys are specified using the *Shortcut* **ComboBox**. All shortcut keys listed in the **Shortcut ComboBox** are predefined by Visual Basic. Programmers may not define their own.

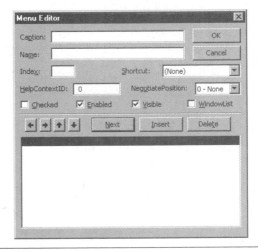

**Fig. 10.30   Menu Editor** dialog.

**Common Programming Error 10.5**

*Attempting to assign a shortcut key to a top-level menu is a syntax error.*

**Look-and-Feel Observation 10.2**

*When assigning shortcut key values, use the well-established industry shortcut keys to ensure a consistent look and feel. For example, use Ctrl + C for copy, not Ctrl + Q.*

The **Menu Editor** dialog also provides several **CheckBox**es for controlling the appearance of menus. The **Checked** **CheckBox** is unchecked (**False**) by default and allows the programmer the option of creating a *checked menu item* (a menu item that acts as a toggle and displays a check mark when selected). Figure 10.32 displays a portion of a menu containing several checked menu items. The **Enabled** **CheckBox** specifies whether or not the menu is grayed (or *disabled*). Menus or menu items are commonly grayed to visually indicate to the user that a feature is not available. The **Visible** **CheckBox** specifies whether or not a menu or menu item is visible. We discuss the **Menu Editor** buttons momentarily.

**Common Programming Error 10.6**

*Attempting to add a check to a top-level menu is a syntax error.*

**Fig. 10.31**    An expanded menu.

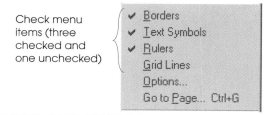

**Fig. 10.32**    Checked menu items.

In our next example, we create two top-level menus, **File** and **Graphics**, using the **Menu Editor**. Building the menus does not require us to write any code. Creating and designing menus is an excellent example of *visual programming* (the ability to create windows GUIs writing only minimal code). In order to make the menus functional, we will of course have to write code. We discuss how this is done in a later example.

Figure 10.33 displays a GUI containing two menus, **File** and **Graphics**—each of which is created using the **Menu Editor**. Note that the separator bars are created by placing a *hyphen*, **-**, in the **Caption TextBox**.

Figure 10.34 shows the **Menu Editor** dialog corresponding to the program of Fig. 10.33. The ***Next*** button allows the next menu or menu item to be edited. ***Insert*** allows a menu or menu item to be inserted between two existing menus or menu items. ***Delete*** removes the selected menu or menu item. The left and right arrow buttons control the indentation of a menu or menu item. The up and down arrow buttons perform insertion in the same manner as **Insert**.

Notice that the top-level menus appear in the left column. Any submenus or menu items are indented (using the second arrow button). Submenu menu items are indented beneath their respective menus (using the second arrow button). Indentation up to six levels is allowed.

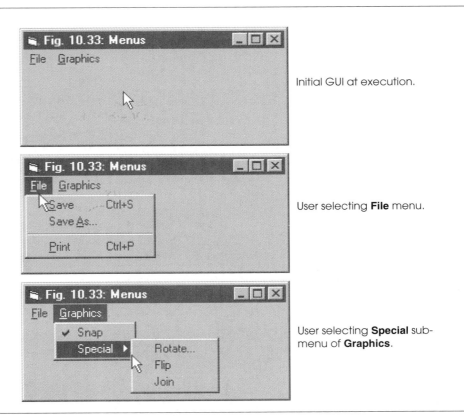

Initial GUI at execution.

User selecting **File** menu.

User selecting **Special** sub-menu of **Graphics**.

**Fig. 10.33**   Program with two menus.

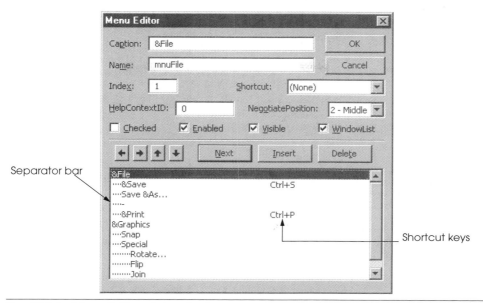

Separator bar

Shortcut keys

**Fig. 10.34   Menu Editor** dialog for the program of Fig. 10.33.

## 10.10  Pop-Up Menus

Pop-up menus are menus that appear when the user right-clicks the mouse. Pop-up menus are created using the **Menu Editor** dialog. A pop-up menu's **Visible CheckBox** should be unchecked in the **Menu Editor** dialog. Method *PopupMenu* displays a pop-up menu. The program of Fig. 10.35 contains a **Label** displaying the word **TEXT**. Right-clicking the form displays a pop-up menu from which the user can select either **Right**, **Center** or **Left** to justify **TEXT**.

Pressing a mouse button on the form results in *Form_MouseDown* being called. When coded, the **MouseDown** procedure is called when any mouse button is clicked. The first argument, *Button*, specifies which mouse button was pressed. The constant *vbRightButton* represents the right mouse button. We discuss mouse events in detail in Chapter 12. If the right mouse button was pressed, then the line

```
Call PopupMenu(mnuPopUp)
```

is executed. The **PopupMenu** method displays the specified pop-up menu. When the user selects a menu item, *Click* is called for that menu item. All menu and menu items have only one event procedure, **Click**, that is called when the item is selected. The **Label**'s *Alignment* property is set to one of three constants: *vbLeftJustify*, *vbCenter* or *vbRightJustify*.

*Look-and-Feel Observation 10.3*

*Having pop-up menus display when only the right mouse button is clicked is the correct look and feel for Windows applications.*

```
1   ' Fig. 10.35
2   ' Demonstrating pop-up menus
3   Option Explicit        ' General Declaration
4
5   Private Sub Form_MouseUp(Button As Integer, Shift As Integer, _
6                           X As Single, Y As Single)
7
8       ' When right button is clicked display pop-up menu
9       If Button = vbRightButton Then
10          Call PopupMenu(mnuPopUp)
11      End If
12
13  End Sub
14
15  Private Sub mnuitmLeft_Click()
16      lblText.Alignment = vbLeftJustify
17  End Sub
18
19  Private Sub mnuitmRight_Click()
20      lblText.Alignment = vbRightJustify
21  End Sub
22
23  Private Sub mnuitmCenter_Click()
24      lblText.Alignment = vbCenter
25  End Sub
```

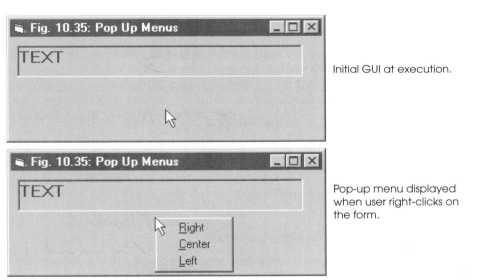

Initial GUI at execution.

Pop-up menu displayed when user right-clicks on the form.

**Fig. 10.35**  Demonstrating pop-up menus (part 1 of 2).

## 10.11 Function MsgBox

Function **MsgBox** displays a custom dialog that provides the user with information about a program's state of execution. The **MsgBox** dialog can be customized to display a text message, a predefined icon, and predefined buttons. Figure 10.36 shows a **MsgBox** dialog

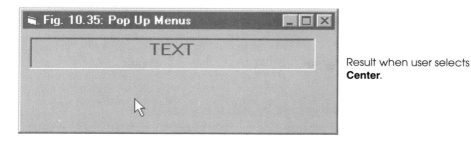

**Fig. 10.35**   Demonstrating pop-up menus (part 2 of 2).

generated by Visual Basic. By calling function **MsgBox**, the programmer can create dialogs similar to Fig. 10.36. Note, however, that the programmer cannot change the position of the buttons, icon or message.

*Look-and-Feel Observation 10.4*

*Function **MsgBox** provides a standard way of displaying application messages to the user across Windows platforms. Windows applications messages have the same look and feel.*

While the **MsgBox** provides the user with information, the user can also provide information to the program by pressing a **MsgBox** button. Types and values for **MsgBox** buttons are listed in Fig. 10.37.

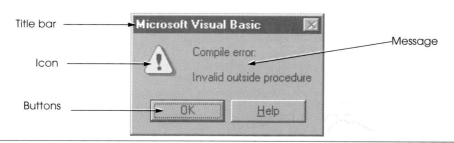

**Fig. 10.36**   **MsgBox** dialog generated by Visual Basic.

| Constant | Value | Description |
|----------|-------|-------------|
| vbOKOnly | 0 | **MsgBox** displays **OK** button. |
| vbOKCancel | 1 | **MsgBox** displays **OK** and **Cancel** buttons. |
| vbAbortRetryIgnore | 2 | **MsgBox** displays **Abort**, **Retry** and **Ignore** buttons. |
| vbYesNoCancel | 3 | **MsgBox** displays **Yes**, **No** and **Cancel** buttons. |
| vbYesNo | 4 | **MsgBox** displays **Yes** and **No** buttons. |
| vbRetryCancel | 5 | **MsgBox** displays **Retry** and **Cancel** buttons. |

**Fig. 10.37**   **MsgBox** constants for specifying the number and type of buttons.

**MsgBox** icons graphically illustrate the nature of the message. Visual Basic provides four predefined icons, listed in Fig. 10.38.

Visual Basic also allows the programmer to specify the severity of the message by specifying its modality. The **MsgBox** dialog is modal to Visual Basic by default. Modal constants are listed in Fig. 10.39.

When the user presses a **MsgBox** dialog button, a value representing the button pressed is returned. Figure 10.40 lists the possible return type values.

The program of Fig. 10.41 presents a series of **OptionButton**s from which the user can decide what the **MsgBox** dialog will look like when it is displayed. The choices are based upon the constants discussed in Figs. 10.37 through 10.39. Clicking the **Display** button displays the modal **MsgBox** dialog. When a **MsgBox** dialog button is pressed, the button is identified and printed in a **Label** at the bottom of the form.

| Constant | Value | Icon | Description |
|---|---|---|---|
| **vbCritical** | 16 | | When serious errors or problems occur, the critical icon is typically displayed. Displays critical icon. |
| **vbQuestion** | 32 | | When the user must make a decision, the question mark icon is typically displayed. Displays question mark icon. |
| **vbExclamation** | 48 | | Displays exclamation mark icon. Typically used to draw the user's attention to the message being displayed. |
| **vbInformation** | 64 | | Displays information icon. Typically used to give the user information about an action. |

**Fig. 10.38**  **MsgBox** constants for icons.

| Constant | Value | Description |
|---|---|---|
| **vbApplicationModal** | 0 | A **MsgBox** is modal—the user cannot interact with other windows in the same application until the **MsgBox** is dismissed. For "application modal" **MsgBox**es, the user ca still interact with other programs. |
| **vbSystemModal** | 4096 | A **MsgBox** is modal—the user cannot interact with other windows in the same application until the **MsgBox** is dismissed. For "system modal" **MsgBox**es, the user also cannot interact with other programs until the **MsgBox** is dismissed. |

**Fig. 10.39**  **MsgBox** constants for specifying the number and type of buttons.

| Constant | Value | Description |
|----------|-------|-------------|
| **vbOK** | 1 | **OK** button was pressed. |
| **vbCancel** | 2 | **Cancel** button was pressed. |
| **vbAbort** | 3 | **Abort** button was pressed. |
| **vbRetry** | 4 | **Retry** button was pressed. |
| **vbIgnore** | 5 | **Ignore** button was pressed. |
| **vbYes** | 6 | **Yes** button was pressed. |
| **vbNo** | 7 | **No** button was pressed. |

Fig. 10.40  **MsgBox** return values.

```
1   ' Fig. 10.41
2   ' Demonstrating Function MsgBox
3   Option Explicit              ' General declaration
4   Dim mButtonType As Integer   ' General declaration
5   Dim mButtonIcon As Integer   ' General declaration
6   Dim mModal As Integer        ' General declaration
7
8   Private Sub Form_Load()
9      mButtonType = vbOKOnly
10     mButtonIcon = vbCritical
11     mModal = vbApplicationModal
12
13     optType(mButtonType).Value = True
14     optIcon(mButtonIcon).Value = True
15     optModal(mModal).Value = True
16  End Sub
17
18  Private Sub cmdDisplay_Click()
19     Dim r As Integer
20
21     r = MsgBox("Visual Basic 6 How To Program", _
22               mButtonType + mButtonIcon + mModal, "VBHTP")
23
24     ' Determine which MsgBox button was pressed
25     Select Case r
26        Case vbOK
27           lblDisplay.Caption = "OK was pressed."
28        Case vbCancel
29           lblDisplay.Caption = "Cancel was pressed."
30        Case vbAbort
31           lblDisplay.Caption = "Abort was pressed."
32        Case vbRetry
33           lblDisplay.Caption = "Retry was pressed."
34        Case vbIgnore
35           lblDisplay.Caption = "Ignore was pressed."
```

Fig. 10.41  Demonstrating function **MsgBox** (part 1 of 3).

```
36          Case vbYes
37              lblDisplay.Caption = "Yes was pressed."
38          Case vbNo
39              lblDisplay.Caption = "No was pressed."
40      End Select
41
42 End Sub
43
44 Private Sub optIcon_Click(Index As Integer)
45      mButtonIcon = Index
46 End Sub
47
48 Private Sub optType_Click(Index As Integer)
49      mButtonType = Index
50 End Sub
51
52 Private Sub optModal_Click(Index As Integer)
53      mModal = Index
54 End Sub
```

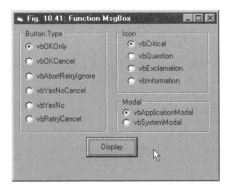

Initial GUI at execution.

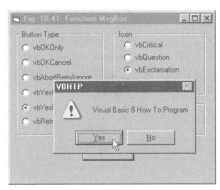

**MsgBox** dialog displayed after the user selects **vbYesNo**, **vbExclaimation** and **vbApplicationModal** and presses **Display**.

**Fig. 10.41**   Demonstrating function **MsgBox** (part 2 of 3).

The **MsgBox** dialog is displayed when the line

```
r = MsgBox("Visual Basic 6 How To Program", _
           mButtonType + mButtonIcon + mModal, "VBHTP")
```

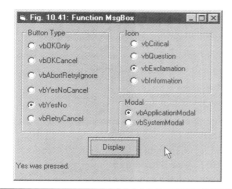

GUI after user dismisses **MsgBox** by pressing **Yes**.

**Fig. 10.41** Demonstrating function **MsgBox** (part 3 of 3).

is executed. The value returned by **MsgBox** is one of the values listed in Fig. 10.42 and is assigned to **r**. The first argument passed is the **String** message. The second argument is a combination of the button type, icon and modality. The third argument is the **String** displayed in the title bar of the **MsgBox** dialog.

Although not demonstrated in the program, Visual Basic also allows the programmer to specify which **MsgBox** button receives the initial focus. This value, like the other for the icon, button type, etc. is added to the third argument in the **MsgBox** function call.

## Summary

- The graphical user interface (GUI) presents a pictorial interface to a program. A GUI (pronounced "GOO-EE") gives a program a distinctive "look" and "feel." By providing different applications with a consistent set of intuitive GUI components, GUIs allow the user to spend less time trying to remember which keystrokes sequences do what and spend more time using the program in a productive manner. Consistent GUIs also enable a user to learn new applications faster. Interaction between the user and the program is through the GUI.

- GUI are built from controls. A control is an object with which the user interacts via the mouse or keyboard. Controls are reusable, predefined GUI components used for visual programming. Controls serve as building blocks that can be quickly combined to create a working application.

- Visual Basic controls exist in two varieties: intrinsic controls and ActiveX controls. Intrinsic controls (also called standard controls) are the controls that ship with all Visual Basic versions.

| Constant | Value | Description |
| --- | --- | --- |
| vbDefaultButton1 | 0 | **MsgBox**'s first button (i.e., the leftmost one) gets the focus. |
| vbDefaultButton2 | 256 | **MsgBox**'s second button gets the focus. |
| vbDefaultButton3 | 512 | **MsgBox**'s third button gets the focus. |
| vbDefaultButton4 | 768 | **MsgBox**'s fourth button gets the focus. |

**Fig. 10.42** **MsgBox** constants for specifying the number and type of buttons.

- ActiveX controls are additional controls that must be loaded into the Visual Basic toolbox with the **Components** dialog, which is displayed when the **Project** menu's **Components** is selected. Checking an ActiveX control and pressing **OK** loads the control.

- Other than the loading process, ActiveX controls are used in the same manner that intrinsic controls are. ActiveX controls have properties, methods and event procedures and when loaded, even display an icon in the toolbox.

- Thousands of ActiveX controls exist. Many independent software venders (ISVs) specialize in creating ActiveX controls. ActiveX controls can be created in languages such as Visual C++, Visual Basic, etc.

- **TextBox**es are intrinsic controls in which text is either input or displayed. The **Change** event is raised every time the **TextBox Text** changes. The **ToolTipText** property displays a text message (called a tool tip) when the mouse pointer rests in the control's area.

- When text is typed or copied into the multilined **TextBox**, the text automatically wraps to the next line when the right edge of the **TextBox** is reached. Text also automatically wraps for multilined **TextBox**es without vertical scrollbars.

- The **MaskEdit** ActiveX control is a specialized version of a **TextBox**. **MaskEdit**s allow for validation of input by ensuring that the correct format is input.

- Most ActiveX controls provide the ability to set control properties through property pages. Once the ActiveX control has been placed on the form, the control's property page is accessed through a pop-up menu. Clicking the control once with the right mouse button displays the pop-up menu.

- When **Properties** is selected, the property page is displayed as a dialog (titled **Property Pages**). Property pages typically contain tabs that group related categories. Properties, including those not listed in the properties page, are accessible in the **Properties** window.

- **MaskEdit** controls are useful for ensuring that information is input in the proper format. The **MaskEdit** control provides this capability by using mask characters. When using a mask, we can exclude certain characters from being input—such as letters or other non-numeric characters. To set the mask, we change the **Mask** property in the **Property Pages** dialog. The parentheses, **( )**, and hyphen, **-**, are literal characters displayed. Any non-masking character is displayed in the **MaskEdit** control. The user cannot modify these characters. The pound sign, **#**, characters specify a mask for required numeric characters. The user does not see the mask characters, only the prompt character in the locations where input is allowed. The **MaxLength** property ensures that the user will not input more characters than allowed.

- The **ComboBox** is an intrinsic control that combines features of a **TextBox** with a short drop-down list. **ComboBox**es can have three different visual appearances (controlled by the **Style** property). The **Style** property is set to either **0** (**vbComboDropDown**), **1** (**vbComboSimple**) or **2** (**vbComboDropDownList**). Style **vbComboDropDown** is the default and allows the user to type data directly into the **ComboBox** and to select items from the drop-down list. Style **vbComboSimple** has the visual appearance of a **TextBox**—a drop-down list never appears. Style **vbComboDropDownList** does not allow the user to enter data in the **ComboBox**. The user can only select items from the drop-down list.

- Clicking the small, down arrowhead on the **ComboBox** displays the drop-down list and gives the **ComboBox** the focus. The user can scroll through the list with the mouse. When the mouse pointer passes over an item, the item is highlighted. A drop-down list member is selected with the mouse by a single click. The selected item appears in the text area of the **ComboBox**. When the focus is directed at another control, the **ComboBox**'s **LostFocus** event is raised.

- **ListBox** intrinsic controls allow the user to view a list of items. **ListBox** controls often allow the user to select one or more items. Visual Basic provides two styles of **ListBox**es. **ListBox** styles are set using the **Style** property. A value of **0**, **vbListBoxStandard**, specifies a standard **ListBox** style that is found in most Window applications. A value of **1**, **vbListBox-CheckBox**, specifies a **ListBox** containing a **CheckBox** in front of each item.

- Property **MultiSelect** determines whether or not the user can select multiple items from a **vb-ListBoxStandard ListBox**.

- Access keys (Alt key plus another key) can be used to execute commands. Access keys are created by preceding a character in the **Caption** property with an ampersand.

- Scrollbar controls are intrinsic controls that allow the user to access a range of **Integer** values. Visual Basic provides two types of scrollbar controls: **HScrollBar** and **VScrollBar**. **HScrollBar**s are horizontal scrollbars and **VScollBar**s are vertical scrollbars.

- The **Slider** ActiveX control provides the same type of a functionality as a scrollbar. **Slider**s do provide a different user interface than scrollbars. Like scrollbars, **Slider**s can either be horizontal or vertical.

- The **TickStyle** property determines whether or not the **Slider** displays tick marks. If tick marks are to be displayed, the **TickStyle** property also specifies where the tick marks are positioned.

- Windows applications provide groups of related commands in menus. These commands depend on the application, but some such as **Open** and **Save** are always found in applications.

- Visual Basic provides an easy way to create menus with the modal **Menu Editor** dialog. The dialog is displayed when **Menu Editor** is selected from the **Tools** menu. The **Menu Editor** dialog can also be displayed by right-clicking the form and selecting **Menu Editor**.

- The **Menu Editor** dialog contains the **TextBox**es **Caption** and **Name**. The value entered in the **Caption TextBox** is the menu name the user sees. The value entered in the **Name TextBox** is the internal name the programmer uses. Every menu must have a **Caption** and a **Name**.

- Expanded menus list various commands (called menu items) as well as other submenus (i.e., a menu in a menu). Menus that are not top-level menus can have shortcut keys (combinations of *Ctrl*, *Shift*, *Alt*, function keys (i.e., *F1*, *F2*, etc.) and letter keys). Shortcut keys are specified using the **Shortcut ComboBox**. All shortcut keys listed in the **Shortcut ComboBox** are predefined by Visual Basic.

- The **Menu Editor** dialog also provides several **CheckBox**es for controlling the appearance of menus. The **Checked CheckBox** is unchecked (**False**) by default and allows the programmer the option of creating a checked menu item (a menu item that acts as a toggle and displays a check mark when selected). The **Enabled CheckBox** specifies whether or not the menu is grayed (or disabled). Menus or menu items are commonly grayed to visually indicate to the user that a feature is not available. The **Visible CheckBox** specifies whether or not a menu or menu item is visible.

- Pop-up menus are menus that appear wherever the user right-clicks the mouse. Pop-up menus are created using the **Menu Editor** dialog. A pop-up menu is created by setting the **Visible CheckBox** to **False**. Calling the **PopupMenu** method displays the pop-up menu.

- Pressing a mouse button on the form results in **Form_MouseDown** being called. When coded, the **MouseDown** procedure is called when any mouse button is clicked. The first argument, **Button**, specifies which mouse button was pressed. The constant **vbRightButton** represents the right mouse button. The **PopupMenu** method displays the specified pop-up menu. When the user selects a menu item, **Click** is called for that menu item. All menu and menu items have only one event procedure—**Click** that is called when the item is selected.

- Function **MsgBox** displays a custom dialog that provides the user with information about a program's state of execution. The **MsgBox** dialog can be customized to display a text message, a predefined icon and predefined buttons.

- While the **MsgBox** provides the user with information, the user can also provide information to the program by pressing a **MsgBox** button. **MsgBox** icons graphically illustrate the nature of the message. Visual Basic provides four predefined icons. When series errors or problems occur, the critical icon is displayed. When the user must make a decision, the question mark icon is displayed. The exclamation mark icon is used to draw the user's attention to the message being displayed. The information icon is used to give the user information about an action.

- **MsgBox**es are modal—the user cannot interact with other windows in the same application until the **MsgBox** is dismissed. The user can still interact with other applications.

## *Terminology*

| | |
|---|---|
| ActiveX control | submenu |
| **Change** event procedure | **TabStop** property |
| **ComboBox** control | **Text** property |
| **Components** dialog | **TextBox** control |
| design-time property | **TickFrequency** property |
| **Enabled** property | **TickStyle** property |
| **GetNumTicks** property | **ToolTipText** property |
| **GotFocus** event procedure | **Value** property |
| **Index** property | **vbAbort** constant |
| intrinsic control | **vbAbortRetryIgnore** constant |
| **LargeChange** property | **vbApplicationModal** constant |
| **ListBox** control | **vbCancel** constant |
| **LostFocus** event procedure | **vbCenter** constant |
| **MaskEdit** control | **vbCritical** constant |
| **Max** property | **vbDefaultButton1** constant |
| menu | **vbDefaultButton2** constant |
| **Menu Editor** dialog | **vbQDefaultButton3** constant |
| menu item | **vbDefaultButton4** constant |
| **Min** property | **vbExclamation** constant |
| **MousePointer** property | **vbIgnore** constant |
| **MsgBox** function | **vbInformation** constant |
| **Orientation** property | **vbLeftJustify** constant |
| run-time property | **vbNo** constant |
| scroll arrows | **vbOK** constant |
| scrollbar | **vbOKOnly** constant |
| scroll box | **vbQuestion** constant |
| **Scroll** event procedure | **vbRetry** constant |
| **SetFocus** method | **vbRetryCancel** constant |
| **sldBoth** constant | **vbRightJustify** constant |
| **sldBottomRight** constant | **vbSystemModal** constant |
| **sldNoTicks** constant | **vbYes** constant |
| **sldTopLeft** constant | **vbYesNo** constant |
| **Slider** control | **vbYesNoCancel** constant |
| **SmallChange** property | **Visible** property |
| **Sorted** property | |

## *Common Programming Errors*

**10.1**    Not setting the ***Multiline*** property to ***True*** for a ***TextBox*** that has its ***Scrollbars*** property set to a non-zero value is a logic error. The scrollbars are not visible.

**10.2**    Attempting to assign a value outside the range of an **Integer** to a scrollbar's **Max** or **Min** property is a run-time error.

**10.3**    Attempting to assign a value outside the range of an **Integer** to a **Slider**'s **Max** or **Min** property is a run-time error.

**10.4**    Not providing a value for either the **Menu Editor**'s **Name** or the **Caption TextBoxes** is a syntax error.

**10.5**    Attempting to assign a shortcut key to a top-level menu is a syntax error.

**10.6**    Attempting to add a check to a top-level menu is a syntax error.

## Good Programming Practices

**10.1**    Prefixing **TextBoxes** with **txt** allows them to be easily identified.

**10.2**    Prefix **MaskEdit** controls with **msk** to allow them to be identified easily.

**10.3**    Prefixing **ComboBoxes** with **cbo** allows them to be identified easily.

**10.4**    Prefixing **ListBoxes** with **lst** allows them to be identified easily.

**10.5**    Prefixing horizontal scrollbars with **hsb** allows them to be identified easily.

**10.6**    Prefixing vertical scrollbars with **vsb** allows them to be identified easily.

**10.7**    Prefixing **Slider**s with **sld** allows them to be identified easily.

**10.8**    Prefixing menus with **mnu** allows them to be identified easily.

## Look-and-Feel Observations

**10.1**    Displaying tick marks gives **Sliders** a more professional appearance.

**10.2**    When assigning shortcut key values, use the well-established industry shortcut keys to ensure a consistent look and feel. For example, use Ctrl + C for copy, not Ctrl + Q.

**10.3**    Having pop-up menus display when only the right mouse button is clicked is the correct look and feel for Windows applications.

**10.4**    Function **MsgBox** provides a standard way of displaying application messages to the user across Windows platforms. Windows applications messages have the same look and feel.

## Self-Review Exercises

**10.1**    Fill in the blanks in each of the following:

a) _____ is the suggested prefix for **ListBox**es.

b) _____ are dialogs that allow the programmer to set ActiveX control properties at design time.

c) Menu separator bars are created by placing a _____ in the **Caption TextBox**.

d) The _____ property displays a tool tip.

e) The _____ property determines whether or not a **Slider** displays tick marks.

f) _____ is the suggested prefix for a horizontal scrollbar.

**10.2**    State which are *true* and which are *false*. If *false*, explain why.

a) **ListBox** items are sorted when the **ListBox** property **Sorted** is **True**.

b) Function **MsgBox** displays a modeless dialog.

c) A **Timer** is an example of an intrinsic control.

d) Visual Basic allows the programmer to create a control array of menus.

## Answers to Self-Review Exercises

**10.1**    a) **lst**.

b) property pages.

c) hyphen (−).

d) **ToolTipText**.

e)  **TickStyle**.
f)  **hsb**.

**10.2**    a)  True.
b)  False.
c)  True.
d)  True.

## Exercises

**10.3**    Fill in the blanks in each of the following:
a)  _____ is the suggested prefix for a **Slider**.
b)  The _____ dialog is used to add ActiveX controls to the toolbox.
c)  Property _____ determines the style of a **ComboBox** or **ListBox**.
d)  _____ is the suggested prefix for a **MaskEdit** control.
e)  _____ is the suggested prefix for a **ComboBox**.

**10.4**    State which are *true* and which are *false*. If *false*, explain why.
a)  **ListBox**es can only contain **String**s.
b)  **Slider**s are considered to be intrinsic controls.
c)  A scrollbar's **Orientation** property determines if it is vertical or horizontal.
d)  Pop-up menus are displayed (i.e., visible) when method **DisplayPopup** is called.
e)  **MaskEdit** controls are considered to be ActiveX controls.

**10.5**    Write a statement or statements to accomplish each of the following:
a)  Display a **MsgBox** containing an exclamation point icon, an **OK** button, "**Installation**" in the title bar, and "**Insert disk #8 and press OK**" as the prompt.
b)  Assign the text in **TextBox txtBx** to **String** variable **s**.
c)  Print the fifth **ListBox** item from **lstBx** on the form.
d)  In **ComboBox cboBx**, make the third item the selected item.

**10.6**    Write a program that allows the user to understand the relationship between Fahrenheit temperatures and Celsius temperatures. Use a vertical **Slider** to scroll through a range of Fahrenheit temperatures. Use a **Label** to display the equivalent Celsius temperature. The **Label** should be updated as the **Slider**'s value changes. Use the following formula:

$$celsius = 9 \ / \ 5 \ \infty \ fahrenheit \ + \ 32$$

**10.7**    Write a program that displays the names of 15 states in a **ComboBox**. When an item is selected from the **ComboBox** remove it.

**10.8**    Modify your solution to Exercise 10.7 to add a **ListBox**. When the user selects an item from the **ComboBox**, remove the item from the **ComboBox** and add it to the **ListBox**. Your program should check to ensure that the **ComboBox** contains at least one item. If it does not, print a message using function **MsgBox** and terminate program execution.

**10.9**    Write a program that allows the user to enter **String**s in a **TextBox**. Each **String** input is added to a **ListBox**. As each **String** is added to the **ListBox**, ensure that the **String**s are in sorted order. Any sorting routine used should be located in a separate code module (i.e., a standard module) for reuse purposes.

**10.10**    Write a program that adds a series of social security numbers to a **ComboBox**. Use a **MaskEdit** control to input the social security numbers using a proper social security number format.

**10.11**  Write a program that plays "guess the number" as follows: Your program chooses the number to be guessed by selecting an **Integer** at random in the range 1-1000. The program then displays in a **Label**:

**I have a number between 1 and 1000 can you guess my number?**
**Please enter your guess.**

A **TextBox** is used to input the guess from the used. As each guess is input the **BackColor** should change to either red or blue. Red indicates that the user is getting "warmer" and blue indicates that the user is getting "colder." A second non-editable **TextBox** displays either "**Too High**" or "**Too Low**" to help the user zero in on the correct answer. When the users guesses correctly, "**Correct!**" is displayed and the input **TextBox** is disabled. Provide a button that allows the user to begin a new game.

**10.12**  Write a program that displays a circle of a random size and calculates and displays the area, radius, diameter and circumference. Use the following equations:

```
diameter = 2 ∞ radius
area = 3.14159 ∞ radius ^ 2
circumference = 2 ∞ 3.14159 ∞ radius
```

All drawing should be done in a **PictureBox** and the results of the calculations should be displayed in a **ListBox**. Each time a button is pressed, a new circle should be displayed.

**10.13**  Enhance your solution to Exercise 10.12 by allowing the user to alter the circle's radius with a scrollbar. The program should work for every radius in the range 100 to 200. As the radius changes, update the values in the **ListBox**. Set the initial radius to 150.

**10.14**  Write a program that uses several **MaskEdit** controls to exercise the **MaskEdit** control's formatting capabilities.

**10.15**  Write a program that contains the series of menus **File**, **Options** and **Help**. The **File** menu contains **Save**, **Print** and **Exit**. **Options** contains a submenu **Colors**. **Colors** contains two submenus **BackGround** and **ForeGround**. The **BackGround** menu contains the colors **white**, **red**, **green** and **blue**. The **ForeGround** menu contains the colors **black**, **yellow**, **cyan** and **gray**. The **Help** menu contains one command—**About**. Provide functionality only for the color commands, **About** and the **Exit** command. Use a **PictureBox** to test the colors. **About** displays a **MsgBox** informing the user that this is Exercise 10.15.

**10.16**  Write program that allows the user to search a **ListBox** for a **String**. Populate the **ListBox** with animal names. When a **String** is found, highlight it. If a **String** is not found, display a **MsgBox** informing the user that the **String** was not found.

**10.17**  Modify your solution to Exercise 10.16 to allow the user to search for **String**s that fit a specified pattern. For example, a user might want to know all the animal names that begin with the letter **c** or they might want to know how many names contain at least one **z**. Provide a second **ListBox** to store any names that match the description.

## Special Section: Building Your Own Computer

In the next several problems, we take a temporary diversion away from the world of high-level language programming. We "peel open" a computer and look at its internal structure. We introduce machine language programming and write several machine language programs. To make this an especially valuable experience, we then build a computer (through the technique of software-based *simulation*) on which you can execute your machine language programs!

**10.18**   (*Machine-Language Programming*) Let us create a computer we will call the Simpletron. As its name implies, it is a simple machine, but, as we will soon see, a powerful one as well. The Simpletron runs programs written in the only language it directly understands, that is, Simpletron Machine Language, or SML for short.

The Simpletron contains an *accumulator*—a "special register" in which information is put before the Simpletron uses that information in calculations or examines it in various ways. All information in the Simpletron is handled in terms of *words*. A word is a signed decimal number such as **+3364**, **-1293**, **7**, **-1**, etc. Each word contains a maximum of four digits. The Simpletron is equipped with a 100-word memory and these words are referenced by their location numbers **00**, **01**, ..., **99**.

Before running an SML program, we must *load* or place the SML program into memory. The first instruction (or statement) of every SML program is always placed in memory location **00**. The simulator will start executing at this location.

Each instruction written in SML occupies one word of the Simpletron's memory (and hence instructions are signed four-digit decimal numbers). We shall assume that the sign of an SML instruction is always plus, but the sign of a data word may be either plus or minus. Each location in the Simpletron's memory may contain either an instruction, a data value used by a program or an unused (and hence undefined) area of memory. The first two digits of each SML instruction are the *operation code* specifying the operation to be performed. SML operation codes are summarized in Fig. 10.43. Each constant is part of **Enum OperationCodes**.

| Operation code | Value | Meaning |
|---|---|---|
| *Input/output operations:* | | |
| **smlRead** | 10 | Read a word from the keyword into a specific location in memory. |
| **smlWrite** | 11 | Write a word from a specific location in memory to the screen. |
| *Load/store operations:* | | |
| **smlLoad** | 20 | Load a word from a specific location in memory into the accumulator. |
| **smlStore** | 21 | Store a word from the accumulator into a specific location in memory. |
| *Arithmetic operations:* | | |
| **smlAdd** | 30 | Add a word from a specific location in memory to the word in the accumulator (leave result in accumulator). |
| **smlSubtract** | 31 | Subtract a word from a specific location in memory from the word in the accumulator (leave result in accumulator). |

**Fig. 10.43** Simpletron Machine Language (SML) operation codes (part 1 of 2).

| Operation code | Value | Meaning |
|---|---|---|
| `smlDivide` | 32 | Divide a word from a specific location in memory into the word in the accumulator (leave result in accumulator). |
| `smlMultiply` | 33 | Multiply a word from a specific location in memory by the word in the accumulator (leave result in accumulator). |
| *Transfer of control operations:* | | |
| `smlBranch` | 40 | Branch to a specific location in memory. |
| `smlBranchNegative` | 41 | Branch to a specific location in memory if the accumulator is negative. |
| `smlBranchZero` | 42 | Branch to a specific location in memory if the accumulator is zero. |
| `smlHalt` | 43 | Halt—the program has completed its task. |

**Fig. 10.43** Simpletron Machine Language (SML) operation codes (part 2 of 2).

The last two digits of an SML instruction are the *operand*—the memory location containing the word to which the operation applies. Let's consider several simple SML programs.

The first SML program (Example 1) reads two numbers from the keyboard and computes and prints their sum. The instruction **1007** reads the first number from the keyboard and places it into location **07** (which has been initialized to zero). Then instruction **1008** reads the next number into location **08**. The *load* instruction, **2007**, puts the first number into the accumulator, and the *add* instruction, **3008**, adds the second number to the number in the accumulator. *All SML arithmetic instructions leave their results in the accumulator.* The *store* instruction, **2109**, places the result back into memory location **09** from which the *write* instruction, **1109**, takes the number and prints it (as a signed four-digit decimal number). The *halt* instruction, **4300**, terminates execution.

| Example 1 Location | Number | Instruction |
|---|---|---|
| 00 | 1007 | (Read A) |
| 01 | 1008 | (Read B) |
| 02 | 2007 | (Load A) |
| 03 | 3008 | (Add B) |
| 04 | 2109 | (Store C) |
| 05 | 1109 | (Write C) |
| 06 | 4300 | (Halt) |
| 07 | 0000 | (Variable A) |
| 08 | 0000 | (Variable B) |
| 09 | 0000 | (Result C) |

The second SML program reads two numbers from the keyboard and determines and prints the larger value. Note the use of the instruction **4107** as a conditional transfer of control, much the same as Visual Basic's **If** statement.

| Example 2 Location | Number | Instruction |
|---|---|---|
| 00 | 1009 | (Read A) |
| 01 | 1010 | (Read B) |
| 02 | 2009 | (Load A) |
| 03 | 3110 | (Subtract B) |
| 04 | 4107 | (Branch negative to 07) |
| 05 | 1109 | (Write A) |
| 06 | 4300 | (Halt) |
| 07 | 1110 | (Write B) |
| 08 | 4300 | (Halt) |
| 09 | 0000 | (Variable A) |
| 10 | 0000 | (Variable B) |

Now write SML programs to accomplish each of the following tasks.

     a)   Use a sentinel-controlled loop to read up to ten positive numbers and compute and print their sum. Input terminates when either ten positive numbers has been input or when a negative number is input.

     b)   Use a counter-controlled loop to read seven numbers, some positive and some negative, and compute and print their average.

     c)   Read a series of numbers and determine and print the largest number. The first number read indicates how many numbers should be processed.

**10.19**   (*A Computer Simulator*) It may at first seem outrageous, but in this problem you are going to build your own computer. No, you will not be soldering components together. Rather, you will use the powerful technique of *software-based simulation* to create a *software model* of the Simpletron. You will not be disappointed. Your Simpletron simulator will turn the computer you are using into a Simpletron, and you will actually be able to run, test and debug the SML programs you wrote in Exercise 10.18. Figure 10.44 shows the initial Simpletron GUI at run time.

When you run your Simpletron simulator, it should display:

```
Welcome to Simpletron! Please enter your SML program one
instruction (or data word) at a time into the TextBox. The SML
memory location is displayed on the button. Press the Done
button when input is completed.
```

The program should display an input **TextBox** in which the user will type each instruction one at a time and a **Done** button for the user to press when the complete SML program has been entered. Simulate the memory of the Simpletron with a one-dimensional array **memory** that has 100 elements. Now assume that the simulator is running and let us examine the GUI as we enter the SML program from Example 2 of Exercise 10.18 (Fig. 10.45).

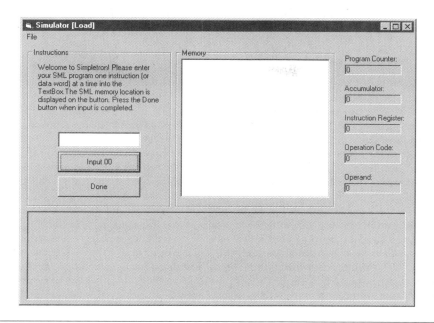

**Fig. 10.44** Simpletron GUI.

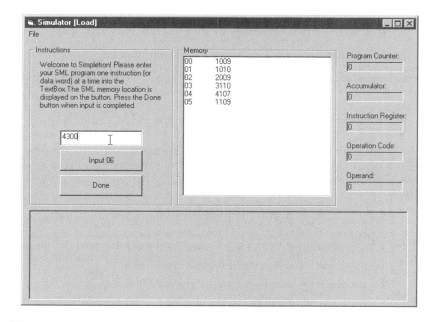

**Fig. 10.45** Entering the program of Example 2.

Your program should use a **CommandButton**'s **Caption** property to display the memory location where the word will be loaded. Each word input by the user is loaded into **memory** and displayed (with its **memory** location) in a **ListBox**. When **Done** is pressed, the title bar displays:

### Simulator [Execute]

The Simulator always displays its state in the title bar. Either **Load**, **Execute** or **Dump** is displayed in the square brackets.

The SML program has now been placed (or loaded) in array **memory**. The Simpletron should provide a **Timer** that—when its event is raised—calls **Execute** to execute one SML instruction. The **Timer** executes an instruction every three seconds (this allows you to see the execution of each instruction in the GUI as it occurs). Execution begins with the instruction in location **00** and, like Visual Basic, continues sequentially unless directed to some other part of the program by a transfer of control (these are discussed shortly). As an instruction is executed, it is highlighted in the **ListBox**.

Use the variable **accumulator** to represent the accumulator register. Use the variable **programCounter** to keep track of the location in **memory** that contains the instruction being performed. Use the variable **operationCode** to indicate the operation currently being performed, i.e., the left two digits of the instruction word. Use the variable **operand** to indicate the **memory** location on which the current instruction operates. Thus, **operand** is the rightmost two digits of the instruction currently being performed. Do not execute instructions directly from **memory**. Rather, transfer the next instruction to be performed from **memory** to a variable called **instructionRegister**. Then "pick off" the left two digits and place them in **operationCode** and "pick off" the right two digits and place them in **operand**. Each of the preceding registers should have a corresponding **Label** in which its current value is displayed at all times. When Simpletron begins execution, the special registers are all initialized to 0 and their corresponding **Label**s should display 0.

Now let us "walk through" the execution of the first SML instruction, **1009** in memory location **00**. This is called an *instruction execution cycle*.

The **programCounter** tells us the location of the next instruction to be performed. We *fetch* the contents of that location from **memory** by using the Visual Basic statement

```
instructionRegister = memory( programCounter )
```

The **operationCode** and the **operand** are extracted from the **instructionRegister** by the statements

```
operationCode = instructionRegister \ 100
operand = instructionRegister Mod 100
```

Now the Simpletron must determine that the **operationCode** is actually a *read* (versus a *write*, a *load*, etc.). A **Select Case** differentiates among the twelve SML operations.

In the **Select Case** structure, the behavior of various SML instructions is simulated as follows (each may require more code than that presented):

*read:*    Display the prompt "**Enter an integer.**" Enable the input **TextBox** so a value can be entered by the user. Read the value entered, convert it to an **Integer** and store it in location **memory( operand )**. See Fig. 10.46.

*load:*    **accumulator = memory( operand )**

*add:*    **accumulator = accumulator + memory( operand )**

*branch:*    We will discuss the branch instructions shortly.

*halt:*    This instruction prints the message
　　　　 **\*\*\* Simpletron execution terminated \*\*\***

The other instructions are left to the reader to implement. When the SML program completes execution, the name and contents of each register as well as the complete contents of **memory** should be displayed. Such a printout is often called a *computer dump*. To help you program your **Dump** procedure, the dump format for Example 2 is shown in Fig. 10.47. Note that a dump after executing a Simpletron program shows the actual values of instructions and data values at the moment execution terminated. These values are displayed in a **PictureBox** in a **Courier** font.

Let us proceed with the execution of our program's first instruction, namely the **1009** in location **00**. As we have indicated, the **Select Case** statement simulates this by prompting the user to enter a value into the input **TextBox**, reading the value, converting the value to an **Integer** and storing it in memory location **memory( operand )**. Because the Simpletron is event driven, it waits for the user to type a value into the input **TextBox** and press button **Enter**. The value is then read into location **09**.

When the user presses **Enter**, simulation of the first instruction proceeds. All that remains is to prepare the Simpletron to execute the next instruction which is done by enabling the **Timer** (so it can raise new **Timer** events). Since the instruction just performed was not a transfer of control, we need merely increment the **programCounter** register as follows:

```
programCounter = programCounter + 1
```

This completes the simulated execution of the first instruction. When the **Timer** interval expires, the entire process (i.e., the instruction execution cycle) begins again with the fetch of the next instruction to be executed.

Now let us consider how the branching instructions—the transfers of control—are simulated. All we need to do is adjust the value in the **programCounter** appropriately. Therefore, the *unconditional branch* instruction (**smlBranch**) is simulated in the **Select Case** as

```
programCounter = operand
```

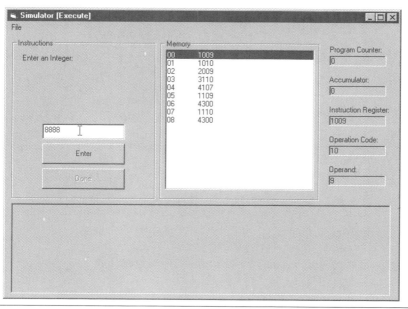

**Fig. 10.46**   Simpletron executing a read instruction.

The conditional *branch if accumulator is zero* instruction is simulated as

```
If accumulator = 0 Then
    programCounter = operand
End If
```

At this point you should implement your Simpletron simulator and run each of the SML programs you wrote in Exercise 10.18. You may embellish SML with additional features and provide for these in your simulator. Figure 10.47 shows the GUI after the Simpletron program finishes executing.

Your simulator should only load and execute one set of instructions. Provide a **File** menu containing an **Exit** command to allow the user to terminate the program.

Your simulator should check for various types of errors. During the program loading phase, for example, each number the user types into the Simpletron's **memory** must be in the range **–9999** to **+9999**. Your simulator should test that each number entered is in this range, and, if not, display a **MsgBox** informing the user to enter a valid instruction.

During the execution phase, your simulator should check for various serious errors, such as attempts to divide by zero, attempts to execute invalid **operationCode**s, **accumulator** overflows (i.e., arithmetic operations resulting in values larger than **+9999** or smaller than **–9999**), and the like. Such serious errors are called *fatal errors*. When a fatal error is detected, your simulator should print an error message in a **MsgBox** such as:

```
*** Attempt to divide by zero ***
*** Simpletron execution abnormally terminated ***
```

and should print a full computer dump in the format we have discussed previously. This will help the user locate the error in the program. You will learn more about error handling in Chapter 13.

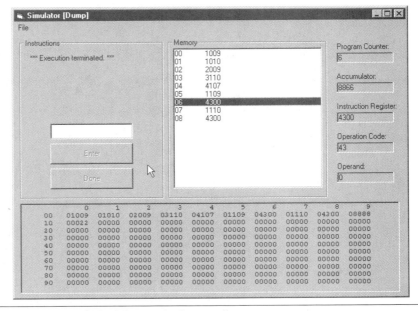

**Fig. 10.47** Simulator GUI at the end of execution.

**10.20** (*Modifications to the Simpletron Simulator*) In Exercise 10.19, you wrote a software simulation of a computer that executes programs written in Simpletron Machine Language (SML). In this exercise, we propose several modifications and enhancements to the Simpletron Simulator. Note: Some of these modifications may conflict with other modifications. For this reason you may choose to implement some of these separately.

a) Extend the Simpletron Simulator's memory to contain 1000 memory locations.
b) Add operation code **34** to allow the simulator to perform modulus calculations.
b) Add operation code **35** to allow the simulator to perform exponential calculations.
c) Modify the simulator to process floating-point values in addition to **Integer** values.
d) Modify the simulator to display a leading **+** or **−** in front of data.

**10.21** (*Simulation: The Tortoise and the Hare*) In this exercise you will recreate one of the truly great moments in history, namely the classic race of the tortoise and the hare.

Our contenders begin the race at "square 1" of 70 squares. Each square represents a possible position along the race course. The finish line is at square 70. The first contender to reach or pass square 70 is rewarded with a pail of fresh carrots and lettuce. The course weaves its way up the side of a slippery mountain, so occasionally the contenders lose ground.

There is a clock that ticks once per second implemented with a **Timer** object. With each tick, your program should randomly adjust the position of the animals according to the following rules:

| Animal | Move type | % of the time | Actual move |
|---|---|---|---|
| Tortoise | Fast plod | 50% | 3 squares to the right |
| | Slip | 20% | 6 squares to the left |
| | Slow plod | 30% | 1 square to the right |
| Hare | Sleep | 20% | No move at all |
| | Big hop | 20% | 9 squares to the right |
| | Big slip | 10% | 12 squares to the left |
| | Small hop | 30% | 1 square to the right |
| | Small slip | 20% | 2 squares to the left |

Keep track of the positions of the animals (values from 1 to 70). Start each animal at position 1 (i.e., the "starting gate"). If an animal slips below position 1, move the animal back to position 1.

Generate the percentages in the preceding table by producing a random integer, $i$, in the range $1 \le i \le 10$. For the tortoise, perform a "fast plod" when $1 \le i \le 5$, a "slip" when $6 \le i \le 7$, or a "slow plod" when $8 \le i \le 10$. Use a similar technique to move the hare.

Begin the race by printing "**BANG!!!!! AND THEY'RE OFF!!!!!**" For each second, print a 70-position line showing the letter **T** in the position of the tortoise and the letter **H** in the position of the hare. Occasionally, the contenders will land on the same square. In this case, the tortoise bites the hare and your program should print **OUCH!!!** beginning at that position. All print positions other than the **T**, the **H**, or the **OUCH!!!** (in case of a tie) should be blank.

After each line is printed, test if either animal has reached or passed square 70. If so, then print the winner and terminate the simulation. If the tortoise wins, print **TORTOISE WINS!!! YAY!!!** If the hare wins, print **Hare wins. Yuch.** If both animals cross the finish line at the same time, you may want to favor the tortoise (the "underdog"), or you may want to print **It's a tie**. Remember to disable the **Timer** when the race finishes. If neither animal wins, continue the simulation. When you are ready to run your program, assemble a group of fans to watch the race. You'll be amazed at how involved your audience gets!

# Advanced Graphical User Interface Concepts

## Objectives

- To understand and be able to create multiple document interface (MDI) programs.
- To be able to create a single document interface (SDI) program utilizing multiple form modules.
- To be able to use template form modules.
- To be able to use the **RichTextBox** control to display formatted text.
- To be able to use the **UpDown** control to select from a list of values.
- To be able to use the **ImageList** control to maintain a set of images for use in an application.
- To be able to use the **ImageCombo** control to select from a list of items displayed with images.
- To be able to use the **FlatScrollBar** control.
- To be able to create native code executables.

*A president is either constantly on top of events or . . . events will soon be on top of him.*
Harry S. Truman

*. . . the wisest prophets make sure of the event first.*
Horace Walpole

*But, soft! what light through yonder window breaks? It is the east, and Juliet is the sun!*
William Shakespeare

*An actor entering through the door, you've got nothing. But if he enters through the window, you've got a situation.*
Billy Wilder

# Outline

## 11.1  Introduction

In this chapter, we continue our study of graphical user interface (GUI) concepts. We begin our discussion with programs that contain multiple form modules—a technique used in more sophisticated applications. We introduce predefined template form modules that encapsulate common program tasks to decrease program development time. Several additional ActiveX controls for enhancing the GUI are discussed. Finally, we demonstrate compiling programs to native code for faster program executables.

## 11.2  Multiple Document Interface (MDI)

In previous chapters, we discussed building applications in Visual Basic that look and act much like other Windows applications (i.e., **Notepad**, **WordPad**, etc.). The applications we developed are called *single document interface (SDI)* applications. When an SDI application such as **Notepad** executes, it can only display one document at a time. Generally, SDI applications have a narrow focus (e.g., Microsoft **Paint** only edits bitmap images).

For example, consider **Notepad** and how it is used. **Notepad** is a simple text editor that allows the user to edit one *document* (e.g., a text file) at a time. To edit multiple documents simultaneously with **Notepad**, the user must execute another instance of **Notepad**. With two separate **Notepad** windows executing simultaneously, the user can view and edit both documents. SDI applications are the most common application type.

An application such as Microsoft **Word** is much more complicated than **Notepad**. **Word** has many more features and a more complex GUI. **Word** allows the user to edit multiple documents simultaneously. Every document opened with **Word** gets its own separate window within **Word**'s GUI. Figure 11.1 shows **Word** with two open documents.

**Word** is an example of a *multiple document interface (MDI)* application (i.e., an application that can have multiple documents open at the same time). **Word** and **Notepad** are two common applications that most Windows users are familiar with and this is why we chose them to introduce SDI and MDI concepts. Keep in mind that a document is not necessarily a text file; a document could also be a bitmap file, a compressed file, etc.

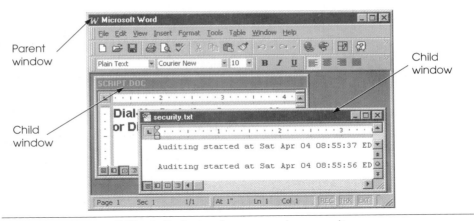

**Fig. 11.1**   Microsoft **Word** displaying two open documents.

*Look-and-Feel Observation 11.1*

*Using an SDI application is often much more intuitive than an MDI application.*

*Software Engineering Observation 11.1*

*MDI applications are usually "feature-rich" and require extensive documentation.*

Each window inside an MDI application is called a *child* window and the application window is called the *parent* window. MDI applications can have many child windows but only one parent window. Child windows behave like any other window (i.e., closing, minimizing, resizing, etc.) with one important difference—a child window can never be moved outside the parent window. A child window's functionality can be different from other child windows. For example, one child window might allow an image to be edited, another child window might allow text to be edited, and a third child window might allow network traffic to be viewed graphically.

Visual Basic allows programmers to quickly and efficiently build MDI applications. An MDI parent window is represented in Visual Basic with an *MDI form.* Selecting the **Project** menu's *Add MDI Form* adds an MDI form to the project. Selecting **Add MDI Form** displays the **Add MDI Form** dialog of Fig. 11.2, which allows the programmer to select a new *MDI Form* or an existing one.

Figure 11.3 shows the MDI form added to the project when **MDI Form** is selected and **Open** pressed. After an MDI form has been added to the project, **Add MDI Form** is disabled. A project can contain only one MDI form.

For discussion purposes, we have enlarged three icons (Fig. 11.4) that represent the three types of forms. We refer to the form type we have been using in previous chapters as a "standard" form. Notice that the MDI forms have two squares and a standard form has only one. The larger of the two squares in an MDI form represents the MDI parent form and the small square represents the MDI child form. One of the squares is always darker than the other—which indicates whether or not it is a parent form or a child form. These icons also display next to the form name in the **Project** window and in the form title bar.

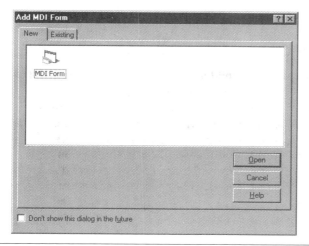

**Fig. 11.2    Add MDI Form** dialog.

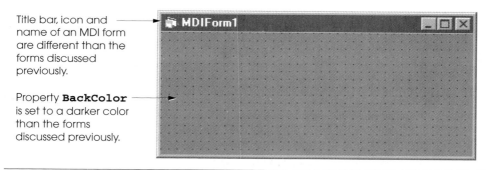

Title bar, icon and name of an MDI form are different than the forms discussed previously.

Property **BackColor** is set to a darker color than the forms discussed previously.

**Fig. 11.3**    An MDI form.

MDI parent form icon     Form icon     MDI child form icon

**Fig. 11.4**    Visual Basic form types.

Creating an MDI application involves using multiple forms (as a minimum the parent form and one child form). Child forms do not exist as a separate form type, but are standard forms with their **MDIChild** properties set to **True**. Additional forms are added to the project by selecting **Add Form** from the **Project** menu. Selecting **Add Form** displays the dialog of Fig. 11.5.

Selecting **Form** adds a new form to the project. Changing the new form's **MDIChild** property to **True** makes the form a child form. The other types of forms listed in the **Add Form** dialog are discussed in Section 11.4.

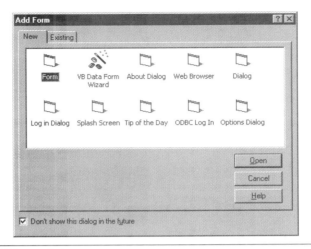

**Fig. 11.5** **Add Form** dialog.

*Common Programming Error 11.1*

*Attempting to execute a form with its **MDIChild** property set to **True** that does not have an MDI parent form is a run-time error.*

Unlike standard forms, MDI parent forms cannot contain the same types of controls. MDI forms can only contain controls that have an **Align** property (e.g., **PictureBox** controls) or controls that are not visible at run-time (e.g., **Timer** controls). The **Align** property describes where a control is located (i.e., top, left, etc.) on a *container* (i.e., a form or **PictureBox**). Figure 11.6 lists the **Align** property constants.

*Common Programming Error 11.2*

*Attempting to add to an MDI parent form a control that does not have an **Align** property or a control that is visible at run-time is a syntax error.*

Figure 11.7 shows a **PictureBox** control **vbAlignTop Align**ed. Notice that the **PictureBox** contains a **ComboBox**. Using a **PictureBox** as a container allows the programmer to indirectly use controls that are not allowed to be placed directly on the MDI parent form. Also notice that the position of the **PictureBox** cannot be affected (i.e., covered) by the child window. A **PictureBox** can be de-emphasized by changing its **BorderStyle** property to **vbBSNone** (**0**) and by changing its **BackColor** to the MDI parent form's **BackColor**.

Like standard forms, both parent forms and child forms can have menus. The **Menu Editor** dialog is used to create the menus (as discussed in Chapter 10). A parent form's menu is displayed only if the *active child window* (i.e., the child form with the focus) does not have any menus. If the active child window has a menu, the parent window displays the child's menu—the parent's menu is not displayed. Figure 11.8 shows how the parent's menu is affected by the child's menu. We do not show any code for this example, because we have a few other MDI issues to discuss. For clarity, we added **(ONE MENU)** and **(NO MENUS)** to the child form title bars. Later in this section we raise this issue again.

| Constant | Value | Description |
|---|---|---|
| **vbAlignNone** | 0 | Control is not aligned. A control placed on an MDI parent form cannot have this value. |
| **vbAlignTop** | 1 | Aligns the control at the top. |
| **vbAlignBottom** | 2 | Aligns the control at the bottom. |
| **vbAlignLeft** | 3 | Aligns the control at the left side. |
| **vbAlignRight** | 4 | Aligns the control at the right side. |

**Fig. 11.6** **Align** property constants.

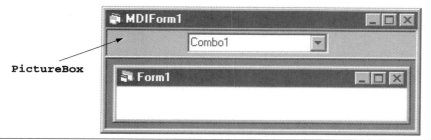

PictureBox

**Fig. 11.7** A **PictureBox** control **vbAlignTop Align**ed.

MDI parent window with two child windows. The MDI parent window contains one menu, **PARENT,** which is displayed because the active child window, **Child window #1**, does not contain any menus.

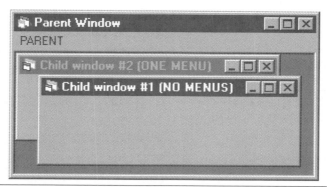

**Fig. 11.8** Demonstrating the MDI parent window/MDI child window relationship (part 1 of 2).

*Look-and-Feel Observation 11.2*

*By convention, MDI applications provide a **Window** menu that allows the user to view and arrange the child windows. Providing a **Window** menu for an MDI application provides a consistent Windows look-and-feel.*

*Software Engineering Observation 11.2*

*In order to avoid confusing the user, MDI parent window menus often duplicate child window menus.*

MDI parent window displaying menu **CHILD2**. **Child window #2** contains one menu, named **CHILD2**, and this menu is displayed as the MDI parent window menu when **Child window #2** becomes the active child window. Visual Basic automatically changes the parent menu.

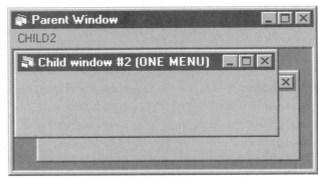

**Fig. 11.8**    Demonstrating the MDI parent window/MDI child window relationship (part 2 of 2).

Child windows can be minimized (by clicking the **_Minimize_** button), maximized (by clicking the **_Maximize_** button) and closed (by clicking the **_Close_** box) independent of each other and the parent window. Figure 11.9 shows two images, one containing a child window maximized and a second containing two child windows minimized. When the parent is minimized or closed, the child windows are minimized or closed.

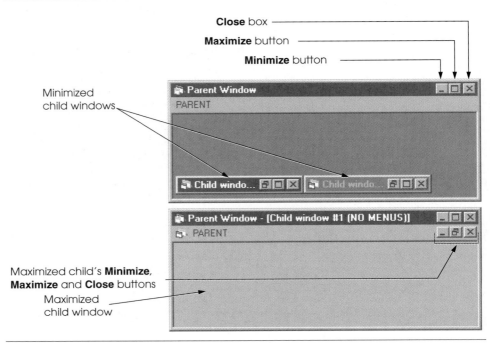

**Fig. 11.9**    Minimized child windows and a maximized child window.

### Look-and-Feel Observation 11.3

*By convention, the MDI parent window* **Caption** *contains the application name, and each MDI child window's* **Caption** *contains the name of its document.*

Notice the title bar in the second image of Fig. 11.9. When a child window is maximized, its **Caption** is automatically combined with the parent window's **Caption**.

Figure 11.10 is an MDI application containing an MDI parent form with three MDI child forms. Each child form contains an **ImageBox** to display an image of a book cover.

```
1   ' Fig. 11.10
2   ' Creating and using MDI
3   Option Explicit        ' General declaration mdiParent
4
5   Private Sub MDIForm_Load()
6      Call Load(frmForm3)      ' Load child frmForm3
7      Call Load(frmForm2)      ' Load child frmForm2
8      Call Load(frmForm1)      ' Load child frmForm1
9   End Sub
10
11  Private Sub mnuItem_Click(Index As Integer)
12     Call mdiParent.Arrange(Index)   ' Arrange children
13  End Sub
14
15  Private Sub mnuC_Click()
16     Call frmForm1.Show     ' Show child frmForm1
17  End Sub
18
19  Private Sub mnuCpp_Click()
20     Call frmForm2.Show     ' Show child frmForm2
21  End Sub
22
23  Private Sub mnuJava_Click()
24     Call frmForm3.Show     ' Show child frmForm3
25  End Sub
26
27  Private Sub mnuExit_Click()
28     Call Unload(frmForm1) ' Unload child frmForm1
29     Call Unload(frmForm2) ' Unload child frmForm2
30     Call Unload(frmForm3) ' Unload child frmForm3
31     End                   ' Terminate execution
32  End Sub
```

**Fig. 11.10**   MDI application (part 1 of 4).

```
33  ' Form frmForm1
34  Option Explicit        ' General declaration frmForm1
35
36  Private Sub Form_Load()
37     imgImage.Picture = LoadPicture("d:\images\ch11\chtp2.gif")
38  End Sub
```

**Fig. 11.10**   MDI application (part 2 of 4).

```
39   ' Form frmForm2
40   Option Explicit      ' General declaration frmForm2
41
42   Private Sub Form_Load()
43       imgImage.Picture = LoadPicture("d:\images\ch11\cpphtp2.gif")
44   End Sub
```

**Fig. 11.10**   MDI application (part 3 of 4).

```
45   ' Form frmForm3
46   Option Explicit      ' General declaration frmForm3
47
48   Private Sub Form_Load()
49       imgImage.Picture = LoadPicture("d:\images\ch11\jhtp2.gif")
50   End Sub
51
52   Private Sub mnuGray_Click()
53       BackColor = QBColor(7)
54   End Sub
55
56   Private Sub mnuWhite_Click()
57       BackColor = vbWhite
58   End Sub
```

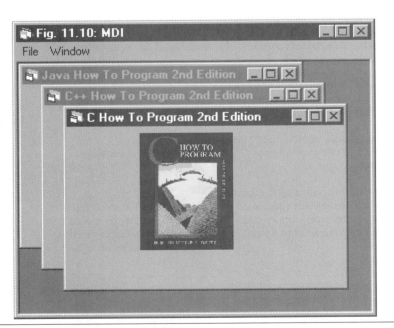

**Fig. 11.10**   MDI application (part 4 of 4).

Since the program uses multiple forms, we must specify in the ***Project Properties*** dialog the ***Startup Object*** (which form is executed when the program runs). MDI applications use the MDI parent form as the **Startup Object**. The **Project Properties** dialog is displayed when ***Project1 Properties*** is selected from the **Project** menu. The project name **Project1** can be altered by changing the contents of the ***Project Name*** TextBox. (Note: If you would like to change the project name later, you can click on the project name in the **Project Explorer** and set its **Name** property in the **Properties** window.) For example, if the contents of the **Project Name** TextBox is changed to **VBHTP**, the **Project Properties**' title bar would read **VBHTP - Project Properties** and the **Project** menu's command to display the **Project Properties** window would read **VBHTP Properties**. Everywhere in the Visual Basic IDE (i.e., **Project** window, title bar, etc.) the name **Project1** is replaced by **VBHTP**. Pressing **OK** closes the dialog.

In the MDI parent form's code, **Option Explicit** forces variable declaration in the form. Since the MDI parent form **mdiParent** is the **Startup Object**, event procedure **MDIForm_Load** is called automatically by Visual Basic to load the parent form into memory. The programmer is responsible for determining when and in what order the child forms are loaded. Lines 6 through 8 use method ***Load*** to load the three child forms into memory. When loading is complete, the child forms are automatically made visible.

The parent form contains two menus, **File** and **Window**. The **File** menu contains the **Exit** command to terminate execution. The **Window** menu contains the menu items **Java**, **C++**, **C**, **Cascade**, **Tile Horizontal** and **Tile Vertical**. The last three items are members of control array **mnuItem** and are used to arrange child forms.

Clicking the **File** menu's **Exit** command results in event procedure **mnuExit_Click** being called. Each form is removed from memory with a call to method ***Unload***. If we do not call **Unload**, Visual Basic will automatically release the form's memory upon termination. The program is terminated when the **End** statement is executed.

*Performance Tip 11.1*

*Methods **Load** and **Unload** allow the programmer to manage program memory. Forms can be **Load**ed and **Unload**ed as they are needed. Calling these methods too frequently can decrease performance.*

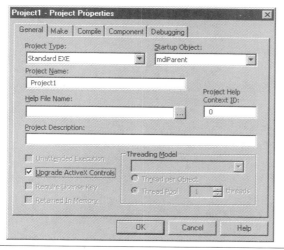

Fig. 11.11   **Project Properties** dialog.

Selecting the **Window** menu's **Java**, **C++** or **C** menu items results in method *Show* being called to display a child form. Although not demonstrated, method *Hide* makes a form invisible—while still retaining the form in memory.

Child windows can be arranged according to the values of Fig. 11.12. MDI parent forms order their child windows with method **Arrange**. Control array **mnuItem**'s selected index (0 - 3) is passed to method **Arrange**. The menu items were arranged such that the index of the menu item also represents the appropriate constant in Fig. 11.12.

As shown in Fig. 11.10, the initial GUI displays the child windows *cascaded* (i.e., the child windows are stacked on top of each other—with all title bars visible). Figure 11.13 shows the child windows tiled horizontally and vertically (the result of selecting **Tile Horizontally** and **Tile Vertically** from the **Window** menu). When *vbArrangeIcons* is used, minimized child forms are arranged at the bottom of the MDI parent window.

The child forms **frmForm1**, **frmForm2** and **frmForm3** all have their **MDIChild** property set to **True**. The code listings for **frmForm1** and **frmForm2** are similar. They both contain an **Image** control that displays the appropriate image. Notice that each form has its own general declaration.

Form **frmForm3** displays an image like **frmForm1** and **frmForm2**. However, **frmForm3** has one menu, **Color**, that contains two commands, **Gray** and **White**. The **Color** menu allows the user to change the **BackColor** of this child form to either gray or white. Figure 11.14 shows **frmForm3** as the active child form after the user has selected **White** from the **Color** menu.

| Constant | Value | Description |
|---|---|---|
| **vbCascade** | 0 | Cascades child windows. |
| **vbTileHorizontal** | 1 | Tiles child windows horizontally. |
| **vbTileVertical** | 2 | Tiles child windows vertically. |
| **vbArrangeIcons** | 3 | Arranges minimized child windows at the bottom of the parent window. |

**Fig. 11.12**  **Arrange** method constants and values.

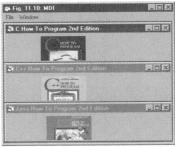
Child windows tiled horizontally.

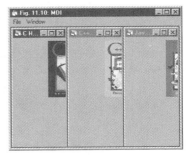
Child windows tiled vertically.

**Fig. 11.13**  Child windows tiled vertically and horizontally.

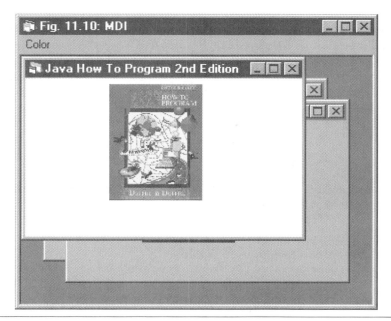

**Fig. 11.14** Form `frmForm3` as the active child form.

Since `frmForm3` is the active child form in Fig. 11.14, its menu **Color** is displayed by the parent form. When a child form that does not have menus is the active child form, the parent form menus are **File** and **Window**.

## 11.3 Multiple Forms

As was demonstrated in the last section, a Visual Basic program can consist of multiple forms. This section focuses on SDI applications that consist of multiple forms. Each form is a standard form that is added to the project using **Add Form** from the **Project** menu. We need not set any special property (as we did for a child form's **MDIChild** property). Each form is customized according to the programmer's preferences.

Like MDI applications, we must specify a **Startup Object** in the **Project Properties** dialog. The startup form is automatically loaded and displayed at execution. Only the startup form is loaded and displayed. As a general rule, this form is used to control when other forms are loaded and displayed.

*Look-and-Feel Observation 11.4*

*Multiple forms can make a program more user friendly, because the amount of information displayed on a single form is reduced. This is preferable to having a single form contain all the GUI features—which can overwhelm the user.*

*Software Engineering Observation 11.3*

*Multiple forms promote software reusability. Each form, once it is created, can potentially be reused by future applications.*

The program of Fig. 11.15 consists of four forms. One form is the startup form, which contains three buttons: **C**, **C++** and **Java**. Pressing **C**, **C++** or **Java** displays one of three *modal* forms (i.e., must be closed before the user can interact with any other Visual Basic form). Each modal form displayed contains one **Image** control, **imgImage**, which displays the image. No code is explicitly written for the three modal forms.

```
1    ' Fig. 11.15
2    ' Using multiple forms
3    Option Explicit                ' General declaration frmStarter
4    Option Base 1
5    Dim mImagesArray(3) As IPictureDisp
6
7    Private Sub Form_Load()
8        ' Load the images into memory
9        Set mImagesArray(1) = LoadPicture("d:\images\ch11\" & _
10                                          "chtp2.gif")
11       Set mImagesArray(2) = LoadPicture("d:\images\ch11\" & _
12                                          "cpphtp2.gif")
13       Set mImagesArray(3) = LoadPicture("d:\images\ch11\" & _
14                                          "jhtp2.gif")
15
16       Call Load(frmForm1)      ' Load frmForm1 into memory
17       Call Load(frmForm2)      ' Load frmForm2 into memory
18       Call Load(frmForm3)      ' Load frmForm3 into memory
19   End Sub
20
21   Private Sub cmdC_Click()
22       frmForm1.imgImage.Picture = mImagesArray(1)
23       Call frmForm1.Show(vbModal)     ' Display the form
24   End Sub
25
26   Private Sub cmdCpp_Click()
27       frmForm2.imgImage.Picture = mImagesArray(2)
28       Call frmForm2.Show(vbModal)     ' Display the form
29   End Sub
30
31   Private Sub cmdJava_Click()
32       frmForm3.imgImage.Picture = mImagesArray(3)
33       Call frmForm3.Show(vbModal)     ' Display the form
34   End Sub
35
36   Private Sub Form_Unload(Cancel As Integer)
37       ' Unload all other forms and terminate execution
38       Call Unload(frmForm1)       ' Unload frmForm1
39       Call Unload(frmForm2)       ' Unload frmForm2
40       Call Unload(frmForm3)       ' Unload frmForm3
41   End Sub
```

**Fig. 11.15**   Using multiple forms (part 1 of 2).

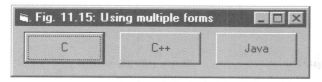

Initial GUI at execution. This form is always visible during execution.

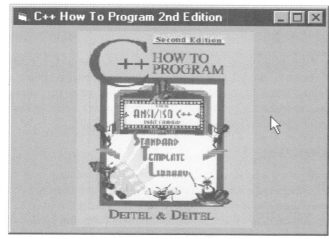

Form that is displayed when user presses **C++**. This form is visible at the same time the image above is. This form is modal—it must be closed before the user can interact with the form containing the three buttons.

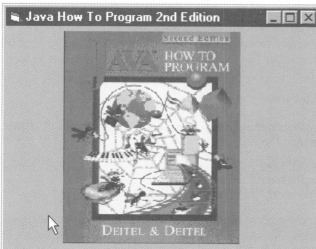

Form that is displayed when user presses **Java**. This form is visible at the same time the first image is. This form is modal—it must be closed before the user can interact with the form containing the three buttons.

**Fig. 11.15**    Using multiple forms (part 2 of 2).

At execution the form specified as the **Startup Object**, **frmStarter**, is loaded into memory and displayed automatically. During the loading process, method **Form_Load** is called. Each element of **IPictureDisp** array **mImagesArray** is assigned an image. We chose **IPictureDisp** as the array type because it is the type returned by function **LoadPicture**. When assigning an **IPictureDisp** variable a value, keyword **Set** is required.

**Common Programming Error 11.3**

*Attempting to assign a value to an **IPictureDisp** variable without using keyword **Set** is a syntax error.*

In **frmStarter_Load**, the other three forms are loaded into memory with calls to method **Load**. The three forms exist in memory, but cannot be seen or interacted with by the user. Pressing a button results in a second form being displayed (in addition to the startup form). Line 12,

```
frmForm1.imgImage.Picture = mImagesArray(0)
```

in **cmdC_Click** assigns an image to the **Picture** property of **imgImage**. When accessing **Public** procedures and controls in another module, the module name precedes the procedure or control. Controls are **Public** by default. Form **frmForm1** is made visible when the line

```
Call frmForm1.Show(vbModal)
```

is executed. Method **Show** displays a modal form and when passed, optional argument **vbModal**. Forms are non-modal, **vbModeless**, by default. If a form has not been previously loaded and method **Show** is called, the form is first loaded and then displayed. **Click** event procedures for **cmdCpp** and **cmdJava** are almost identical in behavior.

Event procedure **Form_Unload** is called when the user presses the **Close** box with the mouse. Each form is removed from memory with a call to method **Unload**. We discuss the use of variable **Cancel** in the next example.

When a program contains many forms it is sometimes difficult to identify the startup form and what is executed at startup. For this purpose Visual Basic provides procedure **Main**. The header for **Main** is

```
Private Sub Main()
```

Procedure **Main** is placed in a standard module (i.e., a **.bas** file) and set in the **Project Properties** dialog as the **Startup Object**.

**Common Programming Error 11.4**

*Specifying **Main** as the **Startup Object** and not providing method **Main** in a standard module is a run-time error.*

Figure 11.16 rewrites the program of Fig. 11.15 to use **Main**. With the exception of execution starting in **Main** and the introduction of event procedure **QueryUnload**, which is used at program termination, program behavior is identical to that of Fig. 11.15.

As the **Startup Object**, **Main** must call for loading and displaying of **frmStarter**—which is accomplished with a call to **Show**. **Main** also loads the three other forms into memory by calling **Load** for each form.

Before a form's **Form_Unload** event procedure is called, event procedure **Form_QueryUnload** is called. **QueryUnload** provides the programmer with a means of preventing a form from unloading. For example, **QueryUnload** might be used to remind the user that they are closing the application without saving the latest changes to their file. The user could then either cancel the close operation, save the file and then exit, or ignore the warning and exit anyway.

**QueryUnload** declares two argument variables, *Cancel* and *UnloadMode*. **Cancel**'s value determines whether or not **Form_Unload** is called. When **Cancel** is **False** (i.e., 0), **Form_Unload** is called and passed **False**. The form is then unloaded. Any **True** (i.e., non-zero) value prevents **Form_Unload** from being called. **Unload-Mode**, although not used in this example, specifies how the **UnLoad** event originated. **QueryUnload** and **Unload** are not called if **End** is executed.

```
1    ' Fig. 11.16 : modMain.bas
2    ' Using multiple forms with procedure Main
3    Option Explicit      ' General declaration modMain
4
5    Private Sub Main()
6       Call frmStarter.Show    ' Display frmStarter
7       Call Load(frmForm1)     ' Load frmForm1 into memory
8       Call Load(frmForm2)     ' Load frmForm2 into memory
9       Call Load(frmForm3)     ' Load frmForm3 into memory
10   End Sub
```

**Fig. 11.16**   Using procedure **Main** as the **Startup Object** (part 1 of 4).

```
11   ' Form frmStarter
12   Option Explicit            ' General declaration frmStarter
13   Option Base 1
14   Dim mImagesArray(3) As IPictureDisp
15
16   Private Sub Form_Load()
17      Set mImagesArray(1) = LoadPicture("d:\images\ch11\" & _
18                                        "chtp2.gif")
19      Set mImagesArray(2) = LoadPicture("d:\images\ch11\" & _
20                                        "cpphtp2.gif")
21      Set mImagesArray(3) = LoadPicture("d:\images\ch11\" & _
22                                        "jhtp2.gif")
23   End Sub
24
25   Private Sub cmdC_Click()
26      frmForm1.imgImage.Picture = mImagesArray(1)
27      Call frmForm1.Show(vbModal)    ' Display the form
28   End Sub
29
30   Private Sub cmdCpp_Click()
31      frmForm2.imgImage.Picture = mImagesArray(2)
32      Call frmForm2.Show(vbModal)    ' Display the form
33   End Sub
34
35   Private Sub cmdJava_Click()
36      frmForm3.imgImage.Picture = mImagesArray(3)
37      Call frmForm3.Show(vbModal)    ' Display the form
38   End Sub
39
```

**Fig. 11.16**   Using procedure **Main** as the **Startup Object** (part 2 of 4).

```
40   Private Sub Form_QueryUnload(Cancel As Integer, _
41                                UnloadMode As Integer)
42      Dim r As Integer
43
44      r = MsgBox("Are you sure you want to exit?", vbYesNo, _
45              "VB6HTP: Fig. 11.16")
46
47      If r = vbNo Then
48          Cancel = True    ' Allow Form_Unload to be called
49      End If
50
51   End Sub
52
53   Private Sub Form_Unload(Cancel As Integer)
54          Call Unload(frmForm1)     ' Unload frmForm1
55          Call Unload(frmForm2)     ' Unload frmForm2
56          Call Unload(frmForm3)     ' Unload frmForm3
57   End Sub
```

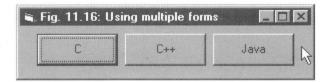

Initial GUI at execution.
This form is always visible
during execution.

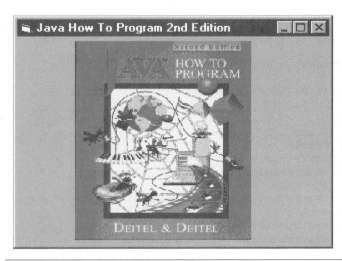

Form that is displayed
when user presses **Java**.
This form is visible at the
same time the image
above is. This form is
modal—it must be closed
before the user can
interact with the form
containing three buttons.

**Fig. 11.16**   Using procedure **Main** as the **Startup Object** (part 3 of 4).

All forms are displayed in the **Forms Layout** window and each one can be individually positioned by the user. Figure 11.17 shows the **Forms Layout** window for the program of Fig. 11.16.

Form that is displayed when user presses **C**. This form is visible at the same time the first image is. This form is modal—it must be closed before the user can interact with the form containing three buttons.

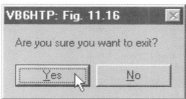

**MsgBox** displayed when the form containing three button's **Close** box is pressed.

**Fig. 11.16**   Using procedure **Main** as the **Startup Object** (part 4 of 4).

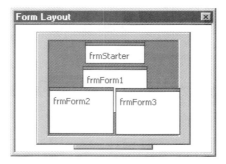

**Fig. 11.17**   **Forms Layout** window displaying multiple forms.

## 11.4  Template Forms

*Template forms* are predefined forms that ship with Visual Basic. The programmer can add these predefined forms to a project. The standard form we have used throughout this book is an example of a template form. Figure 11.18 shows the **Add Form** dialog which displays the template forms. The number of template forms in Fig. 11.18 can vary depending upon the version of Visual Basic being used. Note that each template form is more than just a GUI. Template forms also contain code that the programmer can change to customize the template form.

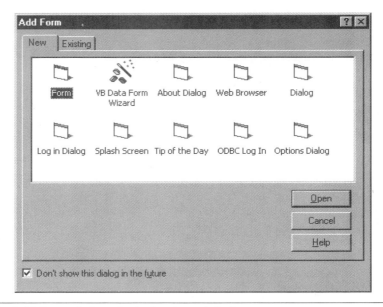

**Fig. 11.18** **Add Form** dialog displaying template forms.

***Software Engineering Observation 11.4***

*Template forms are examples of reusable modules. Common tasks are developed once and reused again in different projects. Template forms reduce development time.*

***Look-and-Feel Observation 11.5***

*Template form GUIs are modeled after the Windows look-and-feel.*

Figure 11.19 shows some common template forms at design time. We provide a brief synopsis next to each template form.

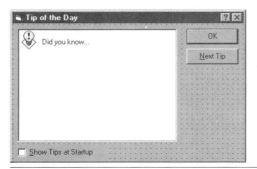

**Tip of the Day**. Displays tips on how to use an applications feature. Typically displayed when an application is loaded.

**Fig. 11.19** Some template forms (part 1 of 2).

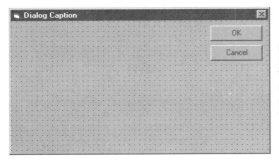

**Dialog.** Allows the program to display information to the user. Since this template form is customizable, it provides greater flexibility than either function **InputBox** or function **MsgBox**.

**About Dialog.** Allows the programmer to display general information about the application. An application usually displays this dialog when the user selects a menu item named **About**.

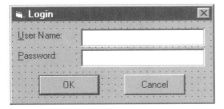

**Login.** Provides a simple GUI for gathering login information.

**Splash Screen.** Used to display information about an application as the application loads.

**Fig. 11.19**   Some template forms (part 2 of 2).

The program of Fig. 11.20 uses the template form **Splash Screen** to display a splash screen. We customize the template form to suit our needs and simulate application loading by creating an artificial time delay. This delay will allow our splash screen to be displayed long enough to be viewed.

```
1   ' Fig. 11.20
2   ' Demonstrating the use of form templates
3   Option Explicit     ' General declaration modMain
4
5   Public Sub Main()
6      Dim delayTime As Double
7      Dim counter As Double
8
9      Call Load(frmSplash)     ' Load frmSplash
10     Call frmSplash.Show      ' Display frmSplash
11     Call Load(frmEmpty)      ' Load frmEmpty
12
13     delayTime = Timer()      ' Get current time
14
15     ' Manufacture a delay to simulate an application
16     ' loading and to give frmSplash a chance to display
17     Do
18        counter = Timer() - delayTime
19        DoEvents
20     Loop While (counter < 10)
21
22     Call Unload(frmSplash)   ' Unload frmSplash
23     Call frmEmpty.Show       ' Display frmEmpty
24  End Sub
```

**Fig. 11.20**   Using a splash screen (part 1 of 4).

```
25  ' Form frmSplash
26  Option Explicit        ' General declaration frmSplash
27
28  Private Sub Form_Load()
29     lblProductName.WordWrap = True
30     lblProductName.Caption = "VB6 How To Program"
31     lblWarning.Caption = ""
32     lblLicenseTo.Caption = ""
33     lblVersion.Caption = "First Edition"
34     lblPlatform.Caption = "Win 95/NT"
35     lblCompany.Caption = "Deitel && Associates, Inc."
36     lblCopyright.Caption = Chr$(169) & "1998. All Rights " & _
37                            "Reserved."
38     imgLogo.Picture = LoadPicture("d:\images\ch11\tbug.gif")
39     lblCompanyProduct.Caption = "Deitel && Deitel / T. R. Nieto"
40  End Sub
```

**Fig. 11.20**   Using a splash screen (part 2 of 4).

```
41  ' Form frmEmpty
42  Option Explicit        ' General declaration frmEmpty
43
44  Private Sub Form_Unload(Cancel As Integer)
45     End
46  End Sub
```

**Fig. 11.20**   Using a splash screen (part 3 of 4).

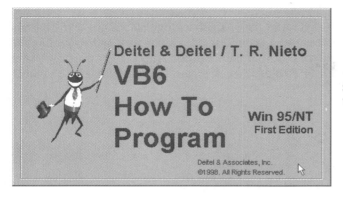

Splash screen displayed
when program is executed.

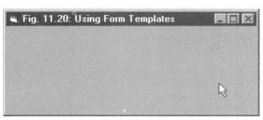

Form displayed when
splash screen disappears.

**Fig. 11.20**  Using a splash screen (part 4 of 4).

In **Main**, methods **Load** and **Show** are called for **frmSplash**. Method **Load** is also called for **frmEmpty**. Form **frmEmpty** is a blank form that represents some application feature that is initially displayed when the application is loaded. Line 13 uses function **Timer** to get the current time, in seconds, since midnight. We use this time to create an artificial delay to simulate other application pieces loading. This also gives our splash screen time to display.

The **Do/Loop While** repetition structure keeps the splash screen displayed as long as 9 seconds has not been exceeded. Function **Timer** is called each iteration of the loop to get the current time. The line

```
DoEvents
```

calls function **DoEvents**, which allows Visual Basic to process other events. If we do not call **DoEvents**, Visual Basic does not respond to events and cannot continue other actions, such as continuing loading the splash screen until the loop terminates execution—and we get inconsistent program behavior. Computational intensive processes, such as looping, consume the processor and make responding to events difficult. **DoEvents** provides a means for the processor to respond to events. After the manufactured delay expires, **frmSplash** is **Unload**ed and **frmEmpty** displayed.

We chose to explicitly set the properties of **frmSplash** at run-time to better illustrate the kinds of control **Name**s the template form contains. We also removed some event procedures that we did not need.

## 11.5 `RichTextBox` Control

The ***RichTextBox*** control is a powerful ActiveX control for manipulating text. Like other ActiveX controls, the **RichTextBox** control is added to the toolbox by selecting ***Microsoft Rich TextBox Control 6.0*** from the **Components** dialog (displayed when **Components** is selected from the **Project** menu). Figure 11.21 shows the **RichTextBox** toolbox icon.

> *Good Programming Practice 11.1*
>
> *Prefixing **RichTextBox** controls with **rtf** allows them to be identified easily.*

The **RichTextBox**, although similar to a **TextBox**, is capable of displaying a special type of formatted text called *rich text*. Rich text is formatted according to a Microsoft standard format called *rich text format* (*RTF*). Rich text files end in **.rtf**. Rich text format stores formatting information along with the text. Figure 11.22 shows a file called **sample.rtf**, which was created with Microsoft **WordPad**.

> *Software Engineering Observation 11.5*
>
> ***RichTextBox** controls have many of the same properties, methods and events associated with a **TextBox**. **RichTextBox** controls of course have additional properties, methods and events that **TextBox**es do not. **RichTextBox**es do not have the 64K-character capacity limit that **TextBox**es do.*

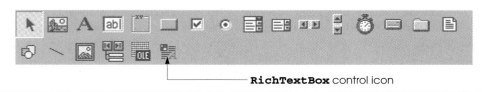

RichTextBox control icon

**Fig. 11.21** **RichTextBox** control toolbox icon.

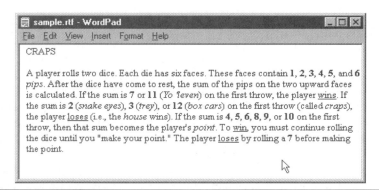

**Fig. 11.22** **WordPad** displaying a rich text formatted file (**sample.rtf**).

Since **WordPad** understands rich text formatted text, the user can edit and format the text. Some editors, such as **Notepad**, are not capable of recognizing rich text format. The result of opening **sample.rtf** in **Notepad** is shown in Fig. 11.23.

If you are already familiar with Hypertext Markup Language (HTML), the rich text format shown in Fig. 11.23 might appear similar. Unlike HTML, a programmer is not expected to code rich text format. When a file is saved as rich text format file, the formatting is written to the file along with the text (Fig. 11.23). Any rich text enabled control or application is capable of displaying the formatted text as shown in Fig. 11.22.

*Portability Tip 11.1*

*Rich text format files are portable to any control or editor capable of understanding rich text format.*

The program of Fig. 11.24 creates a simple rich text editor. The program consists of one **RichTextBox** control, five buttons (three for applying styles, one for a find operation and one for a save operation), one **Label**, one **Frame** and three **CheckBox**es. The user can edit the text, search for words and save the file to disk.

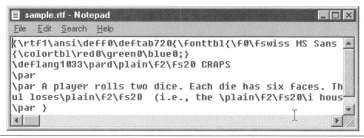

**Fig. 11.23**    **Notepad** displaying an open rich text format file (**sample.rtf**).

```
1   ' Fig. 11.24
2   ' RichTextBox control example
3   Option Explicit
4
5   Private Sub Form_Load()
6       ' Load RTF file into RichTextBox
7       Call rtfTextBox.LoadFile("d:\books\vbhtp\examples\" & _
8                       "chap11\RichTextBox\sample.rtf", rtfRTF)
9
10      ' Allow selected text to be visible even
11      ' after user interacts with RichTextBox
12      rtfTextBox.HideSelection = False
13  End Sub
14
15  Private Sub cmdFind_Click()
16      Dim options As Integer
17      Dim x As Integer, y As Integer
18
```

**Fig. 11.24**    Demonstrating the **RichTextBox** control (part 1 of 3).

```
19        y = chkBoxes.LBound
20        For x = 1 To chkBoxes.Count
21
22            ' Sum the search options
23            If chkBoxes(y).Value Then
24                options = options + y
25            End If
26
27            y = y * 2    ' Adjust y for next control array element
28        Next x
29
30        ' Find text specified in TextBox
31        Call rtfTextBox.Find(txtKey.Text, , , options)
32     End Sub
33
34     Private Sub cmdSave_Click()
35        ' Save file to disk
36        Call rtfTextBox.SaveFile("d:\books\vbhtp\examples\" & _
37                         "chap11\RichTextBox\sample.rtf", rtfRTF)
38     End Sub
39
40     Private Sub cmdBold_Click()
41        rtfTextBox.SelBold = Not rtfTextBox.SelBold
42     End Sub
43
44     Private Sub cmdItalic_Click()
45        rtfTextBox.SelItalic = Not rtfTextBox.SelItalic
46     End Sub
47
48     Private Sub cmdUnderline_Click()
49        rtfTextBox.SelUnderline = Not rtfTextBox.SelUnderline
50     End Sub
```

**RichTextBox** control

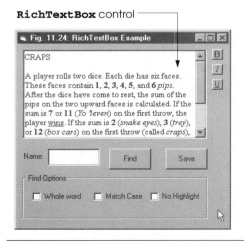

Initial GUI at execution.

**Fig. 11.24**   Demonstrating the **RichTextBox** control (part 2 of 3).

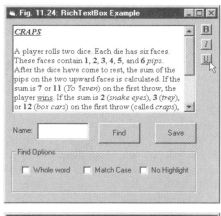

GUI after user has selected the word **CRAPS** and pressed the **B**, **I** and **U** buttons.

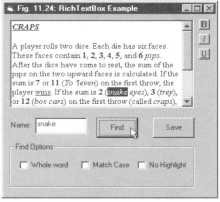

GUI after user has entered **snake** in the **TextBox** and pressed **Find**.

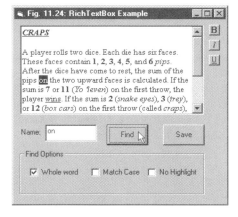

GUI after user enters **on** in the **TextBox**, checks **Whole word** and presses **Find**.

**Fig. 11.24** Demonstrating the **RichTextBox** control (part 3 of 3).

Design-time property **_ScrollBars_** determines whether or not the **RichTextBox** control displays any scrollbars. The default setting is **_rtfNone_**, **0**, which does not display any scrollbars. For this example, the **RichTextBox** has one vertical scrollbar because

**ScrollBars** is *rtfVertical*, **2**. Setting *rtfHorizontal*, **1** displays one horizontal scrollbar and setting *rtfBoth*, **3** displays one horizontal scrollbar and one vertical scrollbar. For **rtfVertical**, **rtfHorizontal** and **rtfBoth**, the *Multiline* property must be set to **True** (the default) in order to see the scrollbars.

When using **rtfHorizontal** or **rtfBoth**, the horizontal scrollbar appears only when the **RichTextBox**'s right margin value (in twips) is greater than or equal to the **RichTextBox**'s **Width**. The *RightMargin* property specifies the right margin. *Note:* A **RightMargin** value slightly less than the **Width** often results in the horizontal scrollbar being displayed. When a horizontal scrollbar is not used, text automatically wraps when the right margin is encountered.

In **Form_Load**, **sample.rtf**'s content is loaded into the **RichTextBox**, **rtfTextBox**, with a call to function *LoadFile*. The first argument passed to **LoadFile** specifies the file name, and the second argument specifies the file type (*rtfRTF*, the default, for rich text format or *rtfText* for text). The statement

**rtfTextBox.HideSelection = False**

sets property *HideSelection* to **False**, which specifies that any text highlighted in the **RichTextBox** should remain highlighted when the **RichTextBox** loses the focus.

Highlighting (i.e., selecting) characters and pressing **B**, **I** or **U** applies bold, italic or underline formats to the highlighted characters. **RichTextBox** properties *SelBold*, *SelItalic* and *SelUnderline* specify whether or not the highlighted text is bold, italic or underlined, respectively. When set to **True**, the formatting is applied.

Pressing **Save** saves the file to disk. Function *SaveFile* takes the same two argument types as **LoadFile**—a file name expressed as a **String** and the format type, which defaults to **rtfRTF**.

 ***Common Programming Error 11.5***

*When using **rtfRTF** in **LoadFile** or **SaveFile**, opening a file type other than a rich text format file is a run-time error.*

The find capability finds the first occurrence of the text typed in the **TextBox**. Finding the next occurrence is left to the reader as an exercise. Each of three **CheckBox**es inside the **Frame** is part of a control array named **chkBoxes**. The **Index** properties are set to the values 2, 4 and 8—which correspond to the constants listed in Fig. 11.25.

In **cmdFind_Click**, variable **y** is assigned **chkBoxes.LBound** (i.e., **2**). Inside the **For** loop, each **chkBoxes** element's **Value** is tested. If **True**, **y**'s value is added to **options**. The value of **y** is then multiplied by **2** such that the next control array element can be accessed. The statement

| Constant | Value | Description |
|---|---|---|
| **rtfWholeWord** | 2 | Match the whole text and not text fragments. |
| **rtfMatchCase** | 4 | Match the exact case. |
| **rtfNoHighlight** | 8 | Do not highlight found text. |

**Fig. 11.25   RichTextBox Find** constants.

```
Call rtfTextBox.Find(txtKey.Text, , , options)
```

calls function *Find* to search for the first occurrence of **txtKey.Text**. The last three optional arguments passed to **Find** are the starting index, the ending index, and the search options. Each character within the **RichTextBox** has a unique **Integer** index; the first character has an index of zero. When the starting index and the ending index are omitted and text is not highlighted, the entire range of indexes is searched. If text is highlighted, the index range of the highlighted text is searched. Options is an **Integer** value corresponding to the sum of one or more of the constants listed in Fig. 11.25. Although not used in this example, function **Find** returns either the index of the found text's first letter or **–1**, indicating that the text searched for was not found.

## 11.6 UpDown Control

An *UpDown* control is an ActiveX control that increments or decrements the value of another control (called a *buddy control*). The **UpDown** control is one of several controls that are added when **Microsoft Windows Common Controls-2 6.0** is selected in the **Components** dialog. Figure 11.26 shows the toolbox, which contains five additional icons (from **Microsoft Windows Common Controls-2 6.0**).

Once an **UpDown** control is placed on the form, its **BuddyControl** property can be set to another control. Figure 11.27, which shows Fig. 11.28's GUI at design-time, shows an **UpDown** control, a **TextBox** control and a **Timer** control. The **UpDown** control consists of two arrows.

UpDown control toolbox icon

**Fig. 11.26  UpDown** control toolbox icon.

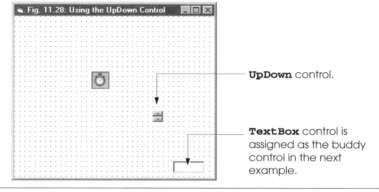

UpDown control.

TextBox control is assigned as the buddy control in the next example.

**Fig. 11.27**   GUI for Fig. 11.28 at design time.

*Good Programming Practice 11.2*

*Prefixing the name of* **UpDown** *controls with* **upd** *allows them to be identified easily.*

The program of Fig. 11.28 modifies an example from Chapter 9 to allow the user to control the drawing rate by using an **UpDown** control. The **UpDown** control sets the number of milliseconds for a **Timer Interval**.

```
1    ' Fig. 11.28
2    ' Demonstrating the UpDown Control
3    Option Explicit
4
5    Private Sub Form_Load()
6       txtSpeed.Text = tmrTimer.Interval
7
8       With updSpeed
9          ' Make txtSpeed the buddy control
10         .BuddyControl = txtSpeed
11
12         .Min = 0         ' Minimum value
13         .Max = 1000      ' Maximum value
14         .Wrap = True     ' When Min is exceeded wrap to 1000
15                          ' and when Max is exceeded wrap to 0
16
17         .Increment = 100  ' Increment/decrement amount
18      End With
19
20   End Sub
21
22   Private Sub DrawShape()
23      Dim x As Single, y As Single
24      Dim totalRadians As Single, r As Single
25      Dim a As Single, theta As Single
26
27      Call Randomize
28      Scale (3, -3)-(-3, 3)           ' Change scale
29      totalRadians = 8 * Atn(1)       ' Circle in Radians
30
31      ForeColor = QBColor(Rnd() * 15)
32
33      a = 3 * Rnd()  ' Offset used in equation
34
35      For theta = 0 To totalRadians Step 0.01
36         r = a * Sin(10 * theta) ' Multi-Leaved Rose
37         x = r * Cos(theta)       ' y coordinate
38         y = r * Sin(theta)       ' x coordinate
39         PSet(x, y)               ' Turn pixel on
40      Next theta
41
42   End Sub
43
```

**Fig. 11.28**   Demonstrating the **UpDown** control (part 1 of 2).

```
44  Private Sub tmrTimer_Timer()
45      Call DrawShape    ' Call when time interval expires
46  End Sub
47
48  Private Sub updSpeed_Change()
49      ' Get UpDown control's value as it is changed
50      ' and assign to Timer's Interval property and
51      ' TextBox's Text property
52      tmrTimer.Interval = updSpeed.Value
53      txtSpeed.Text = updSpeed.Value
54  End Sub
```

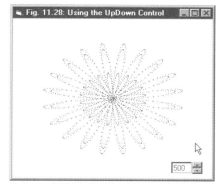

Initial GUI at execution.

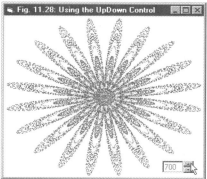

GUI after user clicks the **UpDown** control's up arrow twice. The drawing rate decreases.

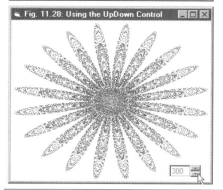

GUI after user clicks the **UpDown** control's down arrow four times. The drawing rate increases.

**Fig. 11.28**   Demonstrating the **UpDown** control (part 2 of 2).

In **Form_Load**, several properties for the **UpDown** control **updSpeed** are set using statement *Width*—which provides a convenient syntax for setting multiple properties for a single control. The **Width** statement can be used with any control and is terminated with keywords *End Width*. **TextBox txtSpeed** is assigned as **updSpeed**'s buddy control with the line

```
.BuddyControl = txtSpeed
```

Once a buddy control is assigned, the **UpDown** control appears at run-time next to the buddy control (its design time position does not change, however). When the buddy control is a **Textbox**, the combination of the **UpDown** control and the **TextBox** control is sometimes called a *spinner control*.

The **UpDown** control also contains another property for setting the buddy control, called *AutoBuddy*. Setting **AutoBuddy** to **True** at design-time causes the **UpDown** control to associate the previous control (based on **TabIndex**) as the buddy control. If a previous control does not exist, the next control (based on **TabIndex**) becomes the buddy control. An **UpDown** control without a buddy control behaves like a simplified scrollbar.

The minimum and maximum values of the **UpDown** control are set with the lines

```
.Min = 0
.Max = 1000
```

Property *Min* sets the minimum value and property *Max* sets the maximum value that the **UpDown** control's *Value* property can have. **Value** cannot exceed **Min** or **Max**. When set to **True**, the *Wrap* property sets **Value** to **Min** when an attempt is made to exceed **Max** and sets **Value** to **Max** when an attempt is made to exceed **Min**. Property *Increment* specifies the increment or decrement of **Value** when an arrow is clicked. If property **Wrap** is **False**, incrementing or decrementing stops when **Min** or **Max** is reached.

*Common Programming Error 11.6*

*Attempting to assign a negative number to **Increment** is a run-time error.*

By default, an **UpDown** control appears to the right of its buddy control because its *Alignment* property is set to constant *cc2AlignmentRight*, **1**. Changing the **Alignment** property to *cc2AlignmentLeft*, **0** displays the **UpDown** control to the left of the buddy control.

By default, an **UpDown** control's arrows point left and right. The *Orientation* property, which defaults to *cc2OrientationHorizontal*, **1**, specifies orientation. Changing the **Orientation** to *cc2OrientationVertical*, **0** results in the **UpDown** control's arrows pointing up and down.

*Common Programming Error 11.7*

*Attempting to set the **Orientation** property at run-time is a run-time error.*

**Sub** procedure **DrawShape** performs the calculations to generate the flower-shaped output. **DrawShape** is called by **tmrTimer_Timer**.

Clicking either of the **UpDown** controls arrows results in *updSpeed_Change* being called. The **Timer**'s **Interval** property and the **TextBox**'s **Text** property are assigned the **UpDown** controls new **Value**.

## 11.7 `ImageList` Control

ActiveX control *`ImageList`* loads and stores a group of images for use by other controls. In the next section, we use an **`ImageList`** control to store the images displayed by an **`ImageCombo`** control. **`ImageList`** is one of several ActiveX controls that are added to the project when *Microsoft Windows Common Controls 6.0* is selected in the **Components** dialog. Figure 11.29 displays the toolbox and labels the **`ImageList`** control.

**Good Programming Practice 11.3**

*Prefixing the name of* **`ImageList`** *controls with* **`ils`** *allows them to be identified easily.*

Like **`Timer`**s and **Common Dialog**s, **`ImageList`** controls are visible only at design time. Figure 11.30 shows a form with an **`ImageList`** control at design time.

Right-clicking the **`ImageList`** control displays a pop-up menu. Selecting **Properties** displays the **`ImageList`**'s **Property Pages** dialog that contains three tabs: *General*, *Images* and *Color*. The tab we are interested in is **Images**, as shown in Fig. 11.31.

**`ImageList`** control toolbox icon ─────────

**Fig. 11.29    `ImageList`** control toolbox icon.

**Fig. 11.30    `ImageList`** control at design time.

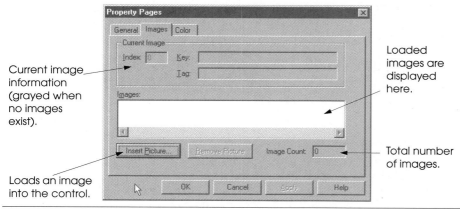

Current image information (grayed when no images exist).

Loads an image into the control.

Loaded images are displayed here.

Total number of images.

**Fig. 11.31  `ImageList` Property Pages** dialog displaying the **`Images`** tab.

Pressing **_Insert Picture..._** displays the **_Select picture_** dialog (Fig. 11.32). The programmer navigates the directory structure, provides the proper file name and presses **Open**. Pressing **Open** closes the dialog and the image is then loaded into the `ImageList` control.

Figure 11.33 shows the results of adding one image to the `ImageList` control. The image is assigned an index of 1.

Figure 11.34 shows the `ImageList` **Property Pages** displaying six images. Each image was added individually by pressing **Insert Picture...**. Pressing **OK** (or **Apply** when it is enabled) closes the **Property Pages** dialog.

The images are now ready for use. The program of Fig. 11.35 randomly draws these images on the form. A `Timer` control is used to control when the next drawing operation occurs.

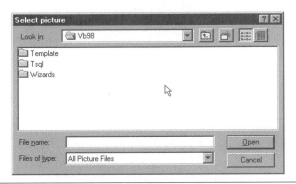

**Fig. 11.32** **Select picture** dialog displayed when **Insert Picture...** is pressed.

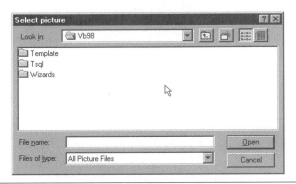

**Fig. 11.33** `ImageList` **Property Pages** displaying a loaded image.

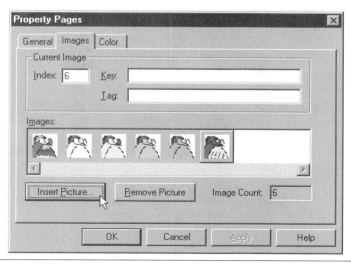

Fig. 11.34 **ImageList Property Pages** displaying six images.

```
1   ' Fig. 11.35
2   ' Using an ImageList control.
3   Option Explicit
4
5   Private Sub Form_Load()
6       Call Randomize
7       tmrClock.Interval = 500    ' Milliseconds
8   End Sub
9
10  Private Sub tmrClock_Timer()
11      Dim r As Integer
12
13      r = Int(6 * Rnd()) + 1
14
15      ' Draw an image from ilsTheImages at a random position
16      ' on the form.
17      Call PaintPicture(ilsTheImages.ListImages(r).Picture, _
18                        Rnd() * Width, Rnd() * Height)
19  End Sub
```

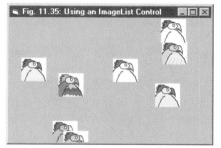

GUI at run-time. Every 500 milliseconds a new image is drawn at a random location on the form.

Fig. 11.35   Using an **ImageList** control.

An image is drawn with the statement

```
Call PaintPicture(ilsTheImages.ListImages(r).Picture, _
                  Rnd() * Width, Rnd() * Height)
```

Method **PaintPicture** draws an image at a specified set of coordinates. The first argument specifies the image to be drawn. Each item stored in the **ImageList** is a **ListImage** object—which encapsulates all the information about the image. These **ListImage** objects are stored in an array-like entity known as a *collection*. To access an individual element in the **ListImages** *collection*, we provide an index. Indexes are assigned when an image is added to the **ImageList** control—which is specified in the **Current Image Frame**'s **Index TextBox** (see Fig. 11.34). The actual image contained in a **ListImage** object is accessed through the **Picture** property. The last two arguments passed to **PaintPicture** are the *x* and *y* coordinates where the image should be drawn on the form (the coordinates indicate the image's upper-left corner).

## 11.8 ImageCombo Control

The **ImageCombo** control is similar to a **ComboBox** control with a few major differences. The primary difference is that an **ImageCombo** can display images next to its items. The **ImageCombo** control is one of the ActiveX controls added to the project when **Microsoft Windows Common Controls 6.0** is selected in the **Components** dialog. Figure 11.29 displays the toolbox and labels the **ImageCombo** control.

*Good Programming Practice 11.4*

*Prefixing the name of **ImageCombo** controls with **imgcbo** allows them to be identified easily.*

The program of Fig. 11.37 uses an **ImageCombo** control to display six images stored in an **ImageList**. When the user selects an **ImageCombo** item, the image associated with the item is displayed in a borderless **PictureBox**.

The assignment

```
imgcboIC.ImageList = ilsImageList
```

associates **ImageList ilsImageList** with **ImageCombo imgcboIC**. Once associated with an **ImageList**, the **ImageCombo** control can use images from the **Image-List**. We will discuss how this is done when we discuss line 27.

Each item in an **ImageCombo** control is a **ComboItem** object—which is part of a **ComboItems** collection. Each **ComboItem** encapsulates all the information about a **ImageCombo** item.

ImageCombo control toolbox icon

**Fig. 11.36   ImageCombo** control toolbox icon.

```
1   ' Fig. 11.37
2   ' Demonstrating the ImageComboBox
3   Option Explicit
4   Option Base 1
5
6   Private Sub Form_Load()
7       Dim x As Integer            ' Looping variable
8       Dim images(6) As String    ' Names of images
9
10      ' User cannot modify contents of ImageCombo
11      imgcboIC.Locked = True
12
13      ' Use images from ImageList ilsImageList
14      imgcboIC.ImageList = ilsImageList
15
16      ' Populate ImageCombo
17      For x = 1 To 6
18          images(x) = "bird" & x & ".bmp"
19
20          ' Specify the index (i.e., x), a name used
21          ' for identification (i.e., id1, id2, etc.),
22          ' and the displayed name (i.e., images(x))
23          Call imgcboIC.ComboItems.Add(x, "id" & x, images(x))
24
25          ' Set the items image (i.e., give id1 the image
26          ' located in ilsImageList(1))
27          imgcboIC.ComboItems("id" & x).Image = x
28      Next x
29
30      ' Display First ImageCombo item
31      imgcboIC.ComboItems.Item("id1").Selected = True
32  End Sub
33
34  Private Sub imgcboIC_Click()
35      Dim i As Integer
36
37      ' Get the index of the selected item
38      i = imgcboIC.SelectedItem.Index
39
40      ' Display the picture that is selected
41      picPicture.Picture = ilsImageList.ListImages(i).Picture
42
43      ' Transfer focus to PictureBox
44      picPicture.SetFocus
45  End Sub
```

Initial GUI at execution. Displayed
item is highlighted by default.

**Fig. 11.37**   Using an **ImageCombo** control (part 1 of 2).

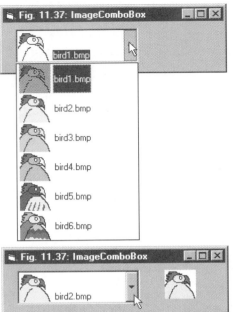

GUI after user clicks the down arrow. The drop-down list displays images and text strings.

GUI after user selects **bird2.bmp**. The selected item's image is displayed in a **PictureBox**.

**Fig. 11.37** Using an **ImageCombo** control (part 2 of 2).

The statement

```
Call imgcboIC.ComboItems.Add(x, "id" & x, images(x))
```

creates and adds a **ComboItem** to the **ComboItems** collection. The first argument passed to method **Add**, **x**, specifies the index within the collection. The second argument specifies the *key* (i.e., a name that can be used in place of the index). The third argument specifies the **ComboItem**'s text.

Each **ComboItem** in the **ComboItems** collection is accessible either by specifying an index or by specifying a key. Line 27's statement,

```
imgcboIC.ComboItems("id" & x).Image = x
```

sets the **Image** for each **ComboItem**. The right side of the assignment, **x**, corresponds to a **ListImage** index—from the associated **ImageList** specified on line 14. Each image need not be specified separately. We could have specified the image as a fourth argument in line 23 as in

```
Call imgcboIC.ComboItems.Add(x, "id" & x, images(x), x)
```

The **ImageCombo**'s selected item is set with the line

```
imgcboIC.ComboItems.Item("id1").Selected = True
```

**ComboItem id1**'s *Selected* property is set to **True**. When the **ImageCombo** control has the focus, the **Selected** item is highlighted.

Selecting an **ImageCombo** item with the mouse results in **imgcboIC_Click** being called. **ComboItems'** *SelectedItem* property contains the selected **ComboItem**. The **ComboItem** index is stored in the *Index* property. The **ListImage Picture** corresponding to the selected **ComboItem**'s index is assigned to **PictureBox picPicture**'s **Picture** property with the statement

```
picPicture.Picture = ilsImageList.ListImages(i).Picture
```

Focus is then transferred to **picPicture** with a call to method **SetFocus**—which results in the item displayed in the **ImageCombo** not being highlighted.

## 11.9 **FlatScrollBar** Control (Professional and Enterprise Editions)

ActiveX control *FlatScrollBar* is an enhanced scrollbar and is one of several controls that are added when *Microsoft Windows Common Controls-2 6.0* is selected in the **Components** dialog. Figure 11.38 labels the **FlatScrollbar** control toolbox icon.

 *Good Programming Practice 11.5*

*Prefixing the name of **FlatScrollbar** controls with **fsb** allows them to be identified easily.*

**FlatScrollbar**s have the same basic functionality as scrollbars, but with a few added enhancements—such as the ability to disable one or both of the scroll arrows and the ability to change the interface of the control (i.e., have a "flat" scrollbar as opposed to a raised 3D look).

Property *Arrows* controls which scroll arrows are enabled. Figure 11.39 summarizes the constants that control enabling and disabling of **FlatScrollBar** scroll arrows.

FlatScrollBar control toolbox icon

**Fig. 11.38 FlatScrollBar** control toolbox icon.

| Constant | Value | Description |
|---|---|---|
| **cc2Both** | 0 | Default. Both scroll arrows are enabled. |
| **cc2LeftUp** | 1 | Only the left scroll arrow is enabled for horizontal **FlatScrollBar**s, and only the up scroll arrow is enabled for vertical **FlatScrollBar**s. |
| **cc2RightDown** | 2 | Only the right scroll arrow is enabled for horizontal **FlatScrollBar**s, and only the down scroll arrow is enabled for vertical **FlatScrollBar**s. |

**Fig. 11.39 Arrows** property constants.

Property **Appearance** specifies the **FlatScrollBar** control interface. Figure 11.40 lists property **Appearance** constants and shows the interface for each constant.

Properties **LargeChange**, **SmallChange**, **Max**, **Min**, **Value** and **Orientation** (either **cc2OrientationVertical** or **cc2OrientationHorizontal**) are the same as a scrollbar control.

Figure 11.41 allows the user to set the color displayed in a **PictureBox** using three **FlatScrollBar**s (which represent the red, green and blue intensities). Three **OptionButton**s allow the user to determine the interfaces for the three **FlatScrollBar**s.

| Constant | Value | Interface | Description |
|---|---|---|---|
| **fsb3D** | 0 | 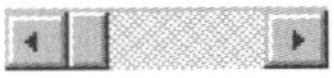 | Interface is 3D. |
| **fsbFlat** | 1 | 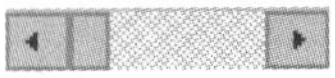 | Default. Interface is flat. |
| **fsbTrack3D** | 2 |  | Interface is flat. Scroll box and scroll arrows are 3D when mouse pointer is placed on top of them. |

**Fig. 11.40  Appearance** property constants.

```
1    ' Fig. 11.41
2    ' Demonstrating FlatScrollBars
3    Option Explicit
4
5    Private Sub Form_Load()
6       Dim x As Integer
7
8       For x = fsbScroll.LBound To fsbScroll.UBound
9
10         With fsbScroll(x)
11            .Min = 0              ' Minimum value
12            .Max = 255            ' Maximum value
13            .LargeChange = 10     ' Large change value
14            .SmallChange = 1      ' Small change value
15         End With
16
17      Next x
18
19   End Sub
20
21   Private Sub fsbScroll_Change(Index As Integer)
22      Dim c(2) As Integer, x As Integer
23
24      ' Read value of each FlatScrollBar into array
25      For x = LBound(c) To UBound(c)
26         c(x) = fsbScroll(x).Value
27      Next x
```

**Fig. 11.41**  Demonstrating **FlatScrollBar**s (part 1 of 2).

```
28
29        picColor.BackColor = RGB(c(0), c(1), c(2))
30   End Sub
31
32   Private Sub optOption_Click(Index As Integer)
33        Dim x As Integer
34
35        ' Change appearance of FlatScrollBars
36        For x = optOption.LBound To optOption.UBound
37           fsbScroll(x).Appearance = Index
38        Next x
39
40   End Sub
```

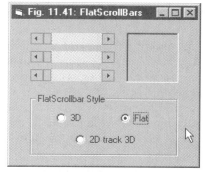

Initial GUI at execution.

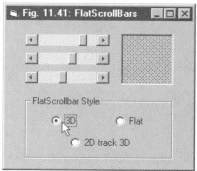

GUI after user has moved scroll boxes and clicked **3D**.

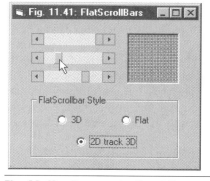

GUI after user has moved the scroll boxes and clicked **2D Track 3D**. The middle **FlatScrollBar**'s scroll box appears raised (i.e., 3D) be-cause the mouse pointer is on it.

**Fig. 11.41**    Demonstrating **FlatScrollBar**s (part 2 of 2).

*Look-and-Feel Observation 11.6*

**FlatScrollBar**s *provide a consistent look for Internet Explorer 4.0 GUIs.*

In **Form_Load**, properties **Max**, **Min**, **LargeChange** and **SmallChange** are set. Clicking a **FlatScrollBar** results in a call to **fsbScroll_Change**. The **Value** of each **FlatScrollBar** is used in the RGB color for the **PictureBox**'s **BackColor**.

Clicking an **OptionButton** results in the **optOption_Click** being called. The **Appearance** property of each **FlatScrollBar** is set to the **OptionButton** control array element's index (0, 1 and 2, respectively) that was clicked.

## 11.10 Native Code Compilation (Professional and Enterprise Editions)

Visual Basic programs by default are compiled to an *intermediate level* of instructions called *p-code*. At run-time, p-code instructions are interpreted by the *run-time engine* **msvbvm60.dll**. Before a p-code statement can be executed, it must be translated to an equivalent set of low-level instructions (called *machine code* or *native code*). Only when a line is about to be executed is it compiled down to native code.

Visual Basic provides the option of compiling directly to native code. Native code compilation often increases execution speed for computation-intensive programs and also allows optimizations that are not possible with p-code. P-code's main advantage over native code is that it is smaller in size.

To change compilation from p-code to native code, select **Compile to Native Code** on the **Project Properties** dialog's **Compile** tab (Fig. 11.42). The **Project Properties** dialog is displayed when **Project Properties** is selected from the **Project** menu.

*Software Engineering Observation 11.6*

*There is often a trade-off between executable size and execution speed.* **Optimize for Fast Code** *can increase execution speed while also increasing the size of the compiled program.* **Optimize for Small Code** *can reduce the compiled program size while reducing execution speed.*

**CheckBox** *Favor Pentium Pro(tm)* provides an option for optimizing code specifically for the Pentium Pro™ microprocessor. **CheckBox** *Create Symbolic Debug Info* provides the option of creating a file for use with debuggers. We do not discuss *Advanced Optimizations* because if not used carefully, many different types of errors can be introduced into a program.

Selecting *Make Project1.exe...* (where **Project1** is the project name) from the **File** menu creates an *executable file* (i.e., a **.exe** file). Selecting **Make Project1.exe...** displays a file dialog titled *Make Project* for specifying the file name and directory location. Pressing **OK** creates a native code executable according to the settings specified in the **Project Properties** dialog. Native code executables still use **msvbvm60.dll** at run-time for certain procedure calls.

Double-clicking the **.exe** file in **Windows Explorer** executes the file. Also, in a DOS command prompt, typing the **.exe** file name at the and pressing *Enter* executes the program if the program is in the current directory specified in the DOS prompt.

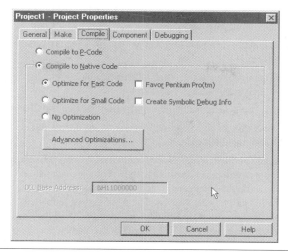

**Fig. 11.42 Project Properties** dialog displaying the **Compile** tab.

## Summary

- When a single document interface (SDI) application executes, it can contain only a single document (i.e., display one document). SDI applications generally have a narrow focus (e.g., Microsoft **Paint** only edits images). SDI applications are the most common application type.

- Multiple document interface (MDI) applications can have multiple documents open at the same time. Documents are text files, bitmap files, compressed files, etc.

- Each window inside an MDI application is called a child window and the application window is called the parent window. MDI applications can have many child windows but only one parent window. MDI parent forms can only contain controls that have an **Align** property (e.g., **PictureBox** controls) or controls that are not visible at run-time (e.g., **Timer** controls).

- Child windows behave like any other window but cannot be moved outside the parent window. A child window's functionality can be different from that of other child windows. Child windows are forms with their **MDIChild** properties set to **True**.

- MDI forms, both child and parent, can have menus. A parent window's menu is displayed if the active child window (i.e., the one with the focus) does not have any menus. If the active child window has a menu, the parent window displays the child's menu—the parent's menu is not visible.

- Child windows can be minimized (by clicking the **Minimize** button), maximized (by clicking the **Maximize** button) and closed (by clicking the **Close** box).

- Programs that use multiple forms must specify in the **Project Properties** dialog a **Startup Object**. MDI applications use the MDI parent form.

- Project name **Project1** can be changed by modifying the **Project Name TextBox**.

- Event procedure **MDIForm_Load** is called when the parent form is loaded into memory. The programmer specifies when and in what order child forms are loaded with method **Load**. When loading is complete, the child form is visible.

- Call to method **Unload** removes a form from memory.

- Method **Show** displays a form. If the form is not loaded and **Show** is called, the form is loaded and then displayed. Method **Hide** makes a form invisible but does not unload the form.

- MDI parent forms order the child windows with method **Arrange**.

- SDI application can have multiple forms.

- **IPictureDisp** is **LoadPicture**'s return type. Assigning an **IPictureDisp** variable a value requires keyword **Set**.

- Passing optional argument **vbModal** to method **Show** results in the displayed form being modal. Forms are non-modal, **vbModeless**, by default.

- Event procedure **Form_Unload** is called when the user presses the **Close** box with the mouse.

- Procedure **Main** is placed in a standard module (i.e., a **.bas** file) and set in the **Project Properties** dialog as the **Startup Object**.

- Before **Form_Unload** is called, event procedure **Form_QueryUnload** is called. **QueryUnload** provides the programmer with a means of preventing a form from unloading. **QueryUnload** declares two variables, **Cancel** and **UnloadMode**. When **Cancel** is **False**, **Form_Unload** is called and passed **False**. The form is then unloaded. A **True** value prevents **Form_Unload** from being called. **UnloadMode** specifies how the **UnLoad** event originated. **QueryUnload** and **Unload** are not called if **End** is executed.

- Template forms are predefined Visual Basic forms that can be added to a project.

- Function **Timer** returns the current time since midnight expressed in seconds.

- Function **DoEvents** allows Visual Basic to process events while a computational intensive process is executing.

- The **RichTextBox** control is an ActiveX control for manipulating text and is added to the toolbox by selecting **Microsoft Rich TextBox Control 6.0** from the **Components** dialog. The **RichTextBox** is capable of displaying a special type of formatted text called rich text. Rich text files end in **.RTF**.

- Design-time property **ScrollBars** determines whether or not the **RichTextBox** control displays any scrollbars. The **RightMargin** property specifies the right margin. Text automatically wraps when the right margin is encountered.

- Function **LoadFile** loads a text file or rich text file into the **RichTextBox**. The **HideSelection** property specifies whether or not any text highlighted in the **RichTextBox** should remain highlighted when the **RichTextBox** loses the focus.

- Properties **SelBold**, **SelItalic** and **SelUnderline** specify whether or not any selected text is bold, italic or underlined, respectively. When set to **True**, the formatting is applied. Function **SaveFile** saves the text file or rich text file to disk. Function **Find** searches a **RichTextBox** for characters and strings.

- ActiveX control **UpDown** increments or decrements the value of another control (which is assigned to the **BuddyControl** property) and is one of several controls that are added when **Microsoft Windows Common Controls-2 6.0** is selected in the **Components** dialog.

- The **With** statement provides a convenient syntax for setting multiple properties for a single control and is terminated with keywords **End Width**.

- Setting **AutoBuddy** to **True** at design-time causes the **UpDown** control to associate the previous control (based on **TabIndex**) as the buddy control. If a previous control does not exist, the next control (based on **TabIndex**) becomes the buddy control. An **UpDown** control without a buddy control behaves like a simplified scrollbar.

- The **Min** property sets the minimum value and the **Max** property sets the maximum value that the **UpDown** control's **Value** property can have. When set to **True**, the **Wrap** property sets **Value** to **Min** when an attempt is made to exceed **Max** and sets **Value** to **Max** when an attempt is made to exceed **Min**. The **Increment** property specifies by how much **Value** will increment or decrement when an arrow is clicked. If the **Wrap** property is **False**, incrementing or decrementing stops when **Min** or **Max** is reached.

• The **ImageList** ActiveX control loads and stores a group of images that can be used by other controls and is one of several ActiveX controls that are added to the project when **Microsoft Windows Common Controls 6.0** is selected in the **Components** dialog.

• Method **PaintPicture** draws an image at a specified set of coordinates—which specify the image's upper-left corner.

• Each item stored in the **ImageList** is a **ListImage** object—which encapsulates all the information about the image. These **ListImage** objects are stored in a collection.

• The **ImageCombo** control can display images next to its items. The **ImageCombo** control is one of the ActiveX controls added to the project when **Microsoft Windows Common Controls 6.0** is selected in the **Components** dialog.

• Each item in an **ImageCombo** control is a **ComboItem** object—which is part of the **ComboItems** collection. Each **ComboItem** encapsulates all the information about a **ImageCombo** item. Method **Add** is used to create and add a **ComboItem** to the **ComboItems** collection.

• The **FlatScrollBar** ActiveX control is one of several controls that are added when **Microsoft Windows Common Controls-2 6.0** is selected in the **Components** dialog. **FlatScrollbar**s have the same basic functionality as scrollbars, but with a few added enhancements—such as the ability to disable one or both of the scroll arrows and the ability to change the interface of the control (i.e., have a "flat" scrollbar as opposed to a raised 3D look). The **Arrows** property controls which scroll arrows are enabled, and the **Appearance** property specifies the interface.

• Visual Basic programs by default are compiled to an intermediate level of instructions called p-code which are interpreted at run-time by **msvbvm60.dll**.

• Visual Basic provides the option of compiling directly to a native code executable (**.exe** file). Native code compilation often increases execution speed for computation-intensive programs and also allows optimizations that are not possible with p-code. Double-clicking the **.exe** file (when viewing with **Windows Explorer**) or typing the **.exe** file name at the DOS command line and pressing Enter executes the file.

• Native code executables still use **msvbvm60.dll** at run-time for certain procedure calls.

## Terminology

| | |
|---|---|
| **.exe** file | **cc2AlignmentRight** constant |
| **.rtf** file | **cc2Both** constant |
| **Add Form** | **cc2LeftUp** constant |
| **Add MDI Form** | **cc2OrientationHorizontal** constant |
| **Add** method | **cc2OrientationVertical** constant |
| **Advanced Optimizations** | **cc2RightDown** constant |
| **Align** property | child form |
| **Alignment** property | collection |
| **Appearance** property | **ComboItem** object |
| **Arrange** method | **ComboItems** collection |
| **Arrows** property | **Compile** tab |
| **AutoBuddy** property | **Compile to Native Code** |
| buddy control | container |
| **BuddyControl** property | **Create Symbolic Debug Info** |
| **Cancel** variable | document |
| cascade child windows | **DoEvents** function |
| **cc2AlignmentLeft** constant | **End With** |

## Common Programming Errors

**11.1**   Attempting to execute a form with its **MDIChild** property set to **True** that does not have an MDI parent form is a run-time error.

**11.2**   Attempting to add to an MDI parent form a control that does not have an **Align** property or a control that is visible at run-time is a syntax error.

**11.3**   Attempting to assign a value to an **IPictureDisp** variable without using keyword **Set** is a syntax error.

**11.4**   Specifying **Main** as the **Startup Object** and not providing method **Main** in a standard module is a run-time error.

**11.5**   When using **rtfRTF** in **LoadFile** or **SaveFile**, opening a file type other than a rich text format file is a run-time error.

**11.6**   Attempting to assign a negative number to **Increment** is a run-time error.

**11.7**   Attempting to set the **Orientation** property at run-time is a run-time error.

## Good Programming Practices

**11.1**   Prefixing **RichTextBox** controls with **rtf** allows them to be identified easily.

**11.2**   Prefixing the name of **UpDown** controls with **upd** allows them to be identified easily.

**11.3**   Prefixing the name of **ImageList** controls with **ils** allows them to be identified easily.

**11.4**   Prefixing the name of **ImageCombo** controls with **imgcbo** allows them to be identified easily.

**11.5**   Prefixing the name of **FlatScrollbar** controls with **fsb** allows them to be identified easily.

## Look-and-Feel Observations

**11.1**   Using an SDI application is often much more intuitive than an MDI application.

**11.2**   By convention, MDI applications provide a **Window** menu that allows the user to view and arrange the child windows. Providing a **Window** menu for an MDI application provides a consistent Windows look-and-feel.

**11.3**   By convention, the MDI parent window **Caption** contains the application name, and each MDI child window's **Caption** contains the name of its document.

**11.4**   Multiple forms can make a program more user friendly, because the amount of information displayed on a single form is reduced. This is preferable to having a single form contain all the GUI features—which can overwhelm the user.

**11.5**   Template form GUIs are modeled after the Windows look-and-feel.

**11.6**   **FlatScrollbar**s provide a consistent look for Internet Explorer 4.0 GUIs.

## Performance Tip

**11.1**   Methods **Load** and **Unload** allow the programmer to manage program memory. Forms can be **Load**ed and **Unload**ed as they are needed. Calling these methods too frequently can decrease performance.

## Portability Tip

**11.1**   Rich text format files are portable to any control or editor capable of understanding rich text format.

## Software Engineering Observations

**11.1**   MDI applications are usually "feature-rich" and require extensive documentation.

**11.2**   In order to avoid confusing the user, MDI parent window menus often duplicate child window menus.

**11.3**   Multiple forms promote software reusability. Each form, once it is created, can potentially be reused by future applications.

**11.4**   Template forms are examples of reusable modules. Common tasks are developed once and reused again in different projects. Template forms reduce development time.

**11.5**   **RichTextBox** controls have many of the same properties, methods and events associated with a **TextBox**. **RichTextBox** controls of course have additional properties, methods and events that **TextBox**es do not. **RichTextBox**es do not have the 64K-character capacity limit that **TextBox**es do.

**11.6**   There is often a trade-off between executable size and execution speed. **Optimize for Fast Code** can increase execution speed while also increasing the size of the compiled program. **Optimize for Small Code** can reduce the compiled program size while reducing execution speed.

## Self-Review Exercises

**11.1**   Fill in the blanks in each of the following:
a)   The MDI form is also called the _____ form.
b)   A **FlatScrollBar**'s interface is determined by its _____ property.
c)   Executable files have _____ as an extension.
d)   The combination of an **UpDown** control and **TextBox** control is often called a _____.
e)   The _____ property determines which **FlatScrollBar** scroll arrows are enabled.
f)   **UpDown** control property _____ makes the previous control, based on **TabIndex**, the buddy control.

**11.2**   State which are *true* and which are *false*. If *false*, explain why.
a)   A program can have only one MDI parent form.
b)   A program can have multiple forms.
c)   SDI is short for Standard Document Interface.
d)   **Optimize for Fast Code** creates the smallest and fastest native code executable possible.
e)   **Optimize for Small Code** creates the smallest p-code executable possible.

**11.3**   Find the error(s) in each of the following and explain how to correct it/them.
a)   `Unload.frmDR44`
b)   `frmBG76.Load = True`
c)   `Hide frmSW78`
d)   `Show frmSM61`
e)   `With picPicture1`
       `.Picture = LoadPicture("c:\myimage.gif")`
       `.Refresh`

**11.4**   Briefly do the following:
a)   List some potential advantages/disadvantages of creating a p-code executable in preference to a native code executable.
b)   Explain the difference between **Load** and **Show**.
c)   Explain the difference between **Visible = False** and **Unload**.

## Answers to Self-Review Exercises

**11.1**   a) parent. b) **Appearance**. c) **.exe**. d) spinner control. e) **Arrows**. f) **AutoBuddy**.

**11.2**   a)  True.

b) True.

c) False. SDI is short for Single Document Interface.

d) False. The smallest possible code in not likely to be generated.

e) False. The smallest native code possible is generated.

**11.3**  a) `Call Unload(frmDR44)`

b) `Call Load(frmBG76)`

c) `Call frmSW78.Hide`

d) `Call frmSM61.Show`

e) `End With` is missing.

```
With picPicture1
    .Picture = LoadPicture("c:\myimage.gif")
    .Refresh
End With
```

**11.4**  a) P-code executables are more compact than native code executables and execute slower than native code executables. P-code executables cannot be optimized for size or speed, whereas native code executables can.

b) Method **Load** loads a form into memory but does not display it. Method **Show** loads a form into memory if it is not already loaded and displays the form.

c) Setting the **Visible** property to **False** hides the form, but the form still resides in memory. **Unload** removes the form from memory.

## Exercises

**11.5**  Fill in the blanks in each of the following:

a) By default, Visual Basic programs are compiled to _____.

b) **LoadPicture** returns type _____.

c) The _____ statement provides a convenient syntax for setting multiple properties for a control.

d) A _____ is a predefined form that is provided with Visual Basic.

e) **RichTextBox** property _____ determines the number and orientation of scrollbars.

**11.6**  State which of the following are *true* and which are *false*. If *false*, explain why.

a) An MDI parent window can contain multiple child windows.

b) MDI is short for multiple document instance.

c) MDI child windows cannot have menus.

d) A **Image** control can be placed directly on an MDI parent window.

e) An MDI child window can never be moved outside its MDI parent window.

f) A form becomes an MDI child window when its **Child** property is set to **True**.

g) In general, SDI applications are not as complex as MDI applications.

h) MDI parent windows can have menus.

**11.7**  Briefly explain the difference between an SDI application and an MDI application. Excluding the SDI and MDI applications discussed in the chapter, list 3 examples of an SDI application and list 3 examples of an MDI application.

**11.8**  Briefly explain why a **Window** menu is important to an MDI parent window.

**11.9**  Take any previous exercise you have solved and create a p-code executable file named **pcode.exe**. Now create a native code executable version (using **Optimize for Fast Code**) of the same program—name it **fast.exe**. How do the two file sizes compare? Now create two additional native code executables (one using **Optimize for Small Code** and the other using **No Optimization**) named **small.exe** and **no_op.exe**, respectively. How do these compare to each other and the other **.exe** files?

**11.10**   Write a program that begins decrementing a loop from 200000000 to 0 in decrements of –1 when a button is pressed. Use function **Timer** to determine how much time the loop required for execution. Although the time is approximate, the value is suitable for a basic performance test. Compile the program to a p-code executable. How much time did it take to execute?

**11.11**   Compile the program of Exercise 11.10 to a native code executable and time each optimization. Also test the **No Optimization** feature. How much execution time did each optimization take? Is this what you expected?

**11.12**   Write a small editor program that performs syntax color highlighting on ANSI C programming language keywords of Fig. 11.43. Each keyword should appear as green. Normal text should appear as black. Use the **RichTextBox** control. Consult the on-line documentation for additional **RichTextBox** properties, methods and events. Provide a button that when pressed changes every ANSI C keyword to green.

**11.13**   Modify the program of Fig. 11.24 to find the next occurrence of the text being searched for by the user. Display a **MsgBox** if the text is not found. Also display the current location (i.e., index) of the cursor. Consult the on-line documentation for additional **RichTextBox** properties, methods and events.

**11.14**   Modify the program of Fig. 11.24 by adding two additional buttons for subscripting and superscripting highlighted text. Also add three additional buttons for aligning the paragraphs. Use constants **rtfLeft**, **rtfRight** and **rtfCenter**. Consult the on-line documentation for additional **RichTextBox** properties, methods and events.

**11.15**   Modify your solution to Exercise 11.13 to provide a find and replace feature. Consult the on-line documentation for additional **RichTextBox** properties, methods and events.

**11.16**   Rewrite the Craps program of Exercise 6.24 to use an **ImageList** control to manage the images.

**11.17**   Create a simple animation using a **PictureBox** control and images from an **ImageList** control.

| C keywords | | | |
|---|---|---|---|
| auto | break | case | char |
| const | continue | default | do |
| double | else | enum | extern |
| float | for | goto | if |
| int | long | register | return |
| short | signed | sizeof | static |
| struct | switch | typedef | union |
| unsigned | void | volatile | while |

**Fig. 11.43**   ANSI C programming language keywords.

**11.18**   Create a simple animation using method **PaintPicture**.

**11.19**   Modify Fig. 11.10 to provide password protection. Use the template form **Login**.

**11.20**   Using method **PaintPicture** to display on the form two **.bmp** images—one flipped horizontally and the other flipped vertically. (Hint: Passing negative values for the fourth and/or fifth arguments flips an image.)

**11.21**   Write a program that plays the game of concentration. Use a series of **PictureBox** controls to display the images. When the user **Click**s on a **PictureBox**, the image associated with that **PictureBox** is displayed. Clicking a second **PictureBox** displays the image associated with the second **PictureBox**. If the images match, they remain displayed. If they do not match, both images should be hidden.

**11.22**   Modify the program of Fig. 11.16 to use template form **Dialog** instead of function **MsgBox**.

**11.23**   A company pays its employees as managers (who receive a fixed weekly salary), hourly workers (who receive a fixed hourly wage for up to the first 40 hours they work and "time-and-a-half," i.e., 1.5 times their hourly wage, for overtime hours worked), commission workers (who receive a $250 plus 5.7% of their gross weekly sales), or pieceworkers (who receive a fixed amount of money per item for each of the items they produce—each pieceworker in this company works on only one type of item). Write a program to compute the weekly pay for each employee. You do not know the number of employees in advance. Each type of employee has its own pay code: Managers have paycode 1, hourly workers have code 2, commission workers have code 3 and pieceworkers have code 4. Enter the appropriate facts your program needs to calculate each employee's pay based on that employee's paycode. Each employee type should be handled as a separate form.

**11.24**   Modify the Simpletron Simulator of Exercise 10.19 to use MDI. The user should be able to independently display windows for loading an SML program, executing the instructions of an SML program and the dump display. Provide checked menu items that allow the user to select which windows are displayed at any time.

# 12

# Mouse and Keyboard

## Objectives

- To recognize mouse events such as **Click**, **DblClick**, **MouseDown**, **MouseUp** and **MouseMove**.
- To determine which of the mouse buttons was pressed.
- To determine whether or not the *Shift*, *Ctrl* and *Alt* keys were held down when a mouse button was pressed.
- To be able to drag-and-drop an object using the mouse.
- To be able to change the mouse pointer icon into shapes appropriate for various contexts.
- To recognize key events such as **KeyPress**, **KeyDown** and **KeyUp**, and to write code to respond to these events.
- To be able to use the **KeyPreview** property to intercept keyboard events.

*Not a creature was stirring—not even a mouse; ...*
Clement Clarke Moore
*A Visit from St. Nicholas*

*Consider the little mouse, how sagacious an animal it is which entrusts its life to one hole only.*
Titus Maccius Plautus

*I would willingly stand at street corners, hat in hand, begging passersby to drop their unused minutes into it.*
Bernard Berenson

# Outline

## 12.1  Introduction

Users interact with Visual Basic programs using the mouse and keyboard. The mouse is used to click buttons, move windows, resize windows, etc. Visual Basic controls are capable of recognizing when the mouse is single-clicked or double-clicked as well as other *mouse events* such as *moving the mouse*, *pressing a mouse button* and *releasing a mouse button*. Like other events, the programmer writes code to perform some action when the event is triggered (or raised). The program can test which mouse button (*left*, *middle* or *right*) was pressed. Also, Visual Basic provides support for *drag-and-drop*—dragging an item on the screen and dropping it on another item.

When a key on the keyboard is pressed, a *key event* occurs. Key events (*pressing a key* and *releasing a key*) are processed at the form level or at the control level. We present key event handling later in the chapter.

## 12.2  Changing the Shape of the Mouse Pointer

A form or control's ***MousePointer*** property determines the shape of the mouse pointer when the mouse pointer enters the area of the control. Visual Basic provides constants for changing the mouse pointer shape (Fig. 12.1). Property **MousePointer** does not perform the actions indicated; rather it provides the user with visual feedback as to what can be done with the mouse. For example, in Microsoft Word, the I-beam cursor indicates that the user can enter text into the document by clicking where the first character should be typed, then typing characters. Note: Users can customize the mouse cursors used by applications on their computer, which may change the cursor icons shown in Fig. 12.1 on their computer.

***Look-and-Feel Observation 12.1***

*A control's default mouse pointer (and all other mouse pointers) can differ from the arrow if it has been set at the system level through the control panel.*

Windows allows the user to specify that a group of animated images (called an *animated cursor*) to be used as the mouse pointer. Animated cursors end in the extension **.ANI**. Animated cursors cannot be used in Visual Basic.

| Constant | Value | Cursor | Description |
|---|---|---|---|
| vbDefault | 0 |  | Default cursor. Describes the default cursor for a form or control. |
| vbArrow | 1 |  | Arrow cursor. Typically used to indicate that selections can be made. |
| vbCrosshair | 2 | 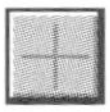 | Crosshair cursor. Typically used to indicate precision. |
| vbIbeam | 3 | 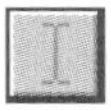 | I-beam cursor. Typically used to indicate that text can be input. |
| vbSizePointer | 5 |  | Sizing cursor. Typically used to indicate that resizing is allowed in all directions. |
| vbSizeNESW | 6 |  | North-East-South-West cursor. Typically used to indicate that resizing is allowed in this direction. |
| vbSizeNS | 7 |  | North-South cursor. Typically used to indicate that resizing is allowed in this direction. |
| vbSizeNWSE | 8 |  | North-West-South-East cursor. Typically used to indicate that resizing is allowed in this direction. |
| vbSizeWE | 9 |  | West-East cursor. Typically used to indicate that resizing is allowed in this direction. |
| vbUpArrow | 10 |  | Up arrow. |
| vbHourglass | 11 |  | Hourglass cursor. Typically used to indicate that the program is busy performing some task. |
| vbNoDrop | 12 |  | No-drop cursor. Typically used to indicate that a drop operation is not permitted. |
| vbArrowHourglass | 13 |  | Arrow hourglass cursor. Typically used to indicate that the program is busy performing some task and that the user can still make selections with the mouse pointer. |
| vbArrowQuestion | 14 |  | Arrow question mark cursor. Typically used to indicate help is available for a feature. |
| vbSizeAll | 15 |  | Size all directions cursor. |
| vbCustom | 99 |  | Custom cursor. Typically used to display a non-Visual Basic cursor). |

Fig. 12.1    **MousePointer** constants.

*Common Programming Error 12.1*

*Attempting to use animated cursors for **MousePointer** images is not allowed.*

The program of Fig. 12.2 changes the form's mouse pointer shape. The GUI consists of a control array containing 16 **OptionButton**s (also called *radio buttons*). **Option-Button**s are similar in behavior to **CheckBox**es in that their **Value**s are either **True** or **False**. However, **OptionButton**s form a group in which at any point in time only one **OptionButton** is **True**. Clicking any **OptionButton** sets it to **True** while setting all other **OptionButton**s in the group to **False**.

```
1   ' Fig. 12.2
2   ' Changing the mouse pointer
3   Option Explicit        ' General declaration
4
5   Private Sub optCursor_Click(Index As Integer)
6       MousePointer = Index
7   End Sub
```

Initial GUI at execution.

GUI after user selects **arrow question**.

**Fig. 12.2**   Demonstrating the **MousePointer** property.

## 12.3 Mouse Events

When a user interacts with the mouse, mouse events are generated. Visual Basic provides five event procedures for handling mouse events *Click*, *DblClick*, *MouseDown*, *MouseUp* and *MouseMove*. Event procedure **Click** is called when a mouse button is clicked once. Event procedure **DblClick** is called when a mouse button is clicked twice in rapid succession. (You can set the double-click speed for your computer in the **Mouse Properties** dialog's **Buttons** tab. Display the **Mouse Properties** dialog by opening the **Mouse** option in the Windows **Control Panel**.) Event procedure **MouseDown** is called when a mouse button is pressed. Event procedure **MouseUp** is called when a mouse button is released and event procedure **MouseMove** is called when the mouse is moved. Visual Basic only recognizes mouse events when they occur on a form or a form's control. The program of Fig. 12.3 demonstrates mouse events.

```
1   ' Fig. 12.3
2   ' Demonstrating mouse events
3   Option Explicit            ' General declaration
4
5   Private Sub Form_Load()
6       Call Randomize          ' Randomize
7   End Sub
8
9   Private Sub cmdClear_Click()
10      Call Cls      ' Clear Form
11  End Sub
12
13  Private Sub Form_Click()
14
15      ' Randomly set Form ForeColor
16      Select Case (1 + Int(Rnd() * 4))
17         Case 1
18            ForeColor = vbBlack
19         Case 2
20            ForeColor = vbMagenta
21         Case 3
22            ForeColor = vbRed
23         Case 4
24            ForeColor = vbBlue
25      End Select
26
27  End Sub
28
29  Private Sub Form_DblClick()
30
31      ' Randomly set Form BackColor
32      Select Case (1 + Int(Rnd() * 4))
33         Case 1
34            BackColor = vbWhite
35         Case 2
36            BackColor = vbYellow
```

**Fig. 12.3**   Demonstrating mouse events (part 1 of 3).

```
37          Case 3
38              BackColor = vbGreen
39          Case 4
40              BackColor = vbCyan
41      End Select
42
43      ' Change chkMove BackColor to Form's BackColor
44      chkMove.BackColor = BackColor
45   End Sub
46
47   Private Sub Form_MouseDown(Button As Integer, _
48                             Shift As Integer, X As Single, _
49                             Y As Single)
50
51      CurrentX = X          ' Set x coordinate
52      CurrentY = Y          ' Set y coordinate
53      Print "MouseDown"
54   End Sub
55
56   Private Sub Form_MouseUp(Button As Integer, _
57                           Shift As Integer, X As Single, _
58                           Y As Single)
59
60      ' Reverse coordinates
61      CurrentX = Y
62      CurrentY = X
63      Print "MouseUp"
64   End Sub
65
66   Private Sub Form_MouseMove(Button As Integer, _
67                             Shift As Integer, X As Single, _
68                             Y As Single)
69
70      ' If checked enable printing operations
71      If chkMove.Value = 1 Then
72         CurrentX = X
73         CurrentY = Y
74         Print "MouseMove"
75      End If
76
77   End Sub
```

**Fig. 12.3**   Demonstrating mouse events (part 2 of 3).

Event procedure **Form_MouseDown** is called when the right or left mouse button is clicked. The form's *CurrentX* and *CurrentY* properties are set to the **X**-coordinate and **Y**-coordinate of where the **MouseDown** occurred. Properties **CurrentX** and **CurrentY** determine where the next **Print** will occur and can only be set at run-time (i.e., **CurrentX** and **CurrentY** are not available in the form's **Properties** window at design-time). The text "**MouseDown**" is printed at the location of the **MouseDown**.

Releasing a mouse button results in **Form_MouseUp** being called. **CurrentX** is set to **Y** and **CurrentY** is set to **X** in order to avoid **Print**ing "**MouseUp**" on top of "**MouseDown**".

Initial GUI at execution.

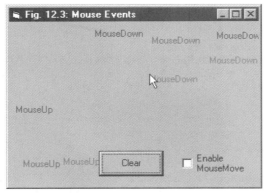

GUI after user has clicked mouse in several different locations.

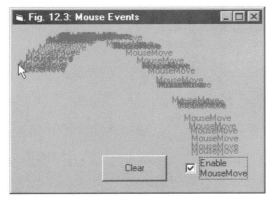

GUI after user has pressed **Clear** and then clicked **Enable MouseMove** and moved the mouse.

**Fig. 12.3**    Demonstrating mouse events (part 3 of 3).

Single-clicking results in **Form_Click** being called to change the **ForeColor** to black, magenta, red or blue. Double-clicking the mouse on the form results in the event procedure **Form_Dblclick** being called and the **BackColor** randomly changing to either white, yellow, green or cyan.

*Portability Tip 12.1*

*The frequency of the **MouseMove** event is system dependent. The triggering of a **Mouse-Move** event is not necessarily continuous as the mouse is moved over objects (some systems may trigger the event more often than others).*

Moving the mouse over the form results in event procedure **Form_MouseMove** being called. If **chkMove** is checked, "**MouseMove**" is **Print**ed at the current mouse location. If **chkMove** is unchecked, event procedure **Form_MouseMove** is still executed but nothing is **Print**ed.

## 12.4  Mouse Buttons

The **Button** argument of **MouseDown**, **MouseUp** and **MouseMove** indicate which mouse button was pressed. A mouse may have one, two or three buttons. A mouse with three buttons has a *left button*, a *middle button* and a *right button*. A mouse with two buttons has a left and a right mouse button. A mouse with one button has a left mouse button.

Figure 12.4 lists the mouse button constants associated with the **Button** argument. **Button** has a value of **1** if the right mouse button is pressed, a value of **2** if the left button is pressed, and a value of **4** if the middle button is pressed. Combinations of buttons can be tested by adding these values. For example, a value of **3** represents the right button and the left button being pressed simultaneously.

The program of Fig. 12.5 determines which mouse button has been pressed and displays an image of a three-button mouse. When a mouse button is pressed, the image changes to indicate which button is being pressed.

| Constant | Value | Description |
|---|---|---|
| **vbRightButton** | 1 | The right mouse button. |
| **vbLeftButton** | 2 | The left mouse button. |
| **vbMiddleButton** | 4 | The center mouse button. |

**Fig. 12.4**   Mouse button constants.

```
1   ' Fig. 12.5
2   ' Mouse buttons
3   Option Explicit        ' General declaration
4
5   Private Sub Form_Load()
6      imgImage.Picture = LoadPicture("d:\images\ch12\mouse0.gif")
7   End Sub
8
9   Private Sub Form_MouseDown(Button As Integer, _
10                          Shift As Integer, X As Single, _
11                          Y As Single)
12      Call SetPressedImage(Button)
13   End Sub
```

**Fig. 12.5**   Determining which mouse button was pressed (part 1 of 3).

```
14
15    Private Sub Form_MouseUp(Button As Integer, Shift As Integer, _
16                            X As Single, Y As Single)
17
18        Call SetReleasedImage
19    End Sub
20
21    Private Sub imgImage_MouseDown(Button As Integer, _
22                                  Shift As Integer, _
23                                  X As Single, Y As Single)
24        Call SetPressedImage(Button)
25    End Sub
26
27    Private Sub imgImage_MouseUp(Button As Integer, _
28                                Shift As Integer, _
29                                X As Single, Y As Single)
30        Call SetReleasedImage
31    End Sub
32
33    Private Sub SetPressedImage(b As Integer)
34        imgImage.Picture = LoadPicture("d:\images\ch12\mouse" & _
35                                      b & ".gif")
36    End Sub
37
38    Private Sub SetReleasedImage()
39        imgImage.Picture = LoadPicture("d:\images\ch12\mouse0.gif")
40    End Sub
```

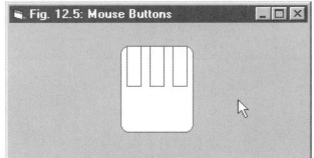

Initial GUI at execution.

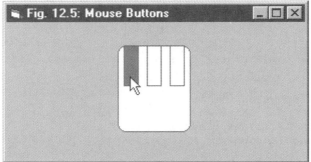

GUI after user presses the left mouse button.

**Fig. 12.5**   Determining which mouse button was pressed (part 2 of 3).

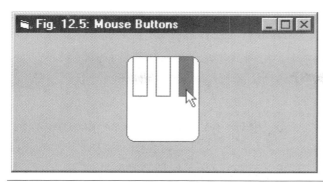

GUI after the user presses the
right mouse button.

**Fig. 12.5**    Determining which mouse button was pressed (part 3 of 3).

When a **MouseDown** event occurs on either the **Image** or the **Form** the line

```
imgImage.Picture = LoadPicture("d:\images\ch12\mouse" & _
                                b & ".gif")
```

in procedure **SetPressedImage** executes. The procedure receives the value of **Button** from the **MouseDown** event procedures as **b** and uses it to determine the image to display. When a mouse button is released, the **MouseUp** event procedures both call **SetReleasedImage** to return the image to its original state.

## 12.5 *Shift, Ctrl* and *Alt* Keys

The status of the *Shift*, *Ctrl* and *Alt* keys can be determined when a **MouseDown**, **MouseMove** or **MouseUp** event occurs. A value representing the status of these keys is stored in variable **Shift**. Figure 12.6 shows the constants associated with variable **Shift**. Like **Button** constants, **Shift** constants can be combined to check for combinations of *Shift*, *Ctrl* and *Alt*.

The program of Fig. 12.7 determines which combination of *Shift*, *Ctrl* and *Alt* is being pressed when the form's **MouseDown** event occurs. The code contains the program code of Fig. 12.5 except for the **Image**'s **MouseDown** and **MouseUp** event procedures. Clicking the image in this example generates **MouseDown** or **MouseUp** events for the image, not for the form. The program uses a control array consisting of three **Label**s to visually indicate the *Shift*, *Ctrl* and *Alt* keys. The control array indexes are **1**, **2** and **4**.

| Constant | Value | Description |
|---|---|---|
| **vbShiftMask** | 1 | Status of the *Shift* key. |
| **vbCtrlMask** | 2 | Status of the *Ctrl* key. |
| **vbAltMask** | 4 | Status of the *Alt* key. |

**Fig. 12.6**    Constants associated with variable **Shift**.

```
1   ' Fig. 12.7
2   ' Mouse buttons
3   Option Explicit        ' General declaration
4
5   Private Sub Form_Load()
6       imgImage.Picture = LoadPicture("d:\images\ch12\mouse0.gif")
7   End Sub
8
9   Private Sub Form_MouseDown(Button As Integer, _
10                             Shift As Integer, x As Single, _
11                             Y As Single)
12
13      Dim a As Integer, c As Integer, s As Integer
14
15      a = Shift And vbAltMask        ' Mask Alt bit
16      c = Shift And vbCtrlMask       ' Mask Ctrl bit
17      s = Shift And vbShiftMask      ' Mask Shift bit
18
19      If (a <> 0) Then       ' Alt
20          lblKeys(a).BackColor = vbGreen
21      End If
22
23      If (s <> 0) Then       ' Shift
24          lblKeys(s).BackColor = vbGreen
25      End If
26
27      If (c <> 0) Then       ' Ctrl
28          lblKeys(c).BackColor = vbGreen
29      End If
30
31      imgImage.Picture = LoadPicture("d:\images\ch12\mouse" & _
32                             Button & ".gif")
33  End Sub
34
35  Private Sub Form_MouseUp(Button As Integer, Shift As Integer, _
36                           x As Single, Y As Single)
37
38      ' Change Label BackColors to Form's BackColor
39      lblKeys(1).BackColor = BackColor
40      lblKeys(2).BackColor = BackColor
41      lblKeys(4).BackColor = BackColor
42
43      ' Load mouse image of unpressed buttons
44      imgImage.Picture = LoadPicture("d:\images\ch12\mouse0.gif")
45  End Sub
```

**Fig. 12.7**    Determining which combination of *Shift, Ctrl* or *Alt* was pressed
(part 1 of 2).

The statement

```
a = Shift And vbAltMask
```

uses *bit manipulation* to determine if the *Alt* key was pressed. Like **Button**, variable
**Shift** represents a *bit field* (a series of related bits) where the three least significant bits

represent the status of *Shift*, *Ctrl* and *Alt,* respectively. Figure 12.8 shows bit fields for both **Button** and **Shift**.

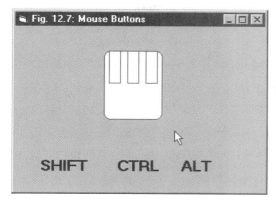

Initial GUI at execution.

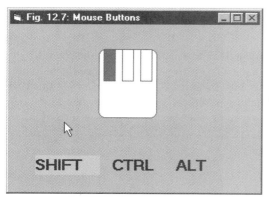

GUI after user presses the left mouse button while *Shift* is held down.

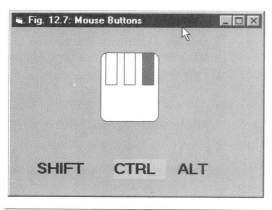

GUI after user presses the right mouse button while *Ctrl* is held down.

**Fig. 12.7**   Determining which combination of *Shift, Ctrl* or *Alt* was pressed (part 2 of 2).

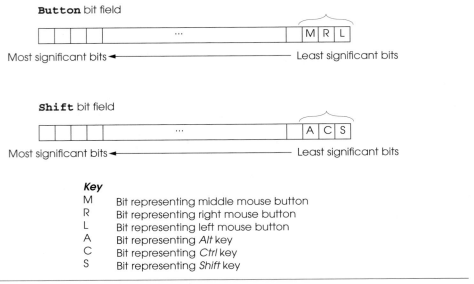

**Fig. 12.8    Button** and **Shift** bit fields.

Constant **vbAltMask** has a value of **4** (which is **00000100** in the lowest byte). When **vbAltMask** and **Shift** are combined using bitwise operator **And**, the individual bit representing *Alt* is isolated—all other bits in **Shift** are *masked off* (hidden) by "**And**ing" with constant **vbAltMask**. The bitwise operation results in either **4** (if the *Alt* bit has a value of 1) or **0** (if the *Alt* bit has a value of 0) being assigned to **a**. Variables **c** and **s** get assigned the result of "**And**ing" **Shift** with **vbCtrlMask** and "**And**ing" **Shift** with **vbShiftMask**, respectively.

## 12.6 Drag-and-Drop

The mouse can be used at run-time for *drag-and-drop* operations. A drag-and-drop operation consists of pressing and holding the left mouse button, moving the mouse and releasing the mouse button (resulting in the event procedure **DragDrop** being called). While a drag-and-drop operation is in progress, mouse events and key events (discussed in the next section) initiated by the user are not recognized. Visual Basic provides *manual drag-and-drop* and *automatic drag-and-drop,* which are specified in a control's **DragMode** property. We first discuss manual drag-and-drop (the default) that has a **DragMode** value of **0**.

Manual drag-and-drop allows the programmer to determine when a drag-and-drop operation should occur and requires the use of method **Drag**. Figure 12.9 summarizes the three values that are used with method **Drag**.

Figure 12.10 demonstrates manual drag-and-drop by allowing the user to drag the knight chess piece around a chess board. The program uses a control array of 64 **PictureBox**es to represent the board. The program introduces the **DragOver** event procedure and the **DragIcon** property. Event procedure **DragOver** executes for a control when a drag-and-drop operation is in progress and the area of the control is entered. Property **DragIcon** displays an image while the drag-and-drop operation is in progress.

| Constant | Value | Description |
| --- | --- | --- |
| `vbCancelDrag` | 0 | Cancels drag-and-drop operation. Event procedure **DragDrop** is not called. |
| `vbBeginDrag` | 1 | Begins drag-and-drop operation. Event procedure **DragDrop** is called. |
| `vbEndDrag` | 2 | Terminates drag-and-drop operation. Event procedure **DragDrop** is called. |

**Fig. 12.9**   Constants used with method **Drag**.

```
1   ' Fig. 12.10
2   ' Demonstrating manual drag-and-drop
3   Option Explicit                    ' General declaration
4   Dim mCurrentCell As Integer        ' General declaration
5
6   Private Sub Form_Load()
7      Dim x As Integer
8
9      mCurrentCell = 2        ' Lower left corner
10
11     For x = 1 To 64
12
13        If x Mod 2 Then
14           picSquare(x).Picture = LoadPicture("d:\images\ch12\" & _
15                                              "w_marble.jpg")
16        Else
17           picSquare(x).Picture = LoadPicture("d:\images\ch12\" & _
18                                              "b_marble.jpg")
19        End If
20
21     Next x
22
23     picSquare(2).Picture = LoadPicture("d:\images\ch12\" & _
24                                        "b_knight.jpg")
25  End Sub
26
27  Private Sub picSquare_MouseDown(Index As Integer, _
28                                  Button As Integer, _
29                                  Shift As Integer, _
30                                  x As Single, Y As Single)
31
32     ' If on the PictureBox displaying the image
33     ' then enable dragging.
34     If Index = mCurrentCell Then
35        picSquare(mCurrentCell).Drag vbBeginDrag
36     End If
37
38  End Sub
```

**Fig. 12.10**   Demonstrating manual drag-and-drop (part 1 of 4).

```
39
40    Private Sub picSquare_DragOver(Index As Integer, _
41                                  Source As Control, _
42                                  x As Single, Y As Single, _
43                                  State As Integer)
44
45       ' Display icon while dragging over a PictureBox
46       picSquare(Index).DragIcon = LoadPicture("d:\images" & _
47                                               "\ch12\knight.cur")
48    End Sub
49
50    Private Sub picSquare_DragDrop(Index As Integer, _
51                                  Source As Control, _
52                                  x As Single, Y As Single)
53
54       ' Draw image at new position
55       If Index Mod 2 Then
56          picSquare(Index).Picture = LoadPicture("d:\images\ch" & _
57                                                 "12\w_knight.jpg")
58       Else
59          picSquare(Index).Picture = LoadPicture("d:\images\ch" & _
60                                                 "12\b_knight.jpg")
61       End If
62
63       ' Remove last image only if the drop is at
64       ' a different location.
65       If mCurrentCell <> Index Then
66          If Source.Index Mod 2 Then
67             Source.Picture = LoadPicture("d:\images\ch12" & _
68                                          "\w_marble.jpg")
69          Else
70             Source.Picture = LoadPicture("d:\images\ch12" & _
71                                          "\b_marble.jpg")
72          End If
73
74       End If
75
76       ' Update current image position
77       mCurrentCell = Index
78    End Sub
```

**Fig. 12.10**   Demonstrating manual drag-and-drop (part 2 of 4).

When executed, **Form_Load** sets **mCurrentCell** that the knight occupies to zero and loads the image representing the knight into **picSquare(2)**'s **Picture** property.

Clicking on any board square results in **MouseDown** being called. When the square currently displaying the knight is clicked, the line

```
picSquare(currentCell).Drag vbBeginDrag
```

initiates the drag-and-drop process on the **PictureBox** displaying the knight. The mouse button must be held in order for the drag-and-drop operation to remain in effect. Method **Drag** is used for manual drag-and-drop operations.

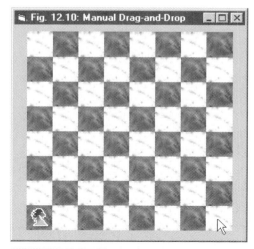

Initial GUI at execution.

GUI when the user is performing a drag operation. Note the change in the mouse pointer. Since a drop has not occurred, the original image is still visible.

**Fig. 12.10**   Demonstrating manual drag-and-drop (part 3 of 4).

Moving the mouse, while the mouse button is still held, over any **PictureBox** results in that **PictureBox**'s **DragOver** event procedure being called. The line

```
picSquare(Index).DragIcon = LoadPicture("d:\images" & _
                                        "\ch12\knight.cur")
```

loads a knight image which is displayed during the drag portion of the drag-and-drop. Only the **PictureBox** beneath the current mouse pointer location displays the **DragIcon** image. If an image is not provided for property **DragIcon**, an arrow surrounded by a hollow square is displayed.

*Common Programming Error 12.2*

*Using a file that is not an icon file (.**ICO**) or a cursor file (.**CUR**) for the **DragIcon** property file is a run-time error.*

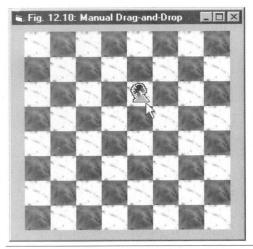

GUI after user drops the knight.

**Fig. 12.10**   Demonstrating manual drag-and-drop (part 4 of 4).

**Common Programming Error 12.3**

*Using a non-existent file for the* **DragIcon** *property file is a run-time error.*

Releasing the mouse button on a control results in that control's **DragDrop** event procedure being called. The **PictureBox** that receives the **DragDrop** event loads and displays the knight image, and if the drag-and-drop operation did not occur on the same **PictureBox**, either the line

```
Source.Picture = LoadPicture("d:\images\ch12\w_marble.jpg")
```

or

```
Source.Picture = LoadPicture("d:\images\ch12\b_marble.jpg")
```

is executed. Parameter *Source* corresponds to the control being dragged. The knight image is cleared from the **Source PictureBox**. The *target* is the control where the **Source** is dropped. Variable **mCurrentCell** is then updated to the **Index**.

Although not used in this example, event procedure **DragOver** provides a *State* parameter that can have three different values: **0** (entered), **1** (exited) and **2** (over). This enables the programmer to control the **DragOver** more precisely.

Unlike manual drag-and-drop, which provides the programmer with control over the entire drag-and-drop, *automatic drag-and-drop* always allows a drag-and-drop operation to occur. Changing a control's **DragMode** property to **1** enables automatic drag-and-drop. Automatic drag-and-drop does not use event procedure **Drag**. The program of Fig. 12.11 demonstrates automatic drag-and-drop. The GUI displays 13 buttons that the user can drag-and-drop around the form to create words or phrases.

In **Form_Load**, each control array element's **DragMode** property is set to **1** (automatic drag-and-drop). When automatic drag-and-drop is set for a control, the control cannot respond to **MouseDown** and **MouseUp** events even if event procedures are provided. Clicking and holding the mouse button will also initiate the drag-and-drop.

```
1    ' Fig. 12.11
2    ' Demonstrating Automatic drag-and-drop
3    Option Explicit          ' General declaration
4
5    Private Sub Form_Load()
6       Dim a As Integer
7
8       ' Set all DragMode properties to Automatic
9       For a = cmdButton.LBound To cmdButton.UBound
10         cmdButton(a).DragMode = 1     ' Automatic
11      Next a
12
13   End Sub
14
15   Private Sub Form_DragDrop(Source As Control, X As Single, _
16                       Y As Single)
17
18      Dim w As Integer, h As Integer
19
20      ' Center control on mouse pointer
21      w = X - Source.Width / 2
22      h = Y - Source.Height / 2
23
24      ' Move button to location where drop occurs
25      Call Source.Move(w, h)
26   End Sub
```

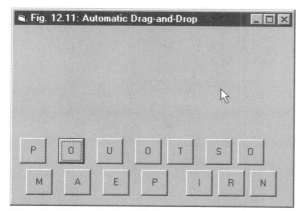

Initial GUI at execution.

**Fig. 12.11**   Demonstrating automatic drag-and-drop (part 1 of 2).

Releasing the mouse button results in event procedure **DragDrop** being called. The lines

```
w = X - Source.Width / 2
h = Y - Source.Height / 2
```

calculate the *x*-coordinate and *y*-coordinate where the dragged button is to be moved. We perform this calculation such that the control is centered on the mouse pointer when dropped. If we do not perform this calculation and use **X** and **Y** for the new coordinates, the top left button corner aligns on the mouse pointer.

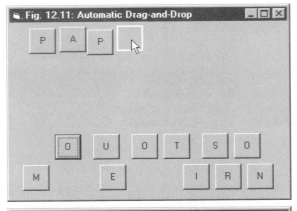

GUI after user has dragged and
dropped three buttons. A drag-
and-drop operation is occurring
on a button.

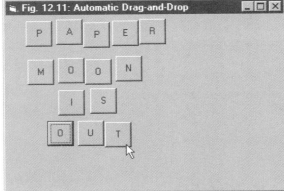

GUI after user has dragged and
dropped all buttons.

**Fig. 12.11**  Demonstrating automatic drag-and-drop (part 2 of 2).

When dragged and dropped, controls do not automatically redraw themselves at the dropped location. The programmer must use method **Move** to accomplish this. Method **Move** draws a control at a new position and removes the control at its initial position.

## 12.7 Key Events

When a user interacts with the keyboard, *key events* (also called *keyboard events*) are generated. Visual Basic provides three event procedures for handling key events: **KeyPress**, **KeyDown** and **KeyUp**. Event procedures **KeyPress** and **KeyDown** are called when a key is pressed, and event procedure **KeyUp** is called when a pressed key is released. **KeyPress** differs from **KeyDown** in that **KeyPress** cannot detect keys such as *Shift*, *Ctrl*, *Alt*, etc. Depending on which key is pressed, all three event procedures may be called. Figure 12.12 lists constants associated with key events.

The program of Fig. 12.13 demonstrates key events. When a key is pressed, both **KeyDown** and **KeyPress** are called. **KeyDown** is used to **Print** the pressed key to the form, and **KeyPress** is used to display the pressed key in the form title bar. **KeyDown** also checks the state of *Shift*, *Ctrl* and *Alt* to change the **ForeColor**. **KeyUp** sets the **ForeColor** to black.

| Constant | ASCII value(s) | Description |
|---|---|---|
| vbKeyA - vbKeyZ | 65-90 | *A* key through *Z* key. |
| vbKeyNumpad0 - vbKeyNumpad9 | 96-105 | Keypad numeric keys *0* through *9*. |
| vbKey0 - vbKey9 | 48-57 | Numeric keys *0* through *9*. |
| vbKeyF1 - vbKeyF16 | 112-127 | Function keys *F1* through *F16*. |
| vbKeyDecimal | 110 | Decimal point key (*Period* key). |
| vbKeyBack | 8 | *Backspace* key. |
| vbKeyTab | 9 | *Tab* key. |
| vbKeyReturn | 13 | *Return* key (or *Enter* key). |
| vbKeyShift | 16 | *Shift* key. |
| vbKeyControl | 17 | *Ctrl* key. |
| vbKeyCapital | 20 | *Caps Lock* key. |
| vbKeyEscape | 27 | *Escape* key. |
| vbKeySpace | 32 | Space bar. |
| vbKeyInsert | 45 | *Insert* key. |
| vbKeyDelete | 46 | *Delete* key. |

**Fig. 12.12**  Common key event constants.

```
1   ' Fig. 12.13
2   ' Demonstrating KeyDown, KeyUp, and KeyPress
3   Option Explicit                 ' General declaration
4   Dim mTitleString As String      ' General declaration
5
6   Private Sub Form_Load()
7      ' Store Caption value for use in KeyPress
8      mTitleString = Caption & Space$(5)
9   End Sub
10
11  Private Sub Form_KeyDown(KeyCode As Integer, Shift As Integer)
12
13     ' Determine which, if any, of the Shift, Ctrl,
14     ' or Alt keys is pressed
15     Select Case Shift
16        Case vbShiftMask                        ' Shift
17           ForeColor = vbYellow
18        Case vbAltMask                          ' Alt
19           ForeColor = vbRed
20        Case vbCtrlMask                         ' Ctrl
21           ForeColor = vbGreen
22        Case vbShiftMask + vbAltMask            ' Shift + Alt
23           ForeColor = vbBlue
```

**Fig. 12.13**  Demonstrating key events (part 1 of 3).

```
24          Case vbShiftMask + vbCtrlMask              ' Shift + Ctrl
25             ForeColor = vbMagenta
26          Case vbAltMask + vbCtrlMask                ' Alt + Ctrl
27             ForeColor = vbCyan
28          Case vbAltMask + vbCtrlMask + vbShiftMask ' All three
29             Call Cls
30       End Select
31
32       ' Test for letter key
33       If KeyCode >= vbKeyA And KeyCode <= vbKeyZ Then
34          Print Chr$(KeyCode);     ' Print the character
35       ElseIf KeyCode = vbKeyReturn Then   ' Return key
36          Print                    ' Print on next line
37       End If
38
39   End Sub
40
41   Private Sub Form_KeyPress(KeyAscii As Integer)
42       ' Update title bar to display the key pressed
43       Caption = mTitleString & "(" & Chr$(KeyAscii) & ")"
44   End Sub
45
46   Private Sub Form_KeyUp(KeyCode As Integer, Shift As Integer)
47       ' When key is released, change ForeColor to black
48       ForeColor = vbBlack
49   End Sub
```

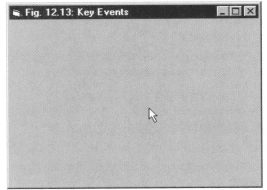

Initial GUI at execution.

**Fig. 12.13**   Demonstrating key events (part 2 of 3).

**KeyDown** parameter **Shift** specifies the status of keys *Shift*, *Ctrl* and *Alt* at the time of the **KeyDown** event. If any combination is pressed when the **KeyDown** event occurs, the **ForeColor** is changed. Parameter *KeyCode*, which contains an ASCII (**Integer**) value representing the key pressed, is checked for a letter. **KeyCode** is case insensitive ("**a**" and "**A**" are treated identically), so the status of the *Shift* key would have to be tested using **Shift** to determine whether or not the "**A**" is uppercase or lowercase. Function *Chr$* is used to convert the characters ASCII value to a **String** representing the character (i.e., **65** is converted to "**A**").

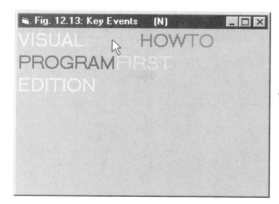

GUI after user has typed text.

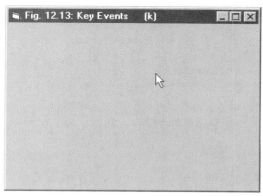

GUI after user has held *Shift, Ctrl* and *Alt* simultaneously to clear the form.

**Fig. 12.13**   Demonstrating key events (part 2 of 2).

Event procedure **KeyPress** also uses **Chr$** to convert the ASCII value to a **String**. **KeyPress** variable **KeyAscii** is case-sensitive. Event procedure **KeyPress** does not contain a **Shift** parameter.

## 12.8 **KeyPreview** Property

If a form contains at least one visible control (i.e., there is a control on the form with its **Visible** property set to **True**) or at least one enabled control, it cannot respond to key events. The form's *KeyPreview* property, when set to **True**, allows a form to receive key events first before they are passed to a control. **KeyPreview** is typically used when several controls need to respond the same way to key events. This allows central handling of the key events, before the events are passed to a control for specialized handling.

The program of Fig. 12.14 demonstrates the **KeyPreview** property by intercepting key events directed at a **TextBox**. **KeyPreview** is used to ensure that only digits are input in the **TextBox** so it can act as a "filter."

Property **KeyPreview** is assigned **True** in **Form_Load**, which allows the form to intercept key events before they are automatically passed to the **TextBox**'s **KeyPress** event procedure. When the user enters data in the **TextBox**, the form's **KeyPress** event procedure is called, which tests for digit characters and updates the **TextBox** display.

```vb
1   ' Fig. 12.14
2   ' Demonstrating the KeyPreview property.
3   Option Explicit                ' General declaration
4
5   Private Sub Form_Load()
6      Call Randomize
7
8      ' Allow Form to get key events first
9      KeyPreview = True
10  End Sub
11
12  Private Sub Form_KeyPress(KeyAscii As Integer)
13
14     ' Only allow numeric keys
15     If KeyAscii >= vbKey0 And KeyAscii <= vbKey9 Then
16        txtInput.Text = txtInput.Text & Chr$(KeyAscii)
17     End If
18
19  End Sub
20
21  Private Sub txtInput_KeyPress(KeyAscii As Integer)
22     KeyAscii = 0    ' Disable event handling
23  End Sub
24
25  Private Sub txtInput_KeyUp(KeyCode As Integer, Shift As Integer)
26
27     Select Case Int(Rnd() * 3)
28        Case 0
29           txtInput.BackColor = vbYellow
30        Case 1
31           txtInput.BackColor = vbCyan
32        Case 2
33           txtInput.BackColor = vbRed
34     End Select
35
36  End Sub
```

Initial GUI at execution.

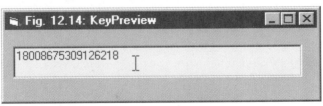

GUI after user enters a series of numbers.

**Fig. 12.14**   Demonstrating property **KeyPreview**.

Rather than having the **TextBox**'s **KeyPress** event procedure do any additional event handling, we disable the handling mechanism with the line

```
KeyAscii = 0
```

Event procedure **KeyUp** is used to randomly change the **TextBox**'s **BackColor** property. Since **KeyUp** has not been disabled, it is called every time a key is released.

## Summary

- Users interact with Visual Basic programs with the mouse and keyboard. The mouse is used to click buttons, move windows, resize windows, etc.

- Visual Basic controls are capable of recognizing when the mouse is single-clicked or double-clicked. Controls are also capable of recognizing other mouse events (such as moving the mouse, pressing a mouse button, and releasing a mouse button).

- Like other events, the programmer writes code to perform some action when a mouse event is triggered.

- Visual Basic also provides the capability to test which mouse button (left, middle, or right) was pressed.

- Visual Basic provides the ability to determine which keyboard key was pressed. The programmer can handle all key events (pressing a key and releasing a key) at the form level or at the control level.

- A form or control's **MousePointer** property determines the shape of the mouse pointer when the mouse pointer enters the area of the control.

- **OptionButton**s form a group in which at any point in time only one **OptionButton** is **True**. Clicking any **OptionButton** sets it to **True** while setting all other **OptionButton**s in the group to **False**.

- Visual Basic provides five mouse-related event procedures: **Click**, **DblClick**, **MouseDown**, **MouseUp** and **MouseMove**.

- Mouse event procedure **Click** is called when a mouse button is clicked once. Event procedure **DblClick** is called when a mouse button is clicked twice in rapid succession. Event procedure **MouseDown** is called when a mouse button is pressed. Event procedure **MouseUp** is called when a mouse button is released, and event procedure **MouseMove** is called when the mouse is moved. Visual Basic only recognizes mouse events when they occur on a form or a form's control.

- Event procedure **Form_MouseDown** is called when the right or left mouse button is clicked. The form's **CurrentX** and **CurrentY** properties are set to the **X**-coordinate and **Y**-coordinate of where the **MouseDown** occurred.

- Moving the mouse over the form results in event procedure **Form_MouseMove** being called.

- The **Button** argument of **MouseDown**, **MouseUp** and **MouseMove** determines which mouse button was pressed. A mouse may have one, two or three buttons. A mouse with three buttons has a left button, a middle button and a right button. A mouse with two buttons has a left and a right mouse button. A mouse with one button has a left mouse button.

- The mouse button constants associated with the **Button** argument are **1** if the right mouse button is pressed, **2** if the left button is pressed and **4** if the middle button is pressed. Combinations of buttons can be tested by adding these values.

- The status of the *Shift*, *Ctrl* and *Alt* keys can be determined when a **MouseDown**, **MouseMove** or **MouseUp** event occurs. A value representing the status of these keys is stored in variable **Shift**. **Shift** constants can be combined to check for combinations of *Shift*, *Ctrl* and *Alt*.

- The mouse can be used at run-time for drag-and-drop operations. A drag-and-drop operation consists of pressing and holding down the left mouse button, moving the mouse, and releasing the mouse button (resulting in the event procedure **DragDrop** being called).

- While a drag-and-drop operation is in progress, mouse events and key events initiated by the user are not recognized.

- Visual Basic provides manual drag-and-drop and automatic drag-and-drop which are specified in a control's **DragMode** property. The default drag-and-drop is manual drag-and-drop, which has a **DragMode** value of **0**.

- Manual drag-and-drop allows the programmer to determine when a drag-and-drop operation should occur and requires the use of method **Drag**.

- Event procedure **DragOver** is called for a control when a drag-and-drop operation is in progress and the area of the control is entered. Property **DragIcon** is used to display an image while the drag-and-drop operation is in progress.

- Moving the mouse, while the mouse button is still held, over any **PictureBox** results in that **PictureBox**'s **DragOver** event procedure being called.

- Only the **PictureBox** beneath the current mouse pointer location displays the **DragIcon** image. If an image is not provided for property **DragIcon**, an arrow surrounded by a hollow square is displayed.

- Releasing the mouse button on a control results in that control's **DragDrop** event procedure being called.

- Event procedure **DragOver** provides parameter **State** that can have values **0** (entered), **1** (exited) and **2** (over). This provides more precise control of a **DragOver** event. Unlike manual drag-and-drop, which provides the programmer with control over the entire drag-and-drop, automatic drag-and-drop always allows a drag-and-drop operation to occur. Changing a control's **DragMode** property to **1** enables automatic drag-and-drop. Automatic drag-and-drop does not use event procedure **Drag**.

- When automatic drag-and-drop is set for a control, the control cannot respond to **MouseDown** and **MouseUp** events even if event procedures are provided. Clicking and holding the mouse button will also initiate the drag-and-drop.

- When dragged and dropped, controls do not automatically redraw themselves at the dropped location. The programmer must use method **Move** to accomplish this. Method **Move** draws a control at a new position and removes the control at its initial position.

- When a user interacts with the keyboard, key events (also called keyboard events) are generated. Visual Basic provides three event procedures for handling key events: **KeyPress**, **KeyDown** and **KeyUp**. Event procedures **KeyPress** and **KeyDown** are called when a key is pressed, and **KeyUp** is called when a pressed key is released. **KeyPress** differs from **KeyDown** in that **KeyPress** cannot detect keys such as Shift, Ctrl, Alt, etc.

- **KeyDown** parameter **Shift** is used to determine the status of the Shift, Ctrl and Alt keys.

- **KeyCode** is case insensitive ("**a**" and "**A**" are treated identically), so the status of the Shift key would have to be tested using **Shift** to determine if a letter is uppercase or lowercase.

- If a form contains at least one visible control (i.e., the control's **Visible** property is **True**) or at least one enabled control, it cannot respond to key events.

- The form's **KeyPreview** property, when set to **True**, allows a form to receive the key events first before they are passed to the control. **KeyPreview** is typically used in situations where several controls need to respond the same way to key events. This allows central handling of the key events before the events are passed to a control for specialized handling.

## Terminology

*Alt* key

**And**ing with a mask

animated cursor (**.ANI** file)

arrow cursor

arrow hourglass cursor

arrow question mark cursor

automatic drag-and-drop operation

**BackColor** property

bit field

bit manipulation

**Button** bit field

**Chr$** function

**Click** event procedure

click the mouse

crosshair cursor

cross mouse pointer

*Ctrl* key

cursor image (**.CUR** file)

custom cursor

**DblClick** event procedure

default mouse pointer

double-click the mouse

drag-and-drop

**DragDrop** event procedure

**DragIcon** property

**Drag** method

**DragMode** property

**DragOver** event procedure

drop operation

**ForeColor** property

**Form_Click** event procedure

**Form_DblClick** event procedure

hourglass cursor

icon image (**.ICO** file)

icon pointer

I-beam cursor

icon mouse pointer

**KeyAscii** variable

keyboard

keyboard events

**KeyCode** variable

**KeyDown** event procedure

key events

**KeyPress** event procedure

**KeyPreview** property

**KeyUp** event procedure

left mouse button

**LoadPicture** function

manual drag-and-drop operation

middle mouse button

mouse

mouse button

**MouseDown** event procedure

mouse event

**MouseMove** event procedure

mouse pointer

**MousePointer** property

**MouseUp** event procedure

move the mouse

no drop mouse pointer

North-East-South-West cursor

North-South cursor

North-West-South-East cursor

press a key

press the mouse button

release a key

release the mouse button

right mouse button

shape of mouse pointer

**Shift** bit field

*Shift* key

size all cursor

size mouse pointer

size NE SW mouse pointer

size N S mouse pointer

size NW SE mouse pointer

size W E mouse pointer

sizing cursor

up-arrow cursor

**vbAltMask** constant

**vbArrow** constant

**vbArrowHourglass** constant

**vbArrowQuestion** constant

**vbBeginDrag** constant

**vbCancelDrag** constant

**vbCrosshair** constant

**vbCtrlMask** constant

**vbCustom** constant

**vbEndDrag** constant

**vbHourglass** constant

**vbIbeam** constant

**vbKey0** through **vbKey9** constants (*0–9*)

**vbKeyA** through **vbKeyZ** constants (*A–Z*)

**vbKeyBack** constant (*Backspace* key)

**vbKeyCapital** constant (*Caps Lock* key)

**vbKeyControl** constant (*Ctrl* key)

**vbKeyDecimal** constant (*Period* key)

**vbKeyDelete** constant (*Delete* key)

**vbKeyEscape** constant (*Escape* key)
**vbKeyF1–vbKeyF16** constants (*F1–F16*)
**vbKeyInsert** constant (*Insert* key)
**vbKeyNumpad0–vbKeyNumpad9** constants
   (*0* key through *9* key)
**vbKeyReturn** constant (*Return* key)
**vbKeyShift** constant (*Shift* key)
**vbKeySpace** constant (spacebar)
**vbKeyTab** constant (*Tab* key)
**vbLeftButton** constant
**vbMiddleButton** constant
**vbNoDrop** constant

**vbRightButton** constant
**vbShiftMask** constant
**vbSizeAll** constant
**vbSizeNESW** constant
**vbSizeNS** constant
**vbSizeNWSE** constant
**vbSizeWE** constant
**vbSizePointer** constant
**vbUpArrow** constant
West-East cursor
**X** variable
**Y** variable

## Common Programming Errors

**12.1**  Attempting to use animated cursors for **MousePointer** images is not allowed.
**12.2**  Using a file that is not an icon file (**.ICO**) or a cursor file (**.CUR**) for the **DragIcon** property file is a run-time error.
**12.3**  Using a non-existent file for the **DragIcon** property file is a run-time error.

## Look-and-Feel Observation

**12.1**  A control's default mouse pointer (and all other mouse pointers) can differ from the arrow if it has been set at the system level through the control panel.

## Portability Tip

**12.1**  The frequency of the **MouseMove** event is system dependent. The triggering of a **Mouse-Move** event is not necessarily continuous as the mouse is moved over objects (some systems may trigger the event more often than others).

## Self-Review Exercises

**12.1**  Fill in the blanks in each of the following:
   a)  A two-button mouse has a _____ button and a _____ button.
   b)  The _____, _____ and _____ keys may be tested for using the **Shift** parameter of the **MouseDown** event procedure.
   c)  The _____ property determines which icon is displayed as the pointer during a drag-and-drop operation.
   d)  The _____ method is used to move an object.
   e)  The _____ event responds to pressing a mouse button down.
   f)  The **MousePointer** property must be set to a value of _____ for the hourglass.

**12.2**  State which of the following are *true* and which are *false*. If *false*, explain why.
   a)  A form is capable of responding to a **MouseMove** event.
   b)  When the mouse is captured by a form or object, the **MouseCapture** event is triggered.
   c)  A mouse always has three buttons (left, center and right).
   d)  The **Button** variable contains information as to which combination of the *Shift*, *Ctrl* and *Alt* keys was pressed.
   e)  The **MousePointer** property can be changed at run-time.

**12.3**  Find the error in each of the following and explain how to correct it.
   a)  **' In form's MouseUp event procedure**

```
     If Shift = 3 Then        ' Test for middle mouse button
        Print "Middle mouse button was pressed."
     End If
```

b) ' Change mouse pointer for the form

```
     Private Sub optDisplayArrow_Click ()
        frmMyForm.MousePointer = Arrow      ' Arrow cursor
     End Sub
```

## Answers to Self-Review Exercises

**12.1**    a) left, right. b) *Shift, Ctrl, Alt.* c) **DragIcon**. d) **Drag**. e) **MouseDown**. f) **vbHourglass** or **11**.

**12.2**    a) True.
   b) False. There is no **MouseCapture** event procedure.
   c) False. A mouse can have one, two or three buttons.
   d) False. Variable **Button** contains information as to which mouse button was pressed.
   e) True.

**12.3**    a) The middle button has a value of **4**. **Shift** should be tested for a value of **4** or **vbMiddleButton**.
   b) Arrow should be **vbArrow** or **1**.

## Exercises

**12.4**    Fill in the blanks in each of the following:
   a) The _____ event is triggered when a pressed mouse button is released.
   b) The process of moving an object with the mouse to another location is called _____.
   c) The **DragMode** property is either _____ or _____.
   d) Movement of the mouse triggers the _____ event.
   e) The **MousePointer** property can have _____ different values.

**12.5**    State which of the following are *true* and which are *false*. If *false*, explain why.
   a) The mouse pointer can be changed using the **MousePointer** property.
   b) Visual Basic allows animated cursors to be used for the mouse pointer.
   c) Method **Move** must be used with manual drag-and-drop.
   d) Operator **And** is often used in bit manipulation for masking.
   e) The status of the *Shift, Ctrl* and *Alt* keys is stored in the most significant bits of the **Shift** bit field.
   f) The status of mouse buttons is stored in the least significant bits of the **Button** bit field.

**12.6**    (*Towers of Hanoi*) Modify your solution to Exercise 6.32 to allow the user to drag-and-drop a disk from one tower to another.

**12.7**    (*Knight's Tour*) Modify your solution to Exercise 7.19 to use the graphical features of Fig. 12.10. As the knight leaves a square, the appropriate move number should be displayed on the square.

**12.8**    (*Knight's Tour*) Modify your solution to Exercise 12.7 to provide a **Hint** button. When **Hint** is pressed, display an asterisk on the square with the lowest accessibility. If the user can no longer make any moves or if the tour is successfully completed, disable the **Hint** button.

**12.9**    (*Eight Queens*) Modify your solution to Exercise 7.22 to allow the user to drag-and-drop each queen on the board. Use the graphical features of Fig. 12.10. Provide eight queen images to the left of the board from which the user can drag-and-drop onto the board. When a queen is dropped on the board, its corresponding image to the left should not be visible.

**12.10**  Write a program that uses the mouse to draw a square on the form. The upper-left coordinate should be the location where the user first pressed the mouse button, and the lower-right coordinate should be the location where the user releases the mouse button. Also display the area in twips in the **Caption**.

**12.11**  Modify your solution to Exercise 12.10 to allow the user to draw different shapes. As a minimum, the user should be allowed to choose from an oval, circle, line and rectangle. Allow the user to select the shape type from a menu.

**12.12**  Modify your solution to Exercise 12.11 to allow the user to specify the shape using the keyboard. The shape drawn should be determined by the following keys: *o* for oval, *c* for circle, *r* for rectangle, *O* for a solid oval, *C* for a solid circle, *R* for a solid rectangle and *L* for line. All drawing is done in the color blue. The initial shape defaults to a circle.

**12.13**  Modify your solution to Exercise 12.10 or Exercise 12.11 to provide a "rubber-banding" effect. As the user drags the mouse, the user should be able to see the current size of the rectangle to know exactly what the rectangle will look like when the mouse button is released.

**12.14**  Modify your solution to Exercise 11.12 to change the ANSI C keywords to green after the word is typed. Remove the button from your solution.

**12.15**  *(Drawing program)* Write a program that allows the user to draw "free-hand" images with the mouse in a **PictureBox**. Provide a button that allows the user to clear the **PictureBox**.

**12.16**  Modify Exercise 12.15 to allow the user to select the drawing color and the pen size.

# Error Handling and Debugging

## Objectives

- To understand errors and how to handle them.
- To be able to use the **On Error** Statement.
- To understand the use of labels in error handling.
- To be able to use the **Resume** statement.
- To be able to use the **Err** object to determine what error occurred.
- To understand error handling and the call stack.
- To understand the debugger elements.

*I never forget a face, but in your case I'll make an exception.*
Groucho (Julius Henry) Marx

*It is common sense to take a method and try it. If it fails, admit it frankly and try another. But above all, try something.*
Franklin Delano Roosevelt

*O! throw away the worser part of it,*
*And live the purer with the other half.*
William Shakespeare

*If they're running and they don't look where they're going I have to come out from somewhere and catch them.*
Jerome David Salinger

*And oftentimes excusing of a fault*
*Doth make the fault the worse by the excuse.*
William Shakespeare

*To err is human, to forgive divine.*
Alexander Pope, *An Essay on Criticism*

# Outline

## 13.1  Introduction

*Error handling* enables programmers to write clearer, more robust, more fault-tolerant programs. Error handling enables the programmer to attempt to *recover* (i.e., continue executing) from infrequent *fatal errors* rather than letting them occur and suffering the
consequences (such as loss of application data). If an error is severe and recovery is not possible, the program can be exited "gracefully"—all files can be closed and notification can
be given that the program is terminating. The recovery code is called an *error handler*.

Error handling is designed for dealing with *synchronous errors* such as an attempt to
divide by zero (that occurs as the program executes the divide instruction). Other common
examples of synchronous errors are memory exhaustion, an out-of-bounds array index, and
arithmetic overflow. Error handling provides the programmer with a disciplined set of
capabilities for dealing with these types of errors.

Error-handling code varies in nature and amount among software systems depending
on the application and whether or not the software is a product for release. Products tend to
contain much more error-handling code than is contained in "casual" software.

*Testing and Debugging Tip 13.1*

*It is best to incorporate your error-handling strategy into a program from the inception of
the design process. It is difficult to add effective error handling after a program has been implemented.*

Usually, error-handling code is interspersed throughout a program's code. Errors are dealt with at the places in the code where errors are likely to occur. The advantage of this approach is that a programmer reading the code can see the error handling in the immediate vicinity of the code and determine if the proper error handling has been implemented.

The problem with this scheme is that code in a sense becomes "polluted" with error handling. It becomes difficult for a programmer concerned with the application itself to read the code and determine if the code is functioning correctly. Error handling often makes the code more difficult to understand and maintain.

*Software Engineering Observation 13.1*

*Flow of control with conventional control structures is generally clearer and more efficient than with error handling.*

## 13.2  When Error Handling Should Be Used

Error handling should be used

- to process only exceptional situations, despite the fact that there is nothing to prevent the programmer from using errors as an alternative form of program control.

- to process errors for components that are not geared to handling those errors directly.

- to process errors from software components such as functions, procedures and ActiveX controls that are likely to be widely used, and where it does not make sense for those components to handle their own errors.

- on large projects to handle error processing in a uniform manner project-wide.

*Good Programming Practice 13.1*

*Use conventional techniques (rather than error handling) for straightforward, local error processing in which a program is easily able to deal with its own errors.*

## 13.3  A Simple Error-Handling Example: Divide by Zero

Now let us consider a simple example of error handling. The program of Fig. 13.1 uses error handling to detect and handle a divide-by-zero error. The GUI consists of two **TextBox**es and three **Label**s. The user enters a value in each **TextBox** and then clicks the **Click Here to Perform Division Label**—which then either displays the result of the division or a message indicating that a divide by zero was attempted.

Before we get into the program's error-handling specifics, we now give a brief overview of how the error handling behaves. If a zero was entered in the second **TextBox**, an error (division by zero) is *raised*. Control is transferred to the error handler, where a message is displayed indicating that a "divide-by-zero error" has occurred and the procedure exits when **End Sub** is executed. If an error handler is not provided in this example and an error is raised, an error message appears in a modal dialog before the program terminates.

Consider the three screen captures. The first shows the GUI as it appears initially at run time. The second shows successful execution. In the third, a zero denominator is input and the program raises and handles the error by displaying the message "**Attempted to divide by zero!**". Without error-handling code, a fatal error occurs, the program displays the dialog of Fig. 13.2 and the program terminates when the user presses **End**. We will discuss what happens with the user presses **Debug** later in this chapter. Pressing **Help** displays help about the error that occurred.

```
1   ' Fig. 13.1
2   ' Divide-by-zero error-handling program
3   Option Explicit            ' General declaration
4
5   Private Sub lblResult_Click()
6       Dim numerator As Double
7       Dim denominator As Double
8
9       numerator = txtInput(0).Text
10      denominator = txtInput(1).Text
11
12      On Error GoTo divideByZeroHandler     ' Set trap
13         lblResult.Caption = "Result is " & numerator / denominator
14
15      Exit Sub     ' Prevents error-handler from being executed
16                   ' if an error is not raised
17
18  divideByZeroHandler:        ' Label for error handler
19      lblResult.Caption = "Attempted divide by zero!"
20
21  End Sub
22
23  Private Sub txtInput_GotFocus(Index As Integer)
24      lblResult.Caption = "Click Here to Perform Division"
25      txtInput(Index).Text = ""    ' Clear TextBox with focus
26  End Sub
```

Initial GUI at execution.

GUI after the user has entered two values and clicked the **Label**.

**Fig. 13.1**   A simple error-handling example with divide by zero (part 1 of 2).

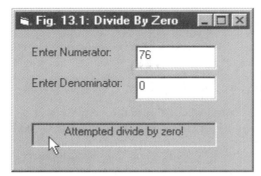

GUI after the user has entered two values (the denominator input is **0**) and clicked the **Label**.

**Fig. 13.1**    A simple error-handling example with divide by zero (part 2 of 2).

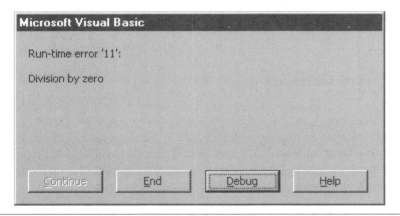

**Fig. 13.2**    Dialog displayed when a division-by-zero error is not handled.

Clicking the **Click Here to Perform Division Label** results in the values input being stored in variables **numerator** and **denominator**. Line 12,

```
On Error GoTo divideByZeroHandler
```

sets or *enables* the *error trap* using **On Error Goto**. The name **divideByZeroHandler** is a programmer-defined *label* where a procedure or function's error-handling code begins. If an error is detected after a trap has been enabled, control is transferred to the label and execution of the error handler's code begins. Although not shown in this example, an error trap in a procedure can be *disabled* with the line

```
On Error Goto 0
```

Raised errors are still detected but not directed to an error handler in the procedure. Disabling error handlers is commonly done when using the Visual Basic debugger, which we discuss later in this chapter.

*Common Programming Error 13.1*

*Specifying in an **On Error GoTo** statement a label that is not in the same procedure or func-tion is a syntax error.*

The statement

```
lblResult.Caption = "Result is " & numerator / denominator
```

divides **numerator** by **denominator** and concatenates the result to a **String**. If the division operation does not *raise* (i.e., generate) an error, the result after implicit conversion and concatenation is assigned to **lblResult**'s **Caption** property. **Exit Sub** is execut-ed next. **Exit Sub** is used to separate the procedure code from the error-handling code. Without **Exit Sub**, the error-handling code is executed—even if an error is not raised.

*Common Programming Error 13.2*

*Forgetting to use the **Exit Sub** or **Exit Function** to prevent error-trapping code from executing unintentionally is a run-time logic error because the error-trapping code will exe-cute even if an error does not occur.*

If the division raises an error, Visual Basic detects the error and transfers control to the label

```
divideByZeroException:
```

Labels (which are not related to **Label** controls) always ends in a colon. Labels are left justified by Visual Basic and cannot be indented by the programmer. Error-handling code follows the label, which in this particular case sets the **lblResult**'s **Caption** to "**At-tempted to divide by zero!**". **End Sub** is then executed and the program returns to an event-monitoring state. Upon exiting the procedure, the error handler is disabled.

*Common Programming Error 13.3*

*Omitting the colon at the end of a label is a syntax error.*

The program also introduces event procedure **GotFocus**, which is called for a form or control that receives the *focus* (i.e., becomes the active control). Clicking a control with the mouse or using the *Tab* key transfers the focus. Event procedure **GotFocus** is used to change **lblResult**'s **Caption** and to clear the **TextBox** that receives the focus. Although not introduced here, the form and most controls provide the event procedure **LostFocus**, which is called just before the form or another control receives the focus.

## 13.4 Nested **On Error** Statements

Figure 13.1 does not handle every type of error that can be raised. Consider the lines

```
numerator = txtInput(0).Text
denominator = txtInput(1).Text
```

which implicitly converts **String**s to **Integer**s. These two lines are not part of the trap, because they precede the **On Error Goto** line. Any errors they raise, such as type mis-match errors (i.e., errors that occur when non-digit characters are input), will not be handled in **divideByZeroError**, which results in a fatal error.

**On Error** statements can be nested (i.e., one inside another) to direct an error to a specific handler. When an error is raised, control is transferred to the nearest trap's error-handler—i.e., the last executed **On Error** statement before the line that raises the error.

The program of Fig. 13.3 modifies the program of Fig. 13.1 to add an additional error-handler for type mismatch errors.

```
1    ' Fig. 13.3
2    ' Divide-by-zero error-handling program
3    Option Explicit            ' General declaration
4
5    Private Sub lblResult_Click()
6        Dim numerator As Double
7        Dim denominator As Double
8
9        On Error GoTo inputHandler
10           numerator = txtInput(0).Text
11           denominator = txtInput(1).Text
12
13           ' Nested On Error statement
14           On Error GoTo divideByZeroHandler
15              lblResult.Caption = "Result is " & _
16                                    numerator / denominator
17
18       Exit Sub      ' Prevents errorhandler from being executed
19                     ' if an error is not raised
20
21   divideByZeroHandler:              ' Label for error handler
22       lblResult.Caption = "Attempted divide by zero!"
23       Exit Sub          ' Prevent next handler from executing
24
25   inputHandler:
26       lblResult.Caption = "Attempted non-numeric input!"
27   End Sub
28
29   Private Sub txtInput_GotFocus(Index As Integer)
30       lblResult.Caption = "Click Here to Perform Division"
31       txtInput(Index).Text = ""    ' Clear TextBox with focus
32   End Sub
```

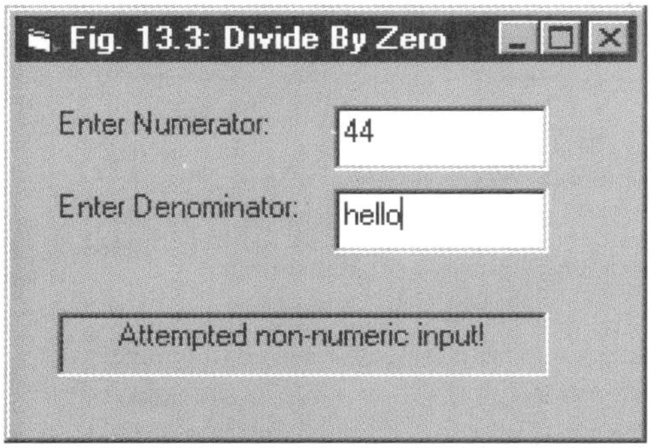

GUI after the user has entered a invalid input and clicked the **Label**.

**Fig. 13.3**    Demonstrating nested **On Error** statements.

Line 9 enables the outer error trap. If an error is raised on either line 10 or line 11, control is directed to the error handler labeled **inputHandler**. Line 14 enables an inner error trap, which specifies where control is transferred if an error is raised. Any error, even a type mismatch error if it could somehow occur, transfers control to the handler labeled **divideByZeroHandler**. Enabling the inner error trap disables the outer trap.

**Exit Sub** is added to the error handler **divideByZeroHandler**, in order to avoid accidentally executing **inputHandler**'s error handler.

In this example, we used another label, named **inputHandler**. Visual Basic also allows *number labels*. For example, we could rewrite line 9 as

```
On Error Goto 8675
```

where the number is any positive non-zero number and rewrite line 25 as

```
8675:
```

For number labels, the colon is optional. If the colon is not provided, **8675** is treated as a line number.

*Common Programming Error 13.4*

*Attempting to set a negative line number or a negative line number label is a syntax error.*

*Common Programming Error 13.5*

*Specifying in an **On Error GoTo** statement a line number or line label that is not in the same procedure or function is a syntax error.*

Nested error handlers often work only for the simplest functions or procedures. More complex procedures and functions can raise the same error type from potentially many locations. Often it is easier to use only one handler for all raised errors. We discuss this in the next section.

## 13.5 **Err** Object

The **Err** object provides information about the raised error in six properties and provides two methods. Using the **Err** object allows the programmer to provide detailed error information. Three of these **Err** properties and both **Err** methods are summarized in Fig. 13.4.

| Property/method | Data type | Description |
|---|---|---|
| *Properties* | | |
| **Description** | **String** | A **String** describing the error. |
| **Number** | **Long** | Internal error number determined by Visual Basic or a component with which the program interacts (such as a control). |
| **Source** | **String** | File name where the error was raised or the source of the error is the error was outside the application. |

**Fig. 13.4**    Common **Err** object properties and methods (part 1 of 2).

| Property/method | Data type | Description |
|---|---|---|
| *Methods* | | |
| `Clear` | | Clears an error—numeric properties are set to 0 and **String** properties are set to empty **String**s. |
| `Raise` | | Raises an error. |

**Fig. 13.4** Common **Err** object properties and methods (part 2 of 2).

*Portability Tip 13.1*

*Err replaces function Error. Do not use function Error because it is obsolete and provided only for backwards compatibility with older versions of Visual Basic. Future versions of Visual Basic may not provide function Error.*

*Portability Tip 13.2*

*The Description property String can differ between versions of Visual Basic.*

Property **Number** is perhaps the most useful of all **Err** properties. If only one error handler is provided in a procedure or function, the **Number** property is normally used to determine which error was raised. Figure 13.5 randomly raises an error and handles the error. **Err** properties **Source** and **Description** are printed and **Err** property **Number**'s value determines the **ForeColor** used for **Print**ing the **Description**.

```
1   ' Fig. 13.5
2   ' Using the Err object
3   Option Explicit          ' General declaration
4
5   Private Sub cmdPrint_Click()
6      Dim num As Integer
7
8      Call Cls          ' Clear form
9      Font.Size = 12    ' Set form Font size to 12 pt.
10
11     On Error GoTo errorHandler   ' Set trap
12
13        ' Randomly manufacture an error
14        Select Case Int(Rnd() * 3)
15           Case 0
16              num = 888888888    ' Overflow error
17           Case 1
18              num = 88 / 0       ' Divide-by-zero error
19           Case 2
20              num = "an Error"   ' Type mismatch
21        End Select
22
23        Exit Sub    ' Exit procedure
```

**Fig. 13.5** Program that uses the **Err** object (part 1 of 2).

```
24
25  errorHandler:
26     Print "Source: " & Err.Source
27     Print "Error: ";
28
29     Select Case Err.Number
30        Case 6      ' Overflow
31           ForeColor = vbYellow
32        Case 11     ' Divide by zero
33           ForeColor = vbWhite
34        Case 13     ' Type mismatch
35           ForeColor = vbBlue
36        Case Else
37           Print "Unexpected error!!!"
38     End Select
39
40     Print Err.Description     ' Print description
41     ForeColor = vbBlack
42  End Sub
```

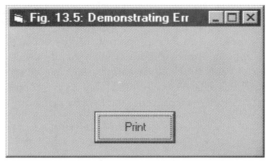

Initial GUI at execution.

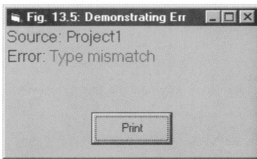

GUI after user clicks **Print**. One of three possible **Description**s is printed.

**Fig. 13.5**    Program that uses the **Err** object (part 2 of 2).

Pressing **Print** clears the form and sets the form's **Font** object property's **Size**. Line 11 sets the error trap. The **Select Case** statement randomly raises an error. Line 23 is never executed and is provided for consistency. The statement

```
Print "Source: " & Err.Source
```

displays the **Err** object's **Source** property. A **Select Case** tests the number contained in the **Err** object's **Number** property for an Overflow error, Divide-by-Zero error, or Type mismatch error and changes. Once the error type is identified, the form's **ForeColor** property is changed. The **Err** object's **Description** property is then **Print**ed.

## 13.6 Resume Statement

The **Resume** statement specifies where in a procedure or function execution continues after an error is handled. Figure 13.6 illustrates the three basic uses of **Resume** in an event handler continuing execution at the line that raised the error, continuing execution at the next executable line following the line that raised the error and continuing at a specified label (which can appear anywhere within the procedure or function). When using **Resume** to re-execute the statement that caused the error, provide a way for the user to terminate the task being performed in the event that the error cannot be handled properly.

*Testing and Debugging Tip 13.2*
_____
**Resume** *label,* **Resume Next** *and* **Resume** *only apply to the current procedure or function.*

*Common Programming Error 13.6*
_____
*Using the* **Resume** *statement outside error-handling code can create logic problems at runtime.*

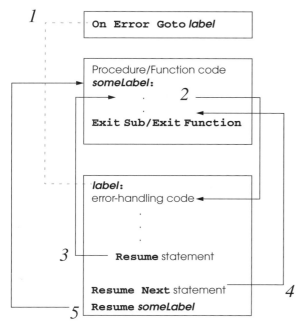

Fig. 13.6    **Resume** flow of control.

Figure 13.7 allows the user to select one of three error-handling responses. Clicking **Go** displays an input dialog using function **_InputBox_**. The dialog prompts the user to enter an **Integer**. Type mismatch errors are raised when non-numeric values are input.

```
1   ' Fig. 13.7
2   ' Resume example
3   Option Explicit              ' General declaration
4
5   Private Sub cmdGo_Click()
6       Dim x As Integer
7       Dim s As String
8
9   resumeLabel:
10      s = "Visual Basic How to Program!"
11      Print s
12
13      On Error GoTo handler
14
15          ' InputBox can raise OverFlow and Type
16          ' mismatch errors
17          x = InputBox("Enter an integer:", s)
18
19          Print "Value of x is " & x
20          Exit Sub
21
22   handler:
23
24      If optResume.Value Then
25          Print "Resume: ";
26          Resume          ' Repeat line that raised error
27      ElseIf optResumeNext.Value Then
28          Print "Resume Next: ";
29         Resume Next  ' Resume at next line after error-raising line
30      Else    ' optResumeLabel
31          Print "Label: ";
32          Resume resumeLabel  ' Resume at label resumeLabel
33      End If
34
35   End Sub
36
37   Private Sub optResume_Click()
38       Call Cls
39   End Sub
40
41   Private Sub optResumeLabel_Click()
42       Call Cls
43   End Sub
44
45   Private Sub optResumeNext_Click()
46       Call Cls
47   End Sub
```

**Fig. 13.7**    Demonstrating **Resume** (part 1 of 3).

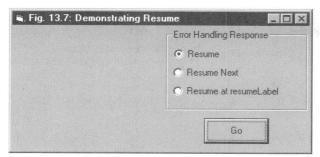

Initial GUI at execution. Pressing **Go** results in a dialog being displayed.

**Close** box

Dialog displayed by function **InputBox**

prompt

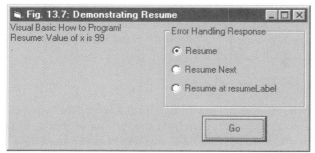

GUI after the user has pressed **Go** and entered valid data in the input dialog. When an error is raised, the input dialog is repeatedly displayed until valid input

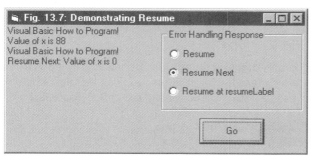

GUI after user has entered a data value of **88** (which does not raise an error) and attempted invalid input (which raises an error). When an error is raised and **Resume Next** is selected, **x** is not assigned a value from the input dialog, therefore **x** has the default initialization of **0**.

**Fig. 13.7**    Demonstrating **Resume** (part 2 of 3).

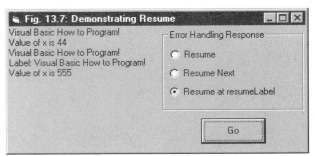

GUI after user has entered a data value of **44** (which does not raise an error) and attempted invalid input (which raises an error). When an error is raised and **Resume at resumeLabel** is selected, the **string Visual Basic How to Program!** is printed and the input dialog repeatedly displays until valid data is input.

**Fig. 13.7** Demonstrating **Resume** (part 3 of 3).

Line 17's statement

```
x = InputBox("Enter an integer:", s)
```

calls function **InputBox**. The first argument sets the **InputBox** prompt and the second argument sets the **InputBox** title bar. The dialog generated by **InputBox** is *modal* (i.e., it must be closed before the user is allowed to interact with any other window in the application). User input is entered in the **TextBox** at the bottom of the dialog. The function returns the converted user input.

Pressing **OK**, **Cancel**, or clicking the **Close** box closes the dialog. If the user inputs the value **4**, an error is not raised and **x** is assigned the **4**. The value of **x** is then **Print**ed. If the user does not enter a value, presses **Cancel**, or enters non-numeric data, a Type mismatch error is raised. If the **Resume OptionButton** is selected, function **InputBox** is called repeatedly until valid input occurs. If the **Resume Next OptionButton** is selected, function **InputBox** is not called again and the next line,

```
Print "Value of x is " & x
```

is executed. Variable **x**'s value is **0**—it does not get a value from **InputBox** because an error was raised when **InputBox** attempted to perform a conversion. If **Resume resumeLabel** is selected, execution continues at the label **resumeLabel**. **String s** is **Print**ed again and the **InputBox** dialog is displayed again.

## 13.7 Error Handlers and the Call Stack

Error handling becomes more complex when multiple calls are made. The programmer must decide which errors, if any, each procedure or each function will handle. Should the calling procedure ("the caller") handle the error or should the called procedure ("the callee") handle the error?

Figure 13.8 shows a typical *call stack*. A call stack is the list of procedures and functions that were called in order to get to the current procedure or current function. In Fig. 13.8, procedure **one** calls procedure **two**, which in turn calls procedure **three**, which calls function **four**. The boxes represent each procedure on the call stack.

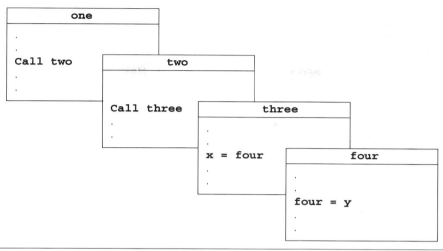

**Fig. 13.8**    A typical call sequence.

If an error occurs in function **four** and **four** does not have an enabled error handler, Visual Basic searches through the call stack—beginning with the caller of function **four**—procedure **three**. If an enabled error handler is found, it is executed—otherwise the caller of procedure **three**—procedure **two** is searched. If procedure **two** has an enabled error handler, it will be executed—otherwise the caller of procedure **two** is searched. If an enabled error handler is found, it is executed—otherwise a fatal error occurs, a dialog box is displayed and the program terminates. Each procedure or function in the call stack must have an error handler. If an error is raised and there is no error handler in the procedure, a fatal error occurs.

The program of Fig. 13.9 demonstrates error handling in the call stack. There are five calls in the call stack and the fifth call raises a run-time error. The GUI allows the user to determine which error handler in the call stack is enabled. The program displays five images, each representing a procedure or function. The image displaying a red 'x' represents the location where the error is raised and the image displaying a green 'x' represents where the error is handled.

```
1   ' Fig. 13.9
2   ' Resume and the call stack
3   Option Explicit              ' General declaration
4   Dim mFlags(4) As Boolean     ' General declaration
5
6   Private Sub Form_Load()
7       Call initializeFlags
8       optSelect(4).Value = True
9   End Sub
10
```

**Fig. 13.9**    Call stack error-handling program (part 1 of 4).

```
11   Private Sub initializeFlags()
12      Dim x As Integer
13
14      For x = LBound(mFlags) To UBound(mFlags)
15         mFlags(x) = False
16         imgImage(x).Picture = LoadPicture("d:\images\" & _
17                                     "ch13\resume1.gif")
18      Next x
19
20   End Sub
21
22   Private Sub setFlag(n As Integer)
23      Call initializeFlags
24      mFlags(n) = True
25   End Sub
26
27   Private Sub cmdBegin_Click()
28
29      If mFlags(0) Then
30         On Error GoTo handler
31      Else
32         On Error GoTo 0   ' Disable error handler
33      End If
34
35      Call one       ' Call procedure one
36      Exit Sub       ' handler's Resume Next executes here
37
38   handler:
39      lblLocation.Caption = "Error handled in cmdBegin_Click"
40      imgImage(0).Picture = LoadPicture(d:\images\" & _
41                                     "ch13\resume3.gif")
42      Resume Next  ' Exit Sub statement
43   End Sub
44
45   Private Sub one()
46
47      If mFlags(1) Then
48         On Error GoTo handlerOne
49      Else
50         On Error GoTo 0   ' Disable error handler
51      End If
52
53      Call two     ' Call procedure two
54      Exit Sub     ' handlerOne's Resume Next executes here
55
56   handlerOne:
57      lblLocation.Caption = "Error handled in one"
58      imgImage(1).Picture = LoadPicture(d:\images\" & _
59                                     "ch13\resume3.gif")
60      Resume Next     ' Exit Sub statement
61   End Sub
62
```

**Fig. 13.9**    Call stack error-handling program (part 2 of 4).

```
63   Private Sub two()
64
65      If mFlags(2) Then
66         On Error GoTo handlerTwo
67      Else
68         On Error GoTo 0   ' Disable error handler
69      End If
70
71      Call three      ' Call procedure three
72      Exit Sub        ' handlerTwo's Resume Next executes here
73
74   handlerTwo:
75      lblLocation.Caption = "Error handled in two"
76      imgImage(2).Picture = LoadPicture(d:\images\" & _
77                                        "ch13\resume3.gif")
78      Resume Next   ' Exit Sub statement
79   End Sub
80
81   Private Sub three()
82      Dim x As Integer
83
84      If mFlags(3) Then
85         On Error GoTo handlerThree
86      Else
87         On Error GoTo 0   ' Disable error handler
88      End If
89
90      x = four()   ' Call function four
91      Exit Sub       ' handlerThree's Resume Next executes here
92
93   handlerThree:
94      lblLocation.Caption = "Error handled in three"
95      imgImage(3).Picture = LoadPicture(d:\images\" & _
96                                        "ch13\resume3.gif")
97      Resume Next   ' Exit Sub statement
98   End Sub
99
100  Private Function four() As Integer
101
102     If mFlags(4) Then
103        On Error GoTo handlerFour
104     Else
105        On Error GoTo 0   ' Disable error handler
106     End If
107
108     ' Draw image representing function raising error
109     imgImage(4).Picture = LoadPicture(d:\images\" & _
110                                        "ch13\resume2.gif")
111
112     Err.Raise Number:=6        ' Cause Overflow Error
113     Print "This is NEVER printed!!!"
```

**Fig. 13.9**   Call stack error-handling program (part 3 of 4).

```
114  handlerFour:
115      lblLocation.Caption = "Error handled in four"
116      imgImage(4).Picture = LoadPicture(d:\images\" & _
117                                  "ch13\resume3.gif")
118  End Function
119
120  Private Sub cmdGo_LostFocus()
121      lblLocation.Caption = ""          ' Clear Label
122  End Sub
123
124  Private Sub optSelect_Click(Index As Integer)
125      Call setFlag(Index)
126  End Sub
```

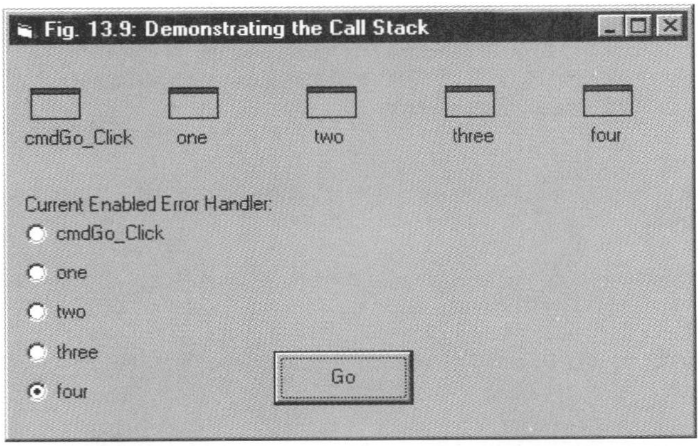

Initial GUI at execution.

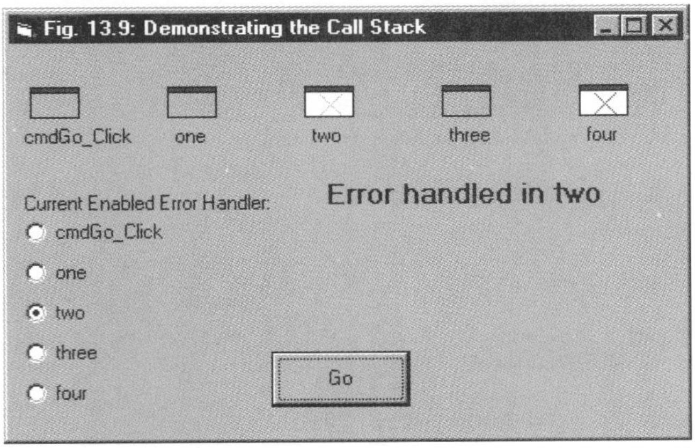

GUI after user selects **two** and presses **Go**.

**Fig. 13.9**    Call stack error-handling program (part 4 of 4).

When an **OptionButton** is selected, one element of array **flags** is set to **True**. Array **flags** determines which handler in the call stack is enabled. When the program begins execution, procedure **Form_Load** enables the error handler in function **four**. Procedures **cmdGo_Click**, **one**, **two**, **three** and **four** each use an **If/Then/Else** to determine if the corresponding element of array **flags** is **True**. If **True**, the error handler in that procedure is enabled with the **On Error Goto** *label* statement. The **On Error**

**Goto 0** statement *disables* the error handler in that procedure (Note: We explicitly disabled the error handler, but this statement can be removed and the program will still execute properly). A disabled error handler cannot trap an error. Note that only the enabled error handler in the call stack executes to handle the error.

A run-time error is generated with line 112 in procedure **four**

```
    Err.Raise Number:=6
```

which uses the **Err** object's ***Raise*** method. A value of **6**, an "overflow error," is assigned to the named argument **Number**. We could also have written the previous line as

```
    Err.Raise(6)
```

*Testing and Debugging Tip 13.3*

*Use method **Raise** during the design process to test error handlers.*

When the **Resume Next** statement is used in an error handler in the call stack, the **Resume Next** statement executes the line after the call that created the error (the callee's error handler must be disabled). For example, if the error handler in **four** is disabled and the error handler in **three** is enabled, the **Resume Next** statement in **three** executes the **Exit Sub** statement in **three**—not **four**.

*Software Engineering Observation 13.2*

*Error handling in a call stack can become quite complex and must be written carefully to ensure that a program executes properly.*

## 13.8 Rethrowing Errors

Once an error has been trapped, it can be *rethrown* (or *reraised*). An error handler might rethrow an error for a variety of reasons such as the error type was unexpected (i.e., not being trapped), the appropriate handler is up the call stack, the error was only partially handled and further handling needs to continue up the call stack, etc. When an error is rethrown, **Err**'s **Raise** method is used.

The program of Fig. 13.10 demonstrates rethrowing an error. The event procedure **cmdRethrow_Click** calls **RethrowTheError** which raises, handles and possibly rethrows the error up the call stack to **cmdRethrow_Click**'s error handler. Procedure **RethrowTheError** only rethrows the error if it is a Type mismatch error. All other errors are handled locally. All program input is accomplished with function **InputBox**.

The *throw point* (i.e., where an error can be raised) in procedure **RethrowTheError** is line 20; the call to function **InputBox**. If an error is raised, it is handled in **localHandler**. Any error other than a Type mismatch is simply output. A "type mismatch" error is rethrown with the line

```
    Call Err.Raise(13)        ' Rethrow error
```

Line 8 in **cmdRethrow_Click** calls **RethrowTheError**. A rethrown error returns to this exact point—looking for an enabled error handler (line 7 is the enabled error handler). Control is transferred to **handler**, where **Resume** is executed. **Resume** continues execution at the line that raised the error, in this case line 8—the call to **RethrowTheError**. Procedure **RethrowTheError** is called again, and the input dialog is displayed for input.

```
1   ' Fig. 13.10
2   ' Demonstrating rethrowing an error
3   Option Explicit
4
5   Private Sub cmdRethrow_Click()
6
7      On Error GoTo handler
8         Call RethrowTheError
9         Exit Sub
10
11  handler:
12     Print "cmdRethrow_Click's error handler executed!"
13     Resume    ' Resume at line that raised error
14  End Sub
15
16  Private Sub RethrowTheError()
17     Dim x As Integer
18
19     On Error GoTo localHandler
20        x = InputBox("Enter a number") ' Error can be raised here
21        Print "You entered " & x
22        Exit Sub
23
24  localHandler:
25
26     If Err.Number = 13 Then    ' Type Mismatch error
27        Print "Rethrowing error..."
28        Call Err.Raise(13)      ' Rethrow error
29     Else
30        Print "Error: " & Err.Description
31     End If
32
33  End Sub
```

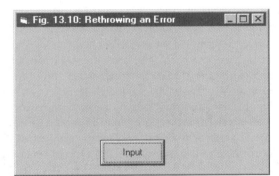

Initial GUI at execution.

**Fig. 13.10**   Rethrowing an error (part 1 of 2).

## 13.9 Break Mode, the Immediate Window, and the `Debug` Object

Until now, we have been developing Visual Basic programs while the integrated development environment (IDE) is in design mode. While in design mode, controls can added from the toolbox and individual control properties can be set in the **Properties** window.

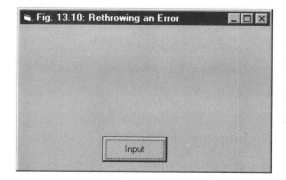

Initial GUI at execution.

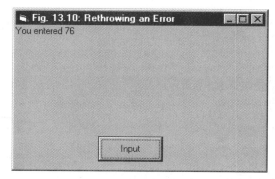

GUI after user has entered valid data in the input dialog.

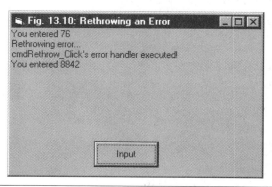

GUI after user attempted invalid input. Error was raised, resulting in input dialog being repeatedly displayed until valid input occurs.

**Fig. 13.10**   Rethrowing an error (part 2 of 2).

We execute our program by placing the IDE in run mode. While in run mode, we can interact with the program GUI, but we cannot access the IDE **Properties** window, most tool bar buttons, and most menu items.

In addition to design mode and run mode, the IDE can also be placed in *break mode* for debugging purposes. While in break mode, program execution is suspended so that code can be checked for logic errors. Break mode allows the programmer to check variable values and confirm overall program logic. Break mode also allows the programmer to edit the code and continue program execution. Figure 13.11 shows three different IDE title bars which specify the IDE's mode.

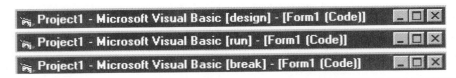

**Fig. 13.11**   Design mode, run mode and break mode title bars.

There are several ways to place the environment in break mode include clicking the **Break** tool bar button (Fig. 13.12), selecting **Run** menu item **Break** (Fig. 13.12), selecting **Debug** menu item **Step Into** (Fig. 13.15), executing the **Stop** statement, or clicking an error dialog's **Debug** button (Fig. 13.13). Later we mention one other way of placing the IDE in break mode.

Like design mode, break mode allows the programmer to use the **Immediate** window, Fig. 13.14, for calculating or testing expressions. The **Immediate** window can be used to a calculate arithmetic expressions, change property values and call procedures. Selecting **Immediate Window** from the **View** menu displays the **Immediate** window.

As shown in Fig. 13.14, either **Print** or a question mark, **?**, displays an expression's or calculation's value in the **Immediate** window.

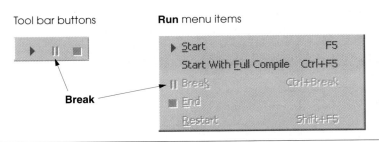

**Fig. 13.12**   **Run** menu items and related tool bar buttons.

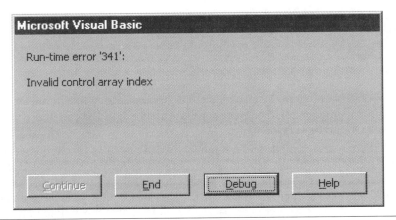

**Fig. 13.13**   Error dialog.

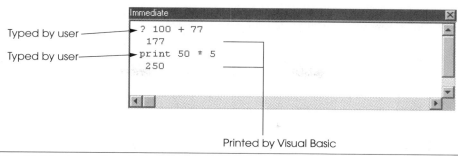

**Fig. 13.14  Immediate** Window.

Program information can also be written to the **Immediate** window by calling the **Debug** object's **Print** method. For example, the statement

```
Debug.Print "VB" & 6
```

would write "**VB6**" to the **Immediate** window. **Debug.Print** statements are executed at run time.

*Software Engineering Observation 13.3*

*When creating a stand-alone executable,* **Debug.Print** *statements are not compiled to machine code.*

The **Debug** object also contains method **Assert**. When passed, **False**, **Assert** places the IDE in break mode. This is useful for testing a condition to ensure that code is executing properly. For example, if variable **x**'s value should always be in the range 0 through 9, the statement

```
Debug.Assert(x >= 0 And x <= 9)
```

tests the value of **x** and, if it is out of range, puts the IDE in break mode so the programmer can debug the problem. If the variable's value is in range, the program continues execution.

*Testing and Debugging Tip 13.4*

*Use* **Assert** *to verify the behavior of conditions during program development.*

*Testing and Debugging Tip 13.5*

**Assert** *statements are not compiled into stand-alone executables.*

## 13.10 First Steps In Bug Prevention

A large number of bugs can be prevented following some simple guidelines. Many of these guidelines have appeared in previous chapters but are summed up here. These guidelines do not require a significant amount of coding. The following list describes these guidelines.

1. Always use **Option Explicit**. As mentioned in Chapter 2, **Option Explicit** should be placed in every form and code module to force explicit declaration of variables, which will eliminate misspelled names at run time.

2. Add comments while you are writing your program. Properly documented code can prevent you as well as someone who is maintaining your code from introducing bugs.

3. Always use the syntax checker. As mentioned in Chapter 2, the syntax checker allows Visual Basic to scrutinize a line of code's syntax when you hit the *Return* key. If there is a syntax error, the line of code turns red and, if the **Auto Syntax Check** option in the **Options...** dialog is checked, a dialog is displayed indicating the syntax error.

4. Use Microsoft's suggested prefixes for objects. The prefixes clearly state the type of the object and should eliminate the possibility of incorrect assignments.

5. Use the tightest scope possible for variables and symbolic constants. Problems with variables and symbolic constants are easier to spot when restricted to one procedure or module.

6. Prefix module variable names to indicate scope. Module variables should be prefixed by **m**.

7. Use the **Private** keyword to limit the scope of a procedure if it is not called outside the code module. This ensures that only a select number of procedures can call a procedure.

8. For variables whose values must be in a specific range, perform range checking in the code (i.e., ensure that the variable's value is in the proper range).

9. Check the validity of variable values before using the values in the program.

## 13.11 Debugging Strategies

In this section we discuss strategies for debugging. Some of these strategies are directly handled by the debugger. We present them here as an alternative method of debugging.

One of the simplest strategies is called *trace debugging*. Trace debugging is used to verify the flow of control in a program. Either **Print** statements or **MsgBox** statements are commonly used. Typically, each procedure and function begins with a statement like

```
Print "Entering procedure calculatePayment."
```

and ends with a statement like

```
Print "Exiting procedure calculatePayment."
```

As each procedure or function is executed, both lines should be displayed. When one of the **Print** lines is not displayed, the procedure or function has a bug. Sometimes the same type of tracing is applied to loops as well. A **Print** statement like

```
Print "Entering Loop"
```

may precede the loops and a statement like

```
Print "Loop is finished"
```

may follow the loop. Adding these lines around a loop can confirm that the loop does terminate. An infinite loop will never reach the **"Loop is finished"** statement.

Specific **Print** statements are commonly added as well, especially to check the values of variables. A statement such as

```
Print "x is " & x%
```

may be written to check the value of a variable. If multiple variables named **x** are being used, the message should specify where the value is. A statement like

```
Print "In procedure calculatePayment: x is " & x
```

would be appropriate.

Trace debugging introduces extra lines of code into a program. When a bug is located and corrected, all the **Print** statements must be commented out or deleted. This can lead to a significant investment of time.

**Testing and Debugging Tip 13.6**

*Trace debugging may not be able to help you locate the exact error. It is possible that the error is being generated by an ActiveX control, a DLL, Windows or even Visual Basic.*

Another strategy for debugging involves writing information to a *log file*. A log file is a text file that has trace-debugging information written to it. Log files are opened in **Append** mode. Information is then written to the log file using **Print #** or **Write #** statements (which we discuss in the file processing chapters). The log file is then immediately closed using the **Close #** statement. The process is then repeated as many times as necessary. The log file can then be viewed in any editor program.

**Common Programming Error 13.7**

*If possible, the log file should use the program name followed by the* **.log** *extension.*

**Testing and Debugging Tip 13.7**

*A log file can preserve information that may not be displayed due to a fatal error.*

Error handlers have four pieces: a *trap* (**On Error Goto** statement), a *label*, *code*, and a **Resume** statement, which specifies where execution is to continue. A generic error handler is illustrated in Fig. 13.15.

```
Sub generalProcedure ()
    ' Local declarations
    ...
    On Error Goto handlerLabel   ' Set trap
    ' Procedure Code inside trap
    ...
    Exit Sub
handlerLabel:    ' error-handler
    ' Code that handles error
    ...
    ' Specify where to resume control
    Resume
End Sub
```

**Fig. 13.15** Demonstrating simple error handling in a procedure.

The programmer encloses in a trap the code that may generate an error. Each trap specifies where the error will be handled. The line

```
On Error Goto handlerLabel
```

"sets the trap." If an error occurs in the trap, control is sent to the error handler **handler-Label**. **HandlerLabel** is the name of a label that appears somewhere in the same procedure or function. A *label* is a location to which control can be directed. If an error does not occur in a trap, the error handler is skipped and program execution continues. Note that the **Exit Sub** line prevents the error handler from being accidentally executed.

*Common Programming Error 13.8*

*Accidentally executing an error handler is a logic error. Error handlers are typically separated from non-error-handling code by **Exit Sub** or **Exit Function**.*

The line

```
Resume
```

uses the **Resume** statement to continue program execution at the statement that caused the error. Once an error has been trapped and corrected, **Resume** can be used to return control to a line preceding the statement that caused the error (**Resume** location), the statement that caused the error (**Resume**), or a line following the statement that caused the error (**Resume Next**). Figure 13.15 illustrates the flow of control for error handling. Either the **End** statement or the **Resume** statement is required in an error handler.

*Testing and Debugging Tip 13.8*

*Do not use error handling as an alternative method of program control. Error handling should only be used to trap fatal run-time errors.*

## 13.12 Debugger

The IDE provides a *debugger* for locating and correcting errors in program logic (called *logic errors*). The debugger is typically used to trace program control, scrutinize variable values, and validate program input and output. The debugger can only be used in IDE break mode. In the following sections we describe debugger elements.

*Software Engineering Observation 13.4*

*Debuggers allow the programmer to confirm the behavior of a program's logic—not to find syntax errors.*

## 13.12.1 Debug Menu and Debug Tool Bar

The ***Debug*** menu and *debug tool bar* contain debugger commands. Both the **Debug** menu and debug tool bar are shown in Fig. 13.16. Some debug tool bar features are the same as some **Debug** menu features. The debug tool bar is displayed when **Debug** is selected from the ***Toolbars*** menu (a submenu of **View**).

The **Start** button executes the program, the **Break** button places the IDE in break mode, and the **End** button terminates program execution. Figure 13.17 summarizes each **Debug** menu item feature of Fig. 13.16.

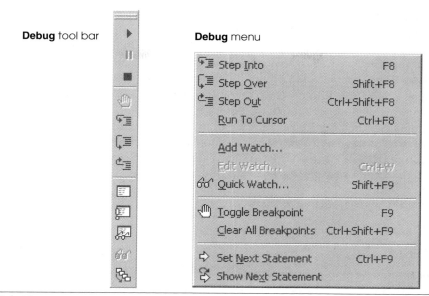

**Fig. 13.16 Debug** menu and debug tool bar.

| Command | Description |
|---|---|
| **Step Into** | Executes the current line. If the current line is a procedure or function call, the procedure or function code is entered. |
| **Step Over** | Executes the current line. If the current line is a procedure or function call, the procedure or function is executed without stepping into its code. |
| **Step Out** | Execute the remaining procedure or function code and continue stepping through the procedure or function caller's code. |
| **Run To Cursor** | Executes all lines of code up to the line containing the cursor. |
| **Add Watch...** | Displays the **Add Watch** dialog. (See Section 13.10.3.) |
| **Edit Watch...** | Displays the **Edit Watch** dialog. (See Section 13.10.3.) |
| **Quick Watch...** | Displays the **Quick Watch** dialog. (See Section 13.10.3.) |
| **Toggle Breakpoint** | Adds or removes a breakpoint. |
| **Clear All Breakpoints** | Removes all breakpoints. |
| **Set Next Statement** | Allows the programmer to specify which statement within the procedure or function is executed next. |
| **Show Next Statement** | Transfers the cursor to the next line to be executed. |

**Fig. 13.17    Debug** menu and debug tool bar commands.

Figure 13.18 shows the effect of selecting **Step Into** after the program of Fig. 13.9 is loaded into the IDE. Selecting **Step Into** places the IDE in break mode with the `Form_Load` header highlighted yellow. For emphasis, a yellow arrow appears to the left of the highlighted line. Normally the next line of code that will execute is highlighted yellow. If a single statement spans multiple lines, all the lines are highlighted. For a single line **If/Then/Else**, the individual sections of the structure are individually highlighted.

Selecting either **Step Into** or **Step Over** executes the current line, resulting in the next line being highlighted (Fig. 13.19). As Fig. 13.19 indicates, the current line to execute is a procedure call. The programmer can choose to **Step Into initializeFlags** or **Step Over initializeFlags**. Stepping into **initializeFlags** highlights the procedure **initializeFlags** header as shown in Fig. 13.20. Selecting **Step Over** executes **initializeFlags** and highlights the next line,

`optSelect(4).Value = True`

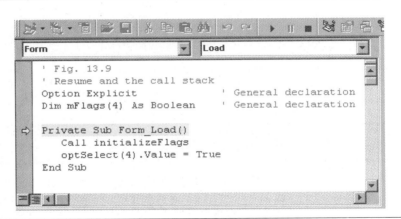

**Fig. 13.18**   Current executable line (in break mode).

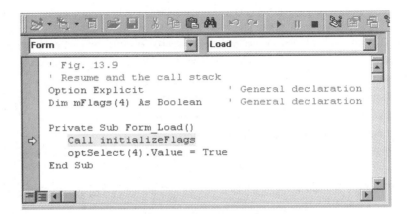

**Fig. 13.19**   Executing a statement (in break mode).

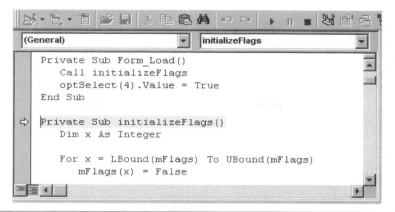

**Fig. 13.20**   Stepping into procedure `initializeFlags`.

Selecting **Step Into** or **Step Over** highlights the next executable line, as shown in Fig. 13.21. Note the value of **x** is displayed when the cursor rests on **x**.

Selecting **Step Into** or **Step Over** repeatedly executes each line of the loop. Sometimes every iteration of the loop need not be verified. The programmer may want to continue debugging at some point after the loop. To accomplish this, click the line of code where execution should next be suspended (i.e., the line that will be highlighted yellow) and select **Run To Cursor**. All code lines between the highlighted line and the cursor are executed. Figure 13.22 shows the result of clicking the **End Sub** line and selecting **Run To Cursor**. Note that we display the value of **x** by positioning the mouse pointer over the variable in the code to confirm that the loop executed in its entirety.

Selecting **Step Into**, **Step Over**, or **Step Out** exits `initializeFlags`. **Step Into** and **Step Over** exit `initializeFlags` because **End Sub** is executed. Selecting **Step Out** at any time within `initializeFlags` exits the procedure and highlights the line

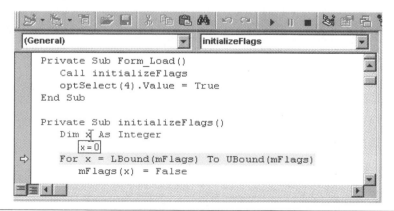

**Fig. 13.21**   Stepping into `initializeFlags`.

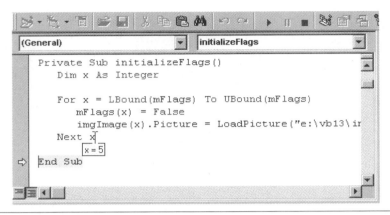

**Fig. 13.22**   Demonstrating **Run To Cursor**.

> `optSelect(4).Value = True`

in **Form_Load**. **Step Out** exits a procedure or function and returns control to the caller.

Sometimes programmers have an idea of the general area where a bug may be located. Stepping line by line may not be the most efficient way to reach that block of code. For this reason, the debugger allows the programmer to set *breakpoints*. Programmers set breakpoints to suspend execution at key lines by clicking a line and selecting **Toggle Break-Point**, by clicking in the *margin indicator bar* (the gray margin indicator at the left of the code window) or by clicking a line and pressing he *F9* key. The programmer can set as many breakpoints as necessary. Figure 13.23 shows a breakpoint. Breakpoint lines are highlighted red and are marked by a solid red circle to the left. Breakpoints can be set during design mode break mode, and run mode.

The breakpoint of Fig. 13.23 was set during design mode and Fig. 13.24 shows the result of clicking **Start**—execution suspends at the breakpoint. Notice that the yellow arrow and red circle overlap as well as the yellow line and red line.

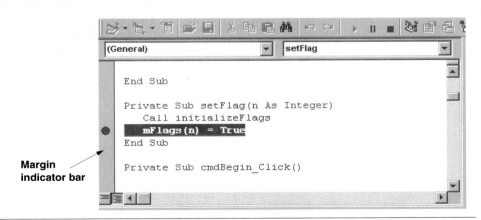

**Fig. 13.23**   A breakpoint.

**Fig. 13.24**  Execution suspending at a breakpoint.

A breakpoint can be removed by clicking the breakpoint line and selecting **Toggle Breakpoint**. All breakpoints can be removed by selecting **Clear All Breakpoints**.

Within a procedure or function, the programmer can decide which line is executed next by clicking a line and selecting **Set Next Statement**. The clicked line is highlighted yellow and the yellow arrow appears to the left. Selecting **Show Next Statement** transfers the cursor to the yellow highlighted line.

## 13.12.2 Locals Window

The *Locals* window displays the current value and data type of all local variables. As a variable's value changes, the **Locals** window is automatically updated by Visual Basic to display the new value. Figure 13.25 shows the **Locals** window when debugging in the program of Fig. 13.9's **initializeFlags** procedure. Notice that the first line in the window indicates "**Me**"—a reference to the current form being manipulated. **Me** allows the programmer to inspect all the form's state information (i.e., its variables) and the states of all objects used in the form (e.g., GUI controls). The **Locals** window is displayed when **Locals Window** is selected from the **View** menu or by clicking the **Locals** button on the **Debug** tool bar.

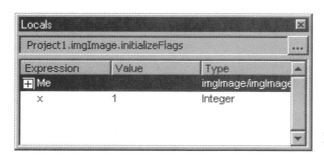

**Fig. 13.25**  **Locals** window.

The form's property settings are accessible through the *Me* keyword by clicking the *plus sign* (+) to the left of **Me** (Fig. 13.26).

For testing purposes, the programmer can change form property values and local variable values by selecting the desired value and entering the new value. Figure 13.27 shows the value of **x** changed to **8**. For demonstration purposes, we selected **8** because it is well outside the maximum value of **x** generated by the **For** loop.

The **Locals** window only allows monitoring of local variables. Once the procedure or function is exited, the local variables are no longer monitored. Module variables cannot be viewed in the **Locals** window.

## 13.12.3 Watch Window

The *Watch* window provides an automated means of monitoring variable values. Local variables and module variables can be **Watch**ed using either *Add Watch* (Fig. 13.28) from the **Debug** menu or by dragging and dropping a variable into the **Watch** window.

The **Add Watch** dialog provides a **TextBox** labeled *Expression* in which to enter the variable name to watch. The programmer selects the procedure and module where the variable resides. The *Watch Type* **Frame** allows the programmer to specify the watch behavior. *Watch Expression* adds the variable to the **Watch** window. *Break When Value Is True* suspends execution when a variable's value is assigned **True**. *Break When Value Changes* suspends execution when the variable's value is modified.

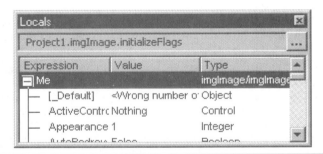

**Fig. 13.26**  **Locals** window showing form properties.

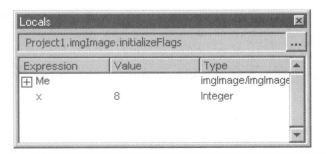

**Fig. 13.27**  Changing a local variable's value.

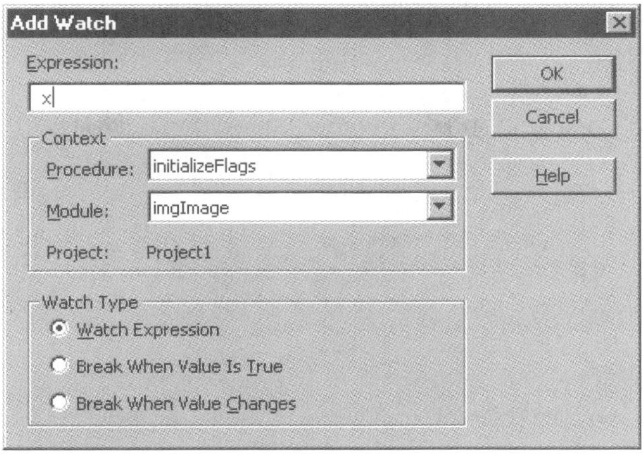

**Fig. 13.28   Add Watch** dialog.

**Watch** window expressions can always be edited by selecting *Edit Watch* from the **Debug** menu. An identical dialog (with the exception of the title bar, which displays **Edit Watch**) to Fig. 13.28 is displayed for editing the expression.

The **Watch** window (Fig. 13.29) is displayed when an expression is added using the **Add Watch** dialog, by selecting **Add Watch** from the **View** menu, or by clicking the **Add Watch** button on the **Debug** tool bar. Variable **x** was added using the **Add Watch** dialog of Fig. 13.28 and `imgImage` was added by a drag-and-drop operation. To perform the drag-and-drop, double-click the variable name in the source code, then drag the variable over the **Watches** window and drop it.

The programmer can also remove **Watch** window expressions by selecting the expression within the **Watch** window and pressing the *Delete* key.

Rather than using the **Watch** window, the programmer can quickly view an expression's value by highlighting the expression and selecting *Quick Watch* from the **Debug** menu. The modal **Quick Watch** dialog is then displayed, as shown in Fig. 13.30 for the variable **x**. Pressing **Add** adds the expression to the **Watch** window.

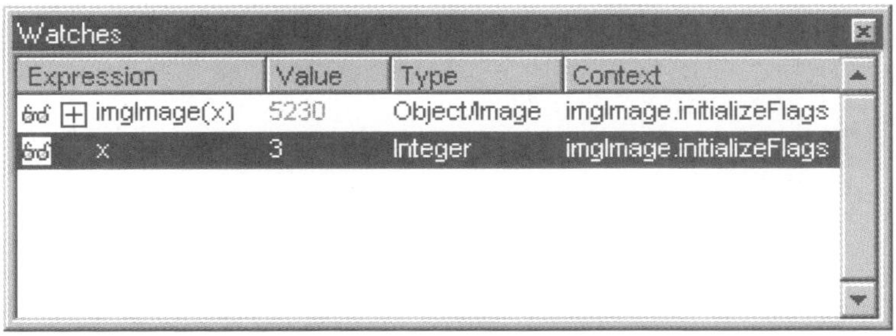

**Fig. 13.29   Watch** window.

**Fig. 13.30    Quick Watch** window.

## 13.12.4 Call Stack Window

The **Call Stack** window allows the programmer to view a list of all the procedures and functions that were called in order to get to the current line. The **Call Stack** window is displayed when **Call Stack** is selected from the **View** menu or when the **Locals** window's **Call Stack** button is pressed (Fig. 13.31). Figure 13.32 shows the **Call Stack** window while debugging in the **initializeFlags** procedure. The procedure or function listed at the top is the current procedure or function being debugged (in this case procedure **initializeFlags**). The bottom procedure or function is the caller of the procedure or function being debugged. In Fig. 13.32, **Form_Load** is the caller of **initializeFlags**. The **Call Stack** window may contain more than two levels—where any particular procedure or function is called by the procedure or function immediately beneath it.

The modal **Call Stack** window contains buttons **Show** and **Close**. Selecting a procedure or function name in the **Call Stack** window and pressing **Show** results in a green triangle being displayed next to the line of code (in the calling procedure or function) that called the current procedure or function. Figure 13.33 shows the result of selecting **Form_Load** in the **Call Stack** window and pressing **Show**.

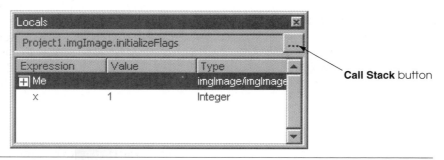

**Fig. 13.31    Locals** window.

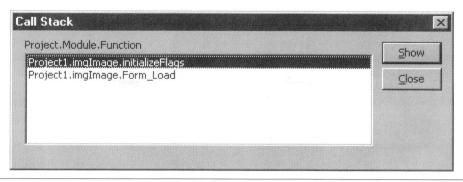

**Fig. 13.32** **Call Stack** window.

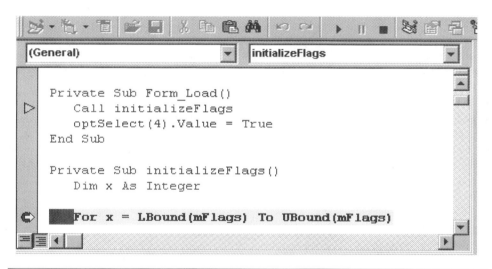

**Fig. 13.33** Green triangle identifying a procedure's calling point.

## 13.13 Debugger and Error Handlers

Code is often difficult to debug with the debugger when error handlers are involved. The most common practice is to have Visual Basic disable the error handlers.

Selecting the **General** tab's ***Break on All Errors*** places the IDE in break mode when a run-time error occurs. The **General** tab is part of the **Options** dialog that is displayed when the **Tools** menu item **Options** is selected. Once in break mode, the debugging techniques discussed earlier can be used. The programmer can also choose to **Break on Unhandled Errors**. The default is **Break in Class Module**.

### Summary

- Error handling gives the programmer the ability to attempt to trap (i.e., continue executing) fatal errors rather than letting them occur and suffering the consequences. If the error is severe enough that recovery is not possible, the program can exit "gracefully"—all files can be closed and notification can be given that the program is terminating. The recovery code is called an error handler.

- Error handling is designed for dealing with synchronous errors such as an attempt to divide by zero (that occurs as the program executes the divide instruction).

- Error handling should be used to process only exceptional situations, despite the fact that there is nothing to prevent the programmer from using errors as an alternate for program control; to process errors for program components that are not geared to handling those errors directly; to process errors from software components such as functions, procedures, and ActiveX controls that are likely to be widely used, and where it does not make sense for those components to handle their own errors; on large projects to handle error processing in a uniform manner project-wide.

- If an error is detected after a trap has been enabled, control is transferred to the label and execution of the error handler's code begins.

- An error trap can be disabled with the statement **On Error Goto 0**. Raised errors are still detected but not directed to an error handler in that procedure. The error returned to the calling procedure for processing.

- Labels (which are not related to **Label** controls) always ends in a colon. Labels are left justified by Visual Basic and cannot be indented by the programmer.

- **On Error** statements can be nested (i.e., one inside another) to direct an error to a specific handler. When an error is raised, control is transferred to the nearest trap's error handler. The nearest trap is the last enabled **On Error** statement above the line that raised the error.

- The **Err** object stores information about the raised error.

- If only one error handler is provided in a procedure or function, the **Number** property is often used to determine which error was raised.

- The **Resume** statement specifies where in a procedure or function execution continues. The three basic uses of **Resume** in an event handler are continuing execution at the line that raised the error, continuing execution at the next executable line following the line that raised the error, and continuing at a specified label (which can appear anywhere within the procedure or function).

- The dialog generated by **InputBox** is modal (i.e., it must be closed before the user is allowed to interact with any other window in that application).

- A call stack is the list of procedures and functions that were called in order to get to the current procedure or current function.

- If an enabled error handler is found, it is executed—otherwise a fatal error occurs.

- Each procedure or function in the call stack must have an error handler.

- A run-time error is generated with the **Err** object's **Raise** method.

- When the **Resume Next** statement is used in an error handler in the call stack, the **Resume Next** statement executes the line after the call that created the error.

- Once an error is trapped, it can be rethrown (or reraised). An error handler might rethrow an error for a variety of reasons, such as the error type was unexpected (i.e., not being trapped), the appropriate handler is up the call stack, the error was only partially handled and further handling needs to continue up the call stack, etc. When an error is rethrown, **Err**'s **raise** method is used.

- While in run mode, we can interact with the program GUI, but we cannot access the IDE **Properties** window, most tool bar buttons and most menu items.

- In addition to design mode and run mode, the IDE can also be placed in break mode for debugging purposes. While in break mode, program execution is suspended so that code can be checked for logic errors. Break mode allows the programmer to check variable values and confirm overall program logic.

- Several different ways exist to place the environment in break mode, including clicking the **Break** tool bar button, selecting **Run** menu item **Break**, selecting **Debug** menu item **Step Into**, executing the `Stop` statement or clicking an error dialog's `Debug` button.

- Like design mode, break mode also allows the programmer to use the **Immediate** window for calculating or testing expressions.

- Either `Print` or a question mark, `?`, displays an expression's or calculation's value in the **Immediate** window. Program information can also be written to the **Immediate** window by calling the `Debug` object's `Print` method.

- The IDE provides a debugger for locating and correcting logic errors. The debugger is typically used to trace program control, scrutinize variable values and validate program input and output. The debugger can only be used in IDE break mode.

- The **Debug** menu and debug tool bar contain debugger commands. The debug tool bar is displayed when **Debug** is selected from the **Toolbars** menu (a submenu of **View**).

- The **Start** button executes the program, the **Break** button places the IDE in break mode and the **End** button terminates program execution.

- **Step Over** executes the procedure or function without stepping into the procedure or function. **Step Out** executes the remaining procedure or function code and continues stepping through the procedure or function caller's code. **Run To Cursor** executes all lines of code up to the line containing the cursor. **Add Watch...** displays the **Add Watch** dialog. **Edit Watch...** displays the **Edit Watch** dialog. **Quick Watch...** displays the **Quick Watch** dialog. **Toggle Breakpoint** adds or removes a breakpoint. **Clear All Breakpoints** removes all breakpoints. **Set Next Statement** allows the programmer to specify which statement within the procedure or function is executed next. **Show Next Statement** transfers the cursor to the next line to be executed.

- **Step Into** places the IDE in break mode with the `Form_Load` header highlighted yellow.

- Selecting **Step Into** or **Step Over** executes the current line.

- Selecting **Step Into** or **Step Over** repeatedly will execute each line of the loop. Sometimes every iteration of the loop need not be verified. The programmer may want to continue debugging at some point after the loop. All the programmer need do to accomplish this is click the line of code where execution should next be suspended (i.e., the line that will be highlighted yellow) and select **Run To Cursor**. All code lines between the highlighted line and the cursor are executed.

- Sometimes programmers have an idea of the general area where a bug may be located. Stepping line by line may not be the most efficient way to reach that block of code. For this reason, the debugger allows the programmer to set breakpoints. Programmers set breakpoints to suspend execution at key lines by clicking a line and selecting **Toggle BreakPoint**. Breakpoint lines are highlighted red and are marked by a solid red circle to the left. Breakpoints can be set during design mode, break mode and run mode.

- A breakpoint can be removed by clicking the breakpoint line and selecting **Toggle Breakpoint**. All breakpoints can be removed by selecting **Clear All Breakpoints**.

- In a procedure, the programmer can decide which line is executed next by clicking a line and selecting **Set Next Statement**. The clicked line is highlighted yellow and the yellow arrow appears to the left. Selecting **Show Next Statement** transfers the cursor to the yellow highlighted line.

- The **Locals** window displays the current value and data type of all local variables. As a variable's value changes, the **Locals** window is automatically updated by Visual Basic to display the new value. The **Locals** window is displayed when **Locals Window** is selected from the **View** menu or by clicking the **Locals** button on the **Debug** tool bar.

- The form's property settings are accessible through the `Me` keyword. Clicking the plus sign, +, to the left of `Me` shows the current property settings.

- The **Locals** window allows monitoring of local variables. Once a procedure exits, the local variables are no longer monitored. Module variables cannot be viewed in the **Locals** window.

- The **Watch** window provides another means of monitoring variable values. Both local variables and module variables can be added to the **Watch** window using either **Add Watch** from the **Debug** menu or by dragging and dropping a variable into the **Watch** window.

- The **Add Watch** dialog provides a `TextBox` labeled **Expression**, where the name of the variable to watch is entered. The programmer selects the procedure and module where the variable resides. The **Watch Type** `Frame` allows the programmer to specify the watch behavior. **Watch Expression** adds the variable to the **Watch** window. **Break When Value Is True** suspends execution when a variable's value is assigned `True`. **Break When Value Changes** suspends execution when the variable's value is assigned another value.

- **Watch** window expressions can be edited by selecting **Edit Watch** from the **Debug** menu.

- The **Watch** window displays when an expression is added using dialog **Add Watch**, by selecting **Add Watch** from the **View** menu, or by clicking the **Add Watch** button on the **Debug** tool bar.

- The programmer can also remove **Watch** window expressions by selecting the expression within the **Watch** window and pressing the Delete key.

- Rather than using the **Watch** window, the programmer can quickly view an expression's value by highlighting the expression and selecting **Quick Watch** from the **Debug** menu. Pressing **Add** adds the expression to the **Watch** window.

- The **Call Stack** window allows the programmer to view a list of procedures and functions that were called to get to the current line. The **Call Stack** window is displayed when **Call Stack** is selected from the **View** menu or when the **Locals** window's **Call Stack** button is pressed. The procedure or function listed at the top is the current procedure or function being debugged. The bottom procedure or function is the caller of the procedure or function being debugged.

- The modal **Call Stack** window contains buttons **Show** and **Close**. Selecting a procedure name in the **Call Stack** window and pressing **Show** results in a green triangle being displayed next to the line of code (in the calling procedure or function) that called the current procedure or function.

- Code is often difficult to debug with the debugger when error handlers are involved. The most common practice is to have Visual Basic disable the error handlers.

- Selecting the **General** tab's **Break on All Errors** places the IDE in break mode when a run-time error occurs. The **General** tab is part of the **Options** dialog that is displayed when the **Tools** menu item **Options** is selected. The programmer can also choose to **Break on Unhandled Errors**. The default is **Break in Class Module**.

## Terminology

| | |
|---|---|
| **Add Watch** dialog | **Clear All Breakpoints** |
| `Assert` method in a `Debug` object | debugger |
| **Break in Class Module** | **Debug** menu |
| break mode | `Debug` object |
| **Break on All Errors** | debug tool bar |
| **Break on Unhandled Errors** | `Description` property of `Err` object |
| breakpoint | disable an error trap |
| Break When Value Changes | disabled error handler |
| **Break When Value Is True** | divide-by-zero error |
| call stack | **Edit Watch** dialog |
| **Call Stack** window | enabled an error trap |
| `clean` method of `Err` object | enabled error handler |

**Err** object
error handler
error trap
fatal error
**Got Focus** event procedure
**Immediate** window
label
line number
**Locals** window
**Lost Focus** event procedure
**Me** keyword
modal dialog
nested **On Error** statements
**Number:** argument
**Number** property of **Err** object
**On Error Goto** statement
**On Error Goto 0** statement
overflow error
**Print** statement
question mark, **?**
**Quick Watch**
raise an error

**Raise** method of **Err** object
recover from an error
reraise an error
**Resume** statement
**Resume Next** statement
rethrow an error
**Run to Cursor**
**Set Next Statement**
Show Next Statement
single-stepping
**Source** property of **Err** object
**Step Into**
**Step Out**
**Step Over**
**Stop** statement
synchronous error
throw point
**Toggle Breakpoint**
Toggle-breakpoint command (F9)
type mismatch error
watch
**Watch** window

## Common Programming Errors

**13.1**   Specifying in an **On Error GoTo** statement a label that is not in the same procedure or function is a syntax error.

**13.2**   Forgetting to use the **Exit Sub** or **Exit Function** to prevent error-trapping code from executing unintentionally is a run-time logic error because the error-trapping code will execute even if an error does not occur.

**13.3**   Omitting the colon at the end of a label is a syntax error.

**13.4**   Attempting to set a negative line number or a negative line number label is a syntax error.

**13.5**   Specifying in an **On Error GoTo** statement a line number or line label that is not in the same procedure or function is a syntax error.

**13.6**   Using the **Resume** statement outside error-handling code can create logic problems at runtime.

**13.7**   If possible, the log file should use the program name followed by the **.log** extension.

**13.8**   Accidentally executing an error handler is a logic error. Error handlers are typically separated from non-error-handling code by **Exit Sub** or **Exit Function**.

## Good Programming Practice

**13.1**   Use conventional techniques (rather than error handling) for straightforward, local error processing in which a program is easily able to deal with its own errors.

## Portability Tips

**13.1**   **Err** replaces function **Error**. Do not use function **Error** because it is obsolete and provided only for backwards compatibility with older versions of Visual Basic. Future versions of Visual Basic may not provide function **Error**.

**13.2**   The **Description** property **String** can differ between versions of Visual Basic.

## Software Engineering Observations

**13.1**    Flow of control with conventional control structures is generally clearer and more efficient than with error handling.

**13.2**    Error handling in a call stack can become quite complex and must be written carefully to ensure that a program executes properly.

**13.3**    When creating a stand-alone executable, **Debug.Print** statements are not compiled to machine code.

**13.4**    Debuggers allow the programmer to confirm the behavior of a program's logic—not to find syntax errors.

## Testing and Debugging Tips

**13.1**    It is best to incorporate your error-handling strategy into a program from the inception of the design process. It is difficult to add effective error handling after a program has been implemented.

**13.2**    **Resume** label, **Resume Next** and **Resume** only apply to the current procedure or function.

**13.3**    Use method **Raise** during the design process to test error handlers.

**13.4**    Use **Assert** to verify the behavior of conditions during program development.

**13.5**    **Assert** statements are not compiled into stand-alone executables.

**13.6**    Trace debugging may not be able to help you locate the exact error. It is possible that the error is being generated by an ActiveX control, a DLL, Windows or even Visual Basic.

**13.7**    A log file can preserve information that may not be displayed due to a fatal error.

**13.8**    Do not use error handling as an alternative method of program control. Error handling should only be used to trap fatal run-time errors.

## Self-Review Exercises

**13.1**    Answer the following questions:
a)  Explain the difference between **Resume** and **Resume Next** in an error handler in the call list.
b)  Explain when conventional techniques should be used to handle errors and when error handling should be used to handle errors.

**13.2**    State which of the following are *true* and which are *false*. If *false*, explain why.
a)  **Err.Raise Number:=11** would create a run-time error.
b)  **Resume 22** regenerates error number **22**.
c)  The label specified in an error trap must be in the same procedure or function as the error trap.
d)  The **Exit Sub** (or **Exit Function**) statement is required in an error handler to avoid syntax errors.

## Answers to Self-Review Exercises

**13.1**    The **Resume** statement returns to the actual line of code that caused the error and executes the entire statement again. The **Resume Next** statement resumes execution with the next statement after the statement that caused the error.

**13.2**    a)  True.
b)  False. This statement resumes program execution at line 22.
c)  True.
d)  False. The **Exit Sub** (or **Exit Function**) statements are not required in error handlers.

## Exercises

**13.3**    Fill in the blanks in each of the following:
   a) Either _____ or _____ disables an active error handler.
   b) The sequence of calls generated to reach a procedure or function is called the_____.
   c) The _____ object is the error object.

**13.4**    State which of the following are *true* and which are *false*. If *false*, explain why.
   a) The **Resume** statement can be placed anywhere a line of executable code is permitted.
   b) An active error handler is always said to be enabled.
   c) The statement **On Error Goto -1** disables an error handler.
   d) Error handlers can be disabled when using the debugger.

**13.5**    List three common errors.

**13.6**    Explain what happens when an error is raised in a procedure or function that does not contain an error handler.

**13.7**    Why are error handlers typically preceded by **Exit Sub** or **Exit Function**?

**13.8**    Briefly describe the three IDE modes.

**13.9**    Modify the program of Fig. 13.9 to allow the user to set the procedure or function where the error is raised.

**13.10**   Modify the Simpletron Simulator of Exercise 10.19 to handle the various errors that can occur (i.e., replace your **MsgBox** function calls with **On Error** statements).

# 14

# Sequential File Processing

## Objectives

- To understand the data hierarchy arrangement of bits, bytes, characters, fields, records, files and databases.
- To be able to use the **FileListBox**, **DirListBox** and **DriveListBox** controls.
- To be able to create and use file system objects **FileSystemObject**, **File**, **Folder** and **Drive**.
- To be able to open, read, write and close sequential files, and to detect the end-of-file condition.

*I can only assume that a "Do Not File" document is filed in a "Do Not File" file.*
Senator Frank Church
Senate Intelligence Subcommittee Hearing, 1975

*I the heir of all ages, in the foremost files of time.*
Alfred, Lord Tennyson

*Open, locks,*
*Whoever knocks!*
William Shakespeare

*Minds are like parachutes.*
*They only function when they are open.*
Sir James Dewar

*Do you know the difference between education and experience? Education is when you read the fine print; experience is what you get when you don't.*
Pete Seeger

# Outline

## 14.1  Introduction

Storage of data in variables and arrays is temporary. Files are used for permanent retention of large amounts of data. Data in files is said to be *persistent*. Computers store files on secondary storage devices such as hard drives, magnetic disks, optical disks and tapes. In this chapter, we explain how data files are created, updated and processed. We consider sequential access files. In the next chapter, we consider random access files.

## 14.2  **DirListBox, FileListBox** and **DriveListBox** Controls

Visual Basic provides three intrinsic controls for representing the directories, files and drives on a system. **FileListBox** visually lists the files in a directory, **DirListBox** visually represents the directory structure and **DriveListBox** visually lists the drive structure. The toolbox icons representing these controls are shown in Fig. 14.1. Note that the **CommonDialog** discussed in previous chapters can also be used to select files, directories and drives. We discuss these features of the **CommonDialog** in Chapter 15.

**DirListBox**es, **FileListBox**es and **DriveListBox**es share many properties and methods, some of which are listed in Fig. 14.2. Note that these controls are not automatically aware of each other on a form; the programmer must write code to "tie" them together. For example, if the user selects a drive from a **DriveListBox**, the program would respond to that event by updating a corresponding **DirListBox** to display the directories from that drive. We demonstrate how this is accomplished in our first example.

When using a **DirListBox** control or a **FileListBox** control, the **Path** property sets the directory path that is displayed. The **Drive** control's **Drive** property specifies which **Drive** is displayed. The primary event procedure of a **DirListBox** and a **DriveListBox** is *Change*—the same event procedure for **ListBox**es and **ComboBox**es. The primary event procedure for a **FileListBox** is *Click*.

DirListBox          FileListBox          DriveListBox

Fig. 14.1  **DirListBox**, **FileListBox** and **DriveListBox** toolbox icons.

**FileListBox**es contain more properties than **DirListBox**es and **DriveList-Box**es. Some of these additional properties are listed in Fig. 14.3.

| Property/method | Description |
| --- | --- |
| *Properties* | |
| **DragIcon** | Icon which is displayed during drag-and-drop operation. |
| **DragMode** | **Integer**. Automatic or manual drag-and-drop. |
| **Enabled** | **Boolean**. Specifies whether or not the user is allowed to interact with the control. |
| **List** | **String** array. Array that stores the **String**s that appear in the controls. |
| **ListCount** | **Integer**. Number of items in the **List** properties array. |
| **ListIndex** | **Integer**. Index of selected **List** property item. Index begins at **0** and is **-1** when a value is not selected. |
| **MousePointer** | **Integer**. Specifies the shape of the mouse pointer when over the control. |
| **Visible** | **Boolean**. Specifies whether or not the control is visible. |
| *Methods* | |
| **Drag** | Starts, terminates, or aborts drag operations. |
| **Refresh** | Forces the control to repaint itself. |
| **SetFocus** | Transfers the focus to the control. |

**Fig. 14.2**    Some **DirListBox**, **FileListBox** and **DriveListBox** common properties and methods.

| Property | Description |
| --- | --- |
| **Archive** | **Boolean**. Specifies whether or not archive attributes are displayed (default is **True**). |
| **Hidden** | **Boolean**. Specifies whether or not hidden attributes are displayed (default is **False**). |
| **MultiSelect** | **Integer**. Specifies whether or not the user can make multiple selections (multiple selection is not allowed by default). |
| **Path** | **String**. Specifies the current path. |
| **Pattern** | **String**. Specifies the type of files displayed in the **FileListBox**. |
| **ReadOnly** | **Boolean**. Specifies whether or not read-only attributes are displayed. |
| **System** | **Boolean**. Specifies whether or not system attributes are displayed (default is **False**). |

**Fig. 14.3**    Some **FileListBox** properties.

The program of Fig. 14.4 allows the user to navigate the system directories. The GUI contains one **FileListBox**, one **DirListBox** and one **DriveListBox**. Selecting a drive from the **DriveListBox** updates the **DirListBox**, which updates the **File-ListBox**.

```
1   ' Fig. 14.4
2   ' Demonstrating FileListBox, DirListBox,
3   ' and DriveListBox controls
4   Option Explicit          ' General declaration
5
6   Private Sub dirDirBox_Change()
7
8       ' Update the file path to the directory path
9       filFileBox.Path = dirDirBox.Path
10  End Sub
11
12  Private Sub drvDriveBox_Change()
13
14      On Error GoTo error handler
15
16          ' Update the directory path to the drive
17          dirDirBox.Path = drvDriveBox.Drive
18          Exit Sub
19
20  errorhandler:
21          Dim message As String
22
23          ' Check for device unavailable error
24          If Err.Number = 68 Then
25              Dim r As Integer
26
27              message = "Drive is not available."
28              r = MsgBox(message, vbRetryCancel + vbCritical, _
29                      "VBHTP: Chapter 14")
30
31              ' Determine where control should resume
32              If r = vbRetry Then
33                  Resume
34              Else    ' Cancel was pressed.
35                  drvDriveBox.Drive = drvDriveBox.List(1)
36                  Resume Next
37              End If
38
39          Else
40              Call MsgBox(Err.Description, vbOKOnly + vbExclamation)
41              Resume Next
42          End If
43
44  End Sub
```

**Fig. 14.4**   Demonstrating controls **DirListBox**, **FileListBox** and **DriveListBox** (part 1 of 2).

Initial GUI at execution.

GUI after user has selected a folder.

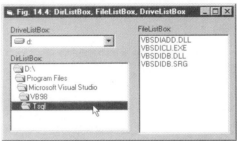

GUI after user has selected a drive.

**Fig. 14.4**    Demonstrating controls **DirListBox**, **FileListBox** and **DriveListBox** (part 2 of 2).

The **FileListBox** is tied to the **DirListBox Path** with the assignment

        **filFileBox.Path = dirDirBox.Path**

in event procedure **dirDirBox_Change**. The **FileListBox** is now "tied" to the **DirListBox**. Every time the user changes the **DirListBox**'s selected directory, the **FileListBox** contents are changed to the contents of that directory.

The **DirListBox** is tied to the selected drive with the assignment

        **dirDirBox.Path = drvDriveBox.Drive**

in event procedure **drvDriveBox_Change**. The **DirListBox** is now "tied" to the **DriveListBox**. Every time the user changes the **DriveListBox**'s selected drive, the **DirListBox** directory structure changes to the contents of that drive. Note that the **a:** drive is usually a floppy drive and that error handlers are often necessary to handle errors associated with accessing this drive.

Accessing the **a:** drive when it does not contain a disk is a common error. The drive is referred to as *not ready*. This specific error is trapped and dealt with, displaying a **MsgBox** dialog that gives the user the opportunity to either **Retry** or **Cancel**. By allowing the user to **Retry**, the user can ensure that a floppy is properly placed in the drive, and by allowing the user to **Cancel**, the attempt to access **a:** is canceled.

**Common Programming Error 14.1**

*Accessing the* **a:** *drive (or similar removable storage drives) when it is not ready is a run-time error.*

When **Cancel** is pressed, the line

```
drvDriveBox.Drive = drvDriveBox.List(1)
```

displays the drive at index **1** (the **a:** drive is at index **0**). Each **Drive** item can be accessed through the **List** property.

**Good Programming Practice 14.1**

*Prefixing* **DirListBox** *controls with* **dir** *allows them to be identified easily.*

**Good Programming Practice 14.2**

*Prefixing* **FileListBox** *controls with* **fil** *allows them to be identified easily.*

**Good Programming Practice 14.3**

*Prefixing* **DriveListBox** *controls with* **drv** *allows them to be identified easily.*

## 14.3 Data Hierarchy

Ultimately, all data items processed by a computer are reduced to combinations of zeros and ones. This occurs because it is simple and economical to build electronic devices that can assume two stable states—one state represents 0 and the other state represents 1. It is remarkable that the impressive functions performed by computers involve only the most fundamental manipulations of 0s and 1s.

The smallest data item in a computer can assume the value 0 or the value 1. Such a data item is called a *bit* (short for "binary digit"—a digit that can assume one of two values). Computer circuitry performs various simple bit manipulations, such as examining the value of a bit, setting the value of a bit, and reversing a bit (from 1 to 0 or from 0 to 1).

It is cumbersome for programmers to work with data in the low-level form of bits. Instead, programmers prefer to work with data in forms such as *decimal digits* (i.e., 0, 1, 2, 3, 4, 5, 6, 7, 8 and 9), *letters* (i.e., A through Z, and a through z) and *special symbols* (i.e., $, @, %, &, *, (, ), -, +, ", :, ?, / and many others). Digits, letters and special symbols are referred to as *characters*. The set of all characters used to write programs and represent data items on a particular computer is called that computer's *character set*. Since computers can process only 1s and 0s, every character in a computer's character set is represented as a pattern of 1s and 0s that is composed of one or more *bytes*. Bytes are composed of eight bits. Programmers create programs and data items with characters; computers manipulate and process these characters as patterns of bits.

Just as characters are composed of bits, fields are composed of characters (or bytes). A *field* is a group of characters that conveys meaning. For example, a field consisting solely of uppercase and lowercase letters can be used to represent a person's name.

Data items processed by computers form a *data hierarchy* in which data items become larger and more complex in structure as we progress from bits, to characters (bytes), to fields, and so on.

A *record* is composed of several fields (also called *members*). In a payroll system, for example, a record for a particular employee might consist of the following fields:

1. Employee identification number

2. Name

3. Address

4. Hourly salary rate

5. Number of exemptions claimed

6. Year-to-date earnings

7. Amount of federal taxes withheld, etc.

Thus, a record is a group of related fields. In the preceding example, each of the fields belongs to the same employee. Of course, a particular company may have many employees, and will have a payroll record for each employee. A *file* is a group of related records. A company's payroll file normally contains one record for each employee. Thus, a payroll file for a small company might contain only 22 records, whereas a payroll file for a large company might contain 100,000 records. It is not unusual for a company to have many files, each containing millions of bytes of information. Figure 14.5 illustrates the data hierarchy.

To facilitate the retrieval of specific records from a file, at least one field in each record is chosen as a record key. A *record key* identifies a record as belonging to a particular person or entity that is unique from all other records in the file. In the payroll record described above, the employee identification number would normally be the record key.

There are many ways to organize records in a file. The most common type of organization is called a *sequential file,* in which records are typically stored in order by the record key field. In a payroll file, records are usually placed in order by employee identification number. The first record in the file contains the lowest employee identification number, and subsequent records contain increasingly higher employee identification numbers.

Most businesses utilize many different files to store data. For example, companies may have payroll files, accounts receivable files (listing money due from clients), accounts payable files (listing money due to suppliers), inventory files (listing facts about all the items handled by the business), and many other types of files. A group of related files is sometimes called a *database*. A collection of programs designed to create and manage databases is called a *database management system* (*DBMS*).

## 14.4 File System Objects

*File System Objects* (*FSOs*) provide the programmer with the ability to manipulate files, directories and drives. FSOs also allow the programmer to read and write text to sequential files. FSOs provide the programmer with power and flexibility for working with files, folders and drives.

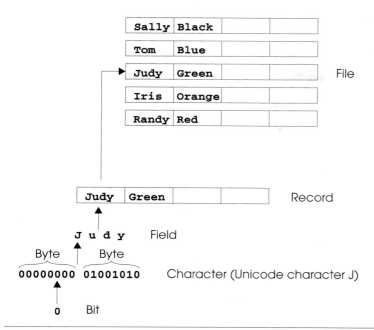

**Fig. 14.5**    Data hierarchy.

FSOs are objects in the *Microsoft Scripting Runtime Library,* which is added to the current project with the ***References*** dialog (Fig. 14.6). Selecting the **Project** menu's **References** command displays the modal **References** dialog.

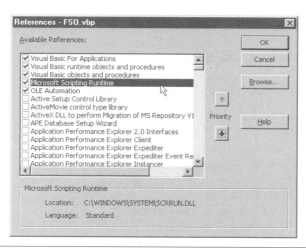

**Fig. 14.6**    **References** dialog with **Microsoft Scripting Runtime** selected.

In Fig. 14.6, we moved the **Microsoft Scripting Runtime** close to the top by selecting it and clicking the ***Priority*** up arrow several times. This allows the programmer to see the references that are used by the current project. Clicking **OK** dismisses the dialog.

***Common Programming Error 14.2***

*Attempting to use an FSO without enabling the Microsoft Scripting Runtime is a compiler error.*

Five FSOs exist: ***FileSystemObject***, ***File***, ***Folder***, ***Drive*** and ***TextStream***. Each object is summarized in Fig. 14.7. In this section we discuss the first four FSOs and discuss **TextStream** in subsequent sections.

**FileSystemObject** allows the programmer to interact with **File**s, **Folder**s and **Drive**s. The programmer can use a **FileSystemObject** to create directories, move files, determine whether or not a **Drive** exists, etc. Some common **FileSystemObject** methods are summarized in Fig. 14.8.

| Object type | Description |
|---|---|
| FileSystemObject | Allows the programmer to interact with **File**s, **Folder**s and **Drive**s. |
| File | Allows the programmer to manipulate **File**s. |
| Folder | Allows the programmer to manipulate **Folder**s (i.e., directories). |
| Drive | Allows the programmer to gather information about **Drive**s (hard disks, RAM disks—computer memory used as a substitute for hard disks to allow high speed file operations, CD-ROMs, etc.). **Drive**s can be local or remote. |
| TextStream | Allows the programmer to read and write text files. |

**Fig. 14.7**    File System Objects (FSOs).

| Methods | Description |
|---|---|
| CopyFile | Copies an existing **File**. |
| CopyFolder | Copies an existing **Folder**. |
| CreateFolder | Creates and returns a **Folder**. |
| CreateTextFile | Creates and returns a text **File**. |
| DeleteFile | Deletes a **File**. |
| DeleteFolder | Deletes a **Folder**. |
| DriveExists | Tests whether or not a **Drive** exists. |
| FileExists | Tests whether or not a **File** exists. Returns **Boolean**. |
| FolderExists | Tests whether or not a **Folder** exists. Returns **Boolean**. |
| GetAbsolutePathName | Returns the absolute path as a **String**. |

**Fig. 14.8**    **FileSystemObject** methods (part 1 of 2).

| Methods | Description |
|---------|-------------|
| GetDrive | Returns the specified **Drive**. |
| GetDriveName | Returns the **Drive** drive name. |
| GetFile | Returns the specified **File**. |
| GetFileName | Returns the **File** file name. |
| GetFolder | Returns the specified **Folder**. |
| GetParentFolderName | Returns a **String** representing the parent folder name. |
| GetTempName | Creates and returns a **String** representing a file name. |
| MoveFile | Moves a **File**. |
| MoveFolder | Moves a **Folder**. |
| OpenTextFile | Opens an existing text **File**. Returns a **TextStream**. |

**Fig. 14.8**   **FileSystemObject** methods (part 2 of 2).

The program of Fig. 14.9 demonstrates using a **FileSystemObject** to add and remove folders. The program builds upon the example of Fig. 14.4.

```
1   ' Fig. 14.9
2   ' Demonstrating FileSystemObjects
3   Option Explicit                           ' General declaration
4   Dim mFileSysObj As New FileSystemObject   ' General declaration
5
6   Private Sub dirDirBox_Change()
7
8       ' Update the file path to the directory path
9       filFileBox.Path = dirDirBox.Path
10  End Sub
11
12  Private Sub drvDriveBox_Change()
13
14      On Error GoTo error handler
15
16          ' Update the directory path to the drive
17          dirDirBox.Path = drvDriveBox.Drive
18          Exit Sub
19
20  errorhandler:
21          Dim message As String
22
23          ' Check for device unavailable error
24          If Err.Number = 68 Then
25              Dim r As Integer
26
27              message = "Drive is not available."
```

**Fig. 14.9**   Using a **FileSystemObject** (part 1 of 4).

```
28              r = MsgBox(message, vbRetryCancel + vbCritical, _
29                      "VBHTP: Chapter 14")
30
31              ' Determine where control should resume
32              If r = vbRetry Then
33                  Resume
34              Else    ' Cancel was pressed.
35                  drvDriveBox.Drive = drvDriveBox.List(1)
36                  Resume Next
37              End If
38
39          Else
40              Call MsgBox(Err.Description, vbOKOnly + vbExclamation)
41              Resume Next
42          End If
43
44   End Sub
45
46   Private Sub filFileBox_Click()
47       Call displayData          ' Update TextBox
48   End Sub
49
50   ' Programmer defined
51   Private Sub displayData()
52       txtDisplay.Text = ""
53       txtDisplay.Text = "GetAbsolutePathName: " & _
54                      mFileSysObj.GetAbsolutePathName( _
55                      filFileBox.Path) & vbNewLine & _
56                      "GetDriveName: " & _
57                      mFileSysObj.GetDriveName( _
58                      filFileBox.Path) & vbNewLine & _
59                      "GetParentFolderName: " & _
60                      mFileSysObj.GetParentFolderName( _
61                      filFileBox.Path) & vbNewLine & _
62                      "GetTempName: " & mFileSysObj.GetTempName
63   End Sub
64
65   Private Sub mnuitmCreateFolder_Click()
66       Dim s As String
67
68       ' Get the Folder name
69       s = InputBox("Enter complete path and folder name:", "CREATE")
70
71       ' Test if the Folder already exists
72       If mFileSysObj.FolderExists(s) Then
73          Call MsgBox("Folder already exists! Cannot create.")
74          Exit Sub
75       End If
76
77       Call mFileSysObj.CreateFolder(s)     ' Create the Folder
78       Call dirDirBox.Refresh               ' Repaint DirListBox
79   End Sub
80
```

Fig. 14.9    Using a **FileSystemObject** (part 2 of 4).

```
81  Private Sub mnuitmDeleteFolder_Click()
82     Dim s As String
83
84     ' Get the Folder name
85     s = InputBox("Enter complete path and folder name:", "DELETE")
86
87     ' Test if the Folder already exists
88     If mFileSysObj.FolderExists(s) = False Then
89        Call MsgBox("Folder does not exist! Cannot delete.")
90        Exit Sub
91     End If
92
93     Call mFileSysObj.DeleteFolder(s)     ' Delete the Folder
94     Call dirDirBox.Refresh               ' Repaint DirListBox
95  End Sub
96
97  Private Sub mnuitmExit_Click()
98     End     ' Terminate execution
99  End Sub
```

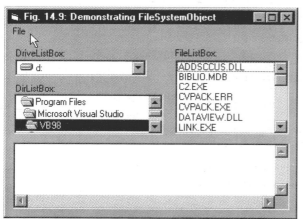

Initial GUI at execution.

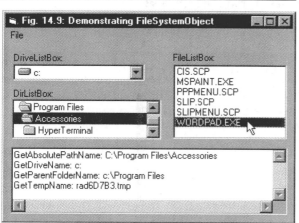

GUI after user has selected **c:** drive and the **Accessories** menu. The **TextBox** displays information about file **WORDPAD.EXE** which the user clicked.

**Fig. 14.9**   Using a **FileSystemObject** (part 3 of 4).

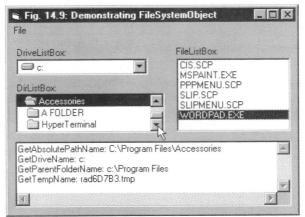

GUI after the user selects **Create Folder** from the **File** menu and enters **c:\program files\accessories\A FOLDER**. Note that the folder is automatically inserted in alphabetical order.

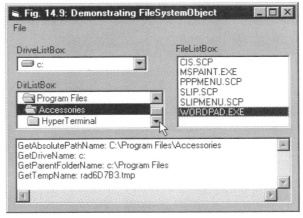

GUI after the user selects **Delete Folder** from the **File** menu and enters **c:\program files\accessories\A FOLDER**.

**Fig. 14.9**    Using a **FileSystemObject** (part 4 of 4).

Before discussing the details of the program, we first take a brief diversion to discuss *objects*. Object orientation is a natural way of thinking about the world and of writing computer programs. We start by introducing some of the key terminology of object orientation. Look around you in the real world. Everywhere you look you see them—*objects*! People, animals, plants, cars, planes, buildings, computers and the like. Humans think in terms of objects. We have the marvelous ability of *abstraction* that enables us to view screen images as objects such as people, planes, trees and mountains rather than as individual dots of color. We can, if we wish, think in terms of beaches rather than grains of sand, forests rather than trees, and houses rather than bricks.

We might be inclined to divide objects into two categories—animate objects and inanimate objects. Animate objects are "alive" in some sense. They move around and do things. Inanimate objects, like towels, seem not to do much at all. They just kind of "sit around." All these objects, however, do have some things in common. They all have *attributes* like size, shape, color, weight and the like. And they all exhibit *behaviors,* e.g., a ball rolls, bounces, inflates, and deflates; a baby cries, sleeps, crawls, walks, and blinks; a car accelerates, brakes, turns; a towel absorbs water; etc.

Humans learn about objects by studying their attributes and observing their behaviors. Different objects can have similar attributes and can exhibit similar behaviors. Comparisons can be made, for example, between babies and adults, and between humans and chimpanzees. Cars, trucks, little red wagons and roller skates have much in common.

*Object-oriented programming (OOP)* models real-world objects with software counterparts. It takes advantage of *class* relationships where objects of a certain class—such as a class of vehicles—have the same characteristics. Object-oriented programming gives us a more natural and intuitive way to view the programming process, namely by *modeling* real-world objects, their attributes and their behaviors. OOP also models communication between objects. Just as people send *messages* to one another (e.g., a sergeant commanding troops to stand at attention), objects also communicate via messages.

OOP *encapsulates* data (attributes) and functions (behavior) into packages called *objects;* the data and functions of an object are intimately tied together. Objects have the property of *information hiding.* This means that although objects may know how to communicate with one another across well-defined *interfaces,* objects normally are not allowed to know how other objects are implemented—implementation details are hidden within the objects themselves. Surely it is possible to drive a car effectively without knowing the details of how engines, transmissions and exhaust systems work internally. For example, throughout the text we have used many controls (**TextBox**, **Label**, **DirListBox**, **Slider**, etc.) without actually knowing how they are implemented. Although it may be interesting to know how a **DirListBox** displays a list of directories, we do not need to know that level of detail about a **DirListBox** object. All we need to know is that when the user selects a directory from the **DirListBox**, we can obtain the selected directory for use in our program. Controls are just one example of objects. Some objects like controls have a graphical representation, whereas others do not (e.g., the **Printer** object).

**FileSystemObject** is one of many different types of Visual Basic objects. Objects, like variables, reside in memory. However, an object must get its memory at run-time (i.e., dynamically). Keyword **New** is used to dynamically allocate objects. We discuss object-oriented programming in detail in Chapter 16. Now let us continue with the details of the program from Fig. 14.9.

Line 4,

```
Dim mFileSysObj As New FileSystemObject
```

*dynamically* creates **FileSystemObject mFileSysObj** using keyword **New**. The object now exists in memory. Like variables, objects have scope and **mFileSysObj** is a module variable.

*Common Programming Error 14.3*

*Attempting to use an object that does not have memory is a run-time error.*

The **DirListBox**, **FileListBox** and **Drive** list boxes are tied together the same exact way as we demonstrated in the program of Fig. 14.4. We have, however, coded the **FileListBox**'s **Click** event procedure to call the programmer-defined procedure **displayData**, which displays information about the file selected. Procedure **displayData** displays the file's absolute path (by calling **GetAbsolutePathName**), drive name (by calling **GetDriveName**) and parent folder name (by calling **Get-ParentFolderName**)—each of which is called for **mFileSysObj**. Method **GetTempName** is also called to display a temporary file name. **GetTempName** creates a name that can be used for a file but does not create a file. Constant *vbNewLine* is used when appropriate to continue printing on the next line.

The program user can decide to create and delete folders by selecting **Create Folder** and **Delete Folder** from the **File** menu. Both **Click** event procedures are almost identical in that they prompt the user for the folder with function **InputBox**, test whether or not the folder exists with **FolderExists**, create with **CreateFolder** or delete with **DeleteFolder**, and call for the **DirListBox** to repaint itself with **Refresh**. Repainting allows the user to see the folder added or removed.

**File**s allow the programmer to gather information about files, manipulate files and open files. Figure 14.10 lists some common **File** properties and methods.

The program of Fig. 14.11 demonstrates using a **File** object. The GUI contains a **DirListBox**, a **FileListBox** and a **TextBox**. When the user clicks a file, information about that file is printed in the **TextBox**. Rather than using the **FileSystemObject** to gather file information, the program uses a **File** object to gather information about the file. Some of the information displayed can only be done through **File** and not directly through **FileSystemObject**.

| Property/method | Description |
|---|---|
| *Properties* | |
| **DateCreated** | **Date**. The date the **File** was created. |
| **DateLastAccessed** | **Date**. The date the **File** was last accessed. |
| **DateLastModified** | **Date**. The date the **File** was last modified. |
| **Drive** | **Drive**. The **Drive** where the file is located. |
| **Name** | **String**. The **File** name. |
| **ParentFolder** | **String**. The **File**'s parent folder name. |
| **Path** | **String**. The **File**'s path. |
| **ShortName** | **String**. The **File**'s name expressed as a short name. |
| **Size** | The size of the **File** in bytes. |
| *Methods* | |
| **Copy** | Copy this **File**. Same as **FileSystemObject** method **CopyFile**. |
| **Delete** | Delete this **File**. Same as **FileSystemObject** method **DeleteFile**. |
| **Move** | Move this **File**. Same as **FileSystemObject** method **MoveFile**. |
| **OpenAsTextStream** | Opens an existing **File** as a text **File**. Returns **TextStream**. |

**Fig. 14.10**   Some common **File** properties and methods.

```
1    ' Fig. 14.11
2    ' Demonstrating File FSO
3    Option Explicit                    ' General declaration
4    Dim mFso As New FileSystemObject  ' General declaration
5
6    Private Sub dirDirectory_Change()
7
8        ' Update filFile's Path when dirDirectory changes
9        filFile.Path = dirDirectory.Path
10   End Sub
11
12   Private Sub filFile_Click()
13       Dim theFile As File
14
15       txtBox.Text = ""      ' Clear TextBox
16
17       ' Determine which file name was selected and return
18       ' its File object.
19       Set theFile = mFso.GetFile(filFile.Path & "\" & _
20                     filFile.List(filFile.ListIndex))
21
22       ' Display File information in PictureBox
23       txtBox.Text = "Created: " & theFile.DateCreated & _
24                     vbNewLine & _
25                   "Last Accessed: " & theFile.DateLastAccessed & _
26                     vbNewLine & "Last Modified: " & _
27                     theFile.DateLastModified & vbNewLine & _
28                     "Drive: " & theFile.Drive & vbNewLine & _
29                     "Size: " & theFile.Size & " bytes" & _
30                     vbNewLine & _
31                     "Path: " & theFile.Path & vbNewLine & _
32                     "Short Name: " & theFile.ShortName
33   End Sub
```

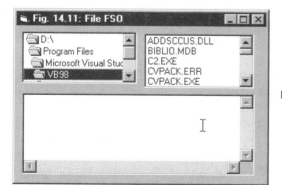

Initial GUI at execution.

**Fig. 14.11**   Demonstrating the **File** FSO (part 1 of 2).

As in the last program, a **FileSystemObject** is created on line 4 and both the **DirListBox Change** event procedure and **FileListBox Click** event procedure are coded.

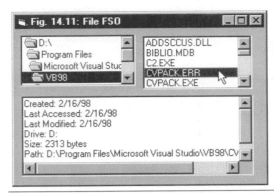

GUI after programmer clicks a file.

**Fig. 14.11**   Demonstrating the **File** FSO (part 2 of 2).

Line 12 declares **File** variable **theFile**. This **File** variable does not refer to any particular file but has a value of **Nothing**. Lines 19 and 20,

```
Set theFile = mFso.GetFile(filFile.Path & "\" & _
                 filFile.List(filFile.ListIndex))
```

assign **theFile** the **File** selected in the **FileListBox**. The **List** property returns a **String** from the **FileListBox** (i.e., a file name). The **ListIndex** property contains the index of the selected **FileListBox** item. The file name selected is then concatenated to the **Path**. Method **GetFile** creates and returns the **File**. Keyword **Set** is used to assign **theFile** to the returned **File**.

*Common Programming Error 14.4*

*Calling **GetFile** for a non-existent file is a run-time error.*

*Common Programming Error 14.5*

*Attempting to assign a **File** variable without using **Set** to the **File** returned by **GetFile** is a run-time error.*

Now that **theFile** refers to a specific **File**, methods can be called to gather information about the file. Property **DateCreated** contains the date the file was created. Property **DateLastAccessed** contains the date the file was last accessed. Property **DateLastModified** contains the date the **File** was last modified. Property **Drive** contains the **Drive** name where the **File** resides. Property **Size** contains the total number of bytes in the **File**. Property **Path** contains the **File**'s path in *long name format* (the operating system does not abbreviate the name when it exceeds the 8-3 format). Property **ShortName** contains, if applicable, the file name in *short name format* (a file name exceeding the 8-3 format is abbreviated). For example, a file name in long name format might be "**ABCD EFG HIJ.doc**." That same file name in short name format might be "**ABCDEF~1.doc**."

**Folder** objects allow the programmer to gather information about folders and to manipulate folders. Figure 14.12 lists some common **Folder** properties and methods.

| Property/method | Description |
|---|---|
| *Properties* | |
| Attributes | **Integer**. Value corresponding to **Folder**'s attributes (read only, hidden, etc.) |
| DateCreated | **Date**. The date the file was created. |
| DateLastAccessed | **Date**. The date the file was last accessed. |
| DateLastModified | **Date**. The date the file was last modified. |
| Drive | **Drive**. The **Drive** where the folder is located. |
| IsRootFolder | **Boolean**. Indicates whether or not a **Folder** is the root folder. |
| Name | **String**. The **Folder**'s name. |
| ParentFolder | **String**. The **Folder**'s parent folder name. |
| Path | **String**. The **Folder**'s path. |
| ShortName | **String**. The **Folder**'s name expressed as a short name. |
| ShortPath | **String**. The **Folder**'s path expresses as a short path. |
| Size | **Variant**. The total size in bytes of all subfolders and files. |
| Type | **String**. The **Folder** type. |
| *Methods* | |
| Delete | Delete this **Folder**. Same as **FileSystemObject** method **DeleteFile**. |
| Move | Move this **Folder**. Same as **FileSystemObject** method **MoveFolder**. |
| Copy | Copy this **Folder**. Same as **FileSystemObject** method **CopyFolder**. |

**Fig. 14.12** Some **Folder** properties and methods.

The program of Fig. 14.13 demonstrates using a **Folder** object. The GUI contains a **DirListBox** and a **TextBox**. When the user clicks a folder, information about that folder is printed in the **TextBox**. The program uses a **Folder** object to gather information about the folder. Some of the information can only be displayed through **Folder**, not directly through **FileSystemObject**.

```
1   ' Fig. 14.13
2   ' Demonstrating the Folder FSO
3   Option Explicit                       ' General declaration
4   Dim mFso As New FileSystemObject       ' General declaration
5
6   Private Sub dirBox_Click()
7       Dim f As Folder
8
```

**Fig. 14.13** Using a **Folder** FSO (part 1 of 2).

```
 9       ' Get a Folder to the selected item
10       Set f = mFso.GetFolder(dirBox.List(dirBox.ListIndex))
11
12       txtDisplay.Text = ""        ' Clear TextBox
13
14       ' Test for the root folder
15       If f.IsRootFolder = False Then
16          txtDisplay.Text = "Root folder: " & f.IsRootFolder _
17                            & vbNewLine & _
18                            "Parent Folder: " & f.ParentFolder & _
19                            vbNewLine & "Size: " & f.Size
20       Else
21          txtDisplay.Text = "Root folder: " & f.IsRootFolder
22       End If
23
24       txtDisplay.Text = txtDisplay.Text & vbNewLine & "Type: " & _
25                         f.Type & vbNewLine & _
26                         "Short Path: " & f.ShortPath & _
27                         vbNewLine & "Path: " & f.Path & _
28                         vbNewLine & "Short Name: " & f.ShortName
29   End Sub
```

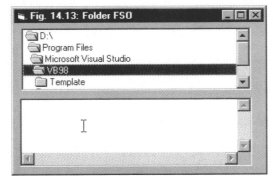

Initial GUI at execution.

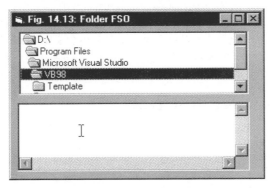

Initial GUI at execution.

**Fig. 14.13**   Using a **Folder** FSO (part 2 of 2).

As in the last program, a **FileSystemObject** is created on line 4 and the **DirL-istBox Change** event procedure is coded.

Line 7 declares **Folder** variable **f**. This **Folder** variable does not refer to any particular folder but has a value of **Nothing**. Line 10,

```
Set f = mFso.GetFolder(dirBox.List(dirBox.ListIndex))
```

assigns **f** the **Folder** selected in the **DirListBox**. The **List** property returns a **String** from the **DirListBox** (i.e., a folder name). The **ListIndex** property contains the index of the selected **DirListBox** item. Method **GetFolder** creates and returns the **Folder**. Keyword *Set* is used to assign **f** to the returned **Folder**.

Property **IsRootFolder** indicates whether or not the folder is the *root folder* for the **Drive**—i.e., the folder that contains everything on the drive. If the folder is not the root folder, method **ParentFolder** is called to print the folder's *parent folder* (i.e., the folder in which the selected folder is contained). Method **Size** is called to print the total number of bytes the folder contains. The size includes *subfolders* (i.e., the folders inside the selected folder) and files.

> **Common Programming Error 14.6**
>
> *Attempting to access the* **ParentFolder** *of a root folder is a run-time error.*

Property **Type** contains the **Folder** type. Property **ShortPath** contains the path as a short path (i.e., each folder name and file name are in the 8.3 format). Property **Path** contains the path in long name format. Property **ShortName** contains the folder name in short name format.

**Drive** objects allow the programmer to gather information about drives. Figure 14.14 lists some common **Drive** properties.

| Property | Description |
| --- | --- |
| AvailableSpace | **Variant**. The amount of available **Drive** space in bytes. |
| DriveLetter | **String**. The letter assigned the **Drive** (e.g., "C"). |
| DriveType | **Integer**. The **Drive** type. Constants **Unknown**, **Removable**, **Fixed**, **Remote**, **CDRom** and **RamDisk** represent **Drive** types and have the values 0 - 5, respectively. |
| FileSystem | **String**. The file system **Drive** description (FAT, FAT32, NTFS, etc.). |
| FreeSpace | **Variant**. Same as **AvailableSpace**. |
| IsReady | **Boolean**. Indicates whether or not a **Drive** is ready for use. |
| Path | **String**. The **Drive**'s **Path**. |
| RootFolder | **Folder**. The **Drive**'s root **Folder**. |
| SerialNumber | **Long**. The **Drive** serial number. |
| TotalSize | **Variant**. The total **Drive** size in bytes. |
| VolumeName | **String**. The **Drive** volume name. |

Fig. 14.14  **Drive** properties.

The program of Fig. 14.15 allows the programmer to display information about a **Drive**. The GUI contains one **DriveListBox** and two **Label**s.

As we have seen before, a **FileSystemObject** is created on line 4 and the **DriveListBox Change** event procedure is coded. Event procedure **Load** calls **Change** initially. Line 11 declares **Drive** variable **d** and line 14 assigns **d** the **Drive** returned from **GetDrive**.

```
1   ' Fig. 14.15
2   ' Demonstrating the Drive FSO
3   Option Explicit                    ' General declaration
4   Dim mFso As New FileSystemObject   ' General Declaration
5
6   Private Sub Form_Load()
7       Call drvBox_Change      ' Call DriveListBox Change
8   End Sub
9
10  Private Sub drvBox_Change()
11      Dim d As Drive
12
13      ' Get the Drive and assign it to d
14      Set d = mFso.GetDrive(drvBox.List(drvBox.ListIndex))
15
16      ' Enable error handler
17      On Error GoTo errhandler
18          lblStats(0).Caption = "Letter: " & d.DriveLetter & _
19                                Space$(3) & "S/N #: " _
20                                & d.SerialNumber & Space$(3) & _
21                                "Free space: " & d.FreeSpace / _
22                                1000000 & " MB"
23          lblStats(1).Caption = "Type: " & d.DriveType _
24                                & Space$(3) & "File System: " _
25                                & d.FileSystem & Space$(3) & _
26                                "Total Size: " & d.TotalSize / _
27                                1000000 & " MB"
28          Exit Sub
29
30  errhandler:
31          Call MsgBox(Err.Description, vbCritical, "ERROR")
32          drvBox.Drive = drvBox.List(1)
33          Exit Sub
34  End Sub
```

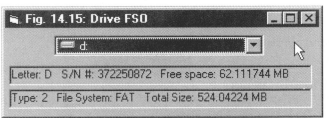

Initial GUI at execution.

**Fig. 14.15**  Using a **Drive** FSO (part 1 of 2).

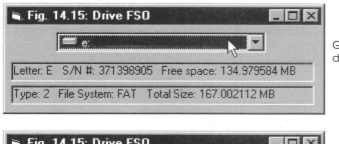

GUI after user selects **e:** drive.

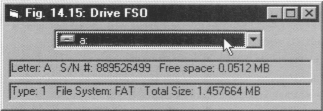

GUI after user selects **a:** drive.

**Fig. 14.15**   Using a **Drive** FSO (part 2 of 2).

Property **DriveLetter** contains the **Drive**'s letter. Property **SerialNumber** contains the **Drive**'s serial number. Property **FreeSpace** contains the number of bytes available. Each of these facts is displayed in the first **Label**.

The second **Label** displays the **Drive** type (i.e., **0** for **Unknown**, **1** for **Removable**, **2** for **Fixed**, etc.), the file system type (i.e., FAT, FAT32, etc.) and the total drive size in bytes. Methods **Type**, **FileSystem** and **Size** are called.

## 14.5  Creating a Sequential Access File

Visual Basic imposes no structure on a file—it views files as sets of bytes on disk that are read or written sequentially from the beginning to the end of the file (also known as reading or writing *streams* of bytes). Thus, notions like "record" do not exist in files. Therefore, the programmer must structure files to meet the requirements of applications. The examples that follow, show how the programmer can impose a record structure on a file.

When working with sequential files, the programmer uses the file system object **TextStream** to read and write file data. A **TextStream** is a stream of characters that are read from a file or written to a file. Figure 14.16 summarizes common **TextStream** properties and methods.

| Property/method | Description |
|---|---|
| *Properties* | |
| **AtEndOfLine** | **Boolean**. Specifies if the position is at the end of the line. |
| **AtEndOfStream** | **Boolean**. Specifies if the position is at the end of the stream. |

**Fig. 14.16**   **TextStream** properties and methods (part 1 of 2).

| Property/method | Description |
|---|---|
| `Column` | **Long**. The current character's position in. |
| `Line` | **Long**. The current line number. |
| *Methods* | |
| `Close` | Closes the **TextStream**. |
| `Read` | Reads a specified number of characters from the **TextStream**. Returns a **String**. |
| `ReadAll` | Reads the entire **TextStream** into a **String**. Returns a **String**. |
| `ReadLine` | Reads a line from a **TextStream**. Returns a **String**. |
| `Skip` | Skips a specified number of **TextStream** characters. |
| `SkipLine` | Skips a line. |
| `Write` | Writes a **String** to a **TextStream**. |
| `WriteBlankLines` | Writes a specified number of blank lines to a **TextStream**. |
| `WriteLine` | Writes a **String** followed by an end-of-line character to a **TextStream**. |

**Fig. 14.16**    **TextStream** properties and methods (part 2 of 2).

The program of Fig. 14.17 allows the user to enter a three-digit account number in a **MaskEdit** control, a last name in a **TextBox** and a balance in a second **TextBox**. When the user clicks **Write**, the account, name and balance are written to a **TextStream**.

```
1    ' Fig. 14.17
2    ' Writing to a sequential text file
3    Option Explicit                         ' General declaration
4    Dim mFileSysObj As New FileSystemObject  ' General declaration
5    Dim mFile As File                        ' General declaration
6    Dim mTxtStream As TextStream             ' General declaration
7
8    Private Sub Form_Load()
9
10       ' Create a text file
11       Call mFileSysObj.CreateTextFile("c:\clients.dat")
12
13       ' Once file is created, reference the file
14       Set mFile = mFileSysObj.GetFile("c:\clients.dat")
15
16       ' Open a text stream for writing to the file
17       Set mTxtStream = mFile.OpenAsTextStream(ForWriting)
18
19       ' Display path in lblFileName
20       lblFileName.Caption = mFile.Path
21   End Sub
```

**Fig. 14.17**    Writing data to a text file (part 1 of 3).

```
22
23    Private Sub cmdWrite_Click()
24
25        ' Write the data to the file
26        Call mTxtStream.WriteLine(mskAccount.Text & " " & _
27                                  txtName.Text & " " & _
28                                  txtBalance.Text)
29
30        ' Clear MaskEdit and TextBoxes
31        txtName.Text = ""
32        txtBalance.Text = ""
33
34        ' Set several properties for mskAccount
35        ' using With statement
36        With mskAccount
37           .Text = "000"      ' Display all zeros in MaskEdit
38           .SelStart = 0      ' Start highlighting at position 0
39           .SelLength = 3     ' Highlight 3 characters
40           .SetFocus          ' Transfer focus
41        End With
42    End Sub
43
44    Private Sub Form_Terminate()
45        Call mTxtStream.Close      ' Close the text stream
46    End Sub
```

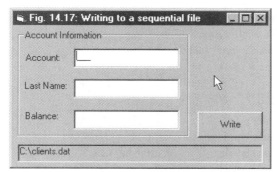

Initial GUI at execution.

GUI as programmer is entering account information.

**Fig. 14.17**   Writing data to a text file (part 2 of 3).

GUI after user clicks **Write**. Focus shifts
to **MaskEdit** where the three digits
are selected.

**Fig. 14.17**   Writing data to a text file (part 3 of 3).

The program of Fig. 14.17 creates a simple sequential access file that might be used in
an accounts receivable system to help manage the money owed by a company's credit clients. For each client, the program obtains an account number, the client's last name and the
client's balance (i.e., the amount the client still owes the company for goods and services
received in the past). The data obtained for each client constitutes a record for that client.
The account number is used as the record key in this application; that is, the file will be created and maintained in account number order. This program assumes the user enters the
records in account number order. In a comprehensive accounts receivable system, a sorting
capability would be provided so the user could enter the records in any order—the records
would then be sorted and written to the file.

In the general declaration, a **FileSystemObject** object named **mFileSysObj**, a
**File** variable named **mFile**, and a **TextStream** variable named **mTxtStream** are
declared. Each are used in the **Form_Load** event procedure.

In **Form_Load**, the text file **clients.dat** is created with the line

```
Call mFileSysObj.CreateTextFile("c:\clients.dat")
```

If the specified file does not yet exist, then a file is created with that filename. If the file
already exists, the file contents are discarded and the file is empty.

The **File** object representing **clients.dat** is assigned to **mFile** with the line

```
Set mFile = mFileSysObj.GetFile("c:\clients.dat")
```

and the line

```
Set mTxtStream = mFile.OpenAsTextStream(ForWriting)
```

opens **clients.dat** as a **TextStream**. The file is opened in *ForWriting* mode.
Text can now be written to the **File** through **mTxtStream**. The file open mode can be
either **ForWriting** to output data to a file or *ForAppending* to append data to the end
of a file (without modifying any data already in the file). Existing files opened in **For-
Writing** mode are *truncated*—all data in the file is discarded. Opening a file establishes
a "line of communication" with the file. Figure 14.18 lists the file open modes. To verify
that the file has been created successfully, in the next section we create a program to read
the file and print its contents.

| File Open Mode | Description |
| --- | --- |
| ForReading | Open the file for reading only. Data cannot be written to the file. |
| ForWriting | Open a file for writing. If the file already contains data, the data are truncated—all data in the file are discarded. |
| ForAppending | Open a file to allow writing at the end of the file. |

**Fig. 14.18**   File open modes.

**Common Programming Error 14.7**

*Opening an existing file for output when, in fact, the user wants to preserve the file; the contents of the file are discarded without warning.* **FileSystemObject** *method* **FileExists** *should be used to test for the existence of the file first.*

When the **Write** button is clicked, the information contained in the **MaskEdit** control and **TextBox** controls is written to the file with the line

```
Call mTxtStream.WriteLine(mskAccount.Text & " " & _
                          txtName.Text & " " & _
                          txtBalance.Text)
```

Method *WriteLine* writes a line of text followed by a new line. The **MaskEdit** is then set to **"000"** and the **TextBox**es are then set to **""**. The **With** statement is used to set four **MaskEdit** properties. The *SelStart* property specifies the index where the selection starts and *SelLength* specifies how many characters are selected (i.e., highlighted). When the user clicks the **Close** box (i.e., the ∞ in the form's upper-right corner), the event procedure *Form_Terminate* is called. **Terminate** allows the programmer to do any necessary clean-up before the program exits—such as closing a file.

**Performance Tip 14.1**

*Explicitly close each file as soon as it is known that the program will not reference the file again. This can reduce resource usage in a program that will continue executing after it no longer needs to be referencing a particular file. This practice also improves program clarity.*

## 14.6  Reading Data from a Sequential Access File

Data stored in files may be retrieved for processing when needed. The previous section demonstrated how to create a file for sequential access. In this section, we discuss how to read data sequentially from a file.

The program of Fig. 14.19 reads records from the file **clients.dat** created by the program of Fig. 14.17 and displays the record contents.

The GUI is similar to the previous program, except a **TextBox** is used instead of a **MaskEdit** control for the account and the button is **Read** instead of **Write**. The program creates and initializes a **FileSystemObject** object and **File** variable in the same exact manner as the previous program. Line 14,

```
Set mTxtStream = mFile.OpenAsTextStream(ForReading)
```

opens **clients.dat** for reading.

```
1    ' Fig. 14.19
2    ' Reading from a sequential text file
3    Option Explicit                               ' General declaration
4    Dim mFileSysObj As New FileSystemObject       ' General declaration
5    Dim mFile As File                             ' General declaration
6    Dim mTxtStream As TextStream                  ' General declaration
7
8    Private Sub Form_Load()
9
10       ' Get the file
11       Set mFile = mFileSysObj.GetFile("c:\clients.dat")
12
13       ' Open a text stream for writing to the file
14       Set mTxtStream = mFile.OpenAsTextStream(ForReading)
15
16       ' Display path in lblFileName
17       lblFileName.Caption = mFile.Path
18    End Sub
19
20    Private Sub cmdRead_Click()
21       Dim s As String
22
23       On Error GoTo handler    ' Set error trap
24
25       ' Read the data
26       s = mTxtStream.ReadLine
27
28       ' Parse String s to get values for MaskEdit
29       ' and TextBoxes
30       Dim mark1 As Integer, mark2 As Integer
31
32       mark1 = 4    ' Location of first space in s
33
34       ' Place only the String portion representing the
35       ' account in the MaskEdit.
36       mskAccount.Text = Trim$(Mid$(s, 1, mark1))
37
38       ' Position to first letter of name
39       mark1 = mark1 + 1
40
41       ' Determine location of second space character and
42       ' add 1 to include the space.
43       mark2 = InStr(mark1, s, " ", vbTextCompare) + 1
44
45       ' Place only the String portion representing the
46       ' name in the TextBox.
47       txtName.Text = Trim$(Mid$(s, mark1, mark2 - mark1))
48
49       ' Place the formatted dollar amount in the TextBox.
50       ' mark2 is positioned at the beginning of the amount.
51       txtBalance.Text = Format$(Mid$(s, mark2, Len(s) - mark1), _
52                                 "Currency")
53       Exit Sub
```

**Fig. 14.19**   Reading from a sequential file (part 1 of 2).

```
54
55    handler:
56        If Err.Number = 62 Then        ' EOF error
57            Call mTxtStream.Close
58            cmdRead.Enabled = False
59            lblFileName.Caption = ""
60        Else
61            Call MsgBox(Err.Description)
62        End If
63
64    End Sub
```

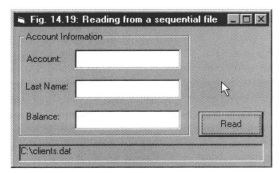

Initial GUI at execution.

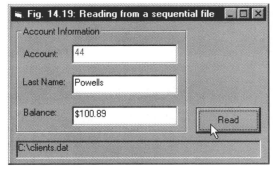

GUI after user clicks the **Read** button once.

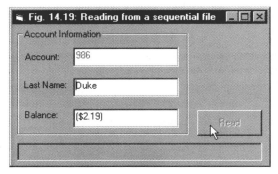

GUI when the last set of information is read.

**Fig. 14.19**   Reading from a sequential file (part 2 of 2).

When **Read** is clicked, the statement

```
s = mTxtStream.ReadLine
```

reads a line of data from the file. After the preceding line executes the first time, **s** contains

```
"044 Powells 100.89"
```

The **String** processing techniques of Chapter 8 are used to extract the individual account, name and balance from **s**. After clicking **Read** multiple times, an attempt to read past the end of file occurs. Visual Basic handles this as a run-time error. The program handles the error by closing the file, disabling the **Read** button and clears the **Label**.

*Common Programming Error 14.8*

*Attempting to read past the end of file is a run-time error.*

To retrieve data sequentially from a file, programs normally start reading from the beginning of the file, and read all the data consecutively until the desired data is found. It may be necessary to process the file sequentially several times (from the beginning of the file) during the execution of a program.

Figure 14.20 enables a credit manager to display the account information for those customers with zero balances (i.e., customers who do not owe the company any money), credit balances (i.e., customers to whom the company owes money) and debit balances (i.e., customers who owe the company money for goods and services received in the past).

```
1    ' Fig. 14.20
2    ' Credit inquiry program
3    Option Explicit                       ' General declaration
4    Dim mFso As New FileSystemObject       ' General declaration
5    Dim mType As Integer                   ' General declaration
6    Const mCREDIT = 0, mDEBIT = 1, mZERO = 2   ' General declaration
7
8    Private Sub cmdButton_Click(Index As Integer)
9      mType = Index    ' Assign cmdButton control array index
10     Call openAndReadFile   ' Open and read file
11   End Sub
12
13   Private Sub openAndReadFile()
14      Dim txtStream As TextStream, s As String
15      Dim balance As Currency, pos As Long
16
17      txtDisplay.Text = "Accounts:"
18
19      ' Get "clients.dat" and open a TextStream for reading
20      Set txtStream = mFso.GetFile("c:\clients.dat"). _
21                      OpenAsTextStream(ForReading)
22
```

**Fig. 14.20**   A credit inquiry program (part 1 of 3).

```
23      ' Loop until end of stream is found
24      Do
25        s = txtStream.ReadLine    ' Read one line
26
27        ' Find the position of the second space
28        pos = InStr(InStr(1, s, " ", vbTextCompare) + 1, s, " ", _
29                    vbTextCompare)
30
31        ' Extract the String that contains the balance
32        balance = Trim$(Mid$(s, pos, Len(s) - pos))
33
34        ' Determine what if anything should be displayed
35        If (mType = mCREDIT And balance < 0) Then
36           txtDisplay.Text = txtDisplay.Text & vbNewLine & s
37        ElseIf (mType = mDEBIT And balance > 0) Then
38           txtDisplay.Text = txtDisplay.Text & vbNewLine & s
39        ElseIf (mType = mZERO And balance = 0) Then
40           txtDisplay.Text = txtDisplay.Text & vbNewLine & s
41        End If
42
43      Loop While (txtStream.AtEndOfStream = False)
44
45      Call txtStream.Close      ' Close TextStream
46   End Sub
```

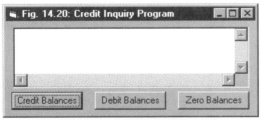

Initial GUI at execution.

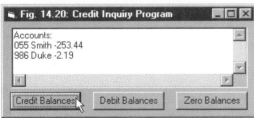

GUI after user has pressed the **Credit Balances** button.

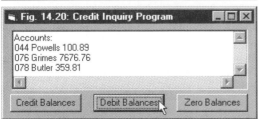

GUI after user has pressed the **Debit Balances** button.

**Fig. 14.20**   A credit inquiry program (part 2 of 3).

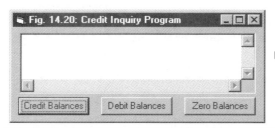

Initial GUI at execution.

**Fig. 14.20**   A credit inquiry program (part 3 of 3).

The GUI contains three buttons, **Credit Balances**, **Debit Balances** and **Zero Balances**, which allow the credit manager to view credit information. **Credit Balances** produces a list of accounts with credit balances. **Debit Balances** produces a list of accounts with debit balances. **Zero Balances** produces a list of accounts with zero balances. All account information is displayed in a multiline **TextBox**.

The account information is collected by reading through the entire file and determining if each record satisfies the criteria for the account type selected by the credit manager. Pressing a button results in **cmdButton_Click** being called to set **mType** to the button **Index**. Event procedure **cmdButton_Click** calls the programmer-defined procedure **openAndReadFile**, which loops through the file reading a line at a time until the end of file is reached. Procedure **openAndReadFile** determines if the current information satisfies the account type requested. Note: If the file is empty, line 25 generates a run-time error. In the exercises, we ask you to modify the program to fix this problem.

## 14.7  Updating Sequential Access Files

Data that is formatted and written to a sequential access file as shown in Section 14.5 cannot be modified without the risk of destroying other data in the file. For example, if the name "**Kaz**" needed to be changed to "**Kaz-Palmer**," the old name cannot simply be overwritten. The record for **Kaz** was written to the file as

        **202 Kaz 0.00**

If this record is rewritten beginning at the same location in the file using the longer name, the record would be

        **202 Kaz-Palmer 0.00**

The new record contains seven more characters than the original record. Therefore, the characters beyond the "**m**" in "**Kaz-Palmer**" would overwrite the beginning of the next sequential record in the file. The problem here is that in the formatted input/output model, fields—and hence records—can vary in size. For example, 7, 14, 117, 2074 and -27383 are all **Integer**s and each is stored in the same number of "raw data" bytes internally, but when these **Integer**s are output as formatted text to the screen or to a file on disk, they become different-sized fields. Therefore, the formatted input/output model is not usually used to update records in place.

Such updating can be done, but it is awkward. For example, to make the preceding name change, the records before **202 Kaz 0.00** in a sequential access file could be copied to a new file, the updated record would then be written to the new file, and the records after **202 Kaz 0.00** would be copied to the new file. This requires processing every record in the file to update one record. If many records are being updated in one pass of the file, then this technique can be acceptable. The preceding problem is one of the primary reasons that database management systems exist. We discussed database management in Chapter 18.

## Summary

- Storage of data in variables and arrays is temporary. Files are used for permanent retention of large amounts of data. Data in files is said to be persistent.

- Computers store files on secondary storage devices such as magnetic disks, optical disks and tapes. In this chapter, we explain how data files are created, updated and processed. We consider sequential access files. In the next chapter, we consider random access files.

- Visual Basic provides three intrinsic controls for representing the directories, files and drives on a system. **DirListBox** visually represents the directory structure, **File-ListBox** visually lists the files in a directory, and **DriveListBox** visually lists the drive structure.

- When using a **DirListBox** control or a **FileListBox** control, the **Path** property sets the directory path that is displayed. The **Drive** control's **Drive** property specifies which **Drive** is displayed. The primary event procedure of a **DirListBox** and a **DriveListBox** is **Change**—the same event procedure for **ListBox**es and **ComboBox**es. The primary event procedure for a **FileListBox** is **Click**.

- Ultimately, all data items processed by a computer are reduced to combinations of zeros and ones.

- The smallest data item in a computer can assume the value 0 or the value 1. Such a data item is called a bit (short for "binary digit"—a digit that can assume one of two values).

- It is cumbersome for programmers to work with data in the low-level form of bits. Instead, programmers prefer to work with data in forms such as decimal digits (i.e., 0, 1, 2, 3, 4, 5, 6, 7, 8 and 9), letters (i.e., A through Z, and a through z) and special symbols (i.e., $, @, %, &, *, (, ), -, +, ", :, ?, / and many others). Digits, letters and special symbols are referred to as characters. The set of all characters used to write programs and represent data items on a particular computer is called that computer's character set. Since computers can process only 1s and 0s, every character in a computer's character set is represented as a pattern of 1s and 0s (called a byte). Bytes are most commonly composed of eight bits. Programmers create programs and data items with characters; computers manipulate and process these characters as patterns of bits.

- A field is a group of characters that conveys meaning.

- Data items processed by computers form a data hierarchy in which data items become larger and more complex in structure as we progress from bits, to characters (bytes), to fields, and so on.

- A record is a group of related fields. A file is a group of related records.

- To facilitate the retrieval of specific records from a file, at least one field in each record is chosen as a record key. A record key identifies a record as belonging to a particular person or entity that is unique from all other records in the file.

- The most common type of file organization is called a sequential file in which records are typically stored in order by a record key field.

- A group of related files is sometimes called a database. A collection of programs designed to create and manage databases is called a database management system (DBMS).

- File System Objects (FSOs) provide the programmer with the ability to manipulate files, directories and drives. FSOs also allow the programmer to read and write text to sequential files.

- FSOs are objects in the Microsoft Scripting Runtime Library, which is added to the current project with the **References** dialog.

- The types of FSOs are **FileSystemObject**, **File**, **Folder**, **Drive** and **TextStream**.

- **FileSystemObject** allows the programmer to interact with **File**s, **Folder**s and **Drive**s, performing operations such as creating directories, moving files, determining whether or not a **Drive** exists, etc.

- An object must get its memory at run-time (i.e., dynamically). Keyword **New** is used to dynamically allocate objects.

- A file's absolute path is obtained by calling **FileSystemObject** method **GetAbsolute-PathName**, a file's drive name is obtained by calling **FileSystemObject** method **Get-DriveName** and a file's parent folder name is obtained by calling **FileSystemObject** method **GetParentFolderName**. **FileSystemObject** method **GetTempName** obtains a temporary file name. **GetTempName** creates a name that can be used for a file but does not create a file.

- **File**s allow the programmer to gather information about files, manipulate files and open files.

- Method **DateCreated** is called to get the date the file was created. Method **DateLastAccessed** is called to get the date the file was last accessed. When the **File** was last modified is determined by calling **DateLastModified**. Method **Drive** is called to get the **Drive** name of where the **File** resides. Method **Size** is called to get the total number of bytes in the **File**. Method **Path** is called to display the **File**'s path in long name format. Method **ShortName** is called to display, if applicable, the file name in short name format.

- Method **IsRootFolder** is called to determine whether or not a folder is the topmost folder on a **Drive**. If a folder is not the root folder, method **ParentFolder** can be called to print the folder's parent folder. Method **Size** prints the total number of bytes the folder contains. Method **Type** is called to get the **Folder** type. Method **ShortPath** is called to get the path as a short path (i.e., each folder name and file name are in the 8.3 format). Method **Path** is called to display the path in long name format. Method **ShortName** is called to display the folder name in short name format.

- **Drive** objects allow the programmer to gather information about drives.

- Method **DriveLetter** is called to get a **Drive**'s letter. Method **SerialNumber** is called to get a **Drive**'s serial number and method **FreeSpace** is called to get the number of bytes available.

- Visual Basic imposes no structure on a file. Thus, notions like "record" do not exist in files. Therefore, the programmer must structure files to meet the requirements of applications.

- When working with sequential files, the programmer uses the file system object **TextStream** to read and write file data.

- The file open mode can be either **ForWriting** to output data to a file or **ForAppending** to append data to the end of a file (without modifying any data already in the file). Existing files opened in **ForWriting** mode are truncated—all data in the file is discarded. Opening a file establishes a "line of communication" with the file.

- When the user clicks the **Close** box (i.e., the ∞ in the form's upper-right corner), the event procedure **Form_Terminate** is called. **Terminate** allows the programmer to do any necessary clean-up before the program exits—such as closing a file.

- To retrieve data sequentially from a file, programs normally start reading from the beginning of the file and read all the data consecutively until the desired data is found.

- The formatted input/output model is not usually used to update records in place.

## *Terminology*

| | |
|---|---|
| **Archive** property | **IsRootFolder** property |
| **AtEndOfLine** property | letter |
| **AtEndOfStream** property | **Line** property |
| bit ("binary digit") | **ListCount** property |
| byte | **ListIndex** property |
| **CDRom** constant | **List** property |
| **Change** event procedure | member of a record |
| character | Microsoft Scripting Runtime Library |
| character set | **MousePointer** property |
| **Click** event procedure | **MultiSelect** property |
| **Close** method | **Name** |
| **Column** property | **New** keyword |
| create a file | parent folder |
| create a folder | **Path** property |
| database | **Pattern** property |
| database management system (DBMS) | persistent data |
| data hierarchy | **RamDisk** constant |
| decimal digit | **ReadAll** method |
| directory | **ReadLine** method |
| **DirListBox** control | **Read** method |
| **DragIcon** property | **ReadOnly** property |
| **Drag** method | record |
| **DragMode** property | record key |
| **DriveListBox** control | record member |
| **Drive** property | **References** dialog |
| **Drive** type | **Refresh** method |
| **Enabled** property | **Remote** constant |
| end of file | **Removable** constant |
| field | **SelLength** property |
| file | **SelStart** property |
| **FileListBox** control | **SetFocus** method |
| file open mode | sequential file |
| file system object (FSO) | **Set** keyword |
| **FileSystemObject** type | **SkipLine** method |
| **File** type | **Skip** method |
| **Fixed** constant | special symbol |
| folder | subfolder |
| **Folder** type | **System** property |
| **ForAppending** | **TextStream** type |
| **ForReading** | truncate a file |
| **ForWriting** | **Unknown** constant |
| **GetAbsolutePathName** | **vbNewLine** constant |
| **GetDrivename** | **Visible** property |
| **GetFile** method | **WriteBlankLines** method |
| **GetParentFolderName** | **WriteLine** method |
| **Hidden** property | **Write** method |

## Common Programming Errors

**14.1**    Accessing the **a:** drive (or similar removable storage drives) when it is not ready is a run-time error.

**14.2**    Attempting to use an FSO without enabling the Microsoft Scripting Runtime is a compiler error.

**14.3**    Attempting to use an object that does not have memory is a run-time error.

**14.4**    Calling **GetFile** for a non-existent file is a run-time error.

**14.5**    Attempting to assign a **File** variable without using **Set** to the **File** returned by **GetFile** is a run-time error.

**14.6**    Attempting to access the **ParentFolder** of a root folder is a run-time error.

**14.7**    Opening an existing file for output when, in fact, the user wants to preserve the file; the contents of the file are discarded without warning. **FileSystemObject** method **FileExists** should be used to test for the existence of the file first.

**14.8**    Attempting to read past the end of file is a run-time error.

## Good Programming Practices

**14.1**    Prefixing **DirListBox** controls with **dir** allows them to be identified easily.

**14.2**    Prefixing **FileListBox** controls with **fil** allows them to be identified easily.

**14.3**    Prefixing **DriveListBox** controls with **drv** allows them to be identified easily.

## Performance Tip

**14.1**    Explicitly close each file as soon as it is known that the program will not reference the file again. This can reduce resource usage in a program that will continue executing after it no longer needs to be referencing a particular file. This practice also improves program clarity.

## Self-Review Exercises

**14.1**    Fill in the blanks in each of the following:

a) Ultimately, all data items processed by a computer are reduced to combinations of _____ and _____.

b) The smallest data item a computer can process is called a _____.

c) A _____ is a group of related records.

d) Digits, letters and special symbols are referred to as _____.

e) Property _____ checks for end-of-stream.

**14.2**    State which of the following are *true* and which are *false*. If *false*, explain why.

a) It is not necessary to search through all the records in a sequential file to find a specific record.

b) Data in sequential access files is always updated without overwriting nearby data.

c) Every data item written to a sequential file is always the same size.

**14.3**    Assume that each of the following statements applies to the same program.

a) Write a statement that creates a **FileSystemObject mFSObject**.

b) Write a statement that creates file **oldmast.dat**.

c) Write a statement that assigns **File** variable **mFileVar** to **oldmast.dat**'s **File** object.

d) Write a statement that creates a **TextStream** variable **tStream**.

e) Write a statement that opens **oldmast.dat** for reading.

f) Write a statement that writes the line "**VB How To Program!**" to **oldmast.dat**.

g) Write a statement that closes the file **oldmast.dat**.

## Answers to Self-Review Exercises

**14.1**   a) ones, zeros. b) bit. c) file. d) Characters. e) **AtEndOfStream**.

**14.2**   a) True.
   b) False. If a record being written contains more bytes than the original record on disk, the new record will partially overwrite the next record in the file.
   c) False. Records in a sequential file can be of many different lengths.

**14.3**   a) `Dim mFSObject As New FileSystemObject`
   b) `Call mFSObject.CreateTextFile("oldmast.dat")`
   c) `Set mFileVar = mFSObject.GetFile("oldmast.dat")`
   d) `Dim tStream As TextStream`
   e) `Set tStream = mFileVar.OpenAsTextStream(ForReading)`
   f) `Call tStream.WriteLine("VB How to Program!")`
   g) `Call tStream.Close`

## Exercises

**14.4**   Fill in the blanks in each of the following:
   a) Computers store large amounts of data on secondary storage devices as _____.
   b) A _____ is composed of several fields.
   c) A field that may contain only digits, letters and blanks is called an _____ field.
   d) Method _____ closes a file.
   e) A group of related characters that conveys meaning is called a _____ .

**14.5**   State which of the following are *true* and which are *false*. If *false*, explain why.
   a) Each statement that processes a **File** in a program explicitly refers to that **File** by name.
   b) Data items represented in computers form a data hierarchy in which data items become larger and more complex as we progress from fields to characters to bits, etc.

**14.6**   Write a program that reads in a series of **Integer**s from a file named **data.dat** and sorts them in descending order with a quick sort.

**14.7**   Modify Exercise 14.6 to write the sorted values to a file called **data.out**.

**14.8**   (*Telephone Number Word Generator*) Standard telephone keypads contain the digits 0 through 9. The numbers 2 through 9 each have three letters associated with them, as indicated in the Fig. 14.21.

   Many people find it difficult to memorize phone numbers, so they use the correspondence between digits and letters to develop seven-letter words that correspond to their phone numbers. For example, a person whose telephone number is 686-2377 might use the correspondence indicated in the above table to develop the seven-letter word "NUMBERS."

   Each seven-letter word corresponds to exactly one seven-digit telephone number. The restaurant wishing to increase its takeout business could surely do so with the number 825-3688 (i.e., "TAKEOUT").

   Each seven-letter phone number corresponds to many separate seven-letter words. Unfortunately, most of these represent unrecognizable juxtapositions of letters. It is possible, however, that the owner of a barber shop would be pleased to know that the shop's telephone number, 424-7288, corresponds to "HAIRCUT." The owner of a liquor store would, no doubt, be delighted to find that the store's number, 233-7226, corresponds to "BEERCAN." A veterinarian with the phone number 738-2273 would be pleased to know that the number corresponds to the letters "PETCARE." An automotive dealership would be pleased to know that the dealership number, 639-2277, corresponds to "NEWCARS."

Write a program that, given a seven-digit number, writes to a file every possible seven-letter word combination corresponding to that number. There are 2187 ($3^7$) such words. Avoid phone numbers with the digits 0 and 1.

**14.9** Modify the program of Fig. 14.4 to provide a **ComboBox** that acts as a filter for the files displayed in the **FileListBox**. Provide as a minimum the following filters in the **ComboBox**:

```
All Files (*.*)
Text Files (*.txt)
Executable Files (*.exe)
```

Use the **FileListBox Pattern** property.

**14.10** Modify the program of Fig. 14.4 to allow the user to drag-and-drop files from one folder into another.

**14.11** Modify the program of Fig. 14.4 to allow the user to drag-and-drop a subfolder from one folder into another.

**14.12** Error handing is an important part of file processing. Modify the Credit Inquiry Program of Fig. 14.20 to prevent a run-time error from occurring if the program attempts to read from an empty file.

| Digit | Letters |
|-------|---------|
| 2 | A B C |
| 3 | D E F |
| 4 | G H I |
| 5 | J K L |
| 6 | M N O |
| 7 | P R S |
| 8 | T U V |
| 9 | W X Y |

**Fig. 14.21** Telephone keypad digits and letters.

# 15

# Records and Random-Access Files

## Objectives

- To be able to create, read, write and update random-access files.
- To become familiar with random-access file processing.
- To be able to specify high-performance unformatted I/O operations.
- To understand the differences between formatted and "raw data" file processing.
- To build a transaction processing program with random-access file processing.
- To be able to use the **CommonDialog** control for opening and saving files.

*I am the voice of today, the herald of tomorrow. . . .I am the leaden army that conquers the world—I am TYPE.*
Frederic William Goudy

*And you yourself shall keep the key of it.*
*Hamlet* [1600–1601]
William Shakespeare

*You Could Look It Up.*
James Thurber

*The used key is always bright.*
*Poor Richard's Almanac* [1744]
Benjamin Franklin

*Do not move the markers on the border of the fields.*
Amenemope

# Outline

## 15.1  Introduction

So far, we have seen how to create sequential-access files and to search through them to locate particular information. Sequential-access files are inappropriate for so-called "instant-access" applications in which a particular record of information must be located immediately. Some popular instant-access applications are airline reservation systems, banking systems, point-of-sale systems, automated teller machines and other kinds of transaction processing systems that require rapid access to specific data.

The bank at which you have your account may have hundreds of thousands or even millions of other customers, yet when you use an automated teller machine, your account is checked for sufficient funds in seconds. This kind of instant access is possible with *random-access files*. Individual records of a random-access file (also called *direct-access file*) can be accessed directly (and quickly) without searching through other records. We consider random-access files in this chapter.

## 15.2  Random-Access Files

As we have said, Visual Basic does not impose structure on a file. So the application that wants to use random-access files must literally create them. A variety of techniques can be used to create random-access files. Perhaps the simplest is to require that all records in a file are of the same fixed length.

Using fixed-length records makes it easy for a program to calculate (as a function of the record size and the record key) the exact location of any record relative to the beginning of the file. We will soon see how this facilitates immediate access to specific records, even in large files.

Figure 11.1 illustrates Visual Basic's view of a random-access file composed of fixed-length records (each record in the figure is 100 bytes long). A random-access file is like a railroad train with many cars—some empty and some with contents.

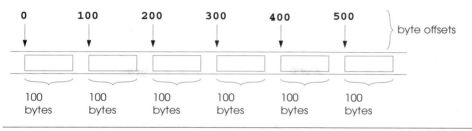

**Fig. 15.1**    Visual Basic's view of a random-access file.

Data can be inserted in a random-access file without destroying other data in the file. Data stored previously also can be updated or deleted without rewriting the entire file. A random-access file has one of three *access types* (Fig. 15.2) associated with it. An access type specifies which operations may be performed on a file. If an access type is not explicitly given, the default access type for the file is **Read Write**.

We will soon see how to create a random-access file, enter data, read the data both sequentially and randomly (i.e., from specific locations in the file), update the data and delete data no longer needed.

## 15.3  Records as User-Defined Types

Visual Basic provides programmers with the ability to create *user-defined types*. User-defined types are collections of related variables—sometimes referred to as *aggregates*—under one name. User-defined types may contain variables of many different data types—in contrast to arrays that contain only elements of the same data type. User-defined data types are commonly used to define fixed-length records to be stored in random-access files.

## 15.3.1 User-Defined Type Definitions

User-defined types are *derived data types*—they are constructed using objects of other types. Consider the following user-defined data type definition:

```
Private Type ClientRecord
    accountNumber As Integer
    lastName As String * 15
    firstName As String * 15
    balance As Currency
End Type
```

| Access type | Description |
| --- | --- |
| **Read** | Open the file in read-only mode. |
| **Write** | Open the file in write-only mode. |
| **Read Write** | Open the file for reading and writing. |

**Fig. 15.2**    Access types available for random-access files.

Keyword **Type** introduces the user-defined type definition. Identifier **ClientRecord** is the *type name*. The type name is used to declare variables of the user-defined type.

**Good Programming Practice 15.1**

*Choose a meaningful type name for user-defined types. This helps make the program self-documenting.*

**Type** definitions must be **Private** when declared in form modules, but can be declared as **Public** or **Private** in standard code modules or class modules (see Chapter 16 for more information on class modules).

**Common Programming Error 15.1**

*Declaring a* **Type** *as* **Public** *in a form module is a syntax error.*

Variables declared in the **Type** definition are called the **Type**'s members. Members of the same **Type** must have unique names.

**Common Programming Error 15.2**

*Declaring multiple members of a* **Type** *with the same name is a syntax error.*

The definition of **Type ClientRecord** contains four members—**Integer accountNumber**, **String**s **firstName** and **LastName**, and **Currency balance**. Notice that **firstName** and **lastName** are both fixed-length **String**s. This is particularly important for maintaining fixed-length records. **Type** members can be variables of basic types (e.g., **Integer**, **String** and **Double**) or aggregate types such as arrays and other **Type**s. For example, a **Type Employee** might contain **String**s for the first and last names and a member of **Type Address** that represents the employee's home address. A **Type** cannot contain an instance of itself.

**Common Programming Error 15.3**

*Declaring a* **Type** *that contains an instance of itself is a syntax error.*

The preceding **Type** definition does not reserve any space in memory; rather, the definition creates a new data type that is used to declare variables. **Type** variables are declared like variables of other types. The declaration

```
Dim oneRecord as ClientRecord, _
    manyRecords(99) as ClientRecord
```

declares **oneRecord** to be of type **ClientRecord** and declares **manyRecords** to be an array with 100 elements (assuming **Option Base 0**) of type **ClientRecord**.

## 15.3.2 Manipulating Members of User-Defined Types

Members of a **Type** definition are accessed like properties using the dot (**.**) operator with a variable of the user-defined type. For example, to assign a value to the **accountNumber** member of **oneRecord** from the previous **ClientRecord** declaration, use the statement

```
oneRecord.accountNumber = 100
```

Variables of the same user-defined type can be assigned to each other in standard assignment statements. For example, if **otherRecord** is a **ClientRecord**, the assignment

```
otherRecord = oneRecord
```

makes a copy of each member of **oneRecord** and assigns it to the corresponding member **otherRecord**.

User-defined types may not be compared because their members are not necessarily stored in consecutive bytes of memory. Sometimes there are "holes" in an instance of a user-defined type because computers may store specific data types only at certain memory boundaries, such as *halfword*, *word* or *doubleword boundaries*. A word is a standard memory unit used to store data in a computer—usually 2 bytes or 4 bytes. Consider the following user-defined type definition:

```
Private Type Example
    c as Byte
    i as Integer
End Type
```

A computer with 2-byte words may require that each of the members of type **Example** be aligned on a word boundary (i.e., at the beginning of a word). Figure 15.3 shows a sample storage alignment for a variable of type **Example** that has been assigned the ASCII character **a** and the integer 97 (the bit representations of the values are shown). If the members are aligned at word boundaries, there is a 1-byte hole (byte 1 in the figure) in the storage for variables of type **Example**. If the members of two variables of type Example are in fact equal, they do not necessarily compare equal because the undefined 1-byte holes are not likely to contain identical values.

> **Common Programming Error 15.4**
>
> *Comparing user-defined type variables is a syntax error because storage alignment requirements can result in undefined areas in each variable.*

## 15.4 Creating a Random-Access File

Random-access file processing programs rarely write a single field to a file. Normally, they write one record at a time, as we show in the following examples.

Consider the following problem statement:

*Create a credit processing program capable of storing up to 100 fixed-length records for a company that can have up to 100 customers. Each record should consist of an account number that will be used as the record key, a last name, a first name, and a balance. The program should be able to update an account, insert a new account, delete an account and list all the account records in a text file for printing.*

| Byte | 0 | 1 | 2 | 3 |
|------|---|---|---|---|
| | 01100001 | | 00000000 | 01100001 |

**Fig. 15.3**    A possible storage alignment for a variable of type **Example** showing an undefined area in memory.

The next several sections introduce the techniques necessary to create this credit processing program. Figure 15.4 illustrates opening a random-access file, defining the record format and writing data to the disk.

```
1   ' Fig. 15.4
2   ' Creating a blank random-access file
3   Option Explicit
4
5   Private Type ClientRecord
6       accountNumber As Integer
7       lastName As String * 15
8       firstName As String * 15
9       balance As Currency
10  End Type
11
12  Sub cmdInitialize_Click()
13      Dim recordLength As Long, x As Integer
14      Dim udtBlankClient As ClientRecord    ' user-defined type
15      Dim filename As String
16
17      ' Determine number of bytes in a ClientRecord object
18      recordLength = LenB(udtBlankClient)
19
20      dlgOpen.ShowOpen
21      filename = dlgOpen.filename
22
23      If dlgOpen.FileTitle <> "" Then
24          ' Open clients.rnd for writing
25          Open filename For Random Access Write As #1 _
26              Len = recordLength
27
28          For x = 1 To 100
29              Put #1, x, udtBlankClient   ' Write empty records
30          Next
31
32          Close #1    ' Close file
33
34          cmdInitialize.Enabled = False   ' Disable button
35          MsgBox ("File initialized. Click Exit to terminate.")
36      Else
37          MsgBox ("You must specify a file name")
38      End If
39  End Sub
40
41  Sub cmdExit_Click()
42      End
43  End Sub
```

**Fig. 15.4**   Writing empty records to a file (part 1 of 2).

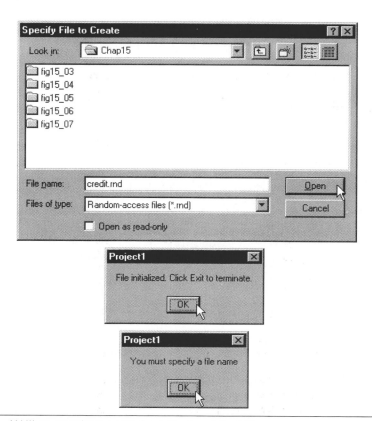

**Fig. 15.4**  Writing empty records to a file (part 2 of 2).

When the program executes, the window in the first screen capture appears. The user specifies the file to create by clicking button **Click here to initialize random-access file** to execute `cmdInitialize_Click` (line 12) and display the common dialog in the second screen capture. Once the user specifies the file name in the **File name** field and clicks the **Open** button, the file is opened for **Random** access and initialized with 100 empty records using the **Put** statement. Each empty record contains 0 for the account number, the null **String** for the last name, the null **String** for the first name and 0 for the balance. Fixed-length **String**s are commonly used with random-access files (where each record should be the same size).

**Common Programming Error 15.5**

*Using variable-length **String**s or **Variant**s with random-access files can lead to logic errors at run-time.*

Once the file has been initialized to 100 empty records, data can be read from or written to a specific location in the file. We will demonstrate this in subsequent examples.

**Good Programming Practice 15.2**

*Use **.rnd** or something similar as the filename extension for a random-access file. The **.rnd** extension should make it clear that the file is not a text file.*

When initialization of the file is complete, the message box in the third screen capture is displayed. If the user does not specify a file name, the message box in the fourth screen capture is displayed.

Lines 13 through 15 of **cmdInitialize_Click**,

```
Dim recordLength As Long, x As Integer
Dim udtBlankClient As ClientRecord    ' user-defined type
Dim filename As String
```

declare several local variables. Variable **recordLength** represents the number of bytes in a record. Variable **x** is a counter to help write 100 records to the file. Variable **udtBlankClient** is a **ClientRecord** object that will be written to the file 100 times. Variable **filename** is the location and name of the file to which the records are written.

Line 18,

```
recordLength = LenB(udtBlankClient)
```

determines the length of a record in bytes using function **LenB**. For user-defined types, function **LenB** determines the number of bytes required to store an instance of that type in memory (which may be more than the sum of the sizes of its members).

Line 20,

```
dlgOpen.ShowOpen
```

displays common dialog **dlgOpen** by calling its **ShowOpen** method. This displays a dialog box for opening files. The user can select a location and a file name to initialize using this dialog. The common dialog also provides a **ShowSave** method to display a **Save As** dialog box. We customized the **DialogTitle** property to display the **String Specify File to Create** and the **Filter** property to display only files that end in **.rnd** (our file-name extension for random-access files). The value of property **Filter** is

```
Random-access files (*.rnd) | *.rnd
```

The **String** to the left of the | is displayed to the user in the **Files of type** area of the dialog box, and the **String** to the right of | is used to filter the files. The filter ***.rnd** indicates that only files ending in **.rnd** should be displayed in the dialog box. *Note:* To use the **CommonDialog** control, it must first be added to the toolbox by selecting **Components...** from the **Project** menu to display the **Components** dialog box. In the dialog box, scroll down and select the option **Microsoft Common Dialog Control 6.0**. When selected properly, a small check mark appears in the box to the left of the option. Click the **OK** button when you are done to dismiss the dialog box. The icon for the **CommonDialog** control will be at the bottom of the toolbox.

Line 21,

```
filename = dlgOpen.filename
```

uses property **filename** of the common dialog **dlgOpen** to get the location and name of the file to initialize.

Line 23,

```
If dlgOpen.FileTitle <> "" Then
```

uses the **FileTitle** property to determine if the user specified a file name. If **FileTitle** is the empty **String**, the user did not specify the name of the file and the message box in the fourth screen capture is displayed. Otherwise, the file specified is opened for output and initialized.

Lines 25 and 26,

```
Open filename For Random Access Write As #1 _
    Len = recordLength
```

uses the **Open** statement to open the file specified by **filename**. The **For Random** keywords specify that the file is to be opened for **Random** access. If the random-access file does not exist, it will be created and given a size of 0. The **Access Write** keywords specify that the file access type is write only. If the **Access Write** is omitted, as in

```
Open filename For Random As #1 Len = length&
```

the default access type is **Read Write**. The **As #1** specifies the file number to be associated with the file. Like sequential files, each random-access file must have a unique file number (between 1 and 255 inclusive) associated with it. The **Len = recordLength** specifies the number of bytes to write to the file. The maximum number of bytes for **Len** is 32,767. If the byte length is omitted, a default of 128 is used.

**Common Programming Error 15.6**

*Assigning a file number to a random-access file less than 1 or greater than 255 is a syntax error.*

**Good Programming Practice 15.3**

*Always use the **Len** clause to specify the number of bytes a record requires to a file.*

The **For** loop at lines 28 through 30,

```
For x = 1 To 100
    Put #1, x, udtBlankClient   ' Write empty records
Next
```

loops 100 times and adds records to the file using the **Put** statement. The argument **#1** specifies the file to which the records are written. The argument **x** specifies the record number so Visual Basic knows where to write the record in the file. The argument **udtBlank-Client** is the variable representing the record to write in the file. The first record position in a file always begins at 1, and the largest possible record number is 2,147,483,647.

**Common Programming Error 15.7**

*Forgetting to precede the file number in a **Put** statement with a **#** is a syntax error.*

**Common Programming Error 15.8**

*Referring to a record number that either does not exist or is out of range is a run-time error.*

**Common Programming Error 15.9**

*Accidentally omitting one or both commas in a **Put** statement is a syntax error.*

*Common Programming Error 15.10*

*Attempting to write an object or array name to a file using the* **Put** *statement is a run-time error.*

Line 32,

```
Close #1     ' Close file
```

uses statement **Close** to close the file. If no file number is specified, all files are closed.

## 15.5 Writing Data Randomly to a Random-Access File

The program of Fig. 15.5 writes data randomly (i.e., directly to a specific position in the file) to a random-access file. The program uses the **Put** statement to store data at exact locations in the file.

```
1   ' Fig. 15.5
2   ' Writing data to a random-access file
3   Option Explicit
4
5   Private Type ClientRecord
6       accountNumber As Integer
7       lastName As String * 15
8       firstName As String * 15
9       balance As Currency
10  End Type
11
12  Dim mUdtClient As ClientRecord    ' user-defined type
13
14  Private Sub Form_Load()
15      cmdEnter.Enabled = False
16      cmdDone.Enabled = False
17  End Sub
18
19  Sub cmdOpenFile_Click()
20      Dim recordLength As Long
21      Dim filename As String
22
23      ' Determine number of bytes in a ClientRecord object
24      recordLength = LenB(mUdtClient)
25
26      dlgOpen.ShowOpen
27      filename = dlgOpen.filename
28
29      If dlgOpen.FileTitle <> "" Then
30          ' Open file for writing
31          Open filename For Random Access Write As #1 _
32              Len = recordLength
33
34          cmdOpenFile.Enabled = False    ' Disable button
35          cmdEnter.Enabled = True
```

**Fig. 15.5**   Writing data randomly to a random-access file (part 1 of 3).

```
36            cmdDone.Enabled = True
37        Else
38            MsgBox ("You must specify a file name")
39        End If
40    End Sub
41
42    Private Sub cmdEnter_Click()
43        mUdtClient.accountNumber = Val(txtAccount.Text)
44        mUdtClient.firstName = txtFirstName.Text
45        mUdtClient.lastName = txtLastName.Text
46        mUdtClient.balance = Val(txtBalance.Text)
47
48        ' Write record to file
49        Put #1, mUdtClient.accountNumber, mUdtClient
50
51        Call ClearFields
52    End Sub
53
54    Sub cmdDone_Click()
55        Close #1
56        cmdOpenFile.Enabled = True
57        cmdEnter.Enabled = False
58        cmdDone.Enabled = False
59    End Sub
60
61    Private Sub Form_Terminate()
62        Close #1
63    End Sub
64
65    Private Sub ClearFields()
66        txtAccount.Text = ""
67        txtFirstName.Text = ""
68        txtLastName.Text = ""
69        txtBalance.Text = ""
70    End Sub
```

**Fig. 15.5**    Writing data randomly to a random-access file (part 2 of 3).

When the program executes the user clicks the **Select a file** button to choose the file to which new records will be written. Once the file is opened, the user can enter a new record by typing an account number (1 to 100), first name, last name and balance in the appropriate **TextBox**es, then clicking the **Add Record** button.

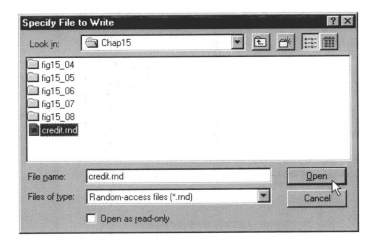

**Fig. 15.5**    Writing data randomly to a random-access file (part 3 of 3).

When the user clicks the **Select a file** button, event procedure **cmdOpen-File_Click** executes. An open file common dialog box is displayed to allow the user to select the file. After the file is selected, lines 31 and 32,

```
Open filename For Random Access Write As #1 _
    Len = recordLength
```

open the file for **Random** access as file **#1** with **recordLength** number of bytes per record.

Each time the button **Add Record** is clicked, event procedure **cmdEnter_Click** (line 42) executes and the data is taken from the **TextBox**es and assigned to the members of **ClientRecord** object **mUdtClient**. Line 49,

```
Put #1, mUdtClient.accountNumber, mUdtClient
```

writes the data in **mUdtClient** to the record location **mUdtClient.accountNumber** of the file.

Here is some sample data for you to use in your file:

| Account | First Name | Last Name | Balance |
|---------|-----------|-----------|---------|
| 29 | Nancy | Brown | -24.54 |
| 33 | Stacey | Dunn | 314.33 |
| 37 | Doug | Barker | 0.00 |
| 88 | Dave | Smith | 258.34 |
| 96 | Michelle | Stone | 34.98 |

You can, of course, enter any information you want into the file. We will use the preceding records in our remaining examples.

## 15.6 Reading Data Sequentially from a Random-Access File

In the previous sections, we created a random-access file and wrote data to that file. In this section, we develop a program (Fig. 15.6) that reads through the file sequentially and displays only those records containing data. These programs produce an additional benefit. See if you can determine what it is; we will reveal it at the end of this section.

```
1   ' Fig. 15.6
2   ' Reading data sequentially from a random-access file
3   Option Explicit
4
5   Private Type ClientRecord
6      accountNumber As Integer
7      lastName As String * 15
8      firstName As String * 15
9      balance As Currency
10  End Type
11
12  Dim mUdtClient As ClientRecord      ' user-defined type
13
14  Private Sub Form_Load()
15     cmdNext.Enabled = False
16     cmdDone.Enabled = False
17  End Sub
18
19  Sub cmdOpenFile_Click()
20     Dim recordLength As Long
21     Dim filename As String
22
23     ' Determine number of bytes in a ClientRecord object
24     recordLength = LenB(mUdtClient)
25
26     dlgOpen.ShowOpen
27     filename = dlgOpen.filename
28
29     If dlgOpen.FileTitle <> "" Then
30        ' Open file for writing
31        Open filename For Random Access Read As #1 _
32           Len = recordLength
33        cmdOpenFile.Enabled = False  ' Disable button
34        cmdNext.Enabled = True
```

**Fig. 15.6**    Reading data sequentially from a random-access file (part 1 of 3).

```
35          cmdDone.Enabled = True
36      Else
37          MsgBox ("You must specify a file name")
38      End If
39   End Sub
40
41   Private Sub cmdNext_Click()
42      ' Read record from file
43      Do
44          Get #1, , mUdtClient
45      Loop Until EOF(1) Or mUdtClient.accountNumber <> 0
46
47      If EOF(1) Then
48          cmdNext.Enabled = False
49          Exit Sub
50      End If
51
52      If mUdtClient.accountNumber <> 0 Then
53          txtAccount.Text = Str$(mUdtClient.accountNumber)
54          txtFirstName.Text = mUdtClient.firstName
55          txtLastName.Text = mUdtClient.lastName
56          txtBalance.Text = Str$(mUdtClient.balance)
57      End If
58   End Sub
59
60   Sub cmdDone_Click()
61      Close #1
62      cmdOpenFile.Enabled = True
63      cmdNext.Enabled = False
64      cmdDone.Enabled = False
65      txtAccount.Text = ""
66      txtFirstName.Text = ""
67      txtLastName.Text = ""
68      txtBalance.Text = ""
69   End Sub
70
71   Private Sub Form_Terminate()
72      Close #1
73   End Sub
```

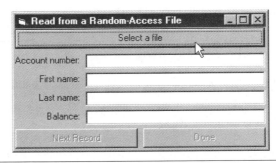

**Fig. 15.6** Reading data sequentially from a random-access file (part 2 of 3).

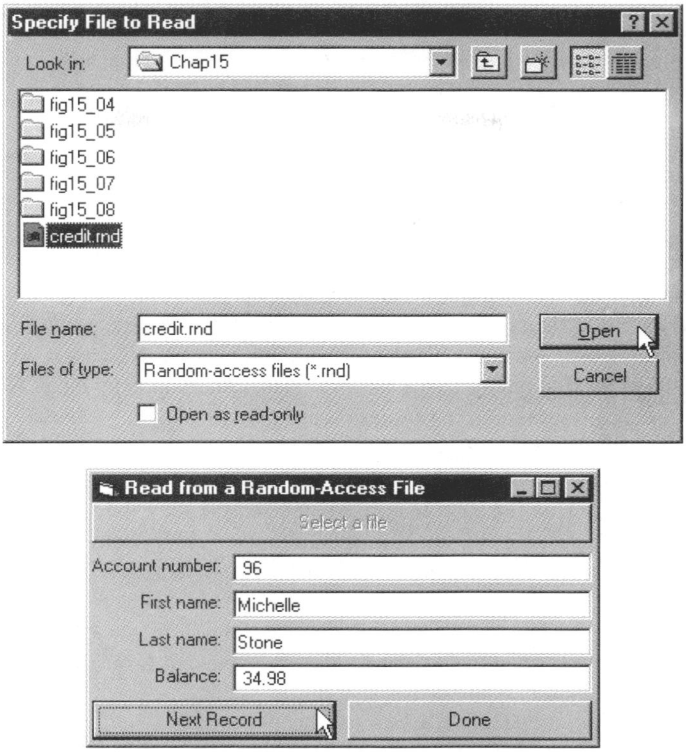

**Fig. 15.6**    Reading data sequentially from a random-access file (part 3 of 3).

When the program executes the user clicks the **Select a file** button to choose the file from which records will be read. Once the file is opened, the user can view each record by clicking the **Next Record** button repeatedly. When there are no more records to read, the **Next Record** button is disabled.

The file is opened with lines 31 and 32,

```
Open filename For Random Access Read As #1 _
    Len = recordLength
```

The access type for the file is **Read** and the number of bytes to be read each time with **Get** is specified by **Len = recordLength**.

When the user clicks **Next Record**, event procedure **cmdNext_click** (line 41) executes. The **Do** loop at lines 43 through 45,

```
Do
    Get #1, , mUdtClient
Loop Until EOF(1) Or mUdtClient.accountNumber <> 0
```

uses the **Get** statement to read the record from the current location of the file into **mUdt-Client**. Like **Put**, **Get** takes three arguments—a file number (**#1**), a record number in the file and a variable into which the information is placed (**mUdtClient**). Since the file is read sequentially in this example, the record location can be omitted. The default starting record position is 1. A *file position pointer* keeps track of the record position in the file. The file position pointer is incremented by one record each time a **Get** statement is executed. The file position pointer retains its last value as long as the file is open.

*Common Programming Error 15.11*

*Accidentally omitting one or both commas in a **Get** statement is a syntax error.*

The loop continues to execute until either **EOF(1)** returns **True**, indicating that the end of the file has been reached or until the account number for the record is not **0**. This allows the next valid record to be located in the file (remember that we created a file of 100 blank records, so some records may still be empty). If a valid record is located, lines 53 through 56 display the data for that record in the **TextBox**es. Otherwise, the **Next Record** button is disabled to indicate that there are no more records in the file.

What about that additional benefit we promised? If you examine the output as you click the **Next Record** button, you will notice that the records are displayed in sorted order (by account number)! This is a simple consequence of the way we stored these records in the file using direct-access techniques. Compared to the bubble sort we have seen (Chapter 7), sorting with direct-access techniques is blazingly fast. The speed is achieved by making the file large enough to hold every possible record that might be created. This means, of course, that the file could be sparsely occupied most of the time, a waste of storage. So here is yet another example of the space-time trade-off—by using large amounts of space, we are able to develop a much faster sorting algorithm.

## 15.7  Reading Randomly from a Random-Access File

Data can be read randomly from a random-access file by providing a specific record location as the second argument to the **Get** statement. This allows a record to be read directly from that location in the file. Figure 15.7 reads data randomly from a random-access file.

```
1    ' Fig. 15.7
2    ' Reading data randomly from a random-access file
3    Option Explicit
4
5    Private Type ClientRecord
6       accountNumber As Integer
7       lastName As String * 15
8       firstName As String * 15
9       balance As Currency
10   End Type
11
12   Dim mUdtClient As ClientRecord    ' user-defined type
13
14   Private Sub Form_Load()
15      cmdGet.Enabled = False
16      cmdDone.Enabled = False
17   End Sub
```

**Fig. 15.7**   Reading randomly from a random-access file (part 1 of 4).

```
18
19   Sub cmdOpenFile_Click()
20       Dim recordLength As Long
21       Dim filename As String
22
23       ' Determine number of bytes in a ClientRecord object
24       recordLength = LenB(mUdtClient)
25
26       dlgOpen.ShowOpen
27       filename = dlgOpen.filename
28
29       If dlgOpen.FileTitle <> "" Then
30           ' Open file for writing
31           Open filename For Random Access Read As #1 _
32               Len = recordLength
33           cmdOpenFile.Enabled = False    ' Disable button
34           cmdGet.Enabled = True
35           cmdDone.Enabled = True
36       Else
37           MsgBox ("You must specify a file name")
38       End If
39   End Sub
40
41   Private Sub cmdGet_Click()
42       On Error Resume Next
43       ' Read record from file
44       If txtAccount.Text <> "" Then
45           Get #1, Val(txtAccount.Text), mUdtClient
46
47           If mUdtClient.accountNumber <> 0 Then
48               txtAccount.Text = Str$(mUdtClient.accountNumber)
49               txtFirstName.Text = mUdtClient.firstName
50               txtLastName.Text = mUdtClient.lastName
51               txtBalance.Text = Str$(mUdtClient.balance)
52           ElseIf mUdtClient.accountNumber = 0 Then
53               txtFirstName.Text = "Record not found"
54               txtLastName.Text = ""
55               txtBalance.Text = ""
56           End If
57       Else
58           MsgBox ("You must specify an Account Number")
59       End If
60   End Sub
61
62   Sub cmdDone_Click()
63       Close #1
64       cmdOpenFile.Enabled = True
65       cmdGet.Enabled = False
66       cmdDone.Enabled = False
67       txtAccount.Text = ""
68       txtFirstName.Text = ""
69       txtLastName.Text = ""
```

**Fig. 15.7**    Reading randomly from a random-access file (part 2 of 4).

```
70        txtBalance.Text = ""
71    End Sub
72
73    Private Sub Form_Terminate()
74        Close #1
75    End Sub
```

**Fig. 15.7**   Reading randomly from a random-access file (part 3 of 4).

The key difference between this example and the sequential-access reading of the file in Fig. 15.6 is that the **Get** statement's second argument is used in this example to specify the exact record to read. When the user clicks the **Get Record** button, event procedure **cmdGet_Click** (line 41) executes. The account number the user types in the **Account number TextBox** is used in the statement

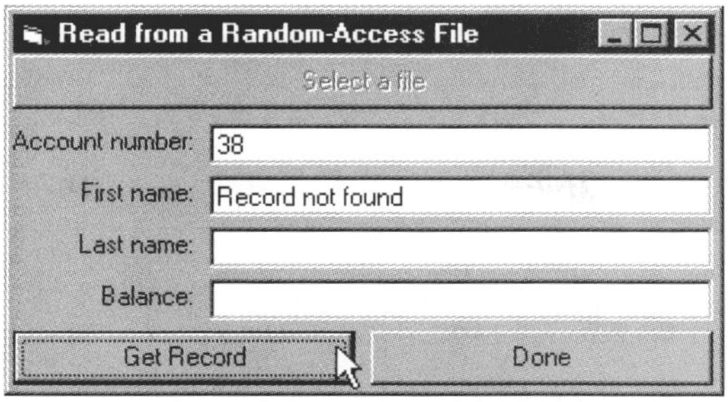

**Fig. 15.7**    Reading randomly from a random-access file (part 4 of 4).

```
Get #1, Val(txtAccount.Text), mUdtClient
```

which specifies that a record should be read from position **Val(txtAccount.Text)**—
the numeric value of the account number **String** the user types. If the specified record
has a non-zero account number, the account information is displayed in the **TextBox**es.
Otherwise, the **First name TextBox** displays the message "**Record not found.**"

## 15.8 Example: A Transaction Processing Program

We now present a substantial transaction processing program (Fig. 15.8) using a random-
access file to achieve "instant" access processing. The program maintains a bank's account
information. The program updates existing accounts, adds new accounts, deletes accounts,
and stores a listing of all the current accounts in a text file for printing. We assume that the
program of Fig. 15.4 has been executed to create a file and that the program of Fig. 15.5
has been executed to insert the initial data in that file. Note: The following application
would typically be implemented using a database to maintain the data. In Chapter 18, Database Management, we overview database concepts and demonstrate Visual Basic's database manipulation capabilities.

```
1   ' Fig. 15.8
2   ' Transaction processing program with random-access files
3   Option Explicit
4
5   Private Type ClientRecord
6       accountNumber As Integer
7       lastName As String * 15
8       firstName As String * 15
9       balance As Currency
10  End Type
11
12  Dim mUdtClient As ClientRecord    ' user-defined type
13
14  Private Sub Form_Load()
15      tabOperations.Enabled = False
16  End Sub
```

**Fig. 15.8**    A transaction processing program (part 1 of 4).

```
17
18   Sub cmdOpenFile_Click()
19      Dim recordLength As Long
20      Dim filename As String
21
22      ' Determine number of bytes in a ClientRecord object
23      recordLength = LenB(mUdtClient)
24
25      dlgOpen.ShowOpen
26      filename = dlgOpen.filename
27
28      If dlgOpen.FileTitle <> "" Then
29         ' Open file for writing
30         Open filename For Random Access Read Write As #1 _
31            Len = recordLength
32         cmdOpenFile.Enabled = False   ' Disable button
33         cmdCloseFile.Enabled = True
34         tabOperations.Enabled = True
35      Else
36         MsgBox ("You must specify a file name")
37      End If
38   End Sub
39
40   ' Create a text file representation of the random-access file
41   Private Sub cmdTextFile_Click()
42      Dim filename As String, balanceString As String
43
44      On Error Resume Next
45      dlgTextFile.ShowOpen
46      filename = dlgTextFile.filename
47
48      If dlgTextFile.FileTitle <> "" Then
49         ' Open file for writing
50         Open filename For Output Access Write As #2
51         Print #2, "Account";
52         Print #2, Tab(10); "First Name";
53         Print #2, Tab(28); "Last Name";
54         Print #2, Tab(46); Format("Balance", "@@@@@@@@@@")
55
56         Seek #1, 1                ' reposition to start of file
57         Get #1, , mUdtClient  ' read first record
58
59         While Not EOF(1)
60            If mUdtClient.accountNumber <> 0 Then
61               Print #2, mUdtClient.accountNumber;
62               Print #2, Tab(10); mUdtClient.firstName;
63               Print #2, Tab(28); mUdtClient.lastName;
64               balanceString = _
65                  Format(mUdtClient.balance, "0.00")
66               Print #2, Tab(46);
67               Print #2, Format(balanceString, "@@@@@@@@@@")
68
69            End If
```

**Fig. 15.8**   A transaction processing program (part 2 of 4).

```
70
71              Get #1, , mUdtClient   'read next record
72          Wend
73
74          Close #2
75      Else
76          MsgBox ("You must specify a file name")
77      End If
78  End Sub
79
80  ' Add a new record to the file
81  Private Sub cmdAddNew_Click()
82      If txtNewAccount.Text <> "" Then
83          Get #1, Val(txtNewAccount), mUdtClient   'read record
84
85          If mUdtClient.accountNumber = 0 Then
86              mUdtClient.accountNumber = Val(txtNewAccount)
87              mUdtClient.firstName = txtNewFirstName.Text
88              mUdtClient.lastName = txtNewLastName.Text
89              mUdtClient.balance = txtNewBalance.Text
90              Put #1, mUdtClient.accountNumber, mUdtClient
91              MsgBox ("Account " & mUdtClient.accountNumber & _
92                      " has been added to the file")
93          Else
94              MsgBox ("Account already exists")
95          End If
96      Else
97          MsgBox ("You must enter an account number")
98      End If
99  End Sub
100
101 ' Update an existing record
102 Private Sub cmdUpdate_Click()
103     Dim account As Integer, transactionAmount As Double
104     On Error Resume Next
105
106     account = Val(InputBox("Enter account number"))
107     Get #1, account, mUdtClient   'read record
108
109     If mUdtClient.accountNumber <> 0 Then
110         txtUpdateAccount.Text = Str$(mUdtClient.accountNumber)
111         txtUpdateFirstName.Text = mUdtClient.firstName
112         txtUpdateLastName.Text = mUdtClient.lastName
113         txtUpdateBalance.Text = Str$(mUdtClient.balance)
114         transactionAmount = Val(InputBox( _
115             "Enter transaction amount. Positive for charge. " & _
116             "Negative for payment."))
117         mUdtClient.balance = _
118             mUdtClient.balance + transactionAmount
119         txtUpdateBalance.Text = Str$(mUdtClient.balance)
120         Put #1, mUdtClient.accountNumber, mUdtClient
```

**Fig. 15.9**     A transaction processing program (part 3 of 4).

```
121        Else
122            MsgBox ("Record " & account & " does not exist")
123        End If
124
125  End Sub
126
127  ' Delete the specified record
128  Private Sub cmdDelete_Click()
129      Dim blankClient As ClientRecord
130      On Error Resume Next
131
132      Get #1, Val(txtDelete.Text), mUdtClient    'read record
133
134      If mUdtClient.accountNumber <> 0 Then
135          Put #1, mUdtClient.accountNumber, blankClient
136          MsgBox ("Account # " & mUdtClient.accountNumber & _
137              " has been deleted")
138      Else
139          MsgBox ("Record does not exist")
140      End If
141  End Sub
142
143  Sub cmdCloseFile_Click()
144      Close #1
145      cmdOpenFile.Enabled = True
146      cmdCloseFile.Enabled = False
147  End Sub
148
149  Private Sub Form_Terminate()
150      Close
151  End Sub
152
153  Private Sub cmdExit_Click()
154      Close
155      End
156  End Sub
```

**Fig. 15.9**    A transaction processing program (part 4 of 4).

The main window has four tabs and three buttons. The **Open File** button (processed by **cmdOpenFile_Click** at line 18) at the bottom of the window must be clicked first so the user can select the random-access file to manipulate in this example. At any time, the user can click the **Close File** button (processed by **cmdCloseFile_Click** at line 143) to close the current file and open a different one. The tabs across the top of the window allow the user to choose the operation to perform. These tabs become active after the user chooses the file to manipulate. On the **Create Text File** tab (shown below), the user clicks the **Click here to specify text file name** button to choose the text file to create. This calls event procedure **cmdTextFile_Click** at line 41, which displays a common dialog top that allows the user to select the file name and location, then creates the text file.

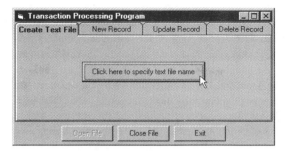

The **Get** statement and sequential file access techniques of Fig. 15.6 are used to input data from the file. The **Print #** statement is used to write data to the specified text file ("**print.txt**" our default). For example, the lines

```
Print #2, "Account";
Print #2, Tab(10); "First Name";
Print #2, Tab(28); "Last Name";
Print #2, Tab(46); Format("Balance", "@@@@@@@@@@")
```

output to file **#2** the column headings. Function **Tab** moves to the specified column in the current line so the next value can be output starting at that column position.

Notice the statement

```
Seek #1, 1              ' reposition to start of file
```

which uses the **Seek** statement to set the file position pointer to the beginning of the file. After clicking on the button the text file contains:

| Account | First Name | Last Name | Balance |
|---|---|---|---|
| 29 | Nancy | Brown | -24.54 |
| 33 | Stacey | Dunn | 314.33 |
| 37 | Doug | Barker | 0.00 |
| 88 | Dave | Smith | 258.34 |
| 96 | Michelle | Stone | 34.98 |

The **New Record** tab (shown below) allows the user to add a new account to the file. The user types the record information into the **TextBox**es, then clicks the **Add New Record** button. This calls event procedure **cmdAddNew_Click** to add the record to the file. If the user enters an account number for an existing account, a message box is displayed informing the user that the account already exists. A new account is added in the same manner as the program of Fig. 15.5.

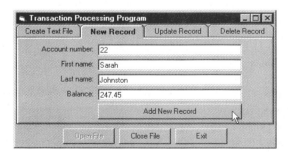

The **Update Record** tab (shown below) allows the user to select an existing record to update. First the user clicks the button **Click here to update** to call event procedure **cmdUpdate_Click**. The user is prompted to enter an account number in an **InputBox**. A record must exist in order to be updated, so the record must be checked for a valid account number. If the account number is valid, the record is read into variable **mUdt-Client** using a **Get** statement, then **mUdtClient.accountNumber** is compared to zero to determine if the record contains information. If **mUdtClient.accountNumber** is zero, a message box is displayed stating that the record does not exist. If the record contains information, the account information is displayed in the **TextBox**es and another **InputBox** is displayed to receive the transaction amount from the user. Once the user enters the amount, the new balance is calculated and displayed in the **Balance TextBox**. Then the record is written to the file with the updated balance.

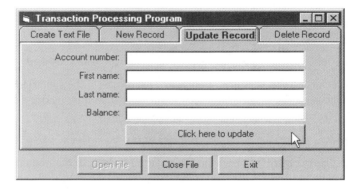

The **Delete** tab (shown below) allows the user to delete a record from the file. The user types the account number in **the TextBox** and clicks the **Delete this account** button to execute event procedure **cmdDelete_Click** (line 128). Only an existing record may be deleted, so if the specified account is empty, a message box is displayed informing the user that the record is empty. If the account exists, it is reinitialized by writing an empty record (**blankClient**) to the file. A message box is displayed to inform the user that the record has been deleted.

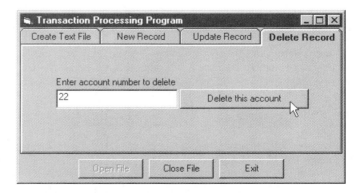

When clicked on, the **Exit** button terminates program execution.

## Summary

- Sequential-access files are inappropriate for so-called "instant-access" applications in which a particular record of information must be located immediately.

- Instant access is possible with random-access (also called direct-access) files.

- Using fixed-length records makes it easy for a program to calculate the exact location of any record relative to the beginning of the file.

- Data can be inserted in a random-access file without destroying other data in the file.

- Data stored previously also can be updated or deleted without rewriting the entire file.

- An access type (**Read**, **Write** or **Read Write**) specifies which operations may be performed on a random-access file.

- User-defined types (derived data types) are collections of related variables—sometimes referred to as aggregates—under one name. User-defined types may contain variables of many different data types—in contrast to arrays that contain only elements of the same data type.

- Keyword **Type** introduces a user-defined type definition.

- **Type** definitions must be **Private** when declared in form modules, but can be declared as **Public** or **Private** in standard code modules or class modules.

- Variables declared in a **Type** definition are called members. A **Type** cannot contain an instance of itself.

- **Type** definitions do not reserve space in memory; rather, the definition creates a new data type that is used to declare variables.

- Members of a **Type** definition are accessed like properties using the dot (**.**) operator with a variable of the user-defined type.

- Variables of the same user-defined type can be assigned to each other in a standard assignment statement.

- User-defined types may not be compared.

- Function **LenB** determines the number of bytes required to store an instance of a type in memory.

- Common dialog method **ShowOpen** displays an **Open File** dialog box. Common dialog method **ShowSave** displays an **Save As** dialog box.

- Common dialog property **DialogTitle** specifies the title of the dialog box.

- Common dialog property **Filter** specifies the types of files the user can see in the dialog box.

- Common dialog property **Filename** specifies the location and name of the file the user chooses in the dialog.

- Common dialog property **FileTitle** specifies the name of the file the user chooses.

- The **Open** statement opens a random-access file. Open mode **Random** (the default) specifies that the file is opened for random access. The access type specifies if the file is opened in **Read**, **Write** or **Read Write** (the default) mode. The **Len** clause specifies the length of each record (maximum of 32,767) in the file.

- The **Put** statement places a record at a specified record number in the file. The first argument is the file number, the second argument is the record number and the third argument is the variable containing the record information.

- The **Close** statement closes the specified file (indicated with the file number). If no file number is specified, all open files are closed.

- The **Get** statement reads a record from a random-access file. The first argument is the file number, the second argument is the record number and the third argument is the variable in which the data should be stored. If the record number is not specified, the record is read from the current position in the file as indicated by the file position pointer.

• Function **EOF** returns true when the end of the specified file is reached.

## Terminology

| | |
|---|---|
| **Access** | **LenB** function |
| access type | **Len =** clause of the **Open** statement |
| aggregate type | member |
| **As** keyword | **Open** statement |
| **Close** | **Put** statement |
| **CommonDialog** control | random-access file |
| **CommonDialog** method **ShowOpen** | **Random** open mode |
| **CommonDialog** method **ShowSave** | **Read** access type |
| derived data type | **Read Write** access type |
| direct-access file | record |
| **EOF** function | transaction processing systems |
| file position pointer | **Type** definition |
| fixed-length record | type name |
| **For Random** | user-defined type |
| **Get** statement | **Write** access type |

## Common Programming Errors

**15.1**   Declaring a **Type** as **Public** in a form module is a syntax error.
**15.2**   Declaring multiple members of a **Type** with the same name is a syntax error.
**15.3**   Declaring a **Type** that contains an instance of itself is a syntax error.
**15.4**   Comparing user-defined type variables is a syntax error because storage alignment requirements can result in undefined areas in each variable.
**15.5**   Using variable-length **String**s or **Variant**s with random-access files can lead to logic errors at run-time.
**15.6**   Assigning a file number to a random-access file less than 1 or greater than 255 is a syntax error.
**15.7**   Forgetting to precede the file number in a **Put** statement with a **#** is a syntax error.
**15.8**   Referring to a record number that either does not exist or is out of range is a run-time error.
**15.9**   Accidentally omitting one or both commas in a **Put** statement is a syntax error.
**15.10**  Attempting to write an object or array name to a file using the **Put** statement is a run-time error.
**15.11**  Accidentally omitting one or both commas in a **Get** statement is a syntax error.

## Good Programming Practices

**15.1**   Choose a meaningful type name for user-defined types. This helps make the program self-documenting.
**15.2**   Use **.rnd** or something similar as the filename extension for a random-access file. The **.rnd** extension should make it clear that the file is not a text file.
**15.3**   Always use the **Len** clause to specify the number of bytes a record requires to a file.

## Self-Review Exercises

**15.1**   Fill in the blanks in each of the following:
     a)  The _____ statement is used to write data randomly to a file.

b) The _____ keywords specify that the file is to be opened as a random-access file.

c) The _____ access specifier is used to specify that a random-access file is to be opened for output to the file.

d) The _____ function returns the number of bytes required to store a variable in memory.

**15.2** State which of the following are *true* and which are *false*. If *false*, explain why.

a) Records are commonly used with random-access files.

b) Data in a random-access file can be updated without overwriting existing data.

c) In random-access file processing a minimum of three records must be searched before a specific record is found.

d) Random-access files may not be read sequentially.

e) Each random-access file opened has a unique file number associated with it.

f) The **LenB** function when applied to a **Variant** returns the number of bytes for the type the **Variant** is currently storing. For example, if a **Variant** is currently storing a **Currency** value, 8 is returned by **LenB**.

**15.3** Assume that each of the following statements applies to the same program. Assume each record length to be 75 bytes.

a) Write a statement that opens file "**old.rnd**" for reading. Use 8 as the file number.

b) Write a statement that opens file "**transact.rnd**" for writing. Use 9 as the file number.

c) Write a statement that opens file "**new.rnd**" for reading and writing. Use 10 as the file number.

d) Write a statement that reads the twenty-second record from the file "**old.rnd**". The record variable **udtRecord** consists of **Integer accountNum**, fixed-length **String name**, and **Currency currentBalance**.

**15.4** Find the error(s) and show how to correct it in each of the following.

a) **Open As Random #1 Len = 90**

b) Record definition to be used with random-access files:

```
Type MedalAwardee
    lastName As String
    branch As String
    rank As String
    yearAwarded As Integer
End Type
```

c) **Close "client.rnd"**

d) **x = LenB udtData      ' Determine size of udtData**

## Answers to Self-Review Exercises

**15.1** a) **Put**. b) **For Random**. c) **Write**. d) **LenB**.

**15.2** a) True.

b) True.

c) False. A record can be found immediately by specifying its record number in the file as part of a **Get** statement.

d) False. Random-access files may be read sequentially using the **Get** statement without a second argument (normally used to specify the exact record number).

e) True.

f) False. The **LenB** function when evaluating a **Variant** argument always returns the number of bytes required to represent the value as a **String**.

**15.3**  a) `Open "old.rnd" For Random Access Read As #8 Len = 75`
       b) `Open "transact.rnd" For Random Access Write As #9 Len = 75`
       c) `Open "new.dat" For Random Access Read Write As #10 Len = 75`
       d) `Get #8, 22, udtRecord`

**15.4**  a) The file name is missing. The **As** should be a **For**. **As** should precede the **#**. The **Access Read Write** is the access type by default.

        `Open "filename" For Random As #1 Len = 90`

       b) The **String** members should be fixed-length **String**s.
       c) A file name may not be used with the **Close** statement. **Close** should either have a file number associated with it or be on a line by itself.
       d) The **LenB** function requires parentheses around the argument.

## Exercises

**15.5**  Fill in the blanks in each of the following:
       a) When opening a file for random access, the _____ specifies the record size.
       b) The _____ access specifier is used to specify that a random-access file is to be opened in read mode.
       c) The _____ statement is used to read data randomly from a file.
       d) The _____ access specifier states that a random-access file can be read from and written to.

**15.6**  State which of the following are *true* and which are *false*. If *false*, explain why.
       a) It is not necessary to search through all the records in a randomly accessed file to find a specific record.
       b) Random-access files are always referred to by name in a program.
       c) When a program creates a file, the file is automatically retained by the computer for future reference.
       d) A program must explicitly close a random-access file before the program terminates.
       e) Fixed-length records should be used with random-access files.
       f) Unlike sequential-access files, random-access files store information as bytes.
       g) A random-access file always has the same size as a sequential-access file.
       h) The **Get** statement always takes three arguments.
       i) Random-access files must end with the `.rnd` extension.

**15.7**  Find the error and show how to correct it in each of the following.
       a) `Get #6, udtCarInformation    ' Store data in record`
       b) `Open #99 For Random Access Append Len = 140`
       c) `Put #33, 15, inventory%    ' inventory is an array name`
       d) `' Open a file for reading and writing`
          `Open "c:\customer.rnd" Access Read+`

**15.8**  Exercise 15.3 asked the reader to write a series of single statements. Actually, these statements form the core of an important type of file processing program, namely, a file-matching program. In commercial data processing, it is common to have several files in each application system. In an accounts receivable system, for example, there is generally a master file containing detailed information about each customer, such as the customer's name, address, telephone number, outstanding balance, credit limit, discount terms, contract arrangements, and possibly a condensed history of recent purchases and cash payments.

      As transactions occur (i.e., sales are made and cash payments arrive in the mail), they are entered into a file. At the end of each business period (i.e., a month for some companies, a week for others and a day in some cases) the file of transactions (called **"trans.dat"** in Exercise 15.3) is applied to the master file (called **"oldmast.dat"** in Exercise 15.3), thus updating each account's record of purchases and payments. During an updating run, the master file is rewritten as a new file (**"newmast.dat"**), which is then used at the end of the next business period to begin the updating process again.

      File-matching programs must deal with certain problems that do not exist in single-file programs. For example, a match does not always occur. A customer on the master file may not have made any purchases or cash payments in the current business period, and therefore no record for this customer will appear on the transaction file. Similarly, a customer who did make some purchases or cash payments may have just moved to this community, and the company may not have had a chance to create a master record for this customer.

      Use the statements written in Exercise 15.3 as a basis for writing a complete file-matching accounts receivable program. Use the account number on each file as the record key for matching purposes. Assume each file is a sequential file with records stored in increasing order by account number.

      When a match occurs (i.e., records with the same account number appear on both the master file and the transaction file), add the dollar amount on the transaction file to the current balance on the master file, and write the **"newmast.dat"** record. (Assume that purchases are indicated by positive amounts on the transaction file, and that payments are indicated by negative amounts.) When there is a master record for a particular account but no corresponding transaction record, merely write the master record to **"newmast.dat"**. When there is a transaction record but no corresponding master record, print the message **"Unmatched transaction record for account number ..."** (fill in the account number from the transaction record).

**15.9**    After writing the program of Exercise 15.8, write a simple program to create some test data for checking out the program. Use the following sample account data:

| Master file account number | Name | Balance |
|---|---|---|
| 100 | Alan Jones | 348.17 |
| 300 | Mary Smith | 27.19 |
| 500 | Sam Sharp | 0.00 |
| 700 | Suzy Green | -14.22 |

| Transaction file account number | Transaction amount |
|---|---|
| 100 | 27.14 |
| 300 | 62.11 |
| 400 | 100.56 |
| 900 | 82.17 |

**15.10**    Run the program of Exercise 15.8 using the files of test data created in Exercise 15.9. Print the new master file. Check that the accounts have been updated correctly.

**15.11**    It is possible (actually common) to have several transaction records with the same record key. This occurs because a particular customer might make several purchases and cash payments during a business period. Rewrite your accounts receivable file-matching program of Exercise 15.8 to provide for the possibility of handling several transaction records with the same record key. Modify the test data of Exercise 15.9 to include the following additional transaction records:

| Account number | Dollar amount |
| --- | --- |
| 300 | 83.89 |
| 700 | 80.78 |
| 700 | 1.53 |

**15.12**    Write a series of statements that accomplish each of the following. Assume that the record

```
Type person
   lastName As String * 15
   firstName As String * 15
   age As String * 3
End Type
```

has been defined, and that the random-access file has been opened properly.

 a) Initialize the file **"nameage.dat"** with 100 records containing **lastName = "unassigned"**, **firstName = ""**, and **age = "0"**.
 b) Input 10 last names, first names and ages, and write them to the file.
 c) Update a record that has information in it, and if there is none tell the user "No info."
 d) Delete a record that has information by reinitializing that particular record.

**15.13**    You are the owner of a hardware store and need to keep an inventory that can tell you what different tools you have, how many of each you have on hand and the cost of each one. Write a program that initializes the random-access file **"hardware.dat"** to one hundred empty records, lets you input the data concerning each tool, enables you to list all your tools, lets you delete a record for a tool that you no longer have and lets you update *any* information in the file. The tool identification number should be the record number. Use the following information to start your file:

| Record number | Tool name | Quantity | Cost |
| --- | --- | --- | --- |
| 3 | Electric sander | 7 | 57.98 |
| 17 | Hammer | 76 | 11.99 |
| 24 | Jigsaw | 21 | 11.00 |
| 39 | Lawn mower | 3 | 79.50 |
| 56 | Power saw | 18 | 99.99 |
| 68 | Screwdriver | 106 | 6.99 |
| 77 | Sledgehammer | 11 | 21.50 |
| 83 | Wrench | 34 | 7.50 |

**15.14**    Modify the card shuffling and dealing program of Fig. 8.31 to use a user-defined type to represent a card (i.e., a face **String** and a suit **String**). Rewrite the shuffling and dealing algorithms to be more efficient. For the shuffling algorithm, make one pass of the array of card objects and swap the current card with a randomly chosen card in the deck. For the dealing algorithm, simply "walk through" the array of cards and display each card.

# Object-Oriented Programming

## Objectives

- To understand encapsulation and data hiding.
- To understand the notions of data abstraction and abstract data types (ADTs).
- To create Visual Basic ADTs, namely classes.
- To add properties, methods and events to classes.
- To be able to create, use and destroy class objects.
- To control access to object variables and methods.
- To use "is-a," "has-a" and "uses-a" relationships.
- To use inheritance with interfaces and delegation.
- To use the **Class Browser** utility.
- To appreciate how polymorphism makes systems more extensible and maintainable.
- To understand interfaces.

*My object all sublime*
*I shall achieve in time.*
W. S. Gilbert

*Your public servants serve you right.*
Adlai Stevenson

*This above all: to thine own self be true.*
William Shakespeare, Hamlet

*Say not you know another entirely, till you have divided an inheritance with him.*
Johann Kasper Lavater

# Outline

## 16.1  Introduction

In this chapter, we introduce the concepts (i.e., "object think") and terminology (i.e., "object speak") of object-oriented programming in Visual Basic. Objects *encapsulate* data (*attributes*) and methods (*behaviors*); the data and methods of an object are intimately tied together. Objects have the property of *information hiding.* This means that although objects may communicate with one another, objects do not know how other objects are implemented—implementation details are hidden within the objects themselves. Surely it is possible to drive a car effectively without knowing the details of how engines and transmissions work. Information hiding is crucial to good software engineering.

In C and other *procedural programming languages,* programming tends to be *action-oriented,* whereas in Visual Basic programming is event-driven and *object-oriented.* In C, the unit of programming is the *function* (functions in objects are called *methods* in Visual Basic). In Visual Basic, the unit of object-oriented programming is the *class* from which objects are *instantiated* (i.e., created). Methods are Visual Basic functions that are encapsulated with the data they process within the "walls" of classes.

Procedural programmers concentrate on writing functions. Data is certainly important in procedural programming, but the view is that data exists primarily to support the actions that functions perform. The *verbs* in a system-requirements document help the procedural programmer determine the set of functions that will work together to implement the system.

Visual Basic programmers can create their own *user-defined types* called *classes.* Classes are also referred to as *programmer-defined types.* Each class contains data as well as the set of methods which manipulate that data. The data components of a class are called *instance variables.* Just as an instance of a built-in type such as `Integer` is called a *variable,* an instance of a class is called an *object.* The focus of attention in object-oriented programming with Visual Basic is on classes rather than methods. The *nouns* in a system-requirements document help the Visual Basic programmer determine an initial set of classes with which to begin the design process. These classes are then used to instantiate objects that will work together to implement the system. The *verbs* in a system-requirements document help the Visual Basic programmer determine what methods to associate with each class.

This chapter explains how to create and use objects, a subject we call *object-based programming (OBP).* We also discuss *inheritance* and *polymorphism*—the key technologies of *object-oriented programming (OOP).*

Visual Basic programmers craft new classes and reuse existing classes. Many *class libraries* exist and others are being developed worldwide. Software is then constructed by combining new classes with existing, well-defined, carefully tested, well-documented, widely available components. This kind of *software reusability* speeds the development of powerful, high-quality software. *Rapid applications development (RAD)* is of great interest today. Visual Basic is the world's premier RAD language.

Actually, you have been using classes and objects throughout this book. From its earliest versions, Visual Basic has been an object-based language. Each control icon represents a class. When you drag a control to the form, Visual Basic automatically creates an object of that class to which your program can send messages. Those objects can generate events. To date, Visual Basic may well be the world's most successful implementation of reuse of classes provided as part of a programming language.

Early versions of Visual Basic did not allow programmers to create their own classes (and controls), but Visual Basic programmers can now develop their own classes, a powerful capability also offered by object-oriented languages like C++ and Java.

Object-oriented programming requires three technologies—encapsulation, inheritance and polymorphism. Visual Basic does not allow inheritance in the sense that C++ and Java do, but it does provide encapsulation and polymorphism. Nevertheless, Visual Basic does enable programmers to realize many of the benefits of inheritance through the use of *interfaces* and a technique called *delegation.*

In procedural programming languages such as C, programmers reuse procedures. The C standard libraries, for example, contain a rich collection of reusable functions that programmers use rather than "reinventing the wheel." But these entities are relatively low level. They do not capture larger units for reuse. So they have not been especially effective in reducing system development time.

Packaging software as classes out of which we make objects makes more significant portions of major software systems reusable. On the Windows platform, these classes have been packaged into class libraries such as Microsoft's *MFC (Microsoft Foundation Classes)* that provide C++ programmers with reusable componentry for handling common programming tasks such as creating and manipulating GUIs.

In this chapter we will see how to create new classes through the mechanism of *class modules.* At the root of Visual Basic's class mechanism is Microsoft's *COM* (Component

*Object Model*). We will discuss COM and the related technologies of DCOM and ActiveX in the next chapter.

Objects are endowed with the capabilities to do everything they need to do. For example, employee objects are endowed with a behavior to pay themselves. Video game objects are endowed with the ability to draw themselves on the screen. This is like a car being endowed with the ability to "go faster" (if someone presses the accelerator peddle), "go slower" (if someone presses the brake peddle) and "turn left" or "turn right" (if someone turns the wheel in the appropriate direction). The blueprint for a car is like a class. Each car is like an instance of a class. Each car comes equipped with all the behaviors it needs, such as "go faster," "go slower" and so on, just as every instance of a class comes equipped with each of the behaviors instances of that class exhibit.

We will discuss how to create classes and how to add properties, methods and events to those classes. We explain the notion of interfaces and how objects can support multiple interfaces. We discuss how Visual Basic supports polymorphism through interfaces. We discuss how Visual Basic enables objects to support multiple interfaces and how this becomes a powerful means of evolving a software system.

Classes can be made *data aware* so that their objects can be bound to databases. A class may be a source of data or a consumer of data. We discuss how to use the **TypeOf** keyword to determine the precise type of an object.

**Software Engineering Observation 16.1**

*It is important to write programs that are understandable and easy to maintain. Change is the rule rather than the exception. Programmers should anticipate that their code will be modified. As we will see, using classes improves program modifiability.*

## 16.2 Data Abstraction and Information Hiding

Classes normally hide their implementation details from the *clients* (i.e., users) of the classes. This is called *information hiding.* As an example of information hiding, let us consider a data structure called a *stack*.

Think of a stack in terms of a pile of dishes. When a dish is placed on the pile, it is always placed at the top (referred to as *pushing* the dish onto the stack). When a dish is removed from the pile, it is always removed from the top (referred to as *popping* the dish off the stack). Stacks are known as *last-in, first-out (LIFO) data structures*—the last item *push*ed (inserted) on the stack is the first item *pop*ped (removed) from the stack. So if we push 1, then 2, then 3 onto a stack, the next three pop operations will return 3, then 2, then 1.

The programmer may create a stack class and hide from its clients the implementation of the stack. Stacks can be implemented with arrays and other methods such as linked lists (see Chapter 21). A client of a stack class need not know how the stack is implemented. The client simply requires that when data items are placed in the stack with *push* operations, they will be recalled with *pop* operations in last-in, first-out order. Describing an object in terms of behaviors without concern for how those behaviors are actually implemented is called *data abstraction,* and Visual Basic classes define *abstract data types (ADTs)*. Although users may happen to know how a class is implemented, users may not write code that depends on these details. This means that a class can be replaced with another version without affecting the rest of the system, as long as the **Public** interface of that class does not change (i.e. every method still has the same name, return type and parameter list in the new class definition).

Most programming languages emphasize actions. In these languages, data exists in support of the actions programs need to take. Data is "less interesting" than actions, anyway. Data is "crude." There are only a few built-in data types, and it is difficult for programmers to create their own new data types. Visual Basic elevates the importance of data. A primary activity in Visual Basic is creating new data types (i.e., *classes*) and expressing the interactions among *objects* of those classes.

An ADT actually captures two notions, a *data representation of the ADT* and the *operations allowed on the data of the ADT*. For example, type **Integer** defines addition, subtraction, multiplication, division and other operations in Visual Basic, but division by zero is undefined. The allowed operations and the data representation of negative integers are clear, but the operation of taking the square root of a negative integer is undefined.

*Software Engineering Observation 16.2*

*The programmer creates new types through the class mechanism. These new types may be designed to be used as conveniently as built-in types. Thus, Visual Basic is an extensible language. Although it is easy to extend the language with these new types, the base language itself cannot be modified.*

## 16.3 Implementing a `Time` Abstract Data Type with a Class

We create each class by building a *class module*. A class module only contains code—it cannot have any GUI elements. Like form modules and standard modules, class modules contain a general declaration. Class modules have only two events associated with them— **Initialize** and **Terminate**. We discuss handling these events later in the chapter.

*Good Programming Practice 16.1*

*Include the **Option Explicit** statement in each class to force all variables to be declared explicitly.*

To add a class module to the project (e.g., the **Standard EXE** we have been using throughout this book) select **Add Class Module** from the **Project** menu which displays the **Add Class Module** dialog (Fig. 16.1). The **Project Explorer** window displays an additional folder (called **Class Modules**) that groups all a project's class files. Each new class module begins with the default name of **Class1**. The programmer can change the class name in the **Name** property.

*Good Programming Practice 16.2*

*Begin each class **Name** with the uppercase letter "**C**" to indicate clearly that it is a class name.*

To use a class, we first create an object of the class and then set its properties and invoke its methods. Keyword **New** is used to create an object. For example, the statement

```
Dim wakeUp As New CTime1
```

might be placed in a **CommandButton**'s **Click** event procedure to create object **wakeUp** as a new instance of class **CTime1**. [Note: Visual Basic does not actually create an instance of an object (e.g., **wakeUp**) until the first time a property is accessed or a method is called. For the remainder of this chapter, we will simply indicate that an object is created when **New** is used.] Once an object is created with **New**, its **Public** methods can be invoked. We now present our first example.

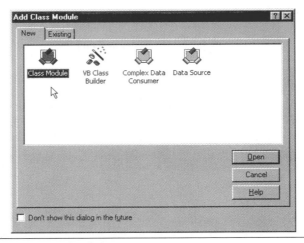

**Fig. 16.1   Add Class Module** dialog.

Figure 16.2 contains a simple definition for class **CTime1**. Class **CTime1** contains three **Integer** variables—**mHour**, **mMinute** and **mSecond**. Normally, we would call these variables module-level variables. In keeping with our object-oriented discussion we call module-level variables within a class *instance variables*.

Class **Integer**'s instance variables **mHour**, **mMinute** and **mSecond** are each declared **Private** making them accessible only to the methods of the class. Instance variables are normally declared **Private** and methods are normally declared **Public**. It is possible to have **Private** methods and **Public** data, as we will see later.

*Testing and Debugging Tip 16.1*

*Using* **Public** *data is uncommon and is a dangerous programming practice.*

Class **CTime1** contains **Public** methods **SetTime**, **ToUniversalTime** and **ToStandardTime**. These **Public** *methods*—or **Public** *services*—of the class comprise the **Public** *interface* of the class. These methods are used by *clients* [i.e., portions of a program that are users (e.g., the form in our example)] of the class to manipulate the data stored in objects of the class.

Method **SetTime** takes three **Integer** arguments and uses them to set the time. Each argument is range checked. For example, the **mHour** value must be greater than or equal to 0 and less than 24 because we represent the time in universal time format (with hours ranging from 0 to 23 and with minutes and seconds ranging from 0 to 59). Any value outside this range is an invalid value and is set to zero. In such a case, the program may want to indicate that an invalid time setting occurred (e.g., possibly by raising an error).

Method **ToUniversalTime** takes no arguments and returns a universal-time-format **String** consisting of six digits—two for **mHour**, two for **mMinute** and two for **mSecond**. For example 083033, represents 8:30:33 AM.

Method **ToStandardTime** takes no arguments and returns a **String**. This method produces a standard-time-format **String** consisting of the **mHour**, **mMinute** and **mSecond** values separated by colons and an **AM** or **PM** indicator, as in **1:27:06 PM**.

```
1    ' Fig. 16.2
2    ' Class definition for CTime1
3    Option Explicit
4    Private mHour As Integer
5    Private mMinute As Integer
6    Private mSecond As Integer
7
8    Public Sub SetTime(ByVal h As Integer, ByVal m As Integer, _
9                       ByVal s As Integer)
10
11       mHour = IIf((h >= 0 And h < 24), h, 0)
12       mMinute = IIf((m >= 0 And m < 24), m, 0)
13       mSecond = IIf((s >= 0 And s < 60), s, 0)
14   End Sub
15
16   Public Function ToUniversalTime() As String
17       ToUniversalTime = Format$(mHour, "00") & ":" & _
18                         Format$(mMinute, "00") & ":" & _
19                         Format$(mSecond, "00")
20   End Function
21
22   Public Function ToStandardTime() As String
23       Dim h As Integer
24
25       h = IIf((mHour = 12 Or mHour = 0), 12, mHour Mod 12)
26
27       ToStandardTime = h & ":" & _
28                        Format$(mMinute, "00") & ":" & _
29                        Format$(mSecond, "00") & " " & _
30                        IIf(mHour < 12, "AM", "PM")
31   End Function
```

**Fig. 16.2**    Abstract data type **CTime1** (part 1 of 3).

```
32   ' Form module used to test class CTime1
33   Option Explicit
34
35   Private Sub Form_Load()
36       Dim t As New CTime1
37
38       Print "Initial Standard time is : " & t.ToStandardTime()
39       Print "Initial Universal time is: " & t.ToUniversalTime()
40
41       Print
42
43       Call t.SetTime(17, 28, 46)
44       Print "Standard time after calling SetTime: " & _
45             t.ToStandardTime
46       Print "Univeral time after calling SetTime: " & _
47             t.ToUniversalTime
48
49       Print
```

**Fig. 16.2**    Form module code that exercises class **CTime1** (part 2 of 3).

```
50
51      Call t.SetTime(5, 44, 99)
52      Print "Standard time after attempting invalid settings: " & _
53           t.ToStandardTime
54      Print "Univeral time after attempting invalid settings: " & _
55           t.ToUniversalTime
56   End Sub
```

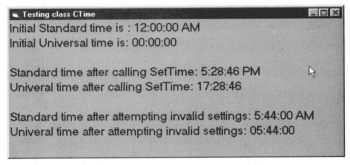

**Fig. 16.2**    Form module code that exercises class **CTime1** (part 3 of 3).

Once the class has been defined, it can be used as a type in declarations such as

```
Dim sunset As New CTime1       ' CTime1 object
Dim timeArray(5) As New CTime1  ' Array of CTime1 objects
```

The client can place these declarations wherever declarations are permitted. The class name is a new type specifier. There may be many objects of a class, just as there may be many variables of a primitive data type such as **Integer**. The programmer can create new class types as needed; this is one of the reasons why Visual Basic is an *extensible language*.

**Form_Load** declares a local variable of class **CTime1** called **t**. The form module can use the **CTime1** class because it is part of the project. Object **t** is instantiated using **New** with the declaration

```
Dim t as New CTime1
```

When the object is *instantiated* (i.e., created using **New**), each **Private Integer** instance variable (i.e., **mHour**, etc.) is initialized to **0** by default. Next, **t**'s **ToStandardTime** method is invoked and the time is printed in standard-time format. **ToUniversalTime** is called to display the time in universal time format. The object's hours, minutes and seconds are then set to valid values using the **SetTime** method and the time is printed in both formats. Method **SetTime** is called again in an attempt to set **mSecond** to an invalid value (**99**). The invalid value is rejected and **mSecond** set to the default value **0**. The time is printed again in both formats.

Note that the instance variables **mHour**, **mMinute** and **mSecond** are declared **Private**. **Private** instance variables of a class are not accessible outside the class. The philosophy here is that the actual data representation used within the class is of no concern to the class's clients. For example, it would be perfectly reasonable for the class to represent the time internally as the number of seconds since midnight. Clients could use the same **Public** methods and get the same results without being aware of this. In this sense, the implementation of a class is said to be *hidden* from its clients. An exercise at the end of this chapter asks you to make precisely this modification to the **CTime1** class of Fig. 16.2 and to show that there is no visible change to the clients of the class.

**Software Engineering Observation 16.3**

*Information hiding can greatly simplify the client's perception of a class.*

**Software Engineering Observation 16.4**

*Clients of a class can (and should) use the class without knowing the internal details of how the class is implemented. If the class implementation is changed (to improve performance, for example), provided the class's interface remains constant, the class clients' source code need not change. This makes it much easier to modify systems.*

It is interesting that the **ToUniversalTime** and **ToStandardTime** methods take no arguments. This is because these methods implicitly know that they are to manipulate the instance variables of the particular **CTime1** object for which they are invoked. This makes method calls more concise than conventional function calls in procedural programming.

**Software Engineering Observation 16.5**

*Using an object-oriented programming approach can often simplify method calls by reducing the number of arguments to be passed. This benefit of object-oriented programming derives from the fact that encapsulation of instance variables and methods within an object gives the methods the right to access the instance variables.*

**Testing and Debugging Tip 16.2**

*Using an object-oriented programming approach reduces the likelihood of passing the wrong arguments, the wrong types of arguments and/or the wrong number of arguments, as often happens with procedural programming languages.*

## 16.4 Class Members

Instance variables may be either **Public** or **Private**. Keywords **Public** and **Private** are called *member access specifiers*. **Public** instance variables and **Public** methods are accessible to every module within the project. **Private** instance variables can be manipulated only by methods of the class. A typical manipulation might be the adjustment of a customer's bank balance (e.g., a **Private** instance variable **mBankBalance** of a class **CBankAccount**) by a method of **CBankAccount** named **ComputeInterest**.

**Common Programming Error 16.1**

*Attempting to declare a **Public Const** instance variable is a syntax error. **Const** instance variables must be **Private**.*

**Private** methods are often called *utility methods* or *helper methods* because they can only be called by other methods of that class and are used to support the operation of those methods. When **Public** or **Private** is omitted, **Property** procedures (which we discuss momentarily), **Sub** procedures, and **Function** procedures default to **Public** and instance variables default to **Private**. Member access specifiers can appear multiple times and in any order in a class definition.

**Good Programming Practice 16.3**

*Every instance variable or method definition should be explicitly preceded by* **Public** *or* **Private**.

**Good Programming Practice 16.4**

*Group* **Public** *members and group* **Private** *members in a class definition for clarity and readability.*

**Common Programming Error 16.2**

*An attempt by a method which is not a member of a particular class to access a* **Private** *member of that class is a syntax error.*

Figure 16.3 demonstrates that **Private** class members are not accessible by name outside the class. Lines 8 and 9 attempt to directly access the **Private** instance variables **mHour** and **mMinute** of **CTime1** object **t**. When this program is compiled, the compiler generates errors stating that the **Private** member specified in each statement is not accessible. Once the error on line 8 is corrected, the error on line 9 occurs. (Note: This program uses the **CTime1** class from Fig. 16.2.)

**Good Programming Practice 16.5**

*Despite the fact that* **Private** *and* **Public** *members may be repeated and intermixed, list all the* **Private** *members of a class first in one group and then list all the* **Public** *members in another group.*

Access to **Private** data should be carefully controlled by the class's methods. For example, to allow clients to read the value of **Private** data, the class can provide a *get method* (also called an *accessor method* or a *query* method).

```
1   ' Fig. 16.3
2   ' Attempting to access Private data
3   Option Explicit
4
5   Private Sub Form_Load()
6      Dim t As New CTime1
7
8      t.mHour = 8             ' Generates Error
9      t.mMinute = 17          ' Generates Error
10
11     Print t.ToStandardTime()
12  End Sub
```

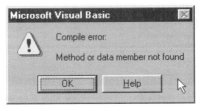

**Fig. 16.3**   Erroneous attempt to access **Private** members of a class.

To enable clients to modify **Private** data, the class can provide a *set method* (also called a *mutator method*). Such modification would seem to violate the notion of **Private** data. But a *set* method can provide data validation capabilities (such as range checking) to ensure that the data is set properly and to reject attempts to set data to invalid values. A *set* method can also translate between the form of the data used in the interface and the form used in the implementation. A *get* method need not expose the data in "raw" format; rather, the *get* method can edit the data and limit the view of the data the client will see.

**Software Engineering Observation 16.6**

*The class designer need not provide* set *and/or* get *methods for each* **Private** *data member; these capabilities should be provided only when it makes sense and after careful thought by the class designer.*

**Testing and Debugging Tip 16.3**

*Making the instance variables of a class* **Private** *and the methods of the class* **Public** *facilitates debugging because problems with data manipulations are localized to the class's methods.*

Classes often provide **Public** methods to allow clients of the class to *set* (i.e., assign values to) or *get* (i.e., obtain the values of) **Private** instance variables. These methods are special methods in Visual Basic called ***Property Let***, ***Property Set*** and ***Property Get*** (collectively these methods and the internal class data they manipulate are called *properties*). More specifically, a method that sets instance variable **mInterestRate** would be named **Property Let InterestRate** and a method that gets the **InterestRate** would be called **Property Get InterestRate**.

**Testing and Debugging Tip 16.4**

***Property*** *procedures should scrutinize every attempt to* set *the object's data and should reject invalid data to ensure that the object's data remains in a consistent state. This eliminates large numbers of bugs that have plagued systems development efforts.*

**Software Engineering Observation 16.7**

***Property Get*** *procedures can control the appearance of data, possibly hiding implementation details.*

Here is how an **Hour** property is defined for a **CTime1** class that stores the hour in universal time as 0 to 23:

```
Private mHour As Integer

Public Property Let Hour(ByVal hr As Integer)
   mHour = IIf(hr >= 0 and hr < 24, hr, 0)
End Property
```

If we have a **CTime1** class object **wakeUp** and we execute the following code

```
wakeup.Hour = -6
```

or the code

```
wakeup.Hour = 27
```

the **Property Let** procedure would reject these as invalid values and set **mHour** to 0.

The **Property Get Hour** procedure is written as follows:

```
Public Property Get Hour() As Integer
    Hour = mHour
End Property
```

Using **CTime1** class object **wakeUp**, we can store the value of **Hour** into **alarm-ClockHourValue** as follows:

```
alarmClockHourValue = wakeup.Hour
```

***Software Engineering Observation 16.8***

*To implement a read-only property, simply provide a **Property Get** procedure but no **Property Set** procedure and no **Property Let** procedure.*

Suppose we have a **CEmployee** class that contains an object **mBirthDate** of class **CDate**. We cannot use a **Property Let** to assign a value to an object. Instead, we must use a **Property Set** as in each of the following **Property** procedures:

```
Public Property Set BirthDay(ByVal bDay As CDate)
    Set mBirthDate = bDay
End Property

Public Property Get BirthDay() As CDate
    Set BirthDay = mBirthDate
End Property
```

Any **Property Get**, **Property Let** or **Property Set** method may contain the ***Exit Property*** statement that causes an immediate exit from a **Property** procedure.

Access methods can read or display data. Another common use for access methods is to test the truth or falsity of conditions—such methods are often called *predicate methods*. An example of a predicate method would be an **IsEmpty** method for any container class—a class capable of holding multiple objects—such as a linked list or a stack (containers we will study in Chapter 21). A program might test **IsEmpty** before attempting to remove another item from a container object. A program might test **IsFull** before attempting to insert another item into a container object.

It would seem that providing *set* and *get* capabilities is essentially the same as making the instance variables **Public**. This is another subtlety of Visual Basic that makes the language desirable for software engineering. If an instance variable is **Public**, it may be read or written at will by any method in the program. If an instance variable is **Private**, a **Public** *get* method certainly seems to allow other methods to read the data at will but the *get* method controls the formatting and display of the data. A **Public** *set* method can—and most likely will—carefully scrutinize attempts to modify the instance variable's value. This ensures that the new value is appropriate for that data item. For example, an attempt to *set* the day of the month to 37 would be rejected, an attempt to *set* a person's weight to a negative value would be rejected, and so on.

***Software Engineering Observation 16.9***

*The benefits of data integrity are not automatic simply because instance variables are made **Private**. Methods that set the values of **Private** data should verify that the intended new values are proper; if they are not, the* set *methods should place the **Private** instance variables into an appropriate consistent state.*

*Software Engineering Observation 16.10*

*Every method that modifies the* **Private** *instance variables of an object should ensure that the data remains in a consistent state.*

Figure 16.4 enhances our **CTime1** class (we call the new class **CTime2**) to include **Property Let** and **Property Get** procedures for the **mHour, mMinute** and **mSecond Private** instance variables. The **Property Let** methods strictly control the setting of the instance variables. Attempts to *set* any instance variable to an incorrect value cause the instance variable to be set to zero (thus at least leaving the instance variable in a consistent state). Validation for **mHour, mMinute** and **mSecond** are implemented in **Private** methods **ValidateHour, ValidateMinute** and **ValidateSecond,** respectively. These methods are designed for internal use and are therefore **Private.** Each **Property Get** procedure simply returns the appropriate instance variable's value.

```
1   ' Fig. 16.4
2   ' Class definition for CTime2
3   ' This class enhances CTime1 by providing Property procedures
4   ' for Hour, Minute and Second properties
5
6   Option Explicit
7
8   Private mHour As Integer
9   Private mMinute As Integer
10  Private mSecond As Integer
11
12  Public Sub SetTime(ByVal h As Integer, ByVal m As Integer, _
13                     ByVal s As Integer)
14
15     mHour = ValidateHour(h)
16     mMinute = ValidateMinute(m)
17     mSecond = ValidateSecond(s)
18  End Sub
19
20  Public Function ToUniversalTime() As String
21     ToUniversalTime = Format$(mHour, "00") & ":" & _
22                       Format$(mMinute, "00") & ":" & _
23                       Format$(mSecond, "00")
24  End Function
25
26  Public Function ToStandardTime() As String
27     Dim h As Integer
28
29     h = IIf((mHour = 12 Or mHour = 0), 12, mHour Mod 12)
30
31     ToStandardTime = h & ":" & _
32                      Format$(mMinute, "00") & ":" & _
33                      Format$(mSecond, "00") & " " & _
34                      IIf(mHour < 12, "AM", "PM")
35  End Function
```

**Fig. 16.4**    Demonstrating **Property Let** and **Property Get** methods (part 1 of 5).

```
36
37   Public Property Get Hour() As Integer
38      Hour = mHour
39   End Property
40
41   Public Property Let Hour(ByVal h As Integer)
42      mHour = ValidateHour(h)
43   End Property
44
45   Public Property Get Minute() As Integer
46      Minute = mMinute
47   End Property
48
49   Public Property Let Minute(ByVal m As Integer)
50      mMinute = ValidateMinute(m)
51   End Property
52
53   Public Property Get Second() As Integer
54      Second = mSecond
55   End Property
56
57   Public Property Let Second(ByVal s As Integer)
58      mSecond = ValidateSecond(s)
59   End Property
60
61   Private Function ValidateHour(ByVal h As Integer)
62      ValidateHour = IIf((h >= 0 And h < 24), h, 0)
63   End Function
64
65   Private Function ValidateMinute(ByVal m As Integer)
66      ValidateMinute = IIf((m >= 0 And m < 60), m, 0)
67   End Function
68
69   Private Function ValidateSecond(ByVal s As Integer)
70      ValidateSecond = IIf((s >= 0 And s < 60), s, 0)
71   End Function
```

**Fig. 16.4**    Demonstrating **Property Let** and **Property Get** methods (part 2 of 5).

```
72   ' Form module that exercises CTime2
73   Option Explicit
74
75   Private mTime As New CTime2
76
77   Private Sub Form_Load()
78      Call mTime.SetTime(txtHour.Text, txtMinute.Text, _
79                         txtSecond.Text)
80      Call UpdateDisplay
81   End Sub
82
```

**Fig. 16.4**    Demonstrating **Property Let** and **Property Get** methods (part 3 of 5).

```
83    Private Sub cmdEnter_Click()
84        mTime.Hour = txtHour.Text
85        mTime.Minute = txtMinute.Text
86        mTime.Second = txtSecond.Text
87        Call UpdateDisplay
88    End Sub
89
90    Private Sub cmdAdd_Click()
91        mTime.Second = (mTime.Second + 1) Mod 60
92
93        If mTime.Second = 0 Then
94            mTime.Minute = (mTime.Minute + 1) Mod 60
95
96            If mTime.Minute = 0 Then
97                mTime.Hour = (mTime.Hour + 1) Mod 24
98            End If
99
100       End If
101
102       Call UpdateDisplay
103   End Sub
104
105   Private Sub UpdateDisplay()
106       lblDisplay.Caption = Space$(12) & "Standard: " & _
107                            mTime.ToStandardTime() & _
108                            "     Universal: " & _
109                            mTime.ToUniversalTime()
110   End Sub
```

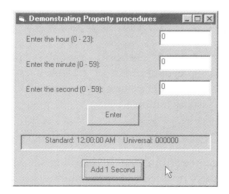

**Fig. 16.4**    Demonstrating **Property Let** and **Property Get** methods
(part 4 of 5).

The program's form module provides a GUI that allows the user to exercise the
methods of class **CTime2**. The user can set the **mHour, mMinute** or **mSecond** values by
typing values in the appropriate **TextBox**es and pressing **Enter**. The user can also press
**Add 1 Second** to increment the time by one second. After each operation, the resulting
time is displayed as a **String**. The screen captures illustrate both before and after the following operations: First, setting **mHour** to 23, setting **mMinute** to 59 and setting
**mSecond** to 59; then incrementing **mMinute** with the **Add 1 Second** button.

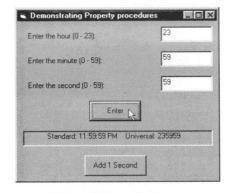

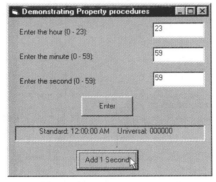

**Fig. 16.4**    Demonstrating **Property Let** and **Property Get** methods
(part 5 of 5).

Note that when the **Add 1 Second** button is pressed, event procedure
**cmdAdd_Click** is called. Procedure **cmdAdd_Click** uses the **Property Let** and
**Property Get** methods to increment **mSecond** properly. Although this works, it incurs
the performance burden of issuing multiple calls.

## 16.5 Composition: Objects as Instance Variables of Other Classes

Classes do not have to be created "from scratch." Forming new classes by including objects
of existing classes as members is called *composition* or *aggregation*. Such *software reuse*
can greatly enhance programmer productivity.

In order to understand composition, the programmer must understand the notion of a
Visual Basic reference. A *reference* is a name that either refers to **Nothing** or refers to an
object. **Nothing** simply means a reference does not refer to an object. Consider the following declarations:

```
Dim t1 As New CTime2
Dim t2 As CTime2
```

Reference **t1** refers to an object because **New** (which actually creates an object) is used.
Reference **t2** refers to **Nothing** because **New** is not used.

The programmer can call methods for **t1** and access properties for **t1**. The programmer cannot call any methods for **t2** or access any properties for **t2** until **New** is used. A statement such as

```
Set t2 = New CTime2
```

**Set**s reference **t2** to refer to a **New** instance of a **CTime2** object. Outside a declaration, the **Set** keyword must be used to assign a reference a value.

**Common Programming Error 16.3**

*Attempting to call a method or access a property for a reference that does not refer to an object (i.e., that refers to **Nothing**) is a run-time error.*

**Common Programming Error 16.4**

*Attempting to assign a reference a value (outside a declaration) without using **Set** is a syntax error.*

A **CAlarmClock** class object needs to know when it is supposed to sound its alarm, so why not include a **CTime2** object (actually an object reference) as a member of the **CAlarmClock** object? Such a capability is called *composition.* A class can have references to objects of other classes as members, just as a car "has a wheel," "has a transmission," "has an engine," etc.

**Software Engineering Observation 16.11**

*One form of software reuse is* composition *(also called* containment *or* aggregation*) in which a class has references to objects of other classes as members.*

Figure 16.5 uses classes **CEmployee** and **CDate1** to demonstrate objects as members of other objects. Class **CEmployee** contains instance variables **mFirstName**, **mLastName**, **mBirthDate** and **mHireDate**. Members **mBirthDate** and **mHireDate** are references to **CDate1** objects that each contain instance variables **mMonth**, **mDay** and **mYear**. The program instantiates a **CEmployee** object and initializes and displays its instance variables.

```
1   ' Fig. 16.5
2   ' Class CDate1 definition
3
4   Option Explicit
5
6   Private mMonth As Integer
7   Private mDay As Integer
8   Private mYear As Integer
9
10  Private Sub Class_Initialize()
11      mDay = 1
12      mMonth = 1
13      mYear = 1900
14  End Sub
15
```

**Fig. 16.5**    Demonstrating an object with member objects (part 1 of 6).

```
16  Public Property Get Day() As Integer
17      Day = mDay
18  End Property
19
20  Public Property Let Day(ByVal dy As Integer)
21      mDay = ValidateDay(dy)
22  End Property
23
24  Public Property Get Month() As Integer
25      Month = mMonth
26  End Property
27
28  Public Property Let Month(ByVal mth As Integer)
29      mMonth = ValidateMonth(mth)
30  End Property
31
32  Public Property Get Year() As Integer
33      year = mYear
34  End Property
35
36  Public Property Let Year(ByVal yr As Integer)
37      mYear = yr    ' Could also be validated by programmer
38  End Property
39
40  Public Function ToString() As String
41      ToString = mMonth & "/" & mDay & "/" & mYear
42  End Function
43
44  Public Sub SetDate(ByVal dy As Integer, _
45                     ByVal mth As Integer, _
46                     ByVal yr As Integer)
47
48      mMonth = ValidateMonth(mth)
49      mDay = ValidateDay(dy)
50      mYear = yr
51  End Sub
52
53  Private Function ValidateMonth(ByVal mth As Integer) As Integer
54      ValidateMonth = IIf((mth > 0 And mth <= 12), mth, 1)
55  End Function
56
57  Private Function ValidateDay(ByVal dy As Integer) As Integer
58      Dim daysPerMonth()
59
60      daysPerMonth = Array(0, 31, 28, 31, 30, 31, 30, 31, 31, _
61                           30, 31, 30, 31)
62
63      If dy > 0 And dy <= daysPerMonth(mMonth) Then
64          ValidateDay = dy
65          Exit Function
66      End If
67
```

**Fig. 16.5**    Demonstrating an object with member objects (part 2 of 6).

```
68        If mMonth = 2 And dy = 29 And (mYear Mod 400 = 0 Or _
69                                       mYear Mod 4 = 0 And _
70                                       mYear Mod 100 <> 0) Then
71           ValidateDay = dy
72           Exit Function
73        End If
74
75        ' An invalid day was passed to ValidateDay
76        ' Set the day to a default value of 1
77        ValidateDay = 1
78     End Function
```

**Fig. 16.5**   Demonstrating an object with member objects (part 3 of 6).

```
79     ' Class CEmployee definition
80     Option Explicit
81
82     Private mFirstName As String
83     Private mLastName As String
84     Private mBirthDate As CDate1
85     Private mHireDate As CDate1
86
87     Private Sub Class_Initialize()
88        Set mBirthDate = New CDate1
89        Set mHireDate = New CDate1
90     End Sub
91
92     Public Function ToString() As String
93        ToString = mLastName & ", " & mFirstName & _
94                    " Hired: " & mHireDate.ToString() & _
95                    " Birthday: " & mBirthDate.ToString()
96     End Function
97
98     Public Property Get Firstname() As String
99        Firstname = mFirstName
100    End Property
101
102    Public Property Let Firstname(ByVal fName As String)
103       mFirstName = fName
104    End Property
105
106    Public Property Get LastName() As String
107       LastName = mLastName
108    End Property
109
110    Public Property Let LastName(ByVal name As String)
111       mLastName = name
112    End Property
113
114    Public Property Get BirthDate() As CDate1
115       Set BirthDate = mBirthDate
116    End Property
```

**Fig. 16.5**   Demonstrating an object with member objects (part 4 of 6).

```
117
118 Public Property Set BirthDate(ByVal bDate As CDate1)
119     Set mBirthDate = bDate
120 End Property
121
122 Public Property Get HireDate() As CDate1
123     Set HireDate = mHireDate
124 End Property
125
126 Public Property Set HireDate(ByVal hDate As CDate1)
127     Set mHireDate = hDate
128 End Property
129
130 Private Sub Class_Terminate()
131     Set mBirthDate = Nothing    ' Release object's memory
132     Set mHireDate = Nothing     ' Release object's memory
133 End Sub
```

**Fig. 16.5**    Demonstrating an object with member objects (part 5 of 6).

```
134 ' Form module to test class CDate1 and CEmployee
135 Option Explicit
136
137 Private Sub Form_Load()
138     Dim employee1 As New CEmployee
139     Dim employee2 As New CEmployee
140
141     With employee1
142         .Firstname = "Bob"
143         .LastName = "Jones"
144         Call .BirthDate.SetDate(9, 8, 1965)
145         Call .HireDate.SetDate(2, 17, 1992)
146     End With
147
148     employee2.Firstname = "Susan"
149     employee2.LastName = "Baker"
150
151     Print employee1.ToString()
152     Print employee2.ToString()
153 End Sub
```

**Demonstrating Composition**

Jones, Bob Hired: 1/2/1992 Birthday: 8/9/1965
Baker, Susan Hired: 1/1/1900 Birthday: 1/1/1900

**Fig. 16.5**    Demonstrating an object with member objects (part 6 of 6).

We begin our discussion with class **CDate1**, which contains three instance variables—**mMonth**, **mDay** and **mYear**. Event procedure *Class_Initialize* is coded to set each instance variable to a default value (for our **Integer**s we want a value different from the default of 0 because we are using dates). Event procedure **Class_Initialize** is called when an instance of the class is created. The **Initialize** event is raised once in an object's lifetime.

**Common Programming Error 16.5**

*Method* **Class_Initialize** *can call other methods of the class, such as* **Property Let** *or* **Property Get** *methods, but because* **Class_Initialize** *is initializing the object, the instance variables may not yet be in a consistent state. Using instance variables before they have been properly initialized can lead to logic errors.*

The class provides **Property** procedures to access the instance variables. **Property Let Day** and **Property Let Month** each call a **Private** method (**ValidateDay** and **ValidateMonth**) to ensure that the object remains in a consistent state at all times. We could have provided a **ValidateYear** method to validate the year as well. Method **ToString** returns a **String** representation of the date. Method **SetDate** is provided to allow the user to *set* the day, month and year with one method call (as opposed to the user setting three different properties). Notice that **SetDate** calls **ValidateDay** and **ValidateMonth**—any method that modifies **Private** instance variables (not just **Property** procedures) should perform validation when necessary.

Class **CEmployee** contains **Private** instance variables **mFirstName**, **mLastName**, **mBirthDate** and **mHireDate**. Notice that both **mBirthDate** and **mHireDate** are references to **CDate1** objects. Since these objects are part of the class definition, we have a "has a" relationship (i.e., composition). Each of these objects is constructed in the **Class_Initialize** event procedure.

**CEmployee**'s **ToString** method prints the employee's name, hire date and birth date. The **ToString** method is called for **mHireDate** and for **mBirthDate** to return the **String** representations of their respective dates.

Property procedures are provided for **FirstName**, **LastName**, **BirthDate** and **HireDate**. When **Property Get** or **Property Set** is called for a **CDate1** object, keyword **Set** is used in the **Property** procedure body because we are using objects.

Event procedure **Class_Terminate** is used by the programmer to "clean up" an object before the object is destroyed. The **Terminate** event is raised when an object's reference goes out of scope and when the last reference referring to an object is **Set** to a different object or **Set** to **Nothing**. We **Set** references **mBirthDate** and **mHireDate** to **Nothing**.

**Good Programming Practice 16.6**

*Always explicitly set a reference to* **Nothing** *before assigning it to another object.*

We use a form to exercise the **CEmployee** and **CDate1** classes. In the **Form_Load** event procedure, we instantiate **CEmployee** objects **employee1** and **employee2**. We set two properties and make two method calls to **SetDate** for **employee1** inside a **With** statement. Although the syntax

```
Call .BirthDate.SetDate(9, 8, 1965)
```

may appear strange, it is correct. When **employee1**'s **BirthDate Get** procedure is called, it returns a **CDate1** object—off which we can call method **SetDate**.

Only the **FirstName** and **LastName** are set for **employee2**. The **BirthDate** and **HireDate** are defaulted to the values in **CDate1**'s **Initialize** event procedure.

## 16.6 Introduction to Object-Oriented Programming

To this point, we have considered *object-based programming* and its key concepts—encapsulation, classes, objects, data abstraction and information hiding. Now we discuss *object-oriented programming (OOP)* and its key concepts—*inheritance* and *polymorphism*.

Inheritance is a form of software reusability in which new classes are created from existing classes by absorbing their attributes and behaviors and extending these with capabilities the new classes require. Software reusability saves time in program development. It encourages the reuse of proven and debugged high-quality software, thus reducing problems after a system becomes operational. These are exciting possibilities.

Polymorphism enables us to write programs in a general fashion to handle a wide variety of existing and yet-to-be-specified related classes. Polymorphism makes it easy to add new capabilities to a system. Inheritance and polymorphism are effective techniques for dealing with software complexity. We discuss polymorphism in Section 16.9.

Even though Visual Basic does not support inheritance in the usual sense—a capability called *implementation inheritance*—we still discuss the general principles of inheritance. We do this for several reasons.

1. It lays the groundwork for a better understanding of the kind of inheritance Visual Basic does support, namely *interface inheritance*. We will also demonstrate a technique called *inheritance by delegation*.

2. It prepares the reader for future study of fully object-oriented languages such as C++ and Java that do support implementation inheritance.

3. It prepares the reader for the possibility that future versions of Visual Basic may eventually support implementation inheritance.

4. It lays the groundwork for understanding how implementation inheritance may reasonably be simulated in Visual Basic 6 by a combination of interface inheritance and a technique called delegation.

Again we remind you that the following general introduction to object-orientation includes a discussion of implementation inheritance—a capability that Visual Basic 6 does not support. When creating a new class, instead of writing completely new instance variables and instance methods, the programmer can designate that the new class is to *inherit* the instance variables and instance methods of a previously defined *superclass*. The new class is referred to as a *subclass*. We say that the subclass is *derived from* the superclass by (implementation) inheritance. Each subclass itself becomes a candidate to be a superclass for deriving future subclasses. We list some simple inheritance relationships in Fig. 16.6.

| Superclass | Subclasses |
|---|---|
| CStudent | CGraduateStudent |
|  | CUndergraduateStudent |
| CShape | CCircle |
|  | CTriangle |
|  | CRectangle |

**Fig. 16.6**     Some simple inheritance examples.

| Superclass | Subclasses |
|---|---|
| CLoan | CCarLoan |
| | CHomeImprovementLoan |
| | CMortgageLoan |
| CEmployee | CFacultyMember |
| | CStaffMember |
| CAccount | CCheckingAccount |
| | CSavingsAccount |

**Fig. 16.6**    Some simple inheritance examples.

With *single inheritance,* a class is derived from one superclass. Visual Basic does not support the complex notion of *multiple inheritance* (as C++ does) but it does support the notion of *interfaces* and allows a class to support multiple interfaces. Multiple interfaces help Visual Basic achieve many of the advantages of multiple inheritance. We discuss the details of interfaces in this chapter with live-code examples that create and use interfaces.

A subclass normally adds instance variables and instance methods of its own, so a subclass is generally larger than its superclass. With single inheritance, the subclass starts out essentially the same as the superclass. The real strength of inheritance comes from the ability to define additions to, or replacements for, the features inherited from the superclass.

Every object of a subclass may also be thought of as an object of that subclass's superclass. However, superclass objects are not objects of that superclass's subclasses. Programmers take advantage of this "subclass-object-is-a-superclass-object" relationship to perform some powerful manipulations. For example, we can link a wide variety of different objects related to a common superclass through inheritance into a linked list of superclass objects. This allows a variety of objects to be processed in a general way—a key thrust of object-oriented programming. [We discuss linked lists in Chapter 21.]

If a procedural program has many closely related special cases, then it is common to see **Select Case** statements that distinguish among the special cases and provide the processing logic to deal with each case individually. We will show how to use inheritance and polymorphism to replace such **Select Case** logic with much simpler logic.

We now distinguish between the *"is a" relationship* and the *"has a" relationship.* "Is a" is inheritance. In an "is a" relationship, an object of a subclass type may also be treated as an object of the superclass type. "Has a" is composition. In a "has a" relationship, a class object has references to objects of other classes as members, just as a car "has a" transmission, "has a" steering wheel, etc.

Because inheritance normally produces subclasses with *more* features than their superclasses, the terms *superclass* and *subclass* can be confusing. There is another way, however, to view these terms that does make perfectly good sense. Because every subclass object "is an" object of its superclass and because one superclass can have many subclasses, the set of objects represented by a superclass is normally larger than the set of objects represented by any of that superclass's subclasses.

Inheritance relationships form tree-like hierarchical structures. A superclass exists in a hierarchical relationship with its subclasses. A class can certainly exist by itself, but it is when a class is used with the mechanism of inheritance that the class becomes either a superclass that supplies attributes and behaviors to other classes, or the class becomes a subclass that inherits those attributes and behaviors.

Let us develop a simple inheritance hierarchy. A typical university community has thousands of people who are community members. These people consist of employees, students and alumni. Employees are either faculty members or staff members. Faculty members are either administrators (such as deans and department chairpersons) or teaching faculty. This yields the inheritance hierarchy shown in Fig. 16.7. Note that the inheritance hierarchy could contain many other classes. For example, students can be graduate students or undergraduate students. Undergraduate students can be freshman, sophomores, juniors and seniors. And so on.

It is possible to treat superclass objects and subclass objects similarly; that commonality is expressed in the attributes and behaviors of the superclass. Objects of all classes derived from a common superclass can all be treated as objects of that superclass. For example, a **CStaff** object can be treated as a **CEmployee** or even more generally as a **CCommunityMember**.

Another substantial inheritance hierarchy is the **CShape** hierarchy of Fig. 16.8. There are abundant examples of hierarchies in the real world but students are not accustomed to categorizing the real world in this manner, so it takes some adjustment in their thinking. Actually, biology students have had some practice with hierarchies. Everything we study in biology is grouped into a hierarchy headed by living things; these can be subclassed into plants or animals, animals are vertebrates or invertebrates, and so on.

One problem with inheritance is that a subclass can inherit methods that it does not need or should expressly not have. When a superclass member is inappropriate for a subclass, that member can be *overridden* in the subclass with an appropriate implementation.

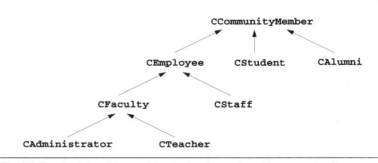

**Fig. 16.7** An inheritance hierarchy for university community members.

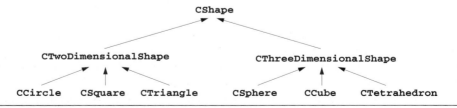

**Fig. 16.8** A portion of a **CShape** class hierarchy.

***Software Engineering Observation 16.12***

*Creating a subclass does not affect its superclass's source code; the integrity of a superclass is preserved by inheritance.*

A superclass specifies commonality. All classes derived from a superclass inherit the capabilities of that superclass. In the object-oriented design process, the designer looks for commonality among a set of classes and factors it out to form desirable superclasses. Subclasses are then customized beyond the capabilities inherited from the superclass.

***Software Engineering Observation 16.13***

*Just as the designer of non-object-oriented systems should avoid unnecessary proliferation of functions, the designer of object-oriented systems should avoid unnecessary proliferation of classes. Proliferating classes creates management problems and can hinder software reusability simply because it is more difficult for a potential reuser of a class to locate that class in a huge collection. The trade-off is to create fewer classes, each providing substantial additional functionality, but such classes might be too rich for certain reusers.*

***Performance Tip 16.1***

*If classes produced through inheritance are larger than they need to be, memory and processing resources may be wasted. Inherit from the class "closest" to what you need.*

## 16.7 Software Engineering with Components

It can be difficult for students to appreciate the problems faced by designers and programmers on large-scale software projects in industry. People experienced on such projects will invariably state that a key to improving the software development process is encouraging software reuse. Object-oriented programming in general (and Visual Basic in particular) certainly does this.

It is the availability of substantial and useful *class libraries* that delivers the maximum benefits of software reuse through inheritance. Organizations develop their own class libraries and can take advantage of other libraries available worldwide. As interest in Visual Basic grows, interest in Visual Basic class libraries will increase. Just as shrink-wrapped software produced by independent software vendors became an explosive growth industry with the arrival of the personal computer, so, too, has the creation and sale of Visual Basic components packaged as classes and ActiveX controls. Someday, most software may be constructed from *standardized reusable components* just as hardware is often constructed today. This will help meet the challenges of developing the vast amounts of ever more powerful software we will need in the future. Application designers build their applications with these components.

## 16.8 Type Fields and `Select Case` Statements

One means of dealing with objects of many different types is to use a **Select Case** statement to take an appropriate action on each object based on that object's type. For example, in a hierarchy of shapes in which each shape has a **mShapeType** instance variable, a **Select Case** structure could determine which **Display** method to call based on the object's **mShapeType**.

There are many problems with using **Select Case** logic. The programmer might forget to make such a type test when one is warranted. The programmer may forget to test all possible cases in a **Select Case** statement. If a **Select Case**-based system is modified by adding new types, the programmer might forget to insert the new cases in existing **Select Case** statements. Every addition or deletion of a class demands that every **Select Case** statement in the system be modified; tracking these down can be time consuming and error prone.

As we will see, polymorphic programming can eliminate the need for **Select Case** logic. The programmer can use Visual Basic's polymorphism mechanism to perform the equivalent logic automatically, thus avoiding the kinds of errors typically associated with **Select Case** logic.

*Testing and Debugging Tip 16.5*

*An interesting consequence of using polymorphism is that programs take on a simplified appearance. They contain less branching logic in favor of simpler sequential code. This simplification facilitates testing, debugging and program maintenance.*

Let us discuss a situation where polymorphism eliminates **Select Case** logic. Suppose we create an inheritance hierarchy in which each of the shape classes **CCircle**, **CTriangle**, **CRectangle**, **CSquare** "is a" **CShape**. In object-oriented programming, each of these classes might be endowed with the ability to draw itself. Although each class has its own **Draw** method, the **Draw** methods for the various shape classes are quite different from one another. When drawing a shape, whatever that shape may be, it would be nice to be able to treat all these shapes generically as **CShape**s. Then to draw any shape, we could simply call method **Draw** of superclass **CShape** and let the program determine which subclass **Draw** method to use. This is precisely what polymorphism is about. We will study two substantial examples and show how objects throughout those hierarchies are manipulated polymorphically.

## 16.9 Polymorphism

With *polymorphism*, it is possible to design and implement systems that are more easily *extensible*. Programs can be written to process generically—as superclass objects—objects of all existing classes in a hierarchy. Classes that do not exist during program development can be added with little or no modifications to the generic part of the program—as long as each of those classes "implements the appropriate interfaces." The only parts of a program that need modification are those parts that require direct knowledge of the particular class that is added to the hierarchy.

As we mentioned earlier, Visual Basic currently does not support implementation inheritance. Visual Basic supports *interface inheritance* (i.e., the ability to inherit the **Public** interface but not the implementation of a class). In languages like Java and C++, a class **CCar** might contain a **Public** method **ParkCar**. Method **ParkCar** would contain code that parks the car. A Java or C++ class named **CToyota** inheriting from **CCar** would get both the **Public** interface and the implementation. With Visual Basic's interface inheritance, **CToyota** gets only the responsibility to implement method **ParkCar** (i.e., **CToyota** does not inherit the code implementation that parks the car). The programmer has to write the implementation for **CToyota** method **ParkCar**. Later in the chapter we will show that we can effectively simulate implementation inheritance with interface inheritance and delegation.

## 16.10 Visual Basic Interfaces

When we think of a class as a type, we assume that objects of that type will be instantiated. However, there are cases in which it is useful to define classes for which the programmer never intends to instantiate any objects. Such classes are called *interfaces*. Objects of interfaces are rarely instantiated; as we will see their methods are normally empty shells with a code body. The sole purpose of an interface is to provide an appropriate superclass from which other classes may inherit interface.

*Good Programming Practice 16.7*

*Begin each interface **Name** with the uppercase letter "**I**" to indicate clearly that it is an interface class.*

We could have an interface **ITwoDimensionalObject** and create classes such as **CSquare**, **CCircle**, **CTriangle**, etc. We could also have an interface **IThreeDimensionalObject** and create classes such as **CCube**, **CSphere**, **CCylinder**, etc. Interfaces are too generic to define real objects; we need to be more specific before we can instantiate objects. Classes that implement the interface provide the specifics that make it reasonable to instantiate objects.

A hierarchy does not need to contain any interfaces, but as we will see, many good object-oriented systems have class hierarchies headed by interfaces. In some cases, interfaces constitute the top few levels of the hierarchy. A good example of this is a shape hierarchy. The hierarchy could begin with interface **IShape**. On the next level down we can have two more interfaces, namely **ITwoDimensionalShape** and **IThreeDimensionalShape**. The next level down would start defining classes for two-dimensional shapes such as **CCircle** and **CSquare**, and classes for three-dimensional shapes such as **CSphere** and **CCube**. Note the differences between the hierarchy we just discussed and the hierarchy of Fig. 16.6.

Any class can serve as an interface for another class. An interface class is created in the same manner as any other class. The **Public** interface usually does not contain any implementation (i.e., the bodies of **Public** methods do not contain any code). Keyword **Implements** is used to implement the interface in another class. For example, we might place the statement

```
Implements IThreeDimensionalShape
```

in the general declaration of class **CCube** to implement **IThreeDimensionalShape**. Each class **Implements** as many interfaces as it needs.

*Software Engineering Observation 16.14*

*With interfaces, implementation is never inherited—even if the interface actually provides implementation.*

*Common Programming Error 16.6*

*Not implementing an inherited method is a syntax error.*

## 16.11 Polymorphism Examples

Here is another example of polymorphism. If class **CRectangle Implements** interface **IQuadrilateral**, then a **CRectangle** object *is a* **IQuadrilateral** object. An operation (such as calculating the perimeter or the area) specified in interface **IQuadrilateral** can be performed on an object of class **CRectangle**. Such operations can also be performed on other "kinds of" **IQuadrilateral**s, such as **CSquare**s, **CParallelogram**s and **CTrapezoid**s. When a request is made through an object reference to use a method, Visual Basic chooses the correct overridden method polymorphically in the appropriate subclass associated with the object.

Here is another example of polymorphism. Suppose we have a video game that manipulates objects of many varieties, including objects of class **CMartian**, **CVenutian**, **CPlutonian**, **CSpaceShip**, **CLaserBeam** and the like. Each of these classes **Implements** interface **IDrawableSpaceObject** that contains method **Draw**. This method must be defined by each class that **Implements** interface **IDrawableSpaceObject**. A Visual Basic screen manager program would maintain some kind of container (such as an **IDrawableSpaceObject** array) of objects of these various classes. To refresh the screen periodically the screen manager would simply send each object the **Draw** message. Each object would respond in its own unique way. A **CMartian** object would **Draw** itself with the appropriate number of antennae. A **CSpaceShip** object would **Draw** itself bright and silvery. A **CLaserBeam** object would draw itself as a bright red streak across the screen. Thus, the same message sent to a variety of objects would take on "many forms"—hence the term *polymorphism.*

Such a polymorphic screen manager makes it especially easy to add new types of objects to a system with minimal impact. Suppose we want to add **CMercurian**s to our video game. We certainly have to build a new class **CMercurian** that **Implements** interface **IDrawableSpaceObject** and provides its own definition of the **Draw** method. Then, when objects of class **CMercurian** need to be drawn, the screen manager need not be modified. It simply sends the **Draw** message to every object in the container regardless of the object's type, so the new **CMercurian** objects just "fit right in." Thus, with polymorphism, new types of objects not even envisioned when a system is created may be added to the system without modifications (other than building the new classes themselves, of course).

Through polymorphism, one method call can cause different actions to occur, depending on the type of the object receiving the call. This gives the programmer tremendous expressive capability. We will see examples of the power of polymorphism in the next several sections.

**Software Engineering Observation 16.15**

*With polymorphism, the programmer can deal in generalities and let the execution-time environment concern itself with the specifics. The programmer can command a wide variety of objects to behave in manners appropriate to those objects without even knowing the types of those objects.*

**Software Engineering Observation 16.16**

*Polymorphism promotes extensibility: Software written to invoke polymorphic behavior is written independent of the types of objects to which messages (i.e., method calls) are sent. Thus, new types of objects that respond to existing messages can be added to such a system without modifying the base system.*

Let us consider more applications of polymorphism. Polymorphism is particularly effective for implementing layered software systems. In operating systems, for example, each type of physical device may operate quite differently from the others. Even so, commands the operating system issues to *read* or *write* data from and to devices can have a certain uniformity. The *write* message sent to a device-driver object needs to be interpreted specifically in the context of that device driver and how that device driver manipulates devices of a specific type. However, the *write* call itself is really no different from the *write* to any other device in the system—simply place some number of bytes from memory onto that device. An object-oriented operating system might use an interface **IDeviceDriver** to provide an interface appropriate for all device drivers. Then, through implementing interface **IDeviceDriver**, specific device driver classes are formed that all operate similarly. The capabilities (i.e., the **Public** interface) to be offered by all device drivers are provided as abstract methods (i.e., empty shells without code bodies) in interface **IDeviceDriver**. The code implementations of these abstract methods are provided in each specific device driver class (i.e., each class that **Implements** the **IDeviceDriver** interface).

It is common in object-oriented programming to define an *iterator class* whose objects can walk through all the objects in a container (such as an array); Visual Basic calls iterators *enumerators*. If you want to print a list of objects in a linked list, for example, an enumerator object can be instantiated that will return the next element of the linked list each time the enumerator is called. Enumerators are commonly used in polymorphic programming to walk through a container (such as an array) of related objects. The references in such a list would all be superclass references (see Chapter 21 for more on linked lists). A list of objects of class **ITwoDimensionalShape** could contain objects from the classes **CSquare**, **CCircle**, **CTriangle**, etc. Sending a **Draw** message to each object in the list would, using polymorphism, draw the correct picture on the screen.

## 16.12 Case Study: `IShape`, `CPoint`, `CCircle`

Now let us consider an interface inheritance example. We create a shape, point, circle hierarchy. First we develop an interface class called **IShape**. Interface **IShape** contains three **Public** methods—**Area**, **Name** and **ToString**. We also develop classes **CPoint** and **CCircle** each of which **Implements** interface **IShape**. We begin our discussion with interface **IShape** (Fig. 16.9).

```
1    ' Fig. 16.9
2    ' IShape interface definition
3    Option Explicit
4
5    Public Function Area() As Double
6    End Function    ' Empty code body
7
8    Public Function Name() As String
9    End Function    ' Empty code body
10
11   Public Function ToString() As String
12   End Function    ' Empty code body
```

**Fig. 16.9**    **IShape** interface definition (part 1 of 6).

```
13   ' CPoint definition
14   Option Explicit
15   Implements IShape
16
17   Private mX As Integer
18   Private mY As Integer
19
20   Private Function IShape_Area() As Double
21      IShape_Area = 0
22   End Function
23
24   Private Function IShape_Name() As String
25      IShape_Name = "Point"
26   End Function
27
28   Private Function IShape_ToString() As String
29      IShape_ToString = "[" & mX & ", " & mY & "]"
30   End Function
31
32   Public Property Let X(ByVal newX As Integer)
33      mX = newX
34   End Property
35
36   Public Property Get X() As Integer
37      X = mX
38   End Property
39
40   Public Property Let Y(ByVal newY As Integer)
41      mY = newY
42   End Property
43
44   Public Property Get Y() As Integer
45      Y = mY
46   End Property
```

**Fig. 16.9**   **CPoint** class definition (part 2 of 6).

```
47   ' CCircle class definition
48   Option Explicit
49   Implements IShape
50
51   Private mX As Integer        ' Cannot inherit from CPoint
52   Private mY As Integer        ' Cannot inherit from CPoint
53   Private mRadius As Double     ' New variable for CCircle
54
55   Private Function IShape_Area() As Double
56      IShape_Area = 3.14159 * mRadius ^ 2
57   End Function
58
59   Private Function IShape_Name() As String
60      IShape_Name = "Circle"
61   End Function
```

**Fig. 16.9**   **CCircle** class definition (part 3 of 6).

```vb
62
63   Private Function IShape_ToString() As String
64      IShape_ToString = "[" & mX & ", " & mY & "], " & _
65                          "Radius: " & mRadius
66   End Function
67
68   Public Property Let X(ByVal xValue As Integer)
69      mX = xValue
70   End Property
71
72   Public Property Get X() As Integer
73      X = mX
74   End Property
75
76   Public Property Let Y(ByVal yValue As Integer)
77      mY = yValue
78   End Property
79
80   Public Property Get Y() As Integer
81      Y = mY
82   End Property
83
84   Public Property Let Radius(ByVal radiusValue As Double)
85      mRadius = radiusValue
86   End Property
87
88   Public Property Get Radius() As Double
89      Radius = mRadius
90   End Property
```

**Fig. 16.9**   **CCircle** class definition (part 4 of 6).

```vb
91   ' Form module that exercises IShape, CPoint,
92   ' and CCircle
93   Option Explicit
94
95   Private Sub Form_Load()
96      Dim p As New CPoint    ' Create a CPoint
97      Dim c As New CCircle   ' Create a CCircle
98      Dim iRef As IShape     ' Create an IShape reference
99
100     p.X = 500     ' Set X via Property Let
101     p.Y = 777     ' Set Y via Property Let
102
103     Set iRef = p ' Assign a CPoint object to an IShape reference
104
105     ' Invoke IShape members of p using iRef
106     Print "Name: " & iRef.Name & " Area: " & iRef.Area, _
107          " ToString: " & iRef.ToString
108
109     Set iRef = c ' Assign a CCircle object to an IShape reference
110     c.Radius = 4 ' Set Radius via Property Let
```

**Fig. 16.9**   **IShape**, **CPoint**, **CCircle** example (part 5 of 6).

```
111       c.X = 11       ' Set X via Property Let
112       c.Y = 812      ' Set Y via Property Let
113
114       ' Invoke IShape members of c using iRef
115       Print "Name: " & iRef.Name & " Area: " & iRef.Area, _
116             " ToString: " & iRef.ToString
117   End Sub
```

```
IShape, CPoint, and CCircle classes                          _ □ X
Name: Point Area: 0        ToString: [500, 777]
Name: Circle Area: 50.26544   ToString: [11, 812], Radius: 4
```

**Fig. 16.9** `IShape`, `CPoint`, `CCircle` example (part 6 of 6).

Interface **IShape** is created and added to the project in the same manner as any other class. Interfaces are classes and still have the **.cls** extension. Each **Public** method of **IShape** is inherited by any class that **Implements** this interface. The class implementing the interface has the responsibility of providing implementation, i.e., the code bodies for the methods. Now we discuss class **CPoint**—that implements **IShape**.

Class **CPoint Implements** interface **IShape** (line 15). When a class implements an interface, the **Object** box in the **Code** window contains the implemented interface's name. The **Procedure** box contains the names of the methods the class must implement. The method names are prefixed with the interface name (**IShape**) and an underscore (_) character. For our example, the names in the **Procedure** box are **IShape_Area**, **IShape_Name** and **IShape_ToString**. Each method defaults to **Private**.

A point has an area of zero, so the implementation of **IShape_Area** simply returns 0. **IShape_Name** returns the **String "Point"** and **IShape_ToString** returns a **String** representing the point's location as an ordered pair delineated with square brackets. **Property** procedures are provided to allow access to **mX** and **mY**.

**CCircle** provides **Property** procedures for accessing **mX** and **mY** and implementations for the three interface methods. **CCircle** adds **Private** instance variable **mRadius** representing the circle's radius and **Property** procedures for accessing **mRadius**.

A circle has a nonzero area, so the implementation of **IShape_Area** calculates and returns 3.14159 times the radius squared. **IShape_Name** returns the **String "Circle"** and **IShape_ToString** returns a **String** containing the center point of the circle followed by the circle's radius. **Property** procedures are provided to allow access to **Private** instance variables **mX** and **mY**.

We use a form to exercise our classes. We create one **CPoint** object **p** and one **CCircle** object **c**. We also create an **IShape** reference.

Lines 100 and 101 assign values to **p**'s **X** and **Y** properties. Line 103 assigns **p** to **iRef** so we can access interface **IShape**'s methods **Area**, **Name** and **ToString**. This assignment is allowed because class **CPoint** (**p**'s type) **Implements IShape** (**iRef**'s type). Recall **CPoint** and **CCircle Private** methods **IShape_Area**, **IShape_Name** and **IShape_ToString** are not accessible outside the classes. By assigning **p** (or **c**) to **iRef** the inherited interface members are allowed to be used. Note also that off **iRef** we can only access **Area**, **Name** and **ToString**. Properties **X** and **Y** cannot be accessed off **iRef**—but can be accessed off **p** (or **c**).

*Common Programming Error 16.7*

*Attempting to assign to a reference an object that does not implement the reference's type is a run-time error.*

## 16.13 Case Study: A Payroll System Using Polymorphism

Let us use interfaces and polymorphism to perform payroll calculations based on the type of employee (Fig. 16.5). We use interface **IEmployee**. The classes that implement **IEmployee** are **CBoss**, who gets paid a fixed weekly salary regardless of the number of hours worked, **CCommissionWorker**, who gets a flat base salary plus a percentage of sales, **CPieceWorker**, who gets paid by the number of items produced and **CHourly-Worker**, who gets paid by the hour with "time-and-a-half" for overtime.

An **Earnings** method call certainly applies generically to all employees. But the way each person's **Earnings** are calculated depends on the class of the employee, and each of these classes **Implements** interface **IEmployee**. So **Earnings** is a **Public** method in interface **IEmployee** and appropriate implementations of **Earnings** are provided in each of the subclasses. Then, to calculate any employee's earnings, the program simply uses an **IEmployee** reference to that employee's object and invokes the **Earnings** method. In a real payroll system, the various **IEmployee** objects might be referenced by individual elements in an array of **IEmployee** references. The program would simply walk through the array one element at a time using an **IEmployee** reference to invoke the **Earnings** method of each object.

Let us consider the **IEmployee** class (Fig. 16.10). The **Public** methods include an **Earnings** method and a **ToString** method that returns the type and name of the employee. Why is method **Earnings** in this interface? The answer is that it does not make sense to provide an implementation of **Earnings** in the **IEmployee** class. We cannot calculate the **Earnings** for a generic employee—we must first know *what kind of* employee it is. By placing the **Earnings** method in the interface we are indicating that we will implement **Earnings** in each class that **Implements IEmployee**.

Class **CBoss Implements IEmployee**. The **Public** methods include a **Property WeeklySalary** to assign/retrieve **mWeeklySalary**'s value, a **Property FirstName**, a **Property LastName**, an **Earnings** method defining how to calculate a **CBoss**'s earnings and a **ToString** method that forms a **String** containing the type of the employee (i.e., **"Boss: "**) followed by the boss's name.

```
1   ' Fig. 16.10
2   ' Interface IEmployee definition
3   Option Explicit
4
5   Public Function Earnings() As Double
6   End Function
7
8   Public Function ToString() As String
9   End Function
```

**Fig. 16.10** **IEmployee** class hierarchy using an interface (part 1 of 10).

```
10   ' CBoss definition
11   Option Explicit
12   Implements IEmployee
13
14   Private mFirstName As String
15   Private mLastName As String
16   Private mWeeklySalary As Currency
17
18   Public Property Let WeeklySalary(ByVal wg As Currency)
19      mWeeklySalary = IIf(wg > 0, wg, 0)
20   End Property
21
22   Public Property Get WeeklySalary() As Currency
23      WeeklySalary = mWeeklySalary
24   End Property
25
26   Public Property Let FirstName(ByVal fName As String)
27      mFirstName = fName
28   End Property
29
30   Public Property Get FirstName() As String
31      FirstName = mFirstName
32   End Property
33
34   Public Property Let LastName(ByVal name As String)
35      mLastName = name
36   End Property
37
38   Public Property Get LastName() As String
39      LastName = mLastName
40   End Property
41
42   Private Function IEmployee_Earnings() As Double
43      IEmployee_Earnings = mWeeklySalary
44   End Function
45
46   Private Function IEmployee_ToString() As String
47      IEmployee_ToString = "Boss: " & mFirstName & " " & _
48                             mLastName
49   End Function
```

Fig. 16.10   **IEmployee** class hierarchy using an interface (part 2 of 10).

```
50   ' CCommissionWorker definition
51   Option Explicit
52   Implements IEmployee
53
54   Private mFirstName As String
55   Private mLastName As String
56   Private mSalary As Currency
57   Private mCommission As Currency
58   Private mQuantity As Long
```

Fig. 16.10   **IEmployee** class hierarchy using an interface (part 3 of 10).

```
59
60   Public Property Let FirstName(ByVal fName As String)
61       mFirstName = fName
62   End Property
63
64   Public Property Get FirstName() As String
65       FirstName = mFirstName
66   End Property
67
68   Public Property Let LastName(ByVal name As String)
69       mLastName = name
70   End Property
71
72   Public Property Get LastName() As String
73       LastName = mLastName
74   End Property
75
76   Public Property Let Salary(ByVal wg As Currency)
77       mSalary = IIf(wg > 0, wg, 0)
78   End Property
79
80   Public Property Get Salary() As Currency
81       Salary = mSalary
82   End Property
83
84   Public Property Let Commission(ByVal com As Currency)
85       mCommission = IIf(com > 0, com, 0)
86   End Property
87
88   Public Property Get Commission() As Currency
89       Commission = mCommission
90   End Property
91
92   Public Property Let Quantity(ByVal qty As Long)
93       mQuantity = IIf(qty > 0, qty, 0)
94   End Property
95
96   Public Property Get Quantity() As Long
97       Quantity = mQuantity
98   End Property
99
100  Private Function IEmployee_Earnings() As Double
101      IEmployee_Earnings = mSalary + mCommission * mQuantity
102  End Function
103
104  Private Function IEmployee_ToString() As String
105      IEmployee_ToString = "Commission worker: " & mFirstName & _
106                          " " & mLastName
107  End Function
```

**Fig. 16.10**    `IEmployee` class hierarchy using an interface (part 4 of 10).

```
108  ' CHourlyWorker definition
109  Option Explicit
110  Implements IEmployee
111
112  Private mFirstName As String
113  Private mLastName As String
114  Private mWage As Currency
115  Private mHours As Integer
116  Private Const mHoursInAWeek As Integer = 168
117
118  Public Property Let FirstName(ByVal fName As String)
119     mFirstName = fName
120  End Property
121
122  Public Property Get FirstName() As String
123     FirstName = mFirstName
124  End Property
125
126  Public Property Let LastName(ByVal name As String)
127     mLastName = name
128  End Property
129
130  Public Property Get LastName() As String
131     LastName = mLastName
132  End Property
133
134  Public Property Let Wage(ByVal wg As Currency)
135     mWage = IIf(wg > 0, wg, 0)
136  End Property
137
138  Public Property Get Wage() As Currency
139     Wage = mWage
140  End Property
141
142  Public Property Let Hours(ByVal hrs As Integer)
143     mHours = IIf((hrs >= 0 And hrs < mHoursInAWeek), hrs, 0)
144  End Property
145
146  Public Property Get Hours() As Integer
147     Hours = mHours
148  End Property
149
150  Private Function IEmployee_Earnings() As Double
151
152     If mHours > 40 Then
153        Dim otHours As Integer
154
155        otHours = mHours - 40
156        IEmployee_Earnings = otHours * 1.5 * mWage + mWage * 40
```

**Fig. 16.10**   **IEmployee** class hierarchy using an interface (part 5 of 10).

```
157        Else
158            IEmployee_Earnings = mWage * mHours
159        End If
160
161    End Function
162
163    Private Function IEmployee_ToString() As String
164        IEmployee_ToString = "Hourly worker: " & mFirstName & " " & _
165                            mLastName
166    End Function
```

**Fig. 16.10    IEmployee** class hierarchy using an interface (part 6 of 10).

```
167    ' CPieceWorker definition
168    Option Explicit
169    Implements IEmployee
170
171    Private mFirstName As String
172    Private mLastName As String
173    Private mWagePerPiece As Currency
174    Private mQuantity As Long
175
176    Public Property Let WagePerPiece(ByVal wg As Currency)
177        mWagePerPiece = IIf(wg > 0, wg, 0)
178    End Property
179
180    Public Property Get WagePerPiece() As Currency
181        WagePerPiece = mWagePerPiece
182    End Property
183
184    Public Property Let FirstName(ByVal fName As String)
185        mFirstName = fName
186    End Property
187
188    Public Property Get FirstName() As String
189        FirstName = mFirstName
190    End Property
191
192    Public Property Let LastName(ByVal name As String)
193        mLastName = name
194    End Property
195
196    Public Property Get LastName() As String
197        LastName = mLastName
198    End Property
199
200    Public Property Let Quantity(ByVal qty As Long)
201        mQuantity = IIf(qty > 0, qty, 0)
202    End Property
203
```

**Fig. 16.10    IEmployee** class hierarchy using an interface (part 7 of 10).

```
204  Public Property Get Quantity() As Long
205     Quantity = mQuantity
206  End Property
207
208  Private Function IEmployee_Earnings() As Double
209     IEmployee_Earnings = mWagePerPiece * mQuantity
210  End Function
211
212  Private Function IEmployee_ToString() As String
213     IEmployee_ToString = "Piece worker: " & mFirstName & _
214                          " " & mLastName
215  End Function
```

**Fig. 16.10   IEmployee** class hierarchy using an interface (part 8 of 10).

```
216  ' Form module to exercise IEmployee,
217  ' CBoss, CComissionWorker, CHourlyWorker,
218  ' and CPieceWorker
219  Option Explicit
220  Private mEmployeeRef As IEmployee
221  Private mBoss As New CBoss
222  Private mCommissionWorker As New CCommissionWorker
223  Private mHourlyWorker As New CHourlyWorker
224  Private mPieceWorker As New CPieceWorker
225
226  Private Sub Form_Load()
227
228     With mBoss
229        .FirstName = "John"
230        .LastName = "Smith"
231        .WeeklySalary = 800
232      End With
233
234     Call Display(mBoss)
235
236     With mCommissionWorker
237        .FirstName = "Sue"
238        .LastName = "Jones"
239        .Quantity = 150
240        .Commission = 3
241        .Salary = 400
242     End With
243
244     Call Display(mCommissionWorker)
245
246     With mHourlyWorker
247        .FirstName = "Karen"
248        .LastName = "Price"
249        .Hours = 40
250        .Wage = 13.75
251     End With
252
```

**Fig. 16.10   IEmployee** class hierarchy using an interface (part 9 of 10).

```
253        Call Display(mHourlyWorker)
254
255        With mPieceWorker
256           .FirstName = "Bob"
257           .LastName = "Lewis"
258           .Quantity = 200
259           .WagePerPiece = 2.5
260        End With
261
262        Call Display(mPieceWorker)
263     End Sub
264
265     Private Sub Display(e As IEmployee)
266        Print e.ToString & " earned " & FormatCurrency(e.Earnings)
267     End Sub
```

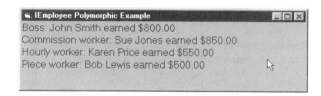

**Fig. 16.10  IEmployee** class hierarchy using an interface (part 10 of 10).

Class **CCommissionWorker Implements IEmployee**. The **Public** methods include a **Property Salary** to assign/retrieve **mSalary**'s value, a **Property Quantity** to assign/retrieve **mQuantity**'s value, a **Property Commission** to assign/retrieve **mCommission**'s value, a **Property FirstName**, a **Property LastName**, an **Earnings** method defining how to calculate a **CCommissionWorker**'s earnings and a **ToString** method that forms a **String** containing the type of the employee (i.e., **"CommissionWorker: "**) followed by the commission worker's name.

Class **CPieceWorker Implements IEmployee**. The **Public** methods include a **Property WagePerPiece** to assign/retrieve **mWagePerPiece**'s value, a **Property Quantity** to assign/retrieve **mQuantity**'s value, a **Property FirstName**, a **Property LastName**, an **Earnings** method defining how to calculate a **CPieceWorker**'s earnings and a **ToString** method that forms a **String** containing the type of the employee (i.e., **"PieceWorker: "**) followed by the pieceworker's name.

Class **CHourlyWorker Implements IEmployee**. The **Public** methods include a **Property Hours** to assign/retrieve **mHours**' value, a **Property Wage** to assign/retrieve **mWage**'s value, a **Property FirstName**, a **Property LastName**, an **Earnings** method defining how to calculate a **CHourlyWorker**'s earnings and a **ToString** method that forms a **String** containing the type of the employee (i.e., **"HourlyWorker: "**) followed by the hourly worker's name.

A form module is used to exercise the classes. In the form's general declaration **IEmployee** reference, **iRef**, is declared. Objects from each of the other class types are created. In event procedure **Form_Load** we set properties for each object and call procedure **Display**—passing an object as an argument. Objects are passed by reference (even if the programmer uses **ByVal**). The object passed to **Display** is assigned to **IEmployee** reference **e**. **Display** calls the object's **ToString** method and **Earnings** method. The **String**s returned are combined into a larger **String** that is printed to the form.

## 16.14 Case Study: Polymorphic Processing of Shapes

Our next example (Fig. 16.11) extends the **IShape**, **CPoint**, **CCircle** hierarchy. We add method **Volume** to **IShape** (and in doing so, we have changed the public interface—so we create a new interface called **IShape2**), add class **CCylinder** to the hierarchy and use an array of **IShape2** references to exercise the classes.

```
1   ' Fig. 16.11
2   ' IShape2 interface definition
3   Option Explicit
4
5   Public Function Volume() As Double
6   End Function    ' Empty body
7
8   Public Function Area() As Double
9   End Function    ' Empty body
10
11  Public Function Name() As String
12  End Function    ' Empty body
13
14  Public Function ToString() As String
15  End Function    ' Empty body
```

**Fig. 16.11**   Polymorphic processing of shapes (part 1 of 9).

```
16  ' CPoint definition
17  Option Explicit
18  Implements IShape2
19
20  Private mX As Integer
21  Private mY As Integer
22
23  Private Function IShape2_Volume() As Double
24      IShape2_Volume = 0
25  End Function
26
27  Private Function IShape2_Area() As Double
28      IShape2_Area = 0
29  End Function
30
31  Private Function IShape2_Name() As String
32      IShape2_Name = "Point"
33  End Function
34
35  Private Function IShape2_ToString() As String
36      IShape2_ToString = "[" & mX & ", " & mY & "]"
37  End Function
```

**Fig. 16.11**   Polymorphic processing of shapes (part 2 of 9).

```vb
38
39  Public Property Let X(ByVal newX As Integer)
40      mX = newX
41  End Property
42
43  Public Property Get X() As Integer
44      X = mX
45  End Property
46
47  Public Property Let Y(ByVal newY As Integer)
48      mY = newY
49  End Property
50
51  Public Property Get Y() As Integer
52      Y = mY
53  End Property
```

**Fig. 16.11**   Polymorphic processing of shapes (part 3 of 9).

```vb
54  ' CCircle class definition
55  Option Explicit
56  Implements IShape2
57
58  Private mX As Integer
59  Private mY As Integer
60  Private mRadius As Double
61
62  Private Function IShape2_Volume() As Double
63      IShape2_Volume = 0
64  End Function
65
66  Private Function IShape2_Area() As Double
67      IShape2_Area = 3.14159 * mRadius ^ 2
68  End Function
69
70  Private Function IShape2_Name() As String
71      IShape2_Name = "Circle"
72  End Function
73
74  Private Function IShape2_ToString() As String
75      IShape2_ToString = "[" & mX & ", " & mY & "], " & _
76                         "Radius: " & mRadius
77  End Function
78
79  Public Property Let X(ByVal xValue As Integer)
80      mX = xValue
81  End Property
82
83  Public Property Get X() As Integer
84      X = mX
85  End Property
86
```

**Fig. 16.11**   Polymorphic processing of shapes (part 4 of 9).

```
87   Public Property Let Y(ByVal yValue As Integer)
88      mY = yValue
89   End Property
90
91   Public Property Get Y() As Integer
92      Y = mY
93   End Property
94
95   Public Property Let Radius(ByVal radiusValue As Double)
96      mRadius = radiusValue
97   End Property
98
99   Public Property Get Radius() As Double
100     Radius = mRadius
101  End Property
```

**Fig. 16.11**   Polymorphic processing of shapes (part 5 of 9).

```
102  ' CCylinder class definition
103  Option Explicit
104  Implements IShape2
105
106  Private mX As Integer
107  Private mY As Integer
108  Private mRadius As Double
109  Private mHeight As Double
110
111  Private Function IShape2_Volume() As Double
112     IShape2_Volume = 3.14159 * mRadius ^ 2 * mHeight
113  End Function
114
115  Private Function IShape2_Area() As Double
116     IShape2_Area = 2 * 3.14159 * mRadius ^ 2 + 2 * 3.14159 * _
117                    mRadius * mHeight
118  End Function
119
120  Private Function IShape2_Name() As String
121     IShape2_Name = "Cylinder"
122  End Function
123
124  Private Function IShape2_ToString() As String
125     IShape2_ToString = "[" & mX & ", " & mY & "], " & _
126                        "Radius: " & mRadius & ", Height: " & _
127                        mHeight
128  End Function
129
130  Public Property Let X(ByVal xValue As Integer)
131     mX = xValue
132  End Property
133
```

**Fig. 16.11**   Polymorphic processing of shapes (part 6 of 9).

```
134  Public Property Get X() As Integer
135      X = mX
136  End Property
137
138  Public Property Let Y(ByVal yValue As Integer)
139      mY = yValue
140  End Property
141
142  Public Property Get Y() As Integer
143      Y = mY
144  End Property
145
146  Public Property Let Radius(ByVal radiusValue As Double)
147      mRadius = radiusValue
148  End Property
149
150  Public Property Get Radius() As Double
151      Radius = mRadius
152  End Property
153
154  Public Property Let Height(ByVal h As Double)
155      mHeight = h
156  End Property
157
158  Public Property Get Height() As Double
159      Height = mHeight
160  End Property
```

**Fig. 16.11**   Polymorphic processing of shapes (part 7 of 9).

```
161  ' Form module that exercises IShape2, CPoint,
162  ' CCircle and CCylinder
163  Option Explicit
164  Option Base 1
165
166  Private Sub Form_Load()
167      Dim k As Integer, shapes(3) As IShape2
168      Dim p As New CPoint, c As New CCircle
169      Dim cy As New CCylinder
170
171      p.X = 333        ' Set X via Property Let
172      p.Y = 444        ' Set Y via Property Let
173
174      c.Radius = 10    ' Set Radius via Property Let
175      c.X = 55         ' Set X via Property Let
176      c.Y = 9          ' Set Y via Property Let
177
178      cy.Radius = 2    ' Set Radius via Property Let
179      cy.Height = 6    ' Set Height via Property Let
180      cy.X = 20        ' Set X via Property Let
181      cy.Y = 88        ' Set Y via Property Let
182
```

**Fig. 16.11**   Polymorphic processing of shapes (part 8 of 9).

```
183   Set shapes(1) = p      ' Create a CPoint
184   Set shapes(2) = c      ' Create a CCircle
185   Set shapes(3) = cy     ' Create a Cylinder
186
187   For k = LBound(shapes) To UBound(shapes)
188      Print shapes(k).Name() & " Area: " & _
189            shapes(k).Area() & " Volume: " & _
190            shapes(k).Volume() & " Attributes: " & _
191            shapes(k).ToString()
192   Next k
193
194 End Sub
```

```
Polymorphism Example                                           _ □ ×
Point Area: 0 Volume: 0 Attributes: [333, 444]
Circle Area: 314.159 Volume: 0 Attributes: [55, 9], Radius: 10
Cylinder Area: 100.53088 Volume: 75.39816 Attributes: [20, 88], Radius: 2, Height: 6
```

**Fig. 16.11**   Polymorphic processing of shapes (part 9 of 9).

The **Form_Load** event procedure declares array shapes to be a three-element array of **IShape2** references. **CPoint** object **p**, **CCircle** object **c** and **CCylinder** object **cy** are instantiated. Properties are assigned to **p**, **c** and **cy**. Each element of **shapes** is assigned an object with the statements

```
Set shapes(1) = p
Set shapes(2) = c
Set shapes(3) = cy
```

Then a **For** statement is used to call the **Name**, **Area**, **Volume** and **ToString** methods for each **shapes** element.

## 16.15 Simulating Implementation Inheritance with Interface Inheritance and Delegation

Implementation inheritance can be simulated in Visual Basic by combining interface inheritance with composition. The superclass (i.e., the class being implemented) contains the appropriate combination of "shell" methods (i.e., methods with empty bodies) and "implemented" methods (i.e., methods with code in their bodies). The subclass **Implements** the superclass—and inherits the superclass's interface. The subclass instantiates a **Private** superclass object using **New**.

The subclass must implement all superclass methods. The superclass "shell" methods are implemented in the same manner as discussed earlier in the chapter. Superclass "implemented" method code is still not inherited—but the interface is. The subclass provides implementation by *delegating* responsibility to the **Private** superclass object for implementation. This means that the superclass methods that contain implementation can be executed using the **Private** superclass object.

*Software Engineering Observation 16.17*

*Implementation inheritance is valuable because it saves code. Common functionality placed at the top of the hierarchy is available to all subclasses. Only one copy of the functionality need be maintained, modified and updated.*

*Software Engineering Observation 16.18*

*A disadvantage of using interface inheritance and delegation is that the subclass must know the superclass implementation.*

The program of Fig. 16.12 redesigns the **IEmployee** example of Fig. 16.10 to use interface inheritance and delegation. The program consists of one superclass named **IEmployee2**, a subclass named **CBoss2**, a subclass named **CCommissionWorker2** and a form module which exercises the classes.

Class **IEmployee2** contains two **Private String** instance variables **mFirst-Name** and **mLastName** for storing the employee's name. **IEmployee2** provides "shell" methods **Earnings** and **ToString** and "implemented" **Property** methods to **Get** and **Let mFirstName** and **mLastName**. All method implementation must be provided by the subclass that **Implements** this interface (i.e., class).

```
1    ' Fig. 16.12
2    ' Interface IEmployee2 definition
3    Option Explicit
4    Private mFirstName As String, mLastName As String
5
6    Public Function Earnings() As Double
7        ' Empty
8    End Function
9
10   Public Function ToString() As String
11       ' Empty
12   End Function
13
14   Public Property Let FirstName(ByVal fName As String)
15       mFirstName = fName
16   End Property
17
18   Public Property Get FirstName() As String
19       FirstName = mFirstName
20   End Property
21
22   Public Property Let LastName(ByVal name As String)
23       mLastName = name
24   End Property
25
26   Public Property Get LastName() As String
27       LastName = mLastName
28   End Property
```

**Fig. 16.12**   Interface inheritance and delegation example (part 1 of 6).

```
29   ' CBoss2 definition
30   Option Explicit
31
32   Implements IEmployee2
33   Private mEmployee As IEmployee2
34   Private mWeeklySalary As Currency
35
36   Private Sub Class_Initialize()
37      Set mEmployee = New IEmployee2
38   End Sub
39
40   Public Property Let WeeklySalary(ByVal w As Currency)
41      mWeeklySalary = IIf(w > 0, w, 0)
42   End Property
43
44   Public Property Get WeeklySalary() As Currency
45      WeeklySalary = mWeeklySalary
46   End Property
47
48   Private Function IEmployee2_Earnings() As Double
49      IEmployee2_Earnings = mWeeklySalary
50   End Function
51
52   Private Property Let IEmployee2_FirstName(ByVal fName _
53                                          As String)
54      mEmployee.FirstName = fName
55   End Property
56
57   Private Property Get IEmployee2_FirstName() As String
58      IEmployee2_FirstName = mEmployee.FirstName
59   End Property
60
61   Private Property Let IEmployee2_LastName(ByVal name As String)
62      mEmployee.LastName = name
63   End Property
64
65   Private Property Get IEmployee2_LastName() As String
66      IEmployee2_LastName = mEmployee.LastName
67   End Property
68
69   Private Function IEmployee2_ToString() As String
70      IEmployee2_ToString = "Boss: " & mEmployee.FirstName & " " & _
71                            mEmployee.LastName
72   End Function
73
74   Private Sub Class_Terminate()
75      Set mEmployee = Nothing
76   End Sub
```

**Fig. 16.12**  Interface inheritance and delegation example (part 2 of 6).

Class **CBoss2 Implements IEmployee2** and also declares a **Private IEmployee2** reference called **mEmployee** (instantiated in **Class_Initialize**). When an **IEmployee2** object is instantiated, it contains the full implementation for the class. The class also contains implementation related to the boss's **mWeeklySalary**. Class **CBoss2** must implement every **IEmployee2** method. **IEmployee2** "shell" methods **Earnings** and **ToString** are implemented to calculate the boss specific information.

```
77   ' CCommissionWorker2 definition
78   Option Explicit
79
80   Implements IEmployee2
81   Private mEmployee As IEmployee2
82   Private mSalary As Currency
83   Private mCommission As Currency
84   Private mQuantity As Long
85
86   Private Sub Class_Initialize()
87      Set mEmployee = New IEmployee2
88   End Sub
89
90   Public Property Let Salary(ByVal w As Currency)
91      mSalary = IIf(w > 0, w, 0)
92   End Property
93
94   Public Property Get Salary() As Currency
95      Salary = mSalary
96   End Property
97
98   Public Property Let Commission(ByVal c As Currency)
99      mCommission = IIf(c > 0, c, 0)
100  End Property
101
102  Public Property Get Commission() As Currency
103     Commission = mCommission
104  End Property
105
106  Public Property Let Quantity(ByVal q As Long)
107     mQuantity = IIf(q > 0, q, 0)
108  End Property
109
110  Public Property Get Quantity() As Long
111     Quantity = mQuantity
112  End Property
113
114  Private Function IEmployee2_Earnings() As Double
115     IEmployee2_Earnings = mSalary + mCommission * mQuantity
116  End Function
117
118  Private Function IEmployee2_ToString() As String
119     IEmployee2_ToString = "Commission worker: " & _
120                           mEmployee.FirstName & _
121                           " " & mEmployee.LastName
122  End Function
```

**Fig. 16.12**    Interface inheritance and delegation example (part 3 of 6).

```
123
124  Private Property Let IEmployee2_FirstName(ByVal fName _
125                                          As String)
126     mEmployee.FirstName = fName
127  End Property
128
129  Private Property Get IEmployee2_FirstName() As String
130     IEmployee2_FirstName = mEmployee.FirstName
131  End Property
132
133  Private Property Let IEmployee2_LastName(ByVal name As String)
134     mEmployee.LastName = name
135  End Property
136
137  Private Property Get IEmployee2_LastName() As String
138     IEmployee2_LastName = mEmployee.LastName
139  End Property
140
141  Private Sub Class_Terminate()
142     Set mEmployee = Nothing
143  End Sub
```

**Fig. 16.12**  Interface inheritance and delegation example (part 4 of 6).

```
144  ' Form module to exercise IEmployee2,
145  ' CBoss2 and CComissionWorker2
146  Option Explicit
147
148  Private mEmployeeRef As IEmployee2
149  Private mBoss As New CBoss2
150  Private mCommissionWorker As New CCommissionWorker2
151
152  Private Sub Form_Load()
153     Set mEmployeeRef = mBoss
154
155     mEmployeeRef.FirstName = "John"
156     mEmployeeRef.LastName = "Smith"
157     mBoss.WeeklySalary = 800
158
159     Call Display(mBoss)
160
161     Set mEmployeeRef = mCommissionWorker
162
163     With mCommissionWorker
164        .Commission = 3
165        .Salary = 400
166        .Quantity = 150
167     End With
168
169     mEmployeeRef.FirstName = "Sue"
170     mEmployeeRef.LastName = "Jones"
171
```

**Fig. 16.12**  Interface inheritance and delegation example (part 5 of 6).

```
172      Call Display(mCommissionWorker)
173   End Sub
174
175   Private Sub Display(e As IEmployee2)
176
177      If (TypeOf e Is CBoss2) Then
178         Print "Type CBoss2"
179      ElseIf (TypeOf e Is CCommissionWorker2) Then
180         Print "Type CCommissionWorker2"
181      End If
182
183      Print e.ToString & " earned " & FormatCurrency(e.Earnings)
184      Print
185   End Sub
186
187   Private Sub Form_Terminate()
188      Set mBoss = Nothing
189      Set mCommissionWorker = Nothing
190      Set mEmployeeRef = Nothing
191   End Sub
```

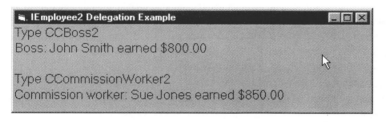

**Fig. 16.12**    Interface inheritance and delegation example (part 6 of 6).

**CBoss2 IEmployee2** "implemented" methods get their implementation from the **IEmployee2** object **mEmployee** (i.e., delegation). Consider the **CBoss2 Get IEmployee2_FirstName** method

```
Private Property Get IEmployee2_FirstName() As String
   IEmployee2_FirstName = mEmployee.FirstName
End Property
```

which simply returns the value of **mEmployee**'s **FirstName**. The other **IEmployee2 Property** methods are implemented in the same manner.

Class **CCommissionWorker2** is structured like **CBoss2** in that it **Implements IEmployee2** and creates **IEmployee2** object **mEmployee**. Delegation is used to **Get** and **Let IEmployee2** properties **FirstName** and **LastName**.

The form module creates **IEmployee2** reference **mEmployeeRef**, **CBoss2** object **mBoss** and **CCommissionWorker2** object **mCommissionWorker**. Reference **mEmployeeRef** (when **Set** to **mBoss**) sets **mBoss**'s **FirstName** and **LastName** and **mEmployeeRef** (when **Set** to **mCommissionWorker**) sets **mCommissionWorker**'s **FirstName** and **LastName**.

Programmer-defined procedure **Display** prints the class name, calls the method **ToString** and method **Earnings**. The procedure receives one **IEmployee2** object and assigns a reference **e** to it. Keyword **_TypeOf_** and operator **_Is_** are used to determine the type of object (e.g., **CBoss2** or **CCommissionWorker2**) that **e** references.

When an object (e.g., **mBoss**) is assigned to a specific reference type (e.g., **IEmployee2**), the Visual Basic compiler is able to check the validity of the assignment. If the assignment is not a proper one—a compiler error occurs. When a valid assignment occurs, the compiler is able to associate the reference with the object—a process called _early binding_. If a reference is declared **_As Object_**, it can hold a reference to any object type. The validity of **Object** references are resolved at run-time—a process called _dynamic binding_ (also called _late binding_).

**Performance Tip 16.2**

_Dynamic binding is much slower than early binding._

## 16.16 Object Browser

_Type libraries_ enable Visual Basic programmers to keep track of the many classes they use while developing programs. Type libraries describe the details of the classes including their methods, events and properties. Programmers use the **_Object Browser_** (Fig. 16.13) to determine what classes are available and what their members are. The **Object Browser** is displayed when **Object Browser** is selected from the **View** menu.

The **_Project/Library_ ComboBox** in the **Object Browser** window lets you choose the project or library to browse. You may select an individual project or library, or you may browse all available projects and libraries.

When a class name in the **_Classes_ ListBox** is clicked, information about that class appears in the description pane at the bottom of the **Object Browser** window and that class's members are displayed in the **_Members_ ListBox**. The displayed members include properties, events, methods and constants. Clicking a member in the **Members ListBox** displays that member's arguments and return values in the description pane.

If you want to view your code, just select your project in the **Project/Library ComboBox** and double-click the name of the module, class or member.

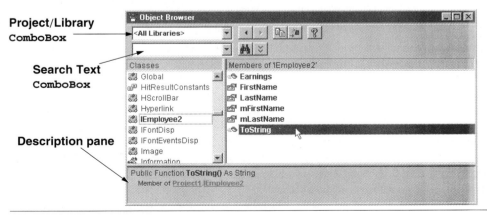

**Fig. 16.13   Object Browser.**

To locate classes and members, enter text in the **Search ComboBox** and press *Enter* [or the ***Search*** button (i.e., the button with binoculars on it)]. Results of the search are listed in the **Search Results Frame**. Clicking an item in the **Search Results Frame**, displays that item's description in the pane at the bottom of the **Object Browser** window. Figure 16.14 shows the results of a search operation.

## 16.17  Events and Classes

Classes can raise events declared in the class. The capability to raise events provides an object with a means of notifying other objects that something happened. Statement ***RaiseEvent*** is used to raise an event; This is also called *triggering an event* or *firing an event*.

An event is declared in the class's general declaration using keyword ***Event***. **Event**s must be declared **Public** (the default if **Event**s are not preceded by an access specifier). **Event** parameters allow the **Event** to pass data to and receive data from the program.

**Common Programming Error 16.8**

*Attempting to declare an **Event** as **Private** is a syntax error.*

Figure 16.15 creates a class called **CEvent** that raises an event. A form module is used to exercise class **CEvent**. Line 6

```
Public Event EventName(s As String, n As Long)
```

declares **Event EventName** with a **String** parameter and a **Long** parameter. The class also defines method **RaisesAnEvent** that simply increments the **Long** instance variable **mNumber** by **1** and raises **EventName** with the statement

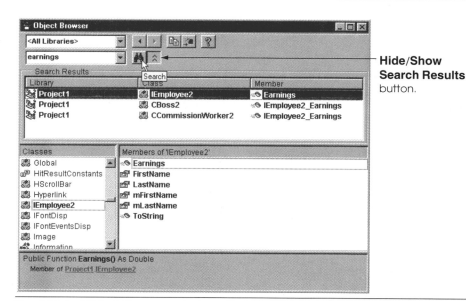

**Fig. 16.14   Object Browser** window displaying the results of a search operation.

```
1   ' Fig. 16.15
2   ' Class that raises an event
3   Option Explicit
4
5   Private mNumber As Long
6   Public Event EventName(s As String, n As Long)
7
8   Public Sub RaisesAnEvent()
9      mNumber = mNumber + 1
10
11     ' Raise the event
12     RaiseEvent EventName("Visual Basic 6 How To Program!", _
13                           mNumber)
14  End Sub
```

**Fig. 16.15**   Demonstrating a class that raises an **Event** (part 2 of 2).

```
15  ' Form module to test CEvent class
16  Option Explicit
17  Private WithEvents mEventRaiser As CEvent
18
19  Private Sub Form_Initialize()
20     Set mEventRaiser = New CEvent
21  End Sub
22
23  Private Sub Form_Load()
24     Dim x As Integer
25
26     For x = 1 To 5
27        Call mEventRaiser.RaisesAnEvent
28     Next x
29
30  End Sub
31
32  Private Sub mEventRaiser_EventName(s As String, n As Long)
33     Print s & " #" & n
34  End Sub
35
36  Private Sub Form_Terminate()
37     Set mEventRaiser = Nothing
38  End Sub
```

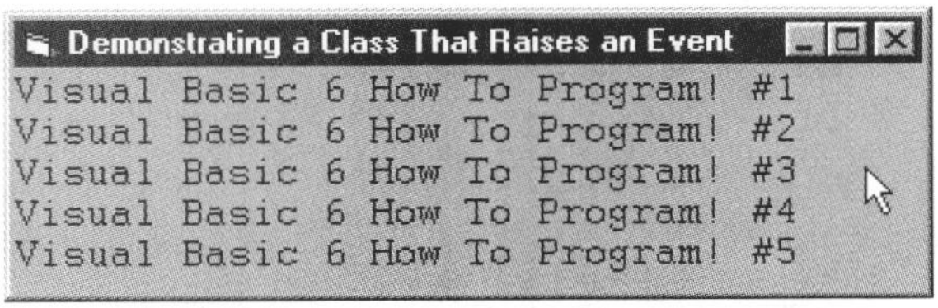

**Fig. 16.15**   Demonstrating a class that raises an **Event** (part 2 of 2).

```
RaiseEvent EventName("Visual Basic 6 How To Program!", _
                     mNumber)
```

The **String** "**Visual Basic 6 How To Program!**" and **mNumber**'s value are used as **EventName**'s parameters. Method **RaisesAnEvent** must be executed for **Event-Name** to be raised.

Line 17

```
Private WithEvents mEventRaiser As CEvent
```

creates a reference to **CEvent** called **mEventRaiser**. Keyword *WithEvents* indicates that this class type has **Event**s associated with it.

 *Common Programming Error 16.9*

*Attempting to use* **WithEvents** *and* **New** *together is a syntax error.*

Line 27

```
Call mEventRaiser.RaisesAnEvent
```

**Call**s **RaisesAnEvent**—which raises **Event EventName**. The form class provides event procedure **mEventRaiser_EventName** to handle the **EventName Event** when it is raised. Event procedure **EventName** appears in the **Code** window's **Procedure Com-boBox** when **mEventRaiser** is selected in the **Procedure ComboBox**.

## Summary

- Objects encapsulate data (attributes) and methods (behaviors) and have the property of information hiding. This means that although objects may communicate with one another, objects do not know how other objects are implemented—implementation details are hidden within the objects.

- In Visual Basic, the unit of object-oriented programming is the class from which objects are instantiated (i.e., created). Methods are Visual Basic procedures that are encapsulated with the data they process within the "walls" of classes.

- Visual Basic programmers can create their own user-defined types called classes. Classes are also referred to as programmer-defined types. Each class contains data as well as the set of methods which manipulate that data. The data components of a class are called instance variables.

- An instance of a user-defined type (i.e., a class) is called an object. The focus of attention in object-oriented programming with Visual Basic is on classes rather than methods.

- Software is then constructed by combining new classes with existing, well-defined, carefully tested, well-documented, portable, widely available components. This kind of software reusability speeds the development of powerful, high-quality software. Rapid applications development (RAD) is of great interest today. Visual Basic is the world's premier RAD language.

- Object-oriented programming requires three technologies—encapsulation, inheritance and polymorphism. Visual Basic does not allow inheritance in the sense that C++ and Java do, but it does provide encapsulation and polymorphism. Visual Basic does enable programmers to realize many of the benefits of inheritance through the use of interfaces and a technique called delegation.

- Classes can be made data aware so that their objects can be bound to databases. A class may be a source of data or a consumer of data. Classes normally hide their implementation details from the clients (i.e., users) of the classes. This is called information hiding.

- An abstract data type actually captures two notions, a data representation of the ADT and the operations allowed on the data of the ADT.

- To add a class module to the project select **Add Class Module** from the **Project** menu which displays the **Add Class Module** dialog.

- **New** is used to create an object. Once created, an object's **Public** methods can be invoked.

- Once the class has been defined, it can be used as a type in a declaration. The client can place these declarations wherever declarations are permitted. The class name is a new type specifier. The programmer can create new class types as needed; thus, Visual Basic is an extensible language.

- Instance variables may be either **Public** or **Private**. The **Public** and **Private** keywords are called member access specifiers. **Public** instance variables and **Public** methods are accessible to every module within the project. **Private** instance variables can be manipulated only by methods of the class.

- Classes often provide **Property** methods to allow clients of the class to set (i.e., assign values to) or get (i.e., obtain the values of) **Private** instance variables. Any **Property Get**, **Property Let**, or **Property Set** method may contain the **Exit Property** statement. When executed, **Exit Property** causes an immediate exit from a **Property** procedure.

- Forming new classes by including objects of existing classes as members is called composition.

- A reference is a name that either refers to **Nothing** or refers to an object. **Nothing** simply means a reference does not refer to an object.

- Event procedure **Class_Terminate** is used to "clean up" an object before the object is destroyed. The **Terminate** event is raised when an object's reference goes out of scope and when the last reference referring to an object is **Set** to a different object or **Set** to **Nothing**.

- Inheritance is a form of software reusability in which new classes are created from existing classes by absorbing their attributes and behaviors and embellishing these with capabilities the new classes require. Polymorphism enables us to write programs in a general fashion to handle a wide variety of existing and yet-to-be-specified related classes. Polymorphism makes it easy to add new capabilities to a system.

- With single inheritance, a class is derived from one superclass. Visual Basic does not support implementation inheritance (either single or multiple) but it does support the notion of interface inheritance (both single and multiple). Multiple interfaces help Visual Basic achieve many of the advantages of multiple inheritance.

- A subclass normally adds instance variables and instance methods of its own, so a subclass is generally larger than its superclass. With single inheritance, the subclass starts out essentially the same as the superclass. The real strength of inheritance comes from the ability to define in the subclass additions to, or replacements for, the features inherited from the superclass.

- Every object of a subclass may also be thought of as an object of that subclass's superclass. Superclass objects are not objects of that superclass's subclasses. Programmers take advantage of this "subclass-object-is-a-superclass-object" relationship to perform some powerful manipulations.

- In an "is a" inheritance relationship, an object of a subclass type may also be treated as an object of the superclass type. In a "has a" composition relationship, a class object has references to objects of other classes as members.

- Inheritance relationships form tree-like hierarchical structures. A superclass exists in a hierarchical relationship with its subclasses. A class can exist by itself, but it is when a class is used with inheritance that the class becomes either a superclass that supplies attributes and behaviors to other classes, or the class becomes a subclass that inherits those attributes and behaviors.

- It is possible to treat superclass objects and subclass objects similarly; that commonality is expressed in the attributes and behaviors of the superclass. Objects of all classes derived from a common superclass can all be treated as objects of that superclass.

- Polymorphic programming can eliminate the need for **Select Case** logic. The programmer can use Visual Basic's polymorphism mechanism to perform the equivalent logic automatically, thus avoiding the kinds of errors typically associated with **Select Case** logic.

- With polymorphism, it is possible to design and implement systems that are more easily extensible. Programs can be written to process generically—as superclass objects—objects of all existing classes in a hierarchy. Classes that do not exist during program development can be added with little or no modifications to the generic part of the program—as long as each of those classes "implements the appropriate interfaces." The only parts of a program that need modification are those parts that require direct knowledge of the particular class that is added to the hierarchy.

- Visual Basic supports interface inheritance (i.e., the ability to inherit the **Public** interface but not the implementation of a class). The sole purpose of an interface is to provide an appropriate superclass from which other classes may inherit interface. Any class can serve as an interface for another class. An interface class is created in the same manner as any other class. The **Public** interface usually does not contain any implementation (i.e., the bodies of **Public** methods do not contain any code). Keyword **Implements** is used to implement the interface in another class.

- Interfaces have the **.cls** extension. The class implementing the interface has the responsibility of providing implementation.

- Implementation inheritance can be simulated in Visual Basic by combining interface inheritance with composition. The superclass (i.e., the class being implemented) contains the appropriate combination of "shell" methods (i.e., methods with empty bodies) and "implemented" methods (i.e., methods with code in their bodies). The subclass **Implements** the superclass—and inherits the superclass's interface. The subclass instantiates a **Private** superclass object using **New**.

- Keyword **TypeOf** and operator **Is** are used to determine the type of object a reference refers to.

- When an object is assigned to a specific reference type, the Visual Basic compiler is able to check the validity of the assignment. When a valid assignment occurs, the compiler is able to associate the reference with the object—a process called early binding. If a reference is declared **As Object**, it can hold a reference to any object type. The validity of **Object** references are resolved at run-time—a process called dynamic binding (also called late binding).

- Type libraries enable the Visual Basic programmers to keep track of the many classes they use while developing programs. Type libraries describe the details of the classes including their methods, events, properties others. Programmers use the **Object Browser** to determine what classes are available and what their members are.

- Classes can raise events declared within the class. Statement **RaiseEvent** is used to raise an event; This is also called triggering an event or firing an event.

- An event is declared in the class's general declaration using keyword **Event**. **Event**s must be declared **Public**. If not preceded by an access specifier, **Event**s default to **Public**. **Event** parameters allow the **Event** to pass data to and receive data from the program.

- Keyword **WithEvents** indicates that this class type has **Event**s associated with it.

## *Terminology*

| | |
|---|---|
| **.cls** filename extension for class module | class |
| abstract data type (ADT) | class hierarchy |
| accessor methods | **Class_Initialize** event procedure |
| **Add Class Module** in **Project** menu | class library |
| aggregation | class module |
| attribute | **Class_Terminate** event procedure |
| behavior | class variable |

client of a class

COM (Component Object Model)

COM interface

component-oriented software construction

composition

containment ("has-a")

control

data member

DCOM (Distributed Component Object Model)

delegation

dot operator

dynamic binding

encapsulation

**End Property**

**Event**

event procedure

**Exit Property**

extensible language

fire an event

"has-a" relationship

hierarchical relationship

implement an interface

implementation hiding

implementation inheritance

implementation of a class

**Implements** an interface

information hiding

inheritance

inheritance hierarchy

initialize a class object

**Initialize** event procedure

instance variable

instantiate an object of a class

interface

interface inheritance

"is-a" relationship

**Is** operator

late binding

**Let** keyword (to assign a value to a property)

message

multiple inheritance

multiple interfaces

mutator method

**New** keyword

**Nothing** keyword

object

**Object** type

**Object Browser**

object-oriented programming (OOP)

object reference

object variable

override a method

persistence

polymorphism

**Private** keyword

programmer-defined type

property

**Property Get** procedure

**Property Let** procedure

**Property Set** procedure

**Public** keyword

**RaiseEvent** statement

rapid applications development (RAD)

reference to an object

reusable classes

services of a class

**Set** a property (to assign an object property)

*set* method

single inheritance

specialization

standardized software components

subclass

superclass

**Terminate** event procedure

trigger an event

type libraries

**TypeOf** keyword

"uses-a" relationship

utility method

verbs (implemented as methods)

**WithEvents** keyword

## Common Programming Errors

**16.1**    Attempting to declare a **Public Const** instance variable is a syntax error. **Const** instance variables must be **Private**.

**16.2**    An attempt by a method which is not a member of a particular class to access a **Private** member of that class is a syntax error.

**16.3**    Attempting to call a method or access a property for a reference that does not refer to an object (i.e., that refers to **Nothing**) is a run-time error.

**16.4**    Attempting to assign a reference a value (outside a declaration) without using **Set** is a syntax error.

**16.5**    Method **Class_Initialize** can call other methods of the class, such as **Property Let** or **Property Get** methods, but because **Class_Initialize** is initializing the object, the instance variables may not yet be in a consistent state. Using instance variables before they have been properly initialized can lead to logic errors.

**16.6**    Not implementing an inherited method is a syntax error.

**16.7**    Attempting to assign to a reference an object that does not implement the reference's type is a run-time error.

**16.8**    Attempting to declare an **Event** as **Private** is a syntax error.

**16.9**    Attempting to use **WithEvents** and **New** together is a syntax error.

## Good Programming Practices

**16.1**    Include **Option Explicit** statement in each class to force all variables to be declared explicitly.

**16.2**    Begin each class **Name** with the uppercase letter "**C**" to indicate clearly that it is a class name.

**16.3**    Every instance variable or method definition should be explicitly preceded by **Public** or **Private**.

**16.4**    Group **Public** members and group **Private** members in a class definition for clarity and readability.

**16.5**    Despite the fact that **Private** and **Public** members may be repeated and intermixed, list all the **Private** members of a class first in one group and then list all the **Public** members in another group.

**16.6**    Always explicitly set a reference to **Nothing** before assigning it to another object.

**16.7**    Begin each interface **Name** with the uppercase letter "**I**" to indicate clearly that it is an interface class.

## Performance Tip

**16.1**    If classes produced through inheritance are larger than they need to be, memory and processing resources may be wasted. Inherit from the class "closest" to what you need.

**16.2**    Dynamic binding is much slower than early binding.

## Software Engineering Observations

**16.1**    It is important to write programs that are understandable and easy to maintain. Change is the rule rather than the exception. Programmers should anticipate that their code will be modified. As we will see, using classes improves program modifiability.

**16.2**    The programmer creates new types through the class mechanism. These new types may be designed to be used as conveniently as built-in types. Thus, Visual Basic is an extensible language. Although it is easy to extend the language with these new types, the base language itself cannot be modified.

**16.3**    Information hiding can greatly simplify the client's perception of a class.

**16.4**    Clients of a class can (and should) use the class without knowing the internal details of how the class is implemented. If the class implementation is changed (to improve performance, for example), provided the class's interface remains constant, the class clients' source code need not change. This makes it much easier to modify systems.

**16.5**    Using an object-oriented programming approach can often simplify method calls by reducing the number of arguments to be passed. This benefit of object-oriented programming derives from the fact that encapsulation of instance variables and methods within an object gives the methods the right to access the instance variables.

**16.6**    The class designer need not provide set and/or get methods for each **Private** data member; these capabilities should be provided only when it makes sense and after careful thought by the class designer.

**16.7**    **Property Get** procedures can control the appearance of data, possibly hiding implementation details.

**16.8**    To implement a read-only property simply provide a **Property Get** procedure but no **Property Set** procedure and no **Property Let** procedure.

**16.9**    The benefits of data integrity are not automatic simply because instance variables are made **Private**. Methods that set the values of **Private** data should verify that the intended new values are proper; if they are not, the set methods should place the **Private** instance variables into an appropriate consistent state.

**16.10**    Every method that modifies the **Private** instance variables of an object should ensure that the data remains in a consistent state.

**16.11**    One form of software reuse is composition (also called containment or aggregation) in which a class has references to objects of other classes as members.

**16.12**    Creating a subclass does not affect its superclass's source code; the integrity of a superclass is preserved by inheritance.

**16.13**    Just as the designer of non-object-oriented systems should avoid unnecessary proliferation of functions, the designer of object-oriented systems should avoid unnecessary proliferation of classes. Proliferating classes creates management problems and can hinder software reusability simply because it is more difficult for a potential reuser of a class to locate that class in a huge collection. The trade-off is to create fewer classes, each providing substantial additional functionality, but such classes might be too rich for certain reusers.

**16.14**    With interfaces, implementation is never inherited—even if the interface actually provides implementation.

**16.15**    With polymorphism, the programmer can deal in generalities and let the execution-time environment concern itself with the specifics. The programmer can command a wide variety of objects to behave in manners appropriate to those objects without even knowing the types of those objects.

**16.16**    Polymorphism promotes extensibility: Software written to invoke polymorphic behavior is written independent of the types of the objects to which messages (i.e., method calls) are sent. Thus, new types of objects that respond to existing messages can be added into such a system without modifying the base system.

**16.17**    Implementation inheritance is valuable because it saves code. Common functionality placed at the top of the hierarchy is available to all subclasses. Only one copy of the functionality need be maintained, modified and updated.

**16.18**    A disadvantage of using interface inheritance and delegation is that the subclass must know the superclass implementation.

### Testing and Debugging Tips

**16.1**    Using **Public** data is uncommon and is a dangerous programming practice.

**16.2**    Using an object-oriented programming approach reduces the likelihood of passing the wrong arguments, the wrong types of arguments and/or the wrong number of arguments, as often happens with procedural programming languages.

**16.3**    Making the instance variables of a class **Private** and the methods of the class **Public** facilitates debugging because problems with data manipulations are localized to the class's methods.

**16.4**    **Property** procedures should scrutinize every attempt to set the object's data and should reject invalid data to ensure that the object's data remains in a consistent state. This eliminates large numbers of bugs that have plagued systems development efforts.

**16.5** An interesting consequence of using polymorphism is that programs take on a simplified appearance. They contain less branching logic in favor of simpler sequential code. This simplification facilitates testing, debugging and program maintenance.

## Self-Review Exercises

**16.1** Fill in the blanks in each of the following:
  a) Class members are accessed via the _____ operator in conjunction with an object of the class.
  b) Members of a class specified as _____ are accessible only to methods of the class.
  c) Method _____ is a special method used to initialize the instance variables of a class.
  d) A _____ method is used to assign values to **Private** instance variables of a class.
  e) Methods of a class are normally made **Public** and instance variables of a class are normally made _____.
  f) A _____ method is used to retrieve values of **Private** data of a class.
  g) Members of a class specified as _____ are accessible anywhere an object of the class is in scope.
  h) Keyword _____ dynamically instantiates an object of a specified type.

**16.2** Fill in the blanks in each of the following:
  a) If the class **CAlpha** inherits from the class **CBeta**, class **CAlpha** is called the _____ class and class **CBeta** is called the _____ class.
  b) Inheritance enables _____ which saves time in development and encourages using previously proven and high-quality software components.
  c) An object of a _____ class can be treated as an object of its corresponding _____ class.
  d) A "has a" relationship between classes represents _____ and an "is a" relationship between classes represents _____.
  e) Using polymorphism helps eliminate _____ logic.

## Answers to Self-Review Exercises

**16.1** a) dot ( . ). b) **Private**. c) **Class_Initialize**. d) set (i.e., **Property Let** or **Property Set**). e) **Private**. f) *get* (or **Property Get**). g) **Public**. h) **New**.

**16.2** a) sub, super. b) software reusability. c) sub, super. d) composition, inheritance. e) **Select Case**.

## Exercises

**16.3** Consider the class **CBicycle**. Given your knowledge of some common components of bicycles, show a class hierarchy in which the class **CBicycle** inherits from other classes, which, in turn, inherit from yet other classes. Discuss the instantiation of various objects of class **CBicycle**. Discuss inheritance from class **CBicycle** for other closely related subclasses.

**16.4** Define each of the following terms: class, **Implements**, interface, superclass and subclass.

**16.5** Distinguish between single inheritance and multiple inheritance. What feature of Visual Basic helps realize the benefits of multiple inheritance?

**16.6** (True/False) A subclass is generally smaller than its superclass.

**16.7** (True/False) A subclass object is also an object of that subclass's superclass.

**16.8** How is it that polymorphism enables you to program "in the general" rather than "in the specific." Discuss the key advantages of programming "in the general."

**16.9**     Discuss the problems of programming with **Select Case** logic. Why is polymorphism an effective alternative to using **Select Case** logic.

**16.10**     How does polymorphism promote extensibility?

**16.11**     You have been asked to develop a flight simulator that will have elaborate graphical outputs. Explain why polymorphic programming would be especially effective for a problem of this nature.

**16.12**     Study the inheritance hierarchy of Fig. 16.7. For each class, indicate some common attributes and behaviors consistent with the hierarchy. Add some other classes (i.e., **CUndergraduateStudent**, **CGraduateStudent**, **CFreshman**, **CSophomore**, **CJunior**, **CSenior**, etc., to enrich the hierarchy).

**16.13**     Write down all the automobile you can think of—both passenger and commercial—and form those shapes into a hierarchy. Your hierarchy should have superclass **IAutomobile** from which class **IPassenger** and class **ICommercial** are derived. Once you have developed the hierarchy, define each of the classes in the hierarchy.

**16.14**     Write an inheritance hierarchy for classes **IQuadrilateral**, **CTrapezoid**, **CParallelogram**, **CRectangle** and **CSquare**. Use **IQuadrilateral** as the superclass of the hierarchy. Make the hierarchy as deep (i.e., as many levels) as possible. Write a program that instantiates and uses objects of each of these classes.

**16.15**     Create a **CDate2** class that can output the date in multiple formats such as

```
MM/DD/YY
June 14, 1992
DDD YYYY
```

**16.16**     Create a class called **CComplex** for performing arithmetic with complex numbers. Write a program to test your class.

Complex numbers have the form

$$realPart + imaginaryPart \infty i$$

where *i* is

$$\sqrt{-1}$$

Use floating-point variables to represent the **Private** data of the class. Provide **Public** methods for each of the following:

a)   Addition of two **CComplex** numbers: The real parts are added together and the imaginary parts are added together.

b)   Subtraction of two **CComplex** numbers: The real part of the right operand is subtracted from the real part of the left operand and the imaginary part of the right operand is subtracted from the imaginary part of the left operand.

c)   Printing **CComplex** numbers in the form **(A, B)**, where **A** is the real part and **B** is the imaginary part.

**16.17**     Create a class called **CRational** for performing arithmetic with fractions. Write a program to test your class.

Use **Integer** variables to represent the **Private** instance variables of the class—**mNumerator** and **mDenominator**. The class should store the fraction in reduced form (i.e., the fraction

$$2/4$$

would be stored in the object as 1 in the **mNumerator** and 2 in the **mDenominator**). Provide **Public** methods for each of the following:

a)   Addition of two **CRational** numbers. The result is stored in reduced form.

b)   Subtraction of two **CRational** numbers. The result is stored in reduced form.

    c)  Multiplication of two **CRational** numbers. The result is stored in reduced form.

    d)  Division of two **CRational** numbers. The result is stored in reduced form.

    e)  Returning **CRational** numbers in the form **mNumerator/mDenominator** (i.e., a **String** with this format).

    f)  Returning **CRational** numbers in floating-point format. (Consider providing formatting capabilities that enable the user of the class to specify the number of digits of precision to the right of the decimal point.)

**16.18**    Modify class **CTime2** (Fig. 16.4) to include method **Tick** which increments the time stored in a **CTime2** object by one second. Name the new class **CTime3**. Also provide method **IncrementMinute** to increment **mMinute** and method **IncrementHour** to increment **mHour**. The **CTime3** object should always remain in a consistent state. Write a program that tests method **Tick**, method **IncrementMinute** and method **IncrementHour** to ensure that they work correctly. Be sure to test the following cases:

    a)  Incrementing into the next **mMinute**.

    b)  Incrementing into the next **mHour**.

    c)  Incrementing into the next day (i.e., 11:59:59 PM to 12:00:00 AM).

**16.19**    Modify class **CDate1** (Fig. 16.5) to perform error checking on the initializer values for instance variables **mMonth**, **mDay** and **mYear**. Name the new class **CDate2**. Also, provide a method **NextDay** to increment the day by one. The **CDate2** object should always remain in a consistent state. Write a program that tests method **NextDay** in a loop that prints the date during each iteration of the loop to illustrate that method **NextDay** works correctly. Be sure to test the following cases:

    a)  Incrementing into the next **mMonth**.

    b)  Incrementing into the next **mYear**.

**16.20**    Combine the **CTime3** class of Exercise 16.18 and the **CDate2** class of Exercise 16.19 into one class called **CDateAndTime**. Modify method **Tick** to call method **NextDay** if the time is incremented into the next **mDay**. Modify methods **ToStandardTime** and **ToUniversalTime** to output the date in addition to the time. Write a program to test the new class **CDateAndTime**. Specifically test incrementing the time to the next **mDay**.

**16.21**    Create a class **CRectangle** that has attributes **mLength** and **mWidth**, each of which defaults to 1. **CRectangle** has methods that calculate the rectangle's **Perimeter** and **Area**. It has *set* and *get* methods for both **mLength** and **mWidth**. The *set* methods should verify that **mLength** and **mWidth** are each numbers larger than 0.0 and less than 20.0.

**16.22**    Create a more sophisticated **CRectangle** class than the one you created in Exercise 16.21. This class stores only the Cartesian coordinates of the four corners of the rectangle. Verify that each set of coordinates is in the first quadrant with no single *x* or *y* coordinate larger than 20.0. Also verify that the supplied coordinates do, in fact, specify a rectangle. Methods calculate the **Length**, **Width**, **Perimeter** and **Area**. The length is the larger of the two dimensions. Include a predicate method **IsSquare** which determines if the rectangle is a square.

**16.23**    Create a class **CHugeInteger** which uses a 40-element array of digits to store **Integer**s as large as 40-digits each. Provide methods **InputHugeInteger**, **OutputHugeInteger**, **AddHugeIntegers** and **SubstractHugeIntegers**. For comparing **CHugeInteger** objects provide methods **IsEqualTo**, **IsNotEqualTo**, **IsGreaterThan**, **IsLessThan**, **IsGreaterThanOrEqualTo** and **IsLessThanOrEqualTo**—each of these is a "predicate" method that simply returns **True** if the relationship holds between the two **CHugeInteger**s and returns **False** if the relationship does not hold. Provide a predicate method **IsZero**. If you feel ambitious, also provide the method **MultiplyHugeIntegers**, the method **DivideHugeIntegers** and the method **ModulusHugeIntegers**.

**16.24**   Create class **CSavingsAccount**. Variable **mAnnualInterestRate** stores the interest rate for each of the savers. Each object of the class contains a **Private** instance variable **mSavingsBalance** indicating the amount the saver currently has on deposit. Provide method **CalculateMonthlyInterest** to calculate the monthly interest by multiplying **mBalance** by **mAnnualInterestRate** divided by 12; this interest should be added to **mSavingsBalance**. Provide method **ModifyInterestRate** that sets the **mAnnualInterestRate** to a new value.

Write a program to test class **CSavingsAccount**. Instantiate two different **CSavingsAccount** objects, **saver1** and **saver2**, with balances of $2000.00 and $3000.00, respectively. Set **mAnnualInterestRate** to 4%, then calculate the monthly interest and print the new balances for each of the savers. Then set the **mAnnualInterestRate** to 5% and calculate the next month's interest and print the new balances for each of the savers.

**16.25**   Create class **CIntegerSet**. Each object of the class can hold **Integer**s in the range 0 through 100. A set is represented internally as an array of ones and zeros. Array element **a(i)** is 1 if **Integer** *i* is in the set. Array element **a(j)** is 0 if **Integer** *j* is not in the set.

Provide the following methods: Method **UnionOfIntegerSets** creates a third set which is the set-theoretic union of two existing sets (i.e., an element of the third set's array is set to 1 if that element is 1 in either or both of the existing sets; otherwise, the element of the third set is set to 0). Method **IntersectionOfIntegerSets** creates a third set which is the set-theoretic intersection of two existing sets (i.e., an element of the third set's array is set to 0 if that element is 0 in either or both of the existing sets; otherwise, the element of the third set is set to 1). Method **InsertElement** inserts a new **Integer** *k* into a set (by setting **a(k)** to 1). Method **DeleteElement** deletes **Integer** *m* (by setting **a(m)** to 0). Method **ToString** returns a **String** containing a set as a list of numbers separated by spaces and prints only those elements that are present in the set or **---** for an empty set. Method **IsEqualTo** determines if two sets are equal. Write a program to test your **CIntegerSet** class. Instantiate several **CIntegerSet** objects. Test that all your methods work properly.

**16.26**   It would be perfectly reasonable for the **CTime1** class of Fig. 16.2 to represent the time internally as the number of seconds since midnight rather than the three **Integer** values **mHour**, **mMinute** and **mSecond**. Clients could use the same **Public** methods and get the same result. Modify class **CTime1** class to implement the time as the number of seconds since midnight and show that there is no visible change to the clients of the class. Name the new class **CTime4**.

**16.27**   Many programs written with inheritance could be solved with composition instead and vice versa. Discuss the relative merits of these approaches in the context of the **CPoint**, **CCircle**, **CCylinder** class hierarchy in this chapter. Rewrite the program of Fig. 16.11 (and the supporting classes) to use composition rather than inheritance. After you do this, reassess the relative merits of the two approaches both for the **CPoint**, **CCircle**, **CCylinder** problem and for object-oriented programs in general.

**16.28**   Rewrite the **CPoint**, **CCircle**, **CCylinder** program of Fig. 16.11 as a **CPoint**, **CSquare**, **CCube** program. Do this two ways—with inheritance and with composition.

**16.29**   Modify the payroll system of Fig. 16.10 to add **Private** instance variables **mBirthDate** (use class **CDate1** from Fig. 16.5) and **mDepartmentCode** (an **Integer**) to class **IEmployee** (name this new class **IEmployee3**) Assume this payroll is processed once per month. Then, as your program calculates the payroll for each **IEmployee3** (polymorphically), add a $100.00 bonus to the person's payroll amount if this is the month in which the **IEmployee3**'s birthday occurs.

**16.30**   Develop a basic graphics package. Use the **IShape** class inheritance hierarchy from Fig. 16.8. Limit yourself to two-dimensional shapes such as squares, rectangles, triangles and circles. Interact with the user. Let the user specify the position, size, shape and fill characters to be used in drawing each shape. The user can specify many items of the same shape. As you create each shape, place a **IShape** reference to each new **IShape** object into an array. Each class has its own **Draw** method. Write a polymorphic screen manager that walks through the array sending **Draw** messages to each object in the array to form a screen image. Redraw the screen image each time the user specifies an additional shape.

**16.31**   Create a class **CTicTacToe** that will enable you to write a complete program to play the game of tic-tac-toe. The class contains as **Private** data a 3-by-3 array of **Integer**s. The array stores 0 for an empty location, 1 for an X location and 2 for a O location. Allow two human players to play the game. Wherever the first player moves, place a 1 in the specified square; place a 2 wherever the second player moves. Each move must be to an empty square. After each move determine if the game has been won, or if the game is a draw.

**16.32**   If you feel ambitious, modify your solution to Exercise 16.31 so that the computer makes the moves for one of the players automatically. Also, allow the player to specify whether he or she wants to go first or second. If you feel exceptionally ambitious, develop a program that will play three-dimensional tic-tac-toe on a 4-by-4-by-4 board (Note: This is a challenging project that could take many weeks of effort!).

# 17

# ActiveX

## Objectives

- To understand the concept of a component in modern software development.
- To understand how ActiveX technologies build upon COM and DCOM.
- To understand the key events in the lifetime of an ActiveX control.
- To be able to create ActiveX controls.
- To be able to use the ActiveX Control Interface Wizard.
- To be able to use the Property Page Wizard to create Property Pages.
- To be able to create ActiveX DLLs.
- To be able to create ActiveX EXEs.

*Well, if you knows of a better 'ole, go to it.*
Bruce Bairnsfather
*Fragments from France* [1915]

*...keep reason under its own control.*
Marcus Aurelius Antoninus
*Meditations*, IX, 7

*An event has happened, upon which it is difficult to speak, and impossible to be silent.*
Impeachment of Hastings [May 5, 1789]
Edmund Burke

*The path of duty lies in what is near, and man seeks for it what is remote.*
Menicius

# Outline

## 17.1 Introduction

In this chapter we discuss a crucial topic, called *ActiveX*, that is at the heart of Microsoft's vision of distributed computing. ActiveX technologies seek to integrate your local machine with the World Wide Web (WWW), the Internet, Intranets, etc. Files and other documents that may seem like they are residing or executing on your machine may actually be stored or executing on a remote machine.

ActiveX covers a wide range of distributed computing technologies and are generally grouped into three broad categories—*ActiveX controls*, *ActiveX documents* and *ActiveX components*. In this chapter we discuss ActiveX controls and ActiveX components (also called *ActiveX servers* or *COM components*).

In Chapter 16, we discussed object-oriented programming. In this chapter and many of the chapters that follow, you will be able to apply the object-oriented techniques you have learned. Most of the features discussed in this chapter are specific to the Professional and Enterprise Editions of Visual Basic.

## 17.2 Components, COM and DCOM

In Chapter 16 we discussed the reuse of source code. In this section we discuss reuse of an application's *binary code* (i.e., machine language). Each reusable binary piece of code is called a *component*.

An application typically consists of one binary file that does not change until the next release replaces it. The next version must be developed, debugged, recompiled and deployed. During the time the next application is being developed, software (e.g., the operating system) and hardware (e.g., microprocessors) are changing—some of which can have a profound effect on the application's behavior. This makes it hard for developers to keep pace with technology—especially as applications become more and more "feature rich."

What if the developers had a way to break these "monolithic" applications into their constituent parts? We can certainly break the application into logical components—a process called *object-oriented analysis and design (OOAD)*. For example, we might break a simple editor application down into logical components (i.e., a spell checker, a thesaurus, a text area, a tool bar, etc.). We can think of each component as an independent, specialized entity that when collectively grouped together form a "super application" called an editor. Each component can be "plugged into" any application that needs it. Software composed of components is often called *componentware*.

Sound familiar? Many of the things that we use in our day-to-day lives use the same concepts—automobiles, computers, light bulbs, shoes, etc. Each is assembled from standard pieces. We can certainly think of an automobile as a series of interchangeable parts.

We can view software as a group of interchangeable components. If our editor's grammar checker becomes obsolete (or if we simply prefer another vendor's grammar checker), we can simply "plug in" a different grammar checker component.

Once developed, these prepackaged components are ready for use—allowing programmers to rapidly build applications using these prepackaged components. This *rapid application development (RAD)* allows applications to be quickly created from proven components in a fraction of the time it would normally take to create the whole application.

At the heart of reusable component development is Microsoft's *Component Object Model (COM)*. COM is a binary-level specification that describes how a series of components—which are possibly written in different programming languages by different vendors—can communicate. This ability of disparate components to intercommunicate is referred to as *interoperability*.

**Software Engineering Observation 17.1**

*COM is not a programming language. COM is a specification that can be implemented by many programming languages, including C++, C, Pascal, etc.*

**Software Engineering Observation 17.2**

*COM is language independent, location independent and compiler independent.*

COM was developed by Microsoft to make applications more dynamic, customizable and flexible. Like most other Microsoft products, Visual Basic uses COM—although the details of COM are hidden from the programmer. We provide a brief introduction to COM and its related technologies because COM provides the foundation for ActiveX.

With COM, applications interact with components through a set of standard methods grouped into *interfaces* (Visual Basic interfaces are modeled after COM interfaces). Many different types of COM interfaces exist—some for ActiveX controls, some for transferring data, some for storing information, etc. The most fundamental COM interface is **IUnknown**. Every COM interface must contain **IUnknown**'s methods—**AddRef**, **Release** and **QueryInterface**. **AddRef** and **Release** are used to control the lifetime of a COM component (e.g., once the COM component is created it has the ability to determine when it should be removed from memory). **QueryInterface** provides a way of asking (at run time) if a COM component supports a particular COM interface (e.g., one COM component may need to determine if another COM component supports a drag-and-drop interface). [Note: As a Visual Basic programmer you will not directly call **AddRef**, **Release**, or **QueryInterface**. They are called "behind the scenes" by Visual Basic.]

*Software Engineering Observation 17.3*

*Visual Basic is one of the most heavily COM-oriented tools in existence.*

Microsoft has been developing an enhancement to COM called *COM+*, which will be released in the near future. COM+ will provide significant enhancements to COM. Since Visual Basic programmers do not work directly with COM, they will not be able to take advantage of COM+ the way C++ programmers will—although "under the hood" Visual Basic will be made COM+ *aware* (i.e., will use COM+). Future versions of Visual Basic are likely to allow programmers to directly access the underlying COM (or COM+) functionality.

*Distributed COM (DCOM)* is a distributed version of COM. DCOM is often described as COM "with a longer wire." DCOM provides the means of executing COM components on remote machines—while hiding all the implementation details from the programmer (i.e., the process of connecting to the remote machine is transparent and the programmer does not have to know how the connecting is actually done). DCOM also adds additional features not provided by COM (e.g., security). DCOM is an essential element in building enterprise-level applications. Communication is accomplished through the same COM mechanisms because DCOM is an extension of COM. DCOM has nothing to do with Visual Basic—but components created with Visual Basic can run remotely using DCOM. DCOM replaces an older technology called *remote automation*. [Note: Remote automation is still used on older versions of Windows that are not DCOM enabled.]

*Software Engineering Observation 17.4*

*COM objects are automatically DCOM objects.*

*Software Engineering Observation 17.5*

*DCOM allows complex problems to be solved using components located on several remote machines. This allows the processing power of several machines to collectively solve a problem.*

Now that COM and DCOM have been introduced, we briefly discuss two higher-level COM technologies—OLE and ActiveX (Fig. 17.1). We first discuss OLE.

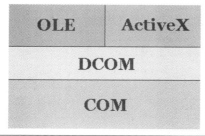

**Fig. 17.1**    ActiveX technologies.

*Object Linking and Embedding* (*OLE*) is a technology that allows applications to work together seamlessly (i.e., the ability to use an **Excel** spreadsheet within **Word**—without having to explicitly open a copy of **Excel**). OLE provides a number of services, including *drag and drop* and *automation* [i.e., the process by which one application can control another application (we provide a short example that demonstrates this at the end of this section)].

ActiveX technologies build upon COM, DCOM and OLE. ActiveX technologies cover a broad range of distributed computing technologies, including ActiveX controls (Section 17.3), ActiveX components (Sections 17.10 and 17.11) and ActiveX documents (not discussed in this book).

To illustrate the power of ActiveX, Fig. 17.2 writes text to a Microsoft **Word** document from Visual Basic using automation. This example requires **Word** be installed (and registered) on the machine. We simply open a **Standard EXE** and add a reference (using the **References** dialog which is displayed when **References...** is selected from the **Project** menu) to the *Microsoft Word 8.0 Object Library*. This library allows our Visual Basic program to control **Word** through automation.

```
1   ' Fig. 17.2
2   ' Demonstrating automation using Word
3   Option Explicit
4   Dim mWord As Word.Application
5
6   Private Sub Form_Initialize()
7       Set mWord = New Word.Application
8   End Sub
9
10  Private Sub cmdWrite_Click()
11      cmdWrite.Enabled = False
12      Call mWord.Documents.Add
13      mWord.Selection.Shading.Texture = wdTexture22Pt5Percent
14      mWord.Selection.Font.Size = 30
15      Call mWord.Selection.TypeText(txtInput.Text)
16      Call mWord.Documents(1).SaveAs("d:\word.doc")
17      Call mWord.Quit
18  End Sub
19
20  Private Sub Class_Terminate()
21      Set mWord = Nothing
22  End Sub
```

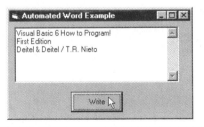

**Fig. 17.2**   Program that creates a **Word** file using automation.

Line 4 creates a **_Word.Application_** reference that we can use to control **Word** (through automation—we will not see **Word**'s GUI). On line 7, we **Set mWord** to a **New Word.Application** object. On line 12, we add a document to the **_Documents Collection_ Word** uses to keep track of documents currently being edited. Since this is the first document, it receives an **Index** of 1. We change the font size with the line

```
mWord.Selection.Font.Size = 30
```

The **_Selection_** object refers to the cursor in the **Word** document we created. We add shading to the background by setting the **_Shading_** object's **_Texture_** property to the constant **_wdTexture22Pt5Percent_**. Method **_TypeText_** is used to write **txtInput**'s **Text** to the **Word** document. We then save the document (which is the first item of the **Documents Collection**) to the file **word.doc** using method **_SaveAs_**. A call to **_Quit_** terminates the **Word** instance.

We run this example and observe that the file **word.doc** is created. If we open **word.doc** (Fig. 17.3) using **Word**, we see the text we entered in Fig. 17.2.

Although not demonstrated here, if you have the Enterprise Edition you can set up this example to run remotely (i.e., on another machine) using the **Automation Manager** and **Remote Automation Connection Manager**. These are Visual Basic tools that ship with the Enterprise Edition and are part of the same group in **Microsoft Visual Studio 6.0** as Visual Basic. The running of the remote component can be handled by either DCOM or remote automation. Consult the on-line Visual Basic documentation for the specifics.

## 17.3 ActiveX Control Types

ActiveX controls are reusable components that can be "plugged" into a Visual Basic program (as well as programs written in other languages). An ActiveX control can be just about anything the programmer can imagine—a calendar, a word processor, an image editor, a card game, etc. ActiveX controls can be visible or invisible to the user. For example, a card game ActiveX control would certainly be visible to allow the user to play the game and a spelling checker ActiveX control would be invisible to the user.

**Fig. 17.3**   Contents of a **Word** file created through automation.

ActiveX controls are the natural evolution of *OLE controls*. Some OLE controls allow *in-place activation* (also called *visual editing*), where the OLE control acts as a *host container* for another control. For example, a Microsoft **Word** document could act as an OLE container and host an **Excel** spreadsheet. This capability allowed the **Word** user to edit an **Excel** spreadsheet without ever opening **Excel** or leaving **Word**. ActiveX controls improve upon OLE controls by providing distributed capabilities (e.g., the ability to be downloaded with a Web page) and by providing a more efficient design (e.g., redesigned to be smaller in size).

Prior to the release of Visual Basic 5.0, ActiveX controls could only be created in languages such as Microsoft Visual C++—not Visual Basic. Beginning with Visual Basic 5.0 (and continuing with Visual Basic 6.0), Visual Basic programmers can now create their own ActiveX controls directly in Visual Basic.

ActiveX controls have their roots in OLE controls and *Visual Basic extension controls* (called *VBX controls*). VBX controls are the predecessor to ActiveX controls. OLE controls and VBX controls have been around for many years and are well understood technologies. Thousands of VBX controls have been created over the years. Many of these VBX controls have been rewritten as ActiveX controls—thus providing a large base of ActiveX controls for developers. VBX controls cannot be used with Visual Basic 5 or Visual Basic 6.

Three different types of ActiveX controls can be created with Visual Basic—*user-drawn controls*, what we call *"enhanced" controls*, and what we call *"aggregate" controls*. User-drawn controls are custom controls developed from "scratch"—which generally makes these the most difficult type of controls to create. User-drawn controls also provide the most design flexibility. An example of a user-drawn control might be a button shaped like a star (a series of calls to method **Line** might be used to create the star).

Enhanced controls add features to existing controls. The **MaskEdit** control is an example of an enhanced control. Aggregate controls contain one or more existing controls [i.e., intrinsic controls, ActiveX controls, third-party controls (i.e., ISV controls)] called *constituent controls*. Aggregate controls are the most common control type. In the sections that follow, we create an aggregate control that contains a **Label** and a **Scrollbar**.

Any one of the three control types is potentially capable of being a *lightweight control* [i.e., a control that does not have a *Windows handle* (i.e., an identification automatically created by the Windows operating system]. A Windows handle is stored in the control's **hWnd** property. Controls with Windows handles are sometimes called *windowed controls*. Some controls, such as **Label** and **Image**, do not have an **hWnd** property and are therefore lightweight controls. Lightweight controls are created by setting the control's **Windowless** property to **True** at design time. Lightweight controls are sometimes referred to as *windowless controls*. Note: The **hWnd** property is a run-time property (i.e., it is not displayed in the **Properties** window) and **Windowless** is a property of a form-like entity called a **UserControl** (discussed in the next section).

***Common Programming Error 17.1***

*Lightweight controls can only contain other lightweight controls. Placing a windowed control on a lightweight control is a syntax error.*

***Performance Tip 17.1***

*Lightweight controls consume fewer resources than controls—but do not necessarily execute any faster.*

*Software Engineering Observation 17.6*

*Lightweight controls were created for distributed applications.*

*Software Engineering Observation 17.7*

*Lightweight controls are not universally supported. If not supported, a lightweight control automatically runs in windowed mode (i.e., it automatically gets assigned a Windows handle). Visual Basic and Internet Explorer 4.0+ support lightweight controls.*

## 17.4 ActiveX Control Lifetime and Events

Throughout the book we have been using ActiveX controls in our programs. As the *developer* (i.e., the people using Visual Basic and ActiveX controls to create applications) we have only been concerned with the properties, methods and events an ActiveX control provides—we have not been concerned with the "under the hood" operations of those ActiveX controls. By discussing these "under the hood" operations briefly, we can gain a better understanding of what is needed to author (i.e., create) our own ActiveX controls. In this section, we discuss the lifetime of ActiveX controls and the key events that occur during the control's lifetime. We will begin authoring controls in the next section.

Double-clicking a toolbox icon, such as the **ImageCombo** ActiveX control, creates an *instance* (more specifically, a *design-time instance*) of the control and *sites* (i.e., places) the control on the *container* (e.g., form). If we were to slow this process down, we would observe the following

1. Double-clicking the toolbox icon creates an instance of the control.

2. Any *constituent controls* (i.e., other visible or invisible controls that the ActiveX control may contain) are created. We discuss constituent controls in Section 17.6.

3. The ***UserControl*** object is created. The **UserControl** object is somewhat similar to a form. Any constituent controls are sited on the **UserControl**.

4. Event procedure ***UserControl_Initialize*** is executed. **Initialize** is only executed once during the control's lifetime and is always the first event.

5. The ActiveX control is sited on its container. If a new instance of the ActiveX control is sited, ***UserControl_InitProperties*** is executed. **InitProperties** initializes the control's properties to their default values. **InitProperties** is only executed once during the control's lifetime. (Note: If an existing form which already contains an instance of the control is opened, **InitProperties** is not called; rather ***UserControl_ReadProperties*** is called. **ReadProperties** retrieves the saved property values.) Special objects called ***Extender*** and ***Ambient*** become available. We will say more about these objects later in the chapter.

6. Next, event procedure ***UserControl_Resize*** is called to size the control. **Resize** is used by constituent controls to determine the layout and size of each control member. User-drawn controls do not use **Resize**.

7. ***Show*** and ***Paint*** events are raised. The control is now visible. User-drawn controls use **Paint** to display their GUI.

At this point we can write code for the various events the control *exposes* (i.e., makes **Public**). We can also use exposed methods and properties. Many of the event procedures we discussed in the numbered list are likely to be **Private**. The control's author decides whether or not the developer needs access to these event procedures.

Let us continue our discussion of the control's lifetime. After the developer has customized the control by setting properties and writing code, the program is executed (i.e., placed in run mode).

8. Running the program closes the form. **UserControl_WriteProperties** is called to save the design-time property settings (only if at least one property value has changed). The properties are written to a copy (in memory) of the form file (**.frm** extension). Saving the project results the **.frm** file on disk being updated to reflect the property changes. If the project is not saved, the **.frm** on disk is not modified.

9. Next, the control is *unsited* (i.e., removed from the container).

10. **UserControl_Terminate** is called.

11. The **UserControl** object and any constituent controls are destroyed.

This marks the end of the design-time instance container and design-time instance control. During execution, a *run-time instance* of the container and a run-time instance of the control are created. Let us continue our observations.

12. **Initialize** is called. Any constituent controls are created. The control is not sited yet.

13. **ReadProperties** is called to retrieve saved property values.

14. The control is sited on the run-time instance of the container. **Extender** and **Ambient** objects are now available. Again, we will say more about these objects later in the chapter.

15. **Resize** or **Paint** events are raised next. The control sizes any constituent controls. User-drawn controls draw themselves.

At this stage, developers can test their applications—which includes setting control properties, calling control methods, and responding to control events. When the developer terminates program execution, the run-time instance of the container and run-time instance of the control are destroyed. **Terminate** is called before the control is destroyed. Any properties set at run-time are not saved. The container and control design-time instances are created again as discussed in list items 2 through 7. Closing the design-time container or closing the project results in **WriteProperties** and **Terminate** being called.

## 17.5 UserControl Object

Creation of ActiveX controls always begins with a form-like object called a **UserControl**. Like a form, a **UserControl** is a container where other controls can be sited. **UserControl**s visually look like a form without a border (Fig. 17.4). We discuss how to load **UserControl**s into the environment in the next section.

As Fig. 17.4 illustrates, a **UserControl** has sizing handles, a grid, a folder in the **Project Explorer** window, and properties (which are listed in the **Properties** window). Customizing a **UserControl** is like customizing a form.

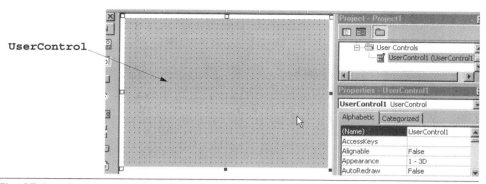

**Fig. 17.4**    A **UserControl** at design time.

As was discussed in the last section, a **UserControl** behaves programmatically different from a form. Form events like **Activate**, **Deactivate**, **Load**, **UnLoad**, **QueryUnload**, etc. do not exist for **UserControl**s. Only **Terminate** and **UnLoad** are somewhat similar. When saved, **UserControl** files get the **.ctl** extension.

> ***Software Engineering Observation 17.8***
>
> *If a **UserControl** contains graphics (e.g., images) that cannot be saved as plain text in the **.ctl** file, a separate file with the same name and extension **.ctx** is created to save the graphics. This is equivalent to what a form does with graphics and **.frx** files.*

## 17.6 Creating an ActiveX Control That Contains Constituent Controls

We are now ready to begin building our first ActiveX control. In this section, we create an ActiveX control that is composed of two constituent controls: a **Label** and a scrollbar. We call this ActiveX control a **LabelScrollbar** (Fig. 17.5). The **LabelScrollbar** is a control that allows the user to scroll through a range of values. The scrollbar value is displayed in the **Label** portion of the control.

In Fig. 17.5, it is important to understand that the developer using the control sees the **LabelScrollbar** as a single control. The developer cannot separate or break apart the control into two separate controls. The developer can resize the control, move it around the form with the mouse, set properties, write event handling code for the control, etc.

ActiveX controls are created using the ***ActiveX Control*** project type as shown in Fig. 17.6. Selecting **New Project** from the **File** menu displays the **New Project** dialog. A similar dialog, unless disabled, is also displayed when Visual Basic is first loaded. We discuss some of the other ActiveX project types later in this chapter.

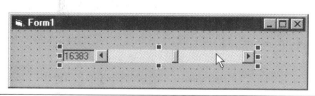

**Fig. 17.5**    **LabelScrollbar** ActiveX control.

**Fig. 17.6**    **New Project** dialog with the **ActiveX Control** project type highlighted.

Figure 17.7 shows the IDE with an open **ActiveX Control** project. The project windows are not much different than that of a **Standard EXE**'s project windows. Unlike **Standard EXE**s, ActiveX control GUIs are not based on forms, but rather on **UserControl**s. Creating an ActiveX control's GUI is similar to creating a **Standard EXE**'s GUI—controls from the toolbox are used to customize the **UserControl**.

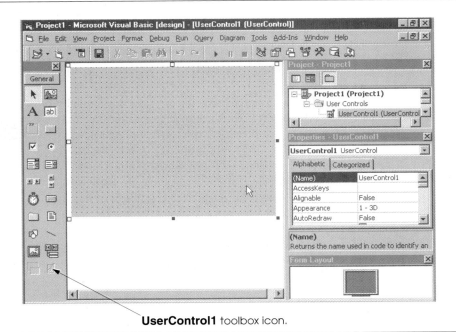

**UserControl1** toolbox icon.

**Fig. 17.7**    IDE displaying an open **ActiveX Control** project.

The toolbox contains an additional icon, named **UserControl1** (the default), that represents the **UserControl** currently being created. The **UserControl**'s name (i.e., **UserControl1**) is set using property **(Name)**. The **UserControl** toolbox icon is disabled at design time because we cannot site an instance of the **UserControl** on itself. We will discuss momentarily when this toolbox icon is enabled.

The author designs the GUI and determines what functionality (i.e., properties, methods, and events) the ActiveX control exposes. The developer can use any exposed properties, methods, and events. As the author of the **LabelScrollbar**, we provide a **Label** and a horizontal scrollbar for the GUI. Figure 17.8 lists the design time property settings for the **UserControl**, **Label** and scrollbar, and Fig. 17.9 shows the **LabelScrollbar** at design time.

> *Software Engineering Observation 17.9*
>
> *Controls containing constituent controls leverage existing GUIs and functionality. The author does not have to redevelop this.*

| Object | Icon | Property | Property setting | Property description |
|---|---|---|---|---|
| UserControl | | (Name) | LabelScrollbar | Identifies the control. |
| | | ScaleHeight | 18 | Scale height. |
| | | ScaleMode | 3 - Pixel | Scale units. |
| | | ScaleWidth | 242 | Scale width. |
| Label | A | Name | lblDisplay | Identifies the **Label**. |
| | | BorderStyle | 1 - Fixed | **Label** border style |
| | | Caption | empty | Text **Label** displays. |
| | | Height | 17 | **Label** height. |
| | | Width | 41 | **Label** width. |
| Scrollbar | ◄ ► | Name | hsbScroll | Identifies the horizontal scrollbar. |
| | | Height | 17 | Scrollbar height. |
| | | Width | 193 | Scrollbar width. |

**Fig. 17.8**    Property listing for **LabelScrollbar** ActiveX control.

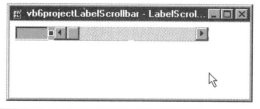

Label and scrollbar are positioned in the upper-left corner of the **UserControl**. The **Label** and scrollbar have the same **Height**. The user control is resized to fit the **Label** and scrollbar.

**Fig. 17.9**    **LabelScrollbar** GUI at design time.

To design the GUI, we simply site a **Label** and horizontal scrollbar on the **User-Control**. Both the **Label** and scrollbar are positioned next to each other and moved to the upper-left corner of the **UserControl**. The **UserControl**'s sizing handles are used to size the **UserControl** to the width and height of the constituent controls it contains (as shown in Fig. 17.9).

*Good Programming Practice 17.1*

*The size of the **UserControl** is the default size the developers using the control will see (unless specified otherwise in the **Resize** or **Paint** event procedure). In general, it is best not to have the control any larger than necessary.*

Now that the GUI is designed, we can focus on authoring the *programmatic interface* (i.e., the code behind the control). Figure 17.10 lists the code for the **LabelScrollbar**. As always, we provide a detailed discussion of the code.

```
1   ' Fig. 17.10
2   ' LabelScrollbar ActiveX control
3   Option Explicit
4   Public Event Change()
5
6   '''''''''''''''''''''''''''''''''''''''
7   ' Event procedures for UserControl   '
8   '''''''''''''''''''''''''''''''''''''''
9   Private Sub UserControl_InitProperties()
10
11      With hsbScroll
12         .Min = 0
13         .Max = 32767
14         .Value = (Min + Max) / 2
15         .SmallChange = 1
16         .LargeChange = 5
17      End With
18
19      lblDisplay.Caption = hsbScroll.Value
20   End Sub
21
22   Private Sub UserControl_ReadProperties(PropBag As PropertyBag)
23
24      With hsbScroll
25         .Value = PropBag.ReadProperty("Value", (Min + Max) \ 2)
26         .Min = PropBag.ReadProperty("Min", 0)
27         .Max = PropBag.ReadProperty("Max", 32767)
28         .LargeChange = PropBag.ReadProperty("LargeChange", 5)
29         .SmallChange = PropBag.ReadProperty("SmallChange", 1)
30      End With
31
32      lblDisplay.Caption = PropBag.ReadProperty("Caption", _
33                                                (Min + Max) \ 2)
34   End Sub
35
```

**Fig. 17.10  LabelScrollbar** code (part 1 of 3).

```vb
36    Private Sub UserControl_WriteProperties(PropBag As PropertyBag)
37       Call PropBag.WriteProperty("Value", hsbScroll.Value, _
38                                  (Min + Max) \ 2)
39       Call PropBag.WriteProperty("Caption", hsbScroll.Value, _
40                                  (Min + Max) \ 2)
41       Call PropBag.WriteProperty("Min", hsbScroll.Min, 0)
42       Call PropBag.WriteProperty("Max", hsbScroll.Max, 32767)
43       Call PropBag.WriteProperty("SmallChange", _
44                                  hsbScroll.SmallChange, 1)
45       Call PropBag.WriteProperty("LargeChange", _
46                                  hsbScroll.LargeChange, 5)
47    End Sub
48
49    Private Sub UserControl_Resize()
50
51       With hsbScroll
52          .Left = lblDisplay.Width
53          .Width = ScaleWidth - hsbScroll.Left
54          .Height = ScaleHeight
55       End With
56
57       lblDisplay.Height = ScaleHeight
58    End Sub
59
60    ''''''''''''''''''''''''''''''''''''''''
61    ' Event procedures for hsbScroll        '
62    ''''''''''''''''''''''''''''''''''''''''
63    Private Sub hsbScroll_Change()
64       lblDisplay.Caption = hsbScroll.Value
65       RaiseEvent Change
66    End Sub
67
68    ''''''''''''''''''''''''''''''''''''''''
69    ' Property methods for hsbScroll        '
70    ''''''''''''''''''''''''''''''''''''''''
71    Public Property Get Value() As Long
72       Value = hsbScroll.Value
73    End Property
74
75    Public Property Let Value(ByVal v As Long)
76       hsbScroll.Value = v
77       Call UserControl.PropertyChanged("Value")
78    End Property
79
80    Public Property Get Max() As Integer
81       Max = hsbScroll.Max
82    End Property
83
84    Public Property Let Max(ByVal m As Integer)
85       hsbScroll.Max = m
86       Call UserControl.PropertyChanged("Max")
87    End Property
88
```

Fig. 17.10 **LabelScrollbar** code (part 2 of 3).

```
89   Public Property Get Min() As Integer
90      Min = hsbScroll.Min
91   End Property
92
93   Public Property Let Min(ByVal m As Integer)
94      hsbScroll.Min = m
95      Call UserControl.PropertyChanged("Min")
96   End Property
97
98   Public Property Get LargeChange() As Integer
99      LargeChange = hsbScroll.LargeChange
100  End Property
101
102  Public Property Let LargeChange(ByVal c As Integer)
103     hsbScroll.LargeChange = c
104     Call UserControl.PropertyChanged("LargeChange")
105  End Property
106
107  Public Property Get SmallChange() As Integer
108     SmallChange = hsbScroll.SmallChange
109  End Property
110
111  Public Property Let SmallChange(ByVal c As Integer)
112     hsbScroll.SmallChange = c
113     Call UserControl.PropertyChanged("SmallChange")
114  End Property
```

**Fig. 17.10  LabelScrollbar** code (part 3 of 3).

Like other module types, a **UserControl** has a general declaration. We use **Option Explicit** to force explicit variable declaration. Any events or properties the control will expose (i.e., make **Public** such that the developer is aware of them and can use them) are placed in the general declaration. **Event**s and properties placed in the general declaration must be **Public** (**Event**s are **Public** by default). Module-level variables may also be placed in the general declaration (module-level variables default to **Private**). The statement

```
Public Event Change()
```

indicates that the control will expose an **Event** called **Change**. The developer using our control will see **Change** as an event procedure listed in the **Code** window's **Procedure ComboBox** (when the **LabelScrollbar** is selected in the **Object ComboBox**). The name **Change** is not some arbitrary name we created, but rather corresponds to an actual event the scrollbar raises. **Event**s, properties, and methods are not exposed unless the author explicitly decides to do so. By exposing **Change**, the developer can write code to handle a **Change** event from our **LabelScrollbar**. We have more to say about how events are raised momentarily.

*Common Programming Error 17.2*

*Attempting to declare an **Event** as **Private** is a syntax error.*

Line 9 begins the *InitProperties* event procedure. **InitProperities**, as its name implies, initializes the user control's properties every time a new instance of the user control is sited on a container (e.g., a form). Event **InitProperties** occurs exactly once in a control's lifetime. We initialize several **hsbScroll** properties and **lblDisplay**'s **Caption** property.

If the control is not a new instance (e.g., a form containing a **LabelScrollbar** is opened), **ReadProperties**—not **InitProperties**—is called to set the control's properties. **ReadProperties** receives exactly one argument of type *PropertyBag*. The **PropertyBag** object (i.e., **PropBag**) enables the state of the control (and any constituent controls) to be retrieved (e.g., read from a **.frm** file). **PropertyBag** method *ReadProperty* reads a single property. The first argument is a **String** containing the name of the **UserControl**'s property. The second argument specifies a default value (which is used if the property does not already have a saved value).

We also provide event handler **WriteProperties** to *persist* (i.e., save to disk) property values when the design-time control instance is destroyed. Event procedure **WriteProperties** receives one **PropertyBag** argument (which is used to save the control's state). **PropertyBag** method *WriteProperty* writes a single property value to disk. The first argument is a **String** containing the property name to write. The second argument specifies the value to save. The third argument specifies a default value. A property value is written only if it is different from the default value.

*Performance Tip 17.2*

*A property value is only written to the container file (i.e., a **.frm** file, **.frx** file, etc.) if it is different from the default value. This saves a write operation as well as reducing the size of the container file.*

The **Resize** event handler contains code that specifies how the constituent controls should size themselves when the control is sited and when the developer resizes the control using the sizing handles. Scrollbar **hsbScroll** is positioned to the immediate left of **lblDisplay** (i.e., no space between the constituent controls). The scrollbar **Width** is calculated by subtracting the scrollbar's **Left** value from the **UserControl**'s **ScaleWidth**. and the scrollbar **Height** is set to the **UserControl**'s **ScaleHeight**. The **Label**'s **Height** is set to the **UserControl**'s **ScaleHeight**.

When the control is resized and made larger by the developer, both the **Label** and the scrollbar stretch to fill the available area both vertically and horizontally. When resized larger horizontally, only the scrollbar grows—the **Label** remains the same size.

By default, constituent control events are hidden within the **UserControl**. The developer cannot directly use them—unless of course the author of the control has exposed them. To expose an event, the event must be declared in the general declaration as **Event** (as we did with **Change** on line 4). The constituent control's event that is being exposed must be coded to *raise* (i.e., *fire*) the event. The line

```
RaiseEvent Change
```

uses statement *RaiseEvent* to raise the **Change** event. By raising the event, we allow the developer using our control to write code to respond to the event. **RaiseEvent** does not have to be the last statement inside the procedure—any code placed after the **RaiseEvent** statement is executed. In **hsbScroll_Change**, we also set **lblDisplay**'s **Caption** to the scrollbar's **Value**.

*Common Programming Error 17.3*

*Raising an event not declared in the general declaration is a syntax error.*

Property **Get** and **Let** procedures are written for **hsbScroll** properties **Max**, **Min**, **LargeChange**, **SmallChange** and **Value**. The **Get** procedures simply return the current **hsbScroll** property settings for the five properties. **Let** procedures set the five property values. Each **Let** procedure calls the **UserControl**'s *PropertyChanged* method to notify the **UserControl**'s container that a property value has changed. This notification allows the **Properties** window to be updated with the new property value and the **WriteProperties** event to be raised.

For our purposes, the control is complete. We are now ready to test it. First, we add a new form to the project. This form will be the container for a **LabelScrollbar**. The form is also set as the start-up object. Using the **LabelScrollbar** toolbox icon, we site a **LabelScrollbar** on the form (as shown in Fig. 17.11).

Notice in Fig. 17.11 that the **UserControl (Name)** property setting is what appears as the tool tip when the mouse pointer rests on the **LabelScrollbar** toolbox icon. If the **LabelScrollbar** object window (visible when **View Object** is pressed while **LabelScrollbar** is highlighted in the **Project Explorer** window) is open while the form object window is open, the **LabelScrollbar** object appears with *hash marks* (Fig. 17.12) and its toolbox icon is grayed. This does not affect the run-time control instance, but affects the design-time instance events and property settings. The control's object window (i.e., the window with the GUI controls) should be closed unless the control's GUI is being modified.

## 17.7 ActiveX Control Example: **Clock** Control

Our next example builds a digital clock ActiveX control, which contains two constituent controls, a **Label** and a **Timer**. The control automatically changes its background color to match the background color of the container. The developer can set the clock's foreground color. Resizing the control results in the clock's digits growing or shrinking. Figure 17.13 shows a run-time instance of the control. Figure 17.14 lists the control's properties, and Fig 17.15 lists the control's code.

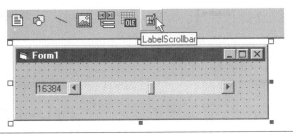

**Fig. 17.11   LabelScrollbar** sited on a form.

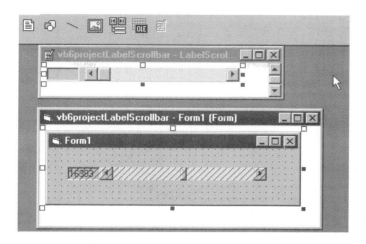

**Fig. 17.12**    Hash marks displayed when both the **LabelScrollbar** object window and form object window are open.

**Fig. 17.13**    **Clock** control at run-time.

| Object | Icon | Property | Property setting | Property description |
|--------|------|----------|------------------|----------------------|
| UserControl | | (Name) | Clock | Identifies the control. |
| | | ScaleHeight | 29 | Scale height. |
| | | ScaleMode | 3 - Pixel | Scale units. |
| | | ScaleWidth | 84 | Scale width. |
| Timer |  | Name | tmrTimer | Identifies the **Timer**. |
| | | Interval | 1000 | **Timer** interval. |

**Fig. 17.14**    Property listing for **Clock** ActiveX control.

```
1    ' Fig. 17.15
2    ' A UserControl ActiveX control
3    ' that represents a clock
4    Option Explicit
5
6    ''''''''''''''''''''''''''''''''''''''''
7    ' UserControl event procedures    '
8    ''''''''''''''''''''''''''''''''''''''''
9    Private Sub UserControl_Show()
10       BackColor = Ambient.BackColor
11   End Sub
12
13   Private Sub UserControl_AmbientChanged(PropertyName As String)
14
15       If PropertyName = "BackColor" Then
16          BackColor = Ambient.BackColor
17       End If
18
19   End Sub
20
21   Private Sub UserControl_Resize()
22       Font.Size = ScaleY(ScaleHeight, vbPixels, vbPoints)
23       Width = 3.95 * Height
24   End Sub
25
26   Private Sub UserControl_WriteProperties(PropBag As PropertyBag)
27       Call PropBag.WriteProperty("ForeColor", ForeColor, vbBlack)
28   End Sub
29
30   Private Sub UserControl_ReadProperties(PropBag As PropertyBag)
31       UserControl.ForeColor = PropBag.ReadProperty("ForeColor", _
32                                                    vbBlack)
33   End Sub
34
35   ''''''''''''''''''''''''''''''''''''''''
36   ' UserControl property methods    '
37   ''''''''''''''''''''''''''''''''''''''''
38   Public Property Get ForeColor() As OLE_COLOR
39       ForeColor = UserControl.ForeColor
40   End Property
41
```

**Fig. 17.15**   Code listing for **Clock** ActiveX control (part 1 of 2).

We code the **Show** event procedure to change the **BackColor** of the **UserControl** object with the line

```
BackColor = Ambient.BackColor
```

The *Ambient* object provides the **UserControl** information about its container (in this case the form) such that the control can "blend" into its container. Figure 17.16 lists properties of the **Ambient** object.

```
42   Public Property Let ForeColor(ByVal c As OLE_COLOR)
43      UserControl.ForeColor = c
44      PropertyChanged "ForeColor"
45   End Property
46
47   ''''''''''''''''''''''''''''''''''''''
48   ' Timer event procedure              '
49   ''''''''''''''''''''''''''''''''''''''
50   Private Sub tmrTimer_Timer()
51      Call Cls
52      Print Abs(Hour(Now) - 12) & ":";
53      Print Format$(Minute(Now), "00") & ":";
54      Print Format$(Second(Now), "00")
55   End Sub
```

**Fig. 17.15**  Code listing for **Clock** ActiveX control (part 2 of 2).

| Properties | | |
| --- | --- | --- |
| BackColor | LocaleID | ShowHatching |
| DisplayAsDefault | MessageReflect | SupportsMnemonics |
| DisplayName | Palette | TextAlign |
| Font | ScaleUnits | UIDead |
| ForeColor | ShowGrabHandles | UserMode |

**Fig. 17.16**  **Ambient** object properties.

When an **Ambient** property changes for a container, the ***AmbientChanged*** event is raised and **UserControl_AmbientChanged** is called to handle the event. The **UserControl_AmbientChanged** event procedure receives a **String** containing the name of the property that changed. All the programmer need do is test to see if the ***PropertyName*** matches an **Ambient** property the **UserControl** is interested in. We test for the **BackColor** property.

Although not explicitly used in this example, Visual Basic also provides the ***Extender*** object for accessing properties, methods, and events controlled by the container. Examples of standard **Extender** properties are **Cancel**, **Default**, **Name**, **Parent**, and **Visible**. Other **Extender** properties, methods, and events are available as well, although some containers may not support them. Some additional **Extender** properties are **Enabled**, **Top**, and **DragMode**. For example, a control may need to position itself relative to the **Top** of its container. The control only knows its internal state but can access the container's **Top** with **Extender.Top**.

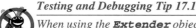

*Testing and Debugging Tip 17.1*

*When using the **Extender** object, write error-handling code in case the container does not support a particular **Extender** property, method or event.*

Event procedure **Resize** specifies the **Font** size for the time drawn on the **User-Control**. Method **ScaleY** converts the **UserControl ScaleHeight** from units of **vbPixels** to units of **vbPoints** (the preferred unit of measurement for fonts). We also indicate that the **Width** of the **UserControl** is always **3.95** times the **Height**.

Both the **WriteProperties** and **ReadProperties** event procedures are coded. These event procedures allow the **UserControl**'s **ForeColor** to be saved and retrieved from disk. We specify **vbBlack** as the default **ForeColor** (although we certainly could have used **Ambient.ForeColor** as the default).

The **UserControl** provides **Property** procedures for property **ForeColor** so users of the control have access to this property. The **Property** procedures use type *OLE_COLOR* to represent the color. Type **OLE_COLOR** is a standard Visual Basic type that represents colors. When the developer uses the **Properties** window and clicks **Fore-Color** (for a **Clock** object), the ellipses button appears in the same manner as it does for forms (or other controls with property **ForeColor**).

The **Timer** control raises the **Timer** event every 1000 milliseconds (i.e., 1 second). The code in the **Timer** event procedure clears the background of the user control and displays the current time formatted as standard time.

We can enhance the control by placing a description for the control in the **Object Browser**. To add the description we

1. Select **Object Browser** from the **View** menu.

2. Right-click the **Clock** control and select **Properties...** from the pop-up menu.

3. Enter a description in the *Member Options* dialog (Fig. 17.17).

4. Press **OK** to close the dialog. When the **Clock** item is selected in the **Object Browser**, the new description is displayed (Fig. 17.18).

We can also set the descriptions for our exposed properties. To do this we

1. Select *Procedure Attributes...* from the **Tools** menu to display the **Procedure Attributes** dialog.

2. Enter a description for the **ForeColor** property (Fig. 17.19). In the **Name ComboBox** all exposed properties, methods and events are listed. Our control only exposes one property—**ForeColor**.

3. Press **OK** to close the dialog.

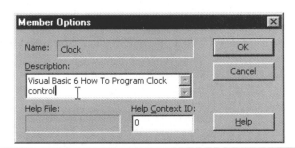

**Fig. 17.17   Member Options** dialog.

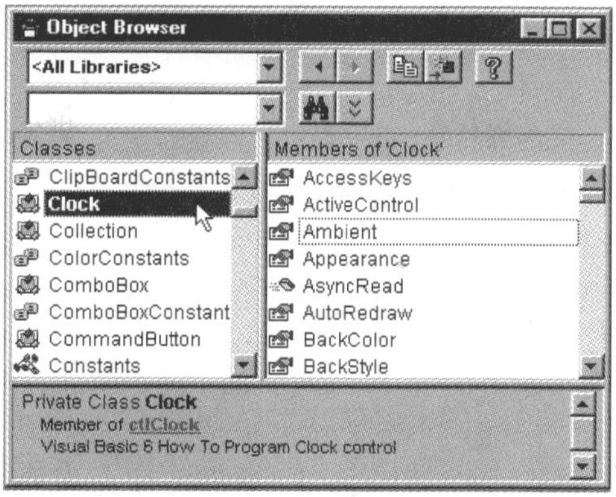


**Fig. 17.18** **Object Browser** displaying the **`Clock`** control's description.

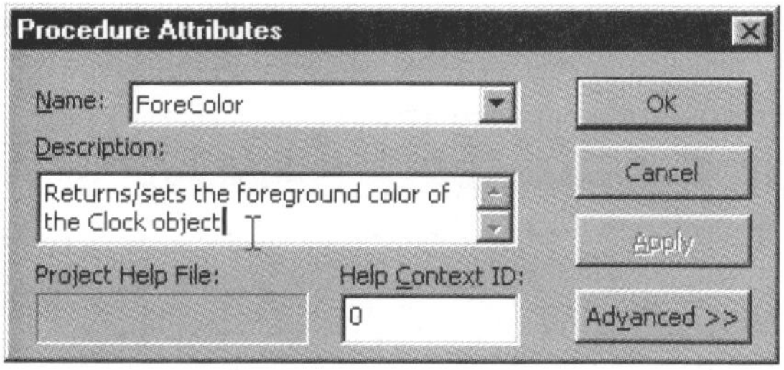


**Fig. 17.19** **Procedure Attributes** dialog.

When the developer selects a **`Clock`** control's **`ForeColor`** property in the **Properties** window, the description entered in the **Procedure Attributes** dialog is displayed (Fig. 17.20).

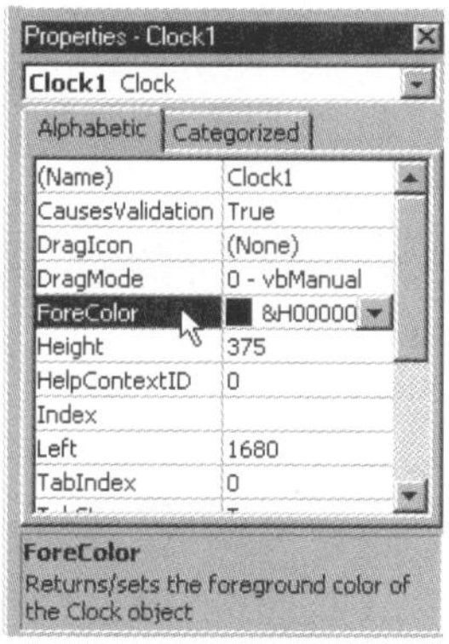


**Fig. 17.20** **Properties** window with a **`Clock`**'s **`ForeColor`** property selected.

The bitmap image used for the toolbox icon can be created using almost any graphics program (we used Microsoft **Paint**). The toolbox bitmap size is 16-by-15 pixels. A control's toolbox bitmap is set with property **ToolboxBitmap**.

Once we have tested our control and are satisfied that it is working properly, we create a version of the control that can run outside the IDE. These stand-alone controls have a **.OCX** extension. To create the **.OCX** file, we do the following:

1. Remove any forms used to test the control.

2. Open the **Project Properties** dialog (Fig. 17.21) by selecting **Project Properties** from the **Project** menu.

3. Select **ActiveX Control** in the **Project Properties** dialog's **Project Type** **ComboBox** and select **(None)** in the **Project Properties** dialog's **Start Up** **ComboBox**. We set the **Project Name** to **ctlClock** and set the *Project Description* to **VB6HTP1 Clock ActiveX Control**. The **Project Description** is the name that will appear in the **Components** dialog (Fig. 17.23).

4. Close the **Project Properties** dialog by pressing **OK**.

5. Set the control's *Public* property to **True** (in the **Properties** window). The **Public** property allows the ActiveX control to be shared with other applications. The **Public** property defaults to **True**.

6. Select the **File** menu's **Make VB6HTP1 Clock.ocx...** command. This displays the *Make Project* dialog shown in Fig. 17.22.

7. Select the location where the **.OCX** control will be saved. Pressing **OK** creates the control in the specified directory. Visual Basic automatically *registers the control* (i.e., makes Windows aware of the control) such that we can use the control with programs such as Visual Basic. We save our **.OCX** on the **D:** drive, but you may save the control wherever you want.

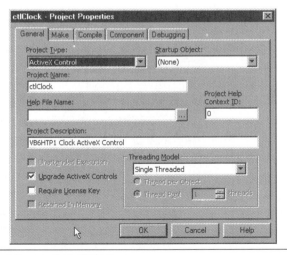

**Fig. 17.21    Project Properties** dialog.

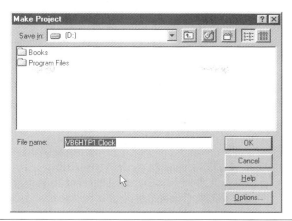

**Fig. 17.22    Make Project** dialog.

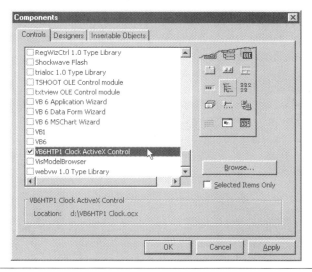

**Fig. 17.23    Components** dialog with **VB6HTP1 Clock ActiveX Control** checked.

8. Close the project and open a **Standard EXE** project. Open the **Components** dialog. Scroll down and check **VB6HTP1 Clock ActiveX Control** (Fig. 17.23). This control is added and used like any other control.

## 17.8  ActiveX Control Interface Wizard

Microsoft Visual Basic 6.0 provides several utilities, called *wizards*, that simplify the process of creating applications, ActiveX controls, etc. In this section we use the *ActiveX control interface wizard* to assist us in the creation of the same **LabelScrollbar** ActiveX control we created earlier. The ActiveX control interface wizard provides a means of quickly generating basic control functionality—leaving programmers to concentrate on programming the more difficult control functionality. Note: Before the ActiveX control interface wizard is used, the control's GUI must be designed (i.e., all controls must be placed on the **User Control**). We deferred this discussion because we wanted the reader to understand how to create an ActiveX control and to understand the key events in the lifetime of the control.

Selecting **Add User Control** from the **Project** menu displays the **Add User Control** dialog of Fig. 17.24. The *VB ActiveX Control Interface Wizard* is part of this dialog.

The **VB ActiveX Control Interface Wizard** can also be accessed by selecting *Add-In Manager...* from the **Add-Ins** menu—which displays the **Add-In Manager** dialog shown in Fig. 17.25. Selecting **VB ActiveX Control Interface Wizard**, checking **Load/Unloaded** and pressing **OK** adds **ActiveX Control Interface Wizard...** to the *Add-Ins* menu. Either double-clicking **VB ActiveX Control Interface Wizard** in the **Add User Control** dialog or selecting **ActiveX Control Interface Wizard** from the **Add-Ins** menu runs the ActiveX control interface wizard.

Figure 17.26 shows the *ActiveX Control Interface Wizard - Introduction* dialog displayed when the ActiveX control interface wizard is run. As its name implies, it provides a brief introduction to the ActiveX control interface wizard. Pressing **Next >** displays the dialog of Fig. 17.27.

The *ActiveX Control Interface Wizard - Select Interface Members* dialog provides a **ListBox** (the left one) of properties, events, and methods from the **User Control**, **Label**, and scrollbar (before running the ActiveX control interface wizard, we placed a **Label** and scrollbar on the **User Control**). A second **ListBox** (the right one) contains a list of all the default properties, methods and events the ActiveX control will expose.

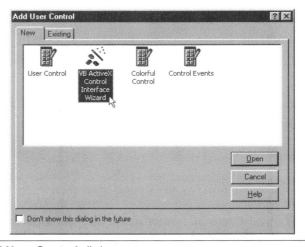

**Fig. 17.24    Add User Control** dialog.

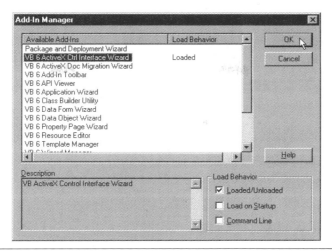

**Fig. 17.25    Add-In Manager** dialog.

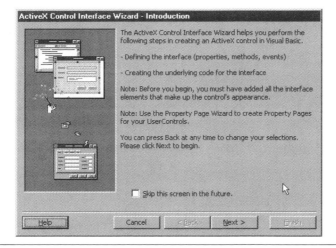

**Fig. 17.26    ActiveX Control Interface Wizard - Introduction** dialog.

Pressing **>>** transfers the entire contents from the left **ListBox** to the right **ListBox** and pressing **<<** transfers the entire contents of the right **ListBox** to the left **ListBox**. Any individual item from the left **ListBox** can be moved to the right **ListBox** by either double-clicking the item or by pressing the **>** button when the item is selected. Multiple items (once they have been selected) can be moved to the right **ListBox** by pressing **>**. Pressing **<** transfers one or more selected items from the right **ListBox** to the left **ListBox**.

For this example we transfer only the **Change** event, **LargeChange** property, **Max** property, **Min** property, **SmallChange** property and **Value** property to the right **ListBox** as shown in Fig. 17.28.

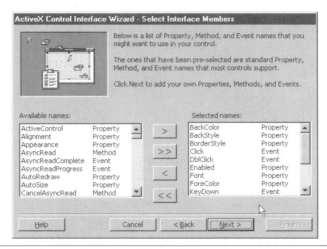

**Fig. 17.27** **ActiveX Control Interface Wizard - Select Interface Members** dialog.

**Fig. 17.28** Selecting properties and events.

Pressing **Next >** displays the **ActiveX Control Interface Wizard - Create Custom Interface Members** dialog (Fig. 17.29). At this stage, the programmer can create custom properties, methods and events. Our **LabelScrollbar** does not have any custom properties, methods or events—so we simply press **Next >**. Note: In the exercises you will be asked to create custom properties—such as how much space appears between the **Label** and scrollbar.

The **ActiveX Control Interface Wizard - Set Mapping** dialog of Fig. 17.30 is displayed next. This dialog lists all of the **Public** properties, methods and events that the control *exposes*. All other properties, methods and events are **Private**. The **Public Name: ListBox** contains properties, methods and events placed in the right **ListBox** of Fig. 17.28. Each property, method and event can be *mapped* to a control listed in the

***Control*** **ComboBox**. Mapping simply means that the property, method or event applies to a certain control. For our **LabelScrollbar**, every item in the **Public Name: ListBox** is mapped to the horizontal scrollbar **hsbScroll**'s equivalent property or event (i.e., **Change** is mapped to **hsbScroll Change**, **LargeChange** is mapped to **hsbScroll LargeChange**, etc.).

Any unmapped members or custom members cause the ***ActiveX Control Interface Wizard - Set Attributes*** dialog to be displayed. This dialog allows the author to set each unmapped member's description and attribute information. Our **LabelScrollbar** does not have any unmapped members or custom members—so this dialog is not displayed.

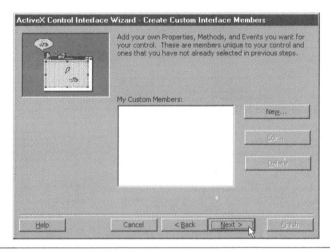

**Fig. 17.29    ActiveX Control Interface Wizard–Create Custom Interface Members** dialog.

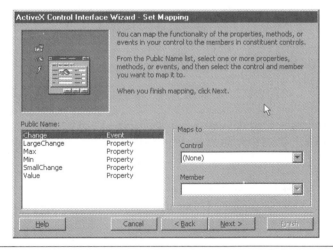

**Fig. 17.30    ActiveX Control Interface Wizard - Set Mapping** dialog.

After items are mapped, pressing **Next >** displays the ***ActiveX Control Interface Wizard - Finished!*** dialog (Fig. 17.31). This dialog contains the ***View Summary Report* CheckBox**, which displays the dialog of Fig. 17.32 when checked. Pressing **Finish** allows the ActiveX control interface wizard to generate code.

Pressing **View Code** in the **Project** window displays the code generated by the ActiveX control interface wizard (Fig. 17.33). The code contains many comments informing the programmer not to edit or remove certain comments—these comments are used by the ActiveX control interface wizard if it is run again (e.g., the programmer may want to add/remove a property). If these comments are removed or edited, the ActiveX control interface wizard may not behave consistently. Note: For presentation purposes we add line-continuation characters—not the ActiveX control interface wizard. We also added the first two comments in the file.

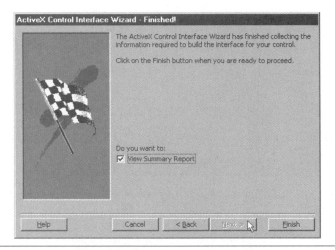

**Fig. 17.31    ActiveX Control Interface Wizard - Finished!** dialog.

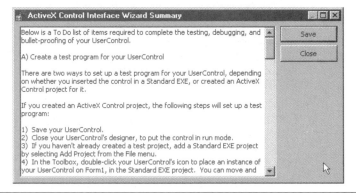

**Fig. 17.32    ActiveX Control Interface Wizard Summary** dialog.

```
1   ' Fig. 17.33
2   ' Code generated by ActiveX Control Interface Wizard.
3   Option Explicit
4   'Event Declarations:
5   Event Change() 'MappingInfo=hsbScroll,hsbScroll,-1,Change
6
7   'WARNING! DO NOT REMOVE OR MODIFY THE FOLLOWING COMMENTED LINES!
8   'MappingInfo=hsbScroll,hsbScroll,-1,LargeChange
9   Public Property Get LargeChange() As Integer
10     LargeChange = hsbScroll.LargeChange
11  End Property
12
13  Public Property Let LargeChange(ByVal New_LargeChange As _
14                                  Integer)
15     hsbScroll.LargeChange() = New_LargeChange
16     PropertyChanged "LargeChange"
17  End Property
18
19  'WARNING! DO NOT REMOVE OR MODIFY THE FOLLOWING COMMENTED LINES!
20  'MappingInfo=hsbScroll,hsbScroll,-1,Min
21  Public Property Get Min() As Integer
22     Min = hsbScroll.Min
23  End Property
24
25  Public Property Let Min(ByVal New_Min As Integer)
26     hsbScroll.Min() = New_Min
27     PropertyChanged "Min"
28  End Property
29
30  'WARNING! DO NOT REMOVE OR MODIFY THE FOLLOWING COMMENTED LINES!
31  'MappingInfo=hsbScroll,hsbScroll,-1,Max
32  Public Property Get Max() As Integer
33     Max = hsbScroll.Max
34  End Property
35
36  Public Property Let Max(ByVal New_Max As Integer)
37     hsbScroll.Max() = New_Max
38     PropertyChanged "Max"
39  End Property
40
41  'WARNING! DO NOT REMOVE OR MODIFY THE FOLLOWING COMMENTED LINES!
42  'MappingInfo=hsbScroll,hsbScroll,-1,Value
43  Public Property Get Value() As Integer
44     Value = hsbScroll.Value
45  End Property
46
47  Public Property Let Value(ByVal New_Value As Integer)
48     hsbScroll.Value() = New_Value
49     PropertyChanged "Value"
50  End Property
51
```

**Fig. 17.33**   Code generated by ActiveX control interface wizard (part 1 of 2).

```
52    'WARNING! DO NOT REMOVE OR MODIFY THE FOLLOWING COMMENTED LINES!
53    'MappingInfo=hsbScroll,hsbScroll,-1,SmallChange
54    Public Property Get SmallChange() As Integer
55       SmallChange = hsbScroll.SmallChange
56    End Property
57
58    Public Property Let SmallChange(ByVal New_SmallChange As _
59                                   Integer)
60       hsbScroll.SmallChange() = New_SmallChange
61       PropertyChanged "SmallChange"
62    End Property
63
64    Private Sub hsbScroll_Change()
65       RaiseEvent Change
66    End Sub
67
68    'Load property values from storage
69    Private Sub UserControl_ReadProperties(PropBag As PropertyBag)
70       hsbScroll.LargeChange = PropBag.ReadProperty( _
71                                   "LargeChange", 1)
72       hsbScroll.Min = PropBag.ReadProperty("Min", 0)
73       hsbScroll.Max = PropBag.ReadProperty("Max", 32767)
74       hsbScroll.Value = PropBag.ReadProperty("Value", 0)
75       hsbScroll.SmallChange = PropBag.ReadProperty( _
76                                   "SmallChange", 1)
77    End Sub
78
79    'Write property values to storage
80    Private Sub UserControl_WriteProperties(PropBag As PropertyBag)
81       Call PropBag.WriteProperty("LargeChange", _
82                                   hsbScroll.LargeChange, 1)
83       Call PropBag.WriteProperty("Min", hsbScroll.Min, 0)
84       Call PropBag.WriteProperty("Max", hsbScroll.Max, 32767)
85       Call PropBag.WriteProperty("Value", hsbScroll.Value, 0)
86       Call PropBag.WriteProperty("SmallChange", _
87                                   hsbScroll.SmallChange, 1)
88    End Sub
```

**Fig. 17.33**   Code generated by ActiveX control interface wizard (part 2 of 2).

**Public Let** and **Get** property methods and **Private** procedures **WriteProperties** and **ReadProperties** are automatically generated based on the mapping setting in Fig. 17.30. **ReadProperties** and **WriteProperties** are **Private** because we did not expose them. This generated code saves the programmer considerable development time. Events or properties listed at the top of the file default to **Public** (the wizard does not precede them with **Public**).

The ActiveX control interface wizard cannot create the complete **LabelScrollbar** control. We must edit and enhance this code to get our desired behavior (Fig. 17.34). We added procedure **InitProperties** and procedure **Resize**. These procedures are identical to the ones we developed earlier in the chapter. We also added code to "tie" the **Label Caption** to the scrollbar **Value** in event procedure **Change**, modified the default values in **ReadProperties** and **WriteProperties**, and added code to **ReadProperties** and **WriteProperties** for the **Label**'s **Caption**.

```
1    ' Fig. 17.34
2    ' Modified code generated by ActiveX Control Interface Wizard.
3    Option Explicit
4    'Event Declarations:
5    Event Change() 'MappingInfo=hsbScroll,hsbScroll,-1,Change
6
7    'WARNING! DO NOT REMOVE OR MODIFY THE FOLLOWING COMMENTED LINES!
8    'MappingInfo=hsbScroll,hsbScroll,-1,LargeChange
9    Public Property Get LargeChange() As Integer
10      LargeChange = hsbScroll.LargeChange
11   End Property
12
13   Public Property Let LargeChange(ByVal New_LargeChange As _
14                                   Integer)
15      hsbScroll.LargeChange() = New_LargeChange
16      PropertyChanged "LargeChange"
17   End Property
18
19   'WARNING! DO NOT REMOVE OR MODIFY THE FOLLOWING COMMENTED LINES!
20   'MappingInfo=hsbScroll,hsbScroll,-1,Min
21   Public Property Get Min() As Integer
22      Min = hsbScroll.Min
23   End Property
24
25   Public Property Let Min(ByVal New_Min As Integer)
26      hsbScroll.Min() = New_Min
27      PropertyChanged "Min"
28   End Property
29
30   'WARNING! DO NOT REMOVE OR MODIFY THE FOLLOWING COMMENTED LINES!
31   'MappingInfo=hsbScroll,hsbScroll,-1,Max
32   Public Property Get Max() As Integer
33      Max = hsbScroll.Max
34   End Property
35
36   Public Property Let Max(ByVal New_Max As Integer)
37      hsbScroll.Max() = New_Max
38      PropertyChanged "Max"
39   End Property
40
41   'WARNING! DO NOT REMOVE OR MODIFY THE FOLLOWING COMMENTED LINES!
42   'MappingInfo=hsbScroll,hsbScroll,-1,Value
43   Public Property Get Value() As Integer
44      Value = hsbScroll.Value
45   End Property
46
47   Public Property Let Value(ByVal New_Value As Integer)
48      hsbScroll.Value() = New_Value
49      PropertyChanged "Value"
50   End Property
51
```

**Fig. 17.34**   Enhancing the code generated by the ActiveX control interface wizard (part 1 of 3).

```
52   'WARNING! DO NOT REMOVE OR MODIFY THE FOLLOWING COMMENTED LINES!
53   'MappingInfo=hsbScroll,hsbScroll,-1,SmallChange
54   Public Property Get SmallChange() As Integer
55      SmallChange = hsbScroll.SmallChange
56   End Property
57
58   Public Property Let SmallChange(ByVal New_SmallChange As _
59                                    Integer)
60      hsbScroll.SmallChange() = New_SmallChange
61      PropertyChanged "SmallChange"
62   End Property
63
64   Private Sub hsbScroll_Change()
65      RaiseEvent Change
66
67      ' NOT generated by ActiveX Control Interface Wizard
68      lblDisplay.Caption = hsbScroll.Value
69   End Sub
70
71   'Load property values from storage
72   Private Sub UserControl_ReadProperties(PropBag As PropertyBag)
73
74      hsbScroll.LargeChange = PropBag.ReadProperty( _
75                                          "LargeChange", 5)
76      hsbScroll.Min = PropBag.ReadProperty("Min", 0)
77      hsbScroll.Max = PropBag.ReadProperty("Max", 32767)
78      hsbScroll.Value = PropBag.ReadProperty("Value", _
79                                          (Min + Max) \ 2)
80      hsbScroll.SmallChange = PropBag.ReadProperty( _
81                                          "SmallChange", 1)
82
83      ' NOT generated by ActiveX Control Interface Wizard
84      lblDisplay.Caption = PropBag.ReadProperty("Caption", _
85                                          hsbScroll.Value)
86   End Sub
87
88   'Write property values to storage
89   Private Sub UserControl_WriteProperties(PropBag As PropertyBag)
90      Call PropBag.WriteProperty("LargeChange", _
91                                 hsbScroll.LargeChange, 5)
92      Call PropBag.WriteProperty("Min", hsbScroll.Min, 0)
93      Call PropBag.WriteProperty("Max", hsbScroll.Max, 32767)
94      Call PropBag.WriteProperty("Value", hsbScroll.Value, _
95                                 (Min + Max) \ 2)
96      Call PropBag.WriteProperty("SmallChange", _
97                                 hsbScroll.SmallChange, 1)
98
99      ' NOT generated by ActiveX Control Interface Wizard
100     Call PropBag.WriteProperty("Caption", _
101                                lblDisplay.Caption, _
102                                (Min + Max) \ 2)
103  End Sub
```

**Fig. 17.34**   Enhancing the code generated by the ActiveX control interface wizard (part 2 of 3).

```
104
105   ' NOT generated by ActiveX Control Interface Wizard
106   Private Sub UserControl_InitProperties()
107
108       With hsbScroll
109           .Min = 0
110           .Max = 32767
111           .Value = (Min + Max) / 2
112           .SmallChange = 1
113           .LargeChange = 5
114       End With
115
116       lblDisplay.Caption = hsbScroll.Value
117   End Sub
118
119   ' NOT generated by ActiveX Control Interface Wizard
120   Private Sub UserControl_Resize()
121
122       With hsbScroll
123           .Left = lblDisplay.Width
124           .Width = ScaleWidth - hsbScroll.Left
125           .Height = ScaleHeight
126       End With
127
128       lblDisplay.Height = ScaleHeight
129   End Sub
```

**Fig. 17.34**   Enhancing the code generated by the ActiveX control interface wizard (part 3 of 3).

## 17.9 Property Pages and the Property Page Wizard

ActiveX controls often have tabbed dialogs—called *property pages*—associated with them. Property pages allow the user to view and set an ActiveX control's properties. Property pages allow the author of the ActiveX control to conveniently group related properties (as opposed to having them scattered throughout the **Properties** window—which can make it difficult for the developer to see which properties are related). Property pages are optional for ActiveX controls.

An ActiveX control's property pages are displayed by double-clicking the *(Custom)* property in the **Properties** window, clicking once with the right-mouse button on the ActiveX control (once it has been sited on an object such as a form) and selecting *Properties* from the popup menu, or by selecting the ActiveX control and selecting *Property Pages* from the **View** menu. Figure 17.35 shows the property pages for the **MaskEdit** ActiveX control we introduced in Chapter 10.

Property pages are added to the ActiveX control project with the *Add PropertyPage* dialog (displayed when *Add Property Page* is selected from the **Project** menu) shown in Fig. 17.36.

The **Add PropertyPage** dialog allows the programmer to either create a new property page or open an existing one. New property pages are created by either selecting *Property Page* or *VB Property Page Wizard*. **Property Page** allows the programmer to create every element of the property page—a process similar to customizing a form. A programmer might choose to use **Property Page** when creating property pages that have special GUI elements (e.g., graphics) that do not conform to the conventional property page GUI (i.e., tabbed dialogs). **Property Page** is likely to be used by experienced ActiveX control developers to provided "polished" property pages.

The **VB Property Page Wizard** provides a fast and convenient means of creating property pages. In this section we use the **VB Property Page Wizard** to create a property page for the **LabelScrollbar** ActiveX control created in Section 17.6.

Opening the **VB Property Page Wizard** displays the *Property Page Wizard - Introduction* dialog shown in Fig. 17.37. This dialog provides the user with a few instructions. Pressing **Next >** displays the dialog of Fig. 17.38.

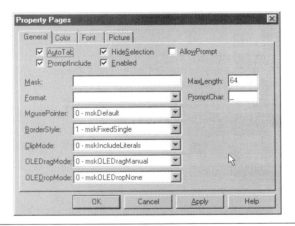

**Fig. 17.35**   Property pages for the **MaskEdit** ActiveX control.

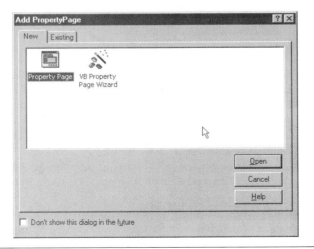

**Fig. 17.36**   **Add PropertyPage** dialog.

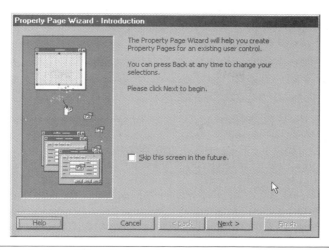

**Fig. 17.37    Property Page Wizard - Introduction** dialog.

The **Property Page Wizard - Select the Property Pages** dialog allows the programmer to either add an existing property page or to create a new one. Existing property pages (if they exist) are displayed in the **ListBox**. The arrows to the right of the **ListBox** allow the programmer to determine the order of the property pages. If the **ListBox** does not contain any property pages, as is the case in Fig. 17.38, the **Rename...** button is disabled. The **Rename...** button allows the programmer to rename an existing property page. Pressing **Add** displays the dialog of Fig. 17.39.

The **Property Page Name** dialog allows the programmer to enter the name that will appear on a property page tab. The default name is **PropertyPage1**. For the example in this section, we set the name to **Scroll**. Pressing **OK** closes the dialog.

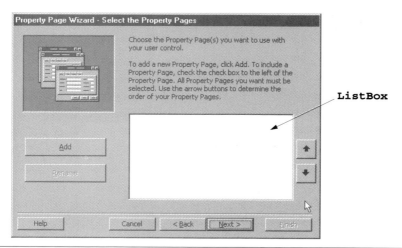

**Fig. 17.38    Property Page Wizard - Select the Property Pages** dialog.

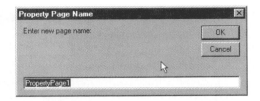

**Fig. 17.39    Property Page Name** dialog.

Figure 17.40 shows the **Property Page Wizard - Select the Property Pages** dialog after **Scroll** is entered in the **Property Page Name** dialog. The **CheckBox** to the left of **Scroll** indicates whether or not the property page is included. When checked, the property page is included (i.e., displayed when the developer displays the property pages). Note that the **Rename...** button is enabled because the **ListBox** contains at least one property page. Pressing **Rename...** displays the **Property Page Name** dialog of Fig. 17.39. At least one property page must be added before the **Next >** is pressed; otherwise, a dialog is displayed, indicating that a property page must be selected.

After the **Next >** is pressed, the *Property Page Wizard - Add Properties* dialog of Fig. 17.41 is displayed. This dialog displays the property page tabs and allows the programmer to associate properties with a specific property page.

The *Available Properties* **ListBox** contains the properties that can be placed on the property pages. An individual property can be placed on a property page by either double-clicking the property, dragging-and-dropping the property or by pressing the **>** button. Multiple properties can be placed on a page by highlighting them and dragging and dropping. All the available properties can be placed on the property page by pressing **>>**. For this example, we select all available properties and add them to the property page. Pressing **Next >** displays the **Property Page Wizard - Finished!** dialog shown in Fig. 17.42.

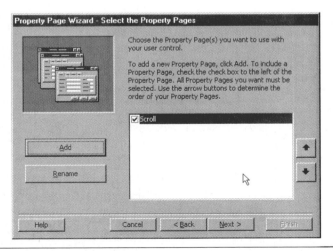

**Fig. 17.40    Property Page Wizard - Select the Property Pages** dialog.

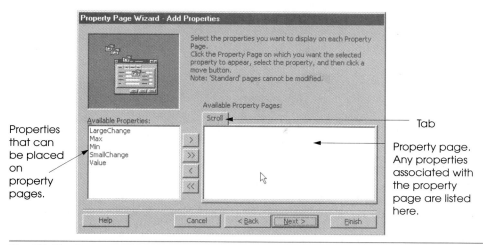

Properties that can be placed on property pages.

Tab

Property page. Any properties associated with the property page are listed here.

**Fig. 17.41    Property Page Wizard - Add Properties** dialog.

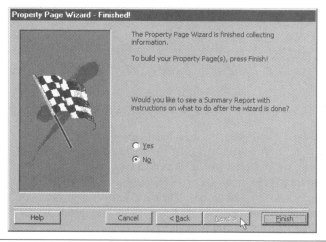

**Fig. 17.42    Property Page Wizard - Finished!** dialog.

The **Property Page Wizard - Finished!** dialog provides the programmer with the option of viewing a summary report after the property pages are created. Figure 17.44 displays the **_Property Page Wizard Summary Report_** dialog. Property pages are created by pressing **Finished** (which results in the **_Property Page Created_** dialog of Fig. 17.43 being displayed). If **Yes** has been selected for the summary report, the **Property Page Wizard Summary Report** dialog is displayed after the dialog of Fig. 17.43 is closed.

Once property pages are created, the **Project Explorer** window displays a new folder titled **Property Pages**. Property page code and the property page GUI can be viewed by selecting the property page in the **Project Explorer** window and pressing **View Code** and **View Object**, respectively. Viewing the property page code and property page GUI provides insight into what is need to create property pages. The programmer can also further customize the property pages by adding code or other GUI elements.

**Fig. 17.43    Property Page Created** dialog.

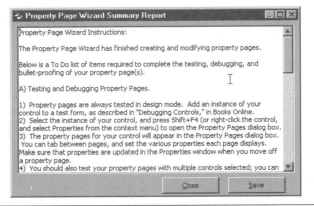

**Fig. 17.44    Property Page Wizard Summary Report** dialog.

At design time, we can set a **LabelScrollbar** ActiveX control's properties using either the **Properties** window or the property pages we just created. First we add a form to the project and place a **LabelScrollbar** control on it. Next we double click the **LabelScrollbar**'s **(Custom)** property to display the property pages that we created using the **Property Page Wizard** (Fig. 17.45).

## 17.10  ActiveX DLLs

Visual Basic allows the programmer to create another type of COM-based object which is not executable by itself—but is intended to be used by another application. This *ActiveX component* (i.e., a unit of executable code) is called an *ActiveX dynamic link library (DLL)*. ActiveX DLLs are a complex topic and this section is an introduction to the basics of creating and using ActiveX DLLs.

Every Windows application that is executed must reside in memory. ActiveX DLLs are loaded into the same *process* (i.e., memory) as the application that uses the ActiveX DLL. For this reason, ActiveX DLLs are often called *in-process components*. Figure 17.46 illustrates two applications in their own *private address spaces* (i.e., an area of memory not accessible to other running applications—this is automatically set up by Windows 95, Windows 98, and Windows NT).

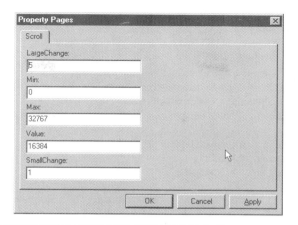

**Fig. 17.45**   **Property Pages** created with the **Property Page Wizard**.

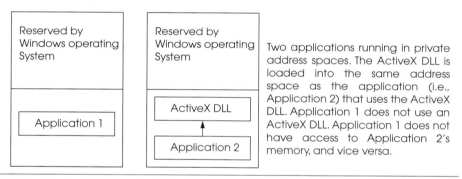

Two applications running in private address spaces. The ActiveX DLL is loaded into the same address space as the application (i.e., Application 2) that uses the ActiveX DLL. Application 1 does not use an ActiveX DLL. Application 1 does not have access to Application 2's memory, and vice versa.

**Fig. 17.46**   ActiveX DLL loaded into the same address space as its calling application.

We are now ready to create a simple example that creates and uses an ActiveX DLL. Figure 17.47 lists code for an ActiveX DLL that provides one **Function** procedure called **SpellCheckWord** that uses Microsoft **Word**'s spell checker. We also create a **Standard EXE** application that uses the ActiveX DLL to verify that it is working properly.

To create an ActiveX DLL, we open an ***ActiveX DLL*** project. By default an **ActiveX DLL** project contains one class module. Inside this class module, we can write code precisely as we did earlier in this chapter as well as in Chapter 16. Note: **ActiveX DLL**s can contain visual elements (i.e., forms)—although we do not use them in this example.

```
1  ' Figure 17.47
2  ' ActiveX DLL example
3  Option Explicit
4  Private mWordRef As Word.Application
```

**Fig. 17.47**   ActiveX DLL code (part 1 of 2).

```
 5
 6  Private Sub Class_Initialize()
 7      Set mWordRef = New Word.Application
 8  End Sub
 9
10  ' Function returns False if s is spelled incorrectly
11  Public Function SpellCheckWord(ByVal s As String) As Boolean
12      SpellCheckWord = mWordRef.CheckSpelling(s)
13  End Function
14
15  Private Sub Class_Terminate()
16      Call mWordRef.Quit
17      Set mWordRef = Nothing
18  End Sub
```

**Fig. 17.47**  ActiveX DLL code (part 2 of 2).

Line 4 creates a **Word.Application** reference. Line 7 sets **mWordRef** to a **New Word.Application** object. Reference **mWordRef** allows us to access the functionality of **Word**. Programmer-defined **Function** procedure **SpellCheckWord** takes one **String** argument and checks the spelling in the **String** with the statement

```
SpellCheckWord = mWordRef.CheckSpelling(s)
```

Method **CheckSpelling** takes a **String** argument and returns a **Boolean** value. If the contents of the **String** are misspelled, **CheckSpelling** returns **False** and if the contents of the **String** are spelled correctly, **CheckSpelling** returns **True**. The value returned by **CheckSpelling** is returned by **SpellCheckWord**. Figure 17.48 lists the names we give the **ActiveX DLL** project members.

Like ActiveX controls, we need to create a stand-alone file that can be used independently of the Visual Basic IDE. ActiveX DLL files end in the extension **.DLL**. To create the **.DLL** we select **Make SpellChecker.dll...** from the **File** menu, which displays the **Make Project** dialog (Fig. 17.22). We save our **.DLL** to the **D:** drive, but you can save yours wherever you want. After saving the **.DLL**, we close the project. Once we have created the **.DLL** we can use it in other applications by adding a reference to it (using the **References** dialog as shown in Fig. 17.49).

We can now test the **.DLL** by opening a **Standard EXE** and adding a reference to the **.DLL** using the **References** dialog of Fig. 17.49. After adding the reference we can begin writing code to use our **SpellChecker.dll**. This code is shown in Fig. 17.50.

| Member | Value |
|---|---|
| Class (Name) | CWordChecker |
| Project (Name) | SpellChecker |
| Project Description | VB6HTP1 ActiveX DLL SpellChecker |

**Fig. 17.48**  Names used in our **ActiveX DLL** project.

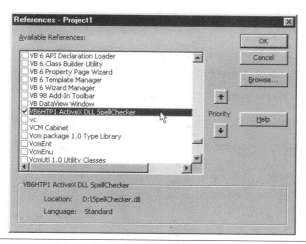

Fig. 17.49    **References** dialog displaying our ActiveX DLL.

```
1   ' Fig. 17.50
2   ' Form module to exercise SpellChecker DLL
3   Option Explicit
4   Private mChecker As CWordChecker
5
6   Public Sub Form_Initialize()
7      Set mChecker = New CWordChecker
8   End Sub
9
10  Private Sub cmdCheck_Click()
11
12     If mChecker.SpellCheckWord(txtInput.Text) Then
13        lblDisplay.Caption = txtInput.Text & _
14                            " is spelled correctly."
15     Else
16        lblDisplay.Caption = txtInput.Text & _
17                            " is spelled incorrectly."
18     End If
19
20  End Sub
21
22  Private Sub Form_Terminate()
23     Set mChecker = Nothing
24  End Sub
```

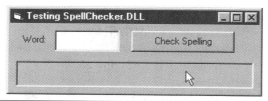

Fig. 17.50    A **Standard EXE** which uses the **SpellChecker.dll** (part 1 of 2).

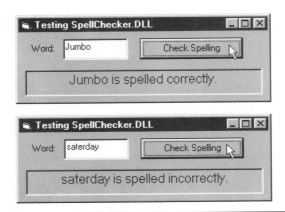

**Fig. 17.50**   A **Standard EXE** which uses the **SpellChecker.dll** (part 2 of 2).

On line 4 we create a reference (called **mChecker**) to a **CWordChecker** type. On line 7 we **Set mChecker** to a **New** instance of a **CWordChecker**. In the **cmdCheck_Click** event procedure, we call **mChecker**'s **SpellCheckWord** procedure passing it **txtInput**'s **Text**. When **True** is returned, **lblDisplay**'s **Caption** indicates that the word is spelled correctly. Otherwise, **lblDisplay**'s **Caption** indicates that the word is spelled incorrectly.

## 17.11  ActiveX EXEs

Visual Basic provides the ***ActiveX EXE*** project type for creating applications that can either run as stand-alone applications or can be executed through automation (locally or remotely). **Word** is a common example of an ActiveX EXE. In this section we provide a brief introduction to ActiveX EXEs.

Unlike ActiveX DLLs, ActiveX EXEs do not run in-process. Each ActiveX EXE runs in its own private address space. If the ActiveX EXE needs to access the resources of another EXE, it must use *marshaling* (i.e., *interprocess communication*). Marshaling translates values from one EXE's process into another EXE's process, and vice versa.

***Performance Tip 17.3***

*ActiveX EXEs usually execute slower than equivalent ActiveX DLLs because they must use marshaling.*

***Software Engineering Observation 17.10***

*EXEs must use marshaling because Windows forbids one process from directly communicating with another process.*

ActiveX EXEs are created using **ActiveX EXE** projects. When an **ActiveX EXE** project is opened, it contains one class module by default. ActiveX EXEs can have GUIs—although the GUI typically is not displayed when the ActiveX EXE is being automated. Earlier in the chapter, we used automation to create a **Word** document—**Word**'s GUI was not displayed.

In Fig. 17.52, we create an ActiveX EXE version of the ActiveX DLL spell checker we developed in Section 17.10. The ActiveX EXE class module code is identical to the

ActiveX DLL's class module code. Figure 17.51 lists the project module names and the project description.

| Member | Value |
|--------|-------|
| **Class** (**Name**) | `CSpellCheckerEXE` |
| **Module** (**Name**) | `modStartup` |
| **Project** (**Name**) | `SpellCheck` |
| **Project Description** | **VB6HTP1 SpellCheck ActiveX EXE** |

**Fig. 17.51**   Names used in our **ActiveX EXE** project.

```
1    ' Fig. 17.52
2    ' ActiveX EXE example
3    ' Class CSpellCheckerEXE
4    Option Explicit
5    Private mWordRef As Word.Application
6
7    Private Sub Class_Initialize()
8       Set mWordRef = New Word.Application
9    End Sub
10
11   ' Function procedure returns False if the word is
12   ' spelled incorrectly
13   Public Function SpellCheckWord(ByVal s As String) As Boolean
14      SpellCheckWord = mWordRef.CheckSpelling(s)
15   End Function
16
17   Private Sub Class_Terminate()
18      Call mWordRef.Quit
19      Set mWordRef = Nothing
20   End Sub
```

**Fig. 17.52**   ActiveX EXE Executing as a stand-alone EXE (part 1 of 3).

```
21   ' Form module
22   Option Explicit
23
24   Private Sub Form_Initialize()
25      Set mChecker = New CSpellCheckerEXE
26   End Sub
27
28   Private Sub cmdCheck_Click()
29
30      If mChecker.SpellCheckWord(txtInput.Text) Then
31         lblDisplay.Caption = txtInput.Text & _
32                               " is spelled correctly."
```

**Fig. 17.52**   ActiveX EXE Executing as a stand-alone EXE (part 2 of 3).

```
33        Else
34            lblDisplay.Caption = txtInput.Text & _
35                                " is spelled incorrectly."
36        End If
37
38    End Sub
39
40    Private Sub Form_Terminate()
41        Set mChecker = Nothing
42    End Sub
```

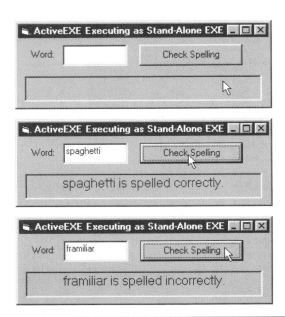

**Fig. 17.52**    ActiveX EXE Executing as a stand-alone EXE (part 3 of 3).

Stand-alone ActiveX EXEs use **Main** for a start-up object. Therefore, a standard module must be added to the project. In **Main**, the lines

```
If App.StartMode = vbSModeStandalone Then
   Call frmCheck.Show
Else    ' vbSModeAutomation
   Set mChecker = New CSpellCheckerEXE
End If
```

test the **App** object's **StartMode** property to determine if the ActiveX EXE began execution as a stand-alone application (**vbSModeStandalone**) or as an ActiveX component (**vbSModeAutomation**). The programmer can use the **App** object to get information about the application that is currently executing.

If the ActiveX EXE is executed as a stand-alone application, method **Show** is called to load **frmCheck** and display the GUI. If the EXE is executed via automation, an instance of **CSpellCheckerEXE** is created and assigned to the reference **mChecker**. We will discuss controlling the ActiveX EXE through automation in greater detail momentarily.

The form module contains three event procedures: **Form_Initialize**, **cmdCheck_Click** and **Form_Terminate**. **Form_Initialize** creates an instance of **CSpellCheckerEXE**. Reference **mChecker** is assigned this **New** instance. In **cmdCheck_Click**, **txtInput**'s **Text** is passed to **SpellCheckWord**. The **Label**'s **Caption** then displays whether or not the text is spelled correctly. Event procedure **Form_Terminate** Sets **mChecker** to **Nothing**.

To execute the ActiveX EXE as a stand-alone application, we

1. Select **ActiveX EXE** as the **Project Type** and **Sub Main** as the **Startup Object**. (These are listed on the **Project Properties** dialog's **General** tab.)

2. Select **Standalone** for the **Start Mode** on the **Project Properties** dialog's **Component** tab (Fig. 17.53).

3. Press **OK** to close the **Project Properties** dialog.

4. Execute the program.

We can also use automation to control the ActiveX EXE we just created. In order to allow the ActiveX EXE to be controlled via automation, we

1. Set the **Start Mode** to **ActiveX Component** in the **Project Properties** dialog's **Component** tab.

2. Select **ActiveX EXE** as the **Project Type** and **Sub Main** as the **Startup Object** in the **Project Properties** dialog's **General** tab.

3. Press the **OK** button to close the **Project Properties** dialog.

4. Run the program. The GUI is not displayed.

Now we create a second program (i.e., a **Standard EXE**) to control the ActiveX EXE. To create the **Standard EXE** we perform the following steps.

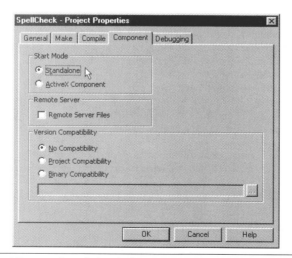

**Fig. 17.53**   **Project Properties** dialog's **Component** tab.

5. Run a second copy of Visual Basic and open a **Standard EXE** project. The ActiveX EXE should still be running in the first copy of Visual Basic as an **ActiveX Component**. At this point two copies of Visual Basic should be open.

6. Set a reference to **VB6HTP1 SpellCheck ActiveX EXE** using the **References** dialog.

7. Write a program to control the ActiveX via automation. Figure 17.54 lists the **Standard EXE**'s code we use. The program displays a **ListBox** containing various words—some of which are deliberately misspelled. The user selects a word and presses **Check Spelling**. **SpellCheckWord** is called and a **MsgBox** is displayed indicating whether or not the word is spelled correctly.

8. Run the program.

In order to ensure that our client application (i.e., the **Standard EXE**) will retain a proper reference to the ActiveX EXE, we

1. Compiled the ActiveX EXE to native code.

2. Selected the *Binary Compatibility* option [in the *Version Compatibility Frame* (Fig. 17.53)].

3. Specified the location and name of the **.exe** (created in Step 1) in the **TextBox** beneath the **Binary Compatibility** option.

```
1   ' Fig. 17.54
2   Option Explicit
3   Private mChkRef As CSpellCheckerEXE
4
5   Private Sub Form_Initialize()
6       Set mChkRef = New CSpellCheckerEXE
7   End Sub
8
9   Private Sub Form_Load()
10      Call lstWords.AddItem("Hello")
11      Call lstWords.AddItem("yllow")
12      Call lstWords.AddItem("venus")
13      Call lstWords.AddItem("ROOT")
14      Call lstWords.AddItem("Mondy")
15      Call lstWords.AddItem("water")
16  End Sub
17
18  Private Sub cmdCheck_Click()
19
20      If mChkRef.SpellCheckWord(lstWords.Text) Then
21          Call MsgBox("Spelled correctly.", vbInformation)
22      Else
23          Call MsgBox("Spelled incorrectly!", vbCritical)
24      End If
25
26  End Sub
```

**Fig. 17.54** **Standard EXE** that uses an ActiveX EXE for spell checking (part 1 of 2).

```
27
28    Private Sub Class_Terminate()
29        Set mChkRef = Nothing
30    End Sub
```

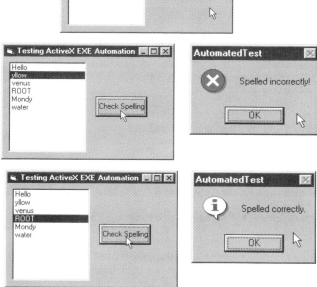

**Fig. 17.54**   **Standard EXE** that uses an ActiveX EXE for spell checking (part 2 of 2).

    4.  Pressed **OK** to close the dialog.

    5.  Saved the project.

If we do not do this, the client may not be able to find the proper reference—which would then have to be added again. For a detailed discussion of this *version compatibility* issue, see the section "*Version Compatibility in ActiveX Components*" in the on-line documentation.

## 17.12  Friend Access

Visual Basic provides a third access specifier—called **Friend**—for sharing functionality within an ActiveX component. Like **Public** access, **Friend** access allows methods to be accessible to all modules within the project. Unlike **Public** access, **Friend** access is not available outside the project (i.e., is not exposed). **Friend** access can only be applied to a procedure within a class module.

**Common Programming Error 17.4**

*Declaring a variable with **Friend** access is a syntax error.*

**Common Programming Error 17.5**

*Declaring a procedure with **Friend** access in a standard module is a syntax error.*

Figure 17.55 modifies the ActiveX EXE introduced in the last section by adding a **Friend** procedure called **GetName**. The GUI is enhanced to display the **String** returned from **GetName**. We execute the ActiveX EXE as a stand-alone executable.

```
1   ' Fig. 17.55 ActiveX EXE example
2   ' Class CSpellCheckerEXE2
3   Option Explicit
4   Private mWordRef As Word.Application
5   Private mString As String
6
7   Private Sub Class_Initialize()
8       Set mWordRef = New Word.Application
9   End Sub
10
11  ' Function procedure returns False if word is
12  ' spelled incorrectly
13  Public Function SpellCheckWord(ByVal s As String) As Boolean
14      mString = s
15      SpellCheckWord = mWordRef.CheckSpelling(mString)
16  End Function
17
18  ' Friend method is only visible within the current application
19  Friend Function GetCaption() As String
20      GetCaption = mWordRef.Caption
21  End Function
22
23  Private Sub Class_Terminate()
24      Call mWordRef.Quit
25      Set mWordRef = Nothing
26  End Sub
```

**Fig. 17.55**  Demonstrating **Friend** access within an application (part 1 or 4).

```
27  ' Standard module used as Startup object
28  ' Module modStartup
29  Option Explicit
30
31  Public mChecker As CSpellCheckerEXE2
32
33  Public Sub Main()
34
35      If App.StartMode = vbSModeStandalone Then
36          Call frmCheck.Show
```

**Fig. 17.55**  Demonstrating **Friend** access within an application (part 2 or 4).

```
37        Else    ' vbSModeAutomation
38            Set mChecker = New CSpellCheckerEXE2
39        End If
40
41    End Sub
42
43    Private Sub Class_Terminate()
44        Set mChecker = Nothing
45    End Sub
```

**Fig. 17.55**   Demonstrating **Friend** access within an application (part 3 or 4).

```
46    ' Form module
47    Option Explicit
48
49    Private Sub Form_Initialize()
50        Set mChecker = New CSpellCheckerEXE2
51
52        ' Call Friend method in CSpellCheckerEXE2
53        lblSuggest.Caption = mChecker.GetCaption()
54    End Sub
55
56    Private Sub cmdCheck_Click()
57
58        If mChecker.SpellCheckWord(txtInput.Text) Then
59            lblDisplay.Caption = txtInput.Text & _
60                                 " is spelled correctly."
61        Else
62            lblDisplay.Caption = txtInput.Text & _
63                                 " is spelled incorrectly."
64        End If
65
66    End Sub
67
68    Private Sub Form_Terminate()
69        Set mChecker = Nothing
70    End Sub
```

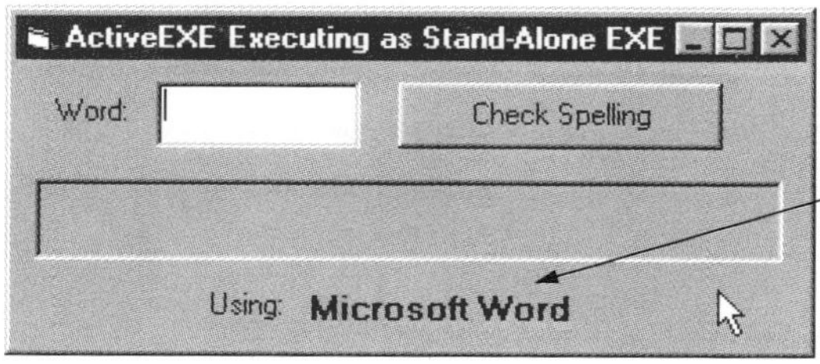

Word's **Caption** displayed in a **Label**.

**Fig. 17.55**   Demonstrating **Friend** access within an application (part 4 or 4).

**Function** procedure **GetCaption**

```
    Friend Function GetCaption() As String
        GetCaption = mWordRef.Caption
    End Function
```

has **Friend** access and returns the **Word**'s **Caption** (which is **Microsoft Word**). When executing as a stand-alone ActiveX EXE, the form module calls **GetCaption** with the statement

```
lblSuggest.Caption = mChecker.GetCaption()
```

**GetCaption** is accessible to the form module because it is declared with **Friend** access. If **GetCaption** were declared **Private**, it could not be called from the form module. If **GetCaption** were declared **Public**, **GetCaption** could be called from the form module. However, **Public** access would make **GetCaption** available to client programs using our ActiveX server (i.e., the ActiveX EXE) via automation.

Figure 17.56 shows *auto quick info* for a **Standard EXE** automating **CSpellCheckerEXE2**. **GetCaption** is not available because it has **Friend** access.

Figure 17.57 shows the result when **GetCaption** is given **Public** access. An application automating **CSpellCheckerEXE2** can call **GetCaption**.

Figure 17.58 summarizes the **Public**, **Private** and **Friend** access modifier visibilities when applied to a method of a class.

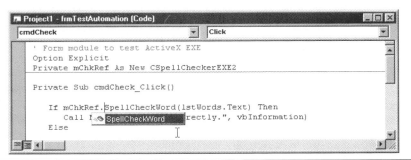

**Fig. 17.56**  Procedures with **Friend** access are not available to executables automating **CSpellCheckerEXE2**.

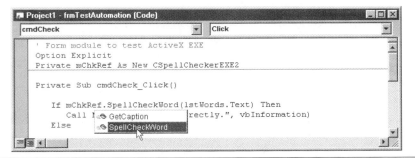

**Fig. 17.57**  Procedures with **Public** access are available to executables automating **CSpellCheckerEXE2**.

| Method access | Accessible within the same project | Accessible outside of the project |
|---------------|-----------------------------------|-----------------------------------|
| **Public**    | yes                               | yes                               |
| **Friend**    | yes                               | no                                |
| **Private**   | no                                | no                                |

**Fig. 17.58** Visibility of access modifiers.

## Summary

- ActiveX technologies cover a wide range of distributed computing technologies and are generally grouped into three broad categories—ActiveX controls, ActiveX documents and ActiveX components.

- A reusable binary piece of code is called a component. Software composed of components is often called componentware.

- COM is a specification that describes how a series of components—which are possibly written in different programming languages by different vendors—can communicate.

- Visual Basic uses COM—although the details of COM are hidden from the programmer.

- With COM, applications interact with components through a set of standard methods grouped into interfaces (Visual Basic interfaces are modeled after COM interfaces). The most fundamental COM interface is **IUnknown**. Every COM interface must contain **IUnknown**'s methods—**AddRef**, **Release** and **QueryInterface**.

- Microsoft has been developing an enhancement to COM called COM+ which will provide significant enhancements to COM.

- Distributed COM (DCOM) is a distributed version of COM. DCOM provides the means of executing COM components on remote machines—while hiding all the implementation details from the programmer. DCOM also adds additional features not provided by COM (e.g., security).

- OLE is a technology that allows applications to work together seamlessly (i.e., the ability to use an **Excel** spreadsheet within **Word**—without having to explicitly open a copy of **Excel**).

- ActiveX technologies build upon COM, DCOM and OLE. ActiveX technologies cover a broad range of distributed technologies, including ActiveX controls, ActiveX code components and ActiveX documents.

- ActiveX controls are reusable components that can be "plugged" into a Visual Basic program (as well as programs written in other languages). An ActiveX control can be just about anything the programmer can imagine—a calendar, a word processor, an image editor, a card game, etc. ActiveX controls can be visible or invisible to the user.

- VBX controls are the predecessor to ActiveX controls and cannot be used with Visual Basic 5 or Visual Basic 6.

- Programmers can create their own ActiveX controls directly in Visual Basic.

- Three different types of ActiveX controls can be created with Visual Basic—user-drawn controls, "enhanced" controls, and "aggregate" controls. User-drawn controls are custom controls developed from "scratch." Enhanced controls add features to existing controls. Aggregate controls contain one or more existing controls called constituent controls.

- ActiveX controls have design-time and run-time instances which are repeatedly created and destroyed as the author changes the IDE from design-mode to run-mode (and vice versa).

- ActiveX controls are created using the **ActiveX Control** project type. ActiveX stand-alone controls have a **.OCX** extension.

- Property **Public** allows the ActiveX control to be shared with other applications. The **Public** property defaults to **True**.

- ActiveX controls often have tabbed dialogs, called property pages, associated with them. Property pages allow the developer to view and set an ActiveX control's properties. Property pages are displayed by double-clicking the **(Custom)** property.

- The author designs the GUI and determines what functionality (i.e., properties, methods and events) the ActiveX control exposes. The developer can use any exposed properties, methods and events. A control exposes properties, methods, and events by making them **Public**.

- Event **Initialize** is only executed once during a control's lifetime and is always the first event raised. Event procedure **InitProperties** initializes a control's properties. **InitProperties** is only raised once during the control's lifetime. If an existing form which already contains an instance of the control is opened, **InitProperties** is not raised—**ReadProperties** is.

- Event procedure **Resize** is used by constituent controls to determine the layout and size of each constituent control member. User-drawn controls do not use **Resize**. User-drawn controls use **Paint** to display their GUI.

- Event procedure **ReadProperties** retrieves properties from the container's file. Event procedure **WriteProperties** saves property values to disk.

- A **UserControl** behaves programmatically different from a form. Form events like **Activate**, **Deactivate**, **Load**, **UnLoad**, **QueryUnload**, etc. do not exist for **UserControl**s. Only **Terminate** and **UnLoad** are somewhat similar. When saved, **UserControl** files get the **.ctl** extension. A **UserControl**'s name is set using the **(Name)** property.

- A **UserControl** has a general declaration. Any events or properties the control will expose are placed in the general declaration. **Event**s and properties placed in the general declaration must be **Public** (**Event**s are **Public** by default). Module-level variables may also be placed in the general declaration (module-level variables default to **Private**).

- Constituent control events are hidden within the **UserControl**. The developer cannot directly use them unless the control's author has exposed them. The constituent control's event that is being exposed must be coded to raise the event using **RaiseEvent**.

- The **Ambient** object provides the **UserControl** information about its container such that the control can "blend" into its container. When an **Ambient** property changes for a container, the **AmbientChanged** event is raised.

- The **Extender** object accesses properties, methods and events controlled by the container.

- Type **OLE_COLOR** is a standard Visual Basic type that represents colors.

- The toolbox bitmap size for a control is 16-by-15 pixels (set with property **ToolboxBitmap**).

- Wizards simplify the process of creating applications, ActiveX controls, etc. The ActiveX control interface wizard provides a means of quickly generating basic control functionality—leaving programmers to concentrate on programming the more difficult control functionality.

- Visual Basic allows the programmer to create a special type of COM-based object called an ActiveX DLL—which is not executable by itself—intended to be used by another application. ActiveX DLLs are loaded into the same process as the application that uses the ActiveX DLL. ActiveX DLL files end in the extension **.DLL**.

- Visual Basic provides the **ActiveX EXE** project type for creating applications that can either run as stand-alone applications or can be executed through automation (locally or remotely). ActiveX EXEs do not run in-process. Each ActiveX EXE runs in its own private address space. If the ActiveX EXE needs to access the resources of another EXE, it must use marshaling. Marshaling translates values from one EXE's process into another EXE's process, and vice versa.

- Stand-alone ActiveX EXEs use **Main** for a start-up object. Therefore, a standard module must be added to the project.

- The **App** object's **StartMode** property determines if the EXE began execution as a stand-alone application or as an ActiveX component.

- **Friend** methods are accessible to all modules within a project. **Friend** methods are not accessible to other applications.

## Terminology

.ctl  
.ctx  
.dll  
.exe  
.frm  
.frx  
.ocx  
.pag  
**(Custom)** property  
**(Name)** property  
ActiveX  
ActiveX components  
ActiveX control  
ActiveX control interface wizard  
**ActiveX Control** project type  
**ActiveX DLL** project type  
ActiveX document  
**ActiveX EXE** project type  
ActiveX server  
ActiveX technologies  
**Add-In Manager** dialog  
**Add-Ins** menu  
**Add PropertyPage** dialog  
**Add User Control** dialog  
**AddRef**  
address space  
aggregate control  
**Ambient** object  
**AmbientChanged** event  
**App** object  
author  
automation  
**Automation Manager** tool  
binary-level specification  
**Binary Compatibility** option  
COM  
COM component  
COM+  
constituent control  

container  
DCE  
DCOM  
design-time instance of a control  
developer  
**Documents** collection  
dynamic link library, DLL  
enhanced control  
**Event**  
expose a method  
expose an event  
expose a property  
**Extender** object  
fire an event  
**Friend** access modifier  
hash marks on a control  
host container  
**hWnd** property  
**InitProperties** procedure  
in-place activation  
in-process component  
**IUnknown**  
lightweight control  
local servers  
**Make Project** dialog  
mapping a property  
marshaling  
**Member Options** dialog  
object linking and embedding  
OLE  
**OLE_COLOR** type  
persist a property  
private address space  
**Procedure Attributes** dialog  
programmatic interface  
**PropertyBag** object  
**PropertyChanged** method  
property page  
property page wizard

**Property Pages** menu command
**Public** property
**Quit** method
**RaiseEvent**
**ReadProperties** event
**ReadProperty** method
Realse
**Remote Automation Connection Manager**
remote servers
**Resize** event
run-time instance of a control
**SaveAs** method
**Selection** object
**Shading** object
siting a control
stand-alone executable
**StartMode** property
**Terminate**
**Texture** property
**TypeText** method

unsiting a control
**UserControl**
user-drawn control
**vbSModeAutomation** constant
**vbSModeStandalone** constant
VBX control
version compatibility
**Version Compatibility Frame**
Visual Basic extension control
visual editing
**wdTexture22Pt5Percent** constant
windowed control
windowless control
**Windowless** property
Windows handle
wizard
**Word**
**Word.Application**
**WriteProperties** procedure
**WriteProperty** method

## Common Programming Errors

**17.1**  Lightweight controls can only contain other lightweight controls. Placing a windowed control on a lightweight control is a syntax error.

**17.2**  Attempting to declare an **Event** as **Private** is a syntax error.

**17.3**  Raising an event not declared in the general declaration is a syntax error.

**17.4**  Declaring a variable with **Friend** access is a syntax error.

**17.5**  Declaring a procedure with **Friend** access in a standard module is a syntax error.

## Good Programming Practice

**17.1**  The size of the **UserControl** is the default size the developers using the control will see (unless specified otherwise in the **Resize** or **Paint** event procedure). In general, it is best not to have the control any larger than necessary.

## Performance Tips

**17.1**  Lightweight controls consume fewer resources than controls—but do not necessarily execute any faster.

**17.2**  A property value is only written to the container file (i.e., a **.frm** file, a **.frx** file, etc.) if it is different from the default value. This saves a write operation as well as reducing the size of the container file.

**17.3**  ActiveX EXEs usually execute slower than equivalent ActiveX DLLs because they must use marshaling.

## Software Engineering Observations

**17.1**  COM is not a programming language. COM is a specification that can be implemented by many programming languages, including C++, C, Pascal, etc.

**17.2**   COM is language independent, location independent and compiler independent.

**17.3**   Visual Basic is one of the most heavily COM-oriented tools in existence.

**17.4**   COM objects are automatically DCOM objects.

**17.5**   DCOM allows complex problems to be solved using components located on several remote machines. This allows the processing power of several machines to collectively solve a problem.

**17.6**   Lightweight controls were created for distributed applications.

**17.7**   Lightweight controls are not universally supported. If not supported, a lightweight control automatically runs in windowed mode (i.e., it automatically gets assigned a Windows handle). Visual Basic and Internet Explorer 4.0+ support lightweight controls.

**17.8**   If a **UserControl** contains graphics (e.g., images) that cannot be saved as plain text in the **.ctl** file, a separate file with the same name and extension **.ctx** is created to save the graphics. This is equivalent to what a form does with graphics and **.frx** files.

**17.9**   Controls containing constituent controls leverage existing GUIs and functionality. The author does not have to redevelop this.

**17.10**   EXEs must use marshaling because Windows forbids one process from directly communicating with another process.

## Testing and Debugging Tip

**17.1**   When using the **Extender** object, write error-handling code in case the container does not support a particular **Extender** property, method or event.

## Self-Review Exercises

**17.1**   State whether the following are *true* or *false*. If *false*, explain why.
   a) An ActiveX control's property pages can only be accessed at run-time.
   b) An ActiveX DLL usually executes faster than an equivalent ActiveX EXE.
   c) COM is short for Computer Object Model.
   d) The ActiveX control interface wizard is a tool that creates the basic functionality for an ActiveX control.
   e) Properties set (at run-time) for an ActiveX control are not saved to disk.

**17.2**   For each of the following ActiveX controls, select the type (constituent control, custom control or enhanced control) that best describes the ActiveX control. For example, **LabelScrollbar**'s type is constituent control.
   a) **MaskEdit**.
   b) **Rich TextBox**.
   c) **CircularButton**.
   d) **TextFieldScrollbar**.
   e) **AnalogClock**.

**17.3**   Fill in the blank for each of the following.
   a) Property _____ specifies an ActiveX control's toolbox bitmap.
   b) Event procedure _____ draws a user-drawn control.
   c) Double-clicking an ActiveX control's _____ property displays the ActiveX control's property pages (if the control has property pages).
   d) Object _____'s **StartMode** property determines if an application is running stand-alone.
   e) _____ is a distributed version of COM.
   f) _____ controls are the predecessor to ActiveX controls.

## *Answers to Self-Review Exercises*

**17.1**  a)  False. They can only be accessed at design time.
       b)  True.
       c)  False. COM is short for Component Object Model.
       d)  True.
       e)  True.

**17.2**  a)  Enhanced control.
       b)  Enhanced control.
       c)  User-drawn control.
       d)  Constituent control.
       e)  User-drawn control.

**17.3**  a)  **ToolboxBitmap**.
       b)  **Paint**.
       c)  **(Custom)**.
       d)  **App**.
       e)  DCOM.
       f)  VBX.

## *Exercises*

**17.4**   Write a program that verifies the order in which events (discussed in Section 17.4) occur for the **UserControl**. Use **Debug.Print** statements to display the name of each event as it occurs.

**17.5**   Modify the **Clock** ActiveX control of Fig. 17.7 to display the current date as a tool tip when the mouse pointer rests on the control.

**17.6**   Modify the **Clock** ActiveX control of Fig. 17.7 to add a custom property called **Format**. The **Format** property should allow either a setting of **0 – 24 Hour** or **1 – 12 Hour**. These settings should be part of an enumeration. The **1 – 12 Hour** format should display either **AM** or **PM**. Also write a second custom property called **DisplaySeconds**. The **DisplaySeconds** property, when **True**, results in the control displaying seconds. When **False**, seconds are not displayed.

**17.7**   Write a user-drawn control that displays an analog clock. Use the **Circle** and **Line** methods to graphically draw the clock and its hands. Do not use the ActiveX control creation wizard.

**17.8**   Write a user-drawn control that allows the user to draw "freehand" pictures with the mouse.

**17.9**   Create a property page for the **Clock** ActiveX control of Exercise 17.5.

**17.10**   Create a control that "ties" together constituent controls **DirListBox**, **DriveListBox** and **FileListBox**.

**17.11**   Modify the **LabelScrollbar** control (Section 17.6) to provide a toolbox icon and attribute descriptions for properties **Min**, **Max**, **SmallChange**, **LargeChange** and **Value**.

**17.12**   Enhance your solution to Exercise 17.11 to add a custom property called **Spacing**. Property **Spacing** determines how much space is between the **Label** and the scrollbar. **Spacing** is a design-time property.

**17.13**   Enhance your solution to Exercise 17.12 to add a **BackColor** property. The **BackColor** property specifies the color of the spacing that appears between the **Label** and the scrollbar.

**17.14**    Write an ActiveX DLL that contains procedures for converting hexadecimal to octal, decimal to binary, octal to hexadecimal, binary to hexadecimal, etc.

**17.15**    Modify the **Clock** ActiveX control to raise an **OnHour** event every time the clock "strikes" the hour.

**17.16**    Create a user-drawn control that displays a "star" button. Use method **Line** to draw the button.

**17.17**    Write an "enhanced" **TextBox** control that only accepts numeric input.

**17.18**    Write a control that displays images specified by the developer. The control should automatically display a different image after a specified number of seconds. Provide special effects options (e.g., inverse, etc.). Provide a minimum of one property page for the control.

**17.19**    Write a "ruler" user-drawn control. The control should display tick marks in units of inches, centimeters, pixels, and points. Set the ruler's **BackColor** to yellow. The ruler should have a horizontal orientation.

**17.20**    Enhance your solution to Exercise 17.19 to allow the developer to set either a vertical or horizontal orientation.

**17.21**    Enhance your solution to either Exercise 17.20 or 17.19 to allow the user to move the ruler next to an object on a form to measure it.

# 18

# Database Management

## Objectives

- To understand the relational database model.
- To use the **ADO Data Control** to access a database.
- To use the **DataGrid**, **Hierarchical FlexGrid**, **DataCombo** and **DataList** controls with the **ADO Data Control** to view and manipulate data in a database.
- To understand basic database queries using Structured Query Language (SQL).
- To use Data Environment Designer to quickly create data-driven applications.

*It is a capital mistake to theorize before one has data.*
Arthur Conan Doyle

*Now go, write it before them in a table, and note it in a book, that it may be for the time to come for ever and ever.*
The Holy Bible: The Old Testament

*Let's look at the record.*
Alfred Emanuel Smith

*True art selects and paraphrases, but seldom gives a verbatim translation.*
Thomas Bailey Aldrich

*Get your facts first, and then you can distort them as much as you please.*
Mark Twain

*I like two kinds of men: domestic and foreign.*
Mae West

# Outline

## 18.1  Introduction[1]

In Chapter 14 we discussed sequential file processing, and in Chapter 15 we discussed random access file processing. Sequential file processing is appropriate for applications in which most or all of the file's information is to be processed. Random access file processing is appropriate for applications—especially transaction processing—in which it is crucial to be able to locate and possibly update an individual piece of data quickly, and in which only a small portion of a file's data is to be processed at once. Visual Basic provides solid capabilities for both types of file processing.

---

1. Portions of Sections 18.1, 18.2, 18.3 and 18.6 based on Deitel, H. M., *Operating Systems, 2/E*, pp. 404–409 (De90). Reading, MA: Addison-Wesley, 1990. [See bibliography on p. 807.]

One problem with each of these schemes is that they simply provide for accessing data—they do not offer any capabilities for querying the data conveniently. Database systems provide file-processing capabilities, but organize data in a manner to facilitate satisfying sophisticated queries. The most popular style of database system on the kinds of computers that use Visual Basic (i.e., personal computers) is the *relational database*. A language called *Structured Query Language (SQL)* is almost universally used among relational database systems to make *queries* (i.e., to request information that satisfies given criteria). Visual Basic enables programmers to write code that uses SQL queries to access the information in relational database systems. Some popular relational database software packages include Microsoft Access, FoxPro, dBase, Paradox, Oracle and SQL Server.

## 18.2 Database Systems

The availability of inexpensive massive direct access storage has caused a tremendous amount of research and development activity in the area of *database systems*. A *database* is an integrated collection of data. A database system involves the data itself, the hardware on which the data resides, the software (called a *database management system* or *DBMS*) that controls the storage and retrieval of data, and the users themselves.

### 18.2.1 Advantages of Database Systems

Date (Da81) lists several important advantages of database systems.

- Redundancy can be reduced.
- Inconsistency can be avoided.
- The data can be shared.
- Standards can be enforced.
- Security restrictions can be applied.
- Integrity can be maintained.
- Conflicting requirements can be balanced.

In conventional non-database systems, each distinct application maintains its own files, often with considerable redundancy and a variety of physical formats. In database systems, redundancy is reduced by integrating separate files.

Sharing is one of the most important benefits of database systems. Existing applications can reference the same data.

Centralized control makes it possible to enforce standards rigidly. This becomes particularly important in computer networks in which data migration between systems occurs.

Security is an intriguing issue in database systems. The data may actually be more at risk because it is collected and retained in a central location rather than being dispersed throughout physically separate files in many locations. To counter this, database systems must be designed with elaborate controls.

### 18.2.2 Data Independence

One of the most important aspects of database systems is *data independence* (i.e., applications need not be concerned with how the data is physically stored or accessed). An application is said to be *data dependent* if the storage structure and accessing strategy cannot be changed without affecting the application significantly.

Data independence makes it convenient for various applications to have different *views* of the same data. From the system's standpoint, data independence makes it possible for the storage structure and accessing strategy to be modified in response to the installation's changing requirements, but without the need to modify functioning applications.

## 18.2.3 Database Languages

Users access a database via statements in some form of database language. Application programs may use a conventional high-level language like Visual Basic, C, C++, Java, COBOL, PL/I or Pascal; a user may make requests of the database in a specially designed *query language* that makes it easy to express requests in the context of a particular application.

Such languages are referred to as host languages. Each host language ordinarily includes a *database sublanguage (DSL)* concerned with the specifics of database objects and operations. Each data sublanguage generally is a combination of two languages, namely a *data definition language (DDL)* that provides facilities for defining database objects, and a *data manipulation language (DML)* that provides features for specifying the processing to be performed on database objects. The popular query language *SQL (Structured Query Language)* that we discuss in Section 18.6 provides both DDL and DML.

## 18.2.4 Distributed Database

A distributed database (Wi88) is a database that is spread throughout the computer systems of a network. Ordinarily in such systems each data item is stored at the location in which it is most frequently used, but it remains accessible to other network users.

Distributed systems provide the control and economics of local processing with the advantages of information accessibility over a geographically dispersed organization. They can be costly to implement and operate, however, and they can suffer from increased vulnerability to security violations.

## 18.3 Relational Database Model

Three different database models have achieved widespread popularity: (1) hierarchical database, (2) network database and (3) relational database. In this text, we concentrate on the most popular of these models—the relational database model—but all can be accessed using Microsoft's *ActiveX Data Object (ADO)* technology discussed in this chapter.

## 18.3.1 Relational Database

The relational model developed by Codd (Co70) (Co72) (Bl88) (Co88) (Re88) is a logical representation of the data that allows the relationships between the data to be considered without concerning oneself with the physical implementation of the data structures.

A relational database is composed of *tables*. Figure 18.1 illustrates a sample table that might be used in a personnel system. The name of the table is EMPLOYEE and its primary purpose is to demonstrate the relationships of various attributes of each employee with that employee. Any particular row of the table is called a *record* (or *row*). This table consists of six records. The employee number field of each record in this table is used as the *primary key* for referencing data in the table. The records of Fig. 18.1 are ordered by primary key.

Each column of the table represents a different *field*. Records are normally unique (by primary key) within a table, but particular field values may be duplicated between records. For example, three different records in table EMPLOYEE contain department number 413.

Different users of a database are interested in different data items and different relationships between the data items. Some users want only certain subsets of the table columns. Other users wish to combine smaller tables into larger ones to produce more complex tables. Codd calls the subset operation *projection* and the combination operation *join*.

Using the table of Fig. 18.1, for example, we might use the projection operation to create a new table called DEPARTMENT-LOCATOR whose purpose is to show where departments are located. This new table is shown in Fig. 18.2. In Visual Basic, a table is manipulated as a **Recordset** object.

The relational database organization has many advantages over the hierarchical and network schemes.

1. The tabular representation used in the relational scheme is easy for users to comprehend and easy to implement in the physical database system.

2. It is relatively easy to convert virtually any other type of database structure into the relational scheme. Thus, the scheme may be viewed as a universal form of representation.

## Table: EMPLOYEE

| | Number | Name | Department | Salary | Location |
|---|---|---|---|---|---|
| | 23603 | JONES, A. | 413 | 1100 | NEW JERSEY |
| | 24568 | KERWIN, R. | 413 | 2000 | NEW JERSEY |
| A record | 34589 | LARSON, P. | 642 | 1800 | LOS ANGELES |
| | 35761 | MYERS, B. | 611 | 1400 | ORLANDO |
| | 47132 | NEUMANN, C. | 413 | 9000 | NEW JERSEY |
| | 78321 | STEPHENS, T. | 611 | 8500 | ORLANDO |

Primary key                    A column

**Fig. 18.1**    Relational database structure.

## Table: DEPARTMENT-LOCATOR

| Department | Location |
|---|---|
| 413 | NEW JERSEY |
| 611 | ORLANDO |
| 642 | LOS ANGELES |

**Fig. 18.2**    A table formed by projection.

3. The projection and join operations are easy to implement and make the creation of new tables needed for particular applications easy to do.

4. Searches can be faster than in schemes requiring following a string of pointers.

5. Relational structures are easier to modify than hierarchical or network structures. In environments where flexibility is important, this becomes critical.

6. The clarity and visibility of the database improves with the relational structure. It is much easier to search tabular data than it is to unwind possibly arbitrarily complex interconnections of data elements in a pointer mechanism.

Stonebraker (St81) discusses various operating system services that support database management systems, namely buffer pool management, the file system, scheduling, process management, interprocess communication, consistency protocol and paged virtual memory. He observes that because most of these features are not specifically optimized to DBMS environments, DBMS designers have tended to bypass operating system services in favor of supplying their own. He concludes that efficient, minimal operating systems are the most desirable for supporting the kinds of database management systems that do supply their own optimized services.

Database systems are sometimes incorporated into operating systems to provide users with more powerful capabilities than are available in conventional file systems. This enables a more synergistic relationship between the operating system and the database management system than is possible when the DBMS is supplied separately.

## 18.4  Introducing the Microsoft ADO Data Control 6.0 and Microsoft DataGrid Control 6.0

Visual Basic provides a variety of data-aware controls for displaying and manipulating data in databases (Fig. 18.3). The data-aware controls each contain several key properties, as shown in Fig. 18.4. In this section, we illustrate how simple it can be to create data-aware applications in Visual Basic. For this purpose, we will use two controls—the *ADO (ActiveX Data Object) Data Control* and the ***DataGrid*** *control*.

| Control | Description |
|---|---|
| **CheckBox** control | Can be attached to a boolean field in a table. |
| **ComboBox** control | Can be populated by a column in a table. |
| **DataCombo** control | Similar to the standard **ComboBox** control. The **DataCombo** control also allows a selected field to be passed to another data-aware control (new in Visual Basic 6). |
| **DataGrid** control | Allows an entire table or the result of a query to be displayed and manipulated (new in Visual Basic 6). |
| **DataList** control | Similar to the standard **ListBox** control. The **DataList** control also allows a selected field to be passed to another data-aware control (new in Visual Basic 6). |

**Fig. 18.3**   Data-aware controls (part 1 of 2).

| Control | Description |
| --- | --- |
| **DataRepeater** control | Allows the programmer to create a new control for data display, then use it repeatedly in a scrollable area to display multiple records from a database (new in Visual Basic 6). |
| **DateTimePicker** control | Similar to the **MonthView** control, but it displays dates in a text box. When the user clicks the text box, a graphic calendar drops down from which the user can select a new date (new in Visual Basic 6). |
| **Hierarchical FlexGrid** control | Allows entire tables to be displayed. It also provides support for hierarchical cursors created with the Data Environment (both are new in Visual Basic 6). |
| **Image** control | Displays images in the following formats: bitmap, icon, metafile, enhanced metafile, JPEG and GIF. |
| **ImageCombo** control | Similar to the standard **ComboBox** control and can display images in the drop-down list. |
| **Label** control | Can be used to display the value of a field in a table. |
| **ListBox** control | Can be populated by a column in a table. |
| **Masked Edit** control | Similar to a **TextBox** control except that it allows the programmer to restrict the format of the data entered in the field. This control can be populated with a field of a table. |
| **MonthView** control | Displays dates in calendar format (new in Visual Basic 6). |
| **Microsoft Chart** control | Displays an array of data as a graph. When this control is used as a data-bound control, the information retrieved from the database is treated as an array. |
| **PictureBox** control | A more elaborate version of the **Image** control. |
| **RichTextBox** control | Allows richly formatted text to be displayed and edited by the user. |
| **TextBox** control | Allows text to be displayed and edited by the user. |

**Fig. 18.3**   Data-aware controls (part 2 of 2).

| Property | Description |
| --- | --- |
| **DataSource** | Used to set or get the source of data for a control. This can be set at design time or at run time to any valid data source. Valid sources include: **Recordset**s produced via queries through **ADO Data Control**, ADO code-based queries, **DataEnvironment** objects created with the **Data Environment Designer**, a user-defined class that is created as a data source or a data source control. For more information on the last two options, see the on-line documentation. |

**Fig. 18.4**   Common properties of most data-aware controls (part 1 of 2).

| Property | Description |
|----------|-------------|
| **DataMember** | Used to set or get the data set that contains the data to be manipulated. For example, the **ADO Data Control** specifies a table, query or stored procedure (a frequently executed query that can receive parameters) in the database that will produce the **Recordset**; and the **Data Environment Designer** allows creation of multiple **Command** objects that each specify a table, query or stored procedure in the database that will produce the **Recordset**. In either case, Visual Basic displays a list of the available data sets. |
| **DataField** | Used to set or get the specific field in the **Recordset** to which a data-aware control is bound. Visual Basic displays a list that contains all fields in the **Recordset**. |
| **DataFormat** | Used to specify automatic data formats for data retrieved from the data source. |

**Fig. 18.4**   Common properties of most data-aware controls (part 2 of 2).

The **ADO Data Control** is one way to manage access to a database by a Visual Basic program, and the **DataGrid** control displays in a table format (and possibly allows the user to manipulate) the data requested from the database. Later in this chapter we introduce several Visual Basic 6 data-aware controls that make use of ActiveX Data Objects (ADOs).

The program of Fig. 18.5 requires no programming to connect to the **Biblio.mdb** database's **Authors** table and display the contents of that table to the user. The form consists of two controls—an **ADO Data Control** and a **DataGrid** control.

The **ADO Data Control** manages the *connection* between an application and a database and allows the data-aware controls to view and manipulate the data in a database. The **DataGrid** control provides easy access to the contents of a **Recordset** for both viewing and editing the data in the database. In this example, we disabled the user's ability to edit the data by setting the **AllowUpdate** property of the **DataGrid** to **False**.

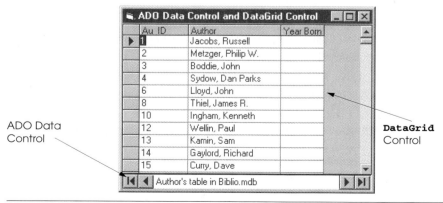

**Fig. 18.5**   Demonstrating the **ADO Data Control** and **DataGrid** control.

When a **DataGrid** is attached to an **ADO Data Control**, the **DataGrid** automatically displays the rows, columns and field names for the table attached to the **ADO Data Control**. Let us now assemble the program.

The **ADO Data Control** and the **DataGrid** control are not intrinsic controls displayed in the Visual Basic toolbox, so they must be added. To add these controls to the toolbox, select **Components...** from the **Project** menu to display the **Components** dialog box. In the dialog box, scroll down and select the option **Microsoft ADO Data Control 6.0**. When the option is selected, a small check mark appears in the box to the left of the option. Next, scroll down and select the option **Microsoft DataGrid Control 6.0**. Click the **OK** button when you are done to dismiss the dialog box. The **ADO Data Control** and the **DataGrid** control will be the last two controls in the toolbox. Note that when you position the mouse over the **ADO Data Control**, a tool tip containing **Adodc** will appear. This helps identify which icon represents the **ADO Data Control**.

We are now ready to connect to the **Biblio.mdb** database from Visual Basic. You may want to make a backup copy of **Biblio.mdb** in case you want to make changes to this database, then start with the original data again in the future.

To access the database using the **ADO Data Control**, we must create a connection to the database. The database can reside either on the same computer as the program or on the network. Add one **ADO Data Control** (automatically named **Adodc1**) and one **DataGrid** control (automatically named **DataControl1**) to the form and position them as shown in Fig. 18.5. The properties for each of these controls at design time can be accessed either by the property sheet for each control or by right-clicking on the control and selecting **ADODC Properties** for the **ADO Data Control** or **Properties...** for the **DataGrid** control.

The following steps create a connection to the **Biblio.mdb** database (this process is often referred to in the Visual Basic documentation as creating an *OLE DB data source*):

1. Right click the **ADO Data Control** and select **ADODC Properties** from the popup menu to display the **ADO Data Control**'s **Property Pages** dialog.

2. In the **Source of Connection** frame, select the **Use Connection String** option and press the **Build...** button to display the **Data Link Properties** dialog. This dialog allows the programmer to build a *connection string*. A connection string provides information that the **ADO Data Control** uses to connect to the database. The connection string includes the *database provider*—the database management system type—the database name and location, and other information. The **Biblio.mdb** database is a Microsoft Access database. Microsoft Access databases normally use the **Microsoft Jet 3.51 OLE DB Provider**.

3. On the **Data Link Properties** dialog's **Provider** tab, select **Microsoft Jet 3.51 OLE DB Provider**.

4. Click the **Data Link Properties** dialog's **Connection** tab. In Step 1, **Select or enter a database name**, you can select the database to which the **ADO Data Control** will connect. Press the **...** button at the right side of the **TextBox** to display the **Select Access Database** dialog.

5. Locate **Biblio.mdb** on your system. The default location is normally

   **c:\Program Files\Microsoft Visual Studio\VB98**

Once you locate the directory, click **Biblio.mdb** then press the **Open** button. A string containing the location and name of the database now appears in the **Select or enter a database name TextBox**. Press the OK button to dismiss the **Data Link Properties** dialog.

6. In the **Property Pages** dialog's **RecordSource** tab, select **2 – adCmdTable** from the **Command Type ComboBox** to specify that a table in the database will be the source of the data. Select **Authors** from the **Table or Stored Procedure Name ComboBox** to specify that the data will be retrieved specifically from the **Authors** table in the database. [Note: These properties can also be set programmatically to allow the **ADO Data Control** to manipulate different tables at execution time.]

7. Click the **Test Connection** button to determine if the connection succeeded. If the connection is successful, a dialog box appears with the message "Test connection succeeded"). Click the **OK** button to dismiss the message. If the connection fails, repeat the preceding steps.

[*Note:* Later in this chapter we illustrate a more flexible mechanism for database connections using the **Data Environment Designer**.]

Once the connection string is specified, set the properties for the controls in this example via the property sheet as shown in Fig. 18.6.

Once the properties are set as in Fig. 18.6, execute the application. Notice that the current row of the grid has a small black arrow in the gray rectangle at the left side of the row. Clicking on a cell in the grid makes that row the current record.

Try manipulating the **DataGrid** control in the following ways:

- Use the *left-arrow* key and *right-arrow* key to move from field to field.

- Use the *up-arrow* key and *down-arrow* key to move from record to record. Press and hold the *down-arrow* key to scroll rapidly down through the records. Press and hold the *up-arrow* key to scroll rapidly up through the records.

- Use the *Page Up* key and *Page Down* key to jump through a *page* of records. A page of records is determined by the number of visible records in the **DataGrid** control. In our example, 11 records are visible initially, so *Page Up* and *Page Down* display the previous 11 records and the next 11, respectively. Press and hold the *Page Down* key to jump rapidly down through the records. Press and hold the *Page Up* key to jump rapidly up through the records.

| Control | Property | Setting |
|---------|----------|---------|
| Adodc1 | Caption | **Authors table from Biblio.mdb** |
| DataGrid1 | DataSource | Select **Adodc1** from the drop-down list. |
| | AllowUpdate | Select **False** from the drop-down list—the user of this application will be able to view the data, but the user will not be able to edit the data. |

**Fig. 18.6**    Property settings for the program of Fig. 18.5.

- Use the vertical scrollbar at the right side of the window to scroll up and down through the records.

- Resize the columns by positioning the mouse over the vertical bar between column names, holding the left mouse button down and dragging the bar to increase or decrease the width of the column. If the three columns of the table do not fit in the window, notice that a horizontal scrollbar appears to allow you to scroll horizontally through the data in each record.

- Resize the rows by positioning the mouse over the horizontal bar between rows (this must be done with the lines between the gray boxes at the far left side of the grid), holding the left mouse button down and dragging the bar to increase or decrease the height of the rows.

- Use the navigation buttons on the **ADO Data Control** (Fig. 18.7) to move between records. The **ADO Data Control** provides buttons to move to the first record, previous record, next record and last record in the table.

If **AllowUpdate** is set to **True** for the **DataGrid**, modifying the data in a cell causes the data in the database to change when another record becomes the current record.

***Software Engineering Observation 18.1***

*Set the **AllowUpdate** property of **DataGrid** to **False** (the default is **True**) to prevent the user from changing the contents of the grid cells.*

Try changing the **AllowUpdate** property of the **DataGrid** to **True** and run the program again. Note that you now have direct access to the data in the database and you can modify the data. For example, you can change the name of an author simply by clicking in the appropriate field and typing the new name, then moving to another record. When another record is made the current record, any changes you performed are written to the database. Try changing the **RecordSource** property to one of the other tables in the **Biblio.mdb** database (**Publishers**, **Title Author** and **Titles**) and run the program again to display the contents of the new table.

## 18.5 Relational Database Overview: The Biblio.mdb Database

In this section we provide an overview of *Structured Query Language (SQL)* in the context of a sample database provided by Microsoft with Visual Basic. Before we get into SQL, we overview the tables of the **Biblio.mdb** database located in your **VB98** directory. We will use this database throughout the chapter to introduce various database concepts, including the use of SQL to obtain useful information from the database and to manipulate the database.

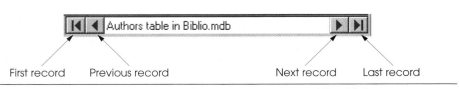

**Fig. 18.7**    The **ADO Data Control** from the program of Fig. 18.5.

The database consists of four tables—**Authors**, **Publishers**, **Title Author** and **Titles**. The **Authors** table (Fig. 18.8) consists of three fields that maintain each author's unique ID number in the database, name and the year in which the author was born.

The **Publishers** table (Fig. 18.9) consists of 10 fields that maintain each publisher's unique ID value, address and phone information and a general comments field.

The **Title Author** table (Fig. 18.10) consists of two fields that maintain each ISBN number and its corresponding author's ID number. This table will help link the names of the authors with the titles of their books.

| Field | Description |
|---|---|
| **Au_ID** | The author's ID number in the database. The ID is the primary key field for this table. |
| **Author** | The author's name as a single string in the form "last name, first name." |
| **Year Born** | The author's year of birth. |

Fig. 18.8   **Authors** table from **Biblio.mdb**.

| Field | Description |
|---|---|
| **PubID** | The publisher's ID number in the database. This is the primary key field for this table. |
| **Name** | The short name for the publisher. |
| **Company Name** | The expanded name for the publisher. |
| **Address** | The publisher's street address. |
| **City** | The publisher's city. |
| **State** | The publisher's state. |
| **Zip** | The publisher's zip code. |
| **Telephone** | The publisher's telephone number. |
| **Fax** | The publisher's fax number. |
| **Comments** | A field for maintaining comments on each publisher. |

Fig. 18.9   **Publishers** table from **Biblio.mdb**.

| Field | Description |
|---|---|
| **ISBN** | The ISBN number for a book. |
| **Au_ID** | The author's ID number, which allows the database to connect each book to a specific author. The ID number in this field must also appear in the **Authors** table. |

Fig. 18.10   **Title Author** table from **Biblio.mdb**.

The **Titles** table (Fig. 18.11) consists of eight fields that maintain general information about each book in the database including the title, year published, ISBN number and the publisher's ID number.

Figure 18.12 illustrates the relationships between the tables in the **Biblio.mdb** database. The field name in bold in each table is that table's *primary key*. A table's primary key uniquely identifies each record in the table. Every record must have a value in the primary key field—*Rule of Entity Integrity*—and the value must be unique.

*Common Programming Error 18.1*
*When a field is specified as the primary key field, not providing a value for that field in every record breaks the Rule of Entity Integrity and is an error.*

*Common Programming Error 18.2*
*When a field is specified as the primary key field, providing duplicate values for multiple records is an error.*

| Field | Description |
| --- | --- |
| **Title** | Title of the book. |
| **Year Published** | Year in which the book was published. |
| **ISBN** | ISBN number of the book. |
| **PubID** | The publisher's ID number. This value must correspond to an ID number in the **Publishers** table. |
| **Description** | The price of the book. |
| **Notes** | General notes about the book. |
| **Subject** | Keywords for the subject matter of the book. |
| **Comments** | Description of the book. |

**Fig. 18.11**   **Titles** table from **Biblio.mdb**.

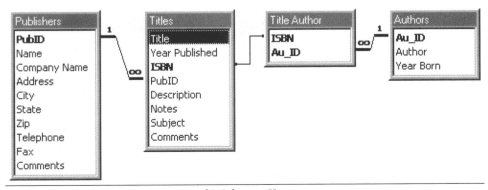

**Fig. 18.12**   Table relationships in **Biblio.mdb**.

The lines between the tables represent the relationships. For example, consider the line between the **Publishers** and **Titles** tables. On the **Publishers** end of the line there is a **1**, and on the **Titles** end of the line there is an infinity symbol. This indicates that for every publisher in the **Publishers** table there can be an infinite number of books from that publisher in the **Titles** table. This relationship is often referred to as the *one-to-many relationship*. The **PubID** field is referred to as a *foreign key*—a field in a table for which every entry has a unique value in another table and where the field in the other table is the primary key for that table (i.e., **PubID** in the **Publishers** table). Foreign keys are specified when creating a table. The foreign key concept helps maintain the *Rule of Referential Integrity*—every value in a foreign key field must appear in another table's primary key field. Foreign keys enable information from multiple tables to be joined together and presented to the user. There is a one-to-many relationship between a primary key and its corresponding foreign key.

The line between the **Title Author** and **Authors** tables indicates that for every author in the **Authors** table there can be an infinite number of books that author wrote in the **Title Author** table. The **Au_ID** field in the **Title Author** table is a foreign key of the **Au_ID** field of the **Authors** table.

Finally, the line between the **Titles** and **Title Author** tables illustrates a one-to-many relationship that does not enforce referential integrity—a title can be written by any number of authors.

## 18.6 Structured Query Language

In this section we provide an overview of *Structured Query Language (SQL)* in the context of the **Biblio.mdb** sample database provided with Visual Basic. You will be able to use the SQL queries discussed here later in the chapter to test the data-aware controls.

The SQL query keywords (Fig. 18.13) are discussed in the context of complete SQL queries in the next several sections. Note that there are other SQL keywords that are beyond the scope of this text. For more information on SQL, please refer to your on-line documentation or to one of the many books on SQL.

| SQL keyword | Description |
|---|---|
| **SELECT** | Select (retrieve) fields from a table or several tables. |
| **WHERE** | Criteria for selection that determine the rows to be retrieved. |
| **FROM** | Tables from which to get fields. Required in every **SELECT**. |
| **GROUP BY** | How to group records. |
| **HAVING** | Used with the **GROUP BY** clause to specify criteria for grouping records in the query results. |
| **ORDER BY** | Criteria for ordering of records. |

**Fig. 18.13**  SQL query keywords.

### 18.6.1 Basic SELECT Query

Now, we will consider several SQL queries that allow us to extract information from the **Biblio.mdb** database. We will use each of these queries in the upcoming sections as we describe each of the data-aware controls.

A typical SQL query "selects" information from one or more tables in a database. Such selections are performed by *SELECT* *queries*. The simplest format of a **SELECT** query is

> **SELECT * FROM** *TableName*

In the preceding query, the asterisk (**\***) indicates that all fields from *TableName* should be selected and *TableName* specifies the table in the database from which the fields will be selected. For example, to select all fields of the **Authors** table, use the query

> **SELECT * FROM Authors**

To select specific fields from a table, replace the asterisk (**\***) with a comma-separated list of the field names to select. For example, to select only the fields **Au_ID** and **Author**, use the query

> **SELECT Au_ID, Author FROM Authors**

*Software Engineering Observation 18.2*

*If a field name contains spaces, it must be enclosed in square brackets ( **[]** ) in the query.*

### 18.6.2 WHERE Clause

Often it is necessary to locate records in a database that satisfy certain *selection criteria*. Only records that match the selection criteria are actually selected. SQL uses the optional *WHERE* *clause* to specify the selection criteria for the query. The simplest format of a **SELECT** query with selection criteria is

> **SELECT * FROM** *TableName* **WHERE** *criteria*

For example, to select all fields from the **Authors** table where the author's **Year Born** is greater than or equal to **1950**, use the query

> **SELECT * FROM Authors WHERE [Year Born] >= 1950**

It turns out that most of the 6246 records in the **Authors** table do not specify the year born, so the preceding query returns only eight records. Notice in the preceding query the use of square brackets ( **[]** ) around the field name **Year Born** because it contains a space.

*Performance Tip 18.1*

*Using selection criteria improves performance by selecting fewer records from the database.*

The condition in the **WHERE** clause can contain operators **<, >, <=, >=, =, <>** and **Like**.

Operator **Like** is used for *pattern matching* with wildcard characters *asterisk ( **\*** )* and *question mark ( **?** )*. Pattern matching allows SQL to search for similar strings. An asterisk

(**\***) in the pattern indicates any number of characters in a row at the asterisk's location in the pattern. For example, the following query locates the records of all the authors whose last names start with the letter **d**:

```
SELECT * FROM Authors WHERE Author Like 'd*'
```

Notice that the pattern string is surrounded by single-quote characters.

**Portability Tip 18.1**

*SQL is case sensitive on some database systems.*

**Portability Tip 18.2**

*Not all database systems support the **Like** operator.*

**Good Programming Practice 18.1**

*By convention, SQL keywords should use all capital letters on systems that are not case sensitive to make the SQL keywords stand out in an SQL query.*

A question mark (**?**) in the pattern string indicates a single character at that position in the pattern. For example, the following query locates the records of all the authors whose last names start with the letter **d** followed by any letter (specified with **?**) followed by the letter **i** followed by any number of additional characters (specified with **\***):

```
SELECT * FROM Authors WHERE Author Like 'd?i*'
```

The preceding query can be specialized to allow any character in a specific range of characters in the position where **?** appears in the preceding pattern string. This is accomplished by replacing the **?** with a range of characters in the form

[*startValue–endValue*]

where *startValue* indicates the first character in the range and *endValue* represents the last value in the range. For example, the following query locates the records of all the authors whose last names start with the letter **D** followed by any letter in the range **a** to **e** (specified with the **?**) followed by the letter **i** followed by any number of additional characters (specified with **\***):

```
SELECT * FROM Authors WHERE Author Like 'd[a-e]*'
```

## 18.6.3 ORDER BY Clause

The results of a query can be arranged in ascending or descending order using the optional ***ORDER BY*** *clause*. The simplest format of an **ORDER BY** clause is

```
SELECT * FROM TableName ORDER BY field ASC
SELECT * FROM TableName ORDER BY field DESC
```

where **ASC** specifies ascending (lowest to highest) order, **DESC** specifies descending (highest to lowest) order and *field* represents the field that is used for sorting purposes.

For example, to obtain the list of authors in ascending order by last name, use the query

```
SELECT * FROM Authors ORDER BY Author ASC
```

To obtain the same list of authors in descending order by last name, use the query

```
SELECT * FROM Authors ORDER BY Author DESC
```

Multiple fields can be used for ordering purposes with an **ORDER BY** clause of the form

```
ORDER BY field1 SortingOrder, field2 SortingOrder, ...
```

where *SortingOrder* is either **ASC** or **DESC**. Note that the *SortingOrder* does not have to be identical for each field.

The **WHERE** and **ORDER BY** clauses can be combined in one query. For example, to locate the records of all the authors whose last names start with the letter **d** and order those records in ascending order by last name, use the query

```
SELECT * FROM Authors
WHERE Author Like 'd*'
ORDER BY Author ASC
```

Note: When we construct a query for use in Visual Basic we will simply create one long string containing the entire query. When we display queries in the text, we often use multiple lines and indentation for readability.

## 18.6.4 Using INNER JOIN to Merge Data from Multiple Tables

Often it is necessary to merge data from multiple tables for analysis purposes into a single view. This is often referred to as *joining* the tables. This can be accomplished using an **INNER JOIN** operation in the **FROM** clause of a **SELECT** query. An **INNER JOIN** merges records from two or more tables by testing for matching values in a field that is common to both tables. The simplest format of an **INNER JOIN** clause is

```
SELECT * FROM Table1 INNER JOIN Table2 ON Table1.field = Table2.field
```

The **ON** part of the **INNER JOIN** clause specifies the fields from each table that should be compared to determine which records will be selected. For example, to merge the **Author** field from the **Authors** table with the **ISBN** field from the **Title Author** table in ascending order by **Author** so you can see the ISBN numbers for the books that each author wrote, use the query

```
SELECT Author, ISBN
FROM Authors INNER JOIN [Title Author]
ON Authors.Au_ID = [Title Author].Au_ID
ORDER BY Author ASC
```

Notice the use of the syntax *TableName.FieldName* in the **ON** part of the **INNER JOIN**. This syntax is used to specify the fields from each table that should be compared to join the tables. The "*TableName.*" syntax is only required if the fields have the same name in both tables. The same syntax can be used in a query any time it is necessary to distinguish between fields in different tables that happen to have the same name.

As always, the **FROM** clause (including the **INNER JOIN**) can be followed by **WHERE** and **ORDER BY** clauses.

## 18.6.5 All Titles Query from Biblio.mdb

The **Biblio.mdb** database contains one predefined query that produces a **Recordset** containing the book title, ISBN number, author's name, author's year born and publisher's name for each book in the database. For books with multiple authors, the query produces a separate composite record for each author. The query is as follows:

```
SELECT Titles.Title, Titles.ISBN, Authors.Author,
       Titles.[Year Published], Publishers.[Company Name]
FROM
Publishers INNER JOIN
   (Authors INNER JOIN
       ([title author] INNER JOIN Titles
           ON [title author].ISBN = Titles.ISBN)
   ON Authors.Au_ID = [title author].Au_ID)
ON Publishers.PubID = Titles.PubID
ORDER BY Titles.Title
```

The indentation in the preceding query is simply to make the query more readable. Let us now break down the query into its various parts. The lines

```
SELECT Titles.Title, Titles.ISBN, Authors.Author,
       Titles.[Year Published], Publishers.[Company Name]
```

indicate the fields to be presented in the results of the query and the order in which they should be displayed left to right. This query will select the **Title** and **ISBN** fields from the **Titles** table, the **Author** field from the **Authors** table, the **Year Published** field from the **Titles** table and the **Company Name** field from the **Publishers** table. The lines

```
FROM
Publishers INNER JOIN
   (Authors INNER JOIN
       ([title author] INNER JOIN Titles
           ON [title author].ISBN = Titles.ISBN)
   ON Authors.Au_ID = [title author].Au_ID)
ON Publishers.PubID = Titles.PubID
```

specify the **INNER JOIN** operations that will be used to combine information from the tables. Notice that there are three nested **INNER JOIN** operations. Remember that an **INNER JOIN** is performed on two tables. It is important to note that either of those two tables can be the result of another query or another **INNER JOIN**. Parentheses are used to nest the **INNER JOIN** operations and the parentheses are always evaluated from the innermost set of parentheses first. So, we begin with the **INNER JOIN**

```
([title author] INNER JOIN Titles
    ON [title author].ISBN = Titles.ISBN)
```

that specifies the **Title Author** table, and the **Titles** table should be joined **ON** the condition that the **ISBN** number in each table matches. The resulting temporary table will contain all the information about each book and the author who wrote it. Remember that the **Title Author** table may have multiple entries for each **ISBN** number if there is more than one author for that book.

Moving to the next outermost set of parentheses, an **INNER JOIN** is performed on the **Authors** table and the result of the preceding **INNER JOIN** using

```
(Authors INNER JOIN
    ([title author] INNER JOIN Titles
        ON [title author].ISBN = Titles.ISBN)
    ON Authors.Au_ID = [title author].Au_ID)
```

This **INNER JOIN** specifies that the **Authors** table and the temporary table from the prior **INNER JOIN** should be joined **ON** the condition that the **Au_ID** field in the **Authors** table matches the **Au_ID** field from the **Title Author** table.

The outermost **INNER JOIN**

```
Publishers INNER JOIN
    (Authors INNER JOIN
        ([title author] INNER JOIN Titles
            ON [title author].ISBN = Titles.ISBN)
        ON Authors.Au_ID = [title author].Au_ID)
    ON Publishers.PubID = Titles.PubID
```

specifies that the **Publishers** table and the temporary table from the previous **INNER JOIN** should be combined **ON** the condition that the **PubID** field in the **Publishers** table matches the **PubID** field in the **Titles** table. The result of all these **INNER JOIN** operations is a temporary table from which the appropriate fields will be selected for the results of this query.

Finally, the line

```
ORDER BY Titles.Title
```

indicates that all the titles should be sorted in ascending order (the default).

## 18.7 Revisiting the ADO Data Control and DataGrid Control

Now that we have introduced the **Biblio.mdb** database, we revisit the *ADO Data Control* and the *DataGrid* control. Figure 18.14 describes some of the key properties, methods and events for the **ADO Data Control**. We use several of these in the examples in this chapter.

| Property, method or event | Description |
|---|---|
| *Properties* | |
| **ConnectionString** | Specifies a string containing parameters to pass to the **ADO Data Control** indicating how to connect to the database. |
| **UserName** | Specifies the user name for connecting to the database. |
| **Password** | Specifies the password for connecting to the database. |
| **RecordSource** | Specifies the query or statement used to retrieve data (e.g., the name of a table or a string containing a query). |

**Fig. 18.14**    Important properties of the **DataGrid** control (part 1 of 2).

| Property, method or event | Description |
|---|---|
| **CommandType** | Specifies the type of command used in the **RecordSource** (e.g., **adCmdTable** for a table, **adCmdText** for a query). |
| **LockType** | Specifies how to lock records to prevent multiple users from modifying the data in a record at the same time. |
| **Mode** | Specifies the permissions for connecting to the database (e.g., read-only, write-only, read/write, etc.) |
| **MaxRecords** | Specifies the maximum number of records to return in a **Recordset**. |
| **ConnectionTimeout** | Specifies the length of time to wait for a connection before generating an error that the attempt to connect failed. |
| **CacheSize** | Specifies the number of records in a **Recordset** to cache in local memory. |
| **BOFAction** | Specifies what to do when the beginning of a **Recordset** is reached. |
| **EOFAction** | Specifies what to do when the end of a **Recordset** is reached. |
| *Methods* | |
| **Refresh** | Refreshes the data in the **Recordset** based on any property changes to the **ADO Data Control**. |
| **UpdateControls** | Resets the data in the currently bound controls to the current record in the **Recordset**. |
| *Events* | |
| **EndOfRecordset** | Called on an attempt to move past the **Recordset**'s end. |
| **FetchComplete** | Called after all the records have been retrieved into the **Recordset**. |
| **FetchProgress** | Called periodically during a lengthy query to report how many rows have been retrieved into the **Recordset**. |
| **WillChangeField** | Called before an operation changes the value of one or more fields in the **Recordset**. |
| **FieldChangeComplete** | Called after the value of one or more fields changes. |
| **WillChangeRecord** | Called before an operation changes the value of one or more records in the **Recordset**. |
| **RecordChangeComplete** | Called after the value of one or more records changes. |
| **WillChangeRecordset** | Called before an operation changes the **Recordset**. |
| **RecordsetChangeComplete** | Called after the **Recordset** changes. |
| **WillMove** | Called before an operation changes the current position in the **Recordset**. |
| **MoveComplete** | Called after the current position in the **Recordset** changes. |

**Fig. 18.14** Important properties of the **DataGrid** control (part 2 of 2).

We will now create a program that allows the user to enter the SQL queries discussed in the previous section, processes the query and displays the results. A key feature of the **ADO Data Control** is that SQL statements can be specified for the **RecordSource** property at execution time. This allows dynamic changing of the data that are manipulated by the **ADO Data Control**.

The program of Fig. 18.15 allows the user to type an SQL query into a textbox and display the results of the query in a **DataGrid** control. The properties set at design time for the controls in this program are shown in Fig. 18.16.

When the form loads, **txtUserQuery.Text** and **Adodc1.Caption** are both set to **Adodc1.RecordSource** (lines 6 and 7)—the text of the default query to be displayed. This places the text of the default query—**SELECT * FROM Authors**—in both the **TextBox** and the caption area of the **ADO Data Control**. The user can type a new query at any time in the **TextBox** at the top of the window. When the user clicks the "**Submit User-defined Query**" button, event procedure **cmdQuery_Click** (lines 10–16) disables the button temporarily, sets **Adodc1.RecordSource** to the string the user typed in the textbox and calls **Adodc1.Refresh** to submit the query to the database (i.e., refresh the **Recordset**). When the query completes, the results are automatically displayed in **DataGrid1** and event procedure **Adodc1_MoveComplete** (lines 18–24) enables the button so the user can submit another query.

```
 1   ' Fig. 18.15
 2   ' Querying the Biblio.mdb database through an ADO Data Control
 3   Option Explicit
 4
 5   Private Sub Form_Load()
 6       txtUserQuery.Text = Adodc1.RecordSource
 7       Adodc1.Caption = Adodc1.RecordSource
 8   End Sub
 9
10   Private Sub cmdQuery_Click()
11       On Error Resume Next
12       cmdQuery.Enabled = False
13       Adodc1.RecordSource = txtUserQuery.Text
14       Call Adodc1.Refresh
15       Adodc1.Caption = Adodc1.RecordSource
16   End Sub
17
18   Private Sub Adodc1_MoveComplete( _
19           ByVal adReason As ADODB.EventReasonEnum, _
20           ByVal pError As ADODB.Error, _
21           adStatus As ADODB.EventStatusEnum, _
22           ByVal pRecordset As ADODB.Recordset)
23       cmdQuery.Enabled = True
24   End Sub
```

**Fig. 18.15**  Querying the **Biblio.mdb** database (part 1 of 2).

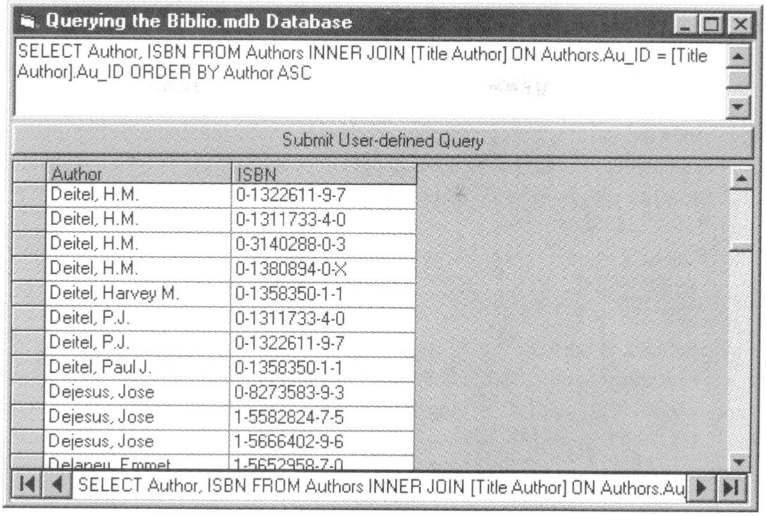

**Fig. 18.15**   Querying the **Biblio.mdb** database (part 2 of 2).

| Control | Property | Setting |
|---------|----------|---------|
| Adodc1 | ConnectionString | Follow the steps discussed with Fig. 18.5 for specifying the connection string. |
| | RecordSource | Click the **...** button for this property. In the **Record Source** area for **Command Type** select "**1 - adCmdText**" and for **Command Text (SQL)** type "**SELECT * FROM Authors.**" |
| DataGrid1 | DataSource | Adodc1 |
| cmdQuery | Caption | Submit User-defined Query |
| txtUserQuery | Multiline | True |
| | ScrollBars | 2 - Vertical |

**Fig. 18.16**   Property settings for the program of Fig. 18.13.

If the **AllowAddNew** property for the **DataGrid** is set to **True** (the default is **False**), the last row of the **DataGrid** can be used to enter a new record of information. If the **AllowDelete** property of the **DataGrid** is set to **True** (the default is **False**), the user can delete an entire record by clicking the gray rectangle to the left of the row to select that row in the table and pressing the *Delete* key on the keyboard. Remember that the **AllowUpdate** property can be set to **False** (the default is **True**) to prevent the user from modifying the data.

*Common Programming Error 18.3*

*Attempting to modify a record such that either the Rule of Referential Integrity or the Rule of Entity Integrity is compromised results in an error message and program termination if the error is not trapped by the program.*

The **Recordset** produced via an SQL query of the database can limit the fields that are actually displayed in the **DataGrid**. Try using some of the queries discussed in Section 18.6 to access the database and limit the fields that are displayed.

## 18.8 Hierarchical FlexGrid Control

The **Hierarchical FlexGrid** control is similar to the **DataGrid** control, but the user can only view the data through a **FlexGrid**. The program of Fig. 18.17 requires no programming. We set the properties via the property sheet as shown in Fig. 18.18.

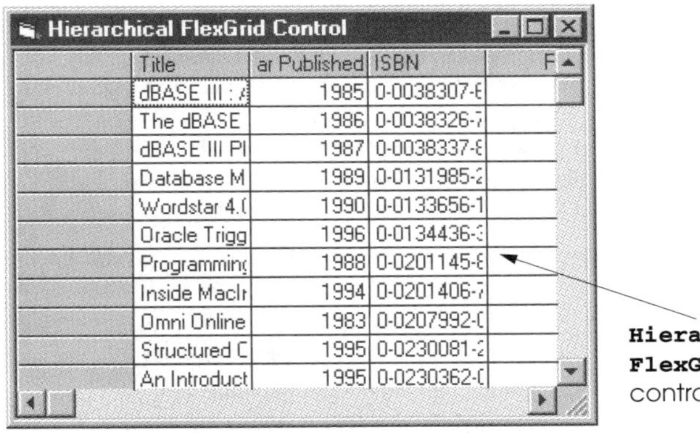

**Fig. 18.17**  Demonstrating the **Hierarchical FlexGrid Control**.

| Control | Property | Setting |
|---------|----------|---------|
| **Adodc1** | **Visible** | **False** |
| | **ConnectionString** | Follow the steps discussed with Fig. 18.5 for specifying the connection string. |
| | **RecordSource** | Click the **...** button for this property. In the **Record Source** area for **Command Type** select "**2 - adCmdTable**" and for **Table or Stored Procedure Name** select "**Titles**." |
| **MSHFlexGrid1** | **DataSource** | **Adodc1** |

**Fig. 18.18**  Property settings for the program of Fig. 18.17.

The program consists of two controls—the **ADO Data Control** and the **Hierarchical FlexGrid** control. These are not intrinsic controls, so they must be added to the toolbox by selecting **Components...** from the **Project** menu and to display the **Components** dialog box. In the dialog box, scroll down and select the option **Microsoft ADO Data Control 6.0**, then scroll down and select the option **Microsoft DataGrid Control 6.0**. Click **OK** when you are done to dismiss the dialog box. The **ADO Data Control** and **Hierarchical FlexGrid** control will be the last two controls in the toolbox.

Next, add one **ADO Data Control** (automatically named **Adodc1**) and one **Hierarchical FlexGrid** control (automatically named **MSHFlexGrid1**) to the form. The properties for each of these controls at design time can be accessed either by the property sheet or by right-clicking on the control and selecting **ADODC Properties** for the **ADO Data Control** or **Properties...** for the **Hierarchical FlexGrid** control.

Once the properties are set as in Fig. 18.18, execute the application and try manipulating the **Hierarchical FlexGrid** control like the **DataGrid** from Fig. 18.5.

## 18.9  DataList and DataCombo Controls

This section introduces the *DataCombo* and *DataList* controls. Each of these controls is capable of being populated automatically using the data from one field of a **Recordset**. The controls look and operate like the standard **ComboBox** and **List** intrinsic controls, but they provide several properties that make them more flexible than the intrinsic controls for database applications. We present two examples in this section—one to simply introduce the two new controls and one that takes advantage of the new properties. Some of the key properties of the **DataList** and **DataCombo** controls are shown in Fig. 18.19.

| Property | Description |
| --- | --- |
| BoundColumn | The field in one **Recordset** that is supplied to another **Recordset**. |
| BoundText | The value of the **BoundColumn** field. |
| DataField | A field name in the **Recordset** produced by the **DataSource**. |
| DataSource | The name of the data control to which the control is bound. |
| IntegralHeight | Specifies whether the control maintains a height that causes only complete rows to be displayed or allows partial rows to be displayed. |
| ListField | The name of the field in the **Recordset** produced by the **DataSource** that is used to populate the list. |
| MatchEntry | Specifies how to search the entries in an active **DataList** or **DataCombo** as the user types characters. |
| RowSource | The name of the data control that provides the data to populate the list. |
| SelectedItem | Returns a **Bookmark** for selected item's row in the **Recordset**. This can be used to keep track of a location in the **Recordset** and return to that location at a later time. |
| VisibleCount | The number of visible items in a list. |

**Fig. 18.19**  Important properties of the **DataCombo** and **DataList** controls.

## 18.9.1 Example: Using the DataCombo and DataList Controls

The program of Fig. 18.20 demonstrates some of the basic capabilities of the **DataCombo** and **DataList** controls. In the program, the user can select an author from the **Data-Combo** control or open the **DataCombo** and type the last name of the author to allow the **DataCombo** to search for the name as the user types. When the user clicks the **Retrieve Books** button, the **DataList** is populated with a list of ISBN numbers for books written by that author. When the user clicks on an ISBN number in the **DataList**, a **DataGrid** appears to display the book's title, publisher and year published. The properties for the controls in this program were set as shown in Fig. 18.21.

```
1   ' Fig 18.20
2   ' Demonstrating DataCombo and DataList controls
3   Option Explicit
4   Dim bookQuery, allInfoQuery As String
5
6   Private Sub Form_Load()
7      On Error Resume Next
8      bookQuery = _
9         "SELECT Authors.Author, [Title Author].ISBN " & _
10        "FROM Authors INNER JOIN [Title Author] ON " & _
11        "Authors.Au_ID = [Title Author].Au_ID " & _
12        "WHERE Authors.Author = "
13     allInfoQuery = _
14        "SELECT DISTINCT Titles.Title, Publishers.Name, " & _
15        "Titles.[Year Published] " & _
16        "FROM (Publishers INNER JOIN Titles ON " & _
17        "Publishers.PubID = Titles.PubID) INNER JOIN " & _
18        "(Authors INNER JOIN [Title Author] ON " & _
19        "Authors.Au_ID = [Title Author].Au_ID) ON " & _
20        "Titles.ISBN = [Title Author].ISBN WHERE " & _
21        "Titles.ISBN = "
22  End Sub
23
24  Private Sub cmdRetrieve_Click()
25     On Error Resume Next
26     DataGrid1.Visible = False
27     adoBooks.RecordSource = bookQuery & _
28        "'" & DataCombo1.Text & "'"
29     Call adoBooks.Refresh
30  End Sub
31
32  Private Sub DataList1_Click()
33     On Error Resume Next
34     adoAllInfo.RecordSource = allInfoQuery & _
35        "'" & DataList1.Text & "'"
36     adoAllInfo.Refresh
37     DataGrid1.Visible = True
38  End Sub
39
```

**Fig. 18.20**  Demonstrating the **DataCombo** and **DataList** controls (part 1 of 2).

```
40   Private Sub Form_Resize()
41      ' set dimensions of GUI components on scaling of window
42      DataCombo1.Width = ScaleWidth - cmdRetrieve.Width
43      DataList1.Height = ScaleHeight - DataCombo1.Height
44      DataGrid1.Width = ScaleWidth - DataList1.Width
45      DataGrid1.Height = DataList1.Height
46      cmdRetrieve.Left = ScaleWidth - cmdRetrieve.Width
47   End Sub
```

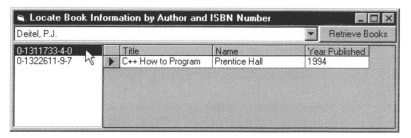

**Fig. 18.20**   Demonstrating the **DataCombo** and **DataList** controls (part 2 of 2).

| Control | Property | Setting |
| --- | --- | --- |
| Form1 | Caption | Locate Book Information by Author and ISBN Number |
| adoAuthorName | CommandType | 1 - adCmdText |
| | ConnectionString | Follow the steps discussed with Fig. 18.5 for specifying the connection string. |
| | RecordSource | SELECT Author, Au_ID FROM Authors ORDER BY Author ASC |
| adoBooks | CommandType | 1 - adCmdText |
| | ConnectionString | Follow the steps discussed with Fig. 18.5 for specifying the connection string. |
| | RecordSource | Provide any simple query here. It will be replaced at execution time. By setting a temporary query, you prevent an error message indicating "no RecordSource specified." |
| adoAllInfo | CommandType | 1 - adCmdText |
| | ConnectionString | Follow the steps discussed with Fig. 18.5 for specifying the connection string. |
| | RecordSource | Provide any simple query here. It will be replaced at execution time. By setting a temporary query, you prevent an error message indicating "no RecordSource specified." |
| cmdRetrieve | Caption | Retrieve Books |
| DataCombo1 | DataSource | adoAuthorName |
| | RowSource | adoAuthorName |
| | ListField | Author |
| | Text | Select an Author |
| DataList1 | DataSource | adoBooks |
| | RowSource | adoBooks |
| | ListField | ISBN |
| DataGrid1 | DataSource | adoAllInfo |
| | AllowUpdate | False |

**Fig. 18.21**   Property settings for controls in the program of Fig. 18.20.

When the program is initially executed, the **DataCombo** and **DataList** controls are displayed as shown in the first screen capture of Fig. 18.20. The **DataGrid** is not displayed until the user selects an author from the **DataCombo** control (as shown in the second screen capture), then selects an ISBN number for a book from the **DataList** control (as shown in the third screen capture). Once an ISBN number is selected, the **Data-Grid** control is displayed with the title of the book, name of the publisher and the year in which that book was published. The program's code is discussed below.

Line 4,

```
Dim bookQuery, allInfoQuery As String
```

creates the strings **bookQuery** and **allInfoQuery**. These strings are modified in response to the user's interactions with the GUI to populate the **DataList** and **DataGrid**, respectively.

Lines 8 through 12,

```
bookQuery = _
    "SELECT Authors.Author, [Title Author].ISBN " & _
    "FROM Authors INNER JOIN [Title Author] ON " & _
    "Authors.Au_ID = [Title Author].Au_ID " & _
    "WHERE Authors.Author = "
```

specify the **INNER JOIN** query that locates all the ISBN numbers associated with a particular author. The query selects the **Author** field from the **Authors** table and the **ISBN** field from the **Title Author** table with the **INNER JOIN** condition, which compares the **Au_ID** field in each table. At execution time, the name of the author is appended to this string to complete the query string. When the **adoBooks Recordset** is refreshed with this query, the complete list of ISBN numbers for books by the specified author is available to be displayed in the **DataList**.

Lines 13 through 21,

```
allInfoQuery = _
    "SELECT DISTINCT Titles.Title, Publishers.Name, " & _
    "Titles.[Year Published] " & _
    "FROM (Publishers INNER JOIN Titles ON " & _
    "Publishers.PubID = Titles.PubID) INNER JOIN " & _
    "(Authors INNER JOIN [Title Author] ON " & _
    "Authors.Au_ID = [Title Author].Au_ID) ON " & _
    "Titles.ISBN = [Title Author].ISBN WHERE " & _
    "Titles.ISBN = "
```

specify the **INNER JOIN** query that locates book information for the ISBN number selected by the user from the **DataList**. The query selects the **Title** field from the **Titles** table, the **Name** field from the **Publishers** table and the **Year Published** field from the **Titles** table. Notice the use of SQL keyword **DISTINCT** to ensure that unique book titles are displayed. The **Publishers** and **Titles** tables are **INNER JOIN**ed on the **PubID** field. The **Authors** and **Title Author** tables are **INNER JOIN**ed on the **Au_ID** field. The results of those two **INNER JOIN**s are then **INNER JOIN**ed on the **ISBN** field retrieved from both the **Titles** and **Title Author** tables. At execution time, the **ISBN** selected by the user is appended to this string to complete the query string. When the **adoAllInfo Recordset** is refreshed with this query, the title, publisher and year published for the selected book are displayed in the **DataList**.

Selects an author from **DataCombo1**, then click **cmdRetrieve** to invoke event procedure **cmdRetrieve_Click** (lines 24 through 30). This procedure hides **DataGrid1**, then assigns **adoBooks.RecordSource** a new string value with the statement

```
adoBooks.RecordSource = bookQuery & _
    "'" & DataCombo1.Text & "'"
```

that appends a single-quote character, the string currently selected in **DataCombo1** and another single-quote character to the end of string **bookQuery**. Next, **adoBooks.Refresh** is invoked to refresh the **Recordset**. **DataList1** is automatically updated to display a list of ISBN numbers based on the author selected in **DataCombo1**.

Select an ISBN number from **DataList1**, to invoke the **DataList1_Click** event procedure (lines 32 through 38). This procedure assigns **adoAllInfo.RecordSource** a new string value with the statement

```
adoAllInfo.RecordSource = allInfoQuery & _
    "'" & DataList1.Text & "'"
```

which appends a single-quote character, the string currently selected in **DataList1** and another single-quote character to the end of string **allInfoQuery**. Next, **adoAllInfo.Refresh** is invoked to refresh the **Recordset**. **DataGrid1** is automatically updated to display the title, publisher and year published based on the ISBN number selected in **DataList1**. **DataGrid1**'s **Visible** property is set to **True** to display the grid.

## 18.9.2 Using the BoundColumn Property

A key feature of the **DataCombo** and **DataList** controls is their ability to use their **BoundColumn** property to update a field value of a record in another **Recordset**. Let us assume that the publisher names associated with many books in the database are incorrect and that we would like to create an application that allows the user to select a title and change its publisher. For example, our publisher—Prentice Hall—has nine unique IDs in the **Publisher**s table and we may want all Prentice Hall books to be associated with the same publisher ID. If you look at the **Titles** table of **Biblo.mdb**, you will notice that this table does not include the publisher's name for each book; rather, it includes only the publisher's ID. This value is an unfriendly integer value—to change the publisher for a book, you would have to know each publisher's unique ID value. Using the **BoundColumn** feature of the **DataCombo** (or **DataList**) control, we can hide the unfriendly ID value from the user and display a list of actual publisher names from which the user can select the new publisher name.

The program of Fig. 18.22 requires no programming. The properties of the controls were set as shown in Fig. 18.23. We discuss these properties shortly. In the first screen capture, we located our Prentice Hall textbook *C++ How to Program*. When a book is selected in **DataGrid1**, its publisher is automatically displayed in **DataCombo1**. Also, notice that the current value for **PubID** is **715**.

If you open **DataCombo1**, you will notice that there are nine different entries for Prentice Hall. In the second output window, we selected the entry **PRENTICE HALL**.

When the user selects another record as the current record, field **PubID** is automatically updated to the new publisher we selected. The third screen capture shows the new value of **2** for field **PubID** after we made another record the current record. We made the *C++ How to Program* record the current record again to highlight it in the screen capture.

We use two **ADO Data Control**s in this example—**adoPublishers** and **adoTitles**. Control **adoPublishers** queries the **Publishers** table of **Biblo.mdb** to retrieve all the **Company Name**s and corresponding **PubID** values. Control **adoTitles** queries the **Titles** table to retrieve the **Title** and **PubID** of each book in the database. The **DataGrid1** control displays the results of the query done by **adoTitles**.

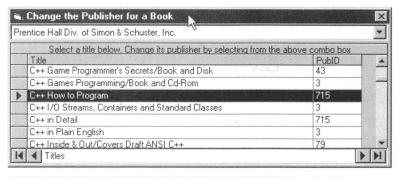

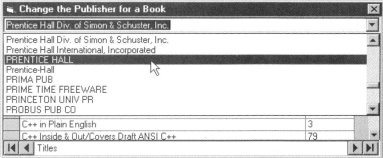

**Fig. 18.22**  Using the **BoundColumn** property of the **DataCombo** control.

| Control | Property | Setting |
| --- | --- | --- |
| **Form1** | **Caption** | **Change the Publisher for a Book** |
|  | **BorderStyle** | **1 - Fixed Single** |
| **adoPublishers** | **CommandType** | **1 - adCmdText** |
|  | **ConnectionString** | Follow the steps discussed with Fig. 18.5 for specifying the connection string. |

**Fig. 18.23**  Property settings for controls in the program of Fig. 18.22 (part 1 of 2).

| Control | Property | Setting |
|---------|----------|---------|
|  | RecordSource | SELECT [Company Name], PubID FROM Publishers ORDER BY Name ASC |
|  | Visible | False |
| adoTitles | CommandType | 1 - adCmdText |
|  | ConnectionString | Follow the steps discussed with Fig. 18.5 for specifying the connection string. |
|  | RecordSource | SELECT Title, PubID FROM Titles ORDER BY Title ASC |
| DataCombo1 | DataSource | adoTitles |
|  | DataField | PubID |
|  | RowSource | adoPublishers |
|  | BoundColumn | PubID |
|  | ListField | Company Name |
|  | Text | Select a Publisher |
| DataGrid1 | DataSource | adoTitles |
|  | AllowUpdate | False |
|  | Caption | Select a title below. Change its publisher by selecting from the above combo box |

**Fig. 18.23**   Property settings for controls in the program of Fig. 18.22 (part 2 of 2).

The key control in this example is **DataCombo1**. It uses both the **adoTitles** and **adoPublishers** controls. The company names displayed in **DataCombo1** are retrieved from the **adoPublishers** control specified as the value for the **RowSource** property. The **ListField** property specifies that the **Company Name** field—one of the fields in the **RowSource Recordset** managed by **adoPublishers**—should be used to populate **DataCombo1**. The **BoundColumn** property is one of the fields in the **Row-Source Recordset**—**PubID** in this example. This is the field that is used to update a field in the **DataSource Recordset**. The **DataField** property specifies the field that is updated by the **BoundColumn** value. When the user selects a new value in **DataCombo1** (i.e., a new publisher for the current book), the value of the **BoundColumn** field is automatically passed from **DataCombo1** to the **DataSource** and used as an updated value for the corresponding field in the **DataSource**'s **Recordset**. As soon as the user makes another record the current record, the updated value is stored in the **Data-Source**.

## 18.10 Using the Data Environment Designer

This section illustrates how the *Data Environment Designer* enables the programmer to rapidly design and implement data-driven applications in Visual Basic. In addition, this section discusses common features of data-bound controls and shows how the **Data Environment Designer** can create a connection to a database and provide a set of data-bound controls that are automatically attached to the fields of a `Recordset` object.

To begin using a **Data Environment Designer**, we must first add one to our project. In the **Project** menu, position the mouse over **More ActiveX Designers...** and click the **Data Envrionment** option in the pop-up menu. The **Data Environment Designer** window in Fig. 18.24 appears. The default name for a data environment is `DataEnvironment1`.

By default, you are provided with one `Connection` object called `Connection1`. A `Connection` object manages the connection between the Visual Basic program and the database. `Connection` objects also allow you to specify properties of the connection at design time and dynamically at execution time.

Next, we associate the `Connection1` object with the `Biblio.mdb` database. Right-click `Connection1` in the **Data Envrionment Designer** and select **Properties...** from the pop-up menu to display the **Data Link Properties** dialog. On the **Provider** tab, select **Microsoft Jet 3.51 OLE DB Provider**. In Step 1 of the **Connection** tab, click the **...** button to display the **Select Access Database** dialog and select the `Biblio.mdb` database from your `VB98` directory. Confirm the connection to the database by clicking the **Test Connection** button. If set up properly, a small dialog appears with the message "**Test connection succeeded.**" Click **OK** to dismiss this dialog and click **OK** again to dismiss the **Data Link Properties** dialog. These steps we just performed are identical to creating a connection string as discussed with Fig. 18.5.

The **Data Environment Designer** is flexible in that it allows multiple `Command` objects to be associated with a `Connection` object. `Command` objects specify operations on the database such as an SQL query or simply viewing a table in the database. These `Command` objects can be used interchangeably during execution of the program.

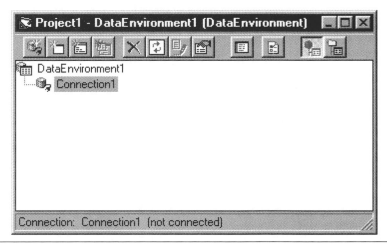

**Fig. 18.24**  The **Data Envrionment Designer** window.

Next, we create a **Command** object (called **Command1** by default) with the **Titles** table of the database. Right-click **Connection1** in the **Data Environment Designer** and select **Add Command** from the pop-up menu. This adds a **Command** object called **Command1** to the **Connection1** object. Right-click **Command1** and select **Proper-ties...** from the pop-up menu. In the **Data Source** area of the **General** tab, select **Table** from the **Database Object** combo box. In the **Object Name** combo box select the **Titles** table. The **Command1** object is now associated with the **Titles** table of the **Biblio.mdb** database.

Perhaps the handiest feature of the **Data Environment Designer** is the ability to drag a **Command** object from the designer onto a form and instantly create a user interface in which to present the **Recordset** data for the associated **Command**. Right-click the **Command1** object and drag it over the form. When you let go of the right mouse button, a pop-up menu appears with three options—**Data Grid**, **Hierarchical Flex Grid** and **Bound Controls**. To display the data in a table format, select either **Data Grid** or **Hier-archical Flex Grid**. Because we demonstrated both of these controls earlier in the chapter, we chose **Bound Controls** here. This automatically produces a set of controls and attaches them to the form as shown in Fig. 18.25. The controls are already attached to specific fields in the **Titles** table associated with the **Command1** object. You can repo-sition and size the controls as necessary.

We added the **First**, **Previous**, **Next** and **Last** buttons at the bottom of the form to allow manipulation of the records in the **Recordset** object. Clicking these buttons will allow the user to view the first record, previous record, next record and last record, respec-tively. Depending on the current position in the **Recordset**, the **Previous** or **Next** button may be temporarily disabled.

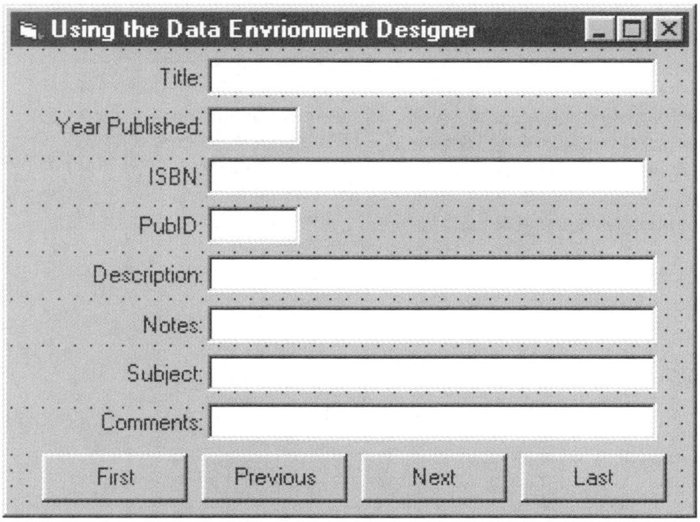

**Fig. 18.25**    The bound controls added to the form by the **Command1** object when it is dragged and dropped onto the form.

The drag-and-drop functionality for creating a user interface of the **Data Envrionment Designer** has a bug in it with respect to field names that contain spaces. For such fields, click the bound control on the form (such as the **TextBox** associated with the **Year Published** field) and modify its **DataField** property by selecting the appropriate field from the drop-down list for the property. This will fix the problem. Notice that the property value displayed now contains the space character.

The code for the four command buttons we added to the user interface is shown in Fig. 18.26.

When the user clicks button **cmdFirst**, the event procedure at line 5 executes. The statement

```
DataEnvironment1.rsCommand1.MoveFirst
```

```
1   ' Fig. 18.26
2   ' Using the Data Environment Designer
3   Option Explicit
4
5   Private Sub cmdFirst_Click()
6      DataEnvironment1.rsCommand1.MoveFirst
7      cmdPrevious.Enabled = False
8      cmdNext.Enabled = True
9   End Sub
10
11  Private Sub cmdLast_Click()
12     DataEnvironment1.rsCommand1.MoveLast
13     cmdPrevious.Enabled = True
14     cmdNext.Enabled = False
15  End Sub
16
17  Private Sub cmdNext_Click()
18     DataEnvironment1.rsCommand1.MoveNext
19     cmdPrevious.Enabled = True
20
21     If DataEnvironment1.rsCommand1.EOF = True Then
22        cmdNext.Enabled = False
23     End If
24  End Sub
25
26  Private Sub cmdPrevious_Click()
27     DataEnvironment1.rsCommand1.MovePrevious
28     cmdNext.Enabled = True
29
30     If DataEnvironment1.rsCommand1.BOF = True Then
31        cmdPrevious.Enabled = False
32     End If
33  End Sub
```

**Fig. 18.26**　Using the **Data Environment Designer** (part 1 of 2).

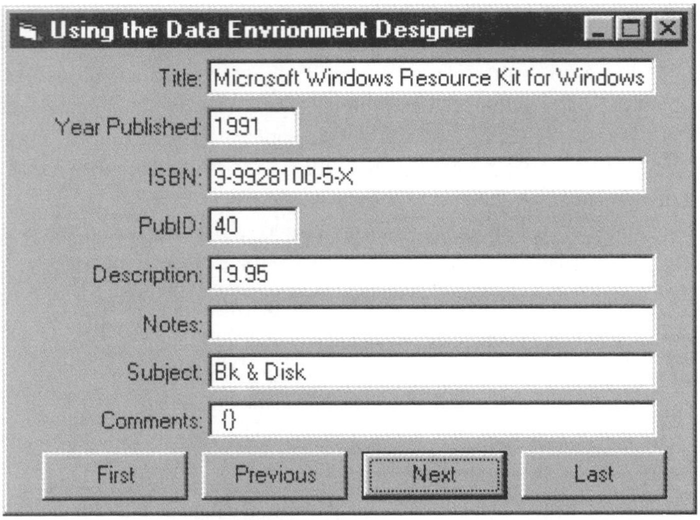

**Fig. 18.26**    Using the **Data Environment Designer** (part 2 of 2).

at line 6 uses **DataEnvironment1**'s **rsCommand1** object to move to the first record in the **Recordset**. Object **rsCommand1** is the **Recordset** object created when **Command1** interacts with the database and returns a **Recordset** for use in the program. Procedure **MoveFirst** indicates that the current record in the **Recordset** should be the first record. Note that the **cmdPrevious** button is disabled in this case because there is no previous record. Note that the data-bound controls are automatically updated when the current record is changed programmatically with the **MoveFirst** procedure (or any of the other **Move** procedures discussed in the next several paragraphs).

When the user clicks **cmdLast**, the event procedure at line 11 executes. The statement

```
DataEnvironment1.rsCommand1.MoveLast
```

at line 12 uses **DataEnvironment1**'s **rsCommand1** object to move to the last record in the **Recordset**. Procedure **MoveLast** indicates that the current record in the **Recordset** should be the last record. Note that the **cmdNext** button is disabled in this case because there is no next record.

When the user clicks **cmdNext**, the event procedure at line 17 executes. The statement

```
DataEnvironment1.rsCommand1.MoveNext
```

at line 18 uses **DataEnvironment1**'s **rsCommand1** object to move to the next record in the **Recordset**. Procedure **MoveNext** indicates that the current record in the **Recordset** should be the next record. A test is performed at line 21 to determine if the end of the **Recordset** has been reached. If the end-of-file indicator

```
DataEnvironment1.rsCommand1.EOF
```

is **True**, the **cmdNext** button is disabled because there is no next record.

When the user clicks button **cmdPrevious**, the event procedure at line 17 executes. The statement

```
DataEnvironment1.rsCommand1.MovePrevious
```

at line 18 uses **DataEnvironment1**'s **rsCommand1** object to move to the previous record in the **Recordset**. Procedure **MovePrevious** indicates that the current record in the **Recordset** should be the previous record. A test is performed at line 21 to determine if the beginning of the **Recordset** has been reached. If beginning-of-file indicator

```
DataEnvironment1.rsCommand1.BOF
```

is **True**, the **cmdPrevious** button is disabled because there is no previous record.

## 18.11 Other Programmatic Capabilities of Recordsets

As you have seen, a **Recordset** is used to manipulate the records in a table or query result. **Recordset**s provide a number of capabilities that are accessible programmatically.

**Fields** objects allow the program to manipulate columns of data in a **Recordset**. For example,

> *[Data control]*.**Recordset.Fields(**"*FieldName*"**)**

returns a ***Field*** object that represents the value in the current record for the column called *FieldName*. This can also be accomplished with

> *[Data control]*.**Recordset(**"*FieldName*"**)**

because **Fields** is the default property assumed by Visual Basic for a **Recordset**. Other common properties of a **Field** object are **Attributes**, **Size**, **Type** and **Value**.

The **Bookmark** property of a **Recordset** can be used to maintain a reference to a specific record for quick access. To store a reference to the current record, simply declare a variable of type **Variant** and assign it the **Bookmark** value. For example, assuming that **bookmarkLocation** is of type **Variant**, the statement

> **bookmarkLocation =** *[Data control]*.**Recordset.Bookmark**

stores the location of the current record in the **Recordset**. This location can be restored at any time using

> *[Data control]*.**Recordset.Bookmark = bookmarkLocation**

## 18.12 Transaction Processing

If the database supports *transaction processing*—changes made to the database can be undone. Visual Basic provides transaction processing in the form of procedures ***BeginTrans***, ***CommitTrans*** and ***Rollback***. **BeginTrans** starts logging changes to the database for possible *rollback* later. Up to five **BeginTrans** calls can be nested. Invoking **CommitTrans** makes all the changes since the most recent **BeginTrans**. For nested transactions, changes are not performed until all transaction logs are closed. Invoking **RollBack** undoes all the changes since the most recent call to **BeginTrans**.

## Summary

- Database systems provide file-processing capabilities but organize data in a manner to facilitate satisfying sophisticated queries.
- The most popular style of database system on personal computers is the relational database.
- Structured Query Language (SQL) is almost universally used to make relational database queries.
- A database is an integrated collection of data which is centrally controlled.
- A database management system (DBMS) controls the storage and retrieval of data in a database.
- A distributed database is a database that is spread throughout the computer systems of a network.
- A relational database is composed of tables manipulated as a **Recordset** objects in Visual Basic.
- Any particular row of the table is called a record or a row.
- Each column of the table represents a different field.
- Some users want only certain subsets of the table columns (called projections). Other users wish to combine smaller tables into larger ones to produce more complex tables (called joins).
- Visual Basic provides a variety of data-aware controls for manipulating data in data-bases.
- The **ADO Data Control** manages access to a database by a Visual Basic program.
- The **DataGrid** control displays the data requested from a database in a table format.
- A table's primary key uniquely identifies each record in the table. Every record must have a value in the primary key field—Rule of Entity Integrity—and the value must be unique.
- A foreign key is a field in a table for which every entry has a unique value in another table and where the field in the other table is the primary key for that table. The foreign key concept helps maintain the Rule of Referential Integrity—every value in a foreign key field must appear in another table's primary key field. Foreign keys enable information from multiple tables to be joined together and presented to the user.
- A typical SQL query "selects" information from one or more tables in a database. Such selections are performed by **SELECT** queries. The simplest format of a **SELECT** query is

  > **SELECT * FROM** *TableName*

  where the asterisk (**\***) indicates that all fields from *TableName* should be selected and *TableName* specifies the table in the database from which the fields will be selected. To select specific fields from a table, replace the asterisk (**\***) with a comma-separated list of the field names to select.
- SQL uses the optional **WHERE** clause to specify the selection criteria for the query. The simplest format of a **SELECT** query with selection criteria is

  > **SELECT * FROM** *TableName* **WHERE** *criteria*
- The condition in the **WHERE** clause can contain operators **<**, **>**, **<=**, **>=**, **=**, **<>** and **Like**. Operator **Like** is used for pattern matching with the wildcard characters asterisk (**\***) and question mark (**?**).
- The results of a query can be arranged in ascending or descending order using the optional **ORDER BY** clause. The simplest format of an **ORDER BY** clause is

  > **SELECT * FROM** *TableName* **ORDER BY** *field* **ASC**
  > **SELECT * FROM** *TableName* **ORDER BY** *field* **DESC**

  where **ASC** specifies ascending (lowest to highest) order, **DESC** specifies descending (highest to lowest) order and field represents the field that is used for sorting purposes.
- Multiple fields can be used for ordering purposes with an **ORDER BY** clause of the form

  > **ORDER BY** *field1 SortingOrder, field2 SortingOrder,* **...**

  where *SortingOrder* is either **ASC** or **DESC**.

- The **WHERE** and **ORDER BY** clauses can be combined in one query.
- An **INNER JOIN** merges records from two tables by testing for matching values in a field that is common to both tables. The simplest format of an **INNER JOIN** clause is

  **SELECT * FROM** *Table1* **INNER JOIN** *Table2* **ON** *Table1.field* = *Table2.field*

- The **ON** part of the **INNER JOIN** clause specifies the fields from each table that should be compared to determine which records will be selected.
- The syntax **TableName.FieldName** is used in a query to distinguish between fields in different tables that have the same name.
- Statements can be specified for **ADO** property **RecordSource** at execution time.
- Set the **AllowAddNew** property for the **DataGrid** to **True** (the default is **False**) to use the last row of the **DataGrid** to enter a new record of information.
- Set the **AllowDelete** property of the **DataGrid** to **True** (the default is **False**) to allow the user to delete an entire record by clicking the gray rectangle to the left of the row and pressing the Delete key on the keyboard.
- Set the **AllowUpdate** property to **False** (the default is **True**) to prevent the user from modifying the data.
- The **Hierarchical FlexGrid** control is similar to the **DataGrid** control, but the user can only view the data through a **FlexGrid**.
- The **BoundColumn** property of the **DataCombo** and **DataList** controls specifies the field in one **Recordset** that will be supplied to another **Recordset**.
- The **BoundText** property of the **DataCombo** and **DataList** controls specifies the value of the **BoundColumn** field.
- To begin using a **Data Environment Designer**, add one to the project by selecting **More ActiveX Designers...** from the **Project** menu. Click the **Data Envrionment** option in the pop-up menu that appears.
- A **Connection** object manages the connection between the Visual Basic program and the database. **Connection** objects also allow you to specify properties of the connection at design time and dynamically at execution time.
- The **Data Environment Designer** is flexible in that it allows multiple **Command** objects to be associated with a **Connection** object.
- **Command** objects specify operations on the database such as an SQL query or simply viewing a table in the database.
- Perhaps the handiest feature of the **Data Environment Designer** is the ability to drag a **Command** object from the designer onto a form and instantly create a user interface in which to present the **Recordset** data for the associated **Command**.
- **Recordset** procedures **MoveFirst**, **MovePrevious**, **MoveNext** and **MoveLast** enable the first, previous, next and last records in the **Recordset** to be specified as the current record in the **Recordset**.
- **Recordset** property **EOF** indicates when the end of the **Recordset** is reached. **Recordset** property **BOF** indicates when the beginning of the **Recordset** is reached.
- **Fields** objects allow the program to manipulate a column of data in a **Recordset**.
- The **Bookmark** property of a **Recordset** can be used to maintain a reference to a specific record for quick access.
- Visual Basic provides transaction processing in the form of procedures **BeginTrans**, **CommitTrans** and **Rollback**.

## Terminology

| | |
|---|---|
| **ADO Data Control** | **INNER JOIN ... ON ...** |
| **AllowAddNew** property of **DataGrid** control | joined table |
| **AllowDelete** property of **DataGrid** control | join two relational database tables |
| **AllowUpdate** property of **DataGrid** control | **Like** operator in a criteria clause |
| ANSI (American National Standards Institute) | Microsoft Access |
| ANSI-89 SQL | **MoveFirst** method |
| **ASC** (ascending order) | **MoveLast** method |
| asterisk (**\***) wildcard character | **MoveNext** method |
| **BOF** (beginning-of-file) property | **MovePrevious** method |
| connect a Visual Basic program to a database | navigation arrows (first, last, previous, next) |
| **Connect** property of data control | **ORDER BY ... ASC** clause |
| criteria clause | **ORDER BY ... DESC** clause |
| current record | primary key field of a record in a table |
| data-aware controls | Professional Edition of Visual Basic |
| database | question mark (**?**) wildcard character |
| database file | record as row of table in relational database |
| database management system (DBMS) | record (row of a table) |
| **DatabaseName** property of a data control | **Recordset** |
| data control | **RecordSource** property of a data control |
| data control icon | **Refresh** method of a data control |
| **DataCombo** control | relational database |
| **DataFields** property | row of a table (record) |
| **DataGrid** control | **RowSource** property |
| **DataList** control | Rule of Entity Integrity |
| data normalization | Rule of Referential Integrity |
| **DataSource** property | **SELECT ... FROM ...** SQL statement |
| **DESC** (descending order) | **SELECT ... FROM ... WHERE ... ORDER BY ...** |
| dynaset | snapshot |
| **EOF** (end-of-file) property | SQL (Structured Query Language) |
| field | square brackets (**[]**) |
| field as column of table in relational database | table in a database |
| Fields | Unique |
| **FindFirst** method | Update |
| **FindLast** method | **Validate** event procedure |
| **Find** method | Validation event |
| **FindNext** method | view in a relational database |
| **FindPrevious** method | **WHERE** clause of **SELECT** statement |
| foreign key | wildcard characters |
| **INNER JOIN** clause of **SELECT** statement | |

## Common Programming Errors

**18.1** When a field is specified as the primary key field, not providing a value for that field in every record breaks the Rule of Entity Integrity and is an error.

**18.2** When a field is specified as the primary key field, providing duplicate values for multiple records is an error.

**18.3** Attempting to modify a record such that either the Rule of Referential Integrity or the Rule of Entity Integrity is compromised results in an error message and program termination if the error is not trapped by the program.

## Good Programming Practice

**18.1**    By convention, SQL keywords should use all capital letters on systems that are not case sensitive to make the SQL keywords stand out in an SQL query.

## Performance Tip

**18.1**    Using selection criteria improves performance by selecting fewer records from the database.

## Portability Tips

**18.1**    SQL is case sensitive on some database systems.

**18.2**    Not all database systems support the **Like** operator.

## Software Engineering Observations

**18.1**    Set the **AllowUpdate** property of **DataGrid** to **False** (the default is **True**) to prevent the user from changing the contents of the grid cells.

**18.2**    If a field name contains spaces, it must be enclosed in square brackets (**[]**) in the query.

**18.3**    SQL is not case sensitive.

## Self-Review Exercises

**18.1**    Fill in the blanks in each of the following:
a) The most popular database query language is _____.
b) A table in a database consists of _____ and _____.
c) Tables are manipulated in Visual Basic as _____ objects.
d) The _____ uniquely identifies each record in a table.
e) SQL keyword _____ is followed by the selection criteria that specify the records to select in a query.
f) SQL keyword _____ specifies the order in which records are sorted in a query.
g) SQL keyword _____ is used to merge data from two or more tables.
h) ADO property _____ specifies the database provider and database to which the **ADO Data Control** should connect.
i) The _____ control displays the contents of a **RecordSet** in read-only format.
j) The _____ enables the programmer to rapidly design and implement data-driven applications.

**18.2**    State whether the following a e *true* or *false*. If the answer is *false*, explain why.
a) Data displayed in a **DataGrid** can always be modified.
b) ADO can only be used to connect to relational databases.
c) There can be multiple **Command** objects associated with each **Connection** object in the **Data Environment Designer**.

## Answers to Self-Review Exercises

**18.1**    a) SQL.  b) rows, columns.  c) **RecordSet**.  d) primary key.  e) **WHERE**.  f) **ORDER BY**.
g) **INNER JOIN**.  h) connection string.  i) **Hierarchical FlexGrid**.  j) **Data Environment Designer**.

**18.2**    a) False. The **AllowUpdate** property of the **DataGrid** control can be set to **False** to prevent data modification.
b) False. ADO can be used to connect to any type of database.
c) True.

## Exercises

**18.3**   Modify the program of Fig. 18.5 to allow the user to select any table from the **Biblio.mdb** database, then display the data in a **DataGrid** control.

**18.4**   Using the techniques shown in this chapter, define a complete query application for the **Biblio.mdb** database. The user should be able to edit existing data and add new data to the database. Provide a series of predefined queries with an appropriate name for each query displayed in a **ComboBox**. Also allow the user to supply their own queries and add them to the **ComboBox**. Provide the following predefined queries:

a) Select all authors from the **Authors** table.
b) Select all publishers from the **Publishers** table.
c) Select a specific author and list all books for that author. Include the title, year and ISBN number. Order the information alphabetically by title.
d) Select a specific publisher and list all books published by that publisher. Include the title, year and ISBN number. Order the information alphabetically by title.
e) Select a publisher and display its address, phone number and fax number.
f) Provide any other queries you feel are appropriate.

For each of the preceding queries, the results should be displayed in an appropriate component. For example, the query that selects all authors from the **Authors** table should be displayed in a **DataGrid** or **Hierarchical FlexGrid** control. The queries in parts (c) and (d) might use both a **DataGrid/Hierarchical FlexGrid** and **TextBox**es for the author or publisher names. Note: If you have the Enterprise Edition of Visual Basic, investigate the **Query Designer**'s capabilities that help you graphically build queries.

**18.5**   Modify Exercise 18.4 to define a complete database manipulation application for the **Biblio.mdb** database. In addition to the querying capabilities, the user should be able to edit existing data and add new data to the database. Allow the user to edit the database in the following ways:

a) Add a new author.
b) Edit the existing information for an author.
c) Add a new title for an author (remember that the book must have an entry in the **Title Author** table). Be sure to specify the publisher of the title.
d) Add a new publisher.
e) Edit the existing information for a publisher.

For each of the preceding database manipulations, design an appropriate GUI to allow the user to perform the data manipulation.

**18.6**   Microsoft **Access** comes with a number of predefined *database wizard templates* (music collection, video collection, wine list, book collection, etc.) that are accessible by selecting **New** from the **File** menu in Microsoft **Access** and choosing a database from **Database** tab. Create a new database using one of the templates of your choice. Perform exercises 18.4 and 18.5 using the new database and its predefined tables. Provide appropriate queries for the database you choose and allow the user to edit and add data to the database.

## Bibliography

(Bl88)   Blaha, M. R.; W. J. Premerlani; and J. E. Rumbaugh, "Relational Database Design Using an Object-Oriented Methodology," *Communications of the ACM*, Vol. 31, No. 4, April 1988, pp. 414–427.

(Co70)   Codd, E. F., "A Relational of Data for Large Shared Data Banks," *Communications of the ACM*, June 1970.

(Co72)   Codd, E. F., "Further Normalization of the Data Base Relational Model," in *Courant Computer Science Symposia*, Vol. 6, *Data Base Systems*. Upper Saddle River, N.J.: Prentice Hall, 1972.

(Co88)   Codd, E. F., "Fatal Flaws in SQL," *Datamation*, Vol. 34, No. 16, August 15, 1988, pp. 45–48.

(De90)   Deitel, H. M., *Operating Systems, Second Edition*. Reading, MA: Addison Wesley Publishing, 1990.

(Da81)   Date, C. J., *An Introduction to Database Systems*. Reading, MA: Addison Wesley Publishing, 1981.

(Re88)   Relational Technology, *INGRES Overview*. Alameda, CA: Relational Technology, 1988.

(St81)   Stonebraker, M., "Operating System Support for Database Management," *Communications of the ACM*, Vol. 24, No. 7, July 1981, pp. 412–418.

(Va97)   Vaughn, W., *Hitchhiker's Guide to Visual Basic & SQL Server, 6th Edition*. Redmond, WA: Microsoft Press, 1997.

(Wi88)   Winston, A., "A Distributed Database Primer," *UNIX World*, April 1988, pp. 54–63.

# 19

# Networking, the Internet and the World Wide Web

## Objectives

- To understand elements of networking.
- To understand and implement clients and servers that communicate with one another.
- To understand how to implement network-based collaborative applications.
- To be able to write programs that "walk the web."
- To be able to use the **WebBrowser**, **Internet Transfer** and **Winsock** controls.
- To be able to use Visual Basic Script (VBScript) to enhance a World Wide Web document.

*If the presence of electricity can be made visible in any part of a circuit, I see no reason why intelligence may not be transmitted instantaneously by electricity.*
Samuel F. B. Morse

*Mr. Watson, come here, I want you.*
Alexander Graham Bell

*What networks of railroads, highways and canals were in another age, the networks of telecommunications, information and computerization . . . are today.*
Bruno Kreisky, Austrian Chancellor

*Science may never come up with a better office-communication system than the coffee break.*
Earl Wilson

*O what a tangled web we weave...*
Sir Walter Scott

# Outline

## 19.1 Introduction

There is much excitement over the Internet and the World Wide Web. The Internet ties the
"information world" together. The Web makes the Internet easy to use and gives it the flair
and sizzle of multimedia. Some organizations see the Internet and the Web as crucial to
their information systems strategies. Visual Basic provides several built-in networking capabilities that make it easy to develop Internet- and Web-based applications. Visual Basic
can enable programs to search the world for information and to collaborate with programs
running on other computers worldwide or just within an organization. Visual Basic can
even enable applications running on the same computer to communicate with one another.

Networking is a massive and complex topic. Computer Science and Computer Engineering students will typically take a full-semester, upper-level course in computer networking and continue with further study at the graduate level. Visual Basic provides a rich
complement of networking capabilities and will likely be used as an implementation
vehicle in computer networking courses. In *Visual Basic 6 How to Program* we introduce
basic networking concepts and capabilities. We provide several live-code examples that
will help the reader create a variety of typical networking applications. The reader is
encouraged to further explore Visual Basic's networking capabilities.

Visual Basic offers *socket-based communications* that enable applications to view networking as streams of bytes similar to file input/output—a program can read from a *socket* or write to a socket as simply as reading from a file or writing to a file. Socket connections are similar to telephone calls—the telephone handset represents the socket. The mouthpiece of the telephone is the output stream and the earpiece of the telephone is the input stream. The call (i.e., connection) continues until one of the participants in the conversation terminates the call by hanging up the phone. We show how to create and manipulate sockets. With *socket-based* networking a process establishes a *connection* to another process. While the connection is in place, data flows between the processes in continuous *streams*. Sockets are said to provide a *connection-oriented service*. The protocol used for transmission is the popular *TCP—Transmission Control Protocol*.

Visual Basic also provides *datagram* networking. With *datagrams*, individual *packets* of information are transmitted. This is not the right protocol for everyday users because unlike TCP, the protocol used, *UDP—the User Datagram Protocol—*is a *connectionless service*, and does not guarantee that packets arrive in any particular way. In fact, packets can be lost, can be duplicated and can even arrive out of sequence. So with UDP, significant extra programming is required on the user's part to deal with these problems (if the user chooses to do so). Sockets and the TCP protocol will be the most desirable for the vast majority of Visual Basic programmers. UDP is commonly used for streaming technologies such as audio and video over the internet where streams of UDP packets are sent to a computer and reassembled into the audio or video clip for playing.

**Performance Tip 19.1**

*Connectionless services generally offer greater performance but less reliability than connection-oriented services.*

**Portability Tip 19.1**

*The TCP protocol and its related set of protocols enable a great variety of heterogeneous computer systems (i.e., computer systems with different processors and different operating systems) to intercommunicate.*

Our discussion of networking focuses on both sides of a *client/server relationship*. The *client* requests that some action be performed and the *server* performs the action returning the result (if any) to the client. The client first attempts to establish a *connection* to the server. The server can *accept* or *deny* the connection. If the connection is accepted, then the client and server communicate through sockets in much the same manner as if they were doing file I/O. When the communication connection is no longer needed, the client and server each close the connection. As an example, consider the use of a World Wide Web browser such as Microsoft's **Internet Explorer** or Netscape's **Communicator**. The user specifies the World Wide Web site from which to retrieve a document or web page. The browser—which is executing on the client computer—connects to the specified World Wide Web server to request the document. The server responds by sending the requested document to the client machine so the document can be displayed by the browser.

## 19.2 Visual Basic Internet Controls

Visual Basic provides several networking controls to facilitate development of network-oriented applications. Each of these controls is summarized in Fig. 19.1 and discussed in the remaining sections of the chapter.

| Control | Description |
|---------|-------------|
| **WebBrowser** control | Enables applications to provide web browsing, local document viewing and file downloading capabilities. This control provides an application with many features of the **Internet Explorer** browser. |
| **Internet Transfer** control | Enables applications to use *HyperText Transfer Protocol (HTTP)* and *File Transfer Protocol (FTP)* for Internet-based applications. An application using this control can retrieve files from an send files to any site that uses one of these protocols. |
| **Winsock** control | Enables client/server application programming using either *User Datagram Protocol (UDP)* or *Transmission Control Protocol (TCP)*. |

**Fig. 19.1**   Visual Basic Internet-related controls.

## 19.3 WebBrowser Control

The Internet offers many *protocols*. The *HTTP protocol (HyperText Transfer Protocol)* that forms the basis of the World Wide Web uses URLs (*Uniform Resource Locators*, also called *Universal Resource Locators*) to locate data on the Internet. Common URLs represent files or directories and can represent complex tasks such as database lookups and Internet searches. For more information on URL formats visit the World Wide Web site:

> **http://www.ncsa.uiuc.edu/demoweb/url-primer.html**

For more information on the HTTP protocol visit the World Wide Web site:

> **http://www.w3.org**

If you know the URL of publicly available *Hypertext Markup Language (HTML)* files anywhere on the World Wide Web, you can access that data through HTTP. Visual Basic makes it easy to manipulate URLs using the **WebBrowser** *control*.

The **WebBrowser** control provides many of the features of the Microsoft **Internet Explorer** browser in your application including browsing the World Wide Web, viewing documents on your local machine and downloading files. Users of an application that provides the **WebBrowser** control can perform web browsing point-and-click hyperlinking. Also, the control supports navigation via URLs. The **WebBrowser** control's history list mechanism allows the user to move backward and forward through previously viewed documents. Some features of the **WebBrowser** control that are beyond the scope of this text are support for Dynamic HTML, hosting ActiveX controls and scripting. The control also provides automatic management of navigation, hyperlinking, history lists, favorites and security (many of these features are accessible through the pop-up menu's **Properties...** option that appears when you right-click on the **WebBrowser** control).

The program of Fig. 19.2 enables the user to enter a URL in the **TextBox** at the top of the window, then click the **Go to URL** button to navigate to the corresponding World Wide Web site. Once a document is loaded with the **WebBrowser** control, the user can click any link—connection to another document—to enable the **WebBrowser** control to load the page to which the link refers.

To use the **WebBrowser** control, it must first be added to the toolbox by selecting **Components...** from the **Project** menu to display the **Components** dialog box. In the dialog box, scroll down and select the option *Microsoft Internet Controls*. When selected properly, a small check mark appears in the box to the left of the option. Click the **OK** button when you are done to dismiss the dialog box. The globe icon for the **WebBrowser** control will be at the bottom of the toolbox.

Figure 19.2 presents a simple web browser using the **WebBrowser** control. The property settings for the form and controls are shown in Fig. 19.3.

```
1   ' Fig. 19.2
2   ' A simple web browser using the WebBrowser Control.
3   Option Explicit
4
5   Private Sub Form_Load()
6       ' When form is loaded, go to home page
7       Call WebBrowser1.GoHome
8   End Sub
9
10  Private Sub cmdGo_Click()
11      ' if txtURL is not empty, go to URL specified in txtURL
12      On Error Resume Next
13
14      If txtURL.Text <> "" Then
15          Call WebBrowser1.Navigate(txtURL.Text)
16      End If
17  End Sub
18
19  Private Sub cmdBack_Click()
20      ' go to previous page
21      On Error Resume Next
22      Call WebBrowser1.GoBack
23  End Sub
24
25  Private Sub cmdForward_Click()
26      ' go to next page
27      On Error Resume Next
28      Call WebBrowser1.GoForward
29  End Sub
30
31  Private Sub cmdHome_Click()
32      ' go to home page
33      On Error Resume Next
34      Call WebBrowser1.GoHome
35  End Sub
36
37  Private Sub Form_Resize()
38      ' set dimensions of txtURL and WebBrowser1
39      On Error Resume Next
40      WebBrowser1.Width = ScaleWidth
```

**Fig. 19.2**    A simple web browser using the **WebBrowser** control (part 1 of 2).

```
41        WebBrowser1.Height = ScaleHeight - WebBrowser1.Top
42        txtURL.Width = ScaleWidth - txtURL.Left
43     End Sub
44
45     Private Sub WebBrowser1_DocumentComplete( _
46          ByVal pDisp As Object, URL As Variant)
47        ' when download complete, display URL in txtURL
48        txtURL.Text = URL
49     End Sub
```

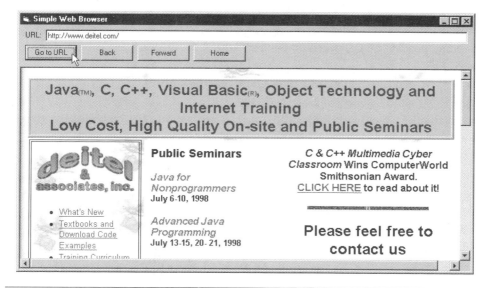

**Fig. 19.2**    A simple web browser using the **WebBrowser** control (part 2 of 2).

| Control | Property | Setting |
|---|---|---|
| frmWebBrowser | Caption | Simple Web Browser |
| | WindowState | 2 - Maximized |
| lblURL | Caption | URL: |
| txtURL | Text | Nothing should be displayed by default. |
| cmdGo | Caption | Go to URL |
| cmdBack | Caption | Back |
| cmdForward | Caption | Forward |
| cmdHome | Caption | Home |
| WebBrowser1 | | Leave default settings. |

**Fig. 19.3**    Property settings for the program of Fig. 19.2.

Our web browser consists of seven controls. Control **lblURL** labels **TextBox txtURL** in which the user can type a URL to display with the **WebBrowser** control. There are four buttons—**cmdGo** displays the URL specified by the user, **cmdBack** moves backward through the previously displayed URLs, **cmdForward** moves forward through the previously displayed URLs and **cmdHome** returns to the home page for the browser. Control **WebBrowser1** displays web pages in response to clicks on the buttons.

Procedure **Form_Load** (lines 5 through 8) is invoked as the program begins execution. Line 7 calls procedure **GoHome** of **WebBrowser1** to load the default web page into the **WebBrowser1** control. The default web page is the page that is specified as your home page in **Internet Explorer**. This can be configured by opening **Internet Explorer**, selecting **Internet Options...** from the **View** menu, and specifying a URL in the **Address TextBox**.

When the user types a URL in **txtURL** and presses **cmdGo**, Visual Basic calls event procedure **cmdGo_Click** (lines 10 though 17). The **If** structure

```
If txtURL.Text <> "" Then
    Call WebBrowser1.Navigate(txtURL.Text)
End If
```

first determines if there is text in **txtURL**. If so, procedure **Navigate** of **WebBrowser1** is called and passed the string in **txtURL**. **WebBrowser1** then displays the document associated with the URL typed by the user (assuming it is a valid URL).

Clicking button **cmdBack** calls event procedure **cmdBack_Click** (lines 19 through 23), which calls procedure **GoBack** of **WebBrowser1** to revisit the previous document in the history list.

Clicking button **cmdForward** calls event procedure **cmdForward_Click** (lines 25 through 29), which calls procedure **GoForward** of **WebBrowser1** to revisit the next document in the history list.

Clicking button **cmdHome** calls event procedure **cmdHome_Click** (lines 31 through 35), which calls procedure **GoHome** of **WebBrowser1** to load the default home page.

When **WebBrowser1** completes the download and display of a URL, event procedure **WebBrowser1_DocumentComplete** (lines 45 through 49). This procedure assigns the value of the **URL** parameter—the currently displayed document's address—to **txtURL.Text** so the URL for the current document appears in **txtURL** for the user to see. Note that the URL displayed may be different from the URL typed by the user; sometimes a web server redirects URLs to new locations.

Resizing the form calls event procedure **Form_Resize** (lines 37 through 43), to resize **txtURL** and **WebBrowser1**. Note that the new **Height** of **WebBrowser1** is adjusted because the top of the **WebBrowser1** control is offset from the top of the form. Similarly, the new **Width** of **txtURL** is adjusted because the left side of **txtURL** is offset from the left of the form.

*Testing and Debugging Tip 19.1*

*Most operations with URLs in the **WebBrowser** control can cause errors that result in program termination.*

*Good Programming Practice 19.1*

*Always provide error-handling code when using the **WebBrowser** control to prevent abnormal program termination.*

The **WebBrowser** control provides a variety of other useful properties, methods and events. Some of these are summarized in Fig. 19.4. For more information on using the **WebBrowser** control and a complete listing of all its properties, methods and events, see the topic "Reusing the WebBrowser Control" in the *Platform SDK* on-line documentation.

| Property, method or event | Description |
| --- | --- |
| *Properties* | |
| **Busy** | A **Boolean** value that is **True** if the control is currently navigating to a document or downloading a file, and **False** otherwise. If **True**, the **Stop** method can be called to cancel the navigation or download. |
| **LocationName** | The name of the document being displayed. For an HTML page, this is the title of the page. For a local folder or file, this is the full path name of the folder or file. |
| **LocationURL** | The location of the document being displayed. For an HTML page, this is the URL of the page. For a local folder or file, this is the full path name of the folder or file. |
| **Offline** | If **True**, the control attempts to read documents from the cache or previously visited pages on disk. Otherwise, the control attempts to locate and read documents from their source on the Internet. |
| *Methods* | |
| **GoSearch** | Causes the control to navigate to the search page specified in the **Internet Explorer** options. |
| **Navigate** | This method provides many features beyond those used in Fig. 19.2, including flags that determine how the **Web-Browser** control operates, target frames in HTML frame sets that indicate where to display the results of navigation, and sending data to the server. |
| **Refresh** | Reloads the current document. |
| **Stop** | Cancels current navigation or file download. |
| *Events* | |
| **DownloadBegin** | Called when navigation begins. This is a good place to display a visual indication of the fact that the application is performing a task. |
| **DownloadComplete** | Called when navigation completes. This is a good place to remove a visual indication of the fact that the application was performing a task. |
| **ProgressChange** | Called when the status of a download is updated by the system. |

Fig. 19.4    Key properties, methods and events for the **WebBrowser** control.

## 19.4 Internet Transfer Control

The **Internet Transfer** control operates at a lower level than the **WebBrowser** control. The **Internet Transfer** control supports two of the most common networking protocols, *Hypertext Transfer Protocol (HTTP)* and *File Transfer Protocol (FTP)*. This control can connect to a web server using HTTP protocol in the same manner as the **WebBrowser** control, but instead of seeing the actual web page displayed automatically, the **Internet Transfer** control simply provides the text of the document being retrieved. This can be useful for custom display of web documents. One of the most common uses of the Internet is file transfer. The FTP protocol enables a program to transfer files between computers on the Internet. The **Internet Transfer** control also provides the option of performing synchronous transfers (the program waits for the transfer to complete) or asynchronous transfers (the program continues executing and an event occurs to notify the program when the transfer is complete).

Some common uses of the **Internet Transfer** control are adding FTP capabilities to an application, creating applications that automatically download files from the Internet and parsing the text of an HTML document for application specific uses such as reading all the URLs in a document.

To use the **Internet Transfer** control, it must first be added to the toolbox by selecting **Components...** from the **Project** menu to display the **Components** dialog box. In the dialog box, scroll down and select the option *Microsoft Internet Transfer Control 6.0*. When selected properly, a small check mark appears in the box to the left of the option. Click the **OK** button when you are done to dismiss the dialog box. The icon for the **Internet Transfer** control will be at the bottom of the toolbox.

### 19.4.1 Hypertext Transfer Protocol (HTTP) Connections

In this section we discuss the specifics of using the **Internet Transfer** control with the HTTP protocol. In the program of Fig. 19.5, the user types a URL in the **TextBox** at the top of the window, then clicks the **Go Get URL** button. The program then displays the contents of the URL in the multiline **TextBox** at the bottom of the window. The properties of the controls are shown in Fig. 19.6.

```
1   ' Fig. 19.5
2   ' Using the Internet Transfer Control to download the contents
3   ' of a file over an HTTP connection.
4   Option Explicit
5
6   Private Sub cmdGo_Click()
7      ' if txtURL is not empty, go to URL specified in txtURL
8      On Error Resume Next
9
10     If txtURL.Text <> "" Then
11        txtOutput.Text = "Retrieving file ..."
12        txtOutput.Text = Inet1.OpenURL(txtURL.Text)
13     End If
14  End Sub
```

**Fig. 19.5    Internet Transfer** control procedure **OpenURL** (part 1 of 2).

```
15
16   Private Sub Form_Resize()
17      ' set dimensions of txtURL and WebBrowser1
18      On Error Resume Next
19      txtOutput.Width = ScaleWidth
20      txtOutput.Height = ScaleHeight - txtOutput.Top
21      txtURL.Width = ScaleWidth - txtURL.Left
22   End Sub
```

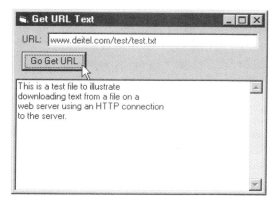

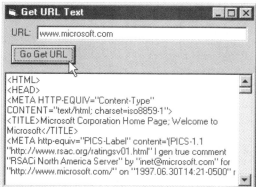

**Fig. 19.5**    **Internet Transfer** control procedure **OpenURL** (part 2 of 2).

| Control | Property | Setting |
|---------|----------|---------|
| frmHTTP | Caption | Get URL Text |
| lblURL | Caption | URL: |
| txtURL | Text | Nothing should be displayed by default. |
| cmdGo | Caption | Go Get URL |

**Fig. 19.6**    Property settings for the program of Fig. 19.5 (part 1 of 2).

| Control | Property | Setting |
|---------|----------|---------|
| txtOutput | Multiline | True |
| Inet1 | | Leave default settings. |

**Fig. 19.6**   Property settings for the program of Fig. 19.5 (part 2 of 2).

Our HTTP download application consists of five controls. The **lblURL** control labels the **txtURL TextBox** in which the user will be able to type a URL to download via the **Internet Transfer** control and display the contents in the **txtOutput TextBox**. The **cmdGo** button displays the URL specified by the user. The **Inet1** control provides access to the URL specified by the user.

Clicking **cmdGo** calls event procedure **cmdGo_Click** (lines 6 through 14). The **If** structure at line 10 determines if there is any text in **txtURL** and, if so, line 12,

```
txtOutput.Text = Inet1.OpenURL(txtURL.Text)
```

invokes method **OpenURL** of the **Internet Transfer** control to download the contents of the URL. The download is performed synchronously—the program does not continue until the download is complete.

When the form is resized, procedure **Form_Load** (lines 16 though 22) sizes the **txtOutput** and **txtURL TextBox**es.

The first output window in Fig. 19.5 illustrates a plain text file being downloaded from **http://www.deitel.com/test/test.txt** and displayed in **txtOutput**. The second output window illustrates the same feature, but for an HTML file (the home page from **http://www.microsoft.com**). Notice that the actual HTML text is displayed in the **TextBox**.

Note: If your program downloads and saves binary files, save the results of method **OpenURL** in a **Byte** array and output the array in binary format to the file. If your program downloads and saves text files, you can read the information and store it directly to a file.

## 19.4.2 File Transfer Protocol (FTP) Connections

In this section we discuss using the **Internet Transfer** control with the FTP protocol. In the program of Fig. 19.7, the user types four pieces of information—the FTP server to which to connect, the name of a file in that server's FTP root directory, the user name and the password. The user clicks the **Get the File** button to retrieve the file. The program then saves the contents of the file to disk in the **c:\temp** directory (Note: This directory must exist before the program executes). The properties of the controls are shown in Fig. 19.8. Notice that **Inet1**'s **Protocol** property is set to **2 - icFTP** to indicate FTP protocol.

```
1   ' Fig. 19.7
2   ' Downloading a text file via FTP
3   Option Explicit
```

**Fig. 19.7**   A simple FTP application to download a text file (part 1 of 3).

```
4
5   Private Sub cmdGetFile_Click()
6      Dim command As String
7
8      Inet1.URL = txtSite.Text
9      Inet1.UserName = txtUserName.Text
10     Inet1.Password = txtPassword.Text
11
12     command = "get " & txtFile.Text & _
13              " C:\temp\" & txtFile.Text
14     txtLog.Text = _
15        txtLog.Text & "COMMAND: " & command & vbNewLine
16     Call Inet1.Execute(, command)
17  End Sub
18
19  Private Sub Inet1_StateChanged(ByVal State As Integer)
20     Select Case State
21        Case icResolvingHost
22           txtLog.Text = txtLog.Text & "Resolving host" & vbCrLf
23        Case icHostResolved
24           txtLog.Text = txtLog.Text & "Host resolved" & vbCrLf
25        Case icConnecting
26           txtLog.Text = _
27              txtLog.Text & "Connecting to host" & vbCrLf
28        Case icConnected
29           txtLog.Text = _
30              txtLog.Text & "Connected to host" & vbCrLf
31        Case icRequesting
32           txtLog.Text = txtLog.Text & "Sending request" & vbCrLf
33        Case icRequestSent
34           txtLog.Text = txtLog.Text & "Request sent" & vbCrLf
35        Case icReceivingResponse
36           txtLog.Text = _
37              txtLog.Text & "Receiving response" & vbCrLf
38        Case icResponseReceived
39           txtLog.Text = _
40              txtLog.Text & "Response received" & vbCrLf
41        Case icDisconnecting
42           txtLog.Text = _
43              txtLog.Text & "Disconnecting from host" & vbCrLf
44        Case icDisconnected
45           txtLog.Text = _
46              txtLog.Text & "Disconnected from host" & vbCrLf
47        Case icError
48           txtLog.Text = txtLog.Text & "Error occurred" & vbCrLf
49        Case icResponseCompleted
50           Dim data As Variant
51
52           txtLog.Text = txtLog.Text & _
53              "Repsonse completed. All data received." & vbCrLf
54
```

**Fig. 19.7**    A simple FTP application to download a text file (part 2 of 3).

```
55              ' write data to a file
56              Open txtFile.Text For Binary Access Write As #1
57
58              ' get a chunk
59              ' Note: can use icByteArray as the second argument
60              ' to receive a binary file like an executable
61              data = Inet1.GetChunk(1024, icString)
62
63              Do While LenB(data) > 0
64                  Put #1, , data
65
66                  ' get a chunk
67                  data = Inet1.GetChunk(1024, icString)
68              Loop
69
70              Put #1, , data
71              Close #1
72          End Select
73
74      txtLog.SelStart = Len(txtLog.Text)
75  End Sub
```

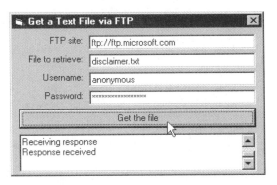

**Fig. 19.7**   A simple FTP application to download a text file (part 3 of 3).

| Control | Property | Setting |
| --- | --- | --- |
| frmFTP | Caption | Get a Text File via FTP |
| lblSite | Caption | FTP site: |
| txtSite | Text | ftp.microsoft.com |
| lblFile | Caption | File to retrieve: |
| txtFile | Text | disclaimer.txt |
| lblUsername | Caption | Username: |
| txtUsername | Text | anonymous |
| lblPassword | Caption | Password: |

**Fig. 19.8**   Property settings for the program of Fig. 19.7 (part 1 of 2).

| Control | Property | Setting |
| --- | --- | --- |
| `txtUsername` | `Text` | Nothing should be displayed by default. |
| `cmdGetFile` | `Caption` | `Get the File` |
| `txtLog` | `Multiline` | `True` |
| `Inet1` | `Protocol` | `2 - icFTP` |

**Fig. 19.8**   Property settings for the program of Fig. 19.7 (part 2 of 2).

When the program executes, the user is presented with the interface shown in the screen capture of Fig. 19.7. We provided default values for the FTP site, file to retrieve and user name so the user has a simple test case they can try. Once the information is entered in the **TextBox**es, the user clicks button **Get the File** to execute **cmdGetFile_Click** (lines 5 through 17). Properties **URL**, **UserName** and **Password** of the **Internet Transfer** control **Inet1** are set with the statements

```
Inet1.URL = txtSite.Text
Inet1.UserName = txtUserName.Text
Inet1.Password = txtPassword.Text
```

Lines 12 and 13 create string **command** containing the FTP *get* command and the name of the file to retrieve. The FTP *get* command requests that a file from the FTP server be downloaded to your machine. The other FTP commands supported by the **Internet Transfer** control are *cd* (change directories), *cdup* (change to parent directory), *delete* (remove a file), *dir* (show a directory listing of the current directory), *mkdir* (make a directory), *put* (send a file to the server), *pwd* (display the current directory name), *quit* (terminate current connection), *recv* (same as *get*), *rename* (change a file name), *rmdir* (remove a directory), *send* (same as *put*) and *size* (get the size of a file). For more information on FTP commands supported by the **Internet Transfer** control see, "Using the Internet Transfer Control" in the *Component Tools Guide* of the on-line Visual Basic Documentation.

Line 16,

```
Call Inet1.Execute(, command)
```

invokes the **Internet Transfer** control's **Execute** method using the **command** string to indicate the request to the FTP server.

Unlike the **OpenURL** method demonstrated in the last section, the **Execute** method performs an *asynchronous transfer*—the program can continue executing as the server responds to the request. The application is automatically notified of responses from the server in event procedure **Inet1_StateChanged** (lines 19 through 75). This event procedure is called for every state change indicated to the **Internet Transfer** control. The **Case**s of the **Select Case** structure at line 20 use constants of the form **ic***State* to indicate the current state of the control. Each of the state changes in this example appends a string to the **txtLog TextBox**.

The most important state is **icResponseCompleted**, which indicates that the request made to the server has completed. In this **Case** (line 49), line 56 opens a file by the name of the file we specified to download. Line 61,

```
data = Inet1.GetChunk(1024, icString)
```

uses the **Internet Transfer** control's **GetChunk** method to retrieve strings up to length **1024**. Note that the second argument can be **icByteArray** for binary data such as images and executable files.

Lines 63 through 68 are a **Do While** loop that puts a chunk of data into the file and gets the next chunk of data. Finally, we put the last chunk of data in the file at line 70 and close the file at line 71.

## 19.5 Other Properties, Methods and Events of the Internet Transfer Control

The **Internet Transfer** control provides a variety of other useful properties and methods. Some of these are summarized in Fig. 19.9. For more information on using the **Internet Transfer** control and a complete listing of all its properties, methods and events, see the topic "Using the Internet Transfer Control" in the *Component Tools Guide* of the Visual Basic on-line documentation (Note: This is for use with the Professional and Enterprise Editions of Visual Basic).

| Property or method | Description |
| --- | --- |
| *Properties* | |
| **AccessType** | Determines how the control communicates with the Internet. Possible values are **icUseDefault** (uses the system's default settings), **icDirect** (direct connection to the internet) or **icNamedProxy** (connect through a proxy server that controls access to the internet). If **icNamedProxy** is used, set the **Proxy** property also. |
| **Proxy** | This is set to the name of the computer that is used as the proxy server. For example, <br><br>    **Inet1.Proxy = "ProxyServer:123"** <br><br>specifies that a computer named **ProxyServer** uses port number **123**. |
| **ResponseCode** | The error number of the error that occurred and caused the **icError** state in the **StateChanged** event. |
| **ResponseInfo** | Text message for the last error that occurred. |
| **StillExecuting** | Indicates **True** if the control is still executing a task; **False** otherwise. |
| *Methods* | |
| **Cancel** | Cancels the last request made to the server and closes the current connections. |
| **GetHeader** | Retrieves header text from an HTML document. |

Fig. 19.9    Important properties and methods for the **Internet Transfer** control.

## 19.6  Winsock Control

The **Winsock** control operates at the lowest level of all the Internet controls, allowing client/server applications to communicate using both *Transmission Control Protocol (TCP)* and *User Datagram Protocol (UDP)*. Communication with TCP is similar to a telephone conversation—there must be a connection between the client and the server before they can communicate. TCP is commonly referred to as a connection-based or connection-oriented protocol. Communication with UDP is similar to sending letters in the mail. A packet—called a datagram—is created, addressed and sent over the network. There is no direct connection between the origin and the destination. UDP is commonly referred to as a connectionless protocol. This section presents examples of using both protocols.

TCP protocol is typically used when large amounts of data are transmitted between a server and a client and when reliability is imperative (i.e., the bytes of information must get to their destination with acknowledgment of their receipt). The connection maintained between the server and the client ensures data integrity. UDP is typically used when small amounts of data are sent or data are sent intermittently.

*Performance Tip 19.2*

*TCP protocol requires more overhead to set up and maintain the connection than UDP connectionless protocol.*

*Software Engineering Observation 19.1*

*Although UDP protocol requires less overhead than TCP protocol, UDP protocol is less reliable.*

## 19.6.1 Establishing a Simple Server (Using TCP Protocol)

Establishing a simple server in Visual Basic requires several steps. Step 1 is to add a **Winsock** control to the form. To use the **Internet Transfer** control, it must first be added to the toolbox by selecting **Components...** from the **Project** menu to display the **Components** dialog box. In the dialog box, scroll down and select the option **Microsoft Winsock Control 6.0**. When selected properly, a small check mark appears in the box to the left of the option. Click the **OK** button when you are done to dismiss the dialog box. The icon for the **Winsock** control will be at the bottom of the toolbox.

In Step 2, the server must be set up to listen for connections from clients on a specific *port number* as specified with the **Winsock** control's **LocalPort** property. Each client will ask to connect to the server on this port. Port numbers are positive integer values up to 65535. Typically, port numbers below 1024 are reserved for system services. The line

```
tcpServer.LocalPort = 5000
```

*registers* with the **Winsock** control **tcpServer** an available port number on the local machine. This line would typically be executed in the **Form_Load** procedure.

*Common Programming Error 19.1*

*Specifying a port number that is already in use results in a run-time error with the error message "Address in use."*

Each client connection is managed with a **Winsock** control. In Step 3, once the **tcpServer** port number is established, the server must be told to listen indefinitely for an attempt by a client to connect. This is accomplished with a call to the **Winsock** control's *Listen* method as in

```
Call tcpServer.Listen
```

This statement is typically placed in the **Form_Load** procedure. When a connection request is received while the server is listening, event procedure **ConnectionRequest** executes.

Step 4 is to accept the request for connection from the client—typically performed in the **ConnectionRequest** event procedure. This is accomplished with the **Winsock** control's *Accept* method as in

```
Call tcpServer.Accept(requestID)
```

where **requestID** is received as an argument to event procedure **ConnectionRequest** and simply passed to the **Accept** method. Once this method is called, there is a connection between the server and the client through which streams of data can be passed.

**Good Programming Practice 19.2**

*Before accepting a connection from a client, check if the state of the **Winsock** control is* **sckClosed** *If not, the previous connection was not closed properly. In this case, invoke the **Close** method on the **Winsock** object, then accept the connection.*

Step 5 is the processing phase in which the server and the client communicate via the connection. When data arrives at the server, the **Winsock** control's *DataArrival* event procedure executes. The statement

```
tcpServer.GetData(message)
```

retrieves string-based information from the client and stores it in the string **message**. Also, two optional arguments can be used to specify the type of data to receive and the maximum length of the data to receive. Data is sent to the client using the **SendData** method. For example, the statement

```
tcpServer.SendData(message)
```

sends the string **message** to the client.

In Step 6 when the transmission is complete and the client closes the connection, the **Winsock** control's *Close* event procedure executes. At this point the server connection should be closed with a statement like

```
tcpServer.Close
```

The server application can be told to listen for a new client connection by invoking the **Listen** method on the **Winsock** object.

**Software Engineering Observation 19.2**

*The **Winsock** control hides much of the complexity of network programming from the programmer.*

**Software Engineering Observation 19.3**

*With Visual Basic's control arrays, we can create servers that can manage many simultaneous connections with many clients.*

*Performance Tip 19.3*

*In high-performance systems in which memory is abundant, a server can be implemented to create a pool of **Winsock** objects that can be assigned quickly to handle network I/O across each new connection as it is created. Thus, when a connection is received, the server need not incur the overhead of **Winsock** object creation.*

## 19.6.2 Establishing a Simple Client (Using TCP Protocol)

Establishing a simple client in Visual Basic requires several steps. Step 1 is to add a **Winsock** control to the form. To use the **Internet Transfer** control, it must first be added to the toolbox by selecting **Components...** from the **Project** menu to display the **Components** dialog box. In the dialog box, scroll down and select the option **Microsoft Winsock Control 6.0**. Click the **OK** button when you are done to dismiss the dialog box. The icon for the **Winsock** control will be at the bottom of the toolbox.

In Step 2, the client-side **Winsock** object must be told the server to which to connect and the port number on that server. This is accomplished with the statements

```
tcpClient.RemoteHost = "localhost"
tcpClient.RemotePort = 5000
```

The value assigned to the ***RemoteHost*** *property* of the **tcpClient Winsock** object is a string indicating either the name of the server (e.g., **www.microsoft.com** or **localhost**) or the Internet IP address for the server (e.g., **127.0.0.1** for the localhost address). Note that the server name **localhost** normally represents the local machine with the IP address **127.0.0.1**. The value assigned to property **RemotePort** of the **tcpClient Winsock** object must match the port number on which the server application is listening; otherwise, no connection can be established between the client and the server.

In Step 3, the connection to the server is established using a call to the **Winsock** object's ***Connect*** method as in

```
tcpClient.Connect
```

If the connection attempt is successful, a connection is established and the client can now communicate with the server; otherwise, a run-time error occurs and the **Winsock** object's ***Error*** *event procedure* executes.

*Common Programming Error 19.2*

*A run-time error occurs if an attempt to connect to a server is unsuccessful. This results in a call to the **Winsock** object's **Error** event procedure.*

Step 4 is the processing phase in which the client and the server communicate via the connection. As with the server, when data arrives at the client the **Winsock** control's ***DataArrival*** event procedure executes. The statement

```
tcpClient.GetData(message)
```

retrieves string-based information from the server and stores it in the string **message**. Data is sent to the server using the **SendData** method. For example, the statement

```
tcpServer.SendData(message)
```

sends the string **message** to the server.

In Step 5 when the transmission is complete and the server closes the connection, the **Winsock** control's *Close* event procedure executes. At this point the client connection should be closed with a statement like

```
tcpClient.Close
```

If the server does not close the connection, the client should still invoke the **Close** method to close its side of the connection.

## 19.7 Example: Client/Server Interaction with the Winsock Control

The applications of Figs. 19.10 and 19.12 use *TCP protocol* to demonstrate a *client/server application*. The server waits for a client connection attempt. Once a connection is established messages are displayed in both the client and server windows indicating that the connection was successful. The user at the client side and the user at the server side can communicate by typing messages in their respective **TextBox**es and pressing their **Send Text** buttons, at which point the message sent will appear in both the client window and the server window with an indication of who sent the message. If the client closes the connection, the server the waits for the next client application to connect.

*We have chosen in this example to demonstrate the client/server relationship by connecting between programs executing on the same computer. Normally, the client would specify the Internet address of another computer to which to connect. If you would like to try this example with two networked computers, run the server on one computer and run the client on another computer. When the client applications prompts you to enter the remote host IP address, type either the name of the server (e.g., **www.microsoft.com**) or the IP address of the server (e.g., **127.0.0.1**).*

## 19.7.1 A Simple TCP-Based Server

The definition of the server is in Fig. 19.10 and its control properties are in Fig. 19.11. The output windows are shown and discussed in Fig. 19.14.

```
1   ' Fig. 19.10
2   ' A simple server using TCP sockets
3   Option Explicit
4
5   Private Sub Form_Load()
6      cmdSend.Enabled = False
7
8      ' set up local port and wait for connection
9      tcpServer.LocalPort = 5000
10     Call tcpServer.Listen
11  End Sub
12
13  Private Sub Form_Resize()
14     On Error Resume Next
15     Call cmdSend.Move(ScaleWidth - cmdSend.Width, 0)
16     Call txtSend.Move(0, 0, ScaleWidth - cmdSend.Width)
```

**Fig. 19.10** Simple TCP server (part 1 of 3).

```
17      Call txtOutput.Move(0, txtSend.Height, ScaleWidth, _
18         ScaleHeight - txtSend.Height)
19   End Sub
20
21   Private Sub Form_Terminate()
22      Call tcpServer.Close
23   End Sub
24
25   Private Sub tcpServer_ConnectionRequest( _
26         ByVal requestID As Long)
27      ' Ensure that tcpServer is closed
28      ' before accepting a new connection
29      If tcpServer.State <> sckClosed Then
30         Call tcpServer.Close
31      End If
32
33      cmdSend.Enabled = True
34      Call tcpServer.Accept(requestID)  ' accept connection
35      txtOutput.Text = _
36         "Connection from IP address: " & _
37         tcpServer.RemoteHostIP & vbCrLf & _
38         "Port #: " & tcpServer.RemotePort & vbCrLf & vbCrLf
39   End Sub
40
41   Private Sub tcpServer_DataArrival(ByVal bytesTotal As Long)
42      Dim message As String
43      Call tcpServer.GetData(message)   ' get data from client
44      txtOutput.Text = _
45         txtOutput.Text & message & vbCrLf & vbCrLf
46      txtOutput.SelStart = Len(txtOutput.Text)
47   End Sub
48
49   Private Sub tcpServer_Close()
50      cmdSend.Enabled = False
51      Call tcpServer.Close   ' client closed, server should too
52      txtOutput.Text = txtOutput.Text & _
53         "Client closed connection." & vbCrLf & vbCrLf
54      txtOutput.SelStart = Len(txtOutput.Text)
55      Call tcpServer.Listen  ' listen for next connection
56   End Sub
57
58   Private Sub tcpServer_Error(ByVal Number As Integer, _
59         Description As String, ByVal Scode As Long, _
60         ByVal Source As String, ByVal HelpFile As String, _
61         ByVal HelpContext As Long, CancelDisplay As Boolean)
62      Dim result As Integer
63      result = MsgBox(Source & ": " & Description, _
64         vbOKOnly, "TCP/IP Error")
65      End
66   End Sub
67
```

**Fig. 19.10**   Simple TCP server (part 2 of 3).

```
68   Private Sub cmdSend_Click()
69      ' send data to the client
70      Call tcpServer.SendData("SERVER >>> " & txtSend.Text)
71      txtOutput.Text = txtOutput.Text & _
72         "SERVER >>> " & txtSend.Text & vbCrLf & vbCrLf
73      txtSend.Text = ""
74      txtOutput.SelStart = Len(txtOutput.Text)
75   End Sub
```

**Fig. 19.10**   Simple TCP server (part 3 of 3).

| Control | Property | Setting |
|---------|----------|---------|
| frmTCPServer | Caption | Simple TCP Server |
| tcpServer | Protocol | 0 - sckTCPProtocol (the default) |
| txtSend | Text | Nothing should be displayed by default. |
| txtOutput | Multiline | True |
| cmdSend | Caption | Send Text |

**Fig. 19.11**   Property settings for the program of Fig. 19.10.

Executing the program calls procedure **Form_Load** (lines 5 through 11) to disable the **cmdSend** button until there is a connection and set up the server to listen for connections with the statements

```
tcpServer.LocalPort = 5000
Call tcpServer.Listen
```

indicating that the server should listen on port **5000** of the local machine for connections from clients.

*Common Programming Error 19.3*

*Specifying a port that is already in use or specifying an invalid port number when binding a **Winsock** object to a specific port results in a run-time error.*

Terminating the application calls procedure **Form_Terminate** (lines 21 through 23), which calls **tcpServer.Close** to ensure that the server is shut down properly. If a client is connected when this application terminates, the client is automatically notified with a call to its **Close** event procedure.

Event procedure **tcpServer_ConnectionRequest** (lines 25 through 39) executes when a client requests a connection. The **If** structure at line 29 ensures that the previous connection to the server was closed properly. Line 34,

```
Call tcpServer.Accept(requestID)   ' accept connection
```

accepts the request for connection from the client. Then, a string is displayed in the **txtOutput TextBox** indicating that a connection is established. The **RemoteHostIP** and **RemotePort** properties are used to display the IP address of the client and the port number the client is using to communicate, respectively.

Event procedure **tcpServer_DataArrival** (lines 41 through 47) executes when data arrives at the server from the client. Line 43,

```
Call tcpServer.GetData(message)    ' get data from client
```

receives the data and stores it in the string **message**.

Event procedure **tcpServer_Close** (lines 49 through 56) executes if the client closes the connection. Line 51,

```
Call tcpServer.Close    ' client closed, server should too
```

ensures that the server is shut down properly. Then, line 55 calls **tcpServer.Listen** to allow the server to wait for the next connection.

If any errors occur on the **Winsock** object, event procedure **tcpServer_Error** (lines 58 through 66) executes. Line 63 and 64,

```
result = MsgBox(Source & ": " & Description, _
    vbOKOnly, "TCP/IP Error")
```

display a message box containing the **Source** of the error and the **Description** of the error that are both passed to the event procedure automatically. The program ends when the user acknowledged the error.

Clicking the **cmdSend** button calls **cmdSend_Click** (lines 68 through 75) to send data to the client. Line 70,

```
Call tcpServer.SendData("SERVER >>> " & txtSend.Text)
```

uses the **SendData** method to send the string typed by the user preceded by an indication that the message is from the server.

## 19.7.2 A Simple TCP-Based Client

The definition of the client is in Fig. 19.12 and its control properties are in Fig. 19.13. The output windows are shown and discussed in Fig. 19.14.

```
1    ' Fig. 19.12
2    ' A simple client using TCP sockets
3    Option Explicit
4
5    Private Sub Form_Load()
6       cmdSend.Enabled = False
7
8       ' set up local port and wait for connection
9       tcpClient.RemoteHost = _
10         InputBox("Enter the remote host IP address", _
11           "IP Address", "localhost")
12
13      If tcpClient.RemoteHost = "" Then
14         tcpClient.RemoteHost = "localhost"
15      End If
```

**Fig. 19.12**   Simple TCP client (part 1 of 3).

```
16
17      tcpClient.RemotePort = 5000   ' server port
18      Call tcpClient.Connect   ' connect to RemoteHost address
19   End Sub
20
21   Private Sub Form_Terminate()
22      Call tcpClient.Close
23   End Sub
24
25   Private Sub Form_Resize()
26      On Error Resume Next
27      Call cmdSend.Move(ScaleWidth - cmdSend.Width, 0)
28      Call txtSend.Move(0, 0, ScaleWidth - cmdSend.Width)
29      Call txtOutput.Move(0, txtSend.Height, ScaleWidth, _
30         ScaleHeight - txtSend.Height)
31   End Sub
32
33   Private Sub tcpClient_Connect()
34      ' when connection occurs, display a message
35      cmdSend.Enabled = True
36      txtOutput.Text = "Connected to IP Address: " & _
37         tcpClient.RemoteHostIP & vbCrLf & "Port #: " & _
38         tcpClient.RemotePort & vbCrLf & vbCrLf
39   End Sub
40
41   Private Sub tcpClient_DataArrival(ByVal bytesTotal As Long)
42      Dim message As String
43      Call tcpClient.GetData(message)   ' get data from server
44      txtOutput.Text = txtOutput.Text & message & vbCrLf & vbCrLf
45      txtOutput.SelStart = Len(txtOutput.Text)
46   End Sub
47
48   Private Sub tcpClient_Close()
49      cmdSend.Enabled = False
50      Call tcpClient.Close   ' server closed, client should too
51      txtOutput.Text = _
52         txtOutput.Text & "Server closed connection." & vbCrLf
53      txtOutput.SelStart = Len(txtOutput.Text)
54   End Sub
55
56   Private Sub tcpClient_Error(ByVal Number As Integer, _
57         Description As String, ByVal Scode As Long, _
58         ByVal Source As String, ByVal HelpFile As String, _
59         ByVal HelpContext As Long, CancelDisplay As Boolean)
60      Dim result As Integer
61      result = MsgBox(Source & ": " & Description, _
62         vbOKOnly, "TCP/IP Error")
63      End
64   End Sub
65
66   Private Sub cmdSend_Click()
67      ' send data to server
68      Call tcpClient.SendData("CLIENT >>> " & txtSend.Text)
```

**Fig. 19.12**  Simple TCP client (part 2 of 3).

```
69        txtOutput.Text = txtOutput.Text & _
70           "CLIENT >>> " & txtSend.Text & vbCrLf & vbCrLf
71        txtOutput.SelStart = Len(txtOutput.Text)
72        txtSend.Text = ""
73     End Sub
```

**Fig. 19.12**   Simple TCP client (part 3 of 3).

| Control | Property | Setting |
|---------|----------|---------|
| frmTCPClient | Caption | Simple TCP Client |
| tcpClient | Protocol | 0 - sckTCPProtocol (the default) |
| txtSend | Text | Nothing should be displayed by default. |
| txtOutput | Multiline | True |
| cmdSend | Caption | Send Text |

**Fig. 19.13**   Property settings for the program of Fig. 19.10.

Executing the program calls procedure **Form_Load** (lines 5 through 19) to disable the **cmdSend** button until there is a connection and set up the client to make a connection. The client is prompted to input the IP address of the remote machine. This value is assigned to property **RemoteHost** (line 9) of the **Winsock** object. If the user does not enter a value for property **RemoteHost**, **localhost** is used. Remember, the **RemoteHost** property can be a string indicating either the name of the server (e.g., **www.microsoft.com** or **localhost**) or the IP address for the server (e.g., **127.0.0.1** for the localhost address).

Lines 17 and 18,

```
tcpClient.RemotePort = 5000   ' server port
Call tcpClient.Connect   ' connect to RemoteHost address
```

indicate that the client should attempt to connect to the server on port **5000** of the remote machine specified by property **RemoteHost**. *Note:* The server port number assigned to **RemotePort** must match the port number at which the server is waiting for connections (sometimes called the *handshake point*); otherwise, the connection attempt will fail.

Terminating the application calls procedure **Form_Terminate** (lines 21 through 23), which calls **tcpClient.Close** to ensure that the client is shut down properly. If the client is connected to the server when this application terminates, the server is automatically notified with a call to its **Close** event procedure.

Event procedure **tcpClient_Connect** (lines 33 through 39) executes when a client makes a successful connection to the server. In this program, the **cmdSend** button is enabled and a message is displayed in the **txtOutput TextBox** indicating the IP address and port number of the server.

Event procedure **tcpClient_DataArrival** (lines 41 through 46) executes when data arrives at the client from the server. Line 48,

```
Call tcpClient.GetData(message)   ' get data from server
```

receives the data and stores it in the string **message**.

Event procedure **tcpClient_Close** (lines 48 through 54) executes if the server closes the connection. Line 50,

```
Call tcpClient.Close  ' server closed, client should too
```

ensures that the client is shut down properly.

If any errors occur on the **Winsock** object, event procedure **tcpClient_Error** (lines 56 through 64) executes. Lines 61 and 62,

```
result = MsgBox(Source & ": " & Description, _
   vbOKOnly, "TCP/IP Error")
```

display a message box containing the **Source** of the error and the **Description** of the error that are both passed to the event procedure automatically. The program ends when the user acknowledges the error.

Clicking the **cmdSend** button calls **cmdSend_Click** (lines 66 through 73) to send data to the server. Line 68,

```
Call tcpClient.SendData("CLIENT >>> " & txtSend.Text)
```

uses the **SendData** method to send the string typed by the user preceded by an indication that the message is from the client.

## 19.7.3 Outputs of the Client/Server Interactions

The output windows in Fig. 19.14 show a series of screen captures for the client and server applications. The first screen capture is the **InputBox**, in which the client can specify the server to which to connect. This provides you with the ability to test these programs on one machine (using the default **localhost** connection) or test them on multiple computers. The second set of screen captures shows the client and the server after the connection is made and when the client is about to send the message "hello." The third set of screen captures shows the client and the server after the message "hello" is sent. Notice that a string is displayed in both windows. The client and server in this example will see a continual log of all the messages sent and received. The fourth screen capture shows the server when it is about to send the message "hi, how are you?" The fifth set of screen captures shows the client and the server after the message "hi, how are you?" is sent. Notice again that a string is displayed in both windows. The last output window shows the server after the client closes its side of the connection.

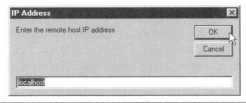

**Fig. 19.14**   Sample outputs of the server and client programs in Figs. 19.10 and 19.12 (part 1 of 2).

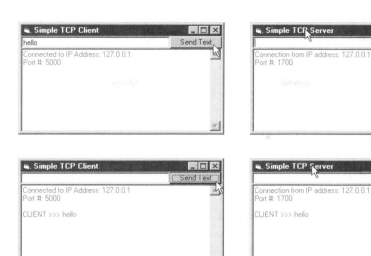

**Fig. 19.14**    Sample outputs of the server and client programs in Figs. 19.10 and 19.12 (part 2 of 2).

## 19.8  Winsock Control and UDP-Based Client/Server Computing

We have been discussing *connection-oriented transmission with streams*. Now we consider *connectionless transmission with datagrams* (also called *peer-to-peer communication*).

Connection-oriented transmission is like the telephone system, in which you dial and are given a *connection* to the telephone you wish to communicate with; the connection is maintained for the duration of your phone call, even when you are not talking.

Connectionless transmission with *datagrams* is more like the way mail is carried via the postal service. If a large message will not fit in one envelope, you break it into separate message pieces that you place in separate, sequentially numbered envelopes. Each of the letters is then mailed at once. The letters may arrive in order, out of order or not at all (although the last case is rare, it does happen). The person at the receiving end reassembles the message pieces into sequential order before attempting to make sense of the message. If your message is small enough to fit in one envelope, you do not have to worry about the "out-of-sequence" problem, but it is still possible that your message may not arrive. One difference between datagrams and postal mail is that duplicates of datagrams may arrive on the receiving computer. As mentioned previously, UDP is commonly used for streaming technologies such as audio and video over the internet where streams of UDP packets are sent to a computer and reassembled into the audio or video clip for playing. The key to this technology is performance, thus the packets are reassembled on the client.

The programs of Figs. 19.15 and 19.17 use datagrams to send packets of information between a client application and a server application. In this client/server interaction, the user of the client or server application types a message into a **TextBox** and presses the **Send Text** button. The message is sent to the other application. The server or client receives the packet and displays the information in the packet, the IP address of the computer that sent the packet, the port number of the computer that sent the packet and the number of bytes received. In this example, the client and server are implemented similarly, thus emphasizing the peer-to-peer relationship. One important difference is that the server must specify the port number to which clients send packets. The client can use any available port. When the server receives the packet, it can use the **RemoteHostIP** and **Remote-Port** properties to determine the client that sent the packet.

### 19.8.1  A Simple UDP-Based Server

The definition of the server is in Fig. 19.15 and its control properties are in Fig. 19.16. The output windows are shown and discussed in Fig. 19.19.

```
1   ' Fig. 19.15
2   ' A simple server using UDP protocol
3   Option Explicit
4
5   Private Sub Form_Load()
6       ' set up local port and wait for connection
7       Call udpServer.Bind(5000)
8   End Sub
9
```

**Fig. 19.15**   Simple UDP server (part 1 of 2).

```
10   Private Sub Form_Terminate()
11      Call udpServer.Close
12   End Sub
13
14   Private Sub Form_Resize()
15      On Error Resume Next
16      Call cmdSend.Move(ScaleWidth - cmdSend.Width, 0)
17      Call txtSend.Move(0, 0, ScaleWidth - cmdSend.Width)
18      Call txtOutput.Move(0, txtSend.Height, ScaleWidth, _
19         ScaleHeight - txtSend.Height)
20   End Sub
21
22   Private Sub udpServer_DataArrival(ByVal bytesTotal As Long)
23      Dim message As String
24      Call udpServer.GetData(message)   ' get data from client
25      txtOutput.Text = txtOutput.Text & _
26         "From: IP address: " & udpServer.RemoteHostIP & _
27         vbCrLf & "Port #: " & Str$(udpServer.RemotePort) & _
28         vbCrLf & "Bytes received: " & Str$(bytesTotal) & _
29         vbCrLf & "Message: " & message & vbCrLf & vbCrLf
30      txtOutput.SelStart = Len(txtOutput.Text)
31   End Sub
32
33   Private Sub cmdSend_Click()
34      Call udpServer.SendData(txtSend.Text)   ' send data to client
35      txtOutput.Text = txtOutput.Text & _
36         "Sent message: " & txtSend.Text & vbCrLf & vbCrLf
37      txtSend.Text = ""
38      txtOutput.SelStart = Len(txtOutput.Text)
39      udpServer.RemotePort = 0
40   End Sub
```

**Fig. 19.15**    Simple UDP server (part 2 of 2).

| Control | Property | Setting |
| --- | --- | --- |
| frmUDPServer | Caption | Simple UDP Server |
| udpServer | Protocol | 1 - sckUDPProtocol |
| txtSend | Text | Nothing should be displayed by default. |
| txtOutput | Multiline | True |
| cmdSend | Caption | Send Text |

**Fig. 19.16**    Property settings for the program of Fig. 19.15.

Executing the program calls procedure **Form_Load** (lines 5 through 8) to bind the server to a specific port for receiving packets. Line 7,

```
Call udpServer.Bind(5000)
```

indicates that the server should wait for packets on port **5000** of the local machine.

Terminating the application calls procedure **Form_Terminate** (lines 10 through 12), which calls **udpServer.Close** to ensure that the server is shut down properly.

Event procedure **udpServer_DataArrival** (lines 22 through 31) executes when a data packet arrives. Line 24,

```
Call udpServer.GetData(message)   ' get data from client
```

receives the data and stores it in the string **message**. Then, a string is appended to the **txtOutput TextBox** indicating the IP address of the computer that sent the packet (**RemoteHost**), the port number of that computer (**RemotePort**), the number of bytes received and the message received.

Clicking the **Send Text** button calls **cmdSend_Click** (lines 33 through 40) to send a packet of information. Line 34,

```
Call udpServer.SendData(txtSend.Text)   ' send data to client
```

uses the **SendData** method to send the string typed by the user.

## 19.8.2 A Simple UDP-Based Client

The definition of the client is in Fig. 19.17 and its control properties are in Fig. 19.18. The output windows are shown and discussed in Fig. 19.19.

```
1   ' Fig. 19.17
2   ' A simple client using UDP protocol
3   Option Explicit
4
5   Private Sub Form_Load()
6       ' determine remote machine
7       udpClient.RemoteHost = _
8           InputBox("Enter the remote host IP address", _
9               "IP Address", "localhost")
10
11      If udpClient.RemoteHost = "" Then
12          udpClient.RemoteHost = "localhost"
13      End If
14
15      udpClient.RemotePort = 5000
16  End Sub
17
18  Private Sub Form_Terminate()
19      Call udpClient.Close
20  End Sub
21
22  Private Sub Form_Resize()
23      On Error Resume Next
24      Call cmdSend.Move(ScaleWidth - cmdSend.Width, 0)
25      Call txtSend.Move(0, 0, ScaleWidth - cmdSend.Width)
26      Call txtOutput.Move(0, txtSend.Height, ScaleWidth, _
27          ScaleHeight - txtSend.Height)
28  End Sub
```

**Fig. 19.17**   Simple UDP client (part 1 of 2).

```
29
30   Private Sub udpClient_DataArrival(ByVal bytesTotal As Long)
31      Dim message As String
32      Call udpClient.GetData(message)   ' get data from server
33      txtOutput.Text = txtOutput.Text & _
34         "From IP address: " & udpClient.RemoteHostIP & _
35         vbCrLf & "Port #: " & Str$(udpClient.RemotePort) & _
36         vbCrLf & "Bytes received: " & Str$(bytesTotal) & _
37         vbCrLf & "Message: " & message & vbCrLf & vbCrLf
38      txtOutput.SelStart = Len(txtOutput.Text)
39   End Sub
40
41   Private Sub cmdSend_Click()
42      Call udpClient.SendData(txtSend.Text)   ' send data to server
43      txtOutput.Text = txtOutput.Text & _
44         "Sent message: " & txtSend.Text & vbCrLf & vbCrLf
45      txtOutput.SelStart = Len(txtOutput.Text)
46      txtSend.Text = ""
47   End Sub
```

**Fig. 19.17**   Simple UDP client (part 2 of 2).

| Control | Property | Setting |
|---------|----------|---------|
| frmUDPClient | Caption | Simple UDP Client |
| udpClient | Protocol | 1 - sckUDPProtocol |
| txtSend | Text | Nothing should be displayed by default. |
| txtOutput | Multiline | True |
| cmdSend | Caption | Send Text |

**Fig. 19.18**   Property settings for the program of Fig. 19.17.

Executing the program calls procedure **Form_Load** (lines 5 through 16) to determine the computer and server port to which packets will be sent. The client is prompted to input the IP address of the remote machine. This value is assigned to property **RemoteHost** (line 7) of the **Winsock** object. If the user does not enter a value for property **Remote-Host**, **localhost** is used. Remember, the **RemoteHost** property can be a string indicating either the name of the server (e.g., **www.microsoft.com** or **localhost**) or the Internet IP address for the server (e.g., **127.0.0.1** for the **localhost** address). Line 15 specifies the **RemotePort** value. *Note:* The server port number assigned to **Remote-Port** must exactly match the port number at which the server is waiting for packets; otherwise, the server will not receive the packets.

Terminating the application calls procedure **Form_Terminate** (lines 18 through 20), which calls **udpClient.Close** to ensure that the client is shut down properly.

Event procedure **udpServer_DataArrival** (lines 30 through 39) executes when a data packet arrives. Line 32,

```
Call udpClient.GetData(message)   ' get data from server
```

receives the data and stores it in the string **message**. Then, a string is appended to the **txtOutput TextBox** indicating the IP address of the computer that sent the packet (**RemoteHost**), the port number of that computer (**RemotePort**), the number of bytes received and the message received.

Clicking the **Send Text** button calls **cmdSend_Click** (lines 41 through 47) to send a packet of information. Line 42,

```
Call udpClient.SendData(txtSend.Text)   ' send data to server
```

uses the **SendData** method to send the string typed by the user.

## 19.8.3 Outputs of the Client/Server Interactions

The output windows in Fig. 19.19 show a series of screen captures for the client and server applications. The first screen capture is the **InputBox**, in which the client can specify the server to which to connect. This provides you with the ability to test these programs on one machine (using the default **localhost** connection) or test them on multiple computers. The second set of screen captures shows the client and the server before any packets are sent.

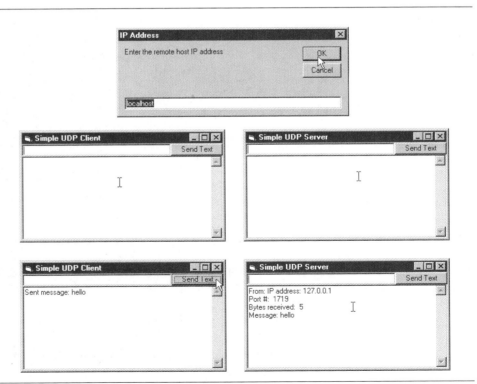

**Fig. 19.19**   Sample outputs for the programs of Figs. 19.15 and 19.17 (part 1 of 2).

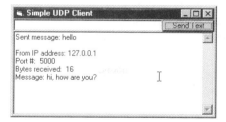

**Fig. 19.19**   Sample outputs for the programs of Figs. 19.15 and 19.17 (part 2 of 2).

The third set of screen captures shows the client and the server after the message "hello" is sent from the client to the server. Notice that a string is displayed in the client window indicating the message that was sent, and several lines of text are displayed in the server window indicating all the information about the packet received. The client and server in this example see a continual log of all the messages sent and received. The fourth set of screen captures shows the client and the server after the message "hi, how are you?" is sent from the server to the client. Notice again that strings are displayed in both windows.

## 19.9 Other Properties, Methods and Events of the Winsock Control

The **Winsock** control provides a variety of other useful properties, methods and events. Some of these are summarized in Fig. 19.20. For more information on using the **Winsock** control and a complete listing of all its properties, methods and events, see the topic "Using the Winsock Control" in the *Component Tools Guide* of the Visual Basic on-line documentation (Note: This is for use with the Professional and Enterprise Editions of Visual Basic).

| Property, method or event | Description |
| --- | --- |
| *Properties* | |
| **BytesReceived** | Number of bytes currently in the buffer that can be retrieved with method **GetData**. |
| **LocalHostName** | The local computer's name. |
| **LocalHostIP** | The local computer's IP address. |
| **LocalPort** | The local computer's port number being used for communication with another application. |
| **State** | The state of the control. One of **sckClosed**, **sckOpen**, **sckListening**, **sckConnectionPending**, **sckResolvingHost**, **sckConnecting**, **sckConnected**, **sckClosing** or **sckError**. |
| *Methods* | |
| **PeekData** | Works like **GetData**, but does not remove the data from the input buffer. |

**Fig. 19.20**   Properties, methods and events for the **Winsock** control (part 1 of 2).

| Property, method or event | Description |
|---|---|
| *Events* | |
| `SendComplete` | Called when a send operation completes. |
| `SendProgress` | Called repeatedly while data is being sent to indicate the progress of the operation. |
| `Connect` | Called when a connection is established. |

**Fig. 19.20**   Properties, methods and events for the **Winsock** control (part 2 of 2).

## 19.10 Visual Basic Script (VBScript®): An Overview

*Visual Basic Script (VBScript)* is a subset of Visual Basic used in World Wide Web *Hypertext Markup Language (HTML)* documents to enhance the functionality of a web page displayed in a web browser (such as Microsoft's **Internet Explorer**) and used on Microsoft's Internet Information Server (IIS) to enhance the functionality of server-side applications. In this section, we discuss client-side VBScript for use in HTML documents.

Note: This section is not meant as a discussion of the features of HTML, but does introduce several HTML concepts to facilitate our discussion of VBScript. For more information on HTML visit the World Wide Web site:

        `http://www.w3.org`

At this site, you will find a complete overview of HTML and its capabilities. Complete details on VBScript can be found on the Microsoft web site at:

        `http://msdn.microsoft.com/scripting/default.htm`

An HTML document consists of text that specifies the content of a web page to be displayed and the format in which to display it. Most of the formatting is specified by using *pairs of tags* of the form *<TAGNAME>* and *</TAGNAME>* that indicate the start and end of the format in the document. For example, the tags *<HTML>* and *</HTML>* are normally used at the beginning and end of an HTML document to specify where the HTML formatting begins and ends, respectively. When the **demo.html** file of Fig. 19.21 is loaded into a browser it displays the string "**Welcome to HTML formatting!**" in plain font then displays the same string in bold font as shown in the screen capture.

*Portability Tip 19.2*

*HTML is not case sensitive.*

*Good Programming Practice 19.3*

*All HTML tags should use uppercase letters to make them stand out in an HTML document.*

Line 2 of the file,

        `Welcome to HTML formatting!<P>`

```
1    <HTML>
2    Welcome to HTML formatting!<P>
3    <B>Welcome to HTML formatting!</B>
4    </HTML>
```

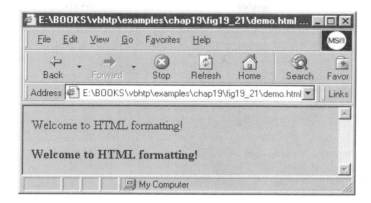

**Fig. 19.21**   A simple HTML document and its appearance in **Internet Explorer**.

specifies that the characters of the string "**Welcome to HTML formatting!**" should be displayed. The tag **<P>** specifies that the next text output should appear on the next line. Note: The tag **<P>** is one of several tags in HTML that do not use the paired tag notation.

   Line 3 of the file,

> **<B>Welcome to HTML formatting!</B>**

uses the bold formatting tags **<B>** and **</B>** to specify that the characters of the string "**Welcome to HTML formatting!**" should be displayed in bold letters. All text between these tags will be formatted in bold.

   Most HTML documents have the basic format shown in Fig. 21.22.

```
1    <HTML>
2    <HEAD>
3    <TITLE>document title here</TITLE>
4    </HEAD>
5
6    <BODY>
7      .
8      .
9      .
10   document content here
11     .
12     .
13     .
14   </BODY>
15   </HTML>
```

**Fig. 19.22**   Typical format of an HTML document.

Lines 2 and 4 are the **<HEAD></HEAD>** tags that delineate the part of the document that is decoded by the browser first. This is commonly where the title of the document is specified (as shown on line 3) and where the programmer places most VBScript code that will be used in the document. Information in this section is not displayed to the users as part of the document. Lines 6 and 14 are the **<BODY></BODY>** tags that delineate the content that is displayed to the user. When incorporating VBScript into an HTML document, the VBScript code can appear in the **<HEAD></HEAD>** section and the **<BODY></BODY>** section. VBScript code that appears in the **<BODY></BODY>** section is called *inline scripting code*. Inline VBScript code is used where it is defined and cannot be called from other parts of the same web page.

VBScript provides only one data type—**Variant**—that is capable of storing data of the types shown in Fig. 19.23 (also known as **Variant** *subtypes*). Section 21.2 provides a more in-depth overview of the **Variant** data type. A **Variant** type variable is interpreted by VBScript in a manner that is suitable to the type of data it contains. For example, if it contains numeric information, it will be treated as a number; if it contains **String** information, it will be treated as a string.

Variables declared at *script level* (similar to module level in Visual Basic) can be declared using **Dim**, **Public** or **Private** and can be accessed throughout the VBScript code in the document.

*Software Engineering Observation 19.4*

*Because all variables are of type* **Variant**, *there is no need to specify the variable type when declaring a variable in VBScript.*

Variables can also be declared simply by using their name in the VBScript code. As in Visual Basic, **Option Explicit** can be used to force all variables to be declared before they are used.

VBScript provides many predefined constants for use in your VBScript code. The constant categories include color constants, comparison constants (to specify how values are compared), date/time constants, date format constants, drive type constants, file attribute constants, file I/O constants, **MsgBox** constants, special folder constants, **String** constants, **VarType** constants (to help determine the type stored in a variable) and miscellaneous other constants. You can also create your own constants using keyword **Const**.

VBScript provides a wide variety of operators for arithmetic operations, equality operations, relational operations, logical operations and string concatenation.

VBScript supports many control structures including: **If/Then/Else**, **Select Case**, **Do/Loop** (all versions), **While/Wend**, **For/Next** and **For Each/Next**.

| Variant subtypes | | | |
| --- | --- | --- | --- |
| Empty | Integer | Single | String |
| Null | Currency | Double | Object |
| Boolean | Long | Date (Time) | Error |
| Byte | | | |

**Fig. 19.23** **Variant** subtypes supported by VBScript.

VBScript provides support for **Sub** procedures and **Function** procedures and includes many intrinsic functions such as **InputBox** and **MsgBox** (a complete listing of the supported intrinsic functions can be found in the on-line VBScript documentation).

The HTML document of Fig. 19.24 includes a VBScript that enables the user to click a button to display an **InputBox** in which they can type an **Integer** to be added to a total. When the **OK** button is pressed, a **MsgBox** is displayed with a message indicating the number that was entered and the sum of all the numbers entered so far.

Line 1, the **<HTML>** tag, indicates the beginning of the HTML formatting. Line 2, the **<HEAD>** tag, begins the header section of the HTML document. Remember, this section of an HTML document is decoded first by the browser. For this reason, VBScript code is normally placed here so it can be decoded before it is invoked in the document.

Line 3 specifies the title of the document. The document title is often displayed in the title bar of the browser window.

Line 4

```
<SCRIPT LANGUAGE="VBScript">
```

```
1   <HTML>
2   <HEAD>
3   <TITLE>Our first VBScript</TITLE>
4   <SCRIPT LANGUAGE="VBScript">
5   <!--
6   Option Explicit
7   Dim intTotal
8
9   Sub Add_OnClick()
10      Dim intValue
11
12      intValue = _
13         InputBox("Enter an integer", "Input Box", , 1000, 1000)
14      intTotal = CInt(intTotal) + CInt(intValue)
15      Call MsgBox("You entered " & intValue & _
16                  "; total so far is " & intTotal, , "Results")
17   End Sub
18   -->
19   </SCRIPT>
20   </HEAD>
21   <BODY>
22   Click the button to add an integer to the total.
23   <HR>
24   <FORM>
25   <INPUT NAME="Add"
26          TYPE="BUTTON"
27          VALUE="Click Here to Add to the Total">
28   </FORM>
29   <HR>
30   </BODY>
31   </HTML>
```

**Fig. 19.24**  Adding **Integer**s on a Web page using VBScript (part 1 of 2).

HTML document title

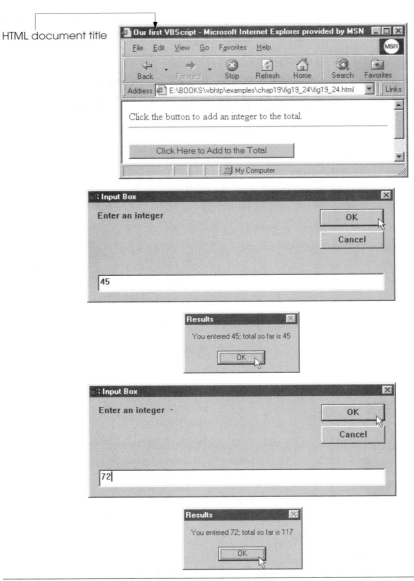

**Fig. 19.24**  Adding **Integer**s on a Web page using VBScript (part 2 of 2).

introduces the script that is embedded into the web page with the **<SCRIPT>** tag. There
are other scripting languages besides VBScript, so the **<SCRIPT>** tag includes an attribute
specifying that the **LANGUAGE** of our script is **VBScript**. This helps the browser understand how to interpret the script code.

The script code is enclosed in an HTML comment using the tags

```
<!--
-->
```

at lines 5 and 18. This is done specifically for browsers that do not support the scripting language to prevent them from accidentally displaying the contents of the script as text in the document. Browsers that do not understand an HTML tag normally ignore the tag, but any other text would be displayed as part of the document contents.

*Good Programming Practice 19.4*

*Always place script code in an HTML comment.*

Lines 6 through 17

```
Option Explicit
Dim intTotal

Sub Add_OnClick()
   Dim intValue

   intValue = _
      InputBox("Enter an integer", "Input Box", , 1000, 1000)
   intTotal = CInt(intTotal) + CInt(intValue)
   Call MsgBox("You entered " & intValue & _
               "; total so far is " & intTotal, , "Results")
End Sub
```

are the VBScript. Note that the code of the script uses the same Visual Basic syntax presented throughout this text. Line 6 uses **Option Explicit** to force declaration of all variables used in the script and line 7 declares the script-level variable **intTotal** that will be used to keep track of the total of all **Integer**s the user enters into the script. Remember there is no need to declare the variable's type because all variables are of type **Variant**.

Lines 9 through 17 define **Sub** procedure **Add_OnClick**. This event procedure responds to the HTML document's **Add** button being pressed by the user. When a button is used on a web page in **Internet Explorer**, the browser automatically looks for an event procedure of the form

*buttonName*_**OnClick**

to respond to each click on the button called *buttonName* (we present the common events later in this section). When the event procedure executes, it displays an **InputBox** in which the user can type an **Integer**. When the user clicks **OK**, the **Integer** is added to the total and the result is displayed in a **MsgBox** as shown in the screen captures.

Line 19 ends the script code with **</SCRIPT>** and line 20 ends the header section of the document with **</HEAD>**.

Line 21 indicates the beginning of the body section of the HTML document with the **<BODY>** tag. The body contains the actual content of the web page that will be displayed. Line 22 displays the text

```
Click the button to add an integer to the total.
```

Line 23 uses the **<HR>** tag (*Horizontal Rule*) to display a line across the web page.

Lines 24 through 28

```
<FORM>
<INPUT NAME="Add"
       TYPE="BUTTON"
       VALUE="Click Here to Add to the Total">
</FORM>
```

use the *<FORM></FORM>* tags to specify an *HTML form*. HTML forms contain GUI components with which the user interacts such as the button used in this example. Most HTML form components are specified with the *<INPUT>* tag. Three attributes are provided by the *<INPUT>* tag—*NAME*, *TYPE* and *VALUE*. Attribute **NAME** is a string representing the form name (**Add** in this example). Attribute **TYPE** specifies the form component type (**BUTTON** in this example). Attribute **VALUE** is a component specific attribute. For a **Button**, **VALUE** is the **Button**'s label. Figure 19.25 lists some common HTML GUI components.

Line 29 displays a horizontal rule. Line 30 ends the body section of the HTML document with the **</BODY>** tag. Line 31 ends the HTML document with the **</HTML>** tag.

Some intrinsic HTML GUI controls are shown in Fig. 19.25. Figure 19.26 lists the events of the intrinsic HTML GUI controls in Fig. 19.26. The basic HTML tag syntax for each control in Fig. 19.25 is shown in Fig. 19.27. These tags must appear between the form tags **<FORM>** and **</FORM>**. Attributes specified in square brackets (*[]*) are optional.

| Control | Description |
|---|---|
| **Button** | A button control similar to a **CommandButton** in Visual Basic. |
| **CheckBox** | A checkbox control. |
| **Password** | A text control that enables the user to enter a password. Characters typed by the user are displayed as asterisks (*) to prevent the characters from being seen on the screen. The control does not protect the password entered in any other way. |
| **Radio** | An **OptionButton**-style control for selecting one of several options. |
| **Reset** | A button control that clears all the **Text** and **TextArea** controls in the current form. This is used to reset a form so the contents can be re-entered by the user. |
| **Select** | A **ComboBox**-style control for selecting from a list of options. |
| **Submit** | A button that submits form contents to a program running on a web server. |
| **Text** | A **TextBox**-style control that allows the user to enter text into a form. |
| **TextArea** | A control similar to the **Text** control that enables multiple lines of user input. |

**Fig. 19.25**  Some intrinsic HTML controls.

| Event name | Description | Raised by |
|---|---|---|
| **OnClick** | Executes when the control is clicked. | **Button, CheckBox, Radio, Reset, Submit** |

**Fig. 19.26**  Common events of intrinsic HTML controls (part 1 of 2).

| Event name | Description | Raised by |
|---|---|---|
| **OnFocus** | Executes when the control receives the focus (i.e., the control becomes active). | **Button**, **CheckBox**, **Password**, **Radio**, **Reset**, **Select**, **Submit**, **Text**, **TextArea** |
| **OnBlur** | Executes when the control loses the focus (i.e., another control becomes active). | **Password**, **Select**, **Text**, **TextArea** |
| **OnChange** | Executes when the control's state changes (e.g., the user makes a selection from a **Select** control). | **Select**, **Text**, **TextArea** |
| **OnSelect** | Executes when the control's contents are selected. | **Text**, **TextArea** |

**Fig. 19.26**   Common events of intrinsic HTML controls (part 2 of 2).

| Control | Syntax |
|---|---|
| **Button** | `<INPUT TYPE="BUTTON"`<br>`        [NAME="`*buttonName*`"]`<br>`        [VALUE="`*buttonLabel*`"]>` |
| **CheckBox** | `<INPUT TYPE="CHECKBOX"`<br>`        [NAME="`*checkboxName*`"]`<br>`        [VALUE="`*checkboxState*`"]`<br>`        [CHECKED]>` |
| **Password** | `<INPUT TYPE="PASSWORD"`<br>`        [NAME="`*passwordName*`"]`<br>`        [VALUE="`*defaultValue*`"]`<br>`        [SIZE="`*numberOfCharactersWide*`"]`<br>`        [MAXLENGTH="`*maximumCharactersAllowed*`"]>` |
| **Radio** | `<INPUT TYPE="RADIO"`<br>`        [NAME="`*radioName*`"]`<br>`        [VALUE="`*uniqueValueToBeSubmitted*`"]`<br>`        [CHECKED]>` |
| **Reset** | `<INPUT TYPE="RESET"`<br>`        [NAME="`*resetName*`"]`<br>`        [VALUE="`*resetLabel*`"]>` |
| **Select** | `<SELECT NAME="`*selectName*`"`<br>`        [SIZE="`*numberOfItemsDisplayed*`"]`<br>`        [MULTIPLE]>`<br>`<OPTION [SELECTED] VALUE="`*value1*`">`*DisplayedItem1*`</OPTION>`<br>`    ...`<br>`<OPTION [SELECTED] VALUE="`*valueN*`">`*DisplayedItemN*`</OPTION>`<br>`</SELECT>` |

**Fig. 19.27**   HTML tags for several intrinsic HTML controls (part 1 of 2).

| Control | Syntax |
|---------|--------|
| Submit | `<INPUT TYPE="SUBMIT"`<br>`[NAME="`*submitName*`]`<br>`[VALUE="`*submitLabel*`]>` |
| Text | `<INPUT TYPE="TEXT"`<br>`[NAME="`*textName*`]`<br>`[VALUE="`*defaultStringContents*`]`<br>`[SIZE="`*numberOfCharactersWide*`]`<br>`[MAXLENGTH="`*maximumCharactersAllowed*`]>` |
| TextArea | `<TEXTAREA [NAME="`*textAreaName*`]`<br>`[ROWS="`*numberOfRows*`]`<br>`[COLS="`*numberOfColumns*`]>`<br>`</TEXTAREA>` |

**Fig. 19.27**   HTML tags for several intrinsic HTML controls (part 2 of 2).

Figure 19.28 provides another VBScript example. The HTML form provides a **SELECT** component to allow the user to select a web site from a list of sites. When the selection is made, the new web site is displayed in the browser as shown in the screen captures. The change of sites is performed by an inline VBScript for the **SELECT** component.

```
1   <HTML>
2   <HEAD>
3   <TITLE>Select a site to browse</TITLE>
4   </HEAD>
5
6   <BODY>
7   Select a site to browse<P>
8   <HR>
9   <FORM>
10  <SELECT NAME="SiteSelector" SIZE="1">
11      <OPTION VALUE="http://www.deitel.com">
12          Deitel & Associates, Inc.
13      </OPTION>
14      <OPTION VALUE="http://www.prenhall.com">
15          Prentice Hall
16      </OPTION>
17      <OPTION VALUE="http://www.phptr.com/phptrinteractive">
18          Prentice Hall Interactive
19      </OPTION>
20  </SELECT>
21  <SCRIPT FOR="SiteSelector"
22          EVENT="OnChange"
23          LANGUAGE="VBScript">
24      Document.Location = SiteSelector.Value
25  </SCRIPT>
```

**Fig. 19.28**   Using inline VBScript code to respond to an event (part 1 of 2).

```
26   </FORM>
27   <HR>
28   </BODY>
29   </HTML>
```

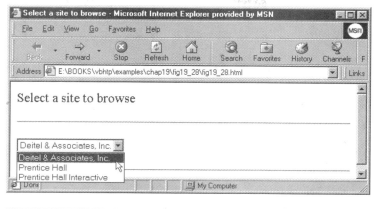

**Fig. 19.28**    Using inline VBScript code to respond to an event (part 2 of 2).

Lines 1 and 27 indicate the start and end of the HTML document with tags **<HTML>** and **</HTML>**. Lines 2 through 4 are the **<HEAD></HEAD>** section of the document in which the title of the document (line 3) is specified. Remember that VBScript is commonly placed in the **<HEAD></HEAD>** section. However, in this example we are demonstrating inline VBScript code. The **<BODY>** of the document is lines 6 through 26. Line 7 displays

> **Select a site to browse**

then starts a new line with the **<P>** tag. Line 8 displays a horizontal rule with tag **<HR>**.

Lines 9 through 24 define a **<FORM>** containing a **SELECT** component. Line 10

> **<SELECT NAME="SiteSelector" SIZE="1">**

introduces the **SELECT** component named **SiteSelector** with the **<SELECT>** tag. Two attributes are specified—**NAME** (the name of the component) and **SIZE** (the number of items displayed at one time). This is a single-selection **SELECT** component (only one item can be selected at a time).

The items presented in the **SELECT** component are specified with the tags **<OPTION>** and **</OPTION>**. For example, lines 11 through 13

```
<OPTION VALUE="http://www.deitel.com">
    Deitel & Associates, Inc.
</OPTION>
```

specify in the starting **<OPTION>** tag that the **VALUE** of the first option is the URL

```
http://www.deitel.com
```

Between the **<OPTION>** and **</OPTION>** tags (line 12) is the string displayed for that **OPTION** in the **SELECT**. We specified three options in this **SELECT**.

Lines 21 through 25

```
<SCRIPT FOR="SiteSelector"
        EVENT="OnChange"
        LANGUAGE="VBScript">
   Document.Location = SiteSelector.value
</SCRIPT>
```

specify an inline VBScript. Lines 21 through 23 are the starting **<SCRIPT>** tag. In inline VBScript code, the **<SCRIPT>** tag's **FOR** attribute indicates the HTML component on which the script operates (i.e., **SiteSelector**), the **EVENT** attribute indicates the event to which the script responds (i.e., **OnChange** which occurs when the user makes a selection) and the **LANGUAGE** attribute specifies the scripting language (i.e., VBScript).

Line 24

```
Document.Location = SiteSelector.Value
```

causes the browser to change to the selected location. This line uses **Internet Explorer**'s *Document* object to change the location. The **Document** object is part of **Internet Explorer**'s *Dynamic HTML* capabilities for dynamically manipulating Web pages and their content. The **Document** object's *Location property* specifies the URL of the page to display. **SiteSelector.Value** gets the **VALUE** of the currently selected **OPTION** in the **SELECT**. When the assignment is performed, **Internet Explorer** automatically displays the Web page for the selected location.

For more information on Dynamic HTML and other technologies, visit the sites

```
http://premium.microsoft.com/msdn/library
http://www.microsoft.com/workshop/default.asp
```

The first site contains the entire Microsoft Developer Network Online Library of documentation (Note: You may need to register for this service, but registration is free). The site includes the complete documentation for Visual Basic and Microsoft's other development tools and technologies (such as Dynamic HTML). The second site—Microsoft's SiteBuilder Network Workshop—provides a detailed overview of many Microsoft Internet technologies including Dynamic HTML.

## Summary

- Visual Basic offers socket-based communications that enable applications to view networking as streams of bytes. The protocol for transmission is TCP—Transmission Control Protocol.

- Visual Basic offers packet-based communications with datagrams. The protocol for transmission is UDP—User Datagram Protocol. UDP is a connectionless service.

- HTTP protocol (HyperText Transfer Protocol) forms the basis of the World Wide Web. URLs (Uniform Resource Locators, also called Universal Resource Locators) locate data on the Internet.

- The **WebBrowser** control provides many of the features of the Microsoft **Internet Explorer** browser, including WWW browsing, viewing local documents and downloading. The control also provides automatic management of navigation, hyperlinking, history lists, favorites and security.

- Procedure **Navigate** of the **WebBrowser** control receives a string representing the URL to display, then displays the document (assuming it is a valid URL).

- **GoBack** revisits the previous document in the **WebBrowser** control's history list.

- **GoForward** revisits the next document in the **WebBrowser** control's history list.

- **GoHome** loads the default web page into the **WebBrowser** control. The default web page is the page that is specified as your home page in **Internet Explorer**.

- When the **WebBrowser** control completes the download and display of a URL, event procedure **DocumentComplete** executes.

- **WebBrowser** property **Busy** is **True** if the control is currently navigating a document or downloading a file. **WebBrowser** property **LocationName** is the name of the displayed document. **WebBrowser** property **LocationURL** is the location of the displayed document. **WebBrowser** property **Offline** should be set to **True** if the control should read documents from the cache and **False** if the control should read documents from their original source.

- **WebBrowser** method **GoSearch** navigates to the **Internet Explorer** search page. **WebBrowser** method **Refresh** reloads the current document. **WebBrowser** method **Stop** cancels the current navigation or download.

- **WebBrowser** event **DownloadBegin** executes when navigation begins. **WebBrowser** event **DownloadComplete** executes when navigation completes. **WebBrowser** event **ProgressChange** executes repeatedly to indicate progress of downloads.

- The **Internet Transfer** control supports two of the most common networking protocols, Hypertext Transfer Protocol (HTTP) and File Transfer Protocol (FTP).

- The **Internet Transfer** control can connect to a web server using HTTP protocol in the same manner as the **WebBrowser** control to read the text of the document being retrieved.

- The FTP protocol enables a program to transfer files between computers on the Internet.

- **Internet Transfer** control method **OpenURL** downloads the contents of a URL. The download is performed synchronously—the program does not continue until the download is complete.

- If a program downloads and saves binary files, it should save the results of the **OpenURL** method in a byte array and output the byte array in binary format to the file.

- **Internet Transfer** control property **URL** is the location of the server to which to connect. **Internet Transfer** control property **UserName** is the user name specified for servers that require users to log in. **Internet Transfer** control property **Password** is the password for the user specified by **UserName** for servers that require users to log in.

- FTP command *get* requests that a file from the FTP server be downloaded to your machine (command *recv* performs the same task). Command *cd* changes directories. Command *cdup* changes directories to the parent directory. Command *delete* removes a file. Command *dir* shows a directory listing of the current directory. Command *mkdir* makes a directory. Command *put* sends a file to the server (command *send* performs the same task). Command *pwd* displays the current directory name. Command *quit* terminates the current connection. Command *rename* changes a file name. Command *rmdir* removes a directory. Command *size* gets the size of a file.

- The **Internet Transfer** control's **Execute** method sends a **command** string to an FTP server to indicate a request. Method **Execute** performs an asynchronous transfer—the program can continue executing as the server responds to the request. The application is automatically notified of responses from the server in event procedure **StateChanged**.

- The **Internet Transfer** control state **icResponseCompleted** indicates that the request made to the server has completed.

- The **Internet Transfer** control's **GetChunk** method retrieves data. The second argument is **icByteArray** for binary data such as images and executable files or **icString** for text data.

- **Internet Transfer** control property **AccessType** determines how the control interacts with the Internet. Possible values are **icUseDefault** (uses the system's default settings), **icDirect** (direct connection to the Internet) or **icNamedProxy** (connect through a proxy server that controls access to the Internet). Property **Proxy** sets the name of the proxy server. Property **ResponseCode** is the error number for the error that results on the **icError** state in the **StateChanged** event. **Internet Transfer** control property **ResponseInfo** is the text message for the error that results on the **icError** state in the **StateChanged** event. Property **StillExecuting** is **True** if the control is still executing its last task.

- **Internet Transfer** control method **Cancel** cancels the last request made to the server and closes the connections. Method **GetHeaders** gets the header text from an HTML document.

- The **Winsock** control allows client/server applications to communicate using both Transmission Control Protocol (TCP) and User Datagram Protocol (UDP).

- TCP protocol is typically used when large amounts of data are transmitted between a server and a client and when reliability is imperative.

- UDP is typically used when small amounts of data are sent or data are sent intermittently.

- Using the TCP protocol, the server must listen for connections from clients on a specific port number as specified with the **Winsock** control's **LocalPort** property. Each client will ask to connect to the server on this port.

- Each client connection is managed with a **Winsock** control.

- The server must be told to listen indefinitely for an attempt by a client to connect by calling the **Winsock** control's **Listen** method.

- When a connection request is received while the server is listening, event procedure **ConnectionRequest** executes.

- To accept a request for connection from the client—typically performed in the **ConnectionRequest** event procedure—call the **Winsock** control's **Accept** method.

- When data arrives at the client or the server, the **Winsock** control's **DataArrival** event procedure executes.

- Data is sent through the **Winsock** control using the **SendData** method. Data is received through the **Winsock** control using the **GetData** method.

- When the transmission is complete and the client closes the connection, the **Winsock** control's **Close** event procedure executes (the same is true on the client side).

- Using TCP protocol, the client specifies the server and port number to which to connect. These are specified with the **RemoteHost** and **RemotePort** properties of the **Winsock** control.

- Connection to the server is established using a call to the **Winsock** object's **Connect** method.

- If a run-time error occurs while processing a connection, the **Winsock** object's **Error** event procedure executes.

- To use UDP protocol, the **Winsock** control's **Protocol** property must be set to **1 - sckUDP-Protocol** (the default is **0 - sckTCPProtocol**).

- The **Winsock** control's **Bind** method binds a UDP server to a specific port to receive packets.

- A UDP client must specify the **RemoteHost** to which packets are sent and the **RemotePort** at which the server expects to receive the packets.

- **Winsock** property **BytesReceived** specifies the number of bytes in the buffer that can be retrieved with **GetData**. Property **LocalHostName** is the local computer's name. Property **LocalHostIP** is the local computer's IP address. Property **LocalPort** is the local computer's port number being used for communication with another application. Property **State** specifies the current state of the control.

- **Winsock** method **PeekData** works like **GetData**, but does not remove data from the buffer.

- **Winsock** event **SendComplete** is called when a send operation completes. Event **SendProgress** is called repeatedly while data is being sent to indicate the progress of the operation. Event **Connect** is called when a connection is established.

- Visual Basic Script (VBScript) is a subset of Visual Basic used in World Wide Web Hypertext Markup Language (HTML) documents and used on Microsoft's Internet Information Server to enhance the functionality of server-side applications.

- An HTML document consists of text specifying the content of a web page to be displayed and the format in which to display it. Most of the formatting is specified by using pairs of tags of the form **<TAGNAME>** and **</TAGNAME>** that indicate the start and end of the format in the document.

- The tag **<P>** specifies that the next text output should appear on the next line. All text between tags **<B>** and **</B>** is displayed in bold letters.

- The **<HEAD></HEAD>** tags delineate the header of the HTML document that is decoded by the browser first. This is commonly where the title of the document and VBScript code are placed.

- The **<BODY></BODY>** tags delineate the content that is displayed to the user.

- VBScript code can appear in the **<HEAD></HEAD>** section and the **<BODY></BODY>** section. VBScript code that appears in the **<BODY></BODY>** section is called inline scripting code.

- VBScript provides only one data type—**Variant**.

- Variables declared at script level can be declared using **Dim, Public** or **Private** and can be accessed throughout the VBScript code in the document.

- **Option Explicit** can be used to force all variables to be declared before they are used in a VBScript. VBScript provides many predefined constants for use in your VBScript code.

- VBScript provides a wide variety of operators for arithmetic operations, equality operations, relational operations, logical operations and string concatenation.

- VBScript supports a number of control structures including: **If/Then/Else, Select/Case, Do/Loop, While/Wend, For/Next** and **For Each/Next**.

- VBScript provides support for **Sub** procedures and **Function** procedures and includes many intrinsic functions such as **InputBox** and **MsgBox**.

- The **<SCRIPT>** tag includes an attribute specifying the **LANGUAGE** of the script. This helps the browser understand how to interpret the script code.

- The script code is enclosed in an HTML comment using the tags

```
<!--
-->
```

so browsers that do not support the scripting language do not accidentally display the contents of the script as text in the document.

- When a button is used on a web page in **Internet Explorer**, the browser automatically looks for an event procedure of the form

    buttonName_**OnClick**

    to respond to each click on the button called buttonName.

- The **<HR>** tag (**H**orizontal **R**ule) displays a line across the web page.

- The **<FORM></FORM>** tags specify an HTML form. HTML forms contain GUI components with which the user interacts such as the button used in this example. Most HTML form components are specified with the **<INPUT>** tag.

- The items in a **SELECT** component are specified with the tags **<OPTION>** and **</OPTION>**.

- In inline VBScript code, the **<SCRIPT>** tag's **FOR** attribute indicates the HTML component on which the script operates, the **EVENT** attribute indicates the event to which the script responds and the **LANGUAGE** attribute specifies the scripting language.

- The **Document** object is part of **Internet Explorer**'s Dynamic HTML capabilities for dynamically manipulating Web pages and their content. The **Document** object's **Location** property specifies the URL of the page to display.

## *Terminology*

accept a connection
**<B></B>**
**<BODY></BODY>**
client
client connects to a server
client/server relationship
close a connection
collaborative computing
computer networking
connection
connectionless service
connectionless transmission with datagrams
connection-oriented service
connection request
connect to a port
connect to a World Wide Web site
datagram
deny a connection
**Document** object
duplicated packets
**<FORM></FORM>**
FTP (File Transfer Protocol)
FTP command *cd*
FTP command *cdup*
FTP command *delete*
FTP command *dir*
FTP command *get*
FTP command *mkdir*
FTP command *put*

FTP command *pwd*
FTP command *quit*
FTP command *recv*
FTP command *rename*
FTP command *rmdir*
FTP command *send*
FTP command *size*
handshake point
**<HEAD></HEAD>**
heterogeneous computer systems
host
HTML (Hypertext Markup Language)
**<HTML></HTML>**
HTTP (Hypertext Transfer Protocol)
**<INPUT></INPUT>**
Internet
Internet address
**Internet Transfer** control
**Internet Transfer** property **AccessType**
**Internet Transfer** method **Cancel**
**Internet Transfer** method **Execute**
**Internet Transfer** method **GetChunk**
**Internet Transfer** method **GetHeaders**
**Internet Transfer** method **OpenURL**
**Internet Transfer** property **Password**
**Internet Transfer** property **Proxy**
**Internet Transfer** **StateChanged** event
**Internet Transfer** property **URL**
**Internet Transfer** property **UserName**

## Common Programming Errors

**19.1**  Specifying a port number that is already in use results in a run-time error with the error message "Address in use."

**19.2**  A run-time error occurs if an attempt to connect to a server is unsuccessful. This results in a call to the **Winsock** object's **Error** event procedure.

**19.3**  Specifying a port that is already in use or specifying an invalid port number when binding a **Winsock** object to a specific port results in a run-time error.

## Good Programming Practices

**19.1**  Always provide error-handling code when using the **WebBrowser** control to prevent abnormal program termination.

**19.2** Before accepting a connection from a client, check if the state of the **Winsock** control is **sckClosed**. If not, the previous connection was not closed properly. In this case, invoke the **Close** method on the **Winsock** object, then accept the connection.

**19.3** All HTML tags should use uppercase letters to make them stand out in an HTML document.

**19.4** Always place script code in an HTML comment.

## Performance Tips

**19.1** Connectionless services generally offer greater performance but less reliability than connection-oriented services.

**19.2** TCP protocol requires more overhead to set up and maintain the connection than UDP connectionless protocol.

**19.3** In high-performance systems in which memory is abundant, a server can be implemented to create a pool of **Winsock** objects that can be assigned quickly to handle network I/O across each new connection as it is created. Thus, when a connection is received, the server need not incur the overhead of **Winsock** object creation.

## Portability Tip

**19.1** The TCP protocol and its related set of protocols enable a great variety of heterogeneous computer systems (i.e., computer systems with different processors and different operating systems) to intercommunicate.

**19.2** HTML is not case sensitive.

## Software Engineering Observations

**19.1** Although UDP protocol requires less overhead than TCP protocol, UDP protocol is less reliable.

**19.2** The **Winsock** control hides much of the complexity of network programming from the programmer.

**19.3** With Visual Basic's control arrays, we can create servers that can manage many simultaneous connections with many clients.

## Self-Review Exercises

**19.1** Fill in the blanks in each of the following:
   a) The _____ property of the **Winsock** control determines if network transmission is performed with TCP or UDP.
   b) The _____ method of the **Winsock** control causes the server to wait for a TCP-based connection from a client.
   c) The _____ event of the **Winsock** control is automatically called when packets of information arrive in a UDP-based application.
   d) The _____ event of the **Internet Transfer** control is used to read data over an FTP connection asynchronously.
   e) The _____ method of the **WebBrowser** control causes the control to change web pages.
   f) The _____ control is used to perform datagram transmission.
   g) The _____ control can be used with both FTP and HTTP connections.
   h) The two protocols supported by the **Winsock** control are _____ protocol and _____ protocol.
   i) The acronym URL stands for _____.
   j) The key protocol that forms the basis of the World Wide Web is _____.

**19.2**     State whether the following are *true* or *false*. If the answer is *false*, explain why.

    a) The **SendChuck** method is used to send data using the **Internet Transfer** control.

    b) UDP is a connection-oriented protocol.

    c) With the **Winsock** control and TCP protocol a process establishes a connection to another process.

    d) A server waits at a port for connections from a client.

    e) Datagram packet transmission over a network is reliable—packets are guaranteed to arrive in sequence.

    f) **Winsock** event procedure **ConnectionRequest** is automatically called when a client attempts to connect to a TCP-based server.

    g) Before a UDP-based server can receive datagram packets, the server must be attached to a specific port number with the **Winsock** control's **Bind** method.

## Answers to Self-Review Exercises

**19.1**     a) **Protocol**. b) **Listen**. c) **DataArrival**. d) **GetChunk**. e) **Navigate**. f) **Winsock**. g) **Internet Transfer** control. h) TCP, UDP. i) Uniform Resource Locator. j) HTTP.

**19.2**     a) False; the **SendData** method is used.  b) False; UDP is a connectionless protocol and TCP is a connection-oriented protocol.  c) True.  d) True.  e) False; packets could be lost and packets can arrive out of order.  f) True.  g) True.

## Exercises

**19.3**     Distinguish between connection-oriented network services and connectionless network services.

**19.4**     How does a client determine the host name of the client computer?

**19.5**     How does a client determine the host name of the server?

**19.6**     How can a client get a line of text from a server?

**19.7**     Describe how a client application can read a file from a server using the **Internet Transfer** control.

**19.8**     Describe how a client connects to a server.

**19.9**     Describe how a server sends data to a client.

**19.10**     Describe how to prepare a server to receive a streams-based connection request from a single client.

**19.11**     How does a server listen for connections at a port?

**19.12**     Use the **Internet Transfer** control to allow a client to specify a file name to the server and have the server send the contents of the file or indicate that the file does not exist.

**19.13**     Modify the preceding exercise to allow the client to modify the contents of the file and send the file back to the server for storage. The user can edit the file in a **TextBox**, then click a *Save Changes* button to send the file back to the server.

**19.14**     Modify program of Fig. 19.2 to show a list of sites in a **ComboBox** object. Allow users to add their own sites to the list and remove sites from the list.

**19.15** Investigate the capabilities of the **Internet Explorer** browser and use the features of the **WebBrowser** control to create your own version of **Internet Explorer**.

**19.16** Develop a client/server tic-tac-toe program. The two users should alternate making moves. Your program should mediate the players moves determining whose turn it is and allowing only valid moves. The players themselves will determine when the game is over.

**19.17** Develop a client/server checkers program. The two users should alternate making moves. Your program should mediate the players moves, determining whose turn it is and allowing only valid moves. The players themselves will determine when the game is over.

**19.18** Develop a client/server chess-playing program modeled after the checkers program in the previous exercises.

**19.19** Develop a client/server black jack card game program in which the server application deals cards to each of the client applications. The server should deal additional cards (as per the rules of the game) to each player as requested.

**19.20** Develop a client/server poker card game in which the server application deals cards to each of the client applications. The server should deal additional cards (as per the rules of the game) to each player as requested.

**19.21** *(Networked Morse Code)* Modify your solution to Exercise 8.26 to enable two applications to send Morse Code messages to each other through a server application. Each application should allow the user to type normal characters in **TextBox**es, translate the characters into Morse Code and send the coded message through the server to the other client. When messages are received, they should be decoded and displayed as normal characters and as Morse Code. The application should have two **TextBox**es, one for displaying the other client's messages and one for typing.

**19.22** In Chapter 11, Section 11.4 discusses the use of template forms. One of the template forms is for a web browser. Rewrite the program of Exercise 19.15 to use the web browser form template.

**19.23** Using the features of Fig. 19.5, the string processing capabilities of Chapter 8 and the **Rich-TextBox** control (see Section 11.5), write your own Hypertext Markup Language (HTML) interpreter that can parse a simple HTML file, format the text in the file and display the formatted text. Visit the World Wide Web site

> **http://www.w3.org/MarkUp/**

for more information on HTML and the formatting tags that are found in HTML documents.

**19.24** *(Dynamic Stock Portfolio Evaluator)* Create a Visual Basic application that will read a file describing an investor's stock portfolio. For each stock the investor owns, the file contains the stock ticker symbol and the number of shares of that stock the investor owns. The application then accesses some stock quotation service available over the Internet (this requires techniques from Chapter 16, Networking) and filters out only those stock transactions for the stocks in the investor's portfolio. As the application fetches new stock prices, it displays a spreadsheet on the screen and dynamically updates the spreadsheet. The spreadsheet shows each stock symbol, the latest price of that stock, the number of shares and the latest total value of shares of that stock. The spreadsheet also totals the latest value of the investor's entire portfolio. An investor could run your Visual Basic application in a small portion of his or her screen while proceeding with other work.

**19.25** *(Networked Simpletron Simulator)* Modify the Simpletron Simulator exercise you created in Chapter 10 by breaking the program into a client application and a server application. Execute the

SML instructions from the server application. Use the **Winsock** control to perform TCP-based communication between the client and the server. The user interface should appear on the client side. After the user enters the SML program, the program should be sent to the server application for execution. As the SML program executes on the server, the results should be sent back to the client application for display in the user interface.

**19.26**    *(Networked Simpletron Simulator)* Modify your solution to Exercise 19.25 to use UDP-based packet communication between the client and the server.

**19.27**    *(Networked Tic-Tac-Toe)* Write a client/server tic-tac-toe game in which two clients connect to a server to play. The first client to connect should be player **X** and the second client should be player **O**. The server should maintain the status of the tic-tac-toe board at all times. Each client's user interface should display the board. When a player clicks a square on the board, a message should be sent to the server and the server should validate the move. If the move is valid, the server should send messages to both clients informing them to update their boards with the appropriate moves. If the move is invalid, the server should send a message to the client indicating the invalid move and requesting that the player move again. Provide the ability to determine who wins and to play again. Use TCP-based communications between the clients and the server.

**19.28**    *(Networked Tic-Tac-Toe)* Modify your solution to Exercise 19.27 to use UDP-based packet communication between the clients and the server.

**19.29**    *(VBScript Compound Interest Calculator)* Create an HTML document that enables the user to calculate compound interest. Provide several **TEXT** components in which the user can enter the *principal amount*, the yearly interest *rate* and the number of *years* (see the compound interest program of Figs. 5.5 through 5.7 for the calculation of interest). Provide a **BUTTON** to cause the VBScript to execute and calculate the interest. Display the result in another **TEXT** component. If any **TEXT** component is left empty, display a **MsgBox** indicating the error. Use a **Function** procedure to perform the calculation.

**19.30**    *(VBScript Compound Interest Calculator)* Modify Exercise 19.30 to use inline VBScript code.

**19.31**    *(VBScript Monthly Compound Interest Calculator)* Modify Exercise 19.29 to calculate the compound interest on a monthly basis. Remember that you must divide the interest rate by 12 to get the monthly rate.

**19.32**    *(VBScript Monthly Compound Interest Calculator)* Modify Exercise 19.31 to use inline VBScript code.

# 20

# Multimedia: Images, Animation, Audio

## Objectives

- To use the **Microsoft Agent** control to add animated characters to an application.
- To use the **Multimedia MCI** control to add audio and video to an application.
- To use the **Animation** control to repeatedly play AVI files.
- To use the **ActiveMovie** control to play a variety of media formats for both audio and video.
- To use the **Marquee** control to scroll images.
- To use the **Real Audio** control to play live audio downloaded from the Internet.

*The wheel that squeaks the loudest . . . gets the grease.*
John Billings (Henry Wheeler Shaw)

*Noise proves nothing. Often a hen who has merely laid an egg cackles as if she had laid an asteroid.*
Mark Twain, *Following the Equator*

*We'll use a signal I have tried and found far-reaching and easy to yell. Waa-hoo!*
Zane Grey

*A wide screen just makes a bad film twice as bad.*
Samuel Goldwyn

*There is a natural hootchy-kootchy motion to a goldfish.*
Walt Disney

# Outline

## 20.1   Introduction

Welcome to what may well become the largest revolution in the history of the computer field. Those of us who entered the field decades ago were primarily interested in using computers to do arithmetic calculations at high speed. But as the computer field evolves, we are beginning to realize that the data manipulation capabilities of computers are now equally important. One area with "sizzle" in Visual Basic is *multimedia*—the use of *sound*, *images*, *graphics* and *video* to make applications "come alive." Today many people consider two-dimensional color video to be the "ultimate" in multimedia. But within the decade, we expect all kinds of exciting new three-dimensional applications. Multimedia programming offers many new challenges. The field is already enormous and will grow rapidly.

People are rushing to equip their computers for multimedia. Most new computers are being sold "multimedia ready" with CD-ROM drives, audio boards and sometimes with special video capabilities.

Among those users who want graphics, two-dimensional graphics no longer suffice. Now many people want three-dimensional, high-resolution, color graphics. True three-dimensional imaging may become available in the next decade. Imagine having ultra-high-resolution, "theater-in-the-round," three-dimensional television. Sporting and entertainment events will take place on your living room floor! Medical students worldwide will see operations being performed thousands of miles away as if they were occurring in the same room. People will be able to learn how to drive with extremely realistic driving simulators in their homes before they get behind the wheel. The possibilities are exciting and endless.

Multimedia demands extraordinary computing power. Until r cently, affordable computers with this kind of power were not available. But today's ultrafast processors like the SPARC Ultra from Sun Microsystems, the Pentium II from Intel, the Alpha from Digital Equipment Corporation and the R8000 from MIPS/Silicon Graphics (among others) are making effective multimedia possible. The computer and communications industries will be primary beneficiaries of the multimedia revolution. Users will be willing to pay more for the faster processors, larger memories and wider communications bandwidths that will be needed to support multimedia applications. Ironically, users may not have to pay more as fierce competition in these industries forces prices down.

This chapter presents a series of "live-code" examples that cover many interesting multimedia controls you can use in your applications. We cover the basics of controls that manipulate images, play animations, play sounds, play videos and display interactive animated characters. The chapter exercises suggest many interesting projects and even mention some "million-dollar" ideas that may help you make your fortune! When we were creating these exercises it seemed that the ideas just kept flowing. Multimedia leverages creativity in ways that we have not experienced with "conventional" computer capabilities.

## 20.2  Microsoft Agent Control

*Microsoft Agent* is a new and exciting technology for *interactive animated characters* in a Windows application or World Wide Web page. The *Microsoft Agent* control provides access to three predefined characters—*Genie*, *Merlin* and *Robby the Robot*. These characters allow users of your application to interact with the application using more natural human communication techniques. The control accepts both mouse and keyboard interactions and also supports speech recognition, so your application can actually respond to voice commands from the user. You can also create your own characters with the help of the *Microsoft Agent Character Editor* and the *Microsoft Linguistic Sound Editing Tool*.

In this section, we discuss some basic capabilities of the **Microsoft Agent** control. For complete details on downloading the **Microsoft Agent** control and taking advantage of the control's capabilities, visit the Microsoft Web site:

**http://www.microsoft.com/workshop/imedia/agent**

In addition to the area of this Web site dedicated to **Microsoft Agent**, there are also discussions of several other multimedia technologies that are available for use in Windows applications and in Web pages. Simply visit

**http://www.microsoft.com/workshop/imedia**

for more information.

The example of Fig. 20.1 demonstrates the **Microsoft Agent** control. The second, third and fourth screen captures illustrate the three predefined characters. *Note:* Before using the **Microsoft Agent** control, you must first download and install the control and the character definitions from the **Microsoft Agent** Web site shown above.

```
1   ' Fig. 20.1
2   ' Demonstrating Microsoft Agent
3   Option Explicit
4   Dim currentCharacter As IAgentCtlCharacter
5   Dim characterLocation As String
6
7   Private Sub Form_Load()
8      ' get the location of the character descriptions
9      characterLocation = _
10        InputBox("Enter Microsoft Agent character location", _
11          "Character Location", _
12          "c:\program files\microsoft agent\characters\")
```

**Fig. 20.1**    Demonstrating **Microsoft Agent** (part 1 of 4).

```
13
14      ' load the characters
15      Call Agent1.Characters.Load( _
16         "Genie", characterLocation & "genie.acs")
17      Call Agent1.Characters.Load( _
18         "Merlin", characterLocation & "merlin.acs")
19      Call Agent1.Characters.Load( _
20         "Robby", characterLocation & "robby.acs")
21
22      ' populate the ComboBox
23      Call cboCharacter.AddItem("Genie")
24      Call cboCharacter.AddItem("Merlin")
25      Call cboCharacter.AddItem("Robby")
26   End Sub
27
28   Private Sub Form_Activate()
29      ' set the current character, move it,
30      ' show it and make it speak
31      Set currentCharacter = Agent1.Characters("Genie")
32      Call currentCharacter.MoveTo( _
33         frmMSAgent.Left \ 20, frmMSAgent.Top \ 20)
34      Call currentCharacter.Show
35      Call currentCharacter.Speak(txtToSpeak.Text)
36   End Sub
37
38   Private Sub Agent1_Click(ByVal CharacterID As String, _
39         ByVal Button As Integer, ByVal Shift As Integer, _
40         ByVal x As Integer, ByVal y As Integer)
41      Call currentCharacter.Speak("Ouch! Why did you do that?")
42      Call currentCharacter.Play("Confused")
43      Call currentCharacter.Play("ConfusedReturn")
44   End Sub
45
46   Private Sub Agent1_DblClick(ByVal CharacterID As String, _
47         ByVal Button As Integer, ByVal Shift As Integer, _
48         ByVal x As Integer, ByVal y As Integer)
49      Call currentCharacter.Play("Alert")
50      Call currentCharacter.Play("AlertReturn")
51      Call currentCharacter.Speak("Stop it!")
52   End Sub
53
54   Private Sub Agent1_DragStart(ByVal CharacterID As String, _
55         ByVal Button As Integer, ByVal Shift As Integer, _
56         ByVal x As Integer, ByVal y As Integer)
57      Call currentCharacter.Play("Alert")
58      Call currentCharacter.Speak("Put me down!")
59      Call currentCharacter.Play("AlertReturn")
60   End Sub
61
```

**Fig. 20.1**    Demonstrating **Microsoft Agent** (part 2 of 4).

```
62  Private Sub Agent1_DragComplete(ByVal CharacterID As String, _
63      ByVal Button As Integer, ByVal Shift As Integer, _
64      ByVal x As Integer, ByVal y As Integer)
65    Call currentCharacter.Speak("Thank you!")
66  End Sub
67
68  Private Sub Agent1_Show(ByVal CharacterID As String, _
69      ByVal Cause As Integer)
70    Call currentCharacter.Play("Acknowledge")
71  End Sub
72
73  Private Sub cboCharacter_Click()
74    ' hide the previous character, set the new character,
75    ' move it, show it and make it speak
76    Call currentCharacter.Hide
77    Set currentCharacter = Agent1.Characters(cboCharacter.Text)
78    Call currentCharacter.MoveTo( _
79      frmMSAgent.Left \ 20, frmMSAgent.Top \ 20)
80    Call currentCharacter.Show
81    Call currentCharacter.Speak(txtToSpeak.Text)
82  End Sub
83
84  Private Sub cmdSpeak_Click()
85    ' make the current character speak again
86    If txtToSpeak.Text = "" Then
87      Call currentCharacter.Speak( _
88        "Please, type the words you want me to speak.")
89    Else
90      Call currentCharacter.Speak(txtToSpeak.Text)
91    End If
92  End Sub
```

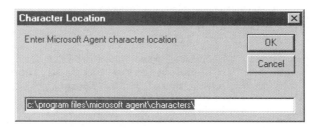

**Fig. 20.1** Demonstrating **Microsoft Agent** (part 3 of 4).

The program consists of four controls—a **TextBox** in which the user types the text for the animated character to speak, a **ComboBox** to choose which character speaks (the default is **Genie**), a **CommandButton** to tell the animated character when to speak and the **Microsoft Agent** control. Note that the **Microsoft Agent** control is only visible in the form of one of the characters displayed on the screen. When the user types a string in the **TextBox** and clicks the **Speak** button, the currently selected character speaks the text the user typed.

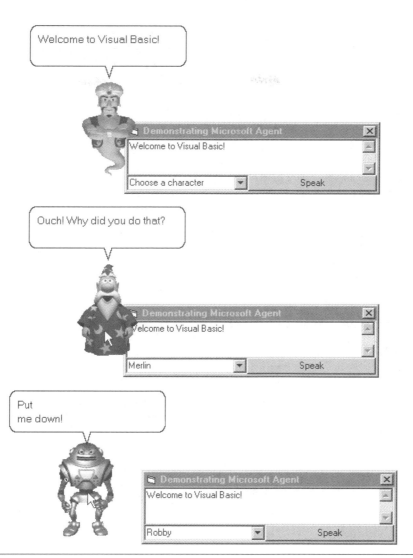

**Fig. 20.1**   Demonstrating **Microsoft Agent** (part 4 of 4).

To use the **Microsoft Agent** control, it must first be added to the toolbox by selecting **Components...** from the **Project** menu to display the **Components** dialog box. In the dialog box, scroll down and select the option **Microsoft Agent Control 1.5**. When selected properly, a small check mark appears in the box to the left of the option. Click the **OK** button when you are done to dismiss the dialog box. The icon for the **Microsoft Agent** control will be at the bottom of the toolbox.

Lines 4 and 5,

```
Dim currentCharacter As IAgentCtlCharacter
Dim characterLocation As String
```

declare two form-level variables for use in this program. Data type **IAgentCtlCharacter** is used to declare variables that refer to **Microsoft Agent** animated characters. At all times during the execution of this program, variable **currentCharacter** refers to the currently selected animated character. Variable **characterLocation** is a **String** that indicates where the animated character description files (these files end with the **.acs** extension) are stored on your system. These files describe the animations that are performed by each character. On our system we installed these files in the directory

```
c:\program files\microsoft agent\characters\
```

Remember, you must download **Microsoft Agent** and the character descriptions from the site **http://www.microsoft.com/workshop/imedia/agent**.

The **Form_Load** procedure (lines 7 through 26) begins by displaying an **InputBox** in which the user can specify the location of the character description files or accept the default location specified above.

Lines 15 through 20,

```
Call Agent1.Characters.Load( _
    "Genie", characterLocation & "genie.acs")
Call Agent1.Characters.Load( _
    "Merlin", characterLocation & "merlin.acs")
Call Agent1.Characters.Load( _
    "Robby", characterLocation & "robby.acs")
```

load the three character descriptions for the predefined animated characters. Property *Characters* of the **Microsoft Agent** control **Agent1** is a **Collection** of the loaded character definitions which are stored as *Character* objects. The *Load* procedure loads a character description using two arguments—a string representing the name used in the program to refer to the character and a string containing the directory and file name for the file containing the character description.

Procedure **Form_Activate** (lines 28 through 36) executes when the form is first displayed on the screen. Line 31,

```
Set currentCharacter = Agent1.Characters("Genie")
```

uses the **Characters** collection object to set the current character to **Genie**. The expression **Agent1.Characters("Genie")** returns a **Character** object that is used to interact with the character.

Lines 32 and 33,

```
Call currentCharacter.MoveTo( _
    frmMSAgent.Left \ 20, frmMSAgent.Top \ 20)
```

use method *MoveTo* of the **IAgentCtlCharacter** interface to indicate the position at which the character is displayed on the screen in pixels from the upper-left corner of the screen. We chose to position the character based on the **Left** and **Top** edges of the form by dividing the number of twips for each by 20. Remember that there are 20 twips per point and 72 points to an inch. We are assuming that a pixel is approximately one point in size.

Line 34,

```
Call currentCharacter.Show
```

uses method *Show* of the **IAgentCtlCharacter** interface to display the character on the screen.

Line 35,

```
Call currentCharacter.Speak(txtToSpeak.Text)
```

uses method *Speak* of the **IAgentCtlCharacter** interface to cause the character to speak the text in the **txtToSpeak TextBox**. At any time, the user can click the **Speak** button to call event procedure **cmdSpeak_Click** (lines 84 through 92) and have the character speak the text in **txtToSpeak**. If the **TextBox** is empty, the character speaks, "**Please, type the words you want me to speak.**"

When a character is initially displayed on the screen, event procedure *Agent1_Show* (lines 68 through 71) is called. Line 70,

```
Call currentCharacter.Play("Acknowledge")
```

uses method *Play* of interface **IAgentCtlCharacter** to play one of the predefined animations associated with the current character. Each animation has a string name that is passed to **Play** to specify the animation to perform, and **Play** immediately plays the animation. In this case, we chose to have the character *Acknowledge* the user with a nod of its head. Genie and Merin have 104 predefined animations; Robby has 94 predefined animations. The majority of the animations are available for each of the predefined characters. We used only common animations in this example. The complete animation sets are listed in the **Microsoft Agent** documentation on the Microsoft Web site.

To have some fun with the animated characters, we decided to use several **Microsoft Agent** control event procedures to have the characters speak in response to mouse interactions. When you click the character (i.e., poking it with the mouse), event procedure **Agent1_Click** (lines 38 through 44) executes. The character speaks, "**Ouch! Why did you do that?**" and two animations are played with lines 42 and 43,

```
Call currentCharacter.Play("Confused")
Call currentCharacter.Play("ConfusedReturn")
```

which specify to play the *Confused* and *ConfusedReturn* animations. Many of the animations are paired such that the character changes its expression or body movements for the first animation in the pair, then the **Return** version of the animation returns the character to its default position. We chose the **Confused** animation here because we wanted the character to appear as if it was not sure why you would poke it with the mouse. By performing these animations, you get a better sense of the interactivity and "social skills" of the characters being presented.

When you double-click the character (i.e., poking it with the mouse twice rapidly), event procedure **Agent1_DblClick** (lines 46 through 52) executes. Two animations are played with lines 49 and 50,

```
Call currentCharacter.Play("Alert")
Call currentCharacter.Play("AlertReturn")
```

which specify to play the *Alert* and *AlertReturn* animations. We chose the **Alert** animation here because we wanted the character to appear annoyed when you poke it twice quickly. The character then speaks, "**Stop it!**"

If you drag the character around the screen with the mouse, event procedure **Agent1_DragStart** (lines 54 through 60) is called at the beginning of the drag operation. The character plays the **Alert** animation again and says, "**Put me down!**" When you drop the character on the screen, event procedure **Agent1_DragComplete** (lines 62 through 66) is called and the character says, "**Thank you!**"

When a character is chosen from the **ComboBox cboCharacter**, event procedure **cboCharacter_Click** (lines 73 through 82) executes. Line 76,

```
Call currentCharacter.Hide
```

hides the current character with **IAgentCtlCharacter** method *Hide*. Line 77,

```
Set currentCharacter = Agent1.Characters(cboCharacter.Text)
```

sets the current character by using the chosen string to select one of the loaded characters from the **Characters** collection of the **Microsoft Agent** control. Lines 78 and 79,

```
Call currentCharacter.MoveTo( _
    frmMSAgent.Left \ 20, frmMSAgent.Top \ 20)
```

use method **MoveTo** of the **IAgentCtlCharacter** interface to determine the starting position on the screen (in pixels from the upper-left corner of the screen) for the selected character. Line 80,

```
Call currentCharacter.Show
```

displays the character with **IAgentCtlCharacter** method **Show**. Line 81,

```
Call currentCharacter.Speak(txtToSpeak.Text)
```

uses method **Speak** of the **IAgentCtlCharacter** interface to cause the displayed character to speak.

Figure 20.2 shows some other **Microsoft Agent** events. For a complete listing of events, see the **Microsoft Agent** documentation at the Microsoft Web site.

Figure 20.3 shows some other properties and methods of the **Character** object. Remember that the **Character** object represents a character that is displayed on the screen and allows interaction with that character. For a complete listing of properties and methods, see the **Microsoft Agent** documentation at the Microsoft Web site.

| Event | Description |
|---|---|
| **BalloonHide** | Called when the text balloon for a character is hidden. |
| **BalloonShow** | Called when the text balloon for a character is shown. |
| **Hide** | Called when a character is hidden. |
| **Move** | Called when a character is moved on the screen. |
| **Show** | Called when a character is displayed on the screen. |
| **Size** | Called when a character's size is changed. |

**Fig. 20.2**    Other events for the **Microsoft Agent** control.

Figure 20.4 shows some speech output tags that can customize speech output properties. These tags are inserted in the text string that will be spoken by the animated character and methods of the **Character** object. Remember that the **Character** object represents a character that is displayed on the screen and allows interaction with that character. Speech output tags generally remain in effect from the time at which they are encountered until the end of the current **Speak** method call. For a complete listing of speech output tags, see the **Microsoft Agent** documentation at the Microsoft Web site.

| Property or method | Description |
| --- | --- |
| *Properties* | |
| **Height** | The height of the character in pixels. |
| **Left** | The left edge of the character in pixels from the left of the screen. |
| **Name** | The default name for the character. |
| **Speed** | The speed of the character's speech. |
| **Top** | The top edge of the character in pixels from the top of the screen. |
| **Width** | The width of the character in pixels. |
| *Methods* | |
| **Activate** | Sets the currently active character when multiple characters appear on the screen. |
| **GestureAt** | Specifies that the character should gesture toward a location on the screen that is specified in pixel coordinates from the upper-left corner of the screen. |
| **Get** | Used to download animation information when the character is downloaded via the World Wide Web using HTTP protocol. |
| **Interrupt** | Interrupts the current animation. The next animation in the queue of animations for this character is then displayed. |
| **Stop** | Stops the animation for the character. |
| **StopAll** | Stops all animations of a specified type for the character. |

**Fig. 20.3**    Other properties and methods for the **Character** object.

| Tag | Description |
| --- | --- |
| **\Chr=**_string_**\** | Specifies the tone of the voice. Possible values for *string* are **Normal** (the default) for a normal tone of voice, **Monotone** for a monotone voice or **Whisper** for a whispered voice. |
| **\Emp\** | Emphasizes the next spoken word. |
| **\Lst\** | Repeats the last statement spoken by the character. This tag must be the only content of the string in the **Speak** method call. |

**Fig. 20.4**    Speech output tags (part 1 of 2).

| Tag | Description |
|-----|-------------|
| **\Pau**=*number*\ | Pauses speech for *number* milliseconds. |
| **\Pit**=*number*\ | Changes the pitch of the character's voice. This value is specified in the range 50 to 400 hertz for the **Microsoft Agent** speech engine. |
| **\Spd**=*number*\ | Changes the speech speed to a value in the range 50 to 250. |
| **\Vol**=*number*\ | Changes the volume to a value in the range 0 (silent) to 65535 (maximum volume). |

**Fig. 20.4**    Speech output tags (part 2 of 2).

## 20.3 Multimedia MCI Control

The **Multimedia MCI Control** (we refer to it as the **MCI Control**) enables a program to interact with any multimedia device connected to the computer that supports the *Media Control Interface (MCI)*—a standard for controlling multimedia devices. Some common devices the MCI control supports are sound boards, MIDI sequencers, CD-ROM drives, audio players, videodisc players and videotape players.

The control provides a series of buttons that correspond to typical buttons on a multimedia device such as a CD player or a VCR. Figure 20.5 shows the **MCI Control** with all of its buttons disabled. When the **MCI Control** is connected to a device, the buttons that are supported by that device are automatically enabled. The control can be customized to display only buttons that are relevant to the current multimedia device.

Figure 20.5 shows key properties and events of the **Multimedia MCI Control**.

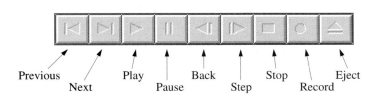

**Fig. 20.5**    The **Multimedia MCI Control**.

| Property or event | Description |
|-------------------|-------------|
| *Properties* | |
| **Command** | A string that specifies the command to execute. Possible values are **Open**, **Close**, **Play**, **Pause**, **Stop**, **Back**, **Step**, **Prev**, **Next**, **Seek**, **Record**, **Eject**, **Sound** and **Save**. |

**Fig. 20.6**    Key features of the **Multimedia MCI Control** (part 1 of 3).

| Property or event | Description |
|---|---|
| DeviceType | A string that specifies the type of device. Possible values are **AVIVideo**, **CDAudio**, **DAT**, **DigitalVideo**, **MMMovie**, **Other**, **Overlay**, **Scanner**, **Sequencer**, **VCR**, **Videodisc** and **WaveAudio**. |
| Notify | When set to **False**, this property disables notification of when the next MCI command completes. Subsequent MCI commands ignore this property until it is assigned another value. |
| Shareable | Determines if the device can be shared between applications (**True**) or should be exclusive to one application (**False**). |
| Track | Specifies the current track. |
| TrackLength | Determines the length of the current track specified by property **Track**. |
| Tracks | Specifies the total number of tracks. |
| UpdateInterval | Specifies the number of milliseconds between calls to the **StatusUpdate** event procedure. |
| Wait | Determines if the next MCI command should complete before returning control to the application (**True**) or if control can be returned before the command completes (**False**). |
| *Button*Enabled | Determines if a button on the control is enabled (**True**) or disabled (**False**). *Button* is one of **Open**, **Close**, **Play**, **Pause**, **Stop**, **Back**, **Step**, **Prev**, **Next**, **Seek**, **Record**, **Eject**, **Sound** and **Save**. |
| *Button*Visible | Determines if a button on the control is visible (**True**) or not visible (**False**). *Button* is one of **Open**, **Close**, **Play**, **Pause**, **Stop**, **Back**, **Step**, **Prev**, **Next**, **Seek**, **Record**, **Eject**, **Sound** and **Save**. |
| Error | Specifies the error code returned from the last MCI command. |
| ErrorMessage | Message for the **Error** returned from the last MCI command. |
| Length | Specifies the length of the media opened by the MCI control. |
| TimeFormat | Specifies the format in which the time information is stored for each of the time-related properties of the MCI control. |
| Frames | Number of **Frames** to move for commands **Step** and **Back**. |
| Mode | Specifies the mode of the MCI device at execution time. Possible values are **mciModeNotOpen**, **mciModeStop**, **mciModePlay**, **mciModeRecord**, **mciModeSeek**, **mciModePause** and **mciModeReady**. |
| Position | Specifies the current position of an open MCI device. |
| TrackPosition | Specifies the current position of the current **Track**. |
| *Events* | |
| StatusUpdate | Called at fixed intervals specified by the **UpdateInterval** property to allow an application to update the display and inform the user about the status of the current MCI device. Status information can be obtained from properties such as **Position**, **Length**, **TrackPosition**, **TrackLength** and **Mode**. |

Fig. 20.6    Key features of the **Multimedia MCI Control** (part 2 of 3).

| Property or event | Description |
|---|---|
| *Button***Click** | Called when a button on the MCI control is clicked. *Button* is one of **Open**, **Close**, **Play**, **Pause**, **Stop**, **Back**, **Step**, **Prev**, **Next**, **Seek**, **Record**, **Eject**, **Sound** and **Save**. |
| *Button***Completed** | Called when a command issued by clicking a button on the MCI control completes. *Button* is one of **Open**, **Close**, **Play**, **Pause**, **Stop**, **Back**, **Step**, **Prev**, **Next**, **Seek**, **Record**, **Eject**, **Sound** and **Save**. |
| *Button***GotFocus** | Called when a button becomes the active button on the MCI control (i.e., gains input focus). *Button* is one of **Open**, **Close**, **Play**, **Pause**, **Stop**, **Back**, **Step**, **Prev**, **Next**, **Seek**, **Record**, **Eject**, **Sound** and **Save**. |
| *Button***LostFocus** | Called when a previously active button becomes inactive on the MCI control (i.e., loses the input focus). *Button* is one of **Open**, **Close**, **Play**, **Pause**, **Stop**, **Back**, **Step**, **Prev**, **Next**, **Seek**, **Record**, **Eject**, **Sound** and **Save**. |
| **Done** | Called when the current command completes. |

**Fig. 20.6**  Key features of the **Multimedia MCI Control** (part 3 of 3).

## 20.3.1 A Multimedia MCI Control CD Player

Figure 20.7 demonstrates the **Multimedia MCI Control** using the computer's CD-ROM device with an audio CD.

When the user loads an audio CD into the computer's CD-ROM device, the **MCI Control** automatically enables the buttons on the **MCI Control** that can be used with audio CDs. For a standard CD-ROM containing an audio CD, the **Back**, **Step** and **Record** buttons are always disabled on the **MCI Control**.

To use the **Multimedia MCI Control**, it must first be added to the toolbox by selecting **Components...** from the **Project** menu to display the **Components** dialog box. In the dialog box, scroll down and select the option **Microsoft Multimedia Control 6.0**. When selected properly, a small check mark appears in the box to the left of the option. Click the **OK** button when you are done to dismiss the dialog box. The icon for the **Multimedia MCI Control** will be at the bottom of the toolbox.

When the program executes, procedure **Form_Load** (lines 6 through 15) executes. Line 7 sets the **MCI Control**'s **Notify** property to **False** to disable the **Done** event procedure from executing after each MCI command completes. Line 8 sets the **MCI Control**'s **Wait** property to **True** to indicate that an MCI command should complete before returning control to the program. Line 9 sets the **MCI Control**'s **Shareable** property to **False** to indicate that only one application at a time can use the specified MCI device (in this case the CD-ROM drive). Line 10 sets the **MCI Control**'s **DeviceType** property to **"CDAudio"** to indicate that this control is used to manage a CD-ROM drive containing an audio CD in this program. Line 12 sets the **MCI Control**'s **Command** property to **"Open"** to indicate that the device should be opened (for a CD this means prepare the CD for playing by opening a connection between the program and the device). Line 13 uses the **MCI Control**'s **Tracks** property to determine the number of tracks on the CD and displays that value in the **txtTotalTracks TextBox**.

```vb
1   ' Fig. 20.7
2   ' Using the Microsoft Multimedia MCI Control
3   ' as an audio CD player.
4   Option Explicit
5
6   Private Sub Form_Load()
7      MMControl1.Notify = False
8      MMControl1.Wait = True
9      MMControl1.Shareable = False
10     MMControl1.DeviceType = "CDAudio"
11
12     MMControl1.Command = "Open"
13     txtTotalTracks.Text = Format$(MMControl1.Tracks, "00")
14  End Sub
15
16  Private Sub Form_Unload(Cancel As Integer)
17     MMControl1.Command = "Stop"
18     MMControl1.Command = "Close"
19  End Sub
20
21  Private Sub MMControl1_NextCompleted(Errorcode As Long)
22     Call UpdateInformation
23  End Sub
24
25  Private Sub MMControl1_PrevCompleted(Errorcode As Long)
26     Call UpdateInformation
27  End Sub
28
29  Private Sub MMControl1_StatusUpdate()
30     Call UpdateInformation
31  End Sub
32
33  Private Sub UpdateInformation()
34     Dim min1 As Integer, min2 As Integer
35     Dim sec1 As Integer, sec2 As Integer
36
37     txtCurrentTrack.Text = Format$(MMControl1.Track, "00")
38     txtTrackLength.Text = _
39        Format$(MMControl1.TrackLength And &HFF, "00") & ":" & _
40        Format$((MMControl1.TrackLength And &HFF00) \ &H10000, _
41           "00")
42  End Sub
```

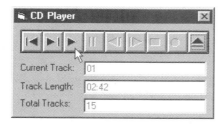

**Fig. 20.7**　　Using the Microsoft **Multimedia MCI Control** to control the CD-ROM drive as an audio CD player (part 1 of 2).

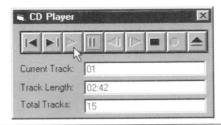

**Fig. 20.7**   Using the Microsoft **Multimedia MCI Control** to control the CD-ROM drive as an audio CD player (part 2 of 2).

Event procedure **Form_Unload** (lines 16 through 19) executes when the application terminates. Lines 17 and 18 set the **MCI Control**'s **Command** property to **"Stop"** and **"Close"** to stop playing the CD and to close the connection to the device, respectively.

Event procedures **NextCompleted** (line 21) and **PreviousCompleted** (Line 25) are called when the command to move to the next track is completed and when the command to move to the previous track is completed, respectively. Event procedure **StatusUpdate** (line 29) is called to indicate the current status of the device to the program. All three procedures call user-defined procedure **UpdateInformation** (lines 33 through 42) to update the **txtCurrentTrack** and **txtTrackLength TextBox**es for the current track on the CD. The **MCI Control**'s **Track** and **TrackLength** properties are used to determine the current track and track length, respectively.

## 20.3.2 A Multimedia MCI Control AVI File Player

Figure 20.8 demonstrates how to add audio and video to an application using the **Multimedia MCI Control** with *AVI (audio-video interleave) files*. Several sample files of this type can be found in the directory

```
C:\Program Files\Microsoft Visual Studio\Common\
Graphics\Videos
```

that is created when you install Visual Basic.

```
1   ' Fig. 20.8
2   ' Using the Microsoft Multimedia MCI Control to
3   ' play AVI files with audio
4   Option Explicit
5
6   Private Sub Form_Load()
7       MMControl1.Notify = False
8       MMControl1.Wait = True
9       MMControl1.Shareable = False
10      MMControl1.DeviceType = "AVIVideo"
11      MMControl1.UpdateInterval = 500
12   End Sub
```

**Fig. 20.8**    Using the **MCI Control** to play AVI files containing audio and video (part 1 of 2).

```
13
14   Private Sub cmdGetAVI_Click()
15       CommonDialog1.Filter = "AVI (*.avi)|*.avi"
16       CommonDialog1.ShowOpen
17       MMControl1.Command = "Close"
18       MMControl1.FileName = CommonDialog1.FileName
19       MMControl1.Command = "Open"
20   End Sub
21
22   Private Sub Form_Terminate()
23       MMControl1.Command = "Close"
24   End Sub
25
26   Private Sub MMControl1_PlayClick(Cancel As Integer)
27       cmdGetAVI.Enabled = False
28   End Sub
29
30   Private Sub MMControl1_StatusUpdate()
31       If (MMControl1.Mode <> mciModePlay And _
32           MMControl1.Mode <> mciModePause) Then
33           cmdGetAVI.Enabled = True
34       End If
35   End Sub
```

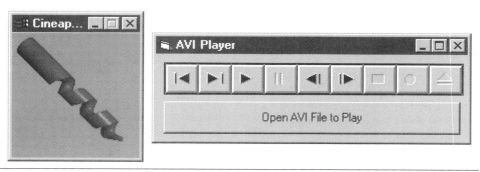

**Fig. 20.8**    Using the **MCI Control** to play AVI files containing audio and video (part 2 of 2).

Remember, the **Multimedia MCI Control** must be added to the toolbox before it can be used in the program.

When the program executes, procedure **Form_Load** (lines 6 through 12) executes. Line 7 sets the **MCI Control**'s **Notify** property to **False** to disable the **Done** event procedure from executing after each MCI command completes. Line 8 sets the **MCI Control**'s **Wait** property to **True** to indicate that an MCI command should complete before returning control to the program. Line 9 sets the **MCI Control**'s **Shareable** property to **False** to indicate that only one application at a time can use the specified MCI device (in this case the AVI player). Line 10 sets the **MCI Control**'s **DeviceType** property to **"AVIVideo"** to indicate that this control is used to manage playing of AVI files in this program. Line 11 sets the **MCI Control**'s **UpdateInterval** property to **500** milliseconds. This causes a call to the **StatusUpdate** event procedure every half second.

When the user clicks the **Open AVI File to Play** button, event procedure **cmdGetAVI_Click** (lines 14 through 20) executes and displays a **CommonDialog** control to allow the user to open an AVI file. Lines 17 through 19,

```
MMControl1.Command = "Close"
MMControl1.FileName = CommonDialog1.FileName
MMControl1.Command = "Open"
```

set the **MCI Control**'s **Command** property to **Close** to shut down the previous AVI file that was playing, set the **MCI Control**'s **FileName** property to the name of the new AVI file to play and set the **MCI Control**'s **Command** property to **"Open"** to open the new AVI file for playing.

When the program terminates, event procedure **Form_Terminate** (line 22) sets the MCI Control's **Command** property to **Close** to shut down the AVI file that was playing (if any) when the application terminated.

When the user clicks the *Play* button on the **MCI Control**, event procedure **MMControl1_PlayClick** (line 26) executes and disables the button **cmdGetAVI** so the user cannot open a new file while the current file is playing.

When the **MMControl1_StatusUpdate** (line 30) event procedure executes, a test is performed to determine if the **MCI Control**'s **Mode** property is **mciModePlay** or **mciModePause**. If the AVI file is not in the playing or paused state, the button **cmdGetAVI** is enabled again so the user can choose a new AVI file.

Note that when an AVI file is played, a separate window automatically appears to display the video.

## 20.4 Animation Control

The **Animation** *control* allows you to create controls that display AVI file animations. The control can play only AVI files that have no sound. Figure 20.9 demonstrates the **Animation** control.

```
1    ' Fig. 20.9
2    ' Using the Animation control to play AVI files
3    Option Explicit
4
5    Private Sub Form_Load()
6        Call SizeComponents
7    End Sub
8
9    Private Sub cmdGetAVI_Click()
10       CommonDialog1.Filter = "AVI (*.avi)|*.avi"
11       CommonDialog1.ShowOpen
12       On Error GoTo errorhandler
13       Call Animation1.Open(CommonDialog1.FileName)
14       Animation1.Play
15       Exit Sub
```

**Fig. 20.9**    Using the **Animation** control to play AVI files (part 1 of 3).

```
16   errorhandler:
17      MsgBox ("Cannot play AVI files containing audio. " & _
18         "Please choose another file.")
19   End Sub
20
21   Private Sub Form_Resize()
22      Call SizeComponents
23   End Sub
24
25   Private Sub SizeComponents()
26      On Error Resume Next
27      cmdGetAVI.Left = 0
28      cmdGetAVI.Width = ScaleWidth
29      cmdGetAVI.Top = ScaleHeight - cmdGetAVI.Height
30      Animation1.Width = ScaleWidth
31      Animation1.Height = ScaleHeight - cmdGetAVI.Height
32   End Sub
```

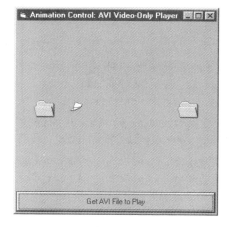

**Fig. 20.9**    Using the **Animation** control to play AVI files (part 2 of 3).

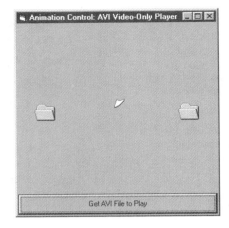

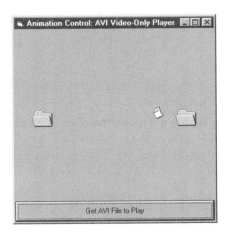

**Fig. 20.9**    Using the **Animation** control to play AVI files (part 3 of 3).

To use the **Animation** control, it must first be added to the toolbox by selecting **Components...** from the **Project** menu to display the **Components** dialog box. In the dialog box, scroll down and select the option **Microsoft Windows Common Controls-2 6.0**. Click the **OK** button when you are done to dismiss the dialog box. The icons for the common controls will be at the bottom of the toolbox. The icon for the **Animation** control looks like a small film strip and displays the tool-tip "**Animation**" when the mouse is positioned over the icon.

When the program executes, the **Form_Load** procedure (line 5) is called, which in turn calls our user-defined procedure **SizeComponents** (line 25) to size the **Animation** control and **CommandButton**. The user can resize the application window at any time to accommodate larger AVI file images. Each resize operation results in a call to **Form_Resize** (line 21), which also calls **SizeComponents**.

When the user clicks the **Get AVI File to Play** button, event procedure **cmdGetAVI_Click** (line 9) executes to load an AVI file and play it. Line 12,

```
On Error GoTo errorhandler
```

indicates that on an error the program should jump to the **errorhandler** label and display a **MsgBox** with an error message.

Line 13,

```
Call Animation1.Open(CommonDialog1.FileName)
```

calls the **Animation** control's **Open** method to open the file the user chose with the **CommonDialog** control. If an attempt is made to open an AVI file containing audio, an error is generated.

Line 14,

```
Animation1.Play
```

calls the **Animation** control's **Play** method to play the loaded AVI file. The **Animation** control automatically loops the animation in the AVI file.

Figure 20.10 shows some key properties and methods of the **Animation** control.

| Property or method | Description |
|---|---|
| *Properties* | |
| **AutoPlay** | If set to **True**, the **Animation** control automatically plays the AVI file when it is opened. Otherwise, the **Play** method must be called to start the animation. |
| **BackStyle** | Specifies if the animation is displayed on a transparent background or on the background specified in the AVI file. This is a design-time-only property. |
| **Center** | If set to **True**, the animation is centered on the **Animation** control. Otherwise, the animation is displayed in the upper-left corner of the control. |

**Fig. 20.10**   Key properties and methods for the **Animation** control (part 1 of 2).

| Property or method | Description |
|---|---|
| *Methods* | |
| Close | Closes the current AVI file in the **Animation** control. |
| Open | Opens the specified AVI file in the **Animation** control. |
| Play | Plays the specified AVI file that is loaded in the **Animation** control. |
| Stop | Stops the current AVI file that is loaded in the **Animation** control. |

**Fig. 20.10**    Key properties and methods for the **Animation** control (part 2 of 2).

## 20.5  RealAudio ActiveX Control Library

The company *Real Networks* has become known for its streaming audio and video capabilities that allow everyone from low-end modem users connecting to the Internet via a phone line to users on high-speed company networks to receive quality audio and video over the Internet. Streaming audio and video allows users to receive portions of a larger audio or video clip, begin playing the clip and continue receiving more of the audio or video clip from the Internet at the same time. By installing Visual Basic, you have also installed Microsoft's Internet Explorer Web browser, which includes the **RealAudio** ActiveX control. This control can be used in standard Windows applications to add capabilities for receiving streaming audio and video. The basic player is also free for download from the Real Networks Web site at

> **http://www.real.com**

Updated versions of the control can be downloaded from this site at any time.

There are many sites on the Internet that are dedicated to live audio, live video and pre-recorded audio and video that can be received with the **RealAudio** control. Several of these sites are listed in Fig. 20.11.

| Site | Description |
|---|---|
| **http://www.timecast.com** | |
| | This site is dedicated to live broadcasts on the Internet with listings of audio and video presentations. |
| **http://www.timecast.com/stations/index.html** | |
| | This area of the TimeCast site is dedicated to radio stations that broadcast on the Internet. |
| **http://www.on-air.com** | |
| | This site is the home of an Internet-only radio station that plays music 24 hours a day without commercials. |

**Fig. 20.11**    Sites that contain listings of streaming audio and video over the Internet (part 1 of 2).

| Site | Description |
|------|-------------|

`http://www.audionet.com`

This site provides samplings of current music in CD-quality sound.

**Fig. 20.11**   Sites that contain listings of streaming audio and video over the Internet (part 2 of 2).

The program of Fig. 20.12 demonstrates the **RealAudio** ActiveX control. For complete details of this control, visit the Real Networks Web site at

`http://www.real.com`

```
1   ' Fig. 20.12
2   ' Demonstrating the RealAudio ActiveX control
3   Option Explicit
4   Option Base 1
5   Dim sites(3, 2) As String
6
7   Private Sub Form_Load()
8       Dim x As Integer
9       sites(1, 1) = "NASA Live"
10      sites(1, 2) = "http://www.spacezone.com/nasa.ram"
11      sites(2, 1) = "CBS SportsLine Live"
12      sites(2, 2) = _
13          "http://chat.sportsline.com/u/audio/radio30.ram"
14      sites(3, 1) = "C-SPAN Radio Live"
15      sites(3, 2) = "http://www.c-span.org/ram/wcsp.ram"
16
17      For x = 1 To 3
18          cboSites.AddItem (sites(x, 1))
19      Next x
20  End Sub
21
22  Private Sub cboSites_Click()
23      RealAudio1.Source = sites(cboSites.ListIndex + 1, 2)
24  End Sub
```

**Fig. 20.12**   Demonstrating the **RealAudio** ActiveX control.

To use the **RealAudio** ActiveX control, it must first be added to the toolbox by selecting **Components...** from the **Project** menu to display the **Components** dialog box. In the dialog box, scroll down and select the option **RealAudio ActiveX Control**. When selected properly, a small check mark appears in the box to the left of the option. Click the **OK** button when you are done to dismiss the dialog box. The icon for the **Real-Audio** control will be at the bottom of the toolbox.

Line 5 declares a two-dimensional array called **sites** in which we store the name and URL for several live audio sites on the Internet. The first row of the array stores the location for *NASA Live*, the second row stores the location of *CBS Sportsline Live* and the third row of the array stores the location for *C-SPAN Radio Live*.

When the program executes, the **Form_Load** procedure (line 7) executes and populates the array with the name and URL of each site listed above. The names of the sites are then added to the **ComboBox cboSites**.

When the user selects a site from **cboSites**, event procedure **cboSites_Click** (line 22) executes. Line 23,

```
RealAudio1.Source = sites(cboSites.ListIndex + 1, 2)
```

sets the **Source** property of the **RealAudio** control to the URL for the site selected by the user. Once the **Source** property is set, the control automatically attempts to connect to the site. If a connection is established, the **Play** button becomes active. The audio can be played simply by clicking the **Play** button. The control then buffers some audio. Once the audio starts playing, the control continues to buffer future audio, thus allowing the control to overcome most situations in which the audio being sent to the program slows down due to traffic on the Internet. With a high-speed connection, it is rare for network traffic to affect the playing of the audio.

## 20.6 Marquee Control Library

The *Marquee Control Library* provides the **Marquee** *control* for scrolling an image from a specified URL in any direction. This control is used mainly with Web pages and is installed on your system when you install the Internet Explorer Web browser. The program of Fig. 20.13 demonstrates the **Marquee** control.

```
1   ' Fig. 20.13
2   ' Using the Marquee control to scroll an image
3   Option Explicit
4
5   Private Sub Form_Load()
6       Marquee1.ScrollDelay = 25
7       Marquee1.ScrollPixelsX = 1
8       Marquee1.ScrollPixelsY = 0
9       Marquee1.WidthOfPage = 180
10
11      Call Marquee1.insertURL(0, "c:\images\deitel0.gif")
12
13      Call cboXStyle.AddItem("Circular")
```

**Fig. 20.13**    Using the Marquee control to scroll an image (part 1 of 2).

```
14        Call cboXStyle.AddItem("Bounce")
15        Call cboYStyle.AddItem("Circular")
16        Call cboYStyle.AddItem("Bounce")
17        txtDelay.Text = Str$(Marquee1.ScrollDelay)
18        txtX.Text = Str$(Marquee1.ScrollPixelsX)
19        txtY.Text = Str$(Marquee1.ScrollPixelsY)
20        txtZoom.Text = Str$(Marquee1.Zoom)
21     End Sub
22
23     Private Sub cmdX_Click()
24        Marquee1.ScrollPixelsX = CInt(txtX.Text)
25     End Sub
26
27     Private Sub cmdY_Click()
28        Marquee1.ScrollPixelsY = CInt(txtY.Text)
29     End Sub
30
31     Private Sub cmdDelay_Click()
32        Marquee1.ScrollDelay = CInt(txtDelay.Text)
33     End Sub
34
35     Private Sub cmdZoom_Click()
36        Marquee1.Zoom = CInt(txtZoom.Text)
37     End Sub
38
39     Private Sub cboXStyle_Click()
40        Marquee1.ScrollStyleX = cboXStyle.Text
41     End Sub
42
43     Private Sub cboYStyle_Click()
44        Marquee1.ScrollStyleY = cboYStyle.Text
45     End Sub
```

**Fig. 20.13**   Using the Marquee control to scroll an image (part 2 of 2).

The program consists of a **Marquee** control to display the image and several **Text-Box**es, **CommandButton**s and **ComboBox**es to allow the user to customize the scrolling of the image.

To use the **Marquee** control, it must first be added to the toolbox by selecting **Components...** from the **Project** menu to display the **Components** dialog box. In the dialog box, scroll down and select the option **Marquee Control Library**. When selected properly, a small check mark appears in the box to the left of the option. Click the **OK** button when you are done to dismiss the dialog box. The icon for the **Marquee** control will be at the bottom of the toolbox.

When procedure **Form_Load** (line 5) executes, lines 6 through 9,

```
Marquee1.ScrollDelay = 25
Marquee1.ScrollPixelsX = 1
Marquee1.ScrollPixelsY = 0
Marquee1.WidthOfPage = 180
```

set several properties of the **Marquee** control. Property **ScrollDelay** indicates the interval in milliseconds at which the image scrolled in the **Marquee** is redisplayed (every **25** milliseconds in this program). Property **ScrollPixelsX** indicates the number of pixels the image moves horizontally to the right at a time (**1** pixel at a time in this program). Setting a negative value for this property results in scrolling to the left. Property **Scroll-PixelsY** indicates the number of pixels the image moves vertically down at a time (the image does not scroll vertically in this program until the user modifies the **ScrollPixelsY** value). Setting a negative value for this property results in scrolling toward the top of the application. Property **WidthOfPage** specifies the width in pixels of the scrolling area—wider **WidthOfPage** values result in less frequent scrolling of the image.

Line 11,

```
Call Marquee1.insertURL(0, "c:\images\deitel0.gif")
```

calls **Marquee** method **insertURL** to add the URL of an image to scroll. The first argument indicates the index in the set of URLs at which the new URL will be added. We specified a local file system URL for a file in the directory **c:\images**. (Note: You may need to change this directory to where you installed this example on your system.) The **Marquee** control's **currentURL** property can be used to cycle through the different URLs to display by specifying the appropriate index number.

Lines 13 through 16,

```
Call cboXStyle.AddItem("Circular")
Call cboXStyle.AddItem("Bounce")
Call cboYStyle.AddItem("Circular")
Call cboYStyle.AddItem("Bounce")
```

populate the two **ComboBox**es—**cboXStyle** and **cboYStyle**—with the strings **"Circular"** and **"Bounce"** that indicate the style of scrolling for the image on the **Marquee** in the *x* and *y* directions (**ScrollStyleX** and **ScrollStyleY**), respectively. The default scroll style is **"Circular"**—when the image hits an edge, the image continues scrolling in the same direction from the opposite edge (i.e., when the image goes off the right side, it continues scrolling from the left side). When the scroll style is set to **"Bounce"**, the image bounces off the edge in the opposite direction.

Lines 17 through 20,

```
txtDelay.Text = Str$(Marquee1.ScrollDelay)
txtX.Text = Str$(Marquee1.ScrollPixelsX)
```

```
txtY.Text = Str$(Marquee1.ScrollPixelsY)
txtZoom.Text = Str$(Marquee1.Zoom)
```

set the our **TextBox**es to the values of properties **ScrollDelay**, **ScrollPixelsX**, **ScrollPixelsY** and **Zoom**, respectively. Property **Zoom** allows the image to be scaled by specifying a percentage of the original image's size. The default percentage is 100%, specified as the integer 100.

The user can change the values of properties **ScrollDelay**, **ScrollPixelsX**, **ScrollPixelsY** and **Zoom** by typing a new value in the appropriate **TextBox** and clicking the **CommandButton** to its right. The user can change the scroll style by selecting a string from one of the **ComboBox**es. The event procedures for clicking the **CommandButton**s and the **ComboBox**es make the changes to the appropriate properties and result in immediate changes in the characteristics of the scrolling image.

Figure 20.14 shows additional properties, methods and events of the **Marquee** control. For a complete listing, see your on-line Visual Studio documentation.

## 20.7 Microsoft ActiveMovie Control

The **ActiveMovie** control enables an application to play video and sound in many multimedia formats, including *MPEG (Motion Pictures Experts Group) audio* and *video*, *AVI (audio-video interleave) video*, *WAV (Windows wave file format) audio*, *MIDI (Music Instrument Digital Interface) audio* and *Apple® QuickTime® video*. Such files can be created with many sound and graphics software packages, and preexisting audio and video can be found all over the Internet. Also, there are quite a number of media files in the directory

| Property, method or event | Description |
|---|---|
| *Properties* | |
| **LoopsX** | Sets the number of times the image scrolls or bounces horizontally. A value of -1 indicates that the looping or bouncing should be infinite. |
| **LoopsY** | Sets the number of times the image scrolls or bounces vertically. A value of -1 indicates that the looping or bouncing should be infinite. |
| *Methods* | |
| **Pause** | Temporarily stops scrolling of the image. |
| **Resume** | Restarts scrolling of the image. |
| *Events* | |
| **OnStartOfImage** | Called just before the image appears in the **Marquee**. |
| **OnEndOfImage** | Called when the image scrolls completely off the screen. |
| **OnBounce** | Called when the scroll style is **"Bounce"** and the image bounces. |
| **OnScroll** | Called when the scroll style is **"Circular"** and the image is about to be scrolled. |
| **OnLMouseClick** | Called when the user clicks the left mouse button in the **Marquee**. |

**Fig. 20.14**   Key properties, methods and events for the **Marquee** control.

```
c:\Windows\Media
```

In fact, you can search your system for files of the types listed above. Figure 20.15 lists the types of files supported by **ActiveMovie** and their typical file name extensions.

The **ActiveMovie** control provides several buttons that allow the user to manipulate the media clip being played. These buttons are shown in Fig. 20.16. Figure 20.17 demonstrates the **ActiveMovie** control for playing media in an application.

| File type | Extension(s) |
| --- | --- |
| MPEG | `.mpg`, `.mpeg` |
| AVI | `.avi` |
| WAV | `.wav` |
| MIDI | `.mid`, `.rmi` |
| Apple QuickTime | `.mov` |

**Fig. 20.15**  File types supported by the **ActiveMovie** control and their typical file name extensions.

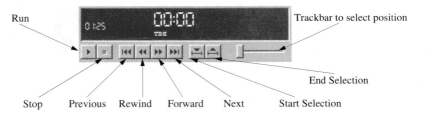

**Fig. 20.16**  The buttons of the **ActiveMovie** control.

```
1    ' Fig. 20.17
2    ' Demonstrating the ActiveMovie control
3    Option Explicit
4
5    Private Sub cmdOpenFile_Click()
6       dlgOpen.Filter = "All files (*.*)|*.*|"
7       Call dlgOpen.ShowOpen
8       ActiveMovie1.FileName = dlgOpen.FileName
9    End Sub
10
11   Private Sub ActiveMovie1_Error(ByVal SCode As Integer, _
12        ByVal Description As String, ByVal Source As String, _
13        CancelDisplay As Boolean)
14      MsgBox ("Invalid file type. Please choose another file.")
15   End Sub
```

**Fig. 20.17**  Using the **ActiveMovie** control to play media files (part 1 of 2).

**Fig. 20.17**   Using the **ActiveMovie** control to play media files (part 2 of 2).

To use the **ActiveMovie** control, it must first be added to the toolbox by selecting **Components...** from the **Project** menu to display the **Components** dialog box. In the dialog box, scroll down and select the option **Microsoft ActiveMovie Control**. Click the **OK** button when you are done to dismiss the dialog box. The icon for the **Active-Movie** control will be at the bottom of the toolbox.

The program consists of three controls—a **CommandButton**, a **CommonDialog** and an **ActiveMovie** control. When the user clicks the **CommandButton**, the **CommonDialog** control is displayed so the user can select a file to play. The **ActiveMovie** control has its **FullScreenMode**, **ShowPositionControls** and **ShowSelectionControls** set to **True** (the default is **False** for all three) at design time. Property **FullScreenMode** determines whether or not video clips take over the entire computer screen when the *Play* button is pressed on the **ActiveMovie** control. Properties **ShowPositionControls** and **ShowSelectionControls** determine whether or not the position controls (buttons *Previous*, *Rewind*, *Forward* and *Next*) and the selection controls (buttons *Start Selection* and *End Selection*) are displayed.

When the program executes and the user clicks the **Open File to Play** button, event procedure **cmdOpenFile_Click** (line 5) executes and line 7 displays the **CommonDialog**. When the user selects a file to play, line 8,

         **ActiveMovie1.FileName = dlgOpen.FileName**

assigns the name of the file to property **FileName** of the **ActiveMovie** control. Now the file can be played by the control. If an error occurs, event procedure **ActiveMovie1_Error** (line 11) executes to indicate that the user chose an invalid file format.

Execute the program and try manipulating the media clip using the buttons on the **ActiveMovie** control. When you press the *Play* button, notice that video clips are displayed using the entire screen.

Figure 20.18 shows several key properties, methods and events of the **ActiveMovie** control. For a detailed listing of all the properties, methods and events of the **ActiveMovie** control, see the on-line documentation.

| Property, method or event | Description |
|---|---|
| *Properties* | |
| **AllowChangeDisplayMode** | Determines if the user can change the display mode between seconds and frames (**True** if so, **False** if not). |
| **AllowHideControls** | Determines if the user can hide the control panel (**True** if so, **False** if not). |
| **AllowHideDisplay** | Determines if the user can hide the display panel at run-time (**True** if so, **False** if not). |
| **AutoRewind** | If **True**, the media clip returns to the starting point when the control reaches the end of the selection. |
| **AutoStart** | If **True**, the media clip automatically plays after it loads. |
| **CurrentPosition** | The current position (in seconds) of the media clip. |
| **CurrentState** | The state of the media clip (stopped, paused or running). |
| **DisplayMode** | Show the current position in seconds (**amvSeconds**) or frames (**amvFrames**). |
| **EnableContextMenu** | If **True**, a shortcut menu is enabled an accessible via a right mouse click on the control. |
| **EnablePositionControls** | Determines if the position buttons are enabled (**True** if so, **False** if not). |
| **EnableSelectionControls** | Determines if the selection buttons are enabled (**True** if so, **False** if not). |
| **EnableTracker** | Determines if the trackbar control is enabled (**True** if so, **False** if not). |
| **MovieWindowSize** | Determines the size of the playback area. |
| **PlayCount** | Determines the number of times the media clip is played. |
| **SelectionEnd** | The ending position in seconds relative to the media clip's beginning. |
| **SelectionStart** | The starting position in seconds relative to the media clip's beginning. |
| **ShowControls** | Determines if the controls panel is displayed (**True** if so, **False** if not). |
| **ShowDisplay** | Determines if the display panel is dispayed (**True** if so, **False** if not). |
| **ShowTracker** | Determines if the trackbar is displayed (**True** if so, **False** if not). |
| *Methods* | |
| **Pause** | Pauses the media clip. |
| **Run** | Runs the media clip. |

**Fig. 20.18**   Key properties, methods and events for the **ActiveMovie** control (part 1 of 2).

| Property, method or event | Description |
|---|---|
| `Stop` | Stops the media clip. |
| `IsSoundCardEnabled` | Determines if the sound card for the computer is enabled. |
| *Events* | |
| `PositionChange` | Called when the user changes the position of the media clip using the buttons of the **ActiveMovie** control. |
| `ReadyStateChange` | Called to indicate changes in the ready state of the control. Possible values are **amvUninitialized** (the control has not been initialized with a file to play), **amvLoading** (the file to play is currently loading), **amvInteractive** (there is enough data to begin playing the file), **amvComplete** (the entire file is loaded and ready to play). |
| `StateChange` | Called to indicate a change in the state of the **ActiveMovie** control (such as from running to stopped). |

**Fig. 20.18**    Key properties, methods and events for the **ActiveMovie** control (part 2 of 2).

## Summary

- Multimedia is the use of sound, images, graphics and video to make applications "come alive."

- Most new computers are being sold "multimedia ready" with CD-ROM drives, audio boards and sometimes with special video capabilities.

- Multimedia demands extraordinary computing power.

- **Microsoft Agent** is a technology for interactive animated characters.

- **Microsoft Agent** provides three predefined characters—Genie, Merlin and Robby the Robot—that allow users of an application to interact with the application using more natural human communication techniques.

- The **Microsoft Agent** control accepts both mouse and keyboard interactions and also supports speech recognition.

- Data type **IAgentCtlCharacter** is used to declare variables that refer to **Microsoft Agent** animated characters.

- Animated character description files (**.acs** extension) describe the animations that are performed by each character.

- Property **Characters** of the **Microsoft Agent** control is a **Collection** of the loaded character definitions which are stored as **Character** objects.

- The **Load** procedure loads a character description into the **Characters Collection**.

- Method **MoveTo** of the **IAgentCtlCharacter** interface indicates the position of the character on the screen in pixels from the upper-left corner of the screen. Method **Show** displays a character. Method **Speak** causes the character to speak the specified text. Method **Hide** hides the current character. Method **Play** plays one of the predefined animations associated with a character. Each animation has a string name that is passed to **Play** to specify the animation to perform.

- When a character is displayed on the screen, event procedure **Show** executes. Clicking a character calls event procedure **Click**. Double-clicking the character calls event procedure **DblClick**.

Dragging the character calls event procedure **DragStart**. Releasing the character after a drag calls event procedure **DragComplete**. Event procedure **BalloonHide** executes when the text balloon for a character is hidden. Event procedure **BalloonShow** executes when the text balloon for a character is shown. Event procedure **Hide** executes when a character is hidden. Event procedure **Move** executes when a character is moved on the screen. Event procedure **Show** executes when a character is displayed on the screen. Event procedure **Size** executes when a character's size is changed.

- **Character** object property **Height** is the height of the character in pixels, and **Width** is the width of the character in pixels. Property **Left** is the left side of the character in pixels from the left edge of the screen, and **Top** is the top side of the character in pixels from the top of the screen. Property **Speed** is the speed of the character's speech.

- **Character** object method **Activate** sets the currently active character. Method **GestureAt** specifies that the character should gesture at a specific location on the screen in pixels from the upper-left corner of the screen. Method **Get** downloads animation information from the Web. Method **Interrupt** interrupts the current animation. Method **Stop** stops the current animation. Method **StopAll** stops all animations a a specified type.

- Speech output tags customize speech output properties.

- The **Multimedia MCI Control** enables a program to interact with any multimedia device connected to the computer that supports the Media Control Interface (MCI)—a standard for controlling multimedia devices.

- The **MCI Control** provides a series of buttons that correspond to typical buttons on a multimedia device such as a CD player or a VCR. The control can be customized to display only buttons that are relevant to the current multimedia device.

- **MCI Control** event **StatusUpdate** is called at fixed intervals specified by the **UpdateInterval** property to allow an application to update the display and inform the user about the status of the current MCI device. Event *Button***Click** is called when a button is clicked on the **MCI Control**. Event *Button***Completed** is called when a command issued by clicking a button on the **MCI Control** completes. Event *Button***GotFocus** is called when a button becomes the active button on the **MCI Control**. Event *Button***LostFocus** is called when a button becomes the inactive button on the **MCI Control**. Event **Done** is called when the current command completes.

- The **Animation** control displays AVI file animations with no sound.

- **Animation** control method **Open** opens the AVI file to play. If an attempt is made to open an AVI file containing audio, an error is generated. Method **Play** plays the loaded AVI file. Method **Close** closes the loaded AVI file. Method **Stop** stops playing the loaded AVI file.

- **Animation** control property **AutoPlay** determines if the **Animation** control automatically plays the AVI file when it is opened. Property **BackStyle** specifies if the animation is displayed on a transparent background or on the background specified in the AVI file. Property **Center** specifies if the animation is centered on the **Animation** control.

- The **RealAudio** ActiveX control can be used in standard Windows applications to add capabilities for receiving streaming audio and video.

- The **Source** property of the **RealAudio** control specifies the URL for the site containing streaming audio content. Once the **Source** property is set, the control automatically attempts to connect to the site. If a connection is established, the **Play** button becomes active. The audio can be played simply by clicking the **Play** button.

- The Marquee Control Library provides the **Marquee** control for scrolling an image from a specified URL in any direction.

- **Marquee** method **insertURL** adds the URL of an image to scroll to the **Marquee**. **Marquee** property **currentURL** can be used to cycle through multiple URLs. Method **Pause** pauses the scrolling of the image. **Marquee** method **Resume** resumes the scrolling of the image.

- **Marquee** event procedure **OnStartOfImage** executes just before the image appears in the **Marquee**. Event procedure **OnEndOfImage** executes when the image scrolls completely off the screen. Event procedure **OnBounce** executes when the image bounces. Event procedure **OnScroll** executes when the image scrolls. Event procedure **OnLMouseClick** executes when the **Marquee** is clicked with the left mouse button.

- The **ActiveMovie** control enables an application to play video and sound in many multimedia formats, including MPEG (Motion Pictures Experts Group) audio and video, AVI (audio-video interleave) video, WAV (Windows wave file format) audio, MIDI (Music Instrument Digital Interface) audio and Apple® QuickTime® video.

- **ActiveMovie** method **Pause** pauses the clip. Method **Run** runs the clip. **ActiveMovie** method **Stop** stops the clip. Method **IsSoundCardEnabled** determines if the sound card is enabled.

- **ActiveMovie** event procedure **Error** executes if an error occurs using the **ActiveMovie** control. Event procedure **PositionChange** is called when the user changes the position of the clip. Event procedure **ReadyStateChange** is called to indicate the ready state of the control for playing a clip. Event procedure **StateChange** is called to indicate state transitions for the control (such as running to stopped).

## Terminology

**Acknowledge** animation
**ActiveMovie** control
**ActiveMovie** property
   **AllowChangeDisplayMode**
**ActiveMovie** property
   **AllowHideControls**
**ActiveMovie** property
   **AllowHideDisplay**
**ActiveMovie** property **AutoRewind**
**ActiveMovie** property **AutoStart**
**ActiveMovie** property **CurrentPosition**
**ActiveMovie** property **CurrentState**
**ActiveMovie** property **DisplayMode**
**ActiveMovie** property
   **EnableContextMenu**
**ActiveMovie** property
   **EnablePositionControls**
**ActiveMovie** property
   **EnableSelectionControls**
**ActiveMovie** property **EnableTracker**
**ActiveMovie** property **FileName**
**ActiveMovie** property **FullScreenMode**
**ActiveMovie** method
   **IsSoundCardEnabled**
**ActiveMovie** property **MovieWindowSize**
**ActiveMovie** method **Pause**
**ActiveMovie** property **PlayCount**

**ActiveMovie** event **PositionChange**
**ActiveMovie** event **ReadyStateChange**
**ActiveMovie** method **Run**
**ActiveMovie** property **SelectionEnd**
**ActiveMovie** property **SelectionStart**
**ActiveMovie** property **ShowControls**
**ActiveMovie** property **ShowDisplay**
**ActiveMovie** property
   **ShowPositionControls**
**ActiveMovie** property
   **ShowSelectionControls**
**ActiveMovie** property **ShowTracker**
**ActiveMovie** event **StateChange**
**ActiveMovie** method **Stop**
**Alert** animation
**AlertReturn** animation
animation
**Animation** control
**Animation** property **AutoPlay**
**Animation** property **BackStyle**
**Animation** property **Center**
**Animation** method **Close**
**Animation** method **Open**
**Animation** method **Play**
**Animation** method **Stop**
audio
AVI (audio-video interleave) file

## Self-Review Exercises

**20.1**     Fill in the blanks in each of the following:
   a)  _____ is a technology for interactive animated characters.
   b)  A _____ is a standard format for an address of a piece of information on the Internet.
   c)  The _____ control provides a series of buttons that correspond to typical buttons on a multimedia device such as a CD player or a VCR.
   d)  The _____ control displays AVI file animations with no sound.
   e)  The _____ control scrolls an image from a specified URL in any direction.
   f)  The _____ control enables an application to play video and sound in many multimedia formats, including MPEG (Motion Pictures Experts Group) audio and video, AVI (audio-video interleave) video, WAV (Windows wave file format) audio, MIDI (Music Instrument Digital Interface) audio and Apple® QuickTime® video.

## Answers to Self-Review Exercises

**20.1**     a) Microsoft Agent.  b) **URL**.  c) **Multimedia MCI**.  d) **Animation**.  e) **Marquee**.
   f) **ActiveMovie**.

## Exercises

**20.2**     *(Story Teller)* Record audio for a large number of nouns, verbs, articles, prepositions, etc. Then use random number generation to forms sentences and have your program speak the sentences.

**20.3**     *(Limericks)* Modify the limerick writing program you wrote in Exercise 8.15 to sing the limericks your program creates.

**20.4**     *(Background Audio)* Add background audio to one of your favorite applications by using the **Multimedia Control** to play the sound in the background while you interact with your application in the normal way.

**20.5**     *(Text Flasher)* Create a Visual Basic application that repeatedly flashes text on the screen. Do this by interspersing the text with a plain background color image. Allow the user to control the "blink speed" and the background color or pattern.

**20.6**     *(Image Flasher)* Create a Visual Basic application that repeatedly flashes an image on the screen. Do this by interspersing the image with a plain background color image.

**20.7**     *(Towers of Hanoi)* Write an animated version of the Towers of Hanoi problem we presented in Exercise 6.32. As each disk is lifted off a peg or slid onto a peg play a "whooshing" sound. As each disk lands on the pile play a "clunking" sound. Play some appropriate background music.

**20.8**     *(Digital Clock)* Implement an application that displays a digital clock on the screen. You might add options to scale the clock; display day, month and year; issue an alarm; play certain audios at designated times and the like.

**20.9**     *(Analog Clock)* Create a Visual Basic application that displays an analog clock with hour, minute and second hands that move appropriately as the time changes.

**20.10**     *(Dynamic Customized Newsletter)* After you complete Chapter 19 you will understand how to develop Internet-based Visual Basic applications that access the World Wide Web. Develop a "newspaper of the future" in which your user uses a graphical user interface to design a customized dynamic newspaper which meets that user's unique information needs. Then have your application harvest information from the World Wide Web at the designated intervals, possibly continuously.

You'll be amazed to see how many popular publications offer computerized versions at no charge on the Web.

**20.11**   *(Dynamic Audio and Graphical Kaleidoscope)* Develop a kaleidoscope application that displays reflected graphics to simulate the popular children's toy. Incorporate audio effects that "mirror" your application's dynamically changing graphics.

**20.12**   *(One-Armed Bandit)* Develop a multimedia simulation of a one-armed bandit. Have three spinning wheels. Place various fruits and symbols on each wheel. Use true random-number generation to simulate the spinning of each wheel and the stopping of each wheel on a symbol.

**20.13**   *(Horse Race)* Create a Visual Basic simulation of a horse race. Have multiple contenders. Use audios for a race announcer. Play the appropriate audios to indicate the correct status of each of the contenders throughout the race. Use audios to announce the final results. You might try to simulate the kind of horse race games that are often played at carnivals. The players get turns at the mouse and have to perform some skill-oriented manipulation with the mouse to advance their horses.

**20.14**   *(Artist)* Design a Visual Basic art application that will give an artist a great variety of capabilities to draw, use images, use animations and the like to create a dynamic multimedia art display.

**20.15**   *(Karaoke)* Create a Karaoke system that plays the music for a song and displays the words for your user to sing at the appropriate time.

**20.16**   *(Calling Attention to an Image)* If you want to emphasize an image, you might place a row of simulated light bulbs around your image. You can let the light bulbs flash in unison or you can let them fire on and off in sequence one after the other.

**20.17**   *(Physics Demo: Kinetics)* If you have taken physics, implement a Visual Basic application that will demo concepts like energy, inertia, momentum, velocity, acceleration, friction, coefficient of restitution, gravity and others. Create visual effects and use audios where appropriate for emphasis and realism.

**20.18**   *(On-Line Product Catalog)* Companies are rapidly realizing the potential for doing business on the Web. Develop an on-line multimedia catalog from which your customers may select products to be shipped. After reading Chapter 19, you are able to handle the networking aspects of this problem. If you have an actual company, you should read the latest articles on secure transmission of credit card IDs over the Internet.

**20.19**   *(Reaction Time/Reaction Precision Tester)* Create a Visual Basic application that moves a randomly created shape around the screen. The user moves the mouse to catch and click on the shape. The shape's speed and size can be varied. Keep statistics on how much time the user typically takes to catch a shape of a given size. The user will probably have more difficulty catching faster moving smaller shapes.

**20.20**   *(Image Zooming)* Create a Visual Basic application that enables you to zoom in on, or away from, an image.

**20.21**   *(Calendar/Tickler File)* Create a general purpose calendar and "tickler" file. Use audio and images. For example, the application should sing "Happy Birthday" to you when you use it on your birthday. Have the application display images and play audios associated with important events. Have the application remind you in advance of important events. It would be nice, for example, to have the application give you a week's warning so you can pick up an appropriate greeting card for that special person.

**20.22**    *(Project: Automated Teller Machine) [Note: This project will require that you use advanced Visual Basic techniques from Chapters 14, 15, 19 and 20. This is an excellent group project.]* One of the authors had the privilege of teaching at the division of one of the largest banks in the United States that builds the hardware and software for the automated teller machines that the bank deploys worldwide. During this teaching engagement the author got a behind-the-scenes peek at the "automated teller machine of the future." Develop the framework of a Visual Basic application that implements an automated teller machine and simulates its interaction with a bank's accounts maintained by another computer. The first version of your application should simulate automated teller machines pretty much as they operate today. Then let your creative juices flow and try to design your own version of the "automated teller machine of the future." Use graphics, animation, sound and any other capabilities of Visual Basic, the World Wide Web and the Internet that you wish to employ.

**20.23**    *(Multimedia-Based Simpletron Simulator)* Modify the Simpletron simulator that you developed in Exercises 10.18 through 10.20 to include multimedia features. Add computer-like sounds to indicate that the Simpletron is executing instructions. Add a breaking glass sound when a fatal error occurs. Use flashing lights to indicate which cells of memory and/or which registers are currently being manipulated. Use other multimedia techniques as appropriate to make your Simpletron simulator more valuable as an educational tool to its users.

# 21

# Data Structures, Collections, Dictionaries

## Objectives

- To be able to form linked data structures using references, self-referential classes and recursion.
- To create and manipulate data structures such as linked lists, queues, stacks and binary trees.
- To understand various important applications of linked data structures.
- To understand how to create reusable data structures with classes and composition.
- To be able to use the Visual Basic **Collection** and **Dictionary** objects.

*'Will you walk a little faster?' said a whiting to a snail,*
*'There's a porpoise close behind us, and he's treading on my*
*tail.'*
Lewis Carroll

*There is always room at the top.*
Daniel Webster

*Push on—keep moving.*
Thomas Morton

*I think that I shall never see*
*A poem lovely as a tree.*
Joyce Kilmer

*Much that I bound, I could not free;*
*Much that I freed returned to me.*
Lee Wilson Dodd

# Outline

## 21.1 Introduction

We have studied fixed-size *data structures* such as single-subscripted arrays and double-subscripted arrays. This chapter introduces *dynamic data structures* that grow and shrink at execution time. *Linked lists* are collections of data items "lined up in a row"—insertions and deletions are made anywhere in a linked list. *Stacks* are important in compilers and operating systems—insertions and deletions are made only at one end of a stack—its *top*. *Queues* represent waiting lines; insertions are made at the back (also referred to as the *tail*) of a queue, and deletions are made from the front (also referred to as the *head*) of a queue. *Binary trees* facilitate high-speed searching and sorting of data, efficient elimination of duplicate data items, representing file system directories and compiling expressions into machine language. These data structures have many other interesting applications.

We will discuss each of the major types of data structures and implement programs that create and manipulate these data structures. We use classes and composition to create and package these data structures for reusability and maintainability. In addition, we demonstrate Visual Basic's pre-defined **Collection** and **Dictionary** data structures.

The chapter examples are practical programs that you will be able to use in more advanced courses and in industry applications. The programs are especially heavy on reference manipulation. The exercises include a rich collection of useful applications.

## 21.2 Type `Variant`

Data type **Variant** is the default data type for variables that are not explicitly declared as a specific data type. **Variant**s can be declared by explicitly using keyword **Variant** as the data type in a declaration. For example, in the declarations

```
Dim anyValue1 as Variant
Dim anyValue2
```

**anyValue1** is explicitly declared as a **Variant** and **anyValue2** is a **Variant** by default. Type **Variant** does not have a type-declaration character.

Data type **Variant** can store any type of data (other than fixed-length **String**s) including instances of user-defined types defined with a **Type** statement and objects. As such, **Variant**s are ideal for building reusable data structures such as linked lists, queues, stacks and trees because the code that manipulates the data structure can be written independent of the data type of the elements that will be stored in the data structure. This is the approach taken by Visual Basic's **Collection** and **Dictionary** objects that are presented at the end of this chapter.

Numeric values stored in a **Variant** must be in the following ranges:

1. **-1.79769313486231E308** to **-4.94066E-324** for negative values

2. **4.94066E-324** to **1.79769313486231E308** for positive values

A number stored in a **Variant** is maintained as its original data type in the **Variant**. When arithmetic is performed on a **Variant** containing a number and the result is outside the normal range of values for the number's actual data type, the result is stored in the **Variant** as the next larger data type (**Byte** becomes **Integer**, **Integer** becomes **Long**, **Long** and **Single** become **Double**).

**Common Programming Error 21.1**

*Attempting to assign a number outside the range of a **Double** to a **Variant** is a run-time error.*

**Performance Tip 21.1**

*Arithmetic is faster with **Integer**s than with **Variant**s. **Variant**s consume more memory resources. They should not be used if the data type is known in advance and is not expected to change at execution time.*

**Performance Tip 21.2**

***Variant**s generally consume more memory (16 bytes each) than other data types.*

The data type in a **Variant** can be determined using functions **VarType** and **Type-Name**. Function **VarType** returns an Integer indicating the type of the value in the Variant. Function **VarType** returns an **Integer** that describes the type. Some **VarType** return values are **vbEmpty** (**0**—uninitialized), **vbNull** (**1**—no valid data), **vbInteger** (**2**), **vbLong** (**3**), **vbSingle** (**4**), **vbDouble** (**5**), **vbCurrency** (**6**), **vbDate** (**7**), **vbString** (**8**), **vbObject** (**9**), **vbBoolean** (**11**), **vbDecimal** (**14**) and **vbByte** (**17**). For example, assuming the following declarations and assignments:

```
Dim var1 As Variant, var2 As Variant, var3 As Variant
var1 = 22890        ' Assign Integer
var2 = "VB6"        ' Assign String
var3 = True         ' Assign Boolean
```

the expressions

```
VarType(var1)
VarType(var2)
VarType(var3)
```

result in **2** (**Integer**), **8** (**String**) and **11** (**Boolean**), respectively.

Function **TypeName** returns a **String** indicating the name of the type for the value stored in a **Variant**. For example, based on the preceding declarations and assignments, **TypeName(var3)** returns the **String** "Boolean."

## 21.3 Self-Referential Classes

A *self-referential class* contains a member that refers to a class object of the same class type. For example, the **CListNode** definition from file **CListNode.cls** of Fig. 21.3,

```
Private mNodeData As Variant
Private mNextNode As CListNode

Public Property Get Data() As Variant
   Data = mNodeData
End Property

Public Property Let Data(ByVal vNewValue As Variant)
   mNodeData = vNewValue
End Property

Public Property Get NextNode() As CListNode
   Set NextNode = mNextNode
End Property

Public Property Let NextNode(ByVal vNewValue As Variant)
   Set mNextNode = vNewValue
End Property
```

defines a class containing two **Private** module variables—**Variant** variable **mNode-Data** and **CListNode** reference **mNextNode**. Member **mNextNode** references an object of class **CListNode**—an object of the same type as the one being declared here, hence the term "self-referential class." Member **mNextNode** is referred to as a *link* (i.e., **mNextNode** is used to "tie" an object of class **CListNode** to another object of the same class). Class **CListNode** also has four property procedures: a **Property Let** procedure **Data** to set the value **mNodeData**, a **Property Get** procedure **Data** to return the value of **mNodeData**, a **Property Let** procedure **NextNode** to set the value of **mNext-Node** and a **Property Get** procedure **NextNode** to return the value of **mNextNode**.

Self-referential objects can be linked together to form data structures such as lists, queues, stacks and trees. Figure 21.1 illustrates two self-referential objects linked together to form a list. A slash—representing a **Nothing** reference—is placed in the link member of the second self-referential object to indicate that the link does not refer to another object. The slash is for illustration purposes; it does not correspond to the backslash character in Visual Basic. A **Nothing** reference normally indicates the end of a data structure.

*Common Programming Error 21.2*

*Not setting the link in the last node of a list to* **Nothing**.

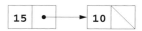

**Fig. 21.1**   Two self-referential class objects linked together.

## 21.4 Dynamic Memory Allocation

Creating and maintaining dynamic data structures requires *dynamic memory allocation*—the ability for a program to obtain more memory space at execution time to hold new nodes and to release space no longer needed. Visual Basic programs do not explicitly release dynamically allocated memory. Rather, Visual Basic performs automatic garbage collection. The limit for dynamic memory allocation can be as large as the amount of available physical memory in the computer or the amount of available virtual memory in a virtual-memory system. Often, the limits are much smaller because the computer's available memory must be shared among many users.

Keyword **New** is essential to dynamic memory allocation. Keyword **New** is followed by the type of the object being dynamically allocated and results in a reference to an object of that type. For example, the statement

```
Set nodeToAdd = New CListNode
```

allocates the appropriate number of bytes to store a **CListNode** object and stores a reference to this memory in **nodeToAdd**. Note that keyword **Set** is required when assigning an object to a reference.

The following sections discuss lists, stacks, queues and trees. These data structures are created and maintained with dynamic memory allocation and self-referential classes.

## 21.5 Linked Lists

A *linked list* is a linear collection of self-referential class objects, called *nodes,* connected by reference *links*—hence, the term "linked" list. A linked list is accessed via a reference to the first node of the list. Subsequent nodes are accessed via the link-reference member stored in each node. By convention, the link reference in the last node of a list is set to **Nothing** to mark the end of the list. Data are stored in a linked list dynamically—each node is created as necessary. A node can contain data of any type, including objects of other classes. Stacks and queues are also linear data structures, and, as we will see, are constrained versions of linked lists. Trees are nonlinear data structures.

Lists of data can be stored in arrays, but linked lists provide several advantages. A linked list is appropriate when the number of data elements to be represented in the data structure at one time is unpredictable. Linked lists are dynamic, so the length of a list can increase or decrease as necessary. The size of a "conventional" fixed-size Visual Basic array, however, cannot be altered, because the array size is set at creation time (remember that Visual Basic does support resizable arrays, but the resizing is not automatic). "Conventional" arrays can become full. Linked lists become full only when the system has insufficient memory to satisfy dynamic storage allocation requests. As we will see later in this chapter, Visual Basic provides the **Collection** object for implementing and manipulating dynamic arrays that can grow and shrink during execution of the program.

*Performance Tip 21.3*

*An array can be declared to contain more elements than the number of items expected, but this can waste memory. Linked lists can provide better memory utilization in these situations. Linked lists allow the program to adapt at run-time.*

*Performance Tip 21.4*

*Insertion into a linked list is fast—only two references have to be modified. All existing nodes remain at their current locations in memory.*

Linked lists can be maintained in sorted order simply by inserting each new element at the proper point in the list. Existing list elements do not need to be moved.

*Performance Tip 21.5*

*Insertion and deletion in a sorted array can be time consuming—all the elements following the inserted or deleted element must be shifted appropriately.*

*Performance Tip 21.6*

*The elements of an array are stored contiguously in memory. This allows immediate access to any array element because the address of any element can be calculated directly based on its position relative to the beginning of the array. Linked lists do not afford such immediate access to their elements.*

Linked list nodes are normally not stored contiguously in memory. Logically, however, the nodes of a linked list appear to be contiguous. Figure 21.2 illustrates a linked list with several nodes.

*Performance Tip 21.7*

*Using dynamic memory allocation (instead of arrays) for data structures that grow and shrink at execution-time can save memory. Keep in mind, however, that references occupy space and that dynamic memory allocation incurs the overhead of procedure calls.*

The program of Fig. 21.3 (whose output is shown in Fig. 21.4) uses a **CList** class to manipulate a list of strings. The data stored in each node of the **CList** is of type **Variant**, so any type of data can be stored. The user interface for the program that tests class CList allows the user to insert values into the list and remove values from the list. After each insertion and deletion operation, the program calls procedure **Display** to display the contents of the list in a **ListBox**. A detailed discussion of the program follows. If an attempt is made to remove an item from an empty list, a **MsgBox** is displayed with the message, "**List is empty**." Exercise 21.20 asks you to implement a recursive procedure that prints a linked list backwards, and Exercise 21.21 asks you to implement a recursive procedure that searches a linked list for a particular data item.

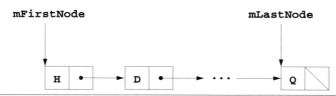

**Fig. 21.2**   A graphical representation of a linked list.

```
1   ' Fig. 21.3
2   ' Class CListNode
3   Option Explicit
4   Private mNodeData As Variant
5   Private mNextNode As CListNode
6
7   Public Property Get Data() As Variant
8      Data = mNodeData
9   End Property
10
11  Public Property Let Data(ByVal vNewValue As Variant)
12     mNodeData = vNewValue
13  End Property
14
15  Public Property Get NextNode() As CListNode
16     Set NextNode = mNextNode
17  End Property
18
19  Public Property Let NextNode(ByVal vNewValue As Variant)
20     Set mNextNode = vNewValue
21  End Property
```

**Fig. 21.3**  Manipulating a linked list (part 1 of 7).

```
22  ' Fix. 21.3
23  ' Class CList
24  Option Explicit
25  Private mFirstNode As CListNode    ' refers to first node in list
26  Private mLastNode As CListNode     ' refers to last node in list
27
28  ' determine if the list is empty
29  Public Function IsEmpty() As Boolean
30     IsEmpty = IIf(mFirstNode Is Nothing, True, False)
31  End Function
32
33  ' insert an element at the beginning of the list
34  Public Sub InsertAtFront(insertItem As Variant)
35     Dim tempNode As CListNode
36
37     If IsEmpty() Then
38        Set mFirstNode = New CListNode
39        Set mLastNode = mFirstNode
40     Else
41        Set tempNode = mFirstNode
42        Set mFirstNode = New CListNode
43        mFirstNode.NextNode = tempNode
44     End If
45
46     mFirstNode.Data = insertItem
47  End Sub
48
```

**Fig. 21.3**  Manipulating a linked list (part 2 of 7).

```
49    ' insert an element at the end of the list
50    Public Sub InsertAtBack(insertItem As Variant)
51       Dim tempNode As CListNode
52
53       If IsEmpty() Then
54          Set mLastNode = New CListNode
55          Set mFirstNode = mLastNode
56       Else
57          Set tempNode = mLastNode
58          Set mLastNode = New CListNode
59          tempNode.NextNode = mLastNode
60       End If
61
62       mLastNode.Data = insertItem
63    End Sub
64
65    ' remove an element from the beginning of the list
66    Public Function RemoveFromFront()
67       Dim removeItem As Variant
68
69       If IsEmpty() Then
70          Call MsgBox("List is empty")
71          RemoveFromFront = Null
72          Exit Function
73       End If
74
75       removeItem = mFirstNode.Data
76
77       If mFirstNode Is mLastNode Then
78          Set mFirstNode = Nothing
79          Set mLastNode = Nothing
80       Else
81          Set mFirstNode = mFirstNode.NextNode
82       End If
83
84       RemoveFromFront = removeItem
85    End Function
86
87    ' remove an element from the end of the list
88    Public Function RemoveFromBack()
89       Dim removeItem As Variant
90       Dim current As CListNode
91
92       If IsEmpty() Then
93          Call MsgBox("List is empty")
94          RemoveFromBack = Null
95          Exit Function
96       End If
97
98       removeItem = mLastNode.Data
99
```

**Fig. 21.3**   Manipulating a linked list (part 3 of 7).

```
100     If mFirstNode Is mLastNode Then
101        Set mFirstNode = Nothing
102        Set mLastNode = Nothing
103     Else
104        Set current = mFirstNode
105
106        While Not current.NextNode Is mLastNode
107           Set current = current.NextNode
108        Wend
109
110        Set mLastNode = current
111        current.NextNode = Nothing
112     End If
113
114     RemoveFromBack = removeItem
115 End Function
116
117 Public Property Get Iterator() As Variant
118     Dim iter As CListIterator
119     Set iter = New CListIterator
120     iter.StartNode = mFirstNode
121     Set Iterator = iter
122 End Property
```

**Fig. 21.3**   Manipulating a linked list (part 4 of 7).

```
123 ' Fig. 21.3
124 ' Class CListIterator
125 Option Explicit
126 Private mBookmark As CListNode
127 Private mFirstNode As CListNode
128
129 Public Property Let StartNode(ByVal vNewValue As Variant)
130     Set mFirstNode = vNewValue
131     Set mBookmark = mFirstNode
132 End Property
133
134 ' return next item in list
135 Public Function NextItem()
136     Dim tempData As Variant
137
138     If mBookmark Is Nothing Then
139        NextItem = Null
140     Else
141        tempData = mBookmark.Data
142        Set mBookmark = mBookmark.NextNode
143        NextItem = tempData
144     End If
145 End Function
146
```

**Fig. 21.3**   Manipulating a linked list (part 5 of 7).

```
147  Public Function HasMoreItems() As Boolean
148     HasMoreItems = IIf(Not mBookmark Is Nothing, True, False)
149  End Function
150
151  ' reset mBookmark to beginning of list
152  Public Sub ResetmBookmark()
153     mBookmark = mFirstNode
154  End Sub
```

**Fig. 21.3**    Manipulating a linked list (part 6 of 7).

```
155  ' Fig. 21.3
156  ' Demonstrating class CList
157  Option Explicit
158  Dim list As New CList
159
160  Private Sub cmdInsertFront_Click()
161     Call list.InsertAtFront(txtInput.Text)
162     Call Display
163  End Sub
164
165  Private Sub cmdInsertBack_Click()
166     Call list.InsertAtBack(txtInput.Text)
167     Call Display
168  End Sub
169
170  Private Sub cmdRemoveFront_Click()
171     txtInput.Text = ""
172     Call list.RemoveFromFront
173     Call Display
174  End Sub
175
176  Private Sub cmdRemoveBack_Click()
177     txtInput.Text = ""
178     Call list.RemoveFromBack
179     Call Display
180  End Sub
181
182  Private Sub Display()
183     Dim elements As New CListIterator
184
185     Call lstOutput.Clear
186     Set elements = list.Iterator
187
188     If elements.HasMoreItems = False Then
189        Call lstOutput.AddItem("The list is empty")
190        Exit Sub
191     End If
192
193     While elements.HasMoreItems
194        Call lstOutput.AddItem(elements.NextItem)
195     Wend
196  End Sub
```

**Fig. 21.3**    Manipulating a linked list (part 7 of 7).

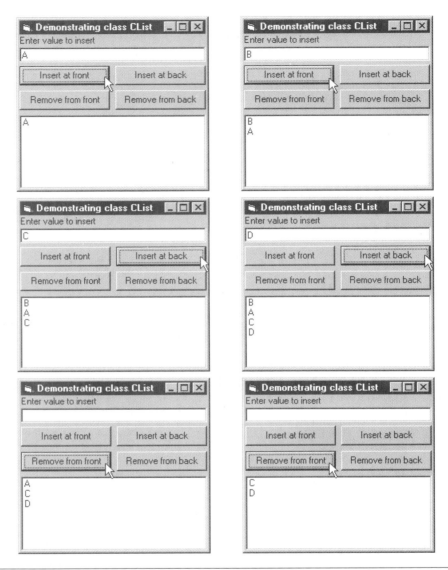

**Fig. 21.4**   Screen captures for the program of Fig. 21.3 (part 1 of 2).

The program of Fig. 21.3 consists of three classes—**CListNode** (lines 1–21), **CList** (lines 22–122) and **CListIterator** (lines 123–154)—and a form to test their capabilities (lines 155–196). Encapsulated in each **CList** object is a linked list of **CListNode** objects. Class **CListNode** consists of **Private** module variables **mNodeData** (type **Variant**) and **mNextNode** (type **CListNode**). Variable **mNodeData** can refer to any object. Variable **mNextNode** stores a reference to the next **CListNode** object in the linked list. Class **CListIterator** provides the ability to maintain a reference into a linked list and use that reference to "walk" the list and manipulate each node in the list.

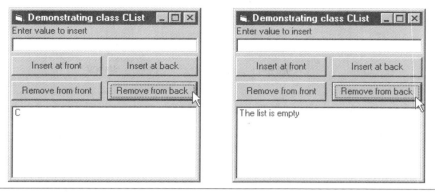

**Fig. 21.4**    Screen captures for the program of Fig. 21.3 (part 2 of 2).

Class **CList** consists of **Private** module variables **mFirstNode** (a reference to the first **CListNode** in a **CList** object) and **mLastNode** (a reference to the last **CListNode** in a **CList** object). When a **CList** is allocated, these variables are set to **Nothing** by default. The primary procedures of the **CList** class are **InsertAtFront**, **InsertAtBack**, **RemoveFromFront** and **RemoveFromBack**. Function **IsEmpty** is called a *predicate function*—it does not alter the list in any way; rather, it determines if the list is empty (i.e., the reference to the first node of the list is **Nothing**). If the list is empty, **IsEmpty** returns **True**; otherwise, **IsEmpty** returns **False**. **Property Get** procedure **Iterator** returns a **CListIterator** object that can be used to walk through a **CList** object (this is also known as *iterating* through the list, thus the name **CListIterator**).

Over the next several pages, we will discuss the procedures of class **CList** in detail. Procedure **InsertAtFront** at line 34 (Fig. 21.5 illustrates the operation) places a new node at the front of the list. The procedure consists of several steps:

1. Call **IsEmpty** to determine if the list is empty (line 37).

2. If the list is empty, set **mFirstNode** to a **New CListNode** (line 38) and set **mLastNode** to refer to the same node as **mFirstNode** (line 39).

3. If the list is not empty, the new node is threaded into the list by setting **tempNode** to refer to the same node as **mFirstNode** (line 41), setting **mFirstNode** to a **New CListNode** (line 42) and setting property **mFirstNode.NextNode** to the node to which **tempNode** refers.

4. Set property **mFirstNode.Data** to the **insertItem** passed as an argument (line 46).

Figure 21.5 illustrates procedure **InsertAtFront**. Part a) of the figure shows the list and the new node during the **InsertAtFront** operation and before the new node has been threaded into the list. (Note that the node is displayed with its new value, but the actual assignment of the data to the node occurs after the node is threaded into the list.) The dashed arrows in part b) illustrate step 3 of the **InsertAtFront** operation, which enables the node containing **G** to become the new first node in the list.

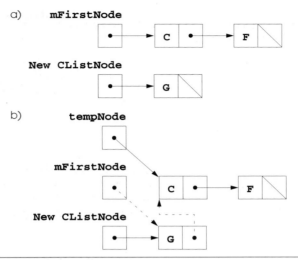

**Fig. 21.5**   The **InsertAtFront** operation.

Procedure **InsertAtBack** at line 50 (Fig. 21.6 illustrates the operation) places a new node at the back of the list. The procedure consists of several steps:

1. Call **IsEmpty** to determine if the list is empty (line 53).

2. If the list is empty, set **mLastNode** to a **New CListNode** (line 54) and set **mFirstNode** to refer to the same node as **mLastNode** (line 55).

3. If the list is not empty, the new node is threaded into the list by setting **tempNode** to refer to the same node as **mLastNode** (line 57), setting **mLastNode** to a **New CListNode** (line 58) and setting property **tempNode.NextNode** to the node to which **mLastNode** refers.

4. Set property **mLastNode.Data** to the **insertItem** passed as an argument (line 62).

Figure 21.6 illustrates an **InsertAtBack** operation. Part a) of the figure shows the list and the new node during the **InsertAtBack** operation and before the new node has been threaded into the list. The dashed arrows in part b) illustrate the steps of procedure **insertAtBack** that enable a new node to be added to the end of a list that is not empty.

Function **RemoveFromFront** at line 66 (illustrated in Fig. 21.7) removes the front node of the list and returns a reference to the removed data. The procedure displays a **MsgBox** with the error message "**List is empty**" if an attempt is made to remove a node from an empty list. Otherwise, a reference to the removed data is returned. The function consists of several steps:

1. If the list is empty (line 69), display a **MsgBox** indicating that the list is empty and return **Null**.

2. If the list is not empty, assign **removeItem** to refer to **mFirstNode.Data** (line 75)—the data being removed from the list.

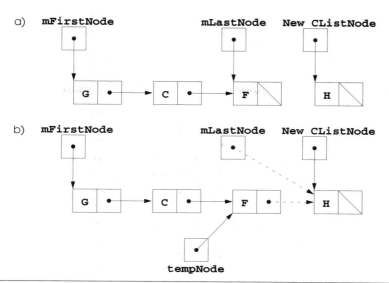

**Fig. 21.6**    The **InsertAtBack** operation.

3. If **mFirstNode** is equal to **mLastNode** (line 77) (i.e., if the list has only one element prior to the removal attempt), then set **mFirstNode** and **mLastNode** to **Nothing** (lines 78 and 79) to dethread that node from the list (leaving the list empty).

4. If the list has more than one node prior to removal, then leave **mLastNode** as is and simply set **mFirstNode** to **mFirstNode.NextNode** (line 81) [i.e., modify **mFirstNode** to reference what was the second node prior to removal (and now, the new first node)].

5. Return the **removeItem** reference (line 84).

Figure 21.7 illustrates procedure **RemoveFromFront**. Part a) illustrates the list before the removal operation. Part b) shows actual reference manipulations.

Function **RemoveFromBack** at line 88 (illustrated in Fig. 21.8) removes the last node of the list and returns a reference to the removed data. The procedure displays a **MsgBox** with the error message "**List is empty**" if an attempt is made to remove a node from an empty list. Otherwise, a reference to the removed data is returned. The function consists of several steps:

1. If the list is empty (line 92), display a **MsgBox** indicating that the list is empty and return **Null**.

2. If the list is not empty, assign **removeItem** to refer to **mLastNode.Data** (line 98)—the data being removed from the list.

3. If **mFirstNode** is equal to **mLastNode** (line 100) (i.e., if the list has only one element prior to the removal attempt), then set **mFirstNode** and **mLastNode** to **Nothing** (lines 101 and 102) to dethread that node from the list (leaving the list empty).

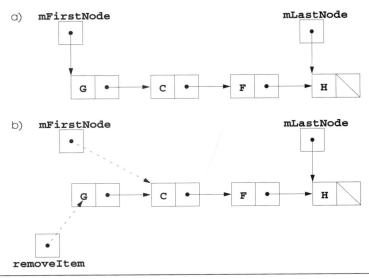

**Fig. 21.7**   The **RemoveFromFront** operation.

4. If the list has more than one node prior to removal, then set **CListNode** reference **current** to **mFirstNode** (line 104).

5. Now "walk the list" with **current** until it references the node before the last node. This is done with a **While** loop (lines 106 through 108) that keeps setting **current** to **current.NextNode** while **current.NextNode** is not **mLastNode**.

6. Set **mLastNode** to **current** to dethread the back node from the list (line 110).

7. Set **current.NextNode** to **Nothing** in the new last node of the list (line 111).

8. Return the **removeItem** reference (line 114).

Figure 21.8 illustrates function **RemoveFromBack**. Part a) illustrates the list before the removal operation. Part b) shows the actual reference manipulations.

**Property Get** procedure **Iterator** (line 117) creates a new **CListIterator** object, sets its **StartNode** property to **mFirstNode** and returns the **CListIterator** object. Class **CListIterator** defines an iterator—an object that allows a program to iterate through (i.e., "walk through") each element of a data structure (a **CList** in this case). Iterators are useful for printing the list as shown in procedure **Display** (line 182) or for applying an operation to each element of a **CList**.

Class **CListIterator** contains two private **CListNode** variables—**mBookmark** and **mFirstNode**. Variable **mFirstNode** maintains a reference to the first node in a **CList** so that the iterator can be reset to the beginning of a **CList** at any time. Variable **mBookmark** maintains the iterator's current position in a **CList**—this is similar to using a bookmark to maintain your position in a book that you are reading. **Property Let** procedure **StartNode** (line 129) initializes the **mFirstNode** and **mBookmark** variables. Function **NextItem** (line 135) returns **Null** if **mBookmark** is **Null** (i.e., there are no

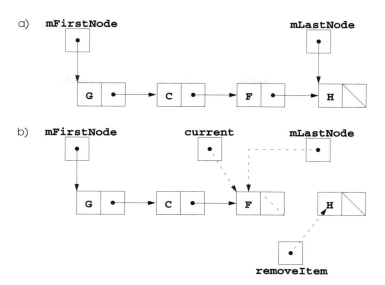

**Fig. 21.8**   The **RemoveFromBack** operation.

more elements in the list). Otherwise, **NextItem** sets **tempData** to refer to **mBookmark.Data** (the data in the current node), sets **mBookmark** to **mBookmark.NextNode** (the next node in the list) and returns **tempData**. Function **HasMoreItems** returns **True** if there are more items in the list; otherwise, **False** is returned. Procedure **ResetBookmark** repositions the iterator to the beginning of the list.

*Software Engineering Observation 21.1*

*If an iterator refers to an item of a list that is subsequently removed, the iterator is no longer valid. A new iterator should be obtained from the list.*

*Common Programming Error 21.3*

*Using an iterator that refers to an element that has been deleted can result in an execution-time error that terminates the application.*

The form in this example provides several buttons that enable the user to insert elements into a list and remove elements from a list by calling the appropriate **CList** methods. Procedure **Display** (line 182) is called after each operation to display the contents of the list after each operation. Line 186 sets **CListIterator** reference **elements** to property **list.Iterator** to obtain an iterator for walking through the elements of the list. Line 188 determines if the list is empty by calling function **elements.HasMoreItems**. If so, the string "**The list is empty**" is displayed in **lstOutput** and procedure **Display** terminates. Otherwise, the while loop at line 193 displays the data in the list. While **elements.HasMoreItems** returns **True**, the loop adds items to **lstOutput** with the statement

```
Call lstOutput.AddItem(elements.NextItem)
```

which calls **elements.NextItem** to get the current node's data value and position the iterator at the next node in the list.

## 21.6 Stacks

A *stack* is a constrained version of a linked list—new nodes can be added to a stack and removed from a stack only at the top. For this reason, a stack is referred to as a *last-in, first-out (LIFO)* data structure. The link member in the last node of the stack is set to **Nothing** to indicate the bottom of the stack.

**Common Programming Error 21.4**

*Not setting the link in the bottom node of a stack to* **Nothing***.*

The primary procedures used to manipulate a stack are **Push** and **Pop**. Procedure **Push** adds a new node to the top of the stack. Procedure **Pop** removes a node from the top of the stack and returns the data from the popped node.

Stacks have many interesting applications. For example, when a procedure call is made, the called procedure must know how to return to its caller, so the return address is pushed onto a stack. If a series of procedure calls occurs, the successive return values are pushed onto the stack in last-in, first-out order so that each procedure can return to its caller. Stacks support recursive procedure calls in the same manner as conventional nonrecursive procedure calls.

Stacks contain the space created for local variables on each invocation of a procedure during a program's execution. When the procedure returns to its caller, the space for that procedure's automatic variables is popped off the stack and those variables are no longer known to the program.

Stacks are also used by compilers in the process of evaluating arithmetic expressions and generating machine language code to process the expressions. The exercises in this chapter explore several applications of stacks.

We will take advantage of the close relationship between lists and stacks to implement a stack class primarily by reusing a list class through composition by including a **CList** object as a **Private** member of a stack class (line 4 of Fig. 21.9). The list, stack and queue data structures in this chapter are implemented to store **Variant** references to encourage further reusability. Thus, any object type can be stored in a list, stack or queue.

Figure 21.9 (output in Fig. 21.10) creates stack class **CStack** through composition of a class **CList** (Fig. 21.3) object. Composition enables us to hide the procedures of class **CList** that should not be in the interface to our stack by providing public interface procedures only to the required **CList** procedures. This technique of implementing each stack procedure as a call to a **CList** procedure is called *forwarding*—the **CStack** procedure invoked *forwards* the call to the appropriate **CList** procedure. Of course, class **CList** contains other procedures (i.e., **InsertAtBack** and **RemoveFromBack**) that we would rather not make accessible through the public interface to the stack class. The stack's procedures each call the appropriate **CList** procedure—procedure **Push** (line 6) calls **list.InsertAtFront**, procedure **Pop** (line 10) calls **list.RemoveFromFront**, **IsStackEmpty** (line 14) calls **list.IsEmpty** and **Iterator** (line 18) calls **list.Iterator**. (Note: Iterators are not normally provided for stacks. We provide iterator capabilities for class **CStack** in this example for demonstration purposes only so we can display the stack contents after each stack operation.)

```
1   ' Fig. 21.9
2   ' Class CStack
3   Option Explicit
4   Private list As New CList
5
6   Public Sub Push(value As Variant)
7      list.InsertAtFront (value)
8   End Sub
9
10  Public Function Pop() As Variant
11     Pop = list.RemoveFromFront()
12  End Function
13
14  Public Function IsStackEmpty() As Boolean
15     IsStackEmpty = list.IsEmpty()
16  End Function
17
18  Public Property Get Iterator() As Variant
19     Set Iterator = list.Iterator
20  End Property
```

**Fig. 21.9**   A simple stack program (part 1 of 2).

```
21  ' Fig. 21.9
22  ' Demonstrating class CStack
23  Option Explicit
24  Dim mStack As New CStack
25
26  Private Sub cmdPush_Click()
27     mStack.Push (txtPush.Text)
28     Call Display
29  End Sub
30
31  Private Sub cmdPop_Click()
32     lblPop.Caption = "Popped: " & mStack.Pop()
33     Call Display
34  End Sub
35
36  Private Sub Display()
37     Dim elements As New CListIterator
38
39     Call lstOutput.Clear
40     Set elements = mStack.Iterator
41
42     If elements.HasMoreItems = False Then
43        Call lstOutput.AddItem("The stack is empty")
44        Exit Sub
45     End If
46
47     While elements.HasMoreItems
48        Call lstOutput.AddItem(elements.NextItem)
49     Wend
50  End Sub
```

**Fig. 21.9**   A simple stack program (part 2 of 2).

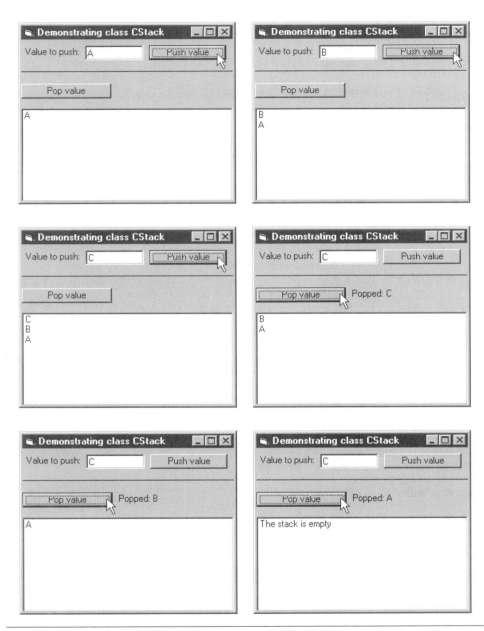

**Fig. 21.10**   Sample output from the program of Fig. 21.9.

Class **CStack** is used in the form to instantiate a stack called **mStack**. The form pro-vides buttons to allow the user to push and pop elements of the stack. The user types values into the **TextBox** and clicks button **Push value** to push an element. Elements are removed with a click of button **Pop value**. Each **Push** and **Pop** operation is followed by a call to **Display** (line 36) to display the stack's current contents.

## 21.7 Queues

Another common data structure is the *queue*. A queue is similar to a checkout line in a supermarket—the first person in line is serviced first and other customers enter the line only at the end and wait to be serviced. Queue nodes are removed only from the *head* of the queue and are inserted only at the *tail* of the queue. For this reason, a queue is referred to as a *first-in, first-out (FIFO)* data structure. The insert and remove operations are known as *Enqueue* and *Dequeue*.

Queues have many applications in computer systems. Most computers have only a single processor, so only one user at a time can be serviced. Entries for the other users are placed in a queue. The entry at the front of the queue is the next to receive service. Each entry gradually advances to the front of the queue as users receive service.

Queues are also used to support print spooling. A multiuser environment may have only a single printer. Many users may be generating outputs to be printed. If the printer is busy, other outputs may still be generated. These are "spooled" to disk (much as thread is wound onto a spool), where they wait in a queue until the printer becomes available.

Information packets also wait in queues in computer networks. Each time a packet arrives at a network node, it must be routed to the next node on the network along the path to the packet's final destination. The routing node routes one packet at a time, so additional packets are enqueued until the router can route them.

A file server in a computer network handles file access requests from many clients throughout the network. Servers have a limited capacity to service requests from clients. When that capacity is exceeded, client requests wait in queues.

Figure 21.11 (output in Fig. 21.12) creates stack class **CQueue** through composition of a class **CList** (Fig. 21.3) object.

```
1    ' Fig. 21.11
2    ' Class CQueue
3    Option Explicit
4    Private list As New CList
5
6    Public Sub Enqueue(value As Variant)
7       list.InsertAtBack (value)
8    End Sub
9
10   Public Function Dequeue() As Variant
11      Dequeue = list.RemoveFromFront()
12   End Function
13
14   Public Function IsQueueEmpty() As Boolean
15      IsQueueEmpty = list.IsEmpty()
16   End Function
17
18   Public Property Get Iterator() As Variant
19      Set Iterator = list.Iterator
20   End Property
```

**Fig. 21.11**   Processing a queue (part 1 of 2).

```
21   ' Fig. 21.11
22   ' Demonstrating class CQueue
23   Option Explicit
24   Dim mQueue As New CQueue
25
26   Private Sub cmdEnqueue_Click()
27      mQueue.Enqueue (txtPush.Text)
28      Call Display
29   End Sub
30
31   Private Sub cmdDequeue_Click()
32      lblDequeue.Caption = "Dequeued: " & mQueue.Dequeue()
33      Call Display
34   End Sub
35
36   Private Sub Display()
37      Dim elements As New CListIterator
38
39      Call lstOutput.Clear
40      Set elements = mQueue.Iterator
41
42      If elements.HasMoreItems = False Then
43         Call lstOutput.AddItem("The queue is empty")
44         Exit Sub
45      End If
46
47      While elements.HasMoreItems
48         Call lstOutput.AddItem(elements.NextItem)
49      Wend
50   End Sub
```

**Fig. 21.11**   Processing a queue (part 2 of 2).

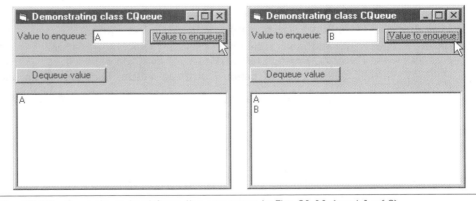

**Fig. 21.12**   Sample output from the program in Fig. 21.11 (part 1 of 2).

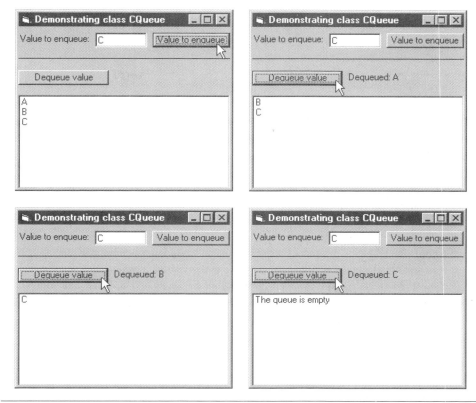

**Fig. 21.12**  Sample output from the program in Fig. 21.11 (part 2 of 2).

The queue's procedures use forwarding—as shown in class **CStack**—to call the appropriate **CList** procedure—procedure **Enqueue** (line 6) calls **list.InsertAt-Back**, procedure **Dequeue** (line 10) calls **list.RemoveFromFront, IsQueue-Empty** (line 14) calls **list.IsEmpty** and **Iterator** (line 18) calls **list.Iterator**. (Note: Iterators are not normally provided for queues. We provide iterator capabilities for class **CQueue** in this example for demonstration purposes only so we can display the queue contents after queue stack operation.)

Class **CQueue** is used in the form to instantiate a stack called **mQueue**. The form provides buttons to allow the user to enqueue and dequeue elements of the queue. The user types values into the **TextBox** and clicks button **Value to Enqueue** to insert an element. Elements are removed with a click of button **Dequeue value**. Each **Enqueue** and **Dequeue** operation is followed by a call to **Display** (line 36) to display the queue's current contents.

## 21.8 Trees

Linked lists, stacks and queues are *linear data structures*. A tree is a nonlinear, two-dimensional data structure with special properties. Tree nodes contain two or more links. This section discusses *binary trees* (Fig. 21.13)—trees whose nodes all contain two links (none,

one or both of which may be **Nothing**). The *root node* is the first node in a tree. Each link in the root node refers to a *child*. The *left child* is the first node in the *left subtree and* the *right child* is the first node in the *right subtree*. The children of a node are called *siblings*. A node with no children is called a *leaf node*. Computer scientists normally draw trees from the root node down—exactly the opposite of the way most trees grow in nature.

***Common Programming Error 21.5***

*Not setting to* **Nothing** *the links in leaf nodes of a tree.*

In this section, a special binary tree called a *binary search tree* is created. A binary search tree (with no duplicate node values) has the characteristic that the values in any left subtree are less than the value in its parent node, and the values in any right subtree are greater than the value in its parent node. Figure 21.14 illustrates a binary search tree with 12 integer values. Note that the shape of the binary search tree that corresponds to a set of data can vary, depending on the order in which the values are inserted into the tree. Figure 21.15 (output in Fig. 21.16) creates a binary search tree of integers and traverses it (i.e., walks through all its nodes) using recursive *inorder, preorder* and *post-order traversals*.

Let us walk through the binary tree program of Fig. 21.15. The form code (lines 126 through 142 create **mTree** as an object of type **CTree** (lines 54 through 125). The user enters numbers in the **TextBox** and clicks button **Insert** to insert each value in the tree with a call to **mTree.InsertNode** (line 132). When the user clicks the **Do traversals** button, the program performs preorder, inorder and postorder traversals (these will be explained shortly) of **mTree**.

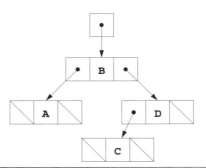

**Fig. 21.13**   A graphical representation of a binary tree.

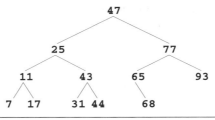

**Fig. 21.14**   A binary search tree.

```vb
1   ' Fig. 21.15
2   ' Class CTreeNode
3   Option Explicit
4   Private mLeft As CTreeNode
5   Private mNodeData As Variant
6   Private mRight As CTreeNode
7
8   Public Property Get Data() As Variant
9      Data = mNodeData
10  End Property
11
12  Public Property Let Data(ByVal vNewValue As Variant)
13     mNodeData = vNewValue
14  End Property
15
16  Public Property Get Left() As Variant
17     Set Left = mLeft
18  End Property
19
20  Public Property Let Left(ByVal vNewValue As Variant)
21     Set mLeft = vNewValue
22  End Property
23
24  Public Property Get Right() As Variant
25     Set Right = mRight
26  End Property
27
28  Public Property Let Right(ByVal vNewValue As Variant)
29     Set mRight = vNewValue
30  End Property
31
32  Public Sub Insert(value As Variant)
33     If value < mNodeData Then
34        If mLeft Is Nothing Then
35           Set mLeft = New CTreeNode
36           mLeft.Data = value
37        Else
38           mLeft.Insert (value)
39        End If
40     ElseIf value > mNodeData Then
41        If mRight Is Nothing Then
42           Set mRight = New CTreeNode
43           mRight.Data = value
44        Else
45           mRight.Insert (value)
46        End If
47     End If
48  End Sub
```

**Fig. 21.15**   Creating and traversing a binary tree (part 1 of 4).

```
49   ' Fig. 21.15
50   ' Class CTree
51   Option Explicit
52   Private mRoot As CTreeNode
53   Private mOutputString As String
54
55   ' Insert a new node in the binary search tree.
56   ' If the root node is null, create the root node here.
57   ' Otherwise, call the insert procedure of class TreeNode.
58   Public Sub InsertNode(value As Variant)
59      If mRoot Is Nothing Then
60         Set mRoot = New CTreeNode
61         mRoot.Data = value
62      Else
63         mRoot.Insert (value)
64      End If
65   End Sub
66
67   ' Preorder Traversal
68   Public Sub PreorderTraversal()
69      mOutputString = ""
70      Call PreorderHelper(mRoot)
71   End Sub
72
73   ' Recursive procedure to perform preorder traversal
74   Private Sub PreorderHelper(node As CTreeNode)
75      If node Is Nothing Then
76         Exit Sub
77      End If
78
79      mOutputString = mOutputString & node.Data & " "
80      Call PreorderHelper(node.Left)
81      Call PreorderHelper(node.Right)
82   End Sub
83
84   ' Inorder Traversal
85   Public Sub InorderTraversal()
86      mOutputString = ""
87      Call InorderHelper(mRoot)
88   End Sub
89
90   ' Recursive procedure to perform inorder traversal
91   Private Sub InorderHelper(node As CTreeNode)
92      If node Is Nothing Then
93         Exit Sub
94      End If
95
96      Call InorderHelper(node.Left)
97      mOutputString = mOutputString & node.Data & " "
98      Call InorderHelper(node.Right)
99   End Sub
100
```

**Fig. 21.15**   Creating and traversing a binary tree (part 2 of 4).

```
101  ' Postorder Traversal
102  Public Sub PostorderTraversal()
103      mOutputString = ""
104      Call PostorderHelper(mRoot)
105  End Sub
106
107  ' Recursive procedure to perform Postorder traversal
108  Private Sub PostorderHelper(node As CTreeNode)
109      If node Is Nothing Then
110          Exit Sub
111      End If
112
113      Call PostorderHelper(node.Left)
114      Call PostorderHelper(node.Right)
115      mOutputString = mOutputString & node.Data & " "
116  End Sub
117
118  Public Property Get Output() As Variant
119      Output = mOutputString
120  End Property
```

**Fig. 21.15**   Creating and traversing a binary tree (part 3 of 4).

```
121  ' Fig. 21.15
122  ' Demonstrating class CTree
123  Option Explicit
124  Dim mTree As New CTree
125
126  Private Sub cmdInsert_Click()
127      mTree.InsertNode (Val(txtInput.Text))
128  End Sub
129
130  Private Sub cmdTraversals_Click()
131      Call mTree.InorderTraversal
132      lblInorderResult.Caption = mTree.Output
133      Call mTree.PreorderTraversal
134      lblPreorderResult.Caption = mTree.Output
135      Call mTree.PostorderTraversal
136      lblPostorderResult.Caption = mTree.Output
137  End Sub
```

**Fig. 21.15** Creating and traversing a binary tree (part 4 of 4).

Now, let us walk through the class definitions and procedures. We begin with class **CTreeNode** class (lines 1 through 48). This class contains three **Private** module variables (lines 4 through 6)—**CTreeNode** reference **mLeft** refers to a node's left subtree, **Variant mNodeData** is the node's value and **CTreeNode** reference **mRight** refers to a node's right subtree. **Property Get** procedure **Data** (line 8) returns the data value in a **CTreeNode**. **Property Let** procedure **Data** (line 12) sets the data value in a **CTreeNode**. **Property Get** procedure **Left** (line 16) returns **CTreeNode** reference **mLeft**. **Property Let** procedure **Left** (line 20) sets **CTreeNode** reference **mLeft** to refer to the specified **CTreeNode**. **Property Get** procedure **Right** (line 24) returns **CTreeNode** reference **mRight**. **Property Let** procedure **Right** (line 28) sets

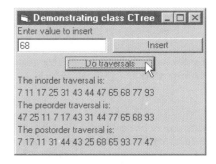

**Fig. 21.16**   Sample output from the program of Fig. 21.15.

**CTreeNode** reference **mRight** to refer to the specified **CTreeNode**. Procedure **Insert** (line 37) is invoked by class **CTree**'s **InsertNode** procedure to insert data into a tree that is not empty. This procedure is discussed in detail shortly.

Class **CTree** (lines 49 through 120) contains two **Private** module variables (lines 52 and 53)—**CTreeNode** reference **mRoot** refers to root node of the tree and **String mOutputString** maintains a **String** used by the traversal algorithms for output purposes (this **String** would normally not be part of class **CTree**). The class has **Public** procedures **InsertNode** (insert a new node in the tree) and **PreorderTraversal**, **InorderTraversal** and **PostorderTraversal**, each of which walks the tree in the designated manner. Each of these procedures calls its own separate recursive **Private** utility procedure to perform the appropriate operations on the internal representation of the tree. By default **mRoot** is **Nothing**, indicating that the tree is empty.

**Tree** procedure **InsertNode** (line 58) first determines if the tree is empty (i.e., **mRoot** is **Nothing**). If so, the procedure sets **mRoot** to a new **CTreeNode** (line 60) and sets the node's property **Data** to the value being inserted in the tree (line 61). If the tree is not empty, **InsertNode** calls **CTreeNode** procedure **Insert** (line 63) to recursively insert a node into the tree. *A node can only be inserted as a leaf node in a binary search tree.*

**CTreeNode** procedure **Insert** (defined at line 32) compares the value to be inserted with the **mNodeData** value in the root node. If the insert value is less than or equal to the root node data, the program determines if the left subtree is empty (line 34). If so, **Insert** sets **mLeft** to a new **CTreeNode** (line 35) and sets property **mLeft.Data** to the value being inserted (line 36). Otherwise, **Insert** recursively calls itself (line 38) for the left subtree to insert the value in the left subtree. If the insert value is greater than the root node data, the program determines if the right subtree is empty (line 41). If so, **Insert** sets **mRight** to a new **CTreeNode** (line 42) and sets property **mRight.Data** to the value being inserted (line 43). Otherwise, **Insert** recursively calls itself (line 45) for the right subtree to insert the value in the right subtree.

Procedures **InorderTraversal**, **PreorderTraversal** and **Postorder-Traversal** call helper procedures **InorderHelper**, **PreorderHelper** and **Post-orderHelper**, respectively, to traverse the tree and print the node values.

Procedure **InorderTraversal** (line 85) sets **mOutputString** to the empty string, then calls **InorderHelper** (line 87). **InorderHelper** (line 91) checks if the **CTreeNode** reference it receives is **Nothing** and, if so, returns immediately with **Exit Sub**. Otherwise, it performs the following steps:

1. Traverse the left subtree with a call to **InorderHelper** (line 96).

2. Concatenate **node.Data** to **mOutputString** for output purposes.

3. Traverse the right subtree with a call to **InorderHelper** (line 98).

The value in a node is not processed until the values in its left subtree are processed. The **InorderTraversal** of the tree in Fig. 21.14 is

```
7 11 17 25 31 43 44 47 65 68 77 93
```

Note that the **InorderTraversal** of a binary search tree prints the node values in ascending order. The process of creating a binary search tree actually sorts the data—and thus this process is called the *binary tree sort*.

Procedure **PreorderTraversal** (line 68) sets **mOutputString** to the empty string, then calls **PreorderHelper** (line 70). **PreorderHelper** (line 74) checks if the **CTreeNode** reference it receives is **Nothing** and, if so, returns immediately with **Exit Sub**. Otherwise, it performs the following steps:

1. Concatenate **node.Data** to **mOutputString** for output purposes.

2. Traverse the left subtree with a call to **PreorderHelper** (line 80).

3. Traverse the right subtree with a call to **PreorderHelper** (line 81).

The value in each node is processed as the node is visited. After the value in a given node is processed, the values in the left subtree are processed, then the values in the right subtree are processed. The **PreorderTraversal** of the tree in Fig. 21.14 is

```
47 25 11 7 17 43 31 44 77 65 68 93
```

Procedure **PostorderTraversal** (line 102) sets **mOutputString** to the empty string, then calls **PostorderHelper** (line 104). **PostorderHelper** (line 108) checks if the **CTreeNode** reference it receives is **Nothing** and, if so, returns immediately with **Exit Sub**. Otherwise, it performs the following steps:

1. Traverse the left subtree with a call to **PostorderHelper** (line 113).

2. Traverse the right subtree with a call to **PostorderHelper** (line 114).

3. Concatenate **node.Data** to **mOutputString** for output purposes.

The value in each node is not printed until the values of its children are printed. The **PostorderTraversal** of the tree in Fig. 21.14 is

```
7 17 11 31 44 43 25 68 65 93 77 47
```

The binary search tree facilitates *duplicate elimination*. As the tree is created, attempts to insert a duplicate value are recognized because a duplicate follows the same "go left" or "go right" decisions on each comparison as the original value did. Thus, the duplicate eventually is compared with a node containing the same value. The duplicate value may simply be discarded at this point.

Searching a binary tree for a value that matches a key value is also fast, especially for *tightly packed* trees. In a tightly packed tree, each level contains about twice as many elements as the preceding level. Figure 21.14 is a tightly packed binary tree. So a binary search tree with *n* elements has a minimum of $\log_2 n$ levels, and thus as few as $\log_2 n$ comparisons would have to be made either to find a match or to determine that no match exists. This means, for example, that when searching a (tightly packed) 1000-element binary search tree, approximately 10 comparisons need to be made because $2^{10} > 1000$. When searching a (tightly packed) 1,000,000-element binary search tree, approximately 20 comparisons need to be made because $2^{20} > 1,000,000$.

In the Exercises, algorithms are presented for several other binary tree operations, such as deleting an item from a binary tree, printing a binary tree in a two-dimensional tree format and performing a level-order traversal of a binary tree. The level-order traversal of a binary tree visits the nodes of the tree row-by-row starting at the root node level. On each level of the tree, the nodes are visited from left to right. Other binary tree exercises include allowing a binary search tree to contain duplicate values, inserting string values in a binary tree and determining how many levels are contained in a binary tree.

## 21.9 Collection Object

In this section we examine the **Collection** *object*, which enables us to create array-like objects that can grow and shrink dynamically as a program's data storage requirements change. We also consider the **Collection** object's capability to iterate through all of its elements using the **For Each/Next** control structure.

Visual Basic provides the predefined data structure **Collection** to maintain a set of related values of any data type. In fact, the elements of a single **Collection** can be of many different data types. **Collection** objects are created using **New** in the same manner as other object types. Members are added to a **Collection** using method **Add** and removed from a **Collection** using method **Remove**. Individual elements are retrieved from a **Collection** using method **Item**. The number of elements in a **Collection** at any time is determined with property **Count**. The program of Fig. 21.17 demonstrates the **Collection** object.

When the user clicks button **Add to Collection**, procedure **cmdAdd_Click** (line 6) adds the value in **TextBox txtAdd** to collection **mMyCollection** with line 7,

```
Call mMyCollection.Add(txtAdd.Text)
```

By default, **Collection** method **Add** places the new element at the end of the **Collection**. Method **Add** has three optional arguments. The second argument is a string that can be used with method **Item** as a key to retrieve the corresponding element from a **Collection** rather than using an explicit index number. The third argument indicates the element *before* which the new element should be added in the **Collection**. The fourth argument indicates the element *after* which the new element should be added in the **Collection**. The before and after arguments can specify an integer index or the string key for an element in the **Collection**. Only the *before* or the *after* argument can be used in a single call to **Add**.

When the user clicks button **Remove from Collection**, the **cmdRemove_click** procedure (line 12) executes. Lines 30 and 31,

```
1   ' Fig. 21.17
2   ' Demonstrating the Collection object
3   Option Explicit
4   Dim mMyCollection As New Collection
5
6   Private Sub cmdAdd_Click()
7       Call mMyCollection.Add(txtAdd.Text)
8       lblRemoved.Caption = ""
9       Call Display
10  End Sub
11
12  Private Sub cmdRemove_Click()
13      Dim index As Integer
14
15      If mMyCollection.Count = 0 Then
16          Call MsgBox("The Collection is empty")
17          Exit Sub
18      ElseIf txtIndex.Text = Null Then
19          Call MsgBox("You must specify the index number to remove")
20          Exit Sub
21      End If
22
23      index = Val(txtIndex.Text)
24
25      If index < 1 Or index > mMyCollection.Count Then
26          Call MsgBox("Invalid index.")
27          Exit Sub
28      End If
29
30      lblRemoved.Caption = "Removed: " & _
31          mMyCollection.Item(index)
32      Call mMyCollection.Remove(index)
33      Call Display
34  End Sub
35
36  Private Sub Display()
37      Dim element As Variant
38      Call lstOutput.Clear
39
40      For Each element In mMyCollection
41          Call lstOutput.AddItem(element)
42      Next
43  End Sub
```

**Fig. 21.17**   Demonstrating the **Collection** object (part 1 of 3).

```
    lblRemoved.Caption = "Removed: " & _
        mMyCollection.Item(index)
```

display the item being removed by setting **lblRemoved.Caption** to the result of the method call **mMyCollection.Item(index)**, which returns the item at position **index** in the **Collection**. If the elements are stored with a *key* using method **Add**, the index argument can specify the key as a **String** and **Item** returns the corresponding value.

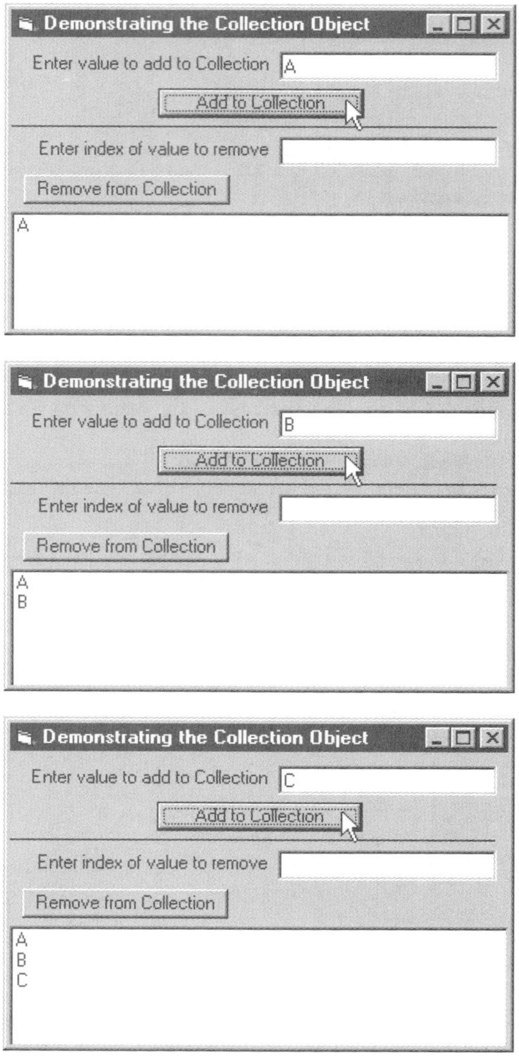

**Fig. 21.17**    Demonstrating the **Collection** object (part 2 of 3).

Line 32,

```
Call mMyCollection.Remove(index)
```

removes the item at position **index** in the **Collection**. If the elements are stored with a *key* using method **Add**, the index argument can specify the key as a **String**, and **Remove** deletes the corresponding element from the **Collection**.

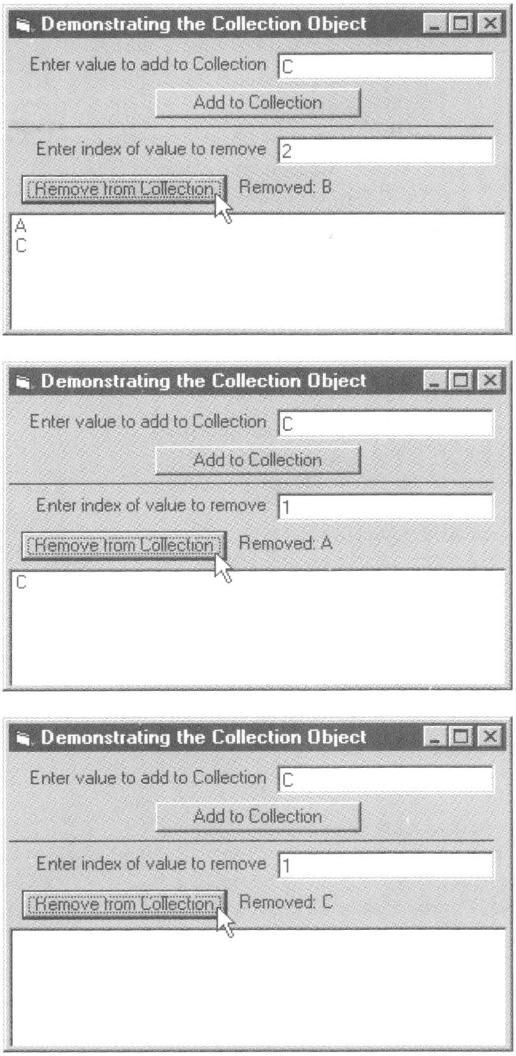

**Fig. 21.17** Demonstrating the **Collection** object (part 3 of 3).

Each **Add** and **Remove** operation results in a call to procedure **Display** (line 36). **Collection**s provide the programmer with the ability to iterate through each element of the **Collection** using the **For Each/Next** statement. Lines 40 through 42,

```
For Each element In mMyCollection
   Call lstOutput.AddItem(element)
Next
```

use **Variant element** to refer to each member of the **Collection**. In the body of the loop, the element is added to a **ListBox** for display purposes.

## 21.10 Dictionary Object

In this section we present the ***Dictionary*** *object*, which provides the framework for storing keyed data in tables and retrieving that data. Data are stored as *key/value pairs*—the *key* specifies where to store the corresponding *value* in the **Dictionary**. When data are retrieved from a **Dictionary**, the *keys* are transformed to *values*—a key is supplied and the **Dictionary** returns the corresponding value.

The program of Fig. 21.18 demonstrates the **Dictionary** object. To use the **Dictionary** object, you must include the *Microsoft Scripting Runtime* in your project. In the **Project** menu, select **References...** and in the **References** window scroll down to **Microsoft Scripting Runtime** and select it (a check should appear in the box to the left of the option). You can now declare **Dictionary** objects in your program.

```
1   ' Fig. 21.18
2   ' Demonstrating the Dictionary object
3   Option Explicit
4   Dim mMyDictionary As New Dictionary
5
6   Private Sub cmdAdd_Click()
7       If mMyDictionary.Exists(txtKey.Text) Then
8           mMyDictionary.Item(txtKey.Text) = txtValue.Text
9       Else
10          Call mMyDictionary.Add(txtKey.Text, txtValue.Text)
11      End If
12
13      Call ListKeys
14      Call ListItems
15  End Sub
16
17  Private Sub cmdExists_Click()
18      If mMyDictionary.Exists(txtKey.Text) Then
19        Call MsgBox("Key '" + txtKey.Text + "' exists. Value is '" _
20            + mMyDictionary.Item(txtKey.Text) + "'")
21      Else
22          Call MsgBox("Key '" + txtKey.Text + "' does not exist.")
23      End If
24  End Sub
25
26  Private Sub cmdRemove_Click()
27      On Error Resume Next
28      Call mMyDictionary.Remove(txtKey.Text)
29      Call ListKeys
30      Call ListItems
31  End Sub
32
33  Private Sub cmdRemoveAll_Click()
34      Call mMyDictionary.RemoveAll
35      Call ListKeys
36      Call ListItems
37  End Sub
```

Fig. 21.18  Demonstrating the **Dictionary** object (part 1 or 4).

```
38
39   Private Sub ListItems()
40      Dim elements() As Variant, i As Integer
41
42      Call lstItems.Clear
43      elements = mMyDictionary.Items()
44
45      For i = 0 To mMyDictionary.Count - 1
46         Call lstItems.AddItem(elements(i))
47      Next
48   End Sub
49
50   Private Sub ListKeys()
51      Dim elements() As Variant, i As Integer
52
53      Call lstKeys.Clear
54      elements = mMyDictionary.Keys()
55
56      For i = 0 To mMyDictionary.Count - 1
57         Call lstKeys.AddItem(elements(i))
58      Next
59   End Sub
```

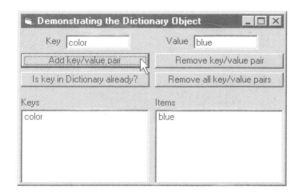

**Fig. 21.18**  Demonstrating the **Dictionary** object (part 2 or 4).

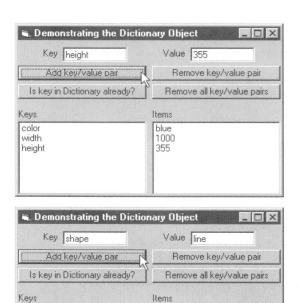

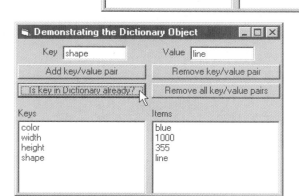

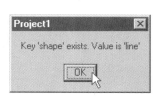

**Fig. 21.18**   Demonstrating the **Dictionary** object (part 3 or 4).

Line 4,

```
Dim mMyDictionary As New Dictionary
```

creates the **Dictionary** object **mMyDictionary**.

When the user types a key and a value in the two **TextBox**es at the top of the window, then clicks the **Add key/value pair** button, procedure **cmdAdd_click** (line 6) executes. This procedure either adds a new key/value pair to the **Dictionary** or replaces the value for a key stored previously. Line 7,

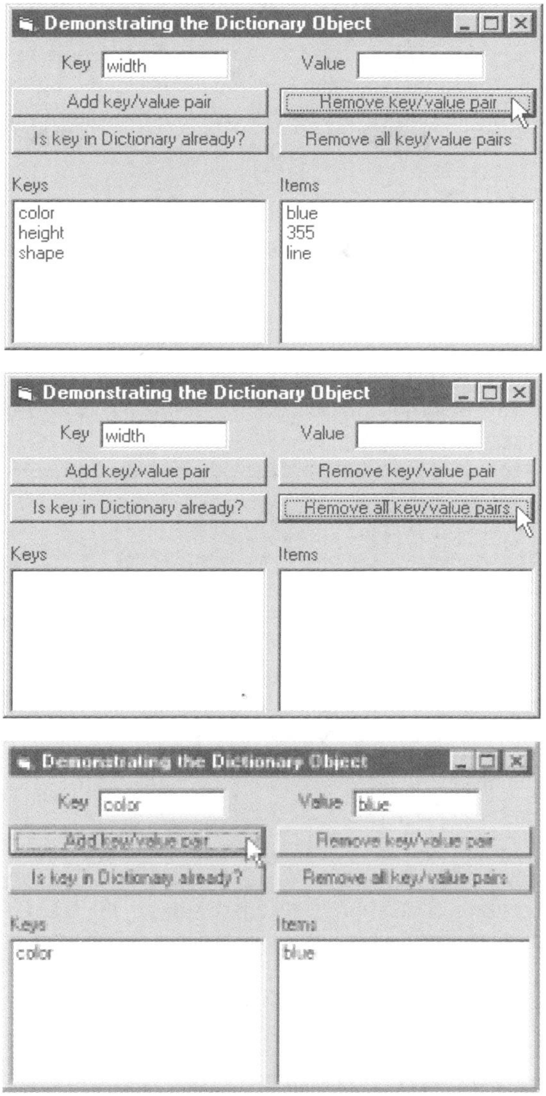

**Fig. 21.18**   Demonstrating the **Dictionary** object (part 4 or 4).

```
If mMyDictionary.Exists(txtKey.Text) Then
```

uses **Dictionary** method **Exists** to determine if the key specified in **TextBox txt-Key** already exists in the **Dictionary**. If so, line 8,

```
mMyDictionary.Item(txtKey.Text) = txtValue.Text
```

uses **Dictionary** property **Item** to insert a new value for the specified key in the **Dictionary**. Note that the key is supplied in parentheses after the **Item** property. If the key is not already in the table, line 10,

```
Call mMyDictionary.Add(txtKey.Text, txtValue.Text)
```

uses **Dictionary** method **Add** to insert a new key/value pair in the **Dictionary**. Method **Add** requires two arguments—the key and a corresponding value. The key can be any data type, but keys are normally integers or strings. The value can be any data type.

Lines 13 and 14,

```
Call ListKeys
Call ListItems
```

call procedures **ListKeys** (line 50) and **ListItems** (line 39) to display the keys and values in the **Dictionary**, respectively.

When the user types a key in the first **TextBox**, then clicks the button **Is key in Dictionary already?**, procedure **cmdExists_Click** (line 17) executes. The procedure uses method **Exists** to determine if the key is in the **Dictionary**, then displays a **MsgBox** with an appropriate message.

Clicking button **Remove key/value pair** executes **cmdRemove_click** (line 26). Line 28,

```
Call mMyDictionary.Remove(txtKey.Text)
```

uses **Dictionary** method **Remove** to delete the key/value pair for the specified key from the **Dictionary**. If the specified key is not in the table, an error occurs. After the key/value pair is removed, procedures **ListKeys** and **ListItems** are called to display the remaining contents of the **Dictionary**.

Clicking button **Remove all key/value pairs** executes **cmdRemoveAll_Click** (line 33). Line 34,

```
Call mMyDictionary.RemoveAll
```

uses **Dictionary** method **RemoveAll** to empty the **Dictionary**.

Procedure **ListItems** (line 39) displays the values in the **Dictionary**. The values are placed in **ListBox lstItems**. Line 43,

```
elements = mMyDictionary.Items()
```

uses **Dictionary** method **Items** to retrieve an array containing the values in the **Dictionary** and assigns the result to **Variant** array **elements**. The **For/Next** structure at lines 45 through 47,

```
For i = 0 To mMyDictionary.Count - 1
   Call lstItems.AddItem(elements(i))
Next
```

uses **Dictionary** property **Count** to determine the number of elements in the **Dictionary** and places each value in **lstItems**.

Procedure **ListKeys** (line 50) displays the keys in the **Dictionary**. The keys are placed in **ListBox lstKeys**. Line 54,

```
elements = mMyDictionary.Keys()
```

uses **Dictionary** method **Keys** to retrieve an array containing the keys in the **Dictionary** and assigns the result to **Variant** array **elements**. The array elements are then displayed in **lstKeys**.

Property **Key** of the **Dictionary** object is not demonstrated by this example. This property is used to change the key associated with a specific value. For example,

```
mMyDictionary.Key("colorvalue") = "color"
```

changes key **colorvalue** to **color**. If the specified key does not exist, an error occurs.

## Summary

- Data type **Variant** is capable of storing any Visual Basic data type. **Variant**s are declared either by explicitly using keyword **Variant** or by not providing a data type in the declaration (**Variant** is the default data type).

- A number stored in a **Variant** is maintained as its original data type in the **Variant**. When arithmetic is performed on a **Variant** containing a number and the result is outside the normal range of values for the number's actual data type, the result is stored in the **Variant** as the next larger data type.

- Function **VarType** returns an Integer indicating the type of the value in a **Variant**.

- Function **TypeName** returns the type name of the value in a **Variant** as a **String** (i.e., In-**teger**, **Byte**, etc.).

- Self-referential classes contain members called links that reference objects of the same class type.

- Self-referential classes enable many class objects to be linked together in stacks, queues, lists and trees.

- A linked list is a linear collection of self-referential class objects.

- A linked list is a dynamic data structure—the length of the list can increase or decrease as necessary.

- Linked lists can continue to grow until memory is exhausted.

- Linked lists provide a mechanism for simple insertion and deletion of data by reference manipulation.

- Stacks and queues are constrained versions of linked lists.

- New stack nodes are added to a stack and are removed from a stack only at the top of the stack. For this reason, a stack is referred to as a last-in, first-out (LIFO) data structure.

- The two primary operations used to manipulate a stack are **Push** and **Pop**. The **Push** operation creates a new node and places it on the top of the stack. The **Pop** operation removes a node from the top of the stack and returns the popped value.

- In a queue data structure, nodes are removed from the head and added to the tail. For this reason, a queue is referred to as a first-in, first-out (FIFO) data structure. The add and remove operations are known as **Enqueue** and **Dequeue**.

- Trees are two-dimensional data structures requiring two or more links per node.

- Binary trees contain two links per node.

- The root node is the first node in the tree.

- Each of the references in the root node refers to a child. The left child is the first node in the left subtree, and the right child is the first node in the right subtree. The children of a node are called siblings. Any tree node that does not have any children is called a leaf node.

- A binary search tree has the characteristic that the value in the left child of a node is less than the value in its parent node, and the value in the right child of a node is greater than or equal to the value in its parent node. If there are no duplicate data values, the value in the right child is simply greater than the value in its parent node.

- An inorder traversal of a binary tree traverses the left subtree inorder, processes the value in the root node, then traverses the right subtree inorder. The value in a node is not processed until the values in its left subtree are processed.

- A preorder traversal processes the value in the root node as the node is encountered, traverses the left subtree preorder, then traverses the right subtree preorder.

- A postorder traversal traverses the left subtree postorder, traverses the right subtree post-order, then processes the value in the root node. The value in each node is not processed until the values in both its subtrees are processed.

- Visual Basic provides the predefined data structure **Collection** to maintain a set of related values of any data type. Members are added to a **Collection** using method **Add** and removed from a **Collection** using method **Remove**. Individual elements are retrieved from a **Collection** using method **Item**. The number of elements in a **Collection** at any time is determined with property **Count**.

- The **Dictionary** object provides a framework for storing keyed data in tables and retrieving that data. Data are stored as *key/value pairs*—the *key* specifies where to store the corresponding *value* in the **Dictionary**. When data are retrieved from a **Dictionary**, the *keys* are transformed to *values*—a key is supplied and the **Dictionary** returns the corresponding value.

- **Dictionary** method **Exists** determines if a key is in the **Dictionary**. **Dictionary** property **Item** inserts a new value for a specified key. **Dictionary** method **Add** insert a new key/value pair in a **Dictionary**. **Dictionary** method **Remove** deletes the key/value pair for a specified key from a **Dictionary**. **Dictionary** method **RemoveAll** empties a **Dictionary**. **Dictionary** method **Items** retrieves an array containing the values in the **Dictionary**. **Dictionary** property **Count** determines the number of elements in a **Dictionary**. **Dictionary** method **Keys** retrieves an array containing the keys in a **Dictionary**. **Dictionary** property **Key** changes the key associated with a specific value.

## *Terminology*

binary search tree
binary tree
binary tree sort
child node
children
delete a node
**Dequeue**
duplicate elimination
dynamic data structures
**Enqueue**
FIFO (first-in, first-out)
head of a queue
inorder traversal of a binary tree
insert a node
leaf node
left child
left subtree
level-order traversal of a binary tree

LIFO (last-in, first-out)
linear data structure
linked list
node
nonlinear data structure
**Null** reference
parent node
**Pop**
postorder traversal of a binary tree
preorder traversal of a binary tree
**Push**
queue
recursive tree traversal algorithms
right child
right subtree
root node
self-referential class
stack

subtree
tail of a queue
top of a stack
traversal
tree
**TypeName** function
**Variant** data type
**VarType** function
**vbBoolean** constant
**vbByte** constant
**vbCurrency** constant

**vbDate** constant
**vbDecimal** constant
**vbDouble** constant
**vbEmpty** constant
**vbInteger** constant
**vbLong** constant
**vbObject** constant
**vbSingle** constant
**vbString** constant
visit a node

## Common Programming Errors

**21.1**  Attempting to assign a number outside the range of a **Double** to a **Variant** is a run-time error.

**21.2**  Not setting the link in the last node of a list to **Nothing**.

**21.3**  Using an iterator that refers to an element that has been deleted can result in an execution-time error that terminates the application.

**21.4**  Not setting the link in the bottom node of a stack to **Nothing**.

**21.5**  Not setting to **Nothing** the links in leaf nodes of a tree.

## Performance Tips

**21.1**  Arithmetic is faster with **Integer**s than with **Variant**s. **Variant**s consume more memory resources. They should not be used if the data type is known in advance and is not expected to change at execution time.

**21.2**  **Variant**s generally consume more memory (16 bytes each) than other data types.

**21.3**  An array can be declared to contain more elements than the number of items expected, but this can waste memory. Linked lists can provide better memory utilization in these situations. Linked lists allow the program to adapt at run-time.

**21.4**  Insertion into a linked list is fast—only two references have to be modified. All existing nodes remain at their current locations in memory.

**21.5**  Insertion and deletion in a sorted array can be time consuming—all the elements following the inserted or deleted element must be shifted appropriately.

**21.6**  The elements of an array are stored contiguously in memory. This allows immediate access to any array element because the address of any element can be calculated directly based on its position relative to the beginning of the array. Linked lists do not afford such immediate access to their elements.

**21.7**  Using dynamic memory allocation (instead of arrays) for data structures that grow and shrink at execution-time can save memory. Keep in mind, however, that references occupy space and that dynamic memory allocation incurs the overhead of procedure calls.

## Software Engineering Observation

**21.1**  If an iterator refers to an item of a list that is subsequently removed, the iterator is no longer valid. A new iterator should be obtained from the list.

## Self-Review Exercises

**21.1**  Fill in the blanks in each of the following:

  a)  A self-_____ class is used to form dynamic data structures that can grow and shrink at execution time.

b) A _____ is a constrained version of a linked list in which nodes can be inserted and deleted only from the start of the list; this data structure returns node values in last-in, first-out order.

c) A function that does not alter a linked list, but simply looks at the list to determine if it is empty, is referred to as a _____ function.

d) A queue is referred to as a _____ data structure because the first nodes inserted are the first nodes removed.

e) The reference to the next node in a linked list is referred to as a _____.

f) A _____ is a constrained version of a linked list in which nodes can be inserted only at the end of the list and deleted only from the start of the list.

g) A _____ is a nonlinear, two-dimensional data structure that contains nodes with two or more links.

h) A stack is referred to as a _____ data structure because the last node inserted is the first node removed.

i) The nodes of a _____ tree contain two link members.

j) The first node of a tree is the _____ node.

k) Each link in a tree node refers to a _____ or _____ of that node.

l) A tree node that has no children is called a _____ node.

m) The four traversal algorithms we mentioned in the text for binary search trees are _____, _____, _____ and _____.

**21.2**   What are the differences between a linked list and a stack?

**21.3**   What are the differences between a stack and a queue?

**21.4**   Perhaps a more appropriate title for this chapter would have been "Reusable Data Structures." Comment on how each of the following entities or concepts contributes to the reusability of data structures:

a) classes
b) composition

**21.5**   Manually provide the inorder, preorder and postorder traversals of the binary search tree of Fig. 21.19.

## Answers to Self-Review Exercises

**21.1**   a) referential. b) stack. c) predicate. d) first-in, first-out (FIFO). e) link. f) queue. g) tree. h) last-in, first-out (LIFO). i) binary. j) root. k) child or subtree. l) leaf. m) inorder, preorder, postorder and level-order.

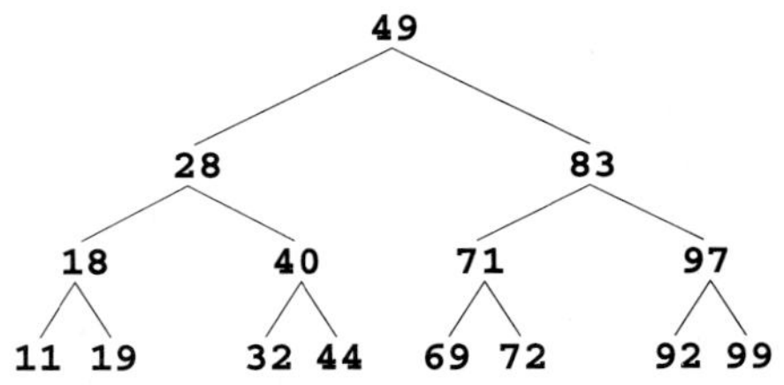

**Fig. 21.19**   A 15-node binary search tree.

**21.2**     It is possible to insert a node anywhere in a linked list and remove a node from anywhere in a linked list. Nodes in a stack may only be inserted at the top of the stack, and removed from the top of a stack.

**21.3**     A queue has references to both its head and its tail so that nodes may be inserted at the tail and deleted from the head. A stack has a single reference to the top of the stack where both insertion and deletion of nodes are performed.

**21.4**     a)   Classes allow us to instantiate as many data structure objects of a certain type (i.e., class) as we wish.

   b)   Composition enables us to reuse code by making a class object data structure a member of a composed class; if we make the class object a **Private** member of the composed class, then the class object's public procedures are not available through the composed object's interface.

**21.5**     The inorder traversal is

           11  18  19  28  32  40  44  49  69  71  72  83  92  97  99

The preorder traversal is

           49  28  18  11  19  40  32  44  83  71  69  72  97  92  99

The postorder traversal is

           11  19  18  32  44  40  28  69  72  71  92  99  97  83  49

## Exercises

**21.6**     Write a program that concatenates two linked list objects of characters. Define procedure **Concatenate**, which takes references to both list objects as arguments and concatenates the second list to the first list. The procedure should return a reference to the concatenated list.

**21.7**     Write a program that merges two ordered list objects of **Integer**s into a single ordered list object of **Integer**s. Define procedure **Merge**, which takes references to each of the list objects to be merged and returns a reference to the merged list object.

**21.8**     Write a program that inserts 25 random **Integer**s from 0 to 100 in order in a linked list. The program should calculate the sum of the elements and the floating-point average of the elements.

**21.9**     Write a program that creates a linked list object of 10 characters, then creates a second list object containing a copy of the first list, but in reverse order.

**21.10**     Write a program that inputs a line of text and uses a stack object to print the line reversed.

**21.11**     Write a program that uses a stack to determine if a string is a palindrome (i.e., the string is spelled identically backwards and forwards). The program should ignore spaces and punctuation.

**21.12**     Stacks are used by compilers to help in the process of evaluating expressions and generating machine language code. In this and the next exercise, we investigate how compilers evaluate arithmetic expressions consisting only of constants, operators and parentheses.

      Humans generally write expressions like **3 + 4** and **7 / 9** in which the operator (**+** or **/** here) is written between its operands—this is called *infix notation.* Computers "prefer" *postfix notation,* in which the operator is written to the right of its two operands. The preceding infix expressions would appear in postfix notation as **3 4 +** and **7 9 /**, respectively.

      To evaluate a complex infix expression, a compiler would first convert the expression to postfix notation and evaluate the postfix version of the expression. Each of these algorithms requires only a single left-to-right pass of the expression. Each algorithm uses a stack object in support of its operation, and in each algorithm the stack is used for a different purpose.

In this exercise, you will write a Visual Basic version of the infix-to-postfix conversion algorithm. In the next exercise, you will write a Visual Basic version of the postfix expression evaluation algorithm.

Write class **CInfixToPostfixConverter** to convert an ordinary infix arithmetic expression (assume that a valid expression is entered) with single-digit **Integer**s such as

$$(6 + 2) * 5 - 8 / 4$$

to a postfix expression. The postfix version of the preceding infix expression is

$$6\ \ 2\ +\ 5\ *\ 8\ 4\ /\ -$$

The program should read the expression into **String infix** and use the **CStack** class implemented in this chapter to help create the postfix expression in **String postfix**. The algorithm for creating a postfix expression is as follows:

a) Push a left parenthesis **'('** on the stack.

b) Append a right parenthesis **')'** to the end of **infix**.

c) While the stack is not empty, read **infix** from left to right and do the following:

If the current character in **infix** is a digit, append it to **postfix**.

If the current character in **infix** is a left parenthesis, push it on the stack.

If the current character in **infix** is an operator,

  Pop operators (if there are any) at the top of the stack while they have equal or higher precedence than the current operator and append the popped operators to **postfix**.

  Push the current character in **infix** on the stack.

If the current character in **infix** is a right parenthesis,

  Pop operators from the top of the stack and append them to **postfix** until a left parenthesis is at the top of the stack.

  Pop (and discard) the left parenthesis from the stack.

The following arithmetic operations are allowed in an expression:

+ addition
− subtraction
* multiplication
/ division
^ exponentiation
% modulus

Some of the procedures you may want to provide are:

a) Procedure **ConvertToPostfix** to convert the infix expression to postfix notation.

b) Procedure **IsOperator**, which determines if **c** is an operator.

c) Procedure **Precedence**, which determines if the precedence of **operator1** (from the infix expression) is less than, equal to, or greater than the precedence of **operator2** (from the stack). The procedure returns **True** if **operator1** has lower precedence than **operator2**. Otherwise, **False** is returned.

d) Procedure **StackTop** (this should be added as a modification to the **CStack** class), which returns the top value of the stack without popping the stack.

**21.13**   Write class **CPostfixEvaluator**, which evaluates a postfix expression (assume that it is valid) such as

$$6\ \ 2\ +\ 5\ *\ 8\ 4\ /\ -$$

The program should read a postfix expression consisting of digits and operators into a **String**. Using class **CStack** implemented earlier in this chapter, the program should scan the expression and evaluate it. The algorithm is as follows:

a) Append a right parenthesis (**')'**) to the end of the postfix expression. When the right parenthesis character is encountered, no further processing is necessary.

b) While the right parenthesis character has not been encountered, read the expression from left to right.

> If the current character is a digit,
>
>> Push its **Integer** value on the stack (the value of a digit character is its value in the computer's character set minus the value of **'0'** in the computer's character set).
>
> Otherwise, if the current character is an *operator*,
>
>> Pop the two top elements of the stack into variables **x** and **y**.
>> Calculate **y** *operator* **x**.
>> Push the result of the calculation onto the stack.

c) When the right parenthesis is encountered in the expression, pop the top value of the stack. This is the result of the postfix expression.

Note: In b) above, if the operator is **'/'**, the top of the stack is **2** and the next element in the stack is **8**, then pop **2** into **x**, pop **8** into **y**, evaluate **8 / 2** and push the result, **4**, back on the stack. This note also applies to operator **'-'**. The arithmetic operations allowed in an expression are

**+** addition
**-** subtraction
**\*** multiplication
**/** division
**^** exponentiation
**%** modulus

The stack should be maintained with the **CStack** class introduced in this chapter. You may want to provide the following procedures:

a) Procedure **EvaluatePostfixExpression**, which evaluates the postfix expression.

b) Procedure **Calculate**, which evaluates the expression **op1 operator op2**.

c) Procedure **Display**, which displays the stack.

**21.14**  Modify the postfix evaluator program of Exercise 21.13 so that it can process **Integer** operands larger than 9.

**21.15**  (*Supermarket simulation*) Write a program that simulates a checkout line at a supermarket. The line should be implemented as a queue object. Customers (i.e., customer objects) arrive in random **Integer** intervals of 1 to 4 minutes. Also, each customer is serviced in random **Integer** intervals of 1 to 4 minutes. Obviously, the rates need to be balanced. If the average arrival rate is larger than the average service rate, the queue will grow infinitely. Even with "balanced" rates, randomness can still cause long lines. Run the supermarket simulation for a 12-hour day (720 minutes) using the following algorithm:

a) Choose a random **Integer** between 1 and 4 to determine the minute at which the first customer arrives.

b) At the first customer's arrival time
Determine the customer's service time (random **Integer** from 1 to 4);
Begin servicing the customer;
Schedule the arrival time of the next customer (random **Integer** 1 to 4 added to the current time).

c)  For each minute of the day:
    If the next customer arrives,
        Say so,
        Enqueue the customer,
        Schedule the arrival time of the next customer.
    If service was completed for the last customer,
        Say so,
        Dequeue next customer to be serviced,
        Determine customer's service completion time (random **Integer** from 1 to 4
           added to the current time).

Now run your simulation for 720 minutes and answer each of the following:
    a)  What is the maximum number of customers in the queue at any time?
    b)  What is the longest wait any one customer experiences?
    c)  What happens if the arrival interval is changed from 1 to 4 minutes to 1 to 3 minutes?

**21.16**    Modify the program of Fig. 21.15 to allow the binary tree object to contain duplicates.

**21.17**    Write a program based on the program of Fig. 21.15 that inputs a line of text, tokenizes the sentence into separate words (use the **String** processing capabilities of Chapter 8), inserts the words in a binary search tree and prints the inorder, preorder and postorder traversals of the tree.

**21.18**    In this chapter we saw that duplicate elimination is straightforward when creating a binary search tree. Describe how you would perform duplicate elimination using only a single-subscripted array. Compare the performance of array-based duplicate elimination with the performance of binary-search-tree-based duplicate elimination.

**21.19**    Write procedure **Depth** which receives a binary tree and determines how many levels it has.

**21.20**    (*Recursively print a list backwards*) Write a procedure **PrintListBackwards**, which recursively outputs the items in a linked list object in reverse order. Write a test program that creates a sorted list of **Integer**s and prints the list in reverse order.

**21.21**    (*Recursively search a list*) Write a procedure **SearchList**, which recursively searches a linked list object for a specified value. Procedure **SearchList** should return a reference to the value if it is found; otherwise, **Null** should be returned. Use your procedure in a test program that creates a list of **Integer**s. The program should prompt the user for a value to locate in the list.

**21.22**    (*Binary tree delete*) In this exercise we discuss deleting items from binary search trees. The deletion algorithm is not as straightforward as the insertion algorithm. There are three cases that are encountered when deleting an item—the item is contained in a leaf node (i.e., it has no children), the item is contained in a node that has one child, or the item is contained in a node that has two children.

If the item to be deleted is contained in a leaf node, the node is deleted and the reference in the parent node is set to **Nothing**.

If the item to be deleted is contained in a node with one child, the reference in the parent node is set to reference the child node and the node containing the data item is deleted. This causes the child node to take the place of the deleted node in the tree.

The last case is the most difficult. When a node with two children is deleted, another node in the tree must take its place. However, the reference in the parent node cannot simply be assigned to reference one of the children of the node to be deleted. In most cases, the resulting binary search tree would not adhere to the following characteristic of binary search trees (with no duplicate values): *The values in any left subtree are less than the value in the parent node, and the values in any right subtree are greater than the value in the parent node.*

Which node is used as a *replacement node* to maintain this characteristic? Either the node containing the largest value in the tree less than the value in the node being deleted, or the node containing the smallest value in the tree greater than the value in the node being deleted. Let us consider the node with the smaller value. In a binary search tree, the largest value less than a parent's value is located in the left subtree of the parent node and is guaranteed to be contained in the rightmost node of the subtree. This node is located by walking down the left subtree to the right until the reference to the right child of the current node is **Nothing**. We are now referencing the replacement node, which is either a leaf node or a node with one child to its left. If the replacement node is a leaf node, the steps to perform the deletion are as follows:

a) Store the reference to the node to be deleted in a temporary reference variable.

b) Set the reference in the parent of the node being deleted to reference the replacement node.

c) Set the reference in the parent of the replacement node to **Nothing**.

d) Set the reference to the right subtree in the replacement node to reference the right subtree of the node to be deleted.

The deletion steps for a replacement node with a left child are similar to those for a replacement node with no children, but the algorithm also must move the child into the replacement node's position in the tree. If the replacement node is a node with a left child, the steps to perform the deletion are as follows:

a) Store the reference to the node to be deleted in a temporary reference variable.

b) Set the reference in the parent of the node being deleted to reference the replacement node.

c) Set the reference in the parent of the replacement node reference to the left child of the replacement node.

d) Set the reference to the right subtree in the replacement node reference to the right subtree of the node to be deleted.

Write procedure **DeleteNode**, which takes as its argument the value to be deleted. Procedure **DeleteNode** should locate in the tree the node containing the value to be deleted and use the algorithms discussed here to delete the node. If the value is not found in the tree, the procedure should print a message that indicates whether or not the value is deleted. Modify the program of Fig. 21.15 to use this procedure. After deleting an item, call the procedures **InorderTraversal**, **PreorderTraversal** and **PostorderTraversal** to confirm that the delete operation was performed correctly.

**21.23**   (*Binary tree search*) Write procedure **BinaryTreeSearch**, which attempts to locate a specified value in a binary search tree object. The procedure should take as an argument a search key to be located. If the node containing the search key is found, the procedure should return a reference to that node; otherwise, the procedure should return a **Null** reference.

**21.24**   (*Level-order binary tree traversal*) The program of Fig. 21.15 illustrated three recursive procedures of traversing a binary tree—inorder, preorder and postorder traversals. This exercise presents the *level-order traversal* of a binary tree, in which the node values are printed level-by-level starting at the root node level. The nodes on each level are printed from left to right. The level-order traversal is not a recursive algorithm. It uses a queue object to control the output of the nodes. The algorithm is as follows:

a) Insert the root node in the queue.

b) While there are nodes left in the queue,

   Get the next node in the queue;

   Print the node's value.

   If the reference to the left child of the node is not **Nothing**,

      Insert the left child node in the queue.

   If the reference to the right child of the node is not **Nothing**,

      Insert the right child node in the queue.

Write procedure **LevelOrder** to perform a level-order traversal of a binary tree object. Modify the program of Fig 21.15 to use this procedure. (Note: You will also need to use the queue-processing procedures of Fig. 21.11 in this program.)

**21.25**   (*Printing trees*) Write a recursive procedure **OutputTree** to display a binary tree object on the screen. The procedure should output the tree row-by-row with the top of the tree at the left of the screen and the bottom of the tree toward the right of the screen. Each row is output vertically. For example, the binary tree illustrated in Fig. 21.19 is output as follows:

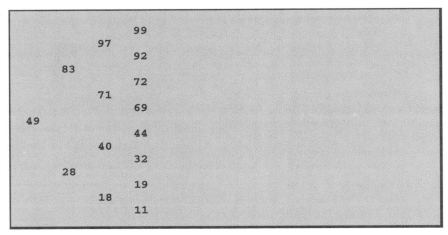

Note that the rightmost leaf node appears at the top of the output in the rightmost column, and the root node appears at the left of the output. Each column of output starts five spaces to the right of the preceding column. Procedure **OutputTree** should receive an argument **totalSpaces**, representing the number of spaces preceding the value to be output (this variable should start at zero so that the root node is output at the left of the screen). The procedure uses a modified inorder traversal to output the tree—it starts at the rightmost node in the tree and works back to the left. The algorithm is as follows:

While the reference to the current node is not **Nothing**,
   Recursively call **OutputTree** with the right subtree of the current node and **totalSpaces** + 5.
   Use a **For** structure to count from 1 to **totalSpaces** and output spaces.
   Output the value in the current node.
   Set the reference to the current node to refer to the left subtree of the current node.
   Increment **totalSpaces** by 5.

**21.26**   (*Insert/Delete Anywhere in a Linked List*) Our linked list class allowed insertions and deletions at only the front and the back of the linked list. These capabilities were convenient for us when we used composition to produce a stack class and a queue class with a minimal amount of code simply by reusing the list class. Linked lists are normally more general that those we provided. Modify the linked list class we developed in this chapter to handle insertions and deletions anywhere in the list.

**21.27**   (*List and Queues without Tail References*) Our implementation of a linked list (Fig. 21.3) used both a **mFirstNode** and a **mLastNode**. The **mLastNode** was useful for the **InsertAt-Back** and **RemoveFromBack** procedures of the **CList** class. The **InsertAtBack** procedure corresponds to the **Enqueue** procedure of the **CQueue** class.

Rewrite the **CList** class so that it does not use a **mLastNode**. Thus, any operations on the tail of a list must begin searching the list from the front. Does this affect our implementation of the **CQueue** class (Fig. 21.11)?

**21.28**    *(Performance of Binary Tree Sorting and Searching)* One problem with the binary tree sort is that the order in which the data are inserted affects the shape of the tree—for the same collection of data, different orderings can yield binary trees of dramatically different shapes. The performance of the binary tree sorting and searching algorithms is sensitive to the shape of the binary tree. What shape would a binary tree have if its data were inserted in increasing order? in decreasing order? What shape should the tree have to achieve maximal searching performance?

**21.29**    *(Indexed Lists)* As presented in the text, linked lists must be searched sequentially. For large lists, this can result in poor performance. A common technique for improving list searching performance is to create and maintain an index to the list. An index is a set of references to key places in the list. For example, an application that searches a large list of names could improve performance by creating an index with 26 entries—one for each letter of the alphabet. A search operation for a last name beginning with 'Y' would then first search the index to determine where the 'Y' entries begin and "jump into" the list at that point and search linearly until the desired name is found. This would be much faster than searching the linked list from the beginning. Use the **CList** class of Fig. 21.3 as the basis of an **CIndexedList** class.

Write a program that demonstrates the operation of indexed lists. Be sure to include procedures **InsertInIndexedList**, **SearchIndexedList** and **DeleteFromIndexedList**.

# Appendix A
## *Operator Precedence Chart*

Operators are shown in decreasing order of precedence from top to bottom with each level of precedence separated by a horizontal line. All operators in Visual Basic associate from left to right.

| Operator | Type |
|---|---|
| ( ) | parentheses |
| ^ | exponentiation |
| – | negation |
| * | multiplication |
| / | floating-point division |
| \ | **Integer** division |
| Mod | modulus |
| + | addition |
| – | subtraction |
| & | **String** concatenation |
| = | equality |
| <> | inequality |
| < | relational less-than |
| > | relational greater-than |
| <= | relational less-than or equal to |
| >= | relational greater-than or equal to |
| Like | pattern matching |
| Is | object reference comparison |
| Not | logical negation |

| Operator | Type |
|----------|------|
| **And** | logical and |
| **Or** | logical or |
| **Xor** | logical exclusion |
| **Eqv** | logical equivalence |
| **Imp** | logical implication |

# Appendix B
## ANSI Character Set

| | 0 | 1 | 2 | 3 | 4 | 5 | 6 | 7 | 8 | 9 |
|---|---|---|---|---|---|---|---|---|---|---|
| 0 | nul | □ | □ | □ | □ | □ | □ | □ | □ | ht |
| 1 | □ | □ | □ | cr | □ | □ | □ | □ | □ | □ |
| 2 | □ | □ | □ | □ | □ | □ | □ | □ | □ | □ |
| 3 | □ | □ | sp | ! | " | # | $ | % | & | ' |
| 4 | ( | ) | * | + | , | - | . | / | 0 | 1 |
| 5 | 2 | 3 | 4 | 5 | 6 | 7 | 8 | 9 | : | ; |
| 6 | < | = | > | ? | @ | A | B | C | D | E |
| 7 | F | G | H | I | J | K | L | M | N | O |
| 8 | P | Q | R | S | T | U | V | W | X | Y |
| 9 | Z | [ | \ | ] | ^ | _ | ' | a | b | c |
| 10 | d | e | f | g | h | i | j | k | l | m |
| 11 | n | o | p | q | r | s | t | u | v | w |
| 12 | x | y | z | { | \| | } | ~ | □ | □ | □ |
| 13 | □ | □ | □ | □ | □ | □ | □ | □ | □ | □ |
| 14 | □ | □ | □ | □ | □ | ' | ' | □ | □ | □ |
| 15 | □ | □ | □ | □ | □ | □ | □ | □ | □ | □ |
| 16 | sp | ¡ | ¢ | £ | ¤ | ¥ | ≠ | § | ¨ | © |
| 17 | ª | « | ¬ | | ® | ¯ | ° | ± | Σ | Π |
| 18 | ´ | µ | ¶ | · | ¸ | ∂ | º | » | π | ∫ |
| 19 | Ω | ¿ | À | Á | Â | Ã | Ä | Å | Æ | Ç |
| 20 | È | É | Ê | Ë | Ì | Í | Î | Ï | √ | Ñ |
| 21 | Ò | Ó | Ô | Õ | Ö | ∞ | Ø | Ù | Ú | Û |
| 22 | Ü | ≈ | ◊ | ß | à | á | â | ã | ä | å |
| 23 | æ | ç | è | é | ê | ë | ì | í | î | ï |
| 24 | ≤ | ñ | ò | ó | ô | õ | ö | ÷ | ø | ù |
| 25 | ú | û | ü | Δ | | ÿ | | | | |

The left digits of each row are the left digits of the character code (0-255) and the top digits of each column are the right digits of the character code (e.g., the code for G is 71). □ represents a code not supported by Windows.

# Appendix C
## *Visual Basic Internet and World Wide Web Resources*

### C.1 Visual Basic Web Resources

[Note: Appendix C was written by Abbey Deitel, a graduate of the Industrial Management program at Carnegie Mellon University and Director of World-wide Marketing at Deitel & Associates, Inc. We would like to thank Thelma Zigman, Barnett Zigman and Josh Deitel for their contributions.]

There is a bounty of Visual Basic information on the World Wide Web. Many people are experimenting with Visual Basic and sharing their thoughts, discoveries, ideas and source code with each other via the Internet. If you would like to recommend other sites, please send an email to

**`deitel@deitel.com`**

and we will put links to the sites you recommend on our web site

**`http://www.prenhall.com/deitel`**

### C.2 Microsoft Visual Basic Web Sites

**`http://msdn.microsoft.com/vbasic/`**
> The *Microsoft Visual Basic* home page contains the latest news, product information and documentation for Visual Basic. You will also find downloads, resources, tips, FAQs, third-party add-ins and technical support.

**`http://msdn.microsoft.com/developer/related/vbasic.htm`**
> The *Microsoft Developer Network Visual Basic* page has links to approximately 30 Visual Basic web sites.

**`http://msdn.microsoft.com/scripting/default.htm`**
**`?/scripting/vbscript/`**
> Visit the *Microsoft Scripting Technologies Visual Basic Script (VB Script)* site for documentation, downloads, links, beta releases, support and samples.

**`http://msdn.microsoft.com/vba/`**
> The *Microsoft Visual Basic for Applications (VBA)* web site. VBA is used in many Microsoft applications to provide enhanced functionality.

**http://msdn.microsoft.com/developer/**
>    The *Microsoft Developer's Network* home page is loaded with product information, downloads, newsgroups and chats, users groups, Microsoft SDKs, development information, links to related sites and third-party software products.

**http://www.microsoft.com/com/default.asp**
>    The *Microsoft COM* home page is a great resource for information on Distributed COM (DCOM), COM+, Microsoft Transaction Server (MTS) and ActiveX controls.

## C.3  Visual Basic Resources

**http://www.developer.com/**
>    *Developer.com* is an excellent resource for programmers. This site covers numerous technologies including Visual Basic.  You will find links to publications, newsgroups, add-ins, on-line help, custom controls, shareware, FAQs, utilities, VBX/OCX controls and links to other VB web sites including over 30 links to sites with information about ActiveX controls.

**http://www.daisy.co.uk/sites/VB/visualbasic001.html#Examples**
>    This site has over 20 Visual Basic code examples as well as lists of Visual Basic newsgroups and other Visual Basic related web sites.

**http://www.cgvb.com/**
>    *Carl and Gary's Visual Basic Homepage* is an excellent resource for Visual Basic information. This site has links to books, games, jobs, mailing lists, news, product information, training information, and more.

**http://www.qns.com/~robinson/vb/vb.html**
>    This site contains a long list of Visual Basic resources including FAQs, downloads, demos, links, technical articles, and much more.

**http://www.vb-world.net/**
>    *VB-World* has lots of valuable information for Visual Basic programmers including demos, books, links to other VB sites, tips and tricks, news and a question-and-answer forum.

**http://www.cetus-links.org/**
>    *Object-Oriented Language: Visual Basic* is a great resource site with plenty of links to Visual Basic FAQs, tutorials, examples and demos, numerous newsgroups, references, conferences, mailing lists, articles, books, magazines and more.

**http://www.vbexplorer.com/**
>    The *Visual Basic Explorer* site is an excellent site for people learning to program in Visual Basic. This site includes tutorials, demos and source code, FAQs, links for other VB sites, book and product information. Check out the VB game programming page for fun. You will find loads of links to game programming sites, tutorials and game products.

**http://www.ookami.com/VB/**
>    The *Visual Basic Game Programming* site is a great resource for game programmers. You will find tutorials, links, suggested books, source code and a discussion group for programmers.

**http://web.inter.nl.net/users/erikkooi/vb.html**
>    The *VB Corner* web site includes web links, FAQs, tools, controls, tips and tricks, samples, add-ins and an extensive list of Visual Basic newsgroups.

**http://www.op.net/~jstrollo/vblinks.html**
>    *Strollo Software's* extensive VB links are divided into groups including books and magazines, ActiveX, VB info, personal pages, third party tools, communications tools, user groups and files.

`http://www.visbasic.co.uk/`

This Visual Basic resource site provides source code, software downloads, links, discussion groups, articles and a list of errors.

`http://web2.airmail.net/gbeene/visual.html`

*Gary Beene's Visual Basic World* includes tutorials, books, magazines, FAQs and downloads.

`http://www.vb-helper.com/`

The *VB Helper* site includes tips and tricks, books, links and source code.

## C.4 FAQs

`http://msdn.microsoft.com/vbasic/`

The *Microsoft Visual Basic* home page contains the latest news, product information and documentation for Visual Basic. You will also find downloads, resources, tips, FAQs, third-party add-ins and technical support.

`http://www.developer.com/`

*Developer.com* is an excellent resource for programmers. This site covers numerous technologies including Visual Basic. You will find links to publications, newsgroups, add-ins, on-line help, custom controls, shareware, FAQs, utilities, VBX/OCX controls and links to other VB web sites including over 30 links to sites with information about ActiveX controls.

`http://www.cetus-links.org/oo_visual_basic.html`

*Object-Oriented Language: Visual Basic* is a great resource site with plenty of links to Visual Basic FAQs, tutorials, examples and demos, numerous newsgroups, references, conferences, mailing lists, articles, books and magazines and more.

`http://www.experts-exchange.com/`

Register at *The Experts Exchange* web site to ask their experts questions on a number of topics including Visual Basic Programming.

`http://www.mvps.org/vbnet/`

The *Visual Basic Developers Resource Centre* includes news, source code, FAQs, and links to other VB sites sorted by subject.

`http://www.vbtt.com/`

The *Visual Basic Tips and Tricks* site has plenty of helpful hints and lists of bugs found in VB component products.

`http://www.ddesoftware.com/`

This site has many Visual Basic programming tips and answers to frequently asked questions (mixed in with the *Tips and Tricks* page and the *Message Board* page). The authors have also provided free source code, add-ins and an extensive list of links to other VB web sites.

`http://surf.to/VbArea`

The *VB Area* web site has lots of programming tips and FAQs plus links, files and a discussion group for VB programmers.

`http://www.inquiry.com/thevbpro/`

Ask the *VB Pro* your programming language questions or check out the extensive list of questions and answers.

`http://home.sol.no/~jansh/vb/default.htm`

The *Visual Basic FAQ* web site has the latest VB news and information, links to other VB web resources and downloadable FAQs.

`http://www.vbexplorer.com/`
> The *Visual Basic Explorer* site is an excellent site for people learning to program in Visual Basic. This site includes tutorials, demos and source code, FAQs, links for other VB sites, book and product information. Check out the VB game programming page for fun. You will find loads of links to game programming sites, tutorials and game products.

## C.5 Tutorials for Learning VB

`http://www.cetus-links.org/`
> *Object-Oriented Language: Visual Basic* is a great resource site with plenty of links to Visual Basic FAQs, tutorials, examples and demos, numerous newsgroups, references, conferences, mailing lists, articles, books, magazines and more.

`http://www.inquiry.com/techtips/thevbpro/`
> Ask *VB Pro* your Visual Basic Programming questions or read the extensive Visual Basic FAQs.

`http://www.cgvb.com/`
> *Carl and Gary's Visual Basic Homepage* is a great resource for Visual Basic information. This site has links to books, games, jobs, mailing lists, news, product information, training information, and more.

`http://www.vbexplorer.com/`
> The *Visual Basic Explorer* site is an excellent site for people learning to program in Visual Basic. This site includes tutorials, demos and source code, FAQs, links for other VB sites, book and product information. Check out the VB game programming page for fun. You will find loads of links to game programming sites, tutorials and game products.

## C.6 VB Newsgroups and Mailing lists

`news:alt.lang.basic`

`news:comp.lang.basic.visual`

`news:comp.lang.basic.visual.misc`

`news:comp.lang.basic.visual.3rdparty`

`news:comp.lang.basic.visual.database`

`news:comp.lang.basic.visual.announce`

`news:microsoft.public.vb.3rdparty`

`news:microsoft.public.vb.addins`

`news:microsoft.public.vb.bugs`

`news:microsoft.public.vb.controls`

`news:microsoft.public.vb.controls.creation`

`news:microsoft.public.vb.controls.databound`

`news:microsoft.public.vb.controls.internet`

`news:microsoft.public.vb.crystal`

`news:microsoft.public.vb.database`

`news:microsoft.public.vb.database.dao`

`news:microsoft.public.vb.database.odbc`

`news:microsoft.public.vb.database.rdo`

`news:microsoft.public.vb.dos`

`news:microsoft.public.vb.enterprise`

`news:microsoft.public.vb.general.discussion`

`news:microsoft.public.vb.installation`

`news:microsoft.public.vb.ole`

`news:microsoft.public.vb.ole.automation`

`news:microsoft.public.vb.ole.cdk`

`news:microsoft.public.vb.ole.servers`

`news:microsoft.public.vb.setupwiz`

`news:microsoft.public.vb.syntax`

`news:microsoft.public.vb.winapi`

`news:microsoft.public.vb.winapi.graphics`

`news:microsoft.public.vb.winapi.networks`

`http://web.inter.nl.net/users/erikkooi/vb.html`
> The *VB Corner* web site includes web links, FAQs, tools, controls, tips and tricks, samples, add-ins, and an extensive list of Visual Basic newsgroups including several Microsoft newsgroups.

`http://www.daisy.co.uk/sites/VB/visualbasic001.html#Examples`
> This site has over 20 Visual Basic code examples as well as lists of Visual Basic newsgroups and other Visual Basic related web sites.

`http://www.cgvb.com/`
> *Carl and Gary's Visual Basic Homepage* is a great resource for Visual Basic information. This site has links to books, games, jobs, mailing lists, news, product information, training information, and more.

`http://peach.ease.lsoft.com/archives/visbas-1.html`
> This mailing list allows Visual Basic programmers to communicate about the Visual Basic programming language.

## C.7  VB Books and Magazines

`http://www.vbonline.com/vb-mag/`
> *Visual Basic On-line Magazine* is a monthly publication with VB news, products and resources.

`http://www.cetus-links.org/oo_visual_basic.html`
> *Object-Oriented Language: Visual Basic* is a great resource site with links to Visual Basic FAQs, tutorials, examples and demos, numerous newsgroups, references, conferences, mailing lists, articles, books and magazines and more.

`http://www.cobb.com/ivb/`
> *Inside Visual Basic* is an on-line magazine with current articles, back issues, code and links.

`http://www.vb-helper.com/`
> The *VB Helper* site includes tips and tricks, books, links and source code.

`http://www.cgvb.com/`
> *Carl and Gary's Visual Basic Homepage* is a great resource for Visual Basic information. This site has links to books, games, jobs, mailing lists, news, product information, training information, and more.

## C.8  VB Products

**http://msdn.microsoft.com/vbasic/**
> The Microsoft Visual Basic home page contains the latest news, product information and documentation for Visual Basic. You will also find downloads, resources, tips, FAQs, third-party addins and technical support.

**http://www.microsoft.com/com/default.asp**
> The Microsoft COM home page is a great resource for information on Distributed COM (DCOM), COM+, Microsoft Transaction Server (MTS) and ActiveX controls.

**http://www.visualstudio6.com/**
> The *DevX Guide to Visual Studio 6* contains news and information about Microsoft Visual Studio 6.0. They have also provided links to download preview editions of the software.

**http://www.vbxtras.com/**
> *Vbxtras* is an extensive on-line catalog for products related to Visual Basic. You will find free product demos, news and resources.

**http://www.cgvb.com/**
> *Carl and Gary's Visual Basic Homepage* is a great resource for Visual Basic information. This site has links to books, games, jobs, mailing lists, news, product information, training information, and more.

**http://www.vbonline.com/vb-mag/**
> *Visual Basic On-line Magazine* is a monthly "publication" with plenty of VB news, products and resources.

**http://www.qns.com/~robinson/vb/vb.html**
> This site contains a long list of Visual Basic resources including FAQs, downloads, demos, links, technical articles, and much more.

**http://www.codeoftheweek.com/index.html**
> For a nominal fee, you can subscribe to the *Visual Basic Code of the Week* mailing list to receive weekly emails with tips, VB classes, etc.

**http://members.xoom.com/vba51/**
> This web site includes information on DirectX, COM and OpenGL.

**http://www.vbexplorer.com/**
> The *Visual Basic Explorer* site is an excellent site for people learning to program in Visual Basic. This site includes tutorials, demos and source code, FAQs, links for other VB sites, book and product information. Check out the VB game programming page for fun. You will find loads of links to game programming sites, tutorials and game products.

# Appendix D
## *Number Systems*

### Objectives

- To understand basic number systems concepts such as base, positional value, and symbol value.
- To understand how to work with numbers represented in the binary, octal, and hexadecimal number systems
- To be able to abbreviate binary numbers as octal numbers or hexadecimal numbers.
- To be able to convert octal numbers and hexadecimal numbers to binary numbers.
- To be able to covert back and forth between decimal numbers and their binary, octal, and hexadecimal equivalents.
- To understand binary arithmetic, and how negative binary numbers are represented using two's complement notation.

*Here are only numbers ratified.*
William Shakespeare

*Nature has some sort of arithmetic-geometrical coordinate system, because nature has all kinds of models. What we experience of nature is in models, and all of nature's models are so beautiful.*

*It struck me that nature's system must be a real beauty, because in chemistry we find that the associations are always in beautiful whole numbers—there are no fractions.*
Richard Buckminster Fuller

# Outline

## D.1 Introduction

In this appendix, we introduce the key number systems that Visual Basic programmers use, especially when they are working on software projects that require close interaction with "machine-level" hardware. Projects like this include operating systems, computer networking software, compilers, database systems, and applications requiring high performance.

When we write an **Integer** such as 227 or -63 in a Visual Basic program, the number is assumed to be in the *decimal (base 10) number system*. The *digits* in the decimal number system are 0, 1, 2, 3, 4, 5, 6, 7, 8, and 9. The lowest digit is 0 and the highest digit is 9—one less than the *base* of 10. Internally, computers use the *binary (base 2) number system*. The binary number system has only two digits, namely 0 and 1. Its lowest digit is 0 and its highest digit is 1—one less than the base of 2.

As we will see, binary numbers tend to be much longer than their decimal equivalents. Programmers who work in assembly languages and in high-level languages like Visual Basic that enable programmers to reach down to the "machine level," find it cumbersome to work with binary numbers. So two other number systems the *octal number system (base 8)* and the *hexadecimal number system (base 16)*—are popular primarily because they make it convenient to abbreviate binary numbers.

In the octal number system, the digits range from 0 to 7. Because both the binary number system and the octal number system have fewer digits than the decimal number system, their digits are the same as the corresponding digits in decimal.

The hexadecimal number system poses a problem because it requires sixteen digits—a lowest digit of 0 and a highest digit with a value equivalent to decimal 15 (one less than the base of 16). By convention, we use the letters A through F to represent the hexadecimal digits corresponding to decimal values 10 through 15. Thus in hexadecimal we can have numbers like 876 consisting solely of decimal-like digits, numbers like 8A55F consisting of digits and letters, and numbers like FFE consisting solely of letters. Occasionally, a hexadecimal number spells a common word such as FACE or FEED—this can appear strange to programmers accustomed to working with numbers.

Each of these number systems uses *positional notation*—each position in which a digit is written has a different *positional value*. For example, in the decimal number 937 (the 9, the 3, and the 7 are referred to as *symbol values*), we say that the 7 is written in the *ones position*, the 3 is written in the *tens position*, and the 9 is written in the *hundreds position*. Notice that each of these positions is a power of the base (base 10), and that these powers begin at 0 and increase by 1 as we move left in the number (Fig. D.3).

| Binary digit | Octal digit | Decimal digit | Hexadecimal digit |
|---|---|---|---|
| 0 | 0 | 0 | 0 |
| 1 | 1 | 1 | 1 |
|   | 2 | 2 | 2 |
|   | 3 | 3 | 3 |
|   | 4 | 4 | 4 |
|   | 5 | 5 | 5 |
|   | 6 | 6 | 6 |
|   | 7 | 7 | 7 |
|   |   | 8 | 8 |
|   |   | 9 | 9 |
|   |   |   | A (decimal value of 10) |
|   |   |   | B (decimal value of 11) |
|   |   |   | C (decimal value of 12) |
|   |   |   | D (decimal value of 13) |
|   |   |   | E (decimal value of 14) |
|   |   |   | F (decimal value of 15) |

**Fig. D.1**   Digits of the binary, octal, decimal, and hexadecimal number systems.

| Attribute | Binary | Octal | Decimal | Hexadecimal |
|---|---|---|---|---|
| Base | 2 | 8 | 10 | 16 |
| Lowest digit | 0 | 0 | 0 | 0 |
| Highest digit | 1 | 7 | 9 | F |

**Fig. D.2**   Comparison of the binary, octal, decimal, and hexadecimal number systems.

| Positional values in the decimal number system | | | |
|---|---|---|---|
| Decimal digit | 9 | 3 | 7 |
| Position name | Hundreds | Tens | Ones |
| Positional value | 100 | 10 | 1 |
| Positional value as a power of the base (10) | $10^2$ | $10^1$ | $10^0$ |

**Fig. D.3**   Positional values in the decimal number system.

For longer decimal numbers, the next positions to the left would be the *thousands position* (10 to the $3^{rd}$ power), the *ten-thousands position* (10 to the $4^{th}$ power), the *hundred-thousands position* (10 to the $5^{th}$ power), the *millions position* (10 to the $6^{th}$ power), the *ten-millions position* (10 to the $7^{th}$ power), and so on.

In the binary number 101, we say that the rightmost 1 is written in the *ones position*, the 0 is written in the *twos position*, and the leftmost 1 is written in the *fours position*. Notice that each of these positions is a power of the base (base 2), and that these powers begin at 0 and increase by 1 as we move left in the number (Fig. D.4).

For longer binary numbers, the next positions to the left would be the *eights position* (2 to the $3^{rd}$ power), the *sixteens position* (2 to the $4^{th}$ power), the *thirty-twos position* (2 to the $5^{th}$ power), the *sixty-fours position* (2 to the $6^{th}$ power), and so on.

In the octal number 425, we say that the 5 is written in the *ones position*, the 2 is written in the *eights position*, and the 4 is written in the *sixty-fours position*. Notice that each of these positions is a power of the base (base 8), and that these powers begin at 0 and increase by 1 as we move left in the number (Fig. D.5).

For longer octal numbers, the next positions to the left would be the *five-hundred-and-twelves position* (8 to the $3^{rd}$ power), the *four-thousand-and-ninety-sixes position* (8 to the $4^{th}$ power), the *thirty-two-thousand-seven-hundred-and-sixty eights position* (8 to the $5^{th}$ power), and so on.

In the hexadecimal number 3DA, we say that the A is written in the *ones position*, the D is written in the *sixteens position*, and the 3 is written in the *two-hundred-and-fifty-sixes position*. Notice that each of these positions is a power of the base (base 16), and that these powers begin at 0 and increase by 1 as we move left in the number (Fig. D.6).

| Positional values in the binary number system | | | |
|---|---|---|---|
| Binary digit | 1 | 0 | 1 |
| Position name | Fours | Twos | Ones |
| Positional value | 4 | 2 | 1 |
| Positional value as a power of the base (2) | $2^2$ | $2^1$ | $2^0$ |

**Fig. D.4** Positional values in the binary number system.

| Positional values in the octal number system | | | |
|---|---|---|---|
| Decimal digit | 4 | 2 | 5 |
| Position name | Sixty-fours | Eights | Ones |
| Positional value | 64 | 8 | 1 |
| Positional value as a power of the base (8) | $8^2$ | $8^1$ | $8^0$ |

**Fig. D.5** Positional values in the octal number system.

| Positional values in the hexadecimal number system | | | |
| --- | --- | --- | --- |
| Decimal digit | **3** | **D** | **A** |
| Position name | Two-hundred-and-fifty-sixes | Sixteens | Ones |
| Positional value | **256** | **16** | **1** |
| Positional value as a power of the base (16) | $16^2$ | $16^1$ | $16^0$ |

**Fig. D.6**     Positional values in the hexadecimal number system.

For longer hexadecimal numbers, the next positions to the left would be the *four-thousand-and-ninety-sixes position* (16 to the 3$^{rd}$ power), the *sixty-five-thousand-five-hundred-and-thirty-six position* (16 to the 4$^{th}$ power), and so on.

## D.2 Abbreviating Binary Numbers as Octal Numbers and Hexadecimal Numbers

The main use for octal and hexadecimal numbers in computing is for abbreviating lengthy binary representations. Figure D.7 highlights the fact that lengthy binary numbers can be expressed concisely in number systems with higher bases than the binary number system.

| Decimal number | Binary representation | Octal representation | Hexadecimal representation |
| --- | --- | --- | --- |
| 0 | 0 | 0 | 0 |
| 1 | 1 | 1 | 1 |
| 2 | 10 | 2 | 2 |
| 3 | 11 | 3 | 3 |
| 4 | 100 | 4 | 4 |
| 5 | 101 | 5 | 5 |
| 6 | 110 | 6 | 6 |
| 7 | 111 | 7 | 7 |
| 8 | 1000 | 10 | 8 |
| 9 | 1001 | 11 | 9 |
| 10 | 1010 | 12 | A |
| 11 | 1011 | 13 | B |
| 12 | 1100 | 14 | C |
| 13 | 1101 | 15 | D |
| 14 | 1110 | 16 | E |
| 15 | 1111 | 17 | F |
| 16 | 10000 | 20 | 10 |

**Fig. D.7**     Decimal, binary, octal, and hexadecimal equivalents.

A particularly important relationship that both the octal number system and the hexadecimal number system have to the binary system is that the bases of octal and hexadecimal (8 and 16 respectively) are powers of the base of the binary number system (base 2). Consider the following 12-digit binary number and its octal and hexadecimal equivalents. See if you can determine how this relationship makes it convenient to abbreviate binary numbers in octal or hexadecimal. The answer follows the numbers.

| Binary Number | Octal equivalent | Hexadecimal equivalent |
|---|---|---|
| **100011010001** | **4321** | **8D1** |

To see how the binary number converts easily to octal, simply break the 12-digit binary number into groups of three consecutive bits each, and write those groups over the corresponding digits of the octal number as follows

| **100** | **011** | **010** | **001** |
|---|---|---|---|
| **4** | **3** | **2** | **1** |

Notice that the octal digit you have written under each group of thee bits corresponds precisely to the octal equivalent of that 3-digit binary number as shown in Fig. D.7.

The same kind of relationship may be observed in converting numbers from binary to hexadecimal. In particular, break the 12-digit binary number into groups of four consecutive bits each and write those groups over the corresponding digits of the hexadecimal number as follows

| **1000** | **1101** | **0001** |
|---|---|---|
| **8** | **D** | **1** |

Notice that the hexadecimal digit you have written under each group of four bits corresponds precisely to the hexadecimal equivalent of that 4-digit binary number as shown in Fig. D.7.

## D.3 Converting Octal Numbers and Hexadecimal Numbers to Binary Numbers

In the previous section, we saw how to convert binary numbers to their octal and hexadecimal equivalents by forming groups of binary digits and simply rewriting these groups as their equivalent octal digit values or hexadecimal digit values. This process may be used in reverse to produce the binary equivalent of a given octal or hexadecimal number.

For example, the octal number 653 is converted to binary simply by writing the 6 as its 3-digit binary equivalent 110, the 5 as its 3-digit binary equivalent 101, and the 3 as its 3-digit binary equivalent 011 to form the 9-digit binary number 110101011.

The hexadecimal number FAD5 is converted to binary simply by writing the F as its 4-digit binary equivalent 1111, the A as its 4-digit binary equivalent 1010, the D as its 4-digit binary equivalent 1101, and the 5 as its 4-digit binary equivalent 0101 to form the 16-digit 1111101011010101.

## D.4 Converting from Binary, Octal, or Hexadecimal to Decimal

Because we are accustomed to working in decimal, it is often convenient to convert a binary, octal, or hexadecimal number to decimal to get a sense of what the number is "really" worth. Our diagrams in Section D.1 express the positional values in decimal. To convert a number to decimal from another base, multiply the decimal equivalent of each digit by its positional value, and sum these products. For example, the binary number 110101 is converted to decimal 53 as shown in Fig. D.8.

| Converting a binary number to decimal | | | | | |
| --- | --- | --- | --- | --- | --- |
| Positional values: | 32 | 16 | 8 | 4 | 2 | 1 |
| Symbol values: | 1 | 1 | 0 | 1 | 0 | 1 |
| Products: | 1*32=32 | 1*16=16 | 0*8=0 | 1*4=4 | 0*2=0 | 1*1=1 |
| Sum: | = 32 + 16 + 0 + 4 + 0 + 1 = 53 | | | | | |

**Fig. D.8**    Converting a binary number to decimal.

To convert octal 7614 to decimal 3980, we use the same technique, this time using appropriate octal positional values as shown in Fig. D.9.

To convert hexadecimal AD3B to decimal 44347, we use the same technique, this time using appropriate hexadecimal positional values as shown in Fig. D.10.

## D.5 Converting from Decimal to Binary, Octal, or Hexadecimal

The conversions of the previous section follow naturally from the conventions of positional notation. Converting from decimal to binary, octal, or hexadecimal also follows these conventions.

Suppose we wish to convert decimal 57 to binary. We begin by writing the positional values of the columns right to left until we reach a column whose positional value is greater than the decimal number. We do not need that column, so we discard it. Thus, we first write:

| Converting an octal number to decimal | | | |
| --- | --- | --- | --- |
| Positional values: | 512 | 64 | 8 | 1 |
| Symbol values: | 7 | 6 | 1 | 4 |
| Products | 7*512=3584 | 6*64=384 | 1*8=8 | 4*1=4 |
| Sum: | = 3584 + 384 + 8 + 4 = 3980 | | | |

**Fig. D.9**    Converting an octal number to decimal.

| Converting a hexadecimal number to decimal | | | |
| --- | --- | --- | --- |
| Positional values: | 4096 | 256 | 16 | 1 |
| Symbol values: | A | D | 3 | B |
| Products | A*4096=40960 | D*256=3328 | 3*16=48 | B*1=11 |
| Sum: | = 40960 + 3328 + 48 + 11 = 44347 | | | |

**Fig. D.10**    Converting a hexadecimal number to decimal.

Positional values:   **64    32    16    8    4    2    1**

Then we discard the column with positional value 64 leaving:

Positional values:          **32    16    8    4    2    1**

Next we work from the leftmost column to the right. We divide 32 into 57 and observe that there is one 32 in 57 with a remainder of 25, so we write 1 in the 32 column. We divide 16 into 25 and observe that there is one 16 in 25 with a remainder of 9 and write 1 in the 16 column. We divide 8 into 9 and observe that there is one 8 in 9 with a remainder of 1. The next two columns each produce quotients of zero when their positional values are divided into 1 so we write 0s in the 4 and 2 columns. Finally, 1 into 1 is 1 so we write 1 in the 1 column. This yields:

Positional values:          **32    16    8    4    2    1**
Symbol values:              **1     1     1    0    0    1**

and thus decimal 57 is equivalent to binary 111001.

To convert decimal 103 to octal, we begin by writing the positional values of the columns until we reach a column whose positional value is greater than the decimal number. We do not need that column, so we discard it. Thus, we first write:

Positional values:   **512   64    8    1**

Then we discard the column with positional value 512, yielding:

Positional values:          **64    8    1**

Next we work from the leftmost column to the right. We divide 64 into 103 and observe that there is one 64 in 103 with a remainder of 39, so we write 1 in the 64 column. We divide 8 into 39 and observe that there are four 8s in 39 with a remainder of 7 and write 4 in the 8 column. Finally, we divide 1 into 7 and observe that there are seven 1s in 7 with no remainder so we write 7 in the 1 column. This yields:

Positional values:          **64    8    1**
Symbol values:              **1     4    7**

and thus decimal 103 is equivalent to octal 147.

To convert decimal 375 to hexadecimal, we begin by writing the positional values of the columns until we reach a column whose positional value is greater than the decimal number. We do not need that column, so we discard it. Thus, we first write

Positional values:   **4096 256   16    1**

Then we discard the column with positional value 4096, yielding:

Positional values:          **256   16    1**

Next we work from the leftmost column to the right. We divide 256 into 375 and observe that there is one 256 in 375 with a remainder of 119, so we write 1 in the 256 column. We divide 16 into 119 and observe that there are seven 16s in 119 with a remainder of 7 and write 7 in the 16 column. Finally, we divide 1 into 7 and observe that there are seven 1s in 7 with no remainder so we write 7 in the 1 column. This yields:

```
Positional values:    256  16   1
Symbol values:         1    7   7
```

and thus decimal 375 is equivalent to hexadecimal 177.

## D.6 Negative Binary Numbers: Two's Complement Notation

The discussion in this appendix has been focussed on positive numbers. In this section, we explain how computers represent negative numbers using *two's complement notation*. First we explain how the two's complement of a binary number is formed, and then we show why it represents the negative value of the given binary number.

Consider Visual Basic's 32-bit **Long** type. Suppose

```
Dim value As Long
value = 13
```

The 32-bit representation of **value** is

```
00000000 00000000 00000000 00001101
```

To form the negative of **value**, we first form its *one's complement* by using Visual Basic's **Xor** operator:

```
onesComplement = value Xor &H7FFFFFFF
```

Internally, **onesComplement** is now **value** with each of its bits reversed—ones become zeros and zeros become ones as follows:

```
value:
00000000 00000000 00000000 00001101

onesComplement:
11111111 11111111 11111111 11110010
```

To form the two's complement of **value** we simply add one to **onesComplement**. Thus

```
Two's complement of value:
11111111 11111111 11111111 11110011
```

Now if this is in fact equal to –13, we should be able to add it to binary 13 and obtain a result of 0. Let us try this:

```
 00000000 00000000 00000000 00001101
+11111111 11111111 11111111 11110011
-----------------------------------
 00000000 00000000 00000000 00000000
```

The carry bit coming out of the leftmost column is discarded and we indeed get zero as a result. If we add the one's complement of a number to the number, the result would be all 1s. The key to getting a result of all zeros is that the twos complement is 1 more than the one's complement. The addition of 1 causes each column to add to 0 with a carry of 1. The carry keeps moving leftward until it is discarded from the leftmost bit, and hence the resulting number is all zeros.

Computers actually perform a subtraction such as

```
x = a - value
```

by adding the two's complement of **value** to **a** as follows:

```
x = a + (onesComplement + 1)
```

Suppose **a** is 27 and **value** is 13 as before. If the two's complement of **value** is actually the negative of **value**, then adding the two's complement of value to a should produce the result 14. Let us try this:

```
a (i.e., 27)                00000000 00000000 00000000 00011011
+(onesComplement + 1)      +11111111 11111111 11111111 11110011
                           -------------------------------------
                            00000000 00000000 00000000 00001110
```

which is indeed equal to 14.

## Summary

- When we write an **Integer** such as 19 or 227 or –63 in a Visual Basic program, the number is automatically assumed to be in the decimal (base 10) number system. The digits in the decimal number system are 0, 1, 2, 3, 4, 5, 6, 7, 8, and 9. The lowest digit is 0 and the highest digit is 9—one less than the base of 10.

- Internally, computers use the binary (base 2) number system. The binary number system has only two digits, namely 0 and 1. Its lowest digit is 0 and its highest digit is 1—one less than the base of 2.

- The octal number system (base 8) and the hexadecimal number system (base 16) are popular primarily because they make it convenient to abbreviate binary numbers.

- The digits of the octal number system range from 0 to 7.

- The hexadecimal number system requires sixteen digits—a lowest digit of 0 and a highest digit with a value equivalent to decimal 15 (one less than the base of 16). By convention, we use the letters A through F to represent the hexadecimal digits corresponding to decimal values 10 through 15.

- Each number system uses positional notation—each position in which a digit is written has a different positional value.

- A particularly important relationship that both the octal number system and the hexadecimal number system have to the binary system is that the bases of octal and hexadecimal (8 and 16 respectively) are powers of the base of the binary number system (base 2).

- To convert an octal number to a binary number, simply replace each octal digit with its three-digit binary equivalent.

- To convert a hexadecimal number to a binary number, simply replace each hexadecimal digit with its four-digit binary equivalent.

- Because we are accustomed to working in decimal, it is convenient to convert a binary, octal or hexadecimal number to decimal to get a sense of the number's "real" worth.

- To convert a number to decimal from another base, multiply the decimal equivalent of each digit by its positional value, and sum these products.

- Computers represent negative numbers using two's complement notation.
- To form the negative of a value in binary, first form its one's complement by using Visual Basic's **Xor** operator. This reverses the bits of the value. To form the two's complement of a value, simply add one to the value's ones complement.

## Terminology

| | |
|---|---|
| base | hexadecimal number system |
| base 2 number system | negative value |
| base 8 number system | octal number system |
| base 10 number system | one's complement notation |
| base 16 number system | positional notation |
| binary number system | positional value |
| conversions | symbol value |
| decimal number system | two's complement notation |
| digit | **Xor** operator |

## Self-Review Exercises

**D.1** The bases of the decimal, binary, octal, and hexadecimal number systems are _____, _____, _____, and _____ respectively.

**D.2** In general, the decimal, octal, and hexadecimal representations of a given binary number contain (more/fewer) digits than the binary number contains.

**D.3** (True/False) A popular reason for using the decimal number system is that it forms a convenient notation for abbreviating binary numbers simply by substituting one decimal digit per group of four binary bits.

**D.4** The (octal / hexadecimal / decimal) representation of a large binary value is the most concise (of the given alternatives).

**D.5** (True/False) The highest digit in any base is one more than the base.

**D.6** (True/False) The lowest digit in any base is one less than the base.

**D.7** The positional value of the rightmost digit of any number in either binary, octal, decimal, or hexadecimal is always _____.

**D.8** The positional value of the digit to the left of the rightmost digit of any number in binary, octal, decimal, or hexadecimal is always equal to _____.

**D.9** Fill in the missing values in this chart of positional values for the rightmost four positions in each of the indicated number systems:

| | | | | |
|---|---|---|---|---|
| decimal | 1000 | 100 | 10 | 1 |
| hexadecimal | ... | 256 | ... | ... |
| binary | ... | ... | ... | ... |
| octal | 512 | ... | 8 | ... |

**D.10** Convert binary **110101011000** to octal and to hexadecimal.

**D.11** Convert hexadecimal **FACE** to binary.

**D.12** Convert octal **7316** to binary.

**D.13** Convert hexadecimal **4FEC** to octal. (Hint: First convert **4FEC** to binary then convert that binary number to octal.)

**D.14** Convert binary **1101110** to decimal.

**D.15** Convert octal **317** to decimal.

**D.16** Convert hexadecimal **EFD4** to decimal.

**D.17** Convert decimal **177** to binary, to octal, and to hexadecimal.

**D.18** Show the binary representation of decimal **417**. Then show the one's complement of **417**, and the two's complement of **417**.

**D.19** What is the result when the one's complement of a number is added to itself?

## Self-Review Answers

**D.1** 10, 2, 8, 16.

**D.2** Fewer.

**D.3** False.

**D.4** Hexadecimal.

**D.5** False. The highest digit in any base is one less than the base.

**D.6** False. The lowest digit in any base is zero.

**D.7** 1 (the base raised to the zero power).

**D.8** The base of the number system.

**D.9** Fill in the missing values in this chart of positional values for the rightmost four positions in each of the indicated number systems:

| | | | | |
|---|---|---|---|---|
| decimal | 1000 | 100 | 10 | 1 |
| hexadecimal | 4096 | 256 | 16 | 1 |
| binary | 8 | 4 | 2 | 1 |
| octal | 512 | 64 | 8 | 1 |

**D.10** Octal **6530**; Hexadecimal **D58**.

**D.11** Binary **1111 1010 1100 1110**.

**D.12** Binary **111 011 001 110**.

**D.13** Binary **0 100 111 111 101 100**; Octal **47754**.

**D.14** Decimal **2 + 4 + 8 + 32 + 64 = 110**.

**D.15** Decimal **7 + 1 * 8 + 3 * 64 = 7 + 8 + 192 = 207**.

**D.16** Decimal **4 + 13 * 16 + 15 * 256 + 14 * 4096 = 61396**.

**D.17** Decimal **177**
to binary:

```
256 128 64 32 16 8 4 2 1
128 64 32 16 8 4 2 1
(1*128)+(0*64)+(1*32)+(1*16)+(0*8)+(0*4)+(0*2)+(1*1)
10110001
```

to octal:

```
512 64 8 1
64 8 1
(2*64)+(6*8)+(1*1)
261
```

to hexadecimal:

```
256 16 1
16 1
(11*16)+(1*1)
(B*16)+(1*1)
B1
```

**D.18**    Binary:

```
512 256 128 64 32 16 8 4 2 1
256 128 64 32 16 8 4 2 1
(1*256)+(1*128)+(0*64)+(1*32)+(0*16)+(0*8)+(0*4)+(0*2)+
(1*1)
110100001
```

One's complement: **001011110**
Two's complement: **001011111**
Check: Original binary number + its two's complement

```
110100001
001011111
---------
000000000
```

**D.19**    Zero.

## Exercises

**D.20**    Some people argue that many of our calculations would be easier in the base 12 number system because 12 is divisible by so many more numbers than 10 (for base 10). What is the lowest digit in base 12? What might the highest symbol for the digit in base 12 be? What are the positional values of the rightmost four positions of any number in the base 12 number system?

**D.21**    How is the highest symbol value in the number systems we discussed related to the positional value of the first digit to the left of the rightmost digit of any number in these number systems?

**D.22**    Complete the following chart of positional values for the rightmost four positions in each of the indicated number systems:

| | 1000 | 100 | 10 | 1 |
|---|---|---|---|---|
| decimal | **1000** | **100** | **10** | **1** |
| base 6 | ... | ... | **6** | ... |
| base 13 | ... | **169** | ... | ... |
| base 3 | **27** | ... | ... | ... |

**D.23** Convert binary **100101111010** to octal and to hexadecimal.

**D.24** Convert hexadecimal **3A7D** to binary.

**D.25** Convert hexadecimal **765F** to octal. (Hint: First convert **765F** to binary, then convert that binary number to octal.)

**D.26** Convert binary **1011110** to decimal.

**D.27** Convert octal **426** to decimal.

**D.28** Convert hexadecimal **FFFF** to decimal.

**D.29** Convert decimal **299** to binary, to octal, and to hexadecimal.

**D.30** Convert the octal **4377** to hexadecimal.

**D.31** Show the binary representation of decimal **779**. Then show the one's complement of **779**, and the two's complement of **779**.

**D.32** What is the result when the two's complement of a number is added to itself?

**D.33** Show the two's complement of **-1** for a 32-bit **Long**.

# Bibliography

(Ai98)    Aitken, P. G., *Visual Basic 6 Programming Blue Book, Vol. 1.* Scottsdale, AZ: The Coriolis Group, 1998.

(Am97)   Amundsen, M., et. al., *Visual Basic 5 Fundamentals Unleashed.* Indianapolis, IN: Sams Publishing, 1998.

(Am97)   Amundsen, M. and C. Smith, *Teach Yourself Database Programming with Visual Basic 5 in 21 Days.* Indianapolis, IN: Sams Publishing, 1997.

(Bl88)    Blaha, M. R.; W. J. Premerlani; and J. E. Rumbaugh, "Relational Database Design Using an Object-Oriented Methodology," *Communications of the ACM*, Vol. 31, No. 4, April 1988, pp. 414–427.

(Bo98)    Box, D., *Essential COM.* Reading MA: Addison Wesley Longman, Inc., 1998.

(Br96)    Brophy, K. and T. Koets, *Teach Yourself VBScript in 21 Days.* Indianapolis, IN: Sams Publishing, 1996.

(Ca98)    Craig, J. C., W. Craig, and J. Webb, *Microsoft Visual Basic 6.0 Developer's Workshop.* Redmond, WA: Microsoft Press, 1998.

(Ch96)    Chappell, D., *Understanding ActiveX and OLE.* Redmond, WA: Microsoft Press, 1996.

(Ci98)    Collin, Simon, *Visual Basic for Network Applications.* Boston, MA: Digital Press, 1998.

(Cl98)    Conley, J. D., and J. Conley, *Teach Yourself Object-Oriented Programming with Visual Basic in 21 Days.* Indianapolis, IN: Sams Publishing, 1998.

(Cm96)  Coombs, T., J. Coombs, and D. Brewer, *ActiveX Sourcebook.* New York, NY: Wiley Computer Publishing, 1996.

(Cn98)   Connell, J., *Beginning Visual Basic 6 Database Programming.* Chicago, IL: Wrox Press Inc., 1998.

(Co70)    Codd, E. F., "A Relational of Data for Large Shared Data Banks," *Communications of the ACM*, June 1970.

(Co72)    Codd, E. F., "Further Normalization of the Data Base Relational Model," in *Courant Computer Science Symposia*, Vol. 6, *Data Base Systems*. Upper Saddle River, N.J.: Prentice Hall, 1972.

(Co88)    Codd, E. F., "Fatal Flaws in SQL," *Datamation*, Vol. 34, No. 16, August 15, 1988, pp. 45–48.

(Cr97)    Cornell, G. and D. Jezak, *ActiveX Visual Basic 5 Control Creation Edition*. Upper Saddle River, NJ: Prentice Hall PTR, 1997.

(Cr98)    Cornell, G. and D. Jezak, *CORE Visual Basic 5*. Upper Saddle River, NJ: Prentice Hall PTR, 1998.

(Cr97)    Cornell, G., *Visual Basic 5 from the Ground Up*. Berkeley, CA: Osborne/McGraw-Hill, 1997.

(Da81)    Date, C. J., *An Introduction to Database Systems*. Reading, MA: Addison Wesley Publishing, 1981.

(De90)    Deitel, H. M., *Operating Systems, Second Edition*. Reading, MA: Addison Wesley Publishing, 1990.

(Dn96)    Denning, A., *ActiveX Controls Inside Out: Second Edition*. Redmond, WA: Microsoft Press, 1996.

(Ed97)    Eddon, G. and H. Eddon, *Active Visual Basic 5.0*. Redmond, WA: Microsoft Press, 1997.

(Ed98)    Eddon, G., and H. Eddon, *Programming Components with Microsoft Visual Basic 6.0*. Redmond, WA: Microsoft Press, 1998.

(Ed98a)    Eddon, G., and H. Eddon, *Inside Distributed COM*. Redmond, WA: Microsoft Press, 1998.

(Fe96)    Fenstermacher, K., *ActiveX for Dummies*. Foster City, CA: IDG Books, 1996.

(Fr97)    Freeze, W., *The Visual Basic 5 Programmer's Reference*. Research Triangle Park, NC: Ventana Communications Group, Inc., 1996.

(Fr98)    Freeze, W., *Expert Guide to Visual Basic 6*. Alameda, CA: Sybex, Inc., 1998.

(Gr97)    Grimes, R., *Professional DCOM Programming*. Olton, Birmingham Canada: Wrox Press, 1997.

(Ha98)    Halvorson, M., *Microsoft Visual Basic Professional 6.0 Step by Step*. Redmond, WA: Microsoft Press, 1998.

(He98)    Hettihewa, S., and G. M. Perry, *Sams' Teach Yourself Visual Basic 6 in 24 Hours*. Indianapolis, IN: Sams Publications, 1998.

(Hi96)    Hillier, S., *Inside Microsoft Visual Basic Scripting Edition*. Redmond, WA: Microsoft Press, 1996.

(Ho96)    Holzner, S., *Web Scripting with VBScript*. New York, NY: M & T Books, 1996.

(Ho98)    Holzner, S., *Visual Basic 6 Black Book, Vol. 1*. Scottsdale, AZ: The Coriolis Group, 1998.

(Ja96)    Jakab, S., et. al., *Instant Visual Basic 5 ActiveX Control Creation*. Olton, Birmingham Canada: Wrox Press, 1996.

(Lh97)    Lhotka, Rockford, *Professional Visual Basic 5.0 Business Objects*. Olton, Birmingham Canada: Wrox Press, 1997.

(Ma97)    Mann, A., *Visual Basic 5 Developer's Guide*. Indianapolis, IN: Sams Publishing, 1997.

(Mc97)     McKinney, B., *Hardcore Visual Basic 5.0: Second Edition.* Redmond, WA: Microsoft Press, 1997.

(Md98)     MacDonald, M., *Exam Cram. Microsoft Visual Basic 5.* Albany, NY: Certification Insider Press, 1998.

(Mn97)     Mandelbrot Set, *Advanced Microsoft Visual Basic 5.* Redmond, WA: Microsoft Press, 1997.

(Mp98)     Microsoft Press and M. Halvorson, *Microsoft Visual Basic: Deluxe Learning.* Redmond, WA: Microsoft Press, 1998.

(Mr97)     Martiner, W., *Visual Basic Programmer's Guide to Web Development.* New York, NY: Wiley Computer Publishing, 1997.

(Ms98)     Microsoft Corporation, *Microsoft Visual Basic 6.0 Programmer's Guide.* Redmond, WA: Microsoft Press, 1998.

(Ms98a)    Microsoft Corporation, *Microsoft Visual Basic 6.0 Reference Library.* Redmond, WA: Microsoft Press, 1998.

(Pa96)     Palmer, S., *VBScript and ActiveX Wizardry.* Scottsdale, AZ: Coriolis Group, Inc., 1996.

(Pe97)     Petroutsos, E., *Mastering Visual Basic 5.* San Francisco, CA: Sybex Inc., 1997.

(Pe98)     Petroutsos, E., *Mastering Visual Basic 6.* San Francisco, CA: Sybex, Inc., 1998.

(Po97)     Potts, A., et. al., *Visual Basic 5 Web & Multimedia Adventure Set.* Scottsdale, AZ: Coriolis Group, Inc., 1996.

(Pp98)     Pappas, C. H., and W. H. Murray, *Visual Basic with the Windows API.* Englewood Cliffs, NJ: Prentice Hall, 1998.

(Pr98)     Perry, G. M., *Sams' Teach Yourself Visual Basic 6 in 21 Days.* Indianapolis, IN: Sams Publications, 1998.

(Re88)     Relational Technology, *INGRES Overview.* Alameda, CA: Relational Technology, 1988.

(Rm97)     Roman, S., *Concepts of Object-Oriented Programming with Visual Basic.* New York, NY: Springer, 1997.

(Ro97)     Rogerson, D., *Inside COM.* Redmond, WA: Microsoft Press, 1997.

(Rs97)     Reselman, B., *Using Visual Basic 5.* Indianapolis IN: Que Corporation, 1997.

(Sa97)     Sankar, Krishna., *Internet Explorer Plug-In and ActiveX Companion.* Indianapolis IN: Que Corporation, 1997.

(Sc98)     Schneider, D., *An Introduction to Programming Using Visual Basic 5.0: Third Edition.* Upper Saddle River NJ: Prentice Hall, 1998.

(Se98)     Sessions, R., *COM and DCOM.* New York, NY: Wiley Computer Publishing, 1998.

(So98)     Scott, D., *Visual Basic for Applications 5 Bible.* Foster City, CA: IDG Books, 1998.

(Sp98)     Spasov, P., *Programming for Technology Students Using Visual Basic.* Englewood Cliffs, NJ: Prentice Hall, 1998.

(St81)     Stonebraker, M., "Operating System Support for Database Management," *Communications of the ACM*, Vol. 24, No. 7, July 1981, pp. 412–418.

(St98)     Stephens, R., and K. R. Stephens, *Ready-To-Run Visual Basic Algorithms.* New York, NY: John Wiley & Sons, 1998.

(Th98)    Thayer, R., *Visual Basic 5 Unleashed: Professional Reference Edition.* Indianapolis, IN: Sams Publishing, 1998.

(Tu96)    Turlington, S., *Exploring ActiveX.* Research Triangle Park, NC: Ventana Communications Group, Inc., 1996.

(Va97)    Vaughn, W., *Hitchhiker's Guide to Visual Basic & SQL Server, 6th Edition.* Redmond, WA: Microsoft Press, 1997.

(Wh98)    Whisler, V. et al, *Visual Basic 6 Bible.* Foster City, CA: IDG Books, 1998.

(Wi88)    Winston, A., "A Distributed Database Primer," *UNIX World*, April 1988, pp. 54–63.

(Wn09)    Wang, W., *Visual Basic 6 for Windows for Dummies.* Foster City, CA: IDG Books, 1998.

(Wr98)    Wright, P., *Beginning Visual Basic 6.* Chicago, IL: Wrox Press Inc., 1998.

# Index